M000086767

The Valley of the Second Sons

Letters of Theodore Dru Alison
Cockerell, a young English naturalist,
writing to his sweetheart and
her brother about his life in
West Cliff, Wet Mountain Valley,
Colorado, 1887-1890

Wm A. Weber

William A. Weber, F. L. S., Editor

I dedicate this book to the memory of Urless Lanham, University of Colorado Museum entomological Professor and curator, a student and disciple of Cockerell who studied the bees of the genus Andrena and published broadly, notably *The Bone Hunters, The Enchanted Mesa, The Fishes,* and *The Sapphire Planet.* It was through Url's enthusiasm about his mentor that I became interested in Cockerell and his life.
William A. Weber

THE VALLEY OF THE SECOND SONS: Letters of Theodore Dru Alison Cockerell, a young English naturalist, writing to his sweetheart and her brother about his life in West Cliff, Wet Mountain Valley, Colorado 1887-1890, William A. Weber, F. L. S., Editor

Copyright © 2004 by Pilgrims Process, Inc.

All rights reserved

Publication of this book was supported, in part, by grants from The University of Colorado Museum, The Friends of the Florissant Fossil Beds National Park, The Florissant Scientific Society, and the Western Interior Paleontological Society. The editor is grateful for their support.

ISBN: 0-9710609-9-1

Library of Congress Control Number: 2003097345

Printed in the United States of America

0 9 8 7 6 5 4 3 2

Set in Palatino 10 pt over 12 pt

Cover and interior design by Gary White

Table of Contents

Introduction

THEODORE DRU ALISON COCKERELL, was one of the last of the great "naturalists" and a member of one of England's famous families. While in his early twenties, he spent three years in the Wet Mountain Valley near West Cliff (now Westcliffe), Colorado (from June, 1887 to June, 1890). The letters forming the substance of this book contain his first-hand impressions of the landscape, its natural history, the people, and how life was lived. Cockerell was a literate, acute observer with a flair for expository writing. The letters, written daily or immediately following events, are accurate accounts of a little-known period on the Colorado frontier, written by a resident rather than by a wealthy traveler.

Cockerell's letters are not characterized by a continuous narrative. They are full of detail, the significance of much of which is lost because the replies were not preserved, so they could not be published complete and unabridged. The letters contain much to interest a student of Victorian times with a penchant for learning just what a young budding scientist would have been reading if he were banished to a "desert island." Every book he read, every newspaper and every letter he received, the weather, his state of health, all are meticulously recorded.

In the later nineteenth century, the promise of restored health and improved fortunes brought many Englishmen to the Colorado Springs region, which offered urban living, or to the Wet Mountain Valley south of the Arkansas River, where ranching, mining, and the clear mountain air beckoned.

Such was the influx of Britons to this part of Colorado that the Colorado Springs area was called "Little England." Robert Athearn, in *Westward the Briton* (1962) describes the phenomenon:

Colorado received higher praise for its climate than any other part of the West. And it received more Englishmen. One of them happily reported that Colorado was almost an English reserve with almost every third ranch belonging to that group of nationals. They came to visit, or perhaps to speculate. Many who had no intention of staying were so attracted by the climate that they settled down permanently. Large numbers of both English and Americans came to improve their failing health. J. E. Liller, the English editor of *Out West*, published at Colorado Springs, estimated in 1872 that one-third of the territory's population consisted of 'reconstructed invalids.' He predicted that within a few years the region would be recognized as the 'Sanitarium of the World.' Rose Kingsley and Isabella Bird both wrote that it was the ideal location for people suffering from pulmonary diseases. Even winter days were not severe and sufferers could spend most days of the year outside.

Theo Cockerell was one of those who came to the Wet Mountain Valley, sometimes called "The valley of the second sons" in search of a cure for tuberculosis. During his few years of enforced residence in the Valley he established the habits of a lifetime of observation, correspondence, teaching, and publication which prepared him for a distinguished career in natural history and at the same time made the remote Colorado Rocky Mountains a vivid vicarious experience

for naturalists the world over. By documenting the wildlife of Colorado in detail he paved the way for scientific study and enjoyment by future generations of amateur and professional scientists. Since these letters illuminate the character of the man as well as the nature of the Valley and its inhabitants, an introduction to Cockerell is in order.

Known as Theo to his family, and later as T.D.A.C. to his colleagues, he was born August 22, 1866, in Norwood, a suburb of London, the eldest of six children of Sidney J. Cockerell and Alice Bennett. His uncle Douglas, who was responsible for the medical diagnosis that sent Theo to Colorado, was Sir Richard Douglas Powell, Bart., an uncle by marriage, who became President of the Royal College of Physicians. Theo's brother Sydney ('Carlie' of the letters), born in 1867, became the brilliant director of the Fitzwilliam Museum at Cambridge and was knighted in 1934. Sir Sydney's son Christopher is known as the 'Father of the Hovercraft' and was knighted by Queen Elizabeth II in 1968. Theo and Carlie were very close as children. Both were passionate collectors of shells, butterflies, insects, fossils, and stamps, and were inseparable field companions vying with each other for the most exciting discoveries. Their brothers and sisters were Olive, a talented artist who worked professionally at book illustration; Douglas, who became a master bookbinder and is noted for his work on the Codex Sinaiticus, Leslie, and Una.

Wilfred Blunt in his 1964 biography of Sir Sydney, entitled simply, *Cockerell*, described the state of the family when Theo turned nineteen:

Meanwhile the Cockerell family was becoming scattered. In 1885, Douglas, then a boy of fifteen, was sent out steerage to Canada 'in the company of terrible riff-raffs — a dreadful experience, to work on a farm [later he got a job in the Imperial Bank of Toronto, where he saved enough money to return to England]. William Morris (the founder of the Kelmscott Press), on being shown a book that Douglas had bound in his spare time, gave him employment, and in due course he became one of the leading bookbinders in England and the author of the principal manual on the subject. He died in 1945. Theo and Sydney were both avid disciples of Morris. Two years later both Theo and Leslie developed consumption and were obliged to go and live abroad. Theo went to Colorado with a former school friend named Payn, who was also tubercular. 'Payn was well-to-do, said Carlie, 'and paid Theo's passage. But he was a rather wild young man. Theo was just the opposite, and they soon parted company.'

Theo was portentously earnest for his age, as is shown by the letters that he wrote to Sydney. They were not so much letters as lectures — lectures on themes such as friendship, love (sub-headed theoretical, aesthetic, Christian, historical, and practical), tolerance and immortality. They contained also, much about Annie Fenn, the girl he had left behind him, and even more about slugs and insects. Theo's exquisite and microscopic calligraphy at that time is hardly distinguishable from Sydney's, and his letters have the added charm of illustration. His industry, in spite of ill-health, was very considerable; in the year 1887, for example, he published no less than 83 papers and notes on natural history subjects in various journals.

As adolescents Theo and "Carlie" came under the spell of William Morris, at whose home they were frequent visitors. Theo's moral attitudes and objective, dispassionate discussions of moral issues, unusual in a youngster, and his lifelong devotion to the principles of British Socialism, testify to the profound impression William Morris made upon his spiritual development. Cockerell's socialistic leanings caused him great difficulty with the father of his fiancée, Annie Fenn.

TDAC and Annie Fenn (about 1891)

In 1887, Theo held a position in the firm of Wm. Klein & Sons, Flour Factors, but because he had contracted what was believed to be a mild case of tuberculosis, his family arranged to send him to Colorado with Payn, his young school chum. Payn's wealthy family paid the passage for both boys. The letters transcribed here indicate that Theo felt a moral obligation to look after Payn. But Payn drifted into morphine addiction and gambling. Theo, after a good deal of soul-searching, finally broke with him. Payn eventually returned to England, in rather bad shape.

Aside from the passage money, Theo was completely on his own and had to earn every penny he needed to survive in the Wet Mountain Valley. The letters tell in detail about his efforts to earn money and find a steady job. For a time he did odd jobs for the local ranchers, but soon he settled at the Cusack ranch where he did chores and became almost one of the family. He also earned small amounts of money by sketching portraits, drawing Valentines for children at the post office, doctoring horses and patching up split lips and cut noses, giving elementary art lessons, tutoring children, digging bulbs for sale to garden suppliers, collecting and selling specimens of insects, snails, and plants to collectors, and acting as custodian of the schoolhouse and church.

Mrs. Cusack was encouraged by Theo to collect botanical specimens, which he curated and identified for her. The Cusack collection eventually went to England, where sets are to be found at Oxford University and the Royal Botanical Garden at Kew.

A young lady, Alice Eastwood, was a school teacher in Denver. She had the great experience of being able to guide Alfred Russel Wallace up to the summit of Gray's Peak (she being the only person in Denver who could be found to have any botanical knowledge). She joined Cockerell's new Colorado Biological Association and visited Theo at West Cliff, becoming the association's secretary before Theo returned to England.

Miss Eastwood and Mrs. Cusack thus were the first resident botanical collectors in Colorado and both found a mentor in Theo Cockerell. Miss Eastwood left Colorado for California in the 1890s and later was appointed curator of the herbarium of the California Academy of Science in San Francisco. She became the first botanical heroine of the world because of her foresight in segregating the precious "Type Specimens" there, which she was able to rescue from the collapsing building during the great earthquake of 1906.

The few years spent in the Wet Mountain Valley were crucial in directing Cockerell's future scientific career and in accustoming him to a Spartan economic life. As soon as he arrived in America he eagerly bought the few books he could find that treated the flora and fauna of the Rocky Mountains. He already had a deep and detailed knowledge of the wildlife of Great Britain, for his letters comment on similarities and differences. When he reached West Cliff he set about compiling catalogues of the fauna and flora of the Rocky Mountain Region, a project that continued for the rest of his life. He collected insects, plants, shells, fossils, and some birds, and he avidly sought out experts all over the world who might be able to identify them for him. The experts, in turn, jumped at the chance of having an alert observer and correspondent in this remote area. In this way Theo established long-lasting ties with future colleagues. Through current books, newspapers, and magazines, he followed developments and controversies in

natural history. He became a strong proponent of the Natural Selection Theory propounded by Charles Darwin and Alfred Russel Wallace. He also read and dissected with Annie and her brother, Frederic, the current Victorian novels, most of them containing moral or uplifting subject matter, He ignored any literature that he considered debasing or depraved. There is no indication that he had much of an ear for music.

Cockerell must have cut an odd and eccentric figure, even as a youth, in the town of West Cliff, though to their credit the frontier folk accepted him in their own way. For his part, he tried to find ways to raise their level of civilization to meet his. To that end he gave art lessons to the local ladies, founded a Literary and Debating Society which met regularly, and established the first Natural History Society in the Rocky Mountain region — the Colorado Biological Association. He solicited memberships from all over the western world and succeeded in building a fair-sized group.

Upon encouragement from his uncle Douglas, who wrote, "you seem to have made a good recovery", Theo returned to England in 1890, where he found a position at the British Museum of Natural History as an assistant to Alfred Russel Wallace. His particular task was to edit the second edition of Wallace's classic of natural history, *Island Life*. The association with Wallace, which continued as long as Wallace lived, must have been a priceless preparatory experience for his future work and thought in systematic zoology. Wallace stands beside Charles Darwin as co-father of the modern theory of evolution. The museum position made it possible for Cockerell to ask for the hand of Annie Fenn, and they were married on June 2, 1891.

With Wallace's help, Cockerell obtained a post as Curator of the Public Museum, Kingston, Jamaica, where he began the next phase of his long research career. He began to specialize on the taxonomy of the scale insects and mealybugs. In Kingston, Annie gave birth to Austin D. Cockerell, who died at age 33 days.

The climate of Jamaica did not agree with Theo, who feared the return of his tuberculosis symptoms. He arranged to trade places with Professor W.H.T. Townsend of the New Mexico Agricultural College at Mesilla Park (now Las Cruces). Here he became State Entomologist for the New Mexico and Arizona territories.

Cockerell suffered a devastating blow when Annie died on September 14, 1893, following the birth of Martin Cockerell on September 9. Also, his political views were not shared by the local people. He left Mesilla Park and moved up to a new college, New Mexico Normal, which had been established at Las Vegas. In 1899, with the cooperation of another biology teacher there, Miss Wilmatte Porter, he established a research station.

But the political climate of New Mexico Territory continued to work against the success of the venture. In 1903 Cockerell was forced to take the only crucial public stand of his career. It is interesting to note, in this respect, that he wrote, many years later, in a note to Dean Hellems of the University of Colorado:

As I review my life, while I recall a certain number of too hasty and impetuous acts which I have lived to regret, I think on the whole that I have erred most in failing to act or speak when action was needed. At any rate, I have very often hesitated, and eventually done nothing, when uncertain what to do, though convinced that something ought to be done.

The one thing that Cockerell could not tolerate was the interference by corrupt political machines in the operation of an institution of higher education. He was not alone, and the faculty, the president, and part of the Board of Regents resigned in a body. The style and content of the manifesto published by the faculty on that occasion in 1903 demonstrates that Cockerell was the spokesman and leader of the fight. His clear and reasoned statement of the nature of a university and the rights of its scholars remains pertinent today.

The University closed down, to reopen a dozen years later as New Mexico Highlands University. Meanwhile Cockerell moved north, back to Colorado, taking charge of the Museum at Colorado College at Colorado Springs. His son, Martin, had died of diphtheria at age 9, and Theo had married Miss Wilmatte Porter, who remained his devoted wife and collaborator until he died. Of the Colorado College appointment he wrote:

My salary there was not enough to live on, and although my wife was teaching, she got no salary at all. Thus it came about that in the fall of 1904 we moved up to Boulder, where we have been ever since, more than thirty years. At first we taught in the Preparatory School (now Boulder High School), the position being given to my wife. My connection with the university was a nominal one, that of a 'lecturer' who did not lecture, but I did have a single graduate student.

In 1906 I was appointed professor, but still with no salary to speak of, and it was only gradually that I became established on the same footing as the regular members of the faculty. Now, [1934] having reached the age limit, I have retired, but am Professor Emeritus, and still have my office in the university. I suppose it would not today be possible to appoint a professor who did not have a university degree. As I look back on my career, I seem to have been well treated on the whole, and it is not without a certain surprise that I find that I have not had to endure injurious or grinding poverty at any time. I have never been obliged to discontinue my researches, and while in the University of Colorado have found opportunity to open up new fields of work, such as fossil insects, the genetics of sunflowers, and the anatomy of rodents. Paleobotany has also taken a good deal of my time.

Perhaps it is legitimate to conclude from all this that one needs enduring interests and a good deal of patience. A good deal of patience, not only with institutions and people, but also with oneself. The people who achieve excellence or make substantial progress in science are those who keep at it month by month, year after year, decade after decade. They correct their own mistakes, which are likely to be numerous. It is an open question whether it is wise to occupy oneself with many different lines of research. Certainly this variety gives one a broader point of view and is valuable as a background for teaching. Probably the same methods are not suitable for all, but I have noticed that those who stick to a single subject are apt to attain a rigidity of mind which may give a comfortable assurance of competence but does not permit much originality. May it not be a good compromise to shift from time to time (say once in ten years) to a related subject, sufficiently different to permit a new outlook? I am inclined to think that this might be recognized as a regular practice by college professors, with advantage to their classes and themselves.

Cockerell's productive career followed the principles he set forth in the above paragraphs. He was one of the last great "naturalists", a peculiar product of the British nineteenth century and a breed that today is considered an anachronism— but perhaps it might be better to say,

he represented a rare and endangered species worthy of conservation!

Theo died in 1948. Wilfred Blunt wrote of the family:

> Leslie had been a highly prosperous mining engineer, but he had a speculative turn and never managed to keep more of his money than his devoted wife insisted on his investing. Una, the youngest of the family (an actress) was a very rare creature with the finest perceptions, but fate was steadily against her. Douglas had a very successful career as a bookbinder, and after his death his business was carried on by his son, Sydney ('Sandy').

> Theo, the last to go, was a recognized authority on bees, but impetuous and rather undisciplined enthusiasm marred much of his work. He was immensely courageous. His brother Douglas once said of him, 'He was never deterred by the possession of only half a lung and corresponding resources, from going, if he heard of a fossil flea 10,000 years old, calling him in central Siberia, to collect it.' He was at Yokohama, on his way home from Siberia with an important collection of bees, when the great earthquake occurred, and it was characteristic of him that he cabled home to anxious relations, 'Bees safe, Theo.'

Editor's Note

Wilmatte died in 1957. After the two Cockerells died and were buried in Columbia cemetery, Boulder, the Department of Biology of the University of Colorado set aside his room in the Hale Science Building to be kept as it was, in perpetuity. A brass plaque was placed on the door. The pressures of needed space in a growing university, however, eventually resulted in his room being emptied, the contents discarded, and the plaque on the wall removed. I happened to enter the room while this was in progress and saved a great amount of material, including

some personal items (a dental plate, a slide ringing device), all of his remaining undistributed reprints, and some books.

It was then that I discovered the letters that he wrote to Annie from West Cliff, tied in red legal tape, together with some black hard-covered notebooks that turned out to be copies of the original letters that Theo had written to Annie's brother Frederic during the period when the two lovers were forbidden to communicate with each other. The earlier letters had been addressed to

May 9th cont.) The time went marvellously quickly in preparations, and it was soon time to go to the schoolhouse. What with microscope, books, diagrams, specimens &c. I had all I could conveniently carry, and when I got half way it began to rain, so I had to put in at the butcher's (Rosenstrauchs) and beg a newspaper to keep the wet off my burden. Arrived at the school-house, I hung my diagrams on a string as at the C.B.A. meeting, but the little table I expected to use for the microscope was not there. But the school-house is also a church, and the minister's reading-desk did excellently for the purpose when moved to the window. Then I sat down and waited, feeling some trepidation lest the thing should be

a failure. 2 o'clock came, and not a soul in sight! 2.5. + still nobody. 2.10.—here is Bertha Humphrey, at any rate. 2.25. Three more (in the interval I showed Bertha some things under the microscope)— Miss Macklebury and the two Alexander girls. Well, it was getting late, and I had 4, so I began. Very soon after Mrs. Chatelat and Anna Gowdy came, making six, and one or two others turned up later. (names unknown to me) I started with explaining the difference between organic and inorganic matter, + between animals and plants, and telling them about protoplasm and cells. I showed them some cells in the seed-vessel of Crompton then being polygonal, + a previous mother sent me in a letter offered a nice example of an elongated cell in one of its hairs. Also, I put under the microscope some blood, and let them see the corpuscles — these being examples of rounded cells. I got along all right, and felt no shyness, + was able to say all I wanted. When I was half through, I saw a lot of ladies (5 I think) coming down the road, and in they came — they were the Ladies Literary Society, which was meeting somewhere near, and had adjourned bodily to attend my lecture! There was Mrs. Stockton, Miss Byington, Mrs. Aldridge, — and I think the other two were Mrs. Humphrey + Mrs. Alexander. I was well pleased to see them, as they are the shining lights of West Cliff. I continued the lecture, speaking of the different divisions of the subject of Botany, and outlining the proposed plan of work. Several of the ladies asked very intelligent questions from time to time, which showed that they understood what I was saying. At half-past 3 I finished, and announced the next lesson or lecture for next Tuesday — we shall see whether they were satisfied by the attendance I got them. Lees came into town soon after, + then Regy + Miss Urquhart. I was rather + surprised to learn that Miss U. was going off to England the next day (i.e. today) + Mrs. Cusack was going with her to Pueblo, (+ thence for a week or so to Colorado Springs, to stay with Mrs. Hamp.) Miss U. goes to England with a Miss Blackmore, an old lady whom she has never seen. Dear me! how I wish I could have changed places with her, + no doubt she would have willingly stayed behind! Lees was going out to Louis', + I thought I would go with him, as I had been asked to go out some day. Afterwards, I found Louis + was giving a sort of little dinner party, and expected the Cusacks (&c. who didn't come). So I felt rather as if I had intruded myself. But it were all right, + there were only Lees, Jack Mackenzie + myself there. I meant to walk back early, as I thought Mrs. Cusack might call at my room, and find me out (which she did, + left a note) but talking &c. the time went, so that it was past 10 before I got back to town.   This morning I walked up to the Cox's (where the Cusacks + Miss U. stayed the night) to say goodbye to Miss Urquhart, as I supposed she would not want me at the station at the last moment. Also, I got the mail of last night — (1.) letter from E.W. Janson. who is to sell my Lepidoptera — but he talks of their being set, which is a bother. (2.) Pall Mall Budget of Oct. 4. -83 — sent by Sherborn — why, I don't know. (3.) Punch: from mother. (4.) "Ati." a little Steppian (Partridge + &c.) magazine I never saw before. containing my article on "Colorado Canons". The paper is well-printed, + well-illustrated for a penny or magazine — but it reeks with religious humbug. Did you ever see it? It would make any sane man turn atheist on the spot, if he thought this was really the best religion had to say for itself!

Facsimile letter

Frederic, who passed them on secretly to Annie, who copied them into the black notebooks, clipping out and pasting the small pen-and-ink sketches alongside the texts. The pasted sketches were often too stained by the glue to be used in this book, but the entire set is preserved in the Archive of the University of Colorado Norlin Library.

For several years this material was stored under the eaves of Norlin Library, which was also short of space. In the meantime, I began to assemble a complete set of Cockerell's published papers, making a special visit to Harvard University to search the Widener Library for those papers that he published in the old Victorian journals. I received a small grant for transportation from the Graduate School, whose dean was very reluctant to support a project which he did not consider to be "research." The result of this work was published in the first and only number of a new biobibliography series of the University of Colorado Studies.

When I opened the letters I realized that this collection constituted a unique record, not only of the formative years of a great biologist and humanitarian, but also of life in a frontier town of Colorado. The transcription onto a manual typewriter took about a decade. The people who helped me are acknowledged in a book published by the University of Colorado Press as a University of Colorado centennial volume (Weber 1976). This book contained portions of the letters that would be of general interest. The rest of the transcript remained fallow until 2002, when I decided to make the entire set available.

Unfortunately, it proved too expensive to scan the transcript, and the scanner did not recognize some of the characters used by the ancient typewriter, so I decided to re-type the entire opus onto the computer, with the result given here. I have included many of the small pen-and-ink drawings that make the letters so delightful, as well as some pertinent photographs given me by Audrey Cusack (see p. xxi).

Cockerell wrote these letters when he was only 21-23 years old. They constitute a remarkable record of the activities, reading habits, wide interests in all of natural biological diversity, and already highly developed personal philosophy of this amazing young man who set out to catalogue *all* of the natural history of the Colorado Rocky Mountains. He later became one of the University of Colorado's most distinguished professors, and the world authority on the wild bees of the world.

It seems strange that Theo never mentioned anything about Annie in his autobiographical writings. He obviously was very much in love with her, and must have been devastated by her early death following the birth of their second child, Martin, which followed shortly after the the death of their first child at birth.

In reading these letters and knowing that Theo remarried, I find it plausible that he rationally decided that he would not marry for love again. His choice of Wilmatte Porter, a fellow teacher at New Mexico Normal University, perhaps might echo Cockerell's earlier experience in the Wet Mountain Valley, where he had found a most satisfactory platonic relationship with Mrs. Cusack, who was obviously sympathetic and with whom he could converse on any subject. Wilmatte seems like an alter ego to Mrs. Cusack, with the addition of a great lifetime devotion to her husband's ideas and his career. It almost seems that Cockerell needed more than anything else a companion who could talk his language and be a sounding board for his ideas. In his letters to Annie he seems to try very hard at being romantic, but his rational mind always gets in the way.

I do not know what happened to the letters written to Theo from Annie; presumably Cockerell discarded them. There are also some gaps in the correspondence.

In the transcription of the letters, I have tried to maintain the essence of the content, if not always the style, of the writer. Cockerell used dashes instead of periods and commas.

His paragraph structure was rarely clean; irrelevant sentences were intercalated occasionally in paragraphs. I have tried to make paragraphs out of blocks of significant discussions, but I rarely took the liberty of transposing a sentence out of a paragraph into its real context. I have maintained the quaintness of his usage, for words such as *waggon* and *atall,* and have kept the English spellings of words like *colour,* and words ending in *-ised.*

I find that some of the scientific names, especially of the animals (snails and insects) mentioned in his complete version of the letters, have been misspelled during the transcription (the original calligraphy was microscopic), but in order to make corrections I would have to have access to specialists. There is no single source for finding the correct spelling of all of the zoological names he used. I also wish I could explain who all of the English men and women were who are mentioned, but these are often family acquaintances who cannot be traced, and it probably is not worth consulting the British equivalents of the *Who's Who* of the time..

The letters have great value. For example, they will be of interest to those who might be related to ancestors in the Wet Mountain Valley and would like to look up their names and learn something about them. For historians the letters tell a great deal about life in the Valley (the local newspapers of the period, I have been told, burned in a fire). For biologists there are gems of anecdotes, and it will amaze some to see the range of Theo's correspondents, which include many of the great figures, scientific, literary and political, of the time.

One of the very interesting features of the letters is Cockerell's obsession with the mail.

He notes almost every letter he received, what it contained, and how he answered it. He knows just when replies to his letters to England are expected and is distressed by any delays. This must come from the fact that, unlike us, the people of that time had no recourse to telephones, radios, or even electricity, and their lives were very lonely, especially a person like Cockerell, who had so little in common with the other residents of the Valley. Mail from his colleagues, friends, and loved ones were terribly important to him and kept him in touch with his beloved England.

For readers who are interested in the literature available during that period there are many tantalizing references. Theo expressed his political views (Socialism), his moral attitudes, and his religious beliefs (he was as much an infidel as his brother Carlie). Some will enjoy the "programmes" of the meetings—either entertainment, debates, picture exhibitions, or celebrations.

Amateur botanists will enjoy his discoveries of the plants that had been seen by very few people before him, his trek across Colorado to the Grand Mesa and back, and his hikes to the Lakes of the Clouds.

Those curious about daily life in frontier Colorado will enjoy his descriptions of tilling the ground, cutting the potatoes, and planting them; how he managed his room, his stove, cooking, and victuals and the prices charged for them; chasing horses; doctoring horses and people in pain; how one worked a one-man mine; surveying property; teaching perspective in art to ladies; tutoring children; and arguing with Mrs., Cusack about religion and politics.

There is something for everyone in these wonderful letters.

Cockerell Chronology

1866. Born August 22 in Norwood, a suburb of London, England, eldest of six children of Sydney J. Cockerell of Beckenham, Kent. Brother (Sir) Sydney C(arlyle) was director of Fitzwilliam Museum, Cambridge; brother Douglas B. "was accepted as the leading artist bookbinder of this country. He made many bindings of rare manuscripts especially for the libraries of Cambridge and Oxford. He bound the *Codex Sinaiticus* for the British Museum." — London Times, November 26, 1945. Brother Leslie M., sisters Una and Olive Juliet.

1877. Father died in his early thirties; family moved to Margate; T.D.A. Cockerell attended private schools, Middlesex Hospital Medical School, but did not take a degree.

1878. First publication at age 12 (cf. obit, *Nature*, unconfirmed).

1879. Trip to Madeira with Henry Dru Drury, great-grandson of the London entomologist Dru Drury, and O. L. Ponder, a wine merchant; found and reported on caterpillar of *Pyrameis indica occidentalis* for the first time.

1882. Beginning of "mollusc phase" of research.

1885. First contribution to political discussion (definition of liberalism, *Pall Mall Gazette*, August 29); attended November 15 meeting of Socialist League in home of William Morris; joined League and attended meetings, 1885-1887.

1887. Contracted a mild case of tuberculosis; gave up position in establishment of Wm. Klein & Sons (flour factors) in London; sailed for America on S. S. Nevada June 15. 1887; arrived at West Cliff, Colorado, in July; lived in the Wet Mountain Valley for three years, founded a Literary and Debating Society and the first Colorado Biological Association; began to catalogue the entire fauna and flora of Colorado, recent and fossil.

1890. Returned to England apparently cured and with a wealth of acquired knowledge; arrived at Bedford Park near London, June 21; worked in British Museum (Natural History) for about a year; edited manuscript of second edition of Alfred Russel Wallace's classic, *Island Life*.

1891. Married Annie S. Fenn, daughter of novelist George Manville Fenn, June 2; Became curator of the Public Museum, Kingston, Jamaica, June; beginning of studies of *Coccidae*; curator for two years.

1892. Birth of Austin D. Cockerell, son, to Annie Fenn Cockerell, at Manchester Cottage, Kingston, Jamaica; death of infant son, aged 33 days, October 21; reappearance of tubercular symptoms.

1893. Moved to Mesilla Park (Las Cruces), New Mexico, via Vera Cruz and Mt. Orizaba, Mexico, exchanging positions with Professor C.H.T. Townsend of New Mexico Agricultural College; professor of entomology and zoology, 1893-1896, 1898-1900; New Mexico Agricultural Experiment Station, 1893-1901; took up study of Hymenoptera; birth of Martin Cockerell, September 9; death of Annie Fenn Cockerell, September 14.

1896. Editor of *New Mexico Educator*.

1898. Became naturalized citizen of U.S.A. in Doña Ana County, New Mexico, October 5.

1900-1903. Teacher of biology, New Mexico Normal University, Las Vegas.

1900. Married Wilmatte Porter, a teacher at New Mexico Normal University, June 19.

1901. Death of Martin Cockerell (date?) Of diphtheria.

1901-1909. Consulting entomologist, Arizona Agricultural Experiment Station.

1902-1918. Wrote reviews for *The Chicago Dial*. Cockerell's reviews were often of more than a single book but several books on a single topic, such as Ultimate conceptions of faith, London, biographies (Hackel, Osler, Wallace, Darwin), replies to criticisms of Darwin, Christianity versus dogma, religious freedom, public versus private management of industry, Socialism, Heredity, and Women's rights. His reviews were carried by the Dial from 1902 through 1918. They resembled reviews of the later Kirtley Mather.

1903. Led a revolt of the faculty, February 11, against the corrupt governor of New Mexico Territory, which resulted in the resignation of the entire faculty and the closing of the school for twelve years, later restored as New Mexico Highlands University.

1903-1904. Curator of the Museum, Colorado College, Colorado Springs.

1904. Teacher, with Wilmatte, at Boulder Preparatory School, lecturer in entomology, University of Colorado, 1904-1906; monograph of the plant genus *Hymenoxys*.

1906. Professor of systematic zoology; collected fossils at Florissant with his wife Wilmatte, William Morton Wheeler, and S. A. Rohwer; beginning of his research on fossils.

1908. Became honorary member of Kansas Academy of Sciences; took up fish scale studies; lecturer on evolution, University of Colorado, 1908-1909.

1909-1912. Lecturer in Comparative Anatomy .

1910. Discovery of the red sunflower by Wilmatte Cockerell; breeding studies begun.

1911. Spent summer at U. S. Bureau of Fisheries, Woods Hole Oceanographic Institution, Woods Hole, Massachusetts.

1912. Professor of Zoology, University of Colorado.

1913. Received the Sc.D., *honoris causa*, Colorado College, Colorado Springs.

1914. Wrote papers on rodent anatomy.

1915. Summer at California Exposition, field work on Coronados Islands, San Diego.

1920. Took leave of absence; visited Isle of Wight and Cambridge; made large collections on island of Porto Santo; published zoology textbook.

1922. Collected shales in Green River, Roan Mountains (summer).

1923. Went to Japan and Vladivostok, on steamer Aleut; had narrow escape in the great Japan earthquake, September 1; was elected president of Entomological Society of America, December 26.

1924. Was University of Colorado delegate to Pan-Pacific Food Conservation Conference, Honolulu, July 31-August 14.

1925. Sailed on S. S. Vestris to Buenos Aires; traveled north to province of Jujuy; camped at Sunchal (summer).

1926. Served as president, Southwest Division, AAAS.

1927. Took leave of absence, academic year; crossed Siberia by Trans-Siberian Railroad, visiting Lake Baikal, Angara River, Irkutsk, Leningrad. Published *Zoology of Colorado*.

1928. Elected member of American Philosophical Society, April 21; took short trip to Australia.

1930.   Went to Morocco, London.

1931.   Cockerell-Mackie-Ogilvie expedition to Africa, last half 1931; took leave of absence, fall semester.

1933.   Awarded National Research Council grant for studies of the bees of Africa ($200).

1934.   Retired, July; spent winters thereafter in California; was appointed Professor of Zoology, Emeritus.

1937.   Undertook natural history study of islands off the coast of Southern California (-1939).

1938.   Appointed University of Colorado Honorary Research Lecturer, May 16; topic: 'Island Life.'

1941.   Became Associate in Zoology, University of Colorado Museum (-1947).

1941-1945. Curator of the Desert Museum, Palm Springs, California, in absence of the regular curator who had joined the staff of a military hospital.

1942.   Awarded the Sc.D., *honoris causa*, University of Denver.

1946.   Worked at the *Escuela Agrícola Panamericana*, Honduras (October 1946--April, 1947); last research was writing a monograph on the bees of Honduras.

1948.   Died January 26, San Diego, California, age 81. Buried in Columbia Cemetery, Boulder.

1957   Death of Wilmatte Porter Cockerell. After Theo's death Wilmatte taught in the Piney Woods School, the largest of four historically black boarding schools, near Jackson, Mississippi.

Biographies, Obituaries, and Notices

Anonymous.

1893. *British Naturalist* 3: 40-41. Portrait.

1923. Boulder pair in quake zone. Professor T.D.A. Cockerell and wife may be among victims, friends fear (with photo — 'Prof. T.D.A. Cockerell, who with his wife is believed lost in Japan catastrophe.') *Denver Times*, Sept. 4, p. 1.

1924. *Digest of the Proceedings of the First Conference of the International Society of Sugar Cane Technologists*. Frontispiece, group photo of representatives includes Cockerell.

1925. Photos of Cockerell at Honolulu meeting) *Mid-Pacific Magazine* 28: (frontispiece), pp.32, 34, 116.

1932. Nomination de membres d'honneur. Cercle Zoologique Congolaise, *Bull.* 9: 2, 3, portrait.

1933. African trip of Cockerells described in *Natural History Magazine* [with two photos of Cockerell in the field]. *Colorado Alumnus*, February, pp. 9, 12.

1948. *Nature* 161: 104; 229-230.

1948. *Pan-Pacific Entomologist* 24: 117-121.

1949. Memorial tablet commemorates career of T.D.A. Cockerell. *Colorado Alumnus* 40 (2): 12.

Benson, Robert B. 1948. *School and Society* 67: 121.

Bonnet, P. 1945. *Bibliographia Araneorum* 1: 62-63.

Calvert, Philip P. 1948. *American Philosophic Society Yearbook*, pp. 247-252.

Carpenter, F. M. 1948. *Psyche* 55:35.

Essig, E. O. 1931. *History of Entomology*, pp. 570-573., portrait.

Ewan, Joseph A. 1950. *Rocky Mountain Naturalists*, Chapter 10, pp.5-137. Univ. Denver Press.

Eyer, J. R. 1949. *Jour. Econ. Entomology* 42: 166-167.

Howard, L. O. 1930. *History of Applied Entomology*, pp. 16, 17, 416, 417, 447, 514.

Jaeger, Edmund C. 1947. Palm Springs Desert Museum, *Report* 3: 30-31, portrait.

James, Maurice T. 1949. *Entomological Society of America, Annals* 412: 235-237.

Leveque, Norma. 1944. Dr. T.D.A. Cockerell, Colorado naturalist. *Trail and Timberline* No. 303: 27-29, 34.

Leveque, Norma. 1948. In Memoriam. An appreciation of Dr. T.D.A. Cockerell. *Colorado Alumnus* 38 (9): 1-13.

Linsey, E. G. 1948. *Brooklyn Entomological Society, Bulletin* 43: 116-118.

Michener, Charles D. 1948. *New York Entomological Society, Journal* 56: 171-174.

Rayment, T. 1948. *Victorian Naturalist* 64: 225-226.

Remington, Charles and Jeanne. 1948. Biographical sketch of T.D.A. Cockerell. *Lepidopterists News* 2(2): 14.

Rohwer, S. A. 1948. *Entomological Society of Washington, Proceedings* 50: 103-108, portrait. (Contains unusual facts not to be found in other obituaries].

Schwarz, H. F. 1948. *Science* 108: 295-296.

Schwarz, H. F. 1948a. *Entomological News* 59: 85-89.

Taft, Robert. 1945. *Kansas Academy of Science, Transactions* 48: 42-44, portrait.

Weber, William A. 1974. *Dictionary of American Biography*, Suppl. 4, 1946-1950: 166-168.

Williams, C. B. 1948-9. *Royal Entomological Society*, London (C) 13: 67.

References

Weber, William A. 1965. *Theodore Dru Alison Cockerell, 1866-1948.* Univ. of Colorado Studies, Series in Biobibliography No. 1: 1-124. This presents the citations of 3,904 papers published during his lifetime. It also contains a chronology of the events in his life.

Weber, William A. 1976. *Theodore D. A. Cockerell: Letters from West Cliff, 1887-1889.* 222 pages, illustr. Colorado Associated University Press. This book contains a selection of portions of the letters, those that were most suitable for general readers, as well as many of the pen and ink drawings that were enclosed with the texts.

Weber, William A. 2000. *The American Cockerell: A Naturalist's Life, 1866-1948.* 352 pages. University Press of Colorado. An annotated collection of Cockerell's autobiographical publications, with a few chapters provided by the editor and other colleagues of Professor Cockerell.

Ancillary References on Theo Cockerell's family

Blunt, Wilfred. 1965. *Cockerell: Sydney Carlyle Cockerell, friend of Ruskin and William Morris and Director of the Fitzwilliam Museum,* Cambridge. 385 pp., 23 illustrations. Knopf, New York.

Corrigan, D. Felicitas. 1985. *The Nun, The Infidel, and the Superman: The remarkable friendships of Dame Laurentia McLachlan* with Sydney Cockerell, Bernard Shaw, and others. 152 pp., John Murray, Ltd., London. Note: A Masterpiece Theatre video called Best of Friends is based on this material.

The Theodore D. A. Cockerell papers are housed in the University of Colorado Norlin Library, Archives Department.

The Cusack Family

During the three years in which Cockerell lived in the Wet Mountain Valley, he was fortunate to have been closely associated, by physical nearness, to an English family who inhabited a small holding at the base of the Sangre de Cristo Mountains west of the town of West Cliff (now called Westcliffe). Their home still stands, now called "The Pines", and is being used for functions of the Wet Mountain Valley Foundation.

In Mrs. Cusack, Cockerell found one person who could be a spiritual companion, and his letters are full of passages about her. If he did not have this close at hand sounding-board to express his opinions and to share his excitement about the flora and fauna of the valley, Cockerell might have succumbed to a terrible loneliness.

I first encountered living members of the Cusack family when I went to West Cliff to become acquainted with the area. One day I happened to find a graveyard in the pine woods near "The Pines," at the base of the Sangre de Cristo mountains. To my surprise, two young ladies were camping there; they happened to be nieces of Audrey B. Cusack Glasgow (a daughter of Regy Cusack). Through Katherine Jensen, of Fowler, Colorado, I learned of Audrey, and thus was able to gain a good deal of information, as well as a few photographs of the family.

Audrey Cusack was born at "The Pines" on June 11, 1903. She had been employed as a teacher in Pueblo, CO, and later was a clerk at Peterson Air Force Base in Colorado Springs, At the time I knew her, she lived in Canyon City. She died at the age of 86 on November 29, 1989 (*vide Wet Mountain Tribune*, Dec. 7, 1989).

On April 10, 1974, Audrey Cusack Glasgow wrote me the following sketch of her recollections of the family:

My father, Reginald Cusack, was born at Abbeyville, Queens County, Ireland, on the family estate, in 1860. He left Ireland in 1864 and went to Bedford, England, where he attended the Bedford Grammar School.

In 1879 he attended Medical School for one year, but had to leave because of very severe asthma. His doctor recommended that he come to Colorado to a high altitude and spend a lot of his time in the open air. He came to Colorado in the 1880s. His first stop was Colorado Springs. He got a job herding sheep so that he could live out of doors. He then came to West Cliff, later ran The Pines Resort.

My mother, Gertrude Edith Urquhart was born at Muzzafarpur in what was then Bengal, India. She was a very frail child and could not stand the heat, so was sent to England when quite young, to live with an uncle and aunt, Henry and Lilly James. Her father was employed by the British government as head of foreign taxes in India. He died at the age of 48, and his wife returned to England with her other children to live at Bedford. Gertrude Urquhart studied to be a teacher, also studying music at the Royal Academy of Music in London. She also had a very bad asthma and her doctor recommended Colorado.

As Mrs. A. S. Urquhart and Mrs. T. B. Cusack knew each other in Bedford it was decided that Gertrude Urquhart should come to Colorado with Mrs. Cusack, who came to Colorado in 1887 to visit her sons, Charles, Francis (Frank), and Reginald (Regy).

Regy Cusack and Gertrude E. Urquhart were married at the Pines, West Cliff, on 2 September, 1889. Father did some ranching and built several houses, and Mother gave music lessons.

Some dates I found in a condensed diary Father had made from Mother's diaries:

1887—2 Nov. Arrived at West Cliff and met the Cusack boys and Louis Howard.

3 Nov. Met Mr. L. de S. Brock.

6 Nov. Met Mr. & Mrs. Beddoes, Mr. & Mrs. C. S. Cox, Mr. G. Payn and Theo Cockerell.

28 Oct. Met Colin Mackenzie.

10 Nov. Met the Harry Farners.

22 Nov. Met Mr. Wheatley.

30 Dec. Met the Ferrises.

31 Dec. Frank Cusack went to Australia.

1889—25 Jan. Met Frank Mackenzie.

27 Jan. Met Mr. Campion and Ronald Ward.

9 May. G. E. Urquhart left West Cliff to go to England for a visit. No date given for return [She returned for the wedding. Ed.]

1890—12 April. Keith Urquhart arrived from England.

23 May. E. T. Pelham arrived.

9 July. Frank Cusack returned from Australia.

(I am assuming you want dates and information for only 1887, 1888, and 1889, when Theo Cockerell was at West Cliff.)

Here is a list of the houses Father [Regy] built, with some dates.

The Pines, Cusack Ranch in Wet Mountain Valley

A log cabin at The Pines built in 1883, the original Pines home.

The Bachelor's Rest, a two-room log cabin built in 1885.

Enlargement of the original Pines cabin in 1890. This is where Mother and Father (Regy and Miss Urquhart of the letters) first lived after they were married.

The Cusach boys and a friend, 1889. Left to Right, Regy, Charley, Louis Howard, Frank. (from the collection of Mrs. Audrey Cusack)

Ladybird Lodge, in 1895. This house was later called Laura and was sold to Pennicuick.

Firmont, which was our permanent home in later years, was built in 1901. We left West Cliff in 1940.

A house at Peck Creek, about 20 miles from Pueblo. This property later was enlarged and was the Lees and Livesey Livestock Co.

Theresa Waddington's cabin, Sydney A. Lang's house, a short distance from The Pines.

Rockmound, for Vernon Urquhart. This was the big house and was the main building for what was The Pines Summer Resort. Regy also built the cabins and the dance hall.

A three-room log cabin for John A. Redmond, his son-in-law.

A log cabin at Birmingham at a mining camp in Huerfano County.

Firmont was our permanent house until we left West Cliff in 1940. The original house on the property where Mrs. Cusack lived with Frank Cusack. In the early 1990s the McKellars bought it from Frank Cusack, who in turn bought the Roberts Ranch.

Reginald Cusack's Lineage

Sir James William Cusack married Frances Elizabeth Bernard.

Sir James was President of the Royal College of Physicians and Surgeon to Queen Victoria when she was in Ireland.

Sir James' son, Thomas Bernard Cusack, married Mary Ellen [surname?]. T. B. Cusack died at age 32. There were five children of the marriage: Robert Oriel, William Henry, Charles Ralph, Francis (Frank) Wilmot, and Reginald (Regy).

Gertrude Urquhart Cusack's Lineage

William Hamilton Urquhart married Alice Smith. W. H. Urquhart was in the Hon. East Indian Co. and held a responsible position in the Muzzarfarpur district, in Opium Excise.

His son, Alexander Shaw Urquhart, married Louisa J. Watkins.

Their children were: Hugh Edward, Kathleen Elizabeth, Gertrude Edith, Mildred Annie, Elsie Vernon, Keith Alexander, and Vernon Watkins.

Regy and Gertrude

Children: Dorothy Mildred, Joan Barbara, Joyce Oriel, Audrey Baskerville, Nancy Bernard, and Geoffrey Urquhart.

Feb. 26. 9. 55 P.M.

morning. Wrote to Foster, Packard, & Hören. & did up spiders for Packard to take to Dr.
Thorell, (who is a great authority on spiders) when he goes to Europe this spring. Thorell is
at Genoa. Wish I were going to Europe! Lucky Packard!

Afternoon. Took numerous notes & extracts from "Canadian Entom."
Evening. Read some of "B.C." - but had supper late (about 8) so "evening" is shorter than
usual. This morning I went out for a while to look for more spiders to fill
up the bottle for Thorell, but found very little. Regy was here this morning, altering
the structure of my door to his better satisfaction. It has been quite fine and warm.
— There - that is all the news whatever. I am terribly behind-hand with my work,
but am gradually eating my way through — things do come down on one in such a heap:
no sooner is one "nearly through" than a lot of letters &c arrive, involving more writing. I like
it, of course, or it would be intolerable. The moral of it all
is, of course, that I must cease to be "lord-high everything"
to the C.B.A., and get some others to help — but there's the rub.

Feb. 27. 8.25. P.M.

I was in a despondent mood last night (perhaps
the result of eating boiled beans, which are rather
indigestible!?) and tonight I smile more complacently
upon the world, my work, and the rest of it. Your spirit has been with me today, to
comfort me. I have been taking notes &c from "Canad. Entomologist" nearly all day.
and have yet more to do. Regy has been working in the empty room part of
the time, & Chamberlain appeared and argued with us (mainly Regy) for a long time
about keeping Sunday and other matters. Chamberlain says he is disgusted with Wet
Mtn. Valley. This afternoon, Lees appeared, and now he is at the Cusacks. I have
just been over there to give him three little drawings of skill. (Player) of which he has
promised to make me woodcuts. Lees is fond of woodcutting, & does it well. When these
are done, I shall try my hand at it — it is a thing one will do well to learn.

10. 10. P.M.

I have finished the notes for "Can. Ents.", and now go to bed. Goodnight, my love!

Feb. 28. "the last day of winter" (?) 8. 55. P.M.

Mostly writing my 12 Report, which is principally about seasonal events - such as
the appearance of the butterflies, blooming of flowers &c. I wonder whether you
went out a-hunting on 16.10, to write on "an English lane". I didn't — although I
said I would. It was the day I walked from town after going to Rosita. I
looked about me, but saw nothing but horned larks - everything being covered with
snow. I meant to go out & search more thoroughly after, but was too tired when
I got home. But you really must write me an article for my C.B.A. report, my
dear, though you did recall your suggestion in a later letter! I won't let you off.
Mrs. Cusack was over here part of the day, also Regy & Miss U... They frequented
the empty room. I read some of "B.C." this evening, and am getting quite interested
in it. Thank goodness the mosquitoes don't bother us here! Here is my list of
Addenda to fauna & flora for Feb. - rather a poor list :-

Middlesex		Colorado		Moths. 45 (and 2 vars.)
Neuroptera. 1.		Birds. 1 var.		Homoptera. 1.
		Mollusca. 1 var. [4 species found]		Diptera. 4.
		Coleoptera. 11.		Arachnida. 3.
		Hymenoptera. 31.		Phanerogams. 3 (and 3 vars)
		Orthoptera. 1.		Fungi. 3.

I shall post this tomorrow - for I am going to town. Now I will write a little
more of my history :- In the autumn of 1879 I went to a boarding school
at Beckenham - Rev. T. L. Phillipps. I remained there (excepting, of course, the holidays)

The Letters

I remember Cockerell telling us how his English friends reacted when he first informed them he was leaving England to live in Colorado: "Colorado? Where is that? Why, that must be the end of the earth! You'll get way out there and — why, you'll die out there!" Then his eyes sparkled and he agreed, "I still expect to die out here." That was about 1932.

— Louise Ireland-Frey, M.D. [letter, June 1975]

North Western Hotel, Liverpool
June 24, 1887

Dear Frederic,

We arrived here safely at about 6:30, and go on board about 10:30 tomorrow morning. Before I started I took Annie's note to the Hemery's and said good-bye to them. They were very kind and sympathetic and made me feel that I had not properly appreciated them. At Wimpole Street Uncle Douglas provided me with a medicine chest and directions for curing all the known diseases, which shall be extremely useful no doubt out in the Wilderness. Olive [sister] and Carlie [brother Sydney Carlyle] saw me off and Mrs. Payn was also there. She begged that I would try to make Payn smoke less, which seems not without reason; he has just spent 22/6d. on cigars! Payn is very good though, on the whole, and I think I shall like him very well. Perhaps he will contrive to lose some of his bad habits under new influences.

On the train we met a man who had been out in Canada and the States with the British Association and knew Sollar the sponge man very well, but was not very scientific himself. Also another man by the name of Crane, who has business in New York and has traveled often to Mexico and all over the States, and knows Denver well. He says it is a very good sort of place, and the neighboring country is very interesting. He is interested in the gold and silver mines in Colorado, and showed us a piece of auriferous quartz from near Denver, We are to give his name to Mr. Rodgers, Superintendent of Mines at Central City, and then he will show us all over and how the thing is done.

I will write again from Queenstown (if not seasick). There seems every prospect of good passage.

Love to Annie. Theo.

[enclosed, a newspaper clipping referring to destinations of steamers from Queenstown]

Union Mail Steamer *Nevada*, off Holyhead,
June 25th, 1887

Dear Frederic,

It seems even now impossible, but we are really off, and the vessel started today a little after twelve. Last night I wrote a postcard from Liverpool with news up to then. So I will tell you what happened today. After breakfast this morning we took a train from Lime St. (where the hotel is) to the Alexandria dock. The train went all round the suburbs of Liverpool and took more than half an hour over it though the docks are only five miles distant as the crow flies. I had seen the Liverpool suburbs before — didn't think any better of them on second acquaintance. The houses are small and ugly and built in rows, and the whole place is full of smoke and hardly anything will grow but *Equisetum arvense*, of which there is any quantity, though there's a good deal of *Leontodon* and dog-daisies on the railway banks.

When we got down to the docks (which are at a place called by the ridiculous name of Bootle) a cart conveyed our luggage to the ship and we walked beside it. The vessel lay up against the quay, which is covered by a great shed where all sorts of goods for import and export are lying; on one side, for instance, a great heap of Indian corn which was being put into sacks.

We went on board about 10:30. Our cabin (we have one all ourselves) is No. 5 and 6, looking into the saloon on the right hand side. I have tried to make a diagrammatic sketch of the cabin and saloon, but not very successfully, and the perspective is all wrong, but I daresay you'll comprehend what it is like.

I went round and carefully inspected all the passengers, though I have not yet talked much with any of them. I don't think much of the saloon people; there are not very many and none seem interesting, but there are 400 steerage passengers of all sorts, mostly Germans, German Jews, and Swedes. Some of them look very interesting, and I mean to try and pick up a few acquaintances before the voyage is over. I wish Annie could come round and see them all, as they sit on the bulwarks, decks, etc., everywhere except at the stern, from which they are barred off by a rope.

At one place, huddled together, are sitting four or five old men, apparently German or Russian Jews. Two of them have ancient books written in Hebrew or something like it — I suppose Hebrew bibles. They look very intelligent, particularly one of them who is a little like Stepniak, only much rougher. Then there is a characteristic German with a round, pink face, pug nose, a pale moustache, a flat hat, a light grey overcoat, and field glasses hung over his shoulder. Another is a nice-looking couple, evidently very poor and very much distressed at having to go. I thought they were English, but I fancy I heard them talking in some other language, though I was not near enough to be certain. One man at starting got out his fiddle and played all the while to keep his spirits up, though I do not think he quite succeeded; another has a concertina.

At parting, the few English ones there are said good-bye to their friends and relations and seemed to feel parting very much, but none of the Germans, etc., seemed to have any friends to leave. I suppose they were all on board or had gone off before. If I get to know any of these people I will introduce you to them (as well as I can under the circumstances) and you shall share my interest in them.

When I got on board I found two letters waiting for me, one from Sherborn 'just for a last shake-hands' and a very nice one from Ponsonby, full of good wishes and encouragement. These letters were very welcome, as I did not expect them. I hope there will be some at Queenstown, where I shall post this. If I had thought of it I would have asked you to write there.

The docks are big places, and it took us some time to get out of them. We had to pass through two quite narrow gates where one might almost have jumped on the quay on either side; when a steamer is not actually passing there is a drawbridge goes over the gate.

There are plenty of sea gulls about on the docks. I saw both *Larus canus* and *L. tridactylus*, but here out in the open sea we have only *L. canus*, several of which follow the vessel to pick up fragments that are thrown overboard. The only other living animal or plant to be seen now is the seaweed, *Fucus vesiculosus*, of which stray detached pieces float by now and again.

As we came down the Mersey, Birkenhead was visible, and later on New Brighton, where there seemed to be a lot of bathing going on, to judge from the number of machines, and the sands were crowded with people. Beyond New Brighton and also on the Lancashire side are great sand hills stretching as far as one could see. These are often mentioned in the *List of Liverpool Coleoptera* in *The Naturalist* as good localities for beetles. After losing sight of the Mersey estuary we saw no more land till Holyhead, Anglesea. First of all a long line of hills was visible, grey in the distance, and later we passed quite close to Holyhead, and we could see the lighthouse and great grey-brown cliffs very distinctly.

Now we have left Holyhead behind and are once more out of sight of land. The sunset has been very beautiful; first of all brilliantly golden, shining on the water, afterwards deep red as it sunk behind the mist. Some of the smoke from our funnel which collected curiously in the distance added to the effect. The purser says such a sunset bodes a hot day tomorrow. The weather has been beautifully fine, and one can hardly feel the motion of the vessel atall, except the quivering caused by the engines and the screw, which makes it difficult for me to write. I do not think anyone has been seasick yet. I have not even *felt* queer.

There is a smoking room on the deck, which Payn frequents. One doubtful-looking individual was very anxious that he should play cards, but to my great relief Payn declined, explaining that he 'did not care for cards!' I played a game of chess with him afterwards by way of consolation. I will not say who won. The Cunard steamship *Umbria* (by which W. Crane, of whom I wrote on postcard, is going) started a little after

we did, but soon caught us up and passed us. She will be in two days earlier than we, as she is a much faster boat.

The *Nevada* is not a very big steamer compared with the other Atlantic boats, nor is it by any means the largest of the Union Line. Payn contrived to get both our passages for £10, which is a very considerable reduction, considering that £20 is the usual price for a single berth.

I hear that we shall be in Queenstown at seven tomorrow morning, so I will end off this. I mean that you shall have an account from me of what happens every day, and I will post you a letter about the rest of the voyage, from New York.

Tell Annie I am full of hope, and give her my best sympathy, and to the others a greeting. Now, farewell, till the next letter.

Mail Steamer *Nevada*
June 24th, 1887

Dear Frederic,
This morning at seven, the first thing visible was the low lying rocky coast of Waterford. Then we passed a light-house (Ballycarry I think it is called) on a small island, and now we are lying off Queenstown (9:15 a.m.). We have caught up the *Umbria*, but she seems not yet to have started, though out of the river, waiting for mails probably. There are plenty of gulls around, I think mostly *Larus argentatus* and some *L. tridactylus*, but there seem to be one or two other species which I cannot quite make out; they may be the others in immature plumage. Other birds seen are two crows, a cormorant, and a small black bird, apparently *Procellaria*. Medusae swarm, some large but mostly small. Queenstown is a rather pretty place from the sea. The houses are all grey or white and lie on a steep slope down to the sea. To the left the river winds round to Cork, 9 miles further up.

Queenstown, June 26th.
As we came to off Queenstown, some boats came alongside with Irish people selling all sorts

of wares: Handkerchiefs, brushes, sweets, oranges and lemons, strawberries, etc., etc. I wondered how they would ever get up the side, but that was easily done. First of all, a boat-hook was fastened above, and with considerable agility the men climbed up it to the deck. Then looped ropes were let down and the women and baskets hoisted up. Now they are having a roaring sale on deck among the steerage passengers. These Irish people look very interesting, and talk very Irish. I do not think I have seen anyone quite so Irish before; the London Irish have lost a good deal of their native manner. The military seem in force down here; there is a camp on one of the hills.

S. S. *Nevada*, Atlantic Ocean
June 26th, 1887

Dear Frederic,

A while ago we lost sight of land and are now out in the Atlantic west of Ireland. No letters for me! We steamed out of Queenstown soon after midday, the 'Flying Irishman' tug first coming alongside with the mails and several Irish emigrants. I like these Irish best of any we have on board; they are so cheerful (after the first grief of parting) and have such pleasant faces. I made the acquaintance of one of them, a youth about my own age who had come from Limerick. He left all his relations behind, but has friends in Chicago where he goes. He is going 'intermediate' as are most of the Irish. Intermediate is between steerage and saloon, rather better than steerage but not very good. Another youth I talked to goes out to Ohio with family. His brother went out before and was very successful and so they are all going. He took me down and showed me his berth in the intermediate; it looked fairly comfortable. We have one addition to the saloon from Ireland, the Rev. O'Donaghue, a grave-looking priest with bald head. On the whole I think he looks nice, certainly the best of the saloon passengers.

At Queenstown *Vanessa atalanta* came flying round, and lots of flies. One looked very curious, a *Tabanus* I think, but I failed to catch it. After leaving Queenstown I think I saw some guillemots in the distance, and two birds flew by which looked like gannets (*Sula bassana* does breed somewhere on the southwest coast of Ireland, *vide* paper in *Zoölogist*), and as we passed Cape Clear a flock of Greater Black-backed gulls (*L. marinus*) followed us.

We passed Cape Clear at about five p. m. today, and at the same time the *Umbria*, which we had left at Queenstown, again overtook us and passed in front. Close by we passed also the Fastnet Lighthouse, going between the Fastnet and Cape Clear. Just now, when I went forward, I found a crowd collected while one man played the concertina and a couple danced (and very well too) to the music.

June 27th. Today has been misty and perfectly calm, the water looking like oil. I am told this is most unusual in the Atlantic. The gulls have deserted us but I saw three Storm Petrels (*Procellaria pelagica*), and we are passing hundreds of medusae, different from those at Queenstown, being yellowish-brown. We passed a sailing vessel from New Brunswick, becalmed, at about three p.m. Although it is so calm, there is a heavy swell which we feel considerably, and both Payn and I have been sick.

June 30th. The last two days have been much the same. The wind got up a bit and we have been under sail. I have not been feeling well enough to write, though only once actually sick, and Payn has been worse. Yesterday I was bold enough to go to breakfast but was immediately sick, after which I thought discretion was the better part of valour and had my meals in the cabin.

I remember when at school we used to learn a song commencing:

To all you ladies on the land
We men at sea indite
But first would have you understand
How hard it is to write.

I never felt the force of that observation till now!

Several sorts of games go on on board. Payn and I play chess (we just now had a game in the cabin, he directing his moves from his berth), and there is a little card-playing, but the chief amusement is a game played with round, flat pieces of wood, thus — [Here a sketch of playing pieces and area. Ed.].

A figure is chalked out on the deck like A, in which are squares marked 1 to 10, and in front a portion marked '10 off.' Then there is a wooden instrument (B) by means of which the flat pieces of wood (C) are sent (pushed) across the deck, and the game is to get them on a square with a high number and to avoid '10 off'; for this, ten is deducted from the score. Another game is a sort of quoits played with rings of rope, which have to be thrown over a short stick.

The saloon passengers do not improve on further acquaintance. We have an old sea captain who was in the American Civil War and tells us tales about it, a Chemistry lecturer, a young man named Leach who has been four years in Philadelphia and had come over for his sister's wedding, and sundry others. I talked with the Rev. O'Donaghue and find him disappointing. In the first place he is Irish only by extraction and has lived all his life in America, and he has not very charitable religious views — thinks Darwin very wicked and all that sort of thing. *Procellaria* still flies round and with them some larger birds, peppery gray on the back. I can't quite make out what they are but am told they come from Newfoundland, which is now only a few hundred miles off. Some porpoises were seen but I missed them, but I saw this morning the water spouted up by a whale, though I could not see the whale itself, it being so far away.

The last two days I have spent most of the time reading. Carlie gave me two books at parting: Black's *Princess of Thule*, and Carlyle's *Sartor Resartus*. I suppose it is very abominable of me, but I quite fail to appreciate *Sartor Resartus* as I should. It is certainly clever, and some things in

it are good, but on the whole I think very little of it. *The Princess of Thule* is interesting, but I think there is somehow an unreality about Black's novels that spoils them. He seems to have mixed with a very miserable lot of people, and perhaps he pictures them fairly accurately, but I never met them myself and do not quite comprehend them. I don't think *The Princess of Thule* is hopeful or elevating anyway. When you are writing I should like to know what Annie thinks of these books, if she has read them both (this particularly because I think any bad opinion of them may be due to my lack of understanding).

Another book I have been reading is called *The Western American*, by a man named Morley Roberts. He traveled over parts of Canada and the States, particularly California and Oregon, doing all sorts of work and often without a cent in his pocket. This book shows up very well the utter folly of supposing that anyone can get plenty of work and good pay in America. Roberts says there are thousands of men out of work in San Francisco, and similarly in all other parts — he himself was often out of work, and when he did get any it was twelve hours a day more or less of hard manual labour. In British Columbia he came across two English missionaries named Small and Edwards, living out in the woods, which made me think of 'Baron Gardner' (Isn't he a missionary somewhere in Canada?)

Now I think of it, I meant to have told you that all my notebooks are in the back room upstairs at 5. Priory [the Cockerell family home. Ed.], mostly on the bookshelf. Some chemicals that will be useful to you are in the drawer in the black table in the same room. I daresay by the time you get this, however, you will have made a raid on 5. Priory and carried all these things off.

July 1st. We are now off the Newfoundland Bank and in a white fog, as is normal in these parts. Every few minutes they blow the fog horn, which does not make a pleasant noise. It is thought possible that we may come across some icebergs as the summer weather breaks up the ice fields and sends the bergs floating southwards to gradually melt. We have seen several more whales, their fins being visible above the water, and the petrels are still about, as also the large peppery kinds already mentioned which we are still doubtful about, but think may be *Anous stolidus* (noddy tern) [very unlikely; probably what he was seeing were fulmars, *Fulmarus glacialis*. Ed.]. A gannet flew close by the vessel this morning.

Last night we had about the most remarkable sunset I ever saw. I don't know how to describe it so as to give you any idea of what it was like, but here are the notes I took down at the time. Sunset, June 30th, 1887. N.W.: Sky, background blue-green on horizon, shading into blue above. Clouds, nearer ones lead-grey, much broken up, with outlines ill-defined. Other clouds behind them further away, pink shading into violet above. S.E.: clouds less broken up, dull grey, at first tinged with lurid pink. Sky near horizon pure deep indigo blue shading into grey of clouds. N.E.: Sky near horizon, at one time very brilliant, shading into blue-green on the N.W. and through grey into indigo on the S.E. Grey clouds above. S.W. dull. Grey clouds, afterwards producing rain.

Towards evening yesterday the fog cleared off and the night was perfectly fine. The moon came out and shone brilliantly (I feel quite an affection for the moon now; it is the nearest object from both Isleworth and America.

A barque has just passed us, in full sail, and we passed a steamer yesterday, and also a number of small fishing vessels. The manner of fishing in these parts is this: A schooner goes out with three or four small boats, which sail from the schooner when arrived at the fishing ground, and return, after fishing, to the vessel, and there leave their fish and go out again, and so until they have sufficient, when they return to port.

This morning I saw a new bird, like a guillemot only larger, black head and wings, white beneath. Perchance it might be *Uria grylla* but I don't know, having no description of that bird at hand [likely this was the Common Murre, *Uria aalge*. Ed.].

Now I will give you some miscellaneous items of information that do not belong to any particular day, as they occur to me. (1.) The captain is an American. Suffers from indigestion and is rather irritable. (2.) The purser is a pleasant sort of man, very big and stout (says he weighs 22 stone!), almost globular. Payn is afraid lest he should capsize the ship by putting all his weight on one side. (3.) The doctor plays cards and chess, is companionable, but I don't like him much. (4.) I am in excellent health, have not coughed once the whole voyage through (except when some of that fog got down my throat). Appetite *enormous*. (5.) Some flies continue with us throughout the voyage, concerning which see Ostern Sachen's remarks about the importation of foreign Diptera into America (*Trans. Ent. Soc.*). There is a charming little cat on board, as pretty as Themistocles. (7.) The *German* with the white overcoat I spoke of in my first letter turns out to be a *Frenchman!* So much for my perception of nationality. But I am consoled by finding that everyone else took him to be a German, until they were told. He is a medical student and is going to America for a holiday. (8.) There is a man on board who got married the day we started and went *intermediate* himself and put his *wife* in the *steerage*. Universal opinion: That he ought to be thrown overboard; but nobody does it. (9.) The steerage people find many ways of amusing themselves. Yesterday there was a grand jumping contest, which provided a great deal of fun. (10.) We travel at the rate of over 300 miles in twenty-four hours. 328 miles is the most we have done. (11.) I was talking to the Chemical lecturer (J. William Jones of University College, Cardiff) concerning the colour of snails. He suggests that it is due to refraction and no pigment at all. This is very suggestive. I had not thought of it before. He says that if there *is* any pigment, the way to get it would be this: Take 50 or so (not fewer) shells, say *Helix hortensis* var. *lutea*, dissolve them in dilute acetic acid; evaporate the solution down, and then dissolve the pigment from the lime by alcohol. If there were any pigment you would then have it in solution. Hardly anything is known of the colours of snails, and it might be very worth while to make the experiment.

We have another new bird flying about in some numbers today, taking the place of the 'noddies', which have disappeared. These new birds are black except on the breast, which is white, and have a considerable expanse of wing. They look not unlike crows flying in the distance. They are probably 'Booby Gannets' (*Sula leucogaster* Bodd). This makes the twelfth (or, counting a doubtful gull, thirteenth) species of bird seen since we started from Liverpool.

Looking over the stern of the vessel, I saw three pieces of seaweed, a sign of land. They seemed to resemble *Fucus* but had much longer capsules (color, yellowish-brown). I also saw a little black fish, about three inches long. It wagged its tail at me!

Sunday, July 3rd. Last night we had another most beautiful sunset, but different from the others. First the sun shone out beautifully through a somewhat misty atmosphere, suffusing the sky with a yellow light. Then a belt of cloud came up and obscured it for a while, till the sky beneath the cloud became dull fiery red, and in due course the sun emerged on the other side, the water appearing silvery-green and golden, changing with the waves. Later on we had a little fog, but it soon cleared off.

This morning it is sunny and warm, with a strong west wind. The sea has got up somewhat and each wave bears a crest of foam; as the waves come in contact with the vessel and break, the spray is thrown into the air and the sun shining on it gives momentary but very vivid rainbow effects.

This being Sunday, we had just now a service, the Captain and the Purser conducting it.

We are passing today quantities of gulfweed (*Sargassum bacciferum*; see Thome, p. 235). It looks like this on the water [sketch]. Its colour is straw-yellow, slightly inclining to brown.

Floating here, the gulf-weed is rather out of its latitude, but I suppose it has drifted.

I have talked with the French medical student. I find him interesting. I will describe him to you. *Homo sapiens* L. variety *Frenchman*. Individual, M. Lancry. Rather short, solidly made, strong. Complexion pink, nose short and pug, eyes intelligent, hair very pale. Medical student of Paris, has been examined by Milne Edwards. Goes to America for holiday, will see Niagara and the sights. Takes notes and will write account of it in return. Will finish his medical education in Dublin. Walks up and down the deck, or sits on bench, converses with everyone. Plays with small boy, in which displaying considerable agility. Takes part in jumping contest, jumps pretty well. Does not understand English very well, but knows Latin and Greek. Is learning English out of an *Ollendorff*. Is much fascinated by Darwin, but doubts if species ever merge into one another. Believes in 'celestial origin' of men, and thinks that does not agree with Darwin's conclusions. *Although he is a Frenchman,* thinks Paris the centre of the world as regards all things relating to Art and Science. Is astonished that I have never been to Paris. Now I have introduced Lancry to you. I hope you will know him if you meet!

Monday, July 4th. Last night a thick white fog came on and still continues, the vessel proceeding at half speed part of the time, and continually blowing the fog horn, which makes a loud but far from melodious noise. It is necessary to be very careful in these fogs because collisions frequently occur. The pilot came on board at about five o'clock this morning. The wind has gone down and the sea is calm. I have noticed several brownish medusae, the largest being about five inches across. They appear to be of the same species as those seen on the 27th of June.

Today is a great holiday in America, being the anniversary of the Declaration of Independence. The pilot brought on board some American newspapers: *The New York Herald, The World, The New York Times,* and Henry George [the land reformer and economist. Ed.] and Father McGy-lyum seem to figure very largely in American politics, considering the amount of space given to reports of their speeches. As we are going west we gain half an hour of daylight every day so that the clock has to be put back.

(Evening). The fog has all cleared off and we are getting along well. Some more of the *Anoüs stolidus* (?) have been flying around, and whales are also to be seen as before. We passed a sailing vessel bound, like us, for New York, but as the wind is very slight, she will not get in till long after us. (We expect to be in New York by about ten a.m. tomorrow.)

This evening I saw them sound the depth of the water twice. First the vessel is stopped, and then a long iron cylinder is let down until it touches the bottom. The end of the cylinder contains some grease to which adheres a portion of the sand (if there is sand). The last sounding gave 28 fathoms and a sandy bottom.

The hotel we are going to in New York for the night is called Everett House, and we shall probably start off the next day to Denver, perhaps breaking the journey for a day at St. Louis or Chicago, whichever route we go. A Mr. Butler, to whom Payn has been written about, will meet us and assist us in various ways.

I shall try to post this as soon as I can after landing in New York so as to catch Wednesday's steamer to England, so I shall leave our experiences there for the next epistle.

I am beginning to feel very lonely, and I look forward eagerly to a letter from you. It will be more than a fortnight since I heard anything of you, as we cannot get a letter earlier than our arrival in Denver. There is a curious sort of satisfaction in writing you all the news in a letter. I feel almost as if I were talking to you, and so I have written all about everything that has interested me, as I mean always to do. My spirits are on the whole excellent. I have all the confidence that things will happen as they should. Going into a new country, there will be innumerable things to interest and occupy my mind and to relate to you, so that the time will pass very quickly and as happily as can be expected.

My hopeful sympathy to Annie. To you a most friendly greeting.

Ever yours, Theo D.A. Cockerell

(Postscript) We have just sighted land, and are about 15 miles from Sandy Hook. Here is a drawing to show you what America looks like at first sight! The land is Long Island, which is very flat, and we cannot see anything but the trees (apparently) by the shore. It is rather misty or we should see more. We lost some time in the night in this wise: One of the men saw something dark in the moonlight, which seemed to be a boat with people in it, so we stopped and steamed round to it. It was, however, lost sight of, and altogether about an hour was spent in the search. When it was discovered it turned out to be nothing more than an old hen-coop that had been thrown overboard from some passing vessel!

Unfortunately the tide is against us, and low water is at one o'clock, so it seems we shall not be able to cross the bar and get into New York till sunset.

We have got over the bar all right after all, and shall be in by one. Just now we passed Sandy Hook, which lies very low and appears to be covered with coarse grass, and has some buildings on it and a lighthouse. There are numbers of sailing vessels at anchor, waiting for a change of wind, and two of the peculiar passenger steamers (as drawn) have passed. We are going down the deep water channel which is about 100 yards wide and is marked by black and white buoys on one side and red ones on the other.

Now we are passing between the Brooklyn end of Long Island and Staten Island. There is a fort on each side to command the entrance to New York. Staten Island is nice and green, and the higher parts are covered with pines and sugar maples. A sailing vessel is just coming in beside us deeply laden with wood.

We are waiting opposite Staten Island for the quarantine Doctor to come to board and see that we have no infectious disease, before we go into New York. At our stern lies an American steamer, the *Niagara*. The green banks of Staten Island look good for snails! I wish I could get at them. The shore is covered with great blocks of grey stone, and the telegraph runs close to the water, the poles being planted amongst the stones. (I write all this in pencil so that I need not go down into the saloon, as I don't want to leave the deck and miss seeing something).

The quarantine official has left us and we proceed. The Brooklyn Bridge and colossal Statue of Liberty have just come in sight, It is coming on to rain.

We are now on the wharf and our baggage is landed. We wait while the Customs official examines our things. Mine have been examined and no duty charged. Payn's have not yet come, as his big chest has not yet been taken out of the hold. It is very hot, and the place swarms with *Musca domestica* (house flies).

The *Wisconsin* (also Union Line) is close by, just ready to sail to England. There are hundreds of bales of raw cotton on the wharf, waiting to be shipped to England. *This* part of New York at any rate looks dirty and uninteresting, but then of course London is not much to look at down at the Docks.

4:30. Here is a nice state of things! Payn's chest has got stowed away ever so far down, and is not out yet, and the Customs people won't pass the rest without it. Payn stands guard over the baggage landed, and I had just come on board to look after the chest when the vessel backed out into the river to make way for the *Wisconsin*, and I don't suppose we shall be back again so that I can land for another hour or so. Probably by the time the chest is landed it will be too late to have it examined, and we shall have to leave all the baggage on the quay. Altogether I feel rather riled, and no doubt Payn more so! Butler, who was to have met us, has not turned up.

Everett House, 5:45. All's well that ends well! The *Wisconsin* soon steamed out, and we in. Meanwhile Butler (I find him a nice man) had arrived, and baggage passed through Customs all right (chest was left on ship, to come in tomorrow). Will write all about it. New York (most curious and somewhat beautiful city) is next. Must get this posted now.

Niagara Falls, July 7th, 1887

I have a letter for you in progress, but we have been traveling about so much that I cannot finish it up to date this evening. We are at Niagara Falls, and have seen everything and have been in the Cave of the Winds under the fall which you shall hear more of. We start from Buffalo for Denver tonight at 12:30. Everything is very new and wonderful. I wish you and Annie could see it all; perhaps some day you may. I like to dream that I shall one day show you all these things that I can now only describe. We came up the River Hudson in the train yesterday evening — scenery beautiful. I have found innumerable insects and plants, but not many snails. *Malva rotundifolia* is one of the commonest weeds here.

Yours, Theo. D.A.C.

Everett House, Union Square, July 5th, 1887

The last epistle (which I consigned to a pillar box on 5th Avenue) gave details up to landing in New York, and this commences with our starting for the hotel. Wm. Butler, who was on the quay with Payn when I finally escaped from the *Nevada*, has been most kind and helpful to us and has shown us some of the principal parts of the town. Leaving the wharf, we got into a tramcar which took us to Union Square (fare five cents, any distance). (Here I was interrupted by the entrance of one Knowles and friend, and Payn and I walking out with him — of which account in due course.)

As I went along in the tramcar from the Docks, I had a good opportunity of seeing what New York was like. It is about as little like London as you can possibly imagine. Most of the houses are brick red (*red-brick* as in London does not convey the same idea) and have green shutters to the windows, giving more the effect of some tropical town than of such a city as London. Trees flourish everywhere, growing luxuriantly by the roadside, particularly the *Ailanthus* tree [of *The Tree grows in Brooklyn* fame. Ed.]. The whole place looks fresh and clean, except that the pavement is bad and the roads consequently muddy. The policemen are most comic-looking creatures and wear grey hats. Letter boxes are not as in England, but are affixed to the lamp posts and at very frequent intervals, and are of course much smaller than ours. Everett House is a very big place, and looks out on to Union Square, which is a large square about the size of Trafalgar Square, only filled with trees and grass.

After leaving our things at Everett House, we went on to Butler's Club House on Fifth Avenue, where he had asked us to dine. This Club House is a most luxurious place and quite different from anything English, but most strange of all was our first American dinner. The first course was *clams*, that is to say, *Mercenaria* dished up raw in its shell, to be eaten thus with salt and pepper, with a sprinkling of lemon juice. Conchologically, they interested me and they were not *very* nasty. Then we had some queer American fish (they call it *basse* over here), and *snipe*, which, being interpreted, is a sandpiper or Johannus — very good eating though.

Then we had a genuinely American drink, and my curiosity overcame my abhorrence of alcohol, and I partook. It is made in this fashion: A glass is filled full of ice, then white wine and Appollinarian water are poured in (to fill up interstices) in about equal proportions. Result, an ice-cold drink tasting of wine, not very bad, but inferior to iced water. To finish up, we had coffee, which is served *very* strong and without milk. After dinner, Butler took us round and showed us Broadway and Fifth Avenue, but it was already getting dark and so we could not see very much. The whole place is lighted up with electric light. Tram cars run everywhere, and overhead is the railway, which, as you know, goes along considerably above the level of the streets. On these railways one can go eight miles for five cents, but five cents is also the minimum charge for any distance. After Butler left us, I sat down to commence this letter when in came Knowles, a somewhat idiotic sort of man who came across with us on the *Nevada*, bringing with him a friend. Payn was going out with him, so I went too, that I might see a little more of the city. We went round in a tram car for a while but did not see much. At one place the car went through a long tunnel under the road, lit up by electric light. Payn, Knowles, and friend went and 'had a drink' and then went off to play billiards. As it was late I came away and wrote more of this. Since then, Payn has returned.

The tram cars here run the whole night through, and business never seems to leave off. Advertising is greatly in favour, and it is characteristic that the side of a house overlooking the best part of the city is covered by a huge advertisement. Telegraph poles of a most primitive kind are in every street, and from them wires, innumerable dangle like a cobweb.

July 6th. Last night there was some lightning, and this morning a heavy thunderstorm, and since then a good deal of rain, for all of which the New Yorkers are thankful since it cools the air and prevents the intense heat they have been suffering of late. After breakfast this morning we went in a tram car (I should say *road* car — they don't call them tram cars here) down Broadway to Butler's office, where we arranged various matters and discussed how we should travel. We shall start from here today by a train leaving a little after six. The General Post Office stands conspicuously in Broadway, and is a very big affair. I found a postcard from Mother waiting there for us, which was very welcome. Afterwards, I went to get some books, but with small success. But I got Coulter's *Manual of Rocky Mountain Botany*, which is a most admirable book, for $1.50. It gives an account of every flowering plant and vascular cryptogam of the district. I have not had much opportunity of noting the fauna and

10

flora of New York: *Passer domestica* [the English sparrow. Ed.] aboundeth, and *Plantago major* occurs in a garden on Fifth Avenue together with some *Polygonum* (I am not sure which species). White butterflies fly about; they look like *Pieris rapae* [the cabbage butterfly, Ed.], but not having caught any I cannot tell. An *Orgyia* abounds on the trees, just as the Vapourer moth does in London — I believe the species is *O. leucostigma* (I have one of the larvae by me; it is pale yellow with a brown head and a red-brown dorsal stripe on the last segments). The only indication of Mollusca I have seen is that some asparagus we had for supper had evidently been gnawed by a slug! Living here is very expensive, and so it is expedient not to stay over another night. Payn has gone out with Knowles to make some purchases.

July 9th (in train, Chicago, Burlington & Quincy RR). The last written dates only to New York. The last day or two we have been traveling all the time and so there was no opportunity for writing, except a postcard from Niagara Falls. On the evening of July 6th at six o'clock we started for Buffalo. Butler came with us to the station and helped us in getting our baggage checked. As I went through the waiting room at the station, someone touched my shoulder and, turning round, there was our friend Lancry, going off to Canada. The train traveled along the east side of the Hudson River all that evening and part of the night. (I attempted to continue this letter on another sheet, but train too jolting, could not write straight, so continue on arrival at Denver.)

Denver, Colorado, July 10th.

(July 6th — continued). That evening we saw the Hudson to advantage, except that it got dark too soon. It is very broad, at places more than a mile across, and on one side the bank is very steep, in some places a cliff, and all along sloping up to a range of mountains behind. All this is overgrown with creepers and herbage, and at the top, trees. And the whole scene, as we saw it from the train on the east bank, was very beautiful. Sailing vessels and steamers were going up and down, and at anchor we saw Jay Gould's yacht, in which this notorious monopolist goes up to town each day. As we went along, I kept a good look out for plants, etc., and saw many strange ones. The British *Chrysanthemum leucanthemum* has become naturalized in America and was very abundant alongside the railroad track. The last thing we saw that night were the lights of Newburgh, and after that we turned in to sleep. We had sleeping cars, as is usual for night journeys, but altogether the American railroad system is so different from the English that I must describe it to you.

First, the engine: You know the appearance of an American engine, the peculiarly shaped funnel, and the pilot or cow-catcher in front, to throw anything off the line. Then there is a large bell, placed close to the boiler, and connected by a string to the driver's seat, so that he may ring the bell whenever crossing a road or coming into the station, to notify that he is coming. These bells sound just like church-bells (when the church has only one) and their constant ringing in the towns as the trains go by is rather disturbing to anyone not used to it. Then, the cars: These are very long, and have doors at the ends, and *never* at the sides. They are all connected together, so that one can walk from one end of the train to the other while it is in motion. The seats are all placed so as to face the engine, and there is a passageway down the middle of the car. Each car is provided with plenty of iced water for drinking, which, in this hot weather, is very much appreciated. The sleeping cars are somewhat different; in the day the beds fold up and the whole apparatus is stowed away so that the bottom of the upper berth forms part of the roof of the car, thus [sketch].

The trains burn very soft coal, and the quantity of cinders and dust arising therefrom is enormous, so that one has the choice of being half roasted by shutting the window in this hot weather, or covered with dust that flies in if the window is opened. The American stations are very strange-looking places; most of them have hardly any or no platform at all, and one just gets off the train on to the ground, which is boarded over in the stations. In England, 'passengers mustn't cross the line' and all that, but in America it would hardly be possible to get to one's train otherwise than by crossing the line, unless the train happened to come up on the nearest rail.

Trains run right through the most crowded thoroughfares of a town just as if they were tram cars, and nobody takes any more notice of them. They go slowly and keep ringing the bell, so it is easy enough to get out of the way. If you buy a ticket (except it is an excursion one or otherwise specially stated) it is good not only for that day, but for any other, instead of being limited to the day of issue as in England. Luggage you give in charge at the station and it is checked right through. Thus, we have checked our boxes from New York to Denver and shall get them there on application, having had no bother on the way about them.

All along the railroad, on every available fence or rock, are innumerable advertisements, mostly of patent medicines. One of the prettiest spots on the Hudson River is covered with a huge advertisement of somebody's pills [probably Lydia Pinkham's. Ed.], painted in capital letters on the face of the rock. I am glad to hear that a law has been enacted making it illegal to thus deface natural scenery, but it seems to be not rigorously enough in force.

It is now getting late, and as I want to get this off so as to go by six o'clock post tomorrow morning. I will give a brief abstract of events up to date and send detailed narrative commencing July 7th, in next letter.

July 7th. Arrived in Buffalo early in morning; spent day at Niagara Falls and saw rapids, etc.; started by 12:30 train from Buffalo.

July 8th. Discovered that our train went into Canada and through St. Thomas, so stopped there and went to Chicago by next train. Had five hours with Douglas; found him well and seemingly on very good terms with everyone there. Saw the bank, and his room there and ev-

erything. Arrived in Chicago at 9:30 that evening and took train (10:40) west.

July 9th. All day in train; got as far as Lincoln (Nebraska) by nightfall.

July 10th. Arrived in Denver at about seven p.m. Went to the American Hotel. All well so far.

We have another day's journey to get to West Cliff (near Pueblo) where Cardwell Lees, to whom we are going, is living. We wait to hear from him before starting. Today being Sunday, we cannot get any letters that are waiting for us at the post office, which is disappointing, but we shall have them first thing tomorrow morning. Farewell! My love to Annie. I hope I shall hear of both of you by post tomorrow, though I suppose we have got here almost as soon as your letter.

Enclosed are seeds of *Rumex salicifolius* Weinmann from McCook, Nebraska. It is a dock with glabrous leaves, not remarkable to look at, but interesting for comparison with the other species. Probably it will grow well at Isleworth.

Denver, July 11th, 1887

Dear Frederic,

(July 7th). On waking early in the morning, I found we had arrived at Rochester, and between six and seven arrived at Buffalo. Here we waited for a train to take us to Suspension Bridge (Niagara rapids and whirlpool) and, while waiting in the station, I captured several species of *Ephemera* (mayflies), some of them large, and also some other insects and a green caterpillar with red spots. The train for Suspension Bridge did not start until more than an hour after the time advertised, at which time all the people had got in. I wonder they waited there so patiently all that time. They seemed to be used to such long delays!

The tickets through to Denver were good to cover the journey to Suspension Bridge, but when the train had started we found that we had got into one belonging to a different line, so we had to pay the fares from Buffalo to Suspension Bridge and back over again, which was very unfortunate. At Suspension Bridge, however, I found a man who had bought a return ticket to go to the races that were on at Niagara and was not going to use the other half, so I got my return ticket at a 28 cent reduction, the full fare being 58 cents. Between Buffalo and Suspension Bridge we passed the end of Lake Erie, looking beautifully blue, and like the sea.

Arrived at Suspension Bridge station, we went down and saw the rapids and the whirlpool. It is necessary to go down the cliff, which is very high and quite perpendicular, in an elevator which lands us at the bottom at the edge of the water. The rapids are very interesting. First the water is clear and smooth, looking like a lake, though there is an immensely strong undercurrent. Then a little farther down, the river narrows and the water breaks up into immense waves crested with foam, and dashes along at frightful speed till at last it flows into the whirlpool, a large, nearly circular basin with nearly smooth water and a strong current. Men bathe in the smooth water above the rapids, but at considerable risk. Only last Sunday one was carried away by the current and drowned.

Everyone at Suspension Bridge talks of Captain Webb and is very anxious that we should know exactly where he was drowned. One man contrived to photograph Webb as he went through the rapids, and they showed us the photograph, with his head and shoulder appearing minute and black in the distance amongst the foam. Down by the rapids there was plenty of vegetation and many curious and interesting flowers I had not seen before. *Oxalis corniculata* was growing close to the water (I sent a specimen in my last letter, for Annie). We also found many insects — beetles, etc., and a few species of butterflies, viz., a *Thecla*, *Pieris rapae* (abundant), *Colias philodice* (very common; this is a sulphur coloured species) and *Anotia plexippus* (= *Danais archippus*) of which last we also got a larva — a curious larva with yellow black and white rings and long black filaments on the body, two anteriorly and two shorter posteriorly. After coming up from the rapids we wandered round for a while, but could not walk much as it was so intensely hot.

At midday we went to an hotel for dinner and both had our hair cut. You remember that my hair was getting long when I left England. Now it is so short that you would think I had just come out of prison. Thus shorn, I present rather a comic appearance, as you will imagine. The barber took a great interest in matters English and questioned us much. He was an Englishman himself though he had not been there since he was a few months old. Everywhere we go we are recognized as English directly we speak, and wherever we meet a fellow-countryman (and we meet many) he always stops to ask all about home and particularly whether we come from his part or know his town. These meetings are very pleasant, and it is very nice to find how willing any Englishman is to assist us and tell us all we want to know, just because we come from the 'old' country.

At the hotel they charged us half-a-dollar each for a meal, which to you will seem a lot, but we really considered it moderate compared to what we had paid before! Meals on the trains, for instance, are a dollar each. Certainly in America a dollar will not buy what two shillings will in England, the difference in prices of almost everything in America being at least a third more than in England, and often more than that. Wages, however, are high, so that to residents the balance is about even, but to those who, like ourselves, have brought all our money from England, prices are quite ruinous here.

After leaving the hotel, we got a man to drive us to the Niagara Falls and on to Goat Island, which is between the American and Horseshoe Falls. I had seen innumerable photographs of the falls and thought I knew exactly what they were like, yet when actually in the presence of these immense masses of water rushing over, it was impossible to feel anything but wonder, and a new interest which photographs and descriptions had not given.

At the foot of the falls are great dark rocks, and the spray dashes up and is drifted away in clouds like steam. The river immediately below widens out into a great basin where the little steamer, *Maid of the Mist*, goes to and fro.

Then we went down through the 'Cave of the Winds' in this manner: At the top of the cliff, by the fall, there is a wooden house, where we took off all our clothes and attired ourselves in woolen shirt and trousers, oilskin jacket, and shoes made in the most primitive fashion out of some substance resembling very thick flannel calculated to hold firm and not slip on the rocks. Thus dressed, we proceeded down a circular flight of steps leading to the bottom of the cliff, and then along a pathway under the cliff at the foot of the fall.

Having arrived close to the fall, the guide led us along a boarded way with rails on each side (as diagram A above railing seen going round, arrow marks where we went, and direction), we came to the end of the railing just where the water came down and the spray dashed up into our eyes so that we could hardly see. Then we got upon the rock and climbed underneath the part of the fall marked X in the diagram and out on the other side. Under the fall the cliff is hollowed out, and this is what is called the Cave of the Winds. As we climbed along, the spray dashed violently against us, and a strong wind, produced by the falling water, blew us against the rock so that we could hardly have fallen into the surging water even had we been so inclined. Coming out on the other side we climbed round and got on to the footway again, and round in front of the fall. Here the spray dashed up and blinded our eyes if we attempted to look in the direction of the fall.

Among the rocks I found some fragments of a species of *Unio*, and further along the moss of which I sent a piece in my last letter was growing abundantly. When once again on the cliff-top,

and in our own clothes, we went round and saw the Horseshoe Falls and Prospect Park, which is the best place from which to see the whole falls. The American government has had the good sense to turn all the ground about Niagara on their side into public property so that every part can be visited by anyone and without payment or hindrance, except that they charge for going down to the Cave of the Winds.

By Niagara I found *Helix alternata* living abundantly, one *Hyalina nitida*, and in the water, *Sphaerium, Planorbis bicarinatus, Physa ancillaria*, etc. All sorts of plants were seen that were new to me, and the familiar *Malva rotundifolia* (which is found in Bedford Park) was a very common weed. I also saw a 'robin', so-called in America — but really a red-breasted thrush, *Turdus migratorius*.

The town of Niagara Falls consists mainly of a single principal street with others branching out. At a shop there they showed us a genuine Indian scalp, which they thought much of, as they are extremely difficult to get; no Indian will sell one or part with one unless killed or taken prisoner. Of course scalping is almost a thing of the past. We went to a hotel for our evening meal and found our host an Englishman from near Birmingham, a most agreeable and kindly man.

At about 9:30 we took the train for Buffalo and waited here till the 12:30 train west started. Waiting at Buffalo, I chanced to look at a railway map of the Michigan Central Railway on which we were to travel, and discovered what I had never dreamt of, that we were going *north* of Lake Erie into Canada, and should pass St. Thomas! So without delay I made enquiries and discovered that there was another train, starting hours later, which, being a fast one, would still be in time to catch the 12:40 train from Chicago next evening. So I arranged with Payn that he should go on the train as already arranged, while I got off at St. Thomas and spent the interval of five hours between this and the next (fast) train with Douglas, following on after that and meeting him at Chicago Station. (N.B. They call railway stations 'depots' here, *never* stations.)

July 8th. The train was advertised to reach St. Thomas at 4:20 so I did not go to sleep that night lest I should miss the station. We did not get there, however, till five, and as the train was running by 'Central Time' it was six by New York time. Of course you will understand that the time is different in various places across the continent, and for convenience they have four different standards of time, each one hour different from the next. Thus, 'Eastern Time' is used in New York and at St. Thomas, 'Central Time' at Chicago, 'Mountain Time' at Denver, and 'Pacific Time' at San Francisco.

Having reached St. Thomas, I found my way to the bank, which is at the other end of the town, and naturally, considering the hour, found it shut. Some side windows, though, were open, and I contrived to attract the attention of a clerk, who was dressing at the time. Having explained who I was, the door was opened and he showed me into Douglas' room. Douglas usually sleeps at the bank, but that night he was at the Boyd's, so I waited while the clerk finished dressing, and then he went with me in search of Douglas, who was considerably astonished to see me, as I had written particularly to say I should not be able to come.

We went to the bank, and Douglas got leave to be out with me till I left, so we went for a walk round the suburbs of the town. I found some shells (Hyalina nitida principally, also Cochlicopa lubrica and Limax agrestis), and saw some interesting birds, particularly a yellow finch, like a siskin, with black markings [goldfinch. Ed.], which is locally called a 'canary'.

We passed by a great women's college where females come from far and near to be instructed. The people of St. Thomas call it 'The Angel Factory'! Two Indian 'squaws' are studying there and are going up for an examination to be held shortly. The whites don't like the idea of being beaten by squaws, they say. I saw a squaw at St. Thomas station; it is not a pretty object.

After our walk, we went to several of the shops in the town where Douglas had to call to collect drafts for the bank, and then we went and had breakfast, for which the charge was only 20 cents, the cheapest meal I have had in America. The train arrived soon after ten and I started off again to Chicago. We went by way of Detroit, and then there is a broad river connecting Lakes Erie and Michigan. As there was no bridge, the whole train was run on to a sort of gigantic ferry boat and ferried over. We got to Chicago punctually at 9:30 and were driven in an omnibus to the station of the Chicago, Burlington & Quincy Railway where we got on the 10:40 train, and as I had had a long day and was tired, I soon got to sleep.

July 9th. Waking early next morning, I looked out of the window and found we were at a place called Gladstone, in Illinois, and very soon we crossed the Mississippi and were at Burlington, Iowa. All that day we traveled in the train. At Chariton, Iowa, we found a very pretty *Chrysomela*, and by the railway track were some very familiar plants: *Brassica sinapis* and *Chenopodium album*. A very pretty lily (*Lilium philadelphicum*) with orange-brown flowers, is very common in the woods, and also near St. Thomas. We changed cars at Pacific Junction and thereafter crossed the Missouri, a great wide muddy river flowing with a strong current, and arrived after dark at Lincoln, Nebraska.

At Chicago we met a man named H. J. Jod, who comes from India (was coffee-planting there) and is also going to West Cliff to see his brother who lives there. He traveled with us and is a very pleasant companion. When we were at Lincoln and had just taken off our shoes preparatory for bed, we were looking at the people of all sorts assembled in the station, and to see better, Jod and I walked down a couple of cars and looked out from the platform of one of them.

After a while, we went back to regain our sleeping car, when what was the horror to find it was detached and had disappeared! Imagine finding ourselves in Lincoln, abandoned without luggage or even shoes or hats. Happily though, we rediscovered our car before it started; it had been shunted to another line, and we thankfully went to bed.

July 10th. Through Nebraska and to Denver! Nebraska is a prairie state different from the others we passed through. For hours we traveled over treeless undulating land with nothing to be seen but herds of cattle and horses and, at intervals, settlers' houses. One of the first places we came to was 'Mystic City', which consisted of about a dozen small wooden houses! They call all these places *cities* in anticipation in America. Then we came to Oxford, where we found *Solanum rostratum*, a very prickly potato-like plant with yellow flowers. Beyond Oxford was Cambridge, where Payn secured a pretty little butterfly called *Nathalis iola*, and a Colorado Beetle, *Leptinotarsus decem-lineata*.

Then we had to wait more than an hour at McCook, and about here found *Pieris protodice*, *Anotia plexippus*, *Nathalis iola* and, among plants, *Rumex salicifolius* (of which I sent seeds), *Setaria viridis* (a Bedford Park species), and *Cnicus* (*Cirsium*. Ed.) *ochrocentrus*. The common sunflower, *Helianthus annuus*, is the commonest weed in Nebraska and Colorado, and lines the railway track for miles. It looks strange to see it growing wild in such profusion. The prairie is in many places covered with cacti, which scarcely rise more than a few inches above the ground, and there are many little piles of earth, on which sit 'prairie dogs' (they are rodents resembling the European marmot somewhat). These are pretty little animals and look very comic sitting each one bolt upright on his mound.

There are numbers of wooden houses of settlers, looking very neat and comfortable, and each with a field or two of Indian corn or wheat or potatoes. I think, though, they must have rather a hard time of it. I should not like to be so isolated as they are. About 6:15 we saw the Rocky Mountains rising high in a long chain in the distance, in places still with snow on them, and at seven we were in Denver, and were driven in an omnibus to the American House Hotel, where we stayed.

July 11th. Next morning I was up early and to the post office, but it did not open till eight, so I went round the town. It is much like other American towns — streets wide with tram cars and electric lit houses, many of them of red brick and many of wood, in long streets, looking irregular because of different heights and sizes, telegraph poles along each road, population rough-looking with broad-brimmed hats (my grey hat is quite the thing here). Many Chinese about, in blue coats; all the washing is done by the Chinese.

At eight I was again at the Post Office, but, alas! no letters (and none have arrived up to the time of writing, six p.m. on July 12th). Perhaps I should not have expected any, as there would be hardly time for them to reach here yet. Then I went to the office of the *Labor Enquirer* (the Socialist League of Denver). The editor was out, but the compositor and another were in, and I called next day and saw the editor. They all welcomed me in the most hearty manner and made all sorts of enquiries about the Socialist movement in England. They seem to be getting on well here. They have an audience of 200 at their Sunday evening lectures, which is distinctly better than at Hammersmith! After breakfast we went out to make some purchases and to arrange about drawing the money ($200 we have) from the bank when we want it.

July 12th. No news from Cardwell Lees yet! We wrote to him from New York, asking him to write at once, and we have telegraphed from here. No doubt, as he is 18 miles from the station, he has not received these messages yet, as he probably does not go to the Post Office for his letters more than once a week. So we have decided to go to West Cliff by the 8:20 a.m. train tomorrow.

Today I went to the Public Library here, but they have no scientific works. I noticed a half-dozen of G. M. Fenn's books down in the catalogue. There is also a sort of Natural History Society here, but they have no meetings. I went to look up the president of it (Dr. Bancroft) and he was out at the time.

I will now finish this up. I write next from West Cliff. So far things have gone fairly well on the whole. Expenses are greater than we expected, and we are rather difficultly placed through having heard nothing from Lees but no doubt we shall find him without difficulty when we get there and it will be all right. My health is excellent, and I do not cough at all. Greetings to Annie

West Cliff, Custer Co., Colorado,
July 14th, 1887

Dear Frederic,

Yesterday morning we started off by train and arrived here in the evening, having passed through Pueblo and changed cars at Cañon City. Between Cañon City and here we passed for miles along a magnificent gorge in the mountains — high rocks on either side and a river flowing in the valley. But I will write about this later. We met a most pleasant and altogether nice man of the name of [C.S.] Cox, with wife and family, in the train. He turned out to be a great friend of Lees, and told us that Lees, not knowing we were coming out so soon, was starting off to British Columbia on a shooting excursion, and it is doubtful whether we shall catch him before starting. So Cox, with great kindness, asked us to go to him while making the necessary arrangements for setting up for ourselves. Cox's ranch is on the slope of the mountains, some miles from here.

We slept last night at the West Cliff Hotel, and go on to Cox's place today. The air here is splendid. We are about 7,800 feet above the level of the sea and surrounded by high mountains, some with snow. The population of this place is about 500, but there are about 1,000 at Silver Cliff, which is quite close. Formerly there was a great rush for the mines at Silver Cliff, and 15,000

people came here. Cox says it is possible to write to England from here and get an answer in about 25 days. The flowers here are very interesting. I have found no Mollusca today.

When I found, in 1887, that I was going to Colorado, I searched for literature on the Mollusca of the Rocky Mountains, and found Ingersoll's report in one of the volumes of the Hayden Survey. As compared with many other countries, the Rocky Mountains are poor in snails and slugs; there is, in fact, only one native species of slug in Colorado. Thus, although I collected what I could, I found it expedient to take up other lines of research, and naturally turned to the very abundant and varied insects.

Recollections of a Naturalist—See Weber(2000).

West Cliff, July 15th, 1887

(Some spell it Westcliffe).
Dear Frederic,

(July 12th) My last letter had this date and gave you account of my doings up till then. We left the American House Hotel on the next day (13th) and took the train for West Cliff. The American House is a large white building standing at the corner of the road. They treated us fairly well, and the charge was 2½ dollars a day each, which, for America, is rather moderate. Do you remember when [Henry] Irving's secretary lectured at Bedford Park, and amused us by telling how he found a notice at one of the American hotels asking people not to *blow out* the gas? At the American House we found a notice up as follows:

'Do not blow out or smother the gaslight. If you don't know how to operate the gas, ring the bell and ask the porter!'

July 13th. Wednesday. The train started at 8:20, and the post office opened at 8:00. I had to be there punctually and hurry to the station. A postcard from Mother dated 27th was the only one for me. H. J. Jod went with us to West Cliff as I think I told you; he is going to live with his brother who lives near West Cliff and has gotten into difficulties with his ranch, and his brother goes to try to set him right again. Jod is a very good sort of man, rather like Richard John Gifford Read in appearance and manner. He had been coffee-planting for many years out in India but was not very successful.

When we left Denver we noticed, near the town, some more *Solanum rostratum*, which seems to be common in all the lower districts of Colorado, and we saw for the first time the Prickly Poppy, *Argemone platyceras*, a large poppy with conspicuous white flowers, prickles all over the stem, and bright yellow juice. This poppy is also abundant near the station at West Cliff. Near Palmer Lake, as the train passes, I saw a specimen of *Ceryle alcyon*, the Belted Kingfisher, which has once or twice been shot in England. At Palmer Lake the common English *Achillea millefolium* [actually *A. lanulosa*. Ed.] was very abundant, and this grows also at West Cliff. The train stopped at Pike View, which is near Pike's Peak, and here I got some beetles and flowers, and two spiders which I have posted off to Rev. O. P. Cambridge (it cost me *one cent* to send these spiders; to send them from London to O.P.C. would cost two cents!) All the while, between Denver and Pueblo, although we were on the plain, we passed close along the mountains and had a good view of them.

At Pueblo we stopped for lunch. It is very funny to see, whenever we stop in traveling for a meal, the competition among the hotel keepers and eating house people to attract customers from the train. At Pueblo, no sooner had the train come to a standstill than gongs were heard loudly sounding from all sides, and at each of the eating houses (about half a dozen) that were in sight, one saw the host at his door, banging away at the gong, trying to make more noise than anyone else and to attract attention!

From Pueblo to Cañon City we passed along the Arkansas River, which is shallow and very muddy — the river shifts a good deal from one course to another — within certain limits, and must formerly have been a much larger stream than now, as can be seen from the formation of its banks. The soil forming the banks of the Arkansas River is in distinct layers, and there can be no doubt that it was formed so by each summer the mud drying hard on the bank, and the next year another layer covering it and also drying, and so on. The same process, indeed, can be seen going on now in some parts of the river.

At Cañon City we changed trains and got into the West Cliff train, which had only one passenger car (the most being trucks and luggage vans), and this very crowded so that we had to ride on the outside platform. After leaving Cañon City we traveled along by Grape Creek, a river which runs through a gorge in the mountains almost all the way between Cañon City and West Cliff. All along here the scenery was magnificent, though rather monotonous from its sameness. At the bottom ran the river and the railway line, and steeply sloping up on either side were the mountains of reddish stone, dotted with bushes of dark green, stunted vines and creepers.

On the train we met C. S. Cox, with wife and baby, and getting into conversation with him found that he lived not very far from Cardwell Lees and was a great friend of his. He told us that Lees was just going away (perhaps had gone already) to British Columbia to hunt, and would not be back for a long while, and therefore Cox, in the most kind manner, asked us to come and stay with him until we could settle down for ourselves, and this we gladly agreed to do.

July 15th. Arriving at West Cliff we went to the Hotel (there is only one) where the host (by name Cox (though no relative of our other friend) treated us kindly and gave us a good dinner, after which we strolled round and talked with some of the people of the place. I got some beetles, etc., and found a very pretty mallow-like flower, *Malvastrum coccineum* [= *Sphaeralcea*] with bright red petals, growing profusely, as also a pretty blue flax, *Linum perenne* [*Adenolinum lewisii*], and large white thistles [*Cirsium canescens*], *Argemone*, and *Potentilla*. So that you may understand the narrative after our arrival at West Cliff, I must now give some account of the district. This map is extremely rough and does not give the distance accurately. It is a little over seven miles from West Cliff to Cox's, but only 3/4 mile from us to Cox's. Wet Mountain Valley is a broad plain, at different points 8,000 feet more or less above the level of the sea, nearly flat, treeless and grassy, surrounded by mountains which rise up to nearly 14,000 feet. Grape Creek runs through its northern portion, and passing with the railway through the cañon, joins the Arkansas River at Cañon City.

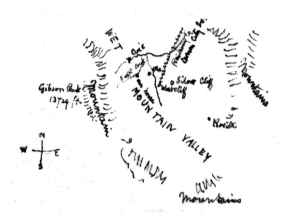

West Cliff district — or Wet Mountain, Colorado

There are four 'towns' in the valley. Rosita is to the south, and I have not yet seen it. I believe it is not much of a place. Ula [pronounced You-lay] consists of three or four houses, or rather huts. It was formerly the 'post town' and so it came to be on the maps. Silver Cliff has about 1,000 inhabitants and boasts a *brick* house, which is a very grand thing in these parts, all the other houses being of wood, mostly painted white.

Silver Cliff is the principal place in the district for silver mining, and some years ago, when the silver was first discovered, there was a great rush for the mines, and about 15,000 people were in the place at one time, but mining was not the success they expected, and very soon what had promised to become a big town dwindled down to its present proportions, a small and insignificant village.

West Cliff, two years ago, consisted of only a few houses, but now the railway has come and the postoffice is there, many houses have been built and there are about 500 residents, with an hotel, a bank, and plenty of shops.

View across the valley to the Wet Mountains

Most of the people are employed in mining or ranching and are a very rough set on the whole. Law, as understood in England, does not exist, and Cox says it is as easy to buy over a judge as to buy one's dinner. Lynching is not very rare, and if a man is killed, usually nothing happens to his murderer than that he has to leave Colorado. Still there is probably more fellow-feeling among these people than in England and they will do much to help one another, though they will also swindle each other to any extent when they get the chance. Horses sometimes get stolen, but petty thieving is extremely rare, and we can leave our cabin with the door open for days without much fear of anything being stolen.

To give an example of the power of the *law* in this place: There is a man named Hugg living close by, and he owes some money which he refuses to pay, so a bailiff went up to seize his property. But when he came to the house, Hugg was at the door with a gun, and told the bailiff he had nothing against him, but if he came a foot nearer he would blow his brains out. So the officer of the law had to retreat, and Hugg remains victorious!

The climate here is excellent. Just now, though, it is the rainy season and we have had a good deal of rain and thunderstorms, and it has been rather cold except when he sun is out. The air is much rarified so that at first it is difficult to breathe, and I soon get out of breath.

The mountains are rocky, but the valley is grassy, with large stones and no trees. There are firs and other trees on the mountains. Antelopes exist, though I have seen none, and also prairie wolves or coyotes (*Canis latrans*) and prairie-dogs. A very pretty rodent, brown and striped, with a long tail, called a chipmunk, is very common all about. Another species called a gopher, grayer and with a short tail, is also very abundant. Jack rabbits are common. There are deer on the hills, and badgers, more than one kind of bear, also pumas or mountain lions, and wild sheep.

Of birds, there are prairie hens, plenty of wild doves, hummingbirds (common), martins, magpies, Turkey buzzards, a sort of plover, etc. Snakes are common, and also a sort of prickly lizard they call a 'horned toad.' Rattlesnakes are by no means rare, and Cox says we are sure to see some before we return. Trout exist in the streams, insects are in great profusion, especially Coleoptera and Hymenoptera. There are plenty of butterflies, *Colias eurytheme* being the commonest. Grasshoppers abound. Mollusca are very rare and I have only got a few species: *Helix pulchella, Hyalina, Comulus, Succinea,* and *Pupa.* Flowers are in great profusion and very beautiful. The evening primrose, *Oenothera biennis* [*O. villosa*] that you see in Bedford Park gardens, grows wild here, and hundreds of flowers I have never seen before.

July 14th. In the morning, Jod, Cox (of the hotel) and I went over to Silver Cliff and saw the mines. I was much interested. They find silver here usually in the form of chloride, which is a sort of olive-green, but also more rarely they get it native. There is also iron and manganese. They have a huge engine for crushing and sifting the ore. First of all, the rock in which the silver is, is hewn out and taken in trucks to the engine house. Here it is put in under a crushing machine which reduces it to powder. Then, together with a stream of water, it is washed onto a machine which moves to and fro and shakes it up, and the water flowing over removes all the lighter particles and leaves behind the black metallic ore, which has a higher specific gravity than the rock. This is then put into sacks and sent to the smelters, most of the smelting being done at Pueblo.

About mid-day Cardwell Lees turned up, not having yet started. He seems a very nice sort of man. (Just at this point Cox came with the cart to ask me to go down to West Cliff, so I left this off, and the other letters I had to write, as I may not be down here again for some days.) We are now in a little three-roomed house near Cox's and on his ranch, which he has let us. We are getting along excellently, but will write all about that next post.

Letters from Mother and Carlie [brother Sydney] at postoffice. None from you. Do write. Greetings to Annie. *Colias eurytheme* enclosed. (Enclosed also): Moss gathered close to Niagara Falls where spray dashes up as one goes down to Cave of the Winds. *Oxalis corniculata*, gathered on the American shore at the Niagara rapids, close to the water. Please give these to Annie.

July 19th, 1887

Dear Frederic,

July 14th. At midday, returning from the mine (see last letter) we found Jod's brother at the hotel. He is quite a different sort of man, taller, hollow-cheeked and thin. He has been here about 14 years and has lately been out of health, and his mental faculties are somewhat impaired. In consequence of this he has been very much swindled and got into considerable difficulties. Our Jod is going to *try* to put matters right again, but he has a hard and depressing task, and I pity him. I hope he will have all success.

In the afternoon Cox was driving up to his ranch, and so I went with him, Payn staying behind to talk with Lees. Cox has let us have a small wooden house on his ranch, well built and with three rooms. Here is a drawing and ground plan of it. By it runs a creek of pure water running from a lake called 'The Lake of the Clouds', right up in the mountains, and on the stream side are plenty of small trees, while the other looks out on to the open prairie, West Cliff and Silver Cliff in the distance.

So our luggage was put on to Cox's vehicle, and he and Mrs. Cox sat on the seat in front while I mounted Payn's great box behind. There was a baby-carriage just in front of me (Mrs. Cox has a baby girl, a year old) which I had to hold with one hand to prevent it slipping off and with the other I held on to the box as best I might. The road, or rather the better part of it, is covered with great stones, and the cart jolted and swayed to and fro, so that I nearly fell off two or three times! But happily we accomplished the seven miles or more in safety, and our luggage is being deposited in our house.

I went up to Cox's house for supper and to sleep. Payn turned up afterwards, having walked all the way, most of it in the dark and in the rain, losing his way more than once. We did not expect that he would attempt to come up that night and it is fortunate that he arrived with nothing worse than a wetting. I also got wet coming up. I succeeded in catching cold. It is the rainy season just now in Wet Mountain Valley, and it rains heavily at times.

The Cox' House. from the South Side.

Now I must introduce you to the family: Firstly Cox, rather tall, slightly made, hair and small moustache dark, face sloping to a point (i.e. tip of nose), features rather sharp and defined, eyes bright, grey coat, hat like mine but with broader brim, and leather strap round in place of a band. Came from Cheshire, had once a good deal of money, and has traveled much, was going into the army but speculated on the Stock Exchange, lost money and had to come out here two years ago. Lived at first in the house

we now occupy, but now has larger and more commodious house 3/4 of a mile further on. Has been fairly successful in ranching and makes sufficient living. Was very fond of hunting in England. Politics conservative, thinks Socialists are a lot of philanthropic idiots. Very nice fellow altogether, manner extremely pleasant, very good-natured. Age 26.

Secondly, Mrs. Cox: Slight and rather thin, pleasant face, not remarkable in any way but altogether very kind and nice, and refined in manner, finds the society here not very congenial, though on excellent terms with everyone, and is going to England some time in the autumn. Is very energetic in domestic duties and care of the baby. Cooks well and gives valuable information as to methods of preparing food.

Thirdly, Baby Cox: A girl, was one year old on Saturday, a companionable child but frequently cries aloud for food and other things.

July 15th. Cox and Payn started off in the morning on an excursion to the south part of the valley and will not return until the next evening. So I, after chopping some wood, went down to our house and commenced to put it straight; cleared out the bedrooms and washed floors and windows. Then went up to lunch at Cox's, and came down again in afternoon and continued cleaning up, so spent all the day and went up and slept the night at Cox's. It rained a good deal that night and next day, but that was in one way an advantage as it kept the air cool.

July 16th. Very wet and rather cold. Finished cleaning out house and got everything straight by the time Payn and Cox returned. They had got drenched and Payn had a bad knee, which got well, however, next day.

July 17th, Sunday. Fine. I rather felt the effects of the rare atmosphere and was a good deal out of breath (have now got over that). We walked round and I got a good many insects, some of them very interesting. We slept in our house for the first time and went down to live there altogether.

"Our house"

July 18th. Monday. Early in the day, just as I was in the middle of a letter to you, Cox turned up with his cart and buckboard and took me down to West Cliff, where I found long letters from Mother and Carlie, and a copy of this week's *Labor Enquirer* waiting for me, and wrote a good many postcards at the postoffice. I spent the rest of the day collecting insects and purchasing stores at West Cliff, returning with Cox in the evening.

July 19th. We had a lot of oranges which were going bad, so I stewed them over the fire and put some pastry over the top with a view to orange pie. It was just fit to eat, but the pastry didn't get properly cooked, as the fire went out. Still I feel a sort of triumph in being able to eat my first pie at all. After that, I washed all our handkerchiefs. We have, of course, had nothing washed since leaving England, so there was a huge pile of dirty things.

Payn was not feeling very well, and had been sick. He had a quinine pill lest he should be going for 'mountain fever' and now he is almost right. Payn shot some of the wild pigeons that are common here and we had them for dinner. They are very good eating. I also shot one myself, but have not yet plucked it.

July 20th. There are a lot of woodpeckers, *Picus villosus*, I think [Hairy Woodpecker], about here. Payn shot one this morning and is skinning it. It is a pretty bird, black, spotted on the breast, with pink marks on the head. Payne has bought two horses, a 'buckboard' (sort of flat cart), harness from Cox, and we shall probably, in about three weeks, start on an excursion to Bear River in the northern part of the state. The reason of this is that game, such as elk, is very plentiful up there, and Payn is very anxious to shoot something big. Cox may very likely go with us, and we shall return towards the end of the year, probably in December. I am not certain what to do about getting letters during the period of our absence. You had best write always to West Cliff, and they will forward letters to me wherever I may be. The postoffice will always forward letters without any trouble or charge to anywhere one wishes.

July 21st. Came down to West Cliff today on our buckboard and I have just got your most delightful letter. Am *so* glad to hear from you. Payn is horribly riled because I *will* read it in the street. Coming down I saw some new insects, including *Vanessa antiopa*. We have some stores and things to get, and when I get back I shall finish chopping wood and preparing evening meal. Will write answer to your letter, though probably may not have opportunity of posting it for some days. Enclosed are some relics for Annie: Feathers of the pigeon I shot (*Columba fasciata*) and leaf of one of the asps that grow in front of our house. Also enclosed some *Grama grass*. This is the best pasture grass here, and grows plentifully all over the meadows.

I expect our money will run out before two years, probably next summer. But if I am not well enough to return, I have no doubt I could earn my living here over the second winter, or longer. They give a dollar a day for working in the hay field, for instance. I hope, though, I shall be all right after a year or so.

July 22nd, 1887

Dear Frederic,

I said I would answer your letter last night, but it was not to be so. Various matters delayed us, and we didn't get home till about half past eight, and when we had finished dinner and washed up and done the necessary work it was late, added to which I had eaten an unripe peach and got a stomachache, so I went to bed. Today we have been round about, up and down Swift Creek, which runs by the house, Payn shooting at birds and securing a few including a hawk, magpie, and nightjar, and I catching insects. I saw a huge black *Papilio* but did not catch it, and also *Vanessa milberti*, which is very like *V. urticae*.

In the evening there came in one Brock, to dine with us. Brock lives close to us, a little further up the mountain. Here is a description of him: Moderate height, tanned face, moustache, straight nose, rather prominent cheekbones, on the whole an agreeable-looking man. Blue clothes, broad-brimmed hat, Englishman. When about ten he was plucked in going up for the army, so came to America and lived years in Iowa, his lungs got bad, so he came out here about two years ago. Means to go back to England some day.

We meant to give Brock a sumptuous repast, so we prepared all sorts of dishes — some rice pudding (only it got burnt), some potatoes (but they weren't quite cooked), some pears

(ditto, etc., etc.), but we ate them, and we being hungry they were not so bad.

Now in answer to your letter: You have no business to 'regret you are not a better letter writer.' You have written me just the best sort of letter possible, because it enables me to imagine all that has taken place almost as if I were on the spot. If I can do as well for you I shall be glad enough. Anyway, I will do my best. I wish you had come to see me off. I thought you would not have been able to get away from Smith's. However, perhaps Carlie and Olive would not have liked it, as you say.

You do seem to have a multitude of callers at Syon Lodge; soon you will know all the aristocracy of Isleworth, and Bedford Park-ites will be looked upon as foreigners! You might ask Mrs. Brodie Clarke what that bird-cage summer house affair is for, just by her gate. I have always been anxious to know. I shall consider that you have introduced all these people to me, and when I return I shall go round Isleworth and look up all my old acquaintances in the flesh, whose ghosts have visited me in Colorado. I hope they will agree with their ghostly forms and not think I am presuming too much in claiming their acquaintance!

As to Olive not quite understanding matters, I daresay not. When she talked about it she evidently did not quite comprehend, and I was at a loss to make her, and did not much try. Of course, they all had somewhat erroneous preconceived ideas of their own.

I am rather amused at Sir John Lubbock's [1834-1913, banker, politician and naturalist, pioneer in the science of animal behavior, cf. *Encycl. Britannica.* Ed.] propositions. Does he believe people are miserable on purpose? Perhaps he would say that some people are happier when they are miserable! I rather suspect he means the duty of pretending to be happy. Certainly children are not particularly happy. When I was a child I used to howl at trifles. They told me I was ever so much happier than grown-up people who had such *serious* things to think about. I said

I didn't believe it, and howled again. I am sure the agonies I have suffered over a broken toy were quite as acute as anything in after life.

Sir John Lubbock's view on friends are probably rather like Carlie's. I suppose he would have one make a friend as he makes a pudding. He should write a book with receipts: 'To make a friend, take an individual with . . . qualities and . . . pedigrees. Treat him in . . . manner, etc.' I hope you wrote abusively to Sir J. L. because I am sure that he never thought properly about the matter. I shall be interested to hear what he has to say in reply. Besides, what friends one has depends just as much on one's own character as anything, and certainly, to choose friends different, or rather, not sympathetic, with oneself would be impossible unless one altered at the time. A key can't choose which lock it will turn.

Did you go to Gardening Fete? On Wednesday you said it was to come off next Saturday, but on Saturday no mention of it. Perhaps it was Saturday week? I like that poem of P. B. Marston's: 'Who can tell how it may be?' Somehow a belief in the future seems to imply also a memory of something in the past, and the future and the past stretch beyond our field of thought but have no certain end than the sea at the horizon, which seems sharply cut against the sky. Yet as we proceed, the horizon recedes and is ever the same distance off. Only the man at the mast-head can see further than other people.

I am very glad that [the] will turned out all right. It would have been very miserable if the family had been obliged to emigrate or do something desperate like that.

It is very tantalizing to hear of Olive and Carlie having a whole Sunday afternoon and evening at Syon Lodge. It may be a hundred Sundays yet before Syon sees me again, but there is always a memory of the past.

I can quite imagine that epistle of Carlie's. I hope you have had your row successfully and are good friends again.

I had rather a row with Payn today 'because I am not sufficiently companionable', which is extremely true. Of course it is impossible that we should ever be friends in the deeper sense of the word, unless we both are considerably modified, which is not likely. On the whole, though, we get on much better than I expected and I daresay we shall do better as time goes on. Of course it is possible that we might disagree, but even in the event of that I do not doubt I could manage to live here all right until I could return.

I wish I could be earning something out here and so be more independent, but Payn is very averse to that, as it would probably involve my working all day and neglecting the house work, that is, cooking, etc., and in this I think he is not unreasonable. As to having plenty of spare time out here, certainly so far I have had less than when I was in England. Perhaps when the winter comes on there will be more.

Next Monday and Tuesday the people of the place will turn out and mend the road leading from West Cliff to here; the latter part of it is strewn with great stones and wants mending badly enough. I expect we shall have two days of hard work, but it is well worth while.

Please thank Mrs. Hemery for her kind remembrances and say I will not on any account forget her advice.

Yesterday I got an epistle from Mother, dated 8th July, enclosing a photograph of myself which I presume resembles me (I don't know what I look like a bit). It has a rather comic expression. I left word that two were to be posted to Syon, and no doubt you have them. Annie went to visit them at 5 Priory on the 7th, Mother writes; no doubt I shall hear of that in your next letter. The *Schoolmistress* has not yet turned up; there would be at least one number to hand by now. I am afraid they do not take much trouble to forward papers, so I have written the postmaster at Denver on the matter. I am looking forward to the next part of Annie's story; it is a long time since the last.

July 23rd, 10:45 a.m. This morning, after breakfast, we went out to catch our horses, as Payn wanted to ride one of them. They were in a large field, or rather portion, of the prairie fenced in by a wire fence (the wire fences they use everywhere here are like the one close to Miss Orme's house at Bedford Park, with sharp points sticking out at intervals. They prevent anything getting through, but animals often cut themselves trying to do so). We went towards the horses slowly and gently but they evidently had no mind to be caught, and commenced trotting round the enclosure, we following them, until at last we got them into a corner by the stream. Here, however, they plunged about, and the chestnut horse continued to cut itself a little on the wire fence, after which they again made off and we almost gave it up as a bad job. Just then, however, Cox came up on his mare and chased the horses round for a long while, nearly catching them once, till at last he caught the chestnut and, having saddled him, rode off after the other (buckskin) horse, after a while securing him also.

It will never do to spend a couple of hours and any amount of breath chasing horses every day! We must get some oats, and then they will come up and feed, and can be easily caught.

Payn and Cox have ridden off to West Cliff and I am left alone for a while, which I rather like as it gives me time to write this and do other things.

There are two customs here that annoy me a great deal. Everyone tells lies to any extent, and they use the word 'damned' about as frequently as a London cabman uses 'bloody' and in the same sort of sense. Unfortunately Payn, on the principle that in Rome one ought to do as the Romans, has taken to these embellishments of conversation, only he seems to think 'whatsoever thy tongue findeth to say, say it with all thy might!' And I think he really tells more lies (generally in the form of gross exaggerations) and damns oftener than the average. But I hope he will be a little more moderate in both respects as time goes on. (Of course I write quite freely to you about everything, but you will know who to show the letter to and who not. If the general public should be curious about this epistle perhaps you had better read them extracts.)

12:45 p.m. I have just been out on a ramble up as far as Cox's place. On the way up, Cox's retriever dog, 'Jim', who was with me, began smelling around a large stone and, lifting it up I saw a gopher underneath. I let the stone down for a minute and went around the other side, and lifting it up again I found I had crushed its head and killed it. A gopher is a pretty little animal, a rodent about 6 ½ inches long including the tail, which is hairy. Its general colour is grey and its back is grey-brown, with six pale grey narrow stripes and five rows of pale grey spots alternating with them. I don't know the scientific name of this or of a chipmunk. If you find out I would rather like to know.

On the way back I caught two specimens of a beautiful sulphur-coloured *Colias*, rather resembling but not identical with *C. philodice*; I don't know the name. (Payn purchased the books on butterflies in New York, but both of them refer only to eastern states and say nothing about species peculiarly western.) I will enclose a specimen so that you may see it yourself. I also got a burying beetle (*Necrophorus*, very like the English *N. ruspator*) under a dead bird, and also a familiar old friend, a real dandelion, just such a one as one might find at Isleworth or Bedford Park. Yesterday I came across a tiger lily, *Lilium philadelphicum*, which grows wild here, and some aconite, *Aconitum columbianum*.

Going out just now I saw a *Vanessa antiopa* flying just by the house. I went in to get my net to catch it, but meanwhile it disappeared. I saw a tomtit [possibly a chickadee, Ed.] sitting on a tree by the stream, as Payn is collecting skins. I fetched the gun to shoot it, but when it was loaded and I was out again, the tomtit had gone and the *antiopa* was back again, so for the second time went out with my net and made a dash at it as it sat on a bush, the result of which was to tear the net and lose the butterfly. So I got neither *Vanessa* nor tomtit.

Looking over some plants I gathered yesterday, I find I have *Saponaria vaccaria* (this is one of those alien plants that spring up in that unused garden in Priory Road. You will find the name in the Bedford Park list).

I expected Cox and Payn back about three, but they have not turned up. I suppose something has delayed them in West Cliff.

There was a new moon last night, just a thin curved streak. I saw it over and a little to the north of Gibson Peak. I wonder whether you saw it at Isleworth.

Here is a rough sketch of my room in our house. It looks comfortable, does it not? The wall marked A is wood whitewashed over. It is a partition wall between my room and Payn's and does not go to the roof. Walls B and C are covered with Willesden paper or something very like it — a thick sort of cardboard substance. The object D in the corner is a roll of this paper, which was not used. The thing marked E on the wall C is a map of the United States.

My room

4:20. Cox and Payn have returned and are playing poker or some similar game, in the next room. Cox doesn't cheat, and Payn has not lost playing with him, but I wish he wouldn't, all the same. Down at West Cliff they play cards to any extent, and cheat universally.

Carlie, in his letter, warned me not to write longer letters to you when I write home, but I fear there is no help for it, as I inevitably must write you at some length, and I don't think I could possibly write to anyone else like I write to you, because I am an abominable correspondent, except on matters conchological, and besides —.

Sunday, July 24th, 3 p.m. We had agreed to go up on the hillside and endeavour to shoot some deer and other game, and Cox was going with us. So we woke up at five, had breakfast and got up to Cox's ranch about half past six. Here, after a consultation, we arranged that Payn should ride up part of the way on the buckskin horse (it is not possible to ride up all the way, as the ground becomes too rough for horses) while Cox and I walked up a shorter way and met him. Payn then departed, and Cox and I started off through the woods. On the way I found under a stone the first slug I have seen since we came out. It is intermediate between *Limax agrestis* and *L. cavis* and is apparently a form of *Limax campestris* Binney.

Further on, going through a pine wood, we found the stump of a tree which had been torn apart on one side by a bear who was no doubt scraping out an ant's nest. The bear itself was not to be seen; bear tracks are more often seen than bears. Presently we came across Payn, who had had a most dismal adventure. Coming along just by a house belonging to one Nathan, there was a dust heap and just there a pig had been killed. Now if there is one thing a horse detests more than another it is a pig, or pig's blood, so this buckskin immediately shied and would not pass. So Payn got off and attempted to lead it past, and somehow contrived to get his arm round the rein in a manner it did not like, whereat it ran, and

Payn fell down and, falling on his rifle, smashed the stock off. This being so, we had nothing to shoot the deer with if we should see them, for although Cox had a rifle, he had hardly any ammunition for it. Payn's cartridges would not fit, so there was nothing for it but to turn back. Then the question arose as to how the rifle was to be mended. We agreed to go down to D. Hugg, who is a gunsmith and metal-worker and lives a little further down the valley, and get him to do it for us. You will remember in a former letter I spoke of one Hug (I think I spelled it wrongly — Hug) who owed money and had offered armed resistance when they attempted to arrest him, and was altogether a very desperate character. Well, this was the man we went to see. He is a Swiss, and works in metal most successfully and is extremely skilled, and also an educated man. His appearance is of the gorilla or orang-utang type. I don't mean he is particularly ugly or really like a gorilla, but he is short and carries his arms in the same sort of way, and his mouth is large and his teeth ditto, and he has a short stumpy rather broad nose and plenty of grey-black hair and a black beard with many grey hairs, for he is getting old. He has been generally treated badly, I believe, and has got rather desperate, and being a dangerous character to begin with, this has made him more so. He has shot more than one man, and has been arrested and locked up eight or nine times. Now he is a regular outlaw and dare not venture into any town or far from his own house, which is well-guarded and has spring guns round to warn him in case of any night attack. All this will seem to you very extraordinary, and yet nobody thinks much of it here, and we went down to get him to mend the rifle as a matter of course.

When we got down there, Hugg was away in the fields working and, seeing us, I suppose he thought we had come to arrest him, as he could not recognize Cox in the distance, and we were of course strangers. So we walked out towards him, but he went round a hedge and we had a regular hunt for him before he was discovered. When we did find him he was very pleasant (desperate characters always are) and talked for a long time about guns. He agreed to mend Payn's gun for $30, which is not considered very dear. And, provided he is not arrested or shot in the meantime, he will have it ready in a fortnight, so we shall not start for Bear River for at least that time.

Leaving Hugg's we went up and had lunch at Cox's and found Jod there, who seems to be getting on very well on the whole. After which we came down here, and all three of them — Payn, Jod, and Cox, are playing cards. while I go to my room and continue this letter. Hanging up in a pan in Hugg's window was a luxuriant growth of *Linaria cymbalaria*, which you know grows very commonly on walls at Isleworth and Kew.

Monday, July 25th. Road mending today, so I was up rather early, and after breakfast went out on to the road. The County obliges each district to mend its own roads, and each one has either to turn out and do two days road mending or instead pay a dollar and a half a day, which is supposed to pay for labour which he has not done. Legally we were not obliged to do road-mending, as the law stipulates that only those who have resided for a certain time are liable. But as we use the road continually in going down to West Cliff, I thought we ought certainly to work.

Payn, however, had a barrel of beer which he bought a few days ago, and he agreed to let those working have free access to his beer on condition of his not working. The barrel was accordingly taken out to the creek where it would be cool, and Payn started off with Jod to West Cliff on the buckboard to get provisions, etc.

There were six of us altogether working on the road: Cox, Brock, Splann (an oldish bearded man), Jim Splann (a youth entirely lacking in wit), Jim Kettle (an Englishman who came out here moneyless six years ago and is now one of the richest men in the valley, and T.D.A.C. The work consisted in removing rocks and stones from the road, many of which were deeply imbedded and had to be taken out with a pickaxe. The work was tolerably laborious, as the sun was hot, but we made a short day of it and so did not work more than six hours. The beer proved a considerable attraction, and Jim Splann contrived to get drunk and had attempted to hit Brock and then throw rocks at him. So Brock knocked him down, where he lay asleep all the afternoon.

When Payn arrived, we sat round — Cox, Brock, Jod, Payn, and I. Payn, extolling the merits of his buckskin horse, idiotically offered to race it against any horse Brock chose to bring within three days, for five dollars either side, added to the inherent foolishness of horse-racing. Cox says Payn will certainly lose that five dollars, which he cannot well afford. After this, Payn offered to race the buckskin for a quarter of a mile against a horse of Brock's, and so they went down to a smooth piece of ground in the valley and raced, Payn losing, but afterwards the same race was run again, only with Cox riding buckskin instead of Payn. This time Cox won, so as regards money nothing was lost or gained on the two races. Sometimes I really wish Payn would lose his money so that he might have to earn some by labour and learn the relation of work to money, only I think he would probably return to England at once if he were moneyless, and nothing would be gained that way.

July 26th. This morning I was rather late, and after breakfast and washing up, it was past ten before I started off across the prairie to the place where the road work was doing — some two miles on. Having arrived, I only found two men there, and the 'road boss' (Jim Kettle) had not arrived. We soon returned, having now made the road fairly passable, and I went up and had lunch at Cox's, afterwards doing a little more road work near there in the afternoon.

Payn and Jod were out shooting nearly all day and secured between them a jack rabbit (more like a hare than a rabbit), a dove, and a magpie. When they got home we spent about two hours preparing supper, Payn having brought up all sorts of luxuries from West Cliff. I made some mince pies, but they were not quite as those things should be. Jod slept at our house last night and is still here.

I have arrived at the following uncharitable conclusions respecting him and Brock. Jod is a very decent sort of fellow, but an utter fool. Brock is an agreeable man when in a good temper, but has no special feeling towards honesty or truthfulness. I think Payn rather likes Jod's company *because* he is a fool, so that Payn can 'show him round' and boss him without any difficulty, and get admired for it.

There is one thing I like about this country: That it makes no difference whatever in the general estimation whether a man has money or not, except that it is rather against a man than otherwise if he is rich, especially if he does not work. All the rich ranch owners, etc., here work as well as anybody and dress in working clothes quite the same as those of a man who hasn't a cent.

We are talking about going on a hunting expedition all next week and so if there should be a rather long interval between my letters, you will know why. We shall probably not be near any postoffice the whole time.

July 27th, 5:30 p.m. Payn, Cox, and Jod went off on horses to West Cliff this morning, and I have spent the day at home looking over my letters and writing to Mother, [William] Morris, and Carrington. I found a beautiful green beetle, *Buprestis nuttalli* I believe, on my window while writing.

9:10 p.m. At dusk I was reading this week's *Labor Enquirer* till it became too dark. When I lay down for a little rest before lighting the lamp, it happened that I dropped off to sleep, and I have just woke up to find the moon shining. Payn has not yet returned from West Cliff. He is very late.

Last night I waited up till eleven, and no signs of Payn or Cox either here or at Cox's house where I went and found all dark and desolate, so I went to bed. Just before doing so, I went out to get some water to drink and found by the stream some luminous wood, shining with a pale glow. The luminosity is, I believe, due to one of the micro-fungi. I enclose a strip of it; you may be able to revive its luminosity if you put it in a damp place.

Payn and Cox turned up this morning; they had slept down at West Cliff. Brock also came by. It seems that he cannot get the horse he meant to race against Payn's, so probably there will be no race and consequent loss of five dollars, which is satisfactory.

Payn brought me up a host of letters and papers which had arrived at the postoffice for me: A letter from Mother, postcards from Carlie and two from Douglas, the *Naturalist* for July, *Pall Mall Budget*, and what I had most been looking forward to, the *Schoolmistress* for June 30th and July 7th. I like the two new bits of Annie's story very much but am rather doubtful as to the effect of mixing up some of mine with it. It is all right so far, but the plot was not quite the same as Annie began with and I like hers best, so hope she won't let mine influence it.

I see she says (page 212): 'There is a great deal in the *order* of shaking hands.' Quite so. I remember I used to wonder why such a ridiculous custom as that of shaking hands was kept up! But more lately I have understood that it has some purpose after all, and is a most blessed custom.

I like Mrs. White's exposition of the 'domestic sideboard theory' in chapter X! I trust the story will tend to refute and demolish those ideas and so have a beneficial effect upon the schoolmistresses who read it. It is very annoying that the story should leave off just at the thrilling moment, though I do not suppose anything *very* dreadful has happened to Douglas. I trust the next number will turn up soon and tell me what had happened. I should think the *School for Wives* (p. 218) ought to be a great success! After such an education they ought to be quite formidable animals. I suppose there will be an examination before marriage, and we will hear unfortunates say

'I was going to get married, only I got plucked in the debating exam,' and so on! But what about a school for husbands?

I enclose a rather amusing advertisement I cut out of the *Labor Enquirer*.

9:30 p.m. Went out this afternoon and found where some bears had been rampaging round about half a mile or rather more from our house. I didn't see anything of them though, which was rather fortunate, as they have cubs about this time and are very savage.

I found two specimens of *Limax campestris* quite close to our house, and also *Vitrina pellucida*, which I had not seen here before. Payn and I picked some wild black currants, which grow plentifully near the stream. They are rather sour.

Payn has got out his banjo and is playing and singing with the skill of a nigger-minstrel (I think he would make a first rate 'nigger' if he should ever find himself hard up in a seaside town). Really, though, the banjo is a pleasant instrument in its way. I wish I could play it myself.

July 19th, 10 a.m. I shall be going down to West Cliff this afternoon and will then post this letter, as it is now a week since I began it. I have been thinking over the definition of 'useful' that Douglas White asks for. Ask Annie how she defines it. I would say that anything is useful which produces happiness or, negatively, prevents misery, using both in the widest sense. Of course it might be argued that a birch-rod is useful but does not produce happiness by any means, but then I would answer that a birch-rod, if applied, is meant as a counter-irritant, like a mustard plaster, and should have a soothing influence in the end. But it might also mean that anything that is used is useful, and if a thing is used wrongly it does not fall within my definition. I do not quite admit this though. I don't think a thumb screw is a useful instrument, for instance, though it is certainly usable. A distinction must be drawn between usable and useful.

I enclose two flowers that I picked by the stream just in front of my house. One is *Geranium fremontii* Torr. The other one, our common English harebell, *Campanula rotundifolia*, which is also common here, is curiously drying; one flower has become white and the other has retained its color. This is very remarkable, I think, and I am at a loss to know why it is so. Should you be going to Kew you might ask Baker if he can explain it, and show him the specimen. The *Geranium* grows white [probably this is *G. richardsonii*. Ed.], though the same species is frequently pink [*G. caespitosum*. Ed.].

In your letter you say that you and Annie have found a lot of new species in the Isleworth fauna. When you are writing, I would like to know the *names* of the principal things you both find, as you get them identified. I have not lost my interest in your fauna and flora books because I am so far away.

6:00 p.m. I have just driven down to West Cliff and am waiting for my letters. Alas! There are none. I do not suppose I shall be here again for some days and till then shall not hear from you, but the *Schoolmistress* I got yesterday is some consolation, and then your long letter of last week will be something to live upon. Goodbye! A most hearty greeting to Annie. I do miss her very much; it is hard to be patient. I must live on hope.

July 30th, 1887, 10:30 a.m.

Dear Frederic,

I did not get home till after dark last night, and got drenched in a heavy fall of rain. I found our house dark and deserted and so drove to Cox's, where I discovered Payn, Cox, and Jod. Cox let me have a change of clothes and so I have not caught cold.

We all slept at Cox's, and got up this morning with the intention of starting off on our hunting excursion, but Payn (who really seems always unfortunate), attempting to bring up a

sack of oats, etc., on the buckskin, got the saddle loose and twisted round, and the horse bolted, kicking Payn on the legs and leaving him on the ground. He managed to walk up to Cox's, but the horse cannot be found. Payn was not very well yesterday, and this shaking has made him worse. I am rather anxious about him.

Yesterday I posted a copy of the *Wet Mountain Tribune* to you. There is another local paper called the *Silver Cliff Rustler*. These papers abuse each other in the most frightful manner and are often very amusing. Advertisements and news are invariably mixed together.

July 11th, 8:15 a.m. Yesterday was spent mostly in a fruitless search after Payn's horse, which seems to have gone right up to the slope of the mountains and to be wandering somewhere among the trees. Today we must have another hunt, and this time I hope we shall be successful. It was a wretched day yesterday — rain and mist all the while, so it is as well that we did not go on our hunting excursion, for we should have been very miserable. Today it promises to be fine.

We found the horse tied up by our house. Someone going by had caught it. Luckily it is not at all hurt though the saddle is rather knocked about. I caught a *Parnassias*, I believe *P. smintheus* Dbl. It is the first I have seen out here.

News reaches us from West Cliff that the two drinking saloon keepers had a quarrel and one, Love, got shot. I bought some whiskey for Cox in Love's place only on Friday. Shooting affairs like this are thought nothing of here. This afterwards was contradicted. Love was not shot after all.

August 1st, 10:00 p.m. At about 3 p.m. yesterday, all having been arranged, Cox, Payn, Jod, and I started off on horseback to hunt out at Horseshoe Bend, which lies round by Gibson Peak. We took blankets, provisions, etc., so that we could sleep there the night and return next day. For a while we passed over fairly level ground, but as we came to enter the gulch, first going over steep inclines covered with rocks, we found ourselves in a tolerably dense wood of asp trees, *Populus tremuloides*, and the trail became very faint.

Coming to a valley at the mouth of the gulch, we rested for a little, and found some wild strawberries. After this, we lost the trail several times and had great difficulty in rediscovering it, as nobody had been there for more than a year, and it was considerably overgrown with vegetation. As the gulch became narrower and higher we came amongst pine trees, and here the trail was easy to see, being marked on each side by pieces of bark being cut off the trees. Under these fir trees and in all sheltered spots above a certain elevation there grew in profusion a beautiful species of columbine, *Aquilegia coerulea* James, not so tall as the garden species, with larger and pale lilac-blue flowers.

At about seven o'clock we arrived in Horseshoe Bend, which is a valley with steep sides, Gibson Peak towering up on one side. Here we found a shanty built of pine logs, and inside it some snow, not yet melted by the summer. By this we made a fire, though not without considerable difficulty, as the logs were wet and no dry wood was forthcoming. Over the fire we made some hot cocoa and got out our salt beef and biscuits and had a good meal, for which the long ride had given us an appetite.

After this we made up a tent to sleep under and had a good night's rest broken only by the necessity of attending to the fire at intervals, for it was bitterly cold and we could hardly have kept comfortably warm without a fire. Mosquitoes were flying round in numbers, but the smoke drove them away and they did not trouble us to any great extent. Payn was rather cantankerous about sleeping and insisted on wrapping up by himself in blankets and sleeping in the open, from which I fear he may have caught a cold.

We were up at five the next morning (today) and walked up the hill in search of game. Here we soon saw a deer in the distance. Payne and

Jod went one way and Cox another to try to get a shot from one side or the other, but without success, the deer disappearing over the mountain crest into the next valley. As I climbed the hill I heard a shot, then another, and another, eight altogether, but I could not see from where I was the end of the valley where the sound came from.

Soon after I heard Cox shouting, and hurried down to tell us that he had seen a bear (of the kind known as 'silver-tip') with two cubs, the old female being a gigantic beast over six feet high he supposed when standing on its hind legs. The bear was a long way off, but he fired and hit her behind the shoulder. After this, seven more shots, after which she disappeared amongst the thick growth of dwarf willows that covers the end of the valley.

We found her trail, and here and there drops of blood, and followed it through the undergrowth, expecting to see the wounded animal jump and make for us at any moment. However, after a long search we failed to discover where she had ultimately disappeared to, and were obliged to give up the search. Our horses had evidently seen her and been scared out of their wits, for they broke away; two went up the mountain and gave us the trouble of a steep climb to secure them.

By the stream, as we were on the search, I came across an abundance of *Primula parryi* Gray, which is something like a crimson purple-flowered Auricula. I also found among the rocks a moss which I cannot distinguish from the English *Webera [= Pohlia] nutans*.

After giving up the bear as a bad job we began to deliberate as to returning home. Payn wanted to stay behind, and me to go down to West Cliff, get sufficient provisions to last for a week, and bring up an experienced hunter of the name of Martin, whose services were available at the rate of two dollars a day. His proposal, however, did not meet with any favour because I could not possibly get provisions and return with Martin before tomorrow night, and there was not enough food to last Payn and Jod (Jod was to stay; we would not leave Payn alone anyway) till then, besides which Payn was not particularly well and it would be very undesirable to have him laid up there — six miles of rocky, hilly, and woody ground away from anybody.

So after a great deal of rather violent moral pressure we got him to return with us, and then if he felt like it in a day or two he could go with anyone and hunt anywhere he pleased, taking plenty of provisions. So we returned, and on the way another fine deer was seen but we failed to get a shot at him, and a squirrel up a tree which Payn fired at and blew to atoms. Jod's horse had wandered off in the night, so Jod had to walk most of the way. No doubt his horse went home as they sometimes will if not tethered at night.

August 2nd. This morning I was up at Cox's at seven and we all had breakfast and, after catching the horses, drove down to West Cliff. On the way, Payn was persuaded to trade his chestnut horse for another buckskin and got rather the worst of the bargain, the new horse being of vast antiquity (17 years).

Coming to the postoffice, I am delighted to find a letter from you, *Schoolmistress* for July 14th, letters from Douglas and W. C. Wetherly, *Labor Enquirer* for July 30th, and *Pall Mall Budget* for July 14th. I am very glad to hear that the families get on all right and that Annie had a pleasant visit at Priory Road. I hoped that it would be so, and that any ill feeling that existed was only temporary and that there was some stronger feeling of friendship beneath.

I am very sorry to hear that Annie has not been very well. Please give her my sympathy in the matter. I am afraid she works too hard at night. I do hope that you will be able to go for the projected holiday together. You would thoroughly enjoy yourselves and it would do you both good, especially Annie. I had often thought before what a good thing such a holiday would be for you but did not imagine that it would be allowed. Go right down into Surrey and walk over the hills and through the valleys, or away to Devonshire or Wales or anywhere you please, only get a good week together in the fresh air right away from work of any kind. I envy you that chalk head of Annie, though Louy [a sister of Frederic and Annie. Ed.] did not catch the proper expression in the one I saw. Could you anyhow persuade Louy to do me one, just a little one? I should be grateful to her.

I am glad to know the common name of Baron Gardner so that I may recognize him should we by any possible chance meet. I think we should be good friends. I think Chapter XI of *Merely Friends* [a story that Annie was composing. Ed.] is very good indeed, quite the best chapter we have had. Please convey my thanks to Annie for writing it. I see in *Chit Chat* Annie says a long dress has a graceful appearance. Does she solemnly and seriously mean this?

I wrote a post card to W. C. Wetherly (well-known American conchologist) to say I was in America, and would he assist me in naming shells. In return I have just received a very nice letter from North Carolina inviting me to go and see him and spend some weeks, which I think is very nice of him considering that I never wrote to him before and he has never seen me, though of course I could almost as easily go to Timbuktoo as North Carolina.

We shall probably go for a week's hunting trip tomorrow, so I will post this while I have the chance.

Aug. 5th, 1887

Dear Frederic,

In my last letter I wrote that we were going on a hunting excursion. We have just returned, and here is the account thereof.

August 3rd. We had not commenced breakfast when Martin, the hunter who was going with us, arrived. Martin is in appearance something like your paternal relation, only boiled down to considerably reduced proportions, baked and dried in the sun. He is very American, and a hunter of very considerable experience, as well as a miner and carpenter, altogether a very well-informed and intelligent man. As soon as he arrived I set about getting the breakfast while Payn and Jod went after the horses and a white mule which Cox had lent us for the expedition. They did not return for a long time, and Martin and I set out in search of them and discovered that the horses had broken down a gate and strayed away. Eventually, though, they were secured, and at 11:30 we started on our journey, well packed with flour, tinned meat, biscuits, cooking utensils, blankets, etc. — four of us altogether, Payne on his buckskin horse, Martin on his mare, Jod on the mule, and myself on the antiquated animal Payn exchanged for his chestnut the day before.

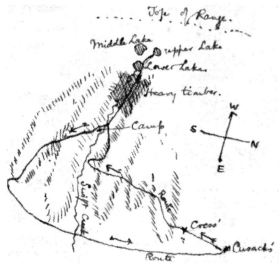

Map of trail to Lakes of the Clouds

We went up Swift Creek Gulch, through which Swift Creek flows after rising in the Lakes of the Clouds. The first part of the gulch is thick with asps, and its sides are covered with dead tree-trunks, some standing and many fallen, the trees having been killed by fire. Here and there are 'prospect holes' where miners have dug deep into the rock in search of ore, sometimes successfully but very often without result.

By the stream we stopped a while for lunch, and here under some bark I found several speci-

mens of a *Sialis*, similar but larger than and not so dark as the *S. lutaria* we found so abundant by the Brent at Isleworth. I also got some shells: a *Pupa* like *marginata* but with three blunt teeth, and a *Helix* which I do not know but think it is new to Colorado. It is something like *rotundata* but larger and without markings. After lunch we passed on up a steep trail through the pine wood where we had a tiring climb, leading our horses over the rocks and fallen timber. In this wood I found plenty of *Aquilegia coerulea*, and *Primula parryi* was growing in the damp places as in Horseshoe Bend.

Lake of the Clouds landmarks

Towards evening we got up to the Lakes of the Clouds, four lakes, one very small, surrounded by pines and dwarf willows, and with steep mountain peaks on all sides but one, where the stream flows out. These lakes are clear and intensely cold, being formed by the melting snow. No fish exist in them but there are water shrimp in great numbers, and caddis-fly larvae, and in the Middle Lake I found quantities of *Pisidium pusillum* (or *P. abditum* as American authors generally call it). This is the first fresh water shell I have found in Colorado.

We camped by the Middle Lake, making a sort of tent out of a waggon sheet, one end being against a rock. As it was early, Payn, Martin, and Jod went out to hunt while I made a fire and prepared a meal. Neither the cooking nor the hunting were particularly successful, as I attempted some biscuit in the frying pan and got it burnt on one side and not cooked enough on the other, and the hunters returned empty-handed, having shot at but missed two mountain wolves (*Canis sp.?*) and a grouse, and seen nothing of interest except that Payn picked up an eagle's feather.

Middle Lake of the Clouds

Mosquitoes were very abundant and troublesome and seemed to have a particular liking for Payn. I hunted a while for shells and found two small *Pupa*, new to me, as well as other species. When evening came and it got dark we made up our beds and went to sleep.

Our camp

Martin would not come under the tent, and we three who slept under it made the mistake of trying to sleep together whereas for warmth we ought to have been wrapped separately in his own blanket, as Martin, wiser by experience, did. At one o'clock I woke up feeling very cold, and finding just the embers of the fire still glowing, contrived to light up a good blaze and, getting a log, sat upon it and warmed myself.

The moon had risen and was very bright, and so I took out a very precious bundle of manuscripts I always carry with me, and read them by its light, thinking of old times and times to come, until Payn, waking up, disturbed me.

August 4. Next morning we left Payn in camp while the other three of us went round to hunt once more, seeing nothing, however, but a black and white woodpecker. The woodpeckers that we had round our house prove to be *Colaptes mexicanus*. This was quite a different species. I found pink *Cyclamen* [*Dodecatheon*. Ed.] growing very abundantly by the smaller streams, and plenty of *Achillea millefolium*. Some large grey birds came around the camp. They are known as 'camp-robbers' because they will steal morsels of food at any moment when nobody is looking.

At about 8 p.m. we packed our horses and started off for Cottonwood Gulch. As we went along we saw some woodchucks (a curious rodent about as big as a small cat) among the rocks, and as we climbed the steep ridge dividing the two gulches, a very pretty dark *Colias* with pink bordered wings was abundant.

When we got to the top, some 13,000 or more feet above sea level we could see right down into Cottonwood Gulch, a large ravine with plenty of timber and a long deep green lake at the bottom, and beyond we saw the San Luis Valley stretching away with a high range of mountains beyond. This ridge divides the two counties, Custer and Saguache — Cottonwood Gulch being in Saguache County. Saguache is an Indian name and is pronounced Si-a-watch.

We rode along the ridge some way and found *Parnassias* very common (probably *P. smintheus*) and forget-me-nots of the most vivid blue I have ever seen in flowers. The species is *Myosotis sylvatica* var. *alpestris Koch* [actually this has to have been *Eritrichum!* Ed.]. I enclose a

34

specimen for Annie; the blue has rather faded on drying. The *type* of *M. sylvatica* is a British plant and has been found in Surrey.

We had a steep climb down the side of the gulch and arrived at our camping place by the lake at about 11:30 a.m. Here we tied up the horses and had lunch; then, being tired and lazy, we went to sleep for a couple of hours. *Aquilegia coerulea* was as common on that side as the other, and I found also several new plants. Under logs by the lake I found some shells, including numbers of *Vitrina pellucida*, which is called *V. limpida* in America. At about five we went right round the gulch in search of game, but found it very hard walking over rocks and fallen tree-trunks, so that we were quite exhausted when we got back again. We did not even *see* any game, though we found deer and bear tracks, the latter very fresh.

On the way, Payn, in his usual impulsive manner, without consulting anyone, offered Martin $150 to take us to Bear River for three months, and it is probable that we shall start very soon. $150 was much more than Payn need have paid, and altogether he considerably repents him of his rash bargain now it is made. I myself am considerably aghast at the prospect of spending three months out with the company of Payn, Jod, and Martin. However, I dare say Payn will give it up before the three months are out. Cox cannot come with us (*will* not anyway, I imagine), which I very much regret, because he is the only person I have as yet come across about here whose company I like better than their room, that is, for any length of time.

I proposed to Payn that as funds are likely to be extremely low by the time we return, would it not be better if I remained behind and earned some money? But he would not hear of it and, of course, under the circumstances I must do as he wishes in the matter, for the present at any rate. I am confident that things will turn out all right in the end, and have by no means lost courage though the immediate future may not be a very happy one.

When evening came, we lay down, each in his own blanket under a big fir tree and slept soundly until the next morning.

Our camp in Cottonwood Gulch

August 5th. As there was no game, and food was running short, we agreed to return home, and accordingly started at about 8:15, climbed up the side of the gulch and down by the Lakes of the Clouds and home by the way we came, getting to our house early in the afternoon.

As we got to the top of the ridge we saw the Wet Mountain Valley covered with white clouds which, owing to our great elevation, we looked down on from above. While it lasted, the sight was a very curious one. But they soon cleared away, and as we got home storm clouds came overhead and a little hail fell, the hailstones being large, as large as currants. By the lakes, Payn shot a woodchuck with a rifle at about 100 yards, which was a decidedly good shot for him.

August 6th, 1:30 p.m. Payn, Cox, and Jod have gone down to West Cliff on the buckboard while I remain at home. I have a lot of letters to write and want to pack off most of my collections before starting for Bear River. I am sending most of the insects to the South London Entomological Society [in care ?]of Billups.

My health is now very good and I have got rid of my cold and do not cough. I feel rather exhausted after much exertion, but considering all things this is natural enough, and doubtless I shall feel stronger after a while.

I have been making enquiries from hunters, etc., as to the Mammalia of this valley and the surrounding mountains, and so far as I can gather, the following seems to be a fairly complete list.

Mountain Lion (Puma). Rare, and considered a great trophy if shot.
Wild Cat. Not uncommon.
Lynx. Fairly common.
Elk, *Cervus alcea*. Uncommon, high on the mountains.
Red Deer. Common.
Spotted Deer. More rare.
Antelope. Formerly common on plains, now only a few at the lower end of the valley.
Brown Bear. The largest species found here (Grizzly Bear is not found here).
Silver-tipped Bear. Rather common.
Black Bear. Not very common. [All these bears belong to the same species! Ed.]
Cinnamon Bear. Commoner here than elsewhere in the states.
Ursus sp. Martin talks of a fifth bear, which he supposes 'may be a cross.'
Wolverine. Extremely rare.
Greyish Fox. (I suppose *Canis virginianus*). Common.
Brownish Fox. (*Canis velox?*). Rare.
Mountain Wolf. Not rare in mountains.
Grey Wolf. Sometimes in packs in winter, more rare in summer.
Jack Rabbit. Abundant. Really a sort of hare.
Rabbit ('Cottontail' it is called). Common, more like English Rabbit.
Beaver, *Castor fiber*. Martin says there are a few down the valley.
Coyote, Prairie Wolf, *Canis latrans*.
Pine Marten. Said to be black. Species?
Badger. Rather common.
Mountain Sheep, *Caprovis canadensis?* Not very rare on high peaks.
Bison, *Bison americanus*. Now extinct, their skulls are sometimes found.
Musquash, *Fiber zybethicus*. Martin thinks there are a few down in the valley.

Woodchuck, Common amongst rocks in the mountains [It is curious he does not mention the pica! Ed.]
Grey Squirrel. Common. [possibly a chickaree? Ed.]
Gopher. Common.
Chipmunk. Very abundant.
House Mouse. There are several in our house.
Field mole, *Arvicola sp.?* Not common.
Shrew, *Sorex sp.* A dead one found.
Mole, *Talpes sp.*, said to be smaller than the English species. Not rare.
Bat. I have seen one. Martin says he knows at least two kinds here.
Skunk. Not rare.

9:45 p.m. Payn returned soon after seven and brought me letters and papers: Letters from Mother, Carlie, and Olive, *Schoolmistress* of July 21st, *Pall Mall Budget*, *Labour Enquirer*, and a St. Thomas paper from Douglas giving account of a railway accident there. Poor Una has been ill, I hear, and Mother tired out looking after her, Carlie and Olive away at Ambleside, but no Ruskin (which must be very tantalising for them). So there was no Cockerellian representation at the gardening fête. Annie was there, though, Mother says, and came in to 5 Priory for just a few minutes. Olive writes me a very nice long letter, four pages. She seems to be thoroughly enjoying Ambleside.

Chapter XII of *Merely Friends* is very good, I think. It calls to mind certain discussions on the subject of delusions, which Annie will remember. I wish I could talk that chapter over with her now, but for that I must wait a long while.

Was W. Imes altogether deluded about Ada? I suppose that the strongest part of her nature was vain and shallow. Might there not also be something better, which he appreciated? Perhaps I am wrong. I do not know how to prove that I am right, but still I cling to the opinion that in such a case it is like the astronomer who looks through a smoked or darkened glass at the sun, and sees a planet (Venus or Mercury) crossing its disc, while others see only the bright solar glare,

TDAC in camp, 1887

per 100 llo., the actual charge on my box being properly 55 cents. I am not sure whether he was telling the truth or not, but it sounds very plausible, & as I have refused the matter in "A1." (p. 408) I have written this morning to the editor asking him to insert Fraser's explanation. I must look into the matter when I have time, and satisfy myself just how it is. Railway monopolies are bad enough, & one does not want to make them appear worse than they actually are. According to Fraser, the D. & R. S. charges will still be over 9 times as heavy as those on other roads.

8.55 P.M.

The snow turned into rain, & that on the ground has melted — but the whole day has been cold and wet — the poor ranchmen, coming into town, have had a rough time, though they affect to regard it as a joke. I have been writing letters, reading "Ihone" &c.; and only went out this afternoon during a lull in the weather to get my paints from the Gowdy's. Really, the only satisfactory thing about today, so far as I am concerned, is this evening's mail — which is "Canad. Entom." and nice letters from Coulter & Galloway. Yes, there is one other good thing — some cabbages have come on the market, & I purchased one for 5 cents, & ate half of it for supper this evening. I am sure I was needing some green food. Respecting those two letters I got today — Coulter writes that he is much obliged for the honor of being elected on council of C.B.A., and he will do all he can. Galloway is the fungus "boss" at the Dept. of Agriculture. He thanks me for some notes I sent for "I. of Mycol." & hopes I will send more; and he joins the Colo. Biol. Assn.. Then he finishes up "Will you have time to collect some fungi for us this summer? We should like to have a collection from your region, including specimens in quantity of all the parasitic species, and especially the Erysipheae, Ustilagineae, Uredineae and Peronosporeae. We have a small sum of money to expend in this work, and if you can help us we shall be obliged." I cannot quite make out from this whether he wants to hire me to get fungi or not, but I must write & find out. He encloses some "penalty envelopes" so that my letters & parcels to him will cost me nothing in postage.

Sunday. May 12". 9.15 P.M.

It is been fine today, so I have been out and about. In the morning, I drew a new sheet of diagrams (leaves & flowers) for my Botany classes, and then went for a stroll down by the creek. I saw a Colias eurytheme intermedia, but having no net, I could not catch it. I found Thermopsis montana in flower, as well as some other things, but nothing very noteworthy. When I got back, I wrote a letter to L.O. Howard of the Dept. of Agriculture, enclosing some specimens (coccid scales &c.). Looking over my galls I have in keeping, I found a most lovely little golden-bronze Hymenopterous (Chalcid) fly had emerged from some galls found on willow. It did not make the galls — they are Dipterous, — but it is a parasite on the gall-maker. I went out to search for more of the galls, & found them, but I fear the flies have already emerged. I hope I shall get more — it is probably a new species. This for second time of going out I found some more flowers — 7 things in flower today altogether. It agrees with your theory about the sequence of colours that all of them are yellow except a Castilleia, which is red. One, Erysimum asperum var. arkansanum, is new for Custer Co., & one or two others wait to be named. I also found a fungus new to me, apparently a Coprinus or allied thereto. It is a good deal like C. micaceus. I got some mail tonight. (1.) "Insect Life". April. It contains a letter from Miss Ormerod about the caterpillars in flour. (E. kühniella). (2.) Form from Cassino, publisher of "Naturalists Directory"; to be filled in with name, address, objects of study &c. (3.) Letter from C. F. Morrison. The poor fellow is only recovering from a very bad illness, & is very shaky yet. He says he is not allowed to write, & only does so because he has escaped the doctors for a moment.

Parasite.

Willow gall.

10.50. P.M.

Senvse came in here a while ago with a "Cosmopolitan" magazine, in which an account of "The Penitent Brothers"; a sect of Mexicans in New Mexico & S. Colorado. They chastise themselves in the most fearful manner every year in lent, & some even are crucified. It often kills them, & 4 young men died on the cross in S. Colorado in 1887! It makes ones blood run cold to think of it — what ghastly barbarity! Let us think of something else: here is our friend the moon looking down upon this letter — it is brilliantly moonlight tonight. It is really very late, and I ought to be going to bed. I sit up to write a letter to Morrison — Goodnight, dear love.

and the planet is to them invisible though most surely there.

If Imes saw clearly the good in Ada's character and none of the overpowering foolishness, he was to some extent deluded, deluded not because he saw falsely but because he did not see enough. I believe that such 'delusions' have many a time been altogether beneficial and that it is possible for good influences combined to conquer bad ones, which cannot combine, as I wrote in my essay on influence long ago.

Of course, in the present instance, Imes himself is not a perfect character, though not a very good type. I mean to say, his ideals would be rather narrow or imperfect, so that acting up to them he would yet fail in some respects. I have expressed this badly but probably you will know what I mean. And so his idealization of Ada would not necessitate perfection in her, but this does not affect the argument. Yet I must admit that it is possible to imagine characters in people that do not exist, though I think this happens less often than is supposed.

I promised Annie that I would keep a diary out here, but I am afraid it is not very full. But as these letters contain all the news and are in diary form, no doubt they will do instead. It is a great deal easier to write my diary to you every day than to write it in a book for myself for your perusal at some distant date.

Sunday, August 7th. Today I have been busy writing and packing up specimens: Letters to Douglas, Olive, Mother, Carlie (the two last enclosed in Olive's short ones), to W. G. Farlow, Cryptogamic botanist of Harvard University, asking whether he will name cryptogamic plants; to Wetherby with a box of shells; to Sutton with some embryo lizards; and to McLachlan with 19 species of Neuroptera in a box.

This afternoon a man named Beddoes came in for a short while with Cox. From what I saw of him and from all accounts I think I shall like him. He is English, a very expert hunter and

mechanic, and lives about four miles from here — some way beyond Hugg's. I mean to make his acquaintance if possible more fully, and will then send you some account of him.

August 8th. Today I have not been well, and as I have been lying down almost all day I have nothing to relate. At first I thought I must have got an attack of jaundice, but now I think it is not that. No doubt I shall be all right in a day or so.

The stove in our house belonged to Brock, it appears, and he came in today and removed it, so we have nothing to cook with except an open fire out of doors.

August 9th. I am not feeling much better today. Payne is also feeling queer. According to arrangements, we are to start for Bear River tomorrow and I must drive down to West Cliff this afternoon. I enclose a pretty little *Chrysis* that is common here. *C. cyanea*, which occurs plentifully at Bedford Park and probably at Isleworth is very much like it.

6 p.m. Have driven down to West Cliff. No letters for me! I hoped to have got your letter of this week before starting tomorrow. Most hearty greeting to Annie.

[The original plan was to go to "Bear" (Yampa) River, but because of Indian troubles to the north, the party took a route that brought them to the Grand Mesa. They began their journey by buckboard and horseback on August 10th, and returned to West Cliff on October 22nd. The route took them to Buena Vista, Twin Lakes, Leadville, Dillon, over what is now Vail Pass to Glenwood Springs, and west to the north base of Grand Mesa. Crossing Grand Mesa, they descended via Surface Creek to Delta and Montrose, then over Blue Mesa via Cerro Summit and Cimarron. A carriage road had recently opened along the Lake Fork of the Gunnison River and they used this to go over the divide from Cebolla Creek into the great sagebrush 'park' to the old Indian Agency, across Cochetopa Pass, and down to Saguache in the San Luis Valley. From Saguache it was a relatively short distance across Poncha Pass to Salida, and thence to the Wet Mountain Valley. Ed.]

August 10th, 1887

Dear Frederic,

Looking round the postoffice (which is also a sort of general store for books, stationery, clothing, etc.) last night, I noted some of the cheap editions of English books. It seemed strange to meet with them in this out-of-the-way place, but there, in paper covers, for 20 cents each, were *Jane Eyre*, *Princess of Thule*, *Story of Ida* (with preface by John Ruskin), *Les Miserables*, etc.

I met Cox down at West Cliff, and we drove home together. This morning, after packing up our things as securely as possible to guard against burglary (my books I left at Cox's) we started off on our journey to Bear River. I was not feeling well and, all things considered, I nearly insisted on staying behind.

Payn and I have been having a good many rows of late about house work, etc. I undertook the cooking, and Payn feels disposed to 'boss it around a bit' and grumbles and is abusive when I don't do things he wants or as he likes them, and the effect of this is to make me less willing to help him than I otherwise should be. If he were more discreet and if I did not fear he would get into difficulties and want some help I would certainly have remained behind. Cox was coming with us, but after going with Payn to Horseshoe Bend he will on no account go with him again, which I am sorry for, as I should have been glad of Cox's company.

Yesterday a small boy came up to our house and told a melancholy tale. He had been traveling with his parents near Cañon City, when a horse strayed away and he was sent to catch it, which he not only failed to do but got lost himself. Getting lifts and walking, he wandered to

Swift Creek, hungry and tired. Payn gave him some food and three dollars and sent him to Cox's, where he slept the night.

As we were traveling the way he wants to go, we took him along. I talked to him a while and found his name was Clarke. He was born in America but family were from Lincolnshire. His father owned a mine. Formerly they had a good deal of money, but his mother was too fond of dressing-up; all the money went and there was very little more forthcoming. He was very curious about the Queen and the Jubilee. Said he 'guessed the Queen didn't do much work, supposed she didn't even do her own washing!' Thought the Queen was the richest woman in the world and wondered if she got as much as four dollars a day. Thought she owned Ireland.

Martin was to meet us where the Ula road (he lives at Ula) joined ours, but we were delayed somewhat and got on the wrong road, so when we did get on the main road Martin had gone on and we could see nothing of him. It came on to rain and hail, thunder and lightning, and we almost thought of stopping for the night at the nearest house or barn. But we had tidings of him and soon found ourselves fixed on to Brush Creek, 2½ miles further, where Martin had gone.

So we went on and found Martin and shelter at the ranch of an Englishman who came out long ago from Devonshire. We are putting in at his barn, very glad of dry lodging, a good meal, and a night's rest.

August 11th. Another wet day! We stopped in our barn all morning, part of the time waiting for Jod to fetch his horse which was in a meadow some distance away, and afterwards to escape a heavy hailstorm followed by rain. At length we packed up and ventured out but had only gone a little way when the rain came on again, more heavily than before. I was riding with Martin on his buckboard and contrived to keep dry, except my feet, by wrapping in a blanket. Payn and Jod rode behind on our buckboard and got rather wet, while the poor Clarke boy, who was riding Jod's horse, got soaked.

So after about six miles we put up at a house (Beckwourth's), now unoccupied except by an old man and his wife as caretakers. Here we found a stove and soon lit a fire and dried the boy by it as best we could, and a meal for us all is now in course of preparation. Payn got the caretaker to sell and cook him two chickens for 75 cents each, and we have ham, corned beef, bread, etc., of our own, so we shall fare sumptuously.

There is a jessamine bush just outside, and a most lovely little hummingbird, ruby-throated with a white breast and green-tinted back, is flying round, at times so near to me that I could almost have caught it with my hand.

August 11th. We started rather late but got along very well and traveled some distance, the weather being fine. The first place we came to was Cold Spring, where there are one or two farms, and we got a drink of fresh milk. While I stopped I got a lovely little fly of the family Dolichopidae, metallic green with speckled wings. After Cold Spring we traveled some time over a very rough district with small hills covered with oak brush, called the Oak Hill district. As we went up the road we saw a coyote or wolf standing in the road ahead. Payn tried to shoot it with a revolver but missed, and the beast made off.

After a while we passed down into Pleasant Valley, a bright-looking valley in the hills at an elevation of about 6,000 feet. We camped in the valley for the mid-day meal, by Cottonwood Creek (not the same Cottonwood as that beyond Lakes of the Clouds). Here was a profusion of flowers, and I got many insects. A bush of hop-vine [*Humulus lupulus*. Ed.] produced some ladybirds (Coccinellidae) and I got some red Lygeids on a yellow-flowered plant which grows very commonly wild here, and is found in gardens at Bedford Park. (There was some by the south fence of our garden at Priory Road; its leaves are very like Michaelmas Daisy).

After leaving Cottonwood Creek, we traveled for a long while along the valley on a gradual upgrade which made it difficult to go fast. The white-flowered poppy, *Argemone platyceras*, appeared by the roadside, evidence that we had descended to a lower level. The Denver and Rio Grande Railway ran close by the road all along, and the trains passing by rather scared our horses and we had some little trouble to hold them in.

The Arkansas River (commonly pronounced Arkansaw) flowed down the valley, and we followed it closely all the latter part of the day. This river is rather wide and very muddy. I could see no traces of Mollusca in it, though *Anodonta dejecta* has been found in it, but I expect that was a long way further down. At the end of the valley we entered a cañon through the mountains where the railway and river also went. We made our night's camp at a place in the cañon called Badger Creek, and put up our tent on an open piece of ground.

August 13th This morning we got off at about nine, and after traveling for a few miles, came to the Hot Springs. These are natural springs, quite warm, rising close to the river. They have been built round, boarded in, and the proprietors of the place charge 50 cents for a bath. Payn, Jod, and I went and bathed, and were much refreshed after traveling. *Physae*, very much like *P. acuta*, were very abundant though small, in the stream flowing from the springs, and some red dragonflies, different from any I have seen before, flew round.

When we emerged from the cañon we had not to travel long before arriving at Salida, a town of over 3,000 inhabitants which has sprung up during the last six years. Just before getting there I found *Helix pulchella* in the rejectamenta of the Arkansas River. Salida, although a new town, has plenty of shops and some good brick buildings. We put up our horses and got lunch.

At the restaurant there was a notice up: 'No vulgar or profane language will be allowed in the
presence of ladies!'

We left the Clarke boy at Salida, as he was
more likely to find tidings of his people there
than anywhere, and there was no use in taking
him farther. After leaving Salida we passed over
a district called 'Adobe', very dry and sandy, but
good soil if irrigated. We have camped by Squaw
Creek, not very far from Salida.

I am quite well again and things are going
more pleasantly than I expected. I ride with Martin and he tells me all about the country and of
his past hunting expeditions.

I am afraid this letter is very incoherent and
disjointed. I write it each day as we travel along,
and in the general hurry and disturbance it is not
very easy to write.

August 14th It has been very hot today and
the road very sandy and difficult to drive over.
We had come some little distance from Squaw
Creek when we found a rattlesnake lying dead
in the road. Someone had killed it and cut off the
rattle. It was a good deal knocked about though
of course easily recognizable and so we left it
there. Perhaps we shall kill one ourselves before
long.

The country is very parched up and we
have had some trouble to get grass for our
horses, but we have camped here at Chalk Creek
in a good grass field. We got here quite early in
the afternoon and meant to have pushed on further but there are trout in the stream and Jod is
anxious to fish, so we wait here the night. I have
just found some *Limnaea*, like *L. palustris*, and
also *Limax campestris*, *Vitrina pellucida*, *Hyalina*,
and *Succinea*.

August 15th. Martin was feeling quite ill
his morning, and altogether we went about the
packing up rather lazily and did not start till 11:
30. We are stopping at Buena Vista, where I shall

post this, for lunch. I enclose wings of a dragon-
fly from Hot Springs and some seeds of various
plants collected on the way. I think you will
grow them best in a rather sandy soil, and in the
greenhouse. Perhaps Annie might take charge of
them and put some in her little red pot. Farewell
till next letter.

P. S. Sunflowers are terrible weeds in this
country. Fields that should be wheat are one yellow blaze of sunflowers, very pretty indeed but
very bad for the farmer.

Aug. 15th, 1887

Dear Frederic,
We got into Buena Vista early this afternoon, where I posted a letter to you. Soon after,
rain came on heavily and seemed likely to last,
and so (as the camping ground will certainly be
very wet if we went on), we decided to stay here
the night, and are now in the 'Commercial' Hotel. The country round here is gradually getting
settled up and railways are being built. Many
very nice-looking houses have by them very
poor and miserable looking log shanties. One
hears that these shanties were the first homes
of the settlers till they obtained enough money,
by keeping cattle and pigs, raising crops, etc., to
build a good house.

Buena Vista is about the same size as Salida.
It is mainly a mining town and would hardly
exist except for the silver mines in the hills, and
the gold to be found in the Arkansas River and
the district generally. There seems to be a good
deal of gambling going on here and the town is
generally 'fast.'

Aug.16th I have suffered the penalty of
sleeping in a Buena Vista hotel. A *Cimex lectu-
larius* was in the bed and bit me all night, so that
for lack of sleep I rose at 5:30. We did not start till
a quarter to nine, but the road was good and we
traveled well, arriving at Granite, 18 miles away.

soon after one o'clock. Granite is in a rather deep cañon of the mountains where the Arkansas River runs, as it did in the cañon at Badger Creek. Two railways run to Granite, side by side. The Denver and Rio Grande was the first, but just this year a new line, the Colorado Midland, has been started, to compete with, and kill the older railway, which it will probably do.

After leaving Granite, we went seven miles, mostly up hill, and arrived at the Twin Lakes. These lakes are the largest in Colorado, one about three miles long, the other rather smaller. They are about 9,000 feet above sea level and surrounded by mountains, much the same as the Lakes of the Clouds. There is an hotel and several houses and a postoffice at Twin Lakes. The place is quite a fishing station also, and several people are camping round to fish for the mountain trout.

August 17th. This morning Payn, Martin, and Jod went out on the lake to fish, but caught nothing. When they returned we packed up and traveled as far as Half Moon Creek, where we camped. Half Moon Creek is a fair-sized stream and produces two species of small trout, one with red spots and the other darker with grey spots. The land on each side of the creek is covered with small birch trees, *Betula glandulosa*, really shrubs rather than trees, with small, rounded leaves. With the birches are dwarf willows and bushy *Potentilla* with bright yellow flowers (*Potentilla glandulosa* Lindley, named by Lindley, who lived at Bedford Park) [Incorrect. This must have been the "shrubby *Cinquefoil*". Ed.] Leadville is not far away and is visible to the extent of a few towers and a great deal of smoke appearing over the hill. Leadville is a large town devoted entirely to mining. The surrounding hills produce immense quantities of metal. It is over 10,000 feet above sea level. This place is 9,000 feet. Soon we shall pass over onto the western slope of the mountains, and in a day or two be at Dillon, where I hope to get some letters forwarded from West Cliff.

August 18th. We packed up and drove into Leadville this morning, where we spent some hours, being delayed while the axle of Payn's buckboard was straightened, for he had bent it by turning too sharply. Leadville is a large town, not so large as Denver but looking a good deal like it in the principal streets, though the suburbs are miserable looking and very dusty. From a distance Leadville reminded me of Warrington because of its many towering chimneys giving out copious smoke — the chimneys of the smelters treat nearly all the ore found about here, though some is actually sent over the Atlantic to Swansea because they have not the proper means of reducing it in America. Fortunes are quickly made and quickly lost in Leadville, and any amount of gambling goes on. There is one gambling place, 'Texas House', which has never been closed, day or night, since it was opened seven years ago.

Leaving Leadville at about five p.m. we drove a few miles and camped close to the East Fork of the Arkansas River, now quite a small stream. We are in a sort of cañon stretching up to Fremont Pass, which we shall cross tomorrow. To the north of us is Zion Mt., and on the other side Prospect Mt., the two railways running along the side of the latter. There is an *Epilobium* very common in wet places in this district, looking like *E. palustre* but with white flowers. It is *E. palustre* var. *albiflorum* [probably this was *E. lactiflorum*. Ed.], the American form of the European species. Probably you will find the type of *E. palustre* at Isleworth.

Just now there is some trouble with the Ute Indians in this state. An old chief named Colorow has started on the war-path with (they say) over 200 warriors, and seems likely to come down on Glenwood Springs or some other place and massacre the inhabitants if measures are not taken to prevent it. Scouts have observed their movements and have seen the squaws making bullets. However, troops have been called out and left Leadville yesterday, so they will doubtless put down the rebellion very quickly and either capture or scatter the Indians. At present I think nobody has been killed, though there are various reports to the contrary. As we propose to hunt just up in Colorow's part of the country, it will be as well for us that it shall be quashed before we arrive.

In Leadville I bought for 15 cents a Ruskin — *The Eagles Nest: Ten lectures on the relation of Natural Science to Art*, given before the University of Oxford in Lent term, 1872 (J. W. Lovell & Co., New York, pirated edition of course). I have read the first three chapters of lectures and like it very much, better than any other Ruskin I have read, perhaps partly because of present circumstances. In the midst of all the cheating and humbug of this country and the not too select conversation of all I come in contact with, it is very refreshing to get into a different, honest, and pure atmosphere, though only from a book. I should like Annie to read this book if she has not already. I am sure she would like it. (I suppose you can get it from Smith's.) I am marking the bits that strike me, and will give you note of them.

The Eagle's Nest, Lecture I. 3. Definitions of Science, Art, and Literature: I don't think these are quite reasonable in a way, because although he defines Science as knowledge of things, he splits the modification of things into Art and Literature, and yet places the three on an equal basis. Should it not be that Art is the modification of things by our power, and Literature is a form of Art?

11. 'Not one person in a hundred is capable of seriously reasoning.' Annie has often said something like this. The following bit is very good, ending, 'and in general all false reasoning', etc. 12 13, 14, 15, about rowing and dancing — good and bad art. 'The higher the art the more capable of degradation.' *Good!* 16, last part: 'Now remember', etc. 17: 'But the true folly. . .is the exertion of our art power in an evil direction.' 18: 'In all cases. . .its absence indicates moria.' [= folly, stupidity. Ed.]. 19, last part: 'And I will', etc. Science, or rather vision: 'Instead of regarding none of the sources of happiness, she regards nothing else, and that she measures all worthiness by pure felicity.' This is the end of the first lecture; it is half past ten and Payn is clamouring

for me to put out the light, so I must postpone further notes until some future opportunity.

August 19th. This morning I collected *Epilobium angustifolium* by our camp. This species is common about here. It occurs in many places in England also, though perhaps hardly native; I think I have seen it near Dorking. When we left camp we passed up the gulch and over Fremont Pass (the border line between the eastern and western slopes of the Rocky Mountains, and also between Lake and Summit counties; the pass is 12,133 ft. high.)

The road was extremely rocky and difficult to drive over. The axle of Payn's buckboard got bent again turning round too sharply, and this added to the difficulty of getting along. Blue gentians were very abundant all along the road in the pass, as well as *Epilobium angustifolium* and other flowers, and some *Rumex salicifolius*. You will remember that I sent you seeds of the *Rumex* from McCook, Nebraska, but up on the pass here it was only just coming into fruit, which difference is I presume due to the altitude.

Passing over the ridge we came to the western slope and the beginning of Ten Mile Creek, which runs into the Blue River and ultimately through the Grand and Colorado rivers into the Gulf of California. A few miles down Ten Mile Creek we came to a mining town called Robinson, where we hunted, and I posted to you a Leadville paper with some account of the Indian troubles. Close to Robinson is another mining town called Kokomo. Both are small and apparently not very prosperous, the mines being hardly worked at present in that neighborhood.

After Robinson the road became just as bad as you can well imagine, up and down hill, covered with rocks, and a steep sloping bank of loose rocks on one side for part of the way. At one place our wheel struck against a great stone, and the whole buckboard narrowly escaped being thrown over the bank and down some 70 feet, where we should certainly have been reduced to a fragmentary condition.

After a while, however, we got out into an open valley full of willow brush, and camped near a place called Wheeler where there is good grass and water in the creek running just by.

Now for a few more Ruskin notes. Lecture II. 26. Prudence and wisdom compared with example of two girls and the stars. I think the examples he gives are very serviceable ones. 27. 'The higher Sophia.' 31. 'In the degree of his wisdom, an artist is unconcerned about his work as his own,' etc. I am very doubtful about this. I think the truest art would be when the artist, knowing or feeling something, deeply wishes to convey his feeling to another or others and so obtain sympathy or to please — in short, to produce happiness. Surely he would he very much concerned about it as his own, or if it were another's, as *his* own. Oft is not the greatest beauty in an artistic product owing to its having been produced and being the expression of particular human beings, not in its mere form or colour? Surely we take most pleasure in *human* art, though for mere form it can never approach a moss or an insect. 32, latter part: I think this is true, in great measure at any rate. 3. 'In a little while the discoveries of which were now so proud will be familiar to all', etc. — the misuse of them. 35. I think it is so. 36, Last part: 'Will you hawk at game or carrion?' Very good!

August 20th. Today we have come up a very narrow and rocky cañon and then to open ground with small willows for a few miles till we reached Dillon, the whole distance being about ten miles. We had not long started when it came on to rain, and it has done so steadily ever since, while the wind blew bitterly cold, making our drive extremely chilly and unpleasant. At one place where we had to cross Ten Mile Creek we found a bridge all broken down on one side, with a notice up in writing: 'This bridge is unsafe for horses and vehicles. Whoever endeavors to cross it does so at his own risk!' Fancy this on the county road, a highway between two towns!

We got over without mishap by careful driving, but that bridge certainly ought to receive the attention of the authorities, seeing that they levy taxes towards the preservation of the roads.

Dillon is quite a small place with scattered houses. It is the end of the railway and thus acquires importance. We hear fresh news about the Indian trouble; it seems there will certainly be a war. I do not think there is any chance of our being able to hunt on Bear River at present at any rate, as we should be exterminated to a certainty if we met any Indians. The Indians fight to great advantage because they know the country perfectly and can shoot from behind trees and brush without being seen. I wonder if you hear anything about these matters in the English papers, and what sort of account they give.

Directly we got to Dillon I rushed to the postoffice and caused (I imagine) some amusement at my appearance — wrapped in a great shawl and dripping wet. I got a grand lot of letters: Yours of — (why don't you date your letters?) with Annie's of July 20th enclosed (which I am altogether delighted to have, and very grateful to you for forwarding it), letters from Mother, Carlie, and Douglas, and a post card of later date from Mother. They appear not to have forwarded my papers, and no *Schoolmistress* or *Pall Mall Budget* turns up.

Now in answer to your letter: *Sartor Resartus*. Of course I admit that most of it is very clever, but still somehow I don't quite like it myself. Probably Annie's explanation of this is the correct one.

We have just been in to dinner — some amusement caused by manner of servant girl who did everything with as much speed as if she had but ten minutes to live, making remarks all the while. She told one unlucky man, before the assembled company, that he had eaten more supper than he had for a month before! They are free and easy in these parts, certainly.

But to return to your letter. Payn doesn't improve particularly on further acquaintance, as I have told you, but he has been much more pleasant since we started on this trip, and we get on pretty well just now by carefully avoiding treading on each other's toes.

Yes, I had just heard of the Nelsons before I started. Annie, I think, had just met Nelson, junior, and did not think much of him. Is not this so? So, far from thinking you have described the Nelsons at too great length, you have not described them enough; appearance, occupation, manners, etc., are omitted, so that I can not really imagine them. You should describe people as if they were new species of snails, and then add further details. Annie describes Forester and Louy in her letter quite in the right sort of way.

I do hope that you and Annie have been down into Surrey together by this time, but if not, I trust you have gone away, at any rate, for a day or two yourself. I am sure you must have needed a change, though it is not pleasant to go entirely by oneself.

Were any of the spiders sent to O.P.C. uncommon? And were they different from the Bedford Park species? I sent some spiders to him from West Cliff myself and hope to hear from him soon. I am glad to hear about the *Ephestia* being the genuine *kuelmiella.* I shall be so interested to see his note on the subject. I presume he will write to the *Entomologist.*

Talking of the *Entomologist,* has any discussion arisen in its pages from my paper on varietal nomenclature?

I am astonished at the proof of that *Science Gossip* paper turning up. I must have written it at least a year ago, and hearing nothing of it (I wrote once asking what they had done with it). I presumed it had gone into the waste paper basket and been oxidised. I almost forget what was in it, but I expect a good deal is stale news by this time, and some may need correction. I rather wish you had sent the proof to me and written them that they must wait till I returned it, but I suppose you have sent it back long ago. I trust it is all right. You and Carlie between you should be able to correct it anyway. There are, or were, some illustrations also.

As to the books, for their sake I sincerely trust you have been to Priory Road and secured them long ago. There is only one important one, the large one with small writing in it, commencing with descriptions by Moquin-Tandon. That book is invaluable and I would not have it lost for anything.

Fancy your reciting in public! I wish I had been there to hear. I really don't know what *Shamus O'Brien* is — comic or tragic? And not getting home till after twelve! Frederic! What was the thrilling story you wrote? Will it be published? If so, mind you send me a copy. I think it would be very good for you all to play Lawn Tennis. I wish I could be there to join you in the game. Never be afraid your letters won't be interesting. I gloat over them. If you were out here and in my position you would understand how precious letters are, and how much they are looked forward to.

I hope Annie will go for another holiday somewhere and write you such another letter as the one you forward. I am the more pleased to have it because it was unexpected and it tells me all about her doings and thoughts at the time.

Lunatics must be very depressing, certainly, but otherwise very interesting. I must go round a lunatic asylum when I get the chance.

I feel rather glad that Annie doesn't care much for *Princess of Thule,* because everyone else I know who has read it likes it considerably, and I felt alone in not caring for it so much.

We have harebells in any quantity here, just as at Sutton, but *Artemisia* takes the place of heath; they call it 'sage brush', and dwarf willows are here instead of furze. Thistles we have but no thyme, though a very strongly scented mint grows by streams.

I think that photograph of Annie with her hair down must look rather queer. But I think I ought to have one, anyway. Do try to procure one for me, or one of her ordinary appearance if it is taken. Carlie says in his letter (from Comiston, July 27th): 'Had a postcard from Frederic yesterday — Annie and Louy at Sutton. F.G.F[enn] to follow later on.' Do I understand from this that you will spend your holidays at Sutton? I hope so, but your next letter will tell me.

August 21st. Though it is Sunday, we have a post as usual, and I have a bundle of papers: *Schoolmistress*, July 28th, with two very nice chapters of *Merely Friends*, for which my particular thanks to Annie. *Journal of Conchology* for July, *Punch*, July 16th, with very good picture of Atherley Jones, and *Pall Mall Budget*.

The *Schoolmistress* is quite right. There are only two things that really give courage and hopefulness, if indeed they can be called two. This is the everlasting human truth which many profess to believe, most ignore at least in part, and very few act up to. When will people understand that they have no real existence except in relation to others?

I think the person who named Niagara 'blue' must have been thinking of the still water under the falls rather than the falls themselves, for they are white with foam.

I see your paper has appeared all right in *Journ. Conch.* Ponsonby is a little behindhand with his *Testacella* found by 'an English clergyman.' I presume Pearce's *Arion sp?* (p. 212) was *subfuscus*. I don't believe in Williams' dextral *Physa*; no doubt it is a thin *P. peregra*. I am pretty sure he wouldn't know the difference. You see, *A. bourgignati* is turning up everywhere: Barmouth, Merionethshire, Handsworth, W. Birmingham.

Some more Ruskin notes. Lecture III. 37, last part: The proper grasp of facts already known essential to a man of science. 38, last part of, and 39: Wise art the expression of wise science. 40: 'but shadows.' 41, first and last parts: 'You will never love art well till you love what she mirrors better' (compare this with 31). 43: The subjects of wise science also the subjects of wise art.

48: W. Gould's collection an example of 'delicate and patient art.' You have seen the hummingbirds at the Museum, and can judge.

To me they seem very bad art just because, to use Ruskin's own argument, they are not arranged in accordance with wise (or true) science. I have seen real hummingbirds over real flowers, and they are quite different, and infinitely more beautiful than W. Gould's glass-cased specimens. To appreciate the Gould collection one must forget the cases and look only at the birds. Of course, Gould as an ornithologist deserves all possible praise though.

Ruskin's account of the bullfinch's nest and comments thereon are very interesting. Question: Whether artists properly appreciate their own work. I think they do, though in a different way from other people. 54, 55, are good. 59: Ruskin's reflections at the bottom of Ludgate Hill. What does it all amount to? 61, middle part: Religious education starting in lies. Quite so. Certain of our masters and pastors seem to think that truth is stranger than fiction, and so, being anxious that we should believe *something*, start with lies as a sort of easy first lesson!

63, last part, and 64: 'Life at Ludgate Hill, or death of the I. of Dogs.' Lecture IV. 66: On a limit to be put to further knowledge owing to lack of understanding what is known. I think Ruskin is wrong here. The man who finds the new titmouse only knows it is new because he is familiar with all present knowledge. To know enough to tell what is not known is surely the fullest knowledge, and I believe it is better to know very much of one thing than very little of all things, for it is very true that to know one thing perfectly is to know the essence of everything.

67. Theology a science, if true. If not a science, false, obviously, yet this would scandalise most theologians! 71, last part, and 73: 'If the ball room is bright and the dresses pretty, what matter how much horror is beneath or around. Nay, this apathy checks us in our highest spheres of thought, and chills our most solemn purposes.' Very, very true. 74, last part: Is it so? This is the end of Lecture IV and as far as I have read at present.

I am sitting in the hotel writing this. Just now some excitement was caused by a horse running away with the cook, but she held on tightly and has got back safe and sound. Ladies know how to ride in this part of the world (there aren't any women in America; they are all 'ladies').

We are going to camp out about a mile and a half from the town, so I will close this up before we start. Enclosed are a gentian from top of Fremont Pass, *Potentilla glandulosa* [see previous note. Ed.] from Twin Lakes, and a daisy (not *Bellis perennis* though; that doesn't grow in America) from Dillon. Please give these to Annie. I am afraid they haven't dried very well. I had them in my purse.

Now farewell — my sympathy to Annie.

Yours always, Theo. D.A.C.

Dillon, Colorado, Aug. 21st, 1887

Dear Frederic,

I posted a letter to you this afternoon, and then we drove on a mile or so from Dillon and camped here by Straight Creek, which runs close by into Blue River. It has been a fine starlight evening with a new moon, and Payn, Martin, and I have been sitting round the fire discussing the Indians. Fresh news is brought by a man just arrived from Bear River district [this is the Yampa Valley. Ed.] that the Indians are in what is called 'Twenty-Mile Park' and are ravaging the country. The settlers are assembling together for mutual protection. The town of Meeker is said to be in danger of attack [but the Meeker Massacre occurred on September 20, 1879. This mention must concern a renewal of hostilities. Ed.].

I have been reading Lecture V of Ruskin's *Eagle's Nest* and have now come to some that I very much disagree with. In 77: 'For the true strength of every human soul is to be dependent . . and to be depended upon', etc. Here is exactly Carlie's theory of friends — you know how much I disagree with it. Truly, I think that the true strength of every human soul is to be co-dependent with others, but rather different than nobler or inferior. I take this as an axiom: That whatever is able to perfectly help or cooperate with another is equal to it, not necessarily in power but in quality. If in a machine one part is better wrought than another, it breaks down, but all and each should be good for its appointed work, none nobler or less than the rest, though indeed it may *occur* that the writer is nobler than his printer, the composer than the instrument maker. Yet I may say that, if each does well, he is equal to the other. Differences in quality are between things of the same kind, not between different [ones]. All our affections, friendships, undertakings — whatever is between one and another — should be like the 'one-hoss shay', made equally strong in every part, though the parts are not alike.

August 22nd. Today is my 21st birthday, and I am 'come of age.' Such an event is usually regarded with a certain amount of pride and importance, though I can scarcely understand why, and for my part I feel rather bewildered to realise that I am 21, or any particular age whatsoever. Yet, if we could be gathered together (and in spirit at least we may be) it might be a time to think over hopes and resolves, not newly made today but old yet unfulfilled.

It is a cold, rainy day, with only here and there a glimpse of the sun, and I lie in the tent reading and thinking, and wondering what is going on at Isleworth. It is now afternoon, but owing to the difference of time between here and England, it must be evening with you. It is Monday, too, so I imagine Annie sitting up in your room, writing *Chit-chat*, by her side a pair of scissors and some old newspapers. You are sitting and arranging some captures of yesterday and entering up the Fauna and Flora. Conversations at intervals. I imagine the cabinet, the books on the mantelpiece. (I trust you have a bookshelf now, and that the books are not so inconveniently crowded.) The aquarium map of Isleworth by the door, boxes of shells; bed, and sober-coloured carpet.

The view out of the window I don't imagine, because it is dark. Yet it rather obtrudes in my visual imagery of the room because I have only been in it by day. I see a Burne-Jones [Sir Edward Burne-Jones, leading painter and designer, designer-illustrator of the Kelmscott (Press) *Chaucer* and close collaborator of William Morris. Ed.] picture on one wall, and a drawing by Annie. The chalk heads of Annie and Kitty I can only half picture because I never saw them and don't know whether they are red or black, and if they hang in black frames on the north wall. The table stands in the middle of the room, rather towards the window, and candles are being used. I do not know what the table is like and this puts me out a little, but I suppose it is round. Have I the picture right? If not, correct me.

Now, you shall imagine me. Spacious tent (ten feet by 14), flies assembled in great numbers on roof (I cannot imagine where so many come from). T.D.A.C. in right hand corner, prostrate on blanket, writing this. Cocoa tin (full of insects in small envelopes) and map of Colorado visible in hold-all, butterfly net behind, cardboard ink bottle in front, Payn's banjo (in blue cloth cover) on one side, two pillows, sponge bag, and Jod's hat. T.D.A.C. in thin grey suit and wearing Payn's high Swiss boots (if I remember right, he came to Isleworth in them), familiar broad-brimmed hat on head (burnt on one side of brim while lighting fire at Nathrop). Jod, also prostrate, in middle of tent, reading paper cover *Alan Quartermain*. Beyond, Martin's gun in red blanket, and his bag and bedding. Two tin plates — knife and fork — and his tin cup on ground (i.e., grass). On shawl in one corner, another tin plate with three small trout Payn caught this morning. Rain pitter-pat on tent. Outside grassy, with willows, firs old and young, and *Potentillae*. Log cabin (not in use), stream (Straight Creek), mountains at some distance all round. I forgot to mention one thing inside: Payn's 'black and tan' dog, Nell, on red rug by my side.

I have been reading more Ruskin, and am very much afraid I have come to the end of the part I like. Lecture V. 82: 'More pleasure taken in small things than in great.' Not always, though it may be often so. I would put it in this way: We take pleasure in a thing in proportion to our appreciation of it, and it is sometimes easier to fully appreciate the good or beauty in small or simple things than in large and complicated ones. 80: 'that which increaseth knowledge, increaseth sorrow.' Yes, or gladness, according to whether the knowledge is used well or ill. 85: 'We must endeavor to do not what is absolutely best but what is easily within our power.' If Ruskin were not ill, I would write and ask him to explain. Does he mean we are not to do the best we can, but only what comes easiest? Surely rather he would say: 'Do that which you are most able, for that is best, but spare no effort.' 94, last portion. I don't think Ruskin can seriously mean all this! 95. I am sure he is quite right here. All true art has been the reflection of the time and not copied from ancient monuments.

August 23rd. Here are the prices of some of Ruskin's books out here (Lovell's Library). *Sesame and Lilies; Crown of Wild Olive; Ethics of the Dust; Unto this Last*, ten cents each. *Stones of Venice*, three volumes, 25 cents each. *Modern Painters*, Volume 1, 20 cents. *Munera Pulvaris, Time and Tide, Lectures on Art*, 15 cents each.

Today has been a little finer, yet not fine enough for me to do much collecting, though I have secured four butterflies of the genera *Lycaena, Argynnis, Pieris,* and *Colias,* the last three new to me although I believe common about here. I walked to Dillon in the afternoon and got caught in the rain coming back, but not much wetted. This evening Martin has been telling us stories of his past experiences in Wet Mountain Valley as we sit round the fire. He says 70 people have been violently killed within 30 miles of West Cliff during the past 15 years, which is a large number considering the size of the population.

August 24th. Early this morning Martin rushed into the tent in a great state of excitement saying that 'Jock', his dog, was after a bear. He ran out again with his gun, and I followed soon after, with Payn and Jod also some distance behind. We lost sight of Martin in the wood and, seeing nothing of the bear after a good search, we returned. After a while Martin came back and told us that he had seen the bear twice (it was a black one) but could not get a shot at it, so it escaped and was probably miles away by then. So we consoled ourselves by eating a good breakfast, and Payn shooting small birds.

It is curious out here that men generally address each other by their Christian names, however little they may be acquainted. Martin seems to think my name is not sufficiently abbreviated into 'Theo' and so calls me 'The', which sounded a little strange until I got accustomed to it.

2:30 p.m. I have just been for a short botanical excursion and secured the following plants: *Epilobium angustifolium*, common by the stream, *Fragaria vesca* (wild strawberry) in abundance, *Ribes oxyacanthoides?* [probably *Ribes inerme*. Ed.], a wild gooseberry plant but not in flower or fruit so cannot be sure of the species, two species of harebell, *Campanula uniflora* [very unlikely at that altitude. Ed.] and *C. rotundifolia* (the last will be the same species as Annie found at Sutton), *Betula glandulosa* (dwarf birch), *Arctostaphylos uva-ursi* (bearberry, an English species, see 'Johns'), *Picea engelmannii* (spruce fir), and a few others I have not succeeded in naming. I also found a beetle very nearly allied to the British *Quedinus fuliginosus*.

5:35 p.m. Coming to the postoffice I was surprised to find among the books for sale on the counter a paper cover 20 cent *Cashel Brown's Profession*. Bernard Shaw should feel proud. Tomorrow, if the weather is fine (very doubtful that!) or at any rate soon, we intend to start off somewhere to hunt. We shall see where to go as we proceed.

The Indian news is more peaceful than before, and we may be able to go to our original locality, Bear River, in safety. It is not unlikely that we shall be for some time out of reach of any postoffice, so if you don't hear from me for an unusually long interval please don't imagine anything has gone wrong, for we haven't the remotest intention of going anywhere or doing anything that is not particularly wise or safe.

I hoped to have some letters today, but the delay in having them forwarded from West Cliff no doubt accounts for their non-arrival. I will post this now although it is quite a short letter, only of four days, since I may not be able to send another for some little while.

Tuesday, August 25th, 1887

Dear Frederic,
Walking up to Dillon yesterday I met a man on horseback and passed him, noticing that he had a rather nice face and wore spectacles. When we came back late in the evening we were surprised to see a fire blazing at our camp, and arriving there found the man in spectacles whom I had met, standing by it. He proved to be a cowboy who had been searching for a lost cow, and being overtaken by the rain, had gone into the log cabin by our tent and lit a fire in front of it. We were glad enough to find such ready means of getting dried and warmed on our return, for it was raining hard. The cowboy departed early this morning between daybreak and sunrise before any of us were up.

Owing to the very wet weather we have decided not to start today but wait until it is tolerably fine. Nothing is more unpleasant than to have to camp in the rain and on wet ground.

9:00 p.m. It has been fine today after all, and we shall start tomorrow. Payn and Martin have just gone up to Dillon to have 'one last game' of billiards before leaving. They have played billiards together the best part of every day that we have been here.

I found a lot of *Equisetum pratense* growing close to the camp today. It is very nearly allied to *E. arvense* which is common at Bedford Park, on the railway bank, etc. *E. arvense* also is found in America but I have not found it here as yet. I have collected a large number of insects today, putting them away in small envelopes duly labeled with locality, etc., for future reference. I find the small envelope method very convenient except for moths. I shall certainly adopt it for my English captures when I return. It is so easy to write data, etc., on the envelope, and they can be packed away very easily.

August 26th, 7:45 p.m. This morning we packed up our things and started again on our travels. The day has been quite fine, and we have traveled along by the Blue River (blue it may have been; now it is yellow with mud because of the gold washing and mining along it, all the refuse mud and sand being thrown into the river). The Blue River is a fairly wide stream but shallow and rocky, bordered by willows round which fly numbers of *Vanessa antiopa* (after always regarding this insect as such a rarity in England, I enjoy the sight of it in such profusion) and also another butterfly, apparently a *Limnetis*, but I have not yet secured one for examination. At one place the road cut through a bank of ancient river-mud, and in it I found thousands of shells of *Patula cooperi* in a sub-fossil state (Ingersoll records *P. cooperi* from the Blue River Valley).

We stopped for lunch at a place called Naomi, a small settlement of six or seven houses by a creek. Here I got a species of *Grapta* new to me, not unlike the English *Grapta c-album* or 'Comma Butterfly.' After Naomi we went a few miles and camped amongst the willows, just where Slate Creek runs into the Blue River. There is a sort of small, swampy ditch close by, which I find swarming with *Pisidium pusillum*, quite like those found in England.

We are in a long valley between two ranges of mountains, the 'Blue River Valley.' To the east of us is a large mountain called Ute Mountain, and above it a break in the range — 'Ute Pass.' To the west some low hills, and beyond a tall peak called 'Powell Peak' and another mountain, very jagged on the top — 'Blue River Mountain.' North of us the valley stretches till the Blue runs into the Grand River, which flows west.

Aug. 27th, 7:30 p.m. Today we have only come a few miles. We intended to camp by Black Lake, and had got as far as the creek running into it and about five miles from the lake, when it came on to rain, so we quickly ran up the tent to get dry ground and cover for ourselves from the wet. As we came along we saw an eagle sitting on a tree the other side of Blue River. Payn shot at it but missed.

Our camp is close to Black Lake Creek, a swift creek running over great stones, with deep pools here and there. Bordering the creek are various trees but mostly 'Quaking Asps', as is usual by creeks at a moderate elevation (about 7,000 ft. more or less to 8,000). Dead shells of *Patula cooperi* are very abundant, and Martin, when he went fishing, saw some living snails which must have been *P. cooperi* also. The trout in this creek are different from the others I have seen. They have obscure transverse bands in additional to the usual markings. Close to the tent I found specimens of a fungus of the genus *Polyporus*, closely allied to, but not identical with the Bedford Park *P. versicolor*.

Jod rode up to Black Lake and reports it a very nice place. Some capitalist (Senator Jones, Martin says his name is) has a house and some land up there which he uses as a summer resort and has friends to hunt and fish.

Sunday, August 28th, 7.45 p.m. We are still by Black Lake Creek, only we have come a good way up the gulch and have camped not very far from the lake. It has been rainy today but not altogether so, and Payn, Jod and Martin have been out fishing in the creek, catching a large number of small trout so that we all had a good meal off them. Our meals out here generally consist of bacon or beef with cocoa and bread. Martin and I do the cooking.

The bread has to be made in this wise: A quantity of flour is mixed in with a little baking powder and a few pinches of salt. This is stirred up with water until liquid enough to pour out. Then a 'Dutch Oven' (a sort of saucepan on legs and with a cover) is heated in the fire, and the bottom greased with bacon fat. The dough is poured in, the oven covered up and placed amongst hot ashes for ten minutes or so. The result is a flat cake of bread, fairly good to eat when you can get no other.

Coming up here we met Senator Jones coming down. He seems a pleasant sort of man.

I have found quite a number of Mollusca by today's camp: *Patula cooperi* (dead shells), *P. striatella* (very young), *Vertigo sp.*, *Pupa sp.* (exactly like *P. marginata*) with three teeth instead of one. *P. marginata* has been recorded from Blue River Valley. Perhaps these were meant, but I consider them a distinct species; *Vitrea pellucida*, *Helix pulchella* var. *costata*, *Succinea* (I think *nuttalliana*), *Limax campestris* (dark variety), *Hyalina fulva*, and *Pisidium fulvum* (in the creek), and some *Hyalina arborea* under logs, etc.

A species of barberry, *Berberis* [*Mahonia*. Ed.] *repens* Lindley grows here. It is very like a species very frequently grown in English gardens, though perhaps not the same one. Probably the garden one is *B. aquifolium*, which is not found in Colorado.

This evening I saw a very beautiful and unusual sunset effect. The sun was behind a hill and out of sight, but it shone red on the opposite hill and on the rain and mist above and beyond it, in strange contrast to the leaden colour of the rest of the sky.

We have not moved camp today. Early this morning Payn and Jod had a great quarrel, over the weather (!), Payn supporting his arguments by all sorts of extraordinary statements. When he appealed to me I told him quite plainly that I thought him the greatest liar I ever came across, whereat he threatened to knock me down, and used the most abusive language you can well imagine. But familiarity breeds contempt and, being about used to his elegant expressions I was not greatly disturbed, and now he is quite peaceful again and fairly agreeable.

After breakfast I walked up to the Black Lake. On the way we met a Swede, six years from Gotland, driving down. He is in the employ of Jones and seems on the whole decidedly a nicer man than his master, though Jones himself is pleasant enough to us. He is 'General' Jones, not Senator. He was captain in the army, on the strength of which he is dubbed General.

Black Lake is somewhat semicircular, about a mile across, very deep, which makes it look black. Jones has a little steam launch on the lake. On the way to and fro from the lake I collected plants, insects, etc. Close to our camp I found two adult *Patula striatella* and saw *Vanessa antiope*. Near the lake, on a stone in the stream, I saw a dipper (*Cichlus*). It is not such a pretty bird as the English one by any means, being brown-grey, and grey instead of white on the breast.

A little further on I came across a small pond swarming with *Limnaea palustris*, quite of the ordinary kind, with a few specimens also of *Moust. decollatum*. The pond also contained quantities of a species of *Sphaerium* just like *S. corneum* only smaller. They may be *S. securum*. On the surface of the water were specimens of *Gerris* [water strider. Ed.] very like the usual English one. (No doubt you can get it at Isleworth. I find I have a note of the occurrence of *Gerris* in your district.) By the pond I saw the first frog I have seen in this country. It was greenish with dark green spots and blotches. Crawling in the road I found a beetle of the genus *Meloë*, I think *M. strigulosus*. It is the first of these curious insects I have seen in Colorado (you will probably find *Meloë* at Isleworth. I once found one, probably *M. proscarabeus*, at Hanwell).

The plants I found included the following: *Geum macrophyllum*, resembling the British *G. urbanum* but taller, *Potentilla hippiana* var. *pulcherrima*, flower like *P. reptans* but on a rather tall stem, leaves whitish beneath, *Gentiana affinis*, deep blue, and *Sidalcea candida*, a white-flowered plant ot the order Malvacea.

August 30th, 12:30 p.m. I have thought over the matter carefully and long and have told Payn that I shall leave him. If we could be even tolerably good friends I would not have done this, but I do not feel obliged in any way to live with him merely to do cooking and odd jobs, and stand any amount of unpleasantness and abuse. Besides which, many of his acts and words are objectionable enough to me when he is trying to please, and of course my manners and customs are equally unsuited to him. I believe I can without difficulty earn an independent living in West Cliff, and if there is nobody there who can be my friend in the deeper sense of the word, there are at least plenty who wish me well and will help me where they can, so that, reasonably circumstanced, and writing to you and hearing from you every week, I may be fairly happy till it is time to return.

As for Payn, he is getting through his money quickly, though he has written for more, and I shall not be surprised if he leaves Colorado before the winter. In any case, I don't think I could be of much use to him, to prevent him from spending overmuch, playing poker, etc. He will do that anyway, and if he should need help during the winter, I shall be living not far from him and will do what I can. I should very much like to hear what you and Annie think of this, whether you think I have done right or wrong, under the circumstances.

Jod has gone off today, as he too is about tired of Payn, and as Payn would be left alone with Martin, and we are out here so far from home, I have agreed to remain with him the rest of the expedition until we return to West Cliff, provided he is not too offensive on the way.

August 31st, 7:45 p.m. We had meant to go down the Blue River still further and then turn west over the range to Piney River and beyond, but we hear that there is no road that we can cross over with our buckboards, so there is nothing for it but to go back to Dillon and to the hunting ground beyond Glenwood Springs by way of Tennessee Pass.

A story reaches us that the Indians led some of the cowboys into an ambush and killed two and wounded others, and altogether, we cannot go safely to Bear River or anywhere north of Grand River. From Black Lake Creek we could see in the distance the range of hills beyond which the Indians are camped, no very great distance away.

We packed up at about 12 o'clock and have got as far on our return journey as Naomi, where we are now camped. Tomorrow we shall pass through Dillon.

Coming by some stony ground this afternoon, we heard a great noise of barking, and found Payn's little dog attacking a great porcupine which had sought shelter in a hole in the rocks. The dog was unwise enough to attempt to bite the animal and as a result got its nose and mouth covered with prickles, which we extracted with considerable difficulty and pain to the dog. Afterwards, Payn got out his gun and shot the porcupine, and now he has skinned it. It is a great beast over 2½ feet long, The bristles are interspersed with and partly hidden by hairs, and not so long as in the African porcupine.

September 1st, 12:45 p.m. We have just arrived at Dillon and found a host of letters from you, and two *Schoolmistress*, etc., etc. I have just rushed through them and now send this off. Will write again in answer to next letter.

Camp at Ten Mile Creek, Dillon,
September 1st. 1887

Dear Frederic,
We came here from Naomi today, arriving at Dillon after a not very eventful journey, the only things to note being that I got a new butterfly, and we came across a place where gold-bearing quartz was to be found, but failed to discover a piece. At Dillon I made for the postoffice, and

to my intense disgust was told that there were no letters for me! But presently the postmaster discovered that he *had* some — a great bundle put aside for me and for the moment forgotten! I snatched them up and proceeded to overhaul them, feeling like a very hungry man suddenly placed before a table full of viands and not knowing what to commence on!

There were two letters from you, bearing Isleworth postmark August 8th, and the other London, postmarked August 2nd; two letters from Mother, letters from Carlie, Olive, and Leslie, postcards from Carlie and Dru Drury, a drinking cup (collapsible) from Douglas, *Schoolmistress* August 4th and 11th, two *Pall Mall Budget*, August *Naturalist*, August *Natural World,* and *Labor Enquirer* August 20th. Is not this a grand lot of letters to have received?

Now I must answer your letters. Figuier's *Day After Death* is a little queer. I don't think it 'amounts to much' as they say in this country. When you mentioned the visits to the Richards', for the moment I imagined them talking to the Professor and his wife, till I suddenly recollected that the Professor, well, did not live at Isleworth! Annie's verdict on the *Princess of Thule* exactly agrees with my idea, which gives me considerable satisfaction. I should like to see that *Pall Mall Gazette* Academy Guide with yours and Annie's marginal notes immensely, though I have not seen the pictures themselves. I envy Olive and Carlie that walk to Kew Bridge. Alas! When again shall I? I don't remember Dr. Beckingsale distinctly though I know the name. It amuses me your saying Vancouver Island is 'but a little further on;' only just about fifteen hundred miles, that is all. I am very glad to hear of Annie's success in selling another picture for £8. I congratulate her, but which was it? Have I seen it?

I feel rather alarmed about Chalto and Windus publishing the uncorrected proofs. I pray, with you, that there are no glaring errors (though the *glaring* errors don't much matter; it is the ones that aren't recognised as such that give all the trouble). I have not yet seen either the July or August *Science Gossip*.

Really, I ought to have one of those photographs of Annie. Surely I may? Can't you send me one?

Poor Nelly Allport. I am sorry she is ill. I think she is a better sort of girl than superficially appears. Just before I started she came and sat for hours sewing on my buttons, tapes with name, mending my shawl, etc., which made me feel rather ashamed of myself because I thought *I* should never have taken so much trouble for *her*. Did you hear of her going to read every day for months to an old blind man? It is strange that such a good creature should be combined with such an utterly ridiculous person as Sally Allport is.

I am glad to hear of you and Annie playing tennis. It will do you both good if you really like it. I wish I could play with you. Theoretically, you certainly should go away for a holiday, but I don't think I should if I were in your place, all the same. I am sorry to hear of Annie not being well that hot Sunday. I wish I could go for a real long holiday somewhere, not merely to a lunatic asylum. Beg her not to work so late at night. It is all very well for the others to sit up to twelve sewing or occupied in handwork, but it won't do for writing, which is much harder and more exhausting, though she may not feel it at the time. I daren't work late even for a few nights, and I am sure it can't be good for Annie. Annie would scold me dreadfully if I did anything so unwise, so I hope she will consider it. There is the future to look to as well as the present.

Yes, I am now 21. Looking back, there is much that might have been and was not, and much also that might not have been, and was, many things to regret, and yet, somehow I would not change those 21 years for anyone else's. If I regret more, I also rejoice more. If many things have done me harm, some things have done me real unalterable good and are yet doing me good. Hope, faith, and love are still with me. 'They have brought me one if not more friends', you write — surely two friends! Frederic, are you not my friend?

I like *Merely Friends* better and better. It does me no end of good. It is almost like a letter every week from Annie, but I am very anxious to see the next chapter, from the way XVIII ends. I have some foreboding as to Douglas' future. I hope nothing bad is going to happen to him. It's no good saying that it's only a story, and it doesn't really matter what happens; in this story the characters are alive to me.

I am much indebted to Annie (*Chit Chat*, p. 282) for the information that the Prince of Wales has dyspepsia!! Should not 'Lady' Cleveland (President's wife) be Mrs. Cleveland? Over here the papers publish it if Mrs. Cleveland buys a new pair of shoes!

I see the printer has put a small 't' to *Totanus*. In such cases the capital should be written very big, as I know from experience the printer has an unaccountable tendency to make it small, but I am very glad to see Annie has introduced some ornithological information.

Perchance we will see something of R. L. Stevenson, but most likely he will frequent the civilised parts — Denver or Colorado Springs, in which case we shall not come across him. Payn *has* spoken to him, but does not think he would recognise him again.

September 2nd, 7:30 p.,m. There is nothing notable to record today. We have come back over the old ground and are camped once more at Wheeler. To our great relief we found that the bridge over Ten Mile Creek that was so dangerous coming up had been repaired at last and was now fairly solid and safe. I saw a species of *Gyrinus* or 'whirligig beetle' in Ten Mile Creek but could not catch it. It seemed very like the English *G. natator*.

You probably will not have seen the *Naturalist*, so I may mention that Roebuck (in List of Lincolnshire Mollusca, p. 249) describes *Arion ater* var. *brunnea* subvar. *pallescens* subvar. nov., very pale brown. This is of no very great importance, but you may as well have note of what

is meant by the name in case you should come across it elsewhere afterwards, and wonder where it was described.

I was very much amused today to read the account of 'The Red Spectre' (otherwise the anarchists) in the *Pall Mall Budget* of August 11th. The writer evidently has a lively imagination (the description of Dave — if you only knew him!). The mildest fellow in the world, a most excellent man, as the King of the London Anarchists (I wonder what a King of Anarchists is, too!) is extremely funny because of its general accuracy with a good sprinkling of blue fire supplied by the author. Mrs. Wilson as an 'English Louise Michel' is almost as good. How they will laugh at this at 13, Farringdon Road!

September 3rd. In answering your letter I meant to have explained how it was impossible that I should see the eclipse of the moon on August 2nd. In the first place, the world goes round from west to east, hence it would be broad daylight here at a time corresponding to 9:30 p.m. at Isleworth. Secondly, we are about a third of the circumference of the globe apart, and hence there is some probability that an object visible to you might not also be visible at the same time in Colorado, though of course it's equally probable that it would be, if far enough off. Under favourable circumstances of time and place, an eclipse of the moon might be seen in both countries at once, but in this case it could not be. The accompanying diagram illustrates the point, only I see I have by accident made it two or three o'clock at Isleworth, instead of 9:35. But shift the globe round and you will see the exact position of your eclipse. I have made Isleworth west and Colorado east, whereas of course it should be the other way round.

Today we have not moved camp. It has been a beautifully clear day though the night was cold enough. Some oatmeal porridge we left outside was frozen hard in the morning. The only botanical find is a gentian new to me: *Gentiana parryi*.

September 4th. The camp tonight is a very interesting spot, not far from Wheeler but right on top of the range at the head of West Ten Mile Creek on the road to Red Cliff. Here, at about 11,500 feet above the sea, is a sort of flat valley between the mountain peaks, full of willow brush with a thick belt of fir trees all round. In the middle of the valley rises a small hill with a few firs and sparse vegetation, and here we have our camp.

This is the old camping ground of the prehistoric people of Colorado, we have discovered. As I was helping to put up the tent, I discovered at my feet, quite by chance, a stone arrowhead and soon after a chip of white, flinty stone which had evidently been chipped off in the manufacture of this or some other similar arrowhead. Further search revealed numbers of chips, some of them of jasper, red or yellow.

Then Martin came across some fragments of ancient pottery, black and dark brown, like that found in the ancient cliff dwellings of southern Colorado. After this all three of us set to work hunting for relics with a will, and all found plenty of chips, some very nice ones, and a little more pottery, of course in a fragmentary state, and I got what seems to be a scraper. But another arrowhead was not to be found, nor any other instrument.

This find of stone implements at such an elevation is very remarkable and interesting. Probably this locality for them has never been discovered hitherto. I shall send some specimens to the Smithsonian Institution in Washington and see what they have to say about it. It seems strange that here, where we are camping, was the workshop of some old savage thousands of years ago, where particularly and carefully, day by day, he carved implements of stone for the slaughter of game in the neighbouring mountains.

September 5th, 7 p.m. Today's journey has brought us to Red Cliff in Eagle County, after a very rough ride over the mountains. At our camp this morning we saw, high up in the air, an eagle pursued by two of the large mountain hawks that are so common here. Not that the hawks could hunt the eagle, but they seemed to fancy they were worrying him and got a good deal of satisfaction from it, until the eagle suddenly flew away to the north-east and left them.

This morning I found a new harebell, *Campanula uniflora*, a species with never more than one flower on each stem [again, not very likely; high altitude *C. rotundifolia* have only one blossom. Ed.].

Our road, for the first two miles lay through what had been a pine forest but now only a forest of poles, for a fire had been through and burnt black and killed all the trees, leaving the tall trunks standing. Curiously, the result of this has been to totally alter the character of the flora of the wood. Instead of low green vegetation, mossy and with few flowers save such as the columbine and mountain primrose, we have in this leafless wood of charred trunks a profusion of flowers, mostly *Epilobium angustifolium* (the leaves of which are now turning red, indicating that the fall of the year has commenced) with small species of sunflowers, aspen, etc.

Soon after, we went over the pass and down a very steep grade for miles till we found Red Cliff lying in the cañon, with the red earth cliff from which it derives its name above it. This pass between Wheeler and Red Cliff seems to have no name. We mean to call it 'Pottery Pass' in honour of the fragments we found on top of it.

At Red Cliff Payn had expected some money he had sent for, but the bank at Denver had not yet forwarded it, so we must wait till tomorrow morning for its arrival. We meant to camp close to the town and come in again in the morning, but Red Cliff being in a cañon there is no camping ground within six miles and therefore, though ill able to afford it, we are obliged to put up for tonight at the Eagle Hotel.

I have been very extravagant and bought three books: *All in a Garden Gate* (Besant) for 20 cents, *The Light of Asia* [Sir Edward Arnold's account of Buddhism, 1878. Ed.], 20 cents, and a little anti-socialism book, *The Principles and Fallacies of Socialism*, for 15 cents. I got the first because I rather like Besant's books and have not read this, the second because I am curious to see what it is like all through (I have only looked at scraps of it hitherto), and the third because I shall amuse and exercise myself by having imaginary discussions with the author in which I shall prove him to be wrong. I also got a Leadville newspaper in which I see the Indians have been defeated in a fight and driven to the reservation, and the country is now safe again.

Unfortunately we have now come almost too far out of the way to Bear River to go there now, so we shall probably go on to the 'Grand Mesa' after all. Payn is very anxious to see some prehistoric cliff-dwellings in the southwest corner of the state and talks of wintering down there. Now as regards the cliff-dwellings, I expect Payn's curiosity is only temporary. having been aroused by yesterday's finds, but there is no doubt that the southwestern corner is a much better part of the state to winter in than Wet Mountain Valley, the latter being extremely bleak and windy. So if Payn ends the expedition there and puts up for the winter, I may probably stay there and not return to West Cliff till the spring.

The credit system is by no means in favour in this country! Nailed up on the wall in this hotel is a big notice in black letters on yellow paper: NO CREDIT. DON'T ASK IT. YOU WILL BE REFUSED, and similar placards are very frequently seen.

I shall post this letter here and probably send the next from Glenwood Springs. I am very anxious to get my letters; quite a number must be waiting for me but I don't know where to have them forwarded to at present. I would of course rather have a little delay than run a risk of losing them. The last news I have of you dates from Sunday 7th August, nearly a month ago, and before we started.

Near Red Cliff, September 6th, 1887

Dear Frederic,

After I posted my last letter to you this morning at Red Cliff, I went into a book store and, looking over some advertisements of books, I came across the following of G. Manville Fenn [Annie's father. Ed.], with prices appended (Seaside Library): *The Rosary Folk*, 10 cents, *Poverty Corner*, 10 cents, *The Parson Dumford*, 20 cents, *The Dark House*, ten cents.

Our tonight's camp is only about six miles from Red Cliff, but our road has been very steep, on the mountainside, with a steep slope or often a precipice on one side, right down for 500 feet or more to the Eagle River. When at length we got down into the valley we put up the tent close to where Two Elk Creek runs into Eagle River, amongst quaking asps and other trees. I went out for a little while botanising here and found a few new plants, and also *Saponaria vaccaria*, the pink flower allied to *Lychnis*, which occurs at West Cliff and also at Bedford Park, though not native in either place.

September 7th, 8:25 p.m. Rain today and a late start, but we made up for that by coming at a good pace, and have reached Squaw Creek and camped there. The road has been close to the Eagle River all along and will be for some time yet. Squaw Creek is a small stream running into the Eagle from the south slope. Not far from here is a lake where we saw a large flock of wild ducks, the first I have seen in Colorado, and I found a *Physa* new to me and quantities of a *Limnaea* allied to *palustris*. In the middle of a field I saw a tall *Verbascum* (*V. thapsus*) with yellow flowers. According to Coulter, no species of *Verbascum* exists in Colorado, so this specimen doubtless arose from an accidentally imported seed. It is very common in the eastern states.

What a memory I have! I commenced to read *All in a Garden Fair* last night and it seemed strangely familiar, when it suddenly flashed upon me that I had read it long ago at Wimpole Street and forgotten the fact. I remember now that I liked it at the time, and as I have forgotten a great part of it I shall probably read it again. Today I have been reading *The Light of Asia*, and rather like it. I note a few passages: Book I. (1) 'Whilst thou sweet queen. . .are grown too sacred for more woe, and life is woe' — 'too good to live', as they say. This seems to typify the most objectionable theory of Buddhism, that of abstention from life because of its hardships and evils, rather than the attempt to remedy them. (2) 'But looking deep he saw the thorns which grow upon this rose of life, how the swart peasant sweated for his wage, toiling for leave to live,' etc., and Buddha was troubled and sought for a remedy. Did he find one? Book II. 'We were not strangers, as to us and all it seemed; in ages long gone by. . .' . . . .'Thus I was he, and she Yasodhara; and while the wheel of birth and death turns round, that which hath been must be between us two,' and the passage Annie first showed me: 'Unto me this was unknown, albeit it seemed half known,' etc.

We have discussed the theory here set forth, but I am glad now to have read all the context and understand its bearing in this particular instance better. The simile 'as hid seed shoots after rainless years' is very good and about the most forcible that could have been chosen.

September 8th, 8:15 p. m. Hot wind, blazing sunshine, toothache, and *Light of Asia* — that is my summary today. Camp near Gypsum, in a dry country, almost treeless, supporting little else than 'sage brush' (*Artemisia*), which grows where nothing else will, five feet high. The soil seems sandy but is really mud, baked in the sun and mostly pulverised, in some places whitish, in others red from the presence of iron oxide. The Eagle River, clear and shallow, in the valley on either side, sometimes close, sometimes far apart, the ranges of mountains with cliffs of deep red sandstone and fir trees scattered up and down.

Toothache has come upon me unawares, and I have no oil of cloves and cannot get any till we get to Glenwood Springs. So I seek what consolation I can in *The Light of Asia*, in which I note a few passages that strike me most:

Book III. 'Here is the common destiny of flesh. The high and the low must die. And then, 'tis taught, begin anew and live. Somewhere, somehow, who knows? And so again, the pangs, the parting, and the lighted pile. Such is man's round.' Book IV. 'That thou may'st know what others will not, that I loved thee most because I loved so well all living souls.' Book IV. 'Mine by chief service — tell him — mine by love! Since there is no hope for man only in man, and none hath sought for this as I will seek who cast away the world to save my world.'

September 9th. It is late and I am too tired tonight to do much. We are camping twelve miles from Glenwood Springs and in Garfield County. Our road today has been over Cottonwood Pass, which is now very beautiful with the autumnal leaves. Imagine a cloudless sky, rising against it grey rocks covered with lichens, and hillsides, all oak scrub, quaking asps, wild cherry and dwarf birch. The oak, some of the brightest green, some vivid red, the asps yellow, wild cherry red, and birch yellow, all intermixed and giving the landscape far more colour than flowers could do.

Coming down from the pass we had an accident. Payn was driving rather carelessly, and the horses went to one side into a steep bank, which resulted in the upsetting of the buckboard on the road. We escaped without hurt, and the horses with a few scratches. They kicked one another when on the ground, and the buckboard and pack, though turned completely over, sustained no damage, so altogether we were very fortunate over our spill.

We have made the acquaintance of a man named Porter who is traveling over the same road and lives near the cliff dwellings in the southwest corner of the state. He seems to be a very nice sort of man in his way, and probably you will hear more of him. He and his family are camped now a mile or so from us, and yesterday we camped quite close together. He has a large waggon drawn by two white horses.

September 10th. Although it froze last night, today has been extremely hot, and the way has been dusty and by cliffs of sandstone rock burning in the sun. We are camped on the hillside above and looking on to the town of Glenwood Springs, the Grand River flowing between us and the town. Glenwood Springs is a fair-sized town with scattered houses and wide streets. It lies in a triangular valley among the mountains, the Grand River, broad and muddy flowing along the base of the triangle, and the Roaring Fork flowing in at the apex and emptying itself into the Grand. Close to the Grand River are the hot springs for which the place is famous — springs bubbling up and flowing close to the river, forming large ponds of decidedly warm water from which odours of sulphuretted hydrogen arise.

The ground on which our camp is placed is covered with sunflowers of the smaller species and looks very pretty though there is no grass for the horses. 'Blue-birds' are very common, small birds not much bigger than sparrows, quite blue on the back. They settle on the fences and stumps and flutter off as we pass. Today I found a beetle of the genus *Paederus*, rather smaller than but almost identical with the English *P. littoralis* (which I have found near Perivale, and you will probably get at Isleworth; it is a pretty beetle).

I have finished *The Light of Asia* and have thoroughly enjoyed it. It is a most beautiful poem. If Buddhism is as E. Arnold represents it, it truly has the spirit of Christianity and the essential nature of a real religion. Even now, though I do not quite understand what is meant by 'Nirvana' unless it corresponds with 'the peace which passes all understanding' of the English Prayer Book. In a sense, Buddha and Christ are the same; they represent the eternal truth breaking through the crust of ignorance and evil that grows on the minds of men. The individual details vary according to the narrator and the period, but the essential spirit remains and must always remain the same.

That Buddhism and Christianity have become degraded into forms of worship and unlimited foolishness is not the fault of Buddha or of Christ but of those who, being unable to openly deny the truth, have succeeded in perverting and destroying it by fraud. Annie had read *The Light of Asia*, but at the time we hardly spoke of it, since I had not read it. I should very much like to hear whether she thinks as I do about it, and if not, how. Will you ask her to tell you this and write me word of it?

Again I copy out a few striking bits: Book VIII: 'Ye suffer from yourselves, none else compels. None other holds you that ye live and die, and whirl upon the wheel and hug and kiss its spokes of agony. Lower than hell, higher than heaven, outside the utmost stars, farther than Brahma doth dwell, before beginning and without an end, as space eternal and as surely sure, is fired a power divine which moves to good. Only its laws endure. Such is the law which moves to righteousness, which none at last can turn aside or stay. The heart of it is Love, the end of it is Peace and Consummation sweet. Obey!'

Today I shall post this, and then we start on our hunting expedition to the 'Grand Mesa.' Probably I shall not be able to post another letter till we arrive in Delta; it may be a fortnight hence, so until then goodbye.

Glenwood Springs, Sunday,
September 11th, 1887

Dear Frederick,
I posted my last letter to you today, and came back to camp to start for Elk Creek, twelve miles further down the Grand River. But it came on to rain and continued pouring all afternoon, so that we would not start today and are still at Glenwood Springs.

American cheap books will certainly ruin me! I have today purchased Darwin on Earthworms for 30 cents, and Volume I of [Gilbert]

White's *Natural History of Selbourne* for ten cents. I have read both Darwin and White before, but long ago (Darwin at Wimpole Street and Gilbert White when I was at Madeira) and I shall be glad to read them again.

> *England is a land of amateur naturalists. . . . As I look back upon the activities of thirty years ago, I marvel at the pure zeal exhibited, the love of nature that could not be suppressed, and then at the lack of organization for the application of all this information to public ends. There was, no doubt, even a certain advantage in the disinterested and socially detached position of most scientific men. They were not in science "for revenue only", as is so commonly the case in America. No, they were free to pursue their studies as they would, tracing the pattern of life without bias and without hindrance. Darwin, the greatest of their kind, regretted that he had not been able to do more direct service to humanity, but who today, for humanity's sake, can wish him to have done otherwise than he did?*
>
> *Recollections*

September 12th, 8:15 p.m. Heavy rain again today, but we were determined to start, and so got away soon after ten and came 18 miles, camping this evening by Divide Creek (see map of route above). The roads are extremely muddy and slippery — 'quite English' — and once we had to make a circuit through the woods because a lot of rock, loosened by the rain, had fallen and blocked up the road. Near Glenwood Springs we passed an eagle's nest, long ago deserted, in a fir tree. Our road lay for the first 13 miles on the north side by the Grand River. Then we crossed the ferry and camped on the south side by Divide Creek, which is at times a big stream but now almost dry.

A man came to our camp this evening who knows some of the people who were in the Ute quarrel recently and told us all about the fight. The feeling here is very much against the Indians, who are regarded almost as vermin, but from all I can gather, it seems to me, if the Indians are treacherous and cruel, the whites are infinitely more so. And while the Indians are naturally inferior to the whites in intellect and many of their customs are barbarous, yet I believe they stand higher morally than the white men of this country and are at least true to their own beliefs. It may be that the Indians are incompatible with 'civilisation' and must go, but can you blame a people robbed of their country, their hunting by which they live, and treated like wild beasts if they revolt at times and do deeds of violence, which under ordinary circumstances would be inexcusable.

September 13th. Yesterday one could hardly see the sky for clouds. Today not a cloud has been visible, nothing but blue sky. A hard frost last night and a hot sun today, hummingbirds still flying about notwithstanding the frost. After breakfast we went down to Divide Creek, and Martin 'panned out' some 'colours', i.e., gold.

The gold pan, a sort of wide, shallow, iron basin, is filled with the auriferous sand (which is to be found along the banks of the creek), and slowly, by shaking the pan in the stream so as to let the water wash all the sand and stones out gradually, a little black sand is obtained at the bottom of the pan, in which glisten minute particles of gold. The gold gets thus left in the pan because it is heavier than the sand, and thus sinks to the bottom.

Martin reckoned the gold in this sand is worth not more than half a cent to a pan, so that it would hardly pay to work it.

Our today's road was for a while by Divide Creek, and then we came to North Man Creek and have camped close to the head of that creek, in a grove of cottonwood trees. We passed the house of a man who has a young elk, tame, and running about the ranch and into the house. It is a pretty creature, as yet without antlers. The man got it last May and intends to keep it until it is fully grown.

In Divide Creek I found some very curious caddis cases made of small fragments of stone cemented together and shaped almost exactly like *Valvata piscinalis*, so that when I first took one out of the water I thought I had found *V. sincera*, which has been recorded from Colorado. The resemblance carried so far that they have a sort of operculum! I must send some to McLachlan, who wrote an illustrated account of some similar cases from Africa in *Entomological Monthly Magazine* some time ago.

We have come over the 'divide' or ridge between the basins of Grand River and Buzzard Creek and are now camped right on the hunting grounds not far from the Grand Mesa. Martin went out hunting this afternoon, but though he saw many deer, and tracks of elk and bear, he did not get a shot at anything. We shall move our camp a little from time to time but shall probably stay in this district a week or ten days or until we have obtained an elk, a bear, and some deer.

I found several snails here this afternoon, including *Hyalina (Cornulus) fulva*, and *Helix pulchella* var. *cisata*, and also a *Hyalina* new to me, very like *crystallina* only duller and larger. It must certainly be new to the Colorado fauna. I found too a beetle, *Tachyporus*, not very unlike the common British *T. chrysomelanus*.

September 15th, 7:30 p.m. This morning Payn and Martin started out on horseback to look for a better place to camp and try to get a shot at an elk if possible or, failing that, to shoot a deer or two. They said that if they had struck the band of elk they very likely might not return tonight, and I trust that they have had this good fortune, since it is now dark and they have not come back.

I, being left alone, have been collecting plants and insects, writing, and reading Darwin's *Earthworms*. There are no earthworms here, and very few in Colorado at all. Some have been found in Wet Mountain Valley, so Martin says. I found two centipedes today, a *Geophilus* and a *Lithobium*, so nearly allied to the common British species that I could hardly see any difference. *Vanessa antiopa* is common here; one was flying around the camp this morning.

'Jock', Martin's dog, is growling and barking outside at something or other — it is too dark to see. Perchance it is a bear, so I have just loaded the rifle and put it close at hand, to be ready if the beast should be over-inquisitive and visit the tent. Now I hear a shout. It is Payn and Martin returning. I wonder how they have fared!

Well, we have just finished a supper of elk steaks. They did strike elk verily, a whole band of them, two bulls with fine horns [Cockerell always speaks of horns rather than antlers. Ed.] and six or seven cows. Both bulls were shot, and several of the cows, but it was getting late and they found only one cow, shot by Payn in the head, before returning. From this they cut plenty of meat and started home, and we shall go tomorrow to look for the rest. They were in very thick brush, and for the most part did not fall exactly on the spot but ran a little after being shot, so it will need some searching to find them.

I should like to have seen the elk, but I would not shoot one unless it were for the sake of meat (elk meat is like beef, only better), though doubtless I would have shot if I had been there, in the excitement of the moment. Elk are getting rapidly killed out and seem likely to be as rare as the bison before long, or quite extinct. So although I sympathize with Payn in his new and (to him) delightful experience, I regret the death of so many elk, since one bull will provide horns as a trophy, and plenty of meat has been cut off one cow, and the rest will be useless.

The meat would be valuable for sale, but there is a law forbidding the killing of game in this season, 'except such as is needed for the hunter's own requirements', to feed him and his party, and therefore anyone selling meat would immediately be arrested and fined for breaking the game law. And indeed if it were to become known that so many had been killed, Payn and Martin would certainly be fined.

Perhaps not so many elk were shot after all, and perhaps the poor beasts, being wounded, ran away to die undiscovered in the woods. At all events, we have spent today looking for them in vain, except that we found a buck of the black-tailed species [Mule deer. Ed.] which was shot by Martin in mistake for an elk.

I have heard more about the elk shooting and will tell you how it happened, as related by Payn and Martin. They were just about to return yesterday evening and, passing through a quaking aspen wood, when they heard an elk call, or 'bugle', as it is called. They looked round and soon saw a fine bull elk about 150 yards away, rubbing his horns against a tree. They both fired at once and saw him fall, then lost sight of him. Immediately after, Martin saw another bull (as he supposed) and got a good shot at it. Then several cows put their heads out of the brush, and both Payn and Martin shot several times. After this they looked for the dead and discovered a cow elk which Payn had shot in the head.

Today we rode up to the place and got a quantity of meat from the cow, as much as we could carry away. It is a grand beast of quite gigantic size compared to an ordinary deer. Then we went to look for the rest, and especially the bull elk, but though we walked over a lot of ground we found nothing, and not an elk at all.

The black-tailed deer is the most common species in Colorado. I don't know what is the scientific name. If you should be at the museum, perchance you might come across a specimen and so find out the name. Here is a description of it: *Cervus* sp. Black-tailed Deer. Five points to each horn. Head and body ashy grey, blackish beneath and on back, and with a black patch on forehead and black spot on each side of under lip. Tail yellowish-white with a black tip. Ears 9½ inches long. Legs tinged with fulvous.

Payn and Martin are just now in the midst of a terrible quarrel, mainly because Martin asked about $75 which will be due him for six weeks from Payn. Payn has written to England for the balance of his money and will soon have it to pay Martin, but meanwhile has barely enough for himself, and Martin consequently becomes a little uneasy and talks of returning, being also somewhat annoyed by Payn's manner, like ev-

erybody else. (This and kindred items of information for you and Annie only, for although I tell you about everything, it would not be right to write of Payn's affairs for general discussion or perusal.)

I saw the tree creeper (*Certhia*) of this country today. It is about the same size as the British species, but grey takes the place of brown. I also saw a tomtit [chickadee, Ed.] more like *Parus ater* than any other British kind.

September 17th. We are still in the same camp, but start for the Grand Mesa and Leon Park tomorrow. No hunting has been done today, and I have been writing and collecting. It is almost too late for flowers now, and I have only found a few: *Sidalcea candida* (which I also found at Black Lake Creek), *Urtica gracilis* (almost indistinguishable at first sight from the English nettle, *U. dioica*), *Galium trifidum* (like *G. aparine* but with smooth seeds), and one or two others.

Just as we were preparing supper we heard a voice in the distance and soon distinguished something about a horse. We got up and saw a horse with a rope around its neck coming along. Martin caught it, and soon the owner came up on another horse in hot pursuit. He turned out to be a man who had passed us early in the afternoon and had afterwards camped six miles further on with some cowboys. His horse, having been raised on the Grand River, felt a longing for home and, not having been properly secured, made off. Roberts (that is the man's name) pursued him on another horse but could not catch him, and seemed likely to have spent all night in pursuit had not Martin caught him.

Horses in this country will often make off for their original home, however far away, and give their owners no end of trouble.

Sunday, September 18th. We struck camp this morning and came ten miles and are camped by Buzzard Creek. The road, though not very rocky, is really only a trail and has never been made, except by waggons, etc., passing over, and so it is very steep in places, and slants so much to one side that the buckboard seems likely to turn over. On the way we passed two dams built by the beavers (now almost extinct) across the creek some time ago.

Buzzard Creek is a pretty stream bordered with willows, and the surrounding country consists of low, rounded hills covered with grey *Artemisia*, oak-brush (now brilliantly red), and here and there patches of quaking asp, turning yellow. When we got here, Martin went out and shot a couple of wild ducks (very like the English species). Payn caught some trout, and I collected many shells new to me, in the stream. *Ancyclus* (something like *lacustris*; the genus is new to Colorado, I believe) and *Physa*, and in rejectamenta, *Cochlicopa lubrica, Planorbis parva* (Sylaber*), Helix pulchella* var. *costata, Vertigo, Pupa, Pisidium, Succinea*, etc.

In a marshy spot here are growing some most extraordinary rushes, apparently some species of *Carex* [probably *Schoenoplectus lacustris*. Ed.] with a long, round, smooth stem, and growing six feet high. Coulter gives no rush so big in his book on the Rocky Mountain Flora, except the bulrush, which is quite different.

It is now just a week since I posted my last letter. It may be more than a week yet before I get a chance of posting this. I have ordered my letters to Delta and am very anxious to get there and find some news. I begin to feel quite uneasy about hearing nothing for so long, though of course there is no help for it. It is so warm tonight that we have not put up the tent but are sleeping in the open.

September 19th, 7:25 p.m. Had the road been straight we should have reached the Grand Mesa by now. As it is, we are camped by Plateau Creek (into which Buzzard Creek runs) with a day's journey to the Mesa still before us. Our camp is close to the creek, and on the sand which once formed its bed, in a grove of tall cottonwood trees (*Populus angustifolia*). The sand by the river, when the sun shines, is alive with beautiful little lizards, one kind with a black back and four pale stripes and a blue tail, the other smaller and with brown interrupted bands on a grey-brown ground. At the same place are innumerable 'tiger beetles' (*Cicindela*) which fly at the slightest alarm, and look, as Wood says in his little book, more like flies than beetles. I also saw a lovely green Chrysid but failed to catch it.

It is now dark, the stars are scarcely out, but there is a new moon shining through the trees. The air is alive with a constant chirping of crickets, a pleasant sound to me, I remember a cricket used to reside in a crack of the pavement just in front of the gate at 5. Priory, and serenade us in the evenings, That was some while ago, but there may be one there still. Have you crickets at Syon?

September 20th. Unfortunately I accidentally left the ink at the last camp, so there is nothing for it but to write in pencil. We came today up the mountainside, a very steep road, so steep that we had to stop to rest the horses every 30 yards or so, and now we are on the Grand Mesa, about 9,500 feet high. The view from the Mesa extends a long way, over mountain ranges and the valley of the Grand River, and even, it is said, into part of Utah. The mountains, in chains one after the other, with scant vegetation, look from above just like the pictures one sees in astronomy books called 'a scene on the moon', only there are no craters.

A little while before we got up the hill it came on to rain, and it has been miserably wet this evening. We luckily came across an old log cabin, built some time ago by a party of Mexicans who were herding sheep up here, and have dry ground to sleep upon.

September 21st. Yesterday's camp was not a very convenient one as the sheep had eaten up all the grass, leaving scarcely anything for our horses, besides which Martin has a curious dislike to the slightest smell of sheep and cannot bear to be where they have been. So today we moved on a mile or so and have found a good camping ground by Clearwater Creek on grassy ground surrounded by spruce firs (*Picea engelmannii*) and a few quaking asps.

Coming along, we saw a footprint of a very large bear and came across a number of grouse, of which Payn shot three. Also there are mountain trout in the creek, so that we are likely to stay here hunting and fishing for about a week. The grouse of these mountains resembles the Scotch species, *Lagopus scoticus*, but is greyer and has the patch above the eye yellow instead of red.

I have been botanising this afternoon and found several plants new to me, but it is almost too late in the year for insects. *Pisidium pusillum* is very abundant in a swamp near here.

We have a visitor tonight, a man riding in an opposite direction to ours. He has a ranch south of here but is not making much money and so goes to work for a couple of months on the railroad near Glenwood Springs to lay up store for the winter months. This morning the clouds came down upon us and enveloped us in mist and rain, making us feel very wet and miserable, but in the afternoon the sun shone out and now the sky is clear and the moon bright.

September 22nd. Our visitor, Drummond by name, slept with us last night and departed in peace this morning. Nothing particular has been doing today. Payn and Martin have done a little fishing, and Martin is reading *Western Avenues*, in which he takes much delight. I have spent most of the day in making a catalogue of the insects collected on this expedition. I did the Neuroptera some days ago. Today I have done the Coleoptera, Lepidoptera, and Orthoptera. I find it an excellent plan to go over the collection in this way, writing down locality and date and a short description of each. It fixes the different species in my mind, whereas merely collecting them day by day and putting them by, one forgets them, and of course the advantage of comparison with

others is lost. Payn shot a couple of grey squirrels today. They are pretty little animals, very common in the Colorado woods.

What is an expedition, and how does it differ from an ordinary holiday trip or journey? It is, I think, distinguished by the definite desire or purpose to make discoveries, to add something to human knowledge. It need not be to a remote country, or of long duration, if this purpose is kept in view. The quite different attitude of a large part of the traveling public has been described in the following lines:

The people wander up and down, they wander up and down,
And when you ask them that they saw, they tell you of a town
Where food was good or drinks were cheap, and how they sped away,
And, stepping on the gas, they did five hundred miles a day.
Recollections

September 23rd, 7 p.m. A most miserable day. This morning it rained for a while and then cleared up. Payn and Martin went off on horseback to hunt. I was feeling rather despondent, and was just starting out to try to walk myself into a better humour when they returned saying that they had found a better camping place by a stream full of fish a mile and a half further on. So we quickly packed up and drove there.

Our new camp is in a small 'park', that is, a piece of ground free from trees and covered with grass and *Potentilla* brush (now dying and gone brown). The 'Mesa' is a tableland and consists of thick spruce and quaking aspen woods with here and there one of these parks, varying from a mile or less in length upwards.

Directly we had got the tent up at our new camping place, a most violent thunderstorm arose with torrents of rain, and for the rest of the afternoon the rain has been pouring down with little intermission. It is very cold, and what I most dread is that the rain will turn to snow, for Martin thinks that if the snow lay deep we could not possibly find our way to Delta, and then how could I get my letters and news of you? When Delta and news is scarcely two days journey away it tortures me to have to stay doing nothing particular here.

I have found one or two new plants today; a *Carex* which I cannot identify with certainty grows by the stream. In the stream I have found *Ranunculus aquatilis* var. *stagnalis.* You have *R. aquatilis* at Isleworth. (I have a note in my diary that it was growing in the Brent on 15th May.)

It has been raining on and off most of today and no game has been found, so we shall probably move on a few miles tomorrow. Provisions are running short. We have only flour to last a few more days, and for meat corned beef and bacon, so if we are to stay here we shall need fresh meat.

I walked up the creek some way and found a puffball fungus (*Bovista*) and, what is more curious, a white-flowered species of marsh-marigold, *Caltha leptosepala*. This is so unlike the familiar golden *C. palustris* that I could hardly realise that it belonged to the same genus. It looks more like a white *Ranunculus ficaria* than a *Caltha*. Coulter says it is 'an excellent potherb', but to me the leaves taste decidedly nasty, so that we do not care to eat it, though a good potherb is just what we want.

I have finished my catalogue of insects, except those captured quite recently and not arranged. I have done the Diptera and Hymenoptera today, and the Hemiptera yesterday.

Sunday, September 25th, 8:25 p.m. Last night we were awakened by as violent a thunderstorm as I ever experienced, together with any amount of rain, and this morning looked all grey, with some sleet and rain. We were all disgusted with the weather by this time and determined to move. So we had breakfast and were about to start when the rain came down upon us with renewed violence and drove us to the tent. After a while it cleared off and we at last packed up when, just at the moment of starting, a dense white fog, as damp and uncomfortable as you can imagine, came down. We drove on, and the fog changed to rain, and that to snow, and that again to rain, and so we passed over the Mesa. When we got some little way down, the rain had stopped and we camped under some smallish spruce firs by Surface Creek (Delta County), which runs down the south side of the mesa into the Gunnison River.

I felt so cold that I thought I should be ill, but I got dry, took some exercise and swallowed a quinine pill and am as right as ever again.

Payn went trout fishing and now plays the banjo, seemingly none the worse. Martin went up the hillside to hunt, and was just about to shoot a fine deer when he heard five shots and found that another man was on the same track and had got the first shot, The deer was killed, and the other hunter turned out to be quite a young man half mad with excitement and delight, for it was the first he had ever shot.

Martin's dog attacked a skunk and has come back smelling like the small animal house at the zoo, only much worse. We won't let him sleep in the tent tonight.

While Martin was away, I saw smoke ascending from the hillside, not far from the top, and supposed that Martin was up there and had lit a fire. So I went up to see what it was and whether he had killed anything, only to discover, after a hard climb, a fir tree burning, presumably struck by lightning, and no Martin, who was at the camp by the time I returned.

Payn wants to stop and hunt here, so Martin is going down to Delta tomorrow, about 20 miles distant, and will return the day after, bringing provisions, etc. I shall give him this to post and I hope he will bring me a great bundle of letters with news of you.

I enclose a moss from Surface Creek, Delta Co., about 8,500 ft. alt. Could you enclose it for me if you are sending any mosses to Kew for identification. Probably Nicholson would be able to recognize it.

Monday, September 26th. Martin started off with his buckboard to Delta at ten o'clock this morning to make various purchases, post letters (including one to you with diary from Glenwood Springs to present date) and get my letters, returning some time tomorrow.

Payn and I, being left to ourselves, went fishing, the result being that he caught five and I one, all of which we consumed this evening for supper. Then, in the afternoon, we went out in search of game, seeing plenty of fresh deer tracks on the hillside, but never a deer. Payn shot a marten (Order Carnivora, Genus *Marten* — you know the kind of beast), somewhat similar to the English pine marten only paler in colour. I found *Comus fulvus*, *Vertigo sp.*, *Pupa sp.*, and a *Pisidium* new to me and to Colorado but which, having no book to tell me, I cannot identify specifically.

September 27th, 7:30 p.m. We have been expecting Martin all the afternoon but he has not yet appeared. I walked some way down the road on the chance of meeting him, and gathered several flowers: *Campanula rotundifolia*, *Aconitum columbianum*, *Veronica serpyllifolia*, *Fragaria virginiana* var. *illinoensis* (a larger species of strawberry than the common one, more like the cultivated kind), *Chenopodium rubrum* [probably *C. capitatum*. Ed.], *Polygonum tenue* [*P. douglasii*. Ed.], etc. I also found *Pisidium pusillum* and *Limnaea truncatula* var. *humilis*, the latter being a new find for me though it has already been recorded for Colorado.

There is a splendid view from our camp, stretching away to the high snowy Uncompahgre Mountains, and in one direction Lone Cone is distinctly visible — a solitary mountain 70 miles away.

September 28th. Martin came back late last night and brought me all the long looked for mail — three letters from you, one from Mother from Ben Rhydding, letters from grandmother and S.C.C. [Carlie], letter from the Smithsonian

Inst. saying that they will be glad to name any specimens from me, one from McLachlan saying (alas!) that a box of Neuroptera I sent him got reduced to powder in the post, one from J. F. Coulter (who wrote a book on the Rocky Mountain Botany, you will remember) saying that he will name my plants most gladly, and furthermore, that an *Aster* I sent him from Twin Lakes is *A. campestris* Nutt., and quite new to Colorado; *Schoolmistress* of August 18th and 25th, *Botanical Gazette* (sent by Coulter, who edits it), *Science Gossip* and *Academy Guide* (for which all thanks to you), *Nat. World*, and three numbers of *Labor Enquirer*.

Now in answer to your letters: (1.) Letter posted August 16th, a delightfully long one with enclosures. I am very much interested in the Isleworth and Sutton fauna and flora lists. Please thank Annie for writing them out for me. Quite a number of plants on the list are also found here in Colorado, as you will have learnt from my letters. Comparing the list with the Bedford Park one, most of the species are common to both, but several Isleworth ones do not occur at Bedford Park and vice versa. The fauna list might of course be easily added to without giving out the garden of Syon Lodge. The *Mus*, if found in the house, would be *M. musculus*, but if in the garden it might have been a field vole (*Arvicola*).

I am sorry your Maidenhead excursion was so unproductive. The only time I was there was one day when I went to see D. Larry (of *European Butterflies* fame) and we went over the river to Dropmore and had an interesting walk through the woods, the principal capture being the butterfly *Argynnis adippe*

In the evening I went for a stroll and found quite a number of snails of which I published a list in *Science Gossip*. The *S. London Ent. & Conch. Record*: (1.) The arrangement of species in the book is after Froebel's *Catalogue*, which I think you have. The districts are mapped out as in the map published by South London Entomological Society, each district being numbered. The manner of entering the records is as already done in the book for *Testacella*. (2.) You will not.

find any record book from which you can copy wholesale. If it were so there would be no need for the present one, but the *Zoölogist* list, which you have, gives all the notable records up to 1885, with many subsequent ones added in ms on the margin. All other records must be sought from various sources and from your own observations, as I sought those from which I compiled the *Zoölogist* list. My *Science Gossip* paper will give you many records of varieties. (3.) Yes, I meant to enter all the bibliographical references, but you will find that nearly all except the very recent ones are duly entered already. (4.) I meant to record not only the marine but also the fossil forms; the marine you will find as nearly up to date as possible in the *Zoölogist*, but perhaps you might let the fossils alone for the present as they want a lot of working up.

The completest list of fossils I have is contained in a black notebook with a limp cover which, unless you have it already, is with the other books at 5. Priory. But this list could not possibly be published without a revision as to synonymy, etc., and very numerous additions. It contains also the Middlesex fossils, which will not come in the S.L.E.S. book. Please do not neglect to ask me anything you want about this record book. If you have any trouble in finding out nomenclature you will find a complete list of S. and W. species and varieties in my large black-covered notebook, and a list of marine ones in a red cardboard cover separate. If everything turns out happily (I trust I shall be back again some time next year) and then, if the list has not been published, no doubt between us we shall soon get it into proper shape.

Your description of the Culverhouses is excellent. They are interesting as specimens but I don't think I should like them very much, no more than the Allports, for instance. That is to say, they would interest me and I should be glad to see them now and then, and I should think of them that they were entirely excellent people. Quite a host of people fall under this same category. I wish I could find a word to express it, but the English language or my knowledge of it is so ridiculously inadequate and unscientific.

I can imagine the little 'Clark' and his wriggling ways! Makes me think of Fox Bourne, junior, only F.B. is, and means to be, only ridiculous, not offensive.

No, Annie, I have not yet arrived at the clay pipe and whiskey stage. It will be a five cent cigar more likely; they don't smoke clay pipes here. It is much more convenient in every way to avoid these things. Payn smokes a good deal more than is good for him, but even he does not drink whiskey except now and then, when he strikes a 'saloon.' I don't think we have any with us now.

I should like to talk to Arthur Nelson about his aspirations and ideas. I wonder what he thinks a clergyman is useful for and what duties attach thereto. Ask him, and let me have his opinion. I fancy a lot of men go into the church with merely a vague kind of idea that it is a respectable and easy calling, and some never wake up from this. Some wake up and wish themselves out of it but dare not say so, and some set themselves earnestly to work, to better the condition of their fellow men in the way that seems to them the best, though often enough this amounts to nothing better than teaching one theology and abusing all others, while the morals and virtues take a back seat and are none too obtrusive.

Well, perhaps it is best I can't talk to A. N. I suspect I should make myself very offensive to him. I am sorry I did not give you enough particulars about my health, but there was no change to report, and the saying is that 'no news is good news.' However, I will in future obey your injunction to give some account in every letter. Present health is excellent except for a cold, now vanishing.

Many thanks to Louy for the excellent portrait of yourself playing tennis. It is unmistakable. Annie, being in the distance, is not so life-like. I am very glad to have the *Pall Mall Picture Guide*, with comments. Payn wishes me to say that he is very much offended because you have put 'very stupid, almost comic' to 627, since R. Lehman is a particular friend of his, but he confesses he doesn't think much of R. L.'s pictures all the same. The sketches given should never have supposed that 426 (Mlle. A. B., otherwise Blanche Culverhouse) was good, to look at the P. M. Cy. engraving. Nor should I have thought that 'Marianna' was good, except the painter's name.

There is only one misprint in the *Science Gossip* paper after all (p. 177, 2nd. column, 6th line from bottom; for 'brown' read 'yellow.' The illustrations, though, don't belong to that part of the paper at all. I don't think I sent the editor the rest of the MS and I cannot rewrite it very well out here, without notebooks, etc., so the illustrations will be rather meaningless. Do you see the advertisement of J. W. Williams' new paper, *The Naturalist's Monthly* (published by Walter Scott, 24 Warwick Lane, Paternoster Row 6)? He seems to have duped a good many people into writing for him, and do you see he is 'M. A.' now? Could you get me a copy of the first number as I ought to see what he is doing. I see also that C. Jeffreys of Tenby has published a list of British Mollusca.

I hope that you and Carlie will be good friends again — surely you will. As to Payn, I think you were rather hard on him as also the kindred but cleverer and stronger-minded spirit, Alec Wise. I fear you will be nearly as uncharitable in condemning people as I am myself. The great fault of Payn is this: That his life is entirely purposeless and he has no moral sense to speak of and is very conceited and thinks he knows more about everything than anybody else. As to his being weak in character, he certainly is that, but I do not know whether to say he is too easily influenced by the wind. The lightest puff blows it away, but try to blow it in any particular direction or in a straight line, and you can't do it; that is Payn.

But Payn is good-natured in a way. He would do nobody a wanton harm and is not revengeful nor has he great dislikes, nor likes either. His main idea seems to be 'I have so long to live, I mean to enjoy myself as well as I can while I am alive, and let everyone else try to do the same. Whatever gives me enjoyment is good and right, and if others suffer it is their lookout.'

Payn's ideal man, as he told me, is a fellow who will join one in any kind of fun or spree, and be jolly under all circumstances, and will help one out of difficulties and scrapes.' I suppose I should class him as a pessimist. He doesn't believe in the future and the power of continued effort for good, but would live for the present enjoyment and have everyone else do the same. On the whole, my opinion of Payn is practically the same as it was on the day of departure.

(2.) Letter posted August 24th. A photograph of Annie, for which my most grateful thanks — and a good one too as far as one can expect of a photograph, and Annie being essentially a human being, is less adapted for photography than some other people who are essentially animals. I am glad I may keep it. It would have been altogether too wretched to have to send it back. I see you ask me to take my choice of the two smaller ones, as if there were any choice. The one I return is a libel. I wish I could keep the photo of you also. Cannot you get Mrs. C. to make another copy for me? Just yourself will do.

I am not so particular about 'The Jar' and all its Culverhouses. It looks like a scene in the 'Forty Thieves', Ethel Culverhouse as Morgiana smothering Ali Baba in oil. Really, though I am glad to see a photograph of the Culverhouses, as it adds life to your descriptions, but not Blanche. I suppose the P. M. Cy. picture must do for now. Please thank Louy for her kind remembrances and for the chalk head, but I have a photograph now, anyway. I like your description of Brougham, Jr.

(3.) Letter posted August 30th. I must certainly see that story of yours when it comes out. Do not fail to send me a copy. Has Annie been writing any more stories, besides *Merely Friends*? And if so, what, and where?

Perhaps Annie is right; the lack of skill on the part of the cook may have had something to do with my feeling out of sorts. I think we were too fond of trying experiments, because Payn is very particular about what he eats, and is always wanting something new. Now we live on bread and meat, and are well.

Merely Friends, Chapter XIX: Very vivid and true for the most part, I think, though I can hardly understand Ada yet. It seems to me that reading the second column that Imes is something like W. Watson. 'I don't flatter myself', etc. is just like Watson, but I always used to doubt whether it was quite genuine in him. Watson would have climbed up the cliff too. Chapters XX and XXI: Poor Corrie! Poor Imes! I wonder what will come of it all. I miss the schoolmistress very much in these three chapters. She has quite disappeared except in Douglas' thoughts.

8:10 p.m. Nothing particular has happened today. I have been busy writing. Martin shot a deer just about dusk, but although nearly sure he killed it, could not find the body tonight. Martin says that he just heard the cry of a 'mountain lion' (a puma, *Felis concolor*) in the distance but could not see it. Mountain lions are common on the Grand Mesa and frequently kill the sheep kept up there.

September 29th, 8:45 p.m. Today I have been busy packing up boxes and writing letters: A box of insects, Mollusca, etc. to the Smithsonian Inst., a box of over 30 species of Neuroptera to Mclachlan, and some plants to Coulter. Beyond this, I have nothing to tell except that I am alone tonight, Payn and Martin having gone off to sleep somewhere up in the woods so as to get a shot at the deer at early dawn. Payn wanted to do this, he said, 'just to say I have done it.'

It is a very cold night and I expect they will be frozen. Having no desire whatever to 'say I had done it', and as someone was wanted to look after the camp, I discreetly stayed here. The deer that Martin shot yesterday got away and was not to be found this morning, leaving nothing but a few drops of blood. Poor beast. I suppose it is dying somewhere.

September 30th, 11:25 a.m. Payn and Martin have returned and have not even got a shot at a deer after all.

Looking over Annie's flora list in comparison to the Rocky Mountain flora, I have made out the following list of species also found in the Rocky Mountain region, as given in Coulter's book. Those I have found myself are marked TDAC. *Potentilla anserina, Galium aparine, Capsella bursa-pastoris, Plantago lanceolata, Plantago major, Epilobium palustre var.* TDAC, *Achillea millefolium* TDAC, *Trifolium pratense, Trifolium repens, Taraxacum officinale* TDAC, *Sonchus oleraceus, Calystegia sepium, Polygonum amphibium, Agrimonia eupatoria* [*A. striata* Ed.], *Equisetum arvense, Campanula rotundifolia* TDAC, *Polygonum aviculare* TDAC.

If Annie does not mind, I should very much like to have note of the species added to her fauna and flora list from time to time so that I might see how it stands. There are three plants found in the Rocky Mountains and also at Isleworth but not on Annie's list: *Urtica dioica, Ranunculus aquatilis* (River Brent) and *Ranunculus sceleratus*, which used to grow in the ditch in the lane leading towards Osterley Park, just by the gate of Syon.

6 p.m. We have moved camp today, a few miles further down and close to a ranch.

October 1st. Yesterday evening a tall, rather shabby-looking man with a moustache and a rather intelligent-looking face came by our camp and I began talking with him, Martin and Payn being out. He turned out, strangely enough, to be an old friend of Martin's, a doctor who had lived in Rosita seven years ago and whom Martin had not seen since. He had been living on the Indian reservation, and he has just been telling us about an Indian funeral he witnessed.

They talk of the 'life hereafter' very much in the English Church, but I imagine few of the Christians have so strong or vivid a faith of it as the Indians. When they buried this Indian they put $500 worth of things: Blankets, guns, etc., into his grave so that he might lack nothing in the 'Happy Hunting Ground', and they would not close up the grave, but only covered it with wickerwork and light earth so that he might easily get out, and they placed food by the grave, to refresh him before starting to his heaven. Last of all, they killed his horses, that their spirits might accompany him and be useful to him in his new life. You may call this superstition if you like, but it is not humbug.

8:35 p.m. We have camped tonight on the east fork of Surface Creek where there is supposed to be plenty of grass. We shall stay here a little while and then go on to Montrose, where I hope to find another bundle of letters. I have not found very much during the last few days. Yesterday afternoon I caught a specimen of *Vanessa milberti* (resembling *V. urticae*) and this morning I saw *V. antiopa*. Yesterday also, I found a wild rose bush with globular berries on it (*R. arkansana*)

Sunday, October 2nd, 8:30 p.m. The hunting has been more successful today. Martin shot a grouse this morning, and this afternoon Payn and Martin each shot a fawn. It seems too bad to shoot these little animals, but we were altogether without fresh meat, and nothing else was seen. It has been very hot today and I have a slight headache, which is unusual with me, so I will not write any more tonight, but go to bed.

October 3rd. There is a little island of stones, about 30 feet by six, surrounded by the waters of Surface Creek, close to our camp. I have been exploring it and making a list of its flora and fauna just to see how many species I could get. The result is, fauna: A wasp, a caddis case, some mayfly (?) larvae in the stream, a green fly (*Lucilia*), a 'bluebottle', a house fly, and another fly, two small spiders, a 'skiptail' (*Podura*), an *Aphis flora-ranunculus*, *Geranium*, *Mimulus*, *Veronica serpyllifolia*, *Rumex*, *Mertensia sibirica* [*M. ciliata*. Ed.], *Sagina decumbens* [*S. saginoides*. Ed.], *Arenaria congesta* var. *subcongesta*, *Epilobium alpinum*,

Salix irrorata, *Carex* (two species), three grasses, and three other unnamed flowering plants, a *Jungermannia* and a *Marchantia*, a moss, two algae and three fungi (two *Peziza* and a mold) — 26 species altogether.

Payn came in this evening with another deer, a doe this time, which he had shot. It seems that he saw five and shot several, only securing this one. I heard a good deal of shooting going on in the distance and supposed he must have come across a bear. Last night (the dogs were growling about something) Payn got up and says he saw some animal moving through the trees (the moon was bright) and he fired two shots at it. It is supposed that it might have been a bear, attracted by the bodies of the fawns, but whatever it was, it got away and left no trace.

October 4th. Today has been very uneventful. I have collected a few specimens and made notes of the lichens (six or seven species) found round here. I wish I knew about lichens! I know less of them even than fungi or algae.

Two wanderers, a man and a boy, rode up and camped close to us this evening. They came all the way from Indian Territory and are traveling 'to see the country.'

Reading a paper by W. G. Farlow in *Botanical Journal* today I came across the following. 'The question is frequently asked whether the species of fungi are more numerous than those of Phanerogams (flowering plants). It is safe to suppose they are, although it is not true that more species of fungi have already been described.' Now Farlow is a very well-known cryptogamic botanist, and his statement comes with authority but seems to me a very remarkable one, almost incredible until one thinks carefully over it. Farlow says that few species of flowering plants are without some special parasitic fungus. A hundred four fungi have been enumerated as parasitic on various species of grape vine! I think I must take up fungi when I return to England. How many Cryptogamia have you down as yet for Isleworth? You ought soon to exceed the

Bedford Park list of these. Annie gives only two, *Equisetum arvense* and *Homalothecium sericeum*.

October 5th. This evening we have camped at a settlement called Marion, consisting of a few ranches not far from Delta on the Gunnison River and less than 5,000 feet above sea level, the lowest altitude we have touched since we started. Our drive of over 20 miles down from last night's camp has been an interesting one, for we have come through six distinct zones of vegetation, and from a cold into a hot climate.

We started from the lower edge of the zone of spruces, past through quaking asps from which the leaves are now rapidly falling; then came to oak-brush, and after that a dry region of piñons (*Pinus edulis*) and 'cedars', so-called (I believe it is a large species of juniper), then sage-brush (*Artemisia*), and last of all, 'greasewood', which has the same general appearance as sage-brush but belongs to the Chenopodiaceae.

We stopped at a ranch in the greasewood zone and got a good meal of eggs with fresh milk and a novelty in the way of jam — 'Squawberry jam' (which has nothing to do with 'strawberry'). It is a berry [*Peraphyllum ramosissimum*. Ed.] they pick in the mountains, very sour uncooked, but making very good jam.

On one side of Surface Creek, there must, thousands of years ago, have been a tremendous volcanic eruption, for the hill stretching from the Mesa almost to the Gunnison River is composed of volcanic sand over which is a layer of lava, and almost all the stones in the neighborhood are volcanic. Under the volcanic mud there is said to be a layer of anthracite coal 30 feet thick, so I suppose that some day this will be a second Northumberland, with its smoke and desolation, but at present it does not pay to work the coal.

The district by the Gunnison River is called the 'dobe — dry, sandy and desolate, with no grass, and vegetation only in patches. The soil is very alkaline and here and there white patches of alkali are seen. The Gunnison River itself is a pretty stream, clear, wide, and smooth. The weather was so warm this evening that I had a bath in the river, which was refreshing. *Physae* are in great profusion in the Gunnison but apparently no other Mollusca.

Last night we were discussing strange beliefs, and I found that Martin actually supposed that the pole star was a sun, and the stars of the 'Great Bear' (or dipper, as he calls it) are planets revolving around it! And yet Martin is a well-read and fairly educated man!

October 6th. Today we have come to Montrose, and I have my mail, of which delightful circumstance more hereafter.

All today has been over a flattish country as miserable as any country could be. Imagine a vast plain, 40 miles or more at its widest, nothing but dried mud, baked and cracked in the sun like an 'Old Master' in a pawnbroker's shop, or a piece of 'Chinese' pottery. On this plain are scattered and solitary plants of the Chenopodiaceae and such like, and stunted cacti, all low, flowerless, and covered with dust. A strong breeze blowing, covering us with dust but tempering the heat of the day, which is very great although snow is visible on the distant mountains, snow that has not melted all the summer, and will not melt.

I will post this now. The next town is Saguache, which we shall not reach for a long while, so do not wonder if no letter arrives next week. Thank you very much for the two letters just arrived and please thank Annie for the pictures of the room. It is just what I wanted. All thanks for *Entomology* and *Entomological Monthly Magazine*, *Science Gossip*, *Fortnightly*, and Williams' paper, and to Annie for sending the *Conch. Exchange*. Will write all about them later. Thank Annie for extracts. Tutt's 'imagines' is all right: *imago*, genitive *imaginis*, plural, *imagines*. *Vide* Latin grammar.

Montrose, October 7th, 1887

Dear Frederic,

Last night we stayed at Lott's Hotel, Montrose, and tonight also, as it has come on to rain so that we cannot proceed.

The mail is the only subject I have to write about, but that is enough. It was a big mail, bigger than usual, so that the postmaster opened his eyes and stared, and asked how I came to have so many letters. Here is what I got. Letters: F.G.F[enn] (2), Mother (3) Una, S.C.C[ockerell] (3), Olive, Ponsonby [and] Roberts (postcards), J. S. Galicia (Malta, enclosed in Carlie's), Thomas (all about Tilein's office — you remember Thomas — a long letter and interesting).

Smithsonian Institution Ethnological Dept. to say the boss of their dept. is in New Mexico and they have forwarded my letter about implements on 'Pottery Pass' to him. Wm. Felix (some one at Chicago whom it appears Mother had met and wrote to about me). Felix wanted to know if he could be of assistance, which was kind, but Chicago is too far away.

Papers: *Schoolmistress* of Sept. 1 and 8, *Conch. Exch., Fortnightly Review* (Aug.), *Sci. Gossip* (Sept.), *Naturalist, Ent. Mo. Mag.* (Aug. and Sept.), *Entomologist, Labor Enquirer* (2), *Pall Mall Budget* (2), *Naturalist's Monthly* (Sept.).

I wrote a number of letters, etc., including (1.) one posted to you up to date Oct. 6, (2.) letter to Douglas at St. Thomas, asking him to send $10 of the $50 he has there of mine. This is that I may not be penniless at the end of this trip. (3.) to Cox, asking him to look out for some work for me when I return. If there is anything to be done he would probably hear of it. (4.) a short paper called 'A Colorado Valley', to *Pall Mall Gazette*. I don't much expect them to accept it, but if by any chance they do and pay me for it I shall be glad, and it might lead to more. It's worth trying and it only took an hour anyway.

In answer to your letters: (1.) postmarked Sept. 6. Yes, I remember Emily Gibson, but not very well. I am afraid I was not thinking very much about Emily Gibson that evening you mention, though I remember the evening well enough. E. G. sat a little to the left of the fire, at an angle of about 45° with the fireplace. What I did think of her was not very favorable, but I supposed I did not know her well enough. I am glad you have a map of Colorado. I am afraid my journey must have been rather unintelligible to you without one. Bear River must be on the map, for it is in the northwest of the state. Perhaps they call it Yampa River, which is another name for it.

Of course *Les Miserables* is grand. I like it best of any novel I know.

I think, as to the magazines, I shall continue to write for them though I feel somewhat that I ought to send American news to the American papers, and in the same way I am already getting quite a host of American correspondents. I have just sent off notes to *Sci. Goss., Ent. Mo. Mag.,* and *Entom.*, however. That 'Trichoptera at Electric Light' in *Ent. Mo. Mag.* was written to Mr. McLachlan and not to the magazine.

To me the proposition, 'on no account to have a friend whose influence is other than beneficial' is senseless, because the mere fact of having a friend is beneficial, that is, supposing it to be a real genuine friend, as I understand the word. I begin to rather like Mrs. B. C., that she wrote to a friend every week for 15 years is conclusive in her favour. I forgive you the description of the Nelsons. I got it into my head that you knew them very well by sight. Under the circumstances I do not see how you could have done better.

I wonder that nearly all the spiders are different from Bedford Park ones. It shows how locally distributed they must be. When you give the spider list, could you also let me know what Saunders has named for you?

I had read the McGlynn excommunication in the American papers. It is perfectly genuine. Is it not a comic document! The pope can have no sense of the ridiculous. It reminds me of *The Little Jackdaw* in Ingoldsby legends, only McGlynn differently from the jackdaw thrives under it. I think Mrs. Fenwick Miller is on the whole right in the scrap Annie sends. I remember how we all looked at the unhappy Mrs. Atherly Jones at the club when A. J. was abusing all sorts and conditions of women in the discussion! Of course, certain 'broad statements' can be made about women, as about men, but they must be broad and illustrated by more than a few examples.

My idea, broadly, is, that as a class, women are superior in goodness or virtue, and men in mental and bodily power, so that I would rather put faith in a woman, while I admit that an approximately perfect man (e.g., Christ) has the greatest human power for good. To all of which numerous exceptions can be stated. But I think that anyone will admit that man is at his best when influenced and helped by woman, and vice versa. The point to consider is not what man and woman can do independently but how they can help one another.

(2.) Letter postmarked Sept. 14. Thank Annie very much for the drawing of the room. I quite imagine how it must be. I see things have shifted round a bit since I last saw them. I wish I could sit at that table in the evening time with you two and do my writing.

Don't you trust Billups! He nearly misled me once or twice, *vide* certain scratchings out in Bedford Park Fauna and Flora book. Saunders is perfectly trustworthy. I expect the S.L.E.S. will make rather a hash of my Colorado insects if they take them up. On second thoughts, I am sending a lot to the Smithsonian where they will fall into more competent hands.

I am glad the play proved such a success. I wish I had been there to see. Your description of the Waterloo to Haymarket walk at night is very good. I know the scene well, and it recalls it all to me.

Of course you are going mad! There is no harm in that. I am sorry you are having such a bother about *Eagle's Nest*. I had no idea it was such a rarity. S.C.C. [Sydney Carlyle Cockerell] writes that he has not read it but is just about

to get it, so perhaps you can borrow his copy. I would send you mine, only they would confiscate it on the way as an infringement of copyright.

You should squeeze a list of Isleworth insects out of the Ormerud before she goes. Williams' paper is not bad, for him, but I expect it will degenerate. Gibson Carmichael (the centipedes) of Chief's Wood, Melrose, N. B. is a good man. You might do well to send him some specimens.

Schoolmistress, Sept. 1. I see we have the Isleworth school treat. Good! I expect Douglas would go to Chilton and tell Olive about Imes. It is quite like him, though not many would have done it. Sept. 8. This is so real that I feel depressed about it. I don't see any way out of the unhappiness for Ada and Imes. I cannot believe now that Ada really loved Imes at all, while I do not know how it is possible to say that Imes did not love her. Alas! The only glimpse of hope in the story is that Douglas does quite genuinely love the schoolmistress, and I don't think he will give that up, whatever happens.

Olive Schreiner's *Three Dreams* is a beautiful story, perhaps more for its idea than the expression of it. I had quite the same feeling myself but couldn't rightly put it into words. The essence of the whole thing is in the sentence, 'He has lisped one word only to me in the desert — "Passion." I have dreamed he might learn to say "Friendship" in that land.' Annie knows how I have thought of this and how I believe the highest love is friendship and the highest friendship love. O. Schreiner's heaven on earth is the true idea, and the same as that preached by Morris John Ball from the cross in the village. Olive Schreiner is a good Socialist of the genuine sort.

October 8th. The weather has cleared up and we shall start this morning. I forgot to write concerning the *Conchologist's Exchange*. It interests me a good deal and gives me a good many interesting notes. I have written to the editor for other copies. I see Ancey is writing in it. He is the man who described *Helix gentianiformis* from Folkestone. I shall post this here as it may be long before I can write again.

October 8th. We started this morning but the fine weather was a fraud. After coming some way through the stickiest mud, it began to rain and got bitterly cold, so that what with the rain, the cold, and the mud, both ourselves and the horses were thoroughly done up when we camped, sooner than we otherwise should have done. I was getting quite drowsy with cold and shivering all over, and only succeeded in getting some life into me by walking instead of driving.

Now we are dry and have a good fire, have had a supper of venison, bread, and muddy water, and feel decidedly better.

October 9th. The effect of the hard traveling yesterday was very injurious to the horses, and one of them quite broke its wind, so that when we started this morning uphill and on a very stiff road, they could hardly drag the buckboard. I happened to be driving, and Payn characteristically began to abuse me for it. I told him he had better drive himself and left him to waste his abuse upon the air, going on foot in front with some magazines to read.

We gradually pulled up to the top of the low range we had to cross [this was Cerro Summit. Ed.], down again for eight miles more to Cimarron (Simaroon they pronounce it), close to where we are camped, on the Cimarron Creek.

Early this morning a great number of 'robins' (so-called. It is *Turdus migratorius*) passed on their migration southward, flying from bush to bush. Today has been quite fine, a contrast to yesterday.

October 10th. We got away about ten this morning and had an easy road until we came to a ranch owned by a pleasant-looking Irishman (so we judged his nationality) where we got oats for the horses, and fresh milk and bread and butter

for ourselves. Then we went up a long gradual slope until we got on the top of the most western of the 'Twin Mesas', in Gunnison County. Coming down from this we crossed the two Blue Creeks, pretty little streams running fast over the stones and bordered by willows, the leafless stems of which have a sort of purplish bloom on them, giving them rather a pleasing appearance in the mass. Leaving the Blue Creeks we have come up on the other Twin Mesa, where we are camped in a little hollow by a spring. Payn wanted to camp further down but Martin declared he would not (since there was not enough grass there for the horses), and started off, and Payn thereupon concluded it best to follow.

It is very desirable to get through this country, as we might get caught in a snowstorm and have to abandon the buckboards and everything we could not ourselves carry, and might even lose the horses, not to speak of the discomfort and danger to ourselves. My chest felt a little uncomfortable this afternoon for a while — nothing to matter — but I don't think the drenchings and freezings we have been having are beneficial.

I forgot to mention that the D. Drury whose book is advertised in *Conch. Exchange*, and whose name is underlined, is (or rather was) great-grandfather of our Dru Drury and a very well known entomologist. He described many American insects.

October 11th. There is hardly anything to tell today, as we have not moved camp, it being thought desirable to rest the horses and let them have a good feed on the excellent grass which grows here. I have been writing and reading, and also had a little search for snails amongst the willows, but could find nothing but *Vitrina*.

Martin told us rather a good story this evening, as follows: Somewhere in the states there was a prison standing close to a river. In the winter the river was frozen over, and most of the young men of the neighborhood used to skate there, some of them being very good skaters. There was a prisoner who had been confined some time, and seemed to want exercise, and someone suggested that he should be taken out to skate. He was asked, could he skate, to which he replied, 'No.' They took him out, however, and tried to teach him, and were amused to see him flounder about, apparently in the greatest difficulty. He was not in any way confined, as they supposed that so bad a skater could always be overtaken at once on the ice. Presently, though, he got 50 or 100 yards away from the rest, when he turned, took off his hat, and said, 'Goodbye, boys', and forthwith made off, having very suddenly discovered how to skate! They set off in pursuit, and the best skater among them followed him closely for five miles or more, but finally he escaped, distancing everybody. So the prisoner was gone, and never afterwards secured.

October 12th. Today's journey has been a rather interesting one. The first thing we were conscious of in the morning was the lowing of a great herd of cattle, some 300 of them, their combined voices going up in a kind of loud continuous roar. They proved to be from Wet Mountain Valley and were going to Utah to winter. After we had started we met the waggons of the cattlemen, and to our astonishment there was the small Clark boy we had left at Salida (see previous letters; you will remember him). This youth was tramping along merrily enough, looking in perfect health and quite brown from the sun. We asked if these were his parents. He said, 'No', and it seems he never came across them. We begin to think he must have run away from his people and does not intend to meet them again if he can help it. But he seems well contented to go off with the cattlemen to Utah, anyway.

After a little while we came to Lake Fork, a swift and shallow stream running down a cañon with sloping sides. This stream runs into the Gunnison River and is quite the most picturesque mountain creek I have seen. We forded Lake Creek and, after passing a place called Allen (merely a few houses) we traveled through a pine wood, which is unusual, most of the woods in Colorado being either fir or quaking asp. Last of all, we arrived at Powderhorn (like Allen, only a settlement of a few houses) and camped there on White Earth or Cebolla Creek (Cebolla is pronounced Seboya) on the grass plot by the side of the road. Near here is a soda spring. I drank some of the water and found it just like inferior soda water.

Thunder clouds came up this evening and we feared a storm, but only a few drops of rain fell. While looking for wood to make a fire I found a pool full of decollate *Physa* and also got a dead shell of *Pisidium pusillum*.

I think I did not mention that Geo. Roberts of Lofthouse near Wakefield writes one postcard: 'We are lost for want of figures and descriptions of continental forms (of shells). If you write to F. Fenn I wish you would get him to send what information he could from your drawings and extracts. We could send him engravings (of *Anodon* and *Unio*, by Wilcock) in return.' I mention this since Roberts wishes it, but probably you have too many other things to do to copy out for Roberts. I used to take some interest in his work and sent him copious extracts from time to time. You will probably remember something about it.

October 13th. Now we are almost in the same latitude as West Cliff and in Saguache County, which borders on Custer. The Sangre de Cristo Range was visible from the top of the range above our camp, in the blue distance. After reaching Cebolla Creek there was a gradual ascent up to 10,000 ft. alt., and then up and down, but pretty much on the same level for several miles (the Summit Park region) until we reached the head of a small tributary of the Pinos Creek, where we camped close to the edge of the wood, which is composed of firs and spruces.

Dark clouds had been above us most of the day, and directly after we camped, a hailstorm came on, but fortunately it did not turn to rain or snow. In Summit Park the rocks assume most fantastic shapes, being ancient and much weather-worn. Some stand up in groups like great tombstones, as sketched here. The high peaks covered with snow are a most beautiful sight, as they stand with a background of white clouds shaded with delicate grey, and above a pure blue sky, below a broad expanse of fir forest, so dark a green as to be almost black.

October 14th. The snow has come at last, cold and drenching. This morning looked grey, and very soon after we started hail and rain came on, though not very violently. It was not very long before we came to the main Los Pinos Creek, and then to the old Los Pinos Indian Agency where the Ute Indians used to live years ago, the agency itself being the representative of the U. S. Government amongst them. (Every Indian reservation has an agency in the same way.) Now that the Indians have moved away the Agency no longer exists as such.

After this we crossed a broad valley called Cochetopa Park, which is surrounded like Wet Mountain Valley with mountains, but is itself nearly flat. There is plain evidence of volcanic action here, and great masses of red and brown lava, covered with many-coloured lichens, abound.

Just as we commenced to ascend the Cochetopa Pass, what had been rain turned to snow. Soon we were covered, and as it was not freezing, the snow melted and ran into every crack and fold of our boots and clothing, making us thoroughly wet. I wrapped myself in a rug, but soon it got wet through. We were feeling very cold and were glad to get out and walk up the hill. The poor horses were almost done up, and struggled with difficulty through the snow and slush.

Sooner than I expected, we came to the top of the Cochetopa range when Martin raised a laugh by turning round and pompously announcing, 'This is the crest of the great American Continent!' So in fact it was, though I fear in our half drowned and frozen condition we did not sufficiently appreciate the grandeur of the idea. Here, on the top of Cochetopa, was snow falling,

the half of it, when melted, to fall into the Atlantic, and the other half into the Pacific, except that, as it happens, the water of Saguache Creek on the Atlantic side never falls into the sea at all but into some lakes that have no outlet.

The worst part of our journey was after leaving the top, for the snow came on more heavily and then turned to a sort of sleet. Added to which, the road was very rough in places, so altogether, wet as we were, we felt sufficiently comfortable. At last we got down to Saguache Creek, and our troubles came to an end at the end of the ranch of a Swiss, where we got a blazing fire, good supper, and food and shelter for the unhappy horses. I do not think I have suffered any great harm from today's journey, though it was not calculated to improve one's health. I coughed just a little in the snow but feel all right again now.

Now I think of it, there is one thing I forgot to tell you about the *S.L.E.S. Conch. Record*. In the Bibliography, each paper or record has a number fixed to it as being the first, second, and so forth of any author. And in the references under each species the number is quoted. Thus, suppose John Smith records *Helix pomatia* for Reigate in *Science Gossip* 1882, p. 8, it is duly entered (that is, the name of the paper or record) in the bibliography, and if it is the fourth entry under his name, the number 4 is affixed to it. Then under *H. pomatia* the record again appears 'Reigate, (J. Smith. 4).' You will see that this saves a great deal of writing, though not at the expense of fullness of detail as to the record.

By the by, Carlie writes that he found *Limax arborum*, '*Arion flavus*', *Helix lapicida,* and *Clausilia laminata* near Seven-Oaks. None of these are new county records except the *Arion* (and I do not know exactly what that may have been) but you had better write them in the record book. Perhaps Carlie will have already sent you word.

October 15th, 2:45 p.m. We are staying here at the ranch today to rest the horses, and I am lying on the tent cloth out of doors, as the weather has cleared up and it is now quite warm and sunshiny.

I have been reading some of the other things in the *Fortnightly* you sent. Coventry Patmore's 'Thoughts on Opinion and Inequality' is clever, for the utter nonsense that it is! My Bennettian grandfather used to say that 'the Tories liked Beaconsfield because nobody could tell their lies for them so well!' The *Fortnightly* seems to be in the same way. It has to convince people that inequality is excellent and necessary, and the question is, who can do it best? But there is only one truth, but an infinite variety of falsehoods; witness the different arguments employed. Yet I suppose *Fortnightly* and company are honest enough in their views. Here is a question for debate: Is the average man more dishonest or more foolish? I think much of the supposed dishonesty is merely honest idiocy, and after all, real dishonesty is merely the outcome of foolishness. (N.B. Idiocy is not the same as madness.)

Saguache Creek, which flows by here, is a pretty stream and full of trout. In a ditch by it I found *Ranunculus aquatilis* and two other familiar plants that you will doubtless get at Isleworth: *Lemna minor* and *Nasturtium officinale* (watercress). The watercress is not a native of Colorado, but was introduced.

The name of the worthy Swiss who owns the ranch is Schaller. He came out to America a long while ago and has been in this place many years. There are six small children in the house. One of them is called Ivy, a name I never heard before. I think it is rather pretty. There is also a girl (whose age I judge to be about seventeen) who does the duty of a cowboy and rides astraddle stirrup-less after the cattle and horses, to drive them in. This would rather astonish people in England, but it is quite the ordinary thing out here!

8:30 p.m. We are sitting round the fire in Schaller's house. Four of the small boys are playing cards. Payn has just been playing the banjo and singing to the assembled host, and I have written a letter to Thomas.

Sunday, October 16th. We are still at Schaller's ranch, as Payn was not disposed to move and also because I have ordered our mail to be sent to Saguache up to the 15th, that is, to arrive there up to the 17th or 18th, and we do not want to be there too soon for it, though if any should come after we left, it could be returned to West Cliff. Payn is expecting money and particularly wants to get it at Saguache. So I have been collecting, reading, drawing, and writing. I found another species of duckweed this morning — *Lemna trisulca*. This is also a common English form.

Last night I was scribbling to amuse the children, and the drawings were exhibited round the house, with the result that the woman of the house (Mrs. Alabama Elizabeth Holmes, a most hardworking creature — comes from Iowa — called 'Ally' by the children) begged that I would make her a picture of the house to send to her sister, which I accordingly did, to her great satisfaction. Then the cowboy girl also wanted a picture, and I did her a smaller one, throwing in the stables, etc. to compensate for size. Who knows but that some day I shall turn traveling artist and draw people's houses in exchange for a meal and lodging? Nobody draws in the wild west, and so the people are easily pleased with a rough sketch.

October 17th. Have just got my mail at Saguache, with your interesting epistles of Sept. 21st and 27th. *Schoolmistress* of Sept. 22nd, and *Punch* (for which all thanks to Annie). Alas! The *Schoolmistress* of September 15th has never turned up! I suppose lost in the post. Can you get me a copy? I see the present number has 'THE END' printed in plain letters beneath it. It has come sooner than I expected. And I shall miss my weekly *Schoolmistress* very much indeed, besides which the story is by no means ended. If its appearance in the *Schoolmistress* is, it is hardly more than begun. Some day, I hope, it will be finished. If Annie writes another periodical story do not fail to let me know, that I may write for copies. And has anything been done about expanding

Merely Friends into a book, as Annie spoke of doing? Why not write the whole story in a book?

Camp at Saguache,
October 17th, 1887

Dear Frederic,

At last we packed up and left Schaller's at 10:00 a.m. We had a downhill and fairly smooth road to Saguache and arrived there early in the afternoon. On the way we passed a Mexican colony, all the houses built out of mud, with generally some framework of wood. These mud houses are characteristic of the Mexicans and have been the same for hundreds of years. Martin says they build of mud even when there is plenty of good wood lying around.

Saguache is a sleepy-looking little town with two principal streets crossing each other at right angles. We camped a little way from the town and walked in again afterwards. Payn and Martin are still in Saguache. I am in the tent writing.

8:45 p.m. Of course the first thing on arrival was the mail, and to post letters. I found waiting for me two letters from you (as you know from my letter to you posted then). Sunday letters from Mother, Carlie, and Olive, a post card from Sherborn, a letter from Billups about my insects. He says the blue *Chrysis* is *cyanea*, I see. I doubt it though it is very near to it. *Schoolmistress,* Sept. 22nd, three *Pall Mall Budget,* two *Labor Enquirer, Punch* (with review of *The Barrister), Naturalist,* Oct., and *Sci. Gossip,* July.

I am now rather tired and sleepy tonight, so I won't answer any letters now or write about other matters I have in mind. In any case this letter will not be posted for some days so it will not matter if I write tomorrow instead.

October 18th, 5 p.m. There is no news of interest to tell today. We have driven over a sandy and almost flat road for about 18 or 20 miles to Villa Grove, and have camped close to the town.

The country round here is barren, treeless and flat. To the south the plain of the San Luis Valley stretches away beyond vision, and some mountains on the other side of the Rio Grande are visible to the southwest.

On the east, rising abruptly from the plain, is the great Sangre de Cristo range, looking grander with its snowy peaks than I have ever seen it before. Villa Grove is a small town, only important as being the terminus of the railroad in the valley.

Now, in answer to your letters: (1.) Letter of Sept. 21st. Yes, I think it is a pity Payn should have more money. When we got to Saguache he had hardly any left, but the £50 that he had written for was awaiting him at the postoffice, and he is once more wealthy. I had rather hoped that his people would not have sent it, or so much, except that Martin had to be paid the amount due to him for his services on this trip.

As to leaving Payn, I feel considerably perplexed as to what I ought to do. When he gets back, Lees will be still away and Cox probably also gone, and I feel some doubts, notwithstanding my previous resolve and everything, whether I should be justified in abandoning him altogether. Also, of late he has really done his best to be pleasant, I think, and is certainly anxious that I should live with him and willing to put up with my (to him) peculiar ideas and unsociability. Nevertheless, I should be extremely unwilling to lose any opportunity of earning an independent living, and if anything offered, it would be really hard not to accept it. Perhaps some compromise might be found, some means of earning my own living without abandoning Payn. Thank Annie for her opinion. I will bear it well in mind.

Speaking of loneliness, it sounds paradoxical, but the only times I have not felt lonely out here have been when I was alone. You write that Percy Hemery was at West Cliff. I asked Martin (who knows almost everybody about there) whether he had ever heard of him, and he said that there was a photographer from Cañon City named Emery who used to come frequently to

West Cliff and was frequently seen in the post-office store there. I described P. Hemery, and Martin says he feels no doubt it is the same man though he is sure that in all his advertisements, etc., he was Emery and not Hemery. You might ask Kate Hemery about it when you next see her, whether he called himself 'Emery.'

With respect to Murray vs. Darwin on coral reefs, I always thought the idea that the islands slowly and steadily subsided an improbable one, only Darwin made his explanation necessary by the generally accepted statement that the coral polyps could not build otherwise. I do not know Murray's facts to show that what he states is true, but on the face of it, it appears infinitely more probable to me. I have no great opinion of the Duke of Argyll, but Murray probably knows what he is about.

I am glad to have note of the four new plants to flora which you and Annie found at Spring Grove. H[ieracium? Ed.] nodiflorum and Epilobium hirsutum (but E. hirsutum was not new; it is on Annie's Isleworth Flora list sent to me before) were to be expected. (E. hirsutum is extremely abundant in the garden of 5 Priory and all over Bedford Park.) Samolus valerandi I have never found myself; a variety of it (var. americanus) grows in the Rocky Mountain district, according to Coulter. Genista tinctoria I have found in profusion on Horsedon Hill near Perivale, but it is very local in Middlesex. E. hirsutum was one of the very first plants I found when I began to collect plants. I found one near Chislehurst and sent it to Wm. West, of Bradford, who named it for me (I had no book in those days).

(2.) Letter of (i.e., posted) Sept. 27. I am glad to hear that Annie does not sit up later than 10:30. I had an idea that she worked later, though that is rather late. Probably she knows what is best for herself, and I ought to have enough faith to believe she will act accordingly, but your reports of ill health troubled me.

I thoroughly enjoyed going with you to Buffalo Bill's show and thank you much for taking me. It seems to be very American!

The Switchback Railway is to some extent a fraud. If the impetus of descent were sufficient to carry the car to the top of the ascent, you would have perpetual motion, which is unknown, but a light impetus given artificially at either end could no doubt suffice if the grades were carefully made (see the article 'Perpetual Motion' in Chamber's *Encyclopedia*), or perhaps the whole line has a downward grade, the ascents being shorter than the descents.

Mrs. Brodie Clark's idea about books is queer! There is just a shadow of truth in it, but I think that altogether it will not hold at all. If a book is really good, it is good always and at all times. In this respect books are like people. And will Mrs. C. say that one ought not to like the same people continuously? It would be a hard world if it were so.

But Mrs. C. will answer that the people one likes advance at the same rate as oneself and are not always the same, while books are, to which I answer that there are changeable and unchangeable virtues, and the true virtue of a good book, as of a good friend, has nothing to do with years or times or seasons, but is above all things human and everlasting, good in the past, present, ever increasing, never decreasing. Yet, superficially, the mind in a state of activity has different wants, one following and extinguishing the other, and thus the book of today is thrown aside tomorrow if it is superficial (and much that we read is superficial) and retained always if it has made a deep impression. Our mind is like a sieve; small particles pass through constantly, larger ones are constantly retained, and woe to that mind if it becomes clogged with the dust of superficiality and nonsense, and woe to it if the meshes are so wide that nothing is retained. Can Mrs. C. defend her theory? Or did she mean it only as I have written? What has Annie to say about it? You do not give her opinion.

It may seem strange that a scientific writer should put first the question of religion. If by religion we mean our fundamental philosophy of life, an attitude which transcends the immediate time and space and links it with the universe and eternity, no political system can do without it. Such philosophy quickly leads us to the borders of the unknown and incomprehensible, but it gives us the assurance that what we do today means more than the immediate results would suggest. Had we been present at the crucifixion of Jesus, we should probably have remarked that this young reformer, a worthy man, had come to a bad end, and all his efforts had failed. History tells us a different story.

Recollections

I haven't seen the inside of a church since I have been out here. They haven't any churches out here to speak of. I wish I could go just once, even to hear that ridiculous old Wilson, for old recollection's sake. Mr. Andrew's sermon illustrates the joy with which we all hail the smallest grains of sense from the pulpit, which uttered elsewhere would seem commonplace truisms. Really, the clergy ought to make more of their opportunities.

I should like to have a list of your fungi, when Massee has named them, and I wish you would ask him what *Fissidens purpureus* is. He gave me the name for a Bedford Park moss, but it does not appear in any of the books etc. [I suggest it was *Ceratodon purpureus*. Ed.].

Schoolmistress Sept. 22nd. As you know from previous letter, the number for Sept., 15th is unaccountably missing, which is very unfortunate, but I hope you will forward me one. Having got over the disappointment of coming so soon to the end, I think Annie did wisely to stop (in this first edition and for the present) where she did, though I hope there may be some sequel. There is much in the last chapter. Corrie's refusal of Mr. Imes is quite like her, and is heroic in its way. While one admires the rectitude of such a character as Corrie's, one cannot help also pitying. Ada has at length found a suitable partner who does not love her humanly at all, but as a pretty domestic animal meant to please and be pleased. Douglas and the schoolmistress will meet again after a year, and it is at least assured that they will be friends again, perhaps better friends than before. A future exists, as yet unknown. It is sufficient to leave it so for the present, in the confidence that it will one day be revealed.

All my thanks to Annie for this story, which has given me happiness and does me good. I shall remember it always, and read parts of it from time to time when I need its influence, and that is often. If Annie writes another story, do not fail to let me know.

October 19th. Salida once more. Today's journey has been about 26 miles, over the treeless upper end of the San Luis Valley, over the low and easy grade of Poncha Pass (Ponchee they call it), not 9,000 feet high, past Mears, which is a town consisting of about four houses and a postoffice, down Poncha Creek, which is lined with cottonwood trees and oak-brush, through the village of Poncha, not long since partially burnt down, and then over the 'dobe flat to Salida. We have put up our horses and buckboard at the livery stable, which is kept by a friend of Martin's, and we shall sleep in the storeroom or barn above, where I am now writing, Payn and Martin being somewhere in the town playing billiards.

In my yesterday's letter I omitted to speak of *Punch*. I am very pleased to see such a good (it could hardly be better) review of *The Barrister*. The picture is amusing, but the likeness of G.N.P. is not a very good one, I think. I have been looking out for a notice of the play in *Pall Mall Budget* but none has appeared yet.

I found *Polygonum convolvulus* today at Salida (this most certainly will be found at Isleworth). It is not considered a native of Colorado but is supposed to have been introduced.

October 20th. Until past 2 o'clock we stayed in Salida, Payn and Harris playing billiards, I strolling round the town, writing a couple of postcards to Olive and the *Entomologist*, and then going into a book store to explore its contents. This enterprising store is kept by a man and woman, and directly anyone enters, the woman goes to a piano in the corner of the room and strikes up a lively air while the man exhibits his wares. I asked for *Sesame and Lilies*, which Carlie is very anxious I should read, but he had sold his last copy a little while ago and had none of Ruskin's save *Ethics of the Dust* and *Crown of Wild Olive*. He told me he was very fond of reading Ruskin himself. So I ended by buying two little books of Björnson's for ten cents each — *Arne* and *The Happy Boy*.

I read *Arne* while Payn and Martin played billiards, and enjoyed it and was interested, though perhaps it is not as good as *Synnöve Solbakken*, the only other book of Björnson's I have read. *Arne* is a strange story and is not very well translated, the verse being very feeble (a great pity), but nevertheless it is full of great ideas and I commend it to you and Annie if you can easily get it. If Annie reads it, ask her, does Arne seem to her to resemble anybody?

When we did get out of Salida we soon got into the Arkansas River cañon and camped at Wellsville, where the hot springs are. From the map you would imagine that Wellsville is a town, but it is nothing more than a store, the owner of which keeps a postoffice and also owns the hot springs.

Our tent is pitched close to some oak and juniper, and by the river a little way down there is a clump of the familiar reed, *Phragmites communis*, and some of the 'Spanish Bayonet', *Yucca angustifolia* [*Y. glauca*. Ed.].

There are several bits in *Arne* that I have marked so I will not copy them out for you and Annie. Without the context I fear they will lose much of their meaning, but if you can get the book (surely Smith's have it) you will be able to understand.

October 21st. This morning after breakfast we had a good bath in the hot springs, and about midday started off. For a while we passed along the cañon, past Badger Creek (where we camped

on our outward journey) and into Pleasant Valley. In the cañon I saw a butterfly settled by the roadside, which looked exactly like *Vanessa cardui*, but it flew away again before I could be quite certain. *V. cardui* is found in almost every part of the globe, but I do not remember having seen any record of its occurrence in this district. Having crossed Pleasant Valley we camped at its upper end, close to Cottonwood Creek, and under the shade of great cottonwood trees (*Populus angustifolia*). After a meal of eggs, milk, and bread, procured from the ranch close by, we put up the tent, under which I now lie writing. Just before supper I had a little hunt, and found some bees and Hemiptera, and also a plant (*Sidalcea malvaeflora*) [*S. neomexicana*. Ed.] which I had not before identified.

As we rode along today I read Björnsen's *Happy Boy*. It is a most beautiful story almost too good to be fiction. You must read it, and Annie also, for I think it is better than *Arne*. And if Annie reads these two books, or one of them, or perchance has read them already, I should much like to have her opinion of them. As with *Arne*, I quote the passages I have marked.

October 22nd. At last we have reached our cabin and have done camping out, for the present at any rate. We started at about ten in the morning, and after a rather rough up and down road through the oak hill district we found ourselves in Wet Mountain Valley, though still many miles from home. We had not gone very far when we met Dick Oule, the Englishman in whose barn we slept on the first day of our journey, and almost the first thing he said was that I was looking a good deal better than when I started, which is comforting.

We had a long and mostly up hill drive to our cabin, which we did but slowly, for it was, and still is, blowing a gale in the valley, so that it was quite difficult to stand up against it. Wet Mountain Valley is known far and wide for its wind storms in the winter time, and well so if this is a sample of them. Fortunately it was a warm wind or we should have been almost frozen. The snow on the mountain tops blows about like smoke so that one may fancy that some volcanic crater exists up there!

We called at Cox's house and found it in the possession of a caretaker who informed us that Cox was away and would not return for a week or two. Mrs. Cox has already left for England as (you will perhaps remember) she was going to do. Then we went down to the cabin and found the door open, but everything pretty much as we left it. We have no stove now, so we had to make a fire up outside to cook some bread, which was a difficult job because of the wind.

Martin has gone down to his house at Ula. Of course, now that he has been paid, and deducting all expenses, it seems that Payn has about $100 left, so you see it will become necessary to earn something anyway, to tide over the winter. I am glad of this because it will make me independent even though I live with him, and I have decided to give it a fresh trial under these new circumstances, to see if it is possible. As to the means of making money, perhaps I can do something by drawing or writing, and perhaps a little enquiry will lead to something, but I feel confident that some way will be found. Everyone in the valley contrives to earn a living, so why not I?

Sunday, October 23rd. Today has been uneventful. We have been overhauling things and setting them straight, and little else. The wind has gone down but it has turned cold. Martin came up to see about the building of a stone chimney to our house so that we can have an open fire.

I have packed up a box of specimens for the S.L.E.S., which I shall send to you this time instead of to Billups. The Mollusca you might (if you will) exhibit on my behalf, and I enclose a note thereon to be read. The insects you may take up and give to Billups if you like, but better to anyone else who knows more about them, only it is not much use exhibiting them until the names

are discovered. Of course it is not necessary to exhibit them at once or at the same meeting unless convenient. I feel this about Billups, that his names may very likely be wrong, and if he exhibits them under wrong names it is published, and thus a false record made, which is very undesirable. If you care to keep any of the specimens for yourself you are of course welcome to do so.

October 24th. I got up at about eight this morning, in spite of previous intention of rising early, and after getting breakfast set about hauling flat rocks to make our projected chimney. It was very cold (severe frost last night) and my hands began to get numbed so that I put them into a pair of woolen socks (I have some gloves but can't find them). Then I got a thick scarf and a woolen jersey, and was comfortably warm. Most of the rocks were some distance from the house, so I got a box and dragged it with a rope, putting the rocks inside. Payn rode down to West Cliff. I did not give him this letter to post because I am going down myself tomorrow, and I thought he would bring me one of your letters, which I could answer this evening. But he comes back and brings me nothing but *Labor Enquirer*, saying there was no more mail! I cannot understand this unless the mail from England has been somehow delayed, for there must be some letters for me somewhere. I feel very much disappointed but will make enquiries tomorrow and perhaps something will turn up. It may be only a stupid mistake at the postoffice, as Payn says they have a new man there.

Payn has brought up a 20 cent copy of *The Woman in White*, which I have long meant to read, and so am glad to have this opportunity, Martin came up here this evening and is sleeping at our house, so that he may commence on the chimney early tomorrow morning. Brock (do you remember Brock) was here today. The bank at West Cliff has failed and quite a number of people have had heavy losses. Two stores have shut up in consequence.

October 25th. I have ridden down to West Cliff this morning and am much relieved to find that it was a mistake after all, and my mail is here all right: A letter from you (Oct. 4th), *Sci. Goss.* and the *Entom. Mag.* $15 forwarded from Douglas, Carlyle's *Heroes* from Carlie, letter from H. W. Kew, *Commonweal, West American Scientist, Conch. Exchange, Pall Mall Budget,* and a card from Smithsonian acknowledging receipt of specimens. I am very pleased to have Annie's notes on *Light of Asia.* I will compare them with the book when I get one and write further. Thank her for them. I will look out for Stevenson's *Familiar Studies.* I daresay I shall run across a ten cent copy on some bookstall.

I should very much like to have a list of those B. P. insects when you work them out. Species of all the four genera you mentioned are on the list for B. P. You had better get a ticket for British Museum. Get a form at the door and fill it up and get a householder (G.M.Fenn) to sign it. I never had one nor did they make any fuss but I ought to have had one, all the same, according to rules. Museum Diptera names are very unreliable, so Verrall says, and so I think. Get Verrall to name them if you can (address Sussex Lodge, Newmarket) or Meade.

It is hard to think of a subject for Annie's lecture (wish I could hear it). The first thing that occurs to me is 'The influence of environment.' Then I think of 'Flowers.' I am sure a botanical lecture would be most interesting and improving to the audience. Then again it might be another ethnological subject, say 'The characters of Isleworth' or 'A comparative study of cockneys and countrymen.' This exhausts my ideas for the present. If I think of anything else I will write in next letter. Send me full report of the lecture when it takes place. Health report. Am very well, except slight cold brought on by wind.

P.S. Can you get me the *Entomologist* for July?

West Cliff, October 25th, 1887

Dear Frederic,

I rode down to West Cliff this morning and got my mail, as you will know from letter posted to you then. I also posted a box of insects and Mollusca for you to take to the S.L.E.S. or keep, or otherwise dispose of as seems best. I have no duplicates of several of the insects, so it will be well not to let them go out of sight without being named. (I propose ultimately to write a full list of species taken in Colorado.) I told Averell (editor of *Conch. Exchange*), and he wants to know if he can act as agent for its sale if published! The list will probably be in *Journ. Conch.* and if I can get some reprints he may as well sell them if he can. There is a sort of *Science Gossip* (only not so good) paper called *West American Scientist* I have read two copies of (I sent the editor a 'trial subscription' for three months). A note comes from the editor asking me to write for the paper, which I shall very likely do.

When I got home I found the chimney in progress, and helped to haul some more stones. Then we had supper, and now I sit writing. Payn reads *The Woman in White* and Martin has been perusing a little blood and thunder novelette about the early days in Kentucky in which he has discovered something about his grandfather.

I have been through the passages noted by Annie in *Light of Asia* and like all her favorite pieces very much, and all of them more or less, some I had already noted, as Annie knows. I will write more about them later on. The worthy Barker (see S.L.E.S.) must have had an inkling that Billups was not a master of Colorado entomology, since he has not recorded the species in the *Ent. Mag.* I have half a mind to join in that discussion about collecting, in the *Entomologist,* not that I think it does much good, but you and Annie know my fondness for discussion. A. Wallis Kew has moved from Lincolnshire to 95 Evershol Road, Stroud Green, N. He is an excellent naturalist and you ought to know him. I will get him to go to the S.L.E.S.

October 26th. Most of today spent in getting rocks for the chimney, which is in good progress. Martin went to West Cliff this afternoon for some iron pipe to make the upper part of it, and brought me some more letters which had come by yesterday's mail, viz., a letter from you, one from Mother, from S.C.C., and from Harold Hanover, our reptilian young friend who used to be at the Zoöl. Soc. meetings. Do you remember?

I will answer both your letters now. The first one I have partly answered in letter already posted to you. The history of Syon Lodge comes to light bit by bit; evidently it has seen some exciting days. Somebody ought to collect all particulars and write a full account thereof in the *Family Magazine*. The delightful picture of the grandmother-in-law scaling the wall of Syon I had formed in my mind's eye was rudely shattered by the Figure 16 inscribed a little lower down at side of page. At 16 she ought to be able to scale anything with the help of a ladder, but the same thing at 85 would be quite romantic.

Massee is a very good sort of fellow, but not so learned as M. C. Cooke. He wrote a list of Yorkshire fungi in Trans. Y.N.U. if I remember right. Perchance your 'old German' is some well-known entomologist; enquire his name.

(2nd letter, commencing October 5th). I saw that paper of N. F. Layard. I shall look forward to your answer to it, which I trust will be sufficiently crushing. To me the paper seemed almost too absurd to be worth attention or reply. I certainly agree with Tutt about the setting. I remember Saunders, who gave me a nicely-set *Cicindela* which he took from his collection, remarking that he had an un-set one to put in its place. I think, though, that Tutt and the rest of them are rather foolish over the 'Lycaenidae in North Kent' discussion, which has become personal and useless. You might take some eggs and shells to the S.L.E.S. exhibition. I never went to one but I believe it to be a sort of soiree at which ladies are admitted. Therefore why not go and take Annie? I think she would be interested, and you could show her the lights of the Society — Billups, Tutt, Carrington, etc. Family wouldn't veto this, would they? Why don't you write a paper for the S.L.E.S.?

I am very glad to hear that Olive is going to stay at Syon. It was good of Annie to contrive it so. I begin to think you will not lose sight of Olive, anyway (although you see little of Carlie or any of the others) which is good.

I am thankful for the list of addenda to B. P. fauna (which I trust you have duly entered in my record book of fauna). This will bring the B. P. species of *Bombus* to five (and a variety), *Eristalis* to four, and *Syrphis* to two, I think. I have a note of the occurrence of *Bombus harricellus* at Isleworth, but with a query after it. Have you authenticated this for Isleworth?

What does Annie think of Emerson's essays? Mother likes them very much, but I don't care much for them.

The 'black-tailed deer' turns out to be *Cervus macrotis*. Two other species are found in Colorado, viz. *C. alcea* and *C. virginianus*. Now I think of it, will you get and post me a copy of the 1888 Smith's *Small Scribbling Diary* (No. 6?). Any time before Jan. 1 will do, but one really can't get such a good diary out here. Carlie will pay for it out of the fund he has for magazines, so let him know.

October 27th. The chimney finished today. I made the mortar while Martin fixed up the stones. The mortar was only mud, a mud pie on a large scale; we had no lime. Afterwards we cleaned up the rubbish, etc., and put the house in good order. This evening we have lit a fire in our new fireplace and find it smokes very considerably, which is a great bother, but it may possibly be better after a little use.

I have written two letters for the *Conch. Exchange*, one on *Parmacella* and one on *Planorbis umbilicatus* Taylor (var. *mut.*) and a letter to Averell, the editor.

October 28th. Nothing particular has happened today. We have been hauling and chopping wood, and I have been writing. I have just finished a list of the flora of Colorado compiled from Coulter's *Manual* and my own notes. Among other things it includes the following: *Anemone, Thalictrum alpinum, Myosurus minimus* (a sorry plant), *Ranunculus flammea* var. *reptans, R. sceleratus, Lepidium sativum, Viola* (seven species), *Linum perenne, Carex* (49 species including *vulgaris, versicolor*, etc.), *Trifolium* (seven spp.), *Astragalus* (46 spp.), *Rubus* (four spp.), *Potentilla* (11 spp.), *Saxifraga* (14 spp.), *Ribes* (seven spp.), *Oenothera biennis, Solidago* (seven spp.), *Phragmites communis, Lycopodium annotinum, Aster* (17 spp.), *Helianthus* (four spp.), *Artemisia* (ten spp.), *Cnicus* (nine spp.), *Primula farinosa, Gentiana* (ten spp.), *Polemonium coeruleum, Festuca ovina, Aspidium filix mas* var., *Mimulus* (three spp.), *Chenopodium hybridum, C. glaucum, C. rubrum* (all these are Surrey plants, and *C. rubrum* is recorded from Middlesex), *Euphorbia* (13 spp.), *Potamogeton* [illegible], *Equisetum* (three spp.).

October 29th. Last night, after I had written the above, the smoke became so bad that I retreated to my room. Soon, however, that was full of smoke also (the partition only goes halfway to the roof), and I had to open the window, a matter of some difficulty as the last occupant had nailed it up.

Today I have been 'fixing up' my room, putting up two shelves, one for books and papers and one for odds and ends, also a box for letters and another for specimens (shells, etc.) and two tin cans to hold newspapers. I have also pinned up a number of American curios by way of ornament and so that I may become familiar with their characters. My only pictures are four photographs, of Mother, Mr. Morris, R. D. Powell, and the excellent Wilcock. Annie's photograph I keep in my pocket. I do not like to put it up until I can get some sort of a frame, with glass.

I have done up a box of shells his afternoon for the Conch. Soc. I imagine that they come from higher altitudes than any Taylor has seen as yet, so I hope he will appreciate them.

Sunday, October 30th. I am afraid my letters now will be very uninteresting, days being much the same, and of course there is not so much to tell as when we were on the expedition. This morning I was drawing, and later on I wrote a paper, 'Town Life and Competition' for the *Labor Enquirer*, and a few notes on a postcard for *West American Scientist*.

Last night I was thinking that I had done nothing for Socialism for a long while, and I felt rather ashamed of myself, so I thought I would get up some labour statistics and study the subject a little more all round. I therefore went through the *Pall Mall Budget* I had at hand, and found quite a lot of interesting information which I duly copied into a notebook, and the paper for *Labor Enquirer* is the first result. If you come across anything on the subject that you think would be useful to me, would you just send me a reference to title and page so that I can look it up at some future time if necessary?

It strikes me that an enormous amount of really valuable information (together with ten times more that is valueless) is published in the newspapers and is lost. It is not that people haven't enough information, but rather that it isn't arranged so that they can understand it and reason from it. The facts in the *Origin of Species* were old enough for the most part, but the arrangement of them revolutionized science. A house is made of bricks, but bricks aren't necessarily a house.

October 31st. Payn and I have ridden down to West Cliff, and I find for me *Some Private Views* (for which all thanks), *Punch* (from Mother), letter from Leslie (poor fellow). It seems his chest is weak (and he has had to give up business), and letter from Smithsonian enclosing catalogue of their publications. Health report. All right.

[The following is a discussion of the book, *Some Private Views*, written by Payn's father, John Payn. And *Light of Asia*. These pages were evidently an appendage to the above letter. Ed.]

Some Private Views. This book is certainly clever. It contains much that is very true, yet there is a pessimistic view running through it, and even its hopes are somewhat halfhearted. Talking of friends, I don't think that John Payn ever had a friend in my sense of the term, any more than his son. All he says about 'friends' applies admirably to those acquaintances that are so common where each part knows the shallowness of the other, and dare not exceed certain limits of confidence.

Good steel is only known from bad in the testing. Payn's friends are like a lot of steel weapons that look good enough, but he uses them gingerly because he knows within himself they are not genuine and cannot safely be put to the test. For my part (though most people think differently) I would test all, and if they break, one is well rid of them, while if they don't, one knows that he has a friend. (I don't mean to say that I would experimentally try to offend people but that I would not refrain from treating them honestly for fear of losing their friendship.)

J. P., in speaking of the young author 'never hearing the last' of his poem, has in mind one of his own effusions, at which S.F.P. laughed uproariously and caused great offense thereby, he tells me. I am glad he is so hard on 'sham admiration in literature.' What he says is extremely just. I don't particularly admire his five poems from *1½ Magazine*, but then I am not a judge of poetry.

As to the wear and tear of story writing, I think it differs in different individuals. I myself would certainly be less tired after writing a scientific article than a story, but then I am used to the one and tread on familiar ground, while the other is more or less strange. Morris says that for him writing is a very easy work compared to other things, yet one would think that his poetry must require a great exercise of brain power. For myself, in such a familiar thing as letter writing, I know that I can easily write when in the humour without fatigue, and am utterly tired out by it if not in the humour. The attempt to write journalistically (e.g. for *Pall mall*) bores me horribly at present.

Respecting night work, I think there is some truth in it, yet Hamerton says he can always write best when everyone else has gone to bed, and no doubt in this also, each one must judge for himself. What has Annie to say about storytelling and night work; does she agree with me?

Frequently, at night, I know I am too muddled to write letters or invent, and then I can do compilation work from magazines, catalogues, etc., easily enough, and such work is quite necessary and useful to me. I did nearly all my Colorado fauna and flora catalogue under these circumstances.

I don't agree with J. P.'s views about servants, though they are natural enough for himself, an irritable man. The popular writer who won't look at a journal unless he knows who sent it for fear of seeing an unfavorable review is J. P. himself. I generally agree with his views about Relations. There was no cause to fear that Payn might not like his comments if he saw the book, since he has never read it and won't look at it, though I recommend it to him. He cannot read his father's books, he says.

The light of Asia. 'Lo as hid seed', etc. (Book II.) This theory of good following good, and evil evil is surely the right one. Curiously, modern Christians have very generally the idea that it is not so, and that they can escape the just rewards of their deeds, yet Christ himself, as reported in one of the gospels (I haven't the reference by me) expressly said 'Whatsoever measure ye mete, it shall be measured unto you again', etc.

Book III. 'Oh, suffering world', etc. This expresses beautifully the feeling that I think comes to every not entirely callous person sooner or later, but the pity is that so many lack the strong hope and conviction 'For them and me and all, there must be help.'

Book IV. 'Man perished in winter winds', etc. This passage is very good by itself, yet the argument is perhaps a little beside the question. Since the help is not to come from any new invention, not from a new power, but a new direction of it, a new feeling, for after all there is no reason to quarrel with the passage, which comes very naturally in the poem.

Book VI. 'Pity and need make all flesh kin', etc. Very good, but I wish more felt it so. Sujata's answer to Buddha is beautifully written, and the idea of the funeral pile, though barbarous in itself, does not interfere with the sentiment of the speech.

'That fixed decree at silent work which wills', etc. Here is a sufficient definition of God. The essential truth which lies at the bottom of all religious conceptions. We know but cannot as yet grasp the power for good. We call it by a variety of names, most often God, and we are very apt to clothe it with imaginary characters and forget its true nature. Hence the truest religions are always the simplest, and elaborate accounts of the appearance and sayings of the Deity are a sure sign of degeneration. The greater our knowledge the better, but while we know little it is better to say so than invent lies.

Some of the other passages I had already written of in my letter, parts toward the end (and particularly the verses marked as non-favourite) are pessimistic and unhappy, and hardly express the true spirit of Buddha, but there is so much that is very beautiful and true in the book that it is easy to forgive this.

The three years in Colorado during which I lived in Wet Mountain Valley were occupied with various pursuits, whereby I earned enough to keep me going, but always the major interest was natural history. I corresponded with many naturalists, and as early as 1887 began a catalogue of the entire Fauna and Flora of Colorado, recent and fossil. It included every reference I could find in the literature, very many other references kindly supplied by correspondents, and of course such of my own finds as I could get identified.

Recollections

October 31st, 1887

Dear Frederic,

Today Payn and I rode down to West Cliff and I posted the last letter to you. Then we jogged back again. I was on the old mare, and Payn on the horse 'Buckskin.' It is curious about that old mare, that no amount of beating, etc., will induce her to more than shuffle along, but no sooner does Buckskin start trotting or galloping when they are together, than off goes the mare just as fast as she can.

On arriving here we found a fellow called Cusack in our house, and he stopped to supper with us and is now playing cards with Payn. He is an Englishman (from Bedfordshire) and youngish. His face is something like an unfinished Julius Caesar.

Martin's dog has come up to our house. We took it down to Ula today but it came back again, so we threw stones at it, but still it declines to depart. We don't want the dog but cannot tell how to get rid of it.

Looking at *Some Private Views*, I find I read it long ago at Wimpole Street. It is the only thing of John Payn's I ever read. I thought it very good at the time and am glad to have an opportunity of reading it again, especially with Annie's comments. I sent to the Smithsonian for $1.70 worth of their publications, which is very extravagant, but I feel that it is worth any while. They are very cheap and I get quite a number for the money.

November 1st. Payn and Cusack played poker till after midnight yesterday, and I went to bed. This morning we all got up very late, and after breakfast we went up to Cusack's house, which is beyond Cox's and amongst the pine trees. Cusack, it appears, was a student at Guy's

Hospital at one time, but has now been in America for seven or eight years; he must be older than he looks. Up at his house we found his brother Frank, an older and nicer-looking man, something like Robinson Crusoe in the face. Frank had been in Australia and seems to be a man of greater information and general intelligence than his brother, though both are rather above the average of these parts (which is not saying much!). They expect their mother from England tomorrow. I saw her photograph. She looks like a very nice old lady.

I took *some Private Views* up with me and read it through. I will write some notes on it later on. Nearly all day they have been playing cards, and I left them (about 7:45 p.m.) so engaged and came down here to write, calling on the way at Cox's ranch which in his absence is in charge of one Bassick, an agreeable fellow but in no wise remarkable or particularly interesting.

I was talking with Frank Cusack about work. He says that just now almost the only work doing is threshing (includes the manipulation of bundles of corn, etc., for the threshing machine) which he says I could not do unless familiar with it, and it is the hardest work to be had, and potato digging, which can be thought equally hard because of the bending of the back all day. He says, however, that if one is actually 'broke', odd jobs can generally be procured, even at the worst time of year.

Up at the Cusack's I was looking in *Haydn's Dictionary of Dates* and came across several interesting things: p. 463, Mulberry trees. 'The alleged first planted in England are in the gardens of Syon House' (as you said in your former letter). Under Lunacy I read that insanity has been defined as the 'paralysis of the regulating or legislating faculties of the mind', and that lunacy in 1,000 cases can be traced to: Drunkenness, 110 cases; Consequence of disease, 100; Epilepsy, 78; Ambition, 73; Excessive labour, 73; Born idiots, 71; Misfortunes, 69; Old age, 69; Chagrin, 54; Love, 47; Accidents, 39; Religion, 29; and others in less numbers.

Payn stayed at the Cusack's last night, having played cards till the small hours of the morning. I went for a short walk in search of insects (but didn't get any) and met him coming down from there this morning.

The rest of the morning I spent in taking notes, and this afternoon I have been reading *The Woman in White*, in which I am somewhat disappointed. (I have got as far as the beginning of Gilmore's narrative.) It seems to me that the great failing of novelists is their tendency to embellish the scenery at the expense of the characters, like the manager of Drury Lane Theatre. Ordinary people are placed in extraordinary circumstances, and their triumph (on which the success of the novel depends) is in their struggle towards and ultimate achievement of the ordinariness, in spite of circumstances. Whereas, it seems to me that a novel ought rather to be idealistic and show how people may do worthy things and lead remarkable lives under the more ordinary circumstances. The interest ought to be centred in the actors and not in their surroundings or adventures.

The only really good detective story I have read is *Les Miserables*, and here you have truly remarkable enough circumstances, in spite of which the whole interest is centred in the noble character of Jean Valjean. In Charlotte Bronte's *Professor* and *Villette* (I like the *Professor* best, contrary to general opinion) you have types of good stories in which hardly any 'stage effects' are introduced. How does Annie think of all this?

Regy Cusack (he younger one) tells us that he has been for three months in the employment of one Jack Lees, as cook to a hunting expedition similar to ours, and besides having all expenses paid and getting hunting on the way, has gotten back £10 to the good, so I don't feel that I have really been much more expense to Payn than was reasonable, for although I probably did much less (and that not so well) than Cusack, I had only my board without wages.

I have been reading *The Woman in White* mostly, but am so little interested by it that I have been glad to throw it down for notebook work, etc., as a change. I have several papers in view but don't want to be too precipitate with them (as I generally am) and need to take plenty of notes and so have sufficient material to work on.

Payn has started to write a novel! I have one myself in a nebulous state in a corner of my brain, but whether it will come to anything or not I cannot tell. Jod came up here today on horseback mainly to ask the loan of our tent, which was granted.

November 4th. Frank Cusack came down this morning, attired in his working clothes of blue cotton, for Payn had offered him some tools if he would make our chimney, etc. He built a number of rocks into the back of it with the idea of creating a draft, and nailed a piece of tin across the front to keep the smoke in, in spite of which it smokes just as badly as it did before. I really don't know how we can get a fire in our house for the winter days. The smoke is intolerable, and the little stove we have (Brock took away the one we used to use) is a very poor substitute.

I have finished *The Woman in White* today and do not think much better of it than when I had only begun. I cannot say anything better of it than that it is clever.

I tried to write an account of Rocky Mountain animals for Step's *Welcome* this afternoon. If I finish it successfully I will send it to him. Partridge & Co. print an enormous amount of twaddle, and I might be able to suit them. Payn has discontinued his novel for the present; he says it's an awful bore writing a novel and wonders how on earth his 'governor' can do it.

November 5th. I have ridden down to West Cliff and got my mail, and your letter, alas! with bad news. I am extremely sorry about Annie's neuralgia. It is a most miserable thing to have, and she has my strongest sympathy. Notwithstanding her assurance I cannot help feeling a little anxious about her work, for your family is the most industrious one I ever saw, and Annie does more than anyone. Report to me in every letter how she is, and tell me exactly the truth.

The second piece of news is that I ought to stay out here three years! I trust that it is not so. I looked forward so eagerly to my return next summer or at the very latest the year after, and it seems too miserable to have to live in exile so long. Thank Annie for her message. I needed it. If it must be I will see it through successfully somehow, even three years, and I feel, as she does, that it will never do to have to go out again.

Sinistral *H. arbustorum* has been recorded for Colorado from the Continent. What sort of a chap is J.H.A. Jenner? I used to correspond a great deal with him. I am sorry to hear of Mrs. Craik's death, and Olive must be more sorry. I am glad that you and Carlie are once more good friends. Sorry for the late hours at the office. It must be horrible. At Klein's they get away at five now, sometimes! I congratulate you on the discovery of *Testacella* at Syon. I would demonstrate myself if I were in London. You will see I could not post a letter sooner, that is why my delay; very sorry but couldn't help it. (I posted letter at Montrose about 4th October). I have finished the paper for Step's *Welcome*, and posted it. I had a very nice letter from Sutton, also letter from Carlie, with photograph which I don't think very good. Looks as though he had toothache.

My best greeting to Annie. I hope that long before the three years she will be able to write to me and I to her. Is this likely to be possible soon?

November 5th, 1887

Dear Frederic,

Today I posted the last letter to you and got yours commencing October 11th as well as sundry other things: Letter from Carlie, one from Sutton, *Commonweal*, *Pall Mall Budget*, pamphlet (carelessly got up) by J. C. Melville on Mollusca of Manchester District, and postcard from Averell.

Coming home I had to put 30 pounds of oats and ten pounds of potatoes on the horse, beside myself, which was a heavy load, and I had to keep him at a walk. Consequently I did not get home till after dark, and found Payn reading. He had not felt energetic enough to get any supper for himself and me. I discovered a piece of bread, some fragmentary remains of potted meat and some biscuits, and so feasted as best I could. It is so warm in here and so cold outside that I really can't go out now and cook supper. Besides I am tired and shall shortly go to bed.

I saw Mrs. Boulger once at Gardening Society, I think, but I did not get a good look at her or have any opportunity of taking much note of her appearance.

I am on the whole in favor of disturbances because I think that where there is a real evil, nothing but some sort of disturbance is likely to cure it. (I defend toothache on exactly the same grounds.) Therefore I am glad the unemployed are drawing attention to their care, even though a great deal of nonsense may be said and a good deal of humbug go on (and mind, the capitalist press is bound to give a more or less unfair account of the proceedings just as they always do of the opposite party in party politics). Have you ever been to a really great demonstration? I think not. Trafalgar Square or Hyde Park full of people all more or less of one opinion is worth seeing.

You do well to send the Diptera to Verrall. He is a reliable man, but he is busy and takes a long while before answering one's letters. I feel pretty sure South's four-antennaed geometrid will prove a fraud, though the thing is by no means impossible, I suppose, save on the ground that it could not have carried on its duplicate existence in the caterpillar and chrysalis stage.

Sinistral *arbustorum flavescens* is unique, but sinistral *arbustorum* has been taken I believe more than once on the Continent. I am glad you are bossing the Mollusca at the S.L.E.S. for your sake and theirs.

How goes the Conch. record? Carlie and Christabel C. seem to get on together. I fancy they are somewhat alike though I only saw Christabel but once, and then didn't pay much attention to her. I thought I shouldn't care much for her.

I used to be familiar with Boulgerian effusions in *Nat. Hist. Notes* in 1882-3. I always thought he was a sound man, but not original.

Poor Frederic! With the dress clothes! But wherefore won't an ordinary black coat do? With any civilized people it should. Whoever persuaded Olive to collect fungi for you? I didn't think it could be done; she once collected snails for me though, in Switzerland.

That three years haunts me. I know that my uncle Douglas is very eccentric in his statements, When he saw me he said (or rather hinted — he rarely definitely says anything) that two would be amply sufficient. The conversation, so far as I can remember it, was something like this.

T.D.A.C.: 'And if I stay for, say, two winters in Colorado, you think that ought to put me all right again?'

R.D.P.: 'Oh yes, if you take care of yourself and don't run any risks you will get all right again.'

Time will show, anyhow. I must see how I am next summer.

There is a smallish black, shiny, covered, blue-edged thick MS book of mine somewhere, with descriptions of varieties, principally of insects. I think you have it. If so, will you post it to me? I find I need it to help me in working out some things in connection with variation. How is your Isleworth slug list now? Will it compare with that for Bedford Park? You ought to have one more species than B. P., namely *Limax laevis*.

Sunday, November 6th. An uneventful day. I felt lazy this morning and got up late. All the day I have been working. We have put up a stove we have here in place of our smoky chimney and open fire. It is not so good as the one we had, but answers its purpose pretty well and keeps us warm. To our usual bill of fare (tea, bread, bacon, or meat) we have added the luxury of potatoes, which are peeled and cut into long prism-shaped pieces and then fried in grease, the result of which is excellent.

Payn has not been feeling very well, and I have rather a cough, but am otherwise most robust. Nearly everyone we have seen since our return has made some remark on the apparently improved state of my health, and some even insinuate that I am getting fat!

Looking over one of my notebooks I find that Miss Ormerud (*Entomologist* 1878, p. 216) records two beetles from near Isleworth: *Psylliodes chrysocephala* L. and *P. nigricollis* (our only of the latter found). They were probably in your fauna district, but I believe she does not make it quite clear whether this is so. You can easily refer to the record in the library of S.L.E.S. when you are there.

November 7th. We drove down to West Cliff today to fetch fresh meat, bacon, etc. I could not bring up sufficient on the horse on Saturday. Payn, although almost at the end of his money, spent about $17 one way and another, e.g., pipe ($3), whiskey, wine, apples, *Scribner's Magazine* and some books, etc., besides the necessaries. As long as he has money he is bound to spend it, and it is no use interfering, nor do I care to do so. I look forward rather curiously to the time when he will be penniless, when we shall live on the $15 I have and anything I can earn, because you may be sure, when the funds are mine to 'boss', I shall use them economically.

I enquired at postoffice, in case there should be any more mail, and got *Pall Mall Budget* and two *Labor Enquirers*. In *P.M.B.* I see a very interesting account of Morris' play at Farrington Road, and also a notice of the funeral of Mrs. Craik.

Tomkins of the hardware store was good enough to give me a piece of glass to fit over Annie's photograph so that I can now put it up over the table on which I write. The sight of it will encourage me.

If you should happen across any of the following amongst my papers, etc., will you post them out to me? *List of British Birds*; Sharp's *List of British Coleoptera*, Conch. Soc.'s *List of British Land & Fresh Water Mollusca*; Simerville's *List of Marine Mollusca*; S.L.E.S. map of district.

November 8th. Two things have happened. Cox has come home and we have had the first snowstorm here. Cox drove up this afternoon with Charlie Cusack (brother of Frank and Regy, very like the latter in appearance. He lives near West Cliff) and went on with him to the Cusack's house. We went up to Cox's later on to see him, but he was still at the Cusack's, and so we returned. While at Cox's a snowstorm came on.

It was looking dull and threatening yesterday, and this morning it was snowing on the mountains, so we were not surprised that it should do so here. The fall has been only a slight one, and now the sky is clear and the stars shining bright.

A fire is visible on the prairie in the distance and we are speculating as to its nature. I think it must be some of the *Potentilla* brush caught fire. I saw some smoke in that direction this afternoon. While I write, a moth (one of the Noctuidae) undaunted by the cold weather, is flying around the lamp.

November 9th. Cloudless and sunny, all the snow melted except in shady nooks. After breakfast we went up to Cox's and met him halfway, coming with Bassick and a sort of waggon to haul poles wherewith to make a fence round his corral nine feet high, to keep off the snow drifts. We went down with them to the quaking asp thicket, where Bassick cut down the trees and

Cox hauled the poles to the waggon, at which I helped.

Cox told me that he heard of a 'clerking' job at Colorado Springs that he thought would suit me. I wish I could go and take it, but I don't see how I can leave Payn just now. Colorado Springs is a much warmer and nicer place than this, and there are many English out there with consumption (for the winter) and I should doubtless meet some I would like. R. L. Stevenson is probably there, but Cox does not know whether he is, though he described to me a man with long hair, etc., that may be him. Cox talks of going to Colorado Springs (whence he has just come) for the winter himself, and proposes that we go and live in his house, which will be much better than our cabin, since it has no holes in the roof and is warm and there is a good stove.

While we were at Cox's two visitors came: Mrs. Cusack and Miss Urquhart (the girl she brought with her from England). Mrs. Cusack has been out here before, some years ago. She is a very vivacious old lady with a pleasant face. She is short and stout, and the only person I can think of to liken her to is Mrs. Peak, only she is not so stout nor so fat in the face, but her manner is much the same. Miss Urquhart reminded me strongly of someone, but until five minutes ago I would not imagine who it was. Now I know — Miss Sophy Smith! Which is rather peculiar, because her face is only slightly like that of S. S., and I have not heard her talk. Nevertheless, though she is probably not so bad, I feel convinced that we have a Sophy Smith-ite for neighbor.

This evening Cox and Payn are playing poker.

I caught today a *Colias* new to me (pale yellow, something like *lyalli* with rosy fringes to the wings). You would hardly imagine that a butterfly would be about where it snowed only yesterday.

R. Davis, in *Commonweal* quotes W. E. Chadwick that the mean age of the gentry is 50 years; shopkeepers is 27; wage earners is 23 years!

What do you think of this? *Syon Playfair* says that 55 per cent of the children of the working class die under the age of five!

I have been talking further with Cox about the Colorado Springs clerkship. I have resolved to take it if I can get it, and take Payn along with me to the Springs. Cox has promised to do what he can in the matter. The only thing against it is that living (and particularly house rent) is much more expensive there than here, but then I should earn the money and therefore hold the money bag, so Payn would have no chance to spend more than was necessary, and this would quite counterbalance the comparative expensiveness of Colorado Springs. Anyway, it will be better to live on a little there than nothing at all here.

9 p.m. We have just come back from Brock's, where we went to supper. The company consisted of Brock, Mrs. Brock, Brock infant, Preston (a Cheshire man, rather a fool I think), Payn, and myself. I had not seen Mrs. Brock or the child before, and I must introduce them to you.

Mrs. Brock: A thoroughly American type of woman, rather good looking after the manner of the pictures you see in *Harper*. Energetic and a hard worker, pleasant mannered and in no wise intellectual. Comes from Iowa, finds ranch life very hard (and I am sure it is) and feels much the solitary situation. For weeks she sees hardly anyone but Brock, since she has too much work to leave the house much. She has recently been to a visit to her people in Iowa and has only just returned.

Brock, junior. Small boy of about four years, chubby, talkative on almost every subject, decidedly precocious. Chaffs his mother but is fond of her, devours great quantities of peanuts, has great affection for donkeys, of which Brock possesses several. There is no doubt that ranch life, if hard for the men, is doubly so for the women, unless there are two or three in the house.

In the Wet Mountain Valley, Colorado, I found Mrs. M. E. Cusack, an elderly English lady who had always longed to study botany, but had been prevented by the circumstances of an exceptionally difficult life. She now began to form an herbarium, and I assisted her to the best of my ability, using Coulter's Manual of Botany, a very serviceable compilation mainly based on the writings of Asa Gray. Really critical work, such as that done in later years by Aven Nelson of Wyoming and P. A. Rydberg of New York, was out of the question, but we did acquire a fair knowledge of the local flora. The Cusack herbarium was eventually incorporated in that of Kew.

Recollections

November 11th. I am in a rather restless mood this evening because I have been disappointed. Brock went down to West Cliff today, and Preston also, and we asked Preston to bring our mail when he returned, which he entirely forgot to do, hence no mail, and ill temper!

I went out for a hunt today and got one thing new to the county — *Limnaea truncatula* var. *humilis*. They were on rotten wood in a small rivulet quite close to the house.

The forest is on fire on the other side of the valley (in the Wet Mountains). No flame is visible but enough smoke for a volcano. Cox tells us that when we were away he one day caught someone, a stranger, in our house, and he civilly explained to him that he would do well not to remain in the neighborhood, because Cox was often about and carried a gun which was 'liable to go off accidentally.' The stranger accordingly 'made tracks.'

November 12th. I walked down to West Cliff today, catching a lot of beetles on the way, and have got my mail, with yours of the 19th. I am sorry to hear that Annie has not been well again, but you say she is better now, which is satisfactory. Thank her much for additional fauna and flora list. I see she has discovered that interesting vertebrate, *Homo sapiens*, since the last list. *Sitta europaea* is interesting. This bird is very common on the trees in Camden Park, Chislehurst. I used to take much interest in watching them.

Agaricus campestris I have found in Colorado more than once, and *Marasmius oreades* occurs in the U. S., but not that I know of in Colorado. Many of the fungi are like the Bedford Park species I note, but several have not yet been found there. *Coccinella 11-punctata* var. *'diopa'* should I suppose be *dispar*? — the red and black variety. I am glad you will continue my Conch. record book.

Fancy suggesting I have forgotten what Annie's like! You deserve to be kicked. I don't think the photograph is so bad; it might have been better, of course, but 'beggars mustn't be choosers', and I was only too glad to get that. If a better one is done, don't fail to send me one. Contrive somehow that I may see the composite story when published. Will it be a book? And in what respect is it altered from *Merely Friends*?

Olive does seem to have gotten quite interested in fungi. She writes me a nice letter from Chislehurst, with coloured drawings of some fungi she has found (*Agaricus fascicularis, A. oleaginosus ? A. sp.? Hygrophorus? Marasmius?* and *Peziza*).

I have also had a nice letter from Carlie (enclosing letter from Hoyle asking reference to one of my papers from *Zoöl. Record*), and I have a letter from R. H. Meade (Mount Royd, Bradford) asking for Colorado Diptera (which he shall have). Meade is a good man and you might send him some Diptera.

Other mail rec'd: Letter from Mother, postcard from Taylor, *Commonweal, Pall Mall Budget,* and *Harper's Weekly* (the last sent by Felix of Chicago, who wrote to me before).

I see from the paragraph you enclose that someone takes exception to Annie's views concerning Mary, Queen of Scots. Personally I should be inclined to agree that it didn't very much matter, but after all I suppose it does matter to some people, and on that account would perhaps have been better omitted. To me it seems that the real fault of the whole thing was that the 'Chit Chat' was not signed. (Which of course could not be helped.) Editorial and unsigned articles ought not to contain more individual opinion than is necessary; and signed articles ought to be quite outspoken and regardless of anyone's toes; there is the difference.

Soon after you get this it will be Annie's birthday. My love and a birthday greeting, and may she have many happy returns of this, as also of the other 364 days. Health report. Good, cough disappeared. Could you send me the December *Zoölogist* with index? I see *Nat. World* threatens to discontinue.

November 12th, 1887

Dear Frederic,

I had meant to have ridden back with Cox this evening, but as he didn't turn up I walked home. Cox turned up at our house later, not having started until some time after. The walk has done me good and I am in hopeful spirits again, but the receipt of mail probably has a good deal to do with that.

I am sorry to hear that Louy is out of sorts and depressed. Can't you get her to take up some hobby — fungi or anything?

At times I don't think I could bear existence at all if it wasn't for science. That was more so formerly, perhaps not entirely so even now, but three or four years ago it used to seem that the only things worth living for were Science and Socialism, and earlier there was only Science.

(These are my views. I hope Louy won't be offended at my expressing them.) Hope is the necessary condition of happy existence in any but a very low grade frame of mind. I have three principal hopes. The first you know full well. The second is for Science, and the third is for the Social Revolution, three main ends to which I may work, and be happy in working. With others it is different. Some (such as my grandmother) are quite happy in the hope of the next world, and so with others who are happy. There is always a hope at the bottom of it. If I see one unhappy, I say to myself: 'He has lost his hope', and everyone loses a measure of their hope at times.

Indeed it is well said that the most religious man is sometimes an atheist. A brute, either man or beast, is one without the hoping capacity.

Annie once asked me for a definition of man. Here is one: Man is an animal whose actions are based on hope. I see I have wandered entirely away from my original subject, and preached you a sermon!

I am glad that Annie is drawing the Isleworth fungi. It is useless frying to preserve them, and there is nothing like good drawings. Please let me have a list of the moths new to the B. P. list. I suppose they are mostly 'micros'? Your drawing of the abnormal *Melleus* looks like the young of it. We used to find them at B. P. in Peacock's field.

Sunday, November 13th. I have been entering up Annie's finds in my notebook (I keep a record of all Isleworth and B. P. species, and my Middlesex records I came across in a notebook especially for the purpose) and comparing them with the B. P. list. Two of the new fauna are not in B. P. list, but Annie had the *Phyllobium* in the former list. If I remember right, the nuthatch is recorded in F. O. Morris' *British Birds* as having been seen in Kensington Gardens, but it must be a rare bird in Middlesex.

The list of flowering plants contains three (*Medicago sativa, Anthemis nobilis,* and *Samolus*) not on B. P. list, and also three Rocky Mountain species: *Urtica dioica* (not native in Rocky Mountains), *Samolus valerandi* (represented by var. *americanus*) and *Triticum repens.* Also, *Medicago sativa* has been introduced into Utah, Wyoming, etc., but is not yet known from Colorado. *Helosciadium nodiflorum* is now generally placed in the genus *Apium,* I believe (and it is at any time a blessing to cut down the number of the genera of Umbelliferae!).

The list of fungi is very interesting. It resembles the B. P. list very much more than the spider list you spoke of, and this is perfectly natural since the same fungi occur all over the world, whereas spiders are very local. (I believe O. P. Cambridge found nine species peculiar to the Isle of Portland, for instance.) Four of the fungus species are not in B. P. list; one of them (*Agaricus lutipes*) is said to be edible in *Sci. Goss.* Of the four species of *Coprinus*, three are not in B. P. list, but I suspect you sent *deliquescens* to M. C. Cooke, only it deliquesced into gravy along the way (there was such a one, I remember). And as for *micaceus*, I had it down for B. P. but was afterwards doubtful about it and so didn't publish it in the *Journ. Bot.* list. The very first time Annie went collecting fungi, she puzzled some out with the book and gave me a scrap of paper (I have it yet) with the names, and one was *Coprinus micaceus!* No doubt many species of *Peziza* will turn up. I used to find the brilliant *P. aurantia* at Chislehurst. A rare species, *P. summeria* has been recorded for Rockhampton, and I fancy for Chiswick also.

Cox gave me an interesting volume, the *Report of the Commission of Agriculture, U.S.A.* for 1885. In it there is a chapter on U. S. edible fungi, with very many quotations from Worthington Smith. The species appear to be all European, as well as American, e.g. *Marasmius oreades, Coprinus comatus, Agaricus campestris, Boletus edulis,* and such well-known things.

I have spent today in working up Geographical Distribution. I am thinking of writing a paper on that subject for S.L.E.S.

Payn contrived to sprain his foot by kicking a stone yesterday, and limps about in consequence.

November14[th]. Payn went up to the Cusack's this morning and has not yet returned. He is doubtless playing poker and won't be back until tomorrow or very late tonight. I have been busy all day in writing a paper on geographical distribution, the one I meant for the S.L.E.S., only on second thought I shall send it to *Science Gossip*; it seeks to demonstrate that every species common to Europe and America belongs to the ancient circumpolar flora and/or fauna, except

those introduced by some human agency and a few migratory species.

Last night I went up to Cox's and found him and Frank Cusack there (Frank has shaved off his beard and doesn't look like Robinson Crusoe any longer). We had a long discussion, commencing with Socialism and ending on Religion. Over the socialism I was in a minority of one (Cox being Tory and Frank 'sort of a radical') but on the religion we agreed better.

One question raised (but not settled) was: Is there such a thing as a genuine atheist? The opinion of the meeting seemed to be that there wasn't, understanding an atheist to be one who was entirely and at all times convinced of the nonexistence of any higher power. And I think so myself, because I think the religious feeling is an inherited instinct and cannot be entirely eliminated, unless in the case of an idiot, which is not the same as a convinced atheist, by any means.

November 15th, 9:10 a.m. Payn did not return last night and has not yet appeared this morning. Cox came by just now on his way to West Cliff, so I gave him the *Sci. Goss.* paper and a postcard to Roebuck to post, and he will bring back any mail tonight. Cox observed, not without some reason, that if Payn plays poker too often with the Cusacks (who play much better than he does) he is likely to lose every cent that he possesses.

I have been writing and reading Stepniak's *Underground Russia*, which is a very interesting and remarkable book. I had heard a good deal of what is in this book, as also much that is not in it from Stepniak himself when he lectured at Kelmscott House, but I never properly understood nihilism before, particularly as regards origins and development.

November16[th]. Cox never turned up last night and did not come today until about half past ten, when he rode up with Frank Hunter (the excellent Englishman who keeps the stables at West Cliff). He had forgotten to get some books Payn wanted and said there was no mail for me, so I saddled our horse and rode down myself, getting back at about six. I found there was some mail after all: A letter from Averell and a *Labor Enquirer*. Averell sent me (to be returned) Hemphill's list of Utah shells, which I was very glad to see. He wants to publish my list of Colorado Mollusca (when I have it ready) in his *Conch. Exchange*, but I mean to send it to *Journ. Conch.*

The *Labor Enquirer* contains the paper on Competition I wrote for them. It is rather lengthy, two columns and a half. I will send it you to read. I had the bit out of the *Light of Asia*: 'But looking deep he saw the thorns', etc., printed at the top of it, but they have also added a heading of their own, which reminds one of the bills of London papers.

I posted postcards to McLachlan, Francis Galton, and Billups, and a letter to the U. S. Agriculture Dept. asking whether I could conduct an investigation for them out here. Also, I sent five Diptera to Meade.

November 17th. First of all I wrote a letter to Averell, and afterwards read some of Carlyle on *Heroes and Hero Worship*, which I like better than *Labour Researches* decidedly, and except that I quite disagree with him on the main point — the advantage of hero worship. I agree with and appreciate much of what he says.

I think the account he gives of Scandinavian theology quite the true one. All things in nature were to the ancients marvelous and incomprehensible, and they would naturally feel awe for such forces as that of the sun, wind, etc., and would deem that some living being was in them, which they would worship. Then some man, wiser than the rest, should study these phenomena and in some measure explain them and their relation to one another. The gods being in the wind, the man who could forestall a storm would of course be held to be in communication with the gods, and so the hero would be wor-

shiped as the visible representative of the gods, or even as a god.

November 18th, 1:25 p.m. A dull day with a cold wind coming from the mountains. Payn has gone up to the Cusack's. Cox, who went down to West Cliff yesterday, has not returned.

I have written a short note on *Vanessa antiope* for the S.L.E.S., which I enclose. Will you, when you next go, either give it to the Secretary or, if you will, read it yourself?

Cox has come up from West Cliff bringing me a most satisfactory mail: Your letter posted November 3rd, letters from Mother and Carlie, and a long letter from Smithsonian Institution with the names of the things I sent them (one butterfly and two Orthoptera are new to their collection).

Couldn't you post me the various publications that appear with Annie's stories, and the poems. I should much like to see them too? I would return them by next mail in all safety.

I must say that I think the members of the S.L.E.S. do quite right to make much of varieties, Looked at properly, nothing of this kind is unimportant, not even the coalescence of bands in *Helix nemoralis*.

The *Ephestia* were from granary in Blackwell Docks. I don't suppose you will get much information out of Klein. It is not to his interest to make known the fact that his flour (which he is trying to sell) is full of caterpillars. I explained everything at the meeting, and Adkin ought to have known.

Berkeley is not a moss man, is he? I thought he was only fungi.

I am glad to hear Annie has sold another picture. In what points does Annie now disagree with her essay on Delusions? I think I can imagine, but should like to know from her. You may keep the *Labor Enquirer*. I have other copies.

I should like to know what Annie thinks of the article.

The red-brown beetle with a very narrow waist (No. 40) that I sent you is said by Smithsonian Inst. to be a rare species, *Platynum jejunus.* I sent them one from Squaw Creek, Chaffee County. Yours came from Squaw Creek, Eagle County. So I have found it, you see, both on the Atlantic and Pacific slopes. If you exhibit it at S.L.E.S. it will be well to mention these matters. The beetle in envelope 33 (the black one) will probably be a species of *Pachyta.* A *Paederus* I sent them, they say is 'probably *littoralis',* our English species.

Carlie sends a letter from Lamb, of Maidstone, with a list of the shells of that district. I don't trust Lamb's naming, and have written asking him to send specimens to you, that you may include them in S.L.E.S. record book. He sent Carlie three slugs from Maidstone: *Armalia marginata, Limax agrestis,* and *Arion hortensis;* the last is new for that part of Kent.

November 19th. I have walked down to West Cliff and got some papers: *Naturalist, Sci. Goss.* (a copy sent by Carlie, I don't know why. I see therein your article, which seems much to the point), *Nat. Hist. Journal* (sent for a specimen copy), *Pall Mall Budget* (with picture of Morris' play — good portrait of May Morris), *Commonweal,* and *Labor Enquirer.*

November 19th, 1887

Dear Frederic,

A letter was posted to you today, and then I just walked back here and there is nothing more to relate. With regard to Williams' paper in *Sci. Goss.* (p. 244), I may as well say that *Lehmannia* is founded on very slight characters, principally the teeth. I went into the matter one day with E. A. Smith at the Museum and we both agreed that there was no sufficient reason to adopt a new genus. And I would not accept Miller's name *marginata* either, for his description is very

insufficient, while there is no doubt as to what *arborum* is. Roebuck adopted *Lehmannia* but later dropped it.

I forgot whether I ever entered the mite *Phelodromus limacum* (Gmel.) Junius (*Sci. Goss.* p. 243) in the Bedford Park fauna book. If not, please enter it. I found it there.

I see you bring in the term 'vestigial' in your note. It recalls to me the smiling countenance and pug nose of Jeffrey Bell! But it is a good term. A rudiment is essentially a part which no longer is of use or has the same use and is a remnant of a former condition of usefulness, so I should define it, though I have no objection to calling that a vestige instead. To give you a familiar example, you go for a walk and put on a hat. It is then useful and actively employed. You enter the house and immediately the hat becomes a rudiment, and you take measures to get rid of it, which is easier than if it were part of yourself — say, an acquired habit.

Altogether I quite agree with your note and think it sufficiently demolishes N. F. Layard.

Sunday, November 20th. This morning I packed up a box of insects for the Smithsonian. I asked them to lend me some books, but Brown Goode (Secretary of the Museum) writes that it is contrary to rules to do so, but he will send me books for their value in specimens for the museum, which is satisfactory, as I shall be thus getting specimens named and getting books at the same time.

I wrote a short account of gold prospecting this afternoon. I am going to write several short things and send them to 5 Priory and ask Carlie to post them out to various magazines, this because I don't know the address of the papers, and it will be better on the whole to send them altogether. I am not very sanguine about the matter. I don't think I shall ever make anything of a journalist, but the practice of writing will do no harm, at all events.

I had another row with Payn tonight. I really don't see how I can live with him all the winter, anyway. If I get the place at Colorado Springs it may be the occasion of our parting, as it is quite likely he won't come.

November 21st. I have been reading *Sesame and Lilies* and like parts of it very much. In the first lecture he asks whether the love of praise is not the strongest human motive. It seems to me that in a certain way it is the only human motive, that is to say, everyone desires to secure happiness, which is the result of harmony or approval. The real question seems to me to be, whose and what approval does a man desire? Is it the approval of his own sense of right most, or most that of other people and, if the latter, what other people?

Now it becomes evident that a man's 'magnetic center' ought to be in himself to the extent of not being contrary to his own conscience. He ought to be conscious of his own idea of right and obey it even though it secures the disapproval of everyone around him, though at the same time plastic and ready to take in new ideas, though not to use them until they are really and genuinely his own.

How then, if a man is to act entirely in accordance with his conscience, is the approval of others to influence him? Because of this, no man's conscience is undivided; no man can say to himself absolutely: 'I will act so, and I am so certain that it is right that I do not care though the whole universe is against me.' Some may feel so for a time, but I doubt if any human being ever lived entirely so. If he did, he would have the attribute of a god. Rather, the conflict within a man is so severe that without help existence would be hard for him, and quite apart from the correcting counsel of others, which is most important, is the supporting approval of those in whom he believes and has perfect trust, without which, it may be, no great deed was ever done. Even Christ, the strongest figure in all history, had, and needed, his disciples.

And here comes the argument of Lecture II. Ruskin shows that, although the actual deeds of history are done for the most by men, yet they could never have been except for the moral influence of women. Women, or at least the best of them, have a perfectly true instinct of what is right, which may, if it will, so influence the same but none too powerful instinct in men as to turn the scale from wrong to right and change their whole being. The average man is strong for good or for evil, and generally it is the influence of his best friend that decides which it is to be. I believe that much of the barbarity of *this* country is due to the lack of women. Men, left to themselves, have lost their balance and are no longer able to control themselves.

I think the part where Ruskin shows how, as a nation, we 'go on despising literature, despising science, despising art, despising nature, despising compassion, and concentrating our soul on pence' is also very good.

What a monstrous thing that was about the Solenhofen fossils! I never knew of it before.

I have been trying to write a sort of skit on Commercialism, the plot (if you will call it one) of which is this: Grapper is a man of business and has always satisfied his great love of excitement in the competition of commerce, but at length longs for something more and looks about him to see what it may be. Just at this time he spends an evening with Katemcy, who tells him, under a promise of secrecy, that he belongs to a society called 'the society of gentleman burglars', and begs that he will join.

This society has several hundred members who are sworn to burgle and to break into one another's houses, and on the other hand, to endeavor to protect their own premises against their fellow members of the society. The use of fire arms or any other means to prevent burglary is allowed, but the police must not be called, nor is a member, if captured housebreaking, to be given up to the law. Burglary on the premises of non-members is discouraged, but the society cannot protect the members so acting should they fall into the hands of the police.

It is a strict rule of the society that none but gentlemen are admitted. The president (annually elected) is he who has burgled most successfully during the past year.

Grapper is indignant that he, a 'law-abiding' citizen, should be asked to join anything so outrageous, but Katemcy argues the matter with him and convinces him that the principles of the society are only those he has held so dear in business all his life, and in the end he joins and becomes a prominent and successful member, and ultimately president. He and other members have numerous and exciting hours asking about each other's experiences, which are duly related.

There is the idea; as yet I have only written to where Katemcy is explaining the objects and aims of the society, and am rather discouraged from proceeding by my inability to express myself as I would. And it seems rather a matter of doubt whether the thing is worth writing. Anyhow, the notion is a ridiculously mad one.

Later in the afternoon I sorted, arranged, and looked over my letters. It is now 22 Sundays since I was last at Isleworth, and 23 since the last Sunday there!

Did you ever come across, at Smith's, a book called *A Lady's Life in the Rocky Mountains*, by Isabella Bird? A book by the same author on the Sandwich Islands is pretty well known, though I never read it, and this one might be interesting. All I know about it is that it is advertised in the list of books published by Murray at the end of *Descent of Man*.

November 22nd. I went down to West Cliff this afternoon and posted a letter and a box of insects to the Smithsonian, and also got my mail, viz: Bundle of pamphlets. etc. (that I sent for) from the Smithsonian, *Labor Enquirer* (and also some extra copies of the number with my article, one of which I sent to Sutton) and a letter from the editor of *Labor Enquirer* (Callahan) thanking

me for article and asking me to write something more, which I will. The Smithsonian papers proved even more valuable and interesting than I expected. There are lists of North American Coleoptera, Reptiles, Amphibia, Fossil Invertebrates, and Mammalia (Zoological Report for 1884), directions for collecting specimens, etc.

One of my objects in going down to the Cliff was to visit Jod's ranch and get a shotgun Payn had lent to Stratton (who went with Jod on a duck-hunting expedition). I had never been there before, and it proved much further than I thought, so I could not get home before dark. The gun was not at Jod's after all. Stratton has it, but Jod gave me three ducks and a water-hen which he had shot, and these will prove a very acceptable change to our usual diet.

On arriving at the cabin, I found supper just ready and partook thereof. Then I went up to Cox's to take him some mail I had fetched from the Cliff for him. I also took up a copy of my *Labor Enquirer* paper which he thought good, though of course he doesn't agree with it. He suggests that I write to the *Denver Republican*, etc., which perhaps I will do.

Cox says he heard that Stratton has 'skipped', i.e., left the state. If so, I fear Payn's shotgun will have skipped with him.

November 23rd. Yesterday afternoon everyone at the Cliff, when they could think of nothing else to say, said, 'I think we are going to have a snowstorm.' Yesterday evening the prophecy was fulfilled and it began to snow. This morning it was freezing cold, and the ground was covered with snow, and it has been snowing in a desultory fashion all day.

We lit a fire and sat by it, plucking the ducks, which were in some need of cooking, quite odoriferous. One we cut up and fried, one we cut up and boiled, and the other was roasted whole. Then Payn boiled up some dried sliced apples (I got them yesterday at the Cliff — 15 cents a pound), and we also had a stew (onions, potatoes, and odd fragments of meat), so we fared pretty sumptuously together.

I have been busy all day going through the Smithsonian publications I received. They are wonderfully interesting.

November 24th. My Colorado fauna and flora list now stands as follows: Mammalia 17, and one extinct; Birds, 46; Reptiles, one, and two fossil; Mollusca, 43, and four varieties; Coleoptera, 32, and one variety; Acaroptera, 12; Arachnida, one; Crustacea, one; Annelida, two; Hymenoptera, three; Orthoptera, three; Butterflies, 59, and five varieties; moths, only three; Homoptera, seven; Flowering plants, 1,045, and 67 varieties; vascular cryptogams, 22; Fungi, one; Gymnosperms, nine; Algae, Lichens, Mosses, or Hepaticae.

Towards the middle of the day nearly all night's snow had melted, but a heavy snowstorm came in in the afternoon, and now the ground is covered a couple of inches or so deep.

I have written some 'science notes' about grasshoppers, flint implements, fossils, watercress, and minerals, which I shall send to the *Rocky Mountain News* (published at Denver). Jod and an English friend of his (of no interest) rode up here today.

November 25th. The snow fell fast last night and was a foot deep this morning.

I have been writing a paper for *Labor Enquirer* on 'Good versus Evil' (in its various aspects of harmony versus discord, happiness versus misery, socialism versus individualism, God versus Devil, etc.). It is rather sermony, and I shan't think any the worse of the editor if he declines to insert it.

Cox came up from the Cliff this evening and brought mail: Letters from you, Mother, Wetherby, and a very long one from Thomas; *Ent. Mo. Mag., Nat. World* (Oct.), *Schoolmistress*

(Sept. 15th), *Pall Mall Gazette* (Nov. 5th), and four copies of *Malvern Lookeron*.

I am very glad to have Chapter XXIV of *Merely Friends*. It is a very good chapter and it would have been a great pity to have missed it. The passage, 'It was impossible for him to feel the fact that John Imes was dying, except as he thought it affected her' particularly strikes me. I think one does not always understand one's own reasons for being glad or sorry perfectly, and still those of other people. Probably everyone's motives might be resolved into a very few primary ones, the rest following of necessity.

I am delighted with the review of Darwin's book. Of course I must get it, but they are almost certain to publish a cheap edition out here, and I must wait for that.

Payn and I had a little discussion about Darwin's youthful indiscretions. Payn argues, 'All those who accomplish anything in after life are disreputable in their young days.' Payn is disreputable, I am not — obvious moral! (Payn's argument, not mine.) I imagine the fact is this: All men who are able to do remarkable things have a special inclination for them in the days of their youth. It rarely happens that the 'parents and guardians' hit upon this or find it convenient to allow the special tendencies full scope. Therefore rebellion and disreputableness.

Let me congratulate you on the advent of old age! I didn't know of your birthday else I would have done it before. I have introduced the frame of Annie's picture into my imagination of the room, but alas! The picture — you don't say what it is. Whatever it is I envy you the possession of it, though I have one picture of Annie's, the Christmas card of last year, as well as that drawing of William Morris at the club.

Let me know what Annie thinks of *Western Avenues*.

I had a very long letter (six pages) from Thomas. His letters are perhaps better than himself and I like to have them. Thomas writes: 'Last night Sidney (Klein) gave a lecture at the

Chandos rooms on the maggoty flour you wrote of. There is a third of a column in today's *Times* about the meeting' (date of letter is Nov. 9th). So it seems Klein has been lecturing on the *Ephestia*. Thomas sends four copies of the *Malvern Look-eron*, each with a page of 'Notes from Town' by himself. They are not all badly written, for him. It appears from one note that he is greatly delighted by Stevenson's *Underwoods*.

One of Payn's sisters, hearing from Payn that he was going to write a book (which same never was continued after the first night) thought she would write something and, being on the Continent, wrote 'A Health Resort out of Season', which actually appeared in the *Cornhill*, and a proof has been sent out here. It is rather good. I enclose too a note for the S.L.E.S.

You promised me lists of Hymenoptera and Arachnida — Isleworthiana — but they haven't appeared. I don't see anything about your Phalangid in the report of S.L.E.S. in *Ent. Mo. Mag.* (Sept. 22 meeting). Why is that?

Mother writes that the rooms at 20 Woodstock are inhabited — by whom, I wonder? It almost goes against one's feelings that that house should be inhabited by strangers.

November 26th. Not much has been doing today. The snow is still on the ground, and we have been chopping wood, as we keep a fire all day this frosty weather. The snow crystals are most beautiful. They cover the surface of the snow and shine so brightly in the sun that one can hardly bear the intense whiteness. Tomtits are still with us, and a plume moth (*Alucita*) was on the window yesterday. Otherwise there is very little life.

Cox and Bassick came in this afternoon. Cox talks of going down to West Cliff tomorrow, in which case I will get him to post this letter. I was wondering how I should get it posted. I don't want to have to go down in all this snow if I can help it (of course, walking would be out of the question).

Payn has just started up 'Seesaw' on the banjo, and we were both suddenly possessed with a mad desire to waltz, with the result that a weak place in the floor gave way, letting our feet through! Now he is treating the company to a performance of the *Mikado* song which relates how the Lord High Executioner 'drew his snickersnee.' Payn has a remarkable memory for songs.

I am sending you a *Silver Cliff Rustler* and a *Wet Mountain Tribune*. The *Rustler* is the better paper of the two. Do you see it is actually bringing out *Treasure Island*, with illustrations! I have marked the names of people I know, with red. The *Tribune* promises to come out daily about February. Health: Good. How is Annie?

Sunday, 27th November, 1887

Dear Frederic,

Cox called here this morning on his way down to West Cliff, so I gave him a letter to you, and a couple of papers to post.

Afterwards I sat before the fire and read the *History of the Mormons* by J.W. Gunnison — a most interesting account of these queer people. Though they are absurd enough in many ways they have some good points. They hold that no man can be a Christian who does no work and therefore any tendency towards the formation of an idle rich class is checked. Their head priest for instance, was doing manual work in a saw mill at the time the book was written. Also, the land is held by the nation, (or community) and it is a maxim of theirs that every man should do what suits his capacity best, and have the best means of doing it. On this principle, they discourage any rush to mining districts, because it takes men away from their proper work.

Polygamy is defended by reference to the Old Testament and by the extraordinary notion that no woman can enter heaven unless she has a husband to introduce her! And as there are said to be more women than men there would be a surplus of women who would be excluded from heaven under the ordinary arrangement!! But it is said that the Mormon women, in their inmost hearts, would rather run the risk of losing heaven than endure polygamy, but it seems they can't help themselves.

November 28th. According to my list of North American Coleoptera your Isleworth *Aphrodius granarius* is a native of America. I do not know, however, whether it exists here in the West. I have found a closely allied species (*A. vittatus*) in Colorado. The common *A. finotarius* is also American.

Not having much news to send home, I have been interviewing myself, like Grant Allen! Did you see that account of Grant Allen's house, etc., by himself, in the *Pall Mall Gazette* some time ago? I am sending you a 'Denver and Rio Grande time-table', as it contains a good deal of information about places I have been to and may interest. I find the photographic Emery whom I wrote of in a former letter, has nothing to do with Hemery at all. It is Charles E. Emery — you will see his adv't. on cover of the D. and R. G. Timetable.

What a wonderful book the *Descent of Man* is! I was reading it this afternoon. It seems quite inexhaustible. Every time one reads it one comes across a lot of fresh things that were not sufficiently noted before. It is a beautiful night; the moon shining bright upon the snow over valley and mountains, is a remarkable sight.

Brock came by with a buckboard a little while ago and borrowed Payn's rifle. He had evidently taken a little too much in the Cliff, and was decidedly muddled.

If you see Tutt, will you ask him how he is getting on with the papers on Variation in Lepidoptera he showed me the beginning of? It was to appear in the *Entomologist*, most probably, and I am looking forward to it with a good deal of interest, as it will be an important paper. It is a very remarkable thing that although no species of *Clausilia* is at present living in North America (there are some in West Indies and South Ameri-

ca), three species are fossil in Dakota: viz., *C. contraria* M. & H. and *C. vermiculata* M. & H. I fancy some of these names have also been given to living European shells. Would you mind looking in the index to Kobelt to see if this is so; and if so giving me particulars of the European species, as they are given in Kobelt? I feel almost sure there is an Austrian *C. teres*.

November 29th. Today has been spent, besides the ordinary wood-chopping and cooking etc., in drawing and reading the report of the U. S. Department of Agriculture for 1885. This last, although it sounds dry, is a bulky volume full of very interesting information.

Payn has exhausted all his books, even to *The Complete Works of Byron*, and is driven to reading *Some Private Views*. Though it *was* written by his respected relative, he cannot conceal his amusement at it now and then.

A thaw has set in, and the snow is gradually melting away.

November 30th. After breakfast I went off in search of our old mare, as she had not come at the usual time for oats, and some fears were entertained for her safety. However, I found her up by Cox's ranch, where she had been kindly taken in and fed last night.

While I was up there, Cox came home from the Cliff and said that he had left one or two letters for me at our cabin. I accordingly hurried down and found two, both of them satisfactory. One was from the Department of Agriculture (Washington). F.C. Nesbitt, the acting commissioner, writing to say he had dispatched for me copies of the Reports for 1884 and 1886, and also a report on irrigation, which is very kind, as the two reports are bulky illustrated volumes, for which they don't charge anything, and I wanted to have them much. The other epistle was from Conrad Callahan, editor of the *Labor Enquirer*, saying he would be pleased to have me write a critical review of Hill's *Principles and Fallacies of Socialism* (as I had offered to do) for his paper.

My spare time during the afternoon was spent in drawing, and this evening I must set about the paper for the *Enquirer*.

Cox came in this afternoon with Frank Hunter, who, besides being the livery stable man, is sheriff of the county. Cox chaffed me about being an 'anarchist' (as he calls it) and recommended Hunter to take stock of me in view of his coming to arrest me at some future time.

Payn made an attempt at suet pudding this afternoon, and as to the result, I told him 'I don't like suet pudding, but this is pretty good', which, somehow, he didn't take as a compliment!

December 1st. We had intended driving down to the Cliff today, so I went up after breakfast to Cox's to get the horses, which were by his house. I intended to drive them down, but the buckskin horse wouldn't be driven and I couldn't catch him without help so I came back again. It was then getting towards mid-day and Payn didn't care about going up, and we decided therefore not to go till tomorrow. Payn is very anxious to go down because Cox brings word there is a registered letter for him.

The rest of the time I have been sawing wood. reading Carlyle's *Heroes*, and drawing. Here is a sort of diagrammatic sketch of the common room of our house I have made for you. The perspective is not exactly right. The lamp, etc., are much nearer the stove than appears, but had I made them so they would have hidden it.

The various objects are numbered as follows:

1. Towel (very dirty) hanging on door. 2. Harness hanging up. 3. Pistol. 4. Photo of James Payn. 5. Photo of Mrs. Payn. 6. Other photos of

Common Room

Payn's.7. Skull of ox hung up as a hat stand. 8. Stove-pipe. 9. Stew-kettle (almost hidden behind pipe.). 10. Kettle. 11. Saucepan. l2 and 13 are on a sort of side-board arrangement originally made by Martin to sleep upon while he was staying here during the making of the chimney. 12. Pan in which dough for bread is made. 13. Lard tin. 14. Four sacks (one half empty). 15. Pail. 16. Kettle (leaks). 17. Tea pot (iron). 18. Shawl hung over the fireplace that Martin made, to keep out draught. 19. Express rifle. 20. Martin rifle. 21-25. Skins of birds put up by Payn, viz., 21. Sparrow-hawk (*Falco sparverius*). 22. Tomtit. 23. Young 'robin' (*Turdus migratorius*). 24. Woodpecker (*Colaptes mexicanus*). 25. 'Blackbird' (*Scolecopha-gus cyanocephalus*). 26. Payn's banjo. 27. Wood boxes.28. Shelves on which clothes are kept.29. Tin cups. 30. Plate (These on a small table. over which a towel is spread as a cloth). 31-34 are on Payn's big black box, used as a table. 31. Tobacco. 32. *Princess of Thule* (which Payn has been reading).

33. Photograph of Miss Kelvey. This is a girl at Davos, whom Payn pretends to love. You will perhaps remember his talking about her when he was at Syon (I think he did so). She is of the 'pretty' but unintelligent type (to judge from photo) and Payn likes to have the photograph lying about to show to people who come in when remarks are made which would not be particularly gratifying to Miss K. The exact amount of Payn's affection for her may be measured by the fact that he likes to have letters from her, but thinks it an awful bore to write back, and only does so for the reason that she would not otherwise write to him! 34. Gloves (leather). 35. A sort of armchair concern without arms on which Payn sits. 36. A wooden box placed under the stove to elevate it.

Payn went out this afternoon and has not yet returned. I presume he is up at Cox's.

There is an interesting account of Mahomet in Carlyle's *Heroes*. Mahomet seems to have been in many ways an excellent man, yet nothing to compare with Christ or even Buddha. What seems to me the most remarkable thing about him is his wonderful perseverance under condi-

tions that for years seemed quite hopeless. It is very true that the 'survival of the fittest' apply one to the other — and there was the *Origin of Species*!

December 2nd. Cox is just going down to the Cliff and will take this, so must end.

Dec. 2nd , 1887

Dear Frederic,

Payn never turned up at all last night, so I had the evening to myself and spent it in finishing my criticism of Hill's *Principles and Fallacies of Socialism* for the *Enquirer*. If ever I write a book it is likely to take me *ages*, since I find I can't get along with such things as newspaper articles much faster than one or at most two pages an hour, and I don't know how to remedy this state of affairs since my ideas don't flow any faster.

This morning. just as I had finished breakfast, I heard a rumbling of wheels and perceived a vehicle coming along, wherein Cox and Payn in front and Mr. and Mrs. Splann behind (the Splanns live beyond Cox's. I think I have mentioned them in a former letter).They were all going down to West Cliff , so I hastily did up the letter I had for you and some other things for the mail and handed them over to Cox to post.

It is cold again today and windy; I have been sitting in front of the fire finishing Carlyle's *Heroes*.

I certainly like Carlyle better for having read this book, although I disagree with him on the most fundamental points. Carlyle is in some respects more liberal-minded than Ruskin, yet not so well able, I think, to formulate his views. Of course the book has a certain flavour of the time (1840) which comes distastefully to a modern, but this could scarcely have been avoided. The accounts of Dante and Luther seem to me about the best in the book. On page 85 there is a rather notable remark concerning poetry: 'I would advise all men who *can* speak their thought, not to sing it; to understand that, in a serious time, among serious men, there is no vocation in them for singing it.' The description of Cromwell is also good. It occurs to me that Carlyle himself bears a certain sort of likeness to Cromwell.

On page 99 there is a remarkable passage about knowledge: 'Without hands a man might have feet, and could still walk; but, consider it, without morality, intellect were impossible for him A thoroughly immoral man could not know anything at all. To know a thing, what we call knowing, a man must first *love* the thing, sympathise with it. That is, be virtuously related to it. If he have not the justice to put down his own selfishness at every turn, and courage to stand by the dangerous-true at every turn, how shall he know? His virtues, all of them, will be recorded in his knowledge.'

This, I imagine, expresses a general truth, but in a rather incoherent manner. On page 113 a remark of Coleridge's is quoted : 'You do not believe! You only believe that you believe', which I think applies to a good many people. If Annie happens to have read this book, I should like to know what she thinks of it and whether she agrees with my ideas of it.

I forgot to mention in my last letter that the butterfly wings enclosed were those of *Vanessa milberti*. It was to show you how very closely it is related to our British *V. urticae*.

Payn and the Splanns have returned from the Cliff, leaving Cox behind. They have brought my mail, with an abundance of good and pleasant news and interesting matter. There is your letter posted on Nov. 14th, a letter from Mother, one from Carlie, and a very nice one from Olive, announcing that she has got pleasant work that suits her. An epistle from Sherborn (the poor fellow appears to be almost penniless and not very happy, but it is an extremely nice letter) and also post-cards from Carlie and Roberts of Lofthouse. Then there are two *Pall Mall Budgets* and a *Commonweal* as well as the books from the Agricultural Department. Now to discuss these various welcome arrivals.

Your letter: What was Annie's new *Agaric* sent to Worthington Smith? I don't know Mrs.

Collis. Who is she? They all write of Annie's visit to 5 Priory. Carlie's epistle was written while she was there. Carlie says on the last page of his letter that he can't write any more because Annie is talking. Olive volunteers the information that she was very nice, and Mother that she wore a green velveteen dress, so I can quite imagine it all and wish I had been there. Your account of the dance is most interesting but Annie doesn't seem to have been there. I suppose she stayed at home, as you said before that only two were going. I think I should certainly like Mrs. Brodie Clark. Notwithstanding Annie's notes of exclamation, I think what she says is perfectly correct. Several people have noted Annie's face in much the same way, though they have expressed it differently, even my grandmother, after seeing her for less than five minutes (that was months ago.).

I get the *Naturalist* direct from Roebuck at Leeds. *You* told me about the *Aeronyeta* larva — you had forgotten. I wonder how they have published Geddes' other paper — the one we heard. I meant to get it if the price was reasonable. Could you find out about it? Please enlighten the S.L.E.S. as to Williams, privately. Step knows something about him, probably. Anyhow, I don't want to have him in the Society — you may well imagine. You might write to London University and get proof that he is not D.Sc. there, as I did to Durham. It is necessary to quash impostors, or maniacs, for that is what I take J.W.W. to be. I think you are right not to hand the insects over to Billups. I think it is very good for Leslie to go to Madeira as a clerk. I wish I could have done that myself. Madeira is only a week away instead of a fortnight. Thank Annie much for her message. I am very glad she has read and appreciated *Arne*, and how I wish she could write. I keep believing that she will be able to before very long. It seems impossible it should be otherwise! Thank Alice too for her 'kind regards', and shake her hand for me.

Your two fauna lists are extremely interesting. I shall have something to say about them.

The other epistles: Carlie writes to say that I am Darwinian and all brains and no feelings to speak of. However, I don't feel weighed down by the vastness of my intellect; rather by its inability to grasp things as I would have it do. And, after all, I do feel very acutely at times and about certain things. Still, there may be some grain of truth in Carlie's assertion after all. For instance, some fellows used to feel sick or even faint on first seeing operations at the hospital, which I never did, and perhaps this is typical of a certain callousness which seems to have been born with me and which I cannot efface. But I have my recompense that if I don't like or sympathize with so many people as Carlie or even as the average man, I think those I do appreciate I do so the more. Anyway, I wouldn't change with anyone in that matter. Carlie also says I can't understand reverence, which, in fact I can't, to any great extent. Also, that I can't understand poetry, which likely has a great measure of truth though not altogether true. You will think from all this that my brother has handled me somewhat roughly, but quite the contrary; it is a very nice letter indeed.

George Roberts says he is writing to you: I don't know, really, whether the work he is doing will come to much, but he is a good sort of chap anyhow, and persevering. Sherborn encloses a pleasant letter he received from Carlie, and his own is very nice. He says, 'The Middlesex Bug and Beetle Crushers have issued a transactions — a very good one of 141 pages', which means to say that Klein's 'County of Middlesex Natural History Society' has published the said volume. You ought to see it, if possible; no doubt they have it at Zoological Society.

With respect to the same society (Sherborn is secretary. you know), he says 'Live Dukes are as common as /2d. buns on the council, etc., but thank God we have no bishops:' Sherborn's munificent allowance is £25 a year — not much to live upon. He says: 'I have plenty of work but no pay. However. as old Pepys said: 'I have counted up my affairs and find I am worth twopence, whereupon I thank God.' I have a sort of instinctive liking for Sherborn, somehow. I think of that night when we walked up and down till midnight between Bedford Park and Hammersmith discussing Socialism and kindred matters. It gave me an idea what sort of man he was.

I think the way the *Pall Mall* obtained their Darwin review and did not acknowledge its source was very mean. Did you see Francis Darwin's letter thereon in *Daily News*? Carlie sent it me. I see Curninghouse Graham has been arrested for speaking in Trafalgar Square. He is an excellent fellow, a Scotch M. P. Although he has been many years in S. America. I saw him at Morris' one evening when I went in to supper and talk with Carlie.

December 3rd. Cold and windy. Busied myself with going over the new Isleworth and B. P. insects (notes thereon appended) and looking over the books for the Agricultural Dept. The report for 1884 says that *Deilephila lineata* was abundant at Colorado Springs last year. This insect appears to occur all over America as well as Europe.

Payn's registered letter, by the by, turned out to be £5 from his mother — kind of her but I think foolish. Payn had just $10 left when it arrived. Payn also has had a letter from someone in the office in which he was thinking that he ought soon to go back. I don't know whether he will — probably not, but I should feel much relieved if he did. (These items are not for the multitude.)

December 4th. In the morning, I cut wood while Payn put up a sort of calico awning over our rafters, intended to keep out the winter wind. Whether it will do so or not remains to be seen.

Then I wrote a long epistle to the Commissioner of Agriculture about as great a variety of subjects as were talked of by the walrus in the poem (e.g., Loco weed, *Ephestia kuelmiella*, watercress, migration of birds, beetle in tree, etc.) . You see, 'Agriculture', as understood by the U.S. Government, includes a good deal.

Jod came by today, riding, and this evening old Splann and Bassick came driving up from West Cliff, Bassick with some bruises and scratches about his face and quite drunk. He reported that Cox had gone off suddenly to Montrose (I don't know why) and I couldn't get anything more out of him. I expect he has gone about some horse-trade, but it is a long way, and he wouldn't go for anything trivial.

I made two excellent apple dumplings for supper, which was rather a triumph as it was quite experimental. For a long while now we have had only two meals a day, breakfast and supper (about 5 o'clock) and find it very much better than three. When I return I shall very much revolt against the mid-day meal.

Payn and I play a game called 'reverse' now in the evening; it is something like 'drafts.' I don't know much about the game, and Payn always wins, but we never have more than one each evening, so it is a pleasant exercise after supper.

December 5th. Writing, reading, and chopping and sawing wood, cooking, etc., much as usual. Day fine and comparatively warm. Visitors: Regy Cusack and Miss Urquhart, who rode up this afternoon, but didn't come inside the house. Fauna: Tom-tits still very abundant, and a new (brownish) finch, *Emberiza* or near to, seen. That's all today's news.

I have done up *The Happy Boy* to send to you as it perhaps isn't published in England, and in any case they can't do worse than confiscate it if it offends the law of copyright. Let me know if it arrives safely, and of course I want to know what Annie thinks of it.

I enclose a note on *Agrolis* for S.L.E.S. South's list is not perfect by any means, and I have quite a long list of addenda and will give you them to insert in your copy if you like. I always post up all corrections and additions in my lists. You ought to beg, borrow or steal a copy of Trinen and Dyer's *Flora of Middlesex*; it is an excellent book, and I believe Worthington Smith gives a list of Middlesex fungi as an appendix.

December 6th. Warm and sunny, much like yesterday, uneventful.

Bassick came down this afternoon and says that Cox has really gone to Denver, not Montrose, and will be back not later than Saturday. We had another visitor, a stranger who came to look for a black pony that had wandered up here. Brock called early this morning, wearing dark blue spectacles to protect his eyes from the glare of the snow. He was riding down to the Cliff, so I gave him word to bring up any mail there might be, and this evening he accordingly returned with a card from the Smithsonian acknowledging receipt of the box of insects I sent them, and a copy of the *Western Naturalist*. I sent for a sample copy. It is published at Madison, Wisconsin, and proves to be a silly little paper with plenty of misprints in the scientific names.

Not so much as a visitor today. Payn went out this afternoon, and has not yet come back (6: 35). I believe he's up at the Splanns. I am going down to West Cliff tomorrow and shall post this.

This will be my Christmas letter, for it will reach you about the 23rd. What a long time it is since last Christmas, and how much has happened in the interval. Do you remember that Monday evening at 5 Priory Road, when we sat round the fire, Annie in front of it on the ground, Olive to her right, T.D.A.C. to her left, and you and Carlie on either side next the wall? I said next day: 'We shall never have another evening like that', but I hope I was wrong.

Christmas Day was a Sunday and we had to go to Glen Druid. but we bargained to be allowed to escape after the dinner, and got back to B. P. And that was Monday, the day after. This Christmas we cannot meet, but it may be next, or at latest the next after. Out here in exile I can only think of you and wish you a very happy Christmas — you and Annie, and Alice, and

Louy, and Kitty, and Clive, Eva, Winnie and Emily, and Mr. and Mrs. Fenn. I would have written Annie a Christmas letter but it may be wisest not, so I enclose a card instead. If you or Annie see the Hemerys, wish them also a happy Christmas from me.Health: It is wonderful how well I am — no cough or cold , though it is December. The days now are beautifully fine with a warm sun. fresh air and clear blue sky. Certainly I am much better for being here as regards my health.

P.S. Have got your letter, a very interesting one. I am very glad Annie is so pleased with *Happy Boy*; as you have got it I won't send copy mentioned above. I must hurry home or I shall not get there before dark, but will write fully in next letter about everything. Thank Annie for *Standard* with review of Darwin's life. *Entomologists* have arrived, thanks, and also *Journal of Conchology*. I believe J.W.W.'s *Sphaerium* is described by Pascal (see my red-edged big note-book) and write and say so if it proves to be the case. Also look over Locard's vars., in same note-book. Will Annie lend me the stories she has written?

Dec. 8th. 1887.

Dear Frederic,

Payn turned up the last thing last night and said he had been at Cox's — Cox having come home that evening from Montrose as Bassick first stated. He had gone as I expected, about a horse trade.

Payn brought down three papers that Brock had brought up from the Cliff for me but had forgotten to leave at our house, viz., a *Commonweal*, a *Labor Enquirer* and a specimen copy of *The American Monthly Microscopical Journal*. This last proves to be a well got up and generally excellent paper, but entirely devoted to microscopy and so to some extent out of my range.

This morning, after a long tramp through the snow, I managed to drive the buckskin horse that was in Cox's big pasture, into the corral, and having secured him, saddled him and rode down

to West Cliff. It was dreary work going across the prairie. The snow was too deep to go much faster than a walk, and the sun was very hot and the glare of the snow very trying to the eyes.

However, I at length arrived at West Cliff and got my mail and posted my Christmas letter to you (enclosing card for Annie). The mail was a big one — your letter and one from Carlie — *Standard* with Darwin review (for which thanks to Annie) and *Daily News* with same from Carlie; *Entomologist*, July and Nov.; *Journal of Conch.*, Oct.; *Labor Enquirer*, *Commonweal*, and a little Individualist/Anarchist paper called *Lucifer*, published in Kansas and sent to me spontaneously to entice me to subscribe (which I shan't do). About all these things I shall have much to say.

(1.) Your letter. I always meant to talk to Miss Lance and see what she was like, but never did. No, I don't remember Dresser, but of course I know him well enough by name. *Parus britannicus* was described by Sharpe and Dresser, but I believe Sharpe, at any rate, no longer considers it a good species. It is about on a par with *Acredula rosea* Blythe and *Troglodytes lurtensis* Seebohm. Possibly it is too late now, but you might have written something on B. P. fauna and flora for the Annual Rept. of Gardening Society.

I think Geddes' papers are extremely useful, though it may all 'follow naturally.' You see gravitation was a tolerably familiar phenomenon long before Newton, but he made it comprehensible. Geddes helps one to grasp the relations of perfectly familiar phenomena, that is all, but it is much.

I should be disposed to fight shy of that *Entomologist's Club*, but would go over to investigate, certainly. Anything connected with a dinner is more or less loathsome to me. You will probably have to worry Lester Arnold about the insects. I used to bother him about them now and then but without result. About the extract from Darwin's life: It is certain that ultimately all characters are due to environment (using that term in its widest sense) but the question is how much in any given individual is due to direct and how much to transmitted effects of environment, the latter being called instinct, hereditary traits, and so on! I think that, generally speaking, the influence of heredity is greatly under-rated, and therefore argue with the extract.

As Carlyle says, he cannot imagine a really great man who could not have been great at anything, and although I am not of this opinion, I think there is much in it. That is, heredity gives power, and environment decides its direction. A case in point is that of the two Buonapartes. No doubt both men inherited considerable ability but, as it happened, one employed it in slaughtering his fellow men while the other became a distinguished ornithologist.

No, I didn't know Kelsall was going in for the church. I am sorry to hear it; I thought he was meant for better things (for besides the 39 articles and all that, I don't think he is suited for the Church).

I exactly agree with what Annie says both about *Happy Boy* and Emerson, though I never gave the latter very much attention. Björnson, I see, is a Socialist (so good a man must needs be) *vide* the enclosed cutting.

Now about Kobelt and the S.L.E.S. book. I would follow Kobelt in arrangement but keep *Pupa* and *Vertigo* as in Jeffreys' (though I confess I don't think much of the 'generic' distinction between them!), and write *lubrica* and *tridens* under *Cochlicopa* but place *A. acicula* in the genus *Caecilianella*. '*Achatina*' includes shells as big as your fist and nothing like *acicula*.

'The average mortal', I may say, hates reforms, but he must be made to swallow them like nasty medicine, and is glad of it afterwards.

Averell's address is Chestnut Hill, Philadelphia, Pa., but don't you bother about sending for copies. Nothing of mine has come out yet, though there are two notes to be in the November number, which is not yet to hand.

I like Annie's children's stories. Could they not be posted out here? I would return them safely. Beg this of Annie, as I should very much like to read them. I attribute the poem 'So he said to his pard, O', etc. to Clive. Is he not the distinguished author? I am grateful for the news about Annie's health. Please do *always* inform me, as you say. Why has she turned vegetarian? Does it suit her best? I should be doubtful about its advisability in winter time in a cold climate like England, unless one were 'born and bred' so. I believe you are to a great extent right about the advisability of staying out here two years; yet it seems a horribly long time. For the present, I an only wait and see what happens. I am sleepy and more or less muddled tonight, so won't write any more now.

December 9th. Payn brought home five fowls from the Splann's yesterday. We were accordingly busy plucking and cleaning them this morning and had a boiled one for supper this evening. I found a species of bird louse in some abundance on one of them and have duly preserved specimens for the U.S. Agr. Dept.

I will continue my remarks on yesterdays mail. Darwin: I have two reviews of Darwin's life, the *Standard* sent by Annie, and a *Daily News* from Carlie. Both are extremely interesting of course. I note that he says: 'I consider all that I have learnt of any value has been self-taught', and I think Darwin's views about modern education are quite justified. Do you see, too, how bad an opinion he has of the 'professions' when deliberating what to do with his boys? Darwin seems to have been as truly humane a man as ever existed, full of sympathy with all life! It seems characteristic of him that he had such an abhorrence for slavery in the days when it was considered right. A very notable extract is that relating how his religious views changed from orthodox to agnostic, and it does seem to me that his arguments as regarding the miracles, etc., are unanswerable. But I think that his former orthodoxy has misled him into thinking that because *some* things fail in his religion it is therefore essentially [false], and also that the non-Christian religions are quite false. I may misunderstand him from the brevity of the extract, but it would seem that he thought so.

Journ. of Conch. Cooke's account of the sinistral *Limnaea* is important and interesting to me. Can you get me a copy of Chas. Jeffreys' list of Brit. S.L.F.W. Mollusca (four pence)? The reviews in *Journ. Conch.* suggest the probability that the reviewer never read the books. Tryon's 'excellently executed plates' are abominable, as you can see for yourself at Zoöl. Soc. *Helix jaffrayi* (p. 254) is preoccupied by one from New Guinea. I have a notion that J.W.W.'s var. of *S. comenum* was described by Locard or Pascal. Will you look in my note book and see? The best thing in the whole journal is Friedlander's book-catalogue; it will be invaluable to me out here.

The *Entomologist*: The July issue proves a good one, I think there must be some humbug at the bottom of these captures of foreign butterflies in England. *G. cleopetia* in Scotland, *P. delius* in Wales, and now *P. gordius* in Devon; it is absurd! At last the *Lucana* discussion has come to an end and has resulted, so far as I can see, only in exhibiting the foolishness of all who have taken part in it. Jenner Weir's remarks in the November number are very justifiable. I must say, I don't think much of Carrington as an editor.

December 10th. Reading *Pall Mall Budget* today I found the last one (Nov. 17th) particularly interesting, all about the Trafalgar Square business.

Regy Cusack and Miss Urquhart drove down this morning — no other visitors. Payn complains of not feeling well. He has been more or less seedy for some days — rheumatism, etc. I don't exactly know why. It seems quite likely that he will leave Colorado before winter is over. In an indirect manner the cold weather is very beneficial to me because it necessitates a fire, and therefore the chopping of wood, by which I get sufficient exercise every day and that of the best kind. Theoretically I ought to be able to take exercise without any such necessity but as a mat-

ter of fact it is very doubtful whether I should, except a little walking.

Some of the Darwin extracts given in the *Standard* and *Daily News* are also in the *Pall Mall's* premature review, and it is amusing to compare them and note the effect in the *Pall Mall* ones of translating into French and then back again! It does not improve them at all! I think the conduct of the police about the Trafalgar Square business is monstrous, and am of course entirely in sympathy with any measures taken to preserve the right of free speech there. I laughed a good deal over the account of the arrest of the *Telegraph* correspondent and the 'prominent Tory' and, best of all, how the uniformed officers set onto and belaboured those in plain clothes! What lunatics they are!

I have this evening written Chapter 1 of my novel, and enclose it. I should like to know how it strikes you and Annie. I don't think novel writing is very much in my line, but if this little story amuses you two to read it will also amuse me to write. I have written it in the form of a play because it comes easiest to me. I have tried both ways. I hope sending the chapters *as written* won't lead me in to any glaring inconsistency (from forgetting what came before). If so, let me know and I will endeavour to rectify it. Could you send me any little pencil sketches of Annie's — the 'original studies' and anything she doesn't want? I want them to put up on the wall of my room.

Sunday, December 11th. Here is something to enter in the S.L.E.S. Conch. record book (Bibliog.), (*vide* Fried, Catalogue in *Journ. Conch.*) . . . Brander, G. *Fossils Dantoniensia* (fossil shells from Hampshire, described by Solander), 1776; new edition in 1829.

Brock came in for a while this morning, and this afternoon we had Frank Cusack and Cox. Cox has just been to Colorado Springs for a flying visit, only a few hours, but he is going again shortly to stay, and will then see about the clerkship I told you of. I have been indexing up

Friedlander's Catalogue, placing the different authors under the names of the countries they have written of so that I can at once refer to all the papers on any particular country, which will be the greatest advantage to me.

December 12th. Another Bibliog. Item for S.L.E.S. Record Book. Mantell, G. *Fossils of the South Downs* (1812) and *Geology of Sussex* (1827).

I am still busy over the index to Friedlander; it proves a longer affair than I expected but it is necessary to do it. Cox went down to the Cliff this morning and I hope will return with some mail for me. Payn has been up at the Splann's most of the day and I have been writing, so there is no news of any sort to tell you.

December 13th. For the first time in a very long while the sun didn't shine on my wall this morning, the consequence being that I didn't get up till nearly ten. All day it has been snowing, and I suppose we shall be a foot deep in snow again by the morning. It seems really too bad after the last fall had been slowly melting away and was fairly on the way to disappear.

I have finished my index to Friedlander but have done little else today except write a letter to Carlie. I enclose an advertisement cut from the *Denver Republican*. It seems almost incredible that such nonsense can take people in, but I suppose it does, else it wouldn't pay to advertise. And what brazen impudence it must require to bring forward such pretenses!

December 14th. Old Splann came by on his way to the Cliff this morning, so I gave him a postcard to Taylor to post, and asked him to bring my mail. He returned this evening with a big budget of news: Your letter; letters from Wallis Kew and Averell, and postcards from Hoyle and Knicheldorff's; also *Naturalist, Nat. World, West American Scientist* (Oct. and Nov.), *Labor Enquirer*, Knicheldorff's price list and *Pall Mall Budget*. I am pleased to see the favourable criticism of Annie's picture. The 'Whistler-like effects' rather amuses me though. Do you want the cutting back?

The Entom. Club sounds interesting. What sort of a man is Champion? He is a very good butterflyist. I have seen McLachlan. Once Klein sent me down to Van Voorst with a paper he wanted inserted in *Entom. Mo. Mag.* It wasn't, though, and I happened to meet McL. there. I didn't say who I was. though, not being on my own business. McL. told me Morrison had sent him a lot of things from Colorado. About the Neuroptera I sent he hasn't written yet; it is about time he did. I have heard of *Helicopsyche* but had forgotten. These caddises are found also near West Cliff, so I will get you some at earliest opportunity if the place isn't too frozen over.

Yes. I expect there will be a lively debate over the Anti-Darwinist! I don't like the idea of Billups as President; why not Jenner Weir? I have heard nothing yet from Step. I congratulate Kitty on her paper on Arachnida. I think it was extremely enterprising of her to lecture on such an unfamiliar subject. Has Annie yet decided on a subject for her lecture? Certainly you must be very busy, and I would not bother about Roberts except in really spare moments. I used to be glad to name shells and slugs for him. because he often sent remarkable things, and it was pleasant to help him because he is so enthusiastic and diligent. I am very grateful to you for taking so much trouble over my specimens. Atkinson of the museum is a very good sort of chap, but he is mad on Tichborne [cf. *Encycl. Britannica*: Tichborne Claimant. Ed.] 'Won't go to church', he says, 'because they pray for the judges etc., who condemned Tichborne.'

Certainly the Gunnison River *Physae* are *Physa heterotropha*. I ought to have known this species. but the types I had were more slender, and I was therefore uncertain. Some I sent to Smithsonian were named *Heterotropha* however (these were from Gypsum), thus confirming the determination. It is a common species. As to *Physa charpentieri* — the name doesn't appear in my list of North American *Physae*, and I don't know it, so it must for the present remain uncertain. Are you sure it's not a European species? Look in Kobelt.

I remember Annie's last party, a year ago, *very well*! It seems too bad I can't come to this one — haven't even been invited: Tell me how it goes off and all about it. I confess I don't quite see the validity of the argument against inviting Mrs. B.C. I think she ought to have been there.

Payn received another £5 today. It's all very well to abuse Annie's photo when you have the original with you. I wouldn't tolerate a photo, good, bad, or indifferent, with Annie herself in the house, but out here one is glad enough of it. Can't Annie's views about *Eagle's Nest* be communicated somehow? Because what you say only tantalizes me. Thank Alice for her kind regards. Same to her.

December 15th. Last night was the coldest we have had. I was kept awake by chilblains. Which sounds ridiculous but it isn't; it's like toothache in one's toes. Fortunately my hands have escaped. I have yet more to say about yesterday's mail: Wallis Kew wrote a nice long letter in which he says he is going in principally for slugs. The slugs, once so neglected, are having a time of it now. Averell writes on various matters: he says Haldeman considers *Limnaea fragilis* L. to be *L. palustris*; you know Jeffreys calls it a variety of *stagnalis*. I have seen Linné's description of *fragilis* and should be inclined to abandon the name, it being impossible to settle definitely what it is. In this case *L. stagnalis* var. *fragilis* becomes var. *elegans* (Leach) or var. *attenuata* (Say).

Hoyle writes about *Zoöl. Record*. He thinks it would be well if authors always send copies of their papers to Ed. L. R. So do I, if he will pay expenses. He says 17 papers are down to my name for 1886, so he seems to have got hold of most of them, anyhow. Kricheldorff is a Berlin dealer. I sent for his catalogues (which he supplies free) and asked whether he would like to exchange Colorado insects for literature or otherwise. He

replies that he would like *Geodephaga* etc. and so next summer I may do something for him.

Nat. World: December is the last number; I should have liked to have seen it transferred into abler hands, but this failing, it does as well to discontinue, I think. The P.N.S. seems likely to die with it, but the London branch talks of carrying it on and the *Garner* is to be their paper. *Naturalist* is a good number, but nothing remarkable in it. Howard ·Saunders has a paper on the Arctic Tern. *West American Scientists* are not remarkable. The November number has 'Notes from Colorado' by T.D.A.C. It is only a short thing (14 lines) on *Aster campestris, Colias eurytheme,* and *Linum perenne* forma *albiflorum*. I would post it to you but it isn't worth sending. *Labor Enquirer* has a 2½ column article by T.D.A.C. called 'Good v. Evil'. This I will post to you, only return it when finished with (no hurry) as I haven't another copy. *Pall Mall Budget* is very interesting.

I wish the 'S.S.S.' all success. How funny those 'specials' must have looked. Did any of the Smithites volunteer? I expect they would have proved a reckless lot if any collision had taken place between them and the people. You see how well Mrs. Besant is spoken of. She is a person you have branded as desperately wicked, 'immoral', etc., etc., but I must say I think very unjustly. I never enquired into her private life. but have seen a good deal of her in public, and she has always struck me as one of the most honest and best in the movement.

Did you read Bernard Shaw's criticism of W. Besant's [Sir Walter Besant, cf. *Encycl. Britannica.* Ed.] scheme of universal copyright? It struck me as being a very able exposure of the utter greediness of W.B., and I entirely agree with it. Pirated editions of both Shaw's and Besant's books are sold in America, so they are both in the same box in that respect. I quite sympathise with *Nature*'s indignation at the notion of the President of the Royal Society (Stokes) turning M. P. It will not do at all to have science mixing itself up with politics, not because politicians don't need science, but because they are partisan, and science must be kept free from all party spirit and prejudice if it is to be any good.

December 16th. It is quite fine again now and sunny; the snow is slowly melting away.

I went up to see Cox this afternoon. but found only Bassick, who said Cox had gone once more to Colorado Springs to try to sell his horses. He is expected back soon. and then I hope I shall hear something of the clerkship.

I have been writing some notes to send to *West American Scientist*, and will send you a copy when they appear (February number, I suppose). I have cut some more adv'ts. out of *Denver Republican* kindred to the one I have already mentioned. Each one seems more preposterous than the last. One would think honesty had ceased to be a virtue.

Saturday, Dec. 17th, 1887

Dear Frederic,
You will notice signs of unwonted haste about the finish of the last letter. Brock came along this morning on his way to West Cliff, and so I finished up my letters as quickly as I could and gave them to him to post. I need not have been in such a hurry after all, as Payn decided to go down later (he was still in bed when Brock arrived, never gets up till breakfast is nearly ready) and to stay the night in West Cliff, which he has done.

One of Payn's principal reasons for going down was to try to arrange about selling some things (e.g. telescope, gun, etc.) to get money for returning to Europe. He does not know whether he will go to England or Germany (where his sister is) but really seems decided to go in a month or six weeks. He does not want anyone except his mother to know when he is coming back until he actually arrives. From his point of view his mother is better than the rest of the family put together, believing all he tells her, and always ready to assist him out of any difficulties, and

to give sympathy where others would withhold it. I cannot help admiring her for her devotion, while at the same time feeling that the father is distinctly the wiser of the two. (These reflections not for publication, of course).

I am going on with my 'novel' and getting quite interested in it. You never said whether Annie read *Western Avenue* after all, and if so, what she thought of it; you brought it from the library on 5th Nov.

Sunday. December 18th. All alone today, which I rather like. Got up and had breakfast as usual, cut some wood, then washed up a few clothes and boiled a chicken, which Payn had brought from the Splanns, as I mentioned before. This is the last of them, part of which I ate for supper. Wrote a letter to Douglas, and drew a little; that is a summary of today. I have been going through the 'London Catalogue' and marking the species also found in America. It is astonishing what a number there is.

Monday, December 19th. Yesterday three people passed along the road, but today I haven't even seen anybody, and there are no signs of Payn. I have been busy over botany again today, making a list of plants which are found in the states bordering on Colorado but not (so far as I know) in Colorado itself. This has been a cold cloudy day, looking very like a coming snow-storm, the sun only shining very feebly now and then. Magpies (*Pica rustica* var. *andronica*) are very abundant round here just now, being, with the tom-tits, almost the only birds to be seen.

9.45 p.m. It is a bitterly cold night with a high wind. I should think anyone out on the open prairie would die of cold. Unfortunately this house isn't air-tight and cold draughts sweep around the floor, etc., freezing my toes. Payn's little dog Nell (or 'Nellums', she gets called) feels the cold and shivers. The poor little beast is having a bad time just now. All the dog's meat is gone and I have hardly anything to feed her on but bacon, chicken bones, and fragments of bread.

December 20th. It *is* cold this morning. The remains of the chicken were frozen hard and had to be thawed out (that was the last bit of meat I had except bacon). The bread was frozen, the jam frozen, the water in the pail had to be got at by breaking the ice with a hatchet, and a little I spilled on the floor in filling the kettle has turned to ice. Even Swift Creek was frozen over except here and there where the water ran very fast. I really couldn't sit still and write. My feet were so cold notwithstanding two pairs of socks, so I got up and walked to and fro, and danced about. At length, however, I discovered a pair of thick over-socks of Payn's, lined with wool inside, so I took off my boots and put these on, and ever since my feet have kept warm. I fancy the great thing is to get a good circulation in one's feet; the boots with the double pair of socks only retarded this by pressure, more so than if I had had on only one pair, and I was therefore cold. I haven't seen anyone all day. I suppose it is too cold to venture out, and Payn has not come back from West Cliff.

December 21st. On waking this morning I found that my breath had frozen into ice on the pillow, but now the sun is out and the sky clear, and it is warmer.

Brock and Stratton came along from the Cliff this afternoon. Stratton came in for a moment to warm himself (he is the one-armed cowboy Payn lent his gun to). The story of his having 'skipped' (*vide* former letter) was evidently a myth. Stratton said he had seen Payn in West Cliff and he had no intention of coming up at present. No doubt he finds it more comfortable in the hotel down there than up here, especially in this cold weather. Stratton says he has never known it so cold in Colorado. It is quite exceptional, which I am glad to hear, because any long continuation of this temperature would be very trying. Brock is going down again tomorrow, he says, so I have asked him to bring up my mail

and some meat, both of which I am very greatly in need of.

December 22nd. Regy Cusack turned up this morning with a buck-board and a little gray mare. 'Want to come into town?' I said I did, and went accordingly. When we got down there I of course went after mail and got a big bundle, but to my great disappointment no letter from you. This, however. is probably not your fault because all my English letters had printed on them 'miss-sent' though how they could have miss-sent them I can't conceive, since they were all directed in the plainest manner. I suppose your epistle has not yet come back to its proper destination, as also a letter from Mother for this week. I trust they won't get lost anywhere. The mail I received I will refer to later.

Regy said he might not be able to return that day, so as old Splann was just going up I went with him. Therefore I did not have time to go in search of Payn, whom I meant to have looked up. I bought three pounds of meat, but stupidly forgot to take it out of Splann's waggon on reaching our house. I must go up to Splann's for it tomorrow.

I talked to Splann going up and found him very nice and agreeable. He very much disapproved of the English aristocracy and also of the Emigration schemes so much advocated on the other side of the water. He was also very indignant on the subject of General Gordon. I lent him the Agric. Rept. for 1886, which he wasn't interested in.

I had scarcely been a quarter of an hour in our house when I saw someone drive up, and who should it be but Cardwell Lees! I was really glad to see him, as everyone says he is a very nice fellow, and my experience of him quite confirms this opinion. He came in for a little while and talked about Payn, Entomology, Socialism, etc., very pleasantly, and then went on to Cusack's. He had seen Payn in town and understood he was not coming up till Cox returned from the Springs, which might be tomorrow. Payn had actually purchased a side-saddle as a present for Miss Urquhart!! And Cardy Lees was taking it up with him. This is characteristic of Payn.

Cardy Lees said the thermometer during the last few days had been down to between 25° and 30° below zero and some say even more. Everyone agrees that it is a remarkably cold 'snap.' It has clouded over this evening. though and is considerably warmer.

December 23rd. At last the cold snap is over and done with and it is actually so warm this morning that I am doing without a fire. Brock came along and with a piece of meat soon after I had got up. He did not go down to the Cliff yesterday and, not knowing I had gone down, brought a piece from his own place. A double supply. however, won't matter, as it will keep any time this frosty weather.

Brock went on down to the Cliff and will bring back any mail that came last night.

I said nothing about the mail received yesterday and will now tell you about it. There were six letters: one from Carlie saying many things. He is reading *Happy Boy*, and is delighted with it. I am pleased to hear this because I did not expect it. One from McLachlan, a long and pleasant letter, but he doesn't give me the names of my Neuroptera. He says *Helicopsyche* is found in southern Europe. He says his health isn't very good — 'some obscure gastric disturbance' (stomach-ache??). He shouldn't go to Ent. Clubs and eat such big dinners!!).

One from Meade, who only knows the generic names of the flies I sent htm. He says very few American flies have been described. He mentions that you sent him some Diptera. I should like to have a list of them when named. One from Taylor, who also sends a number of copies of rules, etc., of Conch. Soc. (I asked for them for distribution) and his photograph. He is not good looking; no doubt Carlie will have shown you his copy. A spontaneous letter from a D.J.H. Oyster (he ought to be a conchologist, from the name!) of Paola, Kansas. who wants to exchange plants. His handwriting leads me to set him down as an ass. On Oyster's letter there is one of the new issue of two cent stamps, which I enclose in case it may interest Clive, who collects stamps (or used to).

Lastly, there was a very long and nice letter from Norman J. Colman. the U.S. Commissioner of Agriculture, including remarks by the Botanist and Entomologist, G. Vasey and C. V. Riley. (Riley was recently in London, I believe.) A beetle I sent them, *Dicerca prolongata*, one of the Buprestidae, was supposed to be a pine-feeder but my observations prove that it feeds on poplar. The Colorado [potatoe] beetle has been found in Colorado after all; it used to occur on *Solanum rostratum*. *Sirex* has never yet been found in America, and I have some I am almost certain are of this genus, which is interesting. I am going to send one to the Agric. Dept. They say they are very familiar with *Ephestia Kuehmiella*.

The injury done in America by slugs and snails is said to be slight. I also rec'd from the Agr. Dept. a copy of the report of the Botanist for 1886, and Vasey's paper on the grasses of Kansas, Colorado, and Nebraska (which adds two species of grasses to my Colorado list.) They are sending also all the Entom. Reports that are not out of print, but they have not yet arrived.

The papers, etc., rec'd were: Diary for 1888 and lists of marine shells and Coleoptera for which all thanks to you. I see you have sent a clean copy of the Marine list; there is an old copy of mine somewhere with all sorts of notes, additions, etc. You might find it useful if you come across it.

Commonwea of Dec. 3; The *Agassiz Companion* for October (a specimen copy, spontaneously sent); it is a rather silly little Nat. Hist. paper; *Labor Enquirer* of Dec. 17th with my review of Hill's book; also a number of extra copies of Dec. 10th and 17th, so I will send you one of each, which need not be returned. *Conch. Exchange*, Nov., with my notes. There were two copies of *Conch. Exch.*, so I will send you one that you can keep.

There is a certain element of humbug about it which seems to run through all American publications, but in many ways it is not a bad little paper. The three first papers, by Carpenter, Ancey, and March are certainly more elaborately got up than what we are accustomed to seeing in our own *Journ. Conch.* (excepting papers like that of Cooke in last issue, and John Ford's paper (p. 71) is interesting.

5.30 p.m. I trudged up to Splann's through the snow, got the meat and came back again, getting back about two. It was quite warm work walking and I did not light a fire until it was time to cook supper. Cardy Lees and Regy Cusack came by. Lees had been down to the Kettles (you remember Jim Kettle, the 'road boss', to get some hay, and Regy had just come back from the Cliff.

Lees has been in British Columbia and has come back looking quite Canadian, with a blue jacket, red scarf, and moccasins, rather a picturesque costume. Brock went by this evening. but brought no mail. Regy asked me to go Ula to his place this evening, and I had half a mind to have gone, as Lees will be there and the ladies (Mrs. Cusack and Miss Urquhart) are pleasant company once in a while, the species being an excessively rare one in these parts. On thinking the matter over though I concluded I had too many letters to write and it was too far to tramp in the snow. The mountains looked grand today, covered with snow, and the blue sky above and clean atmosphere. I believe old Splann will go down to the cliff tomorrow, and I hope to get this posted by him, so I will end up now so as to have the letter ready in case he comes.

In botany, I rank myself as an amateur, my professional work being zoological. At the same time, I have found that a certain amount of botanical knowledge is extremely useful, almost indispensable perhaps, to a Zoölogist. In the early days, when there used to be professors of Natural Philosophy, it appeared natural to study both plants and animals. Linnaeus was primarily a botanist, but included all known animals. During the nineteenth century, the *two subjects drew apart. The immense labors required to study and classify all the forms of life coming to has necessarily compelled specialization. In order to do anything worth while, one had to concentrate on some part of this vast field, and not only were botanists separated from zoologists, but no one could any longer pretend to cover the whole of either science.*

Recollections

Dec. 24th, 1887

Dear Frederic,

Old Splann went down to West Cliff today, having borrowed our buck board, so I gave him four letters to post, viz., one to you and the other three to Carlie, Averell, and Norman J. Colman. Splann has to wait for the evening train (because he went to fetch Mrs. S. and 'Becky', who have been at Cañon City) but when he comes up he will bring my mail if there is any. This is my last chance of getting any Christmas letters. I have been writing postcards, etc., today, and nobody has called. It is cloudy and not cold.

9.24 p.m. I was on the tiptoe of expectation, and directly I saw Splann coming in the distance (it is a moonlight night) I skipped out of the house and over the snow and got my mail at last. The Christmas letters have come just when most welcome, on Christmas Eve. There is yours, and also letters from Mother and Carlie, and the entomological publications from the Agric. Dept.

Thank Annie for her good wish, the best she could have wished, for it includes all else. If this Christmas were not hopeful, neither would it be in any degree happy. Thank you also for your wish of a happy Christmas. It is not incongruous — forgetting what *might* have been, and remembering what may, and all going well, *shall* be. There is nothing to complain of. I am very well indeed. and I get plenty of letters, telling me all about my friends in England. Really, under the circumstances, what more could one desire? Except that Annie write herself — and this, I keep on believing, is going to be. So it is certainly a hopeful Christmas, and, as things go. a happy one.

I saw the scratching out in your last letter, and perceiving what it was, I had no scruples in attempting to decipher it, which I did without the slightest difficulty. I am sorry you say 'not robust', but I trust Annie will continue to improve. The conditions of life (big garden and so on) at Syon ought to be better than they were at Bedford Park.

I am sorry to hear so many people couldn't come to the party, but sometimes a small gathering is nicer than a large one. I shall look forward to the account of it. Respecting Louy, I confess I don't know anything at all about her, but I fancy you take rather a gloomy view. I've a notion she will wake up and astonish you one of these days — and the same remark applies to Kitty and Clive. I have always regarded these two last, at any rate, as unopened poppy buds destined to bloom some day, but not at present; not even the colour of the flower is visible. Everything is to happen in the future. Clive, another poppy bud, is already beginning to expand. (I smile to think what Clive would say on being told he was an unopened poppy bud!).

You will do extremely well to work out the distribution of British Mollusca. I am working at the boreal (i.e., Europe and American) fauna as well as I can and I think my paper (supposing *Sci. Goss.* prints it) will interest you.

As regards hero worship. I take it to be the better function of the knowing ones to explain their knowledge to the rest. Take religion: Everyone admits that this should be based only on persuasion and not on compulsion (if indeed any true religion could be) and I hold this to apply to everything else. If you like, I am an anarchist. I don't believe in coercion of any sort or kind, not even with the consent of the coerced. I hold that every man is morally bound to form an opinion and to act by it. Nobody has a right to become a parasite. If your 'hero' gets hold of a good idea, and can convince people of its goodness, all

right, only let them be so convinced as to understand what they are about.

I remember Poulton, of course. I have often seen him. I thought his theory about larvae a little far-fetched. There is a great herd of collectors in the S.L.E.S. — that is what it really comes to. By himself, a collector has no sort of scientific value, but he often secures material which may be turned to good account in other hands. E. Collier of Manchester was making great investigations as to varieties of *Limax peregra* and conditions, food etc., but so far he has published nothing.

Carlie's letter is all about duties and rights. He thinks we ought to care more about duties than rights. To me, it seems that any real right must also be a duty, and vice versa. I can't distinguish between them. Of course, legal 'rights' are quite another matter, and very often opposed to duty; e.g. the exorbitant landlord, who is quite within his legal 'rights.'

Christmas Day! Annie, I wish you a happy Christmas! A happy Christmas to you, Frederic! What does it matter, 6,000 miles more or less between us, that I should not wish you a happy Christmas on Christmas Day?

6.30: Well, it hasn't been a 'merry' Christmas, anyway. I haven't seen a human being all day, and have been entirely employed in going over and taking notes from the Agric. Dept. Entom. publications. Nothing has happened whatever except that 'Nell' has just been blessed with puppies, which are squealing while their mother licks them in a corner. I daren't look at them yet.

These Entom. books of the Agric. Department are most admirable, and I am delighted with them. It shows the difference between the British and U.S. Governments, this publishing and sending out of books. I should expect the end of the world if the British Government took to supplying its correspondents with literature. For that matter, if it even condescended to correspond with anybody under the rank of, say, a 'Lord High Executioner'! (N.B. A good title for Sir C. Warren). These books have enabled me to add no less than 50 'grasshoppers' to my Colorado list, and also *Heliothis armigera* (recorded from Denver); this has been taken in England, *vide* Necoman, and two Hymenoptera, one recent and one fossil, all of which is very satisfactory. I am also able to add an Orthopteran to my Middlesex fauna, for the migratory locust. The 'plagues of Egypt' one (*Pachytylus migratorius*) is mentioned as having been captured in London during a flight of these insects.

December 26th. The day began with a pleasant invigorating wind, almost warm, though coming from the mountains, blowing the snow about clouds and drifting it into great banks in places. Later it clouded over and became colder, and then a little snow fell.

Towards the afternoon, someone came riding up on Payn's 'buckskin', which somebody proved to be Cox, returned from Colorado Springs. He had made further enquiries about the clerkship, and the man (I forgot his name) who has the place, naturally enough desires me to write and explain who I am and what I can do, and Cox will take the letter with him when he goes again to the Springs very shortly. (I have referred him to Klein in my letter, who will, I doubt not, give me a good character), and stated generally what I am able to do. On the whole I should think there is some prospect of getting the place. Cox said it had been quite warm at Colorado Springs, and no snow, all the time we were having the cold snap here.

I don't know what is to become of Payn. Cox saw him at West Cliff and tells me that he is looking very ill, has spent all his money, and apparently run into debt. And further wants to borrow money of Cox, who has promised to lend him some if he gets through with some cattle trade he has on which will bring him in some money of Cox. He is doing no good at all out here, and I shall be very thankful when he goes home though he may very likely be no better there. Cox said he would probably return to the Cliff tonight, but if he did not I promised to go up there for the evening. As he did not come by

for some time, I walked up, but found him just ready to start, and so had my walk for nothing. I gave him some things to post, including a packet of papers for you (viz., *Labor Enquirer* of Dec. 10th and 17th and *Conch. Exchange* of Nov., 1887). He will return here tomorrow, he says.

December 27th. Today has been windy; strong, cold wind every now and then blowing the smoke down the stove pipe into the room. The night is fine, with a clear sky and a brilliant moon. The mountains show up dark against the sky, and with the fragments of cloud hanging about their summits look very fine. After all, it is something to have mountains to look at every day.

Those puppies squeal like babies; they are ridiculous-looking little animals.

Thinking over my views on hero-worship (*vide* Dec. 24th), they may want a little modification. I won't say that it is a bad thing that the blind should be led, but I do say it is bad that they should be blind. It is always, I hold, better for a man or a nation to see for himself than to follow the lead of another, so that the 'hero' is at best only a make shift, a crutch so to speak.

I have been culling some interesting things about variation from the Agric. publications. You will see in Newman that the *Abrascas grossulariata* varies from the spotted type to almost white. Well, there is a moth called *Hyphantia cuneata* Drury (this being the ancestor of our H. Dru Drury) in the U.S. which varies just the other way, the type being whitish and without spots, and the extreme spotted variety (*punctatissima* Smith) marked like *Abrascas*. There is another moth, *Anomia texana*, which varies like *Hydrucia nictitans* with the var. *erythrostigma*.

December 28th. An ordinary sort of day. Bassick and 'Steve' Splann (son of old Splann, a bright-looking but I believe rather dull-brained young man with short curly hair, drove down to West Cliff, and I gave Bassick a letter to Norman

J. Colman to post. Bassick says Cox has again gone to Colorado. Springs. He was coming up here again yesterday; probably he will shortly return. However, if he doesn't, I must write to him about the clerkship. I asked him the address of the man when he was up here but he had forgotten it.

A stranger rode up as I was making bread this afternoon, enquiring after Brock, who had, unfortunately for him, gone into town this morning. So the stranger rode down towards town on the chance of meeting him coming back.

I have been working up various entomological matters today. I have a *Sarcophaga* in my collection, I find, allied to *S. sarracenia* Riley and *S. carnaria* (doubtless you know this latter well) but probably a new species. Some of the 'grasshoppers' are very interesting. May I beg of you next summer to catch all kinds of grasshopper you can? They want working up very much, and I mean to study the Colorado sorts next season, so it might be interesting for us to work together, comparing notes of the two countries, while I would send you from time to time specimens from here. The only species I have down for Middlesex at present are: (1.) *Stenobollorus lineatus* Pam., Bedford Park (T.D.A.C.), named from British Museum examples, and therefore liable to doubt. However, Stephens records this and many other species (*vide* appendix to Bedford Park fauna book) from the London district. (2.) *Pachytylus migratorius* London, *Gardeners Chronicle* 1859 (quoted by A.H. Swinton: 8th Rept. U.S. Ent. Com. 1885. (3.) '*Locusta' viridissima*, Willesden. (S.T. Klein). I have seen specimens; in fact I named them for him. It is not a true *Locusta*. I forget the name of the genus it is now placed in. And for the S. Lond. Ent. Soc. district I have (1.) *Gomphocerus rugus* Ch., Reigate (Billups, Proc. S.L.E.S. 1886 p. 69). (2.) '*Locusta' viridissima.*, Margate (T.D.A.C.), Deal (Tutt.). (3.) *Stenobothrys rugipes*, Herne Bay (Waterhouse). (4.) *Pachytylus migratorius*, Herne Bay in 1848 (A.H. Swinton). There are four species of *Stenobothrys* (*S. occipitalis*, *S. coloradus*, *S. brunneus*, and *S. quadrimaculatus*) found in Colorado, and two of *Gomphocerus* (*G. clepsydra* and *G. navicula*.)

December 29th . It was a warm night last night. I classify the nights as 'warm' or 'cold' according to whether the ink freezes or not, and it has been a warm day. In the afternoon a great cloud came over and I expected a snowstorm, but to my great astonishment it came down hail. I believe this is very unusual at this time of year.

Cardwell Lees called in the morning on his way down to West Cliff. I gave him postcards to post to O.P. Cambridge and Coulter, asking what had become of the specimens I sent them long ago, since I have not heard from them.

As I was getting supper, Bassick came up from West Cliff bringing me some mail, which I was of course very glad of. Bassick says Cox went to Pueblo and not to Colorado Springs a few days ago, and is now back at West Cliff. Bassick's statements at various times never seem to agree; he has considerable inventive power and likes variety.

I have been working at variation, and enclose a note for S.L.E.S. which will perchance interest one or two. It is very interesting to me, the light *Colias eurytheme* throws on the origin of *C. cleopatra*.

Bassick did not get the mail that came *last night*, so no letter from you is forthcoming, but what he did bring were very nice. Cardwell Lees just returned from town with more mail, including a letter from you. There is a very nice Christmas letter from Olive, headed by a very good drawing of three juvenile angels (representing 1888). Health and Happiness greeting, an excellent likeness of T.D.A.C., and enclosing a green silk handkerchief. Second, a letter from Carlie, very nice and long; both these letters give an account of Annie's party. Third, an extremely nice letter from Sutton, who says he is sending copies of his papers. He says 'I have just published a startling paper in which I maintain that the brain and spinal cord are to be regarded as a modified piece of bowel!' This beats everything! But no doubt Sutton has plenty of proof. Sutton has been reading Darwin's life and is much astonished to find that Huxley was doubtful at first. I sent him my *Labor Enquirer* paper and he replies: 'There is one road by which all this evil may be gradually mitigated. viz., by an open and intelligent advocacy of the doctrines of Malthus among the poorer classes. and a careful dissemination of the full details relating to the evils of early and improvident marriages', which I suppose even you will admit to be absurd.

There were also some papers, of which hereafter. Now for Cardy Lees' mail: Your letter; Christmas letter from Una, and letter from Thomas. enclosing account of Klein's lecture on Ephestiae from *The Miller* of Dec. 5th . I am getting quite a batch of views on my article. Thomas writes 'Mr. Miller (Salvationist) wishes me to tell you that the solution to the problem, how to make things better, is to get more saved', which. I must say, is at least better than Sutton's.

Now for your letter: I am very glad to hear of the success of Annie's party. It is not very difficult to imagine it or to imagine that I imagine it, for I expect when I come to see some of the Isleworthites face to face I shall find they are not themselves at all as I have pictured them. Of course Mary Anderson is pretty, excessively so. If she were a cat she would take the first prize at all the Crystal Palace shows, but I don't think her face much if at all above the average of intelligence; it's not what I call a 'good' face. The only time I ever saw her was at *Pygmalion and Galatea* long ago. As a beautiful animal she is I think a long way ahead of Mrs. Langtry, Miss Fontescue, etc., etc., who are somewhat repulsive to me, but humanly. I should say she was below Mrs. Kendel or Miss Ellen Terry.

Now, about *Labor Enquirer*. Truly I did not expect you to like it, yet I feel somewhat as though I had hit my head against a wall. I have certain small complaints against the *Enquirer*, but I consider it on the whole a very good paper and well adapted for the end to which it aims. There is so vast a wall of ignorance and prejudice existing about those Chicago 'Anarchists' that it is almost hopeless to explain that not even the prosecution alleged that any of them threw the bomb, that none of them (except Ling, who killed himself) are even supposed to have made bombs, that they were speaking in the most ordinary manner in favour of the eight-hour movement and were murdered by the State of Illinois by an infamous law passed *after* their arrest, the result of sheer panic.

Again. have you ever read any good account of the Commune? Do you not know that all the rioting etc., was done during the destruction of the Commune? That while it lasted Paris was orderly and peaceful? Aye, for everyone killed in the heat of battle by the Communists, the Versailles troops killed hundreds in cold blood!

I see you too are going in for a little Malthusianism, perhaps unknowingly. Well, I won't trot over the well-worn ground again and argue the principles of Socialism. Your views are disgustingly pessimistic. The Bryant and May originated in Laboucheret who published it in *Truth* and was quoted in *Pall Mall Budget*. I believe it is accurate; it was never contradicted. I am sure your figure is much too high for an average. Anyhow, consider the price at which matches are sold and the Company's dividends. No, I don't laugh at what you say. I think it is very miserable that you can't understand what seems so clear to me. If you were a wage-worker in the East End you would notice some difference about the food. Why is it that nearly every kind of food is sold at two or three prices, the cheap one being for the poor?

As to 'lifting up his arm', do you condemn the Northerners who fought the South for the freedom of slaves? Do you condemn Cromwell who fought for Parliamentary freedom? And if not, why condemn any who fight for social freedom? It is useless to attempt any forcible measures, but the time will come in all probability. I do not see how it can be averted.

I hope Annie will believe that she was under a misapprehension about the bombs, that the facts stated above are true. I am sorry that Annie cannot agree with me about Socialism, very sorry, but I do not see that I can do otherwise than express as honestly as I can the views I hold nor do I believe she would have me do so. I would most willingly withdraw from all connections with Socialism if I could do so consistently and rightly, but thinking as I do I cannot; I must not.

I have written two other papers you will like still less, and posted them to you; for however I may risk offending either of you, I feel bound to send anything I write of any consequence. I thank you, I thank Annie for the good wishes for the New Year; that you have wished them goes far towards their realization. In many ways this New Year is not the least bright I have seen, not by any means.

December 30th. Now this is very extraordinary. When I read your letter last night I put you down as a fossilized old Tory. Reading it over again I perceive that you are after all a very revolutionary person and not a Tory at all. The idea of recommending sticks if they want to fight — well, 1 don't go that length. I don't recommend fighting at all just now (though I would excuse fists if it came to that), but I think some action may be taken, a kind of passive resistance. And I see you look forward to something approaching Socialism, but not just now. Of course your 'starvation limit' is preposterous and not in accordance with facts. What about 'over-production'? Some day it may be necessary to artificially control the increase of population but not yet.

5.30 p.m. Another dismal day, misty and hail, but not very cold. Cardy Lees came down with his sledge about half an hour ago to get part of an iron boring (mining) machine that was down here. He asked me, on behalf of Mrs. Cusack, to go up to a New Year dinner they are going to have at the Cusack's tomorrow evening, which I promised I would.

I have only told you about the letters I got yesterday. The other mail was a Christmas Card from Douglas, two *Pall Mall Budgets* (I have not had time to more than glance at them yet), *Com-monweal, Labor Enquirer, Illustrated London News*, Christmas number. (The coloured pictures are none of them good enough to put up in any room.) I expect Bret Harte's story will be interesting. *Punch's Almanack* (a rather good one this year from Carlie), *Garner* (with account of meeting of P.N.S. in London) and the *Variety Note Book*, etc., from Carlie (this I was very glad to get, being much in want of it). The Darwin extracts you sent me are very interesting. I had read the bit about Carlyle in one of the reviews, but the rest was new.

December 31st. The last day of the old year. I want to get this letter posted today but cannot very well do so unless I catch someone going down to the Cliff. If nobody goes before Monday I must ride the old mare down though the poor old creature is scarcely fit for it.

Here is an extract out of my letter to Carlie, which seems to apply equally to you. 'I take it that our points of difference are these: You think villainy is inherent and must be rooted out by moral suasion before the circumstances can be changed. I think it is the reflex of environment for the most part and that it is first necessary to change that and the rest will follow. Perhaps the exact truth lies somewhere midway between these extreme views.' Tell me if I have rightly expressed your view.

Now that I have accepted Mrs. Cusack's invitation, the lamentable fact dawns upon me that I haven't a waistcoat that will button up and am otherwise disreputable. But Payn gave to me free leave to use anything of his in case of emergency, and I daresay I shall discover something decent in the big black box. Anyhow, I have a brand new green tie.

I will end up now so as to have the letter ready. Wishing you and Annie all happiness and good fortune in the New Year.

January 1st, 1888

Dear Frederic,

I thoroughly enjoyed yesterday. After living alone, the company of a few human beings is very pleasant. But here are the full minutes of the proceedings.

At about half-past three I began to look around for the means of making myself decent. I therefore turned out Payn's box, but he seems to have traded away all his respectable clothing and nowhere could I discover a pair of trousers, so I resigned myself to wearing 'overalls.' I did, however, discover in the box a black waistcoat of mine that would actually go on, being made rather large, and I had a black coat to match it. Further, I found a clean collar and actually a snow-white handkerchief; and last but not least, I had Olive's green tie.

Then I bethought that I had to shave, but how should I do this without a razor? I discovered, however, a little surgical knife about 1½ inch long in my medicine chest, and got through pretty well with this and a pair of scissors, getting only one cut on the chin. My hair was abnormally long, but no matter; they might take me for a poet.

Thus magnificently attired, I walked up to the Cusack's and joined the circle round a delightfully warm and cheerful open fire burning pitch pine logs. The evening's company consisted of these: Mrs. Cusack, whom I find a most vivacious and agreeable old lady; Frank Cusack and Regy, whom you know; Cardwell Lees; Miss Urquhart — she is distinctly a better sort than S. Smith after all, much quieter, and though rather negative, in no way objectionable. She seems to do a good deal of the housework. Miss Sidford, a young lady from Beddoes' — of the round-faced smiling sort, in no wise remarkable. Louis Howard; I think I have told you of him before — a young Englishman, used to know Cox in England, pleasant and cheerful manner, rather light hair, moustache, ordinary well-formed features. Brock, Mrs. Brock, and Brock child — quite a goodly company for this part of the world.

There was great sound of preparations for dinner, and the men retired to put on black coats which had possibly not been worn since this time last year.

I discussed the question of snails with Mrs. Cusack as we sat before the fire.

After a time, dinner was announced, and we all trooped into the kitchen, where a long table had been set for dinner. Frank carved a gigantic turkey at one end, while Regy had a goose at the other. I sat between Mrs. Cusack and Brock child and opposite to Cardy Lees and Miss Sidford. The company was a merry one and inclined to laugh at even the semblance of a joke.

When the meat was done, there came in a big plum pudding of excellent quality, which Mrs. Cusack insisted on carving. Here an element of excitement was introduced by the announcement that there was a ring in the pudding, which Louis Howard got on his second helping, whereupon no end of chaff. Then we got up and returned to the other room to form a big circle round the fire. After the pudding, dessert, and a great fuss over the double almonds and 'Bonjour, Philippine.'

The Christmas numbers of the illustrated papers were produced and looked at and talked about for a time, till somebody suggested a song. Now there is a newly arrived instrument, a sort of harmonium organ, and Miss Urquhart, seated on a old box for a music stool, began to play and sing — Regy, Frank, Howard, and Cardy Lees joining in. They sang very badly, but it was very enjoyable all the same. First. there was a new and pretty song about 'Jack' — the words I forget. Then we had 'Just a Song at Twilight', which was full of memories for me; possibly you have heard it at 5. Priory. I know Annie has. Then one or two other songs and finally 'The Vicar of Bray.'

After the singing was over, we sat down again for conversation. First the talk ran on a fancy ball at Colorado Springs, to which Frank and Louis Howard are going. Howard was made to exhibit himself in his fancy costume, a gaudy red Chinese gown with square hat and pigtail. 1888 being leap-year, the ladies will have to ask the men to dance at this ball, and Louis and Frank were practising looking bashful, etc., behind fans with which they were to be provided.

Then someone produced a little book on palmistry and there was a great examination of everyone's hands, which revealed that Cardy Lees was to come to begging and the work-house, and other strange things.

From palmistry, thought reading was suggested. Cardy Lees was blindfolded, while Brock and Howard put their hands on his shoulders and 'willed' that he should take an almond off the organ. But after numerous gyrations he came no nearer than touching the keys of the instrument. Next I was experimented with. I had to take up and open a certain book lying on a side table, but though I took it up I failed to open it. Lastly, they willed Miss Urquhart to sit on Miss Sidford's lap, but she got no further than running up against her, so altogether, the thought-reading was not a success though it was the occasion of some fun.

This over, Brock made some remark to me about the Chicago anarchists from the other side of the room, which commenced a very lively but perfectly fair and good-tempered argument in which the whole company gathered round to make me explain why I didn't think they ought to have been hanged. (Not one advanced that they had anything to do with throwing the bomb.) They were of the opinion that their connection with revolutionary bodies justified their execution, except that Mrs. Cusack thought that 'assault on the police' was the only ground for prosecution, and so the question came to be: 'Ought revolutionary views to be allowed free expression?' And most of them seemed to think: *No*, on the ground that they incited people to violence.

From this, naturally, the talk drifted to the objects and aims of Socialism, and I did my best to expound these, particularly condemning the idea they seemed to have that Socialism meant something like 'three acres and a cow'or 'equal division and then let things go on as before.'

Frank Cusack seemed to comprehend best — and Lees was the most violent in opposition, though in a perfectly pleasant way — while all socialists ought to be hanged.

Meanwhile, the time had been getting on, and Frank, taking out his watch, announced the advent of the New Year. He went to the door at the precise moment and ceremoniously opened it, 'to let him in', while we all drank the health of the newly-arrived 1888. Then we got up and stood round in a circle and sang 'Auld Lang Syne', which seemed more than ever appropriate out here in the 'Wild West.'

Before we broke up, there was another valiant argument, as to whether honesty was the best policy and particularly whether one ought to be honest in a horse trade. Cardy Lees thought yes, but Brock, Regy, and Louis Howard considered that it was folly, since the other man was sure to try to cheat you! It was getting on for one when the Brocks departed to their home, and I came back to our house, promising to come another day.

The New Year has opened fine, but cold. I had to *saw* a piece off the joint this morning — it was freezing so hard , and our knives are none of them very sharp.

6.30 p.m.. It is blowing a gale tonight, the strongest wind we have had.

Monday. January 2nd. I am sorry I couldn't get this letter posted today. it was blowing so hard I couldn't go down on that old mare, and Cardy Lees, who meant to go down today, was probably deterred for the same reason. I am feeling tired and a little out of sorts today, no doubt the effect of the wind and the plum-pudding?

I have been very much interested in reading of Mr. Mill's 'Home Colonization Scheme' in *Pall Mall Budget*. Though I do not think these schemes will solve the difficulty, they are immensely interesting and important as experiments.

Tuesday. January 3rd . I walked down to West Cliff today, thinking that would be warmer than riding, and shall go back on the waggon of one Cress. Got *Athenaeum* and Ent. papers; very many thanks. Also *Science Gossip*, and two very nice pictures from Carlie (viz., Burne Jones' 'Golden Stair' and McWhirter's 'Vanguard'). Also letters from Farlow, Orcutt, Ford of Wichita, Thomas (long epistle), my 'Grannie' (a nice letter for New Year) and postcards from Galizia of Malta and H. Lamb. Also papers (some from Orcutt) *Commonweal, Labor Enquirer*, etc., of which will write later.

Wednesday, Jan. 4th, 1888

Dear Frederic:

I thought I *must* get to town somehow yesterday and post your letter, and so I walked because I can get along quite as fast on my own legs as on the old mare's. And it is much warmer.

I had just crossed the prairie when I met Preston coming along on Payn's buckskin horse, and learned from him that he was coming up to fetch down Payn's things (gun, blankets, etc.) for sale at Silver Cliff. The snow had drifted so deep on the road, however, that it seemed impossible that Preston could ever get through with Payn's team, so he returned to West Cliff with me. One Cress, who lives beyond the Cusack's, did manage to get through the drift with his waggon and two strong horses, and he caught us up and we rode with him the last mile or so into West Cliff. In West Cliff I posted your letter and got mail, of which I will write later.

I also saw Payn, who does not look well. He appears to spend all his time in the 'Lager Beer Hall' playing billiards and having drinks at intervals — enough to knock anyone up I should say. After I had been in town a little while, Cardy Lees and Frank Cusack came driving in. They came part of the way in a sledge and the rest (over the good road) in Lees' buckboard. Frank and Louis Howard were off that evening to Colorado Springs for the ball which, they hear at the last moment to their intense disgust, has been changed from fancy dress into an ordinary swallow-tail affair.

I came back with Cress, who is a strange old man (at 44). He is one of those people who always fancy everyone else is envious or what not, and anxious to do them ill. From this, naturally, he does not get on with anyone and is generally set down as an ill-tempered man, though I think if he would look at things in a better light he would be well enough liked. Coming across the prairie after sundown in Cress' waggon was a terrible business. The wind was blowing its hardest and we were bitterly cold. I had some mail for the Cusacks, but after lighting a fire and eating some supper I *could* not get up resolution enough to face the wind again, so let the mail wait till this morning, but I must go and take it to them now.

Cress came with Bassick this morning and took away all of Payn's saleable things down to West Cliff, Cress' horses being able to haul them through the snow.

5.45 p.m. I have just returned from the Cusack's, calling at Brock's for some meat on the way down. I have been having a long talk with Mrs. Cusack, who has lived in Ireland, and she told me many very interesting stories about the state of affairs in that country from the landlord point of view. The way the people stand by each other for good or for evil seems most wonderful in cases of agrarian outrage, though the whole country knows the culprit and will tell anyone in private conversation. Yet you can't get witnesses to prove it in a law court anyhow! I really haven't had time to attend properly to my mail of yesterday, so will defer consideration of it for the present.

Now that I think of it I am very strongly of the opinion that the 'melanic variety of *Vanessa urticae*' taken in Mexico and exhibited at S.L.E.S. Nov. 10th by W. Druce was *Vanessa milberti*, in which case it is very discreditable to the society that they didn't 'spot' it. I sent you wings of *V. milberti*. I wish you would take them up and convey my sentiments to Tutt or someone who was there that night and ask whether it was not the same thing (if so, of course correct the record and get Barker to insert 'erratum' in the *Proceedings*).

January 5ᵗʰ. I have been writing letters all today. The only thing that happened was Regy Cusack, who called in this morning on his way to the Kettle's. He expressed great admiration for Annie's 1886 Christmas card, which was on the wall of my room. Three of Nell's puppies have died, and Regy killed another this morning, so there are only two left. I am going to take Nell and the two puppies up to the Cusack's at first opportunity. Nell originally belonged to Regy. Cardy Lees came up from the Cliff this evening but forgot to get my mail, so I am disappointed in any expectation of getting a letter from you this evening.

Now for Tuesday's mail: I enunciated the letters etc., in letter posted Tuesday. Farlow (the cuss mentioned in *Sci. Goss.* p. 279 I sent that note) sends the names of two Colorado lichens I sent him. Lamb of Maidstone writes that the shells belong to a friend of his. I have written to tell him to get his friend to send them to you. Lamb thinks *H. fusca* is found in his district. Frank J. Ford (of Wichita, Kansas) sends an interesting list of Kansas shells found by him. *Coch. lubrica* and *Planorbis trivolvis* are the only two shells I know of as found in Kansas, Colorado, and Utah. Kansas is the eastern limit of many species.

Orcutt (Editor of *West Amer. Scientist*) writes a pleasant letter and sends me copies of his lists of Mollusca and plants found in Southern and Lower California, both of which are very interesting. He actually finds *Saxicava rugosa* and *Lasaea rubra* in California, and the list of algae includes *Fucus vesiculosus, Ulva latissima* and such familiar things. Is not that interesting? Their origin must have been Boreal. Orcutt also sent, in exchange for some stamps I sent him (he is one of those people who collect everything 'on spec.') several numbers of *Naturalist's Companion* and *Ornithologist and Oölogist*. The first is a silly little paper,

the other rather good (you can see it any time at Zoöl. Society). A paper by one Morrison on the birds of Colorado in *Orn. and Oöl.* furnishes me with 14 species and one var. new to my list.

Thomas writes an eight page epistle. Of my *Labor Enquirer* paper he says: 'I do not think it 'abominable' but a moderate and well-grounded statement of unfortunate facts', but I submit he doesn't know anything about it! However, Thomas dislikes the *Labor Enquirer itself* very much and, further, although agreeing with the *aims* of Socialism, strongly dissents from the plan of carrying them out as advocated by average Socialists. He thinks Champion's speech at Church Congress is what a Socialist speech *ought* to be. Thomas wants me to try to smuggle some cheap Ruskins, etc., to England for him. He thinks 'being for private use' they might pass. I doubt it, but will see if anything can be done. I take it the same rule applies as to 'Tanchinity'edition.

In *Science Gossip* I see J.W.W. proposes *bourguignati* as a variety of *subfuscus*! I don't think this can be allowed under any circumstances. *Arion albus* is of course only white *Arion ater*, in England at any rate, though possibly white *subfuscus* or something may have been mixed up with it on the continent. I see (p. 283) that Miss Layard is going to reply to your 'rudiments and vestiges.' *Ent. Month. Mag.*: I received a copy of the report reviewed on p. 161 from Agric. Dept. Poulton's experiments on the cocoons are very interesting. I see Klein has been coming out with the *Ephestia* at Ent. Soc.

January 6ᵗʰ. I have been writing all today, and nobody has called. In discussing the mail I did not mention Geddes' lecture. I think his arguments are very good, and I quite agree that natural selection does not account for everything, or perhaps for most things. Perhaps I will write to Geddes.

I see Hammersmith is going in for a free library (if the rate-payers will have it). I wish they may get it. Today and for some days past I have been writing a paper on 'insect variation' which, if I get it published, is going to turn the world upside down. That is to say, it is going to shock the feelings of some of the old fogies. I shall send it to the *Entomologist* and I anticipate that Carrington will show it either to Jenner Weir or South for their opinion. If it is Jenner Weir the paper will be published; if it is South, it won't, so I guess. I shall tell Carrington, in the event of non-publication, to give the manuscript to Tutt, who is to give it to you when he has read it. What sort of a chap is Beeby? I see he was at Linnean Society that night.

Jan. 7th, 1888

Dear Frederic,

I shall make a point of ending up [my letters] on Friday nights unless I am myself going down, because someone generally goes to town on Saturday, and I want to have the letter ready to give them. For some unknown reason neither Lees nor Regy Cusack have gone into town today (though they both said they were going). In fact, nobody at all has been past, one way or the other. The strong winds have ceased, I am glad to say, and it is now still, and not so very cold.

I see in *Pall Mall Budget* of Dec. 8th that the archbishop of Canterbury has summoned all the bishops to attend a conference to discuss, among other things, the attitude of the Church towards Socialism. It really almost seems as if the Church (as a body) were going to wake up at last.

I have today been reading and taking notes from a book on Colorado that I borrowed from the Cusacks. It is called *The Crest of the Continent*, by Ernest Ingersoll, apparently the same Ingersoll that wrote the paper on Colorado shells in Bull. U. S. Geol. Survey and also the paper on 'American shell-money' that recently appeared in *Science Gossip*.

Sunday, January 8th. It has turned fine and cold again, which is decidedly better than wind, because I can sit in comfort before the fire, and the smoke doesn't puff out every two minutes

and cover me with ash. My toes get very cold, but they can be warmed now and then, and altogether I am pretty comfortable. I have started a stew-pot — a big iron pot always on the heat, in which I put bits of meat, onions etc., and by some little boiling produce a very palatable stew. There is this disadvantage, though, that as it is always there and warm I am tempted to partake at odd times of the day, which is not good. The bacon is all gone so I live upon stew morning and evening, with oatmeal occasionally for a change.

I was reading over the advertisements in the *Athenaeum* this morning. Someone offers an MS novel of '100,000 words' for sale, as if the number of words was the only recommendation — a rather doubtful one. I should say. Another man advertises for poems — 'all poems sent will be carefully considered' — rash man! I see 'A Dream of John Ball' is to be published in book form, with an illustration by Burne-Jones, which I am glad of because it was never properly appreciated in *Commonweal*.

Did any of the seeds I sent you in the summer ever grow into anything?

January 9th. I feel miserable! Everything seems to conspire against my getting or posting any mail. Regy Cusack came here this evening. He had ridden down to the Cliff with Miss Urquhart, and the scatterbrained fellow actually forgot both to call here going down to ask if there was anything to post, and to get my mail when down there. I have developed an acute sense of hearing and never fail to hear any vehicle going along the road, or even people walking or riding if they talk, but these two slipped by so silently this morning that, as I wasn't looking out of the window, I missed them. I can't go down. If the old mare would do the journey — both bridle and saddle have gone to town to be sold. And as for walking — fresh snow has fallen since last week, and there and back 14 miles in the snow is impossible. I can stand living up here when I get my letters, but without them it becomes intolerable. You and Annie will be calling me all the bad names you know because no letter arrives at the proper time. But you see, I can't help it anyhow — wish I could. Regy says Cardy Lees isn't well, and that's why he didn't go down on Saturday. I have got a cold and a slight cough these last two days. I don't know why.

Yesterday evening I began Bret Harte's *A Phyllis of the Sierras* in the Christmas *Illustr. London News*. Being Bret Harte, it is interesting but not one of his best; besides, it ends abruptly in the middle of the narrative, as much as to say 'I was paid to write so many volumes, and I've written them and don't intend to do any more for nothing.' After finishing this story this morning, I turned to reading magazines.

There is an excellent paper in the *Ornithologist and Oölogist* on 'The Development and Decay of the Pigment Layer on Birds Eggs', by one D. McAldowie. The author states that the pigment on eggs is derived from the haematin of the red blood corpuscles and is of only three colours: Green (including blue-green), red, and black — the brown, etc., being combinations of these. The primitive colour of eggs was green, and the purpose of it was to protect from the sun's rays. Spots, etc., were afterwards developed so as to make the eggs resemble the surrounding objects. In every case of white eggs, the primitive colour has been lost because the bird built out of the light, and he shows that all eggs laid in the dark are white or whitish. A few birds, however, lay exposed white eggs, but these belong to families in which other species lay concealed eggs, and it is supposed that they formerly concealed their eggs, and once having acquired white eggs, the peculiarity was transmitted after they took to open nests again. Altogether the paper is extremely interesting and suggestive and, as you are an eggologist, I should like to know what your views are on the subject. D. McAldowie lives in England (Staffordshire) so perhaps you know something of him. Couldn't *you* take up the question?

Hitherto your eggs have been little more than a collection of specimens to you, but might you not squeeze a little science out of them? Some

light might be thrown on the variations in birds' eggs. I have note of *blue* eggs of *Fringilla coelebs*, *spotted* eggs of *Gecinus viridis* (McAldowie would call this reversion to ancestral type), *spotless* eggs of *Turdus merula*, *white* eggs of *Linota cannabina* and *Sialia sialis*.

Jan. 10th , 1888

Dear Frederic,

I need not have been on the verge of drowning myself in the pail last night after all, because Brock came along the first thing this morning and took my letters to post, and will, I trust, bring back my mail tonight. So, feeling more cheerful at this prospect, I sat me down to the all-engrossing study of ornithology.

American birds are in many ways interesting, presenting as they do so many 'geographical races', e.g., all the western examples of a species will differ from the eastern in some slight but perfectly constant way. It is remarkable what a number of American birds have been named by the good Sclater of our Zoological Society. I think he must be more ancient than he looks. Bowdler Sharpe, also, has stood godfather for one or two.

On looking at the spoon I use to stir up dough for bread this morning, I noticed that the damp dough in it was covered with red spots, like blood , only the wrong sort of red. A careful examination led me to the conclusion that it was a fungus growth, and I have little doubt that it is the *Protococcus nivalis* or 'red snow' which forms on wet substances in cold weather. I am therefore much interested. *Protococcus* is considered an alga, though, rather than a fungus (see Thome).

This afternoon Miss Urquhart and Regy Cusack rode down to pay me a call, which was nice and neighbourly of them. Regy took off 'Nell' and the two remaining pups with him.

7:45 p.m. I'm afraid Brock isn't coming back tonight, so I shall have to wait yet longer for my mail.

10:15 p.m. What is the matter with Annie? You are so indefinite, and I am miserably anxious. Can't you tell me more precisely? Poor Annie! Give her my best sympathy. I trust she is much better or well by now. Tell me all there is to tell and at once. But I know you will do that. I am grateful for the letter and the post-card rec'd. I wish I were nearer town and could get the letters directly they arrive. You see Brock did come after all and brought a lot of mail, about which I will write tomorrow.

Thanks very much for the *African Farm*. I will let you know my views about it when read.

January 11th. As I read, Brock turned up the last thing last night, and Bassick with him. Poor Bassick was half frozen but he came in and warmed himself and had a cup of hot coffee, and felt better. Except the wretched news about Annie the mail was very satisfactory.

In answer to your letters: J.W.W. knows next to nothing about slugs, of course, but since his paper is a compilation and not original, it is decidedly a useful one notwithstanding the blunders over M. Bourgignat, etc. Probably he got this idea out of Kobelt, whose axioms are in the wildest confusion. I would have written to 'squash' him myself, only *Science Gossip* turned up so very late that my reply could not have been in time even for the February number. Why don't you write? You know all about it.

I still maintain most decidedly that the essential thing about a rudiment is that it is *functionless*, not that it is aborted. That was what I meant by the last illustration.

I am afraid the Lancers are scoffers by nature, but I think *Sesame and Lilies* might have been taken seriously. I suppose *Western Avenues* appeals more directly to people out here who have seen things similar to those described, and to me it was full of interest. I came to the conclusion that I didn't like the commercialism skit myself, and so abandoned it.

I wonder what you and Annie will think of my 'novel' of which I have sent out three chapters. I am almost afraid you won't like it. It does not satisfy me by any means; however, let me know exactly what you think. I am glad to hear Darwin was not so disreputable as I am; there is some hope for me yet. But what Payn meant was 'fast' — poker, drinks, and so on. Of course I am disreputable enough for anything in my own way, but he didn't mean that.

Barker's reports in the magazines are most meagre and unsatisfactory. If you have a chance you should abuse him about it. Barker is a collector, heart and soul. I know those *Adipoda*. You can see them any day at the museum. You will find Jenner Weir's views about *Triphena* in Darwin, *Descent of Man*, p. 313. I enclose a slip with my views on the subject, which you might give to Jenner Weir or, if you are sufficiently interested in the matter might bring the subject up yourself at a meeting of S.L.E.S. and get a reply from J.J.W. in public.

I know the Bloggs' only at second hand. I never saw any of them. The 'matric' is a stiff examination in subjects which are not of much general use. I can't imagine why anyone should go in for exams unnecessarily, as the Bloggs' seem to be doing. At best they only enlarge the mind at the expense of cramping it.

It has been shown that with wild birds the size of the eggs bears a definite proportion to the size of the parent (in the same species). I don't know about those eggs of Bob Read's, though. I suppose in that case some were not properly developed. I should think I *had* heard of 'The Ballad-monger'; Carlie took good care of that, besides which there was a long account in *Pall Mall*.

I am glad Annie is under the care of Dr. Macdonald, who ought to know what he is about. I am anxiously waiting the next letter. It was a pity, too, she couldn't go to the gathering at 5. Priory, but not being well she probably did wisely to stay away. I am glad to hear of the subject of your lecture; it must be an interesting one. I wish I could hear it.

I can't imagine why you got no letter on Dec.17th or 19th. On Dec. 2nd I gave Cox several letters to post, including one to you (and also a Denver and Rio Grande Time Table). Two of the letters, I know, have reached their destination. I cannot tell why yours hasn't. Probably it will turn up sooner or later. The other mail rec'd. was: A nice letter from Mother; one from Douglas, and one from Leslie, who seems to like Madeira; one from C. Vasey (Dept. Agric., Entom.) saying any notes will come in handy for a work on Forest Insects just to be published.

An almost pathetic epistle from Callahan (Editor of *Labor Enquirer*) who says he is terribly troubled with editing, his life having been mostly in the shop and mine, and he has never had the opportunity of fitting himself for the position. He ends up: 'I am given by the comrades credit for honesty of purpose as regards the movement but that don't do the work; ability does. I wish you would write for the paper whenever you feel so disposed. With kindliest greetings, J. J. Callahan.' I feel certain he is genuine, whatever he may be as to ability.

Don't ever tell me there isn't magic in a postcard. The next two letters are the result of postcards written to people I had never corresponded with before. W. H. Edwards: A very nice letter saying he will be pleased at any time to name butterflies for me (he is the boss authority on North American butterflies). He wants me to help him by looking for larvae and eggs of butterflies for figuring in his beautiful work on North American Butterflies (you should see this at Zoöl. Society), which of course I will most gladly do. He further sends three plates from his work 'to show you the way I treat larvae', which form a very acceptable addition to my little picture gallery. The last letter is from E. E. Westgate of Houston, Texas, who says he will take great pleasure in assisting me by any means in his power, and sends a list of mollusca he has taken in Texas. It is very encouraging to receive such kind letters from brother naturalists. Don't you think so?

The other mail was: *Story of an African Farm*, which I will write of when I have read it. (They charged 15 cents duty on it. I shouldn't have thought they would have done that.) *Christmas Carol* from Mother (also German dictionary I had sent for). A bundle of very interesting papers from Sutton, including the ones we heard read at Zoöl. Soc. A Christmas card from Wimpole St., two *Pall Mall Budget*s, *Commonweal* and *Labor Enquirer*.

Brock came along this morning, riding to the Cliff, and a little later the one-armed Stratton came and stayed some time, telling me some important things.

(1.) He says Payn looks worse than ever, and spends his whole time in the drinking saloon. Somebody told him that Payn had been turned out of the hotel because he had no money, and that he had pawned all his clothes etc., at the saloon for drinks. How true this may be I cannot tell.

(2.) He says Frank Hunter has got me a place as clerk at the 'Little Nelly' mine at Rosita, one of the best mines in the valley. 'A bird in the hand is worth two in the bush', and if I don't hear from Cox I shall go for this. Both these things, as well as my anxiety to get a letter from you (unless Brock brings it tonight) demand that I go to town tomorrow and, as Stratton is going down with a waggon, he promises to take me. He is not coming back though, so I shall have to walk unless I go to Rosita to see about the mine and stay the night there. (Rosita is pronounced 'rose-eater.' It is about six miles the other side of West Cliff. There is no railway, but a stage does the distance in a very little while from the Cliff, bringing the mail. The mine is quite close to the town.

The fame of the Socialist discussion at the Cusack's seems to have spread far and wide. Stratton had heard about it and was quite sure there was going to be a revolution himself.

January 12th. Stratton not having turned up, I came down to town with Cardy Lees. Alas! No letter from you, and Annie ill. But there may be one tonight.

Jan. 12th , 1888

Dear Frederic,

As I said, Stratton promised to take me to town this morning. He said he would pass with his waggon at about eight. However, eight came, but no Stratton. Nine, and no Stratton, but at 9:30 Cardy Lees came by on his sledge. So I took that opportunity and jumped on the sledge, and over the prairie we went at a grand rate.

Sleighing is admirable over the snow, faster if anything than a buckboard on bare ground, and of course any wheeled contrivance has to walk when snow is on the ground. At Kettle's we changed the sledge for Lee's buckboard, as the road for the rest of the way is snow free, so Lees keeps his buckboard at the Kettle's in view of this. Lees was going in to meet Frank Cusack by the evening's train (coming from the ball at Colorado Springs) and as the buckboard is a little thing and will only hold two, I had to walk back, which I could easily do, as there was plenty of time.

Directly we got into to town I 'made a break' for the Postoffice, but to my great disappointment found only a letter from the Agric. Dept. (with names of some things I sent them). This, however, was explained by the fact that there had been some accident on the line the other side of Pueblo, in consequence of which no eastern mail had arrived at all on Wednesday night, but it is expected that it will turn up tonight. I therefore left word with Lees to be sure not to forget to bring my mail in the event of its turning up by the evening train, which he promised he would, and I am now expecting them with it every minute. Failing tonight, I should think it is sure to come tomorrow, in which case I must arrange somehow to get down on Saturday or have it brought up.

After I had posted off my mail (including letter to you and box of butterflies to Edwards), I went in search of Payn and found him having dinner with Lees at the hotel. The story of his having been ejected proves fictitious, but he is much in need of money, and I believe Lees is going to lend him what he needs. He is very hoarse and looks very ill.

I was induced to have dinner also at the hotel, which is very extravagant (50 cents) but I reflected that I had to walk home, so the inner man might be the better for a little provender. Indeed, I was very extravagant altogether today. I bought a beautiful pair of bright scarlet woolen gloves (50 cents also) to keep my fingers from the cold and symbolise my bloodthirsty Socialistic tendencies, and I also invested in a bottle of ink and some nibs. (They charge 10 cents for a bottle one would get for a penny in England.) You will have noticed in the last few letters that both pen and ink used in their production were vile.

Meanwhile I made enquiries after Frank Hunter, but he had gone to Rosita that very day, so there was no chance of seeing him, but Cox was expected back that night and would be certain to see Hunter if he also returned (they are fast friends), so I left an epistle for Cox saying how things stood, and begging him to investigate the matter and let me know the result. I keep getting up, thinking I hear Lees coming, but it proves a mistake each time. I doubt whether I should hear the sledge anyhow, but he will call out if there is any mail. It is now half past eight.

After dinner (Payn and Lees finished and went out soon after I began) I went to look for Payn, intending to talk over his affairs with him and Lees, but I discovered Payn in a saloon gambling with dice among a crowd of loafers and Lees was not to be found, so considerably disgusted I gave the matter up.

It was two when I started from town, but I did not get up here till five, as I had to walk against a very strong wind. Coming across the prairie the snow was flying about in clouds and the wind so violent that I had to resort to the plan of taking short runs when the wind lulled, and standing still when the blasts came, with my back turned towards them. I tied my scarf over my hat, so that I presented rather a peculiar appearance. But I got here safe and sound, and having lighted a fire, sat before it and devoted myself to a perusal of the *Pall Mall Budget* for awhile. Ten o'clock. No Lees, no mail. I rather expect they stayed in town the night, not caring to face the wind after dark, when it becomes very cold.

January 13th. Cardwell Lees has turned up this morning, bringing from town your most welcome letter and also a letter from Carlie and a postcard from C. J. Simpson. I am very glad indeed to hear that Annie is doing so well. Indeed from what you say it seems certain that she will soon recover and there is therefore no reason for anxiety. Still, I shall be anxious to hear that she is quite well again, which piece of news I hope for in your next letter, or at latest the one after.

In reply to your letter: I have heard Mrs. Wharton Robinson read and recite; she does it very well. I used to go to school at Wharton Robinson's (or 'Bob', as we called him) at Margate at one time (that is, in autumn, 1882).

I don't quite agree with you about crowds. At the crowd I was at, I found someone to talk to, and in fact enjoyed it very much, whereas in *small* parties no sooner has one commenced to talk than, as likely as not the *whole* room turns round to stare and listen, and either one has to 'shut up' or give a lecture! Moral: Either a party ought to be so big that you can get lost in the crowd, or it ought to be so small that conversation can be carried on, which includes everyone present. The number of them should not, generally speaking, be more than a half dozen.

I am infinitely obliged to Carrington for meaning to write, but since I wrote to him on 29th July, one would think he might have braced himself up to do the deed by now. But I thank him for his good wishes, which are very acceptable. Who are Price and Turner? Their names do not appear in the 1886 list of members. I am very glad that

you are going to give a lecture at the S.L.E.S. It was ingenious of you to choose so comprehensive a title, and settle the subject afterwards. I think 'On the Mollusca of the Society's District' would be much the best subject because (1.) The Society doesn't properly realize it has a district yet, and this would bring it home to them. (2.) It would emphasize your position as recorder and show them that something was really being done, and probably secure you help from numbers. (3.) You have plenty of material for such a paper at hand. (4.) The paper would be of practical value to those who cared anything about the Mollusca in the Society, and perhaps entice some others to attend to the subject. (5.) What you have to say about variation and geographical distribution would be a good deal thrown away before the Society and had much better be published in some magazine so that those who studied these matters might have access to it.

As to the treatment of the subject, you might perhaps best take it in districts, showing the zoo-geographical regions in the district and how they were characterized by peculiar forms. I should be inclined to treat these as follows, but of course you will have your own views thereon. (1.) The Upper Thames region: *Paludina collecta* etc. (2.) The lower Thames region: *P. vivipara, Planorbis lineatus*, etc. (3.) The North Kent region: Rarity of *Planorbis corneus*, presence of *Limnaea glutinosa*. Albinism of *Planorbis* and *Limnaea, Pisidium roseum*. Geological evidence that this was once part of Thames valley. Distribution of *Assim. grayana* here and in North Kent. (5.) Northdown region: Chalk hills extending from middle and east Kent west to Barks; *H. pomatia, Cl. rolphi, Coch. tridens, H. lapicida*, etc. (6.) The Sussex region and Kentish coast: *H. cartusiana, H. virgata*, etc.; difference between W. Sussex — *H. rupestris* in Sussex. (7.) The South Hants region: *H. obvoluta*. The region where *Test. scutulum* and *manger* meet; *Limax arborum*. (8.) The Isle of Wight: *Cochlicella acuta*, etc., and if the society's map be taken as a guide as to limits, (9.) A North Wiltshire region might be added , characterised by abundance of *Limnaea auricularia, Planorbis fontanus*, etc. Then the marine regions would be (1.) North Kent:

Sheppy to Margate. (2.) Pegwell Bay, etc. (3.) E. Sussex: Hastings to Brighton. (4.) W. Sussex, and (5.) Isle of Wight, all characterized by peculiar forms.

Then you might get up a petition to Annie, begging her to do some outline or other diagrams of the more notable species to put on the wall for the enlightenment of those who do not know a *Limnaea* from a *Helix*, and you might do a very rough coloured map just to illustrate the regions. And lastly, it would be expedient to take plenty of specimens to show. Where you could, it might be good to confirm the division of the regions by reference to insects, but the material for this is at present insufficient.

Cox evidently didn't post that letter here at all, but days after, when he was at Colorado Springs, which naturally accounts for its late arrival.

You must not suppose polygamy to be the essential thing about Mormonism; in fact it did not exist when Mormonism was first started. I hear that the 'gentile' population in Salt Lake City is increasing, so I suppose they are giving it up somewhat. But you know in England how people will cling to practises they suffer from out of pure conservatism. They can't have 'a husband apiece' anyhow if, inasmuch as the female population is greater than the male — that was the beginning of it. If you read again any explanation of their religious feeling on the subject you will see that if the sexes were equal in number the very principle on which they practice polygamy now would then force them to abandon it.

Frederic! Fancy comparing this magnificent dwelling to 'an old outhouse'! Really though, I wish it were as solid and air tight as some outhouses I have seen.

The only thing I ever read of Shakespeare's is *Coriolanus*, and that I wrote out to dictation when I was a small boy (in 1878 it must have been). Once I got hold of a book at Wimpole St. to prove that Shakespeare was Bacon (and I must say the arguments seemed almost convincing). I think you are quite right about Williams; so long

as he lays low it is not worthwhile to ferret him out. Carlie writes in his last letter: 'When I say you have no feeling, I mean that you cannot derive pleasure from Poetry or from Painting, or, I believe, from Music, the acts into which feeling enters, except now and then in a casual sort of way', so it seems he meant only artistic feeling.

I don't think the *Pall Mall* is more or perhaps so unprincipled as the other papers, only they are 'honest knaves' and don't conceal it. Take the *Daily News* — the Paris Correspondence every morning looks very respectable and honest, but Crawford will tell you. that the 'interviews with distinguished members of the army, etc., are mostly 'fudge'' — and indeed there is plenty of humbug beneath a very respectable exterior.

You should be very careful not to give me anything but *facts*. It is quite a chance I did not bring that matter of the difference between Bedford Park and Isleworth spiders into a paper I wrote for *Science Gossip*. I only hesitated because I wanted fuller particulars. I published two or three lists of Bedford Park insects in *Entomologist*, etc. Look up the list of my papers where you will find reference to them.

I discovered after I had posted my letter that last Christmas was on Saturday; of course we came home on Sunday, not on Christmas Day. All thanks for your promise to send me one of Annie's stories. I will return it safely and promptly.

It appears, then, that Williams' var. of *S. carneum* will stand. It must be an analogous var. of *S. rivicolor* that Pascal describes. I *know* it is hard work entering up the record book. I always put it off when I got too tired, for fear of making slips. I am very glad of the additions to my Isleworth fauna. The Middlesex Syrphi are now quite numerous. The beetle list is very interesting.. You might send the unknown species of *Aurelizethes* to W. W. Fowler, who is great on this genus; the commonest species is *A. aeneus*. I have two down for Middlesex, *M. angipes* from High Gate and *M. coracinus* from Hampstead, both on Fowler's authority. The *Apions* are terrible little beetles to name, except *A. miniatum,* which you can tell anywhere. *Tachyporus hypnorum* and *Phyllobius argentatus* are recorded for Esher, Surrey, by Brunett, but they are common species. Lewcock also records *Anthonomus rubi* from the Esher district. Your list of *Telephoric* is good. If I remember right I took *T. bicolor* at Maidenhead. *Blaps* used to occur in the kitchen at Wimpole St. along with *Niptus holoencus* and *Pristonuchus serricola.* I think I once took *Nebria brevicollis* in Regent's Park, but this is only from memory. *Serica brunnea* is common at Chislehurst. There is an *Anthonomus (A. musculus)* in the U. S. that does damage to strawberries and is treated at some length in one of the Agric. Reports. I should much like any lists additional to those I have, but I have a longish plant list of Annie's. I suppose you have not many to add to that; and also a few birds down from Annie, and just a few snails on my own authority.

January 14th. To continue what I was saying yesterday: I have not had any Isleworth lists of Hemiptera, Neuroptera or Orthoptera. Have you no records of these? C. J. Simpson, from whom I had a postcard yesterday, is a Nebraska conchologist who wants to exchange shells. I may be able to do something for him next season.

This morning is very cold indeed and more unpleasant because a damp fog hangs over everything.

Cardy Lees came down just now, about Payn's horses. Payn had made some arrangement to have his horses in town today. They are at present up at Cox's, to be examined by a man who proposed to buy them, and further, he owed money which must be paid on Monday, and it was necessary for this that someone should take it down. Lees promised to go down if he could, and I said I would otherwise, although it seems that it involves riding one horse bareback and leading the other, and finally walking back. However, Lees came this morning to say he did not think I could possibly get there in this cold, and Brock and Bassick, who had been going down also, likewise would not venture in

such weather, and as I am no wise anxious to come back minus my nose or ears from frostbite, I decided to wait until tomorrow and see how the weather is then.

Lees is very much disheartened with Payn, and thinks it next to impossible to do anything with him. He offered to let him stay for a time up in his cabin in the mountains, but Payn declared he would rather die than that.

Cardy Lees insisted on refunding me the 50 cents I paid for dinner down in the Cliff, on the ground that he had invited me to partake and therefore ought to pay. I have run out of meat and Lees is going to sell me some mutton which he has to spare, so I must try and get up there and fetch it down today.

At about one o'clock I went up to Bassick's (i.e., Cox's) taking an oil can to borrow some lamp oil of which I have run short. I wrapped up well for it was cold. I found Bassick just preparing lunch, of beans, bread, and coffee, so I stayed and partook. (It seemed a great luxury to be having coffee out of a china cup and with milk in it.) Bassick's conversational powers came out a little and I found him slightly more interesting than hitherto. Bassick had no oil to spare, not enough for himself, so I went on to Brock's and got some there. At Brock's I found also Lees and Frank Cusack, and we all sat round the stove and talked for a time, the subjects of conversation being Australia, pearls, sharks teeth, and the Great Ark. As I was going away Mrs. Brock came and very kindly made me a present of a loaf of bread, which being yeast and not baking-powder bread, is something of a luxury to me. I also got a shoulder and ribs of mutton from Lees, for which he charged the very modest price of 40 cents.

I agreed that if it were at all possible I would take Payn's horses down to town tomorrow, and Lees is going to lend me a saddle to facilitate this. Coming back, my fingers got so cold and numb that I had to go into Bassick's and warm them up by the stove. I hope I shall not get frostbitten tomorrow. If I do it shan't be for lack of wrapping up. It was 15° below zero (Fahrenheit) at the Cusack's this morning. It has been colder, but the damp mist today made it worse than a lower temperature on a dry day.

Sunday, January 15th . It was 22° below zero last night at the Cusack's, but this morning is almost cloudless and very fine and sunny. (Letter broken off, continued on the 16th.)

I went up to Bassick's between eight and nine and afterwards up to the Cusack's, where I borrowed a saddle and bridle of Lees. Securely wrapped up, I started out for West Cliff on the buckskin horse, leading the old mare by a rope. On arriving in town I went to the postoffice and got a paper — the *Industrial Review*, sent by Sherborn, and a letter from Smithsonian to say that they had not been able to reply to my last letter from pressure of work, but hoped I would not think that they had overlooked it, which was considerate of them.

Then I went in search of Frank Hunter, who lives in a neat little green-painted house in West Cliff. He welcomed me kindly and said that probably they would not require anyone at the Little Nellie mine till next week at the earliest, but he had bespoken the place for me and thought I might very probably get it. The work will be keeping the books — account of ore raised and shipped, wages account, making out bills. etc., in fact, much the same as I did at Klein's. He thinks I ought to get $3.00 a day, which would be very good wages for me, since at the outside I suppose any expenses would not exceed $1.00 a day, so I am beginning to build castles in the air at the prospect!

After this I went and saw Payn, who was playing cribbage in the saloon. He said he never asked Lees to bring down the mare, so I had to take her back again, which was hard on her, as she is lame.

I then went back to the postoffice and thought I would write the latest news and post this letter then, but I had only written a line when the office closed (it being Sunday). I could

have finished the letter at one of the shops or the hotel, but thought I had best be getting home, as the evening might be cold, and I could write better and more fully at home. One stupid thing I did was to drop my gloves (I had them and scarf in one hand) and so lost them in the town, which involved the purchase of new ones. So I expended 75 cents this time on a very warm pair of 'mitts', philosophically reflecting that the lost gloves did not keep my hands warm enough, and these certainly would, so probably the loss was a providential arrangement to keep my fingers from being frostbitten. Cox of the hotel told me that it was minus 28E!in the Cliff. Curiously it is colder in West Cliff than here during these cold snaps.

I rode the old mare up until I came to the prairie, and there I got off and walked. I did not go into our house, but went up to Bassick's and then on to Brock's and, being asked to stay to supper, did so. Brock improves vastly on acquaintance and is a very good sort of fellow. When I went away Mrs. Brock gave me a 'corn-loaf' she had made, in which the flour is from Indian corn instead of wheat. It is good for a change. Brock would not let me pay for the meat I had from him. He had kindly asked Payn to go up and stay a little while at his place but he refused. There is evidently no getting him out of town.

Coming home from Brock's I looked in at Bassick's and we sat talking a long while, Bassick telling me all sorts of stories about his early life, both in Maine where he was 'raised', and at sea, for he has been a sailor and owned a vessel which, however, got captured and destroyed during the Civil War. It was nearly eleven when we went to bed. I slept up here, as it was warmer than my little house, and Bassick asked me to stay.

January 16th . It is warmer but windy this morning. I am still up at Bassick's. I shall go down to my house presently to cut wood, etc., but have promised to come back this evening. I don't get any work (that is, my scientific papers, etc.) done up here, but it is so pleasant to be in a warm house with someone to talk to that I like the change for a day or so. I went back to Bassick's yesterday afternoon and spent the evening talking (till past eleven) and reading *African Farm*, of which I will write when I have finished it. I may say now that I like it much. This morning is very windy, but less so down here at my house than at Cox's which is much more exposed.

I see that Alfred Russel Wallace is of the opinion that the colour of *Limax agrestis* is protective owing to its resemblance to small pebbles. and he says that in his garden there were little black flints, yellow inside, which when broken were just like *A. hortensis* with its yellow sole (he does not give the names of the slugs, but from what he says there is no doubt what they are). I myself can hardly see this protective resemblance, inasmuch as these slugs, when at rest, always get out of sight, and when crawling, cannot be mistaken for pebbles.

9:50 p.m. I wish you had not sent me that book. I have read it and it has made me miserable.

January 18th. A nice sunny warm day. Armstrong came in for a minute or so to inspect Payn's harness. He is the man to whom Payn has sold his horses, harness, etc., a big man in a gray cloak with a pleasant face and a beard. He lives some way down the valley. The old mare might have been left in town after all, hence Armstrong has bought her. He took her away today.

Another visitor was Regy Cusack, who was good enough to cut my hair for me, and as it had not been cut for over six months, it needed it. Regy and Frank Cusack cut the hair of all the ranchmen round here. It is an act at which they are quite proficient from much practice.

I enclose some notes on *The Story of an African Farm*. [Partial notes enclosed. Ed.] If I can, I want to get into town tomorrow or at latest the day after, as I want to get your letter. Lees came up from town just now, bringing *Commonweal*,

Labor Enquirer, and a letter from C. F. Morrison with a list of 343 Colorado birds. It appears that he has got up a 'Colorado Ornithological Association' and is going to publish a list of he avifauna of the state.

Jan. 19th, 1888

Dear Frederic,

This *is* disgusting! I have walked down here to get your letter and find no English mail. It does not always come in on Wednesday evening, but I quite expected it, else I would not have walked down. I started to come down with Cress, but we had only got half across the prairie when we met a man coming up to Cress' to haul wood, and so Cress turned back. He is coming in tomorrow instead, but I was impatient and walked down. It is a fine day, sunny and quite hot. All the mail I found was a *Pall Mall Budget* and a letter from a man named Pilsbry of Philadelphia, wanting to exchange shells.

For three reasons I have resolved to stay in town tonight. (1.) When I got down here I felt quite faint and tired and did not feel at all equal to walking back. I think it is the effect of the warm weather after the cold we have had. (2.) Probably your letter will come tonight, and I want to get it. (3.) Frank Hunter says Martin of the 'Little Nellie' mine will probably come to West Cliff tonight, and it will be well to see him.

4:45 p.m. The 'Denver and Rio Grande Timetable' I gave Cox to post more than a month ago, I found lying un-posted at the West Cliff Hotel just now. I will abuse Cox when I see him.

7:15. Bad news! I am so sorry. I thought Annie must get all right again. Do tell me exactly what is the matter, and how she suffers. I wish I could do something to help her. I don't know what I could do if I was on the spot, but I feel so helpless all this distance away. Sympathy is all that I can offer.

Talking of coming home, I *must* get back before three years if I can. I have been thinking that if I got a good situation I might save up enough to go to England for a couple of months in the summer, returning to Colorado before the cold weather. Surely nobody would have much to say against this! *Supposing* I were to turn up one July evening at the gate of Syon? But I must not be too confident in projecting what may never be possible. At the same time, if I *do* see my way to visiting England next summer or the one after, I do not know what could prevent my doing so.

There is an account of Clive's journalist, with a portrait, in *Pall Mall Budget.* In S.L.E.S. book the *recorder* would be of more importance than the finder, but if two people record the same thing I would enter both in Bibliography.

I think my taste for science was mainly inherent. I was devoted to animals when very small, and took great pleasure in an old 'Noah's Ark.' But I owe much to the impulse given my the teaching of Miss Sarah Marshall, a lady you have doubtless heard of if not seen. Of course it was mainly chance that led me to take up the Mollusca. I cannot guess who wrote the 'pard, O!' poems — I give it up.

I must say I *don't* think a man's religion is purely a personal matter any more than his actions the outcome of his religion. I entirely condemn the spirit of indifference or cowardice that will not proclaim its religion to all men. I am inclined to think that the reason why Darwin kept his theological opinions to himself was the same that prevents me from ventilating my views on astronomy, namely ignorance of the subject and consequent lack of views. Darwin felt that the evidence which convinced others was insufficient for him, so he declined to give an opinion, as a judge might when the witnesses failed to turn up.

Whatever made Annie choose Russia for her lecture? A good enough subject but rather *worn*, and one cannot get anything but second-hand information. Roberts sent me a copy of his book; it is lying about somewhere at 5. Priory. I am disposed to think well of the Law and Liberty League. Besides your letter, I got one from Mother, and *The Naturalist* this evening.

9:30. The 'Little Nellie' mine man has not come. I am tired and weary and shall go to bed.

January 20th . This letter will go out by this morning's post. It is a beautiful day. The walk up in such fine weather will do me good.

Payn is looking and feeling much better. He got the money he sent for, but it all went, it seems, to paying debts here. But I daresay he will be able to scrape together enough to get to New York, and there will stay some weeks with some friends.

Friday, Jan. 20th, 1888

Dear Frederic,

As I went out of town this morning the old engine stood at the crossing with its great 'cow-catcher', reflector, and two little American flags in front, all ready to start with the train, for it wanted only a few minutes to half-past nine. I felt quite an affection for the hideous great thing, for it does bring me my letters, and takes those I write on their homeward journey! So today, as I saw it steam out and away towards Cañon City, I knew it bore a letter to you. I walked home, and arrived quite fresh, except that my feet ached, this because my boots are getting too thin to protect my feet. I must get a new pair.

You asked for Wallis Kew's address in your letter, but I did not remember it and could not write it until I got back and referred to his letter. It is 95. Evershot Road, Stroud Green, N.

Since I came in I have been writing up the Colorado bird list from a geographical distributional point of view. Many are very interesting. Here is a list of some of the species; it may interest you: *Cinclus mexicanus* Swainson, *Regulus calendula* L., *Parus montanus* Gambel, *Sitta canadensis* L., *Certhia familiaris* var. *ruga* Bartr., *Troglodytes hiemalis* Vieill., *Cotile riparia* Say, *Loxia curvirostris* var. *americana* Wils., *L. curvirostris* var. *mexicana* Strickl., *L. leucoptera* Gym., *Oligothus cinerea* L., *Plectrophanes lapponicus* L., *Plec-*

trophanes nivalis L., *Saxicola oenanthe* L., *Mergus merganser* var. *americanus* Cass., *M. serrator* L., *Corvus corax* var. *carnivorus* Bartr., *Picus villosus* L., *Picordes tridactylus* var. *dorsalis* Baird, *Scops asio* L., *Nyctea scandica* L. *Coccyzus americanus* L., *Falco peregrinus* var. *naevius* Gmel., *Pandion haliaetus* var. *carolinensis* Gmel., *Ortyx virginiana* L., *Botaurus lentiginosus* Mont., *Archibuteo lagopus* var. *sanctijohannis* Gmel., *Aquila chrysaetus* var. *canadensis* L., *Squatarola helvetica* L., *Oxyechus vociferus* L., *Gallinago media* var. *wilsoni* Tenn., *Larus argentatus* var. *smithsonianus* Coues., *Tringa macula* L., *Numenius borealis*, *Bernicla canadensis* L., *B. branta* Pall., *Chaulelasmus strepens* L., *Dafila acuta* L., *Spatula clypeata* L., *Aix sponsa* L., *Clangula islandica* Gmel., *Fuligula marila* L., *Xena sabini* Sabin, *Sterna fluviatilis* Mann.

So you see several are quite the same as British species, while others are represented by varieties. It is remarkable what a number of sea-birds have straggled into this state from time to time. There are no less than five species of *Larus* and three of *Sterna*, besides examples of *Phalacrocorax*, *Xena*, *Hydrochelidon*, *Stercorarius*. and *Columba*. If you have any idea of taking up the geographical distribution of animals as a regular study, I can supply you with a host of interesting notes thereon.

January 21st, 10 p.m. This morning Frank Cusack came along on his buckboard and offered to take me to town. As he was coming back and I should not have to walk, I went, although I was in only yesterday, since I like the drive on a fine warm day, as today has been. I found at the postoffice a letter from Mother, enclosing one from Leslie all about his voyage to Madeira (a very good letter), and also a long epistle from Carlie, of a controversial nature (and seeming to me highly illogical), *Pall Mall Budget* and *Commonweal*.

I went up to the Cusack's to supper on our return, and have just come down from there. We have had a pleasant evening, sitting round the fire talking, varied by some singing by Miss Urquhart and Regy Cusack.

I see it stated in *Pall Mall* that marriage is on the decrease. Did you see the article? Whatever the cause, this is one of the most depressing signs of the times I have seen for a long time. Yet there are idiots who go about discouraging marriage on the grounds of improvidence and what not. Cardinal Manning says a starving man has a natural right to be fed, and I say he has an equally natural right to a wife and family, and the means of supporting them. This may seem to you an extravagant statement, but I have thought the matter over as carefully as I can, and it seems to me that any check to marriage is injurious to the welfare of the whole community and that the supposed advantages of it are wholly fallacious. If you think otherwise I will do my best to convince you at greater length.

Sunday. January 22nd. A fine warm day, the snow melting fast. I have been reading and writing, and nobody has called.

Do you remember that paper of Sutton's on atavism at Zoöl. Soc.? I have been reading over the reprint of it he lent me, and find I can't agree, so I have written a short paper on the subject and shall send it to Sutton for Zoöl. Soc., if he thinks it worth publishing. Sutton says all cases of atavism are due to germs which normally do not develop. I say they aren't, and instance the reversion of the parts of a flower to leaves, which is called atavism as defined in Sutton's paper. What think you?

I hardly know what to tell you about these lonely days. They are so uneventful and like one another. I have been indexing up my notes on the Lepidoptera of the S.L.E.S. district; that is to say, marking with letters (K for Kent, and so forth) the species in the district in my copy of South's catalogue. I am trying to get this and the London Catalogue and the Coleoptera list marked up in this way as I find it very convenient for reference. It seems almost absurd my bothering about the S.L.E.S. Fauna list out here, but in any case it is not labour lost, and judging from their present rate of movement, even three years is likely to expire before they have anything ready for publication. If you care to send me a London Catalogue and a South's list I will mark them for you in this way, copying from my own, and return them to you.

\

January 24th. Reading and writing, as usual. Brock went to town and was to have brought my mail, but forgot it and his own as well. This evening I went up to Brock's to supper, and talking, the time slipped away so that it was 10:15 when I looked at my watch, whereat I felt somewhat ashamed of myself because I believe they go to bed early, and I must have kept them up.

Mrs. Brock has lent me a number of copies of *The Youth's Companion*, as she thought the stories therein might amuse me. It appears to be something like *Cassell's Magazine* and that sort of thing.

January 25th. Brock went to town today for a load of hay, and I went with him. Going down we met Cox coming up on horseback. He had come into West Cliff by yesterday's train. On arriving in town almost the first person I saw was Ed Martin (the one who went on the hunting trip, not the Rosita Martin) who was loafing about apparently doing nothing.

I got some interesting mail: viz., a letter and two postcards from W. H. Edwards , and also copies of several of his papers (from *Papilio* and *Canad. Ent.*) and four beautiful coloured plates illustrating the genus *Colias*. A list of shells for exchange from R. Jetschin, *Science Gossip, Labor Enquirer* and sample copies of a little Socialist paper called *The Word* (published monthly at Princeton, Massachusetts).

Edwards letter is four sheets (eight pages, larger than 'sermon paper', and written on both sides , all of it extremely interesting. Here are some extracts from this letter. 'The butterflies of Colorado have been so much sought for that I have no idea there can be more than a very few new species in the state. . . .I think the state will show a greater number of species than any other. . . .I have experimented much on cold applied to pupae, and the general result has been a darkening of the forms. . . .Your explanation of the reason for the water forms being darker than the summer ones in North America seems to me reasonable.' (I said I considered the darkening due not to cold but to rapid development in the spring.) I am very glad to find Edwards thus supports my view, as I did not expect he would. When you read full details in the paper I sent to Carrington you 'll see how important this is. The Arctic Argynnids are very dark compared with the same species a few degrees to the south.

Now, *Colias eurytheme* manifests itself under three orange forms and one yellow form, in all four well-separated forms. and *eriphyle* is not only one of the four, but itself is dimorphic. having a spring or summer form and a fall or winter form. And it is this last you send me. I will retain this by your permission, as it is just what I have been seeking for the late sub-form. (This is excessively interesting to me, who know the insects, and I think you will be able to understand. I sent you *eurytheme* in a letter.) I shall give a plate to *eriphyle* soon; this is a most satisfactory case of polymorphism. (He goes on to say that the large sulphur *Colias*, of which I sent you one in a letter, is *C. alexandra* and continues: 'By the way, I named this about 1863, just when the princess came over the seas. and it is as lovely in its way as the princess in hers.! Henry Edwards (an Englishman and actor by profession, no relative of mine, but a close friend) is an authority on moths. If you like, send him examples to name.' So I wrote him a postcard on the subject.

Besides this very interesting letter. he sends reprints of 14 of his papers (one particularly interesting, with plates, on the forms of *Pieris* and its subspecies *oleracea* and *bryoniae*) and coloured plates of *Colias scudderi, C. meadi, C. eurytheme* and forms *keewaydin* and *eriphyle*, and *C. alexandra*. I may write a paper for the S.L.E.S. on these species of *Colias*. I have taken them all myself in Colorado.

Robert Jetschin, Reg. Berz. Oppeln, Germany, sends a printed list of his duplicates, and if I were in England I should certainly try to effect an exchange with him. For one thing, he has *Pisidium roseum* and as the species was described from his district, no doubt the genuine thing. Some doubt has been cast on Jeffreys' *P. roseum*, whether they are really Scholle's species. And if you could manage to get some from Jetschin and so settle the point it would be a great gain. He also has for exchange *H. arbostomum* var. *rudis* and var. *jetschini*, *Hyalina glabra* var. *striata*, *Clausilia laminata* var. *jetschini*, etc.

I see the Layardian reply in *Sci. Goss.* What a terrible fuss there is over the name. There is more breath wasted, I believe, over terms than the discussion of facts, so you did extremely well to resist the temptation of sitting on the Layard once more.

When in town, having in view that my boots were getting altogether too 'airy', I purchased ($1.35) a pair of 'overshoes', India rubber soled, warm-lined shoes that go over the boots and keep in the warmth and keep out the wet. Coming back, it was thawing so much that I got my feet wet coming across the prairie (we walked that part to ease the horses) and so was glad to have the dry overshoes to put them into when I got home. This evening I went up to Cox's, but found that Cox had gone into town again, but would be up here again tomorrow.

I saw Frank Hunter in town, and he had been to Rosita and brought back bad news for me. It seems that Martin of the 'Little Nellie' mine is short of capital and has not even enough to pay the wages of the miners. He expects to get money from the East to work the mine, but at present is so short that he will have to stop work unless he can get funds. Hunter advises me strongly not to engage myself to him until I know he has the means to pay me. And so the matter rests, as you see, in a state of considerable uncertainty. Pending the arrival of the said funds, I shall look out for anything else that may offer, and take the first reasonable thing I can get.

I imagine this is about as uninteresting a letter as I have sent you, but as Brock is going to town again tomorrow it will perhaps be best to let him post it. I hope I shall hear good news of Annie in this week's letter, which I may get tomorrow.

Jan. 26th, 1888, 6.15 p.m.

Dear Frederic,

Brock took the last week's letter to you to post this morning, and I am every moment expecting him back bearing a letter from you.

I have been writing to Edwards and entering up the Colorado butterflies and reading the papers Edwards sent me. Some of these papers are very interesting. I see for one thing that *Chinobas (Aeneis) borealis* has been discovered on the highest peaks of Colorado, and this is an arctic species found also in northern Europe. Two of the butterflies I found here, viz., *Colias alexandra* and *Satyrus charon* had already been recorded from Rosita, one Nash having found them there. One of Edwards' papers is on the forms allied to *Pieris napi*. It seems that the original form is the arctic and alpine *P. bryoniae*, and that this has developed into *P. napi* in Europe and into *P. oleracea* and *P. venosa* in America. The whole thing is worked out by Edwards in the most interesting and elaborate manner. I gather from a report in *Entom.* that Jenner Weir had something to say about this matter at S.L.E.S. once, so perhaps you know about it. I wish you would make a point of collecting specimens of *Pieris* next summer to show the seasonal variation, labeling each specimen with the exact date.

I was visited today by a flock of about a hundred birds, which I take to be a sort of waxwing, *Bombycilla cedrorum*. They all sat on the top boughs of the quaking asp trees, and kept on making one remark, 'Che-e-e-, Che-e-e', the purport of which I could not gather. After a while they all flew away.

8.45. No sign of Brock.

Here is a good bit out of one of Edwards' papers: He is speaking of the value of hobbies: 'I knew of a lawyer who at sixty was ordered by his physician to find some employment out of doors which would occupy his time and thoughts, unless he wished to be speedily gathered to his fathers, and he conceived the idea of making a collection of limestone fossils, as they were abundant in the region in which he lived, though hitherto he had known nothing of fossils or of natural history. And this he followed with delight for years, chiseling out the beautiful fossils as laboriously and as skillfully as if stone-cutting had been his trade, studying them and arranging them in cabinet. He lived twenty happy years after that change of base. and left a collection which is famous for its magnitude and value. And, on the other hand, we have all known men who in the prime of their mental and physical strength have retired from active business and have died from sheer vacuity of mind, after twiddling their thumbs in an arm-chair for a few years, who might have reached fourscore if they had had some hobby to ride. So I commend butterflies to elderly gentlemen or retired gentlemen in need of an occupation. The young need no recommendation. It is always enough to show them the way in any branch of natural history and they follow it with ever increasing enthusiasm. Studies of this kind keep young people out of mischief and old people out of the grave, and that is one good reason for cultivating natural history.' (W. H. Edwards, *Canadian Entomologist*, 1884. p. 82.). What do you think of that?

Edwards says the larvae of *Lymnitis* hybernate in a rolled-up leaf and bind the leaf-stalk on to the bough by silken thread, so that it may not fall off in the autumn. Cute of them.

January 27th, 4.25. p.m. Brock did come home last night at past eleven o'clock, but quite forgot my mail, which is rather too bad of him, as I specially asked him not to forget it. However, he has gone in again today and says he will remember this time, so I hope I may get your letter tonight. If not, I must get into town tomorrow.

I saw Cox this morning. The Colorado Springs place seems to have fallen through, which is very unfortunate, but Cox has written to Pueblo, and thinks he can get me a place there. Lees came down here today, and I walked up to the Cusacks' with him. Up there he showed me a book on birds by Ruskin (stupidly I have forgotten the name, very absurd indeed). Ruskin proposes new scientific names for the birds and shows a most ridiculous ignorance of ornithology. Lees is rather fond of reading Ruskin, but is very angry with his remarks on Darwin, which are, as you know, absurd enough.

When I got up this morning not a cloud was visible anywhere, and the day is quite overpoweringly hot. I am now writing with the door wide open and no fire.

6:00 p.m. This is very disappointing. Brock has returned and brought four letters and a paper (of which more later), but they are all from the U. S .— no letter from you and no English mail at all. Brock says he got no English mail either, so I suppose something has delayed it this week.

January 28th, 9:10 p.m. I have just been reading a most admirable article on *Lathraea squamania* in the Jan. *Science Gossip*. If you have not read it, do so at once.

The mail I got last night was as follows (1.) Letter from Simpson of Ogalalla. Nebraska, with an interesting list of Nebraska shells and a list of species found by him in the N. E. corner of Colorado, including five new to my list. (2.) Letter from Westgate of Houston, Texas, with a list of marine shells found at Galveston, and also addenda to Houston list. He finds *Helix labyrinthica* at Houston. You know this species has been found fossil in England. (3.) A letter from Orcutt of San Diego. He is going to lend me a lot of American scientific magazines. He wants to join the Conch. Soc. if they will take his papers (*W. Am. Sci.*) in place of subscription. (4.) Reprint of paper on the life history of *Argynnis edwardsi* (a Colorado species) from *Canad. Ent.*, Jan. 1888, sent by W. H. Edwards. (5.) Specimen copy of *Common Sense*, the most idiotic of all the idiotic little papers of which I have rec'd. specimen copies.

9:00 p.m. I am disgusted. Brock went to town today and forgot once more to bring my mail. He frequently forgets his own, and he forgot the Cusacks' as well this time, out of pure forgetfulness, but it is very annoying. He expressed his great regret, and offered to take me in on Monday, which seems to be the best thing to be done. Unfortunately I have gone lame in one foot (the result of walking too much in worn out boots) or I would walk into town tomorrow (Sunday). I met old Splann going down to the Cliff, and nearly asked him to fetch the mail in case Brock should forget, but thought I would not.

All today I have been helping Bassick haul oats (as cut with the straw, for food for the horses and cattle). Cox spends all his time in town and leaves Bassick to look after the ranch, and he asked me to help him today.

The oats and hay are stacked on the lower part of the ranch. and it is necessary to haul up some to the barn so as to have something on which to feed the animals in case of a snowstorm. First of all. it was necessary to catch the horses. This having been accomplished with some difficulty, they were hitched on to the hayrack, and we went down and got up a load of oats, which we stowed away in the loft over the stable. Pitching oats or hay is not very hard work, and as a change rather pleasant. As we shall be working again tomorrow. I am staying up at Cox's for the night.

Brock went into town with his wife and child, and they brought back with them a pig in a box. Close by my house they got stuck in a snowdrift, whereat great consternation of Mrs. B. and child, and greater consternation of the pig, who contrived to upset the box it was in, out of the waggon, and make its escape. So Brock came up here to get help in hunting for the lost pig, and Bassick and I went out with him on the search. It is a bright moonlight night, and before very long we espied the porcine animal out on the prairie.

Brock's dog 'Jack' gave chase and caught it by the ear, and held it in spite of all the pig's efforts to escape, although the pig was at least twice as big as the dog. We came up, and Bassick tied the pig's legs together with a rope, and then I held the animal until they had fetched the waggon into which he was put and successfully hauled up to Brock's.

Coming back to the house, an unmistakable odour announced the vicinity of a skunk, but we did not see it. Brock was very anxious that I should not send an account of this pig affair to any of my Socialist papers.

Sunday, January 29th. After breakfast, Bassick and I took the hay-rack and went down to haul a load of oats. It was hot work pitching in the load under a blazing sun. This is a queer climate. There was I down there today, working in my shirt-sleeves and feeling half-roasted. yet for all I can tell, tomorrow may be so cold that I daren't go out without a coat, scarf, and thick gloves. The heat after the previous cold affects everyone and makes them feel tired.

When we had got the load on, the horses could not pull it, as there was some slippery snow and ice just there, and in their endeavours they broke off the tongue of the waggon. So we had to trudge up to the house and get a piece of wood to splice on for a tongue, and a shovel to get the slippery snow away, but finally we got the horses hitched up again and pulled up to the corral. By the time we had stowed the oats away in the barn, it was getting on for evening, so we came into the house and had supper. Afterwards I went up to Brock's to get some Swede turnips (Rutabagas, they call them here) which he had promised to let me have. Walter Stratton came in while I was there, and I left him and Brock discussing a horse-trade. I hear Brock's pig is feeling unwell today, and no wonder!

January 30th. I rode down to town with Brock in his waggon and got your letter at last.

I am very glad to see that the news of Annie is more cheerful, but you say her general health is not very good. Thank Annie much for the additional list of Fauna and Flora. The water-hen in Syon Lodge Garden is a queer find! I once saw one in the Brent at Perivale; no doubt this one came from the Brent. *Rubus fruticans* will I suppose be *discolor*. I am glad you got out a list of addenda to B. P. Fauna. I trust Read will send me a copy of the Annual Report when published. I wrote Read a post card (I fancy two), but he never replied, nor did he say anything about some seeds I sent him via 5 Priory, so I have not written to him since.

You are fortunate to have got the lists from Meyer. What fishes does he record ? And are any of the species remarkable?

Children of Haycombe, I am looking forward to, but it has not yet come. Books are always late.

Clive must feel very much the fate of his employer, It is a sort of thing that haunts one for a long time in a most unpleasant way. As to Pickwick — I never could read it through, though it has amused me for half-an-hour or so at times. On the whole, I do not care much for it; it is not in my line.

As to my American accent, I don't think it is noticeable, but I am afraid I do sometimes 'reckon', etc., when talking to Americans. I must try not to get into habitually talking 'American.' I did not send the *Labor Enquirer* so soon as the letter, so no doubt they will arrive later if Cox posted them.

Tell Annie I do take some exercise, and now the weather is better shall take more. I think I must be taking care of myself sufficiently because I am so very well. All sorts of people round have been feeling queer at times, but I have been well enough to get about and do all I wanted to all along, the lame foot, which is almost right now, being the only thing that has bothered me at all. It is hard to say exactly what the influence of my environment out here is. Perhaps you can judge as well from my letters as I can tell you.

Physically, it improves my health. Mentally, the isolation etc., tends to a slower habit of thought perhaps and rather less mental activity, though it leaves my mind clearer for my work.

I have written a paper on insect variation out here I think I could never have written in England when going to town etc., every day.

It makes me value things in England more, as is natural. At first I felt a good deal disgusted with the dishonesty of people, but I am every day getting more proofs of their real good nature and kindliness, and I feel, though I have no friend out here, properly speaking, that I am a citizen among citizens, and as such shall come to no great harm unless from my own stupidity. So altogether I feel more kindly towards people than I did, and more convinced (the opposite of Carlie's view) that their evil practices are the result of an evil system, and not their innate wickedness. (I except born criminals, whom I class as insane.) I also feel more able to 'rustle' for myself than before, and each new experience adds to this.

Payn has had a telegram from home begging him to stay out a little longer, and so he is going to camp out with Preston for a month, he says. He will not like camping out at this time of year, and Preston is (in my opinion) an ass, and is a born loafer and whiskey drinker. Being alone is not very nice, but it is better than being with Payn, in every way. 1 was heartily glad to get rid of him. Besides, I see a good deal of the neighbours now.

Certainly Annie could improve the story vastly, but I fancy it would need a good deal of 'improving.' The fact is, I don't think I am much of a hand at story-telling anyhow. *My* novel ought to have about ten revised and amended editions before I should get it into shape.

Cold is not so very bad, much better than wind, or even snow. It doesn't interfere with me if I keep a good fire going and put something warm on my feet. Mead never said he was riled.

I think I found *Brachypterus urticae* at B. P. I believe it is very common. I might get temporary work for the Agric. Dept. during the summer, or they might send me to investigate, and pay expenses.

Perhaps, after all, the American 'humbug' is only custom, and a good deal of it no worse than 'Dear Sir' and 'Yours truly' and all that, and harms nobody. It rather staggers anyone fresh from England, though.

Barker hasn't yet sent me the 1888 S.L.E.S. card, but no doubt it will come.

I think Darwin fully enters into 'use and disuse' but cannot give you book and page.

I believe F. R. Fitzgerald asking me to vote for him for committee of P.N.S. and offered to vote for me in return! I think though, he has done a little useful ornithological work. E. Collier was 'working up *Limnaea* but nothing has come of it.

The other mail I got was: Letter from Olive and one from Mother enclosed. Letter from J. A. Singley, with list of shells he has found in Texas (the list includes *Planorbis dilatatus. Hyalina fulva,* etc.). Letter from Lorenzo G. Yates about fossil plants in Colorado. Postcard from Roberts saying that Wilcock has engraved about 80 *Unios* and *Anodons,* including two that you sent. At present he has only printed twelve copies of his work, which is too small an edition to be of any use. Postcard from Smithsonian, notifying receipt of box from me. *Pall Mall Budget, Commonweal,* and *Ent. Mags.* Respecting Matthews' scheme for new Ent. Soc. (*Entom.* p. 10) I should think it would be much better to develop it in connection with one of the existing societies than to start a new one. There are too many competing societies already.

The white *Rummia* (p. 15) is interesting to me. I wish they had said what results Incrifield got in the report of Ent. Soc. You will remember the pamphlet Galton sent me about this. I should like to see Pryer's book on Japanese butterflies. It would much assist my work. Walker's account

of the fauna of Gibralter (*E.M.M.* p. 175) is very interesting. I suppose his naming is to be relied on. The review of *Darwin's Life* by F. P. Pascoe is also of much interest. So much for the mail.

I am staying in town till the mail comes in, as Cox went out with Brock and has left me his horse to ride up on. I could have gone in the waggon, but having an animal to ride on, I thought I might as well stay, as the night will be warm enough to not be unpleasant, and there is a moon.

6:30 p.m. The mail has come in, bringing *Children of Haycombe,* which I am very glad to get, also letter from Averell enclosing December *Conch. Exch.* Letter from F. R. Latchford of Ottawa, wanting to exchange shells, and a letter from Leighton (Sec'y. Kansas Nat. Hist. Soc'y but now at San Diego), and *Labor Enquirer.* As I am here I had better send this.

Jan. 31st, 1888

Dear Frederic,

After posting your letter last night I went to the stable to get the horse Cox had left for me.

'Sam', the young man in charge, directed me to go round to the yard where I should find the horse. Now the yard gate was not latched, and so far as I could make out, could not be fastened, so going in I left it swung to, as I had found it. The horse, seeming disinclined to be ridden, moved away when I went up to him with the halter and got into the corner where was the gate.

> *Were the horse not a common animal, to be seen any day on the streets, it would be regarded with wonder and amazement . . . .. Added to all these are the psychological characteristics—the wonderful combination of intelligence with docility, which makes the animal useful to man. A well-known breeder and lover of horses was so moved by all these excellences, that he declared that the one great error in evolution was the derivation of man from a mischievous, ill-behaved creature of the monkey group, instead of a majestic, sagacious beast such as the horse!*

> *Cockerell, Zoology*

Naturally, the gate swung open, and out went the horse. Sam was very busy hitching up a team and could not come just then, and I found my efforts to catch him unavailing after a chase all round the town. It was easy enough to get to him, but that was a very different matter from catching him. Finally, however, I got him close, and Sam coming out to help, we drove him into a shed and secured him. Now that the horse was caught, there was not much to regret in the delay, since the moon rose at eight (when I started), and I had a ride in the moonlight instead of darkness.

Once on the animal I began to discover his peculiarities. He had only two methods of getting along, one being a walk as if he were going to a funeral, and the other a kind of shuffle, with a motion of the legs as if on a treadmill. The walking pace, clearly, would not get me home before morning so, much against his inclinations, I kept him at the shuffle nearly all the way, and took two hours to get home at that.

Cox, I found, was up at Brock's, so I went up there, having some mail for him. I found Lees also there. Then I came back to my house. It appears that they may be wanting a clerk in connection with the 'busted' bank at West Cliff, but the wages are only $30 a month. If I take any steps in the matter after enquiry, of course you shall have full particulars. Cox is going to see Bell (the manager) about it today. Cox thinks Bell is a knave.

This morning, after I had finished reading *The Children of Haycombe*, I went up to help Bassick haul oats, and have been working there all the rest of the day.

The Children of Haycombe: I like this story very much, except that it ends in a rather melancholy way. As a sermon, I think the effect would have been better if Bee had survived to win the affection and regard of the village children and played with them as an equal, nor do I think this would have been contrary to the probabilities of the case. The moral, that very much of the apparent badness of some people is a reflex of our bad treatment of them is an entirely sound one, and one that might be preached with much reason to others than children. I believe there is no human being who, treated well, will not act kindly in return, except those few who from inherited defects are to be classed among the insane. At the same time, I very fully admit that it is a most difficult thing to know exactly what treatment is good for this one and that, so that half the evil is the result of well-intentioned blundering.

The cruelty of the children towards Bee is not at all exaggerated, as anyone who has been to a boarding school will admit (some schools, though, are exceptions).

There were a lot of Cowen children used to be great friends with the Wimpole St. infants and were continually coming to the house. I think their father was a doctor. There is one thing Messr. Blackie and son ought to be written to strongly about. Why is there no date on the title page? It ought to be made criminal to publish a book without a date.

It occurs to me that you ought to tell Barker, in the reports of S.L.E.S., to call you not 'W. Fenn' but 'W.F.C. Fenn', this because there is a well-known entomologist called C. Fenn, living at Lee, Kent (who described *Monagria brevilinea,*. for one thing).

February 1st. I forgot to mention that while I was away yesterday Payn and Preston came up here and fetched away a few things (axe, clothes, etc.) they needed for their 'camping out', and Payn left a note for Lees, with request to me to deliver it at very earliest opportunity. He also said that if I needed an axe I was to buy one in West Cliff and put it down to him. It amuses me the way he gives away what he has not at present got. I don't at all want an axe, since I saw all my wood now, but if I did I have no idea of helping to increase debts which his people must eventually pay off. However, Payn means it very kindly, no doubt.

I went up to Brock's today to deliver the note to Lees, but he had gone to his cabin in the mountains and would not return till Saturday, so I left the note for him at Brock's. The rest of the day I have been writing up the Middlesex Fauna and Flora book, etc., and writing letters. I bought 50 cents worth of beef when last in town and Brock gave me some Swede turnips, so I have made a big stew today, which is pretty good eating and will last some time. Tomorrow being Thursday I rather thought of going into town, but I shan't unless I can get a lift, as it seems very uncertain whether the English mail came in to-night, judging from the last two weeks.

There are several flocks of bluebirds (*Sialia*) about today, the first I have seen this year.

February 2nd. Everyone said this fine weather could not last, and accordingly this morning broke dull and all day a little snow fell, not enough to lie till the evening, when it came down sufficiently to cover the ground a few inches. Seeing the snow coming, I got in a supply of wood and wrote the rest of the morning.

In the afternoon I went up to the Cusacks', calling at Brock's on the way. Cox and Brock are starting out for Cañon City. They go into town tonight and to Cañon by the morning train. I gave Cox to post, letters to Olive, Singley, etc., which I hope he will not forget. (I specially cau-

tioned him.) I took Mrs. Cusack *The Story of an African Farm* to read. I am rather curious to know how it will strike her. I told her that if I came up soon after she finished it she would abuse me most frightfully, but if I came up about a week after, she would say she was rather glad she had read it. She has been reading *Eagle's Nest* and likes it altogether.

Mrs. Cox is the most cultivated and thoughtful person I have come across out here as yet. I sat talking for a long while until supper was ready, and after supper we had some songs, the most notable one being 'Douglas, Douglas, tender and true' (which was written by Mrs. Craik).

Nell has only one puppy now, another having been killed. This one is quite lively and very fat. It is called by the distinguished name of Hamlet, though the first name proposed was George Washington — because it never told a lie.

February 3rd. The day was very fine and warm, so after breakfast I strolled up towards Cox's, reading a rather pretty story called 'After the war' in the December *Century* (borrowed from the Cusacks).

I had just finished the story when, looking up, I saw old Splann and Bassick coming along, and they met me with the extraordinary piece of news that Payn was up at the Splanns — had driven up yesterday, and very bad with gout. Old Splann was coming down to get some laudanum Payn wanted, to ease the pain. So I went down to the house and got the laudanum, and then over to Splann's, where I found Payn sitting before the fire, wrapped up and looking a regular invalid. He seemed to be in some pain, though I have no doubt he rather exaggerated it. Altogether, I am glad he is at the Splann's. They are kind people, and will take excellent care of him, and he will be in every way better than in town or camping out.

After talking with him a little while, I came back again. The effect of the bright sun on the snow is very beautiful, though very trying to the eyes. I wish you and Annie could see the mountains now. Used to them as I am, I could not help stopping several times to admire them. Old Splann talks of going to town tomorrow, and will bring this week's mail.

February 4th. I have been feeling out of sorts today (dyspepsia) and consequently I have done practically nothing. About midday I took a walk up to Bassick's and got him to bake me some bread. Otherwise I have been sitting by the fire reading the *Century* (Nov. & Dec., 1887) and feeling rather 'low.' The day too, is depressing — cold and cloudy, with every indication of a coming snowstorm. Old Splann did not go to town, no doubt on account of the weather, and so I get no mail; in fact nobody has been by at all since the day before yesterday.

I have been thinking a good deal about your saying that you were dissatisfied and sometimes wish you were out with me. There are three points of view from which this may be regarded, viz., yours, Annie's, and mine. (Other people also would have a good deal to say but that is not to the present purpose.) Now from your point of view: I can quite understand that Smith's is not bliss, but you will not remain forever in Smith's. You cannot tell now what may be your fate, but surely you may hope in time for something satisfactory. Look at Bowdler Sharpe. He was in your place once. Now he is as happily placed as a man can expect to be under existing conditions.

Suppose you came out here. I don't think you would get a much better place than at Smith's (the salary would probably be higher though) and the chances of getting more congenial work would be infinitesimal. I had great objections to Leslie coming out, because his character is not formed, and the influences of this country would be most disastrous for him. I have not that fear on your account, but I think it would be on the whole a very bad thing for you unless you returned in a year or two, in which case. why come at all? This is a farming and a mining country. You are neither a farmer nor a miner. Smith's is clerking work and I imagine honest. What you would get out here would be similar work, and probably dishonest, being in some business firm. The sole and only advantage would be that you would earn money a little faster than in England. Possibly I am prejudiced by my peculiar circumstances, but I cannot conceive any sane man (not being a farmer or a miner) and, knowing this country, coming out here when he can live in England. (unless it were for some special appointment offering peculiar advantages).

From Annie's point of view, I should think it would be an unmixed evil, but she is with you to state her own views. Probably if you were actually to propose to depart she would decline to allow you to do anything of the sort! I hope so. From my point of view of course I should be delighted to have you out here — while I was here, but the time will come for my departure, and then I should be extremely unwilling to abandon you. And, so far as I am concerned, I would much rather forego your companionship out here for a little time than for the years to come after my return. (N.B. Annie would write to you anyway, and I should read those letters, but I should have to write to Annie then!). So altogether, I judge it would be 'out of the frying-pan into the fire' and I don't recommend it.

All the while you have been reading this you have probably been wondering why I take a little passing thought so seriously. Well, it is because the matter seemed a serious one, and you never know whether questions that seem trivial today may not be of practical importance tomorrow. So I want you to know all I can tell you of the facts of the case, so that, should it be needful, you may better judge for yourself what to do.

Sunday, February 5th. Darwin on 'Use and disuse.' Darwin deals pretty fully with this subject in *Origin of Species* (6th Ed., pp. 108-112).

So Herbert Spencer has certainly discovered a 'mare's nest', if the essay you speak of is of recent date.

Today has been fine and sunny, but not warm. I am getting over my ill feeling and shall doubtless be all right tomorrow. It is about time I went into town again, but as yet no opportunity has offered for a lift.

On getting up this morning I found numerous coyote-tracks all round the house, made last night.

I should like to have seen the animals, as at present I have only seen *Canis latrans* in the distance. (This is the same species as the 'wolves' in Epping Forest, you know.)

Feb. 6th, 1888

Dear Frederic,

Seeing that there was no chance of getting a lift, and the day being fine, I decided to walk to town, starting at nine and getting here at eleven. The whiteness of the snow was so blinding that I tied Olive's green silk scarf over my eyes, dulling the glare of the snow, and making the rocks look like pure chloride of silver.

Lees has come into town (from Beddoes') since I arrived, and will take me out. I got a good lot of mail, viz., your letter (enclosing card of S.L.E.S. (for which all thanks).

You should get W. West of Greenwich to look for *Assivinea* and *Hydrobia similis* and *ventrosa* in his district. Also he may find good *H. nemoralis* vars. at Crayford, and white variety of *H. aspersa* at Dartford. Tell him also of the Crayford Pleistocene fossil-pit on the road between Crayford and Erith, to the left hand side going from Erith. I am very glad to hear of your success with the story. How is it to appear? Send me a copy to read. Of course I will come to the children's party, only, by the way, it is on the 25th — a fortnight ago! Why didn't you let me know

in time? I congratulate Clive on his success, though perhaps the *Sportsman* is not the paper it would be most desirable to be on. I am sorry my letters are not regular, but I am afraid it can't be helped.

The other mail rec'd. was letters: (1.) From Mother. I am sorry to hear Miss Plummer is ill. (2.) From Carlie — quite mad on receiving telegram from Ruskin, the latter part of the letter written in J. R.'s lodgings at Sandgate. I am very glad of this good fortune for Carlie and Olive. It must delight them, and they will remember it for a long while after. (3.) From 'Grammie', enclosing letters from Leslie and Douglas. Leslie's a very good one. (4.) Postcard from Taylor. (5.) Letter from Farlow, saying that I sent him a fungus, *Aecidium aquilegiae* Pers., from here 'which has not been recorded before in this country I believe', which is satisfactory. (6.) From O. P. Cambridge, who at present can name only one spider of those I sent him: *Azalena naevia* Hentz., though he gives the generic names of the others. (7.) From Hy. Edwards of New York saying he will be pleased to name Colorado moths. (8.) From Douglas. (9.) From J. M. Fry. (Syracuse. N.Y.) wanting to exchange shells. (10.) From Morrison, of Ft. Lewis., Colorado, a nice letter about the Colorado Ornithological Association Papers. *Pall Mall Budget, Industrial Review* (from Sherborn), *Commonweal*, and *Labor Enquirer*.

Feb. 6th, 1888

Dear Frederic,

I duly posted your letter, and *Children of Haycombe* (which is returned with grateful thanks), and rode home with Cardy Lees. Before starting I expended the vast sum of 20 cents on a 'shin bone', which is said to be first rate for soup.

February 7th, 10 p.m. After breakfast I sat down to write a few letters, and then started out to visit Payn and the Cusacks, intending to get back early in the afternoon. Arriving at

Splann's I found Payn considerably better and more cheerful. The Splanns seem very kind to him. Old Splann brought him a lot of fruit from town the other day, but he cannot eat it. I sat a long while talking to Payn, and did not get away till nearly three. (I found up there an old 1885 *Century* with drawings of the Civil War by Harry Fenn! I suppose this is not the same as the cousin you spoke of?

Then I went up to the Cusacks. Mrs. C. had begun *African Farm* at the wrong end, having read the last three chapters. She seemed interested, but it puzzled her, and we had a long discussion over the theories advanced in the book. She had also been reading *Happy Boy* and liked it very much. Talking over these and other matters the time slipped away until it was supper time, so I stayed for the evening. As usual we had songs after supper, this time 'Darby & Joan', 'Home, Sweet Home', 'He was a little tin soldier', etc. Mrs. Cusack, being a person with ideas, is like an oasis in the desert out here, and an extremely nice old lady anywhere. I wish you could know her personally.

February 8th. I don't know what to tell you about today. I have been in all day (except that I went out to get a fresh supply of wood) writing letters, and packing up moths to Hy. Edwards.

I have written to tell Morrison of Ft. Lewis I will join his Colorado Ornithologists Association, and I am going to try to work up a paper on 'The Insect Food of Birds in Colorado', to be published by the Ass'n., only of course it will be a long while before I can get it finished.

Henry Edwards writes that I shall probably get some new species of moths here, 'especially among the obscure Noctuidae.' I found a pretty little freshwater alga in Swift Creek this morning when I went to get water. I have preserved a specimen for Farlow.

I enclose a cutting out of *Industrial Review* that will amuse you and Annie. You might safely offer a prize to anyone who could read it through

without a slip and without hesitation. At the same time, although I laugh at the names they give 'organic' compounds, I quite recognise the necessity and utility of them. To those who know nothing of chemistry, short names would be no more intelligible, while for chemists it is much easier to comprehend a long name compounded of certain well-known syllables, just on the same principle that a language of words composed of letters is easier and in the end more simple than one in which every word has a separate sign for itself.

To understand the nature of a compound, its components must be carried in the head, and short names would not only fail by not indicating their nature but would be too infinitely numerous (in the case of organic compounds) to be remembered. Of course, whenever a compound comes to be popularly talked about, it must have a short name, e.g., 'dynamite.' The system of varietal nomenclature I proposed in the *Zoölogist* (Dec., 1885 I think it was), was quite on the above principle.

February 9th. Mrs. Cusack wanted me to do her some pictures of the country, for which she would pay me, but I don't know whether I can do anything worth having; scenery is not my forte. However, I thought I would do one today, but found there was not a scrap of suitable paper in the place. So, thinking it over, and having in view the prospect of mail (I meant to go for that tomorrow), I walked down to town and walked back again, except that a man named Samson (native of Lincolnshire) gave me a lift for about three quarters of a mile. I could not get any good paper after all in town, but got some that I think will do.

I was very well pleased with my mail: Letter from you in answer to which: The blizzard didn't bother *me* at all but it might have been the cause of delay of the letter. I know a great many trains were snowed up and mail delayed. The letter was posted a day late (Tuesday).

I found a few slugs at Worthing (see *Naturalist's World*, 1884, account of walking tour in Sussex). Your account of Annie and Sir M. M. is a little confused. You say he had been called away to Osborne, and then continue, 'He prescribed a little fresh treatment', etc. I suppose you mean the other doctor did. If I remember right.

Carlie once found some *Pisidium annicum* at Homslow; ask him about it. I hope Carlie won't knot himself up altogether over the Miss Hill work. I must write to him about it. 1 never heard of Payn, senior, instructing Payn to return; quite the contrary. Whence did Carlie get the idea?

I see you read your lecture. Could you send me the MS to read? I am sure you would like Lady B. if you knew her better. She is quite an ideal Grannie, though a little too behind the times to enter into all our ideas. I think it is rather unkind of Annie to object to your reporting on her health, because she knows I am anxious to know, especially now. Will she say why she objects? Of course I did not think she agreed with all you said, but I like to have her notes on the letter, where she disagrees, so that I may see exactly where it is.

Do you remember the distinction I made between 'actual' and 'moral' right? The same applies to duties. If, as your argument seems to indicate, the *actual* right is a man's rights and the *moral* his duties. That quite alters the argument, though I do not by any means admit it. Even in that case, *right* becomes at the bottom of *more* importance than duty, as duty (so understood) may be a mistake altogether. But, as I said before, to my mind, duty and right are synonymous.

Talking of the clerkship, I went to see Bell at the bank today, and found he would not require anyone at present. I was rather relieved at this. I confess, had he offered anything, I should have felt bound to take it, but from what I hear of him I would rather have nothing to do with him.

You shall have abundant notes on variation. I am glad you are working up the subject. Get Elan Shaw to name your grasshoppers (he is a member of S.L.E.S.).

I won't fight over Mary Anderson. I've nothing in the world against her, except that it seems to me that the necessary thing in a play is good acting rather than good looks, and so when people say, 'I enjoy that play; Mary Anderson is beautiful', I feel rather angry, as if they had said 'I *did* like that book. It *is* so nicely bound!'

The bomb at Chicago was thrown by some idiot in the crowd; obviously the men on the platform didn't throw it! The feeling was, of course, some 'anarchist' threw the bomb. 'These are 'anarchists' and are practically responsible, so we'll hang them!' Which I need not say was foolish and unjust.

I *was* taken aback at your asking for 'The Socialist Creed according to T.D.A.C.' I thought if there was one person whose views on that subject had been crammed down your throat till you were perfectly sick of them, it was the said TDAC. However, I will see what I can do for you.

Every ounce of that is imported into England is exchanged for English goods, and therefore, economically equivalent to an English product. [This sentence was in capital letters! Ed.]

An increase in foreign population means an increase in the demand for ironware, cotton goods, cutlery, etc., all of which are made in England and exchanged for wheat, meat, etc. As a matter of fact, *under natural conditions* population does not increase to starvation limit; experience proves the contrary. Natural selection decreases the average fertility after a certain limit is reached, because one surviving out of many is usually less fit for life than one surviving out of one or two offspring, and hence more highly developed animals do not develop so numerously as those less developed, and vice versa. If you do not understand this, I will go into the matter at some length.

I consider environment of all the importance in the world in determining the character of an animal, e.g., surly or affectionate. Carlie made the absurd blunder of comparing the varieties of dogs (spaniel, pointer, etc.) to good, bad, etc., men. instead of to Negro, Indian, etc. And it seems as if you were on the brink of doing likewise. I believe there are very few if any moral qualities that may not be profoundly affected by environment. You may say that your burglar is just as bad morally when he has no need to burgle and therefore does not (I say nothing of the kind), but practically the evil is cured. You might as well tell me I am just as ill really out here as if I were in London, as I am only well because I don't breathe a fog as thick as pea soup. But don't you see this is a 'reductio ad absurdum' of your 'morality' argument? Why, to argue on that line, I have 'morally' committed several murders, stolen all sorts of things, and done everything that is preposterous, and have 'morally' been hung. drawn and quartered for my offences, for I suppose it is possible to imagine circumstances under which one might do all sorts of wickedness.

I can assure you, there is considerable sense in the Christian prayer — 'to be delivered from temptation.' I am glad Annie is reading *Minister's Charge.* I think it is a very good book, only it 'ends in the middle', like *Merely Friends.* I shall want to know what Annie thinks of it.

I am certainly 'open to conviction.' I wish someone would convince me. 1 get no particular pleasure from contemplating what seems to me the absolutely rotten state of society and commerce, and would be only too grateful to anyone who could persuade me that things were not so radically wrong as they seem. Perhaps in some ways it is well that Annie and I should not agree, because I am certainly indiscreet and hasty in my conclusions sometimes, and Annie helps to keep that in check. Perhaps someday we shall find a common opinion somewhere midway between the views we now hold.

I agree with your opinion of Ruskin. Colorado would suit anyone as far as climate goes. The cutting you enclose about the city man and Baccarat is very good.

The other mail rec'd. today was: Letter from Mother. Letter from Coulter, with names of some plants I sent him. Letter from Tutt, a long and very nice one. He writes on School Board paper which, strangely enough, is scented (and the scent is quite strong even after the fortnight's journey). Query: Why does the Board scent its paper? A matter for the attention of rate-payers — extravagance of Board in the purchase of scent! Must write to the papers about it. Tutt says he was 'half-ashamed' of his share in the '*Lycaena* discussion in *Entom.*'

Postcard from W. H. Edwards. He seems to have a poor opinion of the Smithsonian. He writes, 'Don't waste insects on the Smithsonian. No one there is capable of determining a new species from an old one.' He sends his *Catalogue of the Diurnal Lepidoptera of America North of Mexico* — quite a book, with 95 pages. It is a very full and detailed list and will be of infinite use to me. It was good of him to send it. *Industrial Review* (from Sherborn) and *Young Men's Journal* (sample copies from Orcutt, who publishes it), also *West Amer. Scientist* for December.

February 10th. I have been working up the Colorado butterfly list from Edwards' catalogue, which gives localities. The Colorado list now numbers 139 species and 16 vars., not a bad number for a single state. Some of the genera are very largely represented, e.g., *Argynnis* with 14 species, *Thecla* 10, *Lycaena* 17, *Pamphila* 19, but the Satyridae are not numerous. You may be interested to know that there is a variety of *Papilio machaon* (var. *aliaska* Scud.) found in Oregon, British America, and Alaska.

I have also written a long letter to Tutt in reply to his, giving him notes on the American vars. of British species for his variety paper. Nobody has called today, and except Becky Splann and 'her young man' out riding, nobody has been by.

February 11th. Here is the Socialist creed according to T.D.A.C.:

Axioms.

1. The more perfect and harmonious development of humanity is both desirable and possible.

2. A true society is necessary for such development. Definition. A true society is one in which all having equal opportunities, work together for the common good (and thereby for their own good) to the best of their capacity.

3. The monopoly of land and capital, and all forms of oppression are contrary to true society and ought to be suppressed. The suppression of these is the present aim of the Socialist party. This may be brought about by peaceful discussion.

If force is used to prevent peaceful propaganda, it is permissible to use force to secure that right. Strangely, this is part of the written constitution of the United States, but I am not sure whether it exists in the English constitution. Lincoln recognised the right to rebel as one of the privileges of the American citizen, *vide* also the 'Declaration of Independence.'

If a majority is in favour of a measure. but can by no means convince the minority, it is permissible to boycott.

It shows the wide distribution of Lichens that, of the four Colorado species named for me by Dr. Coulter, *Placodium elegans* has also been found in Scotland, *Parmelia conspersa* is recorded also for California and Yorkshire, and *Peltigera horizontalis* occurs in Westmoreland. The other one, *Collema laciniatum*, I cannot find any British record of. I enclose two lichens for exhibition at the S.L.E.S., together with a note thereon.

Cox, Brock, and Frank Cusack all went to town today. I gave Brock Tutt's letters to post, but not this of yours, as I had not got it ready, and besides, I intend to get into town early next week if I can, and I prefer posting your letters myself.

Talking of Tutt, here is an example of the unwisdom of writing without notes. Tutt wanted to know of any vars. of *Leucania unipuncta* for his variety paper, and I wrote him a hasty postcard in reply, giving him var. *umbrosus* Grote. Now *umbrosus* is a var. of *Heliothis armigera* and has nothing to do with *Leucania*, but I was thinking of *Heliothis* at the time, and stupidly mixed them up. Of course I explained fully in my letter, so no harm will come of it, but if I had not remembered what I had done and corrected the mistake, we should have had Tutt publishing an imaginary var. *umbrosus* of *Leucania*. The moral is obvious.

I made an attempt at a painting for Mrs. Cusack on the paper I got at West Cliff, but it is no use. I must get some drawing paper. This paper is very inferior and very thin. It was the only paper they had without lines. I also packed up a lot of plants for Dr. Coulter.

In the afternoon, not feeling quite up to the mark, I thought a walk would do me good (which it did), so I started out over the prairie. Presently I met Frank Cusack and he had brought me four letters, or at least two and a postcard , viz., a ridiculously Ruskinian letter from Olive, enclosing a more sober one from Mother, wherein I see that R. D. Powell has been made 'Physician extraordinary to the Queen!' and Olive Schreiner is the daughter of an Eastbourne schoolmaster and lives in lodgings with another authoress in London where she is writing another book. Mother thinks *African Farm* is 'strong and clever and intensely interesting, but morbid and rather unwholesome.' I am inclined to agree with her.

Letter from Jas. H. Perriss, of Joliet, Illinois, wanting to exchange shells. Postcard from Douglas, saying that he is sending a *Harpers* in which an account of B. P., and postcard from Walter Homback, an egg collector at Silver Cliff, to whom I wrote. From his handwriting I do not expect much of him, but I must go up and see him one day. Frank Cusack says that Cox has a couple of papers he will bring up for me. I expect they are the *Harpers* and a *Pall Mall Budget*.

Sunday, February 12th. Cox had not appeared at ten last night, so I went to bed, and the first thing this morning went up to his house to see whether he had come and got whatever mail he had for me. I found he had not returned, so I went on to the Splann's and saw Payn, who seems improving but not yet able to get about. He says he finds it very slow up there. Then I went up to Brock's and found that he also had not returned. Frank Cusack was there, and Mrs. Brock and I sat a little while talking, and then went down to my house again.

On the way I met Cox coming up from town and he gave me the two papers, *Harpers* and *Pall Mall Budget*. The *Harpers* (of March, 1881) contained a pretty good account of Bedford Park, with illustrations of Stones and Tabard Club, Lawn Tennis Court, Tower House, etc.

I had a visit from an old chap who runs the mail from Silver Cliff to Cotopaxi, and his son. They came up to fetch Payn's harness, which he sold to Armstrong and it seems Armstrong had sold to him (the mail-carrier). In the afternoon I went up to the Cusacks' and stayed to supper. In the evening we had a sort of little service. Psalms, Collect, Gospel, etc., and hymns, a rather nice idea I thought, only it rather lacked life. I would rather someone had read us a chapter or two of the New Testament or a good sermon or a good bit out of any book. But it is not very easy to get up a good 'service' with only five people unless they are all minded to enter heartily into it.

Miss Urquhart lent me her drawing-block on which to attempt the sketch for Mrs. Cusack. She wants me to do an evening view of Pike's Peak, etc., which is very beautiful in reality but not easy to make so in a drawing. But I must try my best.

February 13th. Warm and windy, beautiful sunrise.

7.30 a.m. How do you like this for an essay on the human mind? The human mind at birth is like a cold clear liquid. absolutely pure. As time goes on it becomes heated and absorbs salts — ideas, which it holds in solution. It reaches the boiling point, and is saturated with dissolved matter. It cools down gradually, and one by one the salts separate out and crystallise, till in old age it is again a clear liquid holding ideas which have crystallised into final shape, and others still in solution, which never crystallise. Sometimes the boiling is so intense as to break the vessel, and the liquid is spilled. Then it evaporates and vanishes into the unknown. but the ideas do not evaporate. but crystallise out and remain as tokens of what has been and what might be. So does the mind also vanish in old age. The liquid life is gone, the thoughts remain. This is the history of all minds, but they differ in their solvent powers. Some will absorb hardly anything, some almost everything. Again, some meet with little to absorb. But all crystallise and, in the end separate. The liquid goes, while the crystals remain to be absorbed and reabsorbed again.

5.15 p.m. The first thing I did was to make a little picture of the sunrise, and then I set out to draw the Pike's Peak view for Mrs. Cusack. I could not see it from here, so I went up and sat in the doorway of Cox's house. There I filled in the outline and painted the sky, but it was too cold and my fingers got numb, so I went up to the Cusacks' and finished the sketch from their kitchen window. Regy Cusack came and sat by me, also sketching. The drawing did not turn out particularly good, but perhaps as well as I could expect, since I have done so little landscape drawing (hardly anything since I was in Madeira), and it pleased the Cusacks. I promised to do another at some other time, and when I can get some drawing paper of my own I will do you and Annie some sketches. Just before I left the Cusacks, Cardy Lees arrived, having come down to fetch Frank Cusack to work with him. 'Wind and weather permitting' as they say on the 'penny steamboats.' I go to town tomorrow.

February 14th. I have walked into town today to post this. I found no mail for me of any consequence — postcards from Averell and F.J. Ford, *Conmonweal* and *Labor Enquirer*.

4:20. The night seems likely to be warm, so I have decided to wait for the evening mail before starting home. I have been up to Silver Cliff to see Walter Hornback, who collects eggs. I found him only a boy of about 15 and I doubt he will be of much use to me, but he has promised to let me have a list of birds he has found in Custer County. After coming back from Silver Cliff, I have been sitting in the store here, reading the American comic papers and also a novelette called *The Golden Incubus* by G. M. Fenn in *Chamber's Journal*. It is rather Wilkie Collinsy and I don't care for it.

Today being Valentine's day a good deal of fun is going on in the postoffice — people coming in to choose, then the writing of the envelope in a feigned hand, and speculations as to how it will be received. Then the getting the Valentine, and wondering who sent it. In fact the whole thing is so funny that I have had a broad grin on my face all the latter part of the afternoon. One little girl, aged about nine, came in and with great and serious deliberation selected a Valentine, then she thought, perhaps — well, she had better go and ask Mamma whether she should send it. So she went, and as she has not come back, I conclude Mamma said 'No.'

The mail has come and brought me a letter from Nash of Pueblo, which encloses a list of butterflies he has taken in Colorado, giving several new to my list, big as it is. He has found *Vanessa atalanta*, *V. cardui*, and *V. hunterae* at Rosita.

There is the old joke about the individual who looked up the horse in a dictionary and found that it was an "equine animal." But the collector of butterflies and moths, who said he had collected a Vanessa atalanta, Eulepia cribrum, and Mania maura, would not be much more intelligible if he explained that his killing bottle contained a Red Admiral, a Speckled Footman, and an Old Lady. Punch once had a picture showing the consternation of a venerable rector when his young curate suddenly vaulted over a fence, excitedly calling out that he saw a Painted Lady. In those days the liberal application of paint to the face was supposed to suggest a disreputable occupation.

Recollections

Feb. 15th, 1888

Dear Frederic,

I had a pleasant enough walk back last night. It was about the warmest night we have had, I suppose very little below freezing, and by the time I got up here I was hot and perspiring. It was darkish, the new moon being obscured by clouds, but there was enough light to see the road, and that was all I needed. I started from West Cliff at 6:15 and got here a little before half past eight. I did not feel like settling down to anything, and besides, having run out of lamp-oil, had no means of illumination but a bit of candle a couple of inches long.

I must get more oil as soon as I can, so, having a letter for Mrs. Cusack, I went up and delivered it, after which I came down again and straightway went to bed. I was just considering (8.30) whether it wasn't about time to get up, when Old Splann came along (this morning) with a sack in which he bore off all Payn's dirty clothes that are down here for Mrs. Splann to wash. I pity Mrs. S. as they are very many and dirty. She will have to boil them an hour or two before she can do anything with them.

This morning I have been entering up Nash's butterflies. The list he gave me adds 39 species and 3 vars. to my Colorado list. I forgot to mention that yesterday I found a lot of smallish Physae at West Cliff in a spring. They are the first of the genus I have found in Custer Co. 'Fresh-water shrimps' (*Gammarus robustus*, I think) swarmed at the same place. I don't know whether to call these Physae a small var. of *P. heterotropha* or a distinct species. If I found them in Europe I should certainly dub them *P. acuta*, and it strikes me that a good many of the American 'species' will one day have to sink as varieties of this. The insects are beginning to appear. I found a very pretty grey marbled Noctuid moth the other day. Yesterday I got two beetles which were crawling near the road by West Cliff, and today I took a *Finca* new to me. Bluebottle flies (not the same as the English species) are also buzzing all about the house.

3:25. Here's a wonder! I was just writing a postcard to Averell when I saw something white out of the corner of my eye on the floor. Can that be a mouse? I thought and turned round and looked. Presently there came the head and shoulders of a most beautiful white ermine from a hole in the floor just by the stove! There is a large space between the floor and the ground underneath, and I hope my visitor will take up his abode there and help to keep under the swarms of mice. I am not quite sure what species he belongs to; he is possibly *Putorius noveboracensis*.

You might add to the Bibliog. at end of B. P. fauna book 'Anon. *Harpers Magazine*, March 1881, p. 489. Nightingale and skylark at Bedford Park.' This will be the earliest record of any species for B.P., I fancy.

February 16th. Old Splann went to town on horseback today, so I gave him some letters to post, and he brought me back a very good lot of mail, including your letter, but as it is now dark and I have only one inch of candle left to depend upon for illumination (I can see by the light of the fire, but hardly write), I must defer reply until tomorrow.

This morning I went up to see Payn and found him in bed and in considerable pain. I therefore came down here again and fetched my hypodermic tabloids and gave him a hypodermic injection of morphia, which I hope will have sent him to sleep. (I did not stay to watch the effect, wishing him left quiet.) If he is again in pain I left instructions with Mrs. Splann to repeat the dose, and showed her how it was done.

It has been a bright, hot day, and the bluebirds (*Sialia*) are sitting on the fences, a sign of good weather to come. They are lovely little birds; look them up at the Museum when you go there. I presume they have specimens.

February 17th. I went up to see Payn last night and, thinking it advisable to get a doctor, rode down to Silver Cliff for one that evening, which was good of him. The doctor will come up some time today. Cox and Bassick went to town this morning, so I asked Cox to get me some lamp oil and provisions. I have been out of meat for the last three or four days. Living on bread and oatmeal is all very well, but I like the luxury of a little meat also. I pity those who only get meat on Sundays. I don't think most people appreciate the hardship of it, but Annie, who turned vegetarian for a whole month, will scoff at this!

Now, about the mail: (1.) Your letter. I am very pleased to hear the doctor's good report of Annie. Personally, I rather like the 'typical B. P. squash.' No, I never heard much of E. Wheelwright; where does she come from? Huxley sometimes writes very great nonsense. I think, though, even his nonsense is more or less worth reading.

Whatever you do, don't abandon science in the pursuit of £.s.d! You will later on be able to get work that will bring you sufficient wealth without needing you to abandon everything for it, and if you turn yourself into a machine now you will remain one to the rest of your days and do no good to yourself or anybody else.

For one thing is clear: Good scientific work is a gain to the world, but whether 'money-making' is, seems doubtful, to say the least. I can understand a man working ten hours in order to be able to devote two to science, but that he should give himself up body and soul to business seems to me worse than annihilation. And from another point of view, the hours you work at Smith's are long enough for anybody, and it is necessary for your physical and mental welfare that you should have a complete and refreshing change when not at the office.

Even from the £.s.d. point of view, it is always necessary for success to be intelligent. And let me ask you, what do you suppose would be the state of your intelligence now if you had always or often devoted your time at home to working for money? Which is the most valuable to you, that which you have learnt at 'work', or that which you have learnt at 'play'?

I don't remember sneering at the scientific study of birds' eggs; if I did I apologise for having done so. I must study the subject to make up for my past misdeeds in that direction.

Why do you give me the name of the Guillemot *U. grylle*. Did you not mean *U. troile*? That is the common species. I only know of one animal that preys on Guillemots' eggs; it is a mammal allied to the higher apes.

I am glad Darwin stands up for my 'hat theory'. Annie shall have more of the story.

Baron Gardner is like one of those trick puzzles that you put together bit by bit. Does he reside in the far northwest and is he converting the Indians? (I may say that, as a matter of fact, the Europeans want a deal more converting in America than the Indians, who have at least a religion they believe in.) I think the extracts from *John Sterling* are extremely good, particularly the 'identity of sentiment, difference of opinion'. These are the known elements of a pleasant dialogue. The last bit: 'If you want to make sudden fortunes', etc. is just like a bit of Ruskin.

The other mail was: (1.) Letter from Mother. (2.) Long letter from Olive. She says there 'were a lot of interesting things' at the B. P. squash. (3.) Long argumentative letter from Carlie, enclosing also notes of Annie's on *Eagle's Nest*, which I am very glad to get. It is rather ridiculous the way Carlie and I argue. There is not the remotest chance of our agreeing. I am afraid we haven't got even 'identity of sentiment', and our opinions are as different as black and white. (4.) Postcard from Leslie, who has found 'three large' *Testacella* on Madeira, and has got them in spirit; probably they are *T. mangei*. (5.) Post-card from Barker of the S.L.E.S. He says my variety

paper will be published, and he will submit the proof to you for correction. (6.) *Naturalist* for Feb., containing an interesting paper by J. G. Barker on the Botany of the Cumberland part of the Pennine range. He found 304 species there in a fortnight, not a bad list. There is also a record by Milne of *Amalia gagales* (type) in Cheshire. (7.) *Science Gossip* containing the beginning of my paper on Geographic Distribution. What do you think of it? They have put it up carefully — only one misprint, which may have been my fault. 'Anticosti Islands' for 'Island.' I see there is a lot more about 'Rudiments and Vestiges', which seems to me rather less profitable than the '*Lycaena* discussion' in *Entomologist*! (8 & 9.) *Commonweal* and *Pall Mall Budget*.

6:35 p.m. I went up to see Payn about midday, and met the doctor (Ellis) coming down after seeing him. He said he thought Payn was certainly suffering from gout, and had given him some salicylate of soda and *Guaiacum* mixture, which, however he would not take. I gathered after from the Splanns that the Doctor had contradicted himself once or twice, and did not seem to know much about it.

I found Payn slightly better. He said the morphine had given him an hour or so of rest but had not sent him to sleep. He had had one more dose that evening and also had been taking some chloroform, which did him no good and naturally upset his stomach. I told him it was absurd to be taking chloroform, and I trust he will take no more.

I had lunch at the Splann's and came at about three. On my way there I found a black caterpillar marked with orange and white which I had not seen before. This evening Bassick came back with the waggon. having left Cox in town. He brought me my much wanted stores, viz., meat, potatoes, onions, dried apples, and lamp oil.

February18[th]. We had a slight snow fall last night, but it has now melted all away. The 'Senator Jones' mentioned on the cutting you sent is I think nothing to do with Jones of Black Lake.

Looking over the contents of my purse I discovered an autograph of William Morris, which I enclose for Annie; she may find some use for it perhaps. It was affixed to a subscription sheet of the Socialist League.

6:15 p.m. I went up to see Payn in the afternoon and found him much as yesterday. He is very fidgety and continually wants the pillows moved, and he objects to being left alone, so altogether he must be a considerable bother to the Splanns, though they seem not to mind. He made a remark today that made me feel very angry. He has Miss Kelvey's portrait up there and, talking of her to one of the Splanns, actually said 'She is much too delicate-minded to stand the people or the life in this country.' I said nothing, fearing to make matters worse, and Lewis Splann did not reply. And, after all, as Mrs. S. said to me, 'It don't do to mind what a sick man says.'

On my way back went up to the Cusacks' and fetched *Eagle's Nest* to compare with Annie's notes, but am rather bothered by the fact that she gives references to pages, and my paging is quite different. For instance, 'You cannot so much as . . . character', p. 184 in the copy she had, is p. 101 in my copy.

I quite think that Ruskin's remarks on the Chartist [a British working-class union for parliamentary reform cf. *Encyclopedia Britiannica*] are preposterous. With all my experience of Socialists (and it amounts to much the same thing), I never met anyone who was impelled by hopes of pecuniary gain to himself, simply because there is not the slightest chance of such; quite the reverse. The basest motive is love of notoriety, which I believe does have some influence with a certain number. The ordinary politician is much more open to the imputation of greed because he may and frequently does get a well-salaried post under Government, but I think it is a rare motive even among politicians.

Sunday, February 19th, 9:45 p.m.. There was more snow last night, enough to stay on the ground all day.

In the morning I wrote Chapter IV of my story, which I enclose. I am afraid you will think the plot is a little too far-fetched, but I don't quite know how to modify it.

In the afternoon I went up to Cox's and found him and Bassick and Brock there. Bassick has got a photograph of his (dead) wife stuck on the wall, horribly coloured and in a ghastly frame, and I not knowing what it was, asked Cox, 'Wherever did you get this ridiculous picture?' Cox burst out laughing, and after some minutes, as soon as he got his breath again, explained who it was. Bassick didn't seem to mind, but it was a very unfortunate thing to have said anyhow, though it amused me also considerably.

From Cox's I went up to the Cusack's, and stayed to supper and psalms in the evening. I took Mrs. Cusack *The Autocrat at the Breakfast Table* to read. When I got up there I found Miss Urquhart lying down with a swollen and very painful thumb. I think she must have run something into it and poisoned it. I suggested that if it was left for a day or two and then lanced, it might get well, but she wanted it done at once if at all, so as to have it over, and so I came down here and fetched my little surgical knife, and went up and lanced it. For a little while after the operation it pained her a good deal, but now she says it is much easier, which is satisfactory.

Close to the Cusacks' today I saw a 'Jackrabbit' in its winter dress, just the colour of the snow. It is a pretty animal.

February 20th, 11:35 p.m. I walked down as far as about a mile from town when a man came along with a waggon and gave me a lift. How strange it is how people crop up unexpectedly. He turned out to be one Kennicott, a relation of Kennicott (now dead), a well known American traveler and naturalist and a fast friend of Spencer F. Baird. He also knew Aiken, a well-known ornithologist who has collected in Colorado and after whom a species of snow-bird, *Junco aikeni*, was named.

Talking of names coming up unexpectedly, Cox was telling me yesterday that Mrs. Cox (now in England) had met J. Cosmo Melvill out at dinner, and he had made some complimentary remarks about me.

The mail I have got today is: (1.) A letter and postcard from W. H. Edwards. The letter encloses a paper on *Colias caesonia* from *Canadian Ent.* Edwards wants me to write my views on seasonal forms to *Canadian Ent.*, which I will do. (2.) Postcard from C.F. Ancey (Algeria) wanting to exchange shells. I may do something with him. (3.) Letter from Douglas. (4.) List of Members, Rules etc. of Practical Naturalist's Soc'y.

Feb. 20th, 1888

Dear Frederic,

Having posted my letters, I discovered Regy Cusack (or rather he discovered me) who had arrived in town sometime after I did, and so I rode out with him. I found *The Professor* (Charlotte Bronte) for 25 cents in the postoffice store, and could not resist buying it, as it is I think the novel I like best after *Les Miserables*, and it is a very long while since I read it (it must have been when we were at Margate). Has Annie read it? If so, does she not like it? If not, I entreat her to do so. I am sure she will like it very much. Later I will send some extracts from it.

February 21st. I was feeling dyspeptic yesterday evening, and passed a bad night, so that I lazily stayed in bed this morning till nearly eleven, when Steve Splann, coming to fetch some nightgowns of Payn's, obliged me to get up. Once up, I took a dose of bicarbonate of soda, which put me all right again. It has been a dismal day, chilly and cloudy, with this evening some snow, so I have not been out except to get wood and water, but have been reading *The Professor* by the fire. A number of plump grey little finches

have appeared near the house. I noticed them first by their chirping.

With regard to *The Professor*, I have enjoyed reading it, and it has interested me perhaps more than when I first read it. At the same time, I feel a trifle disappointed. I think the narrator of the story says too much about himself. I would have liked to hear more about Mlle. Henri. There are a few passages that seemed noteworthy, viz., In Chapter XIV, 'Our likings are regulated by our circumstances', etc. (Query: Are not our circumstances regulated also by our likings?) Chapter XVI, the beginning, about Mlle. Henri. Chapter XVII, 'Why, Monsieur, it is just so. In Switzerland I have done but little', etc. Chapter XIX, the beginning: 'and I loved the movement', etc. Chapter XX, 'From all this resulted', etc. Chapter XXIII, 'When are we quite happy?', etc. Also, 'I like unexaggerated intercourse', etc. Also, 'people who are only in each other's company for amusement', etc. Also, 'I must, then, be a man of peculiar discernment', etc. I don't mean to say that I altogether agree with all these passages, but they made me think.

February 22nd. The snow fell several inches last night, but today has been very warm and sunny. I first wrote my paper on 'Seasonal Dimorphism in Rhopalocera' for the *Canadian Entomologist* (will send you a copy if they print it), and then went over to see Payn, whom I found better though still in bed.

Coming back from Payn I called in at Cox's and found him quite out of sorts. It seems that Payn cabled to his doctor in England yesterday for a prescription, and Cox waited for the answer, and coming up in the middle of the night in a snow storm gave him a chill. He has gone into town again today and says that if he is going to be ill he'll go to Frank Hunter's, where they will take good care of him.

After I had got home again the sky seemed so clear and the mountains looked so well that I got my paints and went up to the Cusacks' to try to do the sunset view of Pike's Peak, which

I promised Mrs. Cusack. However, the sunset would not wait long enough for me to get it finished, and in any case, I almost despair of getting even a tolerable representation of it. One difficulty is that of getting vivid lights — I doubt if water-colours can be made to do justice to a sunset in a clear atmosphere. What does Annie think about this? Has she found this difficulty of obtaining bright light effects in working with water-colours?

It was evening, and I stayed to supper and for a while after. Miss Urquhart has now almost recovered from her bad thumb, and she and Regy were able to give us some songs: 'Tit-Willow', 'The Warrior Bold', 'The Quaker's Daughter', etc. Miss U. is coming out a little more than formerly and seems a very nice sort of girl in her way; she is at present however in the 'poppy-bud' stage, so one can't tell what she is coming to. Like 'Castel Byron', she is very cheerful, and never thinks.

Regy is one of the queerest characters I ever met, very amusing and full of fun — in fact a regular Irishman, though of course without the brogue. He is an entirely good fellow, and now I know more of both of them I think I like him better than Frank.

February 23rd. It was very cold last night; the ink froze, the second time it has done so this month, I think. Today is sunny and bright, but cold. I came into town with Cress, and have got the following mail: (1.) Your letter: Dr. Asa Gray was a *very* first-rate botanist, the J. G. Baker of America. He named hundreds of Colorado plants. I am sorry to hear of Mrs. B. Clark's lack of originality; if she is so I quite agree I should not like her very much. Your riddle is ancient (didn't you get it out of *Temple Bar*?). You would most certainly have walked round the monkey, I should say. The artist was perfectly correct; I had no overcoat; in fact, I don't wear one. This is a scarf and mittens climate, not an overcoat climate, if you can appreciate the difference. Besides, who is going to walk seven miles up-grade

in an overcoat? Not 1! I will send Step any subscriptions as Corresponding Member to S.L.E.S. when I write to him, or if he proposes to give me anything for the *Welcome* paper, he can deduct it from that. Your book *wasn't* an unfortunate present. Now I have got over the shock I am very glad I have read it.

Probably there is a good deal of sense in your remarks about my coming to England in the summer. Anyhow, I don't think there is any great chance of my being able to do so.

Of course Annie is perfectly welcome to use anything in my letters that is of any use to her in any way she pleases. But I should like to see the children's story when published.

(2.) Letter and a pretty blue-green 'Liberty' scarf from Mother. (3.) List of Custer Co. birds from W. Hornback of Silver Cliff. (4.) Letter from Hy. Edwards, announcing that the moths I sent him arrived a good deal damaged, but there are some interesting species. He says, 'Your locality must be a very good one' (5.) Letter from J. A. Singley, of Texas. (6.) Letter from C. F. Morrison of H. Lewis, announcing that he has put me down a member of Colo. Ornith. Ass'n. (7.) *Labor Enquirer*.

I had no intention of posting this today, but I think I will. I am sorry not to have Chapter V. of the story ready. I would have written it sooner had I thought I should be posting this today. This is an abominably uninteresting letter.

P. S. I am getting all *Darwin's Life*, bit by bit. I have just been reading a review in *Knowledge* of it!

Feb. 23rd, 1888

Dear Frederic,

Having gone to DeBord's and purchased (80 cents) a 25 pound sack of flour (it ought to be very good flour at this price — about £3, 2/29d. a pound) from Minnesota (it is only 25d. a sack in England, but Colorado flour is the best in America), I walked home. On the way I met first

Lees driving into town. and then Jod, who had been up to see the Cusacks and Brocks. It was rather slippery work walking on the snow, and the sun was by this time quite hot, so I took some time to get up here.

Having rested for a bit, I went up to the Cusacks' to give them some mail I had brought for them. I found Frank up there. He has been working at the mine with Lees, and came down with him.

I meant to come back and write all the evening, but Mrs. Cusack insisted on my staying to supper, and so I did not get away till nine after all. We had songs as usual and talked about various things. I was telling Mrs. C. about the projected children's story with a Colorado 'background', and she suggested that I ought to explain that nurses, etc., were not usual out here, but children are always allowed to scamper about by themselves, generally bare-footed. This includes 'ladies' children just as much as anyone else. I have no great personal experience of the matter myself but give the information as she gave it me.

If Annie would care to have a real bit of ground to put into the story, I will describe minutely some part of this valley. I suppose I must have given you full details of this particular spot at one time and another but never all together, because I did not take it in myself all at once. I shall be very much interested in this story and should like to hear anything about it that Annie will tell me, and of course read it when done. It might be made an accurate representation of life and manners out here as well as a story, and whatever I can do towards helping to make it so I will. Though the principal characters must of course be Annie's creations, it might be well to put into the background some of the people I have told you about from time to time, or if not them, their circumstances. If she wants anything tragic, I may say one child got lost here and was supposed to have been eaten by a mountain lion, and another losing its way in the woods was frozen to death. Only I would rather avoid such distressing topics in a children's (or perhaps any other) story.

February 24th. It has been a curious day — sunshine and snow. I went over to see Payn in the afternoon, and found him considerably better, and reading some story of Miss Braddon's. I am feeling rather out of sorts tonight and shall go to bed, though it is not yet eight.

Hornback gives me *Charadrius pluvialis* in his list of Custer Co. birds, but I feel certain he is mistaken and that *C. dominicus* was the bird he saw.

February 25th. A cold, cloudy, depressing day. I have sat at home writing letters, etc.

Old Splann went to town, and fetched me some mail, viz., (1.) *All Saints, Isleworth, Magazine*, for which best thanks to Annie. It appears, though, that only the blue cover really pertains to Isleworth, and the rest is a sort of general 'church magazine', not a bad idea either, only one would have thought the Church might have got up something rather better. The Rev. Richards must be rolling in wealth. I see he gaily puts down £50 for the Parish church. I should have supposed that the amount headed 'First list of subscriptions' would have been enough (it is nearly £250) for 'cleaning and decorating the church.' If not, it must be in an awfully dirty state! The 'Right Rev. the Lord Bishop of Chester' (almost as bad a name as that of that organic compound in *Industrial Review*!) seems as if he *might* have written some sense in his paper, but either he thought better of it, or the Editor cut it out.

With regard to 'Crucifying the flesh', there was a very well-reasoned article in the *Commonweal* a little while back, arguing that just as the ideal of an ill man is of necessity health, so that of a hungry man is food, and so on, and therefore ill living, so far from being conducive to higher lines of thought, prevented them. I must say, this seems to me pretty conclusive, though it may be said that the more moderate a man's habits are, the more likely he is to be able to satisfy them and to have time to think of other things.

The article 'Before and After Marriage' is rather amusing. I can't make anything of 'Notes on the Church of England', but people will see it looks very learned, and take its conclusions for granted, I suppose.

As to emigration, I must say I think it's mostly 'out of the frying-pan into the fire', but I quite agree with the Rev. Bridge that farmers and agricultural people are the best to emigrate, if any. I long greatly for the 'master mind bent on mischief' that the Rev. author speaks of. The trouble is that those we have are not 'master-minds.'

I see Kitty came in 4th in the Spelling Competition. These competitions remind me of an anecdote I read, I forget where. Clergyman (to small boy), 'Well my little man, and where did you get that beautiful trumpet?' Small boy, 'Won it at a lottery.' Clergyman (shocked), 'Dear, dear, don't you know it's wrong to go in for lotteries, and games of chance?' Small boy (with a grin), 'It was at your own Church bazaar!'

I cannot imagine anything better calculated to defeat the ends of religion and bring the bible into contempt than the 'Bible Explorations' on p. 48. If there was the remotest chance of getting it inserted, I would write a pretty strong letter to the editor about this. It is pure, unadulterated humbug. You know I don't go in for 'Bible infallibility' and all that. but the Bible is a very good book and worth being treated seriously. What would you think if someone ought to measure your knowledge of botany (say) by asking you what words are spelled differently in 'Thome' and 'Bentham and Hooker', or 'What five botanists desired to become land-owners?' And here we have this Rev. gentleman who is capable of such idiocy. 'Incumbent of St. Mathias, Poplar!' I wonder how he strikes the East-enders? I really think there is a good deal of truth in the saying that to be a clergyman of the Church of England one must be a knave or a fool, but 'mostly fools!'

So you see I have found this church magazine both interesting and amusing, and I may say that I shall always be grateful for a copy when you have one you don't want. (2.) *Journal of Conchology*, Jan., 1888). I see Marshall's *J. papillosa* is a fossil after all, just exactly what I expected and suggested to Marshall in a letter a long while ago. I quite agree with Madison that the Welsh '*Barmetti*' are only *lacustris*. Wotton of Cardiff sent me some, and I sent them back to him as *lacustris*. The same thing is found at Killarney. I see Standinger has turned shell dealer. (3.) *Botanical Gazette*, Jan. and Feb. 1888 from Coulter. This is a very good magazine and I am glad to have these two copies. I have not yet had time to more than glance at them.

(4.) *Commonweal*. In *Bot. Gaz.*, p. 15. F. L. Scribner says he found magnificent growths of *Agaricus melleus* round dead or dying oak trees near Dallas, Texas. He thinks they destroy the trees. You might investigate whether this is so with the species at Isleworth.

February 26th. A fine sunny day. Having done a little writing I started out for a Sunday walk. Going up Swift Creek, I soon came to a bank by the stream, exposed to the sun and free from snow. Here I sat down and searched, and was rewarded by the discovery of numerous specimens of *Succinea*, together with a few *Helix pulchella* var. *costata* and some ants., Homoptera, etc. Proceeding further, the next find was a number of galls (containing living larvae) on the stems of a species of rose (I believe *Rosa arkansana*) and a little later I 'jumped' a Jack-rabbit in his grey-white winter costume. I then got out on the open, and went up as far as Cress' house. and thence into the timber on the slope of the range. Then I found the snow had drifted considerably, and I frequently went in above my knees. I managed to scramble along, though, and in due time found myself at an old house (unoccupied) close to the Cusacks'. Here I found their dog 'Chipper', who was in a frightful state of excitement, having got a 'cotton-tail' (a rabbit very like the English species, brown all the year round) under the boarding of the house, and was not able to get under to catch it himself. I saw a crested blue jay (*Cyanocitta stelleri* var. *macrolopha*) here, but was disappointed in my expectation of seeing other birds.

Then I went on to the Cusacks' and talked for a bit with Mrs. C. about the Isleworth church magazine, which I had in my pocket. She has a very small opinion of clergymen as a class, although holding to the orthodox religion. She asked me to stay to supper, and I said I would continue my walk but come back again.

So I went on, 'Chipper' accompanying me. (Chipper is a black and tan terrier, son of and much like Nell.) I soon found a grassy place under a tree, where a little searching revealed *Hyalina (Cornulus) fulva*, *Patula striatella* and *vitrina*, and I also found a young living specimen of *Patula cooperi*, and little beetles of the genus *Tachypoma*. Chipper contrived to tree a squirrel but could not get up the tree after it and was obliged to let it be. It was tantalising for poor Chipper, first a rabbit and then a squirrel that he could see but not get at.

Going on through the quaking asps and pines, I ascended a bluff from which I got an admirable view of the valley. This bluff had but few pines on its sides, but an abundant growth of dwarf oak (*Quercus undulata*) and other shrubs. The curious seed-cases and pointed leaves of *Yucca angustifolia* ('Spanish bayonet') were also very conspicuous, and among the dead stems of plants I noticed *Achillea millefolium*.

It was not past four, so I retraced my steps and went back to the Cusacks'. Just as I was going down from the bluff a 'robin', *Turdus migratorius*, the first I have seen this year, flew by. Regy Cusack says he saw some several weeks ago, however, and old Splann told me the same.

After supper at the Cusack's we sat round the fire discussing botany and other matters, and then had the usual Sunday evening service. Miss Urquhart sang an anthem, and did it remarkably well. Then we had one of Moody and Sankey's hymns in the middle of which a rap at the door announced Mrs. Brock and child, who sat a little while talking. When they left we finished up with two more hymns, and soon after I came back here again.

February 27th. After packing up some fungi for Farlow, some rose galls (*vide* yesterday) for U.S. Agric. Dept., and some shells for Pilsbry of Philadelphia, I started at about 11:15 to walk down to town. The day is nice and sunny, and warmer than yesterday. A pretty little bird (I don't even know its generic name) is very common, sitting on the railings.

Half way I met Kennicott riding, driving some cattle to Ula. When I got here the only mail was a *Pall Mall Budget* and a *Labor Enquirer*. Beddoes came into the postoffice after I arrived. As it is so fine and warm, and the moon will be up, I shall wait for the evening mail.

7 p.m. No mail came this evening after all. I have just had supper with Cox at the hotel, and am about to start back.

Feb. 27th, 1888, 9:50 p.m.

Dear Frederic,

Leaving the postoffice after posting your letter, I had a very pleasant walk home in the light of a full moon. The air was quite warm (comparatively speaking) and there was a slight breeze from the south.

February 28th, 9:20 p.m. All day it has been blowing a gale, though it is quite warm. After breakfast I went up to Bassick's to ask him to drive in to town and fetch Cox out, and then on to the Cusacks' with some mail for them. I found Mrs. Cox and Miss U. busy pasting pictures from the illustrated papers onto the kitchen walls, as is very generally the custom in this country. Louis Howard was up there, having come up from Beddoes', where he was working. Mrs. C. asked me to come to dinner in the evening, which I said I would, though it seems rather too bad to go to dinner at the Cusacks' so often. However, if they don't mind, I don't. Then I came down here again, and then over to the Splann's to see Payn, whom I found much better. After that, up to the Cusacks' supper, evening, and back again as usual.

February 29th, 3 p.m. A dull, windy day, with hail at intervals. A juvenile mouse came to a tragic end last night by falling into the pail and getting drowned . I gloated over its corpse and wished they might all do likewise (which proves Carlie's contention that I haven't any feelings).

I rearranged my insects in the morning and secured three new (to me) flies on the window-pane. I wish I had the books to work up the Colorado Diptera; I must have no end of new species. Three Splanns (viz., Louis, Steve, and Becky) drove into town this afternoon and will get me mail (if there is any) and meat. For the last day or two I have been living on a mixture of potatoes and broth, which I find excellently adapted to my constitution.

4 p.m. The March winds are a day too early; evidently they have forgotten that it is leap-year! This is a strong little house and is sheltered behind a lot of quaking-asp trees, else it would only blow away. 1 don't envy the Splanns having to come home tonight, but the wind will go down after sunset.

10:40 p.m. The Splanns returned before dark, bringing your letter, and letters from Mother and Douglas. They must have come last night, a very unusual thing for the English mail; tonight is the usual time. The *Ent. Mags.* have not yet turned up. (1.) Your letter: I think I will answer tomorrow, as 1 am tired and sleepy and should not do it justice. I will also defer the rest of today's news.

March 1st. Today it is not very windy. but cold, damp, and haily — very unpleasant

weather indeed. Cardy Lees came along. He went into town without my seeing him, and was going back to his mine. Last night another mouse got drowned in the pail, and this morning I slaughtered three juvenile ones in cold blood. They got into the wood box and I caught them in my hands.

To continue, about your letter: I shouldn't wonder if Housley did some good work with *H. nemoralis* and *hortensis*. He generally is successful with anything he takes up, e.g., the Gibralter shells. Does he understand the band formulae and the nomenclature of the various varieties?

Certainly you must give a lecture at the B. P. club and why not on the B. P. Fauna, illustrated by diagrams? I am glad you agree with me about marriage. (I doubt whether Huxley would.) Perhaps I will send you a paper for S.L.E.S., but 1 have no idea of wasting original work on them unless I can be sure it will be published. I thought the rule as to papers being the property of the society was an ancient one. Barker claimed my variety paper on the strength of it. I don't think there would be any advantage in publishing all the papers read at S.L.E.S. because hardly any are original, but it would be preposterous to claim original matter and then not publish it, though in that case I presume the author would be at liberty to write out his views again and let them be published elsewhere.

Did you read my paper on *Gonopteryx* to the Society? The extract from Darwin's letter to Bates is particularly interesting, though I must say I think it is very expedient to know the names etc., of the beasts one meets with.

I think naturalists appreciate theories much more now than formerly, and certainly more than the general public. I know I could not have written any of my recent papers without access to a good deal of literature on the subject, and now I cannot work out the Diptera for lack of books. I myself place a very high value on systematic work taken in conjunction with intelligent reasoning. And even a mere mechanical systematist is of the utmost value to those of the philosophic school, though they profess to despise them. It is something like bricklayer and architect; one cannot work without the other.

As to *B. garrula* at B. P., I think it must have been Tubby Gray who saw them, but the name will be in the B. P. fauna book. It was only a small flock on migration.

I should very much like to see Annie's pictures and verses; you must send me the books when published (I will return them safely). I have seen a little book of this kind got up by E. Nesbit (alias Mrs. Fabian Bland). It used to be at 5. Priory, and Cox has a copy up at his house. What are Annie's verses about?

I think I must feel 'the gap' more than you do. You have Annie to talk to, and she has you, whereas I have nobody but your letters and my books. Mrs. Cusack is nice enough to talk to, certainly, but as she herself said yesterday, 'We agree to talk together about all sorts of things, but if we went a little deeper. you know very well we should disagree very, very much', and whether wisely or not, she avoids 'going a little deeper.' And then Mrs. C.'s ideas have mostly crystallised long ago.

The leading article (from the *Standard*) about men and women in society is a notable one. I do not know how they behaved formerly, but I quite agree that their present behaviour is ridiculous and abominable, though not altogether for the reasons set down by the writer of the article. So far from objecting to their meeting on familiar terms, I entirely approve of it, but I do think they ought to show more respect for one another than they do. And by showing respect I mean treating each other as though they were intelligent human beings and not born idiots.

Society is I think worse than the individuals composing it. A not entirely foolish man will meet a lady at a ball or elsewhere and talk the most utter nonsense to her, which I do think is the most insulting thing he can possibly do. It is equivalent to saying 'I know you are a fool, and I talk folly to suit you.' And the consequence is that nonsense and an utter lack of any serious

purpose has come to be characteristic of 'Society', and whatever some people there may be take precious good care to avoid mixing in it.

There is such a thing as perfect freedom of manner combined with a feeling of mutual regard, and this, it sees to me, marks the true gentleman and lady, understanding those terms in the better sense. As to calling men 'by their surname. without the prefix of Mr.', and all that sort of thing, I don't think it matters in the least, not being the essential thing.

(2.) Mother's letter: She is greatly concerned lest I should be starving (which I am not) and so has written to Douglas telling him to send me three dollars every week, and he sends the first this week. (You know Douglas had $50 of mine when I left England, and sent me $15 when we came back from the hunting trip.) My expenses, including everything, are only about $1.50 a week, so I really don't need the $3.00, and if I did I don't think it would be particularly wise to send it me.

The Splanns also brought some mail for the Cusacks, and as they don't go by there I took it up. We had a couple of long arguments in the evening, first about the leading article on Society, which I took up and Mrs. C. read aloud. Mrs. C. and Miss Urquhart agreed with it, while Louis Howard and Regy C. took a somewhat opposite view. My own views I have given you above. The second argument arose out of *African Farm*, which Mrs. C. would not allow Miss Urquhart to read, lest it should corrupt her morals. In this case also it was Mrs. C. versus Regy and Louis Howard.

Afterwards, while the other three were singing. I had it out with Mrs. C., and I think we both had to give in a little. I admitted that I would in some cases prevent children from reading books I did not deem good for them (the argument was as to books generally, and not specially the *African Farm*, and Mrs. C. told Miss U. afterwards that she could read the book if she liked. (However, when I went, I took it away with me.)

The whole question is a difficult one, to be settled perhaps more on the merits of each individual case than any general rule one can lay down. Respecting the *African Farm*, it certainly is a strong dose for anyone not accustomed to think. I can conceive its driving a weak-minded person out of his wits altogether!

March 2nd. Today, in contrast to yesterday, has been clear and sunny, though not warm. In the first part of the morning I read *The Origin of Species* for a while, and then went over to the Splanns to see Payn. He was better but quite drowsy from taking morphine. I gave it him to relieve acute pain, but now he takes it much too often and simply to procure sleep. So in spite of his protestations I pocketed the syringe, tabloids, etc., and took them away with me.

I got 10 cents worth of potatoes from the Splanns; they are now at 1½ a lb., but old Splann gave me just as many as I could carry (in fact, I had to put them down and rest several times), which I judge to be very full weight indeed. The potato is an admirable institution.

I have been reading a rather noteworthy paper by Belfort Bax called 'The New Ethic' in *Commonweal*. He argues that all religions which teach the subordination of self to the will of the Deity are at the bottom individualistic and selfish because they regard only the standing of the individual before God. Thus, any 'religious' people think only 'How do 1 stand with God?' and not at all 'What use am I to my fellow men?' The first being answered satisfactorily, all else is considered of no consequence. I cannot help feeling that the argument is a just one myself and, notwithstanding its being entirely contrary to the views of Christ himself, this 'individualistic' religion is excessively common among 'Christians' of the present day, and I myself have often heard it preached from the pulpit.

Yesterday being the beginning of a new month I was totting up the additions to Middlesex and Colorado lists for February. For Middlesex I had only one, a fish recorded in *Sci. Goss*,,

but the Colorado additions were: Rhopalocera 105 and 7 vars., Arachnida 1, Phaeogamia 2 and one var., Fungi 1, and Lichenes 4, which I consider a very unsatisfactory total of addenda, except the butterflies.

There is a curious case of idiosyncracy recorded in *Bot. Gazette* (Jan., 1888, p. 19). A man was afflicted with a rash and other symptoms after eating strawberries or when being in a room with them. He first became thus susceptible at the age of 14 and has been so ever since. A distant relative of his was afflicted in a similar way from his birth. 'On one occasion, when visiting some friends who thought his dread of strawberries was largely or wholly a matter of imagination. the hostess prepared some strawberry shrub which was so disguised with other flavours as to conceal the true nature of the beverage. Of this he drank a moderate amount without knowing what it was, but he was soon taken with the worst symptoms of strawberry poisoning, his illness speedily becoming so serious that his life for a time was despaired of.'

Mrs. Cusack tells me that Regy was afflicted similarly with a rash when a boy after eating oatmeal. These idiosyncrasies are extremely curious and very hard to explain by any known physiological facts.

March 3rd. It has been snowing most of the day, so I have not been out except for wood. After breakfast I read 'Variation under Domestication' in *Origin of Species*, and after that, set to sweeping out the house and putting things tidy. I also sorted and arranged my letters so as to make them handy for reference.

I see Darwin (*Orig. of Sp.*, p. 34) says, 'I have as yet failed to find, after diligent research, cases of monstrosities resembling normal structures in nearly allied forms.' This is strange, because I know of several, and Sutton's book on pathology points out many more. The Conchological examples of this are of course familiar to you.

Sunday, March 14th. As I was having break-fast, Louis Howard came in the Cusacks' buck-board and offered to take me into town, which offer I gladly accepted. But 'there's many a slip twixt the cup and the lip', and while he came in for an instant to warm himself, the horse bolted off with the buckboard. It made for home (the Cusacks') but as it went up the hill a bolt broke, and the buckboard and hind wheels were left be-hind while the horse went off with the shafts and front wheels. It was blowing a most violent gale, the snow flying in one's face, and bitterly cold, but Louis Howard, who had better wind than I, pursued the animal up the hill, though need-lessly, for it arrived safely at the Cusacks', no damage having been done save the broken bolt.

Later on I went up there myself (taking *Sesame and Lilies* for Mrs. C. to read. I also told Miss Urquhart to read the 'Lilies' chapter) and found that Howard, as he could not go into town, had gone back to Beddoes'. Mrs. C. tells me that Howard was reading *Light of Asia* (my copy that I took up the other day) and though professing to think it great rubbish, was evidently very much interested in it, and he is going to get a copy to send home to his mother in England. L. H. is the last person I should have expected to like *Light of Asia*; probably I have not hitherto understood him.

Miss Urquhart says she is going in for bot-any, and Mrs. C. is going to make a collection of pressed Colorado flowers.

Later in the afternoon I went down to see Payn, whom I found sitting up playing cards with three fellows who had come up from West Cliff in a buggy, viz., Preston Schneider, who keeps a butcher's shop, and the man who runs the 'Lager Beer Hall.' Doubtless they find it worth their while to come all this way to play with Payn. I went back to the Cusacks', but at almost five returned to the Splanns to get 2 doz. eggs for Mrs. C. (when I came away she insisted on presenting me with four), and then sup-per at the Cusacks, and evening, including the usual Sunday psalms, hymns, etc. Regy and Miss Urquhart sang the Moody and Sankey 'Hold the

fort, for I am coming', which strikes me as being a good deal better adapted to the populace than most of the ordinary hymns. The tune is decid-edly stirring.

Mrs. C. was showing me a branch of pine on which were growing tufts of a curious parasite (growing mistletoe-fashion) and following her directions I went out and found a lot of it grow-ing on the trees myself. It proves to be *Arceuthobium robustum* Engelm., of the Nat. Order Loran-thaceae, and new to my Colorado list. I enclose a piece so that you may see what manner of plant it is.

Regy and Miss U. talk of driving down tomorrow so I shall probably not go myself (as I had intended). Therefore I will close this letter.

P. S. Have come to town with Bassick, of which details in next letter. No mail for me to speak of — one letter, one paper, and one par-cel.

Tuesday, March 6th, 1888

Dear Frederic,
Yesterday I went to town. Regy had been going down 'if it was fine' and would have post-ed my letters, but the day did not correspond with his idea of 'fine', and he did not go.

I went up to Cox's, therefore, to borrow a horse he promised to lend me if I needed it, but I found he was going to ride to town himself, and so horse, saddle, and bridle would be unavail-able. Bassick was also going in with the hay-rack to haul a load of oats for Frank Hunter, and I ar-ranged to go with him. I did not care about walk-ing down on such a miserable day. I was cold, the whole sky was clouded over, the sun shining through as a bright blob, and all the while it driz-zled snow, if you can understand what I mean.

I went up to the Cusack's to get some letters they wanted posted, and then came down and joined Bassick, who was about to start. We went to the oat stack and pitched on one load and started for town. We went round by Beckwith's ranch (*vide* map), as Cox had advised us, it being a somewhat better road than the other way, but it proved to be also much longer, so that it was not worth our while, had we but known it. We had taken so long in loading up and on the journey that the afternoon was late when we reached West Cliff. Before we got to Ula it stopped snowing and the sun came out, making it a good deal more pleasant.

I was disappointed in finding but little mail, viz., (1.) Letter from Carlie, mainly argumentative. He sticks up for the view he previously brought forward, that the mental and moral differences between men are as great, or greater than those of colour, form. etc. To me the thing is preposterous, because I take it as an axiom that whatever is not due to conditions is inherited, and if there exist among us races characterised by mental and moral characters only, I cannot see how they are kept distinct, for Carlie means to say that the races exist among the same variety of *Homo sapiens*, viz., the people of England. If, on the other hand, the vast difference in morality, etc., which certainly exist are due for the most part to conditions, they are obviously to be avoided by bettering those conditions, and in no other way.

I am sure that any biologist (quite apart from Socialism) would agree that the position I have taken is a sound one, but biologists are few! Of course it would be possible to argue that the human race was morally dimorphic, just as certain butterflies are physically dimorphic, but I do not think Carlie takes this view. I wish you would give this matter of conditions vs. inheritance some careful thought and see whether you can prove me wrong. Although I feel so sure about it, it is of course possible I may be in error. I want you to look at the matter impartially as if it were a problem in Euclid.

(2.) Memoir of Edward Tuckerman, by (and sent by) W.G. Farlow. Tuckerman was the boss lichenologist of U. S. (3.) My box of butterflies, returned by W. H. Edwards. He has very kindly put in male and female specimens of all the four forms of *Colias eurytheme* for me, viz., *eurytheme, keewaydin, ariadne,* and *eriphyle.*

Soon after leaving the postoffice, I met Cox, and he gave me the extraordinary information that Steve Splann had 'skipped' with all Payn's money. I could not believe it at first, but I soon found that the thing was known all over the town, and universally credited as a fact. I got the most intelligent account of the matter from Goldstandt, the postmaster. Payn told me a little time ago that his mother had sent him £30, and I know that Steve Splann went to town on horseback last week, and on Sunday they were wondering why he had not returned. Further, there is no doubt that he and a man named Burns went off on the morning (Monday) train to Cañon City. These are certainly facts.

The rest of the story, as believed in town, is that Payn gave Steve a $100 (some say more) bill to change, but he was wishing to leave the district, and so agreed with Burns to steal the money and depart with it. Old Splann, Lewis Splann, and Becky went into town and met him just as he was about to enter the train. I myself saw them going in with the waggon. They passed my house at 7.30, and I wondered what could take them in at that early hour. Old Splann begged him to give up the money, but he refused to do so, and went off. Nobody interfered to stop him, though they knew it all over the town, and Cox says they wanted him to get a warrant issued so that Steve might be arrested a few hours later on the arrival of the train at Cañon City, but he replied that it was none of his business.

When I arrived in town, the train had long ago arrived in Cañon City and Steve might be anywhere, and I was a little puzzled what to do. It appears that the state of the law is this: (1.) Anyone can apply for a warrant. but without a warrant he cannot be arrested. (2.) It would be considered a 'Breach of Trust', which the law only affords means for the recovery of the money (if possible), and criminal prosecution is impossible. Now I think that he ought to be arrested, and that it is a disgrace to the town that a man should be allowed to decamp with $100,

166

and nobody try to stop him, but obviously Payn is the one person who can prosecute. I would gladly take out a warrant if Payn would act in the matter. However, the feeling is that it is not worth while to go to the expense of prosecution because it seems that under this absurd law he cannot be punished. And as for recovering the money, he will probably have spent it all long before they could catch him.

We waited in town for the evening mail, and I got a letter from the Smithsonian, saying they would very soon send me a list of insects I had sent them, and apologising for the delay. Letter from W. H. Edwards, announcing that he had posted off my box. *Commonweal* and *Labor Enquirer*.

We got back at about nine, and I went up to Brock's and the Cusacks' with mail for them, and then came back and slept at Cox's, as I was to help Bassick haul oats next day. I felt too weary to write any intelligent account of the day's proceedings, so let the matter rest until today.

This morning after breakfast I went over to see Payn, and if possible get the exact truth as to Steve and the money, and see if he would move in the matter. I found him sitting in the kitchen with Mrs. Splann, etc., and I did not like to refer to the affair before them, unless Payn first mentioned it. He said nothing, however, and did not seem to wish me to do anything for htm, so I came away none the wiser. If the story, as told in town, is correct, I do not for a moment suppose that Payn will do anything. and from what I know of Splann, I think it not unlikely that he will himself be answerable for the theft, by deducting the amount from what Payn will owe him for board, lodging, etc., all this while.

I then came back and went down to help Bassick haul his load of oats up to the barn, after which I had supper up there, and came back to my house again.

Monday, March 7th. I wrote letters during the morning, and early in the afternoon went up to the Cusacks', taking 'Thome' and Coulter's *Manual*. It was a very fine day, and so we arranged to go out in search of specimens. I went with Mrs. Cusack towards Cress', and Regy and Miss Urquhart went to the Splann's (whence they had to fetch butter, etc.).

We (Mrs. C. and I) searched around for a while, and although a couple of Coleoptera was all we got new to me, we found many things that interested Mrs. Cusack — six species of Mollusca (*Vitrina, H. pulchella, P. striatella, Pupa, Hyalina arborea,* and *Cornulus fulvus.*), three species of lichens, some mosses (including *Barbula sp.*), spiders of various kinds, *Fragaria vesca* (leaves only) etc.

I told Mrs. C. about them, and when we got home and the others came in she was full of it, and insisted on their looking at the specimens while she explained. They had found almost nothing. In fact they did not do very much searching. After supper we talked the subject over. I am going to get Mrs. C. to start a Fauna and Flora book to record her finds. Notwithstanding her age, Mrs. C. has a good deal more energy about her than Regy or Miss U., or indeed most people.

March 8th. I have just walked to town and got mail.

First, to answer Annie's questions. (1.) All the small farmsteads are called ranches. The word 'farm' is hardly ever used. (2.) Settlers nearly always take a plot (about 200 acres) allowed them by the Government. They build a small log hut, often with only the apartment, and spend their capital in the purchase of cattle, pigs, potatoes, and seed, and generally get also a horse and a gun. Others, like Cox, having a little more money, buy a ranch with a house and barn already built. The owner nearly always works on his ranch, and generally only hires his labour when harvesting, which needs extra hands. (Now I think of it, Bassick said Cox was talking of hiring *me* on his ranch in May. I hope he will, unless I have moved elsewhere by then). Wages are $1.25 or more for hired labour on ranches.

(3.) A man either (if he has no money) begins by seeking work (and in time, if careful, can save enough from wages to set up for himself, though many never care to do so), or else, having money, he takes a plot of land and cultivates it.

He can build his own log hut out of pine trunks, which he has to haul in a waggon from the hills. For this he needs a waggon and two horses. If he cannot buy these, another man will haul the wood for a few dollars. He needs a plough and other farm implements, and here again requires horses, so no ranchman of any pretence lacks three or four of these animals. He builds a stable and a barn, and always a 'corral' to keep the cattle and horses in, though these animals are allowed to run in fine weather. In the winter, most of the cattle go into the foot-hills and shift for themselves.

All animals are branded so that the owner may recognise them. There is either a wire or wooden fence round a ranch. He dresses in 'overall clothing', a kind of stout canvas-like material, very cheap, durable, and fairly warm. If he has no wife, he cooks for himself, and this is called 'batching.'

(4.) A man and a boy might very likely go off camping, as you say, though it is more often two men, who are called 'partners' or 'pardners' (whence 'pard') .They might either each take a horse to ride, and one lead a pack-horse or mule, or else they would take a buckboard (*not* cart) and a couple of horses, and drive. For a long journey; the latter is the usual way. They might sleep under a waggon sheet or a 'wigwam' or 'teepee' or they might take a tent, for which they would require three poles (two upright and one across). They would take a shot gun and a rifle with ammunition, probably a fishing rod, to fish for mountain trout (or willow poles might be used). Blankets to sleep in (no sheets), a change of clothing (perhaps).

Provisions: flour, probably a 50 lb. sack, some tins of corned beef, some tins of condensed milk, baking-powder, a can of lard, sugar, coffee (or tea), salt, pepper, potatoes, onions, knives or forks, tin cups and plates, kettle, stew-kettle, tin coffee pot, frying pan, bacon, axle grease (for the buckboard), shovel (probably), Dutch oven (to bake in), pail, saddles (so that they could leave camp and ride (where the buckboard would not go), dog or dogs. If traveling over 'dobe-land', oats or hay for horses. This is about all I can think of just now.

I am writing at the postoffice and have to get home tonight. but will send further details in next letter. Other mail rec'd. was your letter, a letter from Mother, *Ent. Mo. Mags., Pall Mall Budget,* and several copies of *West Amer. Scientist* with notes of mine in it (I send you a copy). [Re] your letter: Thanks, Annie, much for copying out lists of fauna. I am very glad to have them (notes on them I will send later). The Huxley quotation I have heard before, I forget where.

About retailing gossip in family, I can't quite comprehend how it is impossible to talk on other matters and avoid dullness. But since you say it is so, I think the line should be drawn at harmful gossip, at any rate. I mean to say, you should not amuse yourselves by acting the adverse critic on everybody you have come across. Why not tell each other about those you meet fairly, giving both good and ill, as it has come to your knowledge? I see no harm in this. If you can't, and are amused only by ill-tempered or contemptuous criticism of people behind their backs (which I cannot suppose), better buy a gag apiece, and prevent talking altogether. A woman who has come to devote her whole conversation to 'gossip' (and I know there are such) is about as noxious an animal as exists on the face of the earth. Other matters I must touch on later. I cannot now write.

March 8th, 1888

Dear Frederic,

I walked to town today to get mail, but did not mean to post your letter until I got the request for notes for Annie, and so wrote in the postoffice and sent it off.

On my way down to town I found a cocoon of one of the Saturnoidae, about two inches long and shaped like that of *Saturnia pavonia* (= *carpini*). The pupa is inside (I can hear it rattle) so I shall be interested to see what it comes to.

Regy rode into town, arriving soon after I did, and Brock was in with his waggon. He offered to take me out, but as he was not quite sure he would go, and I saw a storm coming on, I walked out but was overtaken by Brock's waggon close to the Kettle's, and so got a ride the rest of the way. The wind was blowing hard and it was hailing as we went across the prairie, though it was quite fine all the while at West Cliff.

I have more to write in answer to your letter, but will do that tomorrow.

March 9th. This dull weather, all mist and hail, is very depressing. I wish we could have a little fine spring weather so that one could get about and enjoy the sun, but I suppose it will come in time. Now, further remarks on yesterday's mail. I have seen the Ruskin plant book. I see you say I have grown more tolerant. I wonder whether that is altogether a good thing? I am afraid I am vegetating out here. One can't keep up the proper pitch of energy all alone and with nothing but one's own business to occupy the time. Possibly what one does do is done better, but there is a tendency to do it slowly and deliberately — too much so.

Payn was worse than nobody, being a hindrance, but that doesn't prove that it is good to work alone. Respecting my *bad* nature, I didn't mean that I was all bad, but there are (at least) two of me, and one is certainly bad (Annie once said there were six — two she liked and four she didn't like), but I think six is almost too many. Frequently the two of me fall out, and then they just 'raise hell', to use an expressive phrase in vogue out here. I think it is more or less so with many people (if not everybody), though not in the same degree perhaps.

I need not have wasted ink over the 'in my opinion' re Preston's asininity, because the opinion is shared 'by all who know him' except, perhaps, Payn.

What did Annie cook? She must try some of *my* dishes, e.g., flapjacks and frying-pan bread, in case she should ever find herself on a desert island. Nothing like being prepared for everything! My cooking is pretty simple: Fill the pan with water, put in the meat, stand it on the stove, and let it boil. If you have potatoes, turnips, or onions, put them in when the meat is nearly done or cook them separately. Frying-pan bread is just flour, baking powder, and water, to make a stiffish dough, grease frying pan and put it in over a hot fire (but not too much flame). Turn over when one side is done. Flapjacks are similar but thin, and made with semi-liquid dough, like pancakes. Just at present I am trying to make jam by boiling down dried apples, but the result is rather insipid.

(At this moment, 2:30, I look out of the window and see, to my disgust, that it is snowing.)

You might ask Belt, if the Ealing Society publishes anything, to let me have a copy or loan or otherwise. I cannot give any more facts about the birds, I am sorry to say, unless about those I saw myself. Tubby Gray's *Perdix (Caccabis) rufa* was a single specimen in the winter of 1885-6. I am glad Annie likes *Minister's Charge*.

It is rather a pity to send the *Ent. Mag.* so late, as it makes it impossible for me to send anything commenting on papers in them to be in time even for the month after next. I had further notes this time on Colorado beetles, but they cannot appear until the May number. (I am now interrupted by Becky Splann coming down on horseback after some things of Payn's. It is good of Becky to come in this weather, but I can't think how Payn could have sent her.)

What is the subject of the other picture Annie has sold? What are your stories about, and where published? Send me copies. The addenda to B. P. and Isleworth lists are very interesting. The Diptera are all new to my Middlesex list except *Syrph. ribesi* and *S. pipiens* which you gave me before. I am glad to see *Lucilia groenlandica*, because I once saw a bluebottle in Marlborough Road that I took for this species, but it flew away before I could catch it. I suppose, from the name, that it was found in Greenland, but it is not by any means confined to that country.

Phytomyza geniculata will be the second Middlesex species of the genus, as E. A. Fitch records *P.bscurella* Pall. in *Entom.*, 1878, p. 42. Should not *Platycheinis* be *Platycheirus*, as in *Ent. Mo. Mag.*, 1887, p. 67? Would it not be as well to publish this Diptera list, say, in *Ent. Mo. Mag.*? I should hardly be inclined to send dragonflies to Harcourt Bath to name. I have a prejudice against him, perhaps, but I never thought much of him. Besides, you can always send to McLachlan. Some of the Hemiptera I had already on record for B. P.; in fact, the B. P. and Isleworth Hemiptera seem much alike. The *Ent. Mo. Mags.*: The species of Chrysomelidae mentioned in the case of mimicry recorded in *E.M.M.* p. 214, is *Disonycha punctigera* Lec. I once sent you a specimen in a letter. If you got it safely you might exhibit it at S.L.E.S. in connection with the note in *E.M.M.* The list of Lepidoptera from Outer Hebrides in *Entom.* is very interesting. Tutt's paper on variation is first-rate; the only thing wanting is a little more precision in some of the localities. I am very fond of the writings of the Rev. Joseph Greene as a rule (I used to gloat over his *Insect Hunter's Companion*) and am therefore the more sorry to see him writing such unprofitable stuff as his note, *Eupithecia europaea!* I see from Goss's note (p.6) that a fossil butterfly has been found in Colorado. I am sorry to see that G. R. Waterhouse is dead.

March 10th. Today has been very fine, and had I not been so busy I would have gone for a walk. I must do so tomorrow, anyway. I have written a paper on *Colias eurytheme* and its variations for the *West American Scientist*. When it comes out I will send you a copy. The chipmunks (*Tamias*) are coming out from hybernation and were skipping about all over the place this morning; I am glad to see them again.

Regy Cusack and Miss Urquhart drove into town and brought me back some mail, viz., (1.) Letter from L. O. Howard at U. S. Agr. Dept., saying that the rose galls found on Feb. 26th (*vide* my letter of that date) are of an undescribed species. I am therefore sending you some galls for exhibition at S.L.E.S. with a note thereon. Afterwards you can either hand them to Billups or keep them, or do as you think fit. Being a new species, it may be well for someone to carefully breed and preserve the flies, and it might be expedient to publish some description of them. There might also be some secondary parasites.

(2.) Letter from Olive. (3.) Letter from Grannie, enclosing one of Leslie's. He writes first-rate letters; that youth will do wondrous things some day! He has evidently found *Testacella mangei* in Madeira. I want him to send you some to forward to Leeds, or examine yourself. (4.) Letter from W. H. Edwards. He does not believe in Pryer's Japanese discoveries. He thinks the experiments are too carelessly conducted to be conclusive. (5.) Lengthy epistle from Geo. Roberts. He seems to be making pretty free with the nomenclature of the *Unios* and *Anodons*. It appears there is to be a *Unio wilcocki*!

Sunday, March 11th, 9:45 p.m. I went up to the Cusacks' this morning and have only just come down. On my way up there I found plenty of *Rhodites*, and in one of them was fortunate in finding a dead imago of the species. I met Cress and Hugg driving down to Hugg's place. I had a lot of insects with me, and showed it to them. Hugg seemed greatly interested; he is a remarkably pleasant man, and a queer character altogether.

I went for a walk in the pine woods the other side of the Cusack's and saw some interesting things. At one place I lay on the ground catching some small green Homoptera. When looking up into a fir tree just above I saw two great serious-looking eyes gazing at me — most beautiful eyes with yellow insides. The owner of them was a big horned owl, of a mottled-grey colour, so like the colour of the pine boughs that had it not been for the eyes I do not think I should have seen him, though he was quite close. I lay still for some time watching it; it would half-doze off, shutting its eyes, but directly I made any noise it was looking at me again.

I also got a very good view of a squirrel, which was crying 'chut-chut' incessantly in a neighbouring fir. This squirrel was of a sort of blue-gray, white underneath, very pretty. I saw several 'robins', *Turdus migratorius*, in the woods. Up in a quaking asp tree I found a pretty nest, old and broken. Regy thinks it belongs to some bird allied to the Chiff-chaff. It is made of grass.

Later on, Mrs. Cusack, Miss Urquhart, and Regy came out also into the wood and sought for specimens, finding various lichens, beetles, etc. I found a specimen of *Coccinella transversalis*, which is very closely allied to *C. 7-punctata*. I have tried to make a rough sketch of it, but it is not a success, and looks ridiculously like a man's face. After supper I expounded botany and entomology, and wrote the natural orders into Miss Urquhart's book in which she proposes to record her discoveries. Then we had psalms, hymns, etc., and I came down here again. Miss U. has been reading 'Lilies' in *Sesame and Lilies*, and thinks it is 'splendid.' Tomorrow I am going up to help Regy haul wood, as he asked me to do so.

March 12th. I went up to the Cusacks' at ten but found Regy was not going to haul wood after all, as Mrs. Cusack was going to town (the first time this year), and he was to drive her in and leave her at the Charley Cusack's (married son of Mrs. C.), coming back himself in the afternoon.

Today is the hottest day we have had this year. I went out and collected insects, securing a great many beetles new to me, also a few Hemiptera and Diptera. I found one larva, too, like a young *Arctia cana*, only perfectly black all over.

The sun was so warm that I lay for quite a while basking in it, which was very lazy of me.

Regy brought me some mail when he returned this afternoon, viz., (1.) Letter from Pilsbry of the Philadelphia Academy of Science (he is curator of conchology there) saying that two species from Colorado I sent him are *Patula cronkheiti* and *Sphaerium occidentale*. The last is new to Colorado but is recorded from Utah, and the *Patula* Pilsbry thinks is probably to be considered a variety of *P. moderata* Stud., a well-known species which has been found fossil in Britain. (2.) *Labor Enquirer*. (3.) 'The Youth's Leisure Hour' (sample copy).

March 13th. A very hot day. I went for a ramble in the morning and found a good many things, among beetles, species of *Paedarus, Sternus, Tachyporus*, etc. Beetles seem to be locally abundant here; on one side of the creek, for instance, I can get any number of one or two species not observed elsewhere, whereas in the field on the other side I got other species, also peculiar to that place. The obvious moral, of course, is, search everywhere. The quaking asp and prairie region is much more prolific in species than the pine woods, though the latter have of course their peculiar forms.

I found a number of fusiform galls on the stems of *Potentilla*, quite different from anything I have seen before. I have done some up for the Agr. Dept., and shall be curious to see what they make of them. My botanical finds consisted of a fungus of the genus *Nidularia* and some juniper which proves to be *J. communis* L., the British species. In the afternoon, when I went out after wood, I saw the first butterfly of the year. I could not get close enough to see it plainly, but I have no doubt it was a hybernated *Vanessa milberti*. What has become of the insects I sent you?

March 14th. Regy Cusack and Miss Urquhart drove to town this morning and I came in with them, and shall walk out this evening. I have got an eminently satisfactory mail, viz., your letter. You have only read one of Annie's children's stories! Verily 'A prophet is not,' etc. I have only read a few, but that is Annie's fault, not mine. I dont in the least see why you should not make money by writing, if you like it. I don't think I should. That is to say, I hate having to write when I have nothing to say. I knew what *Nitella* was! I wish I had been in England for Carrington's good post — how tantalising! It *is* rather absurd of him not to have read any paper.

I used to recollect a Miss Evans that used to herd with the Allports. I always heard good of her but never talked to her to find out what she was like. I should think you would like the Anthropological Institute. Is it not in the same house (3 Hanover Sq.) as Zoöl. Soc'y? I never saw the little book of Galton's you mention. I hope Annie won't overwork herself with all that work. It is rather a pity it should come just when she is not very well. But I am glad she says she is better. She should certainly go for a holiday when the warm weather begins to come.

Larus canus is a good addition to the fauna; the gulls that come up the river are generally *L. tridactylus* I believe. (2.) Letter from Hy. Edwards, about my moths. Several of the species are new to him, and an *Alcita* he thinks is new to science. He says, 'I shall at all times be pleased to do anything I can to help you.' He confirms a *Nomophila* from Saguache Co. as *N. noctuella*, a species which I have taken abundantly at Margate and in Madeira. It is one of the most widely distributed of moths.

(3.) Letter from Bureau of Ethnology (Smithsonian Inst.) about our find of stone implements on 'Pottery Pass.' It appears that they have not been found at so great an elevation before. (4.) Letter and postcard from Douglas. (5.) Letter from Farlow as to specimens I sent him. The supposed *Protococcus nivalis* (vide former letter) is 'probably *Micrococcus prodigiosus*, the so-called bloody-bread. A *Polyporus* I sent is *P. biformis*. (6.) Letter from Bethune, editor of *Canad. Ent.* He says, 'I am much obliged to you for the contribution (a paper on seasonal dimorphism I sent him)

and hope to receive further papers from you.' (7.) Prints of *Unios* and *Anodons* from Wilcock, with 'portrait of the author!' (8.) *Naturalist* for March; a paper on the Land & Fresh Water Mollusca of Airedale, Yorks., is commenced, in which *Sphaerium rivicola* var. *compressa* Pascal is recorded for Appenley. (9.) *Commonweal*. (10.) *Welcome* for March, with my paper on Rocky Mountain animals. Looking over this effusion, it strikes me as being rather feeble. (11.) *Lancet* of Feb. 18th, from Sutton, with abstract of his lecture at College of Surgeons, on 'Evolution in Pathology.' He figures a case of coalesced tentacles in a snail, from a drawing which I sent him. (12.) *Lancet* of Feb. 25th, with an abstract of second lecture on same subject.

6:10 p.m. Have waited for mail, but only got my box of moths returned by Hy. Edwards, and a sample copy of *Agassiz Companion*. Hearty greeting to Annie.

March 15th, 1888

Dear Frederic,

Yesterday, as I was in the postoffice store, a young man came in and ordered Coulter's *Manual*. Of course I at once pricked up my ears and enquired whether he was a botanist. He was N. T. Smith, and taught school in West Cliff. He said he meant to take up botany in earnest this coming season, but he had done hardly anything up to the present. This week he has started botany classes in the school, and has got a number of copies of one of Asa Gray's excellent little elementary books for the children to learn out of. He seems to be fairly intelligent — I should think must be, to teach school at his age (apparently about 20), and I have hopes that he will turn out a good botanist later on.

In the evening I started homewards and, being overtaken by an empty hay-rack going to Hesterburg's, near the Kettle's, I got a lift for a good half of the way. Today has been dull, and I have been very busy writing. Two visitors have been here, and one has been persuaded to stay. Cox called on his way down to West Cliff, an the other visitor was a poor pussy. As I stood in the doorway peeling potatoes a tabby cat came along mewing pitifully. It was very timid, but I enticed it with scraps of meat (it was evidently very hungry) and soon it was purring on my lap and we were the best of friends. Bassick told me some time ago that he had seen a cat wandering round, and doubtless this is the one. I am well pleased to have it, to eat my mice (it has already devoured two) and the cat, having got over its first shyness, seems glad enough to stay.

I see I must exonerate Wilcock from the charge (see last letter) of proposing a *Unio wilcocki*! It was only a joke of Roberts', for now that the engravings are at hand I see that the number (9.) of *U. wilcocki* corresponds to a photograph of Wilcock, which is enclosed with them! But he should have written 'Wilcockius.'

One of the moths Hy. Edwards sends back is a new species of *Crambus*, so I have written a description for the *Ent. Mo. Mag.* under the title *Crambus ulae*. Of course there is no probability that it is confined to the neighbourhood of Ula, but this name is 'short and sweet', and has not been used before. I might have added the conventional termination and made it *ulaellus*, but this does not sound so well.

March 16th. I was feeling lazy today. Sometimes my muscles are lazy and I sit indoors writing and reading, and think it a nuisance even to go and get wood. Sometimes my brain is lazy and I cannot sit down to anything. I was in this latter unfortunate state today, and so, after a short beetle-catching excursion I resolved to walk to town and post the letters I wrote yesterday.

On the way down I caught a curious moth, new to me, and also many beetles, spiders, and ants. (I took it easy and collected as I went.) I also saw a pretty bird about the size and build of a starling, black, with a bright red head and neck. I believe it is a well-known species, but do not know its name. Arrived in town, I got a letter from Mother and a *Commonweal*. I waited for the evening mail, but nothing came. I also got mail

for Payn and Regy Cusack, but shall not bother to deliver it tonight, as it is nearly ten and I am rather tired.

I saw the schoolmaster Smith again today. He seems to have very reasonable views of teaching. He does not believe in teaching writing out of copy-books, and I quite agree with him. He is teaching the children physiology and health, including the effects of alcohol, tobacco, cold, etc., in fact elementary medical knowledge.

So you see this village school in Colorado is in many ways ahead of the grand-looking 'establishment for the sons of gentlemen' in England, or our own Board schools! (Of course, Smith's is a state school. I don't think there are any private schools in the county.) It appears that several of the states have passed a law enforcing the teaching of elementary facts concerning the effects of alcohol and tobacco on the system in schools, and I must say I think this is more likely to do good than any amount of temperance preaching to adult drunkards. If Annie thinks likewise, it might be well to bring this matter to notice in the *Schoolmistress*.

Last night Preston's horse, with saddle and bridle, was stolen out of the stable. He is of course in a great way about it, and declares he will shoot the thief if he can catch him. No doubt, if he is caught, it will go hardly with him, as horse-stealing is considered a particularly great crime in this country.

March 17th. After breakfast I went up to the Cusacks' and found Regy and Miss Urquhart busy preparing to go to a ball to be held at the West Cliff Hotel tonight. I sat talking for a time, and then went to help Regy get wood, after which I went down and saw Payn. This time I saw him alone and heard from him all about Steve Splann and his money. The account as given in the Cliff is correct in the main. The exact amount Steve ran away with was 116 dollars. Payn says he would not have him arrested if he could, both for Mr. Splann's sake and because he could never recover the money.

After this I returned to the Cusacks', as I had promised to keep Mrs. C. company for the evening while the others were in town, which I did. In the afternoon I read bits out of Carlyle's *Heroes* to Mrs. C. while she worked, but my reading is very abominable for want of practice. Afterwards we discussed a variety of subjects. Mrs. C. said she once had a girl living with her out here who was engaged to three different men at the same time! Verily, women being capable of the utmost good, are also capable of the utmost harm — but what fools those men must have been! Mrs. C. says one of them knew all the time that she was engaged to the other two!

Mrs. C. handed over to me a pair of ancient boots left in their outhouse by someone unknown (lots of people have lived up there at different times and left various things behind them). They have good stout nailed soles and so will be useful to me. Mrs. C. wanted to pay me $1.00 to clear up the rubbish round the house, of which there is a good deal, but I promised to do it for nothing. I shall set to work at it as soon as it has thawed out as little more. At present things are to a considerable extent frozen to the ground.

Sunday, March 18th. Most uneventful. The most noteworthy event is the discovery of several specimens of a beetle new to my collection under an old bone close to my door. It is quite warm now, and the water in the pail has not frozen at night for some time. Everyone opines, though, that there is more snow to come between now and summer. The pussy (what name shall I give it — will Annie stand as its godmother and give it a name?) is almost too affectionate, and continually wants to get on my lap, particularly at meal time. It is the most electric cat I ever came across; when stroked, it crackles.

8:30 p.m. After supper I walked up to the Cusacks' and was sorry to find that Mrs. C. was in bed with a sore throat. She had rather a sore throat day before yesterday but seemed all right yesterday and did not feel it again till the middle of last night. Regy and Miss U. did not come home till this morning, so she had to get up and cook her own breakfast, which did not mend matters. Had I anticipated this, I would have stayed up there last night.

I only stayed about half an hour, and coming home I nearly lost my much beloved old hat. It blew off and vanished in the darkness and, had I not chanced to tread on it, I think my search for it would have been fruitless. (It strikes me that this letter is filled up with very trivial matters, but after all, what else is there to say?)

March 19th, 1 p.m. 'Talk of the devil!' I said yesterday that more snow was expected, and so last night it came, a heavy fall several inches deep. It is quite cold again and no sky is visible, but it will probably be fine again tomorrow.

9:25 p.m. Later on it cleared up and so I went for a walk, first up to Cox's and then on to the Splann's. I found Payn asleep. The Splanns tell me that he sleeps by day and is awake all night — the result of taking morphia, of which he has now some of his own. He will just kill himself if he goes on like this. Besides being no end of a nuisance, poor Mrs. Splann was kept up all last night attending to his petty wants. In fact, every night someone has to stay up with him, and as the Splanns all work hard in the day, it tells hardly on them. I have no authority to interfere, but I do not see that anything can be done with him while he is allowed to have his own way.

After this I returned to Cox's. Cox asked me to stay for the evening, but I said I would go down. I meant to do some writing tonight, but alas, for one's good resolutions—. I thought I would just go and see how Mrs. Cusack was (being half-way there), and she insisted on my staying up *there* the evening, though I explained that my fixed and unalterable determination was to go home and write.

I found Mrs. Cusack considerably better though somewhat hoarse. We sat round the fire, talking as usual, and discussed books, boys, emigration, light, and other kindred subjects.

I saw a flock of red-winged starlings (*Age-laeus*) by Cox's house. Their note is queer: 'Chw, Cr-h-e-e-r', if you can imagine what that stands for.

March 120th. The snow is thawing off as fast as it can reasonably be expected to, and will not hinder me from walking to town tomorrow or Thursday to get the mail. I have been indoors writing all day. During the afternoon I amused myself by deciphering bits of Heynemann's 'Die nackten Landpulmonaten des Erdbodens' with the aid of a German dictionary. Having in mind certain efforts of mine in a similar direction with the paper on *Geomalacus*, you will smile incredulously when I say I made pretty good sense of some of it. But perhaps it is like the inscriptions at Sinai, which half a dozen linguists were perfectly successful in deciphering, only they all got different results!

Annie will be wanting to know why I have stopped the story again. I feel disgusted with the plot or my ability to render it, and it is unsatisfactory to be writing what one knows is rubbish. The plot was this. Joe, being anxious to warn people against the Peabody scheme, finds himself taken up for libel, and as none of the office hands will say what they know, he is quite without means of proving his assertions. He is convicted, but only sentenced for a few months (in default of fine) and, coming out of prison finds his character in England ruined, and so, having married Helen, emigrates with her to America (say, Colorado).

Soon after, the Peabody bubble collapses and ruins, among others, Joseph Turner, who also emigrates to America with wife and child. Finally, Peabody and Henry Turner, fearing prosecution, flee to America and go west. Then, in Colorado, Joe Stiggins meets Joseph Turner, who naturally sympathises with him and they become fast friends and occupy neighbouring ranches. Peabody and Henry Turner go round together and spend all their money, and Pea-body comes to an end (say, killed by a bear, or dies of drinking too much).

Henry Turner, being 'broke' and unable to support himself, begs for food on a strange ranch, which turns out to be that of his brother. Joseph is at first inclined to treat him hardly but, pitying his wretched condition, takes him in and takes good care of him. He is already ill, however, and does not recover but dies at his brother's ranch, as repentant for his past villainy as his bad nature will allow him to be. Various other characters and incidents might, of course, be brought in in the course of the narrative.

March 21st. There is an interesting article in *Lancet* on visual centres in the brain. It seems that it has recently been demonstrated that there are quite distinct centres for visual perception and visual memory, so that if the centre for perception is destroyed by disease, and blindness ensues, it is still possible to dream and 'visualise', and, I suppose vice versa.

I have come to town with Frank Cusack. Got letters from W. H. Edwards, Dept. Agric., etc., but no English mail (must walk in tomorrow if fine).

Wednesday, March 21st, 1888

Dear Frederic,
Today opened cloudy and cold, and I quite expected a snowstorm, but later on it cleared up and was sunny though not very warm. Frank Cusack came by between ten and eleven, and I went into town with him. He did not stay long, so I finished my letter to you somewhat hurriedly and posted it together with sundry others. Your letter will probably arrive by this evening's train, but I thought I would rather return with Frank and walk to town tomorrow if it was fine, than wait for it, as the night promised to be cold.

The mail I did get was: (1.) Letter from W. H. Edwards. (2.) Letter from W. Beutenmuller of New York; he is interested in Tineae, and saw the specimens I sent to Hy. Edwards, and wants me to send him some. He appears to be mainly a collector, but I may find him useful to name specimens. (3.) Letter from C. Hart Merriam, the ornithologist and mammalogist of U. S. Agric. Dept. He confirms the skin of a mouse from this house as *Mus musculus* L., and another as a species of *Hesperomys*. He sends some circulars and schedules as to bird migration to fill up and puts in some of the official envelopes of the Department, which I can use without paying any postage. (4.) *Botanical Gazette* for March, from Coulter. (3.) Drawing block and paint brush from Mother. I am very glad to have these. (6.) *Pall Mall Budget*. (7.) *Labor Enquirer*.

In *Botanical Gazette*, Dr. Farlow has a long notice of Asa Gray. Speaking of his invariable cheerfulness, he says,

> This cheerfulness was not that which arises from mere animal spirits. It came from a deep conviction that everything, whatever it may seem to be, is really good. This faith and abiding hope which sprang from within made itself constantly felt in his intercourse with others, and inspired them, for, while those around him were despondent, he always felt that in the end everything would turn out well.

In *Bot. Gaz.*, p. 67, it is stated that *Chara fragilis* is universal, 'found in every country and clime, in ice-water at the north and in hot springs (boiling water) of the Yellowstone', and on p. 69, the death of Dr. Boswell (Syme) is announced.

March 22nd. I forgot to say that yesterday I met Ed Martin in town, and he told me that he had been back to Saguache Creek, proposed to Mrs. E. Alabama Evans, and brought her back and married her since I last saw him! You will remember Mrs. Evans at Schaller's, where we stayed on our hunting trip. She will probably make him a very good wife.

Today Brock drove to town to fetch his wife and child (who had been staying at Silver Cliff for a week) and took me with him. The mail I got was (1.) Your letter.(2.) Letter from one W. W. Reeves of Brighton, wanting *Spiranthes romanzoffiana*. (3.) Postcard from Adkin. (4.) Copy of *The Star* (O'Connor's paper) from Mother. I am rather disappointed in it. I do not think it will live. (5.) *Science Gossip* for March. This finishes my geographic distribution paper. It is very unkind of you; I wrote this entirely for your edification, and I can't make out that you have even read it! I see the Layard replies once more on rudiments! The account of fossil *Planorbis* is interesting; the author of it, G. E. East, junior, used to go to school with me at Wharton Robinson's at Margate. I always thought him rather an ass. Bob Read appears to have been writing (p. 70) on Ray's wagtail.

It is a warm day today, and there are various signs of summer. I saw a specimen of *Vanessa antiopa*, moths (all of one species) are flying abundantly on the prairie, and the prairie dogs are beginning to be visible.

10:30 p.m. Having some mail for the Cusacks, I went up there about seven, and stayed till a little after nine. Now to answer your letter: I never heard of Gustavsen of Skilback. I knew everyone who came to the committee meetings at (Hammersmith) Soc. League, and there was no Skilback. I am sorry to hear of Mrs. Lance being so ill. I don't know Carlie's McCormick.

As to people doing most good unconsciously, I very greatly doubt it! Good requires an effort, and that a very *conscious* one. It may be consoling to some people to suppose that though they do no good of their own wills, they unconsciously effect a lot, but it isn't true!

I think Sewall in *Minister's Charge* is very life-like; I rather pity him than despise him. I would not have started Wilfred Nelson on Charles Reade, as I do not consider this author a model of sense, but perhaps it was on the principle that he wouldn't read a better book, at least not at first.

I am very glad Annie likes my essay on mind; the question of the liquid being pure at first is a very interesting one, which I cannot at present answer. (I will discuss this subject further tomorrow; it is late and I am muddle-headed, so I had better adjourn.)

March 23rd, 8:45 p.m. To continue: In the case of physical peculiarities, we know that they may be either inherited themselves (e.g., colour of hair) or may exist in the offspring only as a *tendency* (e.g., phthysical) which needs certain conditions for the development of the disease.

Mental peculiarities are, I think we may certainly say, frequently inherited, but is it possible to inherit opinions by what I may call spontaneous inheritance? That is, suppose a parent held certain opinions, would it be possible for the children to develop these views by inheritance, without coming into contact with them during their lives and so having an opportunity to assimilate them? And, if so, to what extent does this take place? You see, in my parable, the solvent powers of the liquid — the nature of the mind , and any impurities or dissolved salts at the commencement would correspond to 'spontaneous' or 'automatic' inheritance of ideas. I should like to know what Annie thinks of this). If she is as doubtful about it as I am, it might be wise to write to Francis Galton and see what light he can throw on the problem.

If I *wanted* to go to the Hemery's, I think I should go, though I had only a sack to go in! I think it is rather absurd of you not to go on account of shabby clothes. Do you suppose the Hemery's take you for a clothes-prop?

The limited range of species is a curious question, but one might just as well ask, why do people smother themselves in a hole like London when there are plenty of other places, not only 'as suitable' but infinitely more so?

Don't forget to send me an abstract of your paper to S.L.E.S. as promised.

All thanks to Annie for the extract from Stevenson on *Les Miserables*; I think it is a very good estimate of the book indeed. I do not know,

though, why the character of Javert is said to be ill-written! I return this extract, since you tell me to (though I really don't see why). You enquire about the letter Annie wrote from Sutton; it is in my pocket, where it means to stay! I have had it so long that I shall claim a 'right of way' to it, so it's no use your claiming it!

The list of epithets applied to Mr. Balfour would make even some Colorado editors envious, I should think. I never thought much of Mrs. Kingsford, M.D., though this letter of hers is interesting. She always seemed to me a little bit of a quack, though an entirely well-meaning one.

10 p.m. After writing the above, I went up to the Cusacks' to help Regy haul wood. First of all we had to find the horse, and in the course of the search Regy came across the brown mare, and by her side a foal newly-born, a queer little beast, all legs, as foals are. Regy proposed to call it 'Agamemnon.' The foal being duly examined and criticised, the grey pony was hitched onto the sledge and we went off to haul wood until lunch time. After lunch, Mrs. Cusack, Miss Urquhart, and I went out and sketched the Cusack's house. I did not finish my sketch, nor am I satisfied with it as far as it goes, but I must finish it as best I can. Afterwards I made a pen and ink drawing which was more satisfactory. In the evening we talked of botany, Australia, ghosts, etc.

March 24th. A dull, warm day. I have been at home, writing. In the morning I skinned and dissected a mouse (*Hesperomys*) that Regy gave me. I was fortunate in finding five embryos in it. Preston came down this morning; he is staying up at the Splanns with Payn for a while. He has found out who stole the horse, but there seems small chance of catching him. Regy drove to town and brought me letters from Mother, Carlie, C. V. Riley, and a *Pall Mall Budget*. I was a good deal disappointed that the *Ent. Mags.* did not turn up, but I see Carlie's letter has taken 21 days to get here, so if the *Mags.* are as slow they may not come for some time.

The mail is annoyingly irregular in its comings and goings, but so far, I do not know that I have lost any letters. I see from Mother's letter that Crawford has been swooping down on B. P. again! What a lot of people are dying just now! Carlie wants me to persuade you not to stay indoors on fine Sunday mornings, and I think he is right. Let the Record book be for a bit and go out fauna-ising (and take Annie with you). I wish I had your perseverance, but nevertheless you must not let it keep you indoors when you can get out. Besides, even from the point of view of utility, work on the fauna and flora is distinctly more valuable to science than the mere compilation work on the fauna and flora record-book, though both are very useful.

Sunday, March 23rd. This is as horrid a day as it could possibly be. Cold, with wind and snow. Generally it does not blow and snow at the same time, so this, I am glad to say, is exceptional. Ranchmen say they want some snow to moisten the earth, but it expected to be 'brillig' a little later on.

6 p.m. Just heard a clap of thunder, the first this year. I am writing a second paper for *Sci. Goss.* 'On the distribution of aquatic forms.'

March 26th. Yesterday at about half past six, my feet got so cold and I was feeling so weary of the day that I could not collect my wits for anything, and so went to bed, resolving to stay there till the weather mended! The night was very cold (the ink froze hard) and when I woke up this morning we were enveloped in a white mist. At about nine, however, it cleared up and the sun shone out, but now it is cloudy again and a little snow is falling.

6:20 p.m. Today has been much more comfortable than yesterday. It has been snowing all the afternoon, but there is no wind and it is not very cold, so I am all right indoors.

I have finished my *Sci. Goss.* paper. It contains another of my startling theories, viz., that the more isolated rivers, etc., are in a country, the fewer species of freshwater animals there will be, but these will be very variable and widely distributed.

I saw Cress go to town this morning, no doubt relying on the appearance of fine weather, but he soon got back again!

March 27th. The weather is improving, today plenty of sunshine (though not much warmth) and very little snow. I got in a new supply of wood, but otherwise have not been out.

In the morning I did up a box for the Agric. Dept. and afterwards translated parts of Heynemann's paper on slugs. It is a very valuable paper, and I much regret that I cannot read it properly. However, I can see what is *likely* to be interesting and so have unearthed several notable things by dint of looking out the words in the dictionary. I daresay, too, by the time I have gone through the whole pamphlet (90 pages) I shall have acquired a knowledge of 'snail German', like I have of 'snail French', if you understand what I mean. Heynemann separates *L. agrestis* and *L. laevis* (under the name of *Agriolimax*) from *Limax*. He says *Agriolimax* is quite a distinct genus, and has more in common with *Amalia* than with *Limax*. The *Limax campestris* of this country (considered by some a subspecies of *laevis*) is also an *Agriolimax*.

March 28th. I came in today with one Chamberlain. He lives near Brock's and is a comparatively newcomer, having arrived in February. I never spoke to him before but, seeing him driving to town, asked for a lift, which was readily granted. Chamberlain proves an agreeable man. In appearance he is not very remarkable: A rather red face, hooked nose, and red beard.

I find very little mail waiting for me in town: Letter from Geo. G. Woolson, Supt. Gardener, Dept. of Public Parks, saying he had read my paper in *Sci. Goss.* and could I get him some Colorado seeds? (which I will.) Magazines returned by C. R. Orcutt (which I had lent him). *Commonweal, Labor Enquirer.* Two insect boxes from C. V. Riley (I asked him to send these for some insects I had to send him).

This is a poor sort of letter, but I had better post it as I do not know whether I may be able to get to town again for a few days. I do not much care to walk while all this snow is on the ground. Greeting to Annie.

March 29th, 1888

Dear Frederic,

As you will see from the last letter, I went to town with Chamberlain yesterday. I talked more with this individual coming back, and lent him *Origin of Species*, which he expressed a great desire to read. Chamberlain reminds me a good deal in appearance and voice of a Mr. Edis who lives in Wimpole Street, and was president of Middlesex Hospital Medical Society, but as you don't know this person, you will have no better idea of Chamberlain from this. On the way to town I saw a hornless cow, and Chamberlain tells me there is a regular breed of hornless cattle. I never saw any before, and was much interested.

Coming back it was blowing hard but not very cold, and the night was quite warm. I went up to the Cusack's when I arrived here, taking some seeds they had asked me to buy for them, and I stayed there the evening. In the *Commonweal* received yesterday there are two items of interest: (1.) the Socialist League has started a branch at Acton, and holds meetings on Turnham Green. (2.) Fred Henderson has published a volume of poems!

9 p.m. I promised Regy I would help him haul wood today, so I went up to the Cusacks' at about 11:30. We could not find the grey pony so we did the hauling ourselves, selecting only such wood as was near to the house. Regy chopped the wood and I carried it to the house, using first the hod and afterwards the sledge, which ran pretty easily over the snow and would take a much bigger load at a time.

When we had finished getting the wood I went down to Brock's to get some eggs for the Cusacks and potatoes for myself, after which I came back here. Mrs. C. almost insisted on my staying to supper, but I wanted to get back and was, for some reason or other, feeling faint and unwell, so much so that I had to sit down and rest twice on the way home. However, when I got here, I lay down for a bit and soon felt better again. Mrs. Brock also asked me to stay to supper there. Brock refused to be paid for the potatoes I got of him. The recent cold weather killed poor little Agamemnon, the foal.

March 30th. I have been to town today and got your letter, the *Ent. Mags.*, and lots of other mail. It is past ten, and I am rather tired, so will defer writing till tomorrow.

March 31st. Regy Cusack came down early yesterday morning with some letters for me to post, but I spent the morning working up my fauna-book, and did not start to town till early in the afternoon. It was very pleasant, warm weather and I took it easy, collecting beetles as I went across the prairie, getting a few new to me and two new to Custer county. While thus occupied I was overtaken by Johnny Walsh, who was driving down to John Burke's (a little beyond Ula), and gave me a lift so far. On the way down I saw a *Vanessa antiopa*.

I was well pleased by the mail received, of which later. I stayed in town for the evening mail and got a letter from Morrison of H. Lewis. It was so warm walking home in the evening that although I had my scarf and gloves with me, I did not put them on. This morning, at a quarter to seven, I heard a tapping on the roof, aand, going out to look, found a red-shafted woodpecker (= flicker. Ed.), *Colaptes mexicanus*, the first seen this year.

10:15 a.m. I must now have breakfast and then take some mail to the Cusacks. The mail received yesterday is as follows: (1.) Your letter. I see you would give Smith and Son 'the sack' and do something better. I quite think you can do this by and by, but I think you will find it better to accept a situation of some sort, rather than work promiscuously for yourself. I should think if you keep an eye open something will turn up.

I'm glad you liked the geographical distribution paper. It is a long while since I read Darwin's *Variation of Animals* and then I rather hurried through it, so I have forgotten the theory of Pangenesis. What was it?

About the meat. When I get a shin bone I put it on in the morning, but it does not commence to boil until nearly mid-day, and then I let it boil on and off till the evening. It is so very tough and gristly that it *has* to be boiled. But I am going to get some meat that I can fry, from Brock tomorrow.

Annie's definition of Rights and Duties is almost exactly the same as one Carlie sent me, and I suppose must be considered accurate. I do not dispute it, but my difficulty is still to draw the line between them. In a case of exchange of goods, for instance, it appears that it is the right of each to see that he is not cheated, and the duty of each not to cheat, but the thing is after all a mutual transaction, and the right involves the duty, and vice versa. That is to say, a right without a duty, or a duty without a right, cannot exist, and this is what I denied to emphasize when Carlie talked of people doing their *duty* and letting their rights *alone*, or clamouring for their rights and saying nothing of duty. I may be mistaken in my idea of what he really meant, and perhaps I have not expressed myself to him on this subject with great clearness, but it does seem to me that the two terms merely express somewhat different aspects of the same thing.

I quite agree that Crimesworth in *The Professor* is too egotistical. You should read *Jane Eyre* and *Villette*; you would like them. You have never sent the lists for me to mark. If you are go-ing to, please do so soon, as I shall probably be at work of some sort or another before very long; at least I hope so. I wish you had sent them while the cold weather lasted, and I had *too* much time on my hands. I am astonished to see the account you enclose of 'The Silent Nuns.' If it is strictly accurate it is perhaps as notable a case of contagious insanity as exists. Poor creatures!

(2.) Letter from Smithsonian enclosing a list of some of the insects I sent them. The list is carelessly compiled and full of errors. I am afraid the Smithsonian people are a clumsy lot. I see they are quite unable to name Diptera or Hemiptera. (3.) Letter from Beutenmuller, as to Colorado Tineae. (4.) Letter from Mother.

(5.) Letter from Carlie. He says, 'Duties and Rights is like uphill and downhill; also, Debts and Credits are not the same thing, though what is one man's debt is another man's credit.' Carlie says he went to hear Sir James Paget on 'Scientific Study', and one good remark he made was 'Many people, and good people, exist, who would not for their lives tell a lie, but who yet appear unable, for their lives, to speak the truth.' Which he attributes to inaccuracy of observation, and of course he is perfectly right.

(6.) Five page letter from W. H. Edwards, about *Colias*. (7.) Letter from Morrison of Ft. Lewis about Colorado birds. (8.) An old catalogue (1853) of Coleoptera of the U. S., from Smithsonian. (9.) *Pall Mall Budget*. (10.) *Commonweal*. (11.) The *Ent. Mags*. Tutt's paper continues excellent. I think S. Webb's remarks on recording varieties are a good deal to the point, though I do not agree with him that single records and imperfect lists are useless. They are so *by themselves*, but they afford material on which to base many generalisations, as you will see when Carrington is good enough to read and publish my paper on variation. Of course, the *Vanessa antiopa* aberration on p. 89 is var. *lintneri* Fitch (var. *hygeia* Hdrch. So W. Werner has discovered a 'mare's nest.' *That* record, with no localities, or anything, is *quite* worthless. I am much interested to see Adkin's note on the 'London form of Melanism.'

This morning, coming down from the Cusacks', I found an anemone (*A. patens* var. *nuttalliana* Gray) in bud. It is something like the English garden anemone and has violet flowers.

5:20 p.m. I have been busily writing all day and have not been out since I came from the Cusacks'. The past month has added 65 moths, 24 beetles, and several other things (114 species in all) to my Colorado Fauna and Flora list.

So it comes to this, that for our modern civilization, if it is to succeed, we must depend very largely on the products of superior minds, of which the supply is limited; but at the same time, also on the thinking of the great intellectual middle class, whose duty and function it is to translate the best knowledge and ideas available into action. This means that such knowledge and ideas must be freely published to the world, in such forms as may be interesting and intelligent, and that error, whether due to ignorance or to willful deceit, must be combatted at every turn."

"What of the women?"
Bios 11:164. 1940

Sunday, April 1st. Very warm but not too hot. Windy in the morning. I sat writing till half past eleven, when I walked up to the Cusack's. On the way up I caught some insects, mostly beetles, new to me, and also a very small *Hyalina*, which I take to be *H. conspecta*. The great find, though, was *Anemone patens* var. *nuttalliana* in full bloom and in abundance between the Cusack's and Brock's. It is the first spring flower in Colorado, and a most lovely one. The flowers develop before the leaves and are delicate whitish lilac with yellow anthers. The whole plant Is covered with soft downy hair.

Later on, I went down to see Payn, on the way getting *Dermestes*, *Silpha*, etc., under the remains of a cow. Payn was well enough to walk about, and talks of returning to England in about a month. I went back to the Cusacks' for supper and evening, There was quite a number of us besides the inhabitants.

After supper we had the Sunday evening hymns, and talked of birds, Greek, and other matters. Also, whether it was proper for two young girls to live together by themselves, without an elderly lady (this arising out of the fact that two of Cox's young sisters, of about 17 and 22, have taken a house and live together, but also keep an old lady for the sake of appearances). Cardy Lees thought it was the 'finest kind of proper', but Mrs. Cusack said no, because it would provoke too much comment from the neighbours and place them in an unpleasant position. I must say I don't see why it should not be perfectly feasible and proper myself, and I suppose it must sometimes be done. What does Annie think?

Pink larvae, like those of *Cossus lignipenda*, only purer pink and not so large, are crawling about. I have got three, and want to see if I can get them to pupate.

April 2nd. Cardy Lees called this morning on his way to town. He seems to be taking quite an interest in ornithology, and wanted me to give him the names of several birds found here. About one o'clock I went up to Brock's for some meat, but my journey was fruitless except that I caught some beetles on the way, as Brock was away from home. The rest of the day I have been at home, writing. I have written a paper on 'The Dimorphisms of Animal Pigments' for *Popular Science monthly*, but I hardly expect to get it put in. From the look of the paper, I should think the *Pop. Sci. Mo.* pay for their contributions. It is a most excellent magazine. I see it occasionally at West Cliff.

April 3rd. I got up at half past six and wrote all the morning, and at about twelve went up to the Cusack's to do a picture of the mountains I had promised Mrs. C. Just as I was about to start I caught a lovely *Vanessa antiopa* just by my door, and on my way there I saw three tiger-beetles (*Cicindela*) but they were not to be caught without a net; they fly at the slightest alarm, just like flies.

I sat sketching the mountains all the earliest part of the afternoon, and Mrs. C. came out and sat by me. I got in the sky and the peaks but must do the foreground some other day. In the evening Miss U. and Regy gave us some nice songs: 'London Bridge', 'Nancy Lee', 'For as Gold Must be Tried by Fire', 'Just a Song at Twilight', 'The Warrior Bold', etc.

Mrs. Cusack was telling me of the extraordinary state of the population of Bedford (where she lived). Bedford, it appears, has about 18,000 inhabitants of whom no less than 700 are widows. (That is, *middle-class* widows; the census includes everyone, of course, but Mrs. C. knows only of the middle class.) There are plenty of boys who go to the schools there, but young men are excessively scarce, and it appears that there are not more than 20 unmarried (middle-class) young men, while there are *thousands* of girls in the town. Altogether the number of women is enormously greater than that of men, as may be judged by the fact that in 37 houses making up the road in which Miss Urquhart lived, there were only *nine* men! Though all of the houses were occupied, and one contained as many as 20 women! Query: Whatever is to become of all this surplus of women? It is a most serious problem. Mrs. Cusack is going to write to Bedford to get me full and exact details of the matter.

Coming home I called at Brock's and got some meat. Brock would on no account allow me to pay for it, which was generous of him. (It is very characteristic of this country. A man will treat you with the utmost generosity and yet would unmercifully cheat you in a horse trade. And this is a good deal better than can be said of the average business-man in England.)

April 4th. I rode to town this morning with Regy Cusack and Miss Urquhart, meaning to wait for the evening mail, but as your letter had already arrived, shall not do so. The other mail I got was: (1.) Letter from Ethnological Dept. of Smithsonian Institution. (2.) Postcard from Ansay (Algeria). (3.) Postcard from Galizia (Malta). (4.) Postcard from Averell. (5.) Two boxes from Beutenmuller in which to send him *Tinea*. (6.) *Labor Enquirer*. I am afflicted (I can't imagine why) with that temporary confusion of sight which usually comes before a headache, and so will not write much now. I am sending a *Botanical Gazette*, thinking you and Annie will like to read Farlow's notice of Asa Gray. You can return it at any time.

So I see that Charlie Codd has not yet departed to Australia to tune pianos! I am glad Kate Hemery is taking up botany; mightn't she and Annie work it together somewhat? I should like to have a copy of the Bedford Park Gardening Report. Mother is completely right. I haven't any common sense to speak of! Regy C. is not exactly Miss U.'s 'young man', but they are very fond of each other and I should *think* will be married one of these fine days. I think they would exactly suit one other. Best greeting to Annie.

Wednesday, April 4th, 1888

Dear Frederic,

As I expected, my temporary confusion of vision at the postoffice was followed by a headache, though not a bad one. These headaches of mine, preceded by semi-blindness, are very curious and are perhaps due to a slight capillary hemorrhage in the optic lobe of the brain, which view is strengthened by the fact that the pain is generally only on one side and confined to one lace. Fortunately, they are rare, and hardly ever occur except then I have been writing or reading too long, a sort of natural provision against overwork. This is the first I have had since I came to Colorado, and I am quite unable to account for it.

As I had got your letter, and it was very windy, and a headache was coming on, I concluded to come home. Regy had a good deal on his buckboard, so I concluded to walk. Before starting I got a gallon of lamp oil (40 cents) and some cardboard boxes in which to put insects;

these Regy brought out. Coming across the prairie, I was overtaken by the Splann's waggon and so got a lift for the last mile. Near Ula I found an unknown plant in flower in some abundance. It has whitish green, much-divided leaves and pale lilac flowers in close umbels, surrounded by bracts which at first sight look like sepals [this was probably *Cymopterus montanus*. Ed.]. I have been all through Coulter and can find nothing like it mentioned. A little further on, I found a ditch swarming with *Limnaea truncatula* (alias *S. truncitis*), and beyond that I found a specimen of *Limax montanus*, which some authors call an American race of *L. laevis*. I shall go to bed early tonight.

April 5th. I have been indoors most of the day, writing and packing up boxes for Farlow and Beutenmuller, and arranging my insects. Early in the afternoon I went for a short walk and caught, among other things, two specimens of *Cicindela*. I meant to have done some sketching, but the day was so dull and the mountains so overcast that I could not do anything, it being also too cold to be comfortable sitting out of doors.

A few notes on your letter: One can hardly imagine Solomon as a *little* man, after his picture of the big man overturning the salad bowl (as 'Robert' described it in *Punch*), though I suppose there is no reason why a little man should *draw* little men! I suppose the fat imitation of Irving wasn't Oscar Wilde?

Get Kate Hemery to work up the cryptogams of the Bedford Park flora; there is a vast field for her. I daresay a few might yet be added to the Phanerogamia. Also, do write a paper on Bedford Park Mollusca with Annie's illustrations; it would be first-rate. I should think the rule as to keeping papers at S.L.E.S. would tend to frighten those who *would* read original papers. Certainly I must see the book Annie is illustrating and writing for; if you don't send one I shall get one out of Kate.

Payne has, I believe, now given up taking morphia, or at any rate so much.

I do not by any means agree with all B. Bax's views on religion, but one hears so much on the one side, it is instructive to have the arguments stated for the other. I think Bax means to attack not so much religion itself as the existing forms of religion.

I will give your message to Mrs. Cusack when next I see her. I am very glad Annie says she is better. The notes from the *Ladies' Pictorial* on Farrar's paper in the *Fortnightly* are interesting, but after all they merely say over again what has been said before — the good old lamentations and the good old shirking of the remedy. People look at the world's misery as they look at a tragedy on the stage. They will be moved to tears, but to step down and interfere? It never occurs to them.

April 6th. About twelve I went out to see Payn, taking him some *Pall Mall Budgets* to read, and from there was going to call on Chamberlain, but met him just by Splann's. Chamberlain says he and his boy have been reading *Origin of Species*, and now they want *Descent of Man*. When I got back again, I sat down outside my house and made the enclosed little sketch, which is for Annie. The outlines will probably strike you as being hard, but they are, if anything, *more* sharply defined, owing to the clearness of the atmosphere. The black mossy-looking growth near the base of the mountain is *timber*. The mountain is partly covered with snow where it is not too steep to hold it.

April 7th, 9:30 a.m. Last night was so warm that I left the door open to see what insects would come to the light, and the result was satisfactory. Some red-brown ichneumons with iridescent wings, a fine *Calacampa*, and another *Noctua*. This morning I blew out two caterpillars; one turned out badly, but the other (one of the red *Cossus* larvae) has made an excellent specimen.

Cardy Lees and Regy Cusack came by just now; they are off to Pueblo for a week. Regy told me he had shot a number of birds (and Miss Urquhart succeeded in shooting a nuthatch!) So I am going up to skin them.

10:15 p.m. I found the birds waiting to be skinned were two nuthatches (apparently *Sitta carolinensis* var. *aculeata*), a waxwing (B. *garrula*), a bluebird (*Sialia*), a 'robin' (*Turdus migratorius*), a blue jay (*Cyanocitta stelleri* var. *macrolopha*) and a bird allied to the linnet, which I could not identify. I spent all the morning skinning the nuthatches, robin, and blue jay, and Mrs. C. skinned the bluebird and waxwing. She does it better than I do, being more deft with her fingers. My hands are unfortunately very clumsy for fine work. I also examined carefully the stomachs, and found out what they feed on, this information being required for the Agric. Dept. The nuthatches eat bark beetles; the waxwings, beetles; the bluebird, ants and beetles; the robin, seeds and beetles; and the blue jay had eaten some wheat which had been thrown out for the fowl.

After doing the birds, I went out and filled in part of the foreground of the mountain sketch I mentioned a few days ago, and after that I spent a couple of hours cleaning up the rubbish in front of the Cusack's house and burning it. This rubbish was in very great quantity (I have only done about half today) and consists of wood chips, empty tins, old clothing, cards, pine needles, etc. Before Mrs. C. came here it was the custom to throw everything that was not wanted out of the front door, hence the litter. I raked it into heaps and conveyed it to the bonfire in a sort of wicker basket.

It has been a warm, sultry day, and this afternoon and evening a little rain fell, the first rain this year.

Sunday, April 8th, 9:55 p.m. Hot and sultry, with some rain and distant lightning. When I got up a notion struck me. I would have a garden! I don't know how long I may be here, and so I shall not think of starting vegetables or anything on a large scale, but the plants are all sprouting now and I want to have them conveniently at hand for observation and comparison. So I dug up a little plot by my window, about two paces each way, and manured it and boarded it round, and then went in search of specimens. I got some anemones, and found three other plants in bud, and got also many other things in leaf, including *Achillea millefolium* and *Fragaria vesca*. I sowed some seeds of Colorado wild flowers I had by me, and found four seeds of poppy (from the garden at 5. Priory) along with some shells (Can't you send me some seeds from the garden at Syon? I should like some, Will Annie collect me a few?).

The garden done, I went up to the Cusack's (and was caught by a hail storm on the way up) and thence to Chamberlain's. I was introduced to Mrs. Chamberlain, who is a plain-looking unremarkable woman, and saw the two sons and daughter. One son and the daughter are children; the oldest boy, about 16, seems intelligent and is greatly interested in engineering. The children brought out their trophies to show me. They had found a lot of agates when living near Salida, and a most beautiful arrowhead of semi-transparent flint (*vide* sketch: The notches on the sides are for the thongs that bind it onto the shaft).

Chamberlain returned my *Origin of Species* (which I lent to Miss Urquhart, who has undertaken to read it), and I lent him *Descent of Man*. Chamberlain is a very enterprising man; he has turkeys, pigeons, and fowls, and is growing young cabbage, turnips, and celery in a frame. If he does not succeed it will not be his fault. He lent me an interesting copy of the *North American Review*, and the son lent me many copies of *Scientific American* and *Scientific American Supplement*, which contain some good reading. I returned to the Cusacks' for supper and evening. We had the Sunday evening service, as usual.

While I have been writing this, I left the door open, and a *Calocampa* and another large *Noctua*, new to me, have come into the night.

April 9th, 10:20 p.m. Today has been a good deal like last Saturday. First of all, I went searching for plants for my garden and got one or two, but this was interrupted by Cox and Bassick coming from town (they went in yesterday) bringing my mail, viz., letters from Mother (enclosing Olive's program for Southwark Concert, which is pretty), Mrs. Blossom (of Kansas, promising a list of plants she found in Colorado), C. V. Riley (enclosing some 'penalty envelopes' to save me postage when sending things to him at the Agric. Dept.), and Farlow (with name of a fungus I sent him), *Pall Mall Budget* (a specially interesting one), *Labor Enquirer* and *Ornithologist and Oölogist* for Jan., Feb. and March (as sample copies, from the editor).

I promised Mrs. Cusack I would go up and paint for her if it was fine, so I did, getting well on with the foreground of the mountain view. After this I did more raking up of rubbish, and had another big bonfire. Mrs. C. would pay me the $1.00 for this job, as she originally proposed, though it seemed a very unnecessary proceeding on her part. Cox came up while I was there. He says he will give me some work on his ranch and pay me for it, which is satisfactory. In the evening we sat round the fire (Mrs. C., Frank, Miss U., and T.D.A.C.) and talked, principally of the *Autocrat at the Breakfast Table*, which I read them bits out of for discussion and comment. Before supper, Frank read us some poetry of Longfellow.

April 10th, 6:30 p.m. I had but one match left this morning; it lit the fire that cooked my breakfast, but it was the last. So I went up and got some from Bassick, who was ploughing. Bassick said that Brock and his wife quarreled last night, and she will leave him, but I don't suppose it is really so. It seems that Brock came home drunk, bringing Preston, also intoxicated, with him, and Mrs. Brock resented it. But as I have said before, Bassick has a lively imagination and can make much out of little or nothing.

I spent most of the day writing letters, but in the afternoon went for a stroll. The chief discovery was a cactus which had the whole of its inside eaten out by a pale yellowish, fat, legless Coleopterous larva which resided in a fort of earthen cocoon beneath. I have packed up the cactus and the larva to send to Prof. Riley.

There is a very interesting paper called 'The Meaning of Song', by Helen Kendrick Johnson, in a *North American Review* (May, 1884) that Chamberlain lent me. Here are some extracts from it:

The Meaning of Song. (The author divides the influence of a song under three headings, (1.) That due to the melody, (2.) That due to the association, (3.) that due to the words.) 'Herbert Spencer says, 'an air from a street piano, heard when one is at work, will often gratify more than the choicest music played at a concert by the most accomplished musician.'' (I think this is so, certainly.) 'Sir Walter Scott says, 'The effect of simply, even rude music is such as cannot be attained by the most learned compositions of the finest masters.'' (As an instance of the power of melody alone, it is related that Prof. Kneeland was greatly affected by Icelandic rhythm the words of which he could not understand.) 'Sweet, solemn, and slightly plaintive . . . brought tears to most eyes, and I'm sure it did into mine.' (Quoting Coleridge.) 'Every human feeling is greater and larger than the exciting cause . . . and this is deeply implied in music, in which there is always something more and beyond the immediate expression. Power of association is attributed to the Scottish air of 'Lochamber no More', which the Highland regimental bands are forbidden to play in foreign lands. Thus it would seem that the power of a song lies in the melody or harmony of tone, in the association, in the beauty of the words. Any of these singly can make a pleasing effect. All of them combined produce that which has moved the heart for ages. A fine illustration of the immortality of an air in spite of words . . . is seen in the British National Anthem, 'God Save the King' (Queen).'

'Mr. Ross went to church with his brain full of the suggestion; he sang gravely through the voluntary and opening hymns, and then settled himself to his task. By the time the minister had reached 'lastly', 'Tippecanoe and Tyler Too' had been set dancing to the tune of 'Little Pigs' (Here is an example of the stimulating influence of a sermon to *another* train of thought, which I think I dwelt on in a former letter.) 'Southern negroes: They have never, in their own habitat, sung what we know as Negro spirituals. Two of the most notable instances of world-famous songs founded almost wholly upon the charm of association are 'Home, Sweet Home' and 'Auld Lang Syne'. The air of 'Home, Sweet Home' is pretty, it is true, but slight and meaningless. The words, I fancy, would not for a moment be defended as poetry. The next topic should be the immortal songs which have lived *solely* on account of the beauty of their words. There are no such songs.'

[The following are instanced as perfect or nearly perfect songs, i.e., having all three requisites, namely melody, association, and good words.) 'Scots who hae wi' Wallace bled' (Burns), 'Old folks at home' and 'Swanee Ribber' (S. C. Foster), 'Rocked in the cradle of the deep' (Mrs. Emma Willard, 'Kathleen Mavourneen' (Crawford), 'Stars of the summer night' (Longfellow), 'All quiet along the Potomac tonight' (R. S. Beers), 'Rock me to sleep, mother' (E. A. Allen)].

If you can get this paper on song from Smith's, you and Annie should read it. It is very interesting and full of ideas.

April 11th. I have come to town with Frank C. and Miss U. Got a good mail, viz., your letter, letters from Mother, Carlie, Olive, Supt. of Public Parks, and Coulter. Box of shells from Ancey. Text of *Colias eurytheme* out of his book, from W. H. Edwards. Porter's *Flora of Colorado*, with plants marked that Woolson wants. Ann. Rep. of B. P. Gardening Soc. *Indust. Review* (from Sherborn), all of which I shall write of fully in next letter. The argument about marrying is very interesting; will deal with it in next letter. Can't now in postoffice. I am inclined to disagree with Miss Evans (and I don't think she will be able to keep her own opinion. Love is as mysterious as life.) I am glad my answers to Annie's questions proved the right thing.

April 11th , 1888

Dear Frederic:

I was in the middle of writing up the Colorado Bibliography when Frank and Miss Urquhart came along and took me to town. As we went along they sang together, *Oh, Laddie, Laddie, Laddie!,* etc., and very pleasing it was to listen to them. It is better still when Regy and Miss Urquhart sing together because Regy knows more songs and knows them better. I walked part of the way coming home, and found a *Meloë* on the prairie and a sort of daisy-like plant in flower [This must have been *Townsendia. Ed.*].

In answer to your letter: Let me know when my paper comes on at Zoöl. Soc. No doubt it is atavism; I sent nothing else.

Now, about marrying, etc. Some things strike me. (1.) Love covers a multitude of things. I wish it could be used only for what I should call *true love*, the highest sympathy. A man may 'fall in love' with a woman solely on account of her beauty, which has nothing in the world to do with sympathy, and I don't think any man is right in marrying on these grounds, often as it is done. If *aesthetic love* (so we may call it) were the basis of marriage, it would be truly absurd to restrict to one wife, or to make marriage permanent, and that is exactly the barbarian idea.

On the other hand, the higher development of humanity being characterised precisely by the presence and possibility of *sympathy (true love)*, marriage becomes a *permanent* union between *one* man and *one* woman, and ought to express the highest *sympathy* possible.

(2.) Using 'love' in the wide popular sense, undoubtedly a man may fall in love very many times, but I doubt very much whether more than one *true love* is possible to anyone. It is like ivy on a tree; the tree may die and the ivy live, and vice versa, but the ivy never deserts the tree, though dead, for another, nor *can* it do so. I think this because I believe that love is a growth, not a mere attraction to the *previous* characters of the lovers entirely, and that to give up a love once held for another would almost necessitate living one's life *backwards* to the old time before love, which is impossible. (This is somewhat incoherent, but I hope it conveys something of my meaning,)

(3.) I am disposed to doubt whether the highest possible friendship can exist between two of the same sex, or between blood relations, for the simple reason that they are *too alike*. (4.) In any case, it seems to me that your best friend's friend *must* also be quite your friend, else you have only half a friend. To what extend friendships or loves of three or more can go I am hardly able to judge, but I feel some doubt. It's a very old saying that 'two is company, three is none.'

(5.) As to three meeting in a future existence, I can't believe that a love once grown can cease for an interval and be renewed. Rather I think that it would continue on both sides *until* the future meeting. Suppose a man 'loves' a woman, goes away and hears nothing of her for years, in the meantime 'loves' another woman, and finally (on earth) the three meet, they will certainly fall out, but *because* it will be plain that in the case of the first woman, at least, his 'love' was a fraud, that is, not *true love*. To me, the separation of death, assuming that death is not annihilation (and I think this may be assumed), is in no way essentially different from the separation of locality upon the earth, and as regards love precisely the same rules holds.

(6.) It is well to remember that, *under certain conditions*, people who are not in love may be reasonably married. For instance, Martin recently married Mrs. Evans of Saguache Creek. Now he *may* very likely have *loved* his first wife, but I do not for a moment suppose that there was any *love* between him and Mrs. Evans. Simply he wanted a pleasant companion who would cook, etc., and *she* wanted a means of living in tolerable happiness, and I cannot blame them for getting married on these terms, *both having been married before*. Now, in a future existence surely the *true love* would claim its own, and the second wife and husband would not for a moment think of claiming one another, any more than a mistress would claim her servant, or vice versa!

(7.) But finally, I must confess that I *know* nothing about it, being only able to judge from myself, who may be quite different from other people. It is all very strange and difficult to understand. Love, Life, Space, and Eternity cannot be defined or reduced to language. The soul is not fully conscious of itself, and feels that it is fathomless.

Does Annie agree with all I have said about love, or most of it, or some of it? She will agree that it is very difficult to write a satisfactory account of other people's feelings, and to say with certainty that this or that never happens or always happens. The study of Humanity is by no means plain sailing as the study of beetles.

Respecting the other mail: Coulter sent me a list of the plants I had sent him, and is going to print some remarks of mine on idiosyncrasies, in *Botanical Gazette*. Woolson sends a copy of Porter & Coulter's *Flora of Colorado* with the plants he wants marked in it. You will remember he is head gardener at the Department of Public Parks, and wants plants for the Central Park at New York, etc. I can get him quite a number, I think, and hope to do a good deal for him (making him pay me, of course). He wants 1,000 plants of *Calochortus gunnisonii*, but I have not yet met with it and fear it may not occur here.

I have been working hard indoors all today with the *Flora of Colorado* that Woolson sent. It gives me very many additions to my Colorado list, and also the localities for most of the species. (The precise localities are not given in Coulter's *Manual*.) It is interesting work, though tiring. I have so far got to the end of the Compositae. When I get finished I will give you some interesting details.

Apr.13th. Just like yesterday, working at the Flora all day. I have got to the end of the flowering plants and hope to finish tonight or early tomorrow. The notes I have taken will be of very great value to me all this summer, when I expect to do a lot of botanising.

A *Vanessa milberti* came flying past my door about midday. Last night a number of moths came in to the light, including a *Depressaria* and one or two others new to me.

Apr. 14th. To my great satisfaction I finished my work on the Colorado flora this morning and went out for a walk, taking my butterfly net with me to capture the insects that are now about. First I went to Cox's to look at his map of Colorado (the one we had was Payn's, and he has taken it away), then to Brock's, and Brock asked me to come and clear up the rubbish round his house (as I have been doing at the Cusacks'), which I said I would do on Monday.

I was just going up to the Cusacks' when Cox met me and asked me to go and do the *post mortem* of a mare of his which had just dropped down dead as he was ploughing (hard times for Cox; he gave $125 for that mare only a little while ago). So I went down and we cut the mare open, and discovered a blood clot in front of the heart — aneurism of the aorta and congestion of the lungs.

After this I went up to the Cusacks' and did some more clearing-up of rubbish (there is plenty of it yet to do) but did not stay to supper. When I left, Mrs. Cusack presented me with a basket of provisions 'as we are going to town for a day or two and the things wouldn't keep.'

I hear that ten cattle have died suddenly over by Jod's so I am going over tomorrow to investigate the matter.

Bassick's yarn about Brock and wife quarreling seems to have been more or less fabulous, as I supposed; at least now they are on the best of terms.

Here are some notes on the *Flora of Colorado*. This work has enabled me to add the following to my Colorado list: Phanerogamia, 293 and 76 varieties; Fungi, 8, and lichens, 4, which is eminently satisfactory. Nothing is said about Hepatics and I have not yet a single species down for Colorado (though I have found some but not named them). The following species on the list of addenda will be interesting to you: *Ranunculus repens* L., *Potentilla anserina* L. (Denver, Colorado Springs, etc.), *Daucus carota* L. (introduced), *Galium aparine* L., *Erigeron canadensis* L., *Pyrola minor* L., *Rumex acetosella* L., *Polygonum viviparum* L., *Juncus bufonius* L., *Typha latifolia* L. (Wet Mt. Valley), *Potamogeton natans* L., *Calystegia sepium* L., *Solanum nigrum* L., *Mimulus luteus* L., *Utricularia vulgaris* L., *Prunella vulgaris* L., *Chenopodium album* L., *Atriplex patula* L., *Panicum crus-galli* L., *Triticum repens* L., *Hordeum vulgare* L., *Polypodium vulgare* L., *Pteris aquilina* L. (Wet Mt. Valley), *Equisetum arvense* L., *Bryum argenteum* L., *Funaria hygrometrica* Hedw., *Webera nutans* Schreb., *Cetraria islandica* Ach., *Agaricus velutinus* Curt. It is mentioned of a Kansas moss (*Phascum carniolicum* W. & M.) that it is so far known from only three localities, viz. Kansas in America, and Carniolia and Sardinia in Europe!

I got up at about six this morning, had breakfast, and started off to examine the defunct cattle, some of which belong to Jod's brother and some to one Kitman, all on the same ranch. The place is about five miles or more away, somewhat in the direction of West Cliff.

I collected on the way, getting various insects: *Cincindela*, 2 spp., *Carabus* sp., *Pompilius* sp., grasshoppers (3 sp.), etc., and I saw two *Pier-*

is *protodice* and a *Grapta*, probably G. *zephyrus*, which I failed to catch. In a field I found numbers of pretty little pale blue gentians in flower, only an inch high; they are *Gentiana humilis*. I also caught a frog (*Rana*) which I have put in spirits.

When I arrived, Jod's brother took me to see the cattle. Dr. Ellis had been sent for from Silver cliff, he told me, and he declared it was poisoning, but I don't think he knows anything about it, and I have no doubt that *Anthrax* is what killed them. Now *Anthrax* is a bacillus, one of the largest bacilli known, and the disease is extremely contagious and very quickly fatal and may be communicated to man. So I had no mind to handle the carcasses but examined them from a short distance. Two had been cut open with axe and scythe and I could see some of the internal organs. Everything pointed to *Anthrax* and to nothing else, and I think the poison hypothesis is wholly untenable. I left them with injunctions to bury the bodies or to burn them, or at least cover them with earth, but I do not know whether they will take this trouble.

Coming home I caught a few more insects, notably a pretty little *Arctia*, and picked a few flowers just coming into bloom, and got back at about two. Just now I found some moss by my house which is either the same or very near to *Webera nutans*. (You remember we collected this at Sandwich, and Annie had some growing in her little pot.)

I went up to breakfast at Brock's (as Mrs. Brock asked me to), and spent the day cleaning up the rubbish round the house, and burning it. I rather enjoyed myself on the whole, as this easy manual labour is quite recreation for me, and I do not doubt that it does me good. I had a rake and a wheelbarrow to work with, and as there was a great deal of rubbish I had a very big fire going all day.

While I was working I saw two white butterflies but did not catch them. I found a number of bottles among the rubbish that will do well for my alcoholic specimens, and I also brought away three very decent (though old) boots that would

otherwise have perished in the flames. Brock offered to pay me for the work done, but I did not think that necessary, so he gave me 20 fresh eggs and promised me some potatoes.

Before leaving I made some arrangements for the future. (1.) I would go up one day and do some 'clearing' for Brock; that is, clear young quaking aspens, etc., off a piece of ground so that he could cut hay there. (2.) On Thursday morning I would take Brock's team and waggon and go to town. Brock asked me to do this because he wanted some groceries brought out, and for my part I was not unwilling to drive instead of walking.

When I returned to my house, I found a letter and a postcard from W. H. Edwards; these had been brought from town by Frank Cusack. In a recent letter from Edwards he said he had often tried to get collectors to go to the southwestern corner of Colorado where he supposed there must be new and interesting butterflies, so I wrote in reply that if we could get ten entomologists to pay $10 each, the resulting $100 would be sufficient to pay expenses for a three month's trip, the said entomologists, however, only to be those who could and would work out properly the material I sent them in return for their money.

Now (postcard rec'd. today) Edwards writes, 'I will look about and see if a club can be formed as you suggest. Perhaps it can.' So it is possible that next month may see me at Fort Lewis or Durango. I would like to know whether you and Annie might think this scheme a wise one. It seemed to me that although it might be less profitable in the money sense than other work, it is very healthy and enjoyable and would add greatly to the natural history of a little-known district, which is worth considering.

Morrison has done a good deal with the birds but, except for this, I believe hardly anyone has collected there except the Hayden government survey. There would be lots of new and interesting things. The railway fare would be the most formidable expense if I go. I can get good board and lodging on a ranch for $20 a month or perhaps less. So I figure it, three months traveling, $30, board and lodging $30, postage, etc., $10, boxes, etc., to be provided by the entomologists. But I mustn't cook my hare before I've caught it!

Yesterday the creek (Swift Creek) by my house ceased to flow. There is water in a pool for the present, but I trust it will soon run again or I shall have to go to Cox's for water. *Man cannot live by bread alone*, and although he can do very well without butter, he *must* have something to drink, not to speak of such little matters as washing!

I see one of the plants Woolson wants is *Adoxa moschatellina*; were I only at Chislehurst I could send him a waggon-load!

Apr. 17th. It rained on the range yesterday afternoon, and this morning it was raining down here, which has had one good result; it has set the creek running again. But this was not the end of it. It rained all the day, turning to sleet in the afternoon, and now it is snowing in right earnest, the ground being already white. It has been quite chilly, so that I have had a fire going and have not been too hot.

I packed up a box for Ancey, finished the Colorado Bibliography, wrote some letters, etc., and so have been fairly busy indoors, but tomorrow I wanted to get out and about and so am sorry to see the snow.

Apr. 18th . It did not snow after dark yesterday, so after all the fall was so slight that it melted all off this morning before midday. Today has been fine, and the butterflies are again about. I caught a *Pieris protodice*.

Soon after breakfast I went up to Brock's and cleared away the ashes of the bonfire; there were about eight or ten waggon loads (I did not count how many), so you may judge that it was a pretty big fire though some of it was only half-

burnt. I had lunch at Brock's and then went out and got a lot of plants (cactus, *Gilia*, *Penstemon*, etc.) for Woolson, which I packed in damp moss in six tins. After this I went up to the Cusacks' (about three) and did some more clearing up rubbish until it was too dark to see properly. Then I went in and we talked, sitting round the fire.

I find that Frank, when he last came from town, left some mail of mine (two papers and a 'parcel of pamphlets') by mistake at the hotel. I feel anxious about them. I shall rage considerably if they are lost.

Mrs. Cusack told me a good story of a very shy man she knew. (He was a music critic, and was so shy that when managers of concerts sent him tickets for a good place, he wouldn't use them but bought other and back-seat tickets so that he might not be noticed!) Well, he sang very well and used to like to sing at church but, being shy, he sat in the back seats, which were free and often contained people who had no hymn-books. Now if anyone came next to him who had no hymn-book, he felt bound to let him look over his, but this was a very great trial to him. So one day he bought a second hymn-book to lend, and went to church with the two in his pocket.

When he got up for the first hymn, he looked at his neighbors — on one side a girl, on the other a horrid-looking old man — and neither of them had hymn-books! Whatever should he do? Should he lend the old man one of his books, and look over with the girl? No! He couldn't do that. He was much too shy to think of that. Should he, then, lend the girl a book and look over with the old man? No, he really couldn't do that. So he kept both the hymn-books in his pocket! Isn't that a good story?

A new arrangement has been made about my going to town tomorrow. Brock wants the harness for use on the ranch tomorrow, so Frank and Miss Urquhart will drive and bring out Brock's provisions in their own buckboard, and I shall ride in on one of Brock's horses.

Apr. 19th. I was up at a quarter to six, had breakfast at Brock's at seven, and got down here (riding) just in time to post letters for the morning outgoing mail. I did not post this, however, because I thought there might be something to answer in your letter just received.

I am glad Annie went to stay at 5. Priory. (Wish she had done that when I was there!) I meant to publish the Addenda to Bedford Park list of Diptera. Immense thanks for addenda to Isleworth fauna and flora. A few odd notes thereon: I have *Cetonia aurata* near Twickenham by the river. *Acherontia atropos* is recorded for Twickenham, I think by Stephens or Curtis. I should almost doubt *Papilio machaon* and *Grapta (Vanessa) c-album* unless bred and let go there.

The other mail received was very satisfactory. The papers left at the hotel were *Pall Mall Budgets*, *Commonweal*, and several numbers of *Bulletin of Washburn College* (Kansas). This last sent by Ford, very interesting and valuable to me (it must be returned, so must spend days copying it out). Other mail is: Your letter, letters from Carlie, Wallis Kew, Douglas (and $15), Beutenmuller, F. J. Ford, C. Hart Merriam (Agric. Dept.), Bethune, and also copy of *Canadian Entomologist*, Jan. 1888, *Labor Enquirer*, *Naturalist*, *Botanical Gazette*.

April 19th, 1888, 9:30 p.m.

Dear Frederic:

Frank came to town in the course of the morning, and brought in my plants for Woolson, which I sent off to New York by rail. The box weighed 13 lbs., and cost $2.25 to send, of which $1.50 is charged by the Denver & Rio Grande R. R. to Pueblo, and 75 cents takes it from *there* to New York! Such is monopoly! Frank and Miss U. took Brock's horse, and gave me their pony to ride on — this because the horse 'Tom' of Brock's was a stronger animal, and they thought it would be better able to pull a somewhat loaded buckboard. I started from town before they did, but as I went slowly, reading as I went, they caught me up, and I rode by them the rest of the way.

When I got up to Brock's, I found that Mrs. Frank Hunter and children were there, and Mrs. B. is going to have a sort of 'afternoon tea' in her honour tomorrow, and asked me to go, which I said I would.

Then I went down to see Payn, having two letters for him. He seemed pretty well and was more cheerful than usual. He insisted on presenting us with some of the Splann's butter and two loaves of bread. I didn't quite like taking them but could not agreeably refuse. Frank had asked me to go to supper up at the Cusacks', and rather unwisely (as I have very much to do at home — six letters to answer, etc.) I said I would. So I turned up there about five, and did about 1½ hours work clearing up rubbish (which seems to be everlasting), had supper, talked for a while, and then came down here.

Wrote in the morning, and in afternoon went up to the Brock's. I was rather curious to see Mrs. Hunter, because Lees and Cox, etc., have such a great admiration for her. (I had seen her on the street, but never to notice.) I found her to be a decidedly 'pretty' woman of the American type, but not able (apparently) to talk and seemingly not very intelligent. On the whole disappointing (though, indeed, I did not expect much).

The Cusacks came (i.e., Mrs. C., Frank, and Miss U.) dressed up for a call, and when they arrived we shook hands quite formally as if utter strangers, but the stiffness of the affair was somewhat broken by the arrival of Cox and Brock in shirt sleeves. When the Cusacks went, I departed with them and went up to their house. I was starting (meaning, to write this evening) when Mrs. C. called me back and made me stay to supper which, of course, meant the rest of the evening. After supper Mrs. C. and I argued for about an hour on the stale question whether an ordinary 'business man' does useful work, or is entitled in justice to the profits he pockets. We did not convince one another.

Apr. 21st, 7:30 p.m. How light the evenings are getting. I have only just lit the lamp! The only event of today is that Lees and Regy came back from Pueblo this evening. Lees has bought a waggon and team and came in that. I have been writing letters and extracts from Washburn College Survey Bulletin all day. When I get the extracts finished I will send you some notes. I have written a paper on *Limax montanus* (the Colorado slug) for *Journ. of Conch.*

Sunday, Apr. 22nd, 3:25 p.m. I wrote all the morning, and got my extracts from Washburn Coll. Bull. done, sooner than I expected. Chamberlain and boy rode down about mid-day and took away Agric. Dept. 1886 and other things to read. I went out a little while ago and found a lovely blue *Mertensia* in flower, as well as some other things.

Here is a list of some of the species recorded in Washburn Coll. Bull. Kansas: *Lycoperdon giganteum* Batsch., *Xylaria hypocyton* Fr. (Isleworth), *Mucor mucedo* L., *Aecidium grossulariae* DC. (a Bedford Park fungus), *Helicopsyche* sp., *Rotifer vulgaris* Schr., *Amoeba proteus* Roesel., *Cystopteris fragilis* Bernh., *Peziza vesiculosa* Bull. (an Isleworthite), *Periplaneta orientalis* L. (one specimen only), *Planorbis parvus* Say, *Bryum argenteum* L., *Morchella esculenta* Pers., *Esox luteus* L. (introduced), *Epaira diadema* Hc., *Oidium fructigenum* Kr. (a B. P. fungus), *Hydra viridis* Anett.

It is a curious thing that *Vitrina*, so abundant in Colorado, is not included in the list of Kansas mollusca. My Colorado list now stands as follows: Mammalia, 20 species and 1 extinct; Aves, 311 and 3 vars.; Reptilia, 1 and 2 fossil; Mollusca, 51 and 4 vars., and 1 fossil; Coleoptera, 61 and 2 vars.; Hymenoptera, 12 and 1 fossil; Orthoptera, 63; Rhopalocera, 178 and 19 vars., and 1 fossil; Heterocera, 106; Diptera, 2; Arachnida, 2; Crustacea, 2; Annelida, 2; Phanerogamia, 1,358 and 149 vars.; Gymnosperms, 15 and 2 vars.; Pteridophyta, 31 and 1 var.; Mosses, 112 and 8 vars.; Fungi, 17; Lichens, 51; Algae, 1; Fishes, 1; Amphibia, Neuroptera, Protozoa, Coelenterata, Myriapoda and Hepaticae, none at all.

5:20 p.m. Only just discovered your card of West Cliff Nat. Hist. Soc.! (It was in a corner of envelope and didn't come out with letter.) Here are a few more notes on your addenda to Isleworth list:

Sphinx convolvuli is recorded from near Ulbridge (Benbow); Holloway (Field); Acton (Woodhams); nr. Isleworth (Powley); Victoria Park Station, Biggs. *Lygaena filipendulae*. I once found this near Ealing. *Odonestis potatona*. Recorded from near Highgate (Lockyer). Common in W. Kent (TDAC). *Aporia crataegi*. Must be quite accidental at Isleworth!

Bird list. I don't think these altogether unlikely, but some must be quite occasional. I expect they are all recorded for Middlesex by Hartling. *Agriotis lineatus*. I think Curtis calls this a destructive insect in the larval state.

10:20 p.m. It being Sunday, I went after supper to the Cusacks', taking some flowers I had found. Afterwards, we had the usual hymns, etc. Louis Howard was here, and Cardy Lees.

Coming home, I looked in at Cox's. Cox asked me to clear up round his house, and I shall probably do so next Friday.

Apr. 23rd, 9:20 p.m. I have been working at Brock's all today. I went up after breakfast, meeting Frank Cusack on the way, just starting for Pueblo. The work I did was clearing a piece of ground of quaking asps (mostly dead), so that the hay could be cut on it. It is hard work, but I didn't work very hard. The dead trees can be pulled down; live ones need chopping of course. There were very many dead ones already fallen. All had to be piled up so that they could be burnt. I made three piles, two of them quite big. There is quite a lot of land to be cleared, and Brock says I can go to work there when I like, and he will pay me for whatever I do. He is also going to get me to help him plant potatoes shortly.

Under stumps etc., I found many snails, including some new to Custer co., viz., *Cochlicopa lubrica*, and *Hyalina radiatula* var. *viridiscenti-alba*, and also var. *alba* (var. nov.) of *Hyalina arborea* in some abundance. The var. of *radiatula*, so rare in England, seems quite common in America. I also saw a *Danais plexippus*, the first this year.

Coming home, I saw Regy coming up from the Cliff, bringing Miss Sidford, who has just come home from Colorado Springs and is going to stay at the Cusacks' for a time. She is said to be a botanist in a small way, so I want to see what she has discovered at the Springs.

Apr. 24th, 9 p.m. I thought I would do some of Cox's clearing-up today, but it rained during the morning, so I arranged my Colorado Mollusca and made a careful comparison of them, which I had never done before. I have still species of *Physa*, *Pupa*, *Limnaea*, and *Hyalina* I cannot identify. Soon after I went up to the Cusacks'. On the way I found wild strawberry (*Fragaria vesca*) and other things in bloom. I asked Miss Sidford about her botany and found she had collected several species of plants at Colorado Springs. I think she will perhaps do some good work, as she seems enthusiastic about it, and I hear that the man she is engaged to (he lives in England, has the distinguished name of Brown) is likewise a botanist, and that stimulates her. She says that she made a large collection of flowers in Wiltshire, Darbyshire, and Guernsey, using 'Johns' to name them.

I am afraid Miss Urquhart will not make much of a botanist. I discovered today that she didn't know fungi were plants, and thought insects had something to do with their production! In the afternoon I went out for a very nice ramble in the woods with Mrs. Cusack, and we collected a lot of mosses, lichens, etc., etc.

Apr. 25th, 4:30 p.m. I walked to town today, starting at about twelve and getting here about two. I found a very pretty white flower, very fragrant and fragile, blooming freely on the prairie. It belongs to Liliaceae and is, I think, *Leucocrinum montanum*. I also got some other flowers and some insects on my way down.

When I got here, I found your letter had not yet come, so I must wait till the evening mail. But the mail I did get was: Letters from (1.) Mother. (2.) Coulter, with names of men to whom I can send mosses and Hepaticae, (3.) C. V. Riley, about some insects I sent him. (4.) Douglas (and a *Harper's Magazine*. Other mail was (5.) Instructions for preparing skins of mammals, from Agric. Dept., (6.) *Science Gossip*. Roberts has found a mare's nest in his *Helix hortensis* var. *fuscolabris*! (7.) *Labor Enquirer*. (8.) The *Ent. Mag.* I posted a good deal of mail, including a note on *Hesperomys sonoriensis* to the *Zoölogist* — you see that magazine at S.L.E.S. and might let me know whether or when the note appears. but you needn't send me the numbers. I enclose a few seeds of *Iris*. I have not seen the flower, but no doubt it is *I. missouriensis* Nutt., as that is the only Colorado species. The flowers should be purplish.

7:45. Got your letter and a *Commonweal* this evening. I am sorry to hear Annie is not looking well. The reports I get are rather conflicting and I hardly know what to think. I wish you could take her for a nice holiday in the country. She wants to be somewhere where she can get out and *ramble*. I think woods are much better than the seaside. I am afraid she has been working too hard of late.

What was the matter with your eyes? And why did you go to Dr. Hogg, of all people? I don't believe in Dr. Hogg. He called my consumption 'a slight bronchial infection!' He is an excellent man, *except* as a doctor.

Now I have got to walk home. There will be a moon. Greeting to Annie, and wish for good holiday and good health.

This is a poor sort of letter. Will try to do better next time.

April 26th, 1888.

Dear Frederic,

Yesterday afternoon, in town, Smith (the school-teacher) took me up into his room and showed me some flowers he had got. I talked a bit with him and think there is a possibility he will do some good work in botany. I walked home in the moonlight after the evening mail had come in, getting home after nine. It was rather chilly, and too windy to be pleasant. The morning opened dull, and it has been snowing on and off all day.

I had some mail for the Cusacks, so I went up there about ten and got talking with Mrs. Cusack and stayed till past four! Mrs. C. gave me a photograph of herself, which is not a good one. She doesn't like it herself, but it gives some idea of what she is like. So I will enclose it, and you may have it over to Annie to keep for me (if she will) till I return.

Mrs. C. showed me, in the weekly edition of *The Times* (April 6, 1888) a long report of Crookes' [this was Sir William Crookes. Ed.] Presidential Address to the Chemical Society, on *Elements and Meta-elements*. It proved to be the most interesting chemical paper I have *ever* read. Crookes commences by showing that not only do some elements (so-called) differ *very* slightly from others, say in the intensity of a spectrum-band or the rapidity of precipitation of their salts, but some, formerly called elements, have been split up into several bodies which, though nearly, are not quite alike. Then he goes back to the *origin* of the elements, and speaks of the 'protyle', by which he means the original homogeneous 'fire-mist' or 'formless stuff' from which, he says, we may suppose 'an infinite number of infinitely small ultimate, or rather ultimatissimate particles gradually accreting, and moving with inconceivable velocity in all directions.' These are the atoms.

Then he goes on to show how it can be proved, by experiment, that objects moving at the same velocity tend to aggregate together, and he considers the elements were formed by such aggregation of atoms having the same, or approximately the same, velocity and temperature. 'We may perhaps conceive two elements as springing from the differentiation of a nearly homogeneous swarm of ultimate atoms.'

He thinks the origin of atoms was on the very edge of the protyle, and their subsequent migrations have always been inwards. 'The centre of the unknown creative force in its mighty journey through space having scattered along its track the primitive atoms — the seeds, if I may use the expression, which presently are to coalesce and develop into the groupings known as (here mentioning a number of elements).'

Finally, as to the source of energy of the atoms, he says, 'If we may hazard any conjectures as to the source of energy embodied in a chemical atom, we may, I think, premise that the heat radiations propagated outwards through the ether from the ponderable matter of the universe, by some process of nature not yet known to us, are transformed at the confines of the universe into the primary, the essential motions of chemical atoms which, the instant they are formed, gravitate inwards and thus restore to the universe the energy which otherwise would be lost to it through radiant heat.' All this, or course, is terribly wild speculation, but it is extremely suggestive, and quite fascinated me. You and Annie should certainly read this address if you can get it.

I was talking with about the origin of things and Crookes' view thereon, with Mrs. Cusack, and it led to a long argument on religion, or rather, beliefs, which was interesting to me though we did not arrive at any definite conclusion. Some of the questions raised were: (1.) What is meant by 'Creation?' I pointed out that in the Genesis account, for instance, only the first verse implies actual *creation*; the rest merely means the modification of the heavens and the earth, already created. Here Mrs. C. agreed with me. (2.) What is a soul? Mrs. C. did not consider the soul to be the same as consciousness, for though obliged to admit the consciousness of animals, she denied them souls. It seemed to me that consciousness was identical in the main with soul, and that it implies existence after death. (3.) Were souls created at each birth, or did they previously exist? Mrs. C. thought they were created. I was inclined to suppose they had some previous existence. (4.) What was the idea of the divine forgiveness of sins? I thought it was the name for a mental or moral process and had nothing to do with physical matters. Mrs. C. seemed to half agree with me, but thought that if a person did wrong unintentionally and was sorry, the divine power would turn it to good. This I couldn't see. (5.) Mrs. C. said she accepted as true what was written in the Bible. I could not accept everything in this way. I did not think it was any sure guide as to the truth of a statement. (6.) Mrs. C. quite agreed with me that in a future existence we should be actively employed, else we should not really exist. (7.) The question was raised as to whether we should be 'perfect' in 'heaven.' I thought decidedly not. Mrs. C. at first thought so, but after talking it over seemed a little doubtful. (9.) Mrs. C. agreed with me that 'eternal torments' was bosh, and further said that she was quite unable to conceive the end of things, so altogether, you can suppose we had a considerable argument.

The conversation was interrupted by the arrival of Mrs. Brock, and soon after, I went down to see Payn. As I was going, Mrs. C. said they were going to have a picnic tomorrow in the woods if fine, and would I come? (I would.) I found Payn pretty well, and stayed to supper at the Splann's, after which I came down here.

Now, in answer to your letter: I am very glad of the note as to birds of Outer Hebrides. I have my eye on those islands and am taking good note of all that is written about them (e.g., recent papers by South). I never read *The Ordeal of Richard Feverel*, but have heard of it. About recommending books, I don't think one would be wise in recommending a book unless one knew something about it, and approved of it, but on the principle that one might recommend ABC to children (though not finding it particularly entertaining oneself), one might also recommend a book to a person, though it was not quite what one liked for himself. This seems to me to be quite obvious, though I rarely do so myself. For instance, I can't imagined myself begging anyone to read Wilkie Collins.

Of course Barnett isn't going to do any *great* wonders with his East End picture gallery, but what influence it has is entirely good. I think it has perhaps more good effect than you might suppose. If it makes the East-Enders want a permanent picture gallery that will be something, and it may have a small effect in causing them to wish for better conditions of existence. The *Catechism for Londoners* is good, and very funny. I wonder, though, that *Punch* publishes such a 'revolutionary' article!

Well! This is extraordinary weather. Yesterday the snow melted almost as fast as it fell, but it has been snowing during the night (it was *raining* at ten when I went to bed) and there are six inches of snow now on the ground, and it is still snowing fast. Yet for all that it is quite warm.

3:25 p.m. It has been snowing all day (has just left off), but I find the snow is still only six inches deep, as it has thawed as fast as it fell. I hope it will soon melt off and let people get to town, because I am just out of everything — out of meat, out of lamp oil, and nearly out of flour and baking powder. Of course I can get them at any of the neighbors in case of need, but would rather get them in town.

I haven't attempted to go out, having just enough fire wood for today, but have been reading all the day. The *Ent. Mags* are good this month, especially the 'monthly.'

I have just got a Neuropteran down for Colorado, but he only scrapes in by the skin of his teeth. It is *Termes flavipes* (white ant), and goes down because I sent Prof. Riley some honey-coated wood from a quaking asp tree, and he says it is done by *T. flavipes*. I have seen some little beasties which seem to be *Termes*, so I dare say he is right. But *Termes* belongs to Pseudoneuroptera (classed by some under Orthoptera) so, granting it to be *Termes* we have to stretch a point to put it in Neuroptera, though many authors have so classed it.

Another insect (a beetle — *Rhagium lineatum*) went down on the strength of fragments found in a nuthatch's stomach, and identified by C. V. Riley, but yesterday Payn gave me a living one which had been caught at the Splann's, so confirming the record. I am sending off an Hepatic to one Lucien M. Underwood, who understands those things, and so hope to be able to put down *one* of this group, at any rate, for Colorado. Did I tell you in a former letter about one of the larvae which I found under a cactus, gnawing out all its vitals? Riley says it is an extremely good specimen of the larva of *Cactophagus validus*.

9:30 a.m. Did you read in *Pall Mall* the report 'by one of the Majesty's Inspectors' on the workwomen of London? It is perfectly ghastly. Quite a number only earn 6/. a week, and then are often out of work. Talk about 'bloody revolutions' and so on, I should think the poor wretches would be almost glad to end their lives, if at least they died for the future, since they have no present to live for. In the face of this, doesn't it strike you that the *pretence* of *religion, humanity,* etc., is just *humbug*? People have got to habitually *pretend* and don't know what it is to be in earnest. To my mind happiness is more important than life; to destroy happiness is perhaps only to change the scene of existence; to destroy happiness is quite another thing. You can't kill existence, but you *can* make it miserable. Do look things in the face and measure the misery of the workers against all other things, which will seem as trifles.

Saturday morning, Apr. 28th. The snow is about ten inches deep now. It has been snowing in the night, and is still snowing. Icicles over a foot long hang all round the roof of the house. The sun looks like a grease-spot in the sky. The snow is packed too solid to sweep. I had to dig my way to the creek for water. I must go up to Brock's and get provisions.

7:30 p.m. It has not snowed to amount to anything today and although the sun has not shone out clear, it has been hot enough to melt perhaps a third of the snow already fallen. I went up to Brock's about midday, It took me an age to get there; one has to lift ones feet so to walk that way is very tiring. There was a foot or more of it in many places.

At Brock's I got three dozen eggs and a little baking powder, for which I did not pay as my work of Monday was put against them. I should have come down again soon, only noticing some copies of the *Field* on the table, I asked about them and found Brock had nearly all those for 1887 and many of 1886 which he had received from a brother of his (I think he said) in Hong Kong, who takes the *Field* and sends it to Brock when done with.

I therefore spent the whole afternoon at Brock's, making a careful examination of the Nat. Hist. columns, taking notes therefrom. In this way I added many things to my Middlesex fauna list, etc. In one number I found a pretty full report of the last S.L.E.S. exhibition in which it is mentioned that you exhibited Mollusca. It seems that others are not rare at Hampton Court and do some damage to the fish in the river. W. H. Hudson writes (1887 p.165) that a 'grasshopper' (*Rhonibalea speciosa* Thunb.) found in La Plata very closely resembles a wasp of the genus *Pepris*. There is recorded (1887 p. 215) by Anthony Belt the occurrence of a bittern at Perivale. Of fish, the roach, dace, perch, and gudgeon are recorded for Twickenham. (How about the Isleworth fish list? Haven't you any down?) Barbel and trout are recorded for Hampton, and chub and jack for Sunbury. Lampreys are recorded for Teddington. I enclose a note on *Sesia culiciformis* for the S.L.E.S. — I think Frohawk comes often to the meetings. It would be desirable to tackle him about it if possible. It *may* just be a misprint for 'yellow-banded' — I have had 'green' misprinted 'grey', and 'white' for 'yellow.' It is a very important matter for me, this of *Sesia*.

Sunday, Apr. 29th, 12:35 p.m. Very sunny today, but cold wind. Snow melting fast. Chamberlain just rode down to borrow something to read and return *Descent of Man*. He is going to town tomorrow, and I with him. In snowy weather it is well to go to town when one can get a ride.

10:15 p.m. In the afternoon I went up to the Cusacks' and stayed for the evening. I took up the *P.M.B.* with report on working-women of London and read parts of it to them, and afterwards had much talk thereon, chiefly with Lees (who was up there). I took up Mrs. C.'s photo and got her to sign her name to it. I have promised Lees that if it is fine, and the snow melts off, I will walk up to his cabin some day this week.

Have come to town with Chamberlain. Got letter from Riley, with list of insects I sent him (some appear to be new species), letter from W. H. Edwards, letter from L. Barnes (offering to name Orthoptera), *West American Scientist, Pall Mall Budget, Labor Enquirer, Ornithologist* and *Oölogist.* I may not be able to post another letter till Wednesday week, but will get to town if I can.

April 30th, 1888

Dear Frederic,

As promised, Chamberlain came and took me to town today. It was quite warm, and the snow, by evening, had melted off in patches by my house, and the road to town was mostly bare of snow and very muddy. I talked to Chamberlain a good deal on the way, but he rather annoys me — having 'jingo' tendencies, and continually going on about the excellence of America. I spent quite a small fortune in town, got a 50 lb. sack of flour ($1.50), a tin of baking powder, lamp oil, and a new pair of overalls.

Riley sends me today a list of insects I sent him. There is a small, black *Aphrodius* here, which Riley says is *A. granarius,* a species you also get at Isleworth. It certainly *looks* quite the same, but one doesn't like to be too sure from memory in a case of this kind. Two of my beetles appear to be undescribed. Riley names an ant as *Formica fusca L.?,* and he confirms a house fly from here as the genuine *Musca domestica.*

Chamberlain lent me *Enoch Arden* [Tennyson. Ed.], and I have just been reading it and like it very much. Yet it seems hard to believe that anyone could have borne what Enoch did, and said nothing. Some men are capable of much

heroism, but that seems almost impossible. Still, the story is none the less beautiful for that. Has Annie read *Enoch Arden?*

It has been a warm day, and most of the snow has gone. I found this morning that a miserable donkey has been walking on my garden; I think I must fence it round. I went up to the Cusacks' and Brock's. At Brock's I got some potatoes. At the Cusacks' I found Mrs. C. and Miss U. doing the washing, and as I had brought up a *Pall Mall Budget* I sat and read to them. Reading out loud is not one of the things I can do best, so I am glad to have someone to practice it on, and as they seem to like it, everyone is satisfied.

First I read about Prince Alexander of Battenburg. [See Encycl. Britannica: Bismarck. Ed.]. The unanimous opinion of the House was that they ought to be allowed to marry, and Mrs. C. was quite enthusiastic over the valour of the Empress in standing up against Bismarck. Then I read of Mrs. Bancroft and of Matthew Arnold's (not very favorable) views of America, and finally I read the review of *Robert Elsmere* [a novel by Mrs. Humphrey Ward, 1888, dealing with 19th century religious problems. Ed.], which seems to be a very notable book. I shall try to get it to read. When the washing was done, I wrote up Mrs. C.'s new Fauna and Flora book in which she proposes to record all the plants, animals, etc., she finds.

Mrs. C. tells me that Lees left word there that he would meet me on my way up to his cabin on Thursday. I rather wish I hadn't promised to go, as the snow will be gone by that time and I might be working at Brock's and Cox's, but I said I would go before I knew anything about Brock's job, or Cox's on clearing up.

May 2nd, 9:20 p.m. So this is the 'merry month of May' — and snow on the ground! I went out this morning, meaning first to go to the Cusacks' and give them some things to take to post (Regy talks of going to town tomorrow) and then go and work the rest of the day at Brock's. However, I was soon overtaken by a hail storm and took refuge at Cox's, and when I got to the Cusacks' the weather was so bad that I did not go to Brock's at all. It cleared up a little later on and I went for a ramble with Mrs. C., getting *Berberis* [*Mahonia repens.* Ed.] in flower and other things. (There is some *Berberis* in the garden at Syon — prickly leaves [probably *B. thunbergii.* Ed.] — not the same species though as the one here.

If it does not get better weather, I don't think I shall go to Lees' tomorrow. Tonight there has been a slight fall of snow, just enough to cover the ground with a film. I wish I could have got your this week's letter today, but there is nothing for it but to wait till I return from Lees'.

May 3ʳᵈ, 8 p.m. Fortunately, today has been perfectly fine and warm, and I was able to come up to Lees', where I now write. I started at eight o'clock, shutting up the house as securely as I could. The road to Lees' is rather a difficult one to find, so Wm. Saunders, an American who is working for Lees, came down and met me on the way, bringing also a horse for me to ride.

Here is a sort of map to give you some idea as to where Lees lives.

The road from Splann's to Beddoes' old ranch is over prairie. Then from Beddoes' ranch to the place marked x is a road along which I found a pretty yellow *Corydalis* [In May this would have been *C. curvisiliqua.* Ed.] growing, and took a specimen of a butterfly (*Pamphila sp.*) new to me. At * the road becomes almost a trail, and here it was that Saunders met me, riding a horse and bringing one for me to ride. (Saunders is a very good sort of fellow indeed, but though an excellent workman, he seems intellectually to be rather poppy-buddy. Lees says he is shy). We rode a very devious path among oak scrub, quaking asps, and spruces, mostly steep, and in about an hour arrived at Lees' cabin. It is quite high in the mountains (about 10,000 ft.) and in a gulch.

The cabin itself is quite small (about four paces by three) but full of tools, cooking utensils, etc., etc., arranged in the neatest manner, There is also a shelf of books, not many, but select (e.g., *Origin of Species,* Darwin's *Beagle; Waterton, Smiles, Lives of the Stevensons, Whitaker's Almanack, etc.*) Then there is a little stable, and in front of the house a forge and anvil, for Lees is something of a blacksmith. A path from the house leads up to the mine — a long tunnel into the granite rock. It is about a hundred feet long, and 30 more have to be done before there will be any chance of striking ore (silver and copper). Saunders was working at the mine all the afternoon, while I helped Lees with his blacksmithing (worked the forge and bellows and so on). He was fixing his waggon for a trip to the northern part of the state he and Regy are going to take.

I have been reading an article in the *Spectator* of Lees, about evolution. The author wants to know why we haven't *inherited* (!) the sense of smell of dogs and birds of carrion, or the various peculiarities of insects, etc., since, 'according to the theory of evolution', we are descended from all these creatures (!), and he thinks we may have inherited the slave-making tendency from the slave-making ants! Would you believe that such utter bosh could appear at this time, and in a paper like the *Spectator,* whose editor may be supposed to have a little education? It's perfectly sickening.

May 4ᵗʰ, 8:20 p.m. A day of new experiences. I have been mining. But Lees wants to go to bed so I will shut up and write my story of today tomorrow.

Concerning yesterday, we were up at about 5:30 and got to work soon after breakfast. First of all we sharpened the drills, and this is done by making the ends hot in the forge and beating them sharp with a hammer. Then we went up to the mine, which is some little way above the house. The method of mining is this. Holes are driven in the rock, and into them is inserted some 'giant-powder' (i.e., nitroglycerine 40 per cent, mixed with sawdust — you get it in sticks, like 'Roman-candles') and also some gunpowder and a fuse, all of which is tightly jammed in so that it may expend its full force on the rock.

Dynamite, you know, will only *burn* if ignited, and, the giant powder being practically the same thing, it is necessary to put in gunpowder to explode it, the gunpowder being exploded of course by the fuse.

The drills are long steel rods, sharp at one end. First we started (Lees and I) on a roof-hole, and took it in turns to hold the drill and strike. It is perhaps harder work holding the drill than striking it, because if it is a long one it is heavy, and it has to be turned about an eighth inch of its circumference after each blow, so that the hole will be round. It is not easy at first to hit the end of the drill with the hammer every time, and although there is no danger of harm when a long drill is being used, it is sometimes possible for one man, missing, to hit the other's hand or arm.

Later in the day, when working with Saunders (or 'Bill', as he is called) I was holding a shortish drill and he was making heavy downward strokes and being, like me, new at the work, he did not always hit the end of the drill fair. I thought, 'If he mashes my writing hand —!' But he didn't.

After the explosion, a lot of rock comes down and has to be taken out of the tunnel in a wheelbarrow, but at first the tunnel is full of smoke and poisonous gas from the explosion, and one has to work a large bellows which blows into a pipe going nearly to the end of the mine, to get fresh air in there again. Lees finds that with two men working, he progresses at the rate of almost nine inches a day. After we had done mining for the day, we exploded three sticks of giant powder by a rock so as to move it from the road. The explosion was not a perfect success, but moved the rock so that it could be taken away by a couple of horses later on.

During the latter part of the afternoon I was busy making a road up to the mine (at present it is but a path). In England, to make a road, they put stones over the earth. Here I had to put earth over the stones! Now I will tell you about today.

This morning I started home. Lees asked me to stay a week, but I said I would come up again. I wanted to get my letters and do the work for Brock and Cox, and so did not feel like staying up there too long just now. I started soon after eight, and walked down. It had been rather stormy yesterday, but although it looked threatening I got down to the Cusacks' all right.

On the way I found some earthworms (*Lumbricus*) at Beddoes' old ranch, the first I have seen in Colorado. They are extremely rare here, and so I was very glad to get them (three specimens). When I passed Chamberlain's, one of the children brought me out two *Cicada* larvae that had been found in digging a cellar.

I went up to the Cusacks', as they had my mail — your letter, letters from Mother (two), Carlie, Nash of Pueblo, Riley, Salmon (Agric. Dept., about anthrax) and a postcard from Williston (he is the American Diptera man — says he will name them for me as soon as he has any spare time). I also got the Whitechapel picture guide (for which best thanks), *Journ. of Conch.* (April), *Pall Mall Budget*, and *Commonweal.*

I found Frank Cusack had returned from Pueblo, and had brought with him one Sid Hamp, an Englishman whom Mrs. C. has known for many years (in England) and a very good fellow indeed. He is rather tall and spare, and has a nice though not very striking face, wears spectacles and has light hair. He has a banjo, and whistles tunes, to accompany his playing, in the most remarkable manner; it sounds almost like a bird. He went with the Hayden Geological Survey in Wyoming in 1872, and knew Coulter (the botany man), who was on the same expedition.

Soon after I got to Cusacks', it began to snow, but it did not last long, and the sun quickly melted it off, so quickly in fact that it rose like steam.

In answer to your letter, *Tussilago* is indigenous in the garden of 5. Priory; I never put any in. Most of the things I planted have been rooted up long ago. I have duly informed the cat that its name is Toby; thanks to Annie for suggesting it.

'Visual Centres' in *Lancet* is Feb. 18, 1888, p.331. I could send it, but I suppose you can get it from the library. I seem to have created some disturbance in raising the question of London melanism, the original thing in *Entom.* was a casual remark of Mr. Randall's that there was no such thing as melanism in London District as there is up north. (Sept., 1886 number, I think it was in). I don't see why Tutt need jump on Carrington for it; it was all Randall's fault; he ought certainly not to have made the assertion. I have not a very high opinion of Randall's intelligence.

I am glad to have the list of additional Arachnida; *Pach. degeeri, Amaur. similis,* and *Opilio agrestis* I have taken myself. You have now three species of *Epeira* down for Isleworth; that is good.

Annie Evans' letter to Annie is interesting — rather a better letter than I thought she would have written. I quite agree with her that the *translations* of Björnson's poetry are not quite what they might be, which is a pity. If one were to find fault with Miss Evans' letter I should say it is not simple and direct enough., One has to read it carefully to arrive at the meaning. I was very pleased with the Whitechapel catalogue, with Annie's marks. There do seem to be very many really good pictures, and some of those we know quite well. However did the Rossetti's come to be marked 'lent by S. C. Cockerell, Esq.' Did Carlie lend them something else and they mixed things up?

There is nothing to tell you about the other mail, I forgot to say that Roberts sent me a packet of his 'Miscellaneous rural notes for 1887', which appear in some Yorkshire paper (I forget which). Taylor's paper on variation in *Journ. of Conch.* is good and interesting if not very original. I suggested to Carlie that on his riverside walks he should take up botany, and to my amazement he seems to think well of the idea. I hope he will take it up.

I see in *P.M.G.* that four men in London will get 4/. for making twelve pairs of boots, the boss of them getting 2/., and the other 3/8d.

each! They work 18 hours a day and 'can't make a living by twelve hours work.' How can life be livable on such terms? Boots had been made as 1/6d. a *dozen*, and these were sold at 1/6d. a *pair*!

I want to get to town tomorrow if fine, but it has been raining tonight.

May 6th, 12:30. Have walked to town and found on the way some plants, including two species of violet, one with violet [probably *V. sororia*. Ed.] and the other with yellow flowers [*V. nuttallii*. Ed.] I got a lift for the last mile. The mail I have got is letter from [George] Vasey (Botanist of Dept. of Agric.), postcard from Averell, Bull. 1 of *Washburn College Survey* (from Ford), *Account of Progress in Zoology* for 1883 (from Smithsonian Inst.) and *Conch. Exchange* (Jan. and Feb.). Greeting to Annie.

May 7th, 1888

Dear Frederic,

Having posted my mail, I started from town soon after one. At Grape Creek, a German (queer fellow but pleasant-mannered; I don't know his name) overtook me and gave me a lift as far as Ula, which I was glad of because my feet had got blistered and it was uncomfortable walking, and also because the weather looked threatening and I did not want to be caught in a storm. As it was, it started to rain just before I got to the house, but nothing to matter. I then sat down to write and, looking up presently, found the rain had turned to snow. It was Sunday evening and I had besides, a letter for Regy, so I wrapped up, took my green-lined umbrella, and went up to the Cusacks' in the snow storm.

I found Lees up there; he had come down from the mine in his waggon. We had hymns, etc., in the evening, as usual. What a miserable collection of verses the church hymn-book is! We have to hunt the whole book through to find even a tolerably decent one that we have not already had many times before. If course I don't agree with the words of many of them, and the music of most of them is not very pleasing, but from any point of view they are more like dirges than hymns. Last night we had as good a selection as it is easy to make with the available material, viz., *Eternal Father, strong to save; O Worship the King; Lead, Kindly Light; Sun of my Soul; Onward, Christian Soldiers*, and one or two others.

It had been snowing all the time, and when I came home was still snowing. I can now appreciate the ease with which one can get lost in a snow storm. After passing Brock's I walked on, seeming to go straight, but presently found that I was going *up hill* instead of down and, in fact, was heading almost direct for Chamberlain's. Turning around, I walked till I found a fence and, following it, got to Cox's all right. After leaving Cox's I again got off at right angles to the proper road without knowing it but, coming to a fence, was stopped, and could follow it down till I got on the road again. This morning there were five inches of snow on the ground, but I am thankful to say it is melting rapidly. With this weather, I don't know *when* I shall be able to do Brock's work; it is very annoying.

I *can't* recollect the paintings of Israels (*vide* Whitechapel catalogue), yet I have seen some, I should think.

2:55 p.m. The snow is going fast. Lees went by on his way home, and Bassick came down to enquire whether I had seen anything of three ducks Cox had lost (I had not). It seems that Mrs. Cox will be back in about three weeks. I have been busy writing and clearing out my bedroom.

The Bulletin of Washburn Coll. I got yesterday has an account of Kansas fungi in it, and the following Middlesex species are recorded for Kansas: *Agaricus dryophilus* Bull., *A. galericulatus* Scop., *A. campestris* L., *Coprinus comatus* Fr., *Polyporus hirsutus* Wulf., *P. versicolor* L., *Daedalea unicolor* Bull., *Stereum hirsutum* Fa., *and Agaricus papilionaceus* and *Stereum purpureum* are given as doubtful. I hope to find most of these in Colorado, but so far I have only met with *A. campestris*.

6:45 p.m. It snowed again towards evening, but it is not freezing. Everything is very wet and sloppy (unusual in this country) and the weather still looks threatening. I wish it would clear up. I am going to do some washing this evening.

May 8th, 6:40 p.m. I have a slight headache and otherwise have not been feeling quite well today and so have not done very much. There were two inches of snow on the ground in the morning, but the day has been fine and sunny, and it has all melted off.

I went up to Brock's early in the afternoon to do some clearing, but I found the place was like a swamp from the melting of the snow, so nothing could be done. Regy paid me a visit this afternoon. He, Frank, and Miss U. had been down to the Kettle's and, as the two last were so slow coming home, he rode ahead and waited here till they caught him up. I saw specimens of *Vanessa antiope* and *V. milberti* by my home today.

May 9th. I came across a rather amusing anecdote the other day: A certain poor man, who lived close to the railway, was much pinched to get himself enough coal during the winter, until an idea occurred to him. He taught his dog to bark vociferously at every passing train, and the impulse of the engine driver was always to throw something at the dog, the coal the engine carried being the only thing available. In this way the owner of the dog had sufficient coal for his needs delivered at his own door without expense throughout the year!

12:45 p.m. I have come to town with Frank Cusack and got: Your letter, letters from Mother, S.C.C. Barnes (moss man), Pilsbry (with names of shells; the *Physa* you called *P. charpentieri* Kuster (?) is *P. elliptica* Lea), Sutton, postcard from Taylor, *Conch. Exchange, Labor Enquirer*, and *Key to Genera of Mosses* (from Barnes). Taylor says they are talking of raising dues to Conch Soc. to 10/6d. or 21/! If so, T.D.A.C. ceases to be a member, for one!

I don't know why the learned zoologists couldn't make head or tail of my views on atavism! I thought I was clear to the extent of being elementary. However, if they print it, it will appeal to a wider circle. Sutton in his letter simply says he has forwarded the paper on atavism to Sclater, and doesn't say whether *he* understood it, but I presume so.

I am very glad to hear of Annie's improved health. She should have a *holiday* to set her quite right again.

Jenner Weir is no judge of American butterflies; Edwards knows more about them than anyone else. I shall probably publish most of the views advanced in the paper I sent Carrington *elsewhere* before he gets out the original. Your yellow Herne Bay *Physa* was, I think, simply a case of dark pigment lacking, and so nothing to do with dimorphism. I will post this now, not because there is nothing in it to read, but because it is Wednesday, and I want to get back into the run of Wednesday letters.

Just before coming to town I caught a specimen of *Pieris oleracea* var. *venosa,* which has not before been found on the Atlantic slope. Greeting to Annie.

May 9th, 1888

Dear Frederic,

I found Payn was in town, staying at the hotel, and apparently well. He wanted me to stay at the hotel with him for a day or two but I didn't seem to see it. He says he will go back to the Splann's very shortly. I came out with Frank Cusack, and nothing particular happened then or since.

Respecting my paper and Zoöl. Soc., it strikes me as a curious thing that when one has worked at a subject for some time, certain things do appear most self-evident, which are not appreciated at all by those who have not followed the same lines of thought. I have repeatedly experienced this, notably in connection with Socialism. It is like getting a focus with the microscope;

if the reader or listener hasn't the same mental focus as the writer or speaker, he cannot appreciate his arguments. In working out a problem in Euclid one is conscious of the effort to attain the right focus of mind. Have you never experienced this?

I heard nothing of Collinge's Conch. paper. When is it coming out? I think a *good* monthly Conch. paper would round out the *J. of C.* altogether. If Carrington doesn't want my variety paper when you have read it, I should like Tutt to see it.

I think 'common sense' mainly means a matter-of-fact, unprejudiced habit of mind, adapting itself to circumstances naturally. Or to put it more tersely, one might say it is 'sense in common things.' I have not this quality largely I think because I am too apt to see one thing at the expense of others. I am not always satisfied with an *average* of good, but suffer in one respect for the sake of increased good in another. I think you will not quarrel with this reasoning, nor Annie.

I too, have been interested in *Robert Elsmere,* knowing it only from the *P.M.G.* review, so I am glad of your account and the cuttings. I shall get the book if I can. Ever since I began to know anything of physical laws, the miraculous in the orthodox religion has seemed to me to be extremely difficult to believe, and I have put it aside as fabulous. At the same time, I never could get into the focus of mind for believing that existence ended with death, and so immortality has been a sort of axiom, though I was not in a position to assert it as a known truth to others.

I should not agree with everybody (Carlie for instance) as to the definition of a poet. To my mind, he is simply a man who, having something to say, writes it in verse. (Wherein the distinction between a poet proper and a songster, the latter expressing his feelings in music, the words being of secondary importance.) What is Annie's definition of a poet?

I do hope the holiday with the Lances will come off; it will do Annie a lot of good and she will be in tolerable company. I don't see why 'the family' should object. The Lances are not disreputable people, like the Cockerells, for instance! I wish *you* could get away for a fortnight's holiday this spring, too; I suspect you want it.

May 10th, 9:45 p.m. I went up to Brock's this morning but found the ground still very damp, so I did only about two hours work and then went on to the Cusacks'. Near Brock's and the Cusacks' I caught three species of butterflies: a *Pamphila,* a *Lycaena,* and a *Thecla* (two specimens). At the Cusack's I did some sketching (finishing a sketch of the mountains, etc.) and cleared up rubbish from the back part of the house. Coming home this evening I called at Brock's and arranged to help him plant potatoes tomorrow. Going up there to breakfast and doing a day of it. On arriving home I found a lovely little *Cerura,* something like *bifida,* had emerged from a cocoon I had. An *Arctia* (subspecies *andarctia*) also emerged this morning.

Heap of potatoes

May 11th, 9:10 p.m. I was up at Brock's before seven, had breakfast there, and then went off with Brock to his potato cellar to cut potatoes for planting. The potato cellar is built much like a log hut except that it is partly below the level of the ground. Its purpose is to keep the potatoes from freezing in the winter, a purpose hardly fulfilled by Brock's cellar, since about one third (at least) of the potatoes have frozen and are therefore rotten. We spent the morning cutting them up, that is, into two or three (or more) pieces, so as to leave an 'eye' to each bit at least, as the 'eyes' are of course the parts that grow.

In the afternoon we went over towards Chamberlain's and ploughed up a piece of land (about 3/4 of an acre) and planted potatoes over it. Brock did nearly all the ploughing and I did most of the planting. First Brock would start with the plough, and I, following, would drop the pieces of potato into the furrow he had made, at about 18 inches apart. Then Brock, coming round next time, would cover up the potatoes with the plough, and plough round three times more before I again dropped potatoes into the furrow, so as to leave enough room for the rows of potatoes when grown. You will see that this is altogether a better way of putting them in in quantity than the old-fashioned method of the hole with the pointed stick (as they do in England).

During the afternoon, the Brock infant, who was looking on at us, disappeared, and we had to hunt for him, but he was eventually discovered at home, whither he had found his way with some difficulty. When all the potatoes were in, Brock harrowed the ground over while I went down to the Splann's to get two pounds of butter for the Brocks. Tomorrow there is to be a picnic up in the woods, which will probably be attended by Cusacks, Brocks, Cardy Lees, Sid Hamp, Miss Sidford, Louis Howard, and T.D.A.C.

May 12th, 10:40 p.m. I have a lot to tell you about today, but as it is late and I am sleepy, I will defer writing it until tomorrow.

Sunday, May 13th, 9:45 p.m. Concerning yesterday: I was up at the Cusacks' before ten, and found that they were ready, but the rest of the company had not arrived. Soon Louis Howard rode up, but without Miss Sidford because the Beddoes' wouldn't let her come (Miss S. is a cousin of Mrs. Beddoes, and came out to do housework for them, being paid for it. It seems that the Beddoes' were very kind to her at first, but lately have been treating her very badly and won't let her go out or anything. Of course, a man under these circumstances would just 'make tracks' and get a job elsewhere, but Miss S. can't do that, so it is hard times for her.

Sid Hamp did not come either, having started for Pueblo by the morning's train. Then Regy went down and fetched Mrs. Brock and child (Brock was ploughing and couldn't come) and we started off into the woods, the ladies going in Lees' waggon. Just before we started off, Louis Howard told me he was thinking of going down into New Mexico about September, and if I would come he would provide the waggon, etc. — all the necessary appliances, I paying only for my share of the food (which would amount to very little). I said, most certainly I would come if nothing prevented, and indeed it would be very good for me, being just at a time when the cold weather was coming on, and work was hardly to be got anyway. It appears that they are going to move the Indians off a reservation in the northwestern corner of New Mexico, and Louis wants to go down there and see if he can get a good ranch. If I go on the other expedition for Edwards and Co., I shall be back here about the end of August and so ready to start off again with Louis.

We went only about 3/4 of a mile and then the waggon was left under a tree, the horses tied out to graze, and we went our various ways. Lees turned up just as we were about to commence the meal. He had been up to his mine that morning, starting about five! After the meal we again rambled off, except Lees, Frank, and Louis, who stayed nearby. Mrs. Brock, Miss U., and Regy went off together while I went 'bug-hunting' with Mrs. Cusack. We had a pretty good time together though we didn't find very much.

For the while before supper we amused ourselves in various ways — trying to see who could step nearest 50 yards, judging the yards by 50 paces of course. (Regy did.) Then Regy and Louis got some ropes and wanted to 'lariat' everybody. And just before supper we got to arguing about levers, and why it is that a large body near the fulcrum is balanced by a small body far from it: [diagram]. If you want to have

this demonstrated I will give you the argument and proof.)

I also tried to see whether anyone could understand the difference between *atavism by growth* and *atavism by arrest of growth or change*. Mrs. Cusack and Frank declared they could, but Lees thought the question was 'involved' and would have to be thought over.

After supper we got talking about debating societies, and agreed to start one of our own. So we drew up the following list of subjects: Emigration: Is it desirable? Fire or Water; Which is the greater power in Nature; Is Honesty desirable; Married versus Unmarried Life; Women's Rights; Mining versus Ranching; The American Civil War; Is life Worth Living? And three others which I forget for the moment. Then, as everyone had to speak, we drew lots as to the order in which we should come, the first speaker moving some proposition. They came in the following order: Frank, Louis, Lees, T.D.A.C., Miss U., Regy, and Mrs. Cusack.

For an experiment we had 'Emigration' then and there, but the debate was rather rowdy and irregular, though everyone spoke except Miss U. The debates are to be on Saturday nights, and the next one is to be 'Is Honesty Desirable?' opened by Louis Howard (if he can come). Lees seemed to have the best idea of speaking of any of us, but we all very much want practice, and, besides being amusing or interesting, the debates will, it is hoped, teach us to express our ideas. It was agreed for the present that no party positions were to be introduced, and I suppose religious subjects will also be excluded.

Coming home, I called in at Brock's and found he had brought me mail: Letters from Douglas (encl. $3.00), Woolson (encl. $3.00, which is $2.25 for cost of sending his plants, and $.75 for my trouble. He says he will be very glad to have more plants. It seems it is an affair of his own and not in connection with his Dept. of Public Parks), Averill, Underwood (naming an hepatic from here as *Marchantia polymorpha* L., a common British species), and postcard from D.

F. Stein, wanting shells. Also *Pall Mall Budget* and *Commonweal*.

It is a lovely summer day today, and it is a shame to be indoors, but I *must* write some letters. I just now saw a *Vanessa atalanta* by my house, and caught a *Lycaena*.

10:05 p.m. I went up to the Cusacks' in the course of the afternoon and stayed for the evening. I had another argument with Mrs. C. about religion, but we arrived at no conclusions. Mrs.C.'s religion is all faith and very little charity, or rather, her practical religion is better than her theoretical.

May 11th, 9:30 p.m. Today has been fine and hot, and I have been working for Brock. I have agreed to work for him for 50 cents a day and meals, not a very vast sum, perhaps, but more than I spend and so altogether satisfactory pending something better. Today I spent in sowing seeds mostly. I laid out Brock's vegetable garden with seeds of onion, carrot, lettuce, parsnip, peas, and spinach, and made an irrigation ditch from the creek to the garden so that plenty of water would get to it. Later on, I sowed turnips and rutabagas (Swedes) in a field. I also fixed up a rabbit trap for Brock, with which he will catch the innocent little cottontail.

Regy went to town and brought me mail: A *Harpers* from Douglas and a postcard from Bethune, with 27 extra copies of my article on 'Seasonal Dimorphism' in *Canad. Entom.* I will send you one, and please don't say you can't understand it! (Annie can, I'm sure, anyway.) I saw the first swallows (*Hirundo erythrogaster*) of the year today; they sat on the fence by Cox's.

May 15th, 9:45 p.m. Working at Brock's. In the morning I was clearing land, getting up old quaking asp trunks with a 'grub-hoe.' These old stumps have large roots, and are often hard to extract (it is just like pulling out teeth!) So that it is rather hard work. In the afternoon I first sowed a row of sunflower seeds; this, not because of

Brock's aesthetic tastes but because the ripe heads are good to feed the chickens. Sunflowers, of course, grow wild here, but only small ones. These were the big kind with heads like a dinner plate.

After that I did some harrowing while Brock sowed barley and rye. All one has to do is to walk behind the horses and guide them and see that the harrow does not get stuck on a rock. It must be tiring, though, when one has to walk after a harrow over ploughed fields all day. Fortunately, the soil here is neither clay nor adobe, but quite light and friable. Just before supper I went down the pasture to fetch a mare of Brock's, and while I was going down a thunderstorm with rain, which had been brewing all the afternoon, burst over me and I got wet. But I soon dried out by the stove and suffered no ill.

This evening I looked in at the Cusacks for a moment, and Mrs. C. gave me some insects she had caught. Regy had found eggs of Blue Jay and 'Robin' today. The egg of the *Cyanocitta* is blue and speckled, that of *Merula [Turdus] migratoria* spotless blue, and somewhat more elongate than that of *Merula merula*.

May 16th, 12:25. I am just going to town. A *Rhodites tuberculator* emerged from gall today, so the ones Billups has ought to be coming out. I caught a tattered *Vanessa cardui* by my house this morning, the first I have seen here. White violets (*V. canadensis*) are flowering and look very lovely under the trees by the creek. The quaking asps are well forward, the young leaves being apple-green. The weather is warm, with thunder and showers — good for the plants. In the *Canadian Ent.* I read the Colorado species are underlined in the lists of insects on pp.90-93.

5:50 p.m. I walked to town this afternoon, getting a letter from Cragin, *Birds of Kansas*, by N. S. Goths, and Chicago *Labor Enquirer*. I am sorry to see that the Denver *Labor Enquirer* has stopped publishing and the Chicago one will be sent instead. Cragin sends me the book on Kansas birds as a present (kind of him). It is an interesting volume, much on the same plan as Roebuck and Clarke's book of Yorkshire Vertebrata.

I found Payn in town; he did not like Lees' mine at all and had come down on the first opportunity. The train has just come in, and I wait in expectation of your letter.

6:45. Have got your letter, also *Science Gossip, Naturalist,* and *Illustrated Weekly Telegraph.* Very best thanks to Annie for the seeds. I am very pleased with them. Yes, I will answer the questions in an hour if you send them (if I can!). Didn't you read my note about the galls to S.L.E.S.? They are *Rhodites tuberculator* Riley, MS n. sp.

May 17, 1888, 10:55 p.m.

Dear Frederic,

I am in a very bad temper because I have wasted an evening I could ill afford to lose, but I will try to calm my ruffled feelings and write to you. It didn't rain last night coming home — that is, not on me, but there were storms all round, coming and going, the clouds ever changing in form and color. I never saw such remarkable cloud phenomena before, but I can't describe it to give you any idea. I forgot to say that I found a genuine mushroom (*Agaricus campestris*) on the way to town. The *Weekly Telegraph* rec'd. turns out to be a Yorkshire paper with an account on *Arion*s by Roebuck. (Roebuck quotes Simroth that all the color variations of *A. ater* are produced from two pigments, black and red.) This morning I found another *Rhodites* in my breeding cage. I was not very anxious to get up, feeling rather tired after yesterday's walk, but had to be at Brock's to breakfast at seven, so there was no help for it.

All the morning I was clearing land, hoeing up stumps (I got quite out of breath over it) and this afternoon I betook me to the potato cellar and amused myself for the space of five hours cutting up potatoes for planting. It was very showery, so I was fortunate to be working under cover, though the job was not a very nice

one, half the potatoes being rotten, and the cellar consequently not very sweet-smelling. Mrs. Brock had gone up to the Cusacks', and Brock was in town so Mrs. C. sent Brock child after me to ask me to supper there. After supper we got discussing the debating society, pictures, and a variety of other things, and so I didn't get home till about ten. I am extremely glad to hear that the proposed new Entomological Society is to be incorporated with the S.L.E.S. So constituted it ought to be a vast success.

May 18th, 9 p.m. The *Rhodites* are coming out in profusion. I have been working for Brock today, in the morning cutting potatoes, and in the afternoon harrowing, etc. I went over to the Splann's to get some butter for Brock, and found Becky there. She had just come from Aspen, where she was getting $30.00 a month just for waiting at table at an hotel! Wish I could get such a lucrative job!

Jim Splann had been good enough to catch a nice hawk-moth for me; I think it is *Deilephla lineata.* I found the fourth species of Custer Co. violet near Brock's: *Viola delphinifolia* [*V. pedatifida.* Ed.], like *V.odorata* somewhat, only with deeply cut and dissected leaves, more like those of *Geranium dissectum* than an ordinary violet.

May 19th, 10:20 p.m. I am too tired, sleepy, and disagreeable to write much tonight. When I got up to Brock's this morning he had brought me out some mail last night: Letters from Jenner Weir (interesting, about Gonapterys. I think I can refute his arguments), H. Strecker (wanting insects) and my Uncle Jack (= J. Mountfield Bennet, of New Zealand) where he says he is having terribly hard times, and wants to come out here), and postcards from Ellis and [Francis] Wolle saying they will name fungi and algae.

In the morning I harrowed, and in the afternoon planted potatoes. It being Saturday I went up for the debate on 'Honesty' at the Cusacks, but neither Howard nor Lees were there, so it didn't come off. I am afraid this society will not survive. Coming back I looked in at Cox's for a few minutes. Cox is expecting his wife shortly.

Sunday, May 20th, 4:45 p.m. I wanted to get out for a good walk today, but have been too busy. This morning I put a fence up round my garden, to keep the cattle, donkeys, etc., from walking on Annie's seeds. Otherwise, I have been writing.

10:15. I have been planting potatoes, harrowing, hauling rocks off land, cutting potatoes, etc., today. I find work so much crowding on me that, although I don't like to do it, I must take tomorrow off (and the next day) and go to town. I *must* write letters, and I ought to be doing some collecting also; it is important to get the spring things. I have a lot to write to you about tonight, but perhaps I had best wait til tomorrow, when I shall be fresh. One can't express one's ideas properly late at night after a day's work, so I find! I found a Cyclamen (*Dodecatheon meadia*) [*D. pulchellum*. Ed.] today.

May 22nd, 6:10 p.m. Frank Cusack and Lees went to town yesterday and brought me some interesting mail: Postcards from Beutenmuller (*Tinea* man) and Willey (lichen man), *Pall Mall Budget, Commonweal, Botanical Gazette* (with a note of mine on strawberry poisoning — and they have printed my name wrong — Cockrell), Index to Ellis' *North American Fungi*, and a number of *Journal of Mycology* from Ellis (fungi man) and paper on 'Butterflies and moths and their relation to horticulture' from Strecker (interesting, but seems to have been rather carelessly written). He says (p. 16) '*Arctia caia* has, in North America, a white collar. In European examples, this adornment is only occasional. . . .In Asia Minor, the female only has orange hind wings; in the male they are pure white.' And last and best is your packet of papers, for which all thanks (and thanks to Annie for the cuttings and the Isleworth magazine). *Woman's World*: The article by O[live] Schreiner ['Probably the most unusual

personality ever to emerge from southern Africa. She had a powerful intellect, advanced and passionately held views on politics and society, and great vitality, somewhat impaired by asthma and severe depression,.' *Encyclopedia Britannica*. Ed.] is very good and true, but it makes one think: How rare a thing 'perfect love' is. Otherwise the paper is not very interesting. *Isleworth Magazine*. Very *churchy*, of course! One would think they might have better illustrations. Farrar's hymn (p. 107) is not bad, as hymns go. The *Bible Explorations* are as ridiculous as before, e.g., 'Give an example that our blessed Lord spoke after the manner not of a scientific botanist, but of a practical horticulturist'! Fancy expounding scientific botany to the Jews for their conversion! I see the Vicar asks for the little sum of £400.

The cuttings. I must say my own experience at school makes me decidedly in favor of a mild form of corporal punishment, say caning on the hand. Boys *must* be punished, and I think impositions that keep them in when they should be out, are much worse. The school board teachers have a hard time of it, one way and another, and it is very unfortunate that any extra difficulties should be placed in their way. The stunting is too horrible and I must say I don't believe it, or at any rate won't take it for granted without further confirmation. The morbid taste for horrors is curious, and I have observed it if anything *more* in educated people than others, but then the educated rich are a poor lot taken as a whole.

The Ent. Mags. These are not very good this month. Jenner Weir's *Anthocharis cardamines* is interesting. He should give the English form a name. Sydney Webb's paper on varieties of butterflies at Dover is full of interesting matter, but it is as unscientific and slipshod a paper as I ever read.

Yesterday evening Cox and Lees came to supper at Brock's, and there was much talk over the affairs of this little society in which we live (i.e. Cusacks, Brocks, Coxes and Splanns). Lees was going to start the next day (that is, today), for Bear River, after a horse he had left there, and was going to be away several weeks. Now some people called Liversey, near Glenwood Springs, had offered Regy Cusack $30 a month to cut wood, draw water, and keep them supplied with fish and game, a job which was exactly to Regy's liking. So it was decided long ago that Regy should go with Lees and leave him at Glenwood Springs to take this job with the Liversey's, but it was not to be.

You remember a while ago you asked whether Regy was Miss U.'s 'young man', and I said I thought it might be so. Well, I don't know about that; I don't think they are actually in love with each other, but certainly Frank has developed a strange passion for Miss U., which, whatever it may be, is not O. Schreiner's 'perfect love.' It has come to this, that he has been excessively jealous of, and consequently disagreeable to, anyone who ventured to speak to the unfortunate girl, not even excepting Mrs. Brock, and has at times, in his anger of jealousy, I suppose, been very rude to Miss U. herself. Perhaps he has treated me better than anyone else who comes to the house, but even I noticed his peculiar manner at times, and Louis Howard and others have been quite flabbergasted. I don't know how he feels, I am sure, and as he is really a very good fellow indeed, I am not inclined to condemn him in the unqualified manner that some do, but it appears (I have no positive information) that some of his family represented to him that he was making himself ridiculous, and prevailed on him to go away with Lees instead of Regy, and he decided that he would, and so has gone today. (They can't both go; one must be at home to chop wood, etc.) Perhaps as you read all this, you will think it is just a storm in a tea-cup, but living so near and seeing so much of the actors in this little tragedy, I have been a good deal exercised about it.

Then another matter is between Cox and the Cusacks. It seems that when Regy and Frank were living alone they constantly went down to Cox's, but since Mrs. Cox has been away, and Cox alone, and Mrs. C. up at the Cusacks', Cox has not once been asked to go up there, and when he has gone has not been treated very courteously. The fact is, the Cusacks don't like

Cox (and only used to go there because there was nobody else) and Cox consequently doesn't like them, but I can't help feeling that they ought to have had the civility to ask him up a few times, under the circumstances.

Today I have taken a day off, to clear up some of my correspondence, and I went for an hour's stroll early in the afternoon, finding among other things a *Morchella*, possibly *M. esculenta*. I also saw my first hummingbird of the year.

May 23, 11a.m. Have just driven in with Regy C., and to my disgust find nothing but a *Chicago Labor Enquirer*, Brock having taken my mail last night and forgotten to give it to me when he passed my house. Goldstandt (postmaster) says he thinks the English mail came last night, so I suppose your letter is at Brock's, and I had better get back as soon as I can.

Thursday, May 24, 1888

Dear Frederic,

I must commence with an account of yesterday. As you will gather from my last epistle Regy took me to town, and when I got there was told that Brock had taken all my letters the night before — about half a dozen of mine and three for the Cusacks — some being foreign letters. Well, I hardly knew what to do, but the Splanns had come into town And would probably go out before Regy, and I thought I would ride back with them, and then if your letter wasn't at Brock's I should have time to walk back to town for the evening mail.

The Splanns had gone up to Silver Cliff, so I sauntered up there to see when they were going to start, but they delayed till about two, and so I thought I had better wait for the mail anyhow. By this time I was getting very cross about my mail and the trouble and uncertainty of it, and so to soothe my feelings I went down to the marshy spot near Grape Creek with a view of catching therein sundry protozoa and much small fry for

Cragin of Topeka, who has undertaken to name them. Then I strolled further, and was pleased to discover two old friends in *Lemna minor* and *L. trisulca* (duck-weeds) and then, better still, a number of *Succineas*, which whatever American authors please to call them (and they are generally dubbed *ovalis*) are nothing else but *Succinea pfeifferi* Rossm., the present specimens being a rather pale and thin variety. After this, feeling hot (it was a very hot day), I walked back to town and got a pound (ten cents) of dried prunes to satisfy my hunger, and mustered what philosophy I could to wait patiently for the next train.

At five, however, Goldstandt (the postmaster) looked up and said the train would be an hour and a half late! That is, it would not be in till 7:30. So I just walked out of the postoffice as fast as I could; I really couldn't wait any longer. I got a lift on an empty hay rack as far as Ula, and had walked almost to where the prairie begins, when I met Brock and a friend of his called Templeman coming to town in a waggon. Of course I asked about my mail, and to my utter dismay Brock declared he had brought out no mail either for me or the Cusacks, and knew nothing about it! At this, all I could do was to jump into Brock's waggon and return to town and see what had become of the mail and who was lying.

On our arrival in town, all three men serving in the postoffice declared positively that they heard Brock ask for my mail, and further that he was intoxicated at the time (he had just been horse-racing with a lot of rowdy fellows and of course they all got drunk) and he was cautioned to take care of the mail *and was seen to put it into his inside coat pocket!* Brock was in Falkenburg's store, so I went across the street and asked for an explanation, but all I could get was that he wore a different coat the day before, and if he had got any mail (he was sure he hadn't), it was still in the pocket! Here was a nice state of affairs! And if that mail was lost!

I waited for the evening mail, and got letters from Mother, and H. Edwards, and also Taylor and Roebuck *On Irish Mollusca, Pall Mall Budget, Commonweal,* and *Academy Notes* (for which great

thanks to Annie for marking and you for sending) but your letter was not there. Brock had evidently taken that. So I walked home and got up to Brock's (I went straight up to see if the mail might be there) at about 10:30. Mrs. Brock had just gone to bed, but she got up again and appeared in a dressing gown, and to my great joy produced the mail. She had discovered it in the pocket of Brock's coat when she went to hang it up! — Your letter and a host of others, of which more later. Mrs. B. was quite distressed about it all and, as I had no supper except the prunes, very kindly insisted on my having it up there.

While she was getting it ready, I took Cusacks their mail — I found them all in bed — and Charley Cusack and his wife and two children were also there. I learned from Regy that they had come out from Silver Cliff (where they live) that day. When I returned to Brock's, I found Brock had come home. When he learned what he had done, he was very much ashamed of himself and declared he would never fetch any more mail for anybody. Clearly, being drunk, he had just forgotten all about it, and the mail was safe enough, but it had caused me a lot of worry and bother.

Today I was up at the Brock's soon after seven, but nobody was up except Templeman (who, with his wife, is now staying at Brock's. I cut some wood and then read some of my letters I had only glanced over last night. Meanwhile the Brocks had got up and breakfast was ready. I meant to cut potatoes and do other work all day today, but the Brocks and Templemans were going for a picnic in the woods and, as they urged me to come I didn't like to refuse, though I did not want to go.

The waggon was got, and we went up beyond the Cusack's (Regy and Miss U. joined us when we passed) and up into the woods. The main object of the picnic was to get a load of spruce trees for Mrs. Templeman, 'to grow by their house in Silver Cliff.' But here I should describe the Templemans.

In appearance, Templeman is fat and red, and wears a billy-cock hat. Mrs. T. is not noticeable; both strike me as fools, and their general appearance and manner sets my mental teeth on edge (you will understand the feeling). Now the getting of these spruce trees was a characteristic and sickening piece of foolery. The trees were *pulled* up so that they had hardly any roots, and everyone knew perfectly well that they could not *possibly* grow, yet with great labour they were hauled into town in the afternoon and will be doubtless planted in Silver Cliff. Everyone tried to assume that they were all right, but, well, people *are* fools!

Coming back, I called in at the Cusacks' and saw Charley Cusack and his family. Mrs. Charley C. is short, dark, and seemingly a pleasant sort of person. The children are both small, and both have red hair (curious case of atavism — neither of the parents have red hair). I didn't feel like working today and so came home at about 1:30 and, feeling very tired, lay down and slept for a little while. Then I wrote till supper time, and since supper have been writing this.

I found a pretty *Anthocharis* (but with no orange tips) up in the woods today. Hummingbirds are now in great abundance all round here.

Now, about the mails, taking the least interesting first: (1.) Letter from Sterki of Ohio, wanting *Pupae*. (2.) Letter from Averell. (3.) Letter from Fernald wanting to see *Crambus ulae* Ckll. (he shall). He is the boss man on *Crambus* and such things in America. (4.) letter from Coulter, with names of plants sent. (5.) Letter of Leslie's (long and interesting) forwarded to me. (6.) Letter from Olive. (7.) Two letters from Mother. (8.) Letter from Hy. Edwards, with names of Lepidoptera I sent him; a *Chrysophanus* is perhaps new.

(9.) Letter from C. V. Riley; a very pleasant letter wherein he urges me to refrain from describing new species. I do not agree with him, but here is his opinion. 'If I were in your place I would not describe the new species of *Longitarsus* (a beetle). There is absolutely nothing to be gained by describing a solitary species in this way and it only complicates matters for a monographer. I notice you are inclined to describe as soon as you think you have something new, which I very much regret. It is very much better to wait, and I dislike to see any person get the descriptive fever. No one, unless he has studied the whole group, is competent to describe single species. Hoping that you will take this suggestion in good part, believe me, yours sincerely, C. V. Riley.' What do you and Annie think? I refrain from describing the beetle for the present, but I must say I think all new species ought to be described without delay.

(10.) Taylor & Roebuck on *Irish Mollusca*. This is the paper read before the Royal Irish Academy. It is nicely got up, but as it only dates down to the end of 1885 it contains nothing new of importance. Roebuck describes *Arion ater* var. *brunnea* var. nov. 'deep brown.' (11.) Your letter: All thanks to Annie for the cuttings and the seeds of sunflower (but they don't look as if they would grow). The *Ent. Mags.* came in excellent time this month — any time not later than the 20th will do very well. *Woman's World* I will return to in a little while.

Yes, I admit there is a certain sort of love which may be all one-sided, but it's a mystery to me. I feel that so far I cannot grasp the subject in its many-sided aspects as it affects all sorts of people. Does Annie feel that she quite understands it all? In reply to your hypothetical case, I would say that to like a person better then anyone else is not necessarily to love. Why I suppose most people (certainly not in love) have a preference for somebody. After all, what *is* love? That it *is*, I can certify, but to call it intense sympathy (the best explanation of it perhaps) is to do little else than change one term for another. Who can deny that there is a part of his existence which he knows to be — indeed it is the axiom of himself, so to speak — yet he cannot tell what it is, or where it came from. It would almost seem as if one could by intelligent research find out the nature of everything — except oneself!

(12.) *Academy Notes*. It was nice of Annie to get and mark this for me (is it to be returned, or may I keep it?). I have enjoyed looking over the pictures. I like the face of the woman in Dicksee's 'Within the Shadow of the Church.' 'Soul's Awakening' by J. Sant (Annie does not mark it) is apparently just spoiled by the expression being theatrical rather than real, but it may not be so in the original. Frank Holl flatters the Prince of Wales; it's not like him. I think the face of Mrs. Arthur Street by H. T. Wells (Annie marks 'nice face') is a little too meaningless. I think an artist who will paint people like Mrs. Lorna Lathrop ought to be boycotted!

'Christiane ad Leones!' strikes one as rather morbid. I don't think the general run of people can get up enough enthusiasm over the heroism of the early Christians to appreciate the picture, but I may be wrong, whereas the horror of it they rather do like (as I was saying the other day, respecting the table made of corpses). Possibly the artist had studied the history of his subject and was otherwise able to appreciate his picture from the right point of view, just as a communard might be enthusiastic over a picture representing the slaughter of his comrades after the fall of Paris, while ordinary people would see nothing but a ghastly scene of bloodshed. Does Annie agree with me here?

Solomon J. Solomon seems to have a taste for the gigantic and the violent (in contrast to himself, I suppose). I should say, with Annie, that 'Niobe' was certainly not pleasing! Yes, I did like Alice Havers' 'Mary with Child' very much (she is not a Jewess, but no matter, it would spoil the picture if she were!). I like all I have seen of A. Havers'. Poynters frame to 'Under the Sea Wall' throws up the picture well. Alfred Gilbert has hit off Her Majesty in the statue very well, and the result, like 'Niobe', is not pleasing!

May 25th. It is nearly one, and as I want to give you a full account of today's experiences (and have to be at Brock's tomorrow morning early) I still think I had better postpone writing till Sunday, which will probably be my first leisure time. Tomorrow evening is the debate at the Cusacks'. All I will say now is that I have spent the day doing the amateur cowboy.

May 26th, 9:50 p.m. Planting potatoes for Brock, and debate at the Cusacks' this evening, of which details I write tomorrow.

Sunday, May 27th, 10 a.m. (1.) Concerning May 25: I went up to Brock's to breakfast, as usual. I heard more about the Templemans from Brock. It seems T. is butcher in Silver Cliff, and they invited *themselves* out to Brock's, to his great disgust. One of the first things I did was to go down to feed the pig when, behold, the pig had torn down part of its stye and escaped in the night. That pig has escaped several times before, and generally goes down to the house of one Browning, who lives below Hugg's, so we got the waggon and drove down there.

Arrived at Browning's, we found him there (he lives alone and batches) and also Joe McGinnis, who is Irish and is said to be a most excellent old fellow. The pig *had* come to Browning's, and he had put it with his own, whereupon they had set upon it and killed it. We went in, and Brock, seeming to be in a trading humor, made two trades with Browning. He exchanged his now defunct pig and a one-year-old bull of his for a couple of donkeys belonging to Browning. This settled, we had to get the bull, and so drove down to Brock's, had lunch, and started out, this time both of us riding. Brock his horse 'Tom' and I the black mare 'Molly.'

We got down to the pasture and tried to drive the bull, but it was evident that we could never get it along unless we took the old cow, its mother, with it. We got them by Splann's, and down towards Hugg's, but thence all the way to Browning's we had no end of bother to get them along. They would get in the brush by the creek, and then rush out across the pasture, and so to and fro, we after them.

Molly knew more about the cowboy business than I did, and would get in front of the animals and turn so quickly that nothing but the law of gravitation kept me on her back. Finally we got them both in Browning's corral, and then went on to Beddoes' to fetch the donkeys, which had strayed down there.

I had long ago promised I would go down and see the Beddoes, so I thought it was a good opportunity to make a call, but Brock went after his donkey, and she wouldn't come in. I found them sitting at supper and so had to partake also, after which I had a great discussion with Beddoes about 'loco' (the plant that poisons horses) and, as he has all the necessary chemicals, etc., down there I am going down one day to see whether I can isolate the poison from the plant. I looked, too, over Beddoes' books (he has some excellent ones) and borrowed Hayden's report of the Survey of Colorado, which I was extremely glad to get, as it will add hosts of species to my fauna and flora list.

By this time, Brock had started off, and I had to hurry to catch him up. It was quite late when we got home, but there was a good moon, and we managed to drive the donkeys and the old cow (which we had left at Browning's) back in safety.

When I got to Brock's I found letters from Vasey and Riley waiting for me, and also some papers by Hy. Edwards. These had been brought out by Charley Cusack, who went to town that day.

(2.) Of May 26th: A windy, chilly day. I was planting potatoes for Brock all day except toward evening when we cut some to plant on Monday. It was the debate on 'Women's Rights' at the Cusacks', so I went up after supper. I took up O. Schreiner's paper, *Woman's World*, for Mrs. Cusack to read, and also 'heading notes.' They were all delighted with Alice Havers' picture, as also the Brocks.

We had a pretty good debate, though neither Mrs. Chas. Cusack nor Miss Urquhart would speak. Louis Howard was there, and

Charley Cusack. At the end, Mrs. C. moved that it was desirable that women should be better educated in the direction of teaching them to think, and this was carried unanimously, for although Louis Howard moved an amendment that women were good enough as they were, he said afterward he was in favor of the original motion.

I forgot to mention that before lunch, Brock, Louis Howard, and I branded several donkeys and a calf. The poor little beasts have to be tied down, and are then branded with a hot iron. It seems cruel, but they *must* be branded, and it is the only way to do it.

(3.) Of today: A nasty, damp morning. Most of the time it has been snowing (though not to stay on the ground) and it is so chilly that I have been obliged to light the fire.

6:30 p.m. It has been snowing in a desultory sort of manner all day and I have been at home writing letters. I shan't go up to the Cusack's tonight.

May 28th. There was a little snow on the ground this morning, but it soon melted. It has been very chilly all day though. In the morning I planted potatoes and harrowed, and cut potatoes in the afternoon; this last I had to do in a very cold and draughty stable, and I felt as though I had caught a chill, but I hope not. Just before supper I went up to the Cusack's for a half hour. Mrs. C. likes O. Schreiner's article in *Woman's World*.

May 29th, 7:30 p.m. Cutting and planting potatoes in some ground Brock has up in the woods near where we had the picnic. It was very fine in the morning, and we took our lunch up and would have planted all day had it not snowed. Soon after three there came on a thunder and 'snail storm' (nothing to do with the mollusc. It is half snow and half hail) which lasted till about six. We therefore came home and had supper rather early, and then I came down here.

Regy talked of going to town tomorrow, and if it is not quite fine I shall get him to post this and get my letters, instead of going in myself, so I will make an ending, to be ready should he come, and I want to give it to him.

May 30th, 3:35 p.m. I came to town this afternoon with Brock. It is a haily and cold unpleasant day. I got your nice letter and sundry other mail — viz., letters from Carlie (who seems very depressed), W. H. Edwards, Coulter (enclosing one of Farlow's about a fungus), Bruner (Orthoptera man), and Dr. P. Radenhausen (wanting cacti). Also postcard from Ancey and box of beetles from Algeria (smashed in the post), *Chicago Labor Enquirer*, and papers about a course of lectures to be given on botany by Prof. Goodale at Boston (why does he send them to me? I can't attend them!). W. H. Edwards says he can't get up the club to send me insect-hunting, so Annie was right!

Best thanks to Annie for note on *Agaricus velutipes*; it is evidently not *velutinus*. Much of your letter is not for postoffice answering, so will write in next letter. Can't you get one of those pocket cameras and take a photograph of Annie when she isn't looking? I don't know what you mean by saying she didn't look '*so* common-place', etc. If I were Annie I would pull your nose or hit you over the head with the poker. I *can't* fling a rock 6,000 miles.

I have seen Kane's *European Lepidoptera*. It is pretty good but was roughly handled in review when it came out. Dr. Lang's is the only really first-rate book on European butterflies. I never read Grant Allen on *Colours of Flowers*.

Shaking hands is a magnificent institution when properly done. I think perhaps the work women suffer as much from lack of joy than misery; no doubt they get callous. It's very bad, anyway. I came away in such a hurry that I forgot to bring *Woman's World* to post, but will do so next time.

May 31st, 1888

Dear Frederic,

We waited for the evening mail yesterday, and I got a letter from Underwood (Hepaticae, etc., man) and reprints of some papers by him, also a postcard from J. W. Taylor, who wants *live* mollusca from here. It rained a good deal while we were driving home, but we were well wrapped up and so did not get wet. Brock asked me to go with him and have supper, so I did, and afterward came down here and wrote till past eleven.

This morning I was up at Brock's to breakfast as usual. The first thing we did was to go and mend the fence between Splann's and Brock's. It is a wire fence, and Splann's cattle are constantly getting through and eating Brock's timothy grass, but now we have made the fence secure enough to keep them out, I think. On the way to the fence I came across a nest of a 'blackbird' (*Scolecophagus cyanocephalus*) [*Euphagus*, the Brewer's Blackbird. Ed.] with eggs. If I can get a little collection of eggs from here would you care to have them?

Then we went up above the Cusacks' and planted potatoes, taking lunch with us and not returning till after four, when I was set to saw wood till supper, after which I came down here. As I went by the Cusacks' Mrs. C. came out with three butterflies she had caught for me: *Anthocharis sp.*, *Pieris oleracea*, and *Pieris sp.* Mrs. C. catches something or other nearly every day; good of her.

June 1st. June 1887-June 1888 — a year has nearly gone! I was up at Brock's as usual this morning, and we went up in the wood and planted potatoes till noon. After lunch, as there was nothing of importance to do, I concluded I would take a half-holiday, and so came down here and spent the afternoon turning my meatsafe into a larva-cage (I don't have meat now, and when I have any it will keep just as well in the house) and in taking notes from the Hayden Survey Report I got from Beddoes. I found a lot of very pretty Arctiid larvae on *Mertensia* by my house, black with yellow stripes and steel-blue tubercles. Payn drove by with Preston this afternoon on his way to the Splann's.

Payn has bought a sort of buckboard buggy and a horse, for which he is to pay, two months hence, $90 and $80 respectively. Cox came down while I was talking to Payn and examined this new rig of his, giving his opinion that he had got the horse cheap (though it is only three years old) and has paid too much for the buggy. I haven't seen the puss, Toby, today. I hope no harm has come to her. Now, in answer to your letter:

The cutting on 'Blonde v. Brunette' is very interesting, particularly with reference to red hair being an aberration and not a variety, I have not gone into the matter enough to give any decided opinion on this point.

If religion is a product of sentiment it will hardly die out because sentiment is quite a fundamental thing in the human character (so I judge), but I would rather say that religion is by no means sentiment. Rather, on the contrary it is one's ground-belief about things, on which everything else hinges. So to say a man has no religion is to say that he has nothing whereby he rules his conduct. In fact, that he is at the mercy of chance external influences. He has no *self* at all, properly speaking. So, from this point of view, also, religion becomes a fundamental thing without which humanity cannot exist.

It is as well to make a distinction between religion and theology, the latter being, so to speak, a *theory* of religion. To take an example, our knowledge that two bodies in space attract each other corresponds to our *religion* on the subject, but any *theory* by which we explain (or try to explain) it corresponds to our theology. So you see one's *religion* may be sound enough, though the *theology* is little short of idiotic, and I think this is often the case.

As to going to church, I doubt whether it does any good. People out here rarely go to church and I doubt if they lose much thereby. To me, church has the rather unfortunate effect (in most cases) of making me despise the whole affair, while there is really some good in it if one thinks of it at leisure. I think it is very good for people to meet together for religious service, certainly, but because I think so the more absurd does it seem that they should put up with the ridiculous proceedings of the church and the wild theories of religion one is asked to believe as proved. I don't say that the *religion* of all the orthodox is wrong, but I do say that their reasoning powers are very stiff for want of use, so that on this subject one is led to put them down as fools. But I shall ramble on forever about religion if I don't stop. It is not a good thing to be diffuse, especially in a letter.

I shall be very glad to see the Ealing Society report (it hasn't appeared yet).

The Hayden Survey Report gives me several records of European insects, etc., in Colorado. For example, the following are reported: *Daphnia pulex, Arctia guenseli* Payk., *Cidaria testata, C. populata, Coremia ferrugata* Cl. (I have taken this), *Gastrus equi, Agrotis islandica* Stgr., *Anarcta melanopa* Thunb., *Larentia casiata* S. V., *Melanippe tristata* L., *M. hastata* L., *Syrphus corolla*.

June 2nd, 10:30 p.m. There is a long irrigation ditch in the course of construction, to irrigate Chamberlain's and Brock's land, and the work of making it has to be divided between them. So Brock and I went up to Chamberlain's, and Brock worked on the ditch till noon, and I the whole day, digging with a grub-hoe. Chamberlain and his two sons were also working. This evening I went up to the Cusacks', but although Louis Howard was there, the discussion on 'Swearing' did not come off.

Sunday, June 3rd, 10:10. p.m. It has been very hot, and I have been feeling tired and so have not 'desecrated the Sabbath' by doing nothing whatever, even writing the letters which I certainly ought to have written. In the morning Chamberlain and his son paid me a visit, but did not stay long. I spent the morning catching butterflies to put into my larva-cage in the hope that they will lay some eggs for W. H. Edwards.

Payn came by towards mid-day. He has bought another horse for $125 (he seems to have lots of money just now). Payn showed me a letter from Robinson, editor of the *Daily News*, complementing him on some things he had written, and recommending him to write more. I think myself that Payn might write pretty good *light* articles if he would persevere. Robinson is going to print some of Payn's 'copy' (about Colorado) in the *Daily News* later on. (It shows how small a chance a thing sent to a big paper has of even being looked at, that Robinson mentions he only read Payn's MS because Payn, Sr., who is a great friend of his, specially asked him to do so — and he even admits the request made him rather cross.)

Most of the afternoon I lay down and read the two latest *Pall Mall Budgets*, which I had only time to glance at before. They are both interesting numbers. Later, Mrs. Cusack, Regy, and Miss U. all came down and paid me a visit, and when they went back I went up with them and stayed for the evening. In an old 'Buffon' [*Histoire Naturelle, 1749-1788.* Ed.] at Chamberlain's I found Gmelin's classification of the genus *Homo* given. It is as follows: Genus *Homo* Linn. *Homo sapiens* L. a., var. *albus* Gmel. = white races; b, var. *badius* Gmel. = brown Asiatic races; c, var. *niger* Gmel. = black African races; d, var. *cupreus* Gmel. = American red men; e, var. *fuscus* Gmel.= Australian and Polynesian.

June 4th, 8:45 p.m. I have been working on the ditch at Chamberlain's for Brock, as I did on Saturday, and Brock and the Chamberlains were also working there all day. It is rather tiring work, with pick, shovel, and grub-hoe, but now the ditch is done, and plenty of water is running along it to irrigate the land. Brock is not going to work any more this week (to speak of) and so I am going to take a holiday and do some bug-catching, letter-writing, etc., things which have got somewhat in arrears.

Today I noticed three instances in which spiders get their living helped by their resemblance to the colour of a flower. No doubt it is the usual custom of this spider (which belongs to *Thomisus* or an allied genus). But I must explain — there is a yellow Umbellifer called *Ligusticum montanum* [*Pseudocymopterus montanus.* Ed.] very common here, and these spiders which are similarly yellow, but a little lighter, sit in the middle of the flower and are thus not noticeable unless one is specially looking for them. The flowers of *L. montanum* are, I know, much visited by insects, and there can be no reasonable doubt that as soon as they alight where the spider is, he straightway makes his dinner off them.

I have been at home writing all day and packing up specimens to send away. I have found a lot of eggs of *Pieris sisymbrii* on the buds of a conifer that grows by my house, and am sending them to W. H. Edwards. Toby has not yet turned up. I fear something (e.g., dog) has happened to her.

I walked to town early this morning and, getting a lift for the last mile and a half, arrived in time to post Edwards' *P. sisymbrii* eggs by the morning's mail. I enclose some seeds of *Cymopterus montanus* Torr. & Gray, a curious little umbellifer which is rather common here. I am returning *Woman's World* with much thanks. The mail I got today is your letter and a letter from Mother. The *Ealing Report* has not turned up.

June 6th, 1888

Dear Frederic,
I started from town at ten, and walked home (getting about half a mile lift near Ula). Near Ula I found three specimens of *Primula farinosa* [not correct. It was *P. incana.* Ed.] in bud, the first I have ever seen growing. I was much pleased

with them, as I have had the plant (dried) from Yorkshire, where it is quite common in places. It is a lovely little primrose.

When I got home I found a lot of mail someone had brought there while I was away: Letter from Wolle (with names of algae, diatoms, etc., I sent him), *West American Scientist* (March and April) — several extra copies, with my papers, *Ornithologist and Oölogist* (a good little paper — would you like to have copies to read?, *Commonweal*, *Chicago Labor Enquirer*, and *Pall Mall Budget*. I caught a grand *Papilio* by my house. Then I went up to the Cusacks' to take them some mail, and found that Regy had brought out all this mail yesterday and had taken it up to Brock's, supposing I was there and, as I wasn't, brought it down to my house this morning.

The Cusacks were going for a drive up in the woods this afternoon, so I went with them, and we rummaged about after specimens, not getting very much. I climbed quite a tall spruce tree after woodpecker's eggs, but found the nest was an ancient one and there were no eggs or anything else for my trouble. Regy shot a skunk, a pretty beast — black and white, with a long hairy tail, but rather too odoriferous to be pleasant! However, he took the skin off roughly and is going to preserve it. Then we came back, had supper, and soon after, I came down here.

June 7th, 9:30 p.m. Mrs. Cox is expected this week from England, so Cox asked me to go and clear up the rubbish round the house before she came, and that is what I have been doing today. I did not make a very good job of it, because it was excessively hot all the morning and very windy all the afternoon, but I have got the place much clearer than it was before. Payn went to town and returned bringing me *Pall Mall Budget* and *Commonweal* but no letters.

June 8th, 8 p.m. I was feeling tired and sleepy this morning and so lay down and read *Pall Mall Budget*, but I took a quinine pill and that has brought me to rights again. Pity quinine isn't a patent medicine. I might send the firm an adv't. So! [sketch]

About mid-day Payn paid me a call and announced that Cox wanted me to go and plant potatoes all the afternoon, 'for cash.' I thought I might be well, and so assented. The place is a clearing by Swift Creek a quarter of a mile above my house. I got there at one but found Cox and Bassick had not yet gone to lunch, so I planted a few and then went up with them, and came down again afterwards with Bassick (Cox went to town) and planted till six. Bassick, all the while he is ploughing, keeps up a continuous storm of curses at the horses, and although I can stand a good deal in that way in a pinch, it rather grates on one's nerves, like a bad German band.

June 9th, 7:20 p.m. Somewhat unwisely, perhaps (as I had much else to do), I promised Cox I would plant potatoes today, working with Bassick, as he was going to Cañon City to meet his wife on her journey from England. Bassick said he would be at the potato field at 7:30, and I was there at that time, but as he did not turn up I went up to Cox's and found that, various things having kept him, he had not even had breakfast yet. Finally we got down there, and the rest of the day to 6:15, except for the break for lunch, was spent planting potatoes, which is quite too uneventful an occupation to say much about, except that it was very hot. During the day I contrived to catch sundry insects, including a nice *Cicada*.

Sunday, June 10th, 10:35 p.m. I wrote during the morning, then got my net and boxes and went out collecting and to the Cusacks'. On the way I caught a 'clear-wing' (*Sesia* or some allied genus) and a specimen of *Colias eurytheme* var. *intermedia* (vide *West Amer. Sci.* that I am sending) and found *Mimulus* in flower by the creek. I found Mrs. C. busy arranging her flowers (she has quite a lot) and so sat and talked and read to her (among other things, I read her Morris' *Aims of Art*, which she liked, though not agreeing with everything in it).

Mrs. Cusack told me a bit of news which greatly surprised, but on the whole pleased, viz., that Miss Sidford and Louis Howard are engaged to be married! Now Miss Sidford's people are very poor, it seems, and a certain rich man called Brown had been courting her for a long time, always being rejected. *She* didn't care a bit for the man, but finally, after some pressure from her people, and thinking she would never fall in love, she agreed to marry Brown, and so they were duly engaged.

Meanwhile, she and Louis contrived to fall in love with each other, and when Louis (knowing she really didn't care for Brown) made bold to declare his love, she wrote to Brown breaking him off, and has decided to marry Louis! No doubt this is a very shabby treatment for Brown. She ought never to have been engaged to a man she didn't love. But one cannot do otherwise than rejoice that since (contrary to her expectations) she *was* to fall in love, it was before and not after her marriage, and in time to avert what would certainly have been acute misery for her, for Brown, and for Louis.

Talking of engagements to be married, these things are managed very loosely in America, and I heard of someone, on getting engaged at Colorado Springs, being solemnly asked: 'Was she engaged for good or only for the season?' And it seems that some of them do actually get 'engaged' for a summer only, without the least idea of getting married! Whether the Americans are greater humbugs than the English, I don't know, but at any rate they are not ashamed of it! And perhaps an 'honest rogue' is better than one who tries to conceal his faults.

In the evening I went for a short stroll with Mrs. Cusack, and we came across a patch of the very pretty *Geum rivale*, with its pinkish petals and brown-pink sepals. It is a British plant also, but I never saw it growing before. On the way home I called at Brock's. He had just returned with Mrs. B. from Rosita where they had been to see some people of the name of Turner.

June 11th, 8:40 p.m. It was very hot this morning, quite too hot to go out, so I wrote for a while, and then took to sketching, (I enclose a little view taken from my bedroom window, for Annie.) The yellow appearance in the foreground is due to the abundance of ragwort (*Senecio sp.*) in flower on the prairie. At about mid-day Louis Howard came by. He called out, and I went out and spoke to him, but said nothing about the engagement, as I did not think I was supposed to know anything about it. (Louis afterwards said I approached him with a broad grin, and he wondered whether I did know about it!) Louis went on up to the Cusacks', and I presently followed him, and arrived there as they were having lunch.

So I then congratulated Louis on his engagement and we all talked the affair over in excellent spirits. Louis says he doesn't think he can marry yet for two years, however, because (1.) He must find a ranch and a home, (2.) Miss Sidford must first go to England and see her people. Respecting Brown, Louis tells me that Miss S. broke off with *him* before he said anything, and it was only when she told him that she had given up all idea of marrying Brown that he declared his love. The next thing is to get Miss Sidford to go up to the Cusacks' for a week for a change, as she isn't very well. Louis is very anxious about this, and so tomorrow Regy and Miss U. are going down with a note from Mrs. C., and will do all they can to persuade Mrs. Beddoes to let her come. Louis will of course also take up his abode at the Cusack's that week.

I collected a few flowers today. including four new to Custer Co., and also found *Parnassias smintheus* (newly emerged) flying in some abundance near the Cusacks'. It is a pretty butterfly, not unlike the European *P. apollo*. I enclose a note and a sketch of a Thomisid spider and its deceiving ways for the S. Lond.. Ent. and Nat. Hist. Soc.

June 12th, 6 p.m. Have walked to town, and am waiting for your letter by this evening's mail. On my way I discovered a colony of *Physa hypnorum*! And I have been by that place dozens of times and never found any before. But *P. hypnorum* is not always to be found where it occurs; it buries itself in the mud. I got sundry mail on arriving here: Letters from Strecker (moth man), Sterki (shell man), Coulter, L.. O. Howard (Dept. of Agric.), and Bruner (grasshopper man), postcard from Ellis (fungi man), *Madame Delphine* from Mother (but I have read it before), and *Chicago Labor Enquirer*. Some *Canadian Entomologist* and *Ann. Rept. of Ent. Soc. of Ontario* came here ages ago addressed to D. Down, but as this person was unknown and did not turn up, the postmaster was about to destroy them. On opening them, however, he saw that they were entomological and so handed them over to me. I am glad to have them, as they contain some Colorado records and other interesting matters.

Have got your letters, also very long and interesting one from Tutt, and letter from Mother. Very glad your paper went off well. I hope they will publish it. I hear from one Frere that caterpillars are eating all his alfalfa (i.e., *Medicago sativa*) crop. I must go tomorrow to investigate if I can. The ranch is near Ula.

June 13th, 1888, 9:50 p.m.

Dear Frederic,

I walked home last night after getting mail, and found on my way, in the damp grassy ground by Ula, multitudes of 'June bugs' (*Noctiluca*, a sort of glow worm) which looked exceedingly pretty flashing light from off the grasses and low herbage. The light undulates, but is very bright, lasting from two to four seconds at a time. I collected several specimens and brought them home. Today I have been down to see the caterpillars on alfalfa, etc., but I am practically asleep, and so will defer writing more until tomorrow.

June 14th, 3:35 p.m. First, about yesterday. I went up to the Cusacks' in the morning, having mail for them, and stayed some while talking to Mrs.C. Miss Sidford had come up (and of course also Louis Howard) to stay a few days. Miss S. and Miss U. had gone to town that morning. I met them as I was going up. In the afternoon, at about three, I walked down to Frere's. It is only about three miles, but a considerable grade, Frere's being I suppose about 600 ft. lower than this. In the fields I got some flowers new to me, including a white iris (a var. of *I. missouriensis*). I found Frere just about to start to the alfalfa field, and so went with him.

He told me he had been here since 1869, and at that time the Ute Indians used to come here every winter, but there were no buffalo.

We found the caterpillars on the young alfalfa (*Medicago*) in great abundance in places and I collected a number. They varied in colour, but were generally speaking dark (black to dark olive) with pale longitudinal lines. So far as one can judge, they belong to the Pyralidae. After getting the caterpillars, I came home, and in the evening went up to the Cusacks', taking some flowers for Mrs. C. to press, as all my papers were full, and those I had in press were too crowded and smelling musty.

Louis was strolling about with Miss Sidford all the evening, of course, and was unmercifully chaffed, but was altogether too happy to mind. They came in some time after nine and said they had been almost to the top of the 'hogback' at the back of the house (I suppose a mile and a half up a considerable incline). 'What for?' 'Oh, Mary (Miss S.) had never been up there before and wanted to see what it was like.' Audible smile amongst the company, for it was pitch dark.) Then Regy told Miss S. the air seemed to agree with her wonderfully, for she 'had quite a colour' — and so on and so on. I should say, though, that Regy deserved chaffing as much as anyone, for nearly all the while Louis had been out with Miss S., he was wandering about with Miss U.

As to today, I woke up this morning and the first thing I became conscious of was my garden fence going down, and a great cow walking thereon. I got up and scared it away without having very much damage done. The seeds are not yet coming up. I fear the garden is too dry, and although I put much water on it, it soon dries up again. I hardly know what to do. I felt very far from A-1 this morning and did not get up till nearly eleven. Then I had breakfast and took some quinine, but was obliged to lie down again, feeling very feverish and uncomfortable so that I did not even care to read. I think it is mainly the effect of the heat, and I am better now.

Now a few notes on your letters: From what publication is the cutting as to Annie's character 'from handwriting' out of? Didn't I see that same in MS once? It might have been worse. On the whole I think the interpreter has got as near as he could reasonably expect to, but had he been anyway sure about it, he would not have ventured on giving so many characters, at least half of which are more or less incorrect.

As I said, I am glad the S.L.E.S. paper was a success and I hope they will publish it, at least the part relating to the S.L.E.S. district. I once went into some elaborate investigations to see how far the mollusca of Surrey, Sussex, and West Kent were influenced by soil, but I don't know where the MS relating thereto have gone. Which of my divisions did you leave out? Would it be possible, I wonder, to let me see your MS. It would come as cheaply as newspaper by post, but perhaps it is best not to incur any risk of loss, especially if it is to be published.

If I have any dinner parties they shall be in the Wild West style — 'Frying pans provided. Everyone to cook his own flapjack!' Would that suit you? I have thought more about your lecture to Gardening Society, and come to the conclusion that perhaps it isn't worth the time it would take you (to prepare it, etc.). It was wise of you to take Louy off to Windsor thus, and I hope Annie may be persuaded to do likewise, only one wishes it could be for a week. When the summer holiday comes, you must go off to New Forest or Devonshire or somewhere, and take Annie, 'whether his mother would let him or no', as the nursery ballad has it.

9:15. I had settled down to my letters, and was getting some fresh-water algae ready to send to Wolle when I heard much shouting and noise outside and, going out, perceived a waggon coming full of people, apparently all intoxicated. But they were sober after all except for a natural exuberance of spirits and the influence of the night air, and proved to be Mrs. Cusack, Mrs. Brock, Miss Sidford, Miss Urquhart, Louis, and Regy! It had suddenly occurred to them, they said, that they would come down and pay me a call. Hence the invasion, and I was pleased to see them anyway. Louis and Miss S. of course went for a stroll, and she contrived to lose her watch. We made some search for it, but without success. I must go over the ground tomorrow by daylight and search carefully.

June 15th, 7:20 p.m. The first thing I did was to look for Miss Sidford's watch, but quite unsuccessfully. Miss S. and Louis came down later in the morning, however, and they discovered it amongst the grass where they had sat down. I had promised to write the names on Miss Sidford's plants, so I went up to the Cusacks' and did so. Miss S. showed me a pretty orchid, *Cypripedium parviflorum*, she had found near there.

I stayed up at the Cusacks' most of the day, as it was very hot, too hot to work intelligently. Most of the afternoon I was reading *Madame Delphine* to Mrs. C., while the rest of the household went off in various directions for an afternoon doze. The Cusacks have now got a young magpie that runs about the house and goes by the name of 'Pete.' It is a most ridiculous creature. It is nearly all mouth [sketch] and reminds you of 'Hookybeak the Raven', if you are acquainted with that illustrious bird. *Achillea millefolium* is just now coming into bloom again here.

June 16th. I have been at home all day, writing and reading. Louis and Miss S. and Regy and Miss U. went to town today and brought me a lot of nice mail: Letters from W. H. Edwards, Radenhausen, Vasey, L. O. Howard (Agric. Dept., with names of insects sent), and Orcutt. The *Ent. Mags.* (many thanks for sending so soon! But you needn't hurry so much; if they arrive by the 20th it will do first rate. Don't you want to read them before sending them off?), *Naturalist* for June, *P. M. Budget*, and *Commonweal*. I see in *Nat.* that Eagle Clarke has gone off to boss the museum at Edinburgh and I suppose will have to give up the *Nat.* and Y.N.V. shortly. I also see that Pallas' Sand Grouse is invading the British Islands once more.

Tutt is excellent in his paper on *Labelling Insects* in *Ent.*, but I would never dare to make such an awful confession as that about destroying the locality labels (p. 146)! However, he has made amends for his wickedness in that direction by now, The way Barker has got it (p.165) about *Gonopteryx*, it looks as if I thought *G. rhamni* and *cleopatra* were one species! Which is hardly fair. I have written Jenner Weir a further argument on this subject. The *Ent. Mo. Mag.* is a good number. I think Stainton is quite right about Haworth's old types; it is ridiculous to resuscitate old names that have nothing in the description to tell them by, because someone finds the 'type' is so-and-so.

Sunday, June 17. I have taken to cooking my own meals over an open fire out of doors now so that I can use the Dutch oven, which makes much better bread than a frying pan. After cooking some bread in this way, and having breakfast, I sat writing all the morning except that I went out every now and then to catch butterflies which were flying near the house. I saw some large black *Papilios* but didn't catch any, but I did catch two specimens of *Terias* (I think *T. ancippe*) — orange-coloured butterflies with black borders, very pretty. I am very pleased with them as I never saw any of this genus alive before. A most beautiful *Arctia* about the size of *caia*, emerged in my breeding cage this morning.

Early in the afternoon I went up to the Cusacks and stayed to supper. I ascertained from Brock that Mrs. Cox had arrived the night before (she would have been here many days sooner, only she was delayed in Pueblo by the children developing whooping cough), so we all went down in the to see her, that is, all the Cusack household. Louis and Miss S., T.D.A.C. Brock, Mrs. B. and child also went down at the same time. We found Mrs. Cox looking pretty well and full of her English experiences, but her hands were pretty full with her two small children (Charlie and Isabel). When the Cusacks went back, I stayed talking at Cox's, meaning to come down here, but I found I had left my butterfly net up at the Cusack's, so went up there again, stayed to evening services, and then came down.

June 18th, 6:30 p.m. I have been at home all day, writing and reading, and so have little or nothing to tell. I have sorted out 51 species of plants to go to Dr. Vasey at Washington to be named. A beautiful Saturniid moth, more nearly allied to *Samia cecropia* than anything I know, emerged today from the cocoon I found months ago on my way to town. Do you remember my telling you of it?

Today is the anniversary of the Gardening Society, to which Annie came, so I commemorate the event by sending her white and pink 'everlastings' (*Antennaria dioica*) [*A. rosea*. Ed.] from this locality, where it grows on the prairie by my house.

8:55 p.m. This evening I went up to the Brock's to get some eggs, and when up there I set my first leg. The said leg belonged to their magpie (they have a young magpie, as well as the Cusacks') and had been broken by one of the chickens. I set it with a piece of rag and a match, tied up with cotton.

June 19th. I was writing and reading and packing my boxes till three, when I started to walk to town. I had got about 2/3 across the prairie when Bassick came along with a waggon, so I got a lift into town. The only mail received is postcard from W. H. Edwards, *Chicago Labor Enquirer*, and notice from Conch. Soc. about alteration of rules. I wait till the evening mail for your letter. I suppose you have also received the circular from Conch. Soc. I'm all too late to vote, but I should say, continue publication in Journ. Conch. and don't increase subscription. Practically speaking, there are magazines enough to publish anything worth publishing, and will do it gratis, so I am not so keen on bulky 'proceedings.' If the subscr. is increased I think I shall resign my membership.

The evening mail is in, and I have got your nice letter. The questions are hardly in line; it will interest you to find how immensely ignorant I am!) Our debating society has ceased to be, but there may be occasional revivals.

J. W. Douglas is the man to know all about *Lecanium pyri*. Males should have wings, I fancy. I believe Carmichael is a pretty good man at Myriapoda; I once saw him in the library of the Zoöl. Society but never spoke to him.

I never read any of Zola. I am glad Annie is reading *John Ball*, and likes it.

Yes, it is almost a year! I can't say I *feel* any older. The past year seems to have had a sort of unreality about it. I have been transplanted but have not taken root, so to speak. I am getting too tired of being here, but there's no help for it at present. One must be patient. Perhaps I can get back a year hence.

I should say no compensation to the publicans, but have not deliberately considered the matter in its various aspects. I will think it over. I can't say I would condemn publicans on moral and intellectual grounds in the wholesale manner you seem to do. I don't think they are any worse than most 'business men.' I think some of them are not such bad fellows altogether, e.g., proprietors of country inns.

Science Gossip has not turned up yet, but I dare say it will soon. I hope you didn't send the *Ealing Report,* because it has not arrived, though I should like to see it.

Wednesday, June 20th, 1888, 10:10 p.m.

Dear Frederic,.

I had an uneventful walk home last night, the first part by daylight and the last by moonlight (twilight lasts a very little while in this clear atmosphere). I went up to the Cusacks' when I got back, to take Mrs. C. a letter, and when I was up there Regy asked me to come and help him get wood for the Kettles, and that is what I have been doing today. But I am too sleepy and muddled to write anything intelligently now, so must postpone account of today till tomorrow.

June 21st, 3:15 p.m. Yesterday morning I went up to the Cusacks', and started off up into the woods with Regy. What we had to do was to get dead quaking asps and pile them up (having knocked off the branches) so that the Kettles could come with waggons and easily throw the poles on and take them off. They want about 15 loads, all for their own consumption as firewood, and pay Regy 50 cents for each load. We had about a mile to walk up a very steep grade before we came to where the wood was, and I got out of breath, which made it difficult for me to work. (Once I lose my breath I do not regain it for a long while.) Regy chopped the trees down and I piled them up, except in places where they had already fallen; there we both piled. We took our lunch up with us, but did not do a day's work, coming home between three and four. I received 50 cents for my exertions.

When we got down to the Cusacks' again, we found Charley Cusack there. He had come out with Louis Howard, who went to town that morning. I stayed up there for the evening, and after supper produced Annie's exam paper, which was slowly read out and answered (on paper) by all of us as well as we could from memory in the course of an hour. You will doubtless be disgusted at the depth of our ignorance, but in a general way one may say that none of us knew anything about it. Mrs. Cusack did best, with 42 answers; Regy knew 35, Charley Cusack 34, and T.D.A.C. 38. Miss Urquhart was part of the time talking to Mrs. Brock who (with Brock and child) turned up in the middle of the exam and so did not do all the exam, but she seemed to know very few of the answers.

I enclose (with some shame) my list of answers, taken down at the time; you are at liberty to laugh at my ignorance. But I would say, however, that the paper is not a very practical one, the knowledge it implies being rather of the nature of educational varnish than real value. It is, though, a pretty good test of observation and memory in some of its questions. I should like to know how many answers were given by the various inhabitants of Syon Lodge when they were examined on it. Many questions were unanswerable by anyone last night, and others remained doubtful or in dispute.

This morning, feeling weary, I lay down and read *Caraners* and afterwards slept a little. Cardy Lees arrived with his waggon in the course of the morning, back from Bear River, etc. Frank C. did not return with him, but had taken an irrigation job in South Park and is not likely to be back for some time. *Caraners*, which I have been reading, is in the little book of Cable's stories (*Madame Delphine, Caraners,* and *Grande Pointe*) which Mother sent me, and I like it very much. Has Annie read it? I think she would like it.

Now a note or two on your last letter. Annie's note on Vegetarianism and the reply thereto are interesting. I am not in favour of it myself, but I think that some step towards it would be advisable; we might eat more vegetable food and less meat. It is hardly necessary to say that, as things go, a lessened expenditure all round would *not* give 'the power of procuring increased pleasures of other kinds.' Quite the contrary.

Lecanium pyri might be interesting to watch. The only *Lecanium* I had down previously for Middlesex is *L. longulum* Dougl., found (introduced) at Harrow and in the Royal Botanical Society's gardens. But *L. beaumonti* Dougl., *L. testudo,* and *L. longulum* have been found in Kew Gardens.

You know of old my ideas about your family, and I hold them still. The principle involved is not unlike the Home Rule question in Ireland, and you know also what I think about the Irish question. For me, who have always been allowed the greatest freedom, it is difficult to understand how you can endure a pressure which is artificial and must be contrary to your own ideas of right. And from the parents' point of view, their faith in their own discretion and want of faith in that of their children is very inexplicable.

Morally, I suppose nobody is to blame, yet there is a strange perversion of ideas somewhere. I know what I should do, compelled by my own nature, but how can I advise you — or Annie? I have sometimes thought that, if, by degrees you would assert your liberties, not forcibly but mildly and with show of meaning it, all that you need might be granted you without any disturbance. But here again, how can I tell? A summer holiday with Annie would be a good test case to begin with. I do not think you will gain anything without asking for it, *without meaning to get it.* Of course, disagreements are unpleasant, but acute disagreement followed by agreement is better than chronic lasting disagreement.

10:10 p.m. Toward sundown I went up to the Brock's for some eggs, calling at the Cox's on the way. Mrs. Cox has brought out a lot of books, including a Newman's *British Moths,* which I have borrowed to look over and take some notes from. I had supper at the Brock's; Brock had gone to town, but Lees was there, and Regy and Miss U. came in after supper. Lees showed us a book of very nice photographs taken by a friend of his while they were traveling in British Columbia and Idaho. Lees' brother, who was with them, has written a book on their adventures, which is shortly to be published. Perhaps you will see it at Smith's.

June 22nd. After breakfast I took some notes from 'Newman' and then set out to go up in the woods to get some butterflies (*Chinobas*), in the hope that they would lay some eggs. I looked in at the Cusacks' on the way, and while I was there Brock came along and asked me to work for him the afternoon, so, as it was already past eleven, I had not time to get to where *Chinobas* lived.

But I had a delightful little ramble in the woods, in a place where there were many little creeks bordered by saxifrage, (*S. punctata* [*Micranthes odontoloma*. Ed.], now in flower, the tall spikes of the green-flowered orchids (*Habenaria hyperborea*) being also conspicuous, and in places Solomon's Seal (*Polygonatum giganteum* [most likely *Streptopus fassettii*. Ed.], new to my Colorado list.

Overhead the tall pines and spruces shut off the direct rays of the sun, and the warm, moist air of the wood was fragrant with the scent of the brake-fern (the very same *Pteris* [*Pteridium*. Ed.] *aquilinum* as we get in England). Insects were abundant, species of *Phycides*, *Colias alexandra*, dragonflies, etc., making an altogether natural and most delightful scene.

I had lunch at the Cusacks, and then went down to Brock's. The first thing I had to do was to move a calf which was tied up in the corral to where there was grass, and unfortunately the rope around its neck had not been made tight enough, so that the animal contrived to slip its head out and escape while I was dragging it along. Then we had no end of a chase after the calf — Brock, Mrs. B., Becky Splann (who was up there helping Mrs. B.), and myself — till finally Brock contrived to lariat it by a hind leg, and it was secured.

After this, Brock and I went out and made an irrigation ditch and planted a number of young cabbages, which lasted us the rest of the afternoon, and after also doing a little work on the vegetable garden, we had supper, and then I came down here. I found today a dove's (*Zenaidura carolinensis*) nest with two young ones. It

was on the ground. I should have expected such a bird to build in a tree or bush.

Anniversary Day. June 23rd, 5:40 p.m. The Splanns and Payn came along in a this morning, and I went to town with them as I wanted to get some mail. All I got, however, was letters from Mother and [C. Hart] Merriam (Agric. Dept.) and postcard from Mrs. Saunders of Ontario to say her husband was away from home; also a box of Orthoptera returned, with names, from Bruner; and *Pall Mall Budget*, *Commonweal*, and an advertisement of a new magazine called *Life Lore*, to be published monthly by W. Mawer (Essex St. Strand), 6/. annually. The name of editor is not stated, but the wording of the adv't. suggests the prolific J. W. Williams! {Probably you will have seen the paper by the time you get this.)

Payn has just got a lot of money, and is spending it with due diligence. For one thing, he presented me with a ham and a lot of meat! But I fear they won't keep till eaten in this weather. That is why I have been eating eggs, Nothing else will keep; everybody finds it so. Payn is going for a week's hunting excursion tomorrow. He seems very well, and appears to have left off morphia/

8:40 p.m. So a year has gone! This evening a year ago we said goodbye, and the goodbye still rings in my ears as though it were yesterday. And the year — it has left us much as we were before, yet with hope for the future as bright as ever, and that is something. Still, I wish that more could have been done, that Annie could have written to me, and that I, for my part, could have found a means of earning more than my bare livelihood, for one *can't* save anything to speak of on this ranch work — especially such as I, who cannot get full wages. These things must come early in the next year — at least I hope they will, and at any rate I ought to be sufficiently thankful that all the while I have been out here, my consumption, if not cured, has made no progress. And here I ought to give my thanks to you, Frederic, for writing so fully and so often. Without your letters (Annie being unable to write) I could not have had any patience in waiting all this while. It cannot be the same for you to write to me as it is for me to write to you — and Annie— so I feel very much your goodness in doing so. Nobody else would have done it, even if they could.

The rosebuds will be again on the tree that climbs under the window where we sat this time last year, and perhaps now you and Annie are sitting there and thinking of it. So I send Annie a rosebud that grew on a little bush of wild roses before my door. I send this as a token, and with it my love.

There are two signs tonight that we are not altogether parted. The moon shines bright, and the constellation of the Great Bear is in the sky, visible as it is with you on the other side of the world.

Goodnight! Goodnight!

Sunday, June 24th. During the morning I wrote letters, etc. Payn passed by, starting on his week's hunting excursion, and Bassick paid me a visit to borrow a hammer and nails to fix up a fence the cattle had broken down close by here. We were talking of hair-cutting, and it struck me that I would see whether I couldn't cut my own, so after he was gone I had 'a cut and shampoo.' The result was certainly to get rid of some hair, but not quite uniformly, so that Mrs. Cusack declares that I look as if I had the ringworm, or mange!

In the afternoon I strolled up to the Cusacks', gathering many flowers and finding several insects new to me on the way. Towards evening, also, I went over to Chamberlain's and got a lot of young cabbages which I planted in the Cusacks' garden till it got too dark. I must put in the rest tomorrow. I had supper at the Cusacks', and we had the customary evening service. Mrs. Cusack made me an offer, which I have accepted, as follows: Regy wants to go to work at Lees' mine for a month, but the women can't be left alone, so I am to go up there while he is away and live in the empty house belonging to

Brock, which is quite close to the Cusacks', and do the 'chaws' in return for which I shall receive my board.

Further, if at any time I want to do a day's work for Brock or anyone, I can. I shall not be absolutely tied to the house. The 'chaws', I should explain, consist of chopping firewood, getting water, looking after the horses, tending the garden, and doing all odd things about the house. For some reasons I would have rather remained down here, but I could not well refuse, and it is a very liberal offer, the work required being very slight. I shall probably have to go up there on Thursday. Tomorrow I can go to clean up the empty house.

June 25th. After breakfast I went up to the Cusacks' and planted the remainder of Mrs. C.'s cabbages and also dusted out my coming residence (the afore-mentioned house of Brock). It will want scrubbing. I shall probably do that on Wednesday. It is a very good house except that it is infested with mountain rats, and that the windows are all broken. For this last I have to thank the Hugg boys who did it out of pure 'cussedness' some time since.

I had lunch at the Cusacks and then went down to Brock's and did half a day's work on an irrigation ditch, working with pick, grub-hoe and shovel much as I did when making the ditch on Chamberlain's ranch. Brock worked with me.

I hear that Becky Splann got married yesterday, but have no details as to who is her husband, and so on. I forgot to tell you yesterday of the excellent 'spinach' the Cusacks made from *Chenopodium album*. We had it for supper and it was certainly as good if not better than the garden spinach. They call it 'lamb's quarter' here and it is eaten by many people. It is not native in Colorado but is a very abundant weed on all cultivated land. This plant is common all round London and, one would think, might be largely utilized. Gather some of it and see whether it is not good.

I enclose a note to be read at the S.L.E.S. I hope it will produce a discussion.

June 26th. As I was having breakfast, I heard someone call and, going out found Cox, who had cut a gash about 1½ inch long in his foot with an axe while cutting down quaking asp for poles. He came in, and I sewed up the wound and bandaged it (fortunately no artery was cut) and since then he has been sitting here reading *Pall Mall Budgets*, etc.

I enclose another note for S.L.E.S. I should like these notes to be read at the next meeting of the society you go to, as I want to hear what anybody has to say about them.

In town, evening. I walked in and caught a snake and some butterflies new to me on the way. The *only* mail is *Science Gossip, Botanical Gazette*, and *Chicago Labor Enquirer*! Your letter has not come, which is queer, and Mrs. C. has her English mail (two letters). I must try to get to town again in a few days, when your letter will doubtless have arrived.

June 28th, 1888.

Dear Frederic,

I came to town with Louis Howard this morning, and just write this to say I have got your letter all right (also one from Carlie). I have W. H. Edwards on my side on the Seasonal Dimorphism question. The soirée must have been interesting, and I am glad you took Annie. The jelly-fish is *Limnocodium sowerbyi* Albu. I should like to have a copy of the Riding photograph of Family. Is it *possible* to let me have one? Carlie says little about Christabel, so I can't tell. I incline to think she is only No. 12 (or whatever number it is).

I think Frank is very good in staying away; he has got work and will probably not return until after haying time. I will write more in the letter. Miss U. is too young to be a woman, though too old to be a child. At present she hardly knows what it is to have a *purpose* in anything. It is a critical time, and she may develop well, or

badly. She has good abilities and ought to be of some use in the world.

As to tropical butterflies, I rather think that *metallic* colours may have the same cause as *darkening*, but I won't assert anything yet. I think Jenner Weir's *Pieris* accords with my theory. It is a suffused duskiness that is characteristic of vernal forms.

Regy isn't going up to Lees' mine till next week, he says, so I shan't have to move up to the Cusacks' today.

June 27th, 1888

Dear Frederic,

The walk home last night was quite uneventful. This morning I wrote an effusion on the subject of Botanical Nomenclature, to be sent to *Botanical Gazette*, though I don't suppose they will publish it. After this, I went up to Brock's, and sawed and chopped a pile of wood for Mrs. B. (Brock being away from home) and then I went and washed out my presumed future residence up by the Cusacks'.

Respecting this house, Regy says he does not think he will go up to Lees' mine till after the 4th of July, so I need not go up tomorrow as I had been asked to do. Personally, I was rather skeptical about his going up there at all, or, if he goes, staying long. I shan't have this house unless I am actually required by the Cusacks', unless Cox moves out (as he talks of doing), in which case I shall probably be obliged to move to the house by the Cusacks'.

This afternoon I worked with Regy, getting wood out for the Kettles as before, only this time we took much larger trees and did not go so far away for them. Louis Howard was at the Cusacks' when we got back. He talks of starting on his trip to New Mexico in a few weeks, but I don't know whether he will, or whether I shall go if he does. I have an idea of going down to Pueblo (walking, and packing a donkey with food, etc.) in search of work, but I do not know whether I can. I can't get suitable work here, and to go to Pueblo by train would 'clean me up.' I think I could get there and back in a fortnight, easily.

Today I found a white Thomisid spider on the flower of a white umbellifer. It had caught a fly much larger than itself. *Vanessa hunteri* is quite common here now.

June 28th. I went to town this morning with Louis Howard and was much satisfied on getting your epistle, and also one from Carlie. Louis went off to call at a ranch, and I went down by Grape Creek and got one or two flowers and a weevil new to me, but it was quite too hot to do much hunting.

When Louis returned to town, we drove to Jod's, as Louis wanted to ask him about the price of his ranch (Louis wants to buy a ranch). Jod wanted $5,000, which was too much. While we were there, the other Jod (the one we met on the train coming here) came, and Louis asked him to go on the expedition to New Mexico. I am very much disgusted at this, as I am afraid he *will* go, and I have had quite enough traveling with Jod. Louis knows very little of him, or I don't think he would have asked him. Louis talks of starting in a fortnight. I can't quite make up my mind whether to go. We did not get back till evening, when I came with Louis up to the Cusacks', where I am now writing. I am feeling very restless and irritable today.

Mrs. Cusack showed me a flower of *Trifolium pratense* she found today, but the plant is not native in this country. This one was probably imported with 'timothy' (*Phleum pratense*) seed.

June 29th. At eight I went and met Louis Howard at Brock's and drove with him part of the way up to Lees' mine, the reason being that he wanted to take some coal for the forge and could not carry it up on horseback, so he borrowed the Cusacks' buckboard and I went to bring it back.

When I got to the Cusacks, I found Miss Sidford and Mrs. Beddoes there; they had driven up for a call. Miss S. is going to leave the Beddoes'; I stay with the Brocks. Regy was up in the wood cutting wood, and Mrs. C. asked me to stay and cut wood for the house. I did this and also read a lot to Mrs. C., viz. the rest of *Madame Delphine* (I read most of it before), *Cavaners*, and most of the last part of *Sesame and Lilies*. I also went for a stroll with Mrs. C., and we got a few flowers. I also found a pretty *Cenera* on a quaking asp stump, just emerged from the cocoon, which was on the same stump. I am still feeling excessively restless and somewhat despondent.

June 30th. A few notes now on your last letter: Do I admire Ray Lankester? Well, it depends upon the way I look at him. When present in the flesh, he is a conspicuous but not absolutely beautiful feature in the scenery. As a man, they say hard things about him, and personally I believe he is not much liked, but as an investigator he is certainly most able and persevering and has done much good and accurate work. He is one of the few men who have taken any pains to find out the nature of animal pigments.

How does Flower account for the origin of the pygmy races of man? I believe in Central Africa there are races living in the same district, the one averaging not five feet in height and the other over six, but I have no notes on the subject and quote form memory.

I have not a very high opinion of *Youth's Companion*, but it suits many people, e.g., the Brocks. As I said in the last letter, I should greatly like a copy of the family photograph. When is Annie going to get photographed?

I wish you would publish a list of Isleworth *insects* in *Entomologist*. It would be a valuable contribution to the Middlesex fauna. I have never read *She*, and am likely to take Annie's advice: 'Don't.' It is much read out here (25 cent edition). I wonder when the 1887 proceedings of S.L.E.S. is going to appear?

Respecting Frank and Miss Urquhart — Frank appears to have gone away, as I think I said, because his jealousy was making him ridiculous, and was also no doubt painful to Miss U., and I judge that for the same reason he stays away. This seems strange on the face of it, yet I can quite understand his going away, feeling perhaps that his liking for the girl was a passion rather than a sympathy (as indeed it must have been) and, having the wisdom to see that it might cause both of them trouble. I think, also, that it does him infinite credit to have acted so, and altogether his conduct in the matter has shown great sense. If he had truly and sympathetically *loved* the girl it would have been quite different. Then he would not have gone away, not would have been thus absurdly jealous, because he would have known and trusted her.

As to Miss U. herself, I have not the least idea that she loved Frank. Of the two, there can be no doubt that she prefers Regy, though I do not think she has yet formed character enough to seriously love anyone. Nevertheless, she and Regy go about together, and anyone would suppose they were confessed lovers, to *look* at them. Regy is old enough to be serious, certainly, but I think it is contrary to his nature, as he himself has remarked in different words.

It is now evening, and I have done practically nothing today, feeling out of sorts and lying down for a time in the middle of the day. I could not collect my wits to read anything scientific, so I amused myself with Jules Verne's *Mysterious Island*, which Payn bought in paper-cover edition and left here. I read this book when quite a small boy and enjoyed it greatly then, for I did not see its ridiculous improbabilities. Anyhow, it is an ingenious story, like most of Jules Verne's.

Sunday, July 1st. I am quite ill today. I don't know what is the matter with me. I have a sort of dull headache and feel faint and weak.

Evening. Towards afternoon I felt better, though rather feverish. Cox looked in on his way to town and told me to go up to his place if I felt bad, which was good of him. At about five I went up to the Cusacks', calling on Mrs. C. on my way. Lees and Louis Howard are at the Cusacks', and Mrs. Brock came up for the evening service.

July 2nd. Today and tomorrow are the days appointed for working out the road tax (it is $3.00 if one does not work). You remember the road work last year? It is rather a farce. We don't work very hard, today only from about 9 a.m. to 4:30. Jim Kettle (the boss) came up to hunt us out and make us work. Cox, Bassick, and Brock were fixing the bridge over the creek and had an easy enough time. Regy and I had the road across the prairie to work on, and there is plenty for us to do there tomorrow also, getting rocks out of the road.

Cardy Lees went to town and brought us a lot of good mail, viz., (1.) Letter from Fernald, to whom I sent type specimen of *Crambus ulae*. He writes, 'I regret to say that Mr. Edwards has led you into redescribing an old and well-known species of *Crambus*. It was first described by Clemens as *C. luteoalbus* [two other synonyms quoted]. I described it as *C. zeeltus* and now you have described it as *C. ulae!* — !!! So I have indeed allowed myself to be led into a blunder. The obvious moral is: Never describe a species as new unless you yourself have investigated the matter. I shall post Fernald's letter to *Ent. Mo. Mag.* and get them to insert a notice of the synonymy. (2.) Two letters from W. H. Edwards about things I sent him. (3.) Letter from C. R. Barnes, about mosses I sent him. (4.) Letter from Wolle with names of algae from here (twelve species, he says, 'all cosmopolitan'). If you will send me a little conferva from a stagnant pool at Isleworth, dried without much squeezing, I will forward it to Wolle and get the names of diatoms, etc. for your Isleworth list. (5.) Letter from L. O. Howard (Dept. Agric.) About caterpillars, etc., sent to him. (6.) *Pall Mall Budget*. (7.) *Commonweal*.

July 3rd. Road work was today, and I worked from nine to eleven, but not another man came, so I got disgusted and gave it up. A man (named Dicks) and a boy came along, tired and hot. Said they had arrived at West Cliff by train from Kansas, had hardly any more money and so they must do the rest of their journey (to near Villa Grove in Saguache County) by crossing the Sangre de Cristo range on foot. Hard lines, for they are not accustomed to walking. So I gave them a frugal lunch (bread and ham) and started them out by the Lakes of the Clouds trail. They should arrive in the San Luis Valley tomorrow.

Then I went up to the Cusacks' to see if I could get Regy to come and work, but it was no go. Mrs. C. says I am to go up there tomorrow, as Regy goes to the mine (Lees') on Thursday. Now it is getting late, and I must start townwards.

In town. I got a ride all the way from the end of the prairie on a load of wood Montgomery was taking to town. Got your letter, also letters from Mother and Henry Edwards (who is in England and writes from Twickenham). He is at Sam'l. French & Son, 89, Strand. Could you get Barker to send him a card of S.L.E.S. and get him to join? He is a good man, barring that *Crambus*!

Ealing Report (bird list very interesting; best thanks for sending), *Orn. & Oölogist, Chicago Labor Enquirer*, and a Dept. of Agriculture report on grasses (interesting). Best thanks to Annie for the good list of addenda to Isleworth Fauna and Flora. I have sent you a further report on *Sesia*, etc. for S.L.E.S. which lets more light on the matter. Your account of the meeting makes me smile! It's all very well for Tutt, Carrington & Co. to go on so, but the rest of the members will wish me at the bottom of the deep blue sea! If it would amuse the S..L.E.S.-ites I would write an account of the natural history, etc., of this place and send specimens to illustrate. I will come to the dinner you speak of, provided everyone cooks his own meal! I am coming to agree with C. V. Riley about naming things (that *Crambus* beats any argument), so shall not describe the *Longitarsus*. There is no signature whatever to your epistle.

July 4th, 1888

Dear Frederic,

The walk home last night produced nothing of interest. Payn turned up just as I was leaving, and wanted me to stay in town with him over the 4th. He did not have a very successful hunting excursion, did not even see a deer. Martin caught me up (driving) near Ula and asked me to stay at his house for the night. I did not, but promised to call next time I went that way. Today I went up to the Cusacks' in the morning, taking mail, and found Regy and Miss Urquhart and Louis and Miss Sidford just starting to town to join in the celebration of the 'glorious 4th' (Declaration of Independence anniversary), that is to say, racing and jollification generally, and a dance in the evening.

Then I went down to my house again and wrote until late in the afternoon. It was very hot, so that one felt tempted to lie down and sleep. Between four and five I came up to the Cusacks' again to cut wood, etc., for Mrs. Cusack. Lees arrived up there from the mine about the same time. I was going down with the buckboard to fetch up my blankets, etc., this evening, but as it is occupied I shall go back tonight to sleep and bring up the things tomorrow.

July 5th, 11:45 a.m. A few notes on Isleworth and Middlesex fauna and flora: Annie's list gives me two birds, one amphibian, one neuropteran, five phanerogams and a fungus new to my Middlesex list. Is *Agraphis* the same as *Scilla*? It astonishes me how nearly alike the Isleworth and Bedford Park floras are, considering that Isleworth is so much more open and has the Thames and the Brent. The Isleworth grasses, sedges, and water plants want working up. I have taken full notes from the *Ealing Report:* The account of the Brent excursion gives me 19 plants, two butterflies and a beetle new to my list. Some of these plants should occur by the Isleworth portion of the Brent.

Anthony Belt's bird list is good, but of course many of the birds and animals are casuals, some very much so — *Agelaeus* and *Bernicla*! He might have given the name of 'the man at Isleworth Ferry'! Tubby Gray was responsible for *Parus palustris* at B. P., I think. I certainly ever saw it. Belt's list gives me 47 additions to my Middlesex list, and the only Middlesex birds I have note of *not* on his list are *Asio otus* (in your Isleworth list), *Oriolus galbula* casual at Harrow (*Graphic*, June 2, 1888., p. 582), *Phalacrocorax carbo* (near Hudson, at the Welsh Harp Water, F. R. Rice, *Field*, 1887, p.478), and *Rissa tridactyla* (casual in Kensington Gardens).

Respecting the cuttings about Lord Wolseley and thrift, it certainly has always seemed to me that those who preached thrift as the cure to the ills of modern 'civilization' were either fools or humbugs. I think Lord W. is a fool on that particular subject. As to whether women are unduly extravagant or not, that is a different matter, but there I should say they were far less so than men. At the same time, most of them spend more than a fair proportion of their money on dress, neglecting other things for its sake.

The other day I was astonished to come across a very sensible leader in a *St. James Budget* belonging to Louis Howard, in which it was clearly recognized that the extremely low wages of work-women in London were the direct outcome of their thrift, which enabled them to endure much and compete very severely in consequence. The question of Chinese labour bears on the same matter. I hope you and Annie agree with me as to the wage-lowering effects of thrift (under competition). It is a most fundamental thing to learn. Were labour free, of course wise thrift would be an unmixed blessing.

I forgot to say, I once tried to read *Robert Falconer* but did not succeed. But I like *Sir Gibble*, also by Geo. MacDonald, very much, and recommend it to you and Annie if you have not read it.

Evening. Late in the afternoon I went up to the Cusacks' and found Regy had departed to Lees', so I would get the buckboard and fetch up my things and stay up there. Now Regy, with characteristic Irishness, has always preferred spending an hour or so catching (or frequently, failing to catch) his horses when they were wanted, than spending a few days in putting up a fence which would keep them on his own ranch. So it was today. The animals were in a great pasture of Cox, and I walked I suppose quite 3/4 of a mile round about after them before I finally got a rope round the neck of the steed whose name is 'Specklewattle.' Regy has three horses; this one, a gray called 'Ferris', and a bay called 'Mary Hampton.'

By this time it was too late to go down and get my things up, so I concluded to return here again for the night and take up my new residence tomorrow. I had just got to the Cusacks' with the horse, when Cox appeared and asked me to go with him to Cress's. Cress and Cox are on the same creek, and Cox complains that Cress takes all the water, leaving him scarcely enough to drink. Cox wanted me to go up to be a witness in case they had a row, but although they argued a very long time, they did not come to blows.

I found at the Cusacks' a letter from L. O. Howard, with names of insects sent (Regy brought it out), and Mrs. C. says that Regy left a *Pall Mall Budget* by accident at Charley Cusack's in Silver Cliff, which is a nuisance as I don't relish the idea of having to walk up there after it next time I go to town.

July 6th, 10:25 p.m. I was up at the Cusacks' the first thing this morning and got 'Specklewattle' and the buckboard and went down straight and brought up a load of my things, which I duly deposited in my new residence. Most of the day I spent in tidying up and putting things into order generally, and in the evening I drove down (taking Mrs. Cusack as far as Cox's, to call on Mrs. Cox), and have now got nearly all my things up here (that is, my new house, the empty house of Brock). This evening I have been reading bits from Oliver Wendell Holmes to Mrs. Cusack.

July 7th, 7:40 p.m. This morning I finished putting my house straight, so that it now looks fairly satisfactory. I meant to have sketched it this afternoon, but violent hail came on, soaking everything, so that one could not sit out-of-doors. I therefore wrote the names of Mrs. Cusack's plants [sketch], and afterwards returned to my house, meaning to write. But I had only just finished putting a latch on my door and was about to commence writing, when Cress appeared, and stayed till six, talking mainly about the dreadful ways in which he imagines he is treated with respect to the water question.

Miss Sidford went to town today and brought me mail (1.) Postcard from W. H. Edwards, (2.) Letter and reprints of papers from Ashmead (Hymenoptera man). (3.) Letter from Strecker. I forget whether I said that Strecker wanted me to collect many moths and butterflies for him, and I said I would if he would agree to my terms. He now writes to say he will agree with said terms, so I shall commence collecting for him. The terms are:

(1.) Insects to be un-set, and if pinned, Strecker to send cork and corked box. (2.) Strecker to pay the cost of carriage. (3.) Strecker to pay five cents for the first example of a species, and two cents for every subsequent one. (4.) Not less than half of those sent to be purchased. (5.) Those not purchased to be returned or exchanged. (6.) Species to be named if I have not been able to identify them.

Sunday, July 8th, 4:30 p.m. Regy and Louis Howard rode down to the Cusacks' last night, so as to be there today. I have not done much today except catch two insects and make the enclosed sketch of this house for Annie. It is not very good, but will give a notion of the appearance of the place.

July 9th, 7:45 p.m. I have been writing all day long, except that I went out about mid-day to catch insects, the best thing I found being a spe-

cies of fly allied to *Trypeta*, which lays its eggs in the buds of thistles. The whole Cusack house, as also the Brocks and Louis and Miss S. and Mrs. Cox went off this morning to see the 'round-up', which is the rounding-up of the cattle (some 500) by cow-boys (50 perhaps) — cattle that have been running loose on the prairie and in the foot-hills all winter. The object of this round-up is that each man may claim his own and that the calves may be branded. From my house the affair looked like a lot of flies on the prairie. I had an idea of going down to see it, but was busy and did not think it worth the walk in this hot weather.

I was writing a paper for *Can. Entom.* when Cox appeared and said he and Mrs. Cox were going to see a play in Silver Cliff (*Saints and Sinners*) by a company on tour, and would I come down and stay in the house the evening so that the children would not be quite alone? So I went down to Cox's to supper, and am there now. The children are in bed and asleep and don't bother me. Miss Urquhart has gone to the play with the Cox's.

Louis Howard went to town today and brought me mail: Letter from Radenhausen, postcard from W. B. Saunders, *Rules of American Botanical Exchange Club* (newly started, and managed by the Dept. of Agriculture), and *Canad. Ent.* for May and June. On the *Can. Ents.* were two half-cent (farthing) stamps which I enclose in case you might find someone who would care to have them. *Can. Ent.*, June, has an interesting paper by Grote *On the Origin of Ornamentation in Lepidoptera*, arguing (as you will remember I have argued) that light had much to do with colouring and marking.

12:50 p.m. Playgoers returned. The play turned out to be *Rip van Winkle* and the acting much better than was expected.

July 10th. Evening. I have driven to town with the grey mare Ferris, and the Cusacks' buckboard. Alas, no English mail, only a postcard from Beutenmuller and *Commonweal* and

Chicago Labor Enquirer. The Splanns were upset coming from town today, and Mrs. Splann had her nose all cut up, as well as tongue bitten and a wound on the forehead. I stitched up the wound with many stitches, and find it so as to quite satisfy the rather idiotic little doctor who came and *looked* at it after I had finished (you see he had to be sent to town for). I have to sew up her tongue tomorrow, which is a more difficult matter. But full details of this in next letter.

July 11th, 1888

Dear Frederic,

I must go back to yesterday and give you an account of the various and strange proceedings thereof, but perhaps I had better postpone the narrative for the present, as it is time to go down with Mrs. Splann.

July 12th. About July 10th, it was morning and I was at the Cusacks' when Mrs. Brock came up saying that someone was hurt at Cox's, and I was wanted to sew him up. So I got my materials and went down, to find Sam, Frank Hunter's ostler, with two cuts on his forehead, and to learn that Mrs. Splann and Becky had contrived to get upset between Cox's and Splann's, driving a sort of light waggon, and that Mrs. Splann was very bad indeed.

Therefore, I did not wait to sew up Sam, but rushed over to the Splann's, and there found Mrs. Splann terribly cut about, having fallen on her face on the sharp rocks. Her nose was quite split up and there was a wound on the forehead. Also, as we found out afterwards, she had bitten her tongue badly. I settled down to the work of sewing it up, which Mrs. Splann bore bravely, for it must have been painful. It was a very complicated affair and I suppose I must have put in at least 15 stitches. Meanwhile, Miss Urquhart came down and made herself very useful by threading my needles and getting various things as I required them.

At last it was over, and I bandaged her up and turned to Becky, who fortunately only had a bad bruise resulting in a headache. Then I went over to look after Sam at Cox's, but on the way out met Dr. Björnson, who had been sent to West Cliff for, and returned with him to the Splann's. This doctor is a youngish man, well-meaning, but essentially quite ignorant of medicine. He had actually come out to what he *knew* was a surgical case, with no knife or scissors, and his only piece of lint was grey with dirt (fortunately I had some that was clean). The Doctor undid the bandage and examined the wound, but did not interfere with my sewing, remarking that I had made a very good job of it. The tongue I promised to sew up the next day, as he was not coming, and Mrs. S. did not feel equal to having it done then. Then we went over to Cox's and had lunch, and Dr. Björnson sewed up Sam's wounds, and departed.

It being Tuesday, my day for going to town, and as I had to get some groceries for the Cusacks, and was also too tired to walk, I drove the grey mare Ferris in, arriving there about sundown. While I was getting groceries, Preston accosted me with the news that there was a large moth in the Lager-beer saloon, so I went in and we contrived to catch it, somewhat damaged. It proved to be a large Noctuid of the genus *Erelpus* (I think it is), like the *E. strix* figured in Fuguier's book.

I posted your letter, and also the *Ealing Report*, but English letters had not come. I had got everything and was ready to start when I remembered I had to get some jam at Falkenburg's store, so I just tied the reins round a post and went for the jam. I suppose I had been gone five minutes when, on coming out, there was neither horse nor buckboard to be seen!! Well, I am a good deal played out and shall perhaps do best to go to bed now, so will continue narrative tomorrow.

I went (this is continued July 13th) into the postoffice store which was just opposite where I had tied the horse, and asked if they had seen anything. But no, only one suggested that some fellow might have taken the horse and buck-board up to Silver Cliff (several were going then to the theatricals) 'for a lark.' Of course I was greatly concerned, half fearing that someone had stolen it. I walked up to Silver Cliff and exam-ined every 'rig' that was hitched up along the street, but without result. So there was nothing else to do but search around West Cliff (which I did) and then return home, hoping that the horse had managed to get away of its own accord, in which case it would no doubt find its way home-wards.

And so it was, for I discovered Ferris and the buckboard, quite uninjured, in the lane near the Kettle's. The reins had got twisted round the wheels and compelled the animal to stop. I got in, feeling very thankful that no harm was done, and vowing never again to tie the horse up inse-curely, even for five minutes. (You see, with the reins, one can't easily tie a secure knot, but with a rope a very simple knot will prevent any pos-sibility of escape.) In due time I got home, quite tired out.

About July 11th. I went down to the Splann's the first thing in the morning and learnt there that the doctor had changed his mind and would come up after all. I waited some while, but he did not appear, so I returned to the Cusacks'.

Later he came, and Miss U. and I rode down to the Splann's, where we found the doctor sew-ing up the tongue. I was very willing that the doc-tor should do this, as it was a little difficult, and if it did not prove successful he would be blamed, while if I, an amateur, were in any respect to fail, there would certainly be complaints.

After this, I came up here again, and in the evening (having secured a little sleep during the afternoon) went down to stay with Mrs. Splann that night, as I had promised I would. I took down a novel — Court Royal, and I read most of it that night, finding it not so good as I expected. I got very sleepy towards morning and was very glad when at length daylight came.

About July 12th. I had breakfast at the Splann's and then came home and slept till one.

Meanwhile Jim Splann and Ernest Nathan (this last is a young man staying at the Splann's and is a son of the former owner of Splann's place) went to town to get some lint and oil silk, and also brought me out mail: Your letter (with Annie's quotations; it was nice of her to think of writing me these. I thank her much), and letters from Mother, Carlie (who writes from Abbev-ille, France) and Jenner Weir (on my *Can. Ent.* paper).

After lunch I went down and dressed Mrs. Splann's wounds freshly, That idiot of a doctor had just dabbed on some cotton-wool, which got dry and stuck so that I had no end of trouble to get it off. Then I came back and found Charley Cusack up here, but he did not stay long. After supper I commenced writing some of this let-ter, but as you will see, broke off, feeling utterly weary, and went to bed.

July 13th. This morning Miss Urquhart and I drove down to the Splann's, I to dress Mrs. Splann's wounds, and she to stay with her for the day, as she had undertaken to do. Before I started, Brock came up and asked me to hoe potatoes with him this afternoon, and I said I would, but I really did not feel equal to it, and so looked in on my way back from the Splann's and excused myself. The last few days seem to have exhausted all my vitality.

I was reading an interesting paper on dreams in the June *Century* this morning, in which it states that people blind from birth *never* dream that they see, not do the congenitally deaf that they hear, just what one might suppose, but interesting as bearing out the theory that dreams are always built up of *past* experiences.

In answer to your letter: The additions to Hymenoptera are good. *O. rufa* and *A. albicans* are, I believe, common in Middlesex. *Andrena nigrooenica* was found at Woking by F. Enoch. I am sorry to hear that Grandmother was ill. I trust she has now recovered.

July 14th. This morning Miss Urquhart had to go down to the Kettle's to give music lessons, and I drove down with her, and while the lessons were going on I went to town, as some things were wanted from there. The only mail I got was a letter saying that Fernald was away from home, and that a letter I sent him had been forwarded. But the first thing this morning I got some mail, Ernest Nathan having brought it from town yesterday, viz., letter from Jenner Weir (about the *Gonopteryx* question, long and interesting, in which he admits the possibility of my theory being correct, though he still is not in any wise convinced), postcards from G. Roberts (and also a Yorkshire paper about Y.N.U., etc.), Carlie, and W. H. Edwards, and *Pall Mall Budget*.

At the Kettle's I made a little collection of grasses, and got Kettle to tell me which he valued for food for cattle (this for the Agric. Dept., who have been paying special attention to this subject and have published an excellent report thereon). We were delayed some while at the Kettle's by violent rain in which I got wet while putting up the horse, and did not get home till nearly suppertime. After supper I went down to the Splann's, and found Mrs. S. a good deal better; she had walked out as far as the barn this morning. The swelling is much gone down and there is no inflammation or fever.

I never finished *Court Royal*, but glanced at the ending. It seemed to me a very poor sort of a story, and who can possibly be interested in the foolishness of a lot of dukes, etc.? For that is what it is about. There is not a character in the whole book to be admired.

Sunday, June 15th. It was hot today, but towards evening it rained and has been pleasantly cool. The morning was taken up in going to the Splann's. I drove down with Miss U. We found Mrs. Splann getting on well; she could not be better, considering circumstances. In the afternoon I meant to write many letters, but the heat or something exhausted me so much that I had to lie down for a while, and only got two done after

all. It is very ridiculous for me to collapse in this way, but I soon get over it, and it can't be helped. Lees, Louis, and Regy came down from working at Lees' today, and are here now. It is needless to add that, Louis being here, Miss Sidford has come up from Brock's. We have just had the evening service, and everyone is attempting to write letters amidst a considerable exuberance of spirits, productive of jokes and laughter.

July 16th. Lees and Regy have gone, but Louis is still here, and Miss Sidford. This morning I got Ferris and drove the buckboard down to Beddoes' to get a black cat named 'Agrippa' and a road scraper for Lees. Lees came with me part of the way, it being on the way to his mine. At Beddoes' I had lunch and also looked over the books (Beddoes has an excellent library), bearing away a copy of Geikie's *Textbook of Geology* which belongs to Lees. While I was there one of the children brought in some larvae of *Papilio asterias*, very pretty things, not unlike those of *P. machaon*.

I put the road scraper on behind, and Agrippa in a sack, and so came home, arriving in the course of the afternoon just too late to escape a sharp shower of rain, which commenced soon after I left the Splann's. (I called at the Splann's on the way back. Mrs. S. seems much as before, but complains that her tongue hurts her.)

There is talk now of sundry picnic excursions, up towards Lees' mine and down to the Hardscrabble, towards Pueblo, but one never knows whether these projects will really be carried out. Beddoes asked me to go for a day up on the mountains with him, but I don't much think I shall. Louis Howard's New Mexico journey will never come off, I think.

July 17th, 9:40 p.m. Today is really the day to go to town, but I go tomorrow instead because I expected it would rain this evening, which, however, it didn't. This morning Mrs. Cusack, Miss Urquhart, and I went for a stroll in the woods, the chief capture being a *Limnitis* not unlike *L. sybilla*. In the afternoon I wrote letters, and in the evening went down to Splann's to get milk and butter and to see Mrs. Splann. On the way back I found a white-flowered plant of *Campanula rotundifolia* — very pretty. This evening I have been reading part of *Les Miserables* to Mrs. Cusack. It was at the store in town and I persuaded her to get it, as she had not read it.

July 18th. Have driven to town, but no letter; the train did not come in last night because there was a wash-out on the line between here and Cañon City (line washed away). It is raining now. All the mail I got is letters from Orcutt and Sterki, and *Chicago Labor Enquirer*, also Tuckerman's *North American Lichens*, sent on loan by Orcutt. Orcutt wants me to be Associate Editor of *West American Scientist*. I suppose I may as well.

July 18th, 1888

Dear Frederic,

As you will gather from the letter posted today, my going to town today was fruitless as regards its main purpose, for there had been a 'wash-out' on the line, and the English mail was therefore delayed. Today has been exceedingly rainy and at the same time cold. In fact it has been snowing a little on the top of the range at 13,000 feet and above. The rain storm followed behind me as I went to town, but I got in in time to escape most of it. While I was in town it rained and kept me there long, till finally it cleared up and I got home (I was driving, with Specklewattle) soon after five.

While in town, Payn came up and said that if I wanted *anything* I was to get it and put it down to him, but I said my only want just then was mail. However, he came into the postoffice store later and bought me a pair of high boots (making me look like Puss-in-Boots) and some socks (the boots cost him $30), which was very good of him, although I was not altogether willing that he should do so.

July 19th. Mrs. Cusack was doing 'a wash' this morning, so I brought over some of my shirts and pocket handkerchiefs and washed them at the same time. Under Mrs. C.'s directions I was more successful than hitherto, and to my great amazement the handkerchiefs turned out *white*!! While I was washing, Regy turned up. He had had a row with Lees, and 'quit.' Regy now being home, I shall not have to cut wood, etc., for the Cusacks any longer, so the question arose: Should I go back to my house down below or stay at Brock's house? The house below is nearer town, and handier for water, but Cox talks of moving it, and it is very cold in winter, while this house of Brock's is a good deal better one, being, they say, very warm in winter, and is nearer the Cusacks', which is convenient. So I concluded to reside in the Brock house for the present, at any rate. I shall have to get fresh windows in place of the broken ones, but I believe Brock has such — the windows of the other rooms of the house (which have been removed).

This afternoon I rode down to my house below, with Mrs. Cusack, and brought up the remainder of my goods — the food, etc., and cooking utensils, and Regy had lent me an excellent stove he has but does not use, so I am quite ready to start 'batching' again.

July 20th, 10 p.m. Have been to town and feel very pleased, because I have got lots of mail, including your letter, but, alas, I feel very tired, so will write account of today tomorrow.

July 21st. About July 20th. In the morning I went down to the Splann's and took out all the stitches from Mrs. Splann's nose except one, and that she said pained her when I attempted to cut it (my knife being somewhat blunt), so I let it be for the present. The nose is healing up quite as well as one would expect, and I trust, except for a scar, will soon be all right again.

Soon after I came up from the Splann's I caught a fine Sesiid moth; it looked just like a wasp when flying. In the afternoon Regy and Miss U. want to call on Mrs. Quincy (a person I never saw; she lives near Jod's), and so I went with them as far as where the road turns off to town, and then walked the rest of the way to town. It rained on the way, but I did not get very wet, but there was much rain after I got to West Cliff.

In town I got lots of mail: Your letter, and letters from Mother, W. H. Edwards, Strecker, Saunders (of *Can. Ent.*), Dr. John Hamilton (beetle man), Browning's *Poems* (for which all thanks; will mark and return), *Ent., Mags., Naturalist, Commonweal*, and some cork from Strecker, also *Canadian Entomologist*.

The train was late, and I did not start from town till nearly dusk. I drove out in a 'sulky' (a two-wheeled sort of cart, very light, and only having room for one) of Payn's, as he wanted a horse of his (a bay colt) brought out to be put in Cox's pasture. It was very chilly coming home, and I was very glad when I finally arrived at about half past nine.

About July 31st. This morning I was writing, and early in the afternoon went down to Cox's, and then to Brock's, where I got a dozen eggs and also a window which Brock had by (not in use). It will perhaps do in place of the broken window in my house (the front one).

Sunday, July 22nd, 12:10. Rain, Rain! It has been raining nearly all the morning and looks as if it would all the afternoon as well. We are having very rainy weather now. The rats are getting very troublesome here now. They have been gnawing my shawl and nibbling at my slippers. I really must get some 'Rough on Rats' and poison them.

Mrs. Brock, who has been to Rosita, says she thought I might have got the job of looking after the postoffice there (one makes $20-$25 a month, she says) as the postmaster was leaving, but a man named Thomas turned up unexpectedly and it seems he had (for some reason or other) the prior right to the place. The government is supposed to appoint postmasters, and I think Thomas had been so appointed but had under-let the job to the man (Turner) who is now leaving. In any case, I do not know whether I could have taken the place without becoming an American citizen, and although I suppose it doesn't greatly matter what country a person is supposed to be a citizen of, I don't particularly like the idea of being naturalized, especially as I have no idea of residing here permanently. Turner will probably be staying at the Brock's in a short while, and then I can question him about the matter.

Notes on your letter: I once went to an excursion of Ealing Soc'y, at which Nyles was present. I thought him an exceedingly nice fellow. Your Isleworth Hymenoptera are grand. I haven't found nine Bombi in all Colorado! And have only got three (*Bombus borealis, B. rufocinctus*, and *B. ternarius*) down in my record book, but one or two remain unnamed.

I *have* sometimes tried to draw you portraits of the people out here, but can't do it, and it's no use sending you them unless they are recognizable.

Can't you send Burrows to explore some out of the way spots? If he has lots of time and money he might just as well make himself useful in that way. Ireland would very well repay investigation. I wish Annie would get nicely photographed, and by herself instead of in a group. Surely it is worth while! I enclose *Cantharis, Trichodes,* and *Chrysis* for exhibition at the S.L.E.S. with a note about them to be read. You need not go to the trouble of pinning or setting these insects. Just put them on wool in one of your little glass-topped boxes for exhibition.

11:15 p.m. I had just finished taking some notes from Tuckerman's *North American Lichens* (a good little book. It has records of 13 species and 2 vars. of lichens new to my Colorado list), and was about to light my fire to cook supper, when Louis Howard and Miss Sidford appeared with an invitation to supper at the Cusacks'. So I went across, and after supper we had Sunday evening service as usual. After this, we got talking of astronomy, and looking at the moon through Louis' opera-glasses and the Cusacks' telescope, when presently someone noticed that something unusual was taking place — in fact an eclipse, which shortly became total, and is so at the present minute, the moon appearing dull reddish!

When I returned to my house, I at once commenced to examine a trap I had set for mountain rats, and was glad to find I had caught one. The trap was simply a large box turned upside-down, and set (baited) with bread, in the 'figure of four' fashion.

Having got the rat under the box, the question arose, how to kill it? I daren't lift the box, for it would have darted off in an instant. So I bethought me of some wire netting I had, and slipped the box over that and examined the rat. Then I slipped my hand in under the netting and, after some difficulty, managed to kill the rat by knocking it on the head with a small hatchet. set the trap again and have put the body by, to be skinned tomorrow.

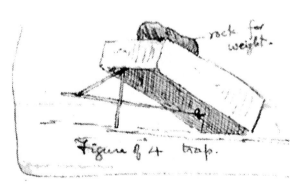

July 23rd, 9:55 p.m. It has been a very electric day — thunder and lightning with showers. Excessive electricity like this makes me feel very restless and uncomfortable. After breakfast I read Browning's poems. Although I like some of them, taken as a whole I cannot say they strike me as good poetry or good sense. Probably my faculties are not of the kind to appreciate what excellence they have, but I cannot escape a decided sense of disappointment in them, always

excepting a few bits which I have marked in pencil in the book.

After the poetry, by way of a change, I borrowed an axe of Regy, and chopped up some wood. In a large quaking asp, I found, on chopping open a bee's (probably *Megachile*) nest made of rose leaves. Interesting!

In the afternoon I wrote, packed up some specimens to send away, and read a little, but after supper could not settle down to do anything, so went over the the Cusacks' and expounded Geology to them out of Geikie's textbook. While I was there, Miss U. astonished and pleased me by starting up a familiar waltzy tune on the organ. It recalled at once the dances at Bedford Park with great vividness. One remembers those dances well enough, to be sure, but it is strange how the memories seem to grow green again under the influence of a tune! I forget the name of the waltz, unless it is 'Myosotis.'

July 24th, 7:15 p.m. Have walked to town and am disappointed to find no English mail has come. All I have got is letters from Wolle (with names of algae) and Morrison (about *Colorado Ornithological Association*), *West American Scientist* (May-June, two very poor numbers) and *Commonweal.*

West Cliff, Custer Co., Colorado
July 25th, 1888

Dear Frederic,

Yesterday morning I walked to town and posted your letter, but got no letter from you, the English mail not having arrived. In fact, the rains have again washed away part of the railway track, and they are now running a mail coach between here and Cañon City while the railway is being repaired. As I walked home, the moon rose full in the east, shining very brightly, and just as I got on the prairie at 9 p.m. a rain storm swept along the Sangre de Cristo range. The result was a lunar rainbow, part only of the arc and scarcely coloured, but still a bright band of light easily enough seen. This phenomenon lasted about a quarter of an hour. I should think it must be rare. I do not remember having heard of such a thing. I have written a note on the subject on a postcard to send to *Nature*. If it is really a rare phenomenon this may excite some interest.

I got home past eleven, feeling very fagged, and did not get up until eight this morning. This morning I wrote letters, etc., and also read a little of Geikie. This afternoon I started to go down to the Splann's but only got as far as Brock's, owing to the rain. I cut some wood for Mrs. Brock, Brock being away. Lees came down from his mine today and I saw him just now when I went across to the Cusacks'.

Cox, also, has returned from a trip to Kansas City. He is very pleased with Kansas and says it looks just like England.

July 26th, 10 p.m. This morning I went down to the Splann's and found Mrs. S. still much improved. Then I returned to the Brock's, where I spent the rest of the morning cutting wood for Mrs. Brock and clearing up the yard. I had lunch there and then returned to my house. At Brock's I found two bundles of *Fields* which had recently arrived (end of 1887 and part of 1888). These I borrowed and have taken therefrom many interesting notes. Hastings, in a paper on Kensington Garden birds, adds three to my Middlesex list, viz., Lesser tern, raven, and kite, but the last two only occurred there long, long ago. Regy and Miss U. went to town, and to my great satisfaction brought me your letter, as well as letter from Mother, postcard from Carlie, and *Chicago Labor Enquirer*.

The line has been destroyed by falling rocks and torrents somewhere between here and Canon City so that the train won't run for three weeks, but they are running mail coaches so that the mail will come every day as usual.

Best thanks to Annie for the forget-me-not and mignonette seeds. I do trust these will come up, the forget-me-nots at any rate. (The Cusacks

Wood.

had some mignonette which they kept well watered, but it failed all the same.) I have put some of these forget-me-not and mignonette seeds in a tin can which I will keep outside the window; others are in a wooden box placed near the creek, and some I keep back in case these fail. If they *will* come up at all here they ought to now. Thanks also for the invitation to 'At Home' (i.e., garden party) but unfortunately I cannot come! Alas, if I *could* would I be allowed to?

About religious beliefs, of course the orthodox religion embraces a great many beliefs which are scarcely compatible with what one may reasonably suppose to be truth, but I do not generally feel moved to attack these absurdities because, after all, they do not have much influence on conduct. If Mrs. Cusack, for instance, believes that the walls of Jericho collapsed when and because Joshua and company shouted, it really makes no difference to anybody but myself, and it were a hopeless task to demonstrate to her the natural improbability of such a thing. But when she states, as she did the other day, that the people of Ireland who refuse to pay exorbitant rents are dishonest, then I am free to argue the matter, which I did with some vigour!

If you want to rewrite your paper you will have some trouble to rescue it from Barker — I warn you! Barker wrote they were going to republish my variety paper, but I am giving up all hope of the 1887 Proceedings ever being published. I think your divisions of the S.L.E.S. district are good. I may remark though that (if I remember right) *one* of the West Kent estuary species (*Hydrobia similis*) does not occur in East Kent. I think Isle of Wight will have to be separated as a division from South Hants. Chas. Ashford used to insist upon this, and he knows most about those parts. I agree that South Hants and West Sussex are not separable. It is curious that *Hyalina glabra* is not (or is very rare) in Sussex. My three papers in *Nat. World*, with list of species found on walking tour in Kent, Surrey, and Sussex, will give you some useful details as to the distribution of the species. Will write more when I get the map.

I never got the counter-circular of Conch. Soc. Only one came to me, but I think I can imagine the other. *Conch Soc.* has three sections, like society — Aristocracy (museum-ites), Bourgeoisie (Taylor and company), and Proletariat (the multitude, including T.D.A.C. when he was in England). However, I can't take part in these quarrels from here, and very likely shall give up membership, except that one wants to see *Journal of Conchology*.

I hope Annie's birthday will really happen this time. So many things are projected and hoped for in the way of holidays and yet don't come off. Another thing, I hope when she goes, before you join her, she will write you a lengthy epistle about it, which said epistle will find its way to me!

I hear from Mother that Leslie is off to Canada, has started in fact by now! I hope he will fall on his feet all right but have no doubt that he will. Physically, I expect him to do well. Mentally

and morally he should be able to take care of himself, but to me the intellectual (or rather non-intellectual) atmosphere of St. Thomas (what I know of it) is depressing. Even this barbarous country is better.

Carlie writes enthusiastically from Beauvais; 'Ruskin climbed to topmost parapet (of the cathedral) with us (C. and Detmar) yesterday, and he proposes that we should all be photographed there from below. We shall look like bacilli! . . . Ruskin is in splendid spirits. I have just come from a feast of strawberries and raspberries and cream in his room.' Carlie found 24 species of Mollusca at Beauvais in half an hour. He gives names — they are all ordinary species.

July 27th, 9:40 p.m. I stayed up writing last night till nearly midnight, and the consequence was that when Regy came round at eight this morning to ask me to help him to get wood (loads of wood for the Kettles, etc., as before) I was still in bed. However, I got up and ate a cold breakfast and soon started off with him. We worked till twelve. While I was working I chanced across a few insects, etc., one of the most notable being a *Saltiens* (spider) about the size of the common English Scenicus (*Epiblemum scenicum*) and resembling it except that the whole of the *back* of the abdomen is *bright red*. I am now puzzling my brain to account for this — its origin and use. Can you suggest anything?

After lunch at the Cusacks', I went down and cut Mrs. Brock some wood. Then I returned to the Cusacks' and read some of *Les Misérables* to Mrs. C., after which I came to my house and took many notes from Tuckerman's lichen book.

Just as I was getting supper, Cox rode up and said that Mrs. Brock wanted me. So after supper I went down to Mrs. B.'s and found what she wanted was for me to go to the Splann's and get her some eggs, as she had made a cake (I think it was) all except the eggs, and then found she hadn't any. I was a little angry at being sent for for such a thing, as she might easily have gone herself, or Miss Sidford. However, I went and got the eggs.

Mrs. Splann told me she had actually ridden on horseback to town today and brought me mail: Letter from W. H. Edwards and postcard from J. B. Ellis (fungi man). As I write, moths come to the light of the lamp and I catch them. Most of them will have to go to Strecker.

July 28th, 9:25 p.m. Felt quite ill this morning but am all right again now. In the morning Louis Howard came with a message from Mrs. Brock that she would like me to come down and help her, but I went out hunting fungi for Ellis (very unsuccessfully, however) and did not go down to the Brock's till nearly four, when I spent an hour or so clearing up their yard. It is now finally decided that an excursion to the Hardscrabble shall take place next Monday (day after tomorrow) consisting of Cusacks, Louis Howard, Miss Sidford, Frank Hamp (brother of Sid Hamp who stayed at the Cusack's — I haven't seen Frank yet), and T.D.A.C., seven in all, and Lees to follow after, making eight. I suspect it will be enjoyable enough, but one feels a kind of anxiety about it.

Sunday, July 29th, 4:40 p.m. I have been getting things ready for starting tomorrow, or rather I should say before starting, as I have been chiefly clearing up my correspondence and such. I enclose a note on *Anthocharis* for the S.L.E.S. (I have written a paper on the same subject for the *Entomologica Americana*.) Louis Howard has been to town and has brought me a letter from Ellis (about fungi), *Science Gossip* and *Commonweal*. It seems that one of the *Ecidimus* I sent Ellis is an undescribed species but has been found before in California (at least it is probably the same as the Californian one).

10.45 p.m. Sunday evening as usual with the Cusacks. Lees came down for a little while but went away again, but before he went it was

arranged that we should all start together, and on Tuesday instead of tomorrow.

July 30th, 7:10 p.m. Today I have been writing, and also collecting fungi for Ellis. Ellis is issuing specimens of *North American Fungi* in an edition of 60 specimens of each, and so I got him 60 examples of three species of *Aecidium* this morning. It is a good thing that types should be sent out in this way; it is so much easier to name fungi from actual specimens than from descriptions. I enclose three fungi from here — two species of *Aecidium* and a fungus on grass, possibly *Scolecotrichum graminis*. Other specimens of these are going to Ellis, so I will let you have the correct names when he writes about them.

Could you not keep an eye open for micro-fungi at Isleworth? At present I have only three species of parasitic micro-fungi known from Middlesex, viz: *Trichobasis suaveolens* and *Aecidium grossialare* DC. from Bedford Park, and *Uredo parallela* Peck, recorded from Kensington (M. J. Berkeley. *English Flora* V, 375). For Colorado I have also only a small list (but several yet to be named), viz., *Puccinia porteri* Peck, *P. mirabilissima* Peck, *Phacidium medicaginis* Lasch., *Aecidium aquilegiae* Pers., *A. monoicum* Peck, *A emphortia* Gmel., *Peronospora arthuri* Farlow, *Uromyces stellatus* Schrank, *Ustilago segetum* Lam., and *Claviceps purpurea* Fr. Those I have found myself I have marked *. The Reverend Hilderic Friend (lives at Carlisle now, I think) will always name micro-fungi for you.

We shall be starting early tomorrow, I expect, so will end up this letter now, so as to have it ready to post as we pass through town.

July 31st. In town. We are started. I came in with Louis and Miss S. in a buckboard; Regy and Mrs. C. have gone on ahead. Lees and Miss S. to follow. No mail for me.

Odd Notes on Colorado

Vegetation: The pine trees begin at about 8,500 feet alt., and go over 11,000 feet. Quaking asps are about 6,000 to 9,500 ft. Piñons (a kind of small pine) are at about 6,000 to 7,000 ft. A ranch might well be by a stream in the quaking asp zone (like Cox's). Here it would be prairie, except by the stream, where are thick brush of willows, birch, quaking asp, etc. Scrub oak grows as high as 8,000, but is best at about 6,000 ft.

Climate: Summer is warm. Autumn lasts long, the cold weather hardly coming before November. Winter lasts more or less till March. It does not snow and blow at the same time, but generally blows *after* a snow storm, and the snow is then whirled about in clouds, which is most blinding. Sometimes there is a fine or warm week in the middle of winter, and the snow nearly melts all away. *Some* snow stays on the mountains all the year round.

Social relations: Men are very generally called by their Christian names (or 'given' names as they say here). The labourer who is hired is generally on the same social footing as his boss — works for him and has meals with him. The term 'servant' is not in use in the country districts. The word 'boy' is used to indicate adult individuals as much as juvenile ones, particularly in the plural 'boys'. It is quite the right thing to go to any ranch and demand a meal and you are expected to offer 50 cents for it on leaving, though they generally will not take anything. If you are 'broke' you can nearly always get a meal, etc., either free or in exchange for a little work, for example, chopping wood. Most of the people have been 'broke' some time or other, so they can sympathise with those who are in this condition better than they otherwise would. There is no sentimental charity: it is 'pitch in and eat' — and the recipient does so. The young men in town fraternise with the girls and take them to dances, picnics, etc. But generally each one has a favourite and styles her his '4th of July girl' — this being the great day in America when everybody displays his best! Manners, generally, are 'free and easy.'

Sale of Ranch Produce: Butter and eggs can be sold in town or to neighboring ranches; similarly potatoes, etc. Hay and oats are also sold as well as grown for consumption on the ranch. Horse trading is profitable to those who know about horses. It is held no disgrace to cheat in a horse trade, and friends will so cheat one another. Cattle may be sold alive or as meat. Pigs are rather a good investment.

Hauling wood: Those who have saws frequently make some money in the spring and autumn by hauling wood from the hills into town. This is only done, however, when there is nothing to do on the ranch.

Mrs. Cusack's Opinions: I showed Mrs. Cusack the questions yesterday and asked her opinion thereon. She thought the man and boy would very likely *not* take a buckboard but a spring waggon because they would already have purchased a waggon to work on the ranch, and a buckboard would be a kind of luxury. Also, she thought that they would probably not take a tent — simply blankets, or perhaps a sheet, and sleep in the open as we did in Cottonwood Gulch (see letter of last August). This of course is perfectly easy in the summer time, and eliminates a good deal of bother with tent poles, etc.

Regy Cusack, being asked what he would take if going for a week into the mountains, gave the following list: Axe, hunting knife, fork, tin cup, coffee pot, frying pan, bacon, sugar, salt, coffee, flour, blankets, rifle, and ammunition. I think that is all he said.

Mrs. Cusack was rather amused at the question as to 'farm servants.' Also, she told me to particularly state that if a girl is hired for a bit on a ranch to help with the work, she is *never* called a servant but is alluded to either by her name or as 'the girl', and people talk of 'getting a girl to help', not 'hiring a servant.' The same with labouring men; they are 'hired hands.' I suppose it would be as offensive to call a hired worker a 'servant' out here as to call a black man a 'nigger.' Coloured gentleman is the proper term. I may mention that there are few black men in Colorado, and Indians are not to be seen at all except on the reservations allotted to them. There are many Germans, who are always called 'Dutchmen.' English are of course very numerous, more so perhaps than Americans.

Cottonwood Springs, Pueblo Co.
Aug. 4th, 1888

Dear Frederic,

Here we are in Pueblo County, camped at a place called Cottonwood Springs — just a few cottonwoods (tall poplars) by a spring in the foothills. Tomorrow we move on twelve miles and shall camp near the place where the Liverseys, cousins of Lees, are living, while Lees and Louis go on to Pueblo. I thought of sending on my letter up to date (to be posted in Pueblo), but I will just send this postcard, and letter with full details of the camping expedition shall follow when I return to West Cliff.

The first night after we started we camped where there had been a mining camp called Comargo, but now there is only a ranch. Then we went down Hardscrabble Canyon and reached a low elevation on the extreme eastern border of Custer County, and now we have come on a mile or so and are just in Pueblo County. So far we have got on very well. I am especially so and have an immense appetite.

I caught a grand *Smerinthus* here; I believe it is called *S. occidentalis*, pale brown with pinkish, or rather pink-madder, underwings. Grasshoppers are very numerous and varied, and I have taken sundry other insects. From near here one can see a magnificent view of the mountains, foothills, and the flat plains stretching far east and looking like the sea. I cannot find *any* Mollusca here, of any kind, except two species of fossil shells in a slaty formation on the bluffs. Hearty greeting to Annie.

Yours, Theo. D.A.C.

August 4th, 1888

Dear Frederic,

I started on this expedition without ink, thinking I would write in pencil and copy out afterwards in ink. But of this I repented, when it was too late, and was lamenting that I could get none, when I found Miss Urquhart had brought some along, which I have borrowed (though she wouldn't lend it to me until I promised to paint her a picture). So now I copy from my pencilled letter, anything added today being in square brackets. (I include also my notes on species found; it will show you what sorts of things I am finding.)

July 31st. I was up and over at the Cusacks' at five this morning and found that Regy had driven Mrs. Cusack to town yesterday evening so that she would not have so long a journey and be so tired today. [I wish I had a decent pen.!] Lees had not yet arrived but was down at Cox's and was going to drive Miss Urquhart in his buckboard, following the waggon when he was ready. It is Lees' waggon, the one he had traveled in before, when he went off with Frank, This time Louis drove, and by his side sat Miss Sidford, while I sat behind on the bedding and general baggage, of which there is an abundance. Frank Hamp did not turn up; he is at Beddoes' and we did not much expect him to come. We did not start till past seven, so many things had to be done at the last moment.

In West Cliff, we waited to get one of the horses shod, and I posted your letter and others, but got no mail. At Silver Cliff, we found Regy and Mrs. Cusack at the Charley Cusack's (where I also got the *Pall Mall Budget* Regy left by accident long ago), and they came with us in their buckboard with Specklewattle. A few miles beyond Silver Cliff we got into a district of low hills, rocky and barren, sparsely covered with pines, and this has continued so up till now. Near Bassickville (where is the famous 'Bassick Mine', discovered by a relation of Ed Bassick at Cox's). [The mine is chloride of silver.] We stopped for lunch, getting some milk and watering the horses at a ranch close by, owned by an old Irish-woman. Then we passed on, going up hill more or less all the time (that is, up the slope of the Wet Mountain Range) till we came to a large open grassy space called Silver Park. After crossing this, we descended somewhat and camped at Comargo, which I believe was once a mining camp but is now only a ranch. Lees and Miss Urquhart caught up with us about a mile before the camping place, and passed us, getting there first.

We are camped on a grassy slope among small pines. There are quaking asps on the opposite hill. Plants, etc., are not numerous, but here and the way here we have met with several new to us. Here, among other things, are *Potentilla anserina*, *Achillea millefolium*, and *Agaricus campestris*. [Mushrooms are quite numerous by the ranch, but the people there did not seem to reckon them edible, so we gathered them.]

Species found near Bassickville (* = new to Custer Co.): *Anosia plexippus, Solanum trifidum, Chenopodium album, Populus tremuloides, Potentilla glandulosa, Agaricus sp., Lecanora rubina, Polygonum aviculare, Clematis douglasii, Epilobium angustifolium, Achillea millefolium, Campanula planiflora, C. rotundifolia, Bouteloua oligostachya, Colias eurytheme var. pallida, Potentilla anserina*, Quercus undulata, Placodium murorum miniatum., Arctostaphylos sp., Zenaidura macroura, Agaricus campestris, Campanula uniflora, Geranium fremontii.* At Silver Park, *Otocorys sp., Bovista circumscissa, Geranium fremontii.* At Comargo, *Agaricus campestris, Potentilla anserina, Achillea millefolium, Campanula planiflora, Anosia plexippus, Colias eurytheme, Clematis douglasii, Polygonum aviculare, Bouteloua oligostachya.* At Hardscrabble Canyon, *Anosia plexippus, Papilio chlorulus, Linum perenne, Limenitis wiedemeyeri, Sidalcea malvaeflora, Vanessa antippe, Pyrameis cardui, Colias eurytheme.* [To all these add many species not named yet.]

Aug. 1st. After supper last night I wandered around but did not find much. One thing, however, was a blue-flowered plant of Nat. Order Borraginaceae which smelled just like a skunk! I brought some into camp, and Miss U. proceeded to play a joke upon Louis and Miss S., putting a bit into the waggon in their absence, and no sooner did they return than of course they raised the cry of 'SKUNK!' and it was some minutes before they discovered that it was only a plant. I found a pitch pine stump and got some wood full of resin, so that when it got dark we sat by a bright fire for a little while. A few moths, *Arnarta*

cliveseana, etc., came to the light of it, but soon we went to bed.

This morning we were up soon after 5:30 but did not get off till nearly nine. Nobody was feeling very well for some unexplained reason, but during the day we mostly recovered, though Regy seems still out of sorts. Our road during the morning ran down the Hardscrabble Cañon, a rocky downward road with steep banks reaching high on each side, topped with picturesque rocks and partly covered with scrub oak, small pines, etc. Butterflies were very numerous, chiefly *Pyrameis cardui, Limenitis wiedemeyeri* and later *Nathalis iole*, and all along *Colias eurytheme*.

We 'nooned', that is, had lunch, and watered the horses at a place near the end of the cañon in among the willows and narrow-leaved cottonwoods, close to a rock called the Templar Rock, supposed to resemble the face of a man, which it does to some extent. All this while we were descending rapidly, and now began to get into low altitudes where it is quite hot, and Indian corn was seen growing well. After noon we crossed and left the Hardscrabble Creek [this runs down the cañon] and then went up a rather steep hill.

Half way up, Specklewattle suddenly became cantankerous and absolutely failed to proceed in spite of being beaten with a stick. Finally he lay right down, so there was nothing for it but to take him out of the shafts and put Lees' spare horse, 'Ben' to the buckboard. So Ben took the buckboard to the top of the hill, and Specklewattle was led behind. Then Regy chastened his horse somewhat and again hitched him up. But it was deemed wise that Miss U. should ride with Regy lest the horse should do anything obstreperous and there should be any necessity to jump out of the buckboard. So she went with Lees. Louis, Miss S., and I rode in the with Regy. Specklewattle behaved perfectly all the rest of the way, and late in the afternoon we reached a camping place by an old and empty house that belonged to one Babcott.

We are camped in a sort of amphitheatre, a flattish space surrounded by low hills. The road is on one side, and on another a branch of Red Creek, now quite dry except that at one place there is a little spring where very clear and good water can be got, but it has to be dipped up with a tin cup. There is not room to put the pail in. It is quite warm but windy every now and then. I hope it won't rain, as I am sleeping in the open. But it's now dark, and Lees protests that I cannot *possibly* write in the dark. It's absurd!

Templar Rock: *Populus angustifolia, Quercus undulata, Colias eurytheme, Nathalis iole, Oxalis corniculata** (brought in by Miss U.).

By Babcott's old house: *Thecla sp., Nathalis iole, Quercus undulata, Solanum rostratum, Boutelous oligostachya, Pyrameis hunteri, Eupatoria clandia, Colias eurytheme keewaydin**, *Juniperus virginiana, Limenitis wiedemeyeri, Achillea millefolium, Amosia plexippus, Agaricus sp., Zenaidura macroura, Lasiocampa** *larvae, Cyanocitta stelleri macrolopha?*, Solpugidae sp.

[Aug. 4th. It is getting twilight, and I have hardly time to copy my pencil letter up to date, so will write in pencil till I catch up.]

[Continued in ink, Aug. 5th.]

Aug. 2nd. I got up at 5:30 this morning and cooked the breakfast, after which Lees in his buckboard, and Regy and Miss U. riding, went off to look for another and better camping place where we shall stay for some days. Miss Sidford commenced a sketch in oils of the camp (the result was ghastly) and Mrs. Cusack had gone down the creek after ferns. I followed after to find her but somehow must have missed her and came on a mile or two, and have climbed to the top of the cliff above the creek. On this cliff I found some grasshoppers new to me and also sundry cacti, including one arborescent one they call the chandelier cactus, a peculiar-looking branched plant with the branches upright.

I am now at the top of this cliff and have the grandest view I have seen in all Colorado.

The ground slopes steeply down and is clothed with small trees until it meets the plains, which stretch, grassy and treeless, far east till they seem to end in the horizon, a pale gray unbroken level line.

To the north is Pike's Peak and the whole 'front range', and then the foothills clothed with junipers and dark piñon trees. It looks indeed like some mighty cliffs bounding a vast ocean, the foothills seeming to be seaweed-covered rocks stretching far out at the low tide. And the plain is almost blue. I have seen the sea as brown and as level to appearance as water. So from here it slopes right down to the Atlantic (but that is the Gulf of Mexico, for the Alleghany Mts. are between here and the eastern seaboard, and the Atlantic is between here and England). It is the way home!

Evening. Well, I returned to camp, and soon Regy, Miss U. and Lees came back saying they had found a camping place down the stream about a mile and a half away, but before we could take the waggon there it would be necessary to do some work on the road. So after lunch, Lees, Regy, Louis and I went off and graded the road in some specially bad places, and we hope the waggon will not upset tomorrow when we go along there. This evening I cooked the dinner, and afterwards went for a short stroll with Mrs. C., and now it is almost dark. It is warm and fine, and the air resounds with the cries of crickets, while bats fly overhead.

Aug. 3rd. Afternoon. Today we are in Pueblo County at what we call Cottonwood Springs. After breakfast we packed up and drove here along a very rough road down the cañon of the creek, which we were mending yesterday. We got here, about a mile (or rather more) from last camp, in all safety, Mrs. C. and Miss U. walking on before, as it was too rough for them driving. The camp here is in a grove of cottonwood trees — the broad-leaved kind. There is a good big creek, but it is dry, and what water there is trickles out from little springs and loses itself in the sand.

Therefore we dug a well a foot or two deep and about the same width, and so got enough water, though not of the clearest [it afterward became clear, but cattle *would* drink out of it and make it muddy].

After lunch, Lee and Regy started off to see Jim Liversey and family — very large cattle people and cousins of Lees — and will not return till tomorrow. Now it is afternoon, and Mrs. C., Miss U., and I are under the 'teepee' (i.e. tent) in the shade, while Louis and Miss S. have gone out for a walk.

The cottonwoods here are very productive of insects — a *Cavus* bores the large ones, and larvae of a hymenopterous insect live in dead stumps, and these last are parasitized by big yellow and brown ichneumons with tremendously long ovipositors. We found some in the act of putting these organs down the holes in the stumps in search of larvae wherein to lay eggs. Beside these, Bombycid larvae live in extensive webs in the boughs, and I find pupa skins of a *Catocala* (near to *nupta*) under the bark, with the characteristic purple tinge, and I chased also one of the moths from tree to tree but failed to catch it.

But the greatest prize of all was a glorious *Smerinthus*, larger than any English species, with pale sandy brown fore-wings, and hind wings shaded with madder red and dark blotches to mark the situation of the ocelli in such species as *ocellatus*. (I believe this species is *S. occidentalis*).

Aug. 4th. Last night the horses suddenly stampeded, and Louis going after them fancied he saw something (possibly mountain lion, but probably not) which might have scared them. After this, though, the horses returned, but this morning again they had disappeared — all except Specklewattle who, having a loose rope around his neck, had managed to tie himself up in the bushes. So, Louis riding and I walking, set off after the horses. On my way I caught a lizard and sundry insects, and at length met Louis, who had just caught the horses about half way

to the last camping place. We rode back, and I spent the rest of the morning drawing in sepia a small picture of this camp for Mrs. C. As we were finishing lunch Lees and Regy returned from the Liversey's, and counseled that we should go and camp near there — some twelve miles from here — and that is what we are going to do tomorrow.

Aug. 5th. Last night, at dusk, Regy rushed into camp saying he saw a deer, and rushed out again after it with a rifle, but he did not get a shot at it, in fact, did not see it again. We sat round the camp fire for some time, talking. This morning, after breakfast, we packed up and started off to the proposed camp by the Liverseys. The road lay over a country consisting of low hills, with some scrub oak, some cacti, and other plants looking parched-up, and not a drop of water anywhere. We had not gone far when we saw, on the hill to the right of us, a fine deer — a buck with two horns, and possibly the same one seen by Regy last night. Lees quickly got out his rifle and went off up the hill at a pace that would have taken all the wind out of *my* body in about ten minutes. The deer went over the rise, however, and was not seen again, so that Lees got no shot at it.

Near what is called Pack Creek (but it seems no water in it) we met Jim Liversey coming along to meet us in a covered waggon, and at this point Lees and Louis parted from us and went off in Lees' buckboard to Pueblo. Some while after, having gone through numerous gates, we came to the Liverseys and had lunch there, and started our camp. But I will not say more now (except that I don't think a great deal of the new camp), because I can write it when I catch up with the pencil copy in ink.

Jim Liversey is perhaps a little of the type of the English 'country gentleman' — tallish, well-built, strong, with decided yet not too expressive features, a prominent Roman nose, moustache, whiskers, and dark hair. His voice is gruff, and he laughs somewhat gurglingly at nearly everything without much appearance of genuine amusement. I do not think he has and very decided opinions or tastes. (Politically he seems to be Whig if anything, but takes the 'Mail' edition of the *Times* and also the *Pall Mall Budget*, 'to see both sides of the question.') He is an agreeable, cheerful man, but possibly an uninteresting one on further acquaintance. Mrs. Liversey is a short woman with long nose, pink face, not good-looking nor ugly. In character, of a common uninteresting type, so far as I can judge.

Our camp is within a hundred yards of the Liverseys, under some pines and close to a wide and deep cañon. Wood is plentiful, but we have to go far for water.

Aug. 6th. I have at length caught up with my pencil copy, but just now it is time to get supper ready, so I must leave off writing. This morning Liversey and Regy went off to haul a horse's body out of Pack Creek (it had died there and was polluting the water) and Miss U. and Miss S. rode with them. I have been writing, reading, etc., and have not been any distance from camp.

To our great astonishment, two people riding up early in the afternoon proved to be Cox and Mrs. Cox, who had come in search of Lees because, Cox said, Payn had got into some mess and wanted Lees (as far as I could make out) either to lend him money or act as surety for him. Cox also said that Payn was on the point of starting on an excursion to White River. The Coxes started from home yesterday afternoon and found their way to a place called Beulah, south of here, where they heard from someone where we were. They only stayed here a little while, and had a little lunch and then started back to Wetmore on their way home. They could not wait for Lees to come back from Pueblo, but I believe left a note with Liversey for him.

Aug. 7. Yesterday evening Jim Liversey sat with us round the camp fire, talking and singing; he rather improves on acquaintance. This morning I have been drawing in sepia, but this afternoon have felt very queer, quite exhausted and my pulse went up to 104 and then down to 62, where it stayed for some time.

Species found: New to Pueblo Co. are marked, but nearly everything is new, because I had very few records for this county before. Cottonwood Springs: *Nathalis iole, Juniperus virginiana, Quercus undulata, Polygonum aviculare, Colias eurytheme, Limenitis wiedemeyeri, Bouteloua oligostachya, Vitis sp.* (wild vine with grapes on it grew on the cottonwoods, looking very pretty, *Formica integra, Pica pica hudsonica, Anosia plexippus, Pyraneis hunteri, Eupatoria claudia, Argemone platyceras*, and many species not yet named.

Aug. 8th. Evening, by the camp fire. I spent the morning sketching rocks in the cañon ('Wales' Cañon, it is called) but without very satisfactory results. I have also been reading bits of *Little Lord Fauntleroy* borrowed from Mrs. C. from Mrs. Liversey); it is a rather prettily written story.

Prince Bismarck seems to be 'carrying on.' Lees and Louis returned from Pueblo late this afternoon and brought us an abundance of food, of which we were in some need, being already obliged to borrow provender from the Liverseys. Louis brought Miss S. a very pretty little river tortoise, marked with red underneath; he found it by the Arkansas River. It has been cloudy lately and quite chilly, but is warmer this evening. I am glad to see the Bryant and May girls have won their strike. B. & In. is an abominable firm.

June 9th. After breakfast I went down into Wales Cañon with Mrs. C., and we did not return till afternoon. We found a good many insects and also a snake, which I skinned and set the skin in spirits. I was fortunate, too, in finding some Mollusca, all new to Pueblo Co., viz., *Limax montana, Hyalina radiatula, Hy. arborea, Helix pulchella* var. *costata, Comulus fulans, Vitrina pellucida,* and *Succinea acara.* This afternoon I have been reading aloud to Mrs. C. from *Century* magazine — Cable on *Home Culture Clubs*, an interesting article.

Aug. 10th. Soon after nine we struck camp and made first for the house of a man named Campion, previously known to Lees, who had invited us to lunch. He lives in a log house down Wales Cañon and not far from our last camp, but to get there we had to go round a good way. Campion is an Englishman, son of a Sussex clergyman. He seems a very good sort of man, but the most noticeable thing about him is a drawling mode of speech which is certainly natural to him. From Campion's we came on some ten miles through very pretty country, the St. Charles River, Mace's Hole, etc., and camped rather late.

Aug. 13th. I wrote notes on the last two days in pencil. I can hardly write at all with this pen now; it is so bad.

Aug. 11th. Camped on South Hardscrabble Creek.

Aug. 12th. Camped near Comargo. Much rain in the evening.

Aug. 13th. Three of the horses disappeared. We can't proceed. Am very much disappointed because I hoped to get my mail today. Will write details when I get a decent pen.

Aug. 14th. Am back at my house and have very much to write, but quite incapable of writing it. Am going to bed early and will try to gel up betimes tomorrow, and finish this letter and take it to post.

Aug. 15. I will now go back to Aug. 10th, and write a full narrative.

Aug. 10th. I have written above how we went to lunch at Campion's. There was a youth named Ward there whom Campion was supposed to be instructing in the art of farming (and gets I think $100 for so doing!), and it illustrated the smallness of this globe that he turned out to be the brother of a girl well-known to Miss Urquhart in Bedford. After leaving Campion's we went over some dry and uninteresting country until we struck the St. Charles River, which is an extremely pretty little stream bordered by tall cottonwoods and running in a broad valley called Mace's Hole, which is very green and fresh-looking after the arid plains we had passed, and is studded with ranches where maize and other warmth-loving crops are grown.

We did not camp till about five, and then by the side of the road next to the ranch of a man who may have been a Pole (he had an '-ovski' name but I forget exactly what it was) and who at all events had most gentlemanly manners since he offered us anything we needed, even to an empty but furnished house if we liked it, and at the same time did not intrude his company upon us beyond making himself pleasant and offering his assistance.

Aug. 11th. Louis Howard had bought him a new buckboard in Pueblo, and yesterday it was found that the wheels had been most clumsily fixed on so that two of them had to be taken off, and Lees and Louis spent some time this morning in putting them into proper working order. This made us late starting, but I got off before the rest of them, taking Mrs. Cusack in Lees' buckboard with the black horse, Ben. We traveled in pine woods more or less all the morning, and at about twelve came to a good creek which runs into the main Hardscrabble stream. The waggon and the other two buckboards arrived, and we all sat down to lunch. Lees was not very well, and the rest were tired, so it was decided not to proceed further but stay at this camp the night. The only trouble was that there was nothing on which to feed the horses, grass being very scanty, but I took the buckboard and Ben and went to the ranch of one Blake, where I managed to get some alfalfa (*Medicago sativa*, alias Lucerne). Towards evening a violent thunderstorm came on, with rain, but we got under the teepee and were not wetted more than a little. An interesting find at this camp was a quantity of *Capsella bursa-pastoris*.

Sunday, Aug. 12. We traveled down the Hardscrabble Creek to where it joins the main stream. Then we got once more on the road we had traveled on our outward journey, past the Templar Rock, up the Hardscrabble Canon, where we nooned, and I caught *Pyrameis hunteri* and other things, and on to about two miles from Comargo, making camp in a small gulch very similar to that at Comargo. [See July 31st.] There was hardly time to make camp before a thunderstorm came down upon us, more violent than that of yesterday, with floods of rain. But the teepee was rigged in genuine Indian style, with a hole in the top for a chimney so that we could have a fire inside, and so keep dry and warm. All except Lees and myself went off to a neighboring ranch for supper, after the storm had subsided.

Aug.13th. We were to make West Cliff by noon today, and I was eagerly looking forward to getting my mail. Lees went out after the horses, but returned with his own, saying he could not find the rest! So Louis' two horses and Regy's Specklewattle had disappeared, and we had only the two belonging to Lees! Of course, a search was at once made, and continued all day — Rosita and Querida (alias Bassickville), but no traces were found of the missing horses. It was perfectly disgusting, as Regy said; it just made him 'homesick.' One could do nothing but wait, and I beguiled a little spare time in reading Chapter 1 of Darwin's *Beagle* (a copy Lees had brought with him) to Mrs. Cusack.

Aug. 14th. It was resolved that the morning should be devoted to looking for the horses, and if they were not found, two buckboards should be left at a ranch while Lees' team took the waggon, with one buckboard trailing behind, and so homewards. But I, having no reason for waiting, started for West Cliff on foot at about seven a.m. (it is about 14 miles), Lees walking with me for a couple of miles and then going off into the hills to look for the horses. I walked across Silver Park, and all the while looked for tracks of the horses, but evidently they had not come along that road. About half-way, near Querida, I was overtaken by a man with a waggon, and so got a ride as far as Silver Cliff. It seemed they had a very violent hailstorm here the other day and there is scarcely a house which has not one or more windows broken by the large hailstones that fell.

I hurried on to West Cliff and was delighted to find a big bundle of mail: Your two letters, two letters from Mother, letters from Carlie, Leslie (from St. Thomas), W. H. Edwards (and a postcard), Ellis (and a postcard), Bethune, Morrison, L. O. Howard, Hamilton (beetle man), postcard from Wolle, *Journ. Conch., Orn. & Oöl., Insect Life* (vol. 1 No. 1, issued by Agric. Dept.), *Pall Mall Budget* (two), *Commonweal*, and *Chicago Labor Enquirer* (two). This letter to you, as you will see, was not finished, and I meant to finish it in the postoffice and post it, but I had only just got my mail when Mrs. Splann and Becky came up and said they were that minute starting from town and would take me out if I liked. I was feeling rather tired, and so did like, wherefore I left your letter to be finished and posted the next day, though on second thoughts I had perhaps done better to post it as it was and write another letter with the later details.

I called at Cox's and found Mrs. Cox at home, who told me that Cox had sold their ranch and was at present in Kansas City. I am rather concerned to know what they are going to do, and what is to become of Mrs. Cox and children. Then I went up to Brock's, and then up to my own house, which I reached soon after two, feeling much 'played out', though I had really done nothing to make me so.

Aug. 15th. I shall ride to West Cliff on Ferris this morning, and If I do not meet the rest of the expedition with the horses, I shall go on to Beddoes' and see if Louis' horses have by any chance gone there. Frequently horses will return to where they have been kept. After this I shall return to my house, I won't answer your letters fully now, as I ought to be getting off (it is 8:20), but will write a little.

[In the following lines, Cockerell follows up on his discussion of Annie's family. Ed.]

(Letter of July 11th, etc.) A very nice letter. I will *try* to write a nice letter to your father, for *something* must be done, and if there is *hope* of success it is best perhaps to try it although I cannot honestly say that the method commends itself to me. My point of view has always been, not that the parents were wrong in *objecting* to my writing [to Annie], but that their error (as it seems to me) lay in interfering with the liberty of their children because they did not share their objections — treating them, in fact, as if they had not sufficient discretion to act for themselves.

This is and always has been the policy of your parents — and the principle involved is just the same as that between absolute monarchy and republicanism, or rather I should say democracy, and in no case has it been possible to *persuade* a monarch that he ought not to interfere with the rights of his subjects, even though he is sure in his own mind that his subjects are doing unwisely.

So, truly, I cannot hope to convince the parents that their whole policy in their treatment of their children is a mistake. It only remains, then, to persuade them that I am not quite so objectionable a person as they have supposed — to appeal, not to their sense of justice or of right, but to their feelings of friendship (or whatever one may call it), and seek their approval of me personally. This is a hard thing to do, because I fear that it is my own essential qualities (physical, moral, and mental) that they dislike. And how can I change? Nor, in a letter, can I write other

than what I think (if I *would*, it would be the most transparent of humbug), and that is not all 'soft soap', as they say out here. But I will try, and will be as 'nice' over it as I possibly can.

I think I am a good deal better in health than when I left England but, in fact, I am not strong like other men, and I fear I shall not be. Although no doubt this country is best for consumption, I am by no means clear that it is better than England as regards one's general health. Sometimes I think I should do better at a somewhat lower altitude. But it is really unreasonable to complain of any ill-health, for I have not once been seriously laid up or had any cough of consequence since I came here.

I am very glad Annie liked the rosebud. Now it is 20 past nine and I ought to be going.

11:30. I caught Ferris, but before I had time to start, it commenced raining, and has not yet stopped.

9:20 p.m. Unfortunately, I have not been able to post this letter today after all, but it certainly shall be posted tomorrow. I rode towards town and by the Kettle's met the waggon with Cusacks, etc., and buckboard trailing behind. They had not found the three horses (but heard of their having gone to Rosita) and had left camp yesterday afternoon, reaching Silver Cliff after dark.

Louis asked me to go back to Kent's (which is close to Beddoes') to ask about the horses, and so I never got to town, as that would have been many miles out of my way, and Louis promised to post this letter the first thing tomorrow, when he would pass through town with Regy on a search for the three horses Rosita-wards.

I rode to Kent's uneventfully, and was there told that doubtless Louis' two horses would have gone to the ranch of one Cole, near Rosita, as they were 'raised' there and had gone there once before when they had escaped from the McKircher's (who live at Kent's). Having learned this, I rode home, arriving soon after five, and had supper at the Cusack's, and then a great argument with Lees in which I maintained that no man ought to own what he could not *use*, especially if others could use it. Lees came to the conclusion, as he generally does, that the question was 'involved.'

More notes on your letters: I think Leslie will do well, but I rather wish he had not gone to St. Thomas. I have a poor opinion of the place. I am glad Annie likes *Caramcro*. Thanks to her for answers to exam papers.

When told that one will think differently in later life, one is tempted to reply: 'Yes, we all *start* honest, but the trouble is that so few can *keep* so!' Which, although not literally true, expresses a general truth. Or again: 'Many kinds of fruit are excellent, but some always go rotten in old age.' But this is too sarcastic! As a matter of fact, youth is by no means always right, but I think the natural impulses are. In maturer years the natural impulses tend to be eliminated.

No, I haven't written any more articles for newspapers, or anything but the strictly scientific. I am obliged to Emily for the silk! Wouldn't the children be delighted with some of the big silk caterpillars? *Atlacus cynthia*, *Samia curopis*, etc. — they can be got for a few pence each at Watkins and Doncaster in the Strand. Or eggs can be bought cheaper.

The train isn't going to run for two months (i.e. to Cañon City) so as mail will go by stage it will be a day longer on the journey. It's a pity, but there's no help for it. Groceries, etc., have to be freighted now (on waggons) and prices have 'riz' in consequence.

The hybrid *Verbascum* in your garden is very interesting, but I have not the least idea that it is native. If so, it were an addition to the list as given in *London Cal.* (8th edition). I have found *V. nigrum* (typical) at Orpington, (W. Kent).

West Cliff, Thursday, Aug. 16th, 1888

Dear Frederic,

Louis and Regy rode off this morning to Rosita to search for the lost horses and will not be back until tomorrow. At the same time, Lees went to town and he took your letter to post. Probably he will not be back tonight, but when he does come I hope he will bring your this week's letter. It should have come through by now, even on the coach.

I have been writing up my fauna book, diary, etc., today, and have managed to get things squared off. Tomorrow I shall start on the letters; I have twelve to write, mostly long ones. This afternoon I found and identified two species of *Solidago* and an *Aster* new to my Custer County list, and also another Composite, *Gymnolomia multiflora*.

I had lunch and supper at the Cusack's, and am doing their 'chaws' for the little while that Regy is away. The Dept. of Agric. have started a most admirable monthly magazine of entomology called *Insect Life*. It is to be issued when convenient, but on the average once a month, and is mainly devoted to Economic Entomology. I received No. 1 the other day (July, 1888).

Aug. 17th, 9:40 p.m. Lees quite forgot to get my mail yesterday after all, and so to make amends lent me Ben and his buckboard that I might drive to town and get it myself. Before I went I wrote the letter to your father. I fear it will not altogether please him, but I wrote what I could, and must now await the result. I got into town at about 12:30 and received a good lot of mail: Your letter, letters from Mother (and socks and tie), C. R. Orcutt, Jenner Weir (interesting) and postcard from J. W. Taylor, *Naturalist*, and reprints. Reprints from *Canad. Entom.*, *Entomologist*, and *Ent. Monthly Mag.*, *Commonweal*, *Chicago Labor Enquirer*, and *Botanical Gazette*. I posted copies of reprints of my papers in *Naturalist* and *Canadian Ent.* to you and Annie, and to the S.L.E.S. While I was in town Louis and Regy arrived from Rosita, having found the three missing horses.

Just before I left, the mail came in on the coach. All I got was a manuscript returned from *Pop. Sci. Monthly* together with a paper which I enclose as being something in the manner of refusing manuscripts. It is ingeniously worded, being so polite yet committing them to nothing. (When I said in last letter I had gotten nothing more for 'popular' use, I quite forgot this sent to *Pop. Sci. Mo.*, but indeed it was hardly a popular paper.) While I was in the postoffice one J. Charlton, a nice looking man with reddish beard, came up to me and enquired about my natural history work. He is an analytical chemist and lives at West Cliff. I think I shall like him when I see more of him. His face and voice remind me the least bit of Anthony Belt. I got back safely, except that it poured with rain the last half mile so that I had to change clothes when I got in.

In answer to your letter: So Frohawk's *Sesia* wasn't white after all, notwithstanding his note in *Entom.*! I wish Tutt had been present at the meeting; he would have sat on Frohawk for his inaccuracy. Did you read (or have read) my notes on *Sesia* (the second one) and on insects not knowing between red and yellow?

I haven't seen any vestiges of *Robert Elsmere* out here yet. I am glad that you will see Henry Edwards; Jenner Weir writes that he saw him. It's queer that Carlie should say I've toned down and am not so socialistic! It's true, though, that I do next to no 'propaganda' now because I hardly ever find anyone fresh to discuss the question with. But I can't say I have in any way altered my opinions on the matter.

You were very fortunate in getting so many vars. of *Helix hortensis* at Isleworth. Very few are recorded for Middlesex. Certainly *lutea* 12045 is very uncommon. It was first recorded by Von Martens from the continent. The only specimen I ever saw was a broken one found by Wallis Kew, so far as I remember. It is recorded by Roebuck in his Lincolnshire list in *Naturalist*, Aug. 1887.

Aug. 18th. I have really nothing to tell you about today for I have been busy writing all the time. In the morning I racked my brains to draw up a circular for the *Colorado Biological Association*, which is to be the new development of C. F. Morrison's *Colorado Ornithological Association*. Morrison has gone to Montana and wants to take the thing up and set it going, so I have written a circular and shall send it to Morrison, who will get it printed for me and pay initial expenses. As far as possible, the Association will be after the manner of the *Yorkshire Naturalists' Association*. The subscription is \$1.00 for ordinary members and 25 cents for those resident without the state. I will send you a circular when I get them out.

This afternoon I have written some notes on Custer Co. entomology for *Ent. Mo. Mag.* I included the new *Longitarsus* beetle, taking the somewhat erratic course of easing my mind on the subject by explaining my views and Riley's views and telling them to publish the new species or not, as they see fit. I am much burdened with correspondence just now. Nine packages of specimens to make up and send off, accompanied by long letters, and six other letters, haunt me night and day! I wish I had the faculty of doing correspondence quickly that some people have! I am one of the slowest people I know of.

Sunday, Aug. 19th, 6:45 p.m. Writing again today. I sorted out some fungi for Ellis, etc. (Now I think of it, Ellis says the fungus on grass I sent you is *Oidium monitoides* Lk. and the one on *Aster* leaves is *Aecidium compositarum* Mart. Two of the fungi I sent him he thinks are new species, and proposes to call them *Puccinia bigeloviae* and *Dermatia pruinosa* respectively.)

This afternoon Mrs. Brock came with Mrs. Cusack and asked me to afternoon tea down there, so I went. The Cusacks and Louis and Miss S. were there. Brock was in town. While at

THE COLORADO
Biological Association!

A MEETING

Of the Custer County branch of the C. B. A. will take place at the SCHOOL HOUSE, WESTCLIFFE, COLO., on

Tuesday, Jan. 29, 1889.

A paper will be read by T. D. A. Cockerell on "The Balance of Nature," or Insects and their Parasites.

Mr. T. Charlton will give a demonstration in Chemistry, illustrated by experiments. The meeting to be followed by a discussion.

ALL ARE INVITED.

MEMBERS FREE. NON-MEMBERS 10 CENTS.
MEMBERSHIP SUBSCRIPTION, $1.00

T. D. A. COCKERELL, Secretary.

CUSTER COUNTY COURANT.

Brock's I picked up a little book called *Five Minutes*, compiled by H.F.S. Lear (second edition, London, 1884), being a poem for each day of the year. In general conception it leant towards the foolish, but I found some very nice little bits of poetry in it — some well known, others new to me. I noted a few (if you have the book at Smith's these references will suffice): March 15. Shakespeare; Jan., 12, Longfellow . . . [There follow eight others. Ed.]

Aug. 20th, 7 p.m. In the morning I made a new insect cage; that is to say, a large wooden box with a wire gauze top in which I put a larva of *Papilio asterias* (found by Mrs. Cusack) and a female *Sabyrus charon*, with a request that she lay some eggs on a tuft of grass supplied her. Then I did some writing, and then went down to Cox's to look at 'Newman' and confirm as *Sesia myopaeformis* a *Sesia* sent me by Carlie, from Mister E. Kent (I think it is new to Isle of Thanet). After this I went to Brock's to chop wood for Mrs. B., Brock himself being away at Rosita. After this, and partaking of tea and bun with Mrs. B., I returned to my mansion.

When at Cox's, Mrs. Cox was telling me that she was in town yesterday and found there was a rumour that when Regy and Miss U. went in to a ball the other day they were married! Two people asked her about it and, although no doubt it's nonsense, it has a good deal more likelihood on the face of it than most West Cliff rumours.

Miss U. gets a good deal criticized as a flirt, and no doubt for the most part justly, for she flirts continuously with Regy. Failing him, then with Lees and even with Louis on occasion, but this is always when she is encouraged. Some men like to amuse themselves with flirting, and some girls don't have the sense to object to their doing so, and vice versa. *Homo sapiens* is capable of much foolishness, notwithstanding his name!

Louis and Miss S. went to town today and brought me back a *Provisional Host Index of the Fungi of the United States*, Part 1 (1888) by Farlow and Seymour, sent 'with respects of W. G. Farlow.' This is a most admirable thing, got up and apparently distributed gratis by Farlow. It enumerates all the plants on which parasitic fungi have been found in the U. S., with the names of the fungi found on them. Part 1 extends to *Comaceae*. Part 2 is to appear during the winter, probably. I will send you a list of the number of parasitic fungi found in North America on some species which also grow in England. It may interest you.

It is pouring with rain now, but I think the rainy season is getting over; it doesn't rain as much as it did during the day.

Aug. 21st, 9:35 p.m. I did some writing. I am at length beginning to see my way to the end of my correspondence, and then read the papers for a while. Some interesting matter was discovered in Lees' *St. James Budget* (e.g., articles on 'chinook' and 'pidgin English, etc.), which seems to be much improved under its new proprietor (some German, the *P.M.G.* says). Of course, it has to do the rabid Tory just as always in politics, but otherwise it is becoming very readable and often sensible.

In the afternoon I went down to Brock's to dig some potatoes for the Cusacks. Going down, I met Mrs. B. coming up to get me to cut some more wood (Brock not yet having come back. He turned up after dark tonight). So I dug the potatoes and was about to cut the wood when a considerable rain storm came on, accompanied by considerable cold. In fact, we could see that snow was falling heavily on the range. As it did not abate I went up to the Cusacks' and, finally, after the storm was over, returned to Brock's, where I had supper and chopped Mrs. Brock quite a big pile of wood. Mrs. B. said she would talk to Brock when he returned, about leaving her with no wood cut, and doubtless she did so, as Louis, who saw Brock afterwards, said he was in a great rage.

After leaving the Brock's, I came up to the Cusacks' for a bit and then came over to my house. Lees has gone to town with Mrs. Cox (or meant to). I gave him letters to post, and he will bring out mail. I half meant to give him yours, but I think while the coach is running the mail, I will go in always on Thursdays, getting your letter and posting mine on the same day.

Aug. 22nd, 9:45 p.m. It occurs to me as I put the date to this, that I am 22 years of age. When I woke up this morning, it was cold and pouring with rain, so I reflected that it would be unpleasant to cook breakfast (the stove being on the verandah) and far more pleasant to stay in bed, so I settled down to Geikie's *Geology*, when I was disturbed by Lees, who brought me mail: Letter from Radenhausen, *Bot. Gazette*, *Chicago Labor Enquirer*, and *West American Scientist* (many copies of March, 1888, with my papers on *Colias*) and copies of the numbers from commencement for indexing. The magazine has come to Vol. IV, and there is no index yet, so I told Orcutt (editor) that I would write him an index for all four if he would publish it at the end of Volume IV. There is a short note of mine on *Linum perenne*, white variety, in the August *Botanical Gazette*.

I found it too cold to sit in my house, so came over to the Cusacks' where I have been spending the whole day in indexing the *W. Amer. Sci.* It is a bigger affair than I supposed. I put out some strychnine last night mixed with flour and grease, and this morning discovered a young mountain rat poisoned thereby, but I fear there are more rats yet. Tomorrow I shall try to get to town, but Louis talks of going, and if the weather looks threatening, I may leave it to him to post letters and fetch mail, so in case of this, I will end up.

Aug. 23rd, morning. It looks as if it would be fine, but I think I will get Louis to take this and bring out mail instead of going in myself. If there should be anything particular to answer in your letter I can write a postcard before next week.

Lees' cabin, Aug. 23rd, 1888

Dear Frederic,

I have come up to Lees' place tonight. Before starting, I got your letter enclosing the roses and message from Annie (Thanks, Annie. It couldn't have been nicer. I half hoped you would send me a rosebud from off that tree, but was afraid you would think you oughtn't) and the photograph of Isleworth Church from Louy, for which give her my best thanks. I didn't expect she would think of me and am pleased accordingly, and thank you also for your good wishes. Annie's additions to fauna and flora are welcome and interesting; more of them later. I am exceedingly glad to see that you and Annie are taking a holiday, and in so good a place as Dorset. But it's now nearly ten, and I must reserve further remarks and narrative of today for tomorrow. Lees has gone to bed, and I must too.

Aug. 24th, 9 p.m. I have been working with Lees today, surveying, etc., but this later. Now, of yesterday. Aug. 23rd. Louis went to town, taking your letter to post, and Lees, who was at the Cusack's, went up to his mine. Before going, he asked me to go up with him and help him survey his land, as he wanted to take it up as a 'homestead', including 'Smith's Park', which is about a mile below his cabin. I was to be up there a week, or till the end of next week, so, having agreed to go, I did not go up in the waggon with Lees but concluded to wait until Louis returned from town and brought your letter, and then walk up. But now Lees has gone to bed and I had better put out the light, and do likewise. Will continue this at next opportunity.

Aug. 25th. We have been surveying all day, but are tired, and I will not write details now, especially as tomorrow is Sunday, and I can then write fully, for we shall do no work to speak of.

Sunday, Aug. 26th. As I said before, I was to go up to Lees' place for a week and help him survey the land near his cabin so that he could take it up as a 'homestead', according to the law of the U. S., which allows a man to take up surveyed land after having lived there five years, and own it altogether provided that nobody was there before him. The government, indeed, has to do all the surveying in the first place, and locate districts called 'townships' enclosing smaller areas — 'forties', arranged like squares on a chess board. Lees, having come after the government survey, did not know where the corners of the forties were, and therefore has to re-survey the land to find the original marks made to indicate the corners, which would be somewhere in the woods.

Louis went to town, saying he would be back at about four, and I waited for the mail, writing, going over some flowers, etc., in the meanwhile. Louis did not come back till past six, bringing your nice letter, and letters from Carlie, Olive, Grannie, and Orcutt. (Orcutt says he can sell some Colorado bulbs, cacti, etc., for me, or rather for himself if I first sell them to him. Which reminds me that I sent Woolson of New York some bulbs, but haven't heard from him.

It was a quarter to seven before I could get off to walk to Lees', and they all tried to dissuade me from going, saying I could not possibly find the place in the dark. However, I started, knowing that in any case the worst that could happen would be to have to sleep in the woods and find the way next morning when it was light.

It got dark before I reached Beddoes' old house, and two miles beyond there the road began to be difficult to find. But just then the moon rose and gave me enough light to proceed, and as the road as been now made fit for a waggon to travel on, I easily made my way along it, reaching Lees' cabin soon after nine. Coming up, I was struck by the complete silence of these woods. Elsewhere, in England or at a lower altitude in Colorado, one hears various cries, but in these mountains there is not a sound.

Aug. 24th. We woke up betimes and set to work.

The principle on which we had to work: Lees has a paper on which the sections, duly numbered out as if on a chess board (and all the lines running N, S, E, and W). The first ranch below belongs to one Davis. It is 2½ miles from here along the road, and on it there is in one place (known to Lees) a stone placed and marked with 1 1/4 chiseled on it. Given this one point, the question is to find the others.

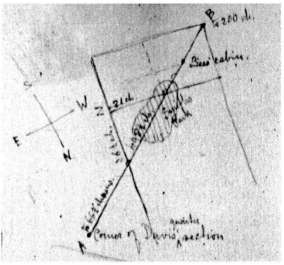

Davis' quarter-section

So Lees went up the gulch to an open space high on the mountainside from whence he could see the place where he knew Davis' corner was, Then he took with his eye a line straight to Davis', and this line diverged 37° 30' from North, and passed by two spruce trees above the cabin and also close to the stable door (as we ascertained exactly by waving handkerchiefs on long poles), and when Lees saw that my pole was just in the line, he fired a shot from his rifle (which he had taken up with him) and I marked the spot. The line A. ·B. on the map here given represents this line diverging 37° 30' from the North (of course Lees ascertained this with a compass). When drawn on the plan, it was found to pass exactly through one corner (at a distance of 200 chains from Davis'. 80 chains = one mile) and in the relation shown to another corner. The map I have drawn is not accurate because it does not allow a proper length to the line as compared with the first part of it, and consequently throws the squares all out of shape, but it will do for a diagram.

For the rest of the morning Lees worked at the forge, while I blew the bellows (quite hard work, this), but after lunch we returned to the surveying. This time we went down to the lower end of Smith's Park and, having ascertained from looking back that we were on the line, proceeded to cut a straight way through the wood for some distance so that in chaining we should not get off the line.

This was done in the following manner. The compass was placed on the line and then turned so that an imaginary line drawn through the slit in A (*vide* sketch) and the hair drawn across B would be 37° 30′ from the north, and consequently a continuation of the line we were tracing. So, by looking through the slit and the hair, one could see into the wood and be sure it was in the right direction.

I looked through the compass while Lees went ahead and cut down the small trees and 'blazed' the larger ones that were on the line (blazing is cutting off a slice of bark so that they can be recognized) until he got too far for me to see, when we moved the compass on and repeated the proceeding. In this way we got a straight line cut through the wood until we arrived at the place where the hill slopes down, and it is possible again to see Davis' corner (marked 1 on the section given).

Then Lees went home to cook supper, while I went on to Davis' to see if I could find Ben, who had strayed off and was supposed to be down there. Lees himself found Ben on his way home, after all, and consequently my journey to Davis' was fruitless except in one respect, that I found an *Aecidium* on *Berberis repens* in some abundance, of which I was especially glad, as it had been reported by few collectors (Tracy, and Galloway) from Colorado, and I had been look-

ing for it all the summer. It is very closely allied to *Aecidium berberidis* (See Thome, pp. 273-264), if not a variety of it.

Aug. 25th. We walked down to Davis' corner and then proceeded to measure up the gulch along the line by means of a chain. I went in front holding one end of the chain, while Lees waited, holding the other. Then, when it was tight, Lees looked over my head at the landmarks (especially a handkerchief on a pole we had put at 1 (See section), and directed me to the right or left until I was exactly in line, when I put a skewer into the ground to mark the place and went on, and we repeated the proceeding.

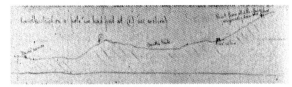

Davis' corner to Lees' cabin

Lees collected the skewers as he went past them, and when I had used them all (there were ten) he came forward and returned them to me, making a note in his note-book that we had gone ten chains. We had very great trouble getting through the willows and brush in many places, and you can judge of this by the fact that though we were diligently at it all day we had only done a hundred chains, or a mile and a quarter, by evening.

During the day I chanced across four species of micro-fungi — three of *Aecidium* and one which is perhaps *Puccinia*.

Aug. 26th. Today being Sunday, we were supposed not to work. Nevertheless, after breakfast, which we had rather late, we went up to the engine at the mouth of the mine, started it, and spent the morning and until about two, grinding axes and cutting wood. The engine is a bottle-shaped affair and will run either a grindstone or a circular saw which projects from a slit in a table. It did not take long to get up steam; a pressure of about six pounds to the square inch was enough to do the axe grinding, Lees holding the axes while I put water and sand upon the grindstone. Afterwards we got up a pressure of 40 pounds to the square inch (nearly) which we let down to 20, cutting wood to burn in the engine. With the circular saw it cuts wood as if it were cheese.

Now your letter: Firstly, Annie's additions to fauna and flora. Surely *Listera ovata* and *Antirrhinum majus* are not very likely to be native! Or at any rate the latter. But I quite agree that it is good to include plants that have escaped and gone wild. *Knautia* and *Artemisia* were a little unexpected by me, and I am glad to hear of them. *Senecio jacobaea* is conspicuous by its absence in Bedford Park, as I noted in the *Entomologist* in connection with *Euchelia jacobaeae*.

Please don't imagine that I am ill. I am very well on the whole, but once in a while I feel a little out of sorts, like most people. I never have been seriously ill in any way since I came out here. In many ways improvement is visible, e.g., I could not have done what I have been doing the last few days a year ago.

As I said, I derive great satisfaction from contemplating the fact that you and Annie are (or were, a fortnight ago) taking a good sensible holiday at Swanage, though I don't quite see why Annie should have to go off to the Boulgers. I trust you have enjoyed yourselves very thoroughly and improved greatly in health (or as greatly as it is possible in so short a holiday).

I hope Annie will send me a list of what she finds. *Pupa secale* is quite a characteristic south coast shell, from Lewes westward. Carlie also met with lots of *Melanagria galatea* somewhere down there (Dorset) when on his walking tour with Leslie if I remember right. Concerning Weymouth and Chesil Bank, *vide* Miss S. Marshall in *Nat. Hist. Notes* for 1882, I have them bound up, but I forget whether you have the volume in keeping. I believe O. F. Cambridge states in *Spiders of Dorset* that nine spiders are peculiar to Portland Island!

Aug. 27th, 8:45 p.m. This day has little to record, surveying all the while. In the morning we chained from Smith's Park (where we left off before) to the cabin, reaching the latter just in time for lunch, having gone through much thick wood — willows and quaking asp. After lunch we did the remaining 50 chains that remained to take us to the end of the 200 chain line and to the supposed situation of the corner of the section.

This last part took us past the mine and far up the gulch through much heavy timber till we finally came to the end on open ground at about 11,500 ft. alt., and about a mile from timber line, a spot where we could see much country, and on one side look into 'Horseshoe Bend', which you will remember from last year. We would have looked longer, but it was already late, and we had to get back to the cabin before dark. It is curious how some of the firs on the top of the rise, where fully exposed to the wind, have grown branched only on one side of the trunk, that opposite to the direction of the wind. The quaking asps up there are reduced to small bushes.

Aug. 28th. We have been looking all today for the corner 2 (in the map given), but without success. The lines we had to chain along (*vide* map) led us into a deep ravine with very steep sides, and the corner mark, which should have been on the further side, has very likely been overthrown by falling rocks and trees. Anyhow, we found nothing except an inscription on a large quaking asp to the effect that one E.C.N. came that way with two horses on June 9th, 1880.

Owing to a lengthy argument with Lees on Socialism — it's now ten and I haven't finished writing!)

A hail storm came on while we were looking for the corner and wetted us somewhat, but not to matter. Lees discovered the remains of a fine buck (*Cervus macrotis*) and is going to keep the horns.

Aug. 29th, 2:50 p.m. After doing some work at the forge, or rather blowing the bellows thereof, I saddled Ben and rode down to the Cusacks' in order to fetch Lees' buckboard for him. I shall soon be going up with the buckboard, and as we may not be down here and to town till next Sunday or Monday, I will leave this letter here to be posted by anyone going to town in the meanwhile.

I found some mail here for me which had been fetched from town in the interval, viz., Letters from Beutenmuller and Douglas, postcard from Geo. Roberts, two *Pall Mall Budgets*, *Commonweal*, and *Science Gossip*. I enclose a specimen of the *Aecidium* on *Berberis repens*.

Lees' cabin, Aug. 30th, 1888

Dear Frederic,

On arriving at the Cusacks' yesterday, I found in addition to the usual inhabitants of the house, Charley Cusack and his wife and two children, Mrs. C. C. being engaged in a clay model ('bas-relief') to be worked in Plaster of Paris afterwards, of the Sangre de Cristo Range. Mrs. Cusack the elder was in her room, not well, but she appeared, looking rather seedy, before I left. I gave them my letter to you to post next time anyone went to town, and then got the buckboard and with no mishap save that I stupidly went off the road for a quarter of a mile or so, arriving at Lees' just about dusk.

This morning we went off again on the surveying business and attempted to find a corner north of here and not very far from Davis'. This time we did no chaining, but with the compass contrived to reach a spot amongst the oak scrub where we judged the corner *ought* to be but, as usual, our most careful search was unavailing to discover any signs of a corner, and we begin to think that the government surveyor scamped his work and didn't mark these corners.

We had lunch down there in the house of an old Irishman named Joe McGinnis, an excellent man of whom all speak well, though rough and uneducated, as he well might be, having wandered for 30 years all over the States, never settling down nor (I believe) having any wife or family. At all events, he lives along in his cabin now, except when he is living with that other solitary man, Browning, of whom I have said somewhat in a former letter.

Leaving McGinnis'— before we went, I, being consulted as to a horse which has a tumor or cyst on its neck, we walked back to Smith's Park and then some way down the road towards the Cusacks', to search for a drill Lees lost there some time ago. But we did not find it, and came back to the cabin, sat discussing a variety of subjects, and then cooked and ate supper. And now I sit writing by the light of a miner's lamp, while Lees studies *The American Settler's Guide* for information as to the finding of lost corners.

Lees was telling me a rather remarkable anecdote, seeming, on the face of it, to indicate thought-transference between a man and a dog.

Lees' brother went to Gibraltar, leaving his dog in England. After a while this brother fell ill, in time seriously so, and at length died. Now for a whole week before he died the dog was howling on and off, and one evening gave a great yelp as if it had been shot, and then ceased howling. This attracted attention, of course, and someone went out to see what had happened to the dog, but found him apparently all right. Lees was there and heard the yelp, and happened to note the time. On comparing times afterward, and allowing for the difference in time at Gibraltar, the time of this yelp was found to correspond exactly with the death of the brother to whom the dog belonged. The dog did not howl at all after this.

Now Lees is not a liar, and no man would be likely to tell lies about the death of his own brother, and Lees was a witness to all this, so altogether the story must have great weight. Thought-transference is the only explanation at present occurring to me, but it opens a curious field of enquiry. Can you give any suggestion?

Aug. 1st, 7:35 p.m. Respecting the story of the dog howling, related yesterday, I should say it could not well be an example of thought transference as generally understood, because there is no reason to suppose that the dying man thought of the dog. The whole question involved is very ill-understood, and one needs to be specially cautious in dealing with it.

After breakfast I went to catch the horses (Ben and Romeo) and then went some way down the road to get out wood (firewood, quaking asp sticks) to be hauled up after lunch with the waggon. We accordingly went down early in the afternoon and loaded up some of the wood I had piled up but, being insecurely tied, the load fell to one side before we got it up to the cabin, and the end of it was that we left half by the roadside to be fetched another day.

Lees, Romeo and Ben

It now began to rain and, wishing to work under shelter, we went up to the mine and spent the rest of the afternoon there, Lees drilling while I took shovel and wheelbarrow and cleared loose rocks out of the tunnel. Lees has been making an enlarged plan of the 'township' and finds that the places where we looked for corners are not exactly where they ought to be, so this may account for our failure to find them.

Sept. 1st, 8:30 p.m. I am very sleepy tonight and shall not write much. We have been working all day and there is little to say about it. In the morning we drove in the buckboard down near to the 'corner' at Davis' and chained to the corner near Joe McGinnis' that we were looking for the other day, with the only result that we confirmed our previous location of the spot where the cor-

ner ought to be, and totally failed to discover any sign of a corner-mark there after much careful searching.

After lunch we went up to the mine. First we both worked in removing part of the dump of rocks where it was obstructing the stream that ran by the mine (the dump consists of rocks taken out of the mine). Then Lees went down to the cabin and I employed myself till suppertime in wheeling a lot of rocks and loose debris out of the tunnel on a wheelbarrow.

Sunday, Sept. 2nd. Lees was going down to Beddoes' today, and thence to town on Monday and to the Cusacks' after. I walked down to my house this morning, and tomorrow I walk into town in the morning, meet Lees, and get him to bring me out, together with some groceries (oatmeal, sugar, bacon) I must buy in town. I did not mention that Lees agreed to pay me 50 cents a day for my work when I was with him, so I shall have a few dollars coming to me from him.

(As I write, the little Cusack child, daughter of Charley C., Mora by name, is leaning on the table looking at me (I am at the Cusack's). She is a very pretty child, rounded pink cheeks, red hair, and most expressive dark grey eyes. I wish I could draw her portrait.)

As I passed the Splanns, coming down here, I found them all seated out on the verandah. They gave me a beetle and a fly Jim had caught, and a dead hummingbird, killed, they said, by the hail. They had preserved it by pressing it in paper as if it were a flower. This afternoon I have been writing up my diary and fauna lists. Annie's mignonette is coming up, but the forget-me-not is represented by only two plants. All are very small as yet.

Sept. 3rd, at home. Have walked to town, and am going out with Lees. Have got your letter and Annie's very good list of Swanage flora, which I shall go through in detail when I get back. I am very glad you and Annie were able to get out and enjoy yourselves at Swanage thus. How one might enjoy these mountains if one were not alone! This is a country full of strange things and beautiful things, but quite too solitary for me.

Mansell Pleydell has a list of Mollusca of Dorsetshire in *Proc. Dorset Club*, which is in the library of S.L.E.S. Other mail I got is: *Pall Mall Budget*, Tanner's *Practice of Medicine* (from Uncle Douglas of Wimpole Street; *Commonweal*, letter from Bruner, letter from Ellis (a fungus I sent him is named provisionally *Uromyces castaneus* sp. nov., letter from Farlow, who says 'I regret to say that it is the habit of some of our mycologists to call everything new off-hand' — doubtless referring to Ellis. Letter from C. V. Riley, letter from Dr. Hamilton, about Custer County beetles. He says four I sent him are new to Colorado, and two were described only from single specimens, and no others were known. Another was known from two specimens, and I sent two more.

West Cliff, Sept. 4th, 1888

Dear Frederic,

I posted your letter yesterday, and henceforth, while the train is not running, shall probably post them on Friday, Saturday, or even Monday, instead of in the middle of the week, so your letter is delayed and does not arrive till the latter end of each week, and so I shall not go in on Tuesday or Wednesday. After leaving the postoffice and also spending a small fortune in groceries (crushed oats 10 lbs, $1.00, make excellent porridge; sugar, 10 lbs, $1.00, and bacon 25 cents).

I drove out from town with Lees. As I was going out with him, he told me two things: (1.) He had heard from Payn, who was at Dillon and wanted $50 sent on to him at Egeria [in Routt Co. Ed.], where he was going. (2.) He had not heard from Cox, who went to Kansas City and has not been heard of for more than a week, to the great distress of Mrs. Cox. Cox is a most reckless man and there is no knowing what he may not do and what consequences may ensue to wife and family. At the present time, he must owe much more money than he has.

Lees found he had no money and had forgotten his cheque book when he got to town, and so went back to his cabin, then down again and to town, and back to Mrs. Cox's at about twelve! As he told me this morning, he must have 'rustled!'

This morning after breakfast I read some of Tanner's *Practice of Medicine* and then meant to do a lot of writing, instead of which I collapsed and had to lie down till about three, after which I wrote letters to Ellis and Farlow, enclosing fungi, and to Beutenmuller, enclosing Tiniae (moths).

10 p.m. I was going through Annie's Swanage list when I heard voices and, on opening the door, let in Mrs. Cusack and Regy, who brought mail which Mrs. Brock had fetched, viz., letters from Wolle, about algae, and Leslie, and *Insect Life* No.2, and *Ornith. and Oölogist*.

Leslie's letter says he has as yet no situation, 'but have got one or two promised in the sweet bye-and-bye.' Then he goes on: 'I am awfully pleased with the climate, as much of it as I have already seen!' Douglas seems both lively and happy. He writes, 'About a week ago, one very hot morning, a cat went mad in the back yard. I, being the only man present, thought it best to kill it, and so took up an axe and committed the murder. In the afternoon, a miserable, stupid, idiot of a boy came and wanted to know whether I had seen a cat — as if I kept cats! It was buried!' You observe, Leslie has a sense of the humorous!

Insect Life is good as before, with notes on every kind of thing. There are two extracts from my letters given (pp. 37-38) about grasshoppers and *Dicerca*. With the mail comes a slip 'for books, duty $1.00, a most appalling announcement! When I get to the postoffice I must inspect books and see whether they are worth it and if not, declare it must be 'someone else of the same name' they were meant for! I can't imagine what books they can be.

Having gone through Annie's Swanage list, I see all her species are marked in my 'London Catalog' as recorded from Surrey except the following: *Pastinaca sativa, Bartonia odontites* var. *verna* (this is given for three counties only in S. Cat. and so should be rare; I never saw it myself, *Carduus marianus* (and I suppose, *Silybum marianum*), *Galium mollugo* var. *scabrum* (this var. is not in L. C.), *Aspidium aculeatum* (unless it is = *lobatum*), *Scandix pecten-veneris, Armeria maritima, Glaucium luteum* (but grows I believe at Deal and near Hastings), *Silene maritima, Eryngium maritimum, Equisetum telmateia* (not in L. C. Is it *E palustre?*). *Marasmius oreades,* and *Agaricus arvensis.* I have no definite Surrey records for them, but they doubtless occur.

Sept. 5th, 7:30 p.m. Have been busy all today over my correspondence, and have made good progress, besides doing more collecting and making some quite remarkable finds in the immediate vicinity of my house. For one thing, a lot of an *Aecidium* I wanted for Ellis' North American Fungi) on *Artemisia*). Then a good spider, but best of all, three kinds of larvae which I have here sketched, not scientifically accurately but so as to give you a some notion of what they are. The first is, I am nearly sure, the larva of *Smerinthus astarte,* which is near to the British species *S. ocellatus.* The larva is very like *S. populi* and feeds on quaking asp. The second is a *Lasiocampa,* rusty grey, hairy, and ridiculous, feeding also on quaking asp. The third I got several of, most extraordinary-looking larvae they are, very conspicuous on willow leaves. They come near to a species called *A. isabella,* and are black in front and behind, and brown in the middle, the black parts having bundles of white hairs interspersed.

Sept. 6th, 7:35 p.m. I have spent the whole of today indexing the *West American Scientist,* so there is nothing whatever to tell you about, except that I chanced on a saw-fly larva new to me — green with a blue-grey dorsal band, on a willow tree by the well when I was going for water. I am glad to get this indexing over. It is a bigger job than I quite expected. It has taken me two whole days, but then there were four volumes to do.

Sept. 7th, 9:10 p.m. I was going to town this morning and, having got ready to start, I went over to the Cusacks' to see if they wanted anything posted, and they mentioned that Mrs. Brock had been to town yesterday and might perhaps have got my mail. So I went down there to see and, sure enough, I met Mrs. Brock coming up, mail in hand, but your letter was not there. What she brought me was: Letters from H. A. Pilsbry (about shells; one of my *Pupae* is possibly a new species), Mother, Bruner (with names of some of my Orthoptera — three new to Colorado list), Radenhausen (with some valuable extracts from papers on Colorado species — list of 31 Colorado spiders, etc.) and Morrison (about the *Colorado Biological Association.* He is going to get circulars printed at once), postcard from Orcutt, *Public Opinion* from Annie (best thanks. It has much in it I shall like to read, but have not yet had time to read it), and *Canadian Entomologist* for Aug. and Sept. (September number has a paper of mine, 'Can insects distinguish red from yellow?').

Mrs. Brock was going into town again today, she said, after groceries, so I gave her a lot of letters to post, but did not go in today myself. Then I went back to my house and wrote, entered up my fauna list, busying myself till suppertime, after which I went down to Brock's, and soon after I got there Mrs. B. returned, bringing your letter and also *Pall Mall Budget, Commonweal,* and three volumes of an excellent book on surgery (Treve's *Manual*) which I was exceeding glad to see, though it did cost me a dollar for duty.

In answer to your letter: I am sorry you couldn't get away to the Klinian Field Day! I am very sorry to hear about the Read child; they must feel bad about it. I care less for poetry than most people, but less for Browning than most poets that I like at all, I must say. I didn't mean to ask you to 'go in for' micro-fungi, but you might cast an eye around for then in your walks abroad (e.g., you are likely to find *Aecidium tussilaginis* on *Tussilago farfara*).

Pall Mall Budget has a lot of discussion on the marriage question. It seems to me it's much like of law — how much ought to be compelled? I suppose that no one would argue that union should be other than permanent. The question is, in cases where it is not naturally so, ought it to be so by compulsion? However, I will read the discussion and let you know what I think of it. Yes, Annie is quite right about your not sending me her letters, though it *is* hard lines, but keep them by for me to read at some future time.

Charley Cusack is going to town tomorrow, and I think perhaps I wil send this by him, although it isn't much of a letter. I may think better of it and take it in myself on Monday, but will end up now so that it will be ready.

Sept. 8th, 1888

Dear Frederic,

I gave the last letter to you to Charlie Cusack to post this morning as he was going to town, and at the same time asked him to bring me out some flour and lamp oil of which I was in need. After breakfast, I thought I would go for a walk, and was going down by Cox's to look at a horse which has a sore on its shoulder, possibly due to diseased bone, and then down as far as my old house by Swift Creek and back. I looked in at the Cusack's on the way, and while I was there a young man generally styled 'The Kid' came riding up and somewhat incoherently stated that 'Cox and horse have falled, and I was to see whether the nose was broken, if I would come down.' I thought he meant the horse's nose, but it turned out to be Cox's.

The nose was not broken, but the nasal bones seemed considerably out of joint, and the nose was quite awry. Cox complained of nothing but the look of it, and so I left him, saying he could apply pressure either now and then with his fingers, or continually with a bandage, and perhaps get it into shape. Cox told me, confidentially (I wasn't to breathe a word to anyone) that it was really done with the butt end of a revolver (doubtless in some quarrel) and he had no fall after all.

After this, I went on my way and down to my old house and back again, but found very little that was new to me, the best thing caught being a male *Colias eriphyle*, which is here the autumn brood of *C. eurytheme*. This afternoon I did up a box of butterflies for W. H. Edwards, read a little, and went out a little, and this evening I took the last *Pall Mall Budget* over to the Cusacks, and having read the views of Mrs. Cair on marriage, discussed them with Mrs. C.

At the outset, one feels one ought to be very careful in dealing with such a question because one's natural prejudices are very liable to make one unfair, although they may be based on reason. The argument as it occurs to me now is this way: (1.) Ideally marriage should be based on sympathy. (2.) Marriage based on sympathy will hold of its own accord, law or no law; it must be permanent. (3.) Many marriages are not based on sympathy and would cease if not obliged to continue by law. Question 1. Ought law to interfere with natural antipathies and cement what was from the beginning a mistake? (4.) Is it possible that many are unable to find anyone they really love, but find some they would associate with for the sake of the comforts of home? Question 2. Ought such to marry? And if so, (5.) Ought marriages, confessedly not based on love (sympathy) to be enforcedly permanent?

So far as I can see, the best laws to govern marriage would be: (1.) Marriage to be a free contract entered in by both parties (The best facilities should be given for the parties to find out whether they did love one another. If they don't, I don't see quite how the state can judge of that. It's like the oaths question). (2.) Separation to be granted at the wish of either party, but this is not to dissolve the bond; that is, the separated parties should not be allowed to marry again, and if the wife has been, owing to her married life, disbarred from learning a trade, the husband ought to support her unless she abandons him for someone else. (3.) No absolute divorce to be granted.

But you must only take this as a temporary suggestion. The whole thing is much too difficult to be settled in this off-hand manner, and I may finally arrive at some quite different opinion. Possibly the most tangible good that can be done at present is in individual cases to try to see that, on the one hand, those who do love can get married, and those who do not, don't. The trouble is that so many girls don't know how they may live unless they marry, and so come to look upon any sort of marriage as desirable.

Men and women ought to have the best facilities for knowing one another, and a real friendship should always be formed before marriage is dreamt of. I wish Herbert Spencer [one of the most argumentative and discussed English thinkers of the Victorian period. Ed.] would state his views on this subject (perhaps he has), as I should think they would afford us the strongest arguments on the non-interference or anarchic side. What do you and Annie think about it?

Sunday, Sept. 9th. A little writing, and some reading of Treve's *Surgery* is all I have really done today. I went down to Cox's in the afternoon to borrow Newman's *Moths* to take notes from, on poplar and willow feeding insects, of which I am making a list, and down there I met Charley Cusack and wife on a visit.

Cox's nose looks better, and he is out and about and apparently quite well.

This evening we had service, it being Sunday, at the Cusacks', to which there turned up also Louis Howard and Miss Sidford, Cardy Lees, and Cox. Miss Sidford is going tomorrow to stay with the Beckwiths, who are cattle people in rather a wholesale way, and own most of the cattle on the prairie in the valley. Another bit of news is that Brock is away in Rosita to see a friend of his, Turner, who used to be postmaster there, now dangerously ill with diphtheria, of which there seems to be just now an epidemic in Rosita. Brock rode to Rosita the other night on hearing of Turner's illness, although he had done a hard day's work. Mrs. Brock is going back to Iowa in about a week on a visit to her people.

Mrs. Charley Cusack has been telling me that she knew a Mr. Manville Fenn, an author, but I can't really make out whether it is really your father or not. Her account of it is this: About nine years ago she lived with her mother near Romford, in Essex (she was a Brantville then) and not infrequently a Mr. Manville Fenn, an author who was blind (!) used to come down from (she thought) London. She frequently saw him, but her mother knew him pretty well. Mrs. Cusack senior tells me that Mrs. Charlie Cusack's memory is not an accurate one, or at least not a good one, and so she may have been mistaken about his being blind. If not, it must be someone else, I suppose. I questioned her closely, but she (though appearing rather uncertain about details) kept to the above. She says she shall write and ask her mother about it.

Sept. 10th. Lees went to town today and brought me out a letter from Strecker and a postcard from C. F. Ancey, and so I have packed up about 50 species (if he buys them, it will be about $2.50) and got them ready to be 'expressed', when I remembered that the train was not running and no one could express anything. I don't know exactly what to do now, whether to send them on by the mail coach and have them expressed from Cañon City or Cotopaxi, or wait (perhaps a month or more) till the train runs again.

Chamberlain came over to my house late this afternoon and told me that he had rented Splann's house from one Harrold, the real owner of it, and was to take possession of it on Oct. 1. But he feared he might have a little trouble in getting the Splanns to leave, and so, according to law, was going to serve a notice on them (that is, if his claim was valid, of course). (In this country you can't turn a man out of a house of which he has possession without a notice of, I think, ten days, even if the house is yours.) It was necessary that someone should witness that this notice was served, so I, at Chamberlain's request, went over with him and saw him duly deliver the document. The Splanns were very irate and declared they wouldn't go, but I did not attempt to get into the rights and wrongs of the question, and will leave that to the parties concerned.

It seems that Mrs. Brock's going away means more than appears on the surface. Brock was telling Mrs. Cusack about his affairs, and says that they cannot live together any longer. I am very sorry that this should be so, but they never quite 'hit it off' together. Both Mr. and Mrs. Brock have their faults, and perhaps the principal fault on each side is inability to put up with the other's failings.

I had another surgical case to attend to today. Regy's horse (the one he got in exchange for Specklewattle) has an abscess on its back, and I was asked to examine and report. It looks as if it might heal, but if not I must investigate for dead bone.

Sept. 11th, 7:30 p.m. I am writing at the Cusacks'. Miss Urquhart went to town and Regy is working for Brock, so Mrs. Cusack being alone, I came over and read to her from *Public Opinion*, and talked for a time. Then we had supper, and just now Miss U. returned and brought me a letter from Hulst (Editor of *Ent. Mag.*) who says he will publish my paper on *Anthocharis* and that he will exchange books for insects, and will name the insects besides.

Mrs. Brock is up here now. Mrs. Cusack went down to see her this afternoon, and thinks she has persuaded her not to go away after all. (I hope so; it will be very bad for Brock if she went.) I dug some bulbs of *Calochortus* [*gunnisonii*. Ed.] today and got some seeds for Orcutt to sell. I enclose some seeds for Annie. It is a pretty flower with three white petals, green at their bases, and slightly tinged with purple.

Sept. 12th, 7:25 p.m. The morning having been devoted to writing letters, early in the afternoon I went down to the Cox's to return 'Newman', which I had borrowed. On my way back from there I found a species of microfungus appearing as orange spots abundantly on the undersides of the leaves of a wild gooseberry bush. (I am nearly sure it is *Uredo ribicola* E. & E.) Later, I went over to Chamberlain's to get some peas and potatoes which he had promised me.

Chamberlain says that the Splanns have become still more obstreperous about the house. Old Splann and Jim threatened him yesterday with pitchforks when he went down there, but Harold, who rented the place to Chamberlain has, it seems, written to tell the Splanns they may stay. So Chamberlain will not attempt to take possession, and of course will not pay his rent (or do the work which was to have been done instead of rent, viz., put up a wire fence).

Chamberlain has an abundance of peas and I was glad to get these from him, as I scarcely ever have any green vegetables. Peas, potatoes, and bacon are boiling together at the present moment.

I am making a list of the insects which frequent species of *Salix* and *Populus*. At present, taking published records only, my list stands as follows: *Populus*: Lepidoptera, 29; Hymenoptera, 6; Coleoptera, 3. *Salix*: Lepidoptera, 37; Hymenoptera, 4; Coleoptera, 6; Hemiptera, 3, of which others are common to *Populus* and *Salix*: Lepidoptera, 13; Hymenoptera, 1. This list is nothing like perfect, but even as it stands it shows how many are the insects frequenting any particular kind of tree.

What has become of the 'country members' scheme of S.L.E.S. Has it collapsed? The country members don't seem to be in any hurry to join! S.L.E.S. wants a good shaking.

Sept. 13th. Have walked to town and got mail, viz., your letter, *Proc. S.L.E.S.*, Longman,

Contemporary 19th Century (for all of which best thanks. Thanks also to Annie for white heather). Other letters are from Clive, Mother, Wallis Kew, and a postcard from W. West asking for algae. Also *Pall Mall Budget*. I enclose *Puccinia bigeloviae*, n. sp. The S.L.E.S. *Proceedings* are good, but I see abundant evidence of clumsy proof-reading even in the hasty look I have had at it. There is one very serious error on p. 89. I enclose a note on it; please do not fail to have it read and tell Barker to correct it in the next *Proceedings*. I cannot think how it can have occurred. *Very* careless of Barker.

[Letter from Annie's father]

Syon Lodge, Isleworth
Sept. 13th, 1888

Dear Mr. Cockerell:

You give me the credit in your letter for having done what I thought was for the best when I forbade any correspondence between you and my daughter Annie. I have no doubt whatever that when you reach my age and position you also will think as I did and will, if you have not already done so, realise the fact that it was your duty to have come direct to the father or mother and spoken out in a frank, manly way respecting your feelings toward the child. There was nothing of this but the whole affair was sprung upon me like a crime after I had been kept in profound ignorance of the matter.

Of course I had noticed your visits and had been told that they were merely those of a companion to my son due to mutuality of tastes. Then just as you were leaving England I learned that you wished to correspond with Annie — but not from you. However, setting aside all ultra notions of etiquette I felt then and I feel now that was right — that it would have been a great mistake for any engagement to be entered into between you and Annie.

Look at your positions. You were, as you say, in bad health, leaving England for an indefinite period without prospects and altogether in a position that should have made you say to yourself, 'It is not fair to the woman I care for to ask her to tie herself to me in any way. If she cares for me she will wait. Let the future settle all that.'

That is my opinion of the matter and I think any parent will agree that it is perfectly just and when you are twenty years older you will be in a better position to judge its correctness though I cannot expect it now.

As to Annie's age, that has nothing to do with it. So long as a girl remains under her parents' charge, they surely have a perfect right to dictate what line of conduct she ought to follow while she resides beneath their roof.

You make one great error in your letter to me. You say I do not like you personally. I *do* and always did, both you and your brother. If I had not liked you, you would not have visited at my house and been made a welcome guest, for I have always been exceedingly particular as to who came to my place, for my children's sake. I always liked you both for your loving study and your variance from the ordinary puppy of everyday life.

What I did not like were your foolish Utopian notions on Socialism all of which I hope you will see must stand in your light if you wish to push your way in the world. Excuse me for speaking so plainly, but I write as Annie's father, the man you seem to wish to make your own by the ordinary tie. I hope, however, more contact with the world is showing you that it cannot be made smooth as Morris and company seek to make it.

However, I need not dwell upon this point as our ideas change vastly as we grow older and I believe that if you had a father always to guide, you would have thought differently.

Now as to this writing — I still think the same. Hold yourself free and leave Annie free. You are constantly hearing of her welfare, she as frequently hearing of yours. You own frankly that you cannot ask her to be your wife for some time to come so wait patiently all you can. If in the future you care for her and she cares for you, come to me and say, 'I can offer her a comfortable house,' well, then, it will be quite time enough to put me to the proof as to what are my feelings toward you.

There, I have written to you simply and sincerely what I believe is right for both of you. Culprits do not agree with their judges but all the same they would be judged. This letter I shall first send to your mother and ask her ideas on the matter, and I have also placed it in Annie's hands.

I am, very truly yours,
Geo. Manville Fenn

P.S. The result of my placing this in Annie's hands she will tell you herself.

Sept. 27th, 1888, 9:05 p.m.

Dear Annie:
At last! I am glad. I got your letter this evening, together with the one from your father.

It is like being let out of prison, to be able to write, and for you to write to me. I cannot complain of your father's letter, considering his point of view; indeed it is far more moderate than I expected. How can I be otherwise than thankful? I wish that you could have written your letter in reply to what I *would* have written to you, but I must be patient for another month, and this letter is a very nice one, after all. I know not what I have wrongly taken for granted, but you see there was no help for it; all I could do was to say what I thought. Long ago I told you how I loved you, and I do not know anything that I wrote or said that I could alter; that I do love you is part of my existence and maybe the best part of it. Whatever it has been to you, it has given *me* hope where I should otherwise have been hopeless, and helped my whole life. Loving you so, It was not easy to go abroad and leave you, and that to a country where I had small chance or wish to make a home, but all the time I have looked forward to my return (as I promised), and hoped when once more in England to find a means of earning enough to support a family. I believe, if no accident befalls, that this time will come in a

year or two, and then, it will only be natural that I shall ask you to be my wife.

In the meanwhile, I hoped that you would write to me, but that could not be, until now. For my part, it has been a great thing to be able to write fully to Frederic and to hear from him constantly about you. I cannot be too grateful to him for his letters. For the future, you will write to me, and until I have made a home in England, I have no right to ask anything further of you.

But, Annie, write all you can; let us be true friends now, working together; though so far apart, encouraging one another. There is a bright hope for the future, but its realisation depends much upon the present, and then, who dare say that this or that *will* be? Love is surely potent for good in times of trouble and endeavor, if at all!

And that you may write as soon as possible, I will not keep you waiting longer than I need; I will post this tomorrow. I have a letter writing to Frederic — the ordinary weekly letter — that I will send to him, but afterwards, they will, of course, go to you.

I have some hope of returning next summer — surely it is time! But I suppose I shall have to do whatever is considered best for my health, and that will no doubt be best for all concerned in the long run. Mother evidently expects me to stay the three years, as she writes of coming out here next spring for a year (but don't tell anyone; she doesn't want it mentioned). What do *you* think about it?

We must, however, face the *possibility* of my not being able to live in England; lots of people out here are unfortunately so, but I do not feel this likely, and whatever the doctors may say about it, I shall, of course, give England a good trial before I give it up. It is not much use talking now of what we might do in this necessity; certainly I would not give up hope, but it is sometimes well to realise what the worst may be.

How I long for a good talk with you! I haven't met a single person to talk to quite openly since June 23, 1887. Sometimes one feels as if there were no real human beings of flesh and blood atall — only animals and angels! Your spirit has kept me company so long that I shall feel quite astonished to find you are a real person on my return!

There is a world of difference between *kindness* and *sympathy*, somehow. All the while I have lived here I have received the greatest kindness possible from all sorts of people, especially Mrs. Cusack, and of course it has been a great thing for me, but it is like giving a thirsty man food only; it leaves him thirsty all the same. It was about this time two years ago that we first became friends. What pleasant days those were!! And what talks and arguments! And how one remembers the "squash" at 5. Priory. When you wanted to know when I was most happy, and I talked some nonsense about chasing butterflies, and finally declined to tell you! And the dance at the Percival Clarke's, when we talked about that 'happiness' paper of mine; then those essays we used to write, and the definitions we concocted. Perhaps Boxing-day evening was the nicest of all, though, but it's hard to say. Once or twice we even walked together, but that was quite exceptional — unfortunately. One nice walk was to the Allport's from 20 Woodstock — and after you had gone to Isleworth, a walk to Sunnersbury — you remember? How nice it was to look forward to the Sunday visits to Syon Lodge, too. Then the last few sad days — the walk to the station and the Gardening Society meeting, and June 23rd — Annie! Annie!

Well, I'll finish for the present,

Yours lovingly, Theo

[The above segment of this letter was evidently private, sent independently of the remainder (below) which was probably intended particularly for Frederic's eyes. Ed.]

Sept. 28th. Thanks muchly for the Swanage Flora and Fauna list. Mightn't you send some notes about Swanage flora to *Science Gossip*? They would be interesting in connection with the recent accounts of Flora of North Downs, South Downs, and Hastings districts, and Arnold's W. Sussex and Devon lists. I see *Glaucium luteum* is recorded for near Hastings in the last *Sci. Goss.* (I said in a former letter I thought it was found that way.) You will see two notes about *Geranium molle* var. *alba* in the last two *Science Gossips*. Is the name *alba* your own? I don't think the variety has any published name yet, and the same may be said for *Origanum vulgare* var. *alba*. I see you also found *Prunella vulgaris alba*; that is surely rare. You must write an account of these white varieties (see my notes on the subject in the last *Sci. Goss.* Of the shells, *Trochus magnus* and *Venus exoleta* are the most interesting. *Hesperia actaeon* was a great find! Dorset is the only county for it in England, I believe.

I have got to dig 750 bulbs of *Calochortus* 'at once', and there is the hardest kind of sod! They are for Orcutt, who sells wholesale. I shall charge $7.50 for them.

12:15. .Mrs. Cusack just came over and asked me to lunch, and poured forth her troubles *re* Miss Urquhart. As she says, Miss U. is a *flirt*. Here is Frank apparently in love with her, and he doesn't flirt with her, but Regy, who cares only to amuse himself, flirts all the time. And as for her, she seems to be willing to flirt with anyone if she gets a chance. Today Louis and Miss S., Miss U., and Raynor have gone up to the Lake of the Clouds, and Mrs. C. says Miss U. is flirting with Raynor. What would you do in Mrs. C.'s place? I don't envy her. I think I would be disposed to ship Miss U. right back to her mother without delay. Miss U. is a good girl in some respects, but seems to have no stability of character or purpose. Yet Mrs. C. says she is impossible to influence by argument or entreaty, so as to do some permanent good. Of course, the men around here, being nearly all flirts themselves, are no doubt responsible for most of the trouble. How foolish otherwise excellent people can be!

4:00 p.m. Have walked to town. No mail for me.

8:30 p.m. Dear Annie,

Having just finished a repast of bread, bacon fat, oatmeal and tea, I proceed to tell you what little there is since I posted your letter. On my way to town, I was fortunate in finding a quantity of the thistle fungus, *Puccinia suaveolens*, which is found also at Bedford Park on the thistles. And on *Bigelovia* (that is something akin to *Senecio*, [= *Chrysothamnus*. Ed.] there was plenty of the new species, *Puccinia bigeloviae*, and aphids that looked exactly like the fungus (being black) except on close inspection. Query: Was it protective resemblance?

In town I posted your letter, also letters to your father and Frederic. I got permission to gum one of my Colorado Biological Association circulars up in the window of the postoffice store for the edification of the multitude. I found Mrs. Brock disconsolate at the hotel, with the child. She had no means of getting home. Brock was at Rosita, and Cox, who promised to take her out, had disappeared in company with a certain Humphrey, and she didn't know when she could go. I offered to return to town with any rig I could borrow, and fetch her out, but she said she had no doubt Cox would take her some time this evening — and if not, Lees goes to town tomorrow. You see, staying at the hotel is expensive. Mrs. B. had already run up $4.50.

I didn't wait for the evening mail but walked out, and as I walked it grew dark, and I reached the Cusacks' at about 7:30, where I took a rest. I found Lees there.

Sept. 29th, 7 p.m. Before six this morning I was awakened from my slumbers by Lees, who wanted to know whether I would go and hunt for the horse, 'Romeo', who was lost somewhere up by Gibb's Peak. Now this would involve walking nearly if not quite as far as to Lees' cabin, and I was a little stiff from yesterday's walk to town. Besides, my boots are getting alarmingly thin about the soles. Then there were those bulbs for Orcutt. — 'No, I really couldn't go and hunt for Romeo. Very sorry.' — And then went to sleep

again, or rather, dozed, until I got up, feeling very lazy, at half past eight.

Breakfast over, I went down to see what had become of Mrs. Brock (if she hadn't returned she wanted me to feed the magpie, she said yesterday) but there she was, having come out with Cox last night after all. Mrs. Brock says Brock is going freighting for three months, and so she is going back to her home in Iowa for the winter, but will return in the spring. They want to sell their ranch and go elsewhere if possible.

After this, I came up to my house and started digging *Calochortus gunnisonii* bulbs for Orcutt (he wants 750; I charge a cent each). In about two hours I dug 50, and then had lunch. After lunch I dug about 20 or thereabouts and was stopped by rain coming on. As I get only 50 cents and board for a whole day's work ranching, digging these bulbs really pays better.

It was chilly towards evening, so I went over and sat by the Cusacks' fire reading *Pall Mall Budget*, coming back here at about 20 to six, when I cooked supper as quickly as I could, for it was getting dark (and you know the stove is out on the verandah). When I am in a hurry I cook a meal up in this wise: Three things on the fire, (1.) Kettle to boil water for tea. (2.) Frying pan to fry slices of potato in grease. (3.) Skilly to boil bacon (three slices) to get rid of its saltiness; then fry it, and after that, fry a flapjack in the bacon grease. This makes a first rate supper and takes very little time. Try it!

I found a parasitic grass fungus growing right in front of my house, and just up the path to the well, yet I never saw it until today when I chanced upon it while digging bulbs! How things do grow right under one's nose without being noticed!

9:40 p.m. Have been going more carefully through the Swanage list, and am ever more persuaded some account of it should be published. I notice some more plants not found in Surrey (*vide* my comments on the first list): *Aster tripolium*, *Crataegus oxyacantha* var. *monogyna*, *Drosera longifolia* (is this *anglica*?), *Plantago maritima*,

Pinguicula lusitanica (this last is a good find). But isn't it rather better to arrange a catalog according to natural orders than alphabetically? It gives one a better grasp of its features.

Sunday, Sept. 30th, 7 p.m. Most of the morning was spent in writing letters, and doing up some 65 species of beetles to be named by Dr. Hamilton. This afternoon I dug about 30 more *Calochortus* bulbs, making about 100 with those already dug. Then I read a couple of chapters of the *Surgery Manual* and settled down to a letter to Carlie, when I was interrupted by Mrs. Cusack, bringing copies of *Times* (weekly edition) for me to cut bits out of.

8:25. I am at the Cusacks' and was interrupted by the prayers and singing. When Mrs. Cusack came over to my house she further unburdened her mind on the subject of Miss Urquhart. Mrs. C. had been speaking to her on the subject of flirting, and especially with Raynor (who has departed. Lees took him to town the other day and he went off by train). She seemed to think she had not acted otherwise than she should, but would reform in future. I must say I think the men are more to blame than she is. She is, at present, as far as one can see, exceedingly wanting in 'common sense' and has not the natural instinct to do wisely.

Cox and Mrs. Cox have just come up with Lees. Cox paid me $2.50 for the picture I painted, though it is not yet quite finished. I must try to finish it tomorrow. (It's rather difficult to write with everyone talking in the room.) Cox pays me now a further $2.50 for the picture of the house (not yet commenced) as he is going away and will not be able to pay me later.

I found another grass fungus new to me by my house today. It is Ergot (*Claviceps purpurea*) or something very near it (see account of ergot in 'Thome'). Ergot has already been recorded for Colorado.

I have just been totting up my additions to my Colorado and Middlesex flora and fauna lists for September, with the following results: Colorado: birds, 1, and 1 var., Coleoptera, 34 and one fossil; Orthoptera, 5, and 1 fossil; Neuroptera, 1 fossil; Diptera, 1 fossil; Homoptera, 1, and 2 fossil; Arachnida, 31, Phaenogamia, 4 vars.; Fungi, 12. Middlesex: Trichoscolices, 1; Coleoptera, 6; Lepidoptera (Heterocera), 4; Hymenoptera, 6; Mollusca, 2 vars.; Mammalia; 1 fossil. Many of the Colorado additions (including all the fossils) were taken from extracts from published records furnished me by Radenhausen, of Davenport, Iowa.

Oct. 1st, 6:45 p.m. Immediately after breakfast I got a few things ready for the post, as Louis Howard is going to town (he has not yet returned), and then I went down to the Cox's and finished their picture of the mountains and commenced one of the house, getting the drawing done, and the roof in colours.

Talking of sketching, there is an amusing anecdote in a recent *St. James Budget*. An artist relates he was painting in the country, when a rustic came up and remarked, 'Well! I wonder a man of your health and strength isn't ashamed of having no occupation!'

Most of the afternoon (till four) I devoted to digging *Calochortus* bulbs, and dug some 60. After that I read the chapter on burns in *Manual of Surgery*, and then it was about time for supper. I also did a little collecting this afternoon, the principle result being a beetle-and-a-half new to me (the half is a fragmentary *Aphodius*).

Frank Cusack departed today, taking 'Ferris', which is his horse, with him. He goes to work for a month at the Hamp's in Pueblo County. His stay at home has been short, but Mrs. C. thinks that, owing to Miss U.'s flirtatious ways, he no longer cares for her (which is a good thing for him). Of course, at no time did he have any real sympathy for the girl.

Oct. 2nd, 7:45 p.m. Was feeling quite out of sorts when I woke up this morning, but cooked and ate breakfast and was better. Then I went down to Brock's to see whether he had any money (I want the $5.50 he owes me for work in the spring; he hadn't, but would get some to-day). Then I returned to my house and donned some additional clothing (for it was cloudy and a bit chilly) and went down to the Cox's, where I stayed till a little after four, sketching the house. There is more in this drawing than I thought, but it is easier than the mountains.

Cox shot three jack-rabbits (the hare of this country) and presented me with one. Beside its food use, I am glad of the skin for a specimen. Mrs. Cox wants to go and spend some hours at the Kettle's tomorrow (was invited to 'spend the day') and I want to go to town to post this and get mail, so we have arranged that I drive Mrs. Cox to the Kettle's, go to town, and pick her up on my way back. I borrow the Cusack buckboard and take one of Cox's horses.

Coming up from the Cox's, I looked in at the Brock's, where Mrs. Cusack was helping Mrs. B. pack up; she departs for Iowa in a few days. Soon after I got back to my house, there came on a most violent storm — thunder and much rain — so I could not cook supper till after dark.

I have been reading some interesting things from a report of meeting of British Association (in *Times* weekly edition). I see it stated that more children are born under bad (i.e., town) conditions of life than good, but they are less healthy. I haven't the paper by me, but no doubt you will have read it. It is a point worth noting that a keen struggle for existence does not necessarily result in the survival of the fit, because there are, under very bad conditions, no fit to survive!

I enclose a note for the South London Ent. & Nat. Hist. Soc., which Frederic might take when he next goes to a meeting there.

P. S. Mrs. Cusack says she will give me $1.50 each for as many pictures as I like to do [for] her! I feel I *ought* to do her what she wants for nothing, but she won't have that, and really, in my impecunious condition I can't afford to be *too* grand. Another question arises — how much

ought I to charge for pictures? I think $1.50 each is about what they should be worth, judging by the time taken to do them, but, if so, was I right in taking $2.50 each from Cox because he was pleased to offer it? And also, shall I be right in future in taking more than $1.50 if it is spontaneously offered?

I don't know but that one does most wisely to get all one can in all cases for one's work, seeing that that's the rule of the day, if everyone else does it, but I only defend this as a defensive measure, to enable one to keep the same advantages as others, and not get trodden down. And then, pictures are by no means necessary, and nobody need buy them. But I wish you would tell me what you think about it. Will you not decide for me?

Another thing I sometimes have trouble about is, ought I to charge anything for doctoring? I am frequently called to attend various animals and people (as you will have gathered from letters) and it certainly costs *me* time and trouble, besides much work, as reading up the *Surgery Manual*, etc. But, thinking this over, I have come quite to the conclusion that, not being a professional, I have no reason to charge anything whatever, except, for instance, in such a case as this: Joe McGinnis has a horse with a bad neck, and he said that if the place did not heal, he would send for me to open it and explore for dead bone. Now this would involve a long day's journey, there and back, and I should accordingly charge Joe 50 cents for the trouble of *going there*, and not for the doctoring. It is very necessary to avoid any semblance of quackery, which is already too frequent by far in America.

Have driven Mrs. Cox and infants to the Kettle's, and come on to the town. Got mail: Letter from Frederic. I don't think Lees would like the story of his brother and the dog to be published. The cutting *re* cowboys getting drowned is probably true in the main. It must have been a 'freshet' [we call it a flash flood. Ed.]. I know some were drowned; letter from Mother; letter from Ellis, about fungi. I seem to have sent him a new agaric (*Inocybe*); postcard from Cragin, expressing approval of C. B. Ass'n., and wishing me success; postcard from [Francis] Wolle, with names of some algae sent; *Public Opinion*, for which best thanks to Frederic; *Journal of Mycology*, two numbers, from Ellis; *The Standard*, Henry George's paper. I wonder why sent to me; it comes from the publishers.

Wednesday, Oct. 3rd, 1888, 8:50 p.m.

Dear Annie,

The drive home was uneventful. I stopped for Mrs. Cox and children at the Kettle's. I talked to Mrs. Cox on the way about the church. Seeing that she is the daughter of a clergyman, she holds very liberal views (perhaps a reaction from the parental notions), and quite thinks the whole affair needs reforming most urgently. She has been reading some sermons of Haweis' (some that *I* heard at his church) and thought them very good. Altogether, I found Mrs. Cox to be more thoughtful than I supposed she was, and also more able to present her thoughts. We got back to Cox's at about four, and then I had to take the buckboard up to the Cusacks', and go to the Splann's for some butter for the Cox's, so it got quite late and I stayed to supper at the Cox's.

Cox was there, and he and Ernest Nathan were in hot controversy on the question of the tariff reform (free trade). Cox being a Democrat (free-trader) and Ernest a Republican (protectionist). I must get to one of the political meetings they are having now (over the Presidential election) and give them a little Socialism! I daresay I should be kicked out.

The Cusacks received a *Field* and two *Ladies' Pictorials* today. I have been amused to read the answers about handwriting, etc., in the *L. P.* How ridiculous people can be!

I am nervous and restless tonight, for no particular reason. Except that I found a microfungus on *Solidago* new to me (but known of and previously looked for), the result of today is the fact that I have finished Mrs. Cox's picture of the house, and happily got it so that it pleases her. For my part, I am glad to have it done, as I have already been paid for it and should not have liked to leave it unfinished or spoil it in any way.

It has been a cold, showery day. I suppose I spent almost as much time waiting in the house during the showers as painting. At one time in the afternoon I got disgusted with the weather and started homeward, but had not reached my house before rain turned to sunshine, and enticed me back again. After that it was fine, till about 4:15, when I finished the picture. Mrs. Cox asked me to do her yet another, viz., a view of Swift Creek and the range from near my old house, showing the quaking asps, the oak scrub, and above, the mountain peaks, now white with snow. I shall probably commence on this, weather permitting, tomorrow.

Louis Howard went to town but brought no mail for me. It is getting about time for answers to my C.B.A. circulars to be coming in. Brock paid me the $5.50 he owed me for work in the spring, which was satisfactory.

10:30 p.m. Have been over to the Cusacks', reading (partly aloud to Mrs. C.) a book Lees has lent me — *A study of Religion*, by Dr. Martineau. It is a most interesting book. If it is at Smith's Library, get Frederic to bring it home some time for you to look at. I am a good deal too sleepy and tired to discuss it properly, but will have much to say about it later.

'Weather permitting', I was going to paint Mrs. Cox a picture. However, weather did not permit. The day began cloudy, with a little rain now and then, and I busied myself getting in a supply of wood for burning. I also was fortunate in discovering a pitch pine stump from which I cut numerous chips; they are full of resin and excellent for lighting the fire.

Presently the child Brock came round and said that Mrs. B. was going away this afternoon (to be in town for the train tomorrow morning at 8:53), and wanted me now to go down to the Splanns and get Mrs. Splann to come up so that she could 'settle up' with her. I accordingly did so, and walked back to the Brock's with Mrs. Splann. After this, I went to the Chamberlain's for potatoes. It was raining a little when I started, but I had only just got there when it commenced to *snow*, and with some intermissions it has been snowing all afternoon! So I stayed to lunch at the Chamberlain's and waited then for some time, but as the snow showed no sign of ceasing, I proceeded homewards.

Then I commenced preparing for the winter, as it was evidently coming. Firstly, I brought the stove inside the house (very nearly came to swearing over the pieces of stove-pipe that wouldn't fit together), and then fixed up shelves for the cooking apparatus and made things as handy and comfortable as I could.

Miss Urquhart went to town today with Mrs. Cox, and came back this evening half-frozen — driving in a snow storm is most chilly work indeed. I had experience of this myself last October — bringing me some mail: *Ladies' Pictorial* (for which all thanks), *Pall Mall Budget*, a letter from Horace G. Smith, Jr. of Denver, enclosing $1.00 as his subscription to C.B.A., and writing a hopeful and encouraging letter. This is the first result of my circulars (save Cragin's postcard). Mrs. Brock, owing to the snow storm, has not departed, and will wait till Sunday.

Oct. 6th, 8 p.m. Except for about 3/4 of an hour in the morning, it has been snowing all day. Now the snow has ceased falling, and is melting. There must be about six inches of it on the grounds.

As for me, I went over to the Cusacks' for a few minutes this afternoon (to return their *Times* I had borrowed), but otherwise have stayed at home writing letters and reading the papers. Most of the morning I was writing a list of the Flora of Arapahoe County (Colorado), so far as present known, for H. G. Smith, Jr., of Denver. In the afternoon I got some fungi ready to send to Ellis. I have bought an axe from Regy for $1.00, and chop wood in this snowy weather very comfortably in one of the empty rooms of the house. I keep a fire going, and the room I write in is quite warm.

Ladies' Pictorial, although in some respects quite foolish, appears to have a much broader notion of women's interests than the *Queen*, which I occasionally see. Much in the *L. P.* is really interesting. It is curious how one reads in this *English* paper of 'the great Socialist, Amilcare Cipriani', and the miserably poor condition of the Italian peasantry, which enables the king to give much wealth to his brother's bride, the said wealth having been extracted from the peasantry.

Exactly, but all this is in *Italy*, but not in England — hence the difference! It always seems to me that these laments in the papers over *foreign* evils, although no doubt justified, have much hypocrisy, whether conscious or unconscious, at the bottom of them. The parable of Christ about the beam and the mote applies well to this sort of thing.

Talking of the Parables, I think they are by no means properly understood or appreciated. Everything Christ ever did or said had got so much swaddled-up in humbug and superstition since his day that the point itself is well-nigh lost. There is a humanly pathetic little bit of a story in *L. P.* (Chapters III to V, Part II of 'The Sound of a Voice') that I like. I think it is quite true that great emotion is not always expressed by weeping, and I am sure that copious tears are more often a sign of weakness than anything else. The illustrations in this story are also well done, especially the girl looking into the fire.

I never read any story of J. S. Winter. Did you? (I think I read somewhere that he is a woman, notwithstanding the 'John.') In *Public Opinion* are quoted some remarks on over-reading by Julian Hawthorne which seem to me very sensible, He says: 'The finest Madeira, if swallowed in sufficiently copious doses, will produce delirium tremens, and the most exceptional books, if they are also too numerous, will bring on mental dyspepsia. . . . The mind becomes a mere sack to hold other people's ideas, instead of a machine to generate ideas of its own. *And the ideas so acquired are of no use to it.* The mind has lost the power to work them up into the flesh and blood of wisdom. They remain a heterogeneous and incongruous mess.' Don't you think this is so?

Perhaps, though, the fault is rather in *unsystematic* reading than the abundance of it. And to read properly is quite hard work at times, e.g., that book of Martineau's on religion, which I have not taken up since the other evening. I shall have to get through that book (three big volumes) very gradually. Perhaps I had better reserve my notes on it until I have read more. The argument shows that the natural phenomena we see are effects, and are impossible without a *cause.* And again, he divides things into the constant and the variable, i.e., the non-happening and the happening — and seems to regard God as the *non-happening* cause of all that happens.

But in another part of the book I find the very reasonable argument that nothing is known except by comparison — a constant non-happening cause cannot be compared, and therefore cannot be known or have any practical relations with humanity. Also, if the *cause* were constant, why should not the effect be constant? Surely it *must* be. Then again, the question is discussed: If God is absolute and impartial, how can he be said to love, or show mercy, or have any human qualities? If he 'loves' all *equally*, and dispenses universal *equal* justice, he has nothing to make him different from a blind force of nature, something quite without sympathy. If, on the other hand, he loves with a human sympathy (like Christ) and he is merciful, he is *not* an unvarying constant cause which rules everything absolutely.

I do not remember ever reading an argument, or series of arguments, which required such close thought and careful reasoning, and I cannot at present go atall deeply into the matter. So far, this at least seems to be proved — that *God* the absolute and omnipresent, and *God* the human and sympathetic are totally different things. To my mind God expresses the constructive and harmonic force, and, in the best sense is that influence which binds together and partly

controls all life, which is progressive, tending to perfect harmony, of which we are conscious yet hardly understand. Commonly, we call it *good* — not always thinking that good is really a live thing — that all good has a similar origin. This is a crude idea. I must think more.

One rather shrinks from attacking these problems because of their almost impossibility of solution. I have never had any theological views sufficiently decided to exercise any marked influence over me. For practical purposes, I find that the instinct called conscience, and consideration for the good of humanity, are the best guides, yet not perfect ones even when implicitly followed. (Indeed, I don't believe that ideal conduct is possible at present.)

It's very difficult to tell you all this in a letter and make it plain, but tell me when you write what you think. It is very marvelous to me to consider the enormous force of instinct, or at all events impulses not generated by our *own* wills, in controlling our conduct.

Sunday, Oct. 7th, 2:45 p.m. The day has been warm and sunny, and the snow is melting fast. I went down to Mrs. Brock's to see what she was going to do about going to town, and found Lees was going to take her tomorrow in time to catch the train. I found Miss Sidford at the Cusacks'; Louis had fetched her up from the Beckwiths for Sunday. I met Chamberlain, who, after a long oration on the subject of *Allan Quatermain* (which I haven't read), asked me to work for him part of tomorrow — help him get his potatoes in. Weather permitting, I said I would. Both Lees and Louis are going to town tomorrow, and so perhaps I had better get this posted then, as I may not get a chance of posting it on Tuesday or Wednesday unless I walk to town. Chamberlain tells me that Hugg has departed to Denver, leaving wife and family to get along here as best they can!

It occurs to me that sometimes the references in my letters to various people must be a little puzzling, so I have drawn up a list of *Dra-*

matis personae which may help you to find 'Who's Who' when you do not know.

8:30 p.m. At the Cusacks'. Evening service just over. Lees has come and says that he hears that Martin is back and has left Payn at Steamboat Springs (on Bear River).I don't know what Payn proposes to do, but he can't very well bring his team back here by himself. I must make enquiries. Very likely I shall send another letter before the end of the week, as this goes unusually early.

Yours most lovingly, Theo.
Health. Am excellently well.

Oct. 8ᵗʰ, 7 p.m.

Dear Annie,

This morning I spent in 'fixing up' my house — closing apertures and making it warm and snug. The afternoon has been at Chamberlain's working for him, What we (that is, Chamberlain, two boys and girl, and TDAC) have been doing is getting the potatoes together in heaps in the field and then covering them up with straw and earth so that they will not freeze.

Nearly all the time we carried on an active political discussion, Chamberlain endeavoring to prove that the U. S. was in all respects of equal political virtue as England, a view to which I did not assent.

While working I found a blue beetle quite new to me, and a micro-fungus on the leaves of *Epilobium angustifolium* that I had not seen before. I had supper at the Chamberlain's, and then came over here to my house.

While at supper we were all puzzled by a strong odor of cloves, and on my way home I found to my dismay that I was the culprit. I lent Mrs. Cox my oil of cloves long ago, and when she returned it the other day I put it in my pocket and forgot all about it. The bottle broke this afternoon by some chance, and the oil of cloves flowing out became perceptible to the Chamberlainian and my own nostrils though we had

no idea whence it came! It's very annoying, as I suppose I shall have to go about smelling of oil of cloves for some time.

Louis Howard went to town and posted the letter to you, and brought me a long and interesting letter from C. V. Riley about specimens sent to him. Lees took Mrs. Brock to catch the train, and also saw Ed Martin, who says that *he* brought Payn's team back and left Payn at Steamboat Springs, well and thriving. They had lots of game, including three bears and some elk. Martin stole Payn's morphine and pretended it was lost, and now Payn does without it. Payn does not know whether he will return here for the winter or not.

Oct. 9ᵗʰ, 9:10 p.m. I have been feeling lazy today. I read some of the *Surgery Manual* and then went down to the Cox's to see about their next pictures. When I got there, Mrs. Cox met me with the request that I would add something to the picture of the house, viz., the children. So Charley and Isabel were trotted out where I could see them, and then I painted them in. After that I went down to near my old house on Swift Creek and commenced Mrs. Cox's sketch of the white mountains and yellow autumnal trees. Curiously, at the very spot where I sat down were two micro-fungi new to me, one on *Senecio*, and the other on *Juncus*. I made but little progress with my sketch, and about three I proceeded homewards, taking with me some stove-pipe and an iron pot ('stew-kettle') which were in my old house. I also found some putty there, which I carried off to stop up chinks.

Except getting supper, my whole time since I got back to my house has been spent in putting up insects (over 100 species) for Riley to name. I expect to go to town tomorrow. Chamberlain said he was going in with a load of potatoes and would give me a lift. The fences are down and this place is overrun with cows now. They are a great nuisance. One devoured some bacon over at the Cusacks' last night. It was hanging out in the wood-shed under the verandah. Fortunately, I have nothing outside now for them to devour except the axe and the shovel, and they may eat those if they can!

Oct. 18th, at the Cusacks', 7:30 p.m. At eight I was ready to go to town, and accordingly went over to Chamberlain's and found him getting the waggon ready, and was just in time to help load as many sacks of potatoes as the waggon would conveniently hold. Then Chamberlain and I mounted upon the top of the potatoes, and we proceeded leisurely (for 'twas a heavy load) to town. In town I got a very good lot of mail, of which later. Also I got (for 50 cents) a paper-cover copy of *Robert Elsmere*. The American publisher (Ogilvie) has not only *pirated* it but also had the impudence to *copyright* the printed edition!

`While in town, T. Charlton (an analytical chemist and a very able man, everyone says) came up and enquired after my scientific work, and I gave him one of the C.B.A. circulars, and he straightway joined and paid up his dollar. I stayed a long while in the postoffice and at length went out to see whether Chamberlain was ready to go, when I met Charley Cusack, who told me that Chamberlain had been enquiring for me and had, he thought, driven out.

This dismayed me somewhat, as I was feeling rather tired and not very fit to walk, but after a search round town and finding no Chamberlain, concluded that he *had* really gone, no doubt supposing that I had already started homewards. Wherefore I had to foot it, except that when about 1/4 mile from town, two kind women overtook me with a buckboard and gave me a lift to near Ula. (I don't know who they were.) I reached the Cusacks' just about six, where a cup of tea much revived me, and afterwards, being asked, I stayed to supper and am there yet. Miss U. and Regy were just now singing a song, *Pass Under the Rod* — did you ever hear it? It's a song with an idea and the tune is peculiar and rather pretty.

Now some notes on the mail: (1.) Frederic's letter, enclosing yours from Swanage which I much like to have (should like the other!). It's

a nice letter. In reply to Frederic's letter, yes, *Coriandrum sativum* is a good addition to the B. P. flora but, perhaps, like many B. P. plants, an introduction. The long extract from Lawrence Oliphant is interesting; one has heard something about the idea before. It might even indicate some notion of coming revolution and Socialism, but as stated, I cannot say I think it amounts to more than an expression of indefinite ideas in a rather too definite way. I don't think the 'spiritual wave' is by any means new, but no doubt things are tending to a crisis, and L. O., feeling this, seems to have been rather hasty in giving an explanation of it.

It is quite one thing to point to the natural consequences of competition and dishonesty, and propose a scheme to remedy these evils, and another to endeavor to explain the springs of moral action which move humanity. In the latter case all suggestions are interesting, but I feel more and more that one ought to be cautious in dogmatising on matters pertaining to religion and ethics. I, as you know, have my own ideas on the subject, but I should never think of insisting upon hem in the same tone that I should insist that twice two is four, or if I did, I should acknowledge in wiser moments that I was wrong.

(2.) Letter from Mother. She says she is sending *Robert Elsmere*, which is unfortunate, as I have got it today. I see Miss Plummer is at B. P. (3.) Letter from Orcutt asking me to send the *Calochortus* bulbs in his name to Berger & Co., San Francisco. (4.) Letter from Dr. Geo. H. Horn (boss American beetle man) who says he will gladly name beetles for me. (5.) Letter from Riley, who joins the C.B.A. as a corresponding member, I am very glad to have him as a member. He further confirms as *Claviceps purpurea* (ergot), some specimens from in front of my house — having handed them to Galloway, the mycologist of the Department, who understands these things. (6.) Letter from Beutenmueller, who sends a list of some Colorado Diptera he has copied out of a book by S. W. Williston. (7.) Letter from Leslie, amusing and cheerful, but no work yet. (8.) *Commonweal.* (9.) *Ornithologist & Oölogist.* (10.) Henry George's *Standard*. It seems that

Chicago Labor Enquirer has stopped publication, and the *Standard* is being sent to me instead. I am sorry to see another Socialist paper cease, but if it had been better conducted I should be more sorry. I think a paper should have more *news* in it than most Socialist papers have. 'Views' only, whatever their excellence, get monotonous. (11.) *Canadian Entomologist* is of no special interest or I would send it to you.

This does seem a long month, waiting for your letter at the end of it! Tell me about the story you were writing and refer to in your Swanage letter. You must send copies of what you write now, won't you? I will always return them if required. I want to know all about your work and what you are doing, and your difficulties and successes.

Oct. 11th, 7 p.m. This has not been a satisfactory day. In the morning, after breakfast, I went down to near my old house to sketch for Mrs. Cox the picture I had commenced. On my way I met Templeman of Silver Cliff driving up to see Brock, who, of course, is away from home (at Rosita, I think). T. was very affable, but he is not one of those persons one feels drawn to! I worked on my sketch till about twelve, but made slow progress. I meant to have gone on with it most of the afternoon, but as I was not feeling very well to start with, the hot sun made me rather faint, and I concluded that if I didn't want to ruin the drawing, I had better quit. Which I did, and struggled up to my house and lay down for a longish time, then took some quinine and felt better. After this I sorted some beetles I had put by for a long time and then prepared supper.

11:20 p.m. Time I was in bed! Miss Urquhart has been riding all over the country with Mrs Cox today (went over 30 miles) and, passing through town, got my mail: Letter and postcard from W. H. Edwards (about butterflies sent), *Daily Telegraph* (for which many thanks — have only glanced at it yet), *Pall Mall Budget, West American Scientist* (several copies, with notes of mine, so I am sending you a copy), and *Naturalist* (the

October number; it has come in 12 days, a short time! It has in it an interesting list of Lincolnshire Heteroptera).

Friday, Oct. 13th, 8:30 a.m. Louis Howard is going to town this morning, so I will give him this to post. The next letter will be posted about the middle of next week, I expect. Yours lovingly, Theo.

I have found in a magazine, *Literature*, some remarks of Emerson's on consistency which, although I don't exactly go that far with him, are interesting:

'A foolish consistency is the hobgoblin of small minds, adored by little statesmen and philosophers and divines. With consistency a great soul has little or nothing to do. He may as well concern himself with his shadow on the wall. Speak what you think now, in hard words; and tomorrow speak what tomorrow thinks, though it contradicts everything you said today.'

This is 'coming it rather strong' indeed! I quite agree that if one *is* consistent in ones notions, it's no use pretending to be otherwise. Also, anyone who thinks is bound to alter his opinions as time goes on, but it's a 'consistent inconsistency', as one might say. It's the inconsistency of a tree which has buds today and blossoms tomorrow, if it is of the right sort.

Oct. 17th, 9:30 p.m.

Dear Annie,

How the wind does whistle! It is blowing a hurricane. It is fortunate I came out before the evening; I should have been blown all to bits! I started from town about 3:30, but owing to the slowness of the pony, did not reach the Splann's till after six. I had supper there, and then came up to the Cusacks', where I have been arguing with Mrs. C. about novels and hot bottles. Mrs. C. got a letter from Mother with all sorts of enquiries about me! Miss U. is deep in *Robert Elsmere* and has read 2/3 of it already and finds it very interesting.

Oct. 18th, 6:25 p.m. Two misfortunes have happened to me: (1.) Last night, as I went to bed, knowing that the window was not very secure, I feared somewhat because of the violence of the wind, and knocked a small nail in for additional safety. Unfortunately this was not enough, for I had scarcely been in bed half an hour when there was a great gust of wind, then a bang and a crash of glass, and in came the cold night air! I got up in all haste and found that, after all, only one of the eight panes was broken, so I got hammer and nails and nailed up the window in a rough sort of way and got into bed, feeling sure I had caught cold (but I haven't).

(2.) Yesterday I made me a pot full of tea to last for two or three days, but to my dismay found the corpse of a mouse in it this morning! I am not fastidious, but don't like tea in which a mouse has committed suicide. But the worst part of the business is that it *is* a mouse, because no mice have hitherto infested this house, and I fear this one came not alone.

So much for my grievances; now for today's news. In the morning I went down below and continued Mrs. Cox's picture, but had only been at it an hour and a half when clouds came over the range, and I really thought a snow storm was imminent, wherefore I hurried home as fast as I could, and of course had only just got here when the clouds dissipated and the sun shone out! However, I could not have gone on painting anyway, as it soon clouded over again and has been raining mildly the rest of the day with occasional intermissions.

This afternoon I went over with *Robert Elsmere* to the Cusacks', intending to commence reading it to Mrs. C., but she had gone down to visit Mrs. Cox, so I came back and got to work planning-out Colorado into divisions for botanical and conchological work. (If you haven't heard of this Frederic will explain.) First of all, I

divided Colorado into nine river basins, lettering them from A to I, viz.: A, Platte R., B, Republican R., C, Arkansas R. (this includes Custer Co.), D, Rio Grande, E, San Juan R., F, Rio Dolores, G, Grand R., H, White R., and I, Bear R. — each of course including all the tributaries of the river in question. Then I further divided the state into 78 counties and vice-counties, which I need not enumerate. Custer Co. is divided into E. Custer (= Hardscrabble district) and W. Custer (Wet Mountain Valley).

After this, I did a little work round the house, stopping up cracks and making my pantry as tight as possible so as to exclude the mice. I don't think they can get in now, but it is wonderful how small a hole a mouse will get through.

Oct. 19th, 6:25 p.m. It was so fine this morning that I could not do otherwise than go down and work at Mrs. Cox's picture, although I had meant to read *Robert Elsmere*. I worked at it diligently and got it finished by about 20 to twelve and took it up to Mrs. Cox, who seemed much pleased with it. I told her I should charge only $1.50. I had lunch with the Cox's and while there, Mrs. Cox asked me to do still another picture — one of the ranch for her to give to Cox. I said I would, weather and other circumstances permitting.

On my way back, I looked in at the Cusacks' and had a long talk with Mrs. C. Mother, in her letter to Mrs. C., enclosed $25, 'on no account' to be given to me but Mrs. C. was to spend it in making me comfortable for the winter!! This is, of course, somewhat ridiculous, and we discussed the question at full length. Mrs. C. will write back to Mother and assure her in the most emphatic terms that I *am* comfortable and, as for the $25, part of it will be spent on (1.) blankets for Leslie and myself, (2.) boots which I want, and (3.) glass for my window, while the rest will be kept until Mrs. C. hears further from Mother.

After this, I went up on a bluff towards Cress's, where I had a good view of Cox's ranch. and made a little rough plan of it which I took down to Mrs. Cox for approval. It will not make a *pretty* picture, anyway, but she agreed that the view from the bluff was the best, so I shall get to work on this sketch as soon as I can. Mrs. C. gave me a piece of paper rather larger than my block to do it on, but it is not very good paper and I am not sure whether I can use it. I shall always now have as many pictures bid for as I can do, which is satisfactory, although I am not going to make my fortune over pictures, at the best! I wish I could do portraits.

Oct. 20th, 8:30 p.m. A cold, miserable day, drizzling rain most of the time. Regy and Miss U. went off in the morning — Miss U. to her music lessons at the Kettle's, and Regy, after taking her there, on to town. They came back this evening, half frozen, Regy bringing me welcome mail. Mrs. Cusack, being alone all day, I went over and read *Robert Elsmere* to her, but we talked and discussed so much (on universities, etc.) that I only got as far as Chapter IV. The book is interesting, but too full of description and comments by the author, I should say, but it's no use attempting to criticise until I have read the book through.

Now about the mail. It is: (1.) Frederic's letter, an interesting one; I suppose I may as well answer it in this to you. Thanks for the note on Swanage list, and the hymn extract! Methinks I have heard of Emilie de Gaja; was she not the writer of certain small writing I once saw?

I never would have thought that Horsley was lunatic enough to omit to note localities of his shells! I hope, Frederic, that you have given him a good lecturing on the subject and that he will repent and reform. I don't wonder at your blood running cold; I shiver to think of it!

I have had yellow-mouthed *H. nemoralis* from Cornwall; methinks I described it in *Sci. Gossip*, 1887 as var. *luteolabiata*, but having nothing but memory to depend upon, I may be mistaken. I had it so named in MS, anyway. (I think it was *Sci., Goss.*, March 1887, p. 67, but look it up.) Were the Dover *H. lapicida* 'live' shells? Because see under *H. lapicida* in my list in *Zoölo-gist*, 1885. No, I never saw a variety of *Vanessa* with extra ocelli, but compare with the species of *Tunonia*, especially a Japanese one. Some Indian butterflies are especially variable in their ocelli, I believe. De Niceville says ocelli are better developed in dry season in India (see *Ent. Mo. Mag.*, 1885, p. 237).

I had no idea that the S.L.E.S. was living beyond its means; it was good of Adkin and the others to subscribe.

Respecting Carrington, of course I am going to return to England as soon as I can. I have written this week to Uncle Douglas (R. D. Powell) to ask whether he will give his assent to my returning next summer. I really think I ought to, but if he thinks it absolutely necessary for me to stay another year, and urges good reasons for it, I may have to do so, for it would be better to stay three years in this country and be quite cured, than two and have finally to return. In that case I should be willing to spend the *year* with Carrington. I do want to get back, though, so very much.

It's such a long time to wait! Write and tell me what you think about it, Annie! Shall I be right if I make a *point* of returning next summer, notwithstanding advice? But I will write you what D. P. says, and you shall judge. I have given him an accurate account of my health.

Fred takes the sinistral *Helix nemoralis* very coolly! It's a grand find, new for England. Record it at once! The only locality in British Isles is the north of Ireland, where they *gregare*. So look for more at W. Drayton. *H. arbustorum* is well-known at W. Drayton.

What has come to your eyes? Be careful with them, Frederic! I am very glad, Annie, to hear of the good report from Sir M. M. It's nice of him not to charge because you are not 'professional'. I should think from all accounts he must be a nice man.

The other mail is (2.) Letter from J. B. Ellis, with names of fungi. He also sends the September number of *Journal of Mycology*. (3.)

Letter from Geo. Dimmock, editor of *Psyche* (an entomological paper published at Cambridge, Mass. He sends a sample copy) who encloses a stamped addressed envelope and asks me for a 'brief biographical sketch of TDAC!! Whatever shall I say? I must answer him. I suppose I had better give him one or two dates, etc., to satisfy him. It does not appear what he proposes to do with said 'biographical sketch' when he gets it. (4.) *Science Gossip* — more of 'rudiments and vestiges.' (5.) *Commonweal*; (6.) *Pall Mall Budget*. (7 and 8.) Sample copies of *Science* and *The Swiss Cross*. No *Ent. Mag.* yet.

Sunday, Oct. 21st, 9:15 p.m. Colder and more miserable than yesterday. A few inches of snow fell in the night, and has melted only slightly to-day, while more is falling now, I believe. I kept the stove going at my house, and so was warm, and wrote four letters and read somewhat. I have given Dimmock some dates and a list of my principal publications, which I presume will do for the 'biography.'

It's rather early in the day to be writing one's life history. Almost as if one were to describe a species of moth from the egg and young caterpillar only, and remark, 'the later stages of this insect are unknown.' So far as I am concerned, the past is chiefly valuable in the hope it bears for the future. Probably nobody should ever attempt to 'rest upon his laurels' till the other side of 50.

In the afternoon I came over to the Cusacks', where I still am. Lees turned up for a short while and has just returned from Pueblo. I have been reading *Robert Elsmere* and find it very clever and interesting. But I will not criticise it yet, as I said. I should have said yesterday that Mrs. C. has lent me a small frame of red velvet to put your photograph in. It's not what I want, but it has a glass, and stands up, and I am going to get Frank to make a nice one of wood as soon as he returns.

Oct. 22nd, 7:45 p.m. The snow has not yet all gone off and it has been chilly and unpleasant,

I have been reading *R. Elsmere* to Mrs. Cusack nearly all day, except when we were talking, the only interruption being Ed Bassick, who came after the key of Brock's house (which we hadn't got). It seems he is going to live there while Brock is away. Regy is perfectly disgusted with *R. Elsmere*. He says, 'You people talk about nothing else, and I don't see any sense in the book. So he seeks refuge in *Innocents Abroad*, while Miss U., having finished *R. E.*, is deep in *Jane Eyre*, which, however, she says she finds less interesting.

Despite my resolution, I must talk to you a little tonight about *Robert Elsmere*. I have got to the end of the second book, *Surrey*, and although I must confess I find it a tiresome book, it disturbs me somewhat and is certainly interesting. Catherine I cannot sympathise with — such a narrow nature, yet so true to its own conception of life, and in many ways so Christian. I know such exist, but I cannot feel with them. Robert I like, but not enthusiastically. I feel he is not quite consistent yet; the only consistent person in the book so far seems to be the clergyman Newcombe. I almost sympathise with him though I cannot agree with him. He is at least genuine.

Rose I feel pity for. I wish her the realisation of the hopes she must needs have. I hope she will be able to keep her balance, so to speak, through it all.

Langham is wretched; such indeed do exist — indeed I have my Langham moments myself. Perhaps I might have become just such a one but for you! I think you are the only real power on the loving side of my nature, and so far away! Is it not miserable? You have almost an exuberance of affection. Do you know what it is to feel as if you were a machine, wound up to go so long, to influence people's lives, perhaps, even for good, but like the wind and the sun, mechanically, not lovingly?

Oct. 23rd, What can I tell you about today? I have done nothing but read and think. In the morning I went up the hill to draw Cox's ranch. But it also being very cold up there, down I came, read at my house for a time, then went over to the Cusacks', then back here, but could not keep still, so returned to the Cusacks' to read for a while out loud to Mrs. C. Finally I had a long religious argument with her, had supper over there, and have been reading the rest of the evening. Not a wholesome day; the book troubles me more than I expected.

Langham makes me shudder. I shall be glad when I have finished and done with it all. It's no use expecting much sympathy out of Mrs. C., though she is a good creature, and nobody else is talkable atall. If only you were here, Annie! I wonder what you will think of this book. If you read it, tell me, what would you have done in Catherine's place, I wonder? *You* would have understood and sympathised, I know. One wishes Catherine were more like you.

Oct. 24th, 7:15 p.m. Too cold to be out of doors much. Besides, I have a little cold in my throat. Till some time in the afternoon I was reading *R. Elsmere* and had just finished it and was looking over Gladstone's article on it once more when, to my astonishment and delight, Miss U. came round bringing a handful of mail which Louis Howard, it appeared, had just brought from town.

After reading this, I went over and talked with Mrs. Cusack for some time, then came back and cooked supper, and since then have been reading the *Ent. Mag.* till just now. Tomorrow I must go to town to post this letter, but whether I walk or borrow the Splann's pony depends on how I feel.

Now for the mail: (1.) Frederic's letter, which, as before, I shall answer here. The cuttings are amusing. 'I am Gatis' is not a bad pun! I *am* a good deal flabbergasted at the Paris scheme for [sister] Olive! I had heard of it before, but never took it atall seriously. One thinks of Rose, in *R. Elsmere*, but Olive is a better sort of girl than that. Yet I can't help feeling a little anxious; she is just now developing, and events make a lasting impression. Will that of Paris be good or bad?

One fears, really, only because of her *friends*. She may get more than she wants, and it's not easy for a girl placed as she will be to refuse their well-meant kindness or hospitality. You see, Olive is (or was, when I last saw her) so exceedingly 'green', not atall up in the wiles of the world. However, it is no use protesting now, so let's hope all will be well. Perhaps, after all, it will prove to have been a good step. She will no doubt write me from Paris, and then I shall be more in a position to judge. I can't exactly think it was right never to have consulted Carlie.

I never collected *Helix sericea* myself (it should be called *granulata*, apparently). (2.) Letter from Mother, about Olive and Paris. (3.) Letter from Dr. Horn, naming beetles I sent. (4.) Letter from Kellerman (Prof. of Botany at Kansas Agric. College), joining the C.B.A. (5.) Letter from Radenhausen about his life He is a German chemist. He asked who I was, and I told him, so he sends this account of himself in return. (6.) *Standard* (Henry George). (7.) The *Ent. Mag*s. I see Brunetti comes out with a useful paper in Entom. Tutt on London melanism is interesting. It is rather foolish of Frohawk to be sending the same note (on *V. antiopa*) to *Entomologist, Ent. Monthly Mag.*, and *Sci. Gossip*!

As I said, I finished *R. Elsmere* today, and so I will say what I can about it. It is certainly a remarkable and interesting book, and very true, I think, to life. Catherine is painfully unfit for the circumstances she finds herself in, and is much to be pitied. As for Elsmere, he is a type of many. My own father was in some ways just such a man, and no doubt his work at Harrett's Court was one of the principal causes of his death; he tried to do more than was possible for his strength.

With the new 'Brotherhood of Christ' one could not fail to have sympathy, but I need to say that I do not consider it a remedy for the evils of society, rather at the best a good palliative. Besides, it has always been a question to me whether this hero worship was a fitting basis on which to found moral action. Christ himself said 'Love *one another*', and I think this is more to the point. I do not think we should do things 'in remembrance of Christ', but in remembrance of the needs of our fellow men. Nevertheless, the ideals and aims set before us by Christ are capable of producing enormous effect for good without a doubt, and as an *example* Christ is magnificent. I only protest against the idea of working *for* Christ primarily, and only incidentally for our human fellows. Tell me your ideas on this point.

I see Rose finally gets married, though it does not strike me that she and Flaxman have the least notion of loving, properly speaking. I can't quite understand Elsmere's affection for the squire, though I can that for Grey (who I supposed is meant to be Prof. Greene). The description of London 'society' (of a certain sort) is very true, no doubt, but it makes one shudder to think of it. It reminds me of an evening Carlie and I once spent at Dr. Wilk's. I think you will remember. Now I have done with *Elsmere* I suppose I must tackle Martineau again.

Oct. 25th, in town. Have got your letter, *dear* Annie! I cannot write properly now, but letter shall be posted on Saturday. You say you love me. I am happy, hopeful for the rest.

Yours with all my love, Theo.

Oct. 25th, 1888, 8:30 p.m.

Annie, my love!

I had no idea your letter would have come yet, but here it is! Wherefore, I will answer it. It is the nicest letter I ever had in my life. For the first time, you say you love me! Yet not so well as you ought — if — but you shall not make me sad by this. I love you, and you love me, and when the time comes, I cannot believe you will not love enough. Once, indeed, it seemed impossible that *you* should love *me*, of all people. I have not been much used to be loved, and it seemed to be impossible, and even now, I cannot see any tangible reason for it. Yet ever since the letter you gave me that evening at the gate of Syon, I have felt that our lives were twined together.

What right have I to think such things? None whatever, I confess, but does not love feel that it *must* have some return? Can it believe itself thrown away? And after all, is there no reason in this? Is not love a higher form of friendship — and it takes *two* to be friends! So ever since, and in the future, I have not been and am not without a confident hope, and a sense of happiness to come, if only I can regain my health and secure a prosperous position in England. And even if I should die, I believe in the unknown existence beyond, our souls might once more come together for help and love.

I had not meant to tell you all this, yet I had meant, rather, to wait patiently until I had secured a position for myself, in the meanwhile asking nothing except a continuation of our friendship, and I hoped that it might not be considered wrong that we should correspond. Perhaps I had better wait for your fuller letter before I say more. I think you will know how I feel. From an outsider's point of view, I know I am not worthy of your love, but as I look at it, I should be still less worthy if I gave it up because of difficulties in the way. I owe it to myself and to you to push on hopefully at all times. Now, I have tried to be as plain and matter-of-fact as possible, but have expressed myself badly.

Your diary-letter is grand! About the *Hypochaeris* 'growing' in your book, you see, towards autumn, plants begin to accumulate material for the production of seed. This is stored mainly in the flower head, and therefore seeds may develop even after the flowers have been plucked. I have noticed this especially in such plants as those allied to *Hypochaeris*. It is on much the same principle that bananas which were picked green will ripen.

No doubt the tram-car conductor's complaints were just, and they are worse on the horses than on the men. I have enjoyed that stroll round the garden, Annie! Thank you! I can read your letters quite well on foreign paper, but isn't *my* writing too small? Do you mind? *Cinchona rubra*, of course, is quinine.

I agree with you in the main about the marriage question, only I think, about the 'old-maids', that the idea of calling them failures is that their whole object in life was to get married and, failing at this, they don't know what to do. You see, many girls do aim only at getting married and, if they fail, their life is a failure. But it is also perfectly plain that any woman who has an aim in life, some work to accomplish, need never be any sort of failure because unmarried; often very much the reverse. I cannot help thinking that men would recognise this, if the girls (and their parents) would seek something more independent and reasonable than the general method of bringing-up.

To my mind, a bachelor is, if anything, more to be regarded as a failure than an old maid. I would cry 'pity the poor bachelor' (especially in Colorado) — he does not always have the best of times. From my experience most old maids are persons of much dignity, and greatly respected, though I am bound to except those of the kind that occur at Chislehurst in more abundance, and elsewhere more sparingly. The real fault one has with them is that they are uneducated and without ideas, vastly uninteresting. After all, if parents and guardians would only recognise the fact, the qualities that make a good 'old maid' — intelligence, knowledge, and above all *purpose*, are just those which help to make a good wife.

I need hardly say I agree that the married state is vastly the happier one for most mortals, at any rate, provided they really love one another, but it is obviously better to remain unmarried than to be married to the wrong person. Mlle. de Gaja's ideas about there being a companion for every soul is Swedenborgian, is it not? It's a very fascinating idea and may be true, but one meets with all sorts of difficulties to it on careful examination. It seems to require, in the first place, that souls shall have all pre-existed, which is likewise impossible.

You have drawn me accurately, in your imagination, of the Cusack evening service. Fancy saying you were half-inclined to cut that bit out! — it's one of the nicest bits in the letter! No, I never heard of Emma Jane Worboise. [Dear me, how slowly I write. It is already ten. I must get to the news of today.]

Today's news: The morning broke doubtfully fine, and clouds hung threateningly over. But I decided to go to town, so the Cusacks offered me the loan of their horse and buckboard. But the horse could not be seen, and I rather preferred to ride; it would keep me warm. So I went over to the Splann's and borrowed their pony. I had not got far on the prairie when I saw a big storm sweeping up the valley, so I smote my lethargic beast and we hurried along, and were just in time to get to the John Kettle's soon after the storm commenced and there take shelter. It was a regular blizzard, a freezing cold and most violent wind, with snow, so I was well out of it.

I found Mrs. John Kettle (an uninteresting person) at home and, having put the horse in the stable, sat in her kitchen until the violence of the storm was past (this was about 12:30). Then I proceeded and, arriving in town, got your letter as well as letters from W. H. Edwards (naming a butterfly, and joining the C.B.A.) and Simpson (a conchological correspondent who went ranching in Nebraska (and writes that it ruined him, and he is now trying to retrieve his fortune in Missouri), and *Pall Mall Budget*. I found Ernest Nathan in town with Cox's team and waggon, so I drove out with him, tying my horse on behind. I took the horse back to the Splann's, went to the Chamberlain's with some mail, then to the Cusacks', and finally back here, where I cooked supper, read your letter over again, and have been writing this ever since.

Oct. 26th, 3 p.m. It's like a stormy day at Margate! The wind whistles and sighs among the trees, just like the sea, and minute particles of ice are flying about, blown down from the mountains. *This* stove will burn all right in windy weather, I am glad to say. You remember the trouble I had in this respect last year? I have been writing up my records, and writing a letter, but can't go on; I feel too unsettled. I shall read Martineau's book, I think.

Ernest Nathan came up and asked me to go and help threshing at Cox's next week (Monday or Tuesday). I shall go to see what it is like. It is much too cold and stormy to do Mrs. Cox's picture of the ranch. I have to have a fire going all day.

4:15 p.m. I did not read Martineau after all; I read *Manual of Surgery* instead, and then chopped some wood. This so that I may not become violently insane, *Robert Elsmere* being perhaps enough religious literature for the present!

6:10 p.m. Have just finished supper (bacon, a turnip, bread, and tea). The wind still howls and laments. One is glad to be on terra firma, and not out at sea.

I forgot to tell you about the micro-fungus on *Tussilago*. It is probably orange, is it not? And if it consists of what looks under the magnifying-glass like a number of orange cheese-cakes, minute and crowded like a mass of pollen, it is *Coleosporium tussilaginis*. I used to find both of these at Chislehurst, but never met with them anywhere in Middlesex.

I have a request to make of you. One of these days, when you are not very busy, will you write me your history? You can quite understand that I am greatly interested to know all about you, and the fragments of information I have got so far are all too scattered and disconnected. Won't you do this for me? And not think that I am too inquisitive?

I shall give this letter to Regy to post tomorrow. Probably your letter will not have arrived yet, as the English mail does not often come at the end of the week, but if it has he will bring it out.

Yours most lovingly, Theo.

Saturday, Oct. 27th, 7:35 p.m.

Dear Annie,

There is not much to say about today. It has been fine, and the wind has gone down, and I have been writing and preparing some micro-fungi to send off to the members of the C.B.A. I went down by Brock's and round about in the morning, helping Regy to find his horse. Regy went to town, posted my letter to you, and brought me letters from Orcutt and Bruner, and *Botanical Gazette*. I am afraid your letter will not turn up till next Tuesday, even if posted within a day or two of the last. I shall go for it on Wednesday morning.

Orcutt writes about those *Calochortus* bulbs. He says he is getting only two cents for them and wants 125 more at the one cent rate. He also says he can't pay for about 30 days, till he has received the money for them from his customers. I think I shall send him 125, but shall look for someone else who will pay cash. I rather think of writing to Ware or Veitch, in England. Bruner joins the C.B.A. and undertakes to name all Orthoptera for the Association. He ought to turn up here about the middle of the month.

Sunday, Oct. 28th, 4:30 p.m. It has been gloriously fine and warm, and I ought to have been out, instead of which I have done nothing but write an account of the Mollusca of Colorado for *Journal of Conchology*. Mrs. Cusack and Miss Urquhart. came over to discuss plans for fitting up this house. They have bought it from Brock, and propose some day to live here and abandon their own. This is a very good house, or would be if properly fitted up.

Mrs. C. also talked to me for a long while. She thinks if Carrington comes to America I ought to go to him for a year or so, so as to raise a little money. She doesn't think I shall be able to live in England, but *I* do, and have every intention of doing so.

10:25 p.m. I have been over at the Cusacks' to supper and evening service. When I got there

I found a stranger, a youngish man with rather broad features, sitting by the fire. He rose and greeted me by name — evidently knew me but I had no idea who he might be. He turned out to be Colin Mackenzie, the man who traded the old mare to Payn last year before we went on our hunting trip. I think you will find it mentioned in a letter of that time. He has been near Meeker for the past year, whence he has just come. He is not a particularly interesting person, English, son of a general, Mrs. C. says. He is also nephew of the widow Ramsden, who used to reside in my present house.

Oct. 29th, 8:35 p.m. The morning was spent bulb digging. I dug 160 *Calochortus* bulbs. I meant to commence work on Mrs. Cox's picture of the ranch in the afternoon, but I had lunch at the Cusacks' and, while there, Lees came and told me that the threshing would begin at two at the Cox's this afternoon. So I went down there with Regy, but the machine did not arrive till a few minutes after we did, and they were some time fixing it up. There were, I think, 14 of us altogether: E. Nathan, old Splann and Jim Splann, Regy, Colin Mackenzie, Joe McGinnis, and several men named Cook, Taylor, etc., whom I had not seen before and who are of no particular interest.

I had no idea threshing was such a many-handed job, but we were all employed. The machine is worked by horse power. Ten horses turn a revolving table which is connected by a revolving iron bar with the machine, but the precise mechanism of the affair is not visible on the surface. We worked till about six, and threshed out about 218 bushels of oats. As I was probably the least strong man among us, I had an easy job assigned me, viz., holding the sacks open while they were filled with grain from the half- bushel measures, and handing them to Jim Splann to put into the waggon when full. It was of course frightfully dusty, especially where I was, and I don't think I could have stood it had I not taken the precaution to cover my face with my green silk handkerchief. Poor Mrs. Cox must have been as tired as anyone, having to cook and get things

ready for such a crowd. Mrs. Splann helped her with the cooking, however, and I washed up the things afterward. We have to be down there to breakfast at six tomorrow, so I shall go to bed.

Oct. 30th, 9:15 p.m. We have finished the threshing. Today it was wheat and barley. I pitched a little after lunch, but nearly all the time was holding sacks, so am not tired, but very weary and sleepy, so will not write more tonight.

Oct. 31st, 2:55 p.m. I must give you a better account of yesterday, especially as there is nothing to say about today. I woke up at four and found it moonlight (Mrs. Cox had to get up about this time, poor thing) so I dozed until nearly six, when I dressed and went down to the Cox's. It was just dawn, and I found some of the men already at breakfast. Regy and Colin Mackenzie arrived about a quarter of an hour afterwards. I took *Robert Elsmere* down for Mrs. Cox to read. We got to work about sunrise, worked till twelve and then lunch and a rest, and then work again till dusk (nearly six). I had an easy job so was not tired, but it was very dusty and unpleasant, and wearying. Mrs. Cox had Miss Urquhart to help cook, and they prepared most sumptuous repasts. I wonder what labourers in England would say to being treated that way! And getting $1.50 a day besides!

Just before supper, one Tom Flynn, a saddle and harness maker from Silver Cliff, appeared on the scene, soliciting votes, for he is running as Democrat for the representation of Custer County in the Colorado House of Representatives at Denver. He much regretted he had not whiskey for all 'you boys who must be tired', but he had only two drinks with him, which he had handed to Regy on arrival to distribute, and Regy and Joe McGinnis had 'got away with it' between them, to the disgust of the rest of the crowd. (This would certainly be bribery in England!) Tom Flynn said a good deal about himself, but nothing about his principles, and of course he 'didn't want office, but was only running for it because his friends had urged him.'

Today is an abominable one, wind and rain, and I am not very well. Regy has gone to town and will, I hope, bring your letter. I was going in with him, but he had to take Miss Urquhart to the Kettle's (she is giving music lessons twice a week now) and I did not think they wanted to take me. Besides, I shall have to go in tomorrow or Friday, I expect, to post this letter to you.

8:25 p.m. This *is* disappointing! Regy comes from town and brings mail, but not your letter! No English mail atall has come. But it's no use grumbling. It can't be helped, and if I feel all right and the weather permits, tomorrow I shall of course go in to town; no doubt it will have come tonight.

The mail I have got is (1.) Letter from Leslie. He doesn't seem to know whether to come here or not now. I wish he would make up his mind. He says he hears from Mother that Carlie has measles, and this stops Olive from going to Paris just yet. Not an entire misfortune, perhaps, and probably Carlie will gain more by the enforced rest than he will lose from the measles. (2.) Letter from Strecker; (3.) Letter from L. O. Howard; (4.) Postcard from H. Engelmann about *Zoöl. Anzeiger*. I wrote to ask what the subscription was. It's all in German, but I gather that the subscription is $4.75 a year — $3.75 too much for me! (5.) *Standard*.

Here are the lists of addenda to my fauna and flora lists for October. (These details are perhaps not very interesting, but you may like to see how I am getting along with this branch of my work.) Colorado: Fishes, 1 (introduced); Hymenoptera, 1; Coleoptera, 40 and 1 var.; Diptera, 26; Heteroptera, 2; Homoptera, 1; Moths, 5; Algae, 6; Fungi, 10 and 1 var. Middlesex: Mollusca, 1 var.; Hymenoptera, 1; Diptera, 19; Heterocera (moths), 15 and 9 vars.; Coleoptera, 1; Phaenogamia, 1.

Thursday, Nov. 1st, 2:35 p.m. Sometime this morning I began to question whether life was worth living, but I have recovered spirits a little since then. When I got up, half of the horizon was in clouds and the other half bright. The weather seemed not to have made up its mind what to do (it blew and rained furiously in the night), so I went down after the Splann pony, to go to town, but old Splann had gone visiting on it and so it was not to be had. I went across to the Cox's, and Mrs. Cox would have let me have a horse from there, but by this time it was beginning to rain and looking very stormy, so I shall go with him. At about one it cleared up, but soon clouded over again, and began to hail and thunder, and then to rain. I should have been drenched and half-frozen had I gone to town, but I do wish I could get your letter.

Nov. 2nd, 12:29 p.m. In town. Oh, Annie! If I weren't so far from you I should be quite happy. Did anyone ever get such a nice letter? Well, it's no use trying to answer it here and now. I can't collect my thoughts but will answer by tomorrow if nothing absolutely prevents. I got Frederic's letter also.

Your own lover, Theo.

Hand in hand, Annie, forever! I wish I could write like you do. Some of my letters must be very incomprehensible, to anyone but you.

November 2nd, 1888

Dear Annie,

I was glad to find that the day broke fine, and so after a hasty breakfast I went down to the Cox's to go to town with E. Nathan, but I need not to have been in such a hurry; he did not start till ten. We had a fast team (we road in Cox's light waggon) and were in town soon after eleven, where I got your altogether delightful letter, for which I can only thank you by my life, not by words. The rest of the day's news is of little account. I went up to the *Wet Mountain Tribune* office to get an estimate for printing report of

C.B.A., and found there several old (1877-1883) volumes of the reports of U. S. Commissioner of Agriculture, which I perused with great interest and took notes therefrom. Then we drove out of town and brought Charley Cusack out with us on a visit up here, and since then I have done nothing in particular — supper, entering-up of notes, C.B.A. business, etc., as usual when I come from town.

Your letter commences like many of the days here. One does not know whether to expect sunshine or rain, but since it turns out sunshine altogether, I must not mind that. I don't think, Annie, we have misunderstood one another so very much, after all! When we first became friends, it was difficult, indeed, but now that is all past, and we can be quite frank to one another without any fear of all sorts of calamities. How nice it is to have you telling me about your side of the question. Often have I wondered what you thought, and I dared not ask you, or whenever I did pluck up courage to put a question, I got no answer!

You see, I am a very bashful young man though it may not always appear so. I had no idea that you were astonished at my first taking an interest in you. Do you mean to say nobody ever took any interest in you before? It's perfectly appalling to think that you should not have been properly appreciated before. Did you never feel lonely? I did, before I knew you I would sometimes watch the faces in the streets and wonder why there was not one among so many to love. It seemed very unreasonable altogether. Perhaps you will say you had some women friends, but if so, who? And I remember, once, as you stood outside the gate of 20. Woodstock, you said you seemed only to get the remnants of other people's friends, whereas I felt much like telling you that you were libeling someone's friendship, but discreetly refrained. Perhaps you guessed what I was thinking, and would have qualified your utterance, but you discreetly refrained, also.

No, I didn't suppose you guessed what had made me most happy when you questioned me at the 'squash.' But you will agree with me that

I did wisely not to tell you. For the same reason, I did not always complete the letters and essays I sent you. I suppose it was mean of me, but I wanted to enjoy your friendship as much as possible, and dreaded in consequence lest I should do anything to cause you to draw back and leave me looking like a sea-anemone abandoned by the tide.

If you divined that I loved you, *that* I did not mind, but I was afraid that if I said as much in plain language, you would feel obliged to withdraw all outward manifestations of friendship. In those days, I had not courage to suppose you loved me. And that Louy should have solemnly warned you so early as 1886. I had no notion that it was so plain to the eye as that! Indeed, my love was still growing then. It had not developed so that I quite understood it myself. I only knew that I always looked forward to seeing you, and when you were at hand, could not pay attention to anyone else. Why, even after I had declared my love in June, 1887, I was quite taken aback that Nelly Allport had fathomed the secret and had been discussing it with Mother. For all I know, it was an open secret all over the Park. Louy's warnings were meant in the kindest way, no doubt, but I am very glad they failed to take effect.

Sometimes you used to puzzle me by seeming distant, but you would always make it up next time. It was always particularly annoying, though, when sometimes a whole week would go, and I saw nothing, or next to nothing, of you. I never expected to find myself scolded for not going in at 20. Woodstock! But I was really bashful, and feared dreadfully that my going so often as I did would annoy the 'authorities.' Perhaps your mother didn't mean it, but I always used to feel unwelcome when she greeted me on my arrival uninvited. And often, when I stayed so long, I used to wonder what they all thought of me, Tell me, weren't the family sometimes annoyed?

It used to be a sort of joke between Carlie and me. 'Going over to the Fenns? What's the excuse this time?' And I'm afraid that Domestic of yours used sometimes to think the excuses were rather thin, from the way she used to smile when I asked 'whether Mr. Frederic is in.' Whether he was or not, she always asked me in anyway, and once when I wouldn't enter, she volunteered the information that 'Miss Annie' wanted me to — but I didn't all the same!

From all of this, you will perceive that I am sometimes given to fraudulent practices, but no doubt you knew that before. Does Louy *now* think it a calamity that I love you? I wonder. And what do the others think about it? I never had the least notion what Alice, Kitty, and Olive thought on the subject. Perhaps they didn't think. I suppose Clive is utterly disgusted, to judge from his recent utterances on love, communicated by Frederic.

You ask why and how you made me miserable. It was no fault of yours, or not much your fault. But in those days I did not think you loved me (and you say you didn't!) And was consequently troubled by many thoughts. I wanted to see much of you, and talk much to you, and yet was often disappointed. It will seem to you a trivial matter. but if I looked forward to your coming over on Sunday, say, and you never came, it troubled me all the rest of the week. I felt like going to you and saying, 'Annie, I am lonely. I want your company. I want to talk to you. Do let's try to be friends, and break down all these conventionalities.' Yet of course I dared not, and had I dared, nothing would have come of it but refusal, if no worse.

I recollect one day, what a rage I was in when I came home and found you had just departed to the Whitechapel picture gallery, and I very nearly had gone there myself, and should have met you. I thought of returning to town after you, but it was almost too late. Another disappointment was when we were to have had the chemistry in the studio, and Mother wouldn't let me go because I had a cough, and the next time, when I did go, you weren't there. I wish I had gone the first time now, in spite of entreaties. (I suppose that is quite wrong of me.) All this looks almost ludicrous, as I relate it now, but it wasn't so then, I can tell you.

Now, about marriage. Of course it was sort of ideal, but not until after I had the letter you gave me at the gate of Syon Lodge, did it ever seem to come within the range of possibility, Added to my belief, before then, that you would not marry me in any case, I felt very despondent about my health. I hardly hoped ever to be in any position to marry. I thought it by no means unlikely that I should die, and in this frame of mind, only hoped that if I began to get worse, I might return to England and see you before the end. Since I have been out here, although I have often been despondent, hope has been growing, and now I look to our marriage as *the possibility* of the future to which all effort must tend.

Had you cut me adrift, as you say, when I left England, I hardly know what I should have done. I would not have abandoned you without a fight for it, that is certain, but once abandoned for good, my only hope for existence would have been a close application to science, and you might have met me, years hence, as a highly respected old professor with a brain but no heart, a soul withered up and miserable, or I might have devoted myself to the Socialist propaganda and become 'a villain of the most desperate type' (as the bourgeois papers would say), but my desperation itself might have harmed the cause. In any case, I should have been unhappy.

You call yours an egotistical letter! Mine is very much worse, but who is one to write egotistical letters to, if not to one's love? You cannot really think that I could get any 'good and happiness' by not marrying you, if you will have me! All I am afraid of is that I shall not be what you would have me. I am so limited in many ways, and all too cold-hearted and callous. The very fact that I love you only brings this into relief. You must help me when we are one; humanise me a bit. Indeed, you can do that now. You have done it in the past. Well, Annie, you know my faults, and you know that I love you with my whole love, and that is all there is to know. Yes, Frederic has been very good. I never could have hoped for more trusty friendship. I will write to him, of course.

Unless health absolutely forbids it, I will come back next summer, you may be sure. Alas! I wish I were quite strong and healthy, Why did I say I did not think it was in your power to give me your love? Because I thought you did not love me at the time, and it is in nobody's power to give their love because they wish to; at least I think not. I had long been wishing to love some-one, but never did so until I knew you, and then it took me almost by surprise. Don't you think I was right, thinking as I did? Now that you say you love me, I am not the least afraid that you will cease to do so, even if you want to. Am I right again?

You want to know whether my letters will be just the same as before, with only 'Dear An-nie' prefixed? Wait and see. I fear they will some of them be altogether uninteresting. When I am tired I can only write the facts down in a bald sort of way; I have not the gift of narration. But I will try to make them interesting. I am afraid I shall send you a great deal of nonsense.

Thank you for joining the C.B.A. I have paid in the 25 cents. You ask me, will I help you with my sympathy? I have so often longed to be able to help you, but you never would tell me about yourself or your troubles. Do tell me what you think and feel about things, and let me try to help you. You have helped me so much. I owe you something.

It is now eleven, and I should be going to bed (I never sit up late now. I find I can do no good work much after ten). I must finish the day's news by an account of the other letters received: (1.) Frederic's letter, of which I shall write later. (2.) Letter from Mother. (3.) Letter from Brown Goode of Smithsonian Inst. about the inscription on an old (Spanish?) knife Regy found. They cannot decipher its meaning. (4.) Letter from L. V. Johnson of Illinois, a botanist, who sends $1.00 for C.B.A., and joins. Good of him to send $1.00, as 25 cents is all he need have sent. (5.) *Insect Life*, October. (6.) *Commonweal*.

(7.) *Pall Mall Budget*. I see Sir M. M. has been pitching into the German doctors! (8.) *Life Lore*, two sample copies, July and October, apparently from the publisher. Good night!

Nov. 3rd, 8:45 a.m. Regy is going to town and will post this. I have more to say to you but that must wait till the next letter. About our being of different ages, so far as I am concerned, since I love you, neither difference of age nor any other difference can alter the fact. People don't marry because they are of about the same age, but be-cause they love one another. I have thought that I should not have liked you so well if you had been younger, but perhaps this is because most girls of 20 and thereabouts I have met have been somewhat foolish, and I cannot imagine you any different from what you are. Probably I should have loved you just the same, whatever your age. I am afraid I am very ridiculously young, but I'm getting older, and lots of men marry younger than 22 or 23.

Yours most lovingly, Theo.

Sunday, Jan. 6th, 1889

Dear Annie:

I was up at seven this morning, but it was 20 past eight before I finally got away. It is as-tonishing how little things get away with one's time. There was only breakfast to cook, the horse to feed and saddle up (to catch hm took no time, as he obligingly walked right by my house just when I wanted him), and some letters to get from the Cusacks. Yet that took nearly an hour and a half! It was the Payn horse, and we took it pretty easy. I got to town about a quarter to eleven.

I went more to post letters than to get them, but I found some mail, best of all your two draw-ings, which are quite too good for me; I like them very much, especially the 'Tale in the Woods.' Next time I go to town I shall get glass for them, and put them up. I have not yet decided where they shall go. I must try to make myself some frames. Thank you for them! One of these days I will give you a kiss on account of them, whether you like it or no!

The other mail was (1.) Letter from C. V. Riley. He sends all good wishes for the C.B.A. but is annoyed because I described the new *Longitarsus* beetle in 1st report, and thinks that new species ought not to be described in these reports. (2.) Letter from Dr. Horn, who also urges that new species should not be described in the C.B.A. reports, and respecting the *Longitarsus*, says he has studied this group for 25 years and only now begins to understand them. And how can Riley know whether it is new or not? He asks for the loan of the beetle; I will send it to him. Dr. Horn also joins the C.B.A. (3.) *Pall Mall Budget.* (4.) Report of Entomologist of Agric. Dept. for 1887, from Riley. (5.) Carlyle's *John Sterling* and *Past and Present*, a diary for 1889 from Carlie (I will write about the Carlyle books when I can read them.

I posted a letter to you, and a *Courant* (with 4th report) and the photograph, and lots of letters to different people, and then went round to see Charlton, but he was not at home. Then I started back, and after an uneventful ride got home somewhere between two and three. Now it is evening (7:30 p.m.) and Lees has just been round. I told him about your reading *B. C.*, and he was greatly interested and amused at your remarks about his appearance, which I read to him. *B. C.* is just now down at Beddoes', but he will lend it to me as soon as he gets it back. Lees has another letter from Mrs. Payn, asking all sorts of questions. Now I am going over to the Cusacks' for a bit, as it is Sunday. I did not go there to supper.

Jan. 7th, 9:30 p.m. The wind is blowing to-night, and thick clouds seem to indicate a storm. Frank departed this afternoon; Regy drove him to town. He starts by the train tomorrow morning via San Francisco and Sandwich Islands. I feel quite depressed about his going, not that I care so much for Frank (though I like him well enough), but the reason of his going, and the whole affair, is miserable. Mrs. Cusack tells me that he himself admits that it is fortunate that he cannot marry Miss Urquhart, since her ways would make him wretched, but it is hard for him anyway. Before going, he gave her his horse, Ferris.

This afternoon I wrote an article on 'Thistle Insects' for my 6th report of C.B.A., and afterwards went over to talk to Mrs. Cusack, thinking she might want cheering up and her thoughts diverting. She was alone, sitting by the fire. (Colin Mackenzie, who is staying here, was out making a fence.) This resulted in my staying for supper and the evening. Colin came in before supper, of course. We were talking about a plan to take boarders here. Mrs. C. says she thinks Regy and Miss U. (the future Mrs. Regy) cannot possibly live off the ranch alone, and suggests it would be a good thing to start a summer boarding house and charge $10 a head a week. It depends a good deal on how it was done.

Then Mrs. C. talked about Regy and Miss U., and she thinks that Miss U. is not so fond of Regy as she might be. For instance, she has written him only two letters since she went to Colorado Springs, and one of them is a mere scrap. However, it isn't any use criticising them; they must run their own affair. But if Miss U. really doesn't love him after all, it will be the culmination of the miseries arising from that young woman.

I was impatient to get your two pictures up, so I have put them up without glass pending my next visit to town. They look very nice — the 'Tale in the Woods' is under the McWhirter, and the two girls under the Burne-Jones. They take the place of the butterfly plates, which I have moved. Perhaps I shall alter their position later on.

Jan. 8th, 6:30 p.m. My love, I am fairly at my wit's end! Hulst has sent me all the back volumes of *Papilio* and *Entomologia Americana*, wherein such a wealth of bugilogical information that I feel like a child at a sumptuous dinner party — too much to eat and yet want to eat it all at once! Well, well, I must take it calmly, and by degrees

I shall assimilate the stores of information, or so much of it as I require.

This morning, when I got up, I was half surprised to see snow on the ground, but only about an inch of it. As I Irishly told Mrs. Cusack, I 'expected snow, but didn't think it would come!' Regy came from town at about one o'clock. Lees had asked me to go up to his mine this afternoon and take him his mail, if Regy brought any. I said I would, but wondered at the request. However, now I learn that one of his brothers (in the army, I forget his name) is very seriously ill and he is consequently anxious to get the news. There was no mail for Lees, after all, but I got the above-mentioned back volumes (which I expected long ago) and also three letters, (1.) From Riley, with names of a lot of insects sent. (2.) One from Berthoud, of Golden, Colo., who says he is going away for the winter, but if he returns will join the C.B.A. He is an ornithologist. (3.) From Nash, of Pueblo, who sends some interesting notes about moths, and undertakes to work up the butterflies of Colorado for the C.B.A. He says he is sending me (on loan) the volumes of *Papilio*. This is a pity; it will cost me the carriage, and Hulst has already sent the volumes, He also says that if it fine he is going to stay a few days with Campion! I had no idea that Nash and Campion knew each other.

Jan. 9th, 8:10 p.m. It has been blowing a gale all day. I have done nothing to speak of except to go through the volumes of *Papilio*, reading much and putting slips of paper as markers where I must take notes. I am beginning to see my way through these volumes, but the mass of new facts is quite overwhelming. I wish you were siting near and writing too! I should enjoy my own work so much more. Winds and weather permitting, I go to town tomorrow.

Jan. 10th, 9:50 p.m. I am not feeling very fit today, though there is nothing the matter with me, and this morning I was half disposed to put off going to town. Now I wish I had, for I never

got your letter after all. The English mail has not come.

I drove Payn's horse with the Cusacks' buckboard, and got off between nine and ten. I took Mrs. Cusack as far as the Cox's, as she wanted to see Mrs. Cox. (The Cox's move to town tomorrow for good. They have rented a house half way between Silver Cliff and West Cliff.) It was quite chilly driving, and I had to wrap up well, but fortunately it was fine and the wind of yesterday had quite gone down. All the mail I got was (1.) Letter from Morrison about C.B.A. He is much pleased with the first report. (2.) Odd numbers of magazines from Morrison for library of C.B.A. (3.) Postcard from Ancey, notifying change of address and asking why I haven't sent him any more shells (he shall have some). I delayed because I wanted to get some small Pupae named first, and I wanted to make sure. (4.) Report of U. S. Commissioner for Agriculture for 1887. (5.) Sample copy of *Santa Clara Valley*, a California agricultural paper. (6.) Commonweal. (7.) *Standard*. I was quite disgusted to find your letter had not come, but it can't be helped. If it has been blowing on the Atlantic like it has here, I don't wonder at the English mail being delayed.

After this, I went up to the *Courant* at Silver Cliff and got 5th Rept. of C.B.A. in the paper, and reprints of 4th Rept. Turner seems in a bad way. He can only raise $47 among his friends, and says he must have $75 by next week if he is to keep up the paper. I really think I must get him some money. Douglas has $30 of mine, and I could afford to lend Turner $10, but the trouble is, I might not get it back. Perhaps it is rather selfish of me to have these scruples, but, after all, I can less afford to lose money than almost anyone about here. I must think the matter over before I next go to town. What makes me doubt is this: Turner has to buy a press for $200. If he can raise $75 now he can have his press, and pay the rest later. Query: Suppose he gets his $75, *will* he be able to pay the rest later? He thinks he can, but even he seems a little doubtful. I shall be sorry if the paper stops. I think if I were wealthy enough I would clear him altogether and go partner with him in the paper! Imagine TDAC editing a weekly newspaper! I would get you to write a story for it, to appear as in *Schoolmistress*.

When I returned to West Cliff, I bought some meat and then went to the express office, where I got the volumes of *Papilio* from Nash (which I must return next time I go to town), and from there to Charlton's, and got from him the second part of his paper on Huerfano County fossils. Then I started homeward and got up to the Cusacks soon after sundown. (It was bitterly cold just before sundown.)

I found Mrs. Cox up there. She was relating how the Turner's (i.e. the Brock-ite Turners) dog had been poisoned by strychnine laid on bread and butter down by my old house. Jim Splann is suspected of putting the poison down because his dog was severely hurt by the Turner's the other day (which it deserved, as it began the attack), and the Splann's had been very wroth thereat. I must say, I think it is quite probable that it was Jim. I don't see who else could have done it.

Jan. 11th, 4:15 p.m. Regy has gone to town to-day, and I shall be very much disappointed if he does not bring your letter. I have been talking it over with Mrs. Cusack about lending the money to Turner, She seems to think I had better lend him $25, if any atall. I have a notion of lending it him on condition that he teaches me printing! What do you think of that? It is good to know a trade, even if one is not likely to follow it. Champion, when he turned Socialist and was cut by his own people, earned a living as a printer.

10:25 p.m. Oh, Annie, Annie! Regy has come back, and he waited also for this evening's mail — and no letter! I don't know what can have happened. The boat must have come to some harm, or the train snowed up, or something. Apparently none of the English mail has come. It seems a year since your last letter, and I did feel so sure I would get one this evening. However, one must 'grin and bear it' and go in on Sunday or Monday on the bare chance (though I never knew an English letter to come on Sunday that I remember), and to post this.

I have been going through *Entom. Americana* all this evening as I waited for your letter. Mrs. Cox and her children are still at the Cusacks'. She expected Cox to take her to town today, but he never turned up. Regy brought me a little mail: *Courant*, and *Canadian Ent.* Letters from Leslie, and Douglas *says he* has a bad cough. It's *perfectly abominable* that he does not come here. Says he also has a pain in his chest, and described symptoms. Bronchitis, apparently. He *must* come here. Douglas has been to Toronto to see Leslie and writes just the same. And the ridiculous part of it all is that, for Leslie's long hours, he only gets £20 a year which, Douglas says, 'pays about half his board.' I shall write a letter home and let them know my views. Lending money to the *Courant* must go to the winds, and Leslie must have the money to get here with.

Jan. 12th, 2:30 p.m. It is snowing. I have just written to Leslie about himself, and to Mother about Leslie, and I hope the letters will have the effect of bringing Leslie here inside of three weeks. If he doesn't come after this, I don't know what I can do in the matter.

7:55 p.m. It has left off snowing. If it is anything like decent weather, I go to town tomorrow. Today, besides writing a few letters, I have been employed taking notes from the four volumes of *Papilio* and have now got all the Colorado species mentioned therein duly entered up in my fauna book and in the Colorado bibliography. I will now write a little more of my 'History.'

History of T.D.A.C.

My father died in Dec., 1877. I went to Madeira in Dec., 1878, so there is a year intervening of which I have rather indistinct recollections. Most of it was spent in lodgings at Margate with Mother, Olive, Una, etc. Miss Plummer lived with us all that time. I collected insects but did not do much at them for lack of means of getting the species names, though I knew most of the butterflies by sight. Once, Mother and I went up to London to stay with Uncle Douglas and Auntie I. (then living in Henrietta St., Cavendish Square) and I made much of my opportunities to go to the British Museum, and gloated for hours over the specimens, and named several of mine. I also went to hear Haweis for the first time, I remember.

Then Mr. Dru Drury, who was a great friend of my father and a wine merchant of Madeira, offered to take me out there for six months, 'for the good of my health.' The offer was accepted, and I spent five months in Madeira, which gave me much new and varied experience. I believe you have my Madeira diary among my other books at Syon. It will show you a good deal how I spent my time there.

I started, with Dru Drury and a Mr. Power, in December, 1878, and we went in the S. S. 'Consco' from Liverpool (since then, this vessel has been wrecked and lost). I remember the voyage very well. I was sick the first night after we started, and recovered when we were somewhere in the Bristol Channel, and remember seeing a shoal of porpoises, which interested me greatly.

A day or two after, as we passed the Bay of Biscay, a great storm arose and treated us very roughly. I was quite terrified. For a while we continued on our course, but a sail was torn to shreds, and a wave smashed the captain's cabin (which was rather exposed, on deck) to pieces, while another broke the skylights of the saloon and let the water in upon us. So we stopped, and lay to with the steamer's head to the wind for four hours. After that the storm abated and we proceeded. But still the great waves were there, though the wind had died down, and we rolled so that we could not stand on deck. The waves were estimated to be about 26 feet high, I believe.

I think we were a week on the sea, till one morning Madeira rose grey on the horizon, while the rugged island of Porto Santo was quite close to our left. We coasted along the south-east part of the island, and at length dropped anchor in Funchal Bay, opposite the town of Funchal. ('Funchal' means fennel; it is so-called because fennel grows abundantly there wild. 'Madeira' means wood, in allusion to the forests of pine, chestnut. etc., that clothe the mountain slopes.)

Now I think I must leave the description of Madeira for next time, as I want to go to bed early tonight (to be rested for the walk tomorrow) and I have a little work I want to do. The other day I mentioned that I was not very well, but I am all right again now.

Sunday, Jan. 13th. Came to town, got your letter, no time to write now. Postoffice shutting up. So glad to get your letter!

Yours lovingly, Theo.

Sunday, Jan. 13th, 1889, 10 p.m.

My love,

There is very much to say in answer to your letter (a very nice one, to make up for the delay), but it is now later, and I must tell you only the news of the town. I was puzzled how best to shoe myself, and first tried experimentally two small boards, after the way of snowshoes, but found they would not do. Then I put on shoes, i.e., slippers, four pairs of socks, and overshoes over them, and that did very well. The snow was not too deep, and I got along at a fair pace though I had to wear my green handkerchief over my eyes to keep off the glare.

As I went by John Burke's, J. B. came out in his shirt-sleeves holding a coat in his hand, explaining that all his folks were out, and he had tried three times unsuccessfully to put his coat on, but he had recently hurt his shoulder, and it was stiff, and he couldn't manage it. So I helped him on with his coat. Then he asked if it was I who wrote the articles in the *Courant*, and finally joined the C.B.A., though I don't know whether I shall ever get the $1.00 subscr. from him. J. B. is an oldish, gray-bearded man with much life in him. They say he is an old swindler, but he is an amusing and original old man, and many are the stories told about him.

Soon after I left John Burke's, a light waggon was seen coming along, which proved to be Jim Splann taking Mrs. Cox and children and Becky Splann to town (the latter to assist Mrs. C. in putting her new house straight). So I got a lift the rest of the way, and drove out with Jim Splann. In town I got mail, to my great satisfaction: Your letter, and very soon started home with him, as he had no wish to stay in town. Since I returned, I have been at the Cusacks'. Lees is here. At the present moment Mrs. C., Lees, and Regy are arguing the question of Education. How much influence has it?

The mail I got, besides your letter, was (1.) Letter from Carlie, very long. He says, 'I don't intend to be simply Ruskinian. Every day I become more conscious of his limitations, at the same time more fully appreciating whatever is best and divinest in him.' He says he went to Wimpole St., and Uncle Douglas was 'entirely opposed' to my returning to England! However, of course I shall return, and I think perhaps this is not quite a true statement of his opinions. We must wait for his next letter. (2.) Letter from Dr. Hamilton, with names of beetles. He is pleased with the C.B.A. reports and will 'take great pleasure in contributing to its pages occasionally.' (3.) Letter from Dr. C. H. Merriam, with interesting remarks on a list of Colorado mammals I sent him. He urges the importance of correct localities, in which I cordially agree with him. Writers are continually annoying me by quoting only 'Colorado.' (4.) 'Insects injurious to forest and shade trees' (175 pp.), by and from Packard, for library of C.B.A. (5.) *Commonweal*.

Jan. 14th, 10 p.m. It's lucky I did go to town yesterday, for today it has been snowing almost without intermission, and there must be seven or eight inches of snow on the ground. I have been entering up records from *Ent. Americana* all day, the only event being three visitors this afternoon, Regy, and to my great astonishment, Campion

and young Ward! They arrived at the Cusacks' today. Campion is very pleasant, and talked about Nash and the C.B.A. Ward is the youth who is living with Campion (I think I mentioned him). He does not seem to have much to say for himself.

Now at last I answer your letter. I like what you say about Socialism; it makes our difference of opinion much clearer. We both recognise the same effects, and we both agree that there are two causes producing these effects, namely circumstances and human wrongdoing. We also both agree that one of these is essential and causative, the other secondary and resultant. We disagree as to which is which. You think that humanity is in such bad straits *because* it is wicked; I think it is because it is *foolish*, and being so conducts affairs in such a way as to *produce* what is called wickedness. Am I not stating it rightly?

Well, my love, who shall decide? We each have our opinion, our *theory*, but the solution of this question is not an easy one. It means much observation and study by many people, and that is *why* it has never been solved. We are all theorisers yet; we cannot *prove* what we believe in an infallible manner. Probably we shall do well to think and notice more, and argue less. So I will not go into another dissertation on the subject.

But I might say one thing. You speak of competition as necessary for some men's happiness. Is there no substitute in *emulation*? Well! We will talk it over some day; it is easier talking than writing. We shall understand each other better. I wish I could find you [someone with] a *good* anti-socialistic argument, but I don't know of one. Perhaps Herbert Spencer would like him still less! Essentially, I believe I agree in the main with Herbert Spencer, though he is so down on 'Socialism.'

You ask how I offended Woodward of the Natural History Museum! What has he been saying about me now? I am a perennial cause of offence to B. B. Woodward for several reasons, which I will enumerate. (1.) There are two special occasions on which I greatly offended him, viz., (a.) Once, being greatly disgusted at the general carelessness and foolishness of much of the work at the Natural History Museum, I wrote a long and very strong letter to Prof. Flower on the subject. As I might have expected, I got only an official reply, but next time I went to the Museum I had got all the staff into no end of a scrape for letting the public (i.e., myself) know all about the failings of the Museum and divulging the secrets thereof. The matter occurred years ago, and it isn't worth while going into the details now, but although the rest of the staff readily forgave me (after I had duly apologised, which I think now I need not have done), I don't think B.B.W. ever did. (2.) Once B.B.W. wrote a rather foolish article in the *Zoölogist* on variation in snails, and I wrote and criticised him in the next number, which he certainly didn't like. (3.) B.B.W. knows I don't like him, and therefore probably is not the fonder of me! (4.) To come to the real and fundamental and everlasting reason, I am strongly in favour of studying and *naming* varieties. B.B.W. loathes, abominates, and detests varietal nomenclature, and is pleased to call those who name varieties as 'variety-mongers', meaning thereby to express vast contempt.

You will smile at so small an issue being a cause of disagreement, but it is a very bitter question, this, of varietal nomenclature, and naturalists are constantly in violent conflict about it. When B.B.W. gives his lecture on conchology at the B. P. Club, I hope you and Frederic will be there, and then you will probably hear *his* side of the question stated in plain language. I would like to be there to argue the matter with him! Not to *convince* him, that is out of the question, but I should enjoy pitching into him!

What a brute Mr. Harrison is. I wonder what his wife thinks of him. I *did* feel pangs of remorse because I sent you no Christmas card. I don't like to hear about your turning so hoarse, poor Annie! Thank you for showing me your Christmas cards; certainly I am interested.

The full passage of Uncle Douglas' letter was 'It seems to me that you are on the whole doing well, and although at times you no doubt miss the society and sympathy of near friends, yet you have your health.' It was stupid of me not to give the whole at first.

Dear Annie, I hardly know what to say to the next part of your letter. You write so kindly, so lovingly. *Must* it be that I do not return next summer? Annie, I do not think about it. I still hope and do not weigh the chances yet. Perhaps some way may be found after all. Let us wait and see.

Then you urge that I ought to have regular employment and to be laying by for our home (thank you for saying 'our') in the future. I know you are right; I must somehow. But I seem to hear of nothing. This place is too far from civilisation. If I could, I would move near Pueblo or Denver or Colorado Springs, and I believe I should have a much better chance of getting work. And *you* are saving, my love, but don't. You need your money now, and some day (I hope not far away) I shall have enough for both of us.

I am quite busy now with my C.B.A., and although it brings in no money now, it will help me to get a post later on I expect. It all helps. [Ugh! The wind is blowing, cold, and the snow flies in at the cracks.] Perhaps I may take up some branch of medicine, after all. I read when I have time. But I think pure science must always be the first with me.

I forgive you for 'losing' the beetles and fly. I hadn't the least idea it was you; I expect it was the Custom House people. Jenner Weir says they open boxes. It was a pity though, as the beetle was unique in its way.

Jan. 15th, 6:55 p.m. A gloomy day, with a little snow. Morning, mostly, at the Cusacks', talking to Mrs. C. and Campion. I found also a stranger there, whom they addressed as Jack. I do not know his name, but he is absolutely uninteresting, a man of about 25 with nothing to say for himself.

Campion says he doesn't like *Robert Elsmere*. (There is yet another paper-cover edition of it, in two volumes.) I looked over some books of the Charley Cusacks' which they left behind and which had been brought up here. One is Doré's illustrations of Spain, which I can't say I like. They are not complimentary to the Spanish! There are also two volumes of Spurgeon's sermons. The first place I opened I came across (as nearly as I can remember) 'and what Christian will not *groan* when he considers all that God has done for him in the past.' Why should he groan, I wonder? If this is a fair sample of Spurgeon, I write him down an ass!

Then there is a little volume, *The Psalms of David*. The 'psalms' are by Watts, and in verse. There are also some hymns, but I don't find 'How doth the little busy bee'; isn't that by Watts? There is also a book on the human mind, and a Euclid, a *Vicar of Wakefield*, and *Pilgrim's Progress*. They are a lot of queer books altogether.

This afternoon I have been writing my 7th report of C.B.A. I have to incorporate the second part of Charlton's paper in this, but I don't altogether like it, and have appended some editorial criticism which you will see when the paper comes out. Lees visited me this morning. He went to town in that snow storm yesterday! Today he has gone up to his cabin. I did not say — of course I want to see the book with your illustrations, and will cheerfully pay postage and duty, so please send it. Who is the story by? I hope they have got your name right this time, and not murdered the drawings in printing (or should I say, engraving). I have an idea to do some wood-engraving for my C.B.A. reports. I wonder whether I could.

Jan. 16th, 8:10 p.m. Last night, after I had written the above, I went round to the Cusacks' for a while, and then came back and wrote notes of the *Geological Magazine* that Charlton lent me, because I have had it a long time and ought to return it tomorrow. This morning, when I woke, it was blowing a hurricane and continued to do so till midday. The snow flew in clouds and sifted in at every crevice and aperture in the

house — under the door, at the sides of the windows, and covering part of the floor with a white powder. I spent much of the day in writing to Dr. Merriam and Dr. Hamilton, and sorting out things for them to name. Later, I went over to the Cusacks' and sat talking to Campion. The snow had almost blocked up the Cusacks' front door.

Regy was 'trading' with one McCormick when I got there, selling him the two Payn horses. They were a long while about it, but finally Regy came in (they had been in the kitchen trading) and said he had 'got it fixed up, and only made $7 and a ton of hay by the transaction!' I remarked that Payn would probably rather object to this, but perhaps it could not be helped.

You see, it was this way. Lees had to get the horses sold, but had not time to do it himself, so he valued them (at $50 I think) and I believe told Regy that if he could sell them he might have anything above that sum he could get.. As a matter of fact, I think $50 is probably all they are worth, and all one can say is that Regy swindled McCormick out of the $7 and ton of hay. But this is 'business.'

After that, Regy produced a blanket which he offered to sell me for $3. Now it was certainly worth that, probably $3.50 or $4, so I got Mrs. C. to give Regy $3 out of the money Mother sent her, as the blanket will do very well for Leslie. Afterwards, Regy said that he only paid $1 for this blanket! He got it from Charley Cusack, who didn't want to take it away with him, and not being able to sell it just then, he let Regy have it for a dollar. Here, you see, it is the other way on. Regy gets $2 of 'unearned increment' but at the expense of the original owner and not of the purchaser. These trades are quite interesting from a political economy point of view [I see I dipped my pen in the red ink by mistake]. Then Campion wanted to sell *me* a horse for $30; I could pay in a year's time if I liked! I daresay the horse is worth $30 (I haven't seen it) but I don't think I want to buy it, all the same.

Leaving the Cusacks', I went down to Brock's (hearing from Regy that he was going

294

to town) and arranged to go to town with him tomorrow. It was about half past six when I got back to my house, and then I had to trim the lamp and fill it, make bread, peel some potatoes and cook and eat supper, so it was quite late before I got settled down to this letter.

In town — no letter! Delayed again by storms, no doubt. Well, I must wait!

Yours with much love, Theo.

Jan. 17th, 1889, 9 p.m.

Dear Annie,

Am most ridiculously sleepy tonight. I suppose the effect of the fresh (very fresh, coming home!) air. Anyhow, I can do nothing but go to bed, hoping to wake up some time tomorrow.

Jan. 18, 8:30 p.m. This is a most melancholy state of affairs. Lees has been to town today, and your letter has not come yet! [Interrupted by visit from Lees, to discuss Payn and other matters.] Of course, it is not a week since the last one, but then that was delayed, and this one should come sooner it if is not delayed also.

Yesterday I was down at Brock's at about 8: 30, but he was not yet ready to start, so I fetched some water from the creek and assisted in various ways until 9:30, and we started to town. Soon we met the Splanns returning from an unsuccessful attempt to get to town, saying that the snow had so drifted at the hill near my old house that no team could get through. But we managed to go another way, crossing the creek a little higher up, a very rough place, too rough for the Splann's heavy waggon but passable for us. (But Brock broke a spring over it coming home.) The snow was rather deep across the prairie, but we got along at a fair pace and got to town in about 1 3/4 hours.

I got some mail, but not your letter, and in the postoffice I met Turner, of the *Courant*, who said he was now only $15 short, and later I

saw him again and he told me he had got all the money. I'm glad of that. Then I went to the express office, and expressed to Nash the volumes of *Papilio* he lent me, and then on to Charlton's, returned his volume of *Geological Magazine*. After this, up to Silver Cliff and got reprints of 5th Report of C.B.A. and corrected 6th Report in the paper. I had been hurrying to get all this done, expecting that Brock would soon leave town, but he was delayed, and I had to sit in West Cliff a long time for him. But I had some mail to read, so it did not matter.

The sun went down as we went homewards, and it became very cold, so I got down and walked from the beginning of the prairie, and let Brock go ahead. At length, I got up to the Cusacks', where I spent the rest of the evening, till about nine. Jack, who I mentioned a few days ago, was still there, and proves to be Jack Mackenzie, brother of Colin. I have hardly spoken to him so cannot tell what he is like. Mrs. C. says he is a very good fellow, indeed. Mrs. C. had just heard from Mrs. Urquhart (I brought the letter from town), who declares she cannot possibly consent to marriage of Regy to Miss U., and wants to know what 'settlement' Regy would be able to make on her! When she wrote this, she had not received Mrs. C.'s letter that I concocted, but only one from Regy or Miss U. (I don't know which).

This morning I entered up records, and after this, Lees turned up and went on to town with his sledge, before he went, asking me to chink up his stable (there is a small stable at the Cusacks', built by Louis, which he uses) which is altogether too airy. So I spent most of the afternoon at this, but did not finish it, as it began to get too cold to work, the sun having gone down. After supper, Lees returned from town, bringing me some mail, and also a new axe-handle (cost 35 cents) which I needed, as I broke the handle of my axe cutting wood this morning. Lees came round here again later and interrupted this just as I had begun it.

Now I must tell you about the mail. Yesterday's mail: (1.) Letter from Mother, enclosing

$3 'to buy a book with.' (2.) Letter from Jenner Weir, who says the Customs people have greatly damaged a box of butterflies I sent him, and *abstracted* a beetle I put in, so it was evidently the same wretch that got away with the specimens I sent you! It's a shame. Jenner Weir says he would like to join C.B.A., but how can he send so minute a subscription? So I have put him down anyway. (3.) Letter from J. B. Ellis, with names of fungi I sent. He says some are very interesting. He also sends *Journal of Mycology*, Nov. and Dec. (4.) Letter from C. H. Merriam. (5.) Letter from C. V. Riley. (6.) Postcard from Orcutt. (7.) *West Amer. Scientist*, November, and the Index I compiled, both with misprints which Orcutt excuses by saying he 'forgot to look at the proof.' I sent you copies of these: *Standard, Science Gossip, Pall Mall Budget, Wm. Wesley's* book circular No. 93, *Ornithologist and Oölogist*, and *Custer Courant*.

Today's mail: (1.) Letter from Dr. Horn, who says the *Longitarsus nitidellus*, being pinned, got damaged in transit. (2.) Letter from G. B. Norris, wanting to know whether I have any Colorado bird's eggs for sale (I haven't). Norris is a good man, and I must try to get him some. (3.) Postcard from Smithsonian Inst., announcing receipt of fossils I sent. (4.) Sample copy of *Hawkeye Ornith. & Oöl.*, a rubbishy little paper. (5.) *Naturalist*. Lees also brought a long letter from 'Mary Howard' (one has to think for a moment, who can that be?) Thanking me for picture I sent down byt Lees today. It was the McWhirter that Carlie sent me, and perhaps it was too bad to give it away, but Louis admired it so that I thought it would give them pleasure, and I have had it a long while.

The first event to tell today is a visit from Lees, just as I had finished breakfast. After that, I wrote a letter and two postcards, and then sallied forth to do some more work on Lees' stable. I got two old gunny sacks and cut them into strips, which I rammed into the chinks between the logs and so prevented the entrance of wind and snow. I have now made it passable, and may do a little more to it on other days in the future, at odd times.

At about 2:30 (I think it was) I went into the Cusacks' and found they had just finished lunch. I had been busy over the stable and had had none (I forgot all about it, though I generally eat some bread or something if I am at home). So Mrs. C. insisted of my partaking. After that I washed up the lunch things and then brought my new axe handle and broken axe over there to get Jack Mackenzie to help me fix it. Jack very kindly put on the new handle himself, which is a bigger business than you would imagine. The handle has to be made to fit, and then a peg carefully knocked in to make it tight. In fact one might speak of the art of putting on an axe handle! It took a long time and much trouble, too, to get off the broken remnant of the old handle, which had been fixed in tighter than I imagined. This evening Colin Mackenzie and Campion have appeared at the Cusacks', having come down from Lees.

9:25 p.m. I have just been across to the Cusacks' to give Colin some mail to post (he goes to town tomorrow). It is a very cold night. Regy has just looked at the thermometer and reports eight below zero.

Sunday, Jan. 20th, 8:20 p.m. At the Cusacks'. Colin and Campion have gone to town but have not returned, which disappoints me much, as I expect surely to get your letter today. Campion went in to get some telegram he expected, and perhaps he is waiting for them, though I don't think the telegraph office would be open on Sunday.

This morning I read various things in the bulky report of the U. S. Commissioner of Agriculture for 1887, one especially interesting paper being on the effect of pollination, whereby it appears that hybridization not only affects the seed, but sometimes even the parent plants. For instance, a florist had a particular variety of *Gladiolus* with pure white flowers, which always flowered true to the variety, until one year he planted some red gladioli close by, and then the same bulbs of the white variety, which had produced white flowers thereto, produced *red* and *white* flowers instead! This is really extremely curious.

This afternoon I wrote my 8th Report of C.B.A. I puzzled for a long time what to have the 'leading' article about, and finally settled on 'snails and slugs.' This evening, as it is Sunday, I am at the Cusacks'. Louis and his wife are here. Regy is going to Colorado Springs by Tuesday's train, and goes to town tomorrow, and I with him, to bring back his horse and buckboard. Regy is going to a ball at Colorado Springs, and then brings Miss Urquhart back here.

Jan. 21st, 11:30 a.m. No sign of Colin or Campion yet. Lees was round here this morning. There is no knowing when I shall get my covers for C.B.A. reports, so I sent the separates of the first five reports for you and Frederic. When I get a cover I will send it, and you can tack them together in it.

8:55 p.m. At the Cusacks'. My dear love, I have got your letter, and *such* a nice one! Thank you. I am rather tired tonight, and will not write much., but I shall be able to write before I post this. Immediately after lunch, I left for town with Regy. We had Lees' waggon .With the horses, Ferris and Sleepy Joe. As soon as we got on the prairie, I saw someone coming and thought, it must be Colin, and I shall get my mail. But it was only Cress, after all. But we did meet Colin later, just after we got off the prairie, and he gave me the mail. Nearly al the rest of the way to town I was reading your letter, as Regy was driving and so I was free. I told Regy that he never got such letters, but he said he wouldn't believe me unless he could read yours and see, and that was out of the question!

The first thing I did in town was to go and see Charlton, whom I found at dinner (although it was about two o'clock). I think I said that I had written some criticism of his paper in my last report (now in press) and I wanted to ask him to reply to it if he cared to do so, so that we could get up a bit of an argument. He said he would.

It seems rather ridiculous criticising a man and then asking him to criticise one's criticism, but I think a little discussion will interest people, and Charlton and I certainly do disagree very much on the question of 'natural selection.'

Having finished with Charlton, I went up with Regy and Campion (who was still in town) to Silver Cliff — Regy to get his hair cut, and I went round and saw Grant Turner. The tail end of my report was just being put in type; the proof was not yet ready. Then I went to Mrs. Cox's in her new house between Silver Cliff and West Cliff. It is quite a large house and not quite in order. I found Mrs. Hunter there, talking to her. Cox has gone off to Kansas City, and that is why I went there, for Mrs. Cox does not like to be left alone (naturally) and asked me to stay there till Cox came back.

There was a letter from Cox and a later note from Mrs. Cox about this among the mail Colin gave me. It is perfectly monstrous that Cox should go off and leave his wife like this. Of course I shall go and stay there as she wishes it. She has Regy and Campion there tonight, and besides, I had to bring the team and waggon out, but I shall walk to town tomorrow and probably stay there till Monday. In one way, it is convenient for me. I may perhaps manage to get up a meeting of the C.B.A. but this is to be thought over.

Leaving Regy at Mrs. Cox's, I returned home with the waggon. It was already late, and the sun soon went down. It was dark before I got up here. There was just a breath of air, enough to make it very cold, but I have thawed out and am warm again now! Fortunately, I was very well wrapped up. I borrowed some extra things from Regy — a pea-jacket and a cap to go over the ears and neck, like an Arctic explorer.

I have ever so much to say in reply to your letter, but perhaps it is better first to tell about the other mail. (1.) Letter from C. V. Riley, in answer to one of mine. (2.) Letter from Prof. A. S. Packard, joining C.B.A. and sending subscription, and also a couple of copies of reprints of note of his on 'The larva of a fly in a hot spring in Colo-rado', one for me and one for C.B.A. He also says he will, if we like, send a copy of his 'Monograph of Geometrid Moths', a very valuable work of which we shall be very glad. He says he will also send a copy for me, but if he sends one for the society, that will be enough. I am very glad to get Packard as a member; he is an exceedingly able naturalist. He says he is going back to Italy for a while. (3.) Letter from Prof. Byron D. Halsted, a very good botanist (lives in Iowa), joining C.B.A. He is now making a special study of weeds. (4.) Pall Mall Gazette from Mother, in its new (large) form which I don't like. But there is a very interesting article in it on Spiritualism, by Huxley. Did you see it? (5.) Letter from Nash of Pueblo.

I must just say now, that I think your idea of writing on 'A Middlesex lane in April', for the C.B.A. reports is just grand. Please do, as soon as you can. Never mind its being April. 'A lane in February' will be interesting to everyone, and then you must write the April one later. One is a little puzzled to know where to find a Custer Co. lane to correspond! The things they term 'lanes' here are just open-country roads with a fence on each side, and never a tree anywhere! However, suppose we have got this letter by then. I will go out into the woods (the nearest approach to a lane I can find) on Feb. 10th, and describe what I see. Will you?

It is 20 past ten by my watch, but people here do not go to bed, so I write a little more. Yes, it is *Cantharis nuttalli* Say (i.e., Thomas Say). The printer of *W. Amer. Scientist* is an idiot!) I am very glad you like the C.B.A. report. Yes, it is my mistake in the spelling of 'synonymy'! You facetious creature! I would make the 'Currant Pudding' suggestion to Turner, only, as Regy remarks, they call Currant Pudding 'Plum Duff' out here, and so he wouldn't see the joke!

My poor Annie, I am so sorry to hear you were so ill! 'Will I be patient with you when you are ill and cross?' When you are ill, I hope I shall be *able* to comfort you a little, though up to date, I do not recollect ever being a consolation to any-one, that is, in times of illness and discomfort.

But perhaps I could be nicer to *you* than I usually am. Do you think so?

Jan. 22nd, 10:15 p.m. (By my watch. I think it is not really so late).This has been a rather busy day, and I have only just got at this letter again, while a great pile of letters lies in front of me unanswered! I wrote and prepared for my departure all the morning. Colin went to town at about nine, but I had some things to do before I left and could not go with him. But I handed him a bundle of things, including note books and diary, to take into town for me. At Mrs. Cusacks' invitation, I had !unch at her house, and directly afterwards started townwards, walking. When I got near Ula, I caught up Sam Kettle taking a load of straw to town, and so got a ride. Soon we met Colin coming out and bringing my bundle with him; he forgot to leave it in town! It is lucky I was riding with Kettle, as the bundle would have been heavy to haul the last mile or so to town.

Of course, I went to the postoffice when I got to West Cliff, and there got a postcard from Dr. Hamilton, schedules for recording bird migration from C. H. Merriam, *Pall Mall Budget*, *Commonweal*, and *Standard*. Then I went up to Mrs. Cox's, and from there to Silver Cliff, where I got and corrected the proof of my coming (7th) report. While I was there, Turner produced a number of copies of *Bath Chronicle*, containing full reports of British Association meeting and some reprints of papers by Sherborn, and said they had come to him with a wrapper marked 'from T.D.A. Cockerell to Grant Turner'!! I know nothing about them, but obviously they must originally have been sent to me by Sherborn, who misdirected them probably to Silver Cliff, and somehow they got to Turner by someone knowing I wrote for his paper [I expect this *should* read *'for'*]. Anyhow, it is very queer, but the papers are quite interesting, and I am glad to have got them at last. Grant Turner wants to exchange his paper with some local English weekly, as much like his own as possible. Can you suggest one? I don't know anything about the local papers about Isleworth and Bedford Park, except their names.

This evening I went down to the postoffice for the evening mail (got letters from (1.) Smith of Denver, enclosing $1 subscr. to C.B.A. on behalf of Denis Gale, of Gold Hill, Colo. (2.) Nash of Pueblo, who says he is sending volumes of *Canadian Entomologist* (on loan) by express. I shall be glad to see these. I also got the Nov. and Dec. *J. of Mycology* from Ellis (he sent these before; he must have forgotten that he did so). I found Campion at the postoffice, still awaiting his telegram. I went with him to the telegraph office, and we found that he might wait till Doomsday, because it is not legal for the telegraph operator to forward telegrams which have been mailed (such was the case with Campion's. He wanted a copy of a telegram which had been out in the postoffice for him in Pueblo). Charlton will now have to telegraph to the Pueblo postmaster, I suppose, and will get his telegram.

From the telegraph office I went to Charlton's and gave him a proof of his paper (second part) and my criticisms thereon. Also I partially arranged for a meeting of the C.B,.A. on Saturday. But of this more when I get it satisfactorily settled. Now I am at Mrs. Cox's. Turner (the Brock-ite Turner) is here, nailing up pictures. As he is here it is not necessary, after all, to be here when he goes. It seems Cox won't come back till the middle of next week at the earliest.

I enclose a note for S. London Ent. Soc. Will Frederic take it when he goes? I wanted L. O. Howard to write a note to *Entom.* about it, but said I would write to S.L.E.S. if he liked, and Riley now writes that probably would be the better way, hence the enclosed note.

Now more about your letter. I think the idea about the object falling from an 'infinite distance' to the earth) as I quoted from *Geol. Mag.*) is this. The amount of attraction exercised by the earth decreases at a given ratio as we go away from it, till it becomes inappreciable. Suppose one pound, falling from a distance so great that the earth's influence is practically nil — it would raise so much (as I quoted).

I am glad I can now smile at your having pitied 'the woman who ever marries Theo'! Let us hope you will never have to return to that opinion! You further say 'I thought it would be all right enough for *Carlie's* future wife. How entirely I have reversed my opinions.' Don't you think *now* that Carlie would make a good husband? I never thought much about it, but he is a very excellent person, and if anyone should like him and he like her well enough for them to be married, I would not be anything but pleased.

Glad to know that I am *'really* millions old!' But it is queer that Kitty is older than I am; I did not think she was so ancient. After all, age isn't years, and years don't always make age! I am thankful that you are young and frivolous, though I am so antique! But Kitty's youngness is different; she seems quite a child. Perhaps you are right in saying I don't take Olive simply enough. Quite true, my dear; I fell in love before I knew it. (I would never have done anything so ridiculous if I had known it, but you see when I found out it was hopelessly too late!). I never was in love before, certainly.

You ask what 'she' stood highest in my esteem before we knew one another. I really don't know. I had no 'she' high in my esteem atall, though I had a kindly enough feeling for the gender. I used to have a sort of childish affection for Ida Gibbs when in Madeira, as we were thrown almost entirely on one another's society, but I was only twelve and she was ten. And I don't think I should like her now she is grown up, if I may judge from the tendency of the family, though they are excellent people enough. I don't know what has become of Ida G. now; the last I heard of her was that she was in school in England. Probably I would have loved nobody if I had never met you. I can't imagine how I could.

You see there is no biography again in this, so please scold me. I really must make amends.

The father that would not let his daughters get married, that Mother was speaking about, as you mention, was an old chap named Gardiner, who lived at Hastings. Now he is dead, but there are still two daughters there, old and unmarried. *Excellent* people, but insufferably pious!

Perhaps Charlton is not quite all I hoped, but he is no doubt a good fellow. No, Annie, I won't smoke if you won't! That's a bargain, isn't it? Of course, I don't mind your correcting my spelling. I should blunder forever if nobody pulled me up.

(My watch says five to twelve, and so though I have more today I will end up for to-day). I would not have sat up so late, only that Mrs. Cox and Turner were so interested in the nailing-up of pictures that they forgot about the time, and I thought I might as well write on, especially as I expect to have next to no time tomorrow. So goodnight, my love!

Jan. 23rd, 10:05 a.m. I am going to post this today, so I had better write what I want to now.

About names, Sarah is not one of my favor-ite names, though I don't think it 'very ugly', as you say. But I like 'Annie' very much. Perhaps this is because I always associate the name with you. You speak of our family 'handwriting.' Well, you see, both the parents wrote much alike, and so the writing should be intensified in the children, one would think. Douglas doesn't write a bit like the rest of us, though.

So I haunted you in your dreams. I rarely dream (or if I do, I forget them on waking), but I did have a queer dream about you a few nights ago. As near as I can remember it was like this. I was traveling on a train when the engine broke, or something, and we could not proceed. We were supposed to be ever so far from every-where, and there was great consternation as to what would become of us. However, I had an idea. I knew where there were some houses over a hill, and said so, but nobody would believe me, and they all declared they would stop with the train. So I started out alone. Just then I saw you among the passengers, but as is often the case in dreams, I did not realize who you were. I felt as if I knew you, but, full of doubt, went off and left you. As I got halfway up the hill and out of sight of the train, I suddenly remembered who you were, and, full of remorse for leaving you, ran back. I found you had left the rest, and I met you striking out on your own account. You did not scold me, but took my hands, and I promised I would never leave you again.

So we went on, and presently came to a house, where we asked for food. The man would not let us have any at first, but at length brought some out, and we were going to eat when you said, 'Look, he has poison' — and I saw he had a box marked strychnine in the other hand. So we were afraid, and ate nothing, but went on. After that the dream ceased. It is strange what extraor-dinary events happen in dreams!

This week's bit of your biography is very interesting. I think I should have liked your old grandfather Leake. I have a very vivid picture of him in my mind from your description.

I am going soon to see whether I can get the use of the West Cliff schoolhouse for my meeting of C.B.A. When I go, I will post this, so will now end up.

Your own lover, Theo.

I enclose three English stamps that I found in my purse that seem not to have been used. You can send them back on a letter!

Jan. 23rd, 10:10 p.m.

My dear,

I posted a letter to you today, but have not got yours of this week. Indeed, considering the late erratic ways of the English mails, I hardly ventured to expect it.

I have been quite busy today, and have now definitely arranged for my C.B.A. meeting at the West Cliff Schoolhouse on Tuesday at 8 p.m. Af-ter breakfast, having written a little and helped to fix up a stove and cut up some meat, I went down to the schoolhouse. I found the school-master there, and asked whether I could have the schoolhouse for a meeting on Saturday. He said yes, so far as he was concerned, but I must get the consent of the trustees. The only trustee I knew was Stewart, the blacksmith, so I went and hunted him up and got him to give me leave to use the schoolhouse, saying he would make it right with the other trustees.

Then I went on the Charlton's, and we concocted a bill to be issued. C. was quite ill with a bilious attack and thought he might not be recovered sufficiently to attend by next Saturday (he is to give us some chemistry), so I promised to put off the meeting till Tuesday. C. described his symptoms in detail, and wanted me to prescribe. I told him to take lots of fresh air (i.e., drive out) and do as little work as possible.

Then I had to see Stewart and the schoolmaster again and get leave for the schoolhouse on Tuesday instead of Saturday. This I did, and finally I had to see an old fellow (I forget his name) who superintended the church, which is the same building as the school. He said I might certainly use the building, provided I wasn't going to give them anything immoral! I assured him that it was strictly moral, and invited him to attend, which I think he will. Having thus arranged matters, I came back here (Cox's) for lunch, and then went to Grant Turner's and gave him the manuscript of the circular. He said he would also print me 50 admission tickets, for which he would not charge (very liberal of him, this).

This afternoon I wrote letters to Packard, Nash, and Halsted, and this evening went down to the postoffice for mail, and got (1.) *Entom. Mag.* (2.) Letter from Step — a big letter with a *penny* stamp on it, so I had to pay 16 cents before I could get it! Step says he will send me $1 for my 'Welcome' article of long ago (about time he did!) and wants to know how he can send it! (He might easily have found out; dollar bills would do well enough!) Also, he encloses a number of engravings of places in Colorado, and one of a buffalo's head, and wants me to write two short articles to accompany them. I will do so, but I hope he will pay me sooner than before. I

don't think I am good at this sort of thing by any means, but if he uses the articles I naturally conclude he owes me for them.

Jan. 24th, 10 p.m. I seem to have been very busy all day, but now looking back, I have done almost nothing. But I have got your letter this evening, and so am very well pleased.

In the morning I went down to West Cliff to get some milk for Mrs. Cox, and I called at the express office and found awaiting me a bundle of *Canadian Naturalist*, lent to me by Nash of Pueblo. It is very fortunate for me to have this chance of reading them. I have *looked* them through and find them very interesting indeed, but I expect I cannot get at them to read until after my C.B.A. meeting on Tuesday.

All today Brock and Mrs. Turner were expected in from the ranch, but they never came. This is unfortunate, because Brock was to have hauled some wood for us, ands now we have none, except a few old boards which have to be chopped up. I wrote to Smith of Denver (a long letter) and to Step (a postcard) this afternoon, and this evening went down for the mail, and to my great satisfaction got your letter. The other mail was *Young Naturalist* (sample copy), *Pall Mall Budget*, and *Commonweal*. I think I must answer your letter a little tonight, at any rate. I don't think I ever heard of N. Richardson. There is a Hugh Richardson who is a conchologist.

The Nelsonian ideas about marriage are idiotic. Whether love can be all one-sided, I don't yet know. I don't know, that is to say, what one-sided love may be, whether it is really what I call love. It's very queer and difficult to understand.

Your remark about Regy and Miss U. is very 'cute.' I think, too, that it will (very likely) be presently broken off! I forgive you for telling Louy about the letter to Mrs. Urquhart. Of course, Annie, I trust you, and you can always tell my secrets when you want to, to people who you think are safe. When I write 'don't tell this', I mean, don't speak of it before anyone who might repeat it. You see, the Urquhart mother letter affair, if circulated promiscuously, might somehow reach Miss U., or Regy, or someone concerned, and that would be lamentable. It is astonishing how news will travel when it is not wanted to.

Re the note on *Colias* and the primrose colour, I think I would call a primrose vivid yellow. I did hesitate when writing the note, however. I think a primrose is vivid (sulphur) yellow, and a buttercup vivid (chrome) yellow — different kinds of yellow, but equally vivid. Buttercup colour diluted does not make primrose colour.

I tried to read *R. Falconer* ages ago, but the Scotch was too much for me. But I read *Sir Gibbie*, and enjoyed it immensely.

Thank you for your thoughts on love, dear Annie. So you have grown more sympathetic, but surely you were always so! I send you a kiss, because you are so nice to me, and don't say you won't have it! What is the least I consider people ought to marry on? I don't know. I think a man has a sort of natural right to marry on tuppence if he wants to, but I do not recommend such a course, all the same. Often people condemn the poor for marrying. I don't, but I condemn a society for most of the evils that come from such marriages. On much the same principle, I don't approve of stealing, but I see a man must eat, and if he is starving and steals food I am not going to condemn him. I condemn the causes which made it impossible for him to get food honestly. Don't you agree with me?

I am glad you are jealous of Miss Plummer no longer! I can't imagine why Wm. West does not reply. I am very glad to hear Sir M. M.'s favourable health report. Your biography this week is very interesting.

Jan. 25th, 6:35 p.m. Brock, Mrs. Turner, and the child Hilda turned up today and will stay here tonight. Tomorrow Brock and Mrs. T. go to Rosita, and leave Turner and the child here. I went up to the *Courant* office this morning,

hoping that the circulars might be ready, but they won't till tomorrow. The meeting is not till Tuesday, after all, so there is no hurry. This afternoon I drew two large coloured diagrams for my paper on ichneumons. One is an ichneumon, and the other (not quite finished) is a caterpillar.

Lees is here — *walked* down from his cabin today because his team is busy hauling sawlogs. It is a horrid snowy night, but I think not very cold, and I am going out with Lees in half an hour to Ula. We shall stop at Louis' for the night. Tomorrow we walk to the Cusacks' or, if the weather is bad, I return here. My reasons for going out are (1.) I want to get some specimens to exhibit at the meeting, and figures to enlarge into diagrams, all of which are at my house. (2.) Mrs. Cox has no need for me, I take it, with all these Turners here. I return here probably Sunday morning.

Jan. 26th, 9:15 p.m. Going to bed at twelve or later, and getting up at half past five makes one feel sleepy. I am now half asleep and too muddled to write any sense. I am back at the Cox's. My C.B.A. bills are printed, but I will tell you about it all tomorrow.

Jan. 27th, evening. (My watch is wrong, so I don't know the right time.) My love, it seems an age since I wrote to you, for the little scrawl last night has no right to be called writing. I have to go back to the evening of the day before yesterday when I started out with Lees.

We had supper here, and then left without further delay. It was not such a bad night after all. At the postoffice I found a letter from Leslie, who says he has got a job at the Imperial Bank at $200 a year and so will not come out here. He does not know which branch they will send him to, but he will not stay in Toronto. Of course, I think he ought to be here, but I need not reiterate my views, and I do not see how I can do anything more to get him here. If he won't, I can't make him, only he must suffer the consequences. But it's very wretched.

We got to Ula all right at about half past nine. I had never seen Louis' house and was much pleased with its appearance. The dining room (includes kitchen) and sitting-room were all that I saw, but they are exceedingly comfortable and pleasant-looking, very comfortable indeed. The two seem to thoroughly enjoy their wedded life so far, and are evidently quite happy. May they continue so! I had no bedding with me and so had to sleep in my clothes, but fortunately Louis has in his sitting-room (where Lees and I slept) a very nice stove which is filled with coal in the evening, and burns all night, feeding itself by some mechanism which I do not properly understand. Had it not been for this I should have been very cold.

I sat up till past twelve and Lees also; he was writing letters he had to post in time to go out by the morning train the next day. To get there in time for this, Lees had to be off early, and so we all got up at 5:30 a.m. (it was not yet daylight). Louis and his wife got us a very nice breakfast, and Lees walked off to town while I turned my steps towards my house. It was very cold, with a sort of damp fog, when I started, but afterwards the sun appeared, and things bettered. It took me 2½ hours to get to the Cusacks', as the snow on the prairie made it hard walking.

It was ten when I arrived, and I found the Cusacks just in the middle of breakfast. Lees had by this time had been to town, and walked out the way I had come, up to the Cusacks'. He asked me to tell Jack MacKenzie to take his (Lees') team and the bob-sleigh, and go down to meet him half way, but Jack had not had his breakfast, and was exceedingly slow, so that he was only about to start when Lees turned up an hour and a half later. I was sorry for this and rather angry with Jack, as Lees had had a hard walk, and might have been spared the last part of it.

I sorted out the papers and specimens I wanted for my C.B.A. meeting, and early in the afternoon began to think of getting back to town.

Now Louis' team and a borrowed spring waggon of Sampson's were at the Cusacks', and Regy was to take them down to Louis'. Regy was very loath to go, I think, and so I kindly (!) offered to take them down, and so got a ride instead of having to walk. I took the Cusacks up some mail; among them was a letter from Charley Cusack from Santa Barbara. He reports everything satisfactory and seems delighted with the place. By the way, Miss Urquhart was up there, having returned from Colorado Springs.

Well, having Louis' horses and the waggon I drove off, and reached Ula without adventure. When I got there I found that Louis wanted to go to town to get some coal, so I rode in with him. It was then about five, and before going to the Cox's, I went up to Silver Cliff (got a ride up there in a waggon) to see if the bills for my meeting were printed. They were, so I took them with me and went to Mrs. Cox's and then down to West Cliff again to get some mail and distribute some of my bills. I had posted a bill in the Silver Cliff postoffice, and in West Cliff I posted them in the postoffice, the hotel, and in Falkenberg's, and distributed a number to various people.

I got two letters from Dr. C. H. Merriam, the ornithologist and mammalogist to the Dept. of Agriculture. He joins C.B.A. (I am very glad of this) and sends $1.00 for four years' subscription. It was very cold driving to West Cliff, colder than it was later after dark, and before going up to Silver Cliff I could not resist the temptation of warming myself well by the stove at the postoffice. The result of getting warm, and then going out into the cold air again, as I half expected at the time, has been to give me a bad cold in the head.

Today I have done little else than write my paper on ichneumons for the meeting of C.B.A. I have got it written (I may add more) but do not feel very pleased with it, because I am so stupid about having a cold that my thoughts do not flow as they ought to do. It is now getting on for eleven, and although I have more to say in answer to your letter, I will now go to bed. Goodnight!

Jan. 28th, 1889, 8:55 p.m. A very busy day. After breakfast I worked a little at my diagrams and then went up to Silver Cliff to see whether my admission tickets for the meeting were ready. They were not, so I returned and made a new diagram (of *Thalassa*) and had lunch, and went again to Silver Cliff and got my tickets. Armed with these, and the bills, and two of the diagrams to show what I was going to speak about, I set out on my travels.

I took the main street of Silver Cliff and went into every store. When I got half way down the street, I found to my horror that the *time* of meeting (8 p.m) was not stated on the bills. I had put it in my MS copy and never looked to see whether it was on the bill before. Quite a number of people said they would probably come, but did not buy tickets. One man would take a ticket, but had only a 25 cent piece, and I had no change. Another offered 25 cents for three tickets and I sold them to him.

It was rather amusing going round. At the beer-hall and eating-house they would give me 25 cents apiece if I would deliver my lecture to them there and then! 'But I haven't got the manuscript with me' — 'Oh, we'll pay a boy to go and get the manuscript' — but I didn't accept their offer! Afterwards, I went down to West Cliff; it was now getting dark. Here I was more successful, and sold six tickets.

I waited for the mail, and got (1.) Letter from Morrison, who says he is very pleased with progress of C.B.A. (2.) Letter from J. P. Norris (a good bird man) joining C.B.A. and sending subscription.(3.) Postcard from J. B. Ellis, and *Journal of Mycology* for 1887 for his subscr. to C.B.A. (4.) Standard. (5.) *Insect Life*, January.

Brock and Mrs. Turner have come back from Rosita, and are here. I wish you could advise me now! Turner (that is, the Brock-ite Turner) tells me that the postmaster at Rosita is wishing to resign his place, and probably I could get it if I wished. The arguments are (1.) Pro: Turner says it would probably bring me $30 a month and would leave me plenty of leisure for scientific work, though I should have to be in the office all day. (2.) Con: If the present holder is so anxious to quit, I don't think the job can be worth so much. Also, I should have the greatest difficulty in getting away if I got anything else that suited me better. Letters would be longer reaching me and, lastly, I should have to become a citizen of the U. S. Turner suggests that I should write and offer to take the post as 'deputy' for a while, and then apply for it. Or, if it is really a good thing, I should stand no chance and only be going to useless trouble and expense because the post depends on getting signatures of Rosita people, and of course, residents who were known there would be sure to be preferred to me if they applied. I think perhaps I will offer to go as deputy for a fortnight, and if this is not accepted will not bother further about it. It might be useful to learn the business of postmaster.

Jan. 29th, 10:35 p.m. The meeting is over, and has been as successful as one could expect under the circumstances. 25 came, and we are 75 cents out on the whole affair, which the C.B.A. can well afford. I think I have lots of impudence to get up and address a meeting like this! But I will tell you all about it tomorrow.

Jan. 30th, 11:15 a.m. Yesterday morning Mrs. Cox and Mrs. Turner went out and I was left to mind the children. I employed my time in making a new diagram, of ladybird and cocoon of its parasite (*Megilla maculata* and *Centides*) and of spider attacked by parasitic larvae (*Linyphia* and *Polysphincta*). Then I went up to Silver Cliff (Mrs. Cox having come and relieved me of the care of the children) and gave Turner the name of a new member (Morris) to include in the next report. After this came lunch, and then I went down to West Cliff to arrange for my meeting. I went to see Charlton, and to my horror I found that he could not come! The doctor would not allow him out of the house, even in the daytime! Here was a pretty state of things! I was left to entertain a whole audience all by myself, and when they had paid, too, and had a right to expect something good! Are you not sorry for me?

Well, it was now altogether too late to go back, so I made up my mind to do the thing as best I could, and trust to 'providence.' The next thing was to get a chairman, and I asked Stewart, the blacksmith, he being the most respected man in town. But he had prior business arrangements and could not come. So I looked round for another chairman, but without success, and let the matter 'slide', hoping to get one when the meeting came. I borrowed some chemicals from Charlton, to appease the multitude, as chemistry was on the bill. I also borrowed some bottles for the same purpose from Merriam's drug store.

At about six, I came up here, had tea, and donned a black coat and masher-collar (borrowed; they belong to Cox) and went down to West Cliff again, first to the schoolhouse, to put up the diagrams, then to the postoffice, for mail (I got a letter from Dr. Horn and one from Webster, editor of *Ornithologist and Oölogist*, joining C.B.A. — this is the 35th member). Then back to the schoolhouse (it was now nearly eight) and some people had arrived. I was in despair about a chairman, when I noticed a rather educated-looking man — English-looking too. I was told his name was Wright, and without knowing him, I asked him to be chairman, and he said he would. This was fortunate, for he made as good a chairman as I could have wished.

At a quarter past eight we commenced. There were 25 people (or with myself, 26), about half of them ladies (or rather more than half). Wright made a preliminary speech, apologising on Charlton's behalf, saying that Charlton would perform at a future meeting, to which those who had come to this would be admitted free.

Here is a picture of the performance. The platform is a recess at the back of the building, raised above the floor like any other platform. I had the diagrams suspended on a string tied to the two side lamps, but they were not in a very good light. I commenced with the chemistry, and showed the tests for iron, lead, and copper.

Then I produced a sample of the 'lard' they sell here in tin buckets and which I and many others use. I stated that some people had suggested that it was not lard, and explained that if genuine it would become orange on being added to sulphuric acid; if spurious it would turn black. Of course it turned black, for it is undoubtedly spurious, probably cottonseed oil. This created a good deal of interest, and Mr. Walters, the grocery man of the firm of Kettle and Walters, who was sitting near the door, was looked at with a great deal of suspicion. But, as a matter of fact I got the sample from Falkenberg.

Lecturing

Then I read my paper on ichneumons; that is, I read part of it, but also spoke a great deal because the manuscript I had prepared was not long enough. When I wrote it of course I expected Charlton to be there. I used the blackboards to draw some additional diagrams. I rather expected I should be scared when I came to speak, but I wasn't a bit, and got along all right. My voice also was much better than when I was in England, and I could easily make myself heard.

At about a quarter past nine I left off, the chairman made a short speech, and the meeting broke up. I walked part of the way up the road with Grant Turner. On the whole, the affair went off as well as I hoped, and the people seemed pleased. The old chap who wanted to know 'whether the meeting was to be anything immoral' looked after the door, and took $1.40 in cash. So, with the tickets sold, the meeting brought in $2.25, but it cost $3.00 ($2.00 for printing and a dollar for lighting, etc.), so the association is 75 cents out by it. But I think it was worth while. Do you?

Today I have been up to Silver Cliff to see the proof of the 8th report, and since I came back have been writing up my diary and writing this. I am going away today, or at least as far as Ula. I don't think I need stay here, and the Turners aggravate me exceedingly. Mrs. T. is a most detestable woman. I meant to write about coming home, but perhaps I must wait till next letter, as I have a great deal to do today, and I want to post this before I go. Perhaps I have said enough on the subject in former letters, but I like to talk to you about it, since I cannot help thinking about it. No more biography, either, this time! Will you forgive me, as I have been so busy?

Most lovingly, Your own Theo.

Evening. Got your letter! Am just off to Ula.

Thursday evening, Jan. 31st, 1889

My love,

In the last letter (posted yesterday) you have the news up to yesterday afternoon. After lunch on that day I wrote several letters relating to the C.B.A., and then towards evening collected my goods into two bundles and departed from the Cox's. The larger bundle being heavy, I left it at Goldstandt's to be fetched by anyone coming to town. The smaller, consisting mainly of diary and Fauna and Flora book I carried.

First I went to Charlton's to return his chemicals. I found him rather better, and talked with him about evolution and kindred matters until the evening meal was distributed, when I went to the postoffice and got, to my great satisfaction, a grand letter from you, and also letters from Mother and Wallis Kew, and a postcard from Carrington (who thinks he may come to America in the spring). It must have been about 7:30 when I left town.

It was not a very cold night, and I got to Louis' at Ula comfortably enough, eating my

supper on the way — a huge sandwich of bread and ham that Mrs. Cox had kindly put up for me. I stayed the night at Louis', as I intended to do. It was perhaps rather a shame to jump in upon them in this way, but they asked me to come whenever I liked, and they greeted me very kindly. I found Bernard Sidford there, which is to say, a brother of Mrs. Howard who has just come out to this country for his health. He suffers from asthma. He has only been in Colorado about a week; he seems a very nice fellow, young, perhaps 20, with a rather slightly-built figure and a fair complexion and almost girlish face. But probably he will figure more prominently hereafter.

As soon as I got settled down at the Howards', I read your letter, which I had only glanced through at the postoffice. When I had finished, I discovered that Mrs. Howard had been looking at me all the time 'watching my expression to see me smile when the nice bits came.' She said, 'Isn't it a shame? I shan't read your letters in public any more! The postoffice man, when he saw me open your letter, remarked, 'Ah, that's a real English letter!' So you see, your letters attract a great deal of attention even from afar off, for I don't allow anyone within two or three feet of them.

This morning I walked from Ula up to the Cusacks', and now I am at my house. I brought Mrs. Cusack some letters, one of them being from a young woman named Ethel Tanner (some relation of Mrs. C.) who presumed to make a joke at my expense. Mrs. C. had written to tell her of the engagement of Regy and Miss U., so she writes back, 'We have also been expecting to hear that *you* are engaged to Mr. Cockerell.' Mrs. Cusack was very anxious that this young person should be sat upon for her libelous suggestions, so I wrote an epistle abusing her freely, which Mrs. C. enclosed in hers!

For a long time, Mrs. C. could not find the key of the padlock by which I had secured my door (it was Mrs. C.'s) and I was unable to enter my own mansion, but at last I it was discovered in her purse. Lees is here, and not at all well. He wanted me to go up to his cabin this afternoon to give some instructions to Colin Mackenzie, who is working up there, and bring some things down. But I could not find the horse I was to ride upon, so I did not go. For a while I was employed making and keeping-up a fire by the stable, by which Lees was heating the iron parts of a sledge which he was mending.

Mrs. C. has had another letter from Mrs. Urquhart, who wants Miss U. to go to Colorado Springs for a while, and then return to her in England, while the engagement is to be finally broken off. Miss U. has not yet said much on the subject, but Mrs. C. thinks she will carry out her mother's wishes, and Regy is feeling very miserable about it. Perhaps, though, it is just as well.

I like your account of the Huttonian party. I can well imagine those people. There are so many people like Webster and Coxhead. By the way, I never kept a book stall with you; perhaps it's just as well I didn't, for I do not think I would have paid much attention to the books!

My love, why are you so troubled about the E. Jones poem? It's queer, but *I* thought it was rather mild, and had no notion that you would protest! I agree that the grammar is a little confused; of course, 'how proud they stand' refers to the stalks of grain. But this is not to the point. Ernest Jones was a chartist, and the father of the great Atherley Jones, M.P.! And as a matter of fact, the poem referred metaphorically to the way in which (as he supposed) the 'charter' would give the day-labourers in possession of the grain, the product of their labour. Of course, from a Socialist point of view, we should say that the poem pointed out how the grain of the capitalist or land-owner (as such) was the product of the toil (and often misery) of the day-labourer, and how it was their right to claim it as their own for this reason. No question of 'theft' is raised, except that it is proposed that whoever appropriates what he did not make (supposing it to have been made) does so wrongfully, and vice versa, assuming that the labourer has really need for his product.

I should define a thief as one who by stealth (= stealing) or compulsion (= robbery) deprives another of the product of his labour. In any case, the poem refers to the general position of day-labourers, and of course does not propose to any individual or set of individuals to 'climb fences and steal corn!' Savez? (As they say out here).

Well, so the cat is finally out of the bag now! After all, is it not wonderful that such an 'amusing' event as the engagement between Annie Fenn and Theo Cockerell should have been kept quiet any time atall, assuming that the Allports knew about it? No doubt the Allports got it from 5. Priory. It has probably been creeping all over the Park as a 'great secret; mind you, don't tell anybody!' till someone discovered that they all knew, and so it became public property!

I expected a scolding about the picture of my room. But I hadn't forgotten; I really will do it.

Shyness and bashfulness seem to me, as you say, to convey different ideas. But I dare not attempt to define them separately without thinking them over. Perhaps, we might say that shyness is loss of self-possession and bashfulness is extreme modesty, but I am not sure that is right. I am ashamed to say, that I believe my name, Alison, was a sort of (very bad) pun on 'Alice's son'! Certainly there was no relative or anything, otherwise.

How do you consider colour ought to be spelled? 'Colour' or 'color'? I am very sorry to hear about Frederic's cough. He ought to be examined by a good doctor, and prescribed for. Thank you for the note from Archer ('Young England'); it's very nice. I will burn it, as you wish, though I would rather like to have kept it. Let me see the story when published, won't you? The photo of the cottage is also very nice. I like very much to see where you lived. I will return it soon. Your biography in this last letter is very interesting.

I shall take quite a new interest in Emily Gibson now I know about her people and connection with your younger days. I really *will* send a health report every letter in future, but I felt rather as you did about yourself, that when one is well, nothing need be said. I am very well indeed now and in good spirits. Please do write for C.B.A. report; I am so looking forward to having a paper from you. You really must!

I am not sure that I envy Carlie his connection with the firm of Cockerell's Coals, but I have not yet heard details from him. For instance, if he gets ill and has to leave work, what then? Does he forfeit his rights in the business? Perhaps he can somehow import enough honesty into his business to make it bearable, but it will be an uphill pull, anyway. I wonder how he feels about it. What do you think?

If I can get a scientific post with about £500 a year, I think it will be better than 'business' with even £5,000, I must say. Which would you have me take, supposing I had the option? I am afraid many things in business grate and will grate on Carlie's feelings and sense of right, which would be of no account to most men. Of course, this is all to his credit, but it makes it harder for him.

It is strange that we both have such a vivid recollection of that 'Swedish dance' at the Percival Clark's. I remember how I felt as I held your hands, and half wondered why I enjoyed it so much. Was that one of the times you thought I loved you?

Feb. 1st, 8:15 p.m. I am tired and sleepy and stupid tonight, not because I have done anything to make me tired, but because I have a bad cold and a slight cough, nothing of any consequence, but you know how one feels with a cold. I have written my 8th report of C.B.A. today, relation to bird migration and other things; e.g., I have totted up the accounts of the C.B.A. Here is the result. I will appoint you auditor.

Rec'd, by Subscriptions $3.01 Paid. To postage $2.62
Meeting 2.25   3.00
15.26   5.62

Balance in hand: $9.64.

Yesterday's unwellness was only a temporary affair after all. I feel all right again, though I still have a slight cold. Now you shall have a little more biography, at last!

Scene: Funchal, Madeira. Early in January, 1879, as I said, I arrived in Madeira. Having visited the custom house, we got into a sledge driven with oxen (I forget now what it is called) and went swiftly over the polished stones of the street to Mr. Drury's house, It was a strange experience for me, this new country with its warm weather and semi0tropical vegetation.

The next day I went up to Mrs. Gibbs', the boarding-house where I stayed all the while I was in Madeira. (There are some drawings of the house in some notebooks which I think Frederick had, and there is also a photograph of it somewhere.) Mrs. Gibbs was practically a widow, although her husband was alive. He had been a partner in the wine-making firm of Drury, Rutherford, and Gibbs (I think it was), and had proved himself a thorough scoundrel, and fled finally to the Cape to evade the law. So Mrs. Gibbs was left almost destitute, but with help from the many who sympathised with her (including Drury) managed to set up a boarding house, which at the time I went there was in a very flourishing condition. Mrs. Gibbs had living there a son named George (I am not sure, but I think that was his name. You can verify this and other like matters by reference to my Madeira diary), a young man about 19 with whom I did not greatly fraternise, though I believe he must have been a very good fellow. He was in the telegraph office with another young man named Pearson, who boarded with the Gibbs'. Pearson is now dead, I believe.

There was another son named Leonard, who was in England at the time, and I never saw him that I can remember. Then Mrs. Gibbs had two daughters. The elder one, named Mary, was about 20 (I suppose) and was considered very pretty. She was devoted to tennis, and played much with a young man named Lees, whom she has since married. I wonder what sort of a wife she made him; she was a great flirt. The younger daughter, Ida, was about ten, and full of life. Not atall a serious-minded child though she was occasionally sorrowful. She was practically my only companion there, and although I used to pull her hair and generally ill-treat her, I liked her well enough.

There were several other boarders in the house, some of whom I only dimly remember. A Captain and Mrs. Foster, who were very friendly to me. The captain sketched a great deal, and took photographs. A Miss Crick, a red-faced maiden lady who resides, I think, at Eastbourne. A Mr. Unkel, a German, with whom I often went for walks, He tried to teach me German but without much success, (I think he is in the foreground of the picture of the house — the photograph, I mean.) Mr. Kennedy, half German and half English, Mr. & Mrs. Carlton (I am not sure about this name). Mrs. C. died of consumption while I was there. There were some others, too, but I have forgotten them.

The house was called 'Casa Blanca', which means, of course, 'White House', although, as a matter of fact, it was pale yellow. There was a large garden, and all round were sugar cane fields, which harboured innumerable insects and plants, one or two I specially remember: The wild *Gladiolus (G. segetum)* with pink flowers, the oxalis (*O. corniculata*) with yellow flowers on the end of a long stalk. The commonest butterfly was *Colias edusa. Vanessa callirhoë* was also very abundant. I was the first to describe the caterpillar of this, as is duly noted in the appendix to Lang's *Rhopalocera Europaea*.

I very often went out hunting specimens; otherwise, I chiefly sketched, Madeira is a beautiful place. The sky is so blue, and the sea so blue also, but a different blue. Even in midwinter flowers are everywhere: Geraniums, camellias, bananas, all in the open air. My experiences in Madeira were many, yet there were no events to specially recall; One day went like another. I believe I was an outrageous boy and a general nuisance to everyone.

I returned to England in June with Mrs. Foster, and went then to Margate, where Mother had rented a house in the Ethelbert Road, called Bertha House. That summer I spent at Margate, and then went to school at Beckenham, as you shall hear.

To return to recent events, I shall go to town today or tomorrow; if today, In the evening to wait for the mail. Lees and Regy have called on me this morning, and I have been helping Lees load a log onto two bob-sleighs fastened together, to take down to Beddoes'. I only 'scotched' it, to prevent its rolling back after each pull from the horses. I have also sifted some weed seeds from some oats raised down at Cox's, the object being to get a sample for Prof. Halsted, who is studying weeds. The seeds are mostly those of *Chenopodium album*.

It is a beautiful day, today, but there is still much snow on the ground.

5:15 p.m. Have come to town. Note from Rosita postmaster to say I can have P. O. whenever I want it. Must go and see about it.

Yours lovingly, Theo.

Health. Am very well, except for cold.

Sunday, Feb. 3, 1899, 7:45 p.m.

Dear Annie,
Yesterday I posted a letter to you. That was in the evening, and I came home after dark. There were a lot of things to get for the Cusacks, so I took the buckboard and Ferris, and the dog 'Hamlet' came with me, although he was not asked. I got into town very soon after sundown, posted my letters and got mail, and asked Falkenberg (the grocery man) to put up the groceries I had to get, and then went up to the Cox's for a minute to give Mrs. C. a note from Miss Urquhart. Cox is not yet back from Kansas City, and the Turners and Brock are still there. I should have had to go up to Silver Cliff, but that I met Grant Turner in West Cliff and gave him the manuscript of my 9th report. He has not yet

got his new press, and the old one has been returned to the editor of the *Wet Mountain Tribune*, so there will be no *Courant* issued next week.

By the time I got back to West Cliff, the train had come in, and soon the mail was distributed. I got nothing by the Saturday evening mail. I waited a little while to do shopping, and feed the horse, then left town. There was a new moon, which soon went down, but Venus and the other stars gave me enough light to see the way. It was hard pulling through the snow over the prairie, and I had to walk, so that I was quite out of breath when I got up to the Cusacks'. Fortunately it was not a very cold night.

Today has been sunny and warm. I have been writing up my record books and going through the *Canadian Entomologists* Nash sent me (I think I have gone through about a third of them). They are exceedingly interesting, and in consequence I have to take a great many notes. The mail I got yesterday is: (1.) Letter from Dr. John Hamilton, with names of some beetles; one is new for Colorado. (2.) Letter from Rosita postmaster to say I can take the postoffice whenever I want it. (3.) *Courant*. (4.) *Commonweal*. (5.) *Pall Mall Budget*. Enclosed in the *P.M.B.* was a very pretty Christmas cartoon by Walter Crane. I suppose Carlie put it in, as it seems not to belong to the *Budget*.

I have made enquiries about the Rosita postoffice, and begin to think it will not be of much use to me, though I may go as deputy. The mail has to be sent off from there every morning before daylight, to catch the 8:30 train from West Cliff, and the incoming mail is distributed between nine and ten at night. The pay varies with the number of letters passing through, but it seems that it would never exceed $25 a month on the average, and often be less; and out of that one would have to pay expenses of board and lodging. Except at mealtimes, and some hours on Sunday, one would never be at liberty to leave the office. So altogether, I cannot persuade myself that it is a very enviable job, yet I don't exactly like to let it go. The next question is, about getting to Rosita. I can't walk, because

I must take blankets, etc. Perhaps I will go on the stage, but that costs $1.00 or so each way, I think. However, there is no great hurry, and I'll see what I can do.

About naming species after people, it seems to me rather absurd that any kind of animal should be everlastingly ticketed with any man's name! If course, some such names are well-sounding enough, but what do you think of *Nepticula hodgkinsoni*, *Arion bourguignati*, or *Colias hageni*? *C. hageni* is a synonym of *C. eriphyle*. Now don't you think 'eriphyle' is very much prettier than 'hageni'? So if we call the new *Pentapleura* 'alticola' instead of 'cockerelli', won't it be a blessing to entomologists?

Feb. 4th, 9 p.m. Have been busy over the *Can. Ents.* all day except that early in the afternoon Mrs. Cusack came round and enticed me out for a short walk. It was warm and sunny, but the snow was too deep for much walking. I was pleased to find two 'tortoise beetles' *(Cassida)* new to me, under a log. They are brown and mottled, the first of the genus I have found here.

Feb. 5th, 7:20 p.m. Another uneventful day, taking notes and writing. Yet it has been beautifully fine, and the sunshine so affected me that extraordinary sounds (meant for singing) might have been heard issuing from my house all morning. Fortunately, nobody was near to hear! I have almost finished the *Can. Ents.* and found them vastly interesting, more so than the *Papilio* or *Ent. Amer.* This evening I have written a longish article for *Can. Ent.*, expressing my views of citing localities and giving collectors credit when describing new species. I hope they will print it although I fear (notwithstanding that I have not mentioned names), that I have trodden on some people's toes in it! Here are my addenda to fauna and flora lists for January: Colorado: Butterflies, 3, and 5 vars.; Moths, 26, and one var.; Mammals, 6; birds, 1; Coleoptera, 89 and 2 vars.; Hymenoptera, 5; Moths, 26 and one var.; Homoptera, 1; Heteroptera, 3; Diptera, 4; Phanerogamia, 2 vars.;

Fungi, 5. For Middlesex: Moths, 1; Butterflies, 1 var.; Mollusca, 1 (*Arion subfuscus*, Highgate (Dr Wallis Kew *in litt.*, tell Frederic), and 2 fossil.

I have written several letters today, and if I can get a lift any of the way (there is some talk of Lees or Jack Mackenzie going to Ula) will go to town tomorrow in the expectation of getting your letter, but shall not go on to Rosita this time, I think. Sampson came up here from town today, bringing boards for the Cusacks, to board the empty rooms in this house. Louis Howard came up with him. They went back this afternoon, taking a load of wood with them. Mrs. Cusack is now deep in a book about Socialism — a novel called *Demos* — (do you know it?). She says it is very good and wants me to read it. It is in Tauschnitz Edition, so it must be widely read, I suppose. I think this is all of today's news.

Here is a little more 'Biography.'

I don't exactly remember where I went to directly after returning from Madeira in June, 1879, but at any rate I was very soon at Margate, lodging at Bertha House, which was just one of the lodging-houses transformed. All our neighbors were lodging-house keepers, except a grocer, whose shop I remember was a marvel of neatness, who lived opposite. Carlie was at school at Beckenham (where I went later), and Olive must have been at Miss Hill's, and altogether I was left much to myself that summer. I read books, which we got at 'Smith's' — the railway bookstall, and collected insects.

I fraternised with Lionel Lewis (still at Margate, I believe), the son of a clergyman there, and a bug-catcher like myself. We were both of us in the same state of ignorance, having no proper books, but we took great pleasure in our entomological excursions, for all that. At this time, I was only a bug-hunter, and cared nothing about shells. And now, you see, I am 'reverting to the original type', for most of my present scientific work is entomological.

Those were the days of *Phesia gamma* and *Vanessa cardui* in abundance, and I think it was this summer that one day as I strolled along the cliff, an old lady, seeing me net in hand, drew my attention to a 'rose-beetle' she had found. I secured it, but did not find out till much later that it was the rare *Calosoma sycophanta*. The specimen was exhibited at the Entomological Society years after. I still occasionally hear of Manders through the magazines. He went to Sikkim. In the autumn of 1879 I went to school in Beckenham.

About returning to England for the summer, I must say your five objections are weighty ones, but we shall see. It may be that some means will turn up whereby I can return, but we cannot foretell them. In any case, I always hope that I may be able to do so. I don't believe there is anything very much the matter with my lungs now — that is, any progressive disease.

Feb. 7th, 12:30. Miss Urquhart has just been here to tell me that Lees has come down from his place, and is going to town in an hour and a half, so I shall go with him. This morning I have made you a little sketch in sepia, representing my writing-table, etc. The perspective is not quite what it should be, but it will give some idea of this corner of the room. The table is in a very untidy state, but I mean to clear it off soon.

Your own lover, Theo.
Health. Am well.

In town, 5:30 p.m. Got lots of mail, but not your letter, so shall wait for mail. I think I go to Rosita tomorrow, will see about postoffice. Have got four new members for C.B.A. by this mail.

Feb. 8th, 4:10 p.m.

Dear Annie,

I am just off to Louis', and tomorrow to Rosita. No time now to write anything.

7:40 p.m. Here I am at the Howard's. But yesterday's news remains untold. I cannot write much tonight, and so will defer the account of yesterday's mail. I was writing letters yesterday, and in the afternoon went to town with Lees and Jack Mackenzie. We went in the waggon, and drove four horses as far as Ula, so we came along at great rate. At Louis' two of the horses (i.e., Louis' team) were left, and we went on to town with the other two and waited for the mail, but no sign of your letter, to my great disappointment (the English mail is delayed again).

I found Turner of the *Courant* had moved, with all his things, to West Cliff and set up in what was Lowe's Saloon. This will be convenient for me, as I shan't have to go up to Silver Cliff to give him my manuscript. I came out with Lees in the waggon as far as Ula, but he stopped at Louis', and I walked on, getting home about 9: 30 p.m. I was rather exhausted by the time I arrived, but the Cusacks kindly gave me some hot tea, which revived me.

This morning I got up quite late and decided not to go to Rosita today, not feeling quite equal to it. Lees turned up before noon, and I was to have taken his horse 'Romeo' and Louis' buckboard, which he had brought, back to Ula, as Louis would require it to help move a stable onto his ranch (he has finally bought the ranch near Ula). But as I wasn't going to Rosita, and besides, had many letters to write, I didn't want to go to Ula at midday (as I should have no horse to bring me back, and did not want to go on yet). So I demurred somewhat, and Lees said he did not atall think Louis would want the horse today, so I did not start till about five, writing all my letters first. When I got here, though, I found Louis had wanted the horse, and was a good deal riled at not getting it. However, it's no use grumbling now, and the stable *was* moved all right, all the same. I sleep here tonight, and go to Rosita tomorrow.

Feb. 9th, 9:25 p.m. At the Cox's. Got your letter and have been to Rosita, but too tired to write tonight. I have very much to say.

Feb. 10th, 7:45 p.m. Back at my house; no time now to write. Will tell you about everything tomorrow.

Feb. 11th, 10:50 a.m. At last I can sit down to tell you something about all the things that have happened during the last few days. On Feb. 8th I was at the Howard's, as I have related. After I wrote the above, Mrs. Howard showed me quite an interesting collection of flowers from Wiltshire, Guernsey, and Switzerland, and also some seaweeds. Some of the Wilts. things deserve to be recorded. The pen I have got is not very fine, so I shall write larger.

The next morning (Feb. 9th) Louis and Jack MacKenzie were going with the waggon to Silver Cliff to get some rock for the sides of a wall they were going to make (from the piles of rock you see in the photograph of Silver Cliff). I went with them, and got a lift as far as Grape Creek, when I turned off to West Cliff to get my mail and post letters. I got your letter, which was very nice, but of this more later. I also called on Grant Turner, and he besought me to write him a three column account of Wet Mountain Valley for his paper, to appear in the next issue. I don't know much to write about the Valley, but promised I would try, as I feel rather indebted to him for the printing he does for the C.B.A. He had got his new type, etc., which he showed me.

By this time it was about 11 o'clock, and I started off on foot to Rosita. The road lay through Silver Cliff and beyond, somewhat turning to the right over several miles of open snow-covered prairie (but the road was mostly bare of snow) till I reached the hills which are at the base of the Wet Mountains, which are like those about Querida (Querida is only three miles from Rosita) — barer, with scattered, poor-looking pines. The road ran up and down, winding continually over these hills, till at last, up in an open gulch, I found Rosita, the distance being about nine miles from West Cliff, with about a thousand feet to ascend.

Rosita is a poor-looking sort of a town, with every sign of decrepitude — fences fallen down and not put up again, and so on. It is not as big as West Cliff; I should suppose it might boast 400 inhabitants. I asked my way to the postoffice, and was directed to a long wooden building which proved to be an empty store, with the postoffice in the back part of it, Thomas, the postmaster, was away on his ranch from Saturday to Monday, and another man (name I forget) had taken his place. He was pleasant enough, and told me all he knew, and referred me to an old fellow named McGlochan, who kept a little grocery store over the way. McGlochan seems to be a nice old man; he batches with Thomas, and so knows all about it. I sat talking with him some time, eating apples and gingerbread biscuits for lunch.

Here is a summary of the information obtained from McGlochan and the other man: Thomas claims to make $1.00 a day at the post-office, but probably he does not make so much (Turner did not make that much, and they admit Rosita has 'gone down' since Turner's day; possibly he does not make more than 25 cents a day.) McGlochan said he would take the job if he was 'broke', not otherwise, and he thought a man might *just* live on it if he batched and did his own washing. The *rent* of the place is low, about $1.50 a month, but firewood costs $4.00 a month. Probably it would cost at least $18 a month to live. Thomas has been very anxious to give up the postoffice for a long while, but so far has not been able to induce anyone to take it. So altogether it is not a very enviable job. On the other hand, if I go as deputy, I can leave when I wish, and then perhaps if I sold stationery, etc., in the store, I might make it do. On the whole, with considerable misgivings, I am disposed to make a trial of it for a while. I left a note for Thomas, stating what I should expect him to agree to if I came.

I left Rosita at about 3:20. The walk down was easy, being nearly all down hill. I got to Silver Cliff about six. It is curious that, although there is lots of snow in Wet Mountain Valley, at Rosita, some 1,000 feet higher, it has nearly all melted away, and the roads are dusty. Rosita is very sheltered and on a sunny slope. I forgot to mention that when I got to Rosita I found the people in a great state of excitement over a barn that had just burnt down. In a small place like Rosita this is, of course, quite an event.

I looked in at the Cox's when I got back from Rosita and found Turner still there (Mrs. Turner and Brock up on the ranch) and Cox not yet back. It is a monstrous shame of Cox to abandon his wife in this way. Some (including Lees) fear he may never return.

I had meant to get a bed down in West Cliff, but Mrs. Cox offered me some old coats, etc., for bedding, so I slept at her house, on the floor of the large room. That evening I went down to West Cliff to get the mail. Yesterday (Sunday), after calling at the *Courant* office and getting mail for the Cusacks, I walked out here, reaching the Cusacks' about one and, finding them at lunch, partook thereof. I was a bit tired after all my walking, and did nothing in particular until late in the afternoon, when I settled down to Turner's paper on 'Wet Mountain Valley', which he said he was so anxious to have for next issue that he would rather some up here to fetch it than not get it! However, I only did half of it — he must wait for the rest — and took that down to Brock's for him to take to town today (he said he was going).

Today I sit in my own room. Regy has been putting down the flooring of the empty room, but is now away at lunch. It is storming, wind and some snow, with a putty-colored sky. Now for the mail received since last account: (1,2,3). *Commonweal, Pall Mall Budget, Standard.* (4.) Index to *Botanical Gazette* for 1888. (5.) *Punch*, from Mother. (6.) Letter from T. M. Trippe of Silverton, San Juan County (pronounced 'San Wan', i.e., Saint John), joining C.B.A., and sending his $1.00 subscription. (7.) Letter from I. O. Emerson (California) enquiring about C.B.A., and sending two bird papers for library. (8.) Letter from D. W. Park (Denver), saying he will join C.B.A.. (10.) Postcard from Geo. Roberts (M. Wakefield) joining C.B.A. and urging me to write and sit on W. M. Webb for his Woodward-ite effusion in *Science Gossip* (re. 'variety-mongers'), but he isn't worth it. (11.) Letter from W. H. Ashmead and reprint of paper for C.B.A. library. Ashmead finds eight new species of Hymenoptera in the last lot I sent him. (12.) Letter from C. V. Riley. (13.) Letter from Mother. (14.) Charlton's fossils from Huerfano returned by Smithsonian Institution, some of them with names. (15.) Packard's *Monograph of Geometrid Moths* for library of C.B.A. This is a magnificent work. (16.) Letter from Douglas, who has had a 'rise' and is now getting $400 a year at the bank, which is good. He also sends his photograph and $5.00 out of the money he has of mine. (I didn't ask him to do so, but am not sorry to get it.). (17.) Letter from C. F. Morrison, and *Auk* for April, 1888 (to be returned; this is a very interesting bird magazine), and *Ornithologist and Oölogist*, Dec., 1887 and Jan., 1888, for C.B.A. library. (18.) Last and best, *your* letter (and Frederic's enclosed).

From your list of guests on Jan. 16th, I see I should have been almost a stranger had I been there! However, that would not have mattered, as I should have monopolised *you*! I don't think I could make much of a job with tobacco. Louis scoffingly offered me a piece of land to try! Yes, I will read *Taming of the Shrew*. There is a Shakespeare over at the Cusacks', I think. The men all call me 'Cockerell.' I am very well! I will send an *Open Court*; I wrote to publishers for sample copy, seeing the paper advertised. 'Early Rose' potato has a pink skin, not white. I must send your father a sample. Yes, the one Middlesex fungus was your *Coleosporium*. The Aunt Clarissa is, as you say, a good woman, with a 'repellent kind of goodness.' The step-children certainly do 'shun the step-maternal roof', and I don't wonder. Yes, I do think your mother is a wonderful woman to have done all she has. I have often wondered what differences it would have made to you all, had you been brought up as other children. But one can't argue from your case that children ought always to be taught at home, for we know many mothers could not do it.

Won't you let me have an account of your writings, as they come out? I want to see them. May I not? Or if they are not sent, at any rate I should like to know what they are. I am trying to 'keep track' of what you write, but often cannot find out when published, etc., though you tell me when the MS is written. One wants to be precise in these matters, because if I don't see them now, I shall look them all up when I get the chance.

One of these days I shall insist upon reading everything as soon as written. How I shall plague you!

Yes, Moses' laws were cruelly severe. Yet one can imagine the work he must have had to keep that horde of Israelites in anything like order, and although I do not approve of his extreme measures, it is hard to condemn him when one hardly knows what he could have done otherwise. I am glad you are interested in *Science Gossip*. A 'Micrographic Dictionary' is a dictionary of all those things usually examined with a microscope. It is a useful work. There is a copy down at Beddoes'. The fight between a hedgehog and a snake, in December's *Science Gossip* is without doubt a lie. For one thing, there are no hedgehogs in America! Both *Pall Mall Budget* and *St. James Budget* comment freely on County Council elections, but both refrain from giving the names of the elected! I am hoping to find a list in Mrs. Cusack's *Times*, which has not yet come.

I have not followed the Parnell Commission; it is altogether too tedious reading. I cannot see that it has brought any new facts of importance to light. I think your resolve to see more of people is a very good one, yet I would not make a point of mixing with people if I did not care for them. It is queer how few people that there are that one really likes or knows much about. If I see another photograph worth sending, I think I shall send it, all the same. 25 cents makes no material difference; somehow one doesn't look at it atall as the equivalent of 1/. in England. It is only dollars that count! I don't care for the canned milk, and it is (I think) 30 cents a can, and a can goes very soon. The American Contract Labour Law *is* ridiculous! It seems I only got here just in time! What if the English Government enacts a law refusing the admission into England of 'Anarchists or Socialists'! I will write to Frederic.

Tuesday, Feb. 12th, 7:40 p.m. Fine weather, TDAC writing letters and addressing envelopes for C.B.A. reports, which ought to have gone out a week ago), Regy C. putting down flooring in the empty room, Miss U. assisting (?) him part of the time. That is all that happened today. I should mention, however, that I packed up a lot of Hymenoptera and Hemiptera for Ashmead.

Feb, 13th, 9:40 p.m. A windy day, but warm. They were washing over at the Cusacks', and I went over and washed a few handkerchiefs, a towel, and my large silk necktie (that I used to wear at Bedford Park). This was *red* and had already been washed pale pink. Today I foolishly put it into boiling water, and it has come out straw-color! The rest of the day I have been writing my 10th C.B.A. Report (on Violets of Custer County), and another installment of Grant Turner's Wet Mountain Valley paper, dealing with weather, crops, weeds, etc. I go to town tomorrow with Jack Mackenzie. Goodnight, my love!

Feb,. 14th, in town. Your letter has come; very nice one. No time now to answer.

> Yours most lovingly,
> with a kiss, Theo.

Feb. 14th, 1889. Evening

My love,

Feeling rather depressed, I have come over to the Cusacks' for a change, but do not get much satisfaction out of it.

If two people love each other, and are true to each other, what does the rest matter?' But we cannot help being worried by the troubles which, when we look back after years, will seem nothing in comparison with our great gain! And somehow, perhaps it is good to be anxious and troubled sometimes. Don't you think so? We must encourage one another, but also sympathise with one another, in trouble as in joy.

To give the news: Today opened stormily, with snow, but it partly cleared up and, taking Lees' waggon, Jack Mackenzie and I started to

town about ten. The journey to town has nothing to remember about it. In town, I went, first, of course, to get the mail. Your letter had come, and also other mail, of which later. Then I went to the *Courant* office and gave Turner the MS of 10th report and second part of Wet Mountain Valley paper. He had his new press there (very nice) and the proof of my 9th report (which I corrected) was the first thing printed on it. I also went to Charlton's and gave him his fossils, and to the express office, where I sent off Nash's *Canadian Ent.*, and got what I long had been expecting, Ellis' microscope from Oregon. I had to pay $1.10 on it (express charges), but it is well worth while. Since I came home I have examined it, and it proves to be a very fair one.

We got back towards five, and it had just begun to snow. It snowed some time after, but has now left off. I rather meant to answer your letter tonight, but I won't, as it has much in it to answer, and I am tired and sleepy. I will mention the less important mail: (1.) Letter from Dr. Shufeldt (a good ornithologist who pays much attention to the anatomy of birds), who lives in New Mexico, joining the C.B.A., and enclosing subscr. Dr. S. is very effusive — 'I beg you to accept my most sincere thanks for the honor you do me in making me a corresponding member of the C.B.A. You have my very best wishes for the fullest success in your work and the work of the Association', etc.! (2.) Letter from H. W. Nash; (3.) Postcard from West. Newman & Co. — 'We are much obliged by your paper in *Entomologist*, proof of which is being sent to Mr. Tutt as you wish. We are keeping back your author's copies to stitch them all together, but if you would prefer to have them sent as they appear, this shall be done.' (4.) *Standard*.

Feb. 15th, 7:45 p.m. Such a horrid day; snow and gusts of wind — impossible to do anything out of doors. I got up late and, as I was finishing breakfast Regy appeared and commenced work on the empty room. A good deal of the boarding has been put up, but I found it too cold for me with the doorway between the rooms open, and decided I had better kill two birds with one stone by going over to the Cusacks' to be warm and overhaul some of Mrs. C.'s pressed flowers, which I promised to do long ago. But about then Regy left work and put up the partition doorway so as to satisfy himself, but not to satisfy me, for a gust of wind brought it down five minutes later. However, I fixed it again so that it would stay, inwardly cursing Regy for his carelessness.

All this afternoon I have been examining Mrs. C.'s flowers, which really form a very valuable and interesting collection. Of course, I have only been able to go through a very small part of them, chiefly Gentianaceae, Caryophyllaceae, and Malvaceae. Many species I have newly identified from Coulter's *Manual*. Several are new to Custer County, and a species and a var. of *Stellaria* (*S. longifolia* and *S. longipes* var. *laeta*) are new to my Colorado list.

Perhaps now I have seen a good deal of Jack Mackenzie, I may say what I think of him. In appearance, he is rather tall, dark, with a not attractive face. He sways to and fro when he walks, and brings his feet down so as to make one fear for the stability of the earth's crust. He is a very good-natured and obliging fellow, but as far as I can make out, he has no other virtue. His tastes are vulgar, his interests nil, and he quite lacks refinement and 'education.' In short, he is a good-natured boor. One can't exactly condemn him for his shortcomings, but he is not a very satisfactory person.

Now at last I will answer your letter: About Religion, it is very puzzling. I do not like to talk too freely about it until I have thought carefully what I am going to say and what I really do mean. I cannot *deny* God to be an individual. I think rather that he *must* have an individual and concrete mind, *must* think and have consciousness, yet I find my mind quite unable to grasp the idea. In the same kind of way, I cannot imagine what the centre of the earth is like, though it is a very sure thing that it has a centre! Or to give perhaps a better analogy, you can understand how the cells of our body might feel the compulsion of our will to do this or that, without having the mental power to grasp the idea of our individuality. So, perhaps, we may feel as a *force* the 'will of God' without at present being able to realise quite what that means. I think the creeds mainly err in stating far more than we know: 'I believe in God the Father Almighty, Maker of Heaven and Earth.' Now, even in this sentence there is much that perhaps even deserves to be called *nonsense*. 'Almighty' means the only power, or the all-prevalent power (as I understand it), and yet all Christians acknowledge the power of evil, which cannot be God. Then: 'Maker of Heaven and Earth.' It isn't worth while to pick this phrase to pieces in detail, but you can see how ambiguous and almost senseless it is. What do we understand by 'heaven'? And is 'maker' to read *originator*, or *constructor*? Altogether, I think it is wisest not to affirm too much, and for the conduct of our lives, to recognize the 'Power that moves to good', and act in accordance with it, is surely sufficient! I may have more to say about this later, when I have thought more about it.

Of course, no human being is perfect, but that is because no human being is ever in perfectly suitable environment. I think the old idea of 'heaven' is just one of perfect environment, as against the conflicting influences of this world. I think the verses of Matthew Arnold you quote are exceedingly good; thank you for them.

One does not know what to say about Louy. It is very hard to do anything in such a case.

Now, my own love, with regard to coming out here. Of course, you are right in what you say. I shall not think of giving up the idea of living in England until it is perfectly plain to myself and everyone else that I simply cannot do so. In any case, I shall come back for a time. What would I do if you were not in existence? Perhaps I would not be in existence, either! I don't know exactly what I *would* do, indeed. Of course, when I think of returning to England, I think of it mainly as a time when I shall meet *you* again, and if you happened to reside in New Zealand my thoughts would naturally flow in that direction. If you were *not* , I suppose I should desire to reside in a civilised country, whether it was

England, France, Germany, or the eastern U. S. But now, in any case, I associate England with *you*, and want to live with you *in England*. Do not ever think that because of *you* I am careless of my health! Why, it is because of you that I am so anxious to regain it. If you were not, I might very likely be careless.

'Do the others *never* mention you?' Of course they do; they are not so bad, after all. Leslie is very nice, and also Carlie. I don't think *he* is a very tight 'knot.' It is only Olive and Mother that don't seem to understand.

Yes, Mrs. Cusack is a widow. Mr. Cusack was an Irishman who led her a terrible life and died of alcoholism. That was ages ago. My poor Annie, with the 'knotted string.' But I think we can untie the knots as time goes on. I never read any Tolstoi (I *can't* find that bit I meant to send) but it ought to be worth reading.

Yes, I would have jumped on Allport for his heresies at the vegetarian lecture, though it would probably have been no use.

Thank you for the reminiscence. I remember coming home and finding you in the kitchen; you declared you were the new domestic. I had a sort of presentiment I should find you there, somehow, and hurried from the station. I have a mental picture of you now, treasured up from that occasion. If there was a 'mild remonstration against your going' in my expression, it concealed an unuttered remonstrance that was *not* mild. I was very much disappointed, and remember envying Carlie his extra half-hour or so with you. I certainly was in love then! I wonder whether I shall ever find out *when* it was I 'fell in love'!

I smiled to read the cutting announcing that Foxbourne is secretary of the 'Aborigines Protection Society'! I wish the Aborigines joy of him!

I like the new bit of history. Thank you.

It is late (10 o'clock'), and I must really turn to the one remaining letter to speak of — from Carlie — and a quite memorable one, nice but with a shade of melancholy. He speaks (1.) Of Ruskin, who is ill, and unhappy. You know I am not a Ruskin-ite, but it does strike me as a *most* sad and pathetic thing that, after all Ruskin has done and been, and the help and guide he has been to so many, he is now probably on the point of death, and *miserable*. The more I think of it, the more does the idea weigh upon me; it is full of significance. (2.) Carlie confesses he has 'forebodings and forebodings' about his health, and I cannot help sharing them. He says he would give up his Southwark work (which is really too much for him) if he could get anyone to take his place. I cannot help being anxious about him. I think his health is more likely to break down than my own. (3 and 4.) Of Miss Hill, and the study of Architecture vs. Science. (5.) About *us*, and very nice on the whole, urging that my health is a necessary condition for the realisation of my own wishes, and hoping that we shall get married later on 'and both live happily ever after.' Carlie, I feel sure, will always be nice to us. (6.) About Religion, he says he supposes he agrees with me but gets no satisfaction out of it. But from what he says, I think he does not feel convinced that the individual, as such, survives after death, which I *do* think. (7.) About his partnership in 'Cockerell's Coals.' He pays £2,000 as premium on entering (namely the £1,000 interest in the business given him by his grandfather, and £1,000 from the will), and receives a fourth part of profits: '£500 a year, more or less.' But of this, he only *draws* half, the rest to form *his* capital in the business. He declares the £1,000 given him by Grandpa Cockerell before his death properly belongs equally to *all* of us, and therefore one sixth part (£166 3/4) is coming to me out of the business, but I don't atall see the justice of this, nor do I believe the grandfather intended it so. Certainly I lay no claim to the money.

It is 10:30. This is enough for tonight. Mrs. Cusack sends her love. I don't send mine, as you already have it with you! But I give you a kiss, and say goodnight!

Feb. 16th, 8:30 p.m. Snow all day, and very cold. I have been over at the Cusacks', naming

Mrs. C.'s flowers, like yesterday, only I have come back to my own house in the evening. Louis Howard appeared about midday to get a load of wood from the wood-pile he has heaped up at the Cusacks'. I wonder he cared to face the storm. He says Bernard Sidford has departed, to Pueblo.

There is no news whatsoever to tell, but I forgot to thank you for *Women's Gazette* and the Vegetarian pamphlet. *Women's Gazette* seems to me rather feeble. What do you think? I am not atall clear that it is good to consider women a separate class of beings and give them a paper of their own. If women want to support the Liberal Party and so on, would they not do it better by *joining* with the men, and using the same paper? Not that I think anything of this women's 'liberal' movement; it seems to me (without knowing very much about it), to be on a par with the Primrose League, which I entirely despise. From my point of view, 'liberalism' in a party way is of very small account, and rather a bar to progress than otherwise.

The account of John Wilson (with portrait) is simply the history of an ordinary capitalist politician who is perhaps rather *more* of a humbug than the generality of them! But tell me what you think.

'Vegetarianism Explained' is interesting. There is, no doubt, much to be said in favour of vegetarianism, but I doubt whether it would be wise for the human race to do without meat.

Showcross, in the pamphlet, proves too much: e.g., p. 3. 'Bible References', but on p. 14 it is shown that to quote Bible references is useless (this in answer to those who have quoted adverse references), as the Bible speaks both ways! Again, on p. 9, he quotes Lankester that animal and vegetable food are of the same composition; elsewhere it will be made to appear that vegetable food is greatly superior. I eat a great deal of bread myself and find it excellent food. Mrs. Brock once gave me some of the 'whole meal' (called 'Graham' out here); otherwise I have only used white flour.

Sunday, Feb. 17th, 9:50 p.m. It has snowed very little today, but has been very cold. I have been doing Mrs. Cusacks' flowers. Three varieties in her collection appear to be undescribed. I am calling them *Pyrola rotundifolia* var. *intermedia*, *Rosa blanda* var. *aciculata*, and *R. blanda* var. *sublaevis*. The first is possibly described, and needs further looking into. Did you ever come across a wintergreen in England? I never did, but they occur there.

Lees came down from 'the mine' on snowshoes today, and is going to town on the sleigh tomorrow, so I will give him this, for in this snowy weather I might not be able to get to town myself to post it on Thursday. Wherefore farewell till the next letter.

Your own lover, Theo.

Health: Am excellently well but have a slight toothache just now, or rather, not a toothache but an ache where I extracted a loose tooth yesterday. I caught cold in the gum, I suppose.

Monday, Feb. 18th, 8:40 p.m.

Dear Annie,

Lees has gone to town today, and also Brock. Last night I left a letter to you, and a letter to Shufeldt, and a postcard to Ellis, at the Cusacks', and Lees was to have taken these and some mail of the Cusacks' to post today. But he stupidly forgot, and Brock, coming up later, was given the letters, and it is to be hoped that he has not forgotten to post them. Lees was to have turned up this evening, but he has not done so, so I presume he is stopping at Louis Howard's. I hope I shall get some mail when he does turn up.

I have continued my examination of Mrs. Cusack's flowers, and found some more interesting things among them.

This afternoon I made a trial of Lees' snowshoes. I had never walked on snowshoes before,]. They are convenient things for walking over the snow, especially if it is atall hard.

Feb. 19th, 10 p.m. Lees did come, and brought me some mail, with a letter from you. I thought somehow that I should get one, though it isn't the day they generally come. The night before last was very cold, 8 below zero, but last night was fearful. The thermometer only stood at about zero F., but the wind was blowing hard — a most unusual thing with so low a temperature. Lees and Brock had an awful time crossing the prairie after dark. Lees was half an hour or so ahead of Brock, with his sleigh and the horse, Romeo. He told us that he had to curl up in the blanket on the floor of the sleigh until he began to freeze, and then he would jump out and walk a bit. It was very slow going, for the snow was very deep, and he said he was afraid he would never reach shelter. I did not see him when he arrived, and when I went round to the Cusacks' and found him there he had got warm again, but his chin was half frozen and ached considerably. Brock came later with a load of hay on two bobsleighs joined together, and four horses. Soon after he got on the prairie, he saw it was impossible to get home with the hay, so he unhitched the horses and rode one of them home, leaving the others to follow as best they could.

They got home all right, and Jack Mackenzie, who went down to help Brock, says the tugs [parts of the harness. Ed.] were hanging down. Evidently Brock had been so numb with cold even then that he could not fix them up. When Brock got to his house, he was incapable of doing anything, his feet especially being almost frozen. Today he is in bed and is better, and apparently will not lose any toes or anything from frostbite, but he is quite ill, and Lees is also quite seedy from the effects of yesterday's drive. It makes me shudder to think of it! It has been miserably cold and threatening again today; this weather takes all the life out of one.

I have written most of my 11th report of C.B.A., dealing with Mrs. Cusacks' herbarium, which I shall describe at length.

Now for the mail: (1.) Your letter. I shan't answer if you address me as 'Dear Mr. Cocker-ell'! I know no such person. I think *Corvus monedula* is also recorded in Middlesex from Ealing district and Kensington Gardens. There were some at Beckenham when I was at school there. I am not sure I like your writing paper; it is too liny. I hope Fred didn't spell Pteropods 'Pterapods'! (You see, I have the jump on your spelling when I get the chance!) No, I don't believe in homoeopathy. My Uncle Douglas was amused because one of the Chief homoeopaths, falling ill, came to *him* to be cured, instead of going to another homoeopath! He did not even believe in his own practices when it came to himself!

You need not be jealous of 'Miss Science', my dear. After all, this young woman has been a great comfort to me in very many ways, and I *am* fond of her; it is only natural. And after all, I like *you* best! (Perhaps it is not the quite the same sort of liking; really I could not do without either.) 'Was I ever jealous?' Well, I don't think I have ever been, nor do I quite know the feeling, except that it must be one of the most unpleasant ones possible. I got into quite a rampant state of mind about *you* once or twice, when you went to the Barnett Picture Gallery, and I almost went, and should have met you. And when you went with Carlie to Toynbee Hall. But I cannot call that jealousy. I was never jealous of Carlie, nor anyone else, though I might be envious. If some young man had come and had been allowed to see more of your society than I, I should certainly have been dreadfully jealous, It used to comfort me to think that, after all, I was treated (by the parents) no worse than anyone else. Do you know the feeling of jealousy — I mean, seriously?

I expect Charlton made the 'laying' mistake — yes, he did. I have the MS still by me, but *I* copied it in writing the clean copy without noticing the error.

I have often thought I might get work in the north of England. How would you like to live in the 'north countree'? Yes, it is true, one *is* biased by one's wishes, or tendency of mind. Perhaps nobody was ever absolutely impartial in his judgment, though all honest people try to be so.

The other mail is: (2.) Letter from B. D. Halsted, enclosing subscr. to C.B.A. (3.) Letter from Dr. John M. Coulter, joining C.B.A. (4.) Letter from Mr. Geo. Vasey, joining C.B.A. and enclosing subscr. (5) Letter from Webster, of *Ornith. & Oöl.* (6, 7, 8.) *Pall Mall Budget, Punch, Naturalist.* (9.) *Canadian Entomologist*, wherein notes on some of my beetles, by Dr. Hamilton. (10.) *Science Gossip.* (11.) *Entomologia Americana*, with paper of mine on *Anthocharis*, and reprints of same; I will send you one. (12.) *Courant*, which I will send. It has my 9th report (spelled 'Nineth'' but I am not responsible. It was so amended after I had seen the proof!) And first part of the Wet Mountain Valley paper.

Feb. 29th, 10:15 p.m. Yesterday, going to town, I was overtaken by a man named Low-estrow (am not sure how he spells his name), also riding. He is an acclimatized German, and a ranchman — nothing remarkable about him. We rode together, talking, as far as Ula, when I turned off to deliver Lees' note at the Howard's. Then I went to town, got mail, and came back.

Grant Turner made me quite angry. In the last part of the paper on Wet Mountain Valley were references to hail, loco, etc., and generally the paper was a perfectly impartial account. But that wouldn't do for Turner. He says he wants to 'boom' the valley, and wanted me to write an account, if not exactly full of lies, at least so far dwelling on the advantages and leaving out the disadvantages of the valley as to convey an entirely wrong impression. I told him he need not apply to me for his 'boom' paper. As a compromise I allowed him to omit the paragraphs relating to hail and loco in my last paper, and of course I shall not continue the subject. I don't believe in 'booms' anyway. Aesop's parable about the cow and the frogs is applicable to this subject. I expect Turner will get up his 'boom' account somehow, but I can't help that, only I don't propose to write what practically amount to lies for his or anyone else's benefit.

I posted the *Courant* with 9th report to you, also two copies of my *Anthocharis* paper, and one of these for Frederic. The mail I got was: (1.) Letter from Rev. C.J.S. Bethune (editor *Can. Nat.*) joining C.B.A. and writing, 'I thoroughly agree with what you say [my paper on localities] and shall gladly publish the paper in the next issue of *Canadian Ent.* I trust you will continue to send me contributions. Your papers are always interesting and valuable.' (2.) Letter from Willoughby P. Lowe, joining C.B.A. and enclosing subscr. Lowe is a new Englishman who lives near Campion's in Pueblo Co., and who is interested in birds. (3.) Letter from Hamilton. The supposed *Cassida* I found under the log rejoice in the name of *Ostoma peppingskoldi*! (4.) Note from Ed. of *Open Court*, who says, 'The views presented in the clipping, Physical basis of Society, out of *Commonweal*, are sound!', and sends two more sample copies. (5.) Postcard from Averell — wants me to help resuscitate the Conch. Exchange. I won't. I don't much believe in Averell. (6.) Postcard from Ancey, joining C.B.A. Ancey is very free with his 'new species' and wants to make a new species out of the *Helix pulchella* var. *costata* we have here. I can't see any difference myself.* (7.) *Ent.*, and *Ent. Mo. Mag.* (8.) *Standard.* (*We have re-examined the *H. pulchellae*. They are not quite like English ones, but I think not a good species.)

6:55 p.m. I have been very busy writing letters. Regy and Miss U. have been putting up the ceiling in the empty room. Lees appeared this evening and says he will probably go to town tomorrow. If so, I go with him. The Rosita postmaster has never written to say whether he agrees to my conditions. Perhaps I will write and wake him up.

Feb. 22nd. Have come to town with Lees. Got letters from Mother, Jenner Weir, and Nash, and Bulletin on Injurious Insects from Bruner. Lees says he will be very pleased to call on you when he goes to England. I have got B.C. to read at last.

Ever your lover, Theo.
Health. Am very well.

Feb, 22nd (Friday), 9:30 p.m.

Dear Annie,

Soon after 8:30 we were off, Lees and I on the sleigh, to town, driving tandem. It was easy going over the snow, and we kept at a trot nearly all the way over the prairie. Lees put Ben up at John Kettle's, to be fetched again on the way back, and we went to town with the other horse, Romeo. Near to town, most of the snow had melted off the roads, so that we had considerable difficulty in getting along with the sleigh. After making various purchases, getting and posting mail, we returned, getting back here just in time for me to cut some wood before dark. On the way back, Lees struck across country on foot to Louis' ranch and saw his house, now moved onto the ranch (I believe a mile or less from Ula). I waited, and Lees joined me again near Ula.

Lees, Romeo, and Ben

In town I bought bacon and meat, and called on the *Courant* editor, and posted mail, including seven letters, one of which is to you. I got a letter from Mother, an interesting letter from Jenner Weir, a published report on injurious insects in Nebraska in 1888, by and from Lawrence Bruner (published by the Agricultural Experiment Station of Nebraska), and also a letter from Nash of Pueblo saying he had sent me on loan some more volumes of *Canad. Ent.*, and these I found awaiting me at the express office.

Tomorrow there is to be a meeting at the court house (between West Cliff and Silver Cliff) to 'consider the best means of advertising the county.' It is to be taken part in by people of all politics and sections. I would rather like to go, but cannot conveniently get there. I have no objection to Custer County being 'advertised', provided they do not attempt to get up a 'boom' on false pretenses. But I fear this is rather what they are about.

Last night was the warmest night for a long while; it did not even freeze. Tonight is likewise warm, though, of course, cold enough for me to need a fire. My first attempt at *yeast bread* is in the bread pan, covered with a cloth, and 'rising' only with considerable deliberation. It will be baked tomorrow morning. Regy and Miss U. have been here most of the day working on the empty room. Regy has now put up a door between that room and mine, which is a distinct improvement. I have been writing, and this evening have read *B. C.*, Chapters I–V. It is certainly amusing and interesting. I have written some notes for *Sci. Goss.* today.

Sunday, Feb. 24th, 6:10 p.m. A hot, sultry day, no fire required. Not sunny, but I think the hottest day we have had this year. Mrs. Cusack came round early in the afternoon, and I went with her specimen-hunting. We turned over a lot of stones and found sundry spiders, but *the* find was a small sandy-coloured caterpillar with a forked tail, hybernating under a stone. It is apparently one of the Saturidae butterflies, and probably *Hipparchia ridingsi*, caterpillars of which Wm. Hy. Edwards wants, so I am sending it to him. I have today written an article for Step about Clear Creek Cañon to illustrate some of the pictures he sent. My yeast bread is heavy (to put it mildly), and I baked it this morning, but it is fit to eat. (Heavy bread is more economical. One does not eat so much!)

Feb. 25th, 9:30 p.m. Last night, after supper, I went to the Cusacks' for a while, as it was Sunday. Regy and Miss U. had ridden to town in the morning and never came back, nor did they do so till late this afternoon; they slept at the Cox's. (Cox is not back from Kansas City). Jack Mackenzie, who was at the Cusacks' looking after Mrs. C., had to go up to Lees' to work this morning, so I went over to keep Mrs. C. company. I mostly did her flowers, and found, among other things, a specimen of the common British *Polygonum convolvulus* in her herbarium. She found it near here.

Regy brought me your letter, which was very nice. Both this and the last reached me on a Monday, and must have come, I suppose, by the Saturday mail, or perhaps Friday; that is quite unusual. Regy also brought letter from Packard, very cordial; a moth from Pueblo seems to be a new species. (2.) Letter from Foster of Salida, with some very interesting notes about Lepidoptera. (3.) Postcard from Horn. We get some little beetles here of the genus *Phaedon* which seem to be undescribed (I sent two to Dr. Horn) unless they are the same as the English *P. tumidulum*, which Horn has not seen. *P. tumidulum* is found at Isleworth. Have you or Frederic got a specimen you could send me to compare? As far as I can recollect, they seem quite alike. (4.) Standard.

Now your letter: About B. B. Woodward, perhaps it is not quite fair to speak of it as a 'personal ill-feeling', but I imagine he looks at me in much the same way you can suppose Lord Salisbury looks at Parnell! I do not doubt that many people of Woodward-like views speak in 'an unflattering manner' of your lover, as probably Frederic could tell you. On the other hand, some are unduly flattering, so one has to strike a mean between the two to arrive at the average opinion. What you say about a doctor's work being *anywhere* is very true, and I admit the force of the argument. I don't think you are right about the blanket Regy sold me. (The trade is 'off'; that is, we swap back again). It *was* worth *over* $3, even if he had picked it up in the road. It is *cost* value that honestly and justly determines the price of a thing. The fact that Charley Cusack was willing to sell for $1 does not prove that was the value of the blanket. If so, that I was willing to pay $3 would equally prove that the blanket had 'gone up' in value, which is absurd. The value of the blanket is rightly just what it cost to make it, minus wear and tear. So it seems to me. (By the way, Leslie isn't coming.)

I apologise for bad English in my paper in *West Amer. Sci*, on *Calochortus*. The remark, 'They are particular', etc., was on a postcard to Orcutt for his own private edification, as indeed were the descriptions of varieties, only I added a P.S. 'You can publish the new vars. if you like', which he did. I see I would have gone on spelling 'synonymy' wrong to the end of my days had you not pointed it out!

The references to W. G. Smith's records were written weeks apart. The article 'Among the magazines' represents scraps written at various times, and sent in odd letters. That is why you see TDAC scattered here and there in the middle of it. The *Trypeta ludens* error not my fault. Your notes about the yellow and red gooseberries, and the colours of flowers, are most interesting. Thank you for them. I shall quote these in my next report (though I expect you will scold me for doing so!). I think there is much in it. Yes, *Ephestia kuehniella* (see *Sci. Goss.*) was my flour maggot. And I got mine at Klein's. Did you notice it was Klein who read the paper referred to?

I have put down Kate Hemery a corresponding member of C.B.A.; she is no. 46. Of course I am pleased to have her join if she cares to. I expect it was the photographic-chemical process that Griffith and Farran referred to *re* your picture. Step once explained it to me, but I forget the details. What a ridiculous thing, that christening of a baby, or rather two babies, in Italy, related by G. Nelson! I saw that Atherby Jones has been 'spreading himself' in the *Times re* O'Brien!

Your letter is not dull, my love, so don't make any pretence it is. I am sure this particular epistle of mine is about as insipid and uninteresting as letters are wont to be, but it is only a reflection of myself. Of late I have been doing routine work, copying out of *Can. Bot.*, classifying flowers, etc., and have got into a machine-like groove. No, I haven't grown whiskers and a beard, though the 'fair moustache' that Miss Vincent alluded to still exists as before. Goodnight, love!

Feb. 26th, 9:55 p.m. Morning. Wrote to Foster, Packard, and Horn, and did up spiders for Packard to take to Dr. Thorell (who is a great authority on spiders) when he goes to Europe this spring. Thorell is at Genoa. Wish I were going to Europe! Lucky Packard! Afternoon. Took numerous notes and extracts from *Canad. Entom.* Evening. Read some of *B.C.* but had supper late (about eight) so 'evening' is shorter than usual. This morning I went out for a while to look for more spiders to fill up the bottle for Thorell, but found very little.

Regy was here this morning, altering the structure of my door to his better satisfaction. It has been quite fine and warm. There, that is all the news whatever. I am terribly behind in my work, but am gradually eating my way through. Things do come down on one in such a heap. No sooner is one 'nearly through' than a lot of letters arrive, involving more writing. I like it, of course, or it would be intolerable. The moral of it all is, of course, that I must cease to be 'Lord High Everything' to the C.B.A. and get some others to help, but there's the rub.

Feb. 27th, 8:25 p.m. I was in a despondent mood last night (perhaps the result of eating boiled beans, which are rather indigestible), and tonight I smile more complacently upon the world, my work, and the rest of it. Your spirit has been with me today to comfort me. I have been taking notes from *Can. Ent.* nearly all day, and have yet more to do. Regy has been working in the empty room part of the time, and Chamberlain appeared and argued with us (mainly Regy) for a long time about keeping Sunday, and other matters. Chamberlain says he is disgusted with Wet Mountain Valley. This afternoon, Lees appeared, and now he is at the Cusacks'. I have just

been over there to give him three little drawings of shells (*Physa*) of which he promised to make me woodcuts. Lees is fond of wood-cutting, and does it well. When these are done, I shall try *my* hand at it. It is a thing one will do well to learn.

10:10 p.m. I have finished the notes from *Can. Ent.* and now go to bed. Goodnight, my love!

Feb. 28th, 'the last of winter'? 8:55 p.m. Mostly writing my 12th report, which is principally about seasonal events, such as the appearance of the butterflies, blooming of flowers, etc. I wonder whether you went out a-hunting on Feb. 10th, to write on 'An English Lane.' I didn't, although I said I would. It was the day I walked from town after going to Rosita. I looked about me, but saw nothing but horned larks, everything being covered by snow. I meant to go out and search more thoroughly after, but was too tired when I got home. But you *really* must write me an article for my C.B.A. reports, my dear, though you did recall your suggestion in a later letter! I won't let you off.

Mrs. Cusack was over here part of the day, also Regy and Miss U. They frequented the empty room. I read some of *B.C.* this evening, and am getting quite interested in it. Thank goodness the mosquitoes don't bother us here! Here is my list of addenda to fauna and flora for Feb., rather a poor list.

Middlesex: Neuroptera, 1. Colorado: Birds, 1 var.; Mollusca, 1 var. (4 species fossil); Coleoptera, 11; Hymenoptera, 31; Orthoptera, 1. Moths, 45 (and 2 vars.); Homoptera, 1; Diptera, 4; Arachnida, 4; Phanerogams, 3 (and 3 vars.); Fungi, 3.

I shall post this tomorrow, for I am going to town. Now I will write a little more of my history:

In the autumn of 1879 I went to a boarding school at Beckenham — Rev. T. L. Phillipps'. I remained there (excepting, of course, the holidays) till 1882. Carlie was there when I went, and had been there for some time already, and he left before I did. Having this start of me, he was always higher up in the school than I, and we were never in the same class. Now, of course, Carlie is better 'educated' than I am. The Rev. T.L.P., or 'The Rev.', as we called him, was very fond of Carlie, and was very kind to both of us. When our father died and we became poor, in order that we might attend his school, he took us at reduced rates. He was (and is) an old man, yet vigorous enough to play 'fives' with anyone. A Welshman by birth, a strong conservative with great prejudices, yet much to be respected for his honesty, his justice, and real kindliness. His character might be compared with that of Mr. Horsley, though there are great differences between them. In appearance, he is short and thick-set, with sandy and grey hair and whiskers. I think his fault in school management was that he did not recognise the differences between boys, and considered that they ought to do their work as a duty, without any reference to any pleasure to be taken in it. That sounds well in theory, but as a matter of fact, boys will not work to any purpose unless it is made more or less interesting to them, and at Phillipps' it became the fashion not to work except when obliged.

There is one thing to be said for it; the boys were of a distinctly 'bourgeois' class, and were many of them very difficult to do any good with. Whatever of meanness and prejudice there may be in a class of people, seems to manifest itself most strongly in the boys. On the whole, I cannot say I regard Phillipps' as a good school. The school itself is called 'The Abbey' (a photograph of it is in one of my books that Frederic has, I think). It is a large building in extensive grounds. Things may have changed since my day, but when I was there, we had a playground at the back of the school, with fives-courts, etc., and across the road a large field for cricket and football.

None of the boarders was ever permitted to go outside of the school grounds unless for some special reason (e.g., a relative coming to see a boy might take him for a walk) or on Sundays, when we all had to go out walking under the care of a master. There was a gymnasium, and we all had to practice dumbbells, I think it was twice a week. A little before I left, an excellent swimming-bath was added. I shall have a lot more to say about the school in the next installment.

March 1st. In town. Got your letter. No time to write.

Yours *entirely*, Theo.

March 1st, 1889, 7:45 p.m.

Love,

I am tired tonight, and sleepy, so will you forgive me if I do not write, though I have so much to say? I posted a letter to you and got yours, which was a very pleasant surprise, as it is not a week since the last. *Competitors* also came. I think your pictures are very nice indeed. 'Process' is much better than woodcuts because the woodcuts are generally so carelessly drawn. (Mrs. Cusack also greatly admires your pictures.)

March 2nd, 4:30 p.m. Yesterday I went to town. The Cusacks let me have a horse, 'Sleepy Joe', and buckboard, as they wanted a few things brought out, and I had no flour, coffee, nor baking powder. There is nothing whatever to say about the journey, either way. I started at about ten and got back before dark. It was not cold, though it threatened to snow all day, and a few flakes fell. In town I got mail, of course, and posted several letters, including one to you. I also purchased groceries, and among them got a 25 pound sack of graham flour (whole meal) on the strength of the recommendations in your vegetarian pamphlet. Some is baked into bread; I can't say I like it, but I console myself by fancying it is exceedingly good for me.

I called at the *Courant* office, and corrected a proof. Grant Turner told me that as through impecuniosity he had to drop his 'patent side' (the part of the paper printed in Denver, with all the state and foreign news), he thought he would not have room for my reports for a time. So after the 12th, they will not appear, at least for the present, or only occasionally. I am not altogether sorry for this, as one had not much to say till the spring came round, and things began to 'look alive' again. But if I can, perhaps I will later on make some arrangement with a Pueblo or Cañon City paper, to publish the reports. I dare say the *Rustler* or *Tribune* here would do it, but they are rather blackguard papers, to put it mildly, and I do not care to have anything to do with them.

I shall look forward to your report on the February walk. I am glad you will do it. I can easily write 'Colorado in February', and dwell on the blue jays, jackrabbits and such beasties, though everything has been more or less under snow, and in none of my 'walks abroad' have I seen anything notable, unless the caterpillar I sent to Edwards and the beetle '*Peppingskoldi*.'

Yesterday I felt tired and sleepy, and so did nothing but sit reading the mail received. I find I can read when I can do nothing else. Do *you* not find it so? Today I have written up records, and looked over a few flowers for Mrs. Cusack, but am on the whole not very well satisfied with what I have done. Yesterday's mail was quite a pile. I will go over them with you, leaving your letter till the end, though, of course, it was read first. (1.) Letter from Mother. She joins C.B.A. (2.) Notice from Ent. Soc. Ontario that $1.00 subs. to *Can. Ent.* is due, but they are mistaken; my last subscr. dates from May. (3.) Letter from Step, enclosing money order for 15/. ($3.65) for the long-ago 'Welcome' article. I am glad of the money. This equals 5/. subscr. to S. Lond. Ent. Soc. (1888-1889), to which Step is Treasurer. (4.) Letter from Orcutt, ordering 150 cacti (*Cereus viridiflorus*) at a cent each. The cacti are common enough (I will send you some), but the ground is too frozen to get them just now. The cacti are to be shipped to Germany. (5.) Letter from Morrison, about C.B.A. He is going to send me a lot of fragments of insects from bird stomachs so that we may see what they feed on. (6.) Postcard from Ellis, (7.) Postcard from Ashmead. (8.) *Athenaeum*

— thank you. I note the adv't. of curatorship at Owens College. (I think Boyd Dawkins is the present one) — £250 a year. I hope Frederic has applied. I think we could marry on £250 a year, do not you? Of course it is not much, but many do well on as little. It is very tantalising! (You see what impudence I have, to aspire to step into Boyd Dawkin's shoes.) (9.) *Punch*, from Mother. (10-11.) Two *Pall Mall Budgets*, in one of which Huxley on Agnosticism (out of 19th century) — did you read it? If not, do. It is very interesting. (12.) Thorell on spiders of Colorado, from Packard. This will be extremely useful to me. (14.) *Insect Life* for Feb. (15.) *Custer Courant* with my 10th report, and rest of Wet Mts. paper, deprived of its 'shady side' and looking unreasonably optimistic. (16.) *Journal of Conchology* for Jan. Fred will have this, so no doubt you have seen it. It has TDAC on Colorado Mollusca. It reminds me of some people I used to know. W. Baillie (p. 15) is a poor schoolmaster in north Scotland with £40 a year and consumption, a sort of Thomas Edward, and an admirable fellow. Carlie has corresponded much with him. 'Dr.' J. W. Williams, 'M.A.' (p. 16) used to be at Middlesex Hospital. He is a liar, and is neither Dr. nor M.A. It is a sort of mania with him to adopt false titles. Frederic will tell you about him. I waged war against him and his pretensions in England, but cannot do so well from here, except as in the criticism in last *Sci. Gossip*.

I. Cosmo Melvill (p. 31) is the man Mrs. Cox met in England, do you remember? He spoke of me to her. 'Mr. Rippon, of Norwood' (p. 33) is a queer old chap. Carlie and I call him 'The Ripponite'. He is as poor as can be, and gives his whole soul to collecting shells, insects, etc. He has a (second) wife, and two children (of the first wife), one named Felix, I remember (a baby when I saw it, with six fingers on each hand, I think and the other (a girl) named Fairy! Rippon earns his wealth, such as it is, by drawing plates for scientific works, and by playing on the organ, both of which he does beautifully. He is not much of scientist, and a few beetles I gave him to name he named all wrong (as I afterward found out). He is a talented little man, and it is a great pity he cannot find a good opening for his talents. He lives quite near the Crystal Palace, or did when we knew him.

Edward Collier (p. 40) is a shirt-maker of Manchester. Rev. R.W.J. Smart (p. 57) once came to 5. Priory Road — a very pleasant man, but with some peculiarities. (Rev.) A. H. Cooke (p.8) once called on us at 51. Woodstock Road. Sir David Barclay (p. 58): I once called on him, with an introduction from Miss Marshall, and saw his magnificent collection of shells. He was a most pleasant and enthusiastic old man. He lived in the Holland Road, and would have all the woodwork about the house outside (front door, etc.) painted sea-blue. This was an easy guide in finding the house. It was at his house I first met Ponsonby, and when Ponsonby left I also did so, and we walked together as far as the Albert Hall, and this is how we got to know each other. You have heard of Ponsonby?

Walter Crouch I also know. I used to see him at Zoöl. Soc. and the Nat. Hist. Museum. So you see, *J. of Conchology* reminds me of many people.

Your letter: I once saw Mr. Marshall at Bedford Park, but did not pay much attention to him. It must have been that evening at 20. Woodstock Rd., when I would sit next to you on the sofa, and you said you had not meant me to talk to you all the evening! It *is* nice that those two should be so happy, there at Windsor. The *idea* of giving *your* pictures to Regy and Miss U. when they get married! Not *much*! (Is this an Americanism?) I would not give your pictures to *anybody*, and I don't think even the McWhirter to Regy and Miss U., but I felt very satisfied (!) with the other two — Louis and his wife. They seem to be doing well.

Gunny sacks are hemp sacks of very ordinary make. Is not the word used in England? They cost about five cents each, I think. Thank you for the local papers. I lent them to Grant Turner to look at. I believe you are right about

Horsley letting Mrs. H. over-exert herself, though I did not think of it that way before. I didn't have Charlton's MS in time; that is why it was not continued in next report. You shall most certainly have the photograph, only I think I can only get it done when Emery, the photographer, comes from Cañon City. He comes to West Cliff once in a while, and then everyone rushes to be photographed. Of course I shall use English stamps again! But those I had were getting so dirty that if not used at once they would be spoiled.

About Frederic and Smith's, I am puzzled, but perhaps I *rather* incline to staying at Smith's; yet I don't know. Smith's must not be the end of him, and even if it did not last, the other job would be better while he was looking round for something else. On the whole, thinking it over again, I would say, take the new place. I shall be anxious to hear what he does.

Wretched Horsley baby, to be named 'Stephen Sebastian!' Yes, I know, W. West writes abominably. Either at 5. Priory, or (I think it is) in Fred's keeping, is a *printed list* of British mosses, bound up with a volume of *Natural History Notes*. I am excellently well. I like those pictures in *Competitors* more and more. I like them greatly. Methinks I recognise one or two of the people. The domestic in the picture opposite p. 53 especially makes me smile. Just the kind of look when I asked, 'Is Mr. Frederic at home?', though it may not be the same domestic. It is interesting about your confirmation, No, I never was at Communion Service, nor indeed was I confirmed. I was baptised at home, and so have really no connection with the Church of England, except that I have always been in the habit of attending its services.

Sunday, March 3rd, 9:50 p.m. At the Cusacks. Lees is here. This morning I packed up a lot of Hymenoptera and Hemiptera for Ashmead, and afterwards washed a shirt and several handkerchiefs. This afternoon I took notes from Packards's *Monograph of Geometrid Moths*, and from Packard's plates succeeded in naming three of my moths found here. One is *Larentia caesiata*, also found in England, the others two species of *Cabera*, peculiar to America. (There is so much talking going on that I cannot write to any purpose.)

March 4, 1:25 p.m. My love, prepare yourself to be astonished. Mrs. Cusack has hit upon a plan to solve our difficulties for the time being. She says, since I can't return this summer, why shouldn't *you* come out *here* for a few months! When she first suggested it I could not see how it could be possible, but the idea commends itself to me more and more as I think about it. Will it also commend itself to you?

It is in this wise. Miss Urquhart is going away, and Mrs. C. was going to do without anyone unless she found somebody she would particularly like, and now she thinks that you would be just such a person, and says that if you can be persuaded to come, she will be only too delighted to have you. It would amount to this, that you would live with Mrs. Cox and help a little with the cooking, etc., in return for board and lodging. (The work really amounts to nothing; Miss U. has any amount of leisure time.) But if you think it atall possible , and care to come, I will get her to write all about it. I will try to put the pros and cons of the matter (apart from my own view of the matter). (1.) It would perhaps rather interrupt some of your work in England, but then it would be a most valuable experience to come to a new country for a time. I feel sure you would enjoy it, and always look back on it with pleasure. (2.) The idea will, I fear, scandalise the parents, but perhaps if Mrs. C. writes, they may be mollified. Looking at it from a common sense point of view, I can't see 'why not.'

(3.) Mrs. C. has hitherto paid the traveling expenses of anyone she has had out here, but she had to lend money to Frank and Charley when they went away, and cannot afford the £60 which it would cost for the journey, £30 each

way. (This is how she put it to me herself.) So we should have, somehow or other, to raise £60, which is rather appalling. But I believe I *could* get this from home as a loan to be paid back as soon as possible. (And if anything happened to me I think I have enough property to cover it.)

While you were here there would be no expense. So it seems to me that the matter narrows itself down to two questions: (1.) Will the parents allow it? And, (2.) If so, will you come? Mrs. C. says, if you can come, the sooner the better. And I suppose you could stay practically as long as you liked until Mrs. C. returned to England. (This might be in the autumn.) Now, dear Annie, I have put it all in a very matter of fact way, but you can suppose how absolutely delightful it would be for me. And how I would show you all the things I have been writing about for so long! But what will you be thinking when you have read this? Will you shake your head and say it is all ridiculously impossible? I am very impatient for your answer.

This morning I have been drawing some snails and a fly on a tiny wood-block (boxwood) for Lees to make me some woodcuts. Before drawing, I had to put on a thin coating of Chinese White, as the wood is so smooth and hard. Afterwards I am going to cut it myself.

Regy and Miss U. went to town this morning and took to post an *Open Court* for you. If you are interested I will send more. (I have not properly read any but this one myself yet, but I expect there is much worth reading in them. The paper on dreams is the one I send that interested me.) The reason Regy and Miss U. went to town is that Miss U. is talking of staying at Mrs. Cox's and taking pupils in music, this until she goes to England in April. She has gone today to see whether she can hunt up enough pupils to make it worth while to stay in town. They are not back yet, and I suppose will not be till tomorrow.

I was talking about Ponsonby last night. I see, in *Journ. Conch.*, p. 11, there is a shell named after him — *Trochus ponsonbyi*.

I am rather bothered to think how you will get here if you come. Mrs. Cusack came over here this afternoon, and we were discussing the matter. I would like to meet you in New York, but that would cost too much. Perhaps you could come with someone coming this way. However, it's no use 'cooking one's hare before one has caught it.'

March 5th, 8 p.m. It has been a beautifully sunny day, so that I have been sitting out in the verandah writing, preparing my notes on insect variation for the rest of my paper in *Entomologist*. Besides this, I have written some letters (to Hamilton, Ashmead, and Robinson), and found (not far from the house) a rose gall that may be a new species. I had found the gall before, but only dead and empty. This lot (I got several in a cluster) has living larvae — little white maggots within — and I shall breed the flies. If it is new I shall call it *Rhodites erinaceus*, because the gall is like a hedgehog! But it is possibly *Rhodites bicolor*, a species already described. We shall see.

Regy and Miss U. came from town this evening but did not bring me any mail. I have not yet heard how Miss U. fared about her music class. I hear these things always from Mrs. C., not from Miss U., who never speaks of her affairs in public.

March 6th, 7:50 p.m. Really nothing has happened whatsoever today. I have just been preparing notes on variation all the time (part of the while sitting out on the verandah, but the sun got too hot, so I came in!) I have found some interesting things among the records. For instance, there is a certain kind of bumblebee, the females of which always gather pollen from one kind of *Aconitum*, and the males from two other kinds, the reason being that the mouth-parts of the two sexes are of different lengths, and so each is suited for its particular flower! (This circumstance is recorded by a gentleman named K. W. Dalla Torre, and the bee's name is *Bombus gerstaeckeri*.)

Fritz Müller writes about a flower which turns three different colours, one after the other, and this, he says, gives it a better chance of being cross-fertilised because each colour attracts a host of insects who particularly fancy that tint! Another queer thing is recorded by H. Müller. There is a fly called *Empis punctata*, the male of which lives on nectar. But there are two kinds of females; one eats (or is it drinks?) nectar, and the other is a ferocious devourer of flesh, murdering and sucking the juices of other flies. (N. B. Good subject for a sermon!) Do you know those red hairy galls that are common on wild roses? You surely must have seen them, They are produced by a little gall-fly called *Rhodites rosae*. Now this *R. rosae* (according to Dr. Hagen) must be in the same fix as the Mormons, only more so, for there is only one male to every hundred females! Truly, there are some queer things in this world not known to most people.

March 7th, 10:30 a.m. Another lovely day. I hear from Regy that he is going to have Wheatley up here to board (Wheatley is an Englishman who came to West Cliff recently; I forget whether I spoke of him). I have seen him often but never spoken to him. This will necessitate my turning out, and I am thinking where I will go. The old house on Swift Creek was left by Black (the Canadian who lived there) in a frightful state of filth and chaos, and when he went he took away the stove. Perhaps I will move nearer to town or even to town if I can manage it. I go to town tomorrow, and will see about it. If you do come out (which I hardly dare to hope), I will move back to the Swift Creek house, so as to be near.

Here is a little more history: When I first went to the Abbey school, I was entirely ignorant, and accordingly found myself somewhere about the bottom of the lowest (4th) class. I did not shine as a scholar at any time, and it was long (I forget how long) before I got moved into the 3rd. I was best at Geography and Mathematics, I think, and was considered fairly good at History and (you will be surprised to hear) spelling! But as to my spelling, it was only because the others spelled so very badly. At French and Latin I was atrocious, and later, when I learnt Greek, I never did any good. (Have forgotten all the Greek now, but remember a little Latin and a small smattering of French, not for talking purposes). I got five or six prizes when I was at the school, none of which were of much use to me, as one could not choose one's own books. (I forget exactly how many.) The master of the fourth class was named Forbes. I never liked him. He was rather severe and much given to favoritism. When I first went there he detested me, and continually annoyed me, but after a bit he turned round the other way and favoured me more than the rest. I used to have great fights with him over the catechism, which I would not learn.

We had to learn Catechism, Collect, Epistle, and Gospel, and do Scripture History on Sundays, which always seemed to me exceedingly monstrous. (And still seems more monstrous now, as I think of it.) The third class was under the charge (as regards Latin, which was the principal thing) of one Gulliver, who was an excellent man, on the whole. Always commanding attention, and ever ready to 'spank' unfortunate transgressors, he was at the same time jovial and pleasant, and did not get into a rage (that is, not often). He was also an excellent cricketer, and this of course added to his popularity. Once, in the holidays, Gulliver came down to Margate, and I went for a long walk with him, to the 'Reculvers.' (Part of that ruined church, which had stood for about a century, I pulled down in pursuit of starling's eggs, which was very wrong.)

There was an arithmetic master called Yorker (not much beloved). He was pleasant, as a rule, but had a bad temper and was exceedingly fond of repeating bad and ancient jokes, at which all the fellows were expected to laugh. Williams was a master who taught Greek and Geography, and was an older man than the other masters. He taught fairly well but was in no way remarkable. We liked him pretty well. I never got any higher than the second class, where 'The Reverend'

taught us Greek, and used to be much exercised with me because I *could not* understand the Greek verbs! The French masters I scarcely remember; they were awful fools, I think without exception. (The Rev. would get so disgusted with each one that we had a new one every term or two.)

As to the boys, I never cared much for any of them. When I first went the big boys bullied me, as was the custom with 'new fellows.' Later on the bullying system almost died out, and they say *before* I went it was something frightful. Before I left, I was on excellent terms with all the masters and the boys. I used to fraternise with one Norton, who came from Wakefield, and Payn and I used to sit together during preparation and fritter away our time. There was always a fashion at the school, at one time kites (they got a kite ten feet high, I think) that held a string about a half mile long!), then marbles, tops, etc.

I set the fashion for caterpillars and moths, and until I left the fellows were always hunting for 'pusses', 'kittens', 'blues', 'whites', and the rest of the Lepidoptera— always known by their common names. Stag beetles were also the rage, and they used to be made to fight. Some of the boys kept mice, and these used to be caught with traps under the hot water pipes. The traps were set before prayers each evening, and when the 'Rev.' imagined the fellows to be paying great attention to their devotions, they were really listening intently for the 'click' of a trap!

We also had gardens, to which we devoted great attention. Cricket was in the afternoons in summer, and football in winter. I used rather to like football, but cricket I never cared for, and although it was 'compulsory' to play, I played so badly that they let me off. We slept in 'cubicles', small rooms arranged each side of a long dormitory, partitioned off, a very good arrangement. When I was at this school I first appeared in print! A notice about butterflies and moths at sea, in *Natural History Notes*, early in 1882. Later, I had a list of the Lepidoptera I had observed in Kent.

7:50 p.m. I finished *B.C.* this evening. Mrs. Cusack came over here this afternoon to discuss matters. She is rather exercised about Wheatley, and declared she wouldn't have him in *her* house. So as things are at present arranged, Wheatley and Regy are to live over here, Regy to cook for Wheatley, who seems not to be able (or willing) to do these things for himself. Miss Urquhart's music class scheme fell through, as she could not find any pupils.

March 8th. In town. Got your very nice letter. No time now to write. Poor Claude Jest!

> Yours everlastingly,
> with all love, Theo.

Health, excellent.

March 9th, 4 p.m.

My love,

I had quite a day of it yesterday, but happily found me a dwelling place. I got up at seven and was off a few minutes after eight, walking. Mrs. Cusack wanted me to take a horse, but I fancied Regy was not very willing I should do so (and, in fact, he used the horses to haul wood that day), and I also thought the walk would be good for me, so I walked. The roads were pretty clear, but things are still a good deal frozen up, so that though I took a box with me, I found nothing. About a mile from town, Sam Kettle caught me up and gave me a lift to town, entertaining me meanwhile with his (very sensible) views on farming, and stories of his young life, how he used to be sent out to scare the rooks off the corn fields in Lincolnshire.

Shortly before Kettle caught me up, I examined a little empty house of Kennicott's, opposite John Burke's, to see whether I could live in it, but it has no inside boarding and is used as a barn. In town, I took up my abode in the postoffice fora long time, posting letters to you, Mother, Ashmead (and sent him a lot of Hymenoptera), Hamilton, Dr. Riley, and Morrison, and a post-card to *Journ. of Conchology*. I got lots of mail, of which hereafter. I enquired at the postoffice about rooms in town. Goldstandt, the postmaster, had some to let, but they were $2.50 a month, *too* much for me. I also went to Cassidy's about a stove, but he had no small ones, the cheapest being $18.00. I can get one for a few dollars in Silver Cliff, I expect.

It had occurred to me that Mrs. Cox would perhaps sub-let one of the rooms of her house, which would suit me excellently (she would be very moderate in her charge, I am sure) and it might also be useful to her to have someone on the spot when Cox went away. Of course, I could have my own stove there, and be quite independent. So, after correcting a proof at Grant Turner's (I find now to my disgust that the last two reports have never been corrected in type, though I corrected *proofs,* so they are full of errors.) I went up to Mrs. Cox's. She was not at home, so I sat on her front step and ate my lunch (a piece of bread I had brought with me) and was leaving town when I saw Turner and Wheatley coming up the street.

Turner introduced me to Wheatley, and told me that Mrs. Cox was at the Hunter's for the day. So I went there and found her with Mrs. Hunter. Mrs. Cox said she would be very pleased indeed if I would come, but she could not make any final arrangement till Charley (Mr. Cox) came home. But if I cared to come until he came here, and then arrange with him, I might do so. So in all probability a week or so will see me resident at the Cox's. It will cost a little more than being out here, but I think I shall have a better chance of getting work to do.

After this, I walked homewards, reaching the Cusacks' at about six, where, at Mrs. C.'s invitation, I stayed for supper and evening. Today I have been writing up records, while Mrs. C., Miss U., and Regy have been fixing up the next room for Wheatley.

This is the mail I got yesterday, commencing with the least important: (1.) *Courant.* (2.) *Standard.* (3.) *Pall Mall Budget.* The *Times* seems to be in quite a mess over the Parnell letter business; their 'evidence' appears to be very slight. (4.) Letter from Nash. (5.) Letter from Vasey, and an interesting bulletin of the Dept. of Agric. on grasses and fungi. Vasey says I can deposit specimens from the C.B.A. in the Dept. of Agric. herbarium, which will be useful as we have no museum of our own. (6.) Letter from Orcutt. (7.) Two letters from Morrison. He says our waxwings here are *Bombycilla garrulus*; that is, the same as the English bird. (8.) *Guy's Little Deception*. Thank you. I think it is a very clever little story. The only thing I would object to in it is the way in which she falls in love (?) with him so suddenly. I don't mean to say it is unnatural, but it leaves one with an uneasy feeling that if they marry they will soon discover that they are not so fond of one another after all! Perhaps I have a leaning towards Darwin's view of stories — that they ought always to 'live happily ever after', even though it may not always be the natural thing. On the whole, though, I like the story and much enjoyed reading it.

(9.) 'A Middlesex Ramble in February.' This is very nice indeed. Very best thanks. (Wish I had been with you.) I will still write mine, and they shall be printed as soon as I can manage it, though possibly not in the same report (for want of space). As you say, I may amend it. I will just add a few English names, as the *hoi polloi*, as Regy calls it (to air the only Greek he knows) does not know that *Merula merula* is a blackbird! Also, I think (but am not sure) the term cat-mint only applies to the other species of *Nepeta* — *N. cataria.*

(10.) Your letter, and a very nice one. Step says it is the fault of the office boy that only a one cent stamp was put on that letter. You say, 'writing articles' about a place you know is an excellent way of earning money.' Muchly so, but there's the rub. I have never been to any of the places illustrated by Step's cuts. However, I have written one article, and will prepare another. We will concoct our 'popular science' together some day, as you say. I presume your walk was in Isleworth district? Because *Agaricus velutipes*,

Funaria hygrometrica, Helix rufescens, H. concinna, and *Nasturtium officinale* seem to be new for Isleworth. *Ag. velutipes* is new for my Middlesex list.

When you illustrate a story, do they send you the MS to read, or the proofs? Poor doll's dressmaker! How many of them are like that? No, I never read *Our mutual Friend*. I remember W. G. Smith's drawings of fungi at the Museum quite well. It was nice, going to the herbarium. They are always very kind and obliging to 'students' at the Museum. I will enclose a fungus for you to present to the herbarium next time you go. It is a new species, so they will be glad to have it. There is enough for two specimens, so if you like, of course, you can keep one for yourself.

Our chipmunk here is not *Tamius asiaticus*, but I expect it is much like it. *T. asiaticus* I know nothing about. They are very poor in North American mammals at the Museum. Thank you for the programme of concerts at Bedford Park. I do not remember Mrs. Perugini though I know her very well by name. I would like to put your whole name to the 'Middlesex Ramble', but as you say 'A.S.F.' I suppose I must not. You will have heard all about the Rosita postoffice matter; it has fallen through. You see, a postmaster cannot leave his post until he gets a substitute. That is why the present Rosita postmaster has had such a bother. (I don't know whether he has gotten one yet.) Being a 'citizen' of the U.S. entitles one to vote and hold government office; that is about all. One cannot 'take up' land unless one is a citizen. The trouble would be, that I should *not* be a citizen of Britain when I *returned* if I became naturalised here.

You miserable creature, to have also made the Ethel Tannerian joke! I am glad you prefer the scientific post to the business one. I incline to think about £250 a year is what one *ought* to get to marry to be comfortable in England. What do you think? And I think the £250 ought gradually to rise to £500. (Klein told Sherborn that he would raise me to £500 in course of time, but I don't think I *could* have become Klein's chief villain!)

Thank you for the mosses, which are interesting. Here are notes about them. (7.) *Funaria hygrometrica.* This is found in Colorado, and I have found it at Bedford Park and in Kensington Gardens. (5.) *Hypnum schreberi.* [= *Pleurozium schreberi.* Ed.] I had this from Scotland in my herbarium. (3.) *Sphagnum rigidum.* I never saw this before. (1.) *Sphagnum 'cymbiforme.'* Probably this is *S. cymbifolium,* which I had from Killarney and Yorkshire. (6.) *Dicranum scoparium.* W. West sent me this from Baildon, Yorkshire. (4.) *Campylopus flexuosus.* W. West also sent me this from Baildon, and also (2.) *Leucobryum glaucum.*

It gives me such a queer feeling to read about 'The C. Scott Episode.' It is nice of you to tell me all about it, or let Louy tell me about it, and thank Louy very much for writing it. I like to think that you should have been appreciated, but it's very sad, though I cannot believe C. Scott really loved you altogether. I have known schoolboys get quite fascinated with girls, when one might almost say they don't know how to *love* anyone. I think 'love at first sight' is generally that sort of thing. I think if C. Scott had really loved you he would have not allowed himself to lose sight of you. I can hardly think of what I should have done if you had said you didn't love me, and never could or would do such a thing! Even then I would have insisted on our remaining friends, in fact as well as in theory. In my most despairing times I always thought that was sure. I wonder whether Claude Scott still thinks of you.

Poor things, with that small-pox, and having only three visitors those seven years! What dreary times! I always did detest the north of London, though I think the south-east is worse a good deal.

Sunday, March 10th, 7:50 p.m. At the Cusacks'. Have been overhauling Mrs. C.'s flowers, and am getting toward the end of them. I took notes, and named a few: *Veronica americana, Mentzelia ornata, M. nuda, Plantago patagonica, Veratrum californicum,* etc. Tomorrow I am to go to town with the buckboard and do a little 'prospecting' for myself (get a stove, etc.) and bring out Wheatley, if he wants to come and inspect his future abode, as he said he would.

There was one thing that amused me that I forgot to tell you. The editor of the *Courant,* being at a loss how to get his 'boom' articles on Colorado, took a 'boom' edition of a Kansas paper and just substituted the word 'Colorado' for Kansas, and reprinted *their* remarks, which in either case were perfectly untruthful! If course, nobody is supposed to know the source of this article in the *Courant,* but it happens that Turner showed me the Kansas paper (as 'the sort of thing he wanted') some weeks ago, so I recognized it at once. There is not anything more to tell about now, so I will continue with the 'history.'

When I left the Abbey School in the summer of 1882, I went to Margate, where we were all living, in Ethelbert Road ('Bertha House'). At this time the doctoring scheme began to be talked of, and with a view to passing my preliminary exam at the College of Preceptors, I went to the 'High School' at Margate. It was a boarding school, but as a sort of favour I was allowed to go as a day boy, and at the same time George Harker, eldest son (i.e., step-son) of my Aunt Clarissa, came to stay with us and went to school with me. George was not by any means a bad fellow in his way, but not overburdened with sense (he *would* read penny novelettes, for instance). I may be wrong, but I should think he might be classed with Frederic's friend Christopher Fawkes. He is now, I believe, a clerk to the P. & O. Company.

The High School was under the charge of a man named Wharton Robinson, a learned man though by no means a good schoolmaster, though he had (and this is a great thing) very liberal ideas about education. His wife, Mrs. Wharton Robinson, is a great friend of Mother's. She came and recited once at 5. Priory Road, as you will remember. The school building was large and well-suited for its purpose. It stood on extensive grounds, consisting of a garden in front and a field behind. The master I do not well remember.

There was one Jeffcott, who taught me Greek, Euclid, etc., (and abominated me). He was a very irate man and, for some unknown reason, George Harker was struck with the ludicrousness of his appearance — not that he was so absurd, but George could not help laughing at him. At first Jeffcott took no notice, but after a bit he concluded that it was himself that so tickled George, and used to get fearfully wild about it. Poor George, dreading lest he should laugh, would be saying his lessons quite soberly, when some fellow (everyone knew his failing) would just whisper 'Harker', and he would collapse in a fit of laughter!

Another master was Tossell, a friend of Jeffcott's, a very jovial fellow. He and Jeffcott were compiling various school books together. Tossell used to come and talk to me about his books 'in preparation.' Tossell was pretty well liked, but not so Jeffcott. Just before I went, Jeffcott gave it out that he was going to Australia, and the fellows were so pleased that they gave him a tea-set as a parting gift. However, he never went atall!

While I was there a little Hindoo master came, called Chuckerbutty, a clever little fellow. He taught us zoölogy, though he knew very little about that science himself. I got *Descent of Man* as a prize for zoology at that school. The boys were on the whole a decidedly better set than at the Abbey, not so snobbish, and more given to work. I did not fraternise with any of them much. One of then, Geo. E. East, Jr., writes now and then for *Science Gossip*, and so I hear in that way of him still, but I did not hold him in any esteem at school.

The discipline was very lax. I remember a boy going up to be caned, and he said he *wouldn't* — and he *wasn't*! Robinson had not enough 'grit' to enforce the punishment. But really the fellows worked pretty well, and they were most of them going up for some exam, in which they took a lively interest. We were fed well, and it was both satisfactory for us and an economy for the school that we were allowed to leave meals before the pudding came, and in fact, as soon as we had eaten enough. At Christmas we had great decorations, and a grand dance was given. I sat and looked on, and enjoyed it. Poor George H. had promised he would dance, and unhappily he selected a quadrille or something he knew nothing about, and his gyrations were amusing to the onlookers!

I passed my exam all right at Christmas, but found out too late that I had to include Euclid among my subjects (which I had not done) to make the exam, sufficient for the medical authorities. So I went to a tutor for a while, and went up to London in the spring and passed another exam, which allowed me to be entered as a student at Middlesex Hospital. I must say that the College of Preceptor's exam was ridiculously easy. I passed, for instance, in 'Light and Acoustics', which I only got up in my spare night or two before the exam! The exam was all written. The subjects, as nearly as I can remember, were Latin (Caesar), French, Geography, History, Grammar (including an essay to be written), Zoology, Light and Acoustics, Drawing, Arithmetic, Algebra, Euclid — I think that was all.

The next part of the 'history' will be about my life at Wimpole St. and the Hospital. Mrs. Cusack has just shown me an epistle she has written to you about coming here.

March 11th, 8:50 p.m. I have been to town today with Ferris and the buckboard. Before I started, Chamberlain came round and told me the news that the Parnell letters were admitted to be forgeries after all, and it seems it really is so, for I saw a lot about it in a New York paper in town. I suppose it will just 'break up' the *Times*, but it really serves them right.

It has been a cloudy and threatening day, with a little snow this afternoon. In town I got and posted mail, called on Mrs. Cox, and got some groceries for the Cusacks. I also went up to Silver Cliff to a second-hand store and found a stove which I could have for $2.50, and I shall take it when I go to town. It is the same make as the present one, but a size larger, and rather broken about. (Regy offered me the stove I am now using, for $4.00, but I could get one cheaper in town, you see.) Wheatley was to have come out with me, but Turner was walking out (wanted to see his wife, for a wonder!). And Wheatley walked with him, and I did not catch them up. (I only got here a little before dark.) Lees came to town while I was there, and tonight he stays at Mrs. Cox's and tomorrow comes out here. He told me he had done my engravings.

I got little mail: (1.) Letter from W. H. Edwards, who got the little caterpillar I sent him all right. He thinks it is *Erebia epipsodea*. (2.) Postcard from Dr. F. Spaeth (I don't know him) of Vienna, wanting to exchange beetles. He writes in French, so I can manage to interpret it. (3.) Circular of C.B.A. from Morrison about the ornithological department of C.B.A. (4.) *Courant*. (5.) *Entom. Americana* for March, in which TDAC paper on a caterpillar (and 25 extras of my paper, so you shall have one). (6.) Annual Report, Bulletins, etc., of Agricultural College at Fort Collins.

March 12th, 8:30 p.m. A sunny day but not very warm owing to a breeze. I went out this afternoon cactus-hunting, getting cacti for Orcutt (at a cent each). I dug them up with a spade and put them in a gunny sack. I have not counted them, but there most be from 50 to 75. Otherwise, I have been writing up the record book, and have written one letter, to Prof. Cassidy of the Agric. College at Fort Collins. Lees appeared on the scene this afternoon and brought me mail, and gave me the woodcuts (of shells and a fly) he had done, and they are very nice indeed. Prints from them will appear in the next report, and you will see.

Wheatley is still at the Cusacks. He, Turner, and Regy (mostly Regy!) Are getting up some mysterious game called 'Pharaoh', of which I know nothing except that it is the *worst* kind of gambling. I cannot understand Mrs. Cusack's position with regard to gambling. If they got drunk, she would never forgive them, but they fritter away both senses and money in gambling and she just looks on. To my mind a gambler is

even more abominable than a drunkard. What think you?

Turner wanted me to go in and stay with Mrs. Cox so that he could stay at Brock's for a few days, but as I cannot yet have Lees' waggon to take my things in, I do not care to go and come back again, and I do not think I am bound to do so to oblige Turner.

Lees brought me quite a lot of mail: (1.) Circular from Averell saying he is starting a new conchological magazine called *The Nautilus*, edited by H. A. Pilsbry. (2.) Reprint of a paper on mosses, from Barnes. (3.) *Standard*. (4.) *Canad. Entom.* for March, in which a note of mine and my controversial paper 'on the citation of localities.' (5.) Letter from Dr. Horn, who has further examined my *Longitarsus nitidellus*, and confirms it as a new species. (6.) Letters from Coulter. (7.) A very cordial letter from Dr. Shufeldt.

(8.) Letter from Riley, who writes again about the publication of new species. What occasioned the letter is this: *In Entom.*, December, I refer to a *Sirex* parasitized by *Thalassa* at Cottonwood Springs. Riley examined a specimen, and said it was a new species of *Tremax*. I wrote and said I should probably describe it (calling it *T. hoopesi n. sp.*). He replied he had no objection to my describing it. I then wrote that I would describe it in *Entom.* and asked him to give me the comparative differences of the nearest species, *T. columba*, as I had no *T. columba* to compare with it. Now he replies as follows: 'In looking more carefully at the supposed new species of *Tremax* I have concluded that it is not a new species but simply a marked western form of *T. columba*. I have already intimated quite freely my strong objection to this describing of different species from limited material, and when I mark something 'n. sp.' it simply means that I have not the particular form determined or have not given it the requisite study to be able to name it for you. I cannot too strongly condemn the disposition to grind out isolated descriptions especially in publications not solely devoted to entomology, and the mere fact that you are willing to describe a new species of *Tremax* without having the requisite material for comparison shows an unscientific tendency. Please take this in good part and in the most friendly spirit. I do want you to make a good reputation and not blast it by the species-grinding mania. When it comes to your new species of Hymenoptera you will be surprised when I tell you that we have probably over a thousand un-named species in the National Museum collection here.' Of course, I am pleased to receive such letters, and am no wise offended, but I think that Riley rather exaggerates his point, and he frequently publishes (or has published) isolated descriptions himself.

March 13th, 9:10 p.m. Being afflicted with a toothache, I shall not write much tonight. Jack went to town today and took Wheatley, and Regy has gone down to the Beddoes'. Beddoes came up to the Cusacks' the other day and said Mrs. B. was ill, so would Miss U. go down and help her for a few days? So she went, and now Regy has gone to visit her. Everyone being thus away, Mrs. Cusack was left alone, so she came round here and asked me to come over, which I did, and spent the afternoon preparing a catalog of her flowers. This evening I went over to the Chamberlains to get some potatoes. He owed me ten pounds, but he has given me more like 30.

March 14th, 7:40 p.m. The first event this morning was Chamberlain, who came round to air his views on politics, and especially on the Splanns. Chamberlain and the Splanns are still at deadly enmity, and neither party seems to have anything bad enough to say about the other. They made some contract about building fences, etc., and neither party seems to be fulfilling his part of it, wherefore the Splanns threaten to summons Chamberlain, and Chamberlain says it they do they will regret it, for he will let out what he knows about their killing a bullock of Beckwith's. I don't pretend to know who is in the right, but probably they are both to blame, but the Splanns more than Chamberlain.

Later on, Lees appeared with his waggon, which he left in front of my house, for me to pack my 'truck.' We are going in with said truck on Saturday. I wish I could get in sooner, but if I went in tomorrow it would not leave me time to pack and do all I have to do, and Lees cannot take the waggon in before Saturday. I ought to have posted a letter to you on Monday, in view of such a difficulty. Now this letter, posted on Saturday, will not go till the Monday morning train, and will reach you nine days after the last. I am sorry.

I have continued my catalogue of Mrs. Cusack's plants today, but it is a slow affair, and I shall not have time to finish it. It is very interesting, but it takes a long time to write a description of almost every plant. I have read a little more of Martineau this evening, after neglecting it so long. There is a clever argument to show that there is design in nature. Someone has calculated that the chances are about 2 or three million to one against a given variety being perpetuated by natural selection to form a species. I think the argument overlooks several important points, but it is interesting.

March 15th, 7:55 p.m. I am writing at the Cusacks'. All my things, except bed and cooking material, are packed up in Lees' waggon, ready to start at 7:30 tomorrow. As Oliver Wendell Holmes says, one *dies* out of a house, and I am quite sad at the necessity of leaving my mansion! It is a sort of venture, this going to town. I may find myself 'broke' in a short time, or perchance I may get some sort of a job and make my way pretty well. We shall see.

All this afternoon I have been packing, the books and papers in four boxes, and the clothes in the hold-all, other things here and there where they will fit. Since I came to this country, the clothes have diminished, but the books have greatly increased, so that I have now quite a waggon-load of property instead of scarcely enough to fill a tin-box. How Thoreau would pity me! And perhaps he would be right. My room looks miserably dismal now with all the pictures and books away.

I am not quite sure whether it is wise to go to the Cox's after all. I am rather puzzled. You see, I should have to go through Mrs. Cox's room every time I want to get to my room, and in many ways should be less independent than if I had a room, say, at the postoffice. But I shall go to Mrs. Cox's first, and then move if I want to do so.

Did I tell ? I read *Taming of the Shrew* some days ago. I cannot say I like it, and if it really expresses Shakespeare's views about women, I think those views are monstrous. Surely you would not say that this play is a fair sample? I enclose a ridiculous cutting found in a Pueblo (I think it was) paper. What a number of people must be ready to be humbugged, for this sort of thing to pay!

Saturday. I have to come to town with all my 'truck.' Lees brought me in. I got your letter, but will write all about everything I can. Will probably post another letter before Monday train, but cannot add to this without making it overweight anyhow.

Always your own lover, Theo. Am very well.

Will post another letter before Monday train, but cannot add to this without making it overweight, anyhow.

LETTER FROM MRS. CUSACK TO ANNIE INVITING HER TO COLORADO

My dear Miss Fenn,

Mr. Cockerell and I have been having a chat about you (one of many) in which I told him I should be very pleased if you would come and stay with me for a few months, say six or more. The young lady who has been with me since I came out here goes home next month, so I shall be quite without ladies' society. And from what I hear of you from Mr. Cockerell. I think we might suit each other very nicely, and it would a change

for you and you would see a little of this country, and the queer way of living in the Rocky Mountains. I would gladly pay you a small salary only that my expenses this year have been unusually heavy.

The journey from London or Liverpool costs as nearly as possible £30, including berth in first class steamer (£12), a berth in the train, and food on the journey and, if necessary, sleeping one night in a hotel. Be sure and take a first class ticket for the train; second out here are most objectionable and besides, you can't get a sleeper second class which you cannot do without. You ought not to leave England later than May as the heat after that is very great.

I think you will find no difficulty in the journey, as ladies traveling alone out here always meet with the greatest civility and kindness from men of all classes, even the roughest.

I will enclose a list of things you will find useful out here, and with kind regards, hoping to see you soon, believe me to be

Very sincerely yours,
M. E. Cusack

A list of things to bring out.

A pair or two of good stout walking boots, easy fit (all boots and shoes out here are dear and very bad.

A pair of strong gauntlet gloves (all gloves are very dear), and stockings.

A good warm wrap and a good-sized rug or coloured blanket, which you will want on board.

A cap with ear flaps for windy days.

A large shady hat—three or four.

Two or three large coloured aprons at three pence or four pence a yard skirting.

A few print boddies with a tough, rough skirt for scrambling. Besides this bring only the clothes you have, your very oldest.

If you come, will you bring for me: six briar pipes, two three-bladed pocket-knives 2/6. each, one two-bladed ditto, 1/9. or 1/6. (buck horn), 12 yards of pink or striped flannelette-like pattern for nightgowns. All writing paper, pens, pencils, needles, are dear and bad.

March 16th, 1889. 9 p.m., Saturday

Dear Annie,

I posted a letter to you today, but with only news up to yesterday night. This morning I had a hasty breakfast, and had almost finished when I was interrupted by Lees coming round with his horses ready harnessed, to hitch them on the waggon. This was about 7:10. Hastily but securely, five cooking utensils and bed were fastened on, and at about eight we departed. Lees buckboard was trailing behind the waggon, as he is going (or is now gone) on to the Beddoes' with the buckboard, leaving the waggon in town.

We jolted over the rocks, and I feared for my things, but everything came quite safely and is now deposited in an empty room at the Cox's, where I now write. Lees charged me only 50 cents for bringing the things in, which was exceedingly moderate. Cox was expected back today, but a telegram came this afternoon saying that he could not leave Kansas City till Monday evening, so we shall not see him till Tuesday or Wednesday at the earliest. Therefore, I stay here with Mrs. Cox until then anyway, and when he comes I do not yet know quite what arrangements I shall make.

Turner is here, but Mrs. Cox wants him to go away tomorrow with Brock, as he is said to be coming to town. She is (and justly) angry with him because he comes up from West Cliff and repeats to her all the slander about Cox he hears round the saloons. It is a most outrageous thing for him to do.

This afternoon I went down to West Cliff and sent off a lot of C.B.A. reports, and posted reports to you (and duplicates for Frederic) and a membership list. Please vote for the officers required, and if you can, get Frederic and Miss Hemery also to do so. I called in at the *Tribune* office to see if could make a 'trade' to borrow some type for my reports, but they were using all they had.

I got a lot of mail today, including a nice letter from you. I will not write about it all tonight but will mention the least important things: (1.) *Courant*. (2.) *Naturalist* for March. (3.) *Pall Mall Budgets.* (4.) Letter from Lomax of Liverpool. (5.) Letter from T. H. Hall of Hartford, wanting to exchange or purchase Colorado beetles. (6.) A cordial letter from Hy. Edwards, joining C.B.A. (7.) Reprints of 'Localities' paper in *Can. Entom.* I have sent you one. (8.) Letter from Walsingham, with names of two moths I sent him. (9.) Letter from Mother. (10.) Letter from Morrison, who sends the name of Mrs. Margaret C. Morrison as a new member of C.B.A. I suppose she may be his wife. (11.) Membership lists of C.B.A. from Morrison. He was good enough to get them printed. (12.) Letter from Carrington, joining C.B.A. and enclosing advance sheet of part of my variation article, so that I may continue it without a break (I had forgotten exactly where I had left off). Carrrington wants me to collect some butterflies for him. His letter is a long and interesting one. He says little about coming here. 'My business is going on well but I cannot yet fix date for my arrival on your continent.' These are all the letters except yours and Frederic's, and these must be answered tomorrow.

I forgot to say that some ladies called on Mrs. Cox today, and among them a Mrs. Stockton, who was quite interested in botany. I talked with her and found she was more or less familiar with even the scientific names of the commoner Colorado plants. I shall be interested to see more of her.

Sunday, March 17th, 5:25 p.m. I feel dull and fogged, which I attribute to an incipient cold, due to the draughts of this house. Last night and most of today I have been writing letters and preparing the membership lists and reports of C.B.A. for the post. We have 51 members now, so it becomes quite an undertaking to get the reports, etc., off. I went down to the town this afternoon for three things: (1.) To post letters, but the postoffice was shut. (2.) To see Charlton, but he was out. (3.) To get some milk for Mrs. Cox, which I did. It snowed and blew last night, and it is a cold, raw day today.

Your letter: I am glad you liked the little sketch of my room, but I am more sorry about another bit of news, that your throat was troubling you again. Thank you for the sketches from the 'Kitty' drawings, in this and the last letter. I think they are very nice. I must have seen Mrs. Bowdler Sharpe often enough, but I cannot recall the faintest mind-image of her. Of course I remember Bowdler, and an infinite number of Sharpe girls, all alike (excellent girls, too). I wish I had been there to hear Bowdler sing! It sounds as if it would be comic! Nearly as comic as it must have been at a concert here the other day, where I hear Dr. Björnson (the flimsiest and weakest-looking of men) personated the god Thor! Why did Bowdler say men were made fellows of the Royal Society? Yes, Bowdler is egotistical, but a good fellow all round, I think. His idea about the 'ingratitude' of the Bedford Park-ites is perfectly absurd.

Yes, I quite remember Mrs.Armstrong. I never cared much for her. She took up spiritualism long ago. How foolish she must be! Someone ought to take her in hand and convert her to reasonableness again. That political discussion with Mrs. Collis must have been rather amusing. I never argued with a primrose dame — should like to! That is a nice bit of verse you quote, the end of Macaulay's *Horatius*, is it not? I do not agree with Mr. Collis that he is bound to 'go with one's party in governmental matters.' In fact I think this is just the mistake of most politicians. It is good that they presented Horsley with teapot, etc.; he well deserved it.

Talking of presentations, the Gardening Society offered to donate me a book when I left Bedford Park, but I couldn't choose. When I came to New York, I bought Coulter's *Manual*, and wrote R.J.G.R. that they might consider that to be the book, but I never heard from him.

However, there was no need to give me a book anyway.

Your riddles scare me, but I have puzzled over them, and conclude that six hens would lay in six days 24 eggs, and a brick and a half would weigh 21 pounds. Is that right? The last is a variation of a favourite puzzle of Lees': 'If a horse weighed 500 pounds and half of its own weight, what would it weigh?'

I feel quite an affection for old nurse Turner, after the bit of her letter you quote. Good old soul! May it be as she says. It makes me shudder to think of that small-pox time. Poor things, but the mother lived, and you did not come to harm, so there is much that might have been worse, looking back on it. I wish my father had lived. You are happy to have both parents.

It has always seemed to be that disease and death, so far as they are not the result of human negligence or wrongdoing, ought not to be grumbled at. I don't say I never grumble, but when I do I feel as though I were wrong in doing so. What do you think? It is always possible that there is a natural fitness of things which is best for all concerned, if we only knew it. But I do grumble against gambling and lying and stealing because they constitute a manifestly unnatural unfitness of things, however looked at. There is no supposing that 'poker' is a natural law of the universe.

That intermittent fever you had reminds me of a like experience of my own which happened directly after I had finished with the College of Preceptors exam, as recorded in the last bit of biography. I got laid up with some sort of a fever, and temperature went up to 105 degrees, and I was expected to have congestion of the lungs. Uncle Douglas came down from London (I was at Margat) and prescribed lots of quinine. I lived on milk chiefly, and before long recovered and totally cured myself by walking to St. Nicholas marshes and back, much to everybody's consternation. I had not meant to walk, but I missed the train both going and returning, and there was no help for it.

Monday, March 18th, 9:15 a.m. After all, I did not get this off by the morning's post, as there was so little in it. The post goes out at 7:25 a.m., and I went down this morning in time to post a lot of letters I had written. I did not say that *Little Folks*, *Standard*, and *Daily News* came safely. Thank you very much for them. I like your little story in *Little Folks* and the daily papers are very interesting. I see even the *Standard* is down on the *Times*.

10:35 p.m. I have just packed up some cacti for you. I think they will grow. They should be put in a warm place (hothouse) in a light soil, and not much water after they have revived. The round ones are *Cereus* [*Echinocereus*. Ed.] *viridiflorus* (Engelm.) and have greenish-yellow flowers. The flat and very spiny ones are (I am nearly sure) a form of *Opuntia missouriensis* (De Candolle). I also send a lichen (*Alectoria sp.*[probably a vagant species of *Xanthoparmelia*. Ed.]) which is very common on the prairie here, and a piece of quaking asp bark covered with a fungus called *Valsa nivea* (Fries). I also enclose butterflies, about which I will write to Fred. I forgot to say that *O. missouriensis* has yellow flowers.

9:55 p.m. Plainly, this letter will not go even by tomorrow's train, for I have this evening got quite the nicest kind of a letter from my love, and how can I post this until I have answered it? News first, though, such as it is. Having packed up your cacti, etc., and also written to Walsingham, I went to town to post these things, and to find Charlton (which I did not; he was not at home again) and look for a room for myself. In the latter venture I also failed, and could hear of nothing better than Goldstandt's offer of a room at $2.50 a month.

Cassidy had a room to let, but there was an 'inside' room in the building already let, so the inside party would have to come rushing through my room whenever he wished to communicate with the outside world, unless he got out of the window! Under these circumstances, Cassidy himself advised me not to take the room, and I certainly think he is right. Cassidy, by the way, is the ironmonger of this city.

Regy and Miss Urquhart appeared today, Miss U. staying here for a long while to talk to Mrs. Cox. She departs for England in April. Later on, I commenced a copy of my picture of the Cox's house (on the ranch) which had been 'on the books' for a very long time. I did the drawing, and painted in the sky and part of the roof, but it began to be late, and I left off to cut some wood. After supper this evening I went to town for mail, and got your letter (a very pleasant surprise) and also letter from Mother (enclosing $1.00), postcard from Packard, *Science Gossip*, and *Standard*.

I am tempted to answer your letter now, but it is late. By the way, I am dosing Mrs. Cox with 'literature' — Dickens' *Christmas Carol* (she had never read it) yesterday, *Happy Boy* (Björnson) today. The ladies here have actually a literary society (nine members!). Mrs. Cox has just joined, by special invitation. But good night, love!

March 19th, 11 a.m. I should have said that Turner went back to Brock's yesterday. Some days ago, Turner shot two wild ducks, and this morning I have been plucking and cleaning them. Now they are in the oven, and I sit down to write to you.

Before turning to your letter, there is one thing in Mother's letter I must tell you about. She writes: 'Grandpa B. has entirely parted with his business, and has turned it into a Limited Liability company. We can't get him to settle anything on Grannie, and all the money will go at once.' Now this is abominable. Poor Grannie! Don't tell this to anyone, as I think it is not supposed to be known.

Would it not be Twickenham Ferry you went across with Mrs. Ruston? Do you know the song about Twickenham Ferry? I mistook your meaning about the 'Early Rose' potato. I think you said it was a white potato, and I thought you meant the skin. When boiled, it is, as you say, white tinged with pink. I see I was in too great a hurry about the articles. Of course, a more or less long time always will intervene between the writing and the publishing. I 'pologise.

Supposing the English Government enacts a law refusing Socialists admission into England, what will I do? It would be an extraordinary thing if I could not smuggle myself in the face of any law, but if not, I should have to persuade you to come to America! But of course there is no possibility of such a law being passed. You speak of choice, but do I choose to be a Socialist, anyway? 'It's the nature of the beast', you see. But you know that, barring impossibilities, I *shall* come to England. Supposing a law were enacted that all who were not Roman Catholics were to be boiled in oil! Could you choose to be Roman Catholic? Alas, I fear we should both get boiled!

Did I ever beautify myself for your sake? Perhaps a little, but not much. I always have been a hideous object, and it is one of my chief failings that I do not take enough care of my appearance. You must scold me for it, and insist upon my appearing like a decent member of society. When you saw me was my decentest time!

I do not now remember what I thought when I saw *Les Miserables* at your house, but I was glad you read it.

You know, I always felt, rather, both as regards appearance and manner, that I ought not to try to be nice to you. That is part of the reason that I was so rude to you. I felt that if you were to judge of me you ought to see me as I really was, without any society polish. People I did not care about, I would sometimes try to please.

I rather like *Walden*, but not so much as some do. Myself, I believe in constant companionship for those who love one another. Thoreau perhaps never loved anyone, and in that case he would naturally regard people rather as things to be studied or to be interested in, like specimens. I think everyone is interesting for a little while, for this point of view, but people one cares for are always welcome.

Your last 'Kitty' picture is very pretty. I like it almost better than any. (I mean the girl sitting down, with her hands clasped in front.) I fear I write more carelessly now than I did in the old days, not so good a hand, this because you note how my handwriting has changed. Carlie, also, I think writes not quite so well. I am generally in more of a hurry now than before. You would notice this most in the letters I write to other people. I wrote at the postoffice in East Cheap, where one is supposed to only write telegrams, but nobody interfered with me.

Thank you for all you have written on *African Farm*. No, I did not think you could send me much of an answer through Frederic, but I wanted to ask you, so I did, answer or no answer. Yes, [illegible] in Chapter X is very good and true, but there is also a reverse to it, is there not? Yes, it was association of ideas that made me cry at the parting of Lyndall and Waldo. I nearly cry as I look at it again now.

Oh, Annie! Do you really think that Fred loves Kate Hemery? It is a sort of thing I have thought of only to dismiss it as absurd. Not absurd that he should love her, but absurd that I should think so without any reason atall. But if it really is so, I am not afraid, or at least I would never do anything to interfere. I have contended long enough and often enough that, when people love, it is not good for others to interfere. With flirtation or any of that foolery I would interfere with the severest hand, but love, that is quite another thing. Now, of Fred, I think he is not the one to do otherwise than love, and if he should love her, might it not happen that she also loves him? I can suppose it may make you uneasy, though, and I quite share with you the opinion that it would be very unfortunate if it should prevent his ever marrying, for I want Fred to marry. On the whole, I should think it might be just an intellectual friendship, and not love atall, but then, I have no means of knowing. Tell me, when you get this, whether your fears have been dispelled in the meanwhile.

Whatever was it that I said in my letter that you didn't like atall? I feel very penitent but cannot at all remember what it might have been. Do tell me.

About Mrs. Cusack, how refined and educated is she? Yes, possibly about on the Allport level, only a better sort of person in herself than Mrs. Allport, I should say. I am bound to say that in England I should not have thought much of her, very likely, but out here she is after all a centre of womanliness, civilization, and decency, which is a very great thing indeed. On the whole, she is an excellent person, and from her constant buoyancy of spirits and energy a pleasant person to be with.

Before you get this you will have got her letter asking you to come here. I begin to feel that it is rather selfish of me to want you to come, and I shall not be atall angry if you say 'nonsense' to the whole thing. But it would be very nice! I am very glad our ideas on religion do not clash. After all, that is the groundwork of all other ideas that are opinions.

'Alcoholism' is as old as can be. I don't know who invented it; we used it at the hospital, if I am not mistaken. You can tell a man he is 'suffering from alcoholism', whereas if you said he was a drunkard he might be offended! I am glad to find you agree with me about *Women's Gazette*, etc. *Picadilly* does not yet arrive.

I can quite imagine your flood. I have a good memory of it from what you told me at Bedford Park. I think it must have been the storm I remember at Beckenham, I think, in 1876. I remember the pouring rain and the lightning. A cow was struck dead at Shortlands. I think the picture of O[live] Schreiner you enclose (out of *Star*) must be a fearful libel, don't you? I will mind the 'nine rules for husbands' when 'Someday' comes. But you must write me a special set of rules. I will try to observe them.

I shall post this this afternoon, and will close it up now. I am very well. It is to be hoped that by this time the weather even in England is nice, beautiful spring weather, as it was that spring of 1887. It will do you good, a little nice weather.

> With very much love,
> your Theo.

I enclose a little note for Frederic.

Tuesday, March 19ᵗʰ, 9:30 p.m.

Dear Annie,

Your letter (and one for Fred enclosed) was posted today. The mail I got this evening is only a letter from Smith, of Denver, about C.B.A., and requiring a long answer. Wheatley was here this afternoon, not having yet gone to the Cusacks', because the money he expects from home has not come, and he cannot leave the hotel in town until he pays his bill there. Cox was half-expected tonight, but he comes not. I looked over the rooms over the postoffice, which are to let, this afternoon. They are nice rooms, and I think I must take one of them.

March 20ᵗʰ, 8:05 p.m. We have just heard the whistle of the train, and Mrs. Cox, though apparently absorbed in a magazine, must be on the tiptoe of expectation, for Cox is expected home tonight.

As for me, I have done practically nothing today except mind the children, and I caught myself making the uncharitable reflection that it was a good thing that parents had a natural love for their children, because if left to others, patience could hardly hold out! But this isn't so, and I am very fond of children. For instance, I believe I could look after the Charley Cusack children for any length of time. However, these Cox children, Isabel and Charley, are rather trying. One has to be constantly amusing them, for their own resources are very few, and Isabel is always crying over some trifle. Charley has been a good deal 'spoiled' by his grandparents, who had him under their charge in England. Still, I like them when they are good, and I trust they will improve in time. They are very young now.

This morning I had to go down town to order some groceries for Mrs. Cox, and I took the children with me. It is not much over half a mile away, but I had to walk slow for them, so it took a long while. Charley was very vigorous, running and jumping the whole way, but Isabel had to be carried on my shoulder a good deal. I am afraid Isabel is getting bow-legged. Mrs. Cox had not noticed it until I drew her attention to it. There is not enough lime in the soil here to make bones. Even the snails can't make a decent shell, and Isabel has been (and is) wearing boots that are very much down on one side. It will be a great pity if she suffers any permanent deformity on account of these things. They each had five cents to buy 'googies' (goodies, = sweets), and got some barley-sugar-looking stuff at Falkenberg's, which they have been sucking more or less ever since.

Before lunch, Humphrey came up with a buggy to fetch Mrs. Cox down to the meeting . . . [interrupted by supper., and then expedition to town for mail and milk — continued at 9:25]. As I was saying, Humphrey (a friend of Cox, a speculator or 'business man' — people say a scamp — and as far as I can see, in every way like Mr. Carr of B. P. — came to fetch Mrs. Cox down to his house, where there was to be a meeting of the women's literary society. I was thus left with the children, so I got them (and myself) more lunch, cut wood, played with them, read *Competitors*, and showed them the pictures therein (which they wanted to see several times over), when Mrs. Cox appeared.

She had enjoyed the 'Ladies' Literary', and was full of it. It must be an amusing affair. The subject today was South America, and from what Mrs. Cox says, they must have come with just as much knowledge of the matter as can be gained by looking it up a little beforehand, which is characteristically an American method. In times gone by, they boasted greater magnificence, and Mrs. Cox brought up a copy of rules and proceedings for 1882, nicely printed and testifying to great activity at that time. Mrs. Stockton is secretary, I believe. They have a fair library, and each member takes one or more magazines, which are handed all round the society afterwards, each one having them for a week.

The meetings are weekly and last about five hours, and are devoted to the following subjects in succession: (1.) Art and literature. (2.) Science and education. (3.) History. (4.) Entertainment (= recitations, reading, etc.). Today was History. Mrs. Cox and Mrs. Humphrey have been deputed to arrange for next meeting, which is at Mrs. Freer's. (The meetings are at the house of each member in succession.) Altogether the Society seems to be a most excellent thing, and I wish the men had something similar, but they are not equal to it I fear. 'No money in it', as they say. Curiously, Mrs. Cox says one of the members offered to give *Story of an African Farm* to the library today. We kept supper waiting till 7:30, but no Cox appeared. Poor Mrs. C. was evidently much disappointed, as I could see. I went to West Cliff, and expected there might be a letter for Mrs. Cox explaining Cox's non-arrival, but there was not.

I got a notice from *Standard* that they want some subscription (they make 50 cents to be due now) but I wrote explaining how I came to have it sent to me, and saying that I didn't read the paper as a rule, and they had better send no more, as I was not subscribing. On the way back I got some milk at Mrs. Peters'. It was very dark out, snowing slightly, but not cold.

In an anonymous article in *Atlantic Monthly* (Feb. 1899) I find the following which is worth quoting: 'The more intensely people live in matters of thought and intellect, the more likely are young men of their own accord to marry women older than themselves. . . . It seems as if women, like men, sometimes exercise a fascination [!] which, though magnetic and personal, is not wholly [strange discovery!] dependent on attractiveness of person. . . . The charm of which we speak continues to the end to be just itself and to command intense affection and devotion. Its power is felt by all who come in contact with its possessor; but when that possessor is a woman, it is often more necessary that a man should have some special quality of nature to enable him to enter the sphere of fascination. . . . The fact is that one of the most essential factors to happiness is agreeable companionship. . . etc.' I rather like this, on the whole; do you?

Changing the subject, I am a good deal disgusted because the new Republican government has appointed a new man (Rusk, I think is the name) in place of Colman as chief of the Department of Agriculture. I am disgusted on these grounds, (1.) It is not a political post and ought not to be influenced by politics. (2.) Even the Republicans admit that Colman has been an excellent Commissioner. (3.) The best that his own party have to say for the new man is that he is a 'practical farmer, a business man, and as a magistrate was noted for the way he sat on the Socialists in Wisconsin, and you can well suppose the last two things do not recommend him to me. Wherefore I am disgusted, as I said.

March 21ˢᵗ, 6:10 p.m. Not much of a day, cold and dull. I have been painting Mrs. Cox's picture of the ranch house and taking noted for my variation paper. Brock came in and brought Turner, to Mrs. Cox's great dismay, for he asked to stay here for the night (Brock has gone back to his ranch). I go down presently to meet Cox at the train (if he comes) and to get mail. I hope the *Ent. Mags.* will come tonight, as I have to write a part of my variety paper for the *Entomologist*, and it will be too late unless I do it soon, and I cannot do it until I see the March *Entom.* It snowed a little last night up about the Cusacks', but not down here.

10 p.m. I went down to the train, but no Cox, nor any letter from him by the mail. It is perfectly abominable of him. Poor Mrs. Cox nearly cried when I came back with no news. I was so sorry for her, though I tried to make little of it, not to discourage her too much. Mrs. Cox has tremendous pluck and has borne everything without complaining, and this is the reward — that she is abandoned to do everything for herself and the children, worse than if she had no husband.

I got no letters, but the *Ent, Mags.* arrived, and also *Pall Mall Budget* and *Punch*. The cartoon about the *Times* is exceedingly clever and funny. Did you see it? Mrs. Cox has been reading *African Farm*. I am not sure (you will be astounded to hear) whether I did wisely in offering it to her, but she needs something interesting or she broods over her troubles, which is not pleasant for her. I do not think the pathos of *African Farm* will affect her so as to add another cause of misery, It is curious that if Mrs. Cox had not been married all this while, we should regard her as a very young woman. She is now only 26. And here is Cox wrecking her life almost at its beginning! But this is enough. Dear love, goodnight!

March 2ⁿᵈ, 8:50 p.m. At last! Here is Cox. I commenced the morning with writing up notes and records, and did not begin writing the next part of the variation paper for *Entomologist* till it was rather late, and the consequence was that (often being interrupted) I found late in the afternoon that I should have all I could do to get it done before I went to town this evening. However, I did finish in time and have posted it off to Carrington. It is a summary of and additional remarks on colour variation.

Mrs. Hunter came up here for a little while to talk to Mrs. Cox, and Frank Hunter came to take her away. Turner never came here last night, but here he is tonight, at present playing cards with Cox, or rather, Cox is showing him a new game. Mrs. Cox looks on wearily.

A telegram came about noon from Cox (from Pueblo) saying he would be here tonight, but one did not assume because of this that he *would* arrive. But I went down to the train this evening and there he was, after all. He came up on the bus that goes to Silver Cliff, and I waited for the mail, getting only a letter from Hamilton, with names of two beetles I sent him.

Cox seems to have done no good in Kansas City, and as far as I can make out, is in as bad a financial mess as ever, if not worse. Mrs. Cox said today she did not care what happened, so long as Cox was here to share it with her, but this only makes it more abominable of Cox to treat her so.

March 23rd, 8:50 p.m. I wish you could pay me a call and look at my new (for the time being) home, and advise about the fitting-up. But you will tell me what you think about it if I write all about it to you, and that is what I will do, only not tonight, as I am not yet 'fixed up.'

This morning, after breakfast at the Cox's, I talked to Mrs. Cox about coming to live in her house versus living at West Cliff. Cox said he did not mind my living there atall, and Mrs. Cox seemed to have no objection, but I had thought it well over and felt sure it would be better for all concerned if I went to West Cliff. This settled, I went down and saw Goldstandt (the postmaster) and rented a room in his building for $2.50 a month.

After this, I went three times to the Cox's, each time bringing a load of things which I put in my new room. Many of my things will remain at the Cox's, but I can get them any time, and I have what I immediately need now. The rest of the day has been spent in fixing things up. I have two nice tables, one for writing and one for cooking, which were out in the yard at the back of the house, and I brought them in. I had lots of trouble getting them through the door. The cooking table I thought I had twisted every possible way, and still it would not come through. But I thought at last of another way, and it came. I have not yet got my stove, so I had to buy some tinned tongue this evening for supper. I really must get the stove in tomorrow.

Charlton is back again. He has been away. I spoke to him in the postoffice. The mail I got tonight was *Piccadilly*, a letter from Dimmock, and papers returned from Hamilton.

Sunday, March 24th, 9:40 p.m. Here I have been talking to the Charltons so long that it is quite late, and I meant to do a lot of writing tonight. The first thing this morning was to purchase food — a dozen eggs — which cost me 20 cents in the store below. (Later I found I could have got them for 15 cents at Kettle & Walters.) For breakfast, I finished my tinned tongue and put the eggs by for the next meal. As it was Sunday, I could not get my stove down to Silver Cliff, so the next best thing to be done was to see about getting wood hauled to town. For this reason, I set off to Ula to see whether Louis would do it for me.

I had hardly left town when Walters (of Kettle & Walters) overtook me with a buggy and took me all the way to Ula. Walters is a pleasant man, in appearance rather stout, with a red face and red beard. We found plenty to talk about. For one thing, I told him an idea of mine, to give a series of ten botanical lectures, and charge a dollar for the course. Walters liked the idea and said that he, for one, would attend. I shall want at least 25, though, to make it pay.

Arrived at Ula, I soon found Louis. I had not been to his house since he moved it, and found that he could not get me the wood, as he was using the horses. I stayed to lunch, employing the intervening time in clearing some land of *Bigelovia* brush with a grub-hoe (*Bigelovia* is allied to *Senecio*), while Louis carpentered and Mrs. Howard commenced two oil paintings of the house, working on both at the same time.

While I was there, Regy and Jack Mackenzie drove up, and a little later Colin Mackenzie appeared, riding Romeo. Colin brought a letter from Lees to Louis, which L. read aloud to us, so that we might advise him how to answer it. It is this way: Louis is exceedingly hot-tempered, and the other day these two fell out about something down at Beddoes', and Louis abused Lees in the freest kind of way, and now Lees writes that if he cannot behave differently, he does not want to have anything more to do with him.

Now, it is difficult to know what to say; both of them are excellent fellows, especially Lees, and yet both are without doubt very aggravating at times, and Louis is very apt indeed to fly into a rage over small matters. But neither of them mean half of what they say on these occasions, and generally it ends in smoke. Louis has written urging that he did not get angry without reason, and half apologising for his violence, and I hope they will make it up all right, but I think they made a mistake ever to go into partnership.

Two other bits of news I got from the Mackenzies. (1.) It seems Regy, Jack Mackenzie, and Wheatley have been playing poker up there, and Jack spoke of winning $4.00. It will ruin the Cusacks' boarding house scheme if there is anything of this sort going on there. Colin hinted (I daresay rightly) that Regy's play is not always strictly 'above board' (2.) It is rumoured that Cox had mortgaged his ranch to one man and then *sold* it to another, for which he is liable to be put in the penitentiary. So much for scandal.

I found at Ula, and afterwards nearer town, plenty of *Cymopterus montanus* in flower, earlier than I expected it. At Ula I also saw the first red-winged blackbirds (*Agelaeus phoeniceus*) and a meadow lark (*Sturnella neglecta*). Louis says the *Ag. phoeniceus* arrived at Ula in order that its children may attend school before I left Ula, and he agreed to haul me a load of wood on Tuesday. I have to pay him $3.00, which is 50 cents more than I might perhaps have paid, but Walters tells me that Simpson's loads are so much bigger than other people's that they are well worth the difference.

I walked back to town, finding on the way a *Limnaea truncatula* and a few beetles. When I got here, I had only written a few notes when someone came tapping at the door, 'Come in!' — and in walked Frank Hunter with a message that Cox was ill, and would I go and see him? I went, and found him feverish and feeling ill, and the lymphatic glands below the left ear swollen and painful. He told me he had been using some ointment on his neck a few days ago, and this had been last used for an abscess on a horse, and might be contaminated with the matter from the horse's wound. There was at the same time a slight cut on his neck, made while shaving. The symptoms certainly look like approaching pyaemia or blood-poisoning, and if that is

what it really is, he is in a very dangerous state. Nothing can be done for it, except quinine if the temperature gets very high. I must go up and see him tomorrow.

I took up six of my eggs and got them boiled at the Cox's; three I ate this evening for supper. After supper I put on a black coat and a collar and went round to Charlton's. I found him and Mrs. C. at home, and very pleasant and talkative they were. I discussed chemistry for a long time with Charlton. He tells me that it is really a fact the cobalt and nickel have decomposed and [been] found to contain a third element common to both. This is the most remarkable chemical discovery for a long time.

Charlton says he and some others are getting up a club for debating, and he invited me to join. I most certainly will, unless the subscription is too much. The preliminary meeting is to be some time this week. I think I must post this tomorrow morning, for the train, so will end up. It is not much of a letter, but I have been rather hurried and bothered this last week, so I am sure, my love, you will forgive me — and also, there is no biography.

Your loving lover, Theo.
Health. Am very well.

March 25th, 1889, 9:35 p.m.

Dear Annie,

A letter went to you by the morning mail. Today has been a day of goings and comings, with very little done. This morning, after breakfast (of three eggs and some bread) I went up to the Cox's to see how Cox was, and found him apparently rather better, but unable to do much. So I had to cut wood, chop a bone for soup, and take the insides out of two ducks. At the same time, I got six eggs boiled for myself. I went also up to Silver Cliff and hunted round once more for stoves, and got one for $2.00 that suits me better than the one I saw the first time I went up. It is smaller, and lacks the damper, but I can make one, and if it will bake (as I do hope), it is pretty cheap.

Then I went back to West Cliff and found Lees here with a buckboard and Ben. I went up with him to the Cox's, left him there, and borrowed the buckboard to go up and get my stove. Then when I got back to the Cox's I had to return to Silver Cliff to fetch Mrs. Cox and little Charley, who had walked up there to buy meat. At length I got the stove down here, and 'Doc' Vetter kindly exercised considerable muscular force in helping me to get it upstairs and into my room. It is now fixed up, but I have not yet any stove pipe; I must get some tomorrow.

I hoped your letter might have come this evening, but the English mail did not turn up. I got a letter from W. H. Edwards, one from Cassidy, the botanist of the Ft. Collins Agricultural College, and one from a Dr. E. B. Landis (don't know him) asking what are the terms on which one becomes a corresponding member of C.B.A. I also got a bundle of interesting reprints from Dimmock.

This evening Charlton appeared, to look at my (i.e., Ellis') microscope. He stayed talking a long while. He says that he and his wife will join the botanical lecture class if I will get it up, and he will do all in his power to help me in this and other matters. He seems to be very kindly disposed towards me.

Tuesday, March 26th, 9 p.m. No English letters today. It is disappointing, but they will surely come tomorrow. By way of breakfast I had bread and prunes, but I wanted something more substantial, and so set off for Silver Cliff after stove-pipe. Before I left, I was astonished to see Lees drive in — it was 7:20 a.m., so he must have got up early. He had driven from the Cusacks', and came to register an important letter. He was just in time. The mail closes at 7:25.

I got my stove-pipe at Silver Cliff at the same place that I got the stove. It cost me 60 cents (new, it would have cost $1.75, and it was in no way damaged).

I came galumping back (got a ride part of the way) and found Lees in a great state of mind about one of Payn's horses, which is missing (it was last seen on Cox's ranch) and he had heard a rumour that it was eleven miles south of West Cliff. He half intended to go, and I was to go with him to the place and catch the horse, but he reflected that it would take too long, so it was put off for a day or two, and Lees said he would go from the Cusacks' and get Regy to go with him.

Then another matter came up — the Lees vs. Louis quarrel of which I wrote in the last letter. Lees had got Louis' letter, and this morning wrote him an answer to it but would not go and deliver it himself. So would I go out with him in the buckboard and get off at the turning to Ula and take the note to Louis while he went on to the Cusacks'? I agreed to this, but as I should have to walk back, I said I really must have something substantial to eat first. So he helped me fix up the stove-pipe (it was too long, and one bit had to be cut out at the blacksmith's, and then I lit a fire and boiled three eggs, which I devoured ravenously. The we went out on the buckboard.

All this time the hours had been slipping by, and I found the Howards at lunch (it was twelve). On the way out, I should say. I met Samse coming to town with my load of wood, and a good big load too. I paid him the $3.00 for it, and asked him to 'dump' it behind the house.

Louis told me that a man named Lowestrow (I don't know how he spells his name) had told him that he had just come across a dead horse on his ranch, found by the melting of the snow. It must have been there a long time and nobody claimed it or recognised it. Louis suggested that it was the lost Payn horse, and as Lowestrow's is on Swift Creek between Cox's ranch and Beckwith's, this is exceedingly probable. In the face of this Lees ought to know of it before starting out to the other place where the horse was supposed to be. Wherefore I concluded to walk up to the Cusacks' and tell him about it.

Jack Mackenzie (who is now working for Louis) was just then going to Beddoes' after a load of lumber, so I went with him as far as the Beckwith's, and then walked up Swift Creek to the Cusacks'. The weather was threatening and I feared a storm, but nothing came of it. I looked for insects, and got some beetles (*Paederus* and *Aphodius)*. I called at Lowestrow's but he was not at home, and I could not spare the time to look for the horse.

When I got to the Cusacks', I found Lees had just gone up to his cabin but would be down again tomorrow, so I left a note for him explaining things. Mrs. Cusack was exceedingly gracious to me, and by sheer force compelled me to eat a meal big enough for two elephants. She asked me to stay the night, but I preferred to return to town. I got Mrs. Cusack to vote for the C.B.A. officers. She wanted me to tell her who to vote for, but I think it best that I do not exercise any influence in the election, so she had to choose for herself as best she could.

I left the Cusacks' at about 5:30 and arrived in town at eight. The mail rec'd. is two letters, one from J. P. Norris, voting for TDAC as Secretary of C.B.A. and requesting me to fill in the rest for him at my discretion. But this I shall not do. The other letter was from Riley. In answer to his criticism in the last letter (about naming species), he says, 'I am greatly pleased that you take my critical remarks in the sprit in which they are intended and to find that we agree so nearly in so many points.' He agrees to a proposition of mine that a collection of Colorado insects shall be formed by C.B.A. and kept under his care at U. S. National Museum till we have a museum in Colorado for them, and he sends a signed agreement (two copies) to that effect. He says he agrees fully with my paper in *Can. Ent.* on localities, and lastly, says he will be in Europe all the summer, and sails from New York on 13th of April.

March 27th, ten minutes to ten. Your letter came this evening. I was so glad to get it. It seemed an age since the last. 'Doc' Vetter, of whom more later) has been in here talking, so the time has slipped by, and I cannot now tell you more than the news. Your letter I will answer (I hope) tomorrow. I have been writing letters most of today, and have written several.

Charlton came in this morning and talked for a long time. He greatly pities my lonely condition (!) and invites me to frequently come around to a meal at his house. It is very kind of him, but one feels a bit shy of such a proceeding. However, I expect we shall see a good deal of one another.

It was quite late this afternoon before I got my letters squared up, and then I went after water, and then turned my attention to the wood pile. Samson, to my dismay, had dumped it all in the road, by the fence of our yard, instead of inside the yard. The road is wide enough and the wood will not be in the way, but I am rather afraid lest it should be stolen. So I went out and threw over the fence all the pieces that were at all small, leaving the large logs (almost too big to steal) in the road for the present. This done, I fetched some boxes out of the yard (the yard is littered with empty boxes in which the draperies, etc., come to Goldstandt's store) and made a temporary bookshelf out of them — so: placing one on top of the other. They are long boxes and just a convenient size.

The next business after this was supper — coffee, three eggs, and bread. I was rather anxious to see how the stove would bake, but to my satisfaction it produced as good a loaf as I have ever been able to make out of the whole meal flour. I deserted the cooking at 7:30 to go down and get the mail, and got your letter and letters from Mother and D. W. Park (enclosing $1.00 subscr. to C.B.A.) and entomological pins from Ashmead. These pins are the finest I have seen, and are for pinning very minute insects.

I was just about to write to you when Vetter came in, and talked and looked at my books so long that the evening speedily departed and it was night. Vetter is a pleasant little man. I forgot to tell you Mrs. Cusack has heard from Frank. He has got a carpentering job near Brisbane at £2 a week and board. Not bad to start on.

March 28th, 9 p.m. This morning I continued Mrs. Cox's picture of the ranch house but was interrupted by the appearance of Regy, who had come to town with Lees. They had with them one of Payn's horses which had a bad leg from ill-use and neglect. I had to go and examine the leg. It seems to be the result of an un-cared-for sprain. The horse has been at Aldridge's, a ranch three miles or so the other side of town, and they came in on purpose to fetch it. The dead horse at Lowestrow's proved to be the horse I thought it was, so Lees did not have to go out after it where it was reported to be.

After this, I continued Mrs. Cox's picture and finished it and took it up to the Cox's. I found Mrs. Frank Hunter there. Cox seems much better. When I got back, I began the preparation of an article on the insects I found on the expedition with Payn on the Pacific slope in 1887. The mail this evening is a letter from Shufeldt, a postcard from Averell, and *Pall Mall Budget*.

Now your letter, only I am very sleepy and stupid tonight, so don't be hard on me if I can't say what I would! I have not yet had time to read *Picadilly*, and have not yet finished *Competitors*. Talking of books, Cox has been looking at *African Farm*, and votes it terrible rubbish, but Mrs. Cox likes it as far as she has read.

I think you must have looked very nice in your yellow dress (of which you send sample), only you look nice anywhere. I remember one party-evening at your house. I was talking to Louy (you had escaped me for the moment) and we discussed the 'get-up' of the various people present. At last Louy asked me it I thought you looked nice. I said 'yes', but it seemed quite an extraordinary idea that clothes should be expected to make any difference to *you*. However, to an outsider I suppose a pretty dress does make an improvement.

I notice the difference in other people, whom I do not care much for — for *themselves*. I am very glad that you do not mind the 'North Countree.' I don't know much about it myself, but I think it would be very nice. One is tempted to build castles in the air, and arrange it all in fancy. But in a few years it will surely be *fact*, won't it, love? And that is more important to us than thinking about details, which we shall be able to consider *together* bye and bye.

I quite agree with all you say about the women's movement. I won't order you about! (Daren't!), but you may order me as much as you like. I shall like it, and it will be good for me. Don't you think so?

That was horrid of Bowdler Sharpe, to *force* the wine on his wife, I should have supposed he knew better.

Oh, Annie! I do like your little remembrance of that night at the gate of Syon; you were very nice to me. You pressed my hand and looked at me so that I felt you had not at all given up our friendship. And then I read the letter — what should I have done without that letter? Of course, I was obliged to *write* you a reply!

I presume Stead of the *Pall Mall* was not at that journalistic ball or he would have made a speech that would have astonished some of them. So you were recognized by your resemblance to Clive! The resemblance throughout your family is very strong, but I never noticed that you were especially like anyone, though it is true at one time I did not even know you by sight from Louy and Alice. Sometimes people see likenesses where there can hardly be any. For instance, Charlton the other day so fancied a family resemblance between your photograph and your lover that he could hardly be persuaded that you were not my sister!

Yes, for my part I think I could be as jealous as anyone if I had any cause, but then that is out of the question. When I said, 'It used to comfort me to think that, after all, I was treated (by the parents) no worse than anyone else', I meant this: Almost any girl I met, except the one I loved, seemed (so far as parents went) quite accessible for friendship. And it was certainly unusual that any girls of the age of yourself, Alice, and Louy, should be prevented from fraternising with whom they would, provided that their friends were not in any way objectionable. Therefore, in my selfishness, I was consoled by thinking, 'Well, if *I* mayn't talk to Annie (except almost by stealth) atall events nobody else may.'

Supposing it had been possible that the parents thought that some young man (say, Alex. Wise! — By the way, how does he get on in Australia? Do you ever hear of him?) was eminently suited to be your friend, and had not yet kept up all the old restrictions as regards myself and the rest of the world, might I not have felt jealous? *Now*, I should not feel jealous even in such an event, but *then* I did not know you loved me. Of course, as things were, we got to know each other very well, but it was hardly with the approval of the parents. As to 'de la B.', of course I don't feel jealous, and do not atall mind how many young men you know. Perhaps if I loved you less I might not like it, but I believe in you too much to nourish foolish jealousies.

No, I never got an answer to the second letter to Uncle Douglas. Yes, I should certainly quarrel with G. Turner of the *Courant*, were we partners. I admit the justice of your criticism of what I said about the Apostles' Creed; I did not quite like what I had written when I had written it. It is a curious question, that of belief. As a matter of fact, it is not beliefs that are founded on facts, but facts on beliefs, however paradoxical that may sound. You know, in Euclid, one starts with the definitions and axioms, and these have to be taken for granted before anything can be proved.

Well, it is half past ten, and I must go to bed. Goodnight.

March 29th, 7 p.m. The potatoes are boiling and the bread is in the oven, so just a word or two, love, while I wait. I am not pleased with myself today, for I have done almost nothing After breakfast (Ah, here is the train; I hear its whistle) I prepared some notes on insects and then went up to the Cox's to borrow my picture of the mountains in order to make Miss Urquhart a copy of it. Miss Urquhart offered to buy a picture from me long ago, but I never felt quite sure whether she meant it, but Mrs. Cusack says she was complaining that I did pictures for other people and would not do her one, so I am going to make this copy before she leaves for England.

At the Cox's, Mrs. Cox met me with all sorts of news about the Ladies' Literary Society, and she said she and Mrs. Ommany had been deputed to prepare the program of next week's meeting, which was to relate to 'Art and Literature.' She wanted me to look her up some papers to be read, ands so I went over a lot of the *Pall Mall Budget*s (which are still up there at Cox's) and selected a number of pieces for her to choose from. This took some time, and I stayed to lunch, coming down here early in the afternoon.

On my way up to Cox's I saw a *Vanessa antiopa*, the first butterfly of this year. This afternoon I read *Competitors* for a while, but felt unwell and had to lie down for an hour or two. It was just the same kind of sleepiness or stupor (quite different from genuine sleep) that I have suffered from at intervals ever since I have been consumptive — nothing of any consequence. It does not affect me atall in the cold weather. I take quinine as a remedy.

9 p.m. The only mail was a *Custer Courant*. I supplied a few news paragraphs in this number, about sunshine in Colorado (out of the Ft. Collins Agric. Report), nickel and cobalt, loco, etc. It is very warm this evening. At supper time I had to open the window for fresh air, and in flew three moths to the light.

I did not finish answering your letter. Was it Ella Ferris I saw play the guitar or banjo at the Percival Clarke's one evening? She looked very young, but not pretty, I thought. I can't say I like the notion of Mrs. B. Clarke's Academy (?) pictures. One would suppose the girl would have something to say about the disposal of her soul, and the angel has no business to compromise with the demon. But I suppose it isn't meant to make sense.

Good gracious! What address did you send to the applicant re Female Emigration? I believe most emigration schemes are foolish, and many are downright frauds, so it is very risky to be sending addresses of emigration bureaus about. Half the people that get shipped out here have no more idea of what they are coming to than the man in the moon! And what is good for one is not good for another. Tell me what you think about emigration. Do you believe in the schemes now so numerously advocated?

Couldn't you get a nearer and better child to paint than Jacky Williams? I once saw a very beautiful child in Isleworth Village, a little beyond the church. Paris would be nice for Louy, I should think. It would interest her, and she is older and more able to take care of herself than Olive. I hear Olive has been acting as model to a young woman who smokes cigarettes and [who] offered her one! The girl is a Russian.

Give the Grannie an affectionate greeting from me, and I trust it will be as she says. I always liked your old Grannie though I saw little of her. I return the ridiculous cutting! There was an amusing article on this same prophet business in *Pall Mall Budget*.

Saturday, March 30th, 6:45 p.m. This has been a better day. Having cast up my accounts, to find I am the happy possessor of $7.15, I began the copy of the picture of the range for Miss Urquhart. I worked at this all day until it was dusk and, being in a good frame of mind for painting, made good progress with it. But it is a long business. All the trees have to be put in carefully, and the mountains shaded to give the proper perspective.

I had several interruptions in the course of the day, though. First, Doc Vetter came rushing up, saying that down in the store they had got up an excited discussion about how bananas grow, and would I come and explain the matter? I went down, and found a great bunch of bananas, just arrived, hanging up in the store, and five or six men discussing whether they grew up or down. As I have seen them growing in Madeira I was able to explain that they grow both up and down — the branch down, and the individual fruit up. By the way, the banana is remarkable for being one of the few seedless fruits.

The next interruption was Cox, who wanted me to 'come and look after the kids' for an hour or so this afternoon, as he and Mrs. Cox were both wanting to go out. I promised to do so, and early in the afternoon went up there, taking my painting apparatus with me. The infants were about as docile as could be expected, and I went on with my work all right. While I was there, Lees and Regy turned up, riding. They had driven the locoed horse of Payn's called 'The Sheriff' into town and are going to leave it at Cox's. Mrs. Cox came home towards evening, and soon after, I left. Directly after I got here there was a little storm of RAIN! The first rain this year.

8 p.m. No mail for me this evening, but an extraordinary piece of news in the Denver papers of today. A man actually went into a bank in Denver, asked to see the president privately, and then pulled out a pistol and 'held him up', making him sign a cheque for $21,000, and got it cashed. Then, when he had got the money, the rascal backed out of the bank and made off, and never was caught! It is the 'cheekiest' thing I ever heard of in all my life, and I cannot help chuckling when I fancy the expression of the bank president on finding himself thus robbed in his own bank. One has a sort of sneaking admiration for this bold scamp, like one has for Napoleon Bonaparte, though he is not half such a criminal, morally speaking, as was Napoleon; at least I judge not. Personally, I am always inclined to be more lenient with open robbery than with fraud or stealing.

I hear there is to be a meeting on Monday evening at the school house to discuss the possibility of a getting up a debating club here. I shall go, of course.

Sunday, March 31st, 1:35 p.m. I have done little this morning but write a report on entomological work of C.B.A. from January to March, 1889, for *Psyche*. There was a slight fall of snow last night, but it has all melted by now. The only event this morning is that, as I wrote, my lamp glass cracked quite spontaneously. Wasn't that a queer thing for it to do? Of course, the lamp was not alight.

I will now tell you something about this house. It is situated in the main street. On the other side of the road is a saloon, and a little higher up, Falkenberg's grocery store. The house itself is of wood, with a brick front. It is two-storied, the whole of the ground floor being taken up with the postoffice and grocery, and drapery, etc., store. Out at the back there is a yard. Really, it is two houses joined together, and it is in the upper part of the larger one (see sketch over the page) that rooms are to let. There are four rooms, which are reached by a staircase ending below in a door leading out onto the street, or rather onto the covered wooded platform in front of the store.

Of the four rooms, one front one is occupied by Vetter, and the other empty, save for rubbish. One back room is occupied by TDAC, and the other is unoccupied. My room is eleven feet by ten, and high in proportion. The door has the upper panels of glass. The woodwork is painted white, and the floor is covered by a not objectionable paper, white floral designs on grey, but there is a fearful dado of complicated hideousnesses that defy description. But I am covering it up with bookshelves made of old boxes. The window looks out onto the roof of the hind part of the store, and beyond to the red roof of the National Hotel, and in the distance the prairie, the southern part of the Sangre de Cristo range, and still more distant, the Sheep Mountains.

I have not yet got things in the room finally arranged, but the stove is near the door, the pipe goes into a hole in the wall, near the ceiling, leading into a brick chimney that serves both for me and the store below. The books are arranged against the east wall, and also sundry miscellanea not arranged. The bed, at present, is on the floor. The window boasts two heavy curtains, which I found here. Near the door are pegs on which hang my coats (one brown and three black). But more of all these things hereafter.

The three men who serve in the store below are Goldstandt, Chetelat (called 'Shuttlett'), and Vetter. Goldstandt is a tallish man with rather pug-dog features. They say he is a Jew, but his Christian name is Mark, which doesn't sound Jewish, does it? He is generally unpopular because (1.) He is not an agreeable man. (2.) He seems to care for only one thing — money. But negatively, he has good points, viz.: (1.) His disagreeableness is not obtrusive; he is only not usually agreeable. (2.) He never swears, gambles, or drinks — at any rate, to excess. (3.) I think he is pretty honest.

Chetelat I don't know very well, but he is always pleasant and cheerful. Vetter is a decidedly popular man, always jovial and bouncing. It is quite a pleasure for people to buy from him. He was in Mexico before he came here. He is a short little man, rather stoutly built, with features more like those of President-that-was Cleveland, only much better looking and not so puffed out. On Sundays he is the glory of the town, in his top-hat and spotless black clothes. Vetter and Chetelat always address me as 'brother Cockerell', I don't know why.

6:45 p.m. After I wrote the above I went round to call on Charlton, but he wasn't in. Since then I have been taking notes from *Psyche* on a new system, with separate 'record slips' five inches by two and a half. I think it is a better way than notebooks, though not quite so neat.

9:45 p.m. Feeling restless, I wandered round to Humphrey's and begged that I might look through the astronomical telescope. Humphrey received me very kindly, and got out the telescope and called in some neighbours — the Stocktons and the Alexanders, and gave us all a demonstration in Astronomy. First we looked at Venus. It was beautiful, very brilliant, and now a crescent, like the moon; then the Pleiades, and then the great nebula in Orion. Then lastly, the telescope was pointed upwards, and Humphrey showed me Saturn, with its rings, and one of its satellites.

I was very much interested, for the only other time I ever looked through an astronomical telescope, not a planet was visible. Saturn pleased me most. It looked about as big as I have sketched it. Humphrey is more than ever the double of Mr. Carr, in voice, manner, and appearance.

Now goodnight, and goodbye, love, till next letter.

> Very lovingly, your Theo.
> Health. Very well.

April 1st, 1889, 6:35 p.m.

Dear Annie,

The morning train took a letter to you. There is hardly time now to write about today, as I have to get supper and be off to a meeting at the schoolhouse to discuss the feasibility of getting up a debating and literary club here.

7:20 p.m. The train came in earlier than usual, at a quarter to seven, so I thought the mail would have been sorted by now, but I have just been down, and find they are not half through it. It seems to be very big mail tonight, and I hope your letter may come, though I should not expect it earlier than tomorrow or Wednesday. The only thing put in my postoffice box so far is a pamphlet or something of the kind with French writing on the cover. I expect it will be some advertisement. I have had supper (two eggs, potatoes, bread, coffee) and shall be away to the meeting as soon as I get the mail.

9:45 p.m. The meeting never came to much after all. The pamphlet in French was all the mail I got; it proves to be copies of some papers on snails, from Ancey. To go back to this morning; after breakfast I continued and finished the picture for Miss Urquhart (if she thinks it worth the $1.50) and was able to send it out to her by Lees, as he came to town. Then I went after some paper for my records, but Turner, of the *Courant*, was playing cards in a saloon, so I finally went up to the *Wet Mountain Tribune* office and got some. It is nice paper, but it costs 25 cents.

Then I went round to Charlton's to borrow a volume of *Nature* he has (1879), to go through it for notes. I found him being interviewed by a man named DeKrafft (to whom I had not before spoken), an American who is out here for his health, and seems to be a journalist (sort of a penny-a-liner) by profession. He also plays poker with great skill, I hear. He is the sort of person I abominate — very bumptious, and with nothing particular to recommend him — rather the reverse. In appearance, he is very dark-complexioned, very like a young man that used to be very common at Bedford Park — I forget his name. Charlton was showing DeKrafft a lot of minerals, and when that was finished, he discussed with me about this proposed debating club. It is being got up by Sam Wright (a cowboy — my chairman at the C.B.A. meeting) and no doubt will be a good thing if it is fairly started.

This afternoon I spent in taking notes from *Nature*, finding much of very great interest. Then, this evening, Charlton came up to me in the postoffice, and we went off to the school house together. After this evening's 'meeting' I don't feel so ashamed of my little gathering of 25, especially as these latter had to pay. Tonight there were only seven: Charlton, Sam Wright, DeKrafft, a Mrs. Lowe, Truax (a grumpy old man who looks after the building (the same that I had to apply to, you will remember), an unknown, ugly, and silent youth, and TDAC. I was made chairman, and we elected a committee (Charlton, S. Wright, and Walters) to draw up a set of rules, and another committee (of three ladies; I forget their names) to arrange the programme for a sort of a little concert on Friday next, to entice people to come. We shall see what happens.

April 2nd, 10:20 p.m. Not much of a day for me. In the morning I made a little painting of the Sheep Mountains, for which I shall charge 25 cents if anyone will buy it. I propose to do a series of such, if there is any sale for them. Then I went to Charlton's to discuss and submit proposals for a plan of cooperation between the Custer County branch of C.B.A. and the proposed debating and literary club. Charlton was experimenting and I stayed some while (and to lunch) watching the experiments, which were new and instructive to me. I shall take as much note as I can of this assaying work of Charlton's (and he is very ready to tell me all about it) because it is not only interesting, but a valuable thing to know.

This afternoon I have been copying out notes from *Nature*. To my great disappointment, no mail of any sort came for me this evening. It has been a hot day, and it is quite oppressively warm tonight. Moths of three species (two Noctuidae, one Pyralid, or rather Phycid) are coming to the light of the lamp. I was interested in coming across a list of birds (in *Nature*) collected in the Solomon Islands by a James Cockerell. This is the only man I ever heard of by my name doing any natural history work (outside the family). One bird, *Sauloprocta cockerelli,* was called after this James C. The only natural history Fenn I know outside your family is C. Fenn, who lives in Kent — quite a well-known entomologist. He named a new moth, *Leucania brevilinea* (Fenn).

April 3rd, 6 p.m. I have just finished *Competitors* and posted it off to you with a C.B.A. circular and some of Stead's Tolstoi article that I found in an old *P.M.B.* The Tolstoi bit I particularly wanted I still fail to find.

About *Competitors*, I like the story on the whole, I think, but do not think it is very well told, and it is rather too moral! I could not help thinking that Milly might have enjoyed life more if she had devoted herself to snails, or something! She needed something to satisfy the intellectual side of her nature, and it would not necessarily have interrupted her works of kindness. This,

I think, applies more or less to everyone, don't you?

It has been quite a misty day today, a thing very unusual in this country. I spent most of the morning taking bibliographic notes from *Nature*, and I finished the volume. Lees came to town and, to my dismay, I found that my picture for Miss U., which I gave him to take up to her, remained still under the seat of the buckboard, forgotten and damp! It is rather spoiled, and if it won't do in consequence, I shall feel a good deal like charging it up to Lees! I did a minute sketch this morning, of the mountains in the mist.

Towards eleven I began to suffer from toothache, and so went up to Cox's after the oil of cloves, which was still there among my other things. This subdued it, and I have only had a twinge now and again this afternoon. I saw the *Courant* editor, and he will put a short report into the next issue, but unfortunately he won't allow me space enough for your article unless I were to divide it, and that I dare not do, as it might be so long before the rest could be printed. How I wish I had my own printing press!

7:38 p.m. This *is* disappointing. I made sure of getting your letter tonight, but the English mail has not come, and consequently no letter. I shall try to console myself by reading *Picadilly*, which I have just begun. All the mail I got was a Bulletin of the Botanical Division of Dept. of Agriculture, which I had already received before.

Thursday, April 4th, 3:30 p.m. I sat up late last night, and finished *Picadilly*, but I won't talk about it to you now. This morning, about the first event was Sam Wright, who said he was very busy, and Walters was very busy, and Charlton had gone to Pueblo, so would I draw up a 'Constitution' for the debating society. I thought to myself that it was rather ridiculous that after a committee had been appointed, they should come round to *me* and ask me to do their work for them, but I promised I would, and accordingly set about it, and when done took the MS round to Walters.

I found Will Kettle at Walters' store; he had just come from his legislative duties in Denver. I had not been back in my room long before DeKrafft appeared with a request from Mrs. Lowe (one of the entertainment committee) that I would contribute something to their entertainment! I had sort of promised Sam Wright I would write a little essay, but on second thought I preferred to read someone else's views on this first occasion, and so, after much deliberation, chose Carlyle on Shakespeare in *Heroes* (p.98, ('For, In fact,' etc., to p. 101 — 'very beautiful to me'). Not that I know anything about Shakespeare myself, but I rather like that bit of Carlyle's. I said, though, I wouldn't read if they could fill the programme without me.

Then I went up to Mrs. Cox's to practice reading my Carlyle bit on her (which she bore very patiently), and also I read her some of Carlyle's views on Cromwell (because she seemed to have a prejudice against Cromwell) and also Lord Frank's oration at the missionary gathering, in *Picadilly*. While I was there, Lees appeared. He said Miss Urquhart was very pleased with the picture, which I am glad to hear.

9 p.m. You *dear* creature! I abandoned my cooking this evening to watch them sorting the mail, for I thought your letter would *surely* come. For a long time nothing went into my mail box atall (you see, the boxes are glass-fronted, so one can see the contents without being able to get at them). Then came a letter, evidently American, but it was face downwards and I could not see the writing [it proves to be from Nash of Pueblo], then a very fat envelope which I could not make out atall, but it looked as if it must have come from New York, from the postmark visible, then a *Pall Mall Budget*, and then English mail went into the Cusacks' box and other boxes, and I thought '*Surely* it must come now', but they finished sorting, and no letter. I felt miserable, until they gave me the mail, and the *big envelope* was your letter, after all, bulged out with the sock! So I smiled benevolently on the assembled crowd and quickly pushed my way through up here to my room.

Now I have read it, and had supper, and attended to business in the shape of a reply to Nash's letter, which was about the C.B.A., so now I may talk to you. Firstly, thank you and a kiss for the socks (one of them yet on the Atlantic). It is nice of you, and it fits beautifully, but I shall hate to wear them out. I really must learn to darn, if I never darn another pair. Who taught you to knit so well, or did you find out yourself? Or were you taught a little, and 'growed the rest'? The U. S. Customs officer either wanted to read your letter, or was inquisitive about the sock, for the envelope was open, and on it in red 'Supposed Liable to U. S. Customs Duties', but the supposition was a false one.

So Louy is going to Paris! What a good creature you are, to think of paying for her (did you do so?). I cannot understand your father's position atall. If it were anyone else, I really think I should become abusive about it! It reminds me of what they used to tell me when I was a child, 'Those who ask mayn't have. Those who don't ask don't want!' I must say, I quite believe in Louy myself, though I know so little of her, and can well understand that she would do well under new circumstances. I felt a little afraid when I read that Mrs. Morgan may be 'fast', because there is such a thing as reaction after a period of restraint, but I think Louy has too much sense to act foolishly in this way.

Do I think it proper to talk to strangers in the train? Well, I am puzzled. Theoretically, yes; practically, discretion must be used. I would *never begin* a conversation with a man, not because it is in any way wrong in itself, but because a woman who does so is apt to be suspected of all kinds of wickedness by the undiscerning public (especially in London). But if a man talks to you, and does not appear objectionable, I don't see why you might not reply. With *women*, I should think you might always talk. That is what I think, love. Probably many would say, *never* talk to a strange man atall, but I think that is unreasonable. Tell me now, how you have decided about it.

Thank you for the KISS. I must keep it, though, as you tell me, for the next time of depression. I feel quite gay just now. Now that Louy is going to Paris, who knows that *you* will come for a visit out here! I rather tremble to think what the parents may say (or *have* said, by now), to so bold a suggestion.

I am astonished that Boulger has joined the Church of Rome. I confess I never thought a great deal of his science, and now (you will think this is unreasonable of me) I think less of it that it has permitted him to join the Roman Catholics. It's no use saying (as probably he might) that science and theology are distinct things, not to be mixed up — an honest man (honest to his own faiths) cannot help their influencing one another. I think I must find you an anti-Socialist book! Now it is past ten. Goodnight!

P. S. Though, while I think of it, I do want to see Fred's paper on Pteropods, of course.

April 5th, 5 p.m. I wrote some letters this morning, and then went for an hour's bug-hunting, the result being a few species of beetles new to me. This afternoon I began a paper for Step on the mining towns of Colorado, but somehow could not do anything with it, and have put it by to be finished in a more auspicious moment.

Cox brought me down a sort of wire bedstead from his house today — kind of him. It is one he has had there a long time and does not use; the bed of it is made of a sort of wire netting. Cox also asked me to go up to tea there this evening, and go to a meeting with them and the Humphreys. I am afraid I accepted the invitation because, thinking it over, I would rather go 'on my own hook.'

9:50 p.m. Meeting over, not much of a thing, but will tell you about it tomorrow. (Illustration: One of today's captures. It is a *Gerris*, and spends its time running about on the surface of pools.)

April 6th, 8:10 p.m. There is ever so much to tell you about. I went up to tea at Cox's — found it was quite a grandiose spread in honor of Mrs. Humphrey and Bertha Humphrey (small girl)

who were there. Mrs. H. is a wizened-up oldish lady, but agreeable in manner and nice enough of her kind. These people call their name 'Umphrey', not because they are h-less, but for some similar reason to that for which Cholmondeley is called 'Chumley', I suppose.

Before the meeting came off, I went down to get my mail, and got: (1.) Letter from Smith of Denver, with interesting records of Arapahoe County reptiles and Amphibia, and sending names of three new members of C.B.A., viz., Todenwarth of Denver, Bentley of Denver, and L. Stejneger of Washington. (2.) Letter from a Dr. Landis of Lancaster, Pennsylvania, joining C.B.A. and sending subscr. (3.) Letter from Messrs.Whitall, Tatum, & Co. of Philadelphia, about price of glass tubes. (4.) 'List of the Birds of Oneida Co., N.Y.' by Ralph & Bagg, a nicely got up pamphlet sent, I suppose, for C.B.A. library, but I know neither of the authors. (5.) *Entom. Amer.* for April. (6.) Reprint from *Entom. Amer.* on the Epipaschiinae (a family of moths) of North America, by and from Hulst. Also, just before going up to the Cox's, I got *Custer Courant*, with a very short 13th report of C.B.A., including Lees' woodcut. So much for the mail of yesterday.

The meeting at the school house was hardly a success, though there were some 32 or 33 people present this time, nearly all ladies. Sam Wright was elected chairman, and we began with a vocal duet by Mrs. Lowe and another lady. Then DeKrafft read a comic bit describing a countryman's experience of Rubenstein's playing. Then two youthful persons, a boy and a girl, performed. The boy played a violin and the girl accompanied on harmonium-organ. The next was Bertha Humphrey, who recited some verse about the different ways of saying yes. Then I read the Carlyle Shakespeare bit. I was a little bit nervous, not feeling the same command over my subject as if it had been biological, but I got through all right and made no blunders. It was not comprehended by the audience atall, I fancy. I even thought some of them took it to be comic, and were rather bothered because they 'couldn't see the joke.' The last performance was flute and organ, and then Sam Wright announced five minutes interval before the business meeting.

At this, people began to make for the door, and Sam had to call the meeting to order and commence 'business' at once in order to prevent a general stampede. The 'business' simply consisted of TDAC reading out the Constitution and bye-laws he had drawn up, as the committee appointed to frame these had never even met, and had proved a perfect farce. DeKrafft got up and objected to a bye-law ruling that the club have nothing to do with 'booming' the town. I was all alive at this, and in my wrath made a rather incoherent reply, but he got up again in reply to me, and by then I had collected my wits and was able to reply again plainly and to the point. The rest of the audience sat and grinned, but offered no comments.

(After the meeting, DeKrafft said he quite agreed with me, but only objected to help raise a discussion. But I think he would turn any way that suited him, after the manner of many journalists.) Then one Alexander, being appealed to, said he wished the club success, and Stockton said ditto, but declared he was too busy to have anything to do with it. Then it was proposed to elect a committee to draw up an amended constitution (though no serious objection had been made to mine) and somebody suggested that the old committee be appointed, and this was carried, as nobody had any further remarks to make. Then it was proposed that the old entertainment committee be also re-appointed, and this was only not carried because the committee refused to serve. So three others had to be chosen; these were 'Doc' Vetter, Mrs. Humphrey, and Mrs. Cox. After the meeting, DeKrafft and I walked a little way with Sam Wright, talking about the club, and Sam W. was coming today to discuss the matter with me, but he has not appeared.

A dreadful thing happened here yesterday, which is now the one subject of conversation with everyone. As far as I can learn it was in this wise: There was a certain trunk containing a few things possibly worth two or three dollars,

standing outside a house here. A man (I forget his name) stole that trunk. He was soon detected, and a warrant was put out for his arrest. Hearing this, he left town, having a rifle in his hand. Hal, a negro, followed him but was held off at 50 yards and told that if anyone came to arrest him (the pursued man) he would shoot him. (He expressed it in language I need not repeat.)

Hall, returning to town, met the under-sheriff and two others starting out to arrest the thief and told them what he had said, whereupon they borrowed rifles and went on after him. They followed him over John Burke's and finally caught him up in the fields beyond. Here he ambushed himself behind some willows and would not be approached. It is *said* that the under-sheriff fired the first shot, but at all events the shooting soon became brisk on both sides, but nobody was hit. Later on, several men came out to the place, and it seems that they were shooting at that unhappy man for hours. Someone wounded him in the arm, but *he* hit nobody, until finally one of the crowd (Mac Ormsby, it is said) shot him through the heart.

But not one of those men had the courage to go and see whether he was dead when he fell, and they left him there. Later though, DeBord went and found him dead, shot as I have said. The Coroner's Inquest was held this morning, and the sheriff, etc., were acquitted of blame. Of course, everyone is discussing whether it was murder or justifiable homicide. The version circulated early this morning, made me think it was justifiable, but later reports tend to undermine that view, and there is no doubt that in any case the pursuers are in many ways to blame.

It is difficult to see why the man resisted in the first place, for they could have done very little to him for stealing the trunk (which he did not take away with him). As he resisted, of course it was very difficult to arrest him without shooting him — probably impossible — but then it seems that the under-sheriff fired the first shot, which places him quite in the wrong (and he is known to be a bad character and a gambler himself, so nobody has much to say for him in the matter).

And it is also very questionable whether it was right for a whole lot of men to go out there and shoot at this man in the way they did, although it is true that he was shooting at them all the time.

But the worst feature of all was leaving him after he fell. This is abominable, and nobody pretends to justify it. They say the man leaves a wife and three children in Nebraska. What do *you* think of it all?

This morning, I was fully occupied with C.B.A. work, writing up records and writing letters. This afternoon, I finished (and sent off) the article for Step, and read some of the *Manual of Surgery*. I shall not be disappointed if Step does not accept the article, but if he does use it, I trust he will not wait a whole year before paying me.

Cox brought his two children here for some hours this afternoon, so I was a good deal interrupted by the necessity of looking after them. Isabel is tractable enough, but Charley is difficult to manage.

The mail this evening is a letter from Nash and a second notice from *Can. Ent.* although my subscription is not due until May first, according to their own account. They are abominably un-businesslike in their proceedings. (It is not the Editor's fault; it is the Treasurer, W. E. Saunders. I shall write him a 'strong letter.')

'Doc' Vetter came in here this evening and we have been talking and discussing, so it is now 10:25. Goodnight, love.

Sunday, April 7th, 10:45 p.m. Although it looked stormy for a few days past, I was quite surprised to see that it was snowing when I woke this morning. It has continued to snow ever since, and there will be several inches on the ground, I do not doubt.

I wonder how 'Buckskin' Joe's menagerie likes it. But I had not told you that two days ago there arrived a traveling menagerie here, and pitched its small tent on a bit of open ground opposite this house. They charge 25 cents to see it, so I have contented myself with reading the poster they have put up about town, on which it is announced that they have three bears, an earless pig, black, white, and blue rabbits, a badger, four magpies, two blue jays, some silver-grey foxes. I think that is about all. It is practically certain that the silver-grey foxes are not the genuine thing, as their skins would be worth $50 at least, and they would not be hawked around by a traveling show. (P.S. Vetter has been to see the show, and reports that the foxes 'have escaped', the blue rabbit is not, and the 'earless Rocky Mountain pigs' are Guinea pigs!)

Here are my additions to the fauna and flora lists for March: Colorado: Mammalia, 1; Mollusca, 3; Coleoptera, 18; Hymenoptera, 32; Arachnida, 2 vars.; Algae, 1; Butterflies, 3; Moths, 5, and 1 var., Heteroptera, 2, Diptera, 1, and 1 var.; Trichoscolices, 1, and Birds, 1. Middlesex: Fungi, 1.

12:10 p.m. It has stopped snowing. I think I will not send you any more biography in this letter, although I meant to do so. I will write all about the Hospital time and send it all together when finished.

I have not yet said what I think of *Picadilly*. I am glad to have read it, and I do not doubt that what it says of fashionable society and fashionable religion is perfectly justified. Only, I would urge this, that the society it condemns is by no means the only society, or even a really important one. Bodwinkle is sufficiently foolish, indeed, but probably the real harmfulness of Bodwinkle lay in the ways he employed to *get* his wealth rather than in the way he spent it. Grandon is the only character in the book I really like, and he is too much in the background.

It has left off snowing now, and is quite hot. I have wasted a lot of the morning talking to Vetter, Frere, etc., down in the store.

8:55 p.m. I have been to church this evening! It is not late, but I have a headache and don't feel equal to writing on account of it, so I shall go to bed. This letter goes by the morning post tomorrow so I end up,

With very much love, your
Theo.

Health. Except for the present headache, am very well.

April 8ᵗʰ, 9 p.m

Dear Annie,

To give you the news, I must go back to yesterday (Sunday). Early in the afternoon I went round to call on Charlton. I found him at home and very talkative, and the consequence was that I stayed all the afternoon and to supper. Mrs. Charlton was there, but she went off to Sunday School for an hour or so. 'Doc' Vetter came in later on. I returned Charlton his *Nature* and borrowed a number of odd unbound numbers of the same journal which he had on hand.

Charlton was full of the tragedy of Friday. He knew the man they shot (Potter was his name) and is strongly of the opinion that it was a case of murder. One hears very conflicting stories, but I think the case seems to get worse and worse for those that shot him, although they now try to patch things up. Potter used to haul ore for Charlton, and Charlton says he was a very respectable sort of man. In any case, the men who killed him are known to be a fearfully 'hard' lot, and it will be a very risky thing to take any measures against them. The *Tribune,* like the blackguard paper that it is, makes almost fun of the thing, and heads its account 'Died with his boots on. Game to the last', and some more.

There was to be church in the evening (Presbyterian) at the schoolhouse, and as I had not been to church since I came out here, I thought I had better go. The place was not crowded, and the audience (or, I should say, congregation) was not of much account. The Charltons and Sam Wright seem to be the pillars of the affair. The preacher was a poor-looking little man in a black

coat, with a poorer voice, but he seems an excellent man, all the same.

When we got there (I walked with Charlton) they were singing a hymn. After this the preacher read a little, and then there was a very long prayer which seemed to be meant to show how many times the same thing could be repeated over again in different words. The burden of it was, that we might be allowed to glorify God in our lives. Then another hymn (sung with a vigour that would shame many an English congregation), and then the little man gave out various announcements, one being that they would have no service next Sunday morning, as 'our Lutheran friends' would occupy the building. He said the word *friends* as if he meant it, and I am sure he did not bear them all the envy and malice that one sect generally bears another.

After this came the sermon, delivered from copious notes (apparently), and an excellent sermon it was. The text was from St. Paul, about 'forgetting those things that were behind, and pressing on to those before' (I forget the exact words), and he dealt greatly upon the fact that a converted Christian need not suppose he had henceforth nothing to do, because he had really just *begun* to do what lay before him. He compared piety and wickedness with rowing up, and drifting down, a stream, and enlarged upon the comparison. He scolded the congregation for their laziness in the Christian virtues (*not* beliefs) and I felt like saying 'hear, hear.' He also said that whatever the different sects disagreed in, they at least agreed in some points, which he urged, were really the important ones, and he admitted that there were some things he did not yet himself understand.

He also dwelt on the piety of St. Paul and said that, as Paul, with all his excellence, did not think himself perfect, still less should we imagine that we had attained all that was worth attaining. He said nothing about damnation, nor pious beliefs, and although I, of course, differed with him in several minor points, I thought that he had more common sense than most of the clergymen I had heard, and cannot doubt that his influence is an entirely good one. And yet it is a ridiculous looking little man, with a ridiculous voice, and no ideas of oratory whatever — so after all, a bad speaker may be a good clergyman, which however generally admitted in theory, is not atall allowed in practice, I fancy.

I must have caught cold in my face or something, as most of yesterday afternoon I had three or four teeth all aching at once, and later on it turned into a headache. So when I got home after church I went to bed, and am pretty nearly right, I think, today.

I posted a letter to you this morning, and *Picadilly* this afternoon. This morning I wrote an account of the Friday evening meeting for *Courant*, and also a letter setting forth the things which had been circulated about the people who had killed Potter, and pointing out that the allegations were very serious ones, and if they could not be denied in such a way as to satisfy the public, the affair began to look very much like murder. I showed the letter (which I signed 'Institia') to Vetter, and then took it round to the *Courant*.

Grant Turner told me more that he had learned about the affair, and said that although he thought Potter ought not to have been killed, his own idea was simply to give all the facts as nearly as possible and make no comment but let people judge for themselves. This seemed to me to be good sense, and I did not press the letter, but Turner asked me to leave it with him as he might want it to help him prepare his account. He asked me to try to get subscriptions for the *Courant*, and offered me 25 cents on the dollar discount on any I could get.

The rest of the morning and this afternoon I have been 'bibliographing' Charlton's odd numbers of *Nature* (they are of 1875, 1878, 1881, and 1882). In one of them I found a very interesting paper by Grant Allen on the colours of flowers. This evening's mail brought me a letter from a man named H.P. Wickham (lives in Iowa) wanting to exchange beetles, and Jeffrey Bell's *Comparative Anatomy and Physiology*. This comes

from home. I asked for it, as Mother offered to send me a book of some sort. It is an admirable little work, and will be invaluable to me. I know Jeffrey Bell slightly, and Frederic knows him at least by sight. He is one of the British Museumites.

The snow has all melted, and this evening it rains.

April 9th, 6:45 p.m. Love, I will take your kiss and hand-shake this evening, for I do feel rather depressed. This is because I am rather out of sorts, partly because it has been raining and has been chilly all day (it is pouring with rain still), and partly because I am appalled at the intricacy of even the most ordinary biological problems, and wonder whether I shall ever really understand anything about them. So, in this puzzled and bothered state of mind I find relief only in thinking that, after all, human sympathy is a sure and a true thing, and of that human sympathy which is given to me, whether I ever solve the question of organic pigments or not!

7 p.m. Tonight's mail is being sorted, and I do believe your letter has come! At all events, there is something very like it in my box. It will be a little while before I can get the mail, as there are lots of papers not yet sorted, so meanwhile I will tell you the very scant news of today.

I have been reading Jeffrey Bell most of the time (part of the morning I read sitting by the stove in the store below), but this afternoon I re-read the whole Bulman-Tansley controversy about the colours of leaves and flowers in *Sci. Goss.*, and thought the matter over. I incline rather to side with Bulman, but he does not seem to know anything about Patrick Geddes' views, and he might have brought up also the matter of coloured fruit.

It *was* your letter! No, dear Annie, I'm not atall vexed at your decision. More and more I have been seeing how impossible it was, so I am not even much disappointed. It *would* have been very delightful, but after all, we must wait, and the good times will come after a while, for the rest of our lives. After that, perhaps some day we may pay this country a visit together, though just now I feel as if once I got to England I would *never* leave it any more — not for ten minutes!

To return to common things. I have got acclimatised to the whole meal flour and like it pretty well. Boyd Dawkins is a very tip-top geologist, a very noted man. You dear love, to offer to marry on £150 a year! But if I can't scrape together more than that when I get a job in England, it will be altogether too bad. You had better insist on something better than that! Of course we are not extravagant, but we must have the ordinary needs of life.

I don't know what has become of the Kleinian Thomas; he never answered the last letter I wrote him. *Is* Frederic going to 'study up' on his Diptera? I wish he would, if he can find time. Apart from the Museum, they greatly need study. I quite agree with you about the Mission Service. Where is the veneration bump? Afraid mine is a big hollow. Thank you for the other sock; the U.S. Customs officer didn't examine this one. What hard work you had to do down in Sussex. I know myself that washing is very tiring work. I think we wash here in a more primitive way than you do.

The other letters from this evening's mail are: (1.) Letter from L. O. Howard. (2.) Letter from Mother. (3.) Long and nice letter from Carlie. He writes further about Ruskin. It is very sad. For himself, he says he is in good health and spirits, which I am glad to hear. He finds the business now much more interesting, and says, 'My aim is very different from that of my partners. They think profits are the chief thing, and I am only anxious to make all the machinery efficient, to satisfy the customers, to improve the position of the employees, and to let the profits look after themselves.' In another part of the letter, he says, 'I should like to join C.B.A. and enclose subscription; also a trifle towards salary and maintenance of secretary, who evidently does not make a fortune out of the concern!' He encloses $3.00. Carlie also forwards me *Entom.* of

April, 1885. and Klein on Willesden insects, both of which I am glad to get.

April 10th, 6:55 p.m. I have a bit of news that will amuse you so much that I must tell it you now. I am going to *teach* drawing., and have got a pupil this afternoon in Mrs. Frere! After this, let nobody say I lack impudence!

9:35 p.m. I was writing all the morning and part of the afternoon until Albert DeBord appeared with a note from Cox, asking me to go up and look after the children for an hour or two. So I took Jeffrey Bell and *Manual of Surgery*, Vol. III, and paper for notes from them, and went up. DeBord had a horse saddled, which I rode, and Cox rode it back again to town. (Cox was there at the house, and Mrs. Cox at the Ladies' Literary Club meeting. Cox sent for me because he and DeBord had some 'business' to do in town, and he wanted to leave the house to attend to it.)

I had a pretty peaceful time till about five, when Mrs. Cox returned. She told me that she had been talking about my drawing, and had got me a pupil! (Kind of her to take all this trouble.) This was Mrs. Frere, who wanted to learn drawing, and was quite willing to be taught by me. For the moment, I was rather aghast but, reflecting on the necessity of earning some money, I resolved to see the thing through with a bold face.

While we were talking, who should come along but Mrs. Frere herself, and so Mrs. Cox went out and enticed her in and introduced her to me. She seems a nice sort of woman, rather like an Americanised Mrs. Horsley, if you can imagine such a thing. She told me about her drawing. and seemed quite enthusiastic. She asked me what I would charge. I said, 25 cents a lesson, which she seemed to think very moderate, as she said she expected to have to pay 50 cents. Then — about a day — she liked it to be in the morning, as she felt fresher then, but tomorrow they were going out somewhere all day. Friday — she didn't like to begin on Friday as that was unlucky, but Saturday, yes, so we agreed on Saturday morning for the first lesson. There was a girl named May Alexander she spoke about, who wold probably also take lessons. Thus ended the interview. This evening in the postoffice, Frere came up and spoke to me about teaching his wife (not knowing that I had seen her). I told him what we had arranged, and he seemed pleased.

I got this evening by the mail: *Naturalist*, and *West Amer. Scientist*. The *Nat.* is very early this month. *West Amer. Scientist* has some notes of mine (Custer County Flora, Bibliography, and a note on beetles).

I hear there has been a great landslide at Hillside, down towards Cotopaxi. A man was going to put his horses into his barn or stable one evening as usual, and lo, the whole thing had disappeared down the hill, and an acre or so of land with it! I once heard of a landslide in which one man's ranch (or part of it), house and all, slid onto the top of another's, and those two were ever after disputing who the land belonged to! The law had not provided for the contingency of one ranch getting on top of another.

April 11th, 9:25 p.m. Not much of a day. I have been working up my Geographical Distribution most of the day It is wonderful what a wide distribution the diatoms (microscopic algae) have. I have 13 species down for Colorado, and I know nine of them are found in England, and for all I know to the contrary, the other four as well. You might easily add some diatoms to your Isleworth list by gathering a little green weed and scum off the top of a stagnant pond, *drying without squeezing*, and putting into an envelope and either sending to me (I would send it to Wolle) or to W. Barwell Turner, 53 Reginald Terrace, Leeds, Yorks. (I don't know him, but I am pretty certain he would name for you). I have also written some letters and packed up some flowers to Coulter and to Vasey for names, and this afternoon I was photographed!

Emery, the photographer, is here for four days and has his room in the upper part of the 'Tomkins Building' (used to be a store belonging to Tomkins) on the opposite side of the street. He is a bland little man and apparently very careful with his work. He showed me the negative. It looks very extraordinary, but perhaps the photograph itself will be recognisable. I am to have half a dozen. It is the smallest number I could get, and I don't want any more.

I have been wondering how far I should be justified in taking Mrs. Frere through the theory of light, colour, etc., and the why and wherefore of perspective. It seems to me it can do her nothing but good to learn these things, but I fear she will find it rather dry. I wonder how many people could answer off-hand, for instance, 'Why does an object look larger when it is near than when it is far off? *I* couldn't, until I thought about it! Probably if this drawing-lesson business develops, the chief thing I shall have to contend with will be a tendency to 'rush things' at the expense of thoroughness. And personally, I think it is a bad thing to start in with oil before one has practised atall in water-colours, don't you? I believe it begets carelessness. Another thing, I wonder whether Mrs. Frere or any others will be annoyed at adverse criticism!

Lees came to town today. He thinks the drawing-lesson idea is excellent, but considers 25 cents too little to charge.

April 12th, 6:45 p.m. I wanted to do a lot today, but the whole day has been taken up with the affairs of this West Cliff debating society, and I have not had any time to myself. Sam Wright appeared here the first thing this morning with a book containing constitution, minutes, etc., of the 'Farmer's Literary Society', which exists in a flourishing condition somewhere out by Todd's ranch, boasting some 60 members. Wright read me the rules (constitution and bye-laws) of this society, which he proposed substantially to adopt for the West Cliff Society. The rules are unnecessarily long, and in several respects I desired amendments. In some of these Wright gave way, while others will have to be put to the vote at the meeting. Wright left me the 'Farmer's Lit.

Soc.' book, and also a little manual on debating by a man named Henry, to look over.

I then went round to discuss the matter with Charlton. I found him testing some ore for an old fellow who had come all the way from Pennsylvania about a supposed tin mine he had found here long ago. He had been, of course, at great expense in coming here, and after it all, Charlton had to tell him, after three or four careful experiments, that there was not a vestige of tin in his ore! The old chap bore it philosophically, but I should think he must be badly disappointed.

This all took some time, and as it was getting towards mid-day when Charlton and I got to business over the Constitution and Bye-laws of the Society. We went carefully through them (were interrupted by lunch, which I had at the Charlton's), and Charlton agreed with nearly all my views about it and promised to move amendments in accordance with our ideas when the constitution was voted on. I also got Charlton to subscribe to the *Courant* for a year ($1.50). (Grant Turner offered me 25 cents commission when I gave him the money, but I would not take it, as Charlton's main reason for subscribing was that Turner was poor and had to keep a wife and child.)

I watched some tests in progress and then returned homewards, when I came across Sam Wright, and he got me to go with him to Kettle & Walters' store, and we talked the thing over with Walters, and then I wrote out a copy of the constitution to be used at the meeting tonight. By this time it was evening, and I have been preparing supper ever since.

Saturday, April 13th, 10 p.m. Here I have been squandering the evening in frivolous talk with Vetter and a youth named Samse in the other room (i.e., Vetter's room), and I shall have to postpone the many things I have to tell until tomorrow. The meeting went off pretty well, and the drawing lesson all right. I expect I shall have quite a class. Goodnight!

Sunday, April 14, 10:05 a.m. Now for the news. On Friday evening, after getting my mail (letter from Hulst, letter from A. Convair [?] (can't read his signature) wanting to exchange insects, and a postcard from C. A. Cooper of Denver, about C.B.A.). I went round to the meeting of the Debating Club, now to be called the West Cliff Literary and Scientific Society, at the schoolhouse.

The room was nearly full. I did not count the numbers, but I suppose there must have been between 40 and 50 present. Sam Wright was elected chairman, and I secretary of the meeting. Just before we began I was astonished to see Regy and Miss Urquhart appear. They had been in town all day and were staying at the Cox's. (I believe they are still there.) Regy paid me $1.00 as part payment for Miss Urquhart's picture. Regy was very unruly during the meeting — behaved abominably — voting for and against resolutions, making noises, holding up both hands, drawing on the blackboard at the back of the room, and so on.

As before, the first part of the evening was taken up with an entertainment, the performers being Mrs. Björnson (who read 'The One-hoss Shay'), Miss Alexander (recitation), Dr. Björnson (sung an anthem, but did it well!), Miss Bertha Humphrey (an amusing dialogue on women's rights, called 'The Dockings'), Mrs. Frere (a song, 'Come in the Springtime'), Miss Byington read a very pathetic little poem which I have heard before, but do not remember the name. It is about a soldier at the war who enquires of a comrade fresh from his native town about 'our folks' and, after a good deal of beating about the bush, is told that his love is dead. She did it well.

Following this was the business part of the meeting, and I first read the proposed constitution and bye-laws through, and then each article of them, separately, and it was adopted by a vote. The whole thing was passed as it stood, with a few additions. Charlton, although present, never came to the front with his amendments, but some had been included when I wrote out the constitution at Kettle & Walters, and two others, which I proposed, were lost.

These were (1.) To have no 'critic.' The Farmers' Club have a critic appointed every evening, whose duty it is to criticise the manner of speaking of the various members. This is supposed to fall in with the 'mutual improvement' idea. Myself, I should prefer to leave it to members to emulate those who do better than they, instead of frightening them by calling attention to defects. Mrs. Charlton seconded this amendment. (2.) To put the question debated to the vote of the meeting at the close of the debate, instead of having 'three judges, one to be chosen by the chief disputant on either side, and one to be chosen by the two.'

The constitution having been adopted, nominations for officers were made (to be voted on next meeting). The following were nominated: President, Charleton and Sam Wright. Vice Presidents (two required): Mrs. Humphrey (I don't know whether she will serve), and DeKrafft. (I find this is how he spells his name, not De Craft. I shall vote against him.) Secretary: T.D.A. Cockerell. I suppose I shall have to do the work, though the C.B.A. takes quite enough of my time. I think I shall ask for an assistant-secretary if I am elected. However, I am to have the job of opening the house, lighting the lamps, etc., each week, and they will pay me for that. Treasurer: Miss Byington. She is a young woman, I should think not over 20, the daughter of a sign painter here. She plays, recites, and is generally accomplished, but I don't know much about her, never having spoken to her.

After this, the chairman appointed a committee to arrange for the next meeting, consisting of Walter, Samse, and Miss Lowther. Miss Lowther I don't know, but Samse is a young man who works in the store below here just now, a tallish youth with rather pug-dog features. There is not much to be said about him. Then it was moved that I get a book and enter up the constitution and bye-laws, after which the meeting adjourned until Friday next, the 19th. 17 people joined by signing the constitution, as follows:

Charlton, Sam Wright, C. S. Cox, Mrs. Cox (Cox signed for her. I believe she doesn't want to join, Lotta L. Byington, Mrs. Charlton, W. R. Samse, I. J. Vetter, May Cassidy, John Fraser, Jessie Lowther, Mathias Ulsh, R. S. Stockton, Sydney Bourne, W. H. Fraser, S. DeKrafft, TDAC.

11:55 a.m. Yesterday was the day of the drawing lesson. Taking pencil, pen, drawing-block and 'Academy Notes' I set out and got to the Frere's at about a quarter to nine. (They live now in town near the schoolhouse). Mrs. Frere received me very kindly and showed me some oil paintings of hers. They were all copied from other pictures but showed a very good idea of painting indeed, the perspectives only being rather at fault in places, and the colours a little unnatural.

We soon got to work, and I went into the theory of colour, light and shade, perspective, and so on. I think she quite understood what I was trying to explain, and she is to draw some houses, etc., out of the window, to illustrate the principles of the thing. Then she had some anemones and wanted to draw theme, so we spent some time over those. Her chief difficulty was to get the sepals to fit onto the stalk. I think she was satisfied, because she asked me to come again on Tuesday, and said that she would like her children also to learn, and said I should have a little class by the next lesson.

It is curious how people's names crop up unexpectedly. Mrs. Frere was telling me that she had been taught by Brandegee, who kept a school in Cañon City, and this Brandegee I know well by name, as he was the first to collect plants in this district (he had six species named after him. I think I told you that Mrs. Stockton also knew him.

The lesson took longer than I had bargained for. It was (I think) about half past ten when I left. In future I shall restrict it to an hour unless I have a large class. If I tell them all I know in the first lesson, there will be nothing left for the others!

The rest of the day was mainly taken up with the Lit. & Sci. Soc'y business. I got a book and entered up the constitution, bye-laws, and minutes, and then went for a walk of an hour or so, beetle-catching. I had better success than I expected — found *Physa heterostrophia* (large and typical), some beetles and otther insects and, best of all, three earthworms (*Lumbricus sp.*), which is a very unusual discovery here. I also got some loco for Charlton to analyse.

I called on Charlton, and he told me that he was going to take records of the meteorology here for the Colorado Meteorological Society at Colorado Springs. These will be published and will be very useful. Mrs. Charlton asked me to look her out something on Central America to read at the Ladies' Literary Soc'y. All I could find was a review of Belt's 'Nicaragua' in *Life Love*, but I took that round for her.

Today it is beautifully sunny and warm. I saw three *Vanessa antiopa* chasing each other down the sunset. I got a letter this morning from H. P. Wickham. Yesterday's train did not arrive till midnight, owing to a landslide on the line. Regy and Miss Urquhart have just called on me. Miss U. says Mrs. Cusack had a very nice letter from you.

9 p.m. It has not been a very cheerful Sunday, at least for me. But I have written the section 'Varieties of form' for my variety paper in *Entomologist*, and that is a great thing, When I had finished it I lay lazily on the bed reading the last *Pall Mall Budget*, which is rather interesting. I read until it was too dark to see, and then cooked supper. Vetter came in this evening, bringing two volumes for me. He had been up to Townsend's at Silver Cliff, and Townsend being a member of Congress for Colorado, had an enormous quantity of 'public documents' which were being given away. So Vetter, happening to find two that looked to be in my line, kindly brought them down. One is the '4th Report of the U. S. Ent. Comm.', which I have already, but it will do for C.B.A., and the other is the 'Third annual Report of the Bureau of Animal Industry', which is quite interesting to me.

Frederic is not doing much with the Mollusca now, is he? If he is not using my note book, beginning with extracts from Moquin-Tandon, and containing many lists of varieties and other matter, I should rather like to have it out here for reference. But if you think he needs it atall, don't ask him to send it. I feel a little afraid of trusting it to the post anyway, but everything has come through all right so far, and I expect there is nothing to fear. This will go tomorrow morning, and must be finished now. So goodbye, love, until the next letter.

Your true lover, Theo.
Health. Am very well.

April 15th, 1889, 10:30 p.m.

Dear Annie,
Those are amusing fellows, Vetter and Samse, and I like a little human society once in a while, but it takes up a lot of time. They came into my room this evening and have been chatting all the time, so I could do nothing. I have been taking bibliographical notes up at Townsend's today, but as it is so late, I won't tell you about it until tomorrow. It is drawing lesson tomorrow morning.

April 16th, 9 p.m. Your letter has come! There is much to answer in it, but not now, as it is getting late and I am terribly behind-time with the news. I feel very much ashamed of myself about that long interval you had to wait for a letter.

Yesterday after breakfast I went up to Silver Cliff to see about the public documents at Townsend's. On the way I called at the Cox's to get them to sign in my minute book of the Lit. & Sci. Soc. Mrs. Cox had told me that Mrs. Frere had been talking to her about the drawing lesson, and seemed very pleased with it. This is encouraging.

Now, about Townsend. Townsend (Col. Hosea T.) is, or ought to be, a very important personage, since he is the Member of Congress for all Colorado (this corresponds to Member of Parliament, of course, in a way), but he lives in a very obscure little house (though well-furnished) in the very obscure town of Silver Cliff, and is very little thought of — practically a nonentity — in the Custer County community, so far as I can make out. (I suppose, because 'A prophet hath no honour, etc.')

Now being Congressman, he received a very large number (amounting to about three tons, I believe) of 'Public Documents' to give to his constituents. The said public documents, being a nuisance in the house from the number of them, were given away on Sunday. That is to say, all the ragamuffins, loafers, etc., of Silver Cliff came in and walked off with as many as they could carry. When I went up yesterday there was nothing of value left, except some volumes of statistics which I took, as they will be useful to me. Even then, boys were coming in for the remnant; while I waited, three youths marched in and bore off 'Treaty with the Hawaiian Islands', 'Report of the Military Academy,' etc! What an idiotic waste of public money!

Fortunately for me, Mrs. Townsend received me very kindly and allowed me to examine them all. It made my mouth water to think what I had missed, and of the volumes that were now in the hands of Silver Cliff people who would not and could not use them. Seeing that there was much to interest me, I asked if I might take notes and, being told I could make any notes I wished, I came down here for pen and record-slips, had a hasty lunch (though it was too early for lunchtime) and went up there again and took notes from the volumes all afternoon. I did most of what I wanted, but I shall have to go up there again for some notes I did not have time to take, relating to variation.

The Colonel came in just before I left. He is a very large man and looks much like Dr. Livingstone. I did not see enough of him to judge what he is like. His manner is rather 'official', as is the way with such men, but I daresay if one got to

know him he might prove a good enough sort of man. Mrs. Townsend seems a nice woman.

In the evening, after I came home, I got mail: (1.) Letter from Prof. J. Cassidy (Botanist of Agric. College at Fort Collins), joining C.B.A. and sending subscr. for himself and Dr. O'Brine (chemist to the same place — not a bad name for a student of salts) who also joins. I am very glad to have these men as members. (2.) Letter from Hamilton, with names of beetles. An *Amara* is undescribed. (3.) Letter from Shufeldt. (4.) *Canad. Ent.*, April. (5.) Circular advertising *Tryon's Manual* (conchological works).

This morning, of course, was the second drawing lesson. I had only Mrs. Frere after all, the Frere children being postponed till Thursday, as it clashed with their other lessons today, and one or two others who were coming could not manage it today. Mrs. Frere says there is a Mrs. Conway who wants to learn botany as well. Mrs. F. had done the things I set for her — a perspective drawing of houses and a drawing of anemones. The flowers were pretty fair, but the perspective drawing was not atall as it should be. I don't demand mathematical precision in these things — the more so that I am rather inaccurate myself in drawing, but when the 'perpendicular' lines are at an angle of 20 degrees, and the lines of perspective, instead of converging to a point on the horizon, rush skyward, one has to object.

The Goldstandt Building

The trouble about these said buildings as a study of perspective is that they are so atrociously built that the lines *do* appear most extraordinary. I had the water-colours, and was pleased to find that Mrs. Frere took quite docilely to these. Especially, she said, jokingly, because she had heard that it was more *ladylike* to paint in watercolours. At any rate, it will be good for her, oils or no oils, and when she gets used to it I expect the oils will be abandoned. She is going to get a box of water-colours. She had a Philadelphia catalogue in which Windsor & Newton's paints are advertised at just the same price as they sell in England, so I marked the paints for her to get (18 in number), and they will be sent for without delay. Also drawing-block and brush, etc.

I painted one of the anemones (*A. patens* var. *nuttalliana*) she had drawn, to show her how it was done, and then, as I had again considerably exceeded the hour, I took my leave. I left my paints there for her to practice with. After this, I went on a beetle-catching expedition down by Grape Creek. I found nothing startling, but several insects new to me. In a swamp, I found *Utricularia* with its curious little bladders (see in Thome).

There is a dance tonight at the Hotel, to be paid for by a subscription raised by the men who go. I am invited by Samse, who is one of the promoters of the thing, but I dare not try to dance without practice, and I have no shoes to dance in. Otherwise I would have liked it, for a change. Now it is 10:30, so goodnight, love!

Wednesday, April 17th, 2 p.m. (At the Cox's.) After I finished this letter last night, I had to write up some records, and found it took me longer than I expected, so that it was 11:30 by the time I had done. Before I went to bed, I took a stroll down the street and had a glimpse of the dance through one of the hotel windows. It looked very bright and cheerful. Regy and Miss U. were there. I also saw Dr. & Mrs. Björnson, DeKrafft, Vetter, Fraser, Samse, Goldstandt, etc.

Besides your letter, I got last night the following mail: (1.) Postcard from W. H. Edwards. (2.) Letter from Whitall, Tatum, & Co. about glass tubes. (3.) Letter from Landis, with votes for C.B.A. election. (4.) Letter from Willoughby Lowe with votes for C.B.A. election. (5.) *Science Gossip*. (6.) *Insect Life* for March. (7.) *Punch* from Mother. (8.) Paper from Shufeldt with an account of the North American Insectivora (shrews) for C.B.A. library.

This morning has been spent without much profit. I hunted up Charlton (found him testing some gold) to get his votes for C.B.A., as the voting is in a rather critical state. I also looked up Turner for the same purpose. Grant Turner is quite exercised about the Townsend book affair (I told him about it) and is going to ventilate the matter in his paper. I must say, if Townsend gets into 'hot water' about it with the authorities in Washington, it serves him right.

Now at last I may answer your letter — though, stop! —there is one more thing to relate. Miss Urquhart paid me the remaining 50 cents for the picture I did her this morning, and at the same time gave me a note from Mrs. Cox saying that Cox had gone down to the Huerfano, and it was the Ladies' Literary Society this afternoon, and would I come to lunch and look after the children during the meeting? So here I am. The meeting is here today, and they are all discussing Central America in an adjoining room at the present minute. Mrs. Stockton, one of the members, brought up a *Cymopterus montanus* for me to name.

Now, your letter. (It is difficult to write, with Isabel standing on my toes and clawing at the pen!) I am a little surprised to hear of the poor appearance of the Isleworth children; here is a case illustrating the power of the environment. It is well-recognised, of course, that town populations are inferior in physique to those of the country, but I should not have thought it would have been so very marked at Isleworth. However, the moral is obvious!

I think that Mother was exceedingly right to withdraw from the school the child who had been questioned as to why she had not been to church. Don't you? I am sorry to hear that the play was not quite a success, but it may very easily be that the first night is not a fair test.

Myself, I strongly object to murders and such on the stage, and I should argue it this way. A play, to be good, should as far as possible carry the audience with it — make them feel as if it were real. Now I don't think it is good for people to witness real murders or real executions unless they are able to *prevent* them. I think, therefore, that it is no better for them to witness theatrical murders which, if badly acted, are foolish, and if well-acted, are loathsome. In short, I regard the tendency to love these things is quite the same as that which made the Romans love gladiatorial fights, and now makes the Spaniards love bull fights. It is degrading, and does no good. I see I have put it rather strongly. What think you?

Of course, I might like your father's play, but not for the sensational part of it. From the fact that it did not off very well, one would judge that it was better than such plays generally are, and did not rely on sensation for its effect. I remember seeing a play at Drury Lane that was a great success because it had a bank robbery, a murder, a snowstorm, a railway accident, and a house on fire! There was no acting atall!

Ugh! This place swarms with fleas. I have just caught one on myself and one on Isabel. They are not *Pulex irritans* but they bite all the same! About the spots on Winnie; Una used to be the same. It is nothing to be alarmed about. Regy Cusack, when young, used to have a rash every time he ate oatmeal. Other people are similarly affected by eating strawberries. Do you notice that Winnie's rash ever begins behind the ear?

I am afraid that my lecture to C.B.A. would be no good for the S.L.E.S. club. In the first place, it was partly spoken, and it would be nothing without the diagrams. Then, it refers almost entirely to American species. But Frederic might make a good lecture of his own on a similar subject. Thank you, Annie, for the bit of Matthew Arnold. I *do* like it, though it is so sad. I gave Miss Urquhart the little letter from Mrs. Cusack. I am very glad you approve of my move into town. I am pretty sure, by now, that it was the right thing. I never heard any more from the Rosita postmaster. I believe someone else has now got it, for good. If so, it is very well I did not go, as this would have turned me out, for I would never have been anything but deputy.

What should I have done had you quite failed me? I don't know. It is about as easy to tell as what should I do if I found I had no existence! It never occurred to me that your friendship was unreal, and I can't imagine such a thing now. Of course, there are plenty of people whose 'friendship' I regard mainly as a thing of convenience and of the present. Perhaps I am too untrustful, but there are *very* few (I dare not say how many) that I *quite* rely upon, and none that I believe in so much as you.

As far as I can make out 'Dr.' Allinson (L.R.C.P. is not a 'Dr.') is what one terms a 'faddist' and probably also something of a quack, but in this latter I am perhaps mistaken. At all events, his views on consumption are of no great value, for we read on the slip you send: 'Have the work-room, etc., windows open two inches, night and day, in all weathers. This plan prevents and cures consumption.' — which is an absurd exaggeration of the facts. I generally have my window open two inches, especially at nights. Now it is warm, but I would like to see Allinson try it with the temperature minus 25 degrees! I see he recommends prunes. I patronise this fruit largely now because they are cheap — ten cents a pound. Allinson would greatly approve of my diet, I perceive brown bread with no butter, a weak coffee with no sugar! Well, it suits me well enough. But I *must* have my eggs and bacon! Haricot beans I used to have, but I don't like them. Poached egg I like (only I *fry* it); I see he recommends this. But he would not allow my quinine pills!

As for his comments on my case, he is probably more or less correct, but don't you think I might manage to get a little open air in England? I really do believe that a return to office work in London would be out of the question, but there are alternatives. Sutton quite expected me to return, and even spoke of my assisting him at the College of Surgeons (if he got a post there), so you see *he* even considered London possible for me. So much for Allinson.

Now I turn to what *you* say about it, which is much more important. Love, you are too good to me: I cannot give in in the way you suggest; it would be monstrous of me. I know you want to live in England (and so, indeed, do I), and I am far from being persuaded that this is impossible. But what you say about the chances of my breaking down is of great weight, and one must think very seriously about it. I shall write again to my Uncle Douglas, and try to get an unqualified decisive opinion from him. I think that if I return to England next year, a very few months will decide whether I can stand it or not; in these matters it does not take long to find out.

For instance, Regy, when he went to England, began to have asthma as soon as he got to New York! The openings are so very few here up in the mountains. That is another consideration, although one could never *starve* here, as one might in England.

I *thought* you would scold me for quoting your letter in C.B.A. report! I apologise, but I'm not sorry! I rather thought of quoting your views without putting it as an extract from the letter, but I wanted you to have the credit of it, and could not satisfactorily do anything but quote it as it stood. (I won't publish *all* your letters!)

I am very glad to get the votes. I will not vote for you; that would never do. One thing amazed me rather, why have both you and Fred voted for Ancey? I should have thought you would have greatly disapproved of him, as he is a conchologist of the Bourgnignat school, and besides, it would take about five weeks to get a vote from him in Algeria. The council business would go slowly at that. I am rather glad you voted for Charlton as Treasurer. I voted for Nash, but I believe Charlton would be better, being conveniently at hand. The voting, so far as it has gone at present, indicates as follows: President, probably Morrison; Sec'y., T.D.A.C.; Treas., Charlton; Council, Nash, Merriam, and probably Packard, and D. W. Park — the rest uncertain. Prof. Halsted will run Morrison close for President.

10:05 p.m. I stopped to supper at the Cox's. Mrs. Cox paid me the $1.50 for the picture I did for her. The train was late tonight, but brought me (1.) Postcard from C. F. Morrison, written in pencil, saying he is laid up with pneumonia. I am sorry to hear this. (2.) Letter from Miss Emily L. Morton, of Newburgh, N.Y., joining C.B.A. This is good, as she is an excellent entomologist. It was Nash who persuaded her to join.

April 18th, 9:10 p.m. Snow, Snow, Snow! Snow all day long, and now about a foot deep! And only last night I wrote Morrison, 'We are having sunny weather here now!' It was the drawing lesson this morning: Mrs. Frere, and this time the two little Frere girls. (There is a third, but she is too young to learn.) I started Mrs. Frere on a water-colour drawing of a clump of anemones, and I think she will make a good success of it. The girls, who are quite young, and rather nice children, were shown some points of perspective, and how to shade a pot so as to make it look round. Then I set them to draw and shade a small vase, and they did it better than I expected. The younger one seems to have the most notion of the thing.

After the lesson, I went round to the Stockton's about a key to the schoolhouse. I found Mrs. Stockton in, and talked with her some while on botany. She also showed me the library of the Ladies' Literary Society (she is librarian). They have an admirable set of books. I noticed Darwin, Herbert Spencer, Fiske, Shakespeare, Hawthorne, Proctor, Thoreau (which Mrs. S. is very fond of), Tolstoi, *Chambers' Encyclopedia*, and very many more. It is most creditable to them. Their perseverance and enthusiasm are wonderful.

Most of the afternoon I have been reading Jeffrey Bell in the store below. It is an excellent little book, but I keep coming across errors of nomenclature which are annoying. I must write to J. B. about them. The mail this evening is *Ent. Mags.*, and from West Newman & Co., six reprints of my variety paper, very nicely got up in grey-blue covers, *Pall Mall Budget*, and a letter from Hy. Edwards about some moths I sent him. In *Entomologist*, I see an advertisement:

'Wanted. An active young man who has a real passion for entomology and is not afraid of roughing it, to go to North America this summer to collect Lepidoptera. Must be able to handle micros neatly and write a fair hand. Some knowledge of botany would be an additional recommendation.' Now, that's me, isn't it? I have written about it, and if I am not too late (there are sure to be many applicants) I may make some arrangement with the advertiser. It says to apply to Mr. Porter, Cavendish Square, but I expect someone else is the real advertiser (possibly Leach, or Walsingham?)

April 19th, 5:35 p.m. Reading and writing, and nothing like news atall. The snow is melting fast. Sam Wright called on me just now. The meeting of Lit. & Sci., Society comes off tonight. Bread is now baking in the oven. These are little fragments of what one must do for news in the absence of anything else. I sent you one of my variety-paper reprints, as of course I want you to have a copy. I have also sent copies to Sutton, W. H. Edwards, and Dr. Hamilton. I have been very extravagant today, spending less than 65 cents in the purchase of cotton-seed oil mixture (alias 'lard'), newspaper wrappers, matches, and post-cards, and this morning some biscuits, because the wood was wet and I could bake no bread — at least not conveniently.

11 p.m. The meeting tonight was a perfect farce, chiefly owing to the idiotic behavior of DeKrafft and Samse and the feeble proceedings of Sam Wright as chairman. I will tell you all about it in the next letter, for I shall post this tomorrow.

> Ever your lover, Theo.
> Health. Excellent.

Saturday, April 20th, 1889, 9:30 p.m.

Love,

I posted a letter to you to go by the train this morning. I must tell you about last night's meeting though it was a dreary business.

At 7:30 I went round and opened the school-house and lit the lamps, but the people did not come till after eight, and then only a few — eight of the members, and of non-members, Stewart the blacksmith, Dr. & Mrs. Björnson, the Freres and some others. Charlton was detained on business, and the Cox's did not come. Sam Wright was elected chairman, and the election of officers came on. The two nominated for president were Charlton and Sam Wright, and Charlton got the *whole* vote, which I think Wright did not like. Then Mrs. Humphrey had been nominated first vice-president but would not serve, so DeKrafft and Samse proposed Miss Bellaire to take her place. (Miss B. is a young Englishwoman who is governess at the Frere's. I don't think much of her, but know nothing against her.)

They were then about to elect her when I rose to order, and pointed out that this was directly against the constitution of the society, which stated that officers were to be elected at the meeting following that of nomination. However, DeKrafft and Samse then moved that 'The constitution and bye-laws be suspended for this occasion' and, as Sam Wright was favourable to this, this absurdity was carried through with a mere pretence of voting. I again protested, but it was no use, and Miss Bellaire was elected.

Then DeKrafft was elected second vice-president (six for and two against) and then came the secretary. I stated that I would not stand in the face of the unconstitutional and absurd notion that had just been carried, but as they would not nominate anyone else, I agreed to act if it could be proved that the motion was in accordance with law and usage, or, if not (which of course it isn't) if it were reversed at the next meeting, and it and all the business arising therefrom, be struck out of the minutes. So the matter stands, and if I cannot have this done at the next meeting, of course I shall have nothing further to do with the society. We all agreed to a given constitution, and also arranged an easy way of having it altered if enough of the members required it, and if we cannot stand by what we have thus resolved, it is no use pretending to be organised.

I was unanimously elected secretary, and Miss Byington treasurer. Then followed the 'entertainment,' as it was facetiously called. DeKrafft read a piece out of a newspaper, and read it atrociously. Sam Wright read an essay of his own, called 'Dreams', which was very feeble, and a small red-headed girl, Miss Anna Gowdy, sang a song, playing her own accompaniment, and this she did really well. It was the only satisfactory thing of the evening, this song of little Miss Gowdy.

After this, Miss Bellaire took the chair, and by this time DeKrafft and Samse had got so rowdy that there was no controlling them. Poor Miss Bellaire did not know what to do, and simply sat there and did nothing. Finally she was made to nominate a committee to arrange for next meeting, and she named Miss Byington, Samse, and T.D.A.C. Thus ended the meeting. Afterwards, DeKrafft, Samse, and Vetter were up in Vetter's room here, and I took the occasion to speak pretty strongly to them about their (i.e., DeKrafft's and Samse's) behavior. They apologised and allowed that they had made fools of themselves, but I did not feel mollified, because I expect they will do just the same another time. I hear several people have been abusing them about it today.

To make the best of a bad business, the committee (Miss Byington, Samse, T.D.A.C.) met at the Byington's this morning and we agreed to have a debate at the next meeting, and also a little music. Samse has now sobered down, but I don't trust him. Later I saw Charlton, and he, as president, confirmed the election of the committee (which, having been elected by the pseudo-vice-president, Miss Bellaire, was unconstitutional), and he suggested that the subject for debate be 'Is alcohol, taken as a whole, a blessing or a curse to mankind?' This is agreed to as the subject, so far as I know.

I had to go to open the schoolhouse before the mail was distributed last night, so I got my mail this morning, although there was none for me by this evening's train. The mail I got is (1.) Letter from H. G. Smith, Jr., of Denver enclosing subscription of Miss Alice Eastwood of Denver as a member of C.B.A. She is a teacher and a botanist. (2.) Letter from Cooper, of Denver, joining C.B.A. and enclosing subscr. (3.) Bulletin of the Laboratory of Natural History of the State University of Iowa, sent me by Wickham. It is very nicely printed, 96 pages, and deals with geology, Mollusca, plants, and beetles of Iowa.

Sunday, April 21st, 6:30 p.m. This morning I was wicked enough to 'break the Sabbath' and 'do a wash.' I washed a shirt and vest, a towel, three handkerchiefs, a pair of socks, and a flour sack which I use as a dish cloth. The place where I get my water, the back yard of a house, has now a tenant in the person of Mr. Sam Lee, a 'heathen Chinee' who keeps a laundry and lives in the said house. He makes no objection to my getting the water at his well, so I still continue, but I suppose it is rather impudent on my part, so I must make it up by giving him some more collars to wash, for I cannot starch these myself.

Repenting of my sins about mid-day, I took it easy this afternoon and mostly amused myself by reading *Science Gossip*. I see there is a reference therein (p. 83) to Coulter. I also went round to call on Charlton (he asked me to do so yesterday) but both he and Mrs. C. were away looking after the Sunday School.

The *event* of the day is the arrival of the train, between five and six, with mail! Henceforth, they tell me, it is to come at this hour, and on Sundays as well as week days. I got no mail today. I have not been feeling quite A-1 the last day or so, though I am not ill by any means. I wonder sometimes what I should do if I were taken seriously ill, so as to be unable to look after myself!

April 22nd, 6 p.m. This morning I expended a dollar of the C.B.A.'s funds in the purchase of a book wherein to write list of members, library catalogue, etc., etc. Hitherto everything connected with the C.B.A. has been in my own books, but it is exceedingly necessary to get everything written up in a book that I can turn over to my successor when the time comes. (The mail is in, and I must go down and see if anything has come for me — perchance your letter.)

8:40 p.m. It is now quite late, but having bread to bake, I have not been able to sit down again since I left off at six. Your letter did not come, I am sorry to say, but I got the six photographs from Emery, and a letter from a man called Conradi who wants vars. of *Colias eurytheme*. The photographs are better than I expected, and I enclose one with this. Tell me what you think of it. When I first saw it, it reminded me of my father, and I am supposed to be a good deal like him in appearance. The tie is the self-same red one, now washed almost white, and the coat is one I wore at Bedford Park, but the jersey was got from Colin Mackenzie out here. You will observe the variety of buttons.

To go back to this morning: Having got my C.B.A. book, I first wrote in the membership list, with addresses, then the cash account, then a list of the publications of the C.B.A., and finally got to the library catalogue, which took me nearly all day and is now not quite finished. I had no catalog of the library atall before, and the papers had got all mixed up with my own in moving to town, so I had a good deal of bother to find them all. A few seem to be still among my things at the Cox's, and these cannot be catalogued until I get them. I have 63 entries at present.

Grant Turner seems to be in a bad way. He told me today that he was not even making his board. I got Lees (who was in town) to subscribe 40 cents (for three months) and gave it to him. Turner promised to print my reprints of 13th Report today.

Beddoes came to town and called here, staying a long while talking about chemistry and other things. He is now going to work with Lees up at the mine (as they are getting near the mineral) and he wanted me to go down and live at his place and look after it while he was away. I had half a mind to go, but I refused, as I must push my drawing and botany classes now, and

have too much on hand to go away and just work for my board.

Lees also came to town. He brought me a note from Mrs. Cusack and a box of 'bugs' she had found at the anemone flowers. The letter enclosed your two letters to her. It was nice of her to send these, as, of course, I wanted to see them. She wants to know when I am 'coming up to stay a few days', as she invited me to do. I must go up there soon, if only for a day.

Lees turned up again this evening, having gone to Louis', and walked back to town with Jack Mackenzie. I showed him the photographs (he thought them very good on the whole) and I gave him one to take to Mrs. Cusack. I shall try to 'trade' one or two for other photographs, which I shall send for you to see. Lees promises to look for one of his.

Vetter has been here this evening, talking. We got on the subject of pictures, and so I showed him the Academy Guide for 1888, and he was greatly interested. He wishes he could see the exhibition.

I think I must post this tomorrow morning, so that you will not have to wait for the photograph.

Lovingly, your own Theo.
Health: Good. Have recovered from slight seediness of the other day. I think it was only a touch of dyspepsia.

Tuesday, April 23rd, 1889. 11 p.m.

Dear Annie,

The letter enclosing photograph went by the morning mail. I hoped that your letter would have come this evening, but there was nothing atall for me, and the English mail was not.

It was drawing lesson this morning again. Mrs. Frere commenced some background (scenery, etc.) for her anemones, and had great trouble with the sky, but I think the picture will look nice when done; the anemones are good. The two girls drew and painted a very red apple. The younger one (Maggie) did far the best.

While the lesson was going on a new pupil arrived — Mrs. Chetelat, who lives next door to me here. I gave her a preliminary lesson in perspective, which she knew nothing atall about. She is a plain, good-natured sort of a woman, of cheerful countenance. She reminds me a little of the Margate landlady type. Before I left, I arranged with Mrs. Frere that the lessons should be regularly on Tuesday and Saturdays, and Mrs. Chetelat's (who wants to have separate lessons to begin with, at her house) on Wednesdays and Fridays.

The afternoon was mainly spent in C.B.A. work, and this evening I went round and talked long with Charlton about the Lit. and Sci. Society and other matters. When I got back here, Samse enticed me into his room and began talking about England and asking all sorts of questions about London, etc., and that is why it is so late and I am not in bed. I always like to talk about England, somehow.

I saw a *Vanessa cardui* in West Cliff today; you could not tell it from an English specimen. You have this butterfly at Isleworth, and it has been recorded from Bethnal Green.

The Tomkins building.

April 24th.12 noon. At nine I went round to the Chetelat's and found Mrs. C. ready for her drawing lesson. She had to be taught perspective first, and that took all of this morning's lesson, but I think she now understands it pretty well. To illustrate the principles, I got her to draw the Tomkins Building on the other side of the road, for which purpose we had to sit out in the balcony, which is over the verandah in front of the store here.

I had just got back to my room when I heard a rap at the door, and to my astonishment in walked Mrs. Cusack. She had driven to town with Miss Urquhart. While she was here, Cox appeared, to ask me to look after the children this afternoon. I promised to do so, and must go up there soon. Mrs. Cusack and Miss Urquhart have gone up to Cox's for lunch.

10:5 p.m. Your letter has come, but I will write about it tomorrow.

April 25th, 1:30 p.m. News first. I went up to the Cox's, as arranged, yesterday. Mrs. Cox had to go to a meeting of the Ladies' Literary Society, while Cox had, or pretended to have, some business in town. The meeting of the Ladies' Literary was at his time at a place about five miles from town where one of the members lived. Mrs. Cox was driven there by Mrs. Ommaney, and enjoyed the drive, as she gets out so little now. I took Mrs. Cox one of my photographs, which she thought an excellent likeness, but Mrs. Cusack and Miss Urquhart both considered that the photographs were not nearly so good as they should have been. Mrs. Cox gave me a photograph of herself in exchange, which I will send to you (please keep it for me), but it is not a very good one, and has got rather smashed from being left about.

Mrs. Cox told me that she had had a letter from England, begging her and the children to come home for the summer, and all expenses to be paid, but with characteristic pluck she says, 'Of course not. I can help Charley out here, and I'm not going to leave him now, even if we are hard up.' She deserves someone better than Charley for a husband, indeed!

I took notes from some *Popular Science Monthly*'s that Mrs. Cox had borrowed from the Ladies' Literary, all the afternoon. The children were good and gave next to no trouble. When the train came in, I took them for a walk downtown and got my mail. Isabel walked all the way down. She walks better now than she used to do, which I attribute to exercise and better shoes. I stayed to supper at the Cox's.

This morning, after entering up some records, I went up to the Cox's to get Mrs. Cox to sign her name to the photograph she gave me, and to get some more things of mine that were up there. On the way back, I called at the *Courant* office and found the 13th Report of C.B.A. had been reprinted for me at last, but only 48 copies.

This letter was interrupted at the asterisk by a fit of uncontrollable sleepiness, and I had to lie down for some long while. It is very hot and sultry today. Perhaps that has something to do with it, but it is very annoying to collapse like this.

8 p.m. I feel so foolish today that I hardly like to write. First now I will tell you about the mail other than your letter, for I always like to leave the best for the last, if I am not too impatient. Today I got the interesting copy of *Great Thoughts*. Many thanks. This is a paper one likes to read once and again, but to read it always — no. I have a horror of too many 'great thoughts' because I always think they are but the expression of great facts (or fallacies) in the minds of the thinkers, and those who get the isolated 'thoughts' selected and arranged for their amusement, do, in fact, read the letter but lack the spirit. That is, they never get at the *thoughts* atall. This is not always so, of course, but I think it applies broadly. Now that I have had my growl, I may confess that the said 'thoughts' are quite interesting to me. Nevertheless, I shall perhaps have more to say about this particular paper another time.

I was quite surprised to see Edith Wheelwright coming out on *Robert Elsmere*. Between ourselves, I don't think much of her review, but I do think that Rev. Abbott's, on next page, is decidedly good, rather from what he says than his manner of saying it.

Yesterday's mail was: (1.) *Pall Mall Budget*. (2.) Copies of *Science Gossip* with my 'Variation and abnormal development of Mollusca' papers in them (1885-1886). I asked Carlie to forward them. (3.) Postcard from Carlie. He says Emery Walker (Sec'y. of Hammersmith branch of Socialist League) has been made assistant secretary of *English Illustrated Magazine*. I knew Walker well and liked him much. (4.) Postcard from W. H. Edwards, to say that the *H. ridingsi* larva I sent him is flourishing. This is, I think, the fourth bulletin of the health of this caterpillar I have had from him. The larva ought to feel itself a distinguished personage! It will, of course, be fully described in print later on, being the first larva of the species ever raised to maturity.

(5.) *Punch*, from Mother. I am delighted to read (*Punch*, April 6, 1889, p. 165) that Mr. Punch has been looking at the Exhibition of Lady Artists (one would suppose from the name that the *artists* themselves were on exhibition!) And says, 'Among the best contributions may be noted those of . . . and A. Manville Fenn.' (6.) Letter from Jenner Weir. He urges me to make experiments on Colorado insects 'or you will hereafter regret that you have neglected golden opportunities.' (7.) Two letters from Mother. In one she says, 'Mr. Fenn's play of 'The Balloon' was very funny. Aunt Anna and Christabel went with me, and we had a good laugh over it. It is very well acted, with great spirit, but the theatre was not full.'

Your letter: You write, 'How dissatisfied one feels when it comes to be nearly bedtime, and one has done next to nothing during the day' — that's exactly how I feel at the present minute.

I never had very much to do with the W. C. Bennett family, but I like them well enough. W.C.B. is a thousand times more estimable a man than Sir J. B. Of the two girls, I liked Mary best. Annie!! If you had seen my 'very nice eyes' when I read the bit about my appearance, you would have noticed that they were wide open! How are *you* to tell whether my eyes are nice? I don't see how you can possibly know. I never offer *my* opinion of *your* appearance. If people ask me, I am quite ready to assert that, to *my* mind your face is the nicest and best one I ever saw — but other people, they must judge for themselves. Of course, I know that people do admire your face and am pleased accordingly, but I do not urge them. If someone even said you were hideous, I should probably reply, 'Well, you think so', or 'Our tastes radically differ.'

Now, as to my own appearance, I don't claim to judge of it myself, but I have good reason to believe that people *do* generally regard me as more or less hideous, and so I accept the verdict philosophically and argue to myself that it is better to be hideous than nothing atall! Are these not words of wisdom? About my mouth opening, that is true. I used to be laughed at much for that at school.

I have altered the votes. With Kate Hemery's it will just about turn the scale re Treasurer. It stood before: Charlton six, Smith, one. Now it is Charlton four, Smith four, and I expect Smith will be elected. I told Charlton the other day that he was sure to be elected Treasurer, and he said he was sorry as he had not the time to do it properly, so probably it is as well that Smith will have the post.

I will reform in the spelling of 'surprise.' I am glad you pointed it out. I told Mother about Mrs. Cusack's idea of your coming out here, but told her *only* to tell Carlie of it. C. was very favourable to it. No, I never heard of Thoreau's love affair; I am glad of it, and like him better for it. Yes, I agree with you about 'rules for husbands.' If husband and wife cannot live without fixed rules, it is a pity they were married. Of course, there are rules that a husband should always observe, but if he is 'any sort' of a husband he will do so of his own accord.

Yes, I like evening walks; if only I could walk over to Isleworth and pay you a call now! Yes, I remember your speaking of my patience. I am eccentric in that way. I am sometimes patient for a while, and then I get angry and am very impatient indeed. People cannot understand that wrath may sometimes be accumulating under a placid countenance. The cutting you enclose, 'Hallucinations and Apparitions' is very interesting indeed. Somewhere in the forties, a number of experiments bearing on this matter were related in *Chamber's Journal*. I had the old volumes and read them when I was at school in Beckenham.

April 25th, 6:30 p.m. Not any time to write the news. Drawing lesson this morning for Mrs. Chetelat. She finished Tomkins Building and is to commence on a pot (to study shading). Meeting of Literary and Sci. Society tonight — debate on alcohol. I shall have to speak.

April 27th, 3:45 p.m. How the house shakes; it is blowing a hurricane. I am going up to the Cusacks' for the night, but I don't think the wind will last. The meeting went off well last night, and today was Mrs. Frere's drawing lesson. I have really all today's and yesterday's news to tell you, but that may have still to be put off till tomorrow. However, I shall not post this till Monday morning.

Sunday, April 28th, 9:30 p.m. It has seemed as if I never were going to get time to write the news of the last few days, and even now I am so tired and sleepy that I am more or less incapable.

To commence with Friday: As I said, I gave Mrs. Chetelat a drawing lesson, and was pleased enough with her understanding of perspective as illustrated in the picture of Tomkins Building, though when she began she had no notion of it atall. After this, I prepared my speech for the debate, writing it down, and then went round to Charlton's to discuss the matter. I found him mending a fence, and with him a man named Warren, whom I had never seen before. Warren, who looks like Earl Granville somewhat, was great on 'Prohibition', so we got him to promise to speak on the alcohol debate.

The debate came off in due course in the evening, but owing to a ball being the same night (given by the 'Odd Fellows') at Silver Cliff we had only 16 people present. DeKrafft was not there, for the excellent reason that he has 'skipped the country', leaving nothing behind him but an unpaid bill at the hotel. (Later, Wheatley told me that DeKrafft was not really a professional journalist but had been living at his mother's expense, and it appears that she stopped his supplies and left him to 'rustle for himself', hence his appearance and disappearance here.)

The meeting went off very well indeed. The 'unconstitutional' part of last meeting was struck out or the minutes by unanimous vote, so that we are straight again. Charlton, opening the debate, affirmed 'That alcohol, taken as a whole, is a blessing rather than a curse to humanity.' He read from manuscript, but Sam Wright, who followed in the negative, spoke without preparation. I then took up the affirmative, my main arguments being (1.) I admit that alcohol has its abuses as well as uses. It is only harmful when used foolishly. (2.) We have to consider the future as well as the present, and it is to be hoped that the abuse of it will cease as humanity progresses. (3.) Alcoholism is merely a phase of vice, and to destroy alcohol is not to destroy vice atall. Probably vice would not even be permanently checked by the abolition of alcohol.

After this, Warren spoke against, and finally Charlton replied to close the debate. The 'judges' (three in number) gave a unanimous verdict in favour of the affirmative side. What do you think about it? Do you agree with me? I certainly would not destroy alcohol off the face of the earth had I the power, though I suppose I appreciate the evils of drunkenness as much as anybody. But it is not the *alcohol* I blame.

`Now it is nearly ten, and I will leave off for tonight. Goodnight, love!

April 29th, 11:15 a.m. Snow this morning! But to go back to Saturday. I have Mrs. Frere for a drawing lesson, and also the youngest child (Maggie). Since the last lesson, Mrs. Frere had painted some anemones in oils, and done them very nicely. I helped her to put some rocks into the picture, and then she began to talk of drawing faces; she did so want to learn how to draw faces. So I took her roughly over the exterior bones of the skull, the principal muscles, and the general anatomy of the face, and then got her to try to draw a face. She had a tendency to make the skull bulge out in front too much, and the eye was not always in the right place, and the mouth was wrong, but I think she will do better in time. We found a very pretty face in a paper to copy from, as there was nobody to sit to be drawn.

After the lesson, I was writing up in my room, when Regy appeared. He had driven to the dance. Miss Urquhart had been coming in with him, but she was not well enough. He had stayed at Cox's the night and put Ferris in the corral, and next morning the gate was open, and no Ferris! It is not known whether she escaped, in which case she would almost surely have gone home, or whether she was stolen (later it transpired that another horse was stolen in Silver Cliff the same night, which makes things look suspicious). Now I told Mrs. Cusack that I was coming out to her on Sunday, so I might just as well go on Saturday instead, and bring Ferris (if she could be found) or come out with Regy (he had a 'sulky' in town) on Sunday. This suited Regy well enough, so at about four I started, and got to the Cusacks' at seven. It was very windy when I started, but it did not last, and I had a pleasant walk.

On the way I found many flowers, notably the yellow violet (*V. nuttallii*) in full bloom at the old locality. *Clematis douglasii* [*Coriflora scottii.* Ed.] was just opening; *Leucocrinum* was not. On the prairie I found the remains of a sad tragedy. A poor little 'horned toad' had become defunct, and three burying-beetles had come in their black and orange to bury him. But some bird had pecked out the insides of all the beetles, and there lay all the corpses together! I found Lees and Wheatley up at the Cusacks'. Mrs. C. welcomed me very kindly.

Sunday (i.e., yesterday). In the morning I went for a little walk with Mrs. Cusack in the woods. We found many beetles and snails, and talked a good deal. Mrs. C. does not care atall for Wheatley, and finds him a great nuisance because he won't come punctually to meals. (Of course the idea of having meals over at the other house fell through — I knew they wouldn't do it).

Ferris was not to be seen, so after lunch I got 'Doc', saddled him, and rode to town. I went up to the Cox's, but Regy wasn't there. Later he turned up here, and in the evening drove home. Yesterday I plagued Mrs. Cusack for photographs, and was quite unexpectedly successful, for she gave me a really nice one of herself, a good one of Frank, and a fair one of Mora and Stella (the Charley Cusack children). In this last, Mora's and Stella's hair both look dark, whereas they are red. I shall send these photographs on to you.

I haven't told you about the mail lately received. On Friday I got a letter from Ashmead, enclosing a list of the recorded Colorado Hymenoptera he has made out for the C.B.A. The number of species is enormous, and it must have been a very laborious work; it fills 19 well-covered pages. I also got ten extra copies of *West American Scientist*, April, and I sent you one. Yesterday I got letters from Miss Morton and Hamilton (with names of beetles sent — a 'whirlygig' (*Gyrinus*) is probably a new species, he says, and *Ornith. & Oöl.*, Jan. and March, and papers from Landis for C.B.A. library.

6 p.m. The mail has come in, but nothing for me. I have been talking with Martin a while down in the store. He tells wonderful stories about Payn's inventiveness. He says now that Payn never shot that elk on Mammoth Mountain after all, but I don't know whether that is so or not. It has left off snowing, but it is still cold, with a dull, grey sky.

Your true lover, Theo.
Health. Am very well.

April 30th, 1889

Love,

Your letter has come this evening, and a very nice one. I send you a kiss for it!

The weather has been better today, but it was cold this morning, and I was a little late at the Frere's. Mrs. Frere had painted a head in oils while I was away, and really it was very nice, for a beginning. Maggie also came to draw, but the child was miserable with toothache, so I excused her. Nobody can apply their mind to drawing when they have toothache, I imagine. When I left, Mrs. Frere invited me to come round in the evenings sometimes, which I shall like to do, only that I am quite busy just now. The Freres are not particularly interesting, but a little society at times is both pleasant and improving.

Since the lesson, I have been writing records and letters, and have not been out except a walk up town to get some paper for Mrs. Cusack. Mrs. Cox called, and also Chetelat, bringing a *Vanessa cardui* which he had caught. This evening's mail brings your letter and a letter from Douglas, who forwards $5.00 of the money he has in keeping, on the probability that I may want it. I am not altogether sorry to see it, though I would not have written for it. Then there is also, from Ashmead, a list of Hymenoptera I sent him (four of which are new species) and two papers: *Punch*, from Mother, and *Journal of Mycology*, now published quarterly by the Department of Agriculture.

Your letter: This is alarming, the other two children falling ill. I quite supposed it was nothing contagious, when you wrote of Winnie's illness. But no doubt it will be chicken-pox, and perhaps it is really as well for them to have it now and be done with it, as they would not be likely to quite escape. Did you never have it? I had it at Miss Law's school at Margate; it was short but far from sweet. I would have had a doctor at once, just to corroborate the diagnosis. I am glad Louy 'likes herself' in Paris.

I will send *Cymopterus montanus* in this. I think I can get some, though it has mostly gone to seed. Yes, go to Sutton by all means! I hope you went, for I do think, as I have always said, that you need a holiday as often as you can conveniently have one. But it is queer, that I always feel as if you were not so near to me when you are away from home. I suppose it is because I mentally live a good deal at Syon Lodge, and I can imagine you there with all your surroundings, but when you are away I cannot of course get any clear image, and I miss you accordingly.

What a ridiculous notion! 'If you should die' (don't!) I am to try to induce Louy to take your place! When I read this I laughed, but it is rather a dreadful joke. I like Louy very much indeed, but she is not atall like you. Besides, whatever happens you will not cease to exist, and that is a very happy thing. So long as I have any existence, I am entirely yours. (It is much nicer to be someone else's than to be only one's own; I think everyone finds it so. If there were only one person in the world, I think he could not help going mad — it would be *too* lonely.)

I like what you say about spring. We never have such delightful spring here, somehow, as in England. It is always either hot or cold. As the geography book lucidly put it, 'The climate of North America is excessive!' No, I think a four-lobed primrose is quite rare, but it seems that *Centunculus*, in the same Natural Order is about as frequently four- as well as five-lobed. Probably White's *Selbourne* has been overrated, but it is a good book with a freshness about it. I first read it in Madeira. I have volume I of it here somewhere. I quite agree with you about the footnotes though.

I don't approve of killing even for murder, but if a man commits a brutal murder I would rather see a community lynch him than shrug their shoulders and disclaim all responsibility. Would you not? On the whole, I regard lynching as a hopeful sign. It means 'I will not have my neighbors killed', and that is a right feeling.

I am sorry you are bothered about my health, and I am afraid I rather made too much of it. What little I suffer may be as much indigestion as anything else, and really I am excellently well on the whole; I have never had cause to be anxious since I came to Colorado. You see, I tell *you* everything, but writing to anyone else, my ills are so slight I should not mention them.

Thank you for the bit of biography. What will you think of me, sending you none all this time? Somehow, I have never seemed to find time for it though I think over the events and how I shall put them down. I must write it soon, though. I have also been meaning to write to Frederic for some weeks past. The Labouchère cutting you enclose is amusing.

May 1st, 12:35 p.m. The 'Merrie month of May' begins with snow; it is snowing at this moment. I gave Mrs. Chetelat a drawing lesson this morning, showed her how to shade a pot, which she did not previously understand atall. She is going to paint in oils on a sort of glazed Holland they use here for window blinds. It is cheap (15 cents a yard I think she said) and seems to hold the paint all right, but its colour (ochre yellow) is a disadvantage.

As it was the end of the month, I sat up late last night making up the accounts. My financial position is this:

Balance from March, $7.07
Received April, $11.33
Paid April, $11.85
Balance now in hand, $6.55

Average daily expenditure for April, 39 ½ cents.

I hope to do better next month, and it is to be remembered that I have not yet received the money for any of the drawing lessons; but then, on the other hand, $2.50 comes due for rent on May 5th. I will send a statement of the C.B.A. on another slip so that the other Middlesex members can see it.

The snow has melted about as fast as it fell, or else there would probably be a foot of it on the ground. I shall not be surprised if there is quite a deep fall during the night, though hardly any is falling now.

Today the Lacy's have taken the postoffice. You know it is the idiotic custom in this country to appoint postmasters according to politics, and consequently the most incompetent man may get the place if he has 'done something for the party.' When the new (Republican) government came in, Goldstandt, being a Democrat, had to leave, and applications were made by Vetter, Cassidy, Lacy, etc., for the post. Now it has been given to Mrs. Lacy, which is of course the same thing as giving it to Lacy, who is the editor of that blackguard sheet, the *Wet Mountain Tribune*. They went in charge today and will continue to run the office in this building until a new building now being erected next door to Falkenberg's is finished. I don't like Lacy, but he may run the postoffice well enough. At all events, I won't grumble at him beforehand.

The fauna lists did pretty well last month. Here is a list of the addenda: Colorado: Mammalia, 1; Birds, 1 var.; Reptiles, 3; Amphibia, 2; Fishes, 1; Mollusca, 2 vars.; Coleoptera, 4; Hymenoptera, 749 (these are from Ashmead's list, of course); Phaenogamia, 1, and 5 vars. (and 2 fossil). Middlesex: Mammalia (2 fossil); Mollusca, 5 vars.; Coleoptera, 1; Moths, 56 and 4 vars.; Diptera, 1; Phaenogamia, 1.

Another wretched day, snowing, and the snow melting as fast as it falls. I have been writing all the time (I got up shockingly late) — Hymenoptera records in the morning, and letters this afternoon. I got some mail: 'Rural Notes' (from *Yorkshire Post*) from Geo. Roberts,

and letters from Hy. Edwards and Carrington. Hy. Edwards says a little moth I sent him is a very interesting new species. It is one of the 'clear-wings' (Sesiidae). Carrington's letter is a nice one, and long also. It is quite remarkable for Carrington to fill four pages with close writing. He says, 'I note your request to get you an agent for the sale of your duplicates. I went yesterday to Mr. Janson of firm of Edward Janson and Son (admirable man), Natural History agents of Little Russell St., Bloomsbury, than whom there are none more respectable. I told him what which you needed and he said he would act for you on commission or purchase. He will write to you himself by next mail. Kind of Carrington. wasn't it? Janson is an excellent man and I hope I can trade with him. He is much better than Strecker — I don't like Strecker much. I shall only sell duplicates, however. Carrington goes on to say that the advertisement I saw in *Entom.* and answered (do you remember?) was really Elwes, and it is South who has to choose the man. Carrington says, 'He (Elwes) is such a 'near' fellow, I hear, that it would be no catch to get the appointment. He is one of those who is never satisfied with what is done for him, and would require *all*. Otherwise I should have suggested to South, who is to select the man, that you were asked.'

May 3rd, 7:10 p.m. Must be off to meeting very soon; no time to write.

At last the bad weather seems to have finished, and it was warm and even sunny today. It was Mrs. Chetelat's drawing day but, owing to the bad weather she had not been able to go to Silver Cliff and get some white paint, which is necessary for the picture now in progress, so we postponed the lesson until the paint should be procured.

After writing some letters, I went out, and for the first time this year took my net, though I caught nothing with it. I got several ants and beetles, and a fungus (*Melampsora lini*) new to my Colorado list; it is a yellow fungus like your *Tussilago* one, only it grows on the wild flax. I looked at its spores under the microscope; they are oval, and orange in colour. Later, when I got back, I wrote some C.B.A. letters, informing the various members of council of their election. Regy appeared, and the Beddoes' were also in town. Regy thinks he saw Ferris in a pasture afar off, and is going after her.

This evening we had a meeting of the Lit. & Sci. Society, but only for the transaction of business. Charlton was not there, but Sam Wright, being elected first vice-president, took the chair. A letter was read from DeKrafft, headed Colorado Springs, resigning his position as second vice-president and apologising to me (he should have apologised to the society) for his behavior at the last meeting he attended. Vetter was elected second vice-president in his place. I shall not have to act as door-keeper and lighter-up any more, as each male member is going to take it in turn. Next meeting there is to be an entertainment! I have got to 'read an essay.' (So the programme states!)

The mail I got this evening was letters from Galloway and H. K. Burrison. Galloway is the fungus man at Dept. of Agriculture, and says he will send me *Journal of Mycology* regularly and will be glad of any publications in return. Burrison I don't know, but he writes to ask how he can get to the southwest Colorado district and what he will find there. He encloses a stamp for reply.

Dear me! This is a fearfully uninteresting letter this week. I am in rather a 'mechanical' state of mind.

May 4th, 9:5 p.m. I am not quite up to the mark this evening, so shall write but little. In the morning I gave Mrs. Frere a drawing lesson. We nearly finished the face she is painting, and it does not look atall bad on the whole. I had to change the position of one eye, and paint in the hair. Mrs. Frere's mother was there, an old lady of amiable disposition if narrow views. We got talking on Socialism, the thing being started by a remark of Miss Bellaire, who was in the room, that a brother of Walter Crane was living with her people somewhere up near Denver. This brother objected to Walter on account of the latter's socialistic views. (You see, Walter Crane has to contend both with Mrs. W. C. and his family in the matter of Socialism, and from all accounts they take a very unreasonable position in the matter). However, he is appreciated in other quarters, and he is a most abominable man. What do you think of him?

Mrs. Frere's mother disapproved of 'trusts' but thought it was a glorious thing that in these United States everyone has a chance, 'and even the meanest man may rise to be president.' I told her that I thought it *was* the meanest man; it required quite an uncommon degree of wealth, but then it is only at someone else's expense, and that isn't what we want. We don't want to give the advantage to 'the meanest man!'

After the drawing lesson, I went round and called on Mrs. Stockton and got her to promise that one of her boys should attend the botany classes, the first of which is to be next Wednesday. After lunch I wrote up the minutes of the Lit. & Sci. Society and a letter to Burrison, and then went out to Charlton's and to get some *Cymopterus montanus* for you. (I found a good bit, and it is pressing.)

Just as I was starting, a box arrived at the postoffice for Charlton, evidently containing a grebe sent by Armstrong; some boys had caught it down at his ranch. It is a queer bird with the brightest of red eyes and the strangest feet, and no tail whatever. It is probably *Dytes nigricollis* var. *californicus*, and it is closely allied to the

The grebe.

English Eared Grebe (*Dytes auritus*). It was put in a box, with a pan of water in which it evidently took great delight.

This evening's mail was of the most uninteresting kind, being a 'receipt of subscript.' sent to *Can. Entom.*, and a receipt of shells sent to Smithsonian Inst. I have not had supper yet, and have not much appetite, but must eat before I go to bed.

Sunday, May 5th, 12:15 p.m. I am sending you a *living* pupa of *Papilio asterias* Feb., the large black 'swallow-tail' of this country. If it does not come to any grief you will see the butterfly emerge some time in June, I expect. In the same tube (at the end of it) are some little things for Frederic.

3:30 p.m. You see, I am obeying your instructions, and I mean to take a walk every day, weather permitting, in future. I went down by the creek today and of course looked for specimens, but I was not very successful, the only captures of any consequence being two specimens (male and female) of a pretty little Tineid moth which I never saw before. I saw two more but they eluded me. I shall post this today, so will end up.

With much love, your Theo.
Health. Good, but not quite A-1 today.

P. S. The *Courant* never appeared last week, and Vetter says he thinks it has stopped publication. I shouldn't wonder if it were so.

Monday, May 6th, 8:55 p.m.

Dear Annie,
Nothing particular happened yesterday after I posted the letter to you. The evening mail came in and brought me a copy of *The Great Divide*, a paper published in Denver, and the last number of *The Nautilus*. This last is *The Conchologist's Exchange* come to life again, and greatly improved. It is to appear monthly, with a dollar per annum subscription. It is edited by Pilsbry. This number has a note of mine on the varieties of *Patula cooperi* that I sent ages ago for *Conch. Exch.* and which never appeared owing to the suspension of the paper.

Today, though the air is now quite still, has been remarkable as about the windiest day I have ever known here. It began before sunrise, and the violence of the wind was such that the house rocked, and I even wondered whether I had better cover my head with the pillows or make a rush for the window if the place blew down! Fortunately, no material damage was done anywhere in town, except that three windows of the saloon opposite the Tomkins Building were blown in. The dust blew up in great clouds, high above the houses, and sifted in everywhere. My window was closed, but there was a sediment of dust over everything when I got up. Cassidy subsequently informed me that 'all the houses in town were 'chock full' of dust, but here we must allow for the poetic imagination of our worthy mayor. (Cassidy is the mayor of West Cliff).

I got to work today at the *Entom.* variety paper again and wrote a chapter dealing with variation in size. There was more to be said on the subject than I supposed.

Later, Chetelat appeared, bringing from Charlton's in a paper bag the body of the grebe. The poor creature had departed this life of its own accord. I proceeded to skin it, and found that the breast was fractured, so the only wonder is that it lived so long and endured so much handling. I took the skin round to Charlton, and the body I shall send, I think, to Shufeldt. I boiled it this evening so that it would travel without decomposing.

I forgot to say that about mid-day I went out after some more of the Tineid moths I found yesterday, but the wind must have been too much for them, and they were not. The grasshoppers were in plenty, and I secured three; they are all the same species, *Psoloesoa coloradensis*.

It really is a fact that the *Courant* has stopped publication. Grant Taylor told me about it today.

He says for some time he has been making only about $2.00 a week clear profit, and this of course won't keep him, wife and Caty. And so he is in debt and think he had better make some new move or he will never be able to clear himself. He talks of going to Rosita, where there is at present no paper, and he was going up there tonight to see about it.

May 7th, 7:55 p.m. Dear Annie! A quite satisfactory day has ended most happily with the arrival of your most delightful letter, and I am 'pleased as Punch', if you can imagine how pleased that is. I am tempted to answer your letter now, but I expect I shall not have time to do so tonight. However, I must tell you the news of the day.

By the morning mail, I posted the boiled corpse of the poor grebe to Shufeldt; I hope the postal authorities won't 'smell a rat', or rather a grebe, on the way, and destroy it. Early in the morning Maggie Frere came round to say her mother could not take a drawing lesson today, as they were doing the spring cleaning, which I was rather glad of for I wanted the time to prepare for my botanical demonstrations. So I settled down to diagrams, and did two during the morning.

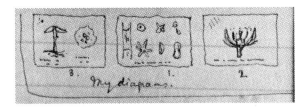

The paper is quite large — 30 x 21 inches. The first one I did represented different forms of galls (in Indian ink, with the nuclei coloured red), and

the other was a diagram of a flower to show stamens, petals, etc.

After this I had lunch and then went round to call on Professor Wright about the botany demonstrations. I wanted his advice as to who I should ask to attend. ('Professor' just means teacher here. Many people call me Professor now.) The Prof. (this is quite a different man from Sam Wright; I think I explained before?) gave me his advice, and off I went on my tour of investigation.

I forget the name of the first people I went to (MacIlhenny, I think it was), but the lady of the house welcomed me very kindly (took me for a Cusack at first) and asked a younger lady (her daughter) whether she would not like to join. She seemed bashful, and said she 'didn't know', but I think she is coming to the 'preliminary center' tomorrow. Then I went to the Alexanders, where Mrs. A. (whom I never remember to have seen before) greeted me as if I were an old friend, and I found Mrs. Stockton and Mrs. Björnson visiting there also. Mrs. A. would *like* to join, but didn't know whether she had time, but an Alexander girl probably would attend the classes.

From the Alexanders over the road to the Frank Hunters. Mrs. Hunter said she would attend directly I mentioned the subject, and while I was there in came Mrs. Gowdy. Mrs. G. is a person of bad repute, and though perhaps libeled to some extent, I judge she cannot be of any great excellence. However, she is has a nice little daughter (aged perhaps 13 — red hair, plain but intelligent face) named Anna, and Anna must certainly go to the botany classes. Also, this very day she had made up her mind to hunt me up and get me to give Anna drawing lessons, so it was fortunate she had met me there. I said I would gladly teach Anna — and then it *must* be that she should begin today, at which I rather demurred, as I wanted to go hunting further for my botany class, but finally I went round with her to her house (it is close to the schoolhouse) and gave the child an hour, and such was her readiness to learn that I got her to draw a box in perspective and to shade a cup fairly well, though she had not the faintest notion of any rules before, as I found by getting her to draw the same box before I expounded the perspective of it, and she got it absolutely wrong.

The lesson over, I went to the Humphrey's and got them to promise that Bertha should come at any rate to the first demonstration, and continue if she liked it). After this I returned home. Now, very likely I shall not more than two or three tomorrow, but I feel satisfied so far, and I think the thing will go all right. It was not yet late. so I did a third diagram representing a lichen and an agaric, prepared my notes for the demonstration, and then read up in 'Thome' the reproduction of algae, fungi and lichens, and got a better understanding of it than heretofore.

After this, the mail — your letter, letters from Mother and Ashmead, and postcard from W. H. Edwards ('The *ridingsi* larva is still alive and healthy') and then supper, after which this letter. The mail was rather late this evening — did not get in till six. Ashmead writes about his list of Colorado Hymenoptera: 'Do not worry about its publication. I will stand the cost of publication, but I shall want it published as emanating from the Colorado Biological Association and do not want the fact of my standing the expense known.' This is very generous of him, and of course I am pleased. As he says, he does not want it known, so don't mention this to anyone. (It will be one of the secret bits to keep from the Grannie!)

You would be puzzled to see the frequent requests in Mother's letters to 'remember Adelina.' However, the said Adelina is Adelina Patti, and it is Mother's delicate way of alluding to Pears' *soap* and the uses thereof!

May 8th, nearly 11 p.m. The end of a full day, and now time to go to bed, as I have to be out at Louis' early tomorrow. The first demonstration was a success beyond my hopes (about 13 present), and this evening I have been out to Louis Howard's so that, with the drawing lesson to Mrs. Chetelat this morning, I have really had no time to myself atall.

May 9th, 8:34 a.m. The minutes must be *very* precious just now to Regy and Miss Urquhart, if they love one another. Miss Urquhart goes to England, and her train starts in about five minutes.

11:50 a..m. I never went out with Louis after all. He asked me to go out with him (he came to town early this morning) and help him write up his accounts, as he has no idea of book-keeping. I promised to do so, but somehow I missed him, and he left town without me. I shall not trouble to walk out to Ula, and I feel rather annoyed at the way he has acted, because I was here in my room, and he ought to have taken the trouble to come and call for me. He could not expect me to follow him about town until he was ready to go! However, I shall scold him about it when next I see him, and tell him I cannot now bother with his accounts.

But I am putting the cart before the horse, since I have told you nothing about yesterday. In the morning I gave Mrs. Chetelat her drawing lesson; she is doing a little painting of a landscape (river scene). Then I commenced preparations for the botany demonstration. I went out towards Charlton's, collecting flowers, getting some *Corydalis, Cymopterus*, etc. Then, when I got back, I tested some things under the microscope and sorted out some dried flowers and the books I needed.

The time went marvelously quickly in preparation, and it was soon time to go to the schoolhouse. What with microscope, books, diagrams, specimens, etc., I had all I could conveniently carry, and when I got half-way it began to rain, so I had to put in at the butcher's (Rosenstraugh's) and beg a newspaper to keep the wet off my burden. Arrived at the schoolhouse, I hung my diagrams on a string as at the C.B.A. meeting, but the little table I expected to use for the microscope was not there. But the schoolhouse is also a church, and the minister's reading-desk did excellently for the purpose when moved to the window. Then I sat down and waited, feeling some trepidation lest the thing should be a failure.

Two o'clock came and not a soul in sight. Two-five and still nobody. Two ten; here is Bertha Humphrey, at any rate. Two twenty-five. Three more (in the interval I showed Bertha some things under the microscope) — Miss MacIlhenny and two Alexander girls. Well, it was getting late, and I had four, so I began. Very soon after Mrs. Chetelat and Anna Gowdy came, making six, and one or two others turned up later (names unknown to me).

I started with explaining the difference between organic and inorganic matter, and between animals and plants, and telling them about protoplasm and cells. I showed them some cells in the seed-vessel of *Cymopterus*, they being polygonal; and a primrose that Mother sent me in a letter offered a nice example of an elongated cell in one of its hairs. Also, I put under the microscope some blood and let them look at the corpuscles, these being examples of rounded cells.

I got along all right and felt no shyness, and was able to say all I wanted. When I was about half-way through, I saw a lot of ladies (five I think) coming down the road, and in they came. They were the Ladies' Literary Society, which was meeting somewhere near and had adjourned bodily to attend my lecture! There was Mrs. Stockton, Miss Byington, Mrs. Aldrich, and I think the other two were Mrs. Humphrey and Mrs. Alexander. I continued the lecture, speaking of the different divisions of the subject of botany and outlining the proposed plan of work. Several of the ladies asked very intelligent questions from time to time, which showed that they understood what I was saying.

At half-past nine I finished, and announced the next lesson or lecture for next Tuesday. We shall see whether they were satisfied, by the attendance I get then.

Lees came into town soon after, and then Regy and Miss Urquhart, I was rather surprised to hear that Miss U. was going off to England next day (i.e., today) and Mrs. Cusack was going with her to Pueblo, ands thence for a week or so to Colorado Springs to stay with Mrs. Stamp. Dear me! How I wish I could have changed places with her, and no doubt she would have willingly stayed behind. Lees was going out to Louis', and I thought I would go with him, as I had been asked to go out some day. Afterwards I found Louis was giving a sort of little dinner party and expected the Cusacks (who didn't come), so I felt rather as if I had intruded myself. But it was all right, as there were only Lees, Jack Mackenzie and myself there.

I meant to walk back early, as I thought Mrs. Cusack might call at my room and find me out (which she did, and left a note), but talking, etc., the time went, so that it was past ten before I got back to town. This morning I walked up to the Cox's (where the Cusacks and Miss Urquhart stayed the night) to say goodbye to Miss Urquhart, as I supposed she would not want me at the station at the last moment.

Also, I got the mail of the night: (1.) Letter from E. W. Janson, who is to sell my Lepidoptera, but he talks of their being *set*, which is a bother. (2.) *Pall Mall Budget* of Oct. 4, 1888, sent by Sherborn; why, I don't know. (3.) Letter from Mother. (4.) *Art*, a little Stepp-ian (Partridge & Co.) magazine I never saw before, containing my article on 'Colorado Cañons.' The paper is well-printed and well-illustrated for a penny magazine, but it reeks with religious humbug! Did you ever see it? It would make any sane man turn atheist on the spot if he thought this was really the best religion had to say for itself!

1:45 p.m. Now I may answer your letter. No, the bedstead I had belonged to the Cusacks (at least it belonged to the house, and when they bought that I presume the bedstead was included), and the one I have now belongs to Cox. In this country, there is never any fear of stuffiness because wooden houses are not so tight as brick ones, and things do not fit closely. In England, of course, it is different, and I think you are right to have the window a little open except when it is foggy. Your room is altogether too small. I said when I saw it I wished you had one of the other rooms. Here, I have the window a little open at night when it is warm. (By the way, a bit of news I forgot to tell is that Regy found Ferris all right.) The idea of your reading my letters to the Grannie! I never should have supposed she would be interested.

About the botanical lectures, your 'Town in the Provinces' notion is rather good! Perhaps I may go down to Cañon City some day and lecture. Lees has heard from Payn recently. He is all right except that his people seem to be sending him more money — a great mistake. About the stove-pipe, you see, I never ate it after all. It was this way: Stove-pipe is not digestible in the raw condition, and I couldn't cook it without a stove and stove-pipe, so I used all my pipe to make the cooking apparatus, and had to cook and eat something else! There was no help for it.

It is true that the grammar and spelling of Morrison's circular is bad, but the circular is all right on the whole. It is queer that some sorts of bad grammar are quite common and correct in America. — notably using 'will' for 'shall.'

The Emigration may have been all right, and I am quite in favour of many people emigrating, only it is certainly true that most migration societies and agencies are either conducted by knaves (such as those who took people to a most unhealthy part of Texas solely for their railroad fares, and those who shipped cheap labour to Australia to build a railway and let it starve)

or fools. I have a good mind to write some plain articles on emigration and try to get them published in some English magazine. Half the men who come out here to ranch know nothing about the business and consequently make a trash of it.

'Doc' Vetter stands for 'Doctor' so-called because he was five years in a drug store.

I think what you say about Socialism is in the main correct, and I have always maintained that 'laws' were useless until the people were prepared to obey them. This, I think, is admitted by all Socialists. But I do believe in cooperative action, and I do think that if the people will 'give themselves a show' they will improve. It is like saying to a man in bad health, 'If you wish to be well, you must observe certain rules; mere wishing won't cure you.' So that mere individual 'piety' is quite beside the question unless the said pious individual is ready to embark on pious ways and urge others to do the same.

Now Socialism, whether good or bad, is a theory of society and you cannot more have Socialism practiced by one man alone than a house built of one brick alone. Therefore a Socialist is bound to seek adherents to his doctrine before he can have the least prospect of carrying it out. Is not this so? Of course, every good life has a most excellent effect for good, but it will not bring about a Socialistic state, because Socialism cannot be taught by precept yet. Therefore, each man's duty is double: (1.) To act as best he can under the circumstances. (2.) To agitate for the bettering of those circumstances. In the latter respect, at least, I have been sadly behind the last year — I must reform!

Your speaking of our taking walks together when I return home brings up visions of happiness. What walks we may have! It was a shame we couldn't walk together before! In the 'some day' we are not going to be as mercenary as John Gilpin, and only get a holiday once in many years, but we must have a delightful time in the woods and fields every year, mustn't we?

Did I ever tell you the clerk's definition of Good Friday? 'Good Friday' is like Sunday without *The Referee*. (I think the referee was the paper named.) I remember the Good Friday time in 1887 very well too,. Klein let me stay away over Saturday but I think the rest of the office had to be there.

I remember that walk to the Allport's; it was one of the few times that I had you to myself, even for a little. The other two went on before, and we walked slowly. The Allport's house was reached much too soon, all the same. The reason I wouldn't come to a decision about where to go was that I didn't want to go anywhere atall. I wanted to see more of *you*, as you knew quite well at the time, didn't you? I grudge that Good Friday away still.

Thank you for quoting Louy's letter about Olive. It is very nice, the account she gives of her, and I can quite imagine everything. Olive herself has not a good idea of writing a descriptive letter. Yes, I read *Alton Locke* and liked it very much; I am glad you are reading it.

Dr. Allinson on consumption is all right in the main, but not atall new, and probably he knows nothing about it. For example, had I used no wraps this winter I should have frozen to death, and so would anyone. You can imagine what 20 degrees below zero, or even zero, means in England! How can Allinson possibly know more about it than, say, R. D. Powell (Uncle Douglas) who has given his life to the study, and sees dozens of patients every day?

It is generally held now that what people inherit is simply a 'phthysical tendency', and the disease is brought about by the *Bacillus tuberculosis* or germ of phthysis, under *unfavourable* conditions. Some diseases are strictly inherited just as if they were features, etc., but phthysis is not one of these. The subject was very fully discussed a few years ago at the Medical Congress at Belfast. At the same time, we are very far from knowing all about it yet. I expect it would be almost impossible for anyone to develop phthysis in this climate, whatever the so-called 'inheritance.'

But I won't give you a lecture on phthysis! I fully agree that [working at] Klein's was enough to develop phthysis in anyone addicted that way.

No, of course I knew you had written that week when the first sack came, but then there is no telling whether your letter might have been delayed somewhere on the way; the mail is very eccentric. Do I remember the snowstorm of Jan. 18th, 1882? Yes, I was at Chislehurst. It was in the holidays just before school-time at 'The Abbey', Beckenham. I remember most of the fellows did not turn up on the first day of school because they said 'the snow prevented them', but mostly they lied, and nobody believed them.

8:30 p.m. It is raining tonight. This afternoon I walked up to the Cox's, partly for a walk, partly by way of a call, and partly to carry a big bundle of my clothes down here. I shall post this tomorrow, although it is not a week since the last one, but there has been an usual amount to say this week.

Everlastingly your own lover,
Theo.
Health, very good.

May 10th, 1889, 6:55 p.m.
Dear love,
I have soon to be off to meeting of Lit. & Sci. Soc., and supper is cooking and must be attended to, so I must tell you about today tomorrow, or later tonight unless I am too tired.

May 11th, 9:35 a.m. It really seems as if spring was never coming this year! It is snowing now as though it were midwinter, and the snow lies already perhaps an inch on the ground.

But of yesterday: I posted a letter to you in the early morning, and at nine it was Mrs. Chetelat's drawing lesson. She has finished her little oil colour river scene and was very proud of it, but it was very shocking, nevertheless. Her clouds had a peculiar tinge of green, the willow tree looked like a green football at the end of a stump, and the water was quite amazing, while the boat was gracefully floating on the very tip of its keel. So I had to affect some notable alterations, and I told Mrs. C. to study willows, boats, and birds pending the next lesson.

In the afternoon, again it was Anna Gowdy's lesson. When I got there I found an assemblage of ladies — Mrs. Hunter and Mrs. Gowdy, only Mrs. Hunter soon left and was supplanted by Mrs. Björnson. The three were working (wool-work), talking, singing, and whistling in the same room as I was teaching all the time, and afforded me a good deal of amusement. Anna had drawn a box, which was not bad but wanted some changes, and then I got her to try to paint a house visible from the window, in water colours.

(The snow is over an inch deep now.) The evening mail I got was: A letter from Hamilton, with names of beetles, and letters from Strecker and Thos. Morgan, wanting to exchange shells. A note reached me from Charlton, saying that he couldn't open the schoolhouse for the meeting, and if I would do so, he would pay me. So I finished my essay, which was on Socialism, and having partaken of two eggs, bread, and coffee, went off to the schoolhouse.

The meeting , in fact, was a glorious success. Charlton was in the chair, and the entertainment was as follows: (1.) Harry Stockton on violin, accompanied by May Alexander on organ — good. (2.) Mrs. Ommaney read a long poem of great sadness about a man who went out west and took his wife, and they lived alone for years in a log cabin, but she pined silently for human society, and he grew restless, till one day, coming home tired, he found the cows had strayed and must be followed. He turned to her and scolded her for the first time in his life and told her she was no use to him. Next morning they did not kiss on parting, but she had put pansies into his lunch basket, and he grew remorseful and hurried home early to ask forgiveness. He found the place deserted, and a note on the table to say she was sorry she had not always been what

he wished, but she had tried hard, and would again, if he would forgive her for the past. Alas, the cows had strayed away again in spite of all she could do, but she had gone to follow them and would bring them back. Just then, raindrops fell, and there came on a terrible thunderstorm which lasted all night. He sought her through the woods and everywhere, and many times returned to his house, hoping to find her there. At last morning broke fine and, as he neared the house once more, he heard the cow-bell and saw the door ajar. He rushed in. She had returned — and died.

Mrs. Ommaney read it very well, and when she had finished, all people could do by way of applause was to scrape their feet a little on the floor, and I noticed tears in many eyes, both men and women. (3.) *The Hunter's Glee*, a quartette well sung, but people were too full of Mrs. Ommaney's reading that I think they paid little attention to it. (4.) Recitation. Miss Katie Aldridge — not badly done, but nothing remarkable. This young lady is going to join my botany class. She is one of the round-faced types. I have not spoken to her yet. (5.) Recitation. *A little girl's wishes*, by Mabel Conway — a very little girl who looked charming and recited wonderfully well, with excellent expression, so that it fairly 'brought down the house.' (6.) T.D.A.C. essay (short but not very sweet) on Socialism. I think people were interested. (7.) Quartette song.

After I got back, Vetter, Fraser, Samse and I were discussing the meeting in Vetter's room. Fraser is the railroad clerk, and I asked him about the D. & R. G. rates. He thinks I must have misunderstood something about the charges on that box of flowers I sent to New York last spring, and suggests that I may have been told '$1,50 to Pueblo' (as I certainly was) without meaning anything more than that the *scale* of charges so far was $1.50 per 100 pounds, the actual charge on my box being properly 55 cents. I am not sure whether he was telling the truth or not, but it sounds very plausible, and as I have referred to the matter in *A-1* (p. 408). I have written this morning to the Editor asking him to insert Fraser's explanation. I must look into this matter when I have time, and satisfy myself just how it is. Railway monopolies are bad enough, and he does not want to make them appear worse than they actually are. According to Fraser, the D. & R. G. charges will still be over nine times as heavy as those on other roads.

8:55 p.m. The snow turned into rain, and that on the ground has melted, but the whole day has been cold and wet. The poor ranchmen coming into town have had a rough time, though they affect to regard it as a joke. I have been writing letters, reading 'Thome', and only went out this afternoon during a lull in the weather to get my paints from the Gowdy's.

Really, the only satisfactory thing about today, so far as I am concerned, is the evening's mail, which is *Canad. Entom.* and nice letters from Coulter and Galloway. Yes, there is one other good thing. Some cabbages have come on the market, and I purchased one for five cents, and ate half of it for supper this evening. I am sure I was needing some green food. Respecting these two letters I got today, Coulter writes that he is much obliged for the honor of being elected on council of C.B.A., and he will do all he can. Galloway is the fungus 'boss' at the Dept. of Agriculture. He thanks me for some notes I sent for *Journal of Mycology* and hopes I will send more, and he joins the C.B.A. Then he finishes up: 'Will you have time to collect some fungi for us this summer? We should like to have a collection from your region, including specimens in quantity of all the parasitic species, and especially the Erysipheae, Ustilagineae, Uredineae, and Peronosporae. We have a small sum to expend in this work, and it you can help us we shall be obliged.' I cannot quite make out from this whether he wants to hire me to get fungi or not, but I must write and find out. He encloses some 'penalty envelopes' so that my letters and parcels will cost me nothing in postage.

Sunday, May 12th, 9:15 p.m. It has been fine today, so I have been out and about. In the morning I drew a new sheet of diagrams (leaves and flowers) for my botany classes, and then went for a stroll down by the creek. I saw a *Colias eurytheme intermedia*, but having no net I could not catch it. I found *Thermopsis montana* in flower, as well as some other things, but nothing very noteworthy.

When I got back, I wrote a letter to L. O. Howard of the Dept. of Agriculture, enclosing some specimens (coccid scales, etc.). Looking over the galls I have in keeping, I found a most lovely golden-bronze Hymenopterous (Chalcid) fly had emerged from some galls found on willows. It did not make the galls; they are Dipterous, but it is a parasite on the gall-maker. I went out to search for more or the galls, and found them, but I fear the flies have already emerged. I hope I shall get more; it is probably a new species.

The second time of going out I found some more flowers. Of things in flower today altogether, it agrees with your theory about the sequence of colours that all of them are yellow except a *Castilleja*, which is red. One, *Erysimum asperum* var. *arkansanum*, is new for Custer Co., and one or two others wait to be named. I also found a fungus new to me, apparently a *Coprinus* or allied thereto. It is a good deal like *C. micaceus*.

I got some mail tonight: (1.) *Insect Life*, April. It contains a letter from Miss Ormerud about the caterpillars in flour (*E. kuhniella*), (2.) A form from Cassino, publisher of *Naturalist's Directory*, to be filled in with name, address, objects of study, etc. (3.) Letter from C. F. Morrison. The poor fellow is only recovering from a very bad illness and is very shaky yet. He says he is not allowed to write, and only does so because he has escaped the doctors for a moment.

Samse came in here a while ago with a *Cosmopolitan* magazine in which an account of the 'Penitente Brothers', a sect of Mexicans in New Mexico and southern Colorado. They chastise themselves in the most fearful manner every year in Lent, and some even are crucified. It often kills them, and four young men died on the cross in southern Colorado in 1887! It makes one's blood run cold to think of it. What ghastly barbarity! Let us think of something else!

Here is our friend the moon looking down upon this letter; it is brilliant moonlight tonight. It is really very late and I ought to be going to bed. I sat up to write a letter to Morrison. Good-night, dear love.

May 13th, 9:40 p.m. Your delightful letter came just when I wanted it (and a day early; this is Monday). I had been feeling out of sorts and depressed, but now I am as jolly as can be and have even been singing to myself. So thank you, Annie!

I had supper very late, and the time has flown, so I can only tell of the news today, such as it is. I spent a long time puzzling out four plants I found on Sunday. I particularly wanted to name them, as I shall have to speak on them tomorrow at the botany class. I got them out all right, and they are *Pedicularis canadensis, Castilleja integra, Lithospermum angustifolium,* and *Ribes aureum.* The last three are new for Custer Co. The *Ribes* is not a bit like a currant, and it gave me more trouble than all the others put together. It is a pretty yellow-flowered shrub, frequently seen also in cultivation, but here wild.

At about one o'clock I was at the Gowdy's, and gave Anna her drawing lesson. She had done some more work since the last, but it was hurried and not atall up to what she can do. I got her to paint a flower — a *Thermopsis,* and she did it fairly well though she needed a lot of help. She is very quick at seeing the theory of things for a child, but she has but a poor idea of proportion and cannot get sufficient control over the muscles of her hand at present. After the lesson, I called at the Frere's to borrow a catalogue of artists' materials. Mrs. Frere showed me a rough sketch of a hand by Miss Bellaire; she has an admirable notion of drawing, and with practice might do very well.

This afternoon, later, I went out but found very little except a curious beetle new to me and some *Hyalina tabiatula* quite like the Middlesex ones. This evening's mail was: (1.) Your letter, of which hereafter. But I must now thank you for the photograph. It is not a very good one, but I like it very much of course. (2.) Letter from Mother. (3.) Letter from Hy. Prime, wanting to exchange shells. (4.) Letter from R.E.C. Stearns from Smithsonian Inst., returning some shells with names. They are new for Colorado. (4.) Letter from H. A. Pilsbry, joining C.B.A. and promising to publish our shell reports in *Nautilus.* (3.) Letter from A. E. Blount about C.B.A. (6.) *West American Scientist,* May. They have reprinted (p. 35) your remarks on colours of flowers from report of C.B.A. with your name attached.

May 14th, 8:10 p.m. The botany class is the only thing about today, but that has kept me busy most of the time. This morning I drew a new sheet of diagrams representing sections of gooseberry, *Ajuga* fruit, poppy capsule, moss theca, and a fungus sporangium. Then I prepared my notes for the lecture, the subject being 'Historical botany' (the history of botanical science), and then I examined a number of things under the microscope to see what would be good to exhibit. Altogether I was rather hurried, and when I got to the schoolhouse it was nearly two, and before I could put up the diagrams, several of the class had arrived.

I had ten altogether, which was very satisfactory: They included Mrs. Ommaney, Mrs. Frere. Mrs. Humphrey, Bertha Humphrey, Anna Gowdy, two Alexander girls, and I think Miss Aldrich, Miss McIlhenney (not spelled 'Macklehenry' as I had it), but I am not certain of the names of the last two — there are so many girls that I get them mixed up. Mrs. Charlton also came. I see I left her out of the list. Mrs. Charlton and Mrs. Ommaney each paid up their $1.00 at the end of the lesson, so I shall hope to see *them* every time, at any rate (though Mrs. C. is not sure whether she can always come).

I had my pot of flowers gathered on Sunday, and some of the class brought flowers. I therefore started in to expound the papilionaceous corolla and so on to other matters, especially pollen, which I exhibited under the microscope, and so the time went, and when I was ready to commence the 'Historical Botany' the hour was just about up, and I could only touch lightly upon it, leaving the most of that subject for next time. They all seemed to take a lively interest, and some asked questions, so I was quite encouraged.

After the lesson, Mrs. Frere asked me to come round to her house and look at a face she had painted, and I went, Mrs. Ommaney also

coming. The face was really very nice, quite the best thing she has done, and she may well be proud of it. She says she will recommence lessons in a few weeks, but I tell her she scarcely needs lessons now and had better get up a class where all those studying help one another. She paid me $1.75 for lessons given. We got to discussing Esoteric Buddhism (!) and kindred matters, and I suppose I was there over half an hour.

I had left my botany things at the schoolhouse and went to fetch them, and then returned home. I met Louis Howard, who had just come to town, and he apologised profusely about going without me the other day, so I did not abuse him much.

This evening's mail: (1.) Long letter from H. G. Smith, Jr., about C.B.A. (2.) Letter from H. K. Burrison. (3.) *Naturalist* for May. I should like to answer your letters now, but there are other things that must be written, and I shall not post this tomorrow anyway.

May 15th, 7:45 p.m. A windy day. Now it is blowing in great gusts, making everything shake. All day long the dust has been flying and I, being busy, made the state of the weather an excuse for not taking my daily walk.

I have been breeding some interesting insects from galls lately, and I spent most of this morning in examining and describing them. There were some little *Cecidomyia* gnats (allied to the famous Hessian fly) which I bred from galls on willow, and a saw-fly parasitic on these. A *Rhodites* of the spiny rose galls, and the little parasite from the willow gall mentioned the other day, and another parasite bred from a rose gall. For the first time in my life I tried to classify these minute Hymenoptera, and with a lens I made out their peculiarities and, to my satisfaction, made out the one from willow to be *Tomocera salicum, n. sp.* and the other one *Perilampus* (probably *P. hyalinus* Say). But I've a notion that it will be like Mrs. Chetelat's picture, and when *my* boss in these matters (Ashmead) comes to see the insects, he will not altogether confirm my views!

Nat. Sise.

Grandfather Peilampus out walking with his sprightly granddaughter, Miss Jamocara. (slightly magnified.)

I ought to have said that I gave Mrs. Chetelat her drawing lesson this morning, and we finished the river scene. It is not very good, but she is immensely proud of it and has bought a magnificent golden frame to put it in! The next thing she is going to do is a picture of the mountains.

This afternoon I had to write a long letter to J. G. Smith, Jr., and turn over to him the Treasury accounts of C.B.A. (he is now Treasurer, you know) and sent him $15.00, keeping the odd dollar or two for current expenses. The mail received this evening was a letter from Miss Eastwood of Denver, about C.B.A., and a sample copy of *Sports Afield*.

Now I really must answer your letter. Poor thing! In that storm at Sutton! I wish I could have appeared and held the umbrella for you! Yes, I think it was Orial Allen that DeKrafft reminds me of. I think the debating society will go all right now. It is certainly true that I should not have read Carlyle to the West Cliff-ites. I don't know how I should feel after killing someone, even if I did it in self-defence and was sure I had done right. I hope I never have to do such a thing; it would surely 'haunt' one, so to speak. It is very interesting, about the lunatics. I should not like to live in an asylum! The photograph, as I said, is not *very* good, but there is a bit of ex-

pression in it different from the other two I have, and I like it very much. It is a pretty process, too. I should like to take hold of the disengaged hand and make you put down the basket and come for a walk and a talk. I don't believe you would refuse me.

No, I certainly could not put my love for you into verse, but then you see, I am not a poet, and although I cannot even fancy a frame of mind in which one would write real love in verse, it is possible that those who are by nature poets may find it the easiest way of expressing themselves. But after all, who can *write* love atall? It is absurd. Would you believe anything about my love if you had nothing but written words to go by? I think not. That is why love letters ought never to be published. Lovers read 'between the lines,' and understand. But to the public, written love, prose, or poetry cannot be as it was to the lovers. Even speech fails. Is it not so, Annie?

I have handed the dollar over to C.B.A. You *shan't* pay the duty on anything you sent — what an idea! Properly, I ought to pay *you* the postage you spent on them, as they were for me. I have therefore paid the 25 cents to C.B.A. as your subscription paid ahead, for 1890. Am I not right?

I will go to church with you often! I like it when there is anything to hear, and the good *spirit* eclipses the often doubtful *letter*. Didn't I go to Haweis' every Sunday evening for a long time? Well! So you don't scoff at me for setting myself up as drawing master after all! I would give you a kiss for that (if you would take it). And thank you for offering to send copies, only please don't, as my one effort is to get them to draw from the real objects. Yes, I read that book, *Idle Thoughts of an Idle Fellow*, and thought it very clever. Of course, it is all nonsense, though, about love. The book is written in rather a cynical vein.

I think that is all, but it is a very nice letter, this last of yours, and I have been feeling happy ever since it came. I shall post this tomorrow, so good-bye till the next.

Your own Theo. Health. Good.

Do you remember my asking you about sending a telegram if ever you should fall seriously ill? You said it would not be right for me to come, even in such a case. But now you will not say no, will you? Will you promise me that a cable shall be sent at once if anything bad happens to you? I should always be ready to come to you in case of need.

May 16, 1899, 10:25 p.m.

Dear Annie,

It is late, but I am not sleepy, so will tell you what news there is. I posted a letter to you this morning, and some insects to Ashmead, and after breakfast settled down to some writing for *West American Scientist*. I am trying them with some C.B.A. work, but if they have it all misprinted they shall never have any more. This took all the morning, and this afternoon I went out.

I had not gone very far when the wind blew cold, and it sprinkled with rain, and I thought myself a duffer for coming out on such a day, and crouched down in a hollow place for shelter. Lo! I immediately saw right under my nose a rose-bush covered with fusiform galls quite new to me! I at once collected a whole boxful of them, well enough pleased with the find, and went on my way. I presently came to more rose-bushes and, on these, little leaf galls, almost certainly a new species of *Rhodites*, and of course a very good find.

I got lots more galls of one sort and another, and a fly (*Gonia exul*) new for Colorado, and some flowers, and returned home. A long time

I spent classifying and arranging my finds, and then went out again and got more (this time I found a *Potentilla anserina* in flower) and when I had done these, the mail had been sorted and I went down to see what there would be for me.

There was quite a lot, viz., (1.) Letter from Elwes; of this more later. (2.) Letter from E. H. Harn wanting to exchange shells. (3.) Letter from *Sports Afield* about C.B.A. They want to print our reports. (4.) *Punch* from Mother. (5.) *Bulletin* on potatoes from Agric. Experiment Station at Fort Collins. (6.) *Science Gossip, Zoölogist, Nature* (two of them), and cutting from S. London Press, from Carlie; of these later. It was nearly nine before I had supper, and later Vetter came in and talked, and that has made me late. Goodnight, Annie!

May 17th, 7:40 p.m. I must now be off to the Lit. & Sci. Society, as it is supposed to meet at 7:30.

11:15 p.m. It was only a business meeting, but of that tomorrow. I fear I have caught cold (P. S., I didn't.)

May 18th, 11:45 a.m. Well — of yesterday. It was a disagreeable day, snow in the morning and again in the afternoon, and cold. The first thing was Mrs. Chetelat's drawing lesson. She had the river scene in the frame with glass over it, and was immensely pleased. It is not so bad, after all. She was to paint the mountains next, but they were covered with clouds, and she couldn't wait, so I gave her a sea scene (Brett, in *Academy Guide*). It is a stormy sea, with a headland, on which a lighthouse. I made the headland red, for I put in some of the sky, headland, and sea, to show her how to get the colours, and so it will be a pretty picture if she does it well.

About lunch time I read *Science Gossip*. I see Mr. Horsley is already president of a Natural History Society at Woolwich! How the 'insect-selection' theory about flowers is being pulled to pieces! I think it was too readily taken for granted.

In the early afternoon I gave Anna Gowdy her drawing lesson, and made her draw a little view in Nova Scotia from the flat, to get her more used to being precise and drawing true lines. She progresses slowly. Mrs. Gowdy paid me for a dollar for the four lessons given so far. I went in to the Freres for a bit after I left the Gowdy's.

The mail that came was three letters on C.B.A. business, from Nash, Denis Gale, *Field and Farm*, and a *Pall Mall Budget*. Nash says he will be at West Cliff early in June. The evening was taken up with the meeting of Literary & Sci. Society. It was Sam Wright's turn to open the building and light up, but he did not come until after eight, so I had to do it. We had only a small meeting (seven present) which was very tedious, being devoted entirely to business, and it was very cold. The law about the opening of the house was abandoned, and I was instructed to do it always, and for this I am to get 25 cents a night. We are to meet at eight, and only fortnightly in future. Further, the meetings are to be devoted, in succession, to Science, Art and Literature, and Entertainment, and permanent committees were appointed to have charge of these branches. Charlton, Fraser, and T.D.A.C. constitute the science committee.

I was going to tell you about Elwes' letter. You remember my applying to the advertisement in *Entom.*, which was really Elwes'? Elwes says that he has already arranged with a collector, but would pay me for anything I got (15 to 25 cents each), especially if I went up through Utah to the Yellowstone Park and beyond. I may send him some things, but I have no idea of wandering over the country as he suggests unless it were for a fixed salary and with expenses paid. He argues that it would pay well, but I am not so sure. What do you think? On the other hand I can get a living here, and butterflies as well.

The cutting from South London Press Carlie sent was a report of the S.L.E.S., a whole column and very full. I see my *Carpocapsa* note was read, and also my paper on *Anthocharis*.

8:45 p.m. Not very much of a day for me. Most of has been spent working out a number of minute Hymenoptera bred from different galls. They are as perplexing as interesting. It looks like a waste of time to spend so long over them, but I think not, as it is very expedient to know something about them, and a knowledge of them is very important in economic entomology, which may mean bread and butter one of these days. Probably you could find some of these little creatures on the windows at Syon Lodge and see what lovely colours they have. If you like to send me any, I will get Ashmead to name them.

This evening I have received a letter from W. A. Marsh, who wants *Patula cooperi*, because he has 'but one specimen in my cabinet', (a state of affairs!). I also got a copy of *Field and Farm*. This is one of the papers that wants to publish the C.B.A. reports, and I see they have taken time by the forelock and announced that *Field and Farm* has become the official medium for the publication of the interesting reports of the Colorado Biological Society, beginning next week with one relating to the thistle insect. These articles are prepared by the most scientific men in Colorado and must necessarily be both entertaining and instructive — !! Of course this is entirely unauthorised, and the article on the 'thistle insect' is simply cut out of the sixth Report, a copy of which I sent them.

Sunday, May 19th, 7:50 p.m. At least we have had a real May day, bright, warm, and sunny. I had a most ridiculous adventure this morning, as depicted in the sketch.

There was a little Braconid (Hymenoptera) on the outside of the window, that I wanted, so I opened the window and sat with my legs inside (as they do when cleaning windows) while I captured the insects. But the window closed down, and I quite forgot there was a catch at about two feet from the bottom to keep the window a few inches open, and was not reminded of the fact until I heard a clink and found myself stuck fast! I could not reach the catch, and the window was

too low to let me draw my knees through and get out! So I rested on the old ladder that is on the roof just under my window, and pondered.

I got a stick that was within reach, and tried to push the catch back, but not successfully. At last, seeing Chetelat down in the road taking his horse to water, I called out and explained the situation. He was immensely amused, and he and Vetter came up to release me. Here, though, was another difficulty. The door was locked! My door has no latch and I have to lock it to keep it shut. However, Chetelat poked his head and arms in at the glass window (which is removable) above the door and with a stick managed to turn the key on the inside, and I was rescued! Of course, I could have escaped at any time by breaking the window-pane and so get at the catch, but I would not do that as it would cost about $2.00 to get a new pane.

I spent the morning working up some new gall insects which have emerged, and writing some letters. I have bred 18 species of gall insects in the last week or so, though some may only be the male and female of the same. This afternoon I went out for an insect-hunting ramble and got many things of interest, notably many species of bees.

May 20, 8 p.m. Another lovely day. I am now going round to call on Charlton, and will write when I get back.

In the morning, much time was taken up putting in papers, labeling the insects taken

yesterday, and writing a catalogue of them. Afterwards I made a diagram of a section of a Composite flower for my botany class. In the afternoon, Lees appeared. He waited for the train as he expected Campion, who did not arrive. The train, by the way, is altered as to time, and now comes in at 6:15 p.m. and does not run on Sundays. This last alteration I am glad of, as although I like to get my mail on Sundays, I think the Sunday train is a bad thing on the whole, and I should not like it atall if I were in the postoffice or working at the depot.

Lees was up here a long time. He showed me a sketch he had done, which was exceedingly nice. Regy and Brock and Mrs. Frere were also in town. This afternoon I went out for a ramble and found a few things new to me, but not much. It was rather windy and the bees were not on the wing to any great extent.

This evening I have been round to Charlton's, talking about the cliff-dwellers and various other matters. The mail tonight was a sample copy of *Oölogist's Exchange*, a little four-page paper, and an interesting paper from Shufeldt for C.B.A. library, on the bones of the ducks and allied birds, with many illustrations. I am beginning to want your next letter very badly, and shall 'just wilt' if it doesn't come tomorrow.

Tuesday, May 21st, 9 p.m. This is miserable! No letter, English mail not come. Well, it must come tomorrow. Today is botany-class day, and that has taken most of the time. In the morning I finished a diagram representing a flower head of a species of Composite, and some cherry flowers, and then I wrote up my notes for the lecture, and after that went out and down by the creek and got a big bunch of flowers — *Potentilla, Thermopsis, Oxytropis, Erysimum,* etc. The demonstration went off all right, but it was exceedingly hot and sultry, and that made us all rather tired, so that I am afraid I was rather dry, and the audience did not pay as good attention as they might.

In view of the mid-day heat of summer we have altered the hour to 3:30 p.m. There were seven present: Mrs. Ommaney, two Alexander girls, Anna Gowdy, Bertha Humphrey, Miss Mc-Ilhenny, and Kate Aldrich. I am getting to know them now. Perhaps K. Aldrich will be my best pupil. She brought many flowers today (which I explained in detail) and evidently means to do well. Miss McIlhenny looks very unpromising; she sits and listens with an inanimate look and gives no sign that she understands. Perhaps it is only on the surface, though, and she may be all right. I think teaching gives one a curious insight into character. One thinks of Charlotte Bronte's *Professor* and *Violette*.

This afternoon, Frere met me in the road, and he wants me to teach his children the three Rs and other things, in fact to take Miss Bellaire's place. I find Miss B. spells her name with two l's). Miss Bellaire has, I think, already left the Freres and gone to the Beddoes'. Frere told me that he liked her well enough but found her too ignorant, and when he discovered she was not able to teach fractions that was the last straw! So she departs. I fear she will not have so good a time with the Beddoes' by any means. The Frere children are nice enough and I have no objection to teaching them, but will see Frere about it again. It will be only for a time, as Frere has booked a governess for some time in June, I think he said.

After the botany class this afternoon, I was lazy and did little else but read a long paper in *Nature* by Prof. Bonney on the oldest known rocks and their probable mode of origin — very interesting indeed.

The mail received tonight is (1.) Letter from L. O. Howard, of Dept. of Agriculture, joining C.B.A. and sending names of some insects. (2.) Letter from H. W. Smith, Jr. (3.) Letter from *Sports Afield* about printing the C.B.A. reports.

May 22nd, 8:5 p.m. Letter has come! This morning was Mrs. Chetelat's drawing lesson. She had been working at the picture, but grew dissatisfied over the sea, and waited until I should come to show her how to do it. So we painted in some sea, and I made a barge with red sails. The picture ought to be finished this week. The rest of the morning I spent working up eight new gall insects which had emerged. One that pleases me best is the fly from the flat leaf-gall on rose. I shall call it *Rhodites rosaefoliae, n.sp.* This afternoon I went out and got an interesting *Chrysomela* and other things. I also wrote some letters. That is the record of today — not at all interesting. The mail this evening was your letter and letters from Carlie (a nice long one) and from Tutt (also a very nice letter).

Now your letter: Thanks for the extracts from *Mr. Isaacs*; they are very nice. They had the book up at the Cusacks' at one time but I never read it. That woman is just like you; I can't see any difference, essentially, and it is the only right kind of woman. Yes, I fear there are not many such, and still fewer ideal men. It is strange, that out of the thousands of people one meets, so few advance atall upon the average, which is itself nevertheless low.

But of loving — after all one does not love an ideal; neither, indeed does one love beauty, not really love. Love is the harmony of two souls, and is always good because it is the expression of the best that is in them. As Carlyle says, nothing absolutely base can love atall. The trouble with Mr. Isaacs was that he did not even know what love meant. We did once listen to 'Just a Song in the Twilight' together, at 5 Priory. Mother sang it. It is the memory of that time that has made it sacred to me.

Your account of the pigs is both amusing and interesting. It is curious their all stopping to listen at the same time, and it would be worth while to publish a note on it, say, in *Nature*. The peculiarity lies in their all knowing when to stop. Some signal must have been made by one of them, or something. It is quite a point in pig-psychology! I think perhaps I shall print it in a report of C.B.A. at some future time.

So the photograph looked at first like a stranger! Well, it is not a very good one, after all, but I don't think that we shall find ourselves really different when we meet. Yes, I remember the 'acting adjectives' at B. P. Fred shall have a photo, certainly. I enclose it now. The asylum chaplain reminds me of the chaplain at Middlesex Hospital, who was a most disagreeable man, cordially detested by everyone. I 'pologise, 'deed I do, and take it all back, re surprise. I'm glad you didn't 'drift' into writing murder stories, but I don't believe you ever would have done so; it is too preposterous. I didn't mean to be severe about Allinson. What you say is certainly all true, only of Allinson especially I should say that 'what is true is not new, and what is new is not true', although there may be much both of truth and originality about him! I don't give way to the temptation of eating poetry! (I don't get the chance, worse luck.) On principle, however, I rarely eat sweets, though (this is a secret) I am very fond of them.

Your voting for C.B.A. was at least as good as anyone else's. The result has been very satisfactory. (By the way, Tutt joins C.B.A. in his letter, received today.) Morrison is good for President, as he was the prime mover of the Colorado Ornithological Association. He is a good sort of fellow, and we can overlook any want of education. I think that *West American Scientist* must have come to you direct from Orcutt, as he has been sending sample copies to members of C.B.A., but I sent you one too.

In speaking of the medical uses of alcohol, perhaps its greatest it its power of extracting various 'essences' from plants; very many valuable medicines are made this way. Yes, I have no doubt I should be looked after very well indeed if really ill.

The 'King's Daughters' here is a society which looks after every case of illness with great care, not excluding even smallpox with all its risks, when no others will venture. It is one more thing that shows that the ladies are the only people here of any account. Did you ever hear of such an association in England where the members *worked* rather than *paid* to have it done, as seems to be the case with most charity organizations?

Yes, the cacti want almost no water atall; I daresay they could get enough moisture out of the damp English air! Thanks for your addition to Sutton flora. The *Carex* I do not know. Perhaps your puzzling Composite was *Hieracium pilosella*? The little Swanage flower is an *Erigeron, E. acre,* I think. We used to get it by the railway station at Chislehurst. The 'daisy' of this country is an *Erigeron.* I will return the *Carex* so that you may be able to get it named by someone else. I never did understand Carices, I am sorry to say. Thank you too, for the Culverhouse photo. It seems a pity to have cut down all those trees! The wood louse which curled itself up into a ball at Sutton was no doubt *Armadillo vulgaris.*

I shall post this tomorrow.

Your lover, Theo.
Health. very good.

Of the Sutton records, the cowslip is the most interesting. This used to grow near Mountfield in Sussex in *one* opening in a wood *only* so far as we knew, and I remember my delight as a child when I first saw them. *Potentilla anserina* we have here, and a var. of *Viola canina.*

May 25th, Sunday, 7 p.m.

Love,

Let me see. I posted a letter to you yesterday and have been gradually progressing towards sanity ever since. Last night, of course, there was the Literary Society. I resigned my secretaryship, and I think a young man named Will Thomson will be elected in my place. Thomson is Stewart's assistant in the blacksmith's shop. He only came here recently. We had the biggest meeting by a good deal than we have ever had. Seats ran short, and many stood, or perched in all sorts of extraordinary places. Here is the program:

Recitation: Doll Cassidy, Gracie Norton. Reading: Mrs., Chetelat, Music: May Cassidy and Fred Haskell. Recitations: Miss Bjerk (An Americanised Swedish school teacher), Mabel Conway, Mrs. Fowler (an oldish lady who doesn't *look* as if she could recite, but she did it remarkably well). Violin and organ duet: Harry Stockton and Ella Etzel.

The Debate: 'Affirmed, that immigrants be not allowed to vote until they have been here (in U. S.) twenty-one years.' Price Walters and Sam Wright took the affirmative. Beaumont and I had the negative. The affirmative spoke well but, I thought, illogically. Beaumont didn't make much of a speech. I was very much in favour of my own side, as you may suppose, and could support the negative with my whole heart. I think I made the best speech I have made before the Literary, or for that matter, anywhere.

The judges chosen were three Americans: L. Tomkins, the banker; DeBord and Schoolfield, and they gave for the affirmative as they were sure to do. (Chetelat was much exercised at this, and vehemently declared to them that he would see they got no 'Dutch votes' at election time!) A show of hands gave entirely for the negative, but not many voted.

At the end, much amusement was caused by Dr. Meyers, a very lively optician, a Frenchman now staying here. The good doctor could not get over what Price Walters and 'Meester President' (Sam Wright) had said on the affirmative, and was very vehement in his defence of the foreigners. Dr. Meyers is 71, but can still jump and talk as if he were 17. Altogether, we had a lively debate, and the people got quite excited about it.

It has been hot today. After breakfast, I went and swept out the schoolhouse, and after that called on Mrs. Humphrey and Mrs. Stockton. They wanted me to go down and talk to and cheer a consumptive young man called Chambers, who is at the hotel. But as I don't know him I feel rather diffident about it, and I don't suppose I could help him much. Afterwards I went

down and saw Mrs. Charlton and the Vances (found them getting breakfast ready). Mrs. Becker turned up while I was there.

I arranged with Mrs. Charlton that when she goes down to Cañon City tomorrow she will find out about the rates, etc., for me, and tell me when she comes back on Wednesday (probably). I think this is the best way. I expect my money from Mother will turn up this week, and if so I shall try to get away at once. I don't want to borrow if I can help it. The way things look, I don't suppose I can leave until next week, after all, at the earliest.

Now I must go and see after that church.

May 26th, 8:45 p.m. Church was very uninteresting last night, though there was a pretty good congregation. When I had lit up, our friend Miss Harsh appeared with two fine geraniums, raised by herself, to decorate the building. They were in tin cans and stood on the organ. I have never had the opportunity of talking to Miss H. after all, so we shall not know what she is like.

The sermon was on 'God's Love', a subject admitting of a good sermon, I should think,. But on this occasion I thought the preacher talked mostly nonsense. I said I would call on the parson sometime, and as I don't think I *will*, I walked up to Silver Cliff with him last night instead. He talked all the way up but said nothing interesting. I fear, taking all things into consideration, we must give him up as a 'bad job.' I don't think he has it in him to rouse any enthusiasm here or anywhere else, and without enthusiasm nothing can be done.

This morning I had many letters to write, but it was so gloriously fine that, obedient to your instructions, I went out for the whole morning. I took net, bottles and boxes, and walking near the creek I captured a great number of insects, some probably new species. Arriving at length at the Conway ranch, I called in, got a glass of water (I was so hot) and talked with Mrs. Conway and

Miss Lowther, who were in the midst of a rather heavy 'wash.'

Passing on, I collected more insects in the meadows beyond, and afterwards returned to the Conways and got some books I had lent them. Miss Lowther produced a great bundle of dried flowers, and I volunteered to name them. When I had finished, they were just about to have lunch, so I, being invited, had lunch with them, and did not get away until past one.

When I got back to town I found the mail was in and there was a letter from you, which was very nice. The other mail consisted of: (1.) Letter from Dr. Sterki. (2.) Letter from *Field and Farm* asking me to reply to a query: Is the Oleander poisonous? I have no idea whether it is or not, but never heard that it was. I can't imagine it is atall. (3.) Letter from Dr. Cooper, with some slugs. (4.) Postcard from Gude, Secretary of Practical Naturalists' Society. He says that society has ceased to exist. (5.) *Field and Farm*.

To answer your letter: That *was* annoying about not meeting Frederic at Waterloo. I never like meeting people; they very often don't turn up. It is kind of your aunt Kitty to invite us. Let's go and call on her, by all means! Yes, Fred is too serious, as also I think is Carlie. Life should be taken as if it were a pleasure. I am glad you heard Gladstone. I should have liked greatly to be there. The only time I ever saw him was once when he wandered down Wardour Street. When I get back you must tell me your ideas on 'protection', and I will try to convert you from any heresies!

Since you confessed that thought of yours about Louy and Bertie Dixon, I will myself admit that I have often thought that it would be a very good thing if Louy would love someone and be loved in return. I never thought of any particular young man in this connection, but I suppose she has an 'affinity' somewhere! (This is likewise in confidence, as I suppose if Louy were to hear it she would never speak to me again!)

This afternoon I have been writing letters. I think I will post this tonight, though it is so short. No, I cannot, for I have looked in my purse and find I have only three cents worth of stamps and it is too late to buy more at the postoffice. It's a pity. I didn't tell you that yesterday I was paid (by Sam Wright) $1.50 for lighting the church. I was glad of the money, as I hadn't a cent.

May 17th, about 7 a.m. I can get this off so as to go by this morning's coach, so will get a stamp and post it. I see Lacy just going to open the postoffice.

Yours lovingly, Theo.
Health, am very well.

May 28th, 1889, 10:25 p.m.

Dear Annie,

This has been a hot day, sunny in the morning and cloudy in the afternoon. One can scarcely believe that less than a week ago it snowed.

All the morning I was out by the creek insect-hunting, and with great success. I got ten male and a female *Colias eryphile* var. *autumnalis* in lovely condition, and a little blue butterfly (*Lycaena oro*). The flowers were also plentiful — *Astragalus hypoglottis* (an English plant), and a dwarf form of the common dandelion. We never see such glorious dandelions here as you have at Syon. Close to the creek, in a very exposed situation, I found a nest of Brewer's Blackbird (see 9th report of C.B.A.). I sent the whole thing — nest and eggs (six of them) to J. P. Norris of Philadelphia. I felt some qualms about robbing so mercilessly, but it is for scientific purposes.

I was half-boiled by the heat when I got home. I had lunch, examined my captures, wrote a little biography, read some *Nature*, dozed for a while, then wrote until the time for supper. There was a good mail for me this evening. After I had looked at it I went round and saw Frere about teaching. He seems to want me to begin next week. Mrs. Frere, I am sorry to hear, had been suffering from a bad headache the last three days. After this I went round to Charlton's to tell him about the letter I got from Shufeldt, and I stayed there some while. Charlton promises ro shoot me some birds for Shufeldt.

The mail received this evening is: (1.) Letters from Mother. (2.) Letter from Douglas, forwarding another $5.00 (at Mother's request). (3.) Postcard from W. H. Edwards: ' The *ridingsi* pupated today at 10 a.m. Best thing done for this year, as this species has given no end of trouble in other years, and always failed.' (4.) Letter from Shufeldt, who says the grebe reached him in good condition, and he is much interested in it. (5.) The *Ent. Mags.* (6.) Six reprints of variety paper in *Entom.* from West, Newman & Co.; I send you one. (7.) *Pall Mall Budget.*

May 24th, 8:10 p.m. Another hot day. Drawing lesson in morning to Mrs. Chetelat; the sea picture almost finished, and looks quite nice. It is decidedly better than this other one (the river scene).

After the lesson was over, I went for an insect hunt for an hour, and although I got but few insects, I was well pleased with the discovery of several plants of *Ranunculus sceleratus*, a plant that I found long ago (before you went to Isleworth) in the little lane leading towards Osterley Park, close to the gate of Syon, though a little more Brentford way.

At 1 p.m. a drawing lesson to Anna Gowdy; she is painting in oils, it being the wish of the parents, and I have given her a little country

scene — distant trees, meadowland, and an old house with a big tree by it. We laboured over the sky mostly today, and Anna did pretty well, though I fear greatly for what she may do when I am away, before the next lesson. During this lesson, I pondered somewhat over the exhibition of pictures I have long thought of, and came to the conclusion that I would get the Literary and Sci. Society to take it up.

Now there is a meeting of the Art and Literature division of the Society on June 14th, and the permanent committee on this matter is Mrs. Charlton, Miss Byington, and Sam Wright. So I went round to Mrs. Charlton's and expounded the idea. She was quite enthusiastic about it and said that she, for her part, was quite willing to have it as I proposed, viz., the pictures exhibited (at the schoolhouse of course) in the afternoon, and left on the walls till the evening when the subject of the meeting would be drawing and painting. *Only local* art to be admitted.

You will wonder how we shall ever get an exhibition of 'local art' here, but I believe we can do it! If course we must not refuse anything, however bad. Mrs. Charlton, while I was there, showed me a bracket of leaves, flowers, and fruit, which she had made entirely out of leather! Perhaps a waste of time, but it was admirably done, and the flowers were quite recognisable, even *Clematis jackmannii*! I never saw anything like it before — did you? It looks something like the Swiss carved woodwork from a distance. I next called on Miss Byington, and she was also very encouraging and promised her support in the matter. I have not seen Sam Wright, but he will not object, so we may regarded it as settled, that there is to be a picture exhibition on the 14th of June.

Later in the afternoon I classified my captures of the morning, and looked at my gall-boxes. More new flies have emerged; there seems to be no end of them! There are about 30 altogether.

The mail this evening is (1.) Letter from Nash, voting in favour of all the propositions submitted to council of C.B.A. (2.) Letter from *Field and Farm*. They want to 'edit' our reports according to their 'style.' I have written to say that if that is so they can have no reports. We cannot allow any 'editing' on any account! (2.) *Sports Afield* for May 23rd. In it is announced the result of C.B.A. election.

10:55 p.m. Have sat up writing C.B.A. letters. I went round to Charlton's for a few moments this evening. We talked of the prevalence of divorce in America. Charlton knew a woman in Missouri who had three divorced husbands and was living with a fourth, all in the same town! Here is a bit of news I think I forgot to relate. Grant Turner has gone to Rosita for good, and the *Courant* has been bought by some people there, and G. Turner (so I understand) retained as editor.

May 25th, at the Cox's, 9:20 p.m. Cox asked me to stay here at his house the night, as he was going away somewhere, so here I am. Mrs. Turner is here, so Mrs. Cox was not alone. They are arranging some clothes in the next room at the present moment.

This has been a field day for me, as I was out in the morning and early afternoon down by the creek and along it southward for some distance. I got an abundance of insects, especially Hymenoptera, and seven examples of a little 'skipper' butterfly I never saw before. They were mostly on the *Erysimum* flowers which are yellow, much like wallflower. On one plant of this was a lovely specimen of *Vanessa cardui*, and down went my net over it, and I on my knees — right into a clump of cacti! The *Vanessa* escaped, and I had to draw out the cactus spines with the forceps when I got home.

I found two kinds of willow galls new to me, and some nice little dragonflies and, among plants, *Polygonum bistorta* (which also grows in England) and an *Astragalus* that may be new, but I have sent it to Vasey, and he will know. After I came in it took me till evening to work up the

specimens caught, and they are by no means finished yet.

This evening's mail is: (1.) Long letter from W. H. Edwards, mostly about getting larvae of *Parnassias smintheus*, which he wants very much. He offers me Vol. I or Vol. II of *Butterflies of North America* with coloured plates and bound if I will get him these larvae. That is liberal! (2.) Letter from J. Morgan, who wants Colorado shells. (3.) *Field and Farm* of May 25th. On page 8 they have a list of officers and new members of C.B.A., and the front page is occupied by a large portrait of a horse, and my article on the thistle-bud fly, reprinted from 6th Report of C.B.A.

Sunday, May 26th, 9:10 p.m. We had breakfast late, and there were many things to wash up from the night before, and then I wasted some time looking at a copy of *Arkansas Ward*, and so it was about eleven before I got down there to my room. Then there were the Hymenoptera of yesterday's catching waiting to be put into papers, and this was quite a long job. I put them into square papers folded three-corner-wise, with the number (referring to my notes), name (if known), locality and date written in red ink on the outside, thus. Then I had my gall-insects to examine, a great lot to sort out under their different species, and five particularly interesting new ones.

Today two more new kinds came out, but I have not worked them up yet. This will make altogether 37 gall-insects bred. I shouldn't wonder it I get 50 before I finish! I must get Ashmead to help to get up an article about them.

That is about all I have done, except that I packed up a little lot of shells for J. Morgan, and went for a walk to get a colony of tent-caterpillars (*Clisiocampa*) which I had seen feeding on a *Ribes aureum* bush. I got them, and have them now in a muslin bag — the food plant being in water and the muslin bag tied over it so that the caterpillars cannot escape, so. This evening I went out after dark to get some beetles (*Lachnasterna*, a sort of cockchafer) for Hamilton if I could, but I found none, and only got a glow-worm of this country (*Pipastomena borealis*). This creature shines brightly, and I found I could intensify the light by squeezing it. I think it has to do with respiration and the supply of oxygen to the part, and the squeezing induces a sort of artificial parting.

The *Wet Mountain Tribune* of yesterday had an allusion to my window adventure, which I enclose. The public knows all about it by this time, else they might suppose from this paragraph that it was the *bug* that caught *me.* Lacy informed me that he would have treated the subject (owing to its importance?!) at quarter length, only Lacy, Jr. had hurt his hand and they could not get the printing done.

Monday, May 17th, 9:20 p.m. This *is* nice, getting your letter today, but I don't like your being ill on May 9th. I send my sympathetic love, though it is all over now. It is so late that perhaps I shall have to confine myself to the news, but I shall answer it tomorrow.

This morning I began a list of the known gall-making insects, and got so interested in it that I had no lunch, and never left off until nearly one, when it was absolutely necessary to give Anna Gowdy her drawing lesson. (Interruption — Vetter came in and talked about the American school system.) There are actually 131 species of gall-making Hymenoptera on oak in North America, which is more than in Europe by a great deal.

I found Anna had done but little to her picture, and that was not good, but I got her to work carefully on it today, and the result was eminently satisfactory. After this lesson I called on the Alexanders. McIlhenneys, Hunters, and Freres (it is spelled Freer, I find, not Frere) about the picture exhibition, and they all promised to exhibit. The McIhenneys are shortly off to Oklahoma, and the Alexanders to Del Norte (where Alexander has got a very good appointment), so I shall lose one of my botany pupils.

I found Mrs. Freer in, and better (she had been very seedy), and she began to talk about my teaching the children.. After discussing for a while as to methods, we arranged that I should come every morning except Saturdays and of course Sundays and give them two hours (nine to eleven), for which I should receive 50 cents each time, beginning tomorrow. This is quite nice for me, don't you think so? I expect I shall now be able to make a little more than bare expenses. Mrs. Cheletat's drawing lessons are to be changed to 2 p.m. (As I afterwards arranged) so as not to clash with the Freer lessons.

When I got back to my room, I spent the rest of the afternoon making two diagrams for my botany class, representing: Types of roots (2.) Potato plants showing tubers. The mail this evening, besides your letter, is (1.) *Truth.* Thank you; I have not read it yet. (2.) Letter from Mother, who likes the photographs much better than the former one. (3.) Two letters from Coulter. (4.) Letter, and a huge Sialid, from Miss Urquhart. This was a great surprise to me, and it was kind of her to send the insect, which is very interesting, and although sent in a match-box, came unbroken and perfect. She writes from Point Leir, near Quebec. It seems that she and Miss Blackmore are 'doing the sights' on their way east. They have been to Niagara, and as far as Quebec. It would just suit Carlie if he wants to come to America, Quebec 'being a quaint old town with houses close upon the water's edge, and from there the slope is a very broad terrace from which one gets an excessively fine view.' When I answer her letter I shall ask her to pay you a visit if she goes to London, and to ask you to show her Kew Gardens! Do you mind? It would give you Colorado from a point of view other than my own.

I don't know when Lees will be off, as the mine is taking him longer than he expected. (5.) Postcard from *Sports Afield* and four copies of the paper to send to council-members of C.B.A. (6.) Reprint of paper on *Arge galathea*, from W. H. Edwards.(7.) Bulletin on diseases of the vine, from Galloway of Dept. of Agriculture.

By the way, if Miss Urquhart calls on you, don't divulge how much of her private history you know! You see, Mrs. Cusack used to tell me everything, and I told it to you, but it's mostly 'private and confidential!' Dear me, it is 20 to eleven. Goodnight, dear Annie.

May 28th, 7:55 p.m. I found I had one more *Sports Afield* than I wanted. so I sent one to you. I have been rather doubtful about the wisdom of having our reports in a sporting paper like this, but the other members seem to wish it in default of something better. What do you think?

This morning was the first lesson-day at the Freers. There are three small girls to teach — Elsie, Maggie, and Mabel — really nice children so far as I can judge. The two elder (Elsie and Maggie) I gave some sums to do, while I tried to see what they knew. They seem to have gone too far without understanding properly all they had done. For instance, Maggie was doing division, and had quite forgotten the multiplication she did before. Elsie had 'finished' the Geography of the United States, but for all that she did not know what states bordered on Colorado.

After the lesson, I had to get some flowers for my botany class, and so I took the two girls down by the creek, and we all gathered as many flowers as we could carry — *Iris, Dodecatheon, Allium* (wild garlic), *Thermopsis*, and many others. I had some biscuits for lunch, and prepared my notes for the botany, and at three, went round to the schoolhouse. I expected to have a very small class, as Miss McIlhenny is busy packing, and Anna Gowdy with some preparations connected with 'Decoration Day', but the others turned up, viz., Mrs. Charlton, Mrs. Ommaney, two Alexander girls, Bertha Humphrey, and Miss Aldrich. I spoke of flowers and inflorescences and sundry other matters, and this took all the time, so that I had to leave the leaves, etc., for next time.

After the demonstration I called in at Mrs. Chetelat's to see how her picture was doing, and found that she had a lot of flowers from near Cañon City, which I examined, a cactus with red flowers [*Echinocereus triglochidiatus*. Ed.] being particularly interesting. It was getting late and she asked me to tea, which I did. Meanwhile the mail came, viz., (1.) A pleasant letter from L. O. Howard. (2.) Letter from C. R. Orcutt about C.B.A.

Now your letter: Please keep the Mrs. Cox photo and regard it as our common property, also the Cusack ones. Carlie *is* ridiculous about the buildings! I suppose I like my insects well enough, but it never entered my head to class them on the same level as friends! However, I suppose C. was only talking nonsense. I like your account of the Foxbourne evening; I can imagine it all so well. Poor Lances! I feel sorry for them; somehow they never seem to have fallen on their feet, so to speak.

Yes, you are quite right about my not being able to teach portrait painting. I told Mrs. Freer how the bones and muscles went, and helped her with the colours and the hair, but when she said she wanted to draw portraits of the children, although I encouraged her ambition, I declined to 'teach' her anything about it. I have not the least idea of drawing a portrait, though of course I can draw some sort of a face.

I must have been thinking of other things when I wrote of Emery Walker — of course it was *Editor*. I think Walker is a very good fellow, but by this time Carlie must know him better than ever I did. That *is* a *sell*, the *Punch* picture being Alice's. I never thought of there being *another* A. Manville Fenn! What sort of things does Alice paint in these days, flowers and birds?

I read a paper at the debate on alcohol. I admitted that it was a curse at present, but argued that it would become a blessing altogether later on, and that even now it was mainly an outlet for the natural foolishness of men which would be bound to express itself, alcohol or no alcohol.

About children and knives. It is queer that the Charley Cusacks go on the principle of letting children handle *anything* so that they may get used to it and learn to avoid its dangers. So one sees Mora and Stella with knives, scissors, needles, and I know not what! So far, no harm has come of it.

That is very good, that article about 'Faith.' About Fred and science, perhaps he is right to give it up as a means of livelihood. Personally I do not care a bit what a man goes in for provided it is *something*, and that seriously. Of course, many men have become most eminent in science while earning their livelihood another way, e.g., Sir John Lubbock. I am only sorry because I do not gather that Frederic *has* found any 'life work.' And of the writing, it may be serious or it may be simply a means of getting shillings and pence — that is, the *means* of doing *real* work but hardly more than a means.

A better instance of what I mean is the life of a clerk, say, At Klein's. Suppose I had devoted my life to the service of Klein, and risen to be head clerk. People would have said that I had done well, but after all, my life would have been *entirely* wasted. It is not necessary to the community that Klein should secure a big share of the profits of the flour business, and that is all it would amount to. In fact, when one comes to think of it, perhaps one-third or more of the occupations of the 'middle-classes' are at the bottom useless ones. I do not complain if anyone embarks on these enterprises, as things are, but I do say that they ought at all events only to be regarded as a *means*.

May 28th, 9:10 p.m. The little Freers' second lesson in the morning. When I got there at nine, the girls were out, having gone on an errand down to the Byingtons' and stopped to gather flowers. So it was nearly half past nine before they were back again and we settled down to lessons. Mrs. Freer was feeling quite ill again. She showed me a lot of medicines she habitually took, and I told her that she should leave off medicines altogether, for the present at any rate, and with that and a little more fresh air and exercise she ought to be all right. She says, though, that her heart is weak, and I fear this altitude is too much for her.

I gave Elsie and Maggie maps of Colorado to draw, and showed them how it was done, and also I set them some sums. Mabel, the little one, did sums and spelling and writing. She seems quite a bright child. They were all very attentive and as industrious as could be expected.

When I got back here, I started out again up to the Cox's to give Mrs. Cox a letter for her which Miss Urquhart enclosed in mine. This letter was a long one, and Mrs. Cox read most of it aloud to me. The poor girl seems to have had no end of trouble to find Miss Blackmore — going to Pueblo, then to Denver, and finally discovering her at Colorado Springs. But they got off all right at last. It is queer that she ends up (I forget the exact words), 'If you see Regy please give him the news about me, as this is the longest letter I have ever written!' One would suppose she might have written the news to Regy! I saw a *postcard* in her writing in the Cusacks' postoffice box!

I talked a good while with Mrs. Cox. She wants me to go up there at nights in a few days while Cox goes to Denver for as week. The reason she is scared is that two burglarious gentlemen endeavoured to break into the McIlhenny's the other night, and are still supposed to be somewhere round about.

It was about noon when I left Mrs. Cox's and went down by the creek insect-hunting. The most notable capture was a moth very like the ordinary English 'gamma' (*Plusius gamma*). The rest of the afternoon I worked at my gall-insects, having several new species to examine.

The mail this evening is not interesting: A letter from *Field and Farm* and a postcard from H. G. Smith, Jr. Cox gave me a *Punch* he took out to the Brocks (he went out there today) by mistake, as it was given him with the Brock and Cusack mail and had been put in the wrong box. This is the first mistake I have found the new postoffice people to make. On the whole they do very well. Mrs. Lacy seems rather a nice woman, and although I don't like Lacy's notions of conducting a paper, he is personally agreeable enough and all right so far as I am concerned. Tomorrow morning is the time to post this, so until the next, farewell.

With all love, your Theo.
Health. Am very well indeed.

May 30th, 1889. 10:7 p.m.

Love,

When I went round to the Freer's at lesson time this morning I found the children ready to go out, and Mrs. F. begged that they might be excused today and take a lesson on Saturday instead, as they wanted to go to the 'Decoration' ceremonies. Mrs. Freer was already feeling better, having taken no medicine since yesterday! I came back to my room and wrote a little of my gall-insect list, and then (it was about 10:20) thought that perhaps I had better go myself and see these ceremonies.

It is in this wise: The 'Grand Army of the Republicans' is an association formed of old soldiers of the Civil War, and others who, on this 'Decoration Day' always ceremoniously place wreaths on the graves of departed soldiers, and make speeches and so on. Now of course there was never any fighting here, but there are many old soldiers, (Interruption. Samse came in to talk about nothing in particular.) and three have died and are up at the Silver Cliff Cemetery. I was rather late, and the cemetery is about half a mile south of Silver Cliff — over a mile from here, and uphill, and it was very hot, so that walking fast all the way I was rather heated when I got there.

There was a great assemblage of buggies hitched up to the fence of the cemetery, and at one point I saw a crowd of perhaps 200 or 300 people, whither I directed my steps. They were standing to form a hollow square in which were three graves of the simplest kind, mere mounds of earth with little flags paced on them for this occasion, and a 'monument', being a very plain, four-sided wooden structure painted white (but the top left rough) and inscribed, OUR UNKNOWN DEAD, and also surmounted by a little flag. At one side was a man in uniform bearing

a large edition of the Stars and Stripes, a regular army flag, and on two of the sides were soldiers in the blue uniform of the American Army, presumably old soldiers who had donned their uniforms, though some were quite too young. Behind the graves was an organ and a choir, and on the side opposite, a row of little girls dressed in white, holding wreaths, each representing one of the states in the Union. Altogether it was a very pretty sight, and I was glad I had not missed it.

When I got there they were singing a hymn — 'Nearer, my God, to Thee' I think it was, after which followed the dedication of the 'monument' by the mayor of Silver Cliff.

The Girls

Then the 'Speaker of the Day' was introduced: 'General' J. T. McNeeley. He made a pretty good speech extolling the deeds of the soldiers in the war, and spoke fluently and distinctly — only the sublime suddenly became transformed into the ridiculous at the end, when he finished up, 'and when the last patriot of them all should die (I quote the words approximately), I would raise to him a monument reaching to the skies, and on that monument I would plant the American flag and inscribe upon its pure white stripes these lines — (long pause) — Well! I've forgotten the lines completely!' Then, aside to the audience, 'Do you remember the lines?' The lines were suggested, and he finished up.

The monument

Fortunately, people were taking the whole thing seriously, so there was no laughter, only a smile all round. Then three volleys were fired over the graves, after which followed a hymn, and then the benediction: 'The Grace of our Lord Jesus Christ', etc. (the wording slightly different from our version) and the proceedings closed. Of course, from some points of view the thing might seem absurd, but the sentiment underlying it is a good one, and I, for one, was altogether pleased.

When the crowd broke up, Mrs. Aldrich came up to me and I talked to her and was introduced to her husband. I am to go to their house (it is about 2½ miles south of West Cliff), to lunch on Saturday. I was a good deal overpowered with the heat by the time I got back, and lay down for a while. Afterwards I finished my list of gall-insects and examined some species recently emerged from galls, and then it was supper time and the mail came in, bringing me only a *Pall Mall Budget* and sample copy of *American Rural Home*. In *P.M.B.* I read, 'Mrs. Lillian Morris has in the press an important poem which Miss Alice Havers has illustrated.'

This evening I was afflicted with a bad toothache which made me squirm. I can generally cure toothache with oil of cloves, but this one jumped from one tooth to the other and *would* not be controlled though I half choked from get-

ting oil of cloves down my throat! But it is all right now.

May 31st, 5:15 p.m. I must write a little now, as I shall be at the meeting of Lit. & Sci. Soc'y tonight.

The first thing in the morning was to get things for breakfast. I was out of provisions and I was extravagant enough to *buy* a loaf of nice white bread at Kettle & Walters! Going into the postoffice, Lacy called out to me and gave me a large registered book that came last night. It proved to be Packard's *Cave Fauna of North America* (156 pages and 27 plates), a grand work just issued by the National Academy of Sciences, giving a full account of all the strange creatures found in caves in America, and also a list of the cave animals of Europe and other parts of the world. I presume it is for the C.B.A. library, and it was kind of Packard to have it sent.

Nine to eleven was the little Freers' lesson. Mabel was worried with toothache and was restless, but the other two did well, and I started Elsie on fractions. Afterwards, I took the Packard book round to show Charlton, and at the same time went over his smelting works.

They are smelting ore down there just now. It was very interesting. The ore, already ground fine, is put in a revolving cylinder of great size, down which it gradually sifts to the furnace, which is kept at about 3000 Centigrade! (Pretty warm, that!) The ore becomes molten, and the copper, silver, and gold unite and, being heaviest, fall to the bottom.

There are two outlets; one you see in the diagram lets out the worthless slag, and the one on the other side gives the metal, being at a lower level. This last is called the 'matt', and has to be sent to Denver to be purified and have the metals separated. Charlton has to boss the thing day and night, and so cannot come to the Lit. & Sci. Soc'y meeting this evening.

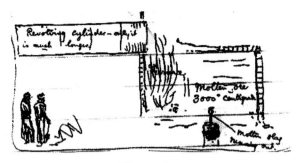

The smelter

This afternoon I have been writing a long letter to L. O. Howard, but was interrupted by Wheatley, who came to take a drawing lesson! I gave him one accordingly and he has given me money to get him some paints, and proposes to do the thing systematically in future.

6:35 p.m. Hurrah! My love, such a letter from R. Douglas Powell. — will quote it later.

9:30 p.m. We had a nice little meeting. Fraser gave a very interesting discourse on the election telegraph. I exhibited *Rhodites rosaefoliae, n. sp.* There are some letters I must answer tonight, so I think I shall have to put off writing about today's very important mail until tomorrow.

June 1st, 9:30 p.m. Quite an exciting day. Lesson to the little Freers in the morning of course. They did very well, and Elsie is getting to understand the addition of fractions. Then, at 20 to twelve, I started out to the Aldrich (not 'Aldridge' — like most of these names, I had the spelling wrong) ranch. It is almost 2½ miles south of West Cliff. I had never been that way before. The last half mile I rode with an old fellow in a waggon, who overtook me. I don't know who he was.

The Aldriches, who always address me as 'Professor' were very kind and hospitable and showed me their pictures, flowers, etc. Among Mrs. A.'s flowers was a new variety of *Lilium philadelphicum* which Mrs. A. proposes to call var. *pulchrum* (at my suggestion). It is a tiger-lily, only pale orange and without any spots. Aldrich showed me a magnificent specimen of native leaf-gold, as a specimen far finer than anything

of the kind I ever saw or heard of. The Aldriches have a nice little house close to Grape Creek, and a good ranch. Aldrich took me over the ranch and showed me with great pride his fish pond, which is a large spring, and has in it hundreds of the eastern species of trout, the progeny of a few little ones he put in a short time ago (that is, a few years ago). Now he can catch all that he wants, and they cost nothing to keep.

I also went out with him in the 'sulky' (a two-wheeled vehicle) after watercress, which has been planted in a damp spot and grows profusely. He told me I could always come and get all I wanted, an offer of which I shall certainly avail myself. I stayed all the afternoon and talked a great deal to Mr. & Mrs. A. and found them exceedingly pleasant and companionable people. Aldrich was one of the very earliest settlers in this valley.

When evening came, the Aldriches had to meet some friends who were coming on the train, and I drove to town in the sulky while Mrs. A. took the buggy, the two sufficing to hold the friends for the return journey.

Mrs. Cusack came home from Colorado Springs by this evening's train and is at the Cox's now. Cox invited me to supper, so I went up with Mrs. C. and carried her bag. She had a lot to say about Colorado Springs, but was glad to be back. For one thing, she had found an Englishman who wanted me to collect seeds for him, but she could not tell me much about it without looking up a paper on which she had his name.

I got down here again after supper at the Cox's just before the mail closed, and got: (1.) Letter from Ashmead with names of Hymenoptera. (2.) Postcard from J. B. Ellis with names of fungi. (3.) 'The osteology of *Amia calva*' (a fish) by Shufeldt, 94 pages and 14 plates, for C.B.A. library. Now I must not write much more tonight, but I must quote from Uncle Douglas' letter (the underlining is mine).

62 Wimpole St. W.,
May 12th, 1889

My dear Theo,

When you rather broke down in health and I carefully overhauled you, I found evidence of incipient but I thought decidedly threatening disease at the apex of one lung. Under the splendid climatic conditions of Colorado you seem to have made a good recovery. Now I do not hesitate to say that on health grounds you will be wise to remain longer there and, if you can find or make an opening, to make it your home. In settling down in this material world the two considerations are to live and to make a living. You can do neither without health. You are under excellent health conditions out there. Do you see any prospect of making a living? I don't mean necessarily of becoming a sleek, wealthy gourmanding alderman, but of making both ends meet and a little margin such as to maintain a wife and possible family. I have never said that you could not live in England atall. I don't think you would maintain your health in London, nor do I see how you could live, that is, make a living, in the country. [Here comes recommendation to get a doctor's degree and practice medicine or get a professorship in comparative anatomy] . I think you have every reason to feel encouraged about your health and about your increasing reputation for good observations on natural history subjects. What you now want is some appointment or work which will bring an income and still leave you a margin of time for your favourite study. Write and tell me what you think, and speak as freely as you can. Your affectionate uncle, R. Douglas Powell

Now, is that not satisfactory, Annie? What do you think of it?

Sunday, June 2nd, 8:30 p.m. Having taken my holiday yesterday, I had to busy myself today and have not even had my usual walk. All the morning I was writing to Ashmead and packing up Hymenoptera for him, as he needs them at once to include in his Catalogue of the Hymenoptera of Colorado. In the afternoon I also wrote, and read a little 'Thome' in preparation for the next botany class. The postoffice has departed from this building and gone over to the other side of the road where Lacy has built a place next to Falkenberg's. I shall post this tomorrow, as I want you to get the news of Friday's mail soon, By the way, I hope you did not send that MS book on Mollusca, because it has never come, but if you still have it at Syon it might be sent on, and I will run any risks there may be.

I have yet to tell you about Friday's mail, which was as follows: (1.) Letter from Uncle Douglas, as given above. I am very pleased, because he evidently thinks I *can* live in England, though not well in London. In the face of his very plainly expressed opinion, I don't see how my family can raise objections to my return, though indeed I cannot help it if they do.

(2.) Letter from Step, enclosing postoffice order which I changed for $9.74, for the two articles I sent him a while ago. I feel quite wealthy! I don't know quite how much I have up to date, as I have not reckoned up last month's accounts. (3.) Letter from Galloway, the fungus man at the Dept. of Agric., who says that if we can arrange on a price he will be perfectly willing to purchase on behalf of the Department 'whatever fungi you may collect.' That is very satisfactory, as I know I can get him a lot of things. This may be the beginning of more paid governmental work. He also undertakes to make descriptions of two species I sent in the last letter, covering two large pages!

(4.) Letter from Morrison about C.B.A. He is much better now, and walked about 12 miles the day before writing. (4.) Letter from W. H. Edwards, about *Colias*. (5.) Letter from Dr. C. H. Horn, with names of some beetles. (7.) Letter from L. O. Howard, in answer to one of mine.

(8.) Long letter from Geo. Roberts of Lofthouse, Yorks. (9.) Letter from C. H. Merriam about C.B.A., and enclosing a little pamphlet on measuring and skinning small mammals. Merriam votes against Norris as Recorder and Referee for Geology for C.B.A. as he says he doesn't think him competent to name 'birds' eggs.' I am surprised at this, but no doubt Merriam knows. But Norris will be elected.

The additions to Fauna and Flora for May are not many, viz., Colorado: Mollusca, 3, and 3 vars.; Coleoptera, 6; Diptera, 3; Homoptera, 1; Moths, 6, and 1 var.; Butterflies, 1 var.; Phaenogamia, 1; fungi, 2. Middlesex: Coleoptera, 1; Diptera, 1.

When I was at the Aldriches, I found that poem read by Mrs. Ommaney at the meeting (in a book). It is called 'The First Settlers' Story', by W. Carlton.

I have just reckoned up my cash account for May; the 'budget' has been more moderate this month. Average daily expenditure, 29 ½ cents (10 cents less than in April). Yet the balance is only $1.42. (Received, $10.60, paid, $9.18.) But I was not so badly off as this looks, for Mrs. Chetelat has yet to pay me for her drawing lessons, and money is owing for Freer's lessons and for botany class. Besides, I have just received the money from Step, so am really quite wealthy.

I hoped to have a letter for Frederick to send with this, but as I anticipate it tomorrow, I am afraid it must wait until the next.

I wonder how you are feeling just now. I am quite exuberant with hope and have a tendency to build castles in the air. I wonder how long it will last! But really, in sober fact, things seem to be looking up.

Yours with everlasting love,
Theo. - Health. Excellent.

June 3ʳᵈ, 1889, 9:15 p.m.

Dear Annie,

At the Cox's tonight, and have promised to come here each night this week, as Cox has gone to Denver. Mrs. Cusack is here. Freers' lesson as usual this morning. Poor little Mabel was suffering so from toothache that she could not do anything, but I took Elsie and Maggie to Geography, Arithmetic, and Reading. (Mrs. Cusack sends her love to you.) Elsie read to me part of 'What the Moon Saw.' I think it is by Hans Anderson, though the 'Reader' in which I found it does not say. Do you know this? It is very pretty.

After the lessons, I took Elsie and Maggie down to the smelter and, afterwards, down by the waterworks, where I got specimens of a fungus, *Ustilago longissima* (I think it is found on Barnes Common) for Galloway. There was scarcely time to get back to my room and put away specimens attained, before I had to go round and give Anna Gowdy her drawing lesson, and then after that I called on Mrs. Stockton and spent a long time talking botany with her and looking at some flowers she has. Writing, etc., occupied the rest of the time till supper.

The mail this evening was: (1.) Letter from Hamilton, with names of beetles. (2.) Letter from Norris, which quite bears out Merriam's opinion of his ignorance on the subject of eggs. I sent him a nest and eggs of *Scolecophagus cyanocephalus* and gave him the proper name, and now he had somehow got hold of this absurd idea that they belong to *Cyanocephalus cyanocephalus*, a totally different bird, and writes to say that they are extraordinary, and differ much from the usual form — as well they might! (3.) Letter from Marsh, a shell man, and a box of shells. (4.) Adv't. of various books in from Webster. One thing is naphthaline, which I want, so have written him tonight for some. He calls it 'cryst. alba.' (5.) A paper on anatomical museums by Shufeldt for C.B.A. library. It looks interesting but I have not had time to read it. (6.) *Custer Courant*, from Rosita, where it has now moved. It contains a notice about my botany classes that I gave him ages ago for the paper when in West Cliff.

June 4th, 9:25 p.m. (Tuesday). I write at the Cox's, being up here for the night again as arranged. I am quite despondent this evening, for the English mail (with your letter) which I quite expected, has not come. It is foolish of me to be so disappointed, I suppose, for it will surely come tomorrow, but I am an impatient creature, as you know.

The little Freers were very good at their lessons this morning, and Mabel was all right again, and to her great pride managed to multiply a whole string of figures by seven and get the sum right. I took Elsie and Maggie on the geography of Europe and told them some of the history — about the French Revolution, Napoleon I, the Franco-Prussian War, and the war between Turkey and Russia. They were interested, and it will make the dry outlines of the map live for them. They also did other things — spelling, etc.

Between the lesson and three p.m. I was preparing for the botany class, writing my MS and drawing a diagram of 'parenchyma' and 'prosenchyma.' The botany demonstration today was mostly about leaves. I was very short of specimens, as I had had no time to get enough myself, and the others brought hardly anything. Mrs. Cusack came down, and I had seven altogether, the others being Mrs. Aldrich, Katie Aldrich, Mrs. Ommaney, one Alexander girl, Bertha Humphrey, and Anna Gowdy.

After the demonstration I wasted about an hour and a half going round town with Mrs. Cusack, talking to her and assisting (?) her to make a number of purchases. I came up here for supper at seven this evening. It is demoralising, as I get no work done in the evenings.

June 5th, 9:30 p.m. At the Cox's. Your letter has come! As for today, it has been warm and I have done much as usual: Freers' lessons in the morning, and after that mostly writing, sending some galls to the British Museum (Nat. Hist.). These are the first things I have sent them, and more especially writing an article for Step on the 'Decoration Day' celebration. By the way, I see in *Silver Cliff Rustler* that the monument was not cut off neatly at the top because it was supposed to represent a 'broken column.'

Besides your letter, there has been another event today, namely the appearance of Nash of Pueblo. He is a shorthand writer to the District Court (Grand Jury) which is sitting here just now, and will be here for a week. Of course he is also an entomologist and a member of Council of C.B.A. He came up to my room and we talked for some time. He is a young man, nice but not remarkable in appearance, and I was well-pleased to see him, for he is the first entomologist I have seen face to face in America. I shall see more of him, and we hope to go out bug-catching together. The only drawback seems to be that he is a collector rather than a scientific man.

The mail this evening was: (1.) Long and very pleasant letter from Thorell, the great spider authority, about spiders which Packard took from me. Thorell is in Italy now. (2.) Letter from Prime, a shell man. (3.) Letter from Dr. John Hamilton, with names of beetles. (4.) Postcard from W. H. Edwards, with names of two butterflies I sent him. (5.) *The Microscope*, sample copy.

It is late, but I think I must answer your letter. I am glad Paris seems to have done Louy good. I don't know why Mrs. Cusack puts drapery round her neck for the photographs; I don't think there is any tangible reason for it. You were right not to send the notebook, but I think I will risk it. I am paying a little attention to the snails now, and feel so lost without my notes. How would it be to *register* it? That could be done.

Yes, I think I quite agree with you about God and creation. Devil *may* be only *not-God* and darkness is not-light, and cold not-heat; he need not have any real existence, I should say. A *reductio ad absurdum* of Mr. Archer's views about matter is that if, for instance, I want my dinner, it avails nothing to say that the dinner *is not*, and only appears, and that my physical need of fuel is only an *apparent* one. Practically, apparent things are real. There is no other real for me. I neither know or care whether things are real in the abstract, only I cannot conceive of their being so. It is just in the same way that matter if it lost its properties would be annihilated, as matter is only known *by* its properties.

If we could reduce all things to *absolute* cold (which would be at 300-and-something degrees below zero, I believe) they would cease to exist — this is allowed by most chemists. Theoretically, they might still exist, but they could have no properties, and evidence of their existence could not be discovered. Theoretically, the world may be full of such property-less bodies! But it is an absurd idea about on a par with the 'fourth dimension' someone wrote a book about. Of course, 'spirit' — the consciousness, is intensely real, and Kant was perfectly right in saying it is the only thing we *know* to be real, only it is nonsense to talk about it, as it is a matter that cannot affect us and we cannot ascertain anything about. It is a theory without facts.

'Trusts' are corporations of capitalists formed to keep up the price of goods. They are organised 'rings.'

I must go to bed now, but more another day in answer to yours before I post this.

June 6th, 19 p.m. No time to write now. Evening all taken up going over butterflies wih Nash. Must go to Cox's.

June 7th, 12:55 p.m. Just discovered that my statement of cash account for May was wrong. I had $7.97 in hand at end of month. I mention this now I think of it.

1:55 p.m. There is not much time for writing now, but I shall be busy with Nash this evening, and so had better tell you the news, such as it is is now.

Of yesterday: Freers' lesson in morning, and then, soon after I got back to my room, Nash called and left me a paper on Colorado butterflies by one Reakirt, published in 1866. I had not seen it before and found it very interesting. Taking extracts from this, and doing other writing, took me practically all the afternoon.

Lees appeared and showed me a letter he had just received from Payn to say that he was ill in bed, and *must* have $250 or $300 before or on June 28th. (Don't tell this to anyone.) Lees and I talked it over and ended by sending a cable on the subject to his (Payn's) people, telling them what he said, and leaving them to do as they pleased.

The mail I got was (1.) Letter from Janson saying that he quite agrees with all my proposals and will sell any insects I send him. (2.) Postcard from Stanley of Margate, wanting shells. He is a little man who was (I think) a tax-collector when I lived in Margate and at that time cared only for coins. He says, 'Your name also is not unknown to me locally, as I believe a relative used to be a resident in our town.' (!!!) (3). *Journal of Conchology*.

Lees came up to the Cox's with me, and afterwards I came down here again and spent some hours going over the Colorado butterflies with Nash, but we did not do half of them. Today I woke with a bad cold, caught I know not how, so I feel both foolish and uncomfortable. The little Freers had their lesson this morning, of course. I taught them a little human anatomy and physiology, for one thing. I must go up this afternoon and examine Mrs. Cusack's Colorado Springs flowers. I wish Cox would come back and leave me free again.

Saturday, June 8th, 10:30 p.m. After I wrote yesterday I went up to the Cox's and examined a lot of flowers Mrs. Cusack had brought from Colorado Springs, some of them being quite interesting. She also had four snails and a moth. In the evening I came down here and finished the work I had to do with Nash at the Colorado butterflies and then went back to the Cox's for the night.

Today I have done very little. I am sorry to say, mostly writing up records and so on, and this afternoon a little painting. Nash has been here again this evening, this time giving me localities for a number of birds; he knows as much about birds as butterflies. I have not gone to the Cox's tonight, as Cox is *supposed* to have come home (I don't know whether he did; the train was three hours late), and Regy is up there.

Chamberlain was in town today and gave me a plant (species of Umbelliferae) which he said had probably poisoned five cattle up near him, four of them being his own. At all events, they had eaten of the plant, and then died, and the plant is quite likely to be poisonous [probably this was *Cicuta*. Ed.]

I was reading today about those floods in Pennsylvania. What a fearful catastrophe! [This was the great Johnstown flood of May 31, 1889. Ed.]

Sunday, June 9th, 9:35 p.m. Fortunately, Cox did get back last night, so I am free again. It has been a miserable sort of day today, with rain in the afternoon and even a little snow this evening. I have been in, writing letters, until this evening, feeling in need of a change, I went round to Charlton's and remained to supper. Later the Charlton's went to church, and I came back here but had not got settled before Nash appeared. He had been out on a picnic with some of the legal lights, and brought in some flowers and butterflies to show me. One of the latter is new to me and to him. It is a *Melitoca*.

My Freer children are supposed to be in Cañon City, a least they were going there when last I saw them, not to return till Monday evening, but I hear they were all at Sunday School today, so I shall have to go and teach them tomorrow as usual, I suppose. I am rather agitated about the picture show on Friday, as I shall have to do most or all the work in connection with it. I hear Mrs. Ommaney has been ill and has gone down to Cañon City for a time, so there goes the best of my botany pupils.

Mrs. Hunter said something to Mrs. Cox about asking me to teach her boys. These boys are the worst boys in town and will need frequent chastisement, but I will undertake it if asked. It would be a blessing to the community to have them out of the way for two hours every day.

More about your letter: Of course, lynching is but a poor makeshift, and it were always better to have cool impartial judgment. But in the case of an atrocious murder, I would rather see the community indignant to the point of lynching the culprit than to be indifferent enough to let him go.

You say, 'It is rather important to me what I make' (as you may suppose!), and I like you to know about it. I *should* like to make more, but am doing better than before. I have almost made up my mind to *buy* bread and have Sam Lee do my washing in future. It is curious that men should hate cooking and washing clothes so much, and I admit I am no exception. How do you account for it?

I have not yet seen 'A plea for Collective Homes' in *P.M.B.*, but it would hardly have reached me yet, anyhow.

I have not that great objection to flogging that some have, yet on the whole I think I would not do it. In a minor way, I approve of caning boys at school, but it should be done carefully, and seriously, without anger.

No, I never heard of any relatives at Winchester. I thought Wharton Robinson had long ago given up that school at Margate. Of course I will keep records of the weather, and have commenced it, on the sixth. It will certainly be interesting. Unfortunately I have no thermometer.

I shall post this tomorrow, but it is a poor sort of letter. Somehow this week I have been feeling stupid or incapable, though except for a cold I am exceedingly well. I have not been out as much as I could have wished.

Lovingly, your own Theo.

Monday, June 10th, 9:45 p.m.

Love,

Today has profited but little. Your letter was posted this morning, and I half hoped that one from you might come this evening, but the English mail is still on the way, so all I got this evening was a letter from Shufeldt (and two numbers of *Forest and Stream* with an interesting paper of his on Carnivora, for C.B.A.; H. G. Smith, Jr. (about C.B.A.). He and Gale object to Morrison and Norris bossing the bird department of C.B.A. and don't want our reports to appear in *Ornith. & Oöl.* (I shall leave the bird men to fight it out themselves), and T. Morgan (a ridiculous small man whose knowledge of grammar is slight. I also got four copies of the June *Nautilus*, one of which I will send you. It has a report of mine on Mollusca of Colorado.

When I went round to the Freer's this morning I found that Elsie and Maggie were ill with sore throats (cause unknown), and Elsie had a headache, so I let them off their lessons and they must make it up by working on Saturday. In a fortnight the governess Freer spoke of will come. It appears that it is a relation of Mrs. Freer who is hard-up and wants to pay for her board by teaching, and so the children will be turned over to her. She will stay two months, and then I shall have them again. Perhaps this is rather good for me, as I may get out and collect specimens, both for science, and duplicates to be sold by Janson. I should like to go on a little tour.

The rest of the morning I spent looking over some *Pall Mall*s for articles on art, and then I took them round to Mrs. Charlton and we made up a programme for Friday night, and I am to read Morris' *Aims of Art*, though I fear they will not understand it.

This afternoon, when engaged on a diagram of a 'section of a palm stem showing fibrovascular bundles' for the botany class, I suddenly remembered that I had forgotten Anna Gowdy's drawing lesson. I went round, and found her at home, so gave her the lesson, or rather, finished up her picture so that it might be ready for the exhibition. She is going to take lessons only on Mondays in future.

Nash goes away tomorrow, which I am rather sorry for I should have liked to have seen more of him. This has been quite a cold day, and wet. The snow was visible on the ground as low down as the Cusacks' early this morning. Lees called in during the day, having just come back from a journey to Birmingham which, notwithstanding its name, is a 'town' of only a few houses somewhere down on the Huerfano.

June 11th, 10:13 p.m. The children were ill again today with the same complaint, a sort of sore throat, which I gather they might have caught from Lana, the hired girl. (They always say 'hired girls' out here, never 'servant.') So they did no lessons though I set them some work to learn for tomorrow. Mrs. Freer is quite out of sorts again. I fear her heart is not in very good condition. I came back to my room and drew a diagram of the hair of a stinging-nettle (from 'Thome') and later on went out by the creek, where I got some caterpillars and other things.

The earlier part of the afternoon I wrote MS for the botany lecture, which came off as usual at 3:30. The subject today was the anatomy of plants. I got some iodine from Charlton to show them the blue reaction with starch, taking a potato for the starch. There were present, viz., Mrs. Charlton, Mrs. Stockton (came in when I was about half through), two Alexander girls,

Bertha Humphrey, Anna Gowdy, Katie Aldrich, and her sister. This Aldrich sister has just arrived from somewhere, and I had not seen her before. She is older than Katie, and I believe her name is Florence.

I see I began the account of today with the Freers, but earlier than that I was up and called on Nash at the hotel and, being invited, had breakfast with him there. We talked over many things, one being starting a monthly magazine for the C.B.A., and Nash departed on the train at 8:30, having work to do in Pueblo. It was a pity he had to go, as today is the first fine day we have had here for some time, and he might have got some insects.

As for mail today: The English mail is not here yet, and I only got *Canadian Entomologist* (in which Dr. Hamilton has a paper containing a few remarks on my beetles), *Amer. Microscopical Journal* (sample copy) and a letter from Coulter with names of plants, two of them new for Colorado. One of these is *Artemisia vulgaris!* I got it down by Davis' Ranch, below Lees', last year, and I never thought of its being *vulgaris* because that is quite new for this region, although I have seen it often enough in England. However, Coulter says he cannot make it anything else, but thinks it must have been introduced. There was plenty of it.

This evening I was at Charlton's for a little while, talking chemistry with him. Feeling a little dyspeptic about supper-time, I deferred that meal until quite late in the evening. Mrs. Chetelat paid me $1.00, being past payment for the drawing lessons. Now that I am wealthy I shall take a few more magazines. Today I sent subscriptions to *Nautilus* and *Bulletin of the Torrey Botanical Club* ($1.00 each), and Nash and I are going to take *Psyche* between us, i.e., $1,00 each. I am to have it first, and forward it to Nash, and he will return it and it will go to library of C.B.A.

Samse has now become teacher at the Ula school; he was teacher somewhere else before. Sometimes I have thought I would do well to get the post of teacher in one of these schools (I don't think there would be any difficulty about it), but

I should have to be a citizen of the U. S., and that I don't want. The pay is said to be about $50.00 a month, but one would have to board out (for lack of time to cook) and school only lasts a few months in the year.

June 12th, 9:35 p.m. Reading your letter, which came this evening, and *Hester's Ambition*, and looking at the pictures, I have enjoyed the evening, but perceive that I shall do no work. Yet I must write a letter or so, and then if it is not very late I shall continue this. Also, I have to shave.

11 p.m. Vetter and Samse came in and talked for some time, so I am late, and now too stupid and sleepy to write. The Freer children were able to have their lessons today although Elsie was evidently still rather seedy. I went out after specimens later on, but got nothing very remarkable. It was very hot.

This afternoon I have been looking at various things with the microscope. I found a most lovely 'spiral cell.' Alas that I did not have it to show to my botany class yesterday, as I was speaking of such.

Of mail, besides that received from you, I got a letter from Mother, a *Punch*, a list of shells for exchange by one Phinney (all common things), and a postcard from publisher of *Amer. Monthly Micro. Journ.* to say he had sent me a sample copy. There is much to say in answer to your nice letter, and the other things, but they must wait until tomorrow. Goodnight, love, and a kiss.

June 13th, 10 p.m. All today gone, and never a line written! The little Freers had their lesson this morning, as usual, and the rest of the day has been devoted to hanging pictures, the exhibition being tomorrow.

It was in this wise: Directly I left the Freer's I went down to the Charltons' and there talked over the matter of the exhibition, and persuaded Mrs. C. to come and help. They asked me to lunch, after which Mrs. Charlton and I started out in the buggy (this is a sort of hybrid between a dog-cart and a hansom cab), and first went to Mrs. Conway's (a ranch on the way to Ula), partly to get some pictures painted by Mrs. Conway (she is away from home just now so did not bring them herself) and partly to get Miss Byington (who is staying out there just now) to come and assist with the hanging. We got the Conway pictures (landscapes and flowers — rather nice, especially some pansies) and although Miss Byington made a bit of a fuss and 'didn't suppose she would be of any use', she agreed to come. Mrs. Charlton and I returned to town, and while I was hanging the Conway pictures, Mrs. C. went back to the Conways' for Miss B. From this time until six and after, we were very busy getting pictures and hanging them. I did the hanging while the others criticised.

We had 33 in all, viz., (1.) Mrs. Conway's five. (2.) Mrs. Freer's: The girl's head and a sea piece, and also the painting of anemones. (3.) Mrs. Aldrich's four. (4.) Frank Hunter, a dog's head; well done. (5.) Mrs. Hunter's three. (6.) Anna Gowdy's, the one she did with me, now framed, and looks quite nice. (7.) Mrs. Bjornson's, lent by Mrs. Gowdy, five. (8.) Mrs. Chetelat's, the two done by me. (9.) Regy Cusack's three little water-colours. (10.) T.D.A.C., five little water-colours borrowed from Mrs. Cox and Mrs. Cusack. There are more yet to be hung tomorrow.

Mrs. Charlton was very kind, going round with her buggy. Mrs. Aldrich turned up with her paintings, and she will bring more. I borrowed a table-cloth from Mrs. Charlton, and piano-cloths (i.e., covers; they are like large table-cloths) from Mrs. Freer and Mrs. Gowdy, and these were excellent as backgrounds for the pictures.

When I finished the picture hanging I went to the postoffice and found letters from Nash and one E. H. Horn, who wants to buy shells, and encloses 20 cents for anything I may be pleased to send him. He shall have a few things. He writes from Pennsylvania and says he has been to see the scene of the Johnstown disaster. He encloses two soiled postcards picked up from the refuse as a memento of the occasion!

Before I had been back to my own room I met Cox in the street, and he asked me to supper. So I went up with him and stayed a while after showing Mrs. Cox the 1889 Picture Guide. I found Mrs. Cox had made a cake to present to me (I have a great partiality for her cakes). That was kind of her. While I was at the Cox's, Lees turned up. He had come to town with the Howards. He brought two charming little sketches of his own for the exhibition, and Mrs. Howard sent a number of water-colour drawings of flowers by herself.

I wish I could have posted this letter tomorrow, but I fear I may not have time to write what I want to until Sunday.

June 14th, 7:209 p.m. The picture show has been quite a success. Must be off to the meeting now very soon, but will write more afterwards if I am not tired.

June 15th, 9:45 p.m. I did not write any more last night you see, and today, for a wonder, I have had a headache and have done nothing but just deliver the pictures to their owners, which this evening led to my staying for a while at the Aldrich's. I shall go to bed in a little while, and hope to wake up tomorrow all right, when I will tell you all about everything.

Sunday, June 16th, 10:40 a.m. All right again today, fortunately. I must go back to Friday and tell you about the exhibition. The little Freers had their lesson in the morning, and after that the picture show took every scrap of time. Before the public was admitted, I had to put up the pictures by Lees and Mrs. Howard and to call on the Alexanders to get from them a little picture by Mattie Alexander, and some they had by Miss McIlhenny (she has a fairly good notion of painting though her works are at present crude). She has been teaching Mattie A. and also May Cassidy.

The Freers, seeing I was busy, very kindly asked me to lunch so that I need not go down to my own room for it. It was quite a sumptuous repast. The show was to be open from two to four, but of course nearly everyone came late and it was about five before I could get away. Altogether we had 45 pictures and 24 people turned up to see them. We should have had more, only the thing had not been advertised, but in any case the men of this town are too absorbed in the pursuit of the almighty dollar to attend to such frivolities. I cannot remember all who came but it included the following: The Freers, Alexanders, Miss Byington, Miss Lowther, Bertha Humphrey, May Cassidy, Regy Cusack (turned up at the last moment with a few odd sketches, which I put up though it was too late for anyone to see them), Miss McIlhenny, Mrs. Humphrey (I can't remember the rest).

I took a census of opinion as to which was the best picture, but unfortunately did not think of it until several had come and gone. But I kept it on till the evening when some fresh people came, so I got 28 votes on the question altogether by dint of worrying people. One of Lees' little water-colour sketches got the most votes (nine) which was satisfactory, as it is a most exquisite little sketch, although I do not doubt myself that Mrs. Aldrich's roses was the best thing in the room. Frank Hunter's dog came second (six votes), then Mrs. Aldrich's roses (four votes), and a few other things got one vote each.

At about five I got back here and from then to 7:30 got supper and mail. The mail I got was: (1.) Letter from Sterki, wanting shells. (2.) Letter from E. A. Southworth (Dept. of Agr.) to say that Galloway is away and hence cannot at once answer a letter I wrote him. (3.) Acknowledgment of shells received, from Smithsonian Inst. (4.) *Pall Mall Budget*. (5.) *Naturalist*, June. (6.) *Science Gossip*, June.

There was a pretty good attendance at the evening meeting (I did not count them). The first thing was an essay on Art by Vetter, I believe his first attempt in this line, and quite good. Then Mrs. Charlton read Walter Crane on the Arts and Crafts Exhibition (in *P. M. Budget*), and I read Morris' 'Aims of Art.' This no doubt astonished many and puzzled more, but I think it was good to read it as it will infuse some notions into the heads of the West Cliff-ites, who are rather backward in their ideas. After this I proposed a vote of thanks to those who had lent their pictures, and the meeting terminated.

As for yesterday, I got up late with a headache, and went round delivering the pictures borrowed from people in West Cliff. After noon I lay down for an hour or two, and later Mrs. Charlton came with the buggy and we took the Conway pictures back. When we returned from there, we met Aldrich, Jr. (a young man with red hair) and I went out to the Aldriches with him in a sort of sulky he was driving, as I had to hold the Aldrich pictures while he drove. It was now getting late, and I stayed to supper and most of the evening at the Aldriches. Nothing today has happened so far; it is very hot. There is a letter, also a parcel for me at the postoffice, I hear, but as it is Sunday I cannot get it yet.

I hear Miss Eastwood, of Denver (botanist and member of C.B.A.) is in town. I went up to the hotel to look for her but she was not to be found.

Not at last I can answer your letter. It was a pity about the *Papilio asterias* but I don't think you were to blame atall for its being a cripple; they will sometimes turn out so. Probably I kept it too dry. It is queer, too, that it should have come out so soon with you. I have not seen a single *P. asterias* here yet this year.

Yes, I like to hear about Louy, but she is a great puzzle. I don't know what to say. As a matter of fact, I expect it would quite wise to send her away somewhere for good, but that will never be allowed. Clive is another anomaly; in some respects he must be almost a child yet. What brings Miss Schafer to America?

Of course, love, all the details of your daily life do interest me, very much — fancy asking! Do mine interest you? I fear they are very dry sometimes, though probably I 'live' as much as most people — certainly more than some. But you are always alive.

I dare not name the Bedford Park *Cerastium* without a book, but may it not be *arvense*? I am pretty sure *C. arvense* grows at B. P. though not down on the list. Look in the flora and fauna book.

I think the 'Woodward' was uncle or something to B.B.W. I am interested in your account of the Woodwardian meeting at B. P. — and amused. I can quite imagine what B. B. Woodward may have had to say about me! It does not really matter though, as I am not greatly concerned personally, and he overdoes it too much to injure my reputation, because his personal animus is so evident. Cheadle of Ealing is another of his abominations.

Look up 'Demonstration' in Webster. Regy seems reconciled to losing Miss Urquhart, or rather, resigned, and she, so far as one can learn, takes things 'philosophically', though certainly sorry to go. It was a pity, sending the 1888 Picture Guide by mistake, but thank you much for both of them. There was a good deal in the '88 one that was new to me, so both were interesting. I meant to write a lot about the pictures for this letter, but I fear now it must wait for the next.

I like what you say about the last two years, only I believe you have really done more than I have. It is strange how much one does without accomplishing anything; I feel this about my work.

Yes, Annie, happiness is in working—working together — there can be no harmony in doing nothing. In one's work, really, there is no end. Any 'end' we can imagine will lead to new and better things. I do not think I could have heart in doing anything if I thought I was only bringing myself to the end of it. But we know the direction in which we must go, and that is everything.

I guessed who the photo was, before I read it in your letter. Thank you for sending it. I can suppose it may not be very flattering. It was good of you to send *Hester's Ambition*, and I like

it very much. It may often be so. Isn't it in *Elsie Venner* that the two parsons argue together with the result that they exchange opinions? Though in this case it was not quite the same. What became of Hester afterwards? You ought to know! Did she ever realize her ambition?

9:40 p.m. I found Miss Eastwood at the hotel at about seven, and have been talking with her ever since. Certainly I have never enjoyed any talk so much since I left England. Miss E. herself is not remarkable to look at, with plain and rounded, though rather interesting, features. Age about 30. But she is utterly different from the people here, and vastly superior, and in her conversation and opinions she quite reminded me of you. First of all, she told me about her botany and her school (she is a teacher), and then we got to talking of evolution, and almost before we knew it, were in the midst of art, socialism, and religion. It was quite delightful to talk and be understood. By the way, with all this talking, I never had any supper. I must get some now, and then to bed, and tomorrow I will post this.

Ever your own lover,
Theo.

Health. All right except for temporary seediness.

Enclosed are some cuttings, one of a buggy, and the other (from *Pall Mall*) because it is just like Wheatley.

Monday, June 17th, 1889

Dear Annie,
'Tis brillig, and has been so all day. My Freer children were ill again. Mabel was supposed to be too ill to work, so she was let off, but Maggie took her lesson though she had a headache. Elsie was all right. I gave them geography and history of the British Isles combined, expounding the outlines of the subject to them as interestingly as I could. I also took them to spelling and the meaning of words. Curiously, I could find no synonym for *suffuse*, and Webster's Dictionary doesn't give any.

After this, I got some biscuits for lunch and ate them as I wandered down by the creek, finding a few plants and insects. After I got back to town I met Miss Eastwood just returning from a morning ramble with a tin bucketful of flowers. We sat down in front of the Tomkins Building and examined the finds. (I suspect we aroused the curiosity of the populace, but nobody had the courage to come and ask what we might be about!) Miss Eastwood had meant to go out for the whole day, but was not very well and didn't feel equal to it. I forgot to mention that this morning before I went to the Freer's, she came round to my room and I showed her the record book, etc. When we finished with the morning's flowers Miss Eastwood went off to her dinner and I busied myself making a new butterfly net (the old one was all in holes) and in looking at a gathering of algae under the microscope. I found many diatoms, but what pleased me most was a quantity of *Spirogyra* showing the spiral bands of chlorophyll very plainly and prettily, as in 'Thome', p. 25, fig. 41. This afternoon was devoted to a pleasant ramble down the creek with Miss Eastwood. She brought her *Coulter's Manual* so we could make out doubtful plants on the spot. We found many plants and I got a few insects.

Coming home, Miss Eastwood told me of her adventures on Gray's Peak with Alfred Russel Wallace. He was out in Colorado some few years ago, and she actually had the good fortune to go botanizing with him on Gray's Peak for several days wherein they found many plants, lost their way, got 'played out', had to subsist on bacon-rind and flour, and had many other equally exciting adventures!

Miss Eastwood doesn't much like the hotel and can't get many plants here at West Cliff, so I sent out a note to Mrs. Cusack by Brock today, asking her to send Regy in with the buckboard tomorrow or the day after and fetch her out there for a few days. I know Mrs. C. will be delighted to have her.

I got some mail tonight: (1.) Letter from Nash. (2.) Letter from *Field and Farm* saying they are going to have sent to me a plant which is said to have poisoned some cattle at Gunnison, as they want it named. (3.) Postcard from Webster and a package of naphthaline crystals which I wrote for. (4.) *West American Scientist* for June, wherein C.B.A. report and notes by T.D.A.C.

June 18th, 12:20 p.m. At the Cusacks'! Very sleepy, doing flowers all the evening with Miss Eastwood and Mrs. Cusack. Will write about it tomorrow.

June 19th. I was up early in the morning and went out (this was up at the Cusacks') and about, getting a great handful of flowers of various sorts. When I got back no one was yet up, but presently Mrs. Cusack appeared, and we made breakfast, and then Miss Eastwood and Regy, and finally, long after the meal was cleared up, Wheatley appeared on the scene.

I was supposed to teach the little Freers that afternoon, and Anna Gowdy's drawing lesson was at one, so I should have started town-wards at about ten a.m., which I didn't do although my conscience rather pricked me on the subject.

Mrs. Cusack, Miss Eastwood and I went over the herbarium all the morning, and Miss E. named a few erroneous identifications of mine, which was very fortunate as there is no telling how long I might have continued to call the plants by their wrong names. Then we had lunch, and after that we went over the *Asters* in the herbarium until about 3:20 I started to walk town-wards. I had a pleasant enough walk, finding various insects and plants, and getting to town about 7:15, when I got my mail.

I did little that evening but read the mail. I went round to the Freers' to apologise for not turning up to teach the children, and on my way back from there I stopped for a quarter of an hour, leaning on the fence alongside Falkenberg's house (of course unobserved) listening to Miss Falkenberg playing dance tunes on the piano. She plays only indifferently, but they were familiar old tunes that reminded me of past times, and so I enjoyed it. (My head seems heavy as lead. I must lie down for a bit. It is too bad, being ill today of all days.)

3:45 p.m. (I took some quinine and am better now, but feel very foolish.)

10:20 p.m. I walked back to town this afternoon, and have got your letter. There is much to write about all sorts of things, but I am too tired and sleepy now.

June 20th. I posted a reprint of last part of variety paper to you by the morning mail. The Freers had their lessons as usual, but after that I did practically nothing, feeling quite 'knocked-up.'

9:45 p.m. I meant to do a lot today, and there is almost nothing done, and I am dreadfully behind in my work. Some correspondents that I have not written to will be greatly disgusted with me. Even to answer your letter and thank you for the sock, I expect I must wait till Monday.

The day before yesterday, after the Freers' lesson I went down the street after flowers for my botany class (it was Tuesday) and there I found Miss Eastwood, and we searched awhile for specimens and finally returned to town.

Later on, Regy and Wheatley arrived in town, the buckboard being sent to fetch Miss Eastwood, as I asked.

It seemed to me that I had better go out to the Cusacks' also, as I might not have another chance of going over Mrs. Cusack's herbarium with someone who was really well-up in the flowers of this region. So after my botany lecture we all went out together.

The botany lecture was given to an audience of only three — Anna Gowdy, Bertha Humphrey and an Alexander. I suppose it was too hot for the rest to come. I had prepared no diagrams this week, and so gave them only a sort of rambling account of various things which, after all, was more amusing and possibly more instructive than the regular lectures.

Directly after the class was over we got ready to depart, and duly reached the Cusacks' in the course of the evening. Regy and Wheatley went down to Brock's after supper, and Mrs. Cusack, Miss Eastwood, and I sat up late looking over the herbarium.

June 21st. Was better. Gave the Freers their lesson and was introduced to the new governess, just arrived, to take my place as teacher on Monday. She is a rather nice-looking girl of the robust type, probably not remarkable in any way, but intelligent, and I daresay a better teacher than myself. Her name is Miss Fowler but they call her 'Bertie.'

Early in the afternoon I gave Anna Gowdy a drawing lesson. She is attempting a big picture of the mountains. We sat outside to get a view and, having drawn the outlines, we began on the sky. Of course it is absurd for her to be attempting such things when she knows practically nothing of drawing or painting, but she would never wait to learn a little more about 'first principles' so I have to help her as well as I can with this. This is the way with all these Americans. Practically, I shall have to do most of the painting myself.

About mail-time, Regy brought Miss Eastwood back from the Cusacks'. I went up to the hotel and found her there, and we talked till nearly ten. First she told me about the numerous flowers she had found up at the Cusacks', and afterwards we talked about Morris' *Aims of Art*, which I had lent her to read. She was quite pleased with it, and had read it three times. She asked for a definition of Art as limited by Morris. I was rather puzzled, but finally gave her 'The expression of ideas in handiwork.' Do you agree with that definition? Miss Eastwood is so entirely sincere and enthusiastic, and never says things 'do not matter', or, 'she doesn't care', and I suppose this is what places her so far above the ordinary run of people here in the West, who are both selfish and superficial. But at the same time she has greater mental capacities than most, which helps her to understand. I should like to introduce her to you. I am sure you would like her. In some ways, she reminds me of Miss Woods, of Bedford Park.

I got so interested in our conversation that I quite forgot to have any supper that evening, and did not remember it until I woke up next morning feeling hungry, and no wonder, for I had had nothing substantial since the breakfast of the day before. Also, what is more important, I forgot to take a list of plants Miss Eastwood had made out for me and which I cannot afford to lose, as it gives me lots of new records. I must write to her for it.

When I got back to my room I was restless, and relieved myself by talking to Vetter (whom I found in his room) of the depravity of the West. Hence it was late when I got to bed.

June 22nd. Miss Eastwood departed by the morning train. I went down to the station to see her off. She goes to Cañon City for a day, then to Denver, and from there to Durango for a while. She talks of returning to this valley in about a month to get the later flowers.

It was the last day of teaching at the Freers (although it was Saturday, they had their lessons to make up for the holiday earlier in the week). I shall quite miss my children, as, apart from the dollars and cents point of view, I enjoyed teaching them. In the afternoon and evening I wrote my variation papers for *Entomologist*.

Mail received: (1, 2.) Your letters, of which hereafter. (3.) Letter from Mother. (4.) Letter from Francis Wolle, with names of some algae. (5.(Letter from Vasey about Chamberlain's supposed poisonous plant. He thinks C. got hold of the wrong plant. (6, 7.) Letters from A. Dean and E. W. Roper, wanting shells. (8). *Report of the Ornithologist and Mammalogist for 1888*, from Merriam. (9.) *Field and Farm*. (10.) *Life Lore* for June. Sample copy, with index. I see they have some remarks about the C.B.A. in one of the back numbers. Boulger has an interesting paper in this number about [John] Ray. (11.) Reprints of variety paper (last part) from West, Newman & Co.

(June 20th). (12.) Postcard from W. H. Edwards. (13, 14.) *Entomological Mags.* (15.) 'Contributions to the Mollusca of Florida' reprint from author (Simpson), two copies, one for myself and one for C.B.A. (16.) *Pall Mall Budget*. (17.) Letter from Bentenmueller. (18.) Letter from N. L. Britton (editor Bulletin of the Torrey Botanical Club) with Bull. Torr. Bot. Club, Jan. to June. (I had subscribed to this, It is a good monthly botanical paper.) (19.) Letter from W. H. Edwards. (20.) Adv't. of *Naturalists Gazette*, a paper published in Birmingham, apparently by Harcourt Bath, although it does not say so. (21.) *Custer County Courant*.

Your letter: (1.) But first of all, I will re-examine and report on the interesting little insects you sent me which flew to the lamp, as I must report on them by daylight. One can't see these things properly at night. They are: Diptera: (1.) *Culex pipiens*. (2.) *Culex aff.?* (head gone). (3.) Small green gnat which I know to be common in London but do not know the name. Seems to be allied to *Chironomus* (4, 5.) Small gnats. (6.) *Diplosis sp.*, apparently. (6.) Gnat sp? (7.) Sp? Allied to the gnats. (8.) *Phora* sp. apparently. (9.) ? Allied to the gnats. (10.) Muscid. Genus? (11.) *Chironomus*? Homoptera: (12.) *Aphis sp.* (13). Braconid; I will send it to Ashmead. You see, here is lots of material for Frederic if he wants to study the Diptera. I always like to see anything you want named, but am sorry I cannot make out the species of these. But nobody knows much about these little gnats.

Now to go on with the letter: Of course, as a matter of fact, babies are not 'born alike.' I should hardly suppose Mr. Payn really thought so. [I see a pretty rainbow out my window.] I wonder what F. Galton would say to such views. So it is *Belgravia* that Fred writes for! He never would tell me. It's a pretty good paper, isn't it? I never saw it, but know the name very well. I think I still have the essay on Socialism; I will look it up and send it. (Now I must cut some wood.)

7:30. I have had supper, and can now go on. No, I never did try talking love, but I don't know how I should do it. I do not think you will find me a very talkative lover when I return, but then you will know what I mean, and that is everything. It will be thought transference! I suppose I must be satisfied about the cable if you were ill, though I should like to have one in any case. I don't think it would matter, if the worst did happen, if I came over uselessly, and it would matter very much if from not hearing in time I was late. But I am not anxious; you are not going to die. It's a queer notion, anyone not being in love, but thinking they are! I can better understand anyone being in love and not knowing it.

Thank you for the socks. I am wearing them at the present moment, and they fit nicely. I should like to get that job of 'Science Demonstrator' at Sheffield of which you enclose cutting. But there's no telling what they mean by 'Science.'

(2.) Yes, the insects generally at the Museum are in a fearful state, but they will never get a good man if they keep up that civil service exam. Am *I* going to be a specialist? Well, I *was*, in England, distinctly (snails and slugs), and now it is *variation*. But I may take up the spiders yet. Darwin used to think it was better not to be too much of a specialist.

I am sorry to hear about your mother being ill. Why not send her off somewhere for a holiday? I am glad you are seeing more of the family. The caterpillar on lilac at B. P. is probably *Uropteryx imbricaria*, though species of *Pericallis* and *Eunomos* feed on lilies, and it might be one of them. But you will have got the moth by the time this reaches you! Tell me what it turns out to be. *Field and Farm* is an old established paper for the West. It is in its seventh volume.

10:5 p.m. I must go to bed now. I have got a weight off my mind, having finished the part of the variety paper in *Entomologist* for the August number.; I hope it will reach them in time. It is about the varieties of caterpillars, a rather difficult subject. I have been quite out of sorts today, as indeed more or less all the past week. A sort of low fever apparently; might be approaching measles, only I know I have had them.

June 23rd, 12 noon. Two years ago!

It is now the evening of the 23rd. Love, I take your hands. It is not necessary to review the past two years; let me think of the future. The next year — what will it bring us? We can scarcely tell. But we know what it is we want, and our hope is real, so we may be happy. So forward!

Your lover, Theo.

Health. Nothing really the matter, but as you see above, rather out of sorts for the time being.

Some notes on the 1889 Picture Guide: p. 1, No. 300. Certainly they will lose their ball! P. 8, No. 74. A pretty scene. P. 5, No. 313. Foolish-looking girls. P. 7, No. 188. Looks as if it would be good. But man seems to be fishing in a hedge. P. 10, No. 266. Very pretty. Everyone likes this. P. 11, No. 535. Methinks I recognise Chamberlain's poisonous umbellifer. Has this young woman been partaking? P. 13, No. 271. Good. No. 301. Pretty. P. 15, No. 272. Very good, and much admired by those who have seen the catalogue. P. 16, No. 760. I don't know whether I like this or not; on the whole I don't. There is something incongruous about it. The angel appears to have the measles badly on her face. P. 17, No. 231. This is amusing! P. 19, No. 230. Very natural. P. 20, No. 200 and p. 21, No. 417. Seem both to be exceedingly good. P. 21, No. 317. I like this. P. 24, No. 629. I don't wonder *Punch* took this off! P. 26, No. 733. This looks good. P. 27, No. 480. Good. P. 28, No. 286. I like this. P. 32, No. 553. Pretty face, rather like Louy. P. 33, No. 419. Mrs. 'Reckitt's blue?' P. 34, No. 1210. This is good. P. 35, No. 1081. Excellent. P. 36, No. 1102. Can't make 'head or tail' of this. P. 37, No. 488. Very nice. No. 1063. Very good indeed and much admired. The best thing Blair Leighton has done. P. 40, No. 1177. Don't like this. P. 41, No. 601. This is good. P. 42, No. 402. Better than last year's. I rather like it. P. 46, No. 4. Very pretty; this is given better in the *Graphic*. P. 51, No. 17. Excellent! No., 61. I rather like this. P. 53, No. 773. The expression and attitude are very well given. P. 62, Nos. 2018 and 2032. These must both be good, also p. 63, No. 2036. P. 64, No. 2089. Very like Katie Aldrich! P. 65, No. 102. Looks well done, but don't understand it. Where is the garden? No. 114. New species of sea monsters! Mrs. N. will certainly fall off. P. 71, No. 228. This looks rather good. P. 79, No. 58. Very pretty. I like this the best of any. P. 82, No. 212. I like this, but who is Betty Lorell? P. 89, No. 10. Stuffed? P. 93, No. 20. What is silver-paint? P. 94, No. 100. Just like little Charlie Cox.

[Enclosed, a flower in a small envelope. Ed.]

June 24th, 11:25 p.m. This *is* nice, another letter so soon! And I have written almost nothing the last few days. Thank you, love, for the rose — I felt sure you would send one — and I had picked one for you, to send on the 23rd, but not such a nice one as yours.

June 24th, 1889

Dear Annie,

A letter-writing day. I have written nine, which is very satisfactory. A letter from you was posted to go by the morning train. I have only been out to give Anne Gowdy her drawing lesson — the picture of the mountains. She had done some sky since the last, but it was too bad to remain, and I had to paint it over. She will only paint her best when I am there to see that she does it. It is a pity. I did up some insects for Janson; I wonder what he will give me for it. It may be worth a dollar or more. It weighed six ounces and cost only three cents postage, about a half cent for a thousand miles of traveling! I also sent off your Isleworth Braconid to Ashmead.

The mail this evening was (1.) Letter from W. C. Roby, a mining engineer of Holy Cross (near Red Cliff) urgently begging me to go up there for two weeks and stay with him, to study the fauna and flora. It is a good locality and I should like to go, but it would cost too much to get there. He also encloses a flower found at 12,000 ft. alt. It seems to be *Polemonium viscosum* Nutt., a very rare flower found, so far as I know,

hitherto only on Gray's Peak. (2.) 'Catalogue of Coleoptera common to North America and Asia', a bulky and very interesting paper by and from Hamilton. (3.) *Oölogist's Exchange,* a sample copy of this foolish paper.

I am quite well again today and have been able to work without interruption. Lees called in this evening. He has heard from Mrs. Payn, and showed me the letter. She sent Payn the $600 he was wanting as soon as she got Lees' cablegram.

June 25th, 8:30 p.m. Letter from Elwes — wants me to go to British Columbia, with advance of £25!

10:30 p.m. Most of the day was taken up in preparation for the botany lecture. It has been very hot, as indeed for many days past. The heat at this altitude seems more trying than a greater temperature lower down, owing to the rarification of the atmosphere. I got out just before the class to get a few plants. This class was more satisfactory than last week's, as Mrs. Ommaney (back from Cañon City, where she has been staying), Florence and Katie Aldrich, and Anna Gowdy were present (or was it Martha Humphrey? I have forgotten whether they were both there or whether Anna or only Bertha). I was in pretty good 'form', and gave them the principles of evolution and a good deal about algae and fungi.

When I got home I was lazy, and read *Grande Pointe* by Cable, just finishing it by suppertime. I had read it before, long ago, but had forgotten it. It is very pretty. Did you ever read it? After this the mail came in, and after that, feeling restless, I went round to the Freers' for a time and talked Socialism and other things with them.

The mail is: (1.) 'Report of the chief of the section of Vegetable Pathology, B. T. Galloway, for the year 1888' from Galloway, 'Author's edition', quite interesting to me, of course. (2.) 'On butterflies of the genus Parnassias', by and from Elwes, from *Proc. Zoöl. Soc.*— very interesting and valuable. (3.) Letter from Mother. (4.)

Nice letter from Jenner Weir, who writes from Lewes. (5.) Letter from Elwes, who says that his previous arrangement with a collector has fallen through, and strongly urging me to go out to British Columbia for him and offering to advance £25 if I will go. It is a very long letter, eight pages. I should like to go, but don't see how it can be done.

June 26th, 9:5 p.m. Here I am, up at Lees'. I walked up today but won't tell about it tonight, as it is about bedtime. I was up early, and they go to bed early here.

June 27th, 9:50 p.m. At the Cusacks'. Have been up in the mountains, above timber line.

June 28th, 11 p.m. Back in town. Meeting of Lit. & Sci. Society was tonight. Got your letter.

June 29th, 8:15 p.m. Such a hot day! I have been quite prostrated, able to do nothing. 88 degrees in the shade at about 6 p.m. according to a thermometer at Merriam's. Could not cook supper, so had it at the hotel (cost 25 cents, which is cheap). Now for an account of my journey to the mountains.

June 16th. Thinking over Elwe's proposal, I resolved to go up and ask Lees to give me an account of his expenditure on the journey to British Columbia, and see whether it was really possible for me to go. At the same time, I would get what insects I could up in the mountains. So I was up soon after five, had breakfast, and started in the cool of the morning at 6:15. On the way I looked for specimens, and even before I had gone a mile I was fortunate in finding an *Hypericum* (St. John's Wort) which I had never seen before in this country, and in taking an interesting male variety of *Vanessa cardui*, of which I saw more later on.

Close to Hesterberg's I met Regy driving to town with Mr. Ferris, the father of the Ferris girls who arrived last Monday, and are staying with the Cusacks. Papa Ferris has a shop (groceries I think) in Denver, and was obliged to be off on the morning train to attend to it. I just shook hands with him. He looked a nice man, in appearance much like Ernest Hart (of Apollinaire's Water, Irish Industries, and British Medical Journal fame). I arrived at the Cusacks' at 9:15 and found them at breakfast, so I got two breakfasts that day, which was not so greatly amiss after all, as I had no lunch. I was introduced to the Ferrises, namely Mrs. (Mama) Ferris, Miss Ferris, and Miss Kitty Ferris. They are all very American, and the two girls have a private school in Colorado Springs. The mother is a short, small woman who looks a great deal meeker and more insignificant than she actually is. She seems a nice little woman. I cannot judge much of them yet, but the Cusacks like them well, and Lees is quite delighted with them. I think it was about eleven when I left the Cusacks' and went on up to Lees'.

This part of the journey I aimed much on catching butterflies, and met with about 20 species of these insects.

T. D. A. C. with butterfly net

421

Altogether, I had a very pleasant walk and felt excellently well, arriving at Lees' not atall tired. It was about 4 p.m. when I got up there, so you see how long I had been on the road. Lees was up at the mine working on a 'fan' — a very ingenious contrivance of his for ventilating the mine. Two men of the name of Musson were there also, mining for him.

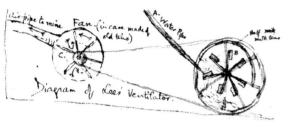

Lee's ventilator

This 'fan' of Lees is curious enough to be worth describing. In the first place, by means of a ditch from a little creek, he gets a head of water, about 50 feet, which comes down an iron pipe (A). This impacts on an arrangement of halved milk tins on a water wheel (B), which is in a case of canvas. The water wheel accordingly revolves, and then by a flywheel (as drawn in red) the power is transmitted to the fan-wheel (C), which revolves 700 times a minute. It is in a case which is so arranged that the air is sucked in in the middle and forced along a pipe to the further end of the mine. The whole thing works by itself and only requires occasional oiling. I was astonished at the amount of work a little water will do. Lees says he saw a similar but rather larger arrangement running a big saw-mill in British Columbia.

As soon as Lees had a little leisure, I asked him about British Columbia, with the result that he immediately demonstrated that it was practically impossible for me to go. In the first place, owing to the very high charges on the western railroad, it would cost at least $100 for the journey each way. When I got there I would find living more expensive than here, and also that it was a sheer impossibility to get about much in the mountains alone. So to make it pay atall I should have to earn at least $5.00 a day the whole

time I was there, which is probably impossible. If Elwes chose to put down £80 in advance and take all risks, it might be a different matter, but I don't think such an arrangement could be worth his while, though no other would do for me. So as I cannot go to British Columbia, I shall get a waggon-sheet and camp out for a while in these mountains, insect-collecting, and I expect I shall get many and interesting things.

Shortly before supper-time, one Davis showed up, a Monmouth-ite man who owns a ranch not very far from Lees', so we had quite a crowd in the little cabin at supper — five altogether. Davis then departed, that is, after supper, and as the Mussons sleep in the teepee which has been put up outside, there was room for me to sleep in the cabin.

June 27th. After breakfast, as Lees was writing a letter for me to post when I went to town. I spent a little time collecting butterflies near the cabin, and after that started up the gulch, meaning to cross the 'hogback' and go back towards town a somewhat different way. But it was so fine and I enjoyed the fresh air so much that I walked up and up, through the quaking asps, in places where it was so steep that I had to hold on to the bushes to help me through the thick timber and, at last, out on the bare mountainside above timber line where the snow was still melting and the flowers and the butterflies were enjoying their springtime. This was about 12,000 feet above the level of the sea.

I hunted round for quite some time and got some butterflies, *Chionobas* and others, and flowers — blue *Polemonium*, the lovely forget-me-not (*Omphalodes* [*Eritrichum*. Ed.]), *Eriogonum*, *Antennaria*, and *Castilleja*, all different from those of lower altitudes. My boxes were stuffed full too soon, and I could only take a small specimen of each. Mountain sheep live up here, and I hoped to see some, but the only 'game' I saw the whole day long was a flock of grouse.

I wandered round towards Gibbs Peak where I could look down into Horseshoe Bend, and in my wanderings found what I am pleased to call *my* mine! It is a 'lead' of quartz and mineral which can be plainly seen on the mountainside, but although I fancied I saw a few specks of native silver in one specimen I took, it is more likely that the ore is only magnetic iron. I had no pencil with me, so I could not 'stake' my claim, i.e., write my name on a stake to indicate that I claimed possession.

After this I descended and got among the trees again in the Horseshoe Bend gulch, meandering down the creek, finding *Primula parryi* just coming into flower, and a lovely *Argynnis* and other butterflies, until I came to an old gateway which stands on the trail a little beyond which one crosses a hog-back, and from there the trail goes down to the old Beddoes road and so on into the valley. But I cut across country and in due time reached the Cusacks'. It was about 5 p.m.

Mrs. Cusack was quite delighted with the alpine flowers, which she had never seen before though she has been in the country so long. I found Miss Bellaire and Ward at the Cusacks'; they had driven up from the Beddoes' and did not start back till after dark. I stopped the night at the Cusacks'. Mrs. C. told me that Cress had killed a bear quite close to their house a few days ago. It had come to the bodies of Chamberlain's poisoned cattle, and Cress lay in wait for it at night.

June 28th. Rather before ten I left the Cusacks' and had an uneventful walk to town where, however, I got my mail, viz., (1.) Your letter. (2.) Letter from Sterki about shells. (3.) Letter from Willoughby Lowe about a scorpion he found. (4.) Letter from J. Bridgeham about caterpillars. (5.) *Punch*.

Anna Gowdy was supposed to have a drawing lesson at one, but I was glad to find that they were moving (they go into the house the Alexanders have just left) and she could not take her lesson, for I was really too tired to have given the matter proper attention.

By the evening mail I got (1.) Letter from Douglas, who has moved to Woodstock, a place some 30 miles from St. Thomas; he seems glad of it. (2.) Report of Botany Department, Kansas Agric. Experiment Station, from Kellerman.

In the evening it was the 'entertainment' meeting of the Literary and Scientific Society. The programme had been mainly arranged by Mrs. Conway and was quite a good one and we had a good attendance of people. Charlton being away, Sam Wright took the chair. The programme was as follows: Duet — Mrs. Conway (organ) and Mrs. Gowdy (violin). (2.) Reading by Bertha Humphrey. (3.) Chorus of little girls, led by Anna Gowdy — quite well done. (4.) Solo — Mrs. Fowler (she has a good voice). (3.) Reading — Miss Byington. (6.) Recitation — Mrs. Becker. (7.) Duet — Miss Louther and Miss Fowler.

Sunday, June 30th, 3:10 p.m. Another hot day. I have been writing letters. I have not yet answered yours. I have a slight headache, so that I do not feel well able to write properly.

The account of the French play (*Le Grouve*) is interesting, because I think [it is] very typical of a certain French style of notions which seem to me entirely 'addled.' But the genuine Frenchman, *not* of Paris, surely is quite different. I forget whether I read the *whole* of *Intellectual Life*, but I think I did. I may have missed a chapter or so.

English mail comes in here about twice a week, sometimes oftener, but I think in most cases only because one mail gets spread out by being partly delayed after reaching America. About the honey fraud, of which you send a cutting, I think they even make artificial honeycomb!

10 p.m. This evening I went round to call on Mrs. Stockton about the Herbarium for the Ladies' Literary Society, and later have been talking to Vetter. I had supper again at the hotel. I am fit for nothing just now, what with the heat, a slight headache, and a greatly swollen face originating in some trouble at the base of the

tooth. It doesn't trouble me but excited a good deal of attention, and I am curious to see what it will develop into.

Thank you for that last bit of biography; it is very interesting. I feel very much ashamed that I have not written more of mine. I wore your socks on my tramp up the mountains, and they were so comfortable, and I came back without blistered feet, a very unusual thing after a long walk. This is a horrid letter.

Your own Theo.

July 2nd, 1889, 9:40 p.m.

Love,

I have just recovered from a little attack of fever — 'Mountain Fever', as they call it here, and am not yet quite well again. It is the first time I have been really laid up since I came to Colorado.

July 3rd, 8:25 p.m. Am much better but am going out to the Cusacks' for a few days to recover. Am waiting now to go with Regy, who is in town, but he and Turner are off somewhere gambling or otherwise playing the fool, and there is no telling when we shall start. Got your delightful letter this evening.

July 4th, 9:15 p.m. At the Cusacks', but just going to bed though it is early. News this morning. Mrs. Cox has a son here, and everything doing as well as can be. I heard it from Cox. I did not come out here until this morning.

July 5th, 9 p.m. There. . . . I wrote one word and that is all, for the talking going on which interrupted me. It has been very hot today and I was rather prostrated until the evening, and now it is nice and cool.

July 6th, 8:50 p.m. A day of almost perfect rest, so that I feel altogether better. Shall go to bed now and hope tomorrow to be all right, and tell you all about the week in this letter which I shall take to town in time for the Monday morning train.

Sunday, July 7th, 12:10 p.m. The whole of this week remains to be recounted. I shall write rather large, as I can write faster that way. Not that I want to write particularly fast, but I seem to have so much to say that I may never end it otherwise.

To begin: Monday, July 1st. Began by feeling out of sorts; I forget what I did or whether I did anything in the morning, only I know that some time Lees turned up, and I mentioned my project for camping out but said that I could not get my 'outfit' taken to the mountains. Whereupon he said that next day the Misses Ferris were going to the Beddoes' for a week and, while there, were coming up with Beddoes to the mine for a sort of picnic; that was to be on Friday. Now he (Lees) was on horseback that day and was not coming to town again before a week or so, so could we arrange for me to take up my own things and also a quantity of 'grub' which Lees required for said picnic?

So we arranged it this way: On Wednesday I was to walk to Louis Howard's and there procure a buckboard and return to town, get Lees' groceries and my camp outfit, drive up to Lees' mine, stay there the night, and the next day drive Louis' horse and buckboard back to him, and then walk back to wherever I might have pitched my camp. I would hardly have made such an arrangement in any case had I thought it well over, as it involved walking about eight miles and driving about 35, to get a few pounds of things carried eight miles or so, but as it happened I was not able to carry it out.

Towards evening I got more feverish and, in fact, quite collapsed so that I could not even cook a few eggs for supper. I struggled down into the store below and explained my melancholy condition, and Mrs. Chetelat, hearing of it, took pity and invited me up to her room where she prepared an excellent meal, which I ate as well as I could, but soon lay down on the sofa and presently retreated to my own room where I spent a restless night. Now all this sounds very pitiful, and I felt bad enough for anything, but had the comfort of knowing that I had nothing worse than 'febricula' or as they say here, 'Mountain Fever', presumably due to the heat, and bound to get well in a little while. But it was humiliating, being the first time since I came here that I had been really laid up.

Tuesday, July 2. (Adjournment for lunch.) I was still more or less incapable and felt quite thankful when Chetelat turned up about breakfast time bearing some breakfast on a tray. What happened that day I do not remember, but it was nothing in particular and I did no work. The Chetelats most kindly brought me both lunch and supper.

Wednesday, July 3. Was better and able once more to cook for myself. But going out to Lees' was an impossibility. In the course of the day Mrs. Beddoes arrived in town with Miss Kitty Ferris, bringing me a list of things to be taken up to Lees (supposing that I should go) — claret, soda-water, etc. It is queer that when some people go out in the mountains for a picnic they cannot be content to drink spring water and eat plain food, devoting their attention to the natural phenomena around them.

I saw Brock. He had been laid-up in the same way as I, at the Cox's. It is perfectly abominable. Mrs. Cox asked Mrs. Turner to come to town and help her (a foolish thing to do, perhaps), and im-mediately Brock comes and *lives* in town, *at the Cox's* (leaving Turner up on the ranch, where he is no earthly use and a great nuisance)! So then Brock gets ill, and Mrs. Turner has to devote herself to nursing him.

Towards evening, to my astonishment, Regy and Turner appeared in town, so I arranged to go out with them to the Cusacks', that I might spend a few days in luxurious idleness and get well again. I got everything ready, but they never went; they stayed in town the night.

Thursday, July 4th. The 'Glorious 4th.' Which one was not likely to forget. At about six in the morning the celebration began — gunpowder being exploded with a deafening sound, most aggravating to me, who had still the ghost of a headache. But I got up, made various preparations and, feeling fairly well, decided to walk out to the Cusacks' and take it easy, supposing that if I should fall by the way, Regy would come along some time and pick me up.

This is just how it happened. I felt a little faint and weary as I got by John Burke's, so I prostrated myself on the grass in a shady place and contemplated things in general until Regy came along, when I took a back seat on the buckboard. Immediately behind I beheld a number of vehicles following, and gathered that it was a company of people coming to picnic in the woods up by the Cusacks'. A few days ago Vetter had asked me whether they could find a place with shade and water up there. When they got nearer one could see who they were: the Conways, Mrs. Becker, Miss Fowler, Miss Cassidy, the Frasers, Vetter, Samse, and so forth. Later, after we got to the Cusacks', the Freers turned up. They all had their picnic in the woods about half a mile to the back of the house.

At the Cusacks' I found Mrs. Ferris still here, but, as I said, the girls were at the Beddoes', a fortunate thing, as I was thus not so much in the way. All the rest of the day I did nothing in particular.

Monday, 7 a.m. In town. I walked to town last night, so you see I am pretty well recovered. This letter is by no means finished, of course, but I must post it now.

> With much love, your own
> Theo.

Tuesday, July 9th, 9:10 p.m.

Dear Annie,

Your letter has come to cheer me this evening, when I most need it. I am going to bed now, and I hope I shall be better tomorrow morning.

July 10th, 10 p.m. Up at the Cusacks' again; came up with Regy today.

July 11th, 7:45 p.m. I shall write up the last week's news on the other sheet so that it may not get mixed up with later events. It is too bad of me to be so much behind, and two letters from you still unanswered as well!

July 12th, 10:35 p.m. Chemistry lecture by Charlton just over; was very good.

July 13th, 10:20 p.m. Just came from the Howard's. Thank goodness this is the last of the festivities, and perchance one may peacefully get to work. I must begin on Monday in earnest.

Sunday, July 14th, 9:20 p.m. Have been quite out of sorts again today, no doubt owing to the intense heat. Have done nothing but read a little except that I struggled round to Charlton's for

a little while this evening, having previously promised to call today.

Monday, July 15th, 7 a.m. This must go this morning, though a more incomplete and unsatisfactory letter would be difficult to imagine. I hope I shall be able to send another letter before the week is out, so that you will forgive me! I ought to have sent the weather report in this, and answered your letters and told you about the mail I have been getting, but —.

How are *you*? Let me see — it was Thursday I went up to the Cusacks' last week, and I wrote up to there in my last letter, so I begin:

Friday, July 5th. This was the day of Lees' picnic up at the mine. He invited me, but of course I didn't go, being by no means equal to such frivolities. Regy and Wheatley went off pretty early in the morning, so Mrs. Cusack, Mrs. Ferris, and myself were left alone here, and we devoted the time to doing nothing in particular. Mrs. Cusack was tired and rather out of sorts.

Mrs. Ferris does not become more interesting on further acquaintance. She seems to be a person with an amiable disposition, a few prejudices, and no ideas, so one does not find conversation very easy or profitable. Possibly she is not as bad as I think, and I don't mean to say I don't like her, because she is an excellent and agreeable woman, only not a very interesting one. Typical of a good many such, don't you think? Regy and Wheatley returned in the course of the evening and reported the picnic a great success. There was quite a multitude up there.

Saturday, July 6th. Very like unto the day before. Was getting better all the time. Read some of *Origin of Species*, which proves as full of novelties as ever. It is an inexhaustible book!

Also looked at Stevenson's *Virginibus Puerisque* which belongs to the Ferrises. Thought it ingeniously written nonsense. I begin to be angry with this sort of literature which thinks fit to play the fool with anything, which is no better than that of the man who uses the word 'bloody' in every sentence to express his contempt for things in general. Will you think I am too hard on this book? I may perchance abate my wrath later, but I do naturally despise such productions.

This day there was a grand dance down at the Beddoes' so that Mrs. Ferris, Regy, and Wheatley went off, and only Mrs. Cusack and T.D.A.C. were left.

Sunday, July 7th. A quite uninteresting day. As it was quite unnecessary to post your letter in time for the Monday morning mail, I settled to walk to town in the evening. Mrs. Cusack made much protest, declaring that I should collapse and never get there. I started about 9:45 and not only got there but made pretty good time, getting to town at 12:15. On the way I saw a lunar rainbow, not very distinct but a rather good one, as the whole arc was visible.

Monday, July 8th. Having duly got rid of the fever, or at least the worst of it, my swollen jaw began to bother, and altogether I was both useless and incapable that day. I had got breakfast and supper at the hotel. (Regy and Frank Hamp are acting dumb-crambo, and it *does* disturb my thoughts.!)

Tuesday, July 9th. Cheek much swollen and painful, Could eat nothing solid, so bought two pounds of oatmeal, and got sugar and milk and, having cooked up the oatmeal (or rather, part of it) devoured great quantities. Later on settled abscess in jaw by lancing it, whereupon it subsided and ceased to trouble.

(Continued, 14th July.)

Wednesday, July 10th. Regy turned up in the course of the day, and asked me to go up to the Cusacks' to witness a theatrical performance and other festivities the next day.

Thursday, July 11th. Performance of 'The Honest Baron, or The Fatal Hairpin' by C. Beddoes, F. Hamp, and R. Cusack. Very amusing, and other entertaining events, which must all be deferred until the next letter, as I cannot now descrbe them in full.

Friday, July 12th. General exodus of visitors from the Cusacks'. I had to be in town to meeting of Literary and Sci. Society, so in the afternoon (towards evening), I went with the Hamps (Sid and Frank) as far as Ula (they went to Louis Howard's) and walked the rest of the way to town. But before we started we went over to the ceremony of afternoon tea at the Ferrises (they have it every afternoon!)

(Continued 7 a.m. Monday.)

Charlton's lecture at Lit. & Sci. Soc'y was very good, on the nature and properties of water, with experiments, as the burning of ice with potassium, the explosion of hydrogen and oxygen (it went off like a pistol), and the burning of phosphorus and other things in oxygen.

Saturday, July 13th. Louis Howard was giving a 'lunch' at Ula (at his house) to which everyone was invited. I said I would go (not knowing quite how to excuse myself) but rather repented doing so. Before I went to Ula I had to go to Silver Cliff to get the Mussons' mail (as requested by Lees). Going to Ula I tried to make a short cut across the fields, but although I got a few flowers and butterflies thereby, I found it longer and more tiring than the road, owing to the number of creeks, swamps, etc., which had to be circumvented or gone through.

At Louis' I found a great multitude. Mrs. Beddoes and children, the three Ferrises (and old Ferris appeared by train in the evening), the

Hamps, Regy Cusack, Lees, Wheatley, Miss Bellaire, Ward — I think that is all, except of course the Howards. We had a sumptuous lunch, and afterwards beguiled the afternoon looking at *Graphics* and talking about nothing in particular. It was not very entertaining, though I think they mostly enjoyed themselves. It was quite late in the evening when I got home.

This seems to me to be pretty good sense: '*Good and evil effects of fiction*. From these reasonings it appears that an habitual attention to exhibitions of fictitious distress is, in every view, calculated to check our moral improvement. It diminishes that uneasiness which we feel at the sight of distress and which prompts us to relieve it. It strengthens that disgust which the loathsome concomitants of distress excite in the mind and which prompts us to avoid the sight of misery. . .' (P. 366, *Elements of the Human Mind*, Dugald Stewart, 1855).

Most lovingly, your own Theo.

Monday, July 15th, 8:40 p.m.

Dear Annie,

My room was really getting unbearably dirty (and I can stand about as much dirt as most people!). So I have today turned everything out into the adjoining uninhabited den and given my own sty a good sweep out, with damp sawdust to collect the dust. Now it has the look of a prison cell, severely plain, with not so much as a book in sight. But it is clean and nice, and I shall have my treasures back by tomorrow. I have done nothing else but this today, except that the early afternoon was so intensely hot as to lay me prostrate exhausted, when I read for a while.

I have read more than usual lately, not because I have had any superfluity ot time for it, but because I can read when I am not fit for anything else. I pondered over my book (20 years hence) on 'Variation', which has been on my mind for some time. I am slowly collecting facts for it. Probably I must give my best brain efforts

to this branch of study during my lifetime. It is a glorious and comparatively unworked field.

The multitude (Cusack, Ferris, Beddoes, and company) was going up to the top of the range today, up the Horseshoe Bend trail. I hope they have had a good time; they will have had all they can do to get there. Lees strongly urged me to go, but though he offered to lend me a horse I thought I was better out of it.

The mail I got tonight is the July *Bulletin of the Torrey Botanical Club*, full of interesting matter. A new species from South America is named in it *Rourea bakerana*, after the Baker of Kew. I am in better health and spirits than since I was taken ill. I hope for a letter from you tomorrow.

I went out this morning to look at some *Yucca*. There is great controversy now as to whether bees visit the flowers. I found one bee on a flower, but it was on the outside, so that hardly counts. Now I am going to take a bath.

July 16th, 9:25 p.m. The principal part of the day (bakingly hot) has been given to copying notes from a very extensive list of Mollusca, with localities, sent me six weeks ago by H. Prine, and which ought to have been returned long ago. I sent it off today with a letter and a few shells. I have got the more needful things back into my room and, indeed, I am loath to bring the others, as they crowd things up so much. But they will have to come.

I hoped for your letter today, but it was not. All that came was *Nautilus* and *West American Scientist*. But I got the mollusca note-book all right, looking just as when I last saw it. It came last night, but being registered, I did not get it until today. It was delayed on the journey by the customs. I am thankful to you for sending it so well.

I had a grand dish of greens for supper this evening, namely 'Lambs Quarter' (*Chenopodium album*, from out of the yard at the back of the house).

July 17th, 9:20 p.m. A satisfactory day. Your letter has gone, and I have done much writing. All the morning I was employed over a list of the moths and Diptera of the Wet Mountain Valley, being the first part of a fauna and flora of this district. It is for the *West American Scientist*. I ought to have got it done long ago, and Orcutt has been clamouring for MS. This afternoon I wrote letters ro Pilsbry, Nash, Webster, and Ashmead, so you see it has been a busy day with little to say about it.

This afternoon I talked to Lacy about the proposed magazine to be printed with his type. If set up it would cost $13 an issue for a thousand copies of newspaper size (small pages would cost much more). We should want about 200 subscribers at $1.00 each to make it pay (issued monthly). What do you think? I think it would not be a bad thing, and might even pay a dividend if semi-popular. I should of course have *entire* control over it. I am rather bothered to think who would be able to carry it on next year, though, when I leave.

It has been cooler today, and now the wind howls; we may expect a change of weather.

I will answer your letter now.

The strawberry jam sounds good. Wish they made it out here; it is not for lack of fruit, but the American mind apparently cannot grasp the idea of jam as we understand it, the stuff they sell as such being the veriest rubbish.

The rose festival is interesting; I never heard of it before; it seems like a May-day in June. No, I never read *Peg Woffington*.

The 'Chair of Logic and Metaphysics' at Toronto sounds good because of the $3,000 a year, but thank goodness I may not get any such, for to become actually a *professor* of these things would deprive me of the last remnants of sanity I may possess. How would you like to marry a professor of metaphysics? I am metaphysical enough, by all odds, as it is!

I should say anaemia was the matter with Louy, and iron, exercises, and open air should put her all right. We had many such cases at the hospital, mostly domestic servants who were confined to the house or the kitchen. Get some dumb-bells for her!

Mr. Montefiore's theory about Florida does sound rather startling. I never heard of it and know not whether it is so.

You are very nice to tell me that everything I tell you interests you, and I feel like kissing you for it. You are the only person who ever would listen to all the nonsense I have to say!

I think Smith and Gale are a bit jealous of Morrison. Norris didn't get elected, you see.

You say, 'Isn't it odd that the people you have liked best since you went away have been women?' No, it seems natural enough. Nearly all men, partly because of their competition one against the other, and partly because of the low standard of morals that prevails among them, have become brutal to some extent and largely callous. Women, on the other hand, are more often sympathetic, more moral in every way, and certainly better members of society. Probably the difference is almost entirely due to difference of environment, as men favourably situated, or able to cope with the situation, are good enough. I can forgive a woman if she is sometimes foolish, sometimes illogical, but I cannot forget or forgive a man whose main motive is one of greed or whose life is mostly given to vice.

These things are perhaps exaggerated in this country, but women must never forget that of most men they see only one side, and that the best one. Men see both sides. Nevertheless, it is perhaps true that I am also biased in favour of women. But you will allow, will you not, that they are mostly better than men? There are certain exceptions, though. I think the doctors in London are a good deal better than their wives, but the doctors are exceptionally good men, while the wives, what I know of them, are exceptionally poor specimens of women.

July 18th, 9:20 p.m. Bad news! Mother writes that 'Dear Grannie is very ill and there is no hope of her recovery; it is cancer of the stomach. She is quite resigned and brave and patient.' Poor Grannie — perhaps it is all over now, and she has found the undiscovered country the thought of which (if not quite like the reality) has done so much to give her courage through a difficult and, in its way, almost heroic life. It is now a long while since death took anyone I cared about, and I had lost some sense of its reality. Shall I write to her on the chance of its being on time? Perhaps better not. The only consolation she would care for would be religious, and in that I could not adopt her views, and it would only trouble her to write otherwise. And why bother her with speculations; she will find out soon enough. I wonder what the Grandfather is feeling, for it is he that has done everything to make her life a misery, and she who has patiently borne it all. Will it sober him, or make him wise? Poor Mother is quite knocked-up by the news.

Well, of other things. I have been rather out of sorts today, with some toothache, and in consequence have done little. It has been very hot.

Beside Mother's letter, the mail was: Letter from W. H. Edwards; reprints of July part of *Entomologist*; Variety paper, from West, Newman, & Co. 'A-1' for July 6th, with my article on 'A mining camp in the Rocky Mountains'; catalogue of school-books in French, for sale by Hachette et Cie. (103 pp.) — why on earth sent to me I can not imagine. I see in this work that Shakespeare wrote a tragedy entitled *Jules Cesar*! I suppose it is all right, but it looks queer. They might have put it M. Jules Cesar!

I shall post this tomorrow, so will end up. I hope I can get out on the mountains some time next week.

Your most loving Theo.

P. S. Please tell Frederic that I wanted to compare the *Helix pulchella* I set him, with English ones, and see if there is any difference. Ancey says they are a new species.

Account of Mail Received.

(1.) Your letter, posted 10th June. A particularly nice letter. Certainly I will go to see Aunt Susanne! No, I don't think the Aldriches claim any relationship to the poet! I saw a volume of his poems the other day. The fly sent in this letter has its head entirely squashed, so I cannot name it though it is different from the others. By the way, I was wrong about the little thing I called a Braconid. Ashmead, to whom I sent it, writes: 'The little Hymenoptera sent by Miss Fenn from Isleworth, England, is not a Braconid but an Ichneumonid belonging to the subfamily Cryptinae, in the genus *Hemiteles*. Braconids have only one recurrent nervure, and this insect has two. Cameron or Marshall could easily identify it specifically. I could not without hours of labor.'

(2.) Your letter posted 26th June. I entirely agree with you about Miss Lord. I cannot see any reason for her notions, however looked at. Does she think the 'process' will cure a hungry man, or a broken leg? It would be good for one thing, I allow — hysteria.

How is your sore throat now? I am rather worried about you, poor thing. You are ever so much more patient when anything goes wrong than I am. 'Cryst. alba' was for keeping the mites from my insects. I will forgive you for signing the anti-Pasteur memorial. More of this perhaps another time. I am rather in the dark about the other mail received that I have not told you of, but I will recall what I can, and if I repeat any, forgive me.

July 1st. Letters from Ford and Pilsbry about shells, and about nothing particular from Roby. Pilsbry seems to think one of my Pupae (*P. coloradensis* Ckll.) is a new species.

July 2nd. Letters from A. Dean (about shells) and Miss Eastwood. This last is quite an extraordinary epistle, and annoyed me a little at the time, though I had no right to be annoyed. She declares that I am going to do lots of good in the world (and so on) and urges me in the strongest terms to take care of my health. Now, I had an idea that I was taking pretty good care of myself, and don't see how she could know in any case. But she meant it excellently well, so I wrote back in the same spirit, assuring her at the same time that she knew nothing about me.

July 3rd. Letters from J. W. Douglas (of Lawisham), Olive, and Ashmead. Ashmead offers $75 towards starting a new magazine here 'if I am sure I can keep it up.' It is very generous of him, but having considered the matter, I think it best not to attempt it, though I may try the newspaper. Ashmead's account of the Hymenoptera was to appear in the new magazine, if started.

July 8th. Letter from G. J. Streator, and postcards from W. H. Edwards and M. B. Williamson. Various papers, including July *Canad. Entom.* in which notes by me on 'a new Myrmophile' and '*Phalangodes robusta* (Pack.)'

July 9th. Letters from Gunther (thanking me for specimens I sent to Nat. Hist. Museum) and Dimmock, saying he thinks the publication of *Psyche* cannot be continued.

July 12th. Letters from Orcutt, Gale, Mother, and E. H. White. Also papers, including the July *Naturalist*, in which the editor has a paragraph speaking favourably of my paper on 'Citation of Localities', which, he says, was sent to him by 'our old and valued correspondent, Mr. T.D.A. Cockerell'!

The Performance of 'The Honest Baron' and Other Events

Let me think what I can remember of that occasion. The day was given to preparations of all sorts which I do not remember in detail, and would not be interesting if I did. There was a great multitude present. Here is a list of them: The Cusacks, the Ferrises, the Beddoes' (Beddoes, Mrs. B., and children), Lees, Louis Howard, T.D.A.C. — 17 in all.

The evening commenced with supper, which was really quite a serious affair, considering the number of people to be fed. In fact, there was quite an overflow, so that Mrs. Cusack, Louis Howard, and myself were sent off to sit at a side table.

I think it was about eight when the play began. This masterpiece of dramatic art (which is really very clever and amusing) was written some time ago by Sid Hamp and Frank Cusack, and has been performed several times at various places, once in public in the theatre at Colorado Springs (in aid of some charity) where they had a crammed house and very appreciative audience. This time they were a good deal handicapped by the absence of the proper dresses, etc., but they made up very well with the materials at their command.

The performance took place in the sitting-room, the audience being seated in the window part. Dramatis Personae: The Baron, Sid Hamp; Anastatia Jane (his daughter), Frank Hemp; Oscar (a knight), Regy Cusack; Pinchbeck (a Jew), Beddoes.

The play opens with the Baron seated at a table, writing in a dressing-gown (which he wears throughout the play). He is looking up his money affairs, which are in a very shaky state. Presently, in came Pinchbeck, the Jew (Beddoes did this extremely well) in a cloak and battered top-hat. After kissing the Baron's door-mat and acting very 'your very 'umble servant' for a bit, he comes down to business and produces a bond on the Baron's cow, and also a claim of 60 cents owing to him, and declares he will go to law unless the money is forthcoming.

The Baron is desperate, as he cannot raise the funds, but the Jew offers to compromise matters by taking the Baron's daughter instead. The Baron gladly assents, and Pinchbeck receives an agreement to this effect. Just then, the Baron discovers a letter on the table, addressed to Anastatia Jane, with the postmark, 'Palestine.' He at once opens it and finds that it is from her lover, Oscar, to say he is coming home at once.

Here is a dilemma, for Oscar will claim the daughter in spite of Pinchbeck. So the Baron and Pinchbeck scheme, and finally agree that the latter is to kill Oscar by stabbing him in the back with a huge tin dagger with which he is provided.. Exit Pinchbeck. Enter, Anastatia Jane (Frank Hemp — and an excellent ugly woman he makes), a hideous creature of great muscularity, and the terror of her father. After some talk, a footstep is heard, and Oscar arrives. Immediately he falls on his knees before Anastatia, who greets him rapturously, but he speedily rises and extracts from his knee a hairpin (!) about two feet long, made of bailing wire, which he declares was on the floor and pierced him when he knelt. Anastatia is very sorrowful over the event, but soon they talk of other things, and he relates his adventures, interspersed with rather far-fetched jokes, e.g.:

Oscar. 'And I killed . . . the sea-green Saracens.'
She: 'Why "sea green Saracens", Oscar?'
He. 'Oh, just for the sake of euphony.'
She. 'You funny man!'

There is a good deal more talk which I will not repeat. Finding the empty envelope of Oscar's letter upon the floor, and the letter gone, they suspect 'a plot to work us ill', and Oscar agrees to wear a shirt of mail.

Scene 2. Just the same scenery, except a 'tree' — a branch of pine planted in an old tin can to indicate that it is a forest.

Baron and Oscar talking. Pinchbeck comes up behind and stabs Oscar in the back. Oscar falls, and the Baron makes away. Pinchbeck jumps round the prostrate Oscar, flourishing his dagger. Oscar cries: 'I die. Farewell, Anastatia Jane, I die!' (Then recovering himself) — 'No I don't! Not a bit of it! I had forgotten, my shirt of mail!' (Rising and discovering that he has really only received a scratch): 'Base Jew, defend thyself!' — he rushes at the now frightened Pinchbeck with his sword (a gigantic wooden structure), while Pinchbeck tries to defend himself with a tattered umbrella and his dagger.

Pinchbeck on his defense

Very soon he is overcome and slain (to the great distress of Margery Beddoes among the audience, who does not like to see her father thus impaled and almost hacked to pieces). Oscar then searches Pinchbeck's pockets and finds the various documents received from the Baron, and also 25 cents (to his delight). Then he throws the

body into a pit (the kitchen) and is preparing to depart when he hears footsteps. He hides behind 'yon spreading beech tree' (the pine bough).

Enter Anastatia Jane, who soliloquises. saying to herself that she had better marry Oscar, as she is 43 (to the horror of Oscar, who supposed her about 20) and remarking that when they may chance to differ, she is 'pretty muscular' and can probably get her own way. Oscar begins to change his mind about marrying Anastatia but does not know how to get out of it. Presently he comes from behind the tree and the two indulge in a lot of ridiculous talk, and finally go off to see the Baron about it.

Scene 3. The Castle. After a great deal of beating about the bush, Oscar gives the Baron to understand that he wants to marry his daughter. Now that the Jew is dead, the Baron sees in this the only way of getting rid of her, so he gleefully consents. They kneel, and he puts his hands on their heads to bless them, when another huge hairpin from Anastatia's hair runs into his finger. Anastatia faints. Oscar, on pretence of going for water, makes his escape. Anastatia, recovering, sees him riding away, and goes in pursuit. The Baron, once she is out of the castle, orders the drawbridge up and declares she will never return. Curtain.

You see, it was an absurd farce, but we all laughed heartily over it, and it was very well done. After this, they had dancing (I did not dance), and later still (about midnight) a great camp fire was lit out of doors, and we all sat round, with singing, banjo, and recitations.

July 19th, 8:45 p.m.

My love,

I *am* a miserable creature, to be sure! Today I have been entirely prostrated by an attack of dyspepsia, which is the more aggravating because I cannot put it down to the weather, heat, or any responsible agency, but know it was entirely my own fault.

Yesterday I bought some liver, for a change and because it is quite cheap. I fancied at the time that it was the least bit high, and yet when cooked it seemed all right, so I ate of it, twice yesterday and this morning for breakfast, as also soup made by boiling liver in the water that cooked the *Chenopodium*. Well, it didn't suit my digestive apparatus, and the said apparatus was careful to let me know it.

Consequently I have done very little today. Nominally, I have been arranging and sorting a lot of insects I had in papers, but the work made little progress. This evening, having had a breakfast I could not digest, and a lunch only of biscuits, I became ravenous and purchased a tin of milk which I entirely devoured. This is very extravagant. It costs 20 cents, but the milk is very good and nutritious. It is a new brand, 'The Highland', of admirable quality though canned, whereas the other brands are quite abominable, being, I believe, mixed with various other things, certainly containing much sugar.

Lees called today. He brought the Ferrises in to depart by the train this morning. I also had a regular bevy of small boys with 'bugs', first two with a couple of big longhorn beetles, and then three with a species of Mutillidae (Hymenoptera). They were common things, but I pretended to be much gratified, and showed them my specimens as a reward.

The mail this evening was a letter from Miss Eastwood, enclosing a list of the plants she found when here, and G. J. Cockerell & Co.'s Coal Circular from Carlie. *Science Gossip* ought to be here by now, but it cometh not.

July 20th, 9:35 p.m. Am all right again today. Have returned to a simple fare of eggs, and for the time being am trying how it is without coffee. I am quite doubtful whether over-much coffee or tea is good for me.

I have been looking over and sorting more insects and doing up some for W. H. Edwards, and writing him a long letter. Otherwise I have been copying out the beginning of a list of the plants found by Miss Eastwood at Denver. They are enumerated in a book which she lent me, and I have not been able to commence copying them out until today. It gives me an enormous number of new localities. The old Fauna and Flora book is overflowing, so I bought a new one today for 75 cents, in which I shall enter the species under the head of localities, and index them up in the old book by pages, thus (in the old book):

Clematis ligusticifolia Nutt. Hardscrabble (M. E. Cusack; Denver (Eastwood); Manitou Springs (Porter & Coulter). 5, 8, 9, 14, 16.

Here, you see, there would be no more room on the line allotted for fresh localities, but I can get in a few numbers which refer to pages in the new book where the other localities are stated.

I went into the drug store today to buy some gum! It is queer how people will waste their money for want of a little sense. They gave little bottles of some detestable and very dirty-looking compound which they sell as mucilage for 20 cents, while for five cents one can get (in the same store) enough gum arabic to make more and clean *good* gum that will answer all the purposes required.

This evening I called round at the Freers. I hear from them that the waterworks that supplied Silver Cliff have stopped working, and all water has to be hauled up there in future in waggons. This will be very inconvenient for the poor Silver Cliff-ites. Freer paid me $8.50, my wages for teaching the children. This will be very useful to me, as my funds were getting low.

Yesterday I was looking up the Grannie's illness in the books. It seems that she may live longer than I supposed. But from what I hear, I should think not long.

It has been very hot today. I hear it has been up in the hundreds at Cañon City. There was no mail for me today.

Sunday. July 21st, 7 p.m. All today has been given to writing the next part of my Variation paper, dealing with variation of pupae and co-coons, and hybrids. The writing did not take so very long, but I had to read a good deal to prepare for it. I changed my mind, and wrote a little letter to the Grannie this evening.

Brock was here today and took away my bedstead, as they want it again at the Cox's. Further (which is more distressing) I have to go up and sleep at the Cox's tonight and probably several other nights. Cox is away in Denver, and Mrs. Cox and her children are left in the care of a nurse of very doubtful character, and Mrs. Cox was afraid she heard someone prowling around the other night who might have been in league with the nurse. Probably it was only fancy, or a cow, but she is afraid all the same. Mrs. Cox is said to be going to stay up in the house that I lived in by the Cusacks', and Cox will be away somewhere. Brock said she wanted me to go and live up there and do the chores, but I don't want to.

I was going to say, about Pasteur, that I never heard of his inoculating with the virus of a mad dog! He uses attenuated viruses from rabbits. However, the scope of Pasteur's work includes the whole germ theory and much else, and it ought to be remembered that the hydro-phobia matter is one of the least of his works. I trust a Pasteur Institute would not confine itself to hydrophobia.

About men cooking and washing; they don't hate it *as a profession* but don't like doing it with other things. It bothers a man to come from his work and *then* have to cook a meal. As a matter of fact, I would rather cook for several than for one.

July 22nd, 8:50 p.m. Today has been given to writing up records in my new book. I have finished all Miss Eastwood's records and done some of my own also. The mail this evening was a letter from Nash and a postcard from Miss Eastwood with a packet of fungi (*Aecidium*) she found on the top of a mountain somewhere near Silverton, where she is now staying. It is quite time that I went up to Mrs. Cox's.

10 p.m. (At the Cox's). I never told you about last night. When I got up here I was introduced to the baby, which I had not seen before. It is not lovely. Mrs. Cox does not claim that, but it is about as good-looking as babies of that age generally are. I have not heard what they propose to call it. The nurse is called Mrs. Howard, a middle-aged woman with a professional air who seems to make herself useful in many ways, and is agreeable. The infant lamented most of the night, so Mrs. Cox was tired from want of sleep this morning, and I left before she was up, first treating Isabel and Charlie to a swing (there is a rough swing outside) to their great delight. Mrs. Cox's father is on his way out here and should arrive in about a week, which will be nice for her, as I suppose she likes him, though from all accounts I imagine I shall not care for him myself. He is a clergyman.

I sat up late last night reading *Mr. Meeson's Will*, by Rider Haggard. You will be astonished at my taking to such very light literature, and Rider Haggard of all things, but it amused me and diverted my thoughts, being therefore restful.

July 23rd, 9:30 p.m. (At the Cox's). When I went to get my mail this evening (hoping for your letter), my jaw dropped to see the Cox house quite empty. The explanation was that there was been a 'washout' on the main line somewhere below Cañon City, and so the mail had not come through. There was a telegram for Mrs. Cox, which I brought up here (and have been here ever since). It was to say that Cox will return tomorrow and that he has got work in Denver, which, if, true, is very satisfactory. I have been writing up my notes all day and have got them so far done that a little work tomorrow will bring them to date. It has been a rainy day, with a thunderstorm.

July 24th, 10:5 p.m. Dear, I am disgusted and in a very bad temper! Wednesday, and the mail not yet arrived! Only a *Punch*, which isn't worth the paper it is printed on. Sympathise with me. I have been writing all day, as usual, mostly over beetles this time. Mrs. Cusack, Lees, and Wheatley called on me. Mrs. C. was looking very well and in very good spirits, and very pleased with herself because she has actually been up to the Lakes of the Clouds! Wheatley wanted me to go camping with him for a little while. Possibly I may, as it will enable me to get well up into the mountains without being left quite alone. (Since I have been ill I feel rather scared about going out quite alone.) Late in the afternoon I came up here and took Isabel and Charley down to meet 'Daddy' at the train. I need hardly say that Daddy did not come, but the walk was good for them.

July 25th, 8:25 p.m. At last the mail has come, with your letter! Today began for me with a slight headache, and I felt rather dull over my writing. But I went out this afternoon to try to find some coccids (*Orthezia sp. nov.*) for J. W. Douglas, to whom I was writing, and although I found no coccids, I was refreshed by the walk and got many insects and a dock (*Rumex*) apparently new for Colorado. and three plants new to the Custer Co. list. As I came homeward a little boy ran after me with such a splendid larva of *Samia gloveri* (one of the great native silk-moths) — as he said, 'a worm as big as your finger!' I told him how to rear it, and he took it home with great glee.

That is all the news except for the mail. I shall not go up to the Cox's tonight until later, as I want to write more of this. The mail was: (l.) Your letter. (2.) Letter from Mother.

(3.) Letter from Carlie. He seems to have enjoyed the garden party, Here is a quotation that will amuse you [from Carlie's letter]: 'Olive was gorgeous in white trousers and a striped cap and blazer, but Frederick, who was more modestly attired, was pronounced by a lady who is a good judge of things to be the most attractive specimen of the unfair sex there present.'

(4.) Letter from Olive, with some *astonishingly* good little French sketches. She will do great things. (5.) Bedford Park Natural History & Garden Society Report. Thank you! (6.) The *Entom. Mags.* (7.) *Science Gossip.* (8.) *Pall Mall Budget.*

Now in answer to yours: I sympathise with you when 'feeling pale.' Mrs. Butler *is* an amusing old creature; she ought to be held up to posterity in a story. Can't you work her in somewhere? No, I didn't hear before of the *Agrostemma.* It will be new for my Isleworth list. I am glad your throat is better. The sketches of the patients at Sir Morell's amuse me; how I can imagine them! It was nice of you to write to Grannie. I remember Hamerton on the dress coat, and I think I agree with the spirit of what he says. Fortunately, I don't mind people laughing at my clothes! So I had long ago forgiven everyone about the 'pink trousers.'

'How little we advance in the labours of a day' is good. But the main thing is to see that we *do* advance. It always seemed to me that so many people were wearing their days and years away, doing — nothing.

I am so sorry you didn't get the letter from me at the right time; I hoped it was not lost. It was posted as usual. What idiots those papers are! I never heard anything about the 'terrific storm in Colorado.' Unless it might have been a little storm and freshet somewhere up by Boulder.

I am quite ashamed of this letter, being so short and uninteresting, but it must be posted tonight. So goodbye, love, till the next.

Your own Theo.

Health. Very better, on the whole.

P.S. I wonder what Cox is up to now. When I went for mail this evening, Mrs. Lacy (the post-

mistress) would only give me a letter addressed to Mrs. Cox, having received a telegram from Cox (which she showed me) to say that *no mail* addressed to *him* was to be given up till he returned. I shan't tell Mrs. Cox about that, as it will only worry her. I must be up to the Cox's now.

July 26th, 10 p.m.

Dear Annie,

Meeting of Literary and Scientific Society (very dull) just over, but must go up to Cox's. No time to write now.

July 27th, 11:30 a.m. It is beautifully fine. I shall look at some flowers I got yesterday and then go out for a walk.

8:50 p.m.. First, about yesterday. I posted a letter to you on Thursday night so that it went by yesterday morning's train. I got away from here rather late. It was very sunny and nice, and I got many insects and a bundle of flowers which I only finished examining this morning. Several are new to the Custer Co. list. Towards evening I sat down and wrote an article on naming varieties of shells, in answer to J. W. Williams in the July *Science Gossip.* I of course take the view that they should be named.

The same evening I got a letter from N. L. Britton, the editor of Torrey Botanical Club Bulletin saying that he will publish an article of mine on naming slight varieties of plants, and will also probably read it before the Botanical Club or the Amer. Assn. for the Advancement of Science (which corresponds to our 'British Assn.) which meets shortly at Toronto.

At the same time I got letters from Morrison, about H. Keogh (who says his health is much better), and from Hy. Prime, who is going to send me a lot of American specimens of *Helix nemoralis* and *H. hortensis* to look at. I forgot to say that N. L. Britton joins the Colorado Biological Association. I also got *Insect Life* for July, in which is a letter from me about a proposed Society of Economic Entomologists, to be called the *American Entomologists Union*.

It was now getting late and I began to prepare supper when Sam Wright appeared and announced that there was to be a discussion on the liquor question that night at the Literary and Scientific Society, and would I find something to read on the subject, as nothing had been done. Now there was just about half an hour before the meeting, and supper to get in at that, so of course I had no time to hunt up anything. We had already had what was practically the same thing before, and as this time the committee had done nothing to get the thing up, the 'debate' was a perfect farce. Charlton spoke first, then I followed, then Sam Wright, and Mrs. Charlton ended up by reading a bit from a newspaper. The only satisfactory thing about the meeting was that we elected five new members.

This morning I had to return here after going down town to bring some permanganate of potash Mrs. Cox wanted, but after that I got back to my room and continued the identification of the flowers found yesterday. When buying the permanganate at Merriam's, I got some beautiful little paper envelopes, about 2½ inches by 1½ that will do splendidly for packing my insects. They were 20 cents a hundred; I got 300.

Although I have many letters waiting to be written, I thought it was a shame to stay in when it was so fine, so I went out for a good ramble

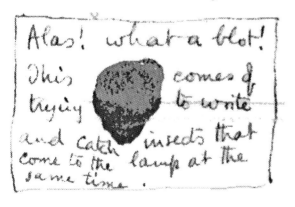

Alas! what a blot! This comes of trying to write and catch insects that come to the lamp at the same time.

and met with multitudes of curious things, the most curious being a fly with most amazing legs — very long, black and white, and almost like wings! I got more plants new to the country list. It took me until mail time to look at them, and now many remain over to be identified tomorrow.

Mrs. Howard (the nurse) departed to Rosita today, and now Mrs. Cox is left along in charge of the three children, which I feel is rather too much for her; the baby is howling at the present minute. Cox is said to be coming back on Monday. He sent Mrs. Cox $50 in a letter today, which she is glad to get. He has gone into the business of real estate in Denver, so I understand. It may be a very good thing for him if he sticks to it. I should think he might make a good agent.

My mail this evening was of no great interest: Postcard from Webster, and a letter from A. Hollick, Sec'y. of the 'Natural Science Association of Staten Island', asking to exchange publications with C.B.A. He sends a sample of their 'Proceedings', which are not very interesting. They are printed on sheets like the C.B.A. reports.

Sunday, July 18th, 8:45 p.m. Today makes me think of Hamerton's remarks on the small results of a day's work. I have not really been lazy, and yet the day seems to have slipped away without any result to show for it. I ran the breakfast this morning, of course, and it was getting late when I got everything washed up and put away. Then I went down to my place and wrote a few notes and then sorted and put by the insects collected yesterday.

After that I began to work up a bundle of plants collected yesterday and, to my astonishment, five o'clock swept down upon me, and I had some yet to be examined. I must have taken at least half an hour over some of the species. However, the results were good. Many species new to the county flora and three new to Colorado. These three are *Amaranthus blitoides*, a plant rather allied to the pigweeds; *Aster commutatus*, a pretty aster with white flowers (and yellow discs), and *Uromyces euphorbiae*, a parasitic fungus on *Euphorbia maculata*.

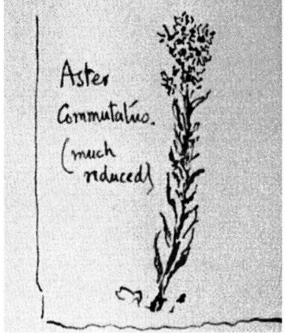

At half-past five I had to come up here again. Mrs. Cox and the children had gone down to the Hunter's for the day and were coming up at six, and I promised to have a fire lit by then so that the baby might come into a warm house. I got my fire lit by then all right, but they never turned up. I read a *Graphic* for a while, and then began a letter to Olive, and by that time it was getting dusk so I waited no longer but had my own supper. Mrs. Cox and children came just as I was finishing. They had been delayed because they could not sooner get a vehicle to ride up in.

This has been a most extraordinarily misty day. This evening the Sangre de Cristo range could not be seen atall. And shortly before that the sun appeared as red as it does on misty days in England. It is reported that the cause of it all is *smoke* from a timber fire on the Greenhorn ranges. I cannot see the fire, but it is quite possible that this is what it is.

Musca domestica is a fearful nuisance in this house. They get into everything and won't let me have a moment's peace.

July 9th, 10:30 p.m. At last Cox is back again. Today is extraordinarily misty, just like a thick sea fog. The range has not been visible atall. There are great speculations as to the cause. Some say it is smoke and talk of a great forest fire near Colorado Springs ('Pikes Peak in eruption' is one story!), while it is even proposed that the great forest fires in Montana are the cause of it. I don't know what to think. It is stated that the same mistiness occurs also at Colorado Springs, Denver, and elsewhere.

I have been naming flowers, writing up records, and writing letters. Towards evening I went up to the Cox's and brought Charley and Isabel down to the station to meet their father. Turner came with Cox. Mrs. Turner and Brock are off at Rosita, I believe. A telegram came from Mr. Wright (Mrs. Cox's father) to say he has just started from New York, so he will be here about Thursday.

My mail this evening was a letter from Dr. John Hamilton about size variations of beetles, and a postcard from W. H. Edwards. This evening I wasted some time talking to Vetter and Samse. They cannot imagine how I can work at science, when (as they suppose) 'there is no money in it.' They are miserable creatures, these two, with no ambition in life except to make sufficient money to take things easy.

July 30th, 9:25 p.m. The first event this morning was Regy. He came to town at about a quarter past eight from Louis Howard's, where he has been working — Mrs. Cusack also staying there. He says Miss Urquhart has written to say that she will call on you if she is in the neighborhood. I hear that Miss Urquhart is bad again with asthma and altogether seems quite unable to live comfortably in England. It is preposterous of her mother to keep her in England under the circumstances.

All this morning I was sorting and packing up a lot of beetles for Hamilton. This afternoon, having had lunch (egg and toast) I set out for Ula to collect specimens, take a walk, and see Mrs. Cusack. On my way I was overtaken by Cress, who had been to town with logs, and I rode some way with him. He was exceedingly amiable — he is generally like a bear with a sore head. When I got to Ula, I met Regy and Mrs. Cusack just driving up to the ranch (I did not know they were going today). Mrs. Cusack asked me to go with them, but I could hardly manage it. She gave me a box of moths she had found and saved for me, as also two *Papilio* pupae Frank Hamp had brought from Pueblo. I hear all those Ferrises (and more) are coming back here in a few weeks!

I went on to the Howard's and found Louis busy making a hayrack while Mrs. H. was doing wool-work. I did not mean to stay, but Louis was very pressing and persuaded me to stay to supper. So with talking, getting specimens round about, and cataloguing the Ula flora (as much of it as I could see) and peeling some onions, the time went until the evening.

When I was sweeping for insects in the meadow, the mosquitoes discovered that I was a very interesting object, and I was obliged to flee to avoid being entirely eaten up! It was after dark when I got back here.

I had only just arrived when I was summoned up to the Chetelat's, where I found an assembly of ladies (Mrs. Chetelat, Mrs. Charlton, Mrs. Vance, and another unknown to me) seated around a table looking at a huge moth that had flown in the window and been caught by Mrs. Charlton under a glass dish. It is a fine creature — an *Erebia*, or owl-moth.

I hope a letter from you may have come this evening, but the postoffice was shut up when I got to town. It is still exceedingly misty. The range was not visible until about sunset, and then very indistinctly.

July 31st, 8:35 p.m. Yes, I found your letter awaiting me this morning at the postoffice, and was pleased accordingly. As I read it the first thing, I will begin the account of the day by answering it. I am sorry you were worried about my being ill. I am afraid in my letters I make things seem worse than they are. You see, you are the only sympathetic person I can grumble to! And also, when one is living alone, one is more bothered by little difficulties which would be forgotten in the society of others. Don't you think so? I am afraid you have been quite as much out of sorts as I have but you don't grumble.

Your dictionary is a duffer! 'Overspread' will never do for 'suffuse' — it comes from *sub* = under and *fundere* = to pour. Bread is not *suffused* with butter!

[Alfred Russel] Wallace is quite old, of course. I once heard him speak on Land Nationalisation. He is a very fine-looking old man with white hair.

Some chrysalids have to be kept in slightly damp moss or in damp soil, etc. This is more necessary. The lilac moth will probably be best dry. It was very nice of you to offer to go and take care of them in case of need. I fear there may be need, soon. Yes, we will go to the Parnell Commission when I get back. Yes, I remember Bob Read.

Carlie says something about the family coming to America, but I don't think they will. I should only advocate such a move on their part in such an event of their becoming entirely impecunious, when they would probably do well out West for a time. But it is not so. Carlie has remunerative work, and the family an income, and I should think it queer if I can't earn a living when I get back!

No, I don't think I will camp out alone, having thought it over. The bears don't make any difference, as they always run away, but it is perhaps best to be with someone in case of accident or illness.

Thank you for the weather report — yours begins much warmer than mine, but mine gets warmer towards the end. I think I like your weather best. Thank you for the insects. The moth found dead on the strawberry bed is very worn, but I think it is *Noctua festiva*. It has been found before in Middlesex, at Highgate (B.Lockyer) and Willesden (S. T. Klein). The little packages are Diptera. Number 1 is much like my 'wound gnat' (figured in 13th report of C.B.A.) but I don't know the genus. No. 2 is perhaps a Tipulid, but too smashed to make out. Frederic is now getting to be an authority on Diptera, is he not? I must write to him and beg him to pay special attention to *Cecidomyia*. Does he want any Diptera from here? The moths are coming in at my window this evening, some nice ones that I had not seen before.

This morning was taken up in sorting and writing notes on the things I got yesterday at Ula. But I spent a little time after breakfast reading the *Pall Mall Budget*. This afternoon I went down by the creek, getting specimens. I found a species of small sunflower (*Helianthus nuttallii*) new for Colorado. It was very hot (about 89 in the shade towards evening) and not so misty as yesterday, the range being visible though indistinct. I got a postcard from W. H. Edwards with names of some butterflies I sent him, and *Pall Mall Budget* and *Punch*.

August 1st, 8:30 p.m. Here is August. Soon it will be autumn! This has been a hot day and as misty as ever. I read in today's paper that there is an enormous tract of country (I think they said 800 square miles) on fire (being all timber, of course) near Glenwood Springs. Supposing this mist to be smoke, it might come from there.

I am not pleased with myself today. I have only written up some notes, written three letters and a review of Hamilton's Coleoptera Catalogue (for *West American Scientist*). This afternoon I lay down for a few hours, being quite faint from the heat. (Not atall ill, of course, but the heat is very trying to everyone, and especially to me. It is so oppressive and dry.)

This evening I got *Little Folks*. Many thanks. *Fritz's Discovery* is a nice story (or anecdote, should one say; it is so very short). I think it served Fritz quite right! I never did like boys, though. I discovered my essay on Socialism today, the one I read before the Literary and Science Society, so I enclose it. What do you think of it? Those eccentric pencil-marks were made during the earlier part of the meeting; I cannot hold a pencil without scribbling. You see the 'essay' is too short to be of much use.

This letter will go tomorrow morning, so I wind up now. I hope to be out in the mountains somewhere before next week, so if by any chance the next letter should be late, will you forgive me? You know I will do all I can to get it posted, but it might be impossible.

Your own lover, Theo.
Health. Good.

I suppose Mrs. Cox's father came today, but I did not see him.

August 2nd, 9:30 p.m.

Dear Annie,

I am up at the Cusacks'. I posted a letter to you by the morning mail. Most of the morning was taken up in sorting some of my things, papers etc., which had been packed away in chaos since I came to town, and in general putting my room straight.

In the early afternoon I packed up some dried flowers and fungi for the Department of Agriculture, and had only just finished doing up the package when Regy arrived and enquired whether I wanted to go up to the ranch. I did, so I hastily did up a few things I required, took some dirty clothes to the Chinaman to wash, and got onto the waggon and was off. We had to sit on a lot of boards, the waggon being full of lumber for boarding one of the rooms in the house I used to live in by the Cusacks'. On our way we met Lees going town-ward. We got out here shortly before suppertime. Mrs. Cusack welcomed me very kindly and was full of enthusiasm about the flowers she had found (some very nice ones), and the cupboard (very neat) she had made for the herbarium, and the insects (some new) she had caught for me.

This evening I read aloud Carnegie's *Gospel of Wealth* or apology for being rich, in *Pall Mall Budget*. Did you see it? It is a very clever defence of his position, but when he argues that it is good for individuals to acquire vast wealth so that they may use it for public purposes, he rather 'gives himself away', as the wealthy men obviously do not and will not so use it — as a class.

Aug. 3rd, 9 p.m. Am so sleepy, though it is not very late. The day seems to have been passed rather superficially, since I have only obtained a few specimens around the house (insects and plants) and examined and identified several alpine flowers found by Mrs. Cusack at the Lakes of the Clouds, and by myself when I went up to timberline from Lees'. Cox was here today at lunch, and Lees came in the afternoon and is here now. The air is beautiful up here compared with that in town.

Aug. 4th, 8:43 p.m. Up at Lees'. Lees was going up to his cabin this morning, and I agreed to go with him. Just before we started he found it would be necessary to send a message to Beddoes about some strayed horses, so we made this arrangement. I was to take Buonaparte (the horse) and the two-wheeled cart and drive to the old Beddoes ranch (which is on the way to the cabin) and there dump the things we had to take up, then drive to Beddoes', come back and meet

Lees (who would walk there) at one o'clock, when we should have lunch and then go on up to the cabin.

I got down to the Beddoes' without incident except that I met a black horse with a saddle, and a rope trailing behind, but no owner had been after it all the morning. Having got through the worst bars (substitute for a gate) I ever saw, I reached the Beddoes', as I said, and delivered my message, but although asked to lunch (they were just sitting down to that meal) did not stay but returned at once. Frank Hamp was there and also Mrs. Hamp from Colorado Springs, whom I had never seen before. It was 20 past one before I could get back to the old Beddoes ranch, and I found Lees already there having his lunch. I likewise fed, and then we proceeded, Lees preferring to walk. He got up here before I did, as I had to walk the horse all the way, and it went very slowly. Since I got here I have been getting what flowers and insects I could round the cabin. There was a refreshing rain at suppertime.

It is not yet nine but I am tired and shall go to bed very soon. I have been up on the mountains above timber line. We got up this morning at about six, and after breakfast Lees and I started out up the gulch to look for a 'corner' but we could not find it (you remember the 'corners' when we were surveying). Then Lees went back to work in the mine, and I went on up the gulch.

It was very steep and I went very slowly, having Coulter's *Manual* with me, and identifying flowers as I went along: Species of *Veronica, Potentilla, Cardamine, Cnicus* [=*Cirsium*. Ed.], *Mertensia, Vaccinium, Saxifraga*, and many other genera. I often sat down, but did at last get up into the thick timber, and at length to timber line. Here I got fresh flowers and insects (some very nice) and then went some way over the rocky and bare but treeless ground. Here grew great woolly thistles with yellow flowers — bright chrome yellow, *Cnicus eriocephalus* [= *Cirsium scopulorum*. Ed.] most curious of all thistles. A bumble bee was visiting the flowers, although bees are supposed to abominate yellow!

I hoped to see some of the great mountain sheep, but all I found of them was a dead and bleached skull. Neither did I see any deer, though I saw where a bear had reposed (this in the gulch), and grouse were plenty. I got back to Lees' at about 5:30, and soon after we had supper, after which I spent some time putting away the numerous specimens gathered during the day.

Aug. 6th, 8:35 p.m. Have come down to the Cusack's. Mrs. Cox was coming up here today and sent for me to be here to help her, but she never arrived. Am very tired, so will write about today tomorrow.

Aug. 7th, 8 a.m. Of yesterday! Up at 6:30. Breakfast. Morning at the cabin and round catching insects (got many) and helping Lees with various odd jobs. But directly after breakfast Lees sent me down to Smith's Park to see if any cattle were there, and gave me a shotgun to shoot them if they were. This sounds rather extraordinary, but it is the only thing to do as, if simply driven away they return and one cannot get near enough to hit them. So they are shot at a distance, and the shot having scattered, make them uncomfortable without really injuring them. These cattle belong to a man named Cowen, who has herded them up onto Lees' place without any justification.

Well, I went down to the Park but found no cattle, so I caught some insects and came back again. After lunch I took the two-wheeled cart and Buonaparte and drove down to the Cusack's to help Mrs. Cox pitch her tent as she had asked me to do. Mrs. Cox never came, and it is not known exactly when she will come, so I had the journey for nothing. This was rather annoying, as she should not have sent for me unless she really knew she would come. I shall go back to Lees' this morning, riding Buonaparte (the cart is to be left here) and shall stay up at this cabin for some time, working every othe day or one day in three for Lees for my board, and the other days

collecting specimens. On Friday I shall walk to town and post this. This morning I was up before six and have had breakfast, and shall start very soon.

8:40 p.m. Up at Lees' again. I rode Buonaparte up today. Have been working in the mine this afternoon.

Aug. 8th, 2 p.m. Concerning yesterday: I was up before six, but having various things to do (this at the Cusacks') did not get off until about 9:20. Before I went Mrs. Cusack kindly put a cloth cover on my Coulter's *Manual*, which I take about the mountains in my hand to identify flowers as they grow; it therefore needs a cover. Mrs. C. had just got a letter from Frank, who is doing excellently well in Australia and has saved nearly enough to repay $100 he borrowed from Frank Hamp to help him get out there. I rode the horse, Buonaparte, packing my bundle on behind. It was after twelve when I got here (to Lees') as I went slowly.

After lunch, I went up with Lees to work in the mine. Water is now coming in at the end, and we were making a channel in the floor for it to flow out. I had to wheel the rocks out in the barrow. Sometimes it was so heavy that I could hardly keep my grip on the barrow handles. While Lees cooked us supper (a grouse and new potatoes) I went down to Smith's Park to see if the cattle were there, but they were not. I caught quite a lot of insects by the mine while Lees was mending the pickaxe, the handle of which had broken.

Aug. 9th, 10:20 p.m. I have come to town and got a very nice letter from you, as also hosts of other letters. I left Lees' place at about 8 a.m. but spent so much time on the road hunting insects and plants that It was nearly four when I reached town. I got a lift the last mile. When I got here I was a little tired so I got some milk and bread as provisions and cooked nothing, but spent the rest of the afternoon perusing the mail at my leisure.

This evening was the concert evening of the Lit. & Sci. Society. We had a full house (only a few seats were vacant) and rather a nice little meeting: Recitations, readings, songs, and so forth. Four new members were proposed.

The train has not come in tonight, owing no doubt to a washout. Do not know whether it will arrive on time to leave at the usual hour tomorrow, but I must have this letter ready in case it does. I will answer some of the things in your letter now.

I sympathise with you about the Fernall Watsons. It is very annoying to have to go to a place when you don't care for it, as I very well know. No, Lees has not struck any ore, but there is the possibility that he will soon. There is of course good ore in the 'lead' above. My 'claim' proved of no value. Of course one could easily tell silver from iron if in any quantity, but the fragment that shone like silver was only microscopic. No doubt it was iron.

I got a few wild raspberries (*Rubus strigosus*) up in the mountains; they are not so good as 'tame' ones and not numerous enough for jam. (They always talk about 'tame' plants instead of saying 'cultivated' out here.) I have often taken *Crocallis elingulata* — it is very easy to recognize if once known. You are very nice about my being ill. I shall treasure it up until the next time I may happen to be out of sorts. At present I am very well. The mountain air has done me much good.

Aug.10, 9:10 a. m. As there is a washout the mail will probably have to go by coach, and I don't know when it will start, but I had better post this so as not to miss it by any chance. I must give an account of the mail I got, in my next. Mother writes that Grandpa B. is worrying the Grannie up to the very last and making himself generally abominable.

Puccinia malvacearum, which you found at Isleworth, is an interesting species, I believe only introduced into England of late years. In parts of South Australia it has been introduced

and nearly caused the extinction of *Lavatera plebeia* (one of the Malvaceae) and this in turn has caused the disappearance of the beautiful beetles called *Lamprima* which used to visit the *Lavatera* flowers in myriads. This is on the authority of Friedrich Ludwig.

I think I will tell you about the mail of yesterday, after all: (1.) Your letter. (2.) Letter from Mother. (3.) Letter from T. C. Curry, wanting shells. (4.) Letter from Tutt Hall of Watford with some interesting notes on variation in beetles. (5.) Letter from Ashmead about Hymenoptera. (6.) Letter from A. Hollick about C.B.A. (7.) Letter from D. McCanne of Gunnison, sending specimens of larkspur which he says is supposed to poison cattle. This was sent to me at the request of the *Field & Farm*. (8.) Letter from Rev. A. Dean, and a box of *Helix nemoralis* and *H. hortensis* for me to name the varieties. (9.) Letter from Leslie, complaining that I have not written to him lately and sending a very remarkable variety of *Physa* he found at Toronto. (10.) Letter from Nash. (11.) Letter from Orcutt. (12.) Postcard from S. Henshaw, about *Psyche*. (13.) *Pall Mall Budget*. (14.) *Insect Life*, a duplicate copy of last number. I will send this to you so that you may see what it is like. It has also a note of mine in it. Can you imagine the British Government publishing such a magazine? (13.) *Journal of Mycology* (also published by the U. S. Government). This number has an article of mine on Custer Co. fungi. (16.) Two *Punch*. In one of them is a very nice and appropriate poem called *Darby and Joan*, on the occasion of Gladstone's Golden Wedding.

Now I will post this, and I hope the next letter will be a better one and posted in better time.

Lovingly, your Theo.
Health. Very good.

Aug. 10th, 10:15 a.m.

Dear Annie,

I shall put down odd notes as they occur to me: (1.) In the list of mail received yesterday (in last letter) I think I forgot to mention *Psyche*, which contains a report on Entomology of the Colorado Biological Association, by T.D.A.C. (2.) *Crocallis elingulata* I had down for two Middlesex localities: London (Meldola) and Willesden (Klein).

8 p.m. This has not been an interesting day. No mail coach and no train. I am afraid you will get the last letter dreadfully late. I have been writing letters the whole day (and packing up specimens) and so got the more important of my correspondence up to date. Lees was here this afternoon. He will not go up to the mine until Tuesday, so I shall stay here until then. For some reason I am extra stupid, tired, and sleepy tonight, so I shall go to bed early.

Sunday, Aug. 11th, 8:30 p.m. At the Cusack's. Stupidly I left yesterday's bit of letter in town, so I begin this on a new sheet. I happened here in this way: Lees appeared this morning and said he was going to Beddoes' but would not go to the mine until Tuesday or later, but we arranged that I should go up today to be there to look out that the cattle did not get in. So I drove with him as far as the Beckwith's and then walked up here. We had lunch at the Howard's. Louis is in the middle of haying, and Ward is working for him. (Campion is away in England.) Walking up here, I hoped to get some specimens on my way, but it soon began to drizzle, and presently it is pouring with rain, so I got pretty well wet through. When I got to the Cusacks', Mrs. C. insisted on my changing everything (which I must have done in any case) and, as my own things are wet, I am stopping here the night instead of going up to the mine.

I found Mrs. Cox was camped by the Brocks', but the rain had come through their tent and drowned them out, so they were at the Brocks' house. I was introduced to old Wright (Mrs. Cox's father) and he was up here tonight. He seems an amiable sort of old fellow. Mrs. Cusack asks me to come here and do chores and odd jobs for board, which I think I will, as I shall like it and it will give me good opportunities for collecting. The railroad is worse washed out than ever and I don't know what they will do. I suppose they will run the coach with the mail tomorrow. A party of Ferrises was due tomorrow but I don't see how they can get here. It was, I think, Mr. and Mrs. Ferris, the two daughters and three cousins, to stay for a week.

Aug. 12th, 7:55 p.m. I am monarch of all I survey — pro tem. I think it was somewhere about nine when I left the Cusacks' to walk up here to Lees' place. I hindered a great deal getting flowers and insects on the way. On Brock's ranch, to begin with, I found *Liatris punctata*, new to me, a species of Compositae with pink flowers and little pits all over the leaves. Then I made descriptions of two varieties of the common *Gilia aggregata* and caught two butterflies, an *Argynnis* new to me and a *Parnassias*.

For the next mile or so, past the old Splann house and across Oak Hollow I got little else than a yellow beetle and some galls on oak, though I did also find come caterpillars on *Gilia* and catch specimens of *Vanessa cardui* and *V. antiopa*, the latter a lovely thing. Beyond, by Greenleaf Creek I found an *Aecidium* (parasitic fungus) new to me, and took a yellow butterfly, *Colias eriphyle*. The next place was Beddoes' old (abandoned) house where I met with a new grass fungus, and had to take shelter a little while from the rain.

Up Beddoes' old road were *Argynnis, Pamphilia*, etc., at the bright yellow flowers of the sunflower-like *Rudbeckia laciniata*, but all this time clouds were gathering, and after picking another new fungus and writing a description of an *Aphis* found on *Clematis* (I *describe* the plant-lice, as they are so hard to keep) I again took shelter from the rain, this time under a fir. Then it cleared up for a time and I pushed on but collected no more. When about a mile (or less) from Smith's Park I heard a cowbell and knew that the Cowen cattle were among the trees to my left. Had it been fine, I would have driven them further away to lessen the chance of their coming to the Park, but a bad storm was gathering, with

444

lightning, hail, and rain. So I pushed on and was only about 100 yards from the cabin when the storm broke, so I soon got shelter.

I was a little tired when I got here, so I made a fire and boiled some Epp's Chocolate and drank it with bread and butter to accompany. It was now about 1:30 p.m. I also read some of Darwin's *Voyage of the Beagle*, which is up here. Like all of Darwin's books, it will stand reading many times and never seems old. It is a very inspiring book, the *Beagle*. I must try some day to write a book on the Rocky Mountains, but the later the better, as a work written now would be crude. Besides, I should want you to be there to help and encourage me.

After this I lay down for a little while and then walked down to Smith's Park to see if perchance the cattle had come in (it was now pretty fine, but it rained shortly after) but they were not to be seen. However, I did not have my walk for nothing, as I got a quantity of *Aecidium* on *Artemisia vulgaris* [probably *A. ludoviciana*. Ed.]. When I got back I walked up to the mine and gathered various flowers which I worked at with the book until dusk, when I had supper — bacon, bread, and chocolate.

I do not know whether Lees will be here tomorrow or the next day. The abscess in my jaw seems to be forming again but does not worry me much. I thought I had got rid of it. I must have a tooth pulled out, I expect, but I believe the West Cliff dentist (Arnold) is such a duffer I don't like to trust him to do it.

Aug. 13th, 8:35 p.m. I did not get up until eight this morning, and then I got interested in naming some flowers (*Aster, Erigeron*, etc.) so that I did not have breakfast until ten. After that, I wandered down beyond Smith's Park where I met Lees coming up, earlier than I expected. This afternoon I have been working in the mine, and later walked down to Smith's Park to get some potatoes (Lees has a crop of them there). I found today a little sunflower by the stable. It is *Helianthus petiolaris*, so far as I know not found in the

Valley. Lees must have brought the seed from Pueblo with oats. Tomorrow I go to town and shall hope for the mail and a letter from you.

Aug.14th, 8:55 p.m. This morning I rode Buonaparte down to the Cusacks' to give Regy a letter of Lees' to post (he was going to town), and perhaps to go with him. On my way down I met Brock and Wright (I shall call him Rev. Wright in future, as there are so many Wrights) riding up to shoot grouse up at Lees'. When I got to the Cusacks' I found Regy had already gone, riding off early before anyone else was up. So I did not go to town but waited at the Cusacks' till his return in the early afternoon, meanwhile naming flowers for Mrs. Cusack. Regy came with no mail, to everyone's disgust, and said that although the West Cliff mail had gone out on the Cotopaxi stage last night, no mail had come in, and it was not known when any would. It is really scandalous that they don't get the mail through better than this.

Then I returned to Lees'. In Beddoes' old road I met Brock and Rev. Wright walking. They had just *seen* a grouse, and their horses had skipped out homeward, so they walked sorrowfully after them. Not far behind them came 'The Sheriff', a sorrel horse belonging to Payn, which had also escaped from Lees, owing to a gate not being shut. Lees brought this horse up the last time he came. I had to drive it back to Lees', which was not very easy, as it is 'locoed' (i.e., poisoned from eating the loco weed, *Oxytropis lambertii*) and consequently very stupid. But I got it back all right, getting to the cabin between five and six. From supper to dark I looked for specimens and found a slug, some agarics, and other interesting things. The Elder here (*Sambucus racemosa*) has bright red berries, but I found a variety this evening with yellow berries.

Aug. 15th, 10:55 p.m. Here I am in town, and have got your letter, but will write a lot and post this tomorrow. Very sleepy now.

Aug. 16th. Morning. Yesterday morning Lees and I had some idea of going up to timber line, but we agreed to defer that expedition until we could get an aneroid from Beddoes to ascertain the altitudes as we went up. I might have stopped and worked in the tunnel (this is, the mine) but I wanted to go to town about the mail, and I do not like working in the mine, as it is very hard work for me to very little purpose. It is not the sort of thing I should ever be likely to do even fairly well.

So I left Lees alone in the mine (feeling a little uneasy, all the same, for were he to come to any harm from falling rock, there would be nobody to help him) and walked over the hog-back into the Horseshoe Bend gulch, getting sundry shells, plants, and insects on the way, the most interesting being a number of little beetles very like the 'Colorado potato beetle' but only half the size.

From the Horseshoe Bend gulch I walked down until I came to Lees' road, which I followed as usual down to the Cusacks'. On my way, to my surprise, I caught two examples of *Neophasia menapia*, a white butterfly which is rare in this part of the world. Close to oak hollow, I heard a bell tinkle, and turning round observed the wearer to be Buonaparte who, with The Sheriff, had left Lees' (as I told him they would) and come down the road until stopped by a fence. I left The Sheriff where he was, but Buonaparte I rode bareback up to the Cusacks'. As I passed the Moore's (that is, the old Splann house now inhabited by people named Moore of whom I know little or nothing), Mrs. Moore came out and told me that Brock had 'left word for you to fix the gate as he fixed it when you went through.'

Now the said gate is between the Moore's and Brock's, and it is only a few very thin sticks tied together by barbed wire (a few nails here and there), so that, when opened, it flops down on one side so the horses and cattle have not infrequently got through. It is illegal as a matter of fact to have a gate there atall, as it is a country road, but it has been tolerated so far, though such an abominably bad one.

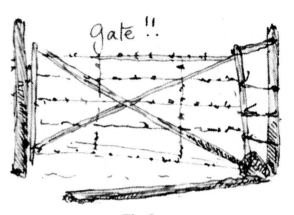

The Gate

Now, when I came to it, I found Brock had wired it up in three places to the post, and put a rock and a log to further keep it from opening! As if people had nothing to do but wire and unwire Brock's faulty gate! Of course I did not 'fix it as he fixed it', when I went through.

I found only Mrs. C. at the Cusacks'; Regy and Wheatley had gone to town. I was a little tired and hot (it was a very hot day) and had a lazy time for an hour or two, besides having lunch of bread and butter and potted meat, with milk (*real* milk) to drink.

Mrs. C. had a story about a three-legged bear that was round there. It seems Cress set a bear trap some time ago, and duly caught a bear by the leg, but like the bear in the legend who got his tail in the ice, It left the member behind and departed. No more was seen of the bear until the Roberts boy rushed in the other day and said he saw a three-legged bear in the pasture (between his place and the Cusacks'), and Wheatley went out with a gun. Sure enough, there were its footprints, but the bear had gone. The same animal came sniffing round the Cox's tent the other night, but they did not know what it was until they saw the footprints in the morning. I suppose Cress will shoot the poor creature before long.

After a while, Regy came from town and said the mail had arrived at last. He had had a letter to say that Miss Urquhart *and her mother* had started for America and would be here in a fortnight or less! I left the Cusacks' at five exactly, and as it was now cool and I was refreshed and in a hurry for my mail, I walked fast and got to town in two hours and a quarter. There was a great lot of mail for me, so that I nearly missed getting my supper by reading it until all the shops were closed. As it was, I had to put up with bread and milk. Today I shall stay in town (and perhaps tomorrow) writing all the time. Besides, my boots are being mended and I have nothing but slippers to wear.

Yesterday's mail is as follows: (1.) Your letter, a nice long one, and mine have been so shockingly short lately! I should like to see 'Garrick', or perhaps I should not like to see it, as it must be very painful to witness. But it must be a very good play if well acted. That Literary Society of the Hamer's sounds rather dreadful! I should have been scared to go! I never could do anything of that sort. My perceptions and ideas work too slowly. Have you not noticed this?

Who are the people you have drawn in your letter? You do not label them! I hope you can go to Swanage again; you must need a holiday. I, like you, very often cannot understand Olive. Indeed, I have never properly understood her. But I have an idea she is not so empty of ideas as one might suppose. I am glad you have been to the academy. I won't answer what you say about the pictures now, and the *Picture Guide* is away at the Cusacks', except today that I agree with you as far as I can see, without the guide.

About my food — I think I live very well on the whole, though I *should* like more variety of food. It has never seemed to me that my food had much to do with any bad health (except very occasionally) but the dry heat and dustiness of West Cliff was exceedingly trying. Really, the winter is much better for my health than the summer. It would be far better for me to be in the mountains *all* the hot weather. Even the Americans, who are used to it, suffer. But I will try to live better in future.

Yes, the Wet Mountain Valley picnics *are* a bit tame. But the *people* are tame, you see.

Other mail was: (2.) Letter from H. G. Smith, Jr., of Denver, about C.B.A. (3.) Letter from I. H. Morrison, of Lexington, Virginia, who sends some *Helix nemoralis* for me to name the varieties. (4.) Letter from H. A. Pilsbry, who sends a lot of American *H. nemoralis* for me to name the varieties, and return. They are very ordinary forms, most of them. (5.) Letter from Dr. Hamilton, with names of a lot of beetles I sent him. One is perhaps a new species. (6.) M. B. Williamson sends a postcard about C.B.A. (8.) Postcard from E. W. Roper, about shells. (8.) Postcard from Carlie. He says he wants me to paint him a $10.00 picture! And will send money. But it must be done in the mountains! (9.) Letter from Mother, who writes, 'I felt sure you were ill. You mustn't stay in that low-lying place, but must go back to Mrs. Cusack's and board with her. I am enclosing five dollars, and will send you some more soon.' At Glen Druid, a sheriff appeared 'and put an officer in possession of the house, for a debt of £18, owed by Grandpa, and he is now living in the drawing room night and day to see we don't take anything away.'

(10.) *Pall Mall Budget*, (11.) *Punch*. (12.) *Science Gossip*. Williams says three of the varieties I named are absurd! However, I am in good company in the matter. You will notice a reference to your Swanage flowers in one of my notes on p. 188. (13.) *Bulletin of the Torrey Botanical Club*. (14.) *Naturalist*. Porritt, in it, says the var. of *Abraxas grossulariae* I called *obscura* was already named *variegata*. But I am not sure he is right. (15.) Interesting paper on the butterflies of the genus *Erebia*, by and from Elwes. (16.) *Psyche*. Jan. to April. (16.) *Dermoids*, a little book of 131 pages, by I. Bland Sutton, 'with the author's kind regards and every good wish.' This is very pleasing to me, and although I am not specially interested in dermoid cysts, anything Sutton writes is always well worth reading.

While they are mending the railroad, the mail goes and comes on the Cotopaxi stage and so arrives at 10 p.m. and leaves at 7 a.m. So I found there was fresh mail for me this morning. (1.) Letter from, Douglas, who seems really to be taking up shells again (a very good thing) and sends a list of what he has found, and says he is sending a box of shells by parcel post for me to name (these have not come yet). He also encloses $3.00. (2.) Letter from W. G. Binney, one of the best authorities on North American shells, sending also a paper of his on shells, which will be of the *greatest* use to me.

Nothing has happened today. I have just finished Pilsbry's *H. nemoralis* and am returning them to him. There was nothing new among them. I shall go to Mrs. Cusack's as soon as I can get my letters answered and one or two other things done.

Lovingly, your Theo.
Health good.

Saturday, Aug. 17th, 8 p.m.
Dear Annie,

I posted the last letter to you yesterday. By the evening mail I got the August *Nautilus*. Today has been spent as follows. Morning, general examination of shells, and letter written to Binney, enclosing some Colorado shells. Afternoon, paper for *Science Gossip* on 'Insects and the Colours of Flowers', not controversial but relating to some of my own observations.

Also, I went round to Charlton's to look at the *Manual of the Mollusca* (Woodward) which C. has got. Mrs. Charlton showed me some work she was doing in gold on china, really very pretty, some of it. Charlton burns it for her to make it permanent. She is doing floral designs on teacups and saucers. I found Charlton assaying. He had just finished his operations, and little globules of silver remained which he had extracted from the ore. When I left, he asked me to come to dinner tomorrow at five. I shall go. Later, I read the first

part of Sutton's book on dermoids and found it very interesting.

I have spent quite a mint of money today. Rent, $2.00. Washing, 30 cents. Mending of boots, $1.10, and nibs, three cents. Equaling three dollars and 95 cents altogether.

Just before supper I was counting up the number of papers and notes I have published since I began to write in 1882. Here is the summary: In 1882, six; 1883, 14; 1884, 19; 1885, 79; 1886, 54; 1887, 32; 1888, 86; 1889 (to Aug. 17), 84. Total: 374. They would make quite a book if all joined together! This list though, is not quite accurate, as separate portions of the same paper if published at different times are numbered separately.

Sunday, Aug. 18th, 8:30 p.m. All this morning I was writing the 'conclusion' of my paper on variations of insects for the *Entomologist*. I am glad to have it finished. Later I read some Darwin (*Descent of Man* — the parts about Hymenoptera and beetles). Last night by the mail I got two copies of *Field and Farm* for the day, with an editorial on the 'poison weed' and my notes on the larkspur. I send you one.

In the afternoon Regy appeared unexpectedly with the buckboard and offered to take me out to the ranch. It was too good a chance to lose, so I went round to Charlton's to say I could not be round to dinner and to apologise, but he was not in. A little later I went again and poked a note in at the door, which I hope they will find when they return. (The house was shut up.) After I was ready, I had to wait some time for Regy. A man named Mott, a sort of cowboy, drove out with us and had supper here at the Cusacks'. He is a friend of Regy, a pretty good sort of fellow, apparently, but utterly uninteresting.

When I got there I found Mrs. Cusack not very well. She told us that the marriage of Regy and Miss Urquhart was now finally decided upon with the Urquhart mother's consent. Regy and Lees are going to drive down to Pueblo and meet Mrs. and Miss Urquhart when they come, and bring them up here. They (Lees and Regy) start on Friday. Mrs. Urquhart says she will only stay here one or two days and then go back to England! Regy and Mrs. Regy-to-be will live in the other house (the one I lived in), while this house will be given over for a time to the Cox's except that Mrs. Cusack will have her room.

Ward was here today. He is getting up a bear hunt on Thursday. We are all to go out and beat up the three-legged bear, which still remains in the neighbourhood, and shoot it. Rather hard on the bear, I think.

Aug. 19th, 8 p.m. A busy day. Entry of Cox's into the Cusack house, and of Regy into the house I used to live in. In future I shall call this the 'old Cusack house' (now occupied by the Cox's) and the other (the one I lived in, to be occupied by Regy and wife) 'Regy's house.' This bit of nomenclature settled, to relate the events of the day.

After breakfast I went down to the Splanns to take some washing for Mrs. Cusack (Mrs. Splann takes washing) and then, coming back to where the Cox's were camped, helped Mrs. Cox get things ready for moving, and later, when Regy came down with the waggon, helped him put the things in. Then I helped Regy get the things into the house he is going to occupy, and one way or another the day went, so that I had no interval to myself except a short one in which I read the last *Pall Mall Budget* (not a very interesting one).

I sleep in the 'workshop', a well-built wooden shanty close to this house, and am to have meals with Regy over at his house. I had supper there this evening. Tomorrow I am to help Regy haymaking. Cress was cutting his hay for him today; Regy has no machine for the purpose.

Mrs. Cusack is quite ill, apparently with 'mountain fever', and Mrs. Cox seems to be sickening for the same thing. There is a hired girl named Bessie Taylor here, who does the cooking for Mrs. Cox and looks after the baby.

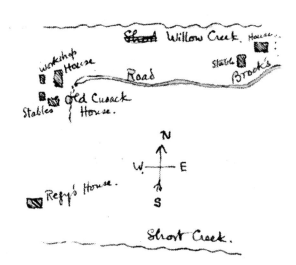

Map showing the old Cusack house, Brock's house, Regy's house, Willow Creek, and Short Creek

Aug. 20th, 9:10 p.m. My dear! Here is your letter, and I never hoped for it so soon. This is very nice. I am so excited about it that my wits have departed from me. Rev. Wright went to town and got the mail. I will just tell you about today and leave the answer to your letter for tomorrow.

First thing was breakfast with Regy at his house (Mrs. Cusack is boarding with the Cox's at present), then over to the old Cusack house where I cut wood and wrote up a lot of notes in my notebook, until towards noon Regy was ready to begin haymaking, and I went out with him. Cress had cut it and was to have raked it with his machine rake, but as he did not appear, we proceeded to rake the hay with the hand rake. Cress came in the afternoon and finished the raking. (Interruption: Dissertation by Mrs. Cusack on subjects various.) Then we (Regy and I) loaded the hay onto the rack and made a stack by the stable. Regy pitched on to the rack while

I trod and smoothed the hay down. It was easy work for me.

Raking hay.
"Quite English, you know!"

It is now 20 to eleven so perhaps I had better 'shut up.' Good night.

Aug. 21st, 7:55 p.m. Up soon after six. Breakfast, and out with Regy to get in a load of hay. This took past eight (possibly past nine) and by that time Wright had had his breakfast and was able to take my place. Rev. Wright is no great hand at these things but he aspired to try his hand, and he and Regy between them got in all the hay that remained in the field. Old Wright seems a pretty good sort of fellow, and I find he takes some interest in flowers, and knows the names of some of the commoner genera.

Most of the middle part of the day I was struggling with a paper on the fauna and flora of the mountains above timber line, to be read on Friday before the West Cliff Lit. and Sci. Society. I may send the paper to Step afterwards. It is very hard to write for these West Cliff people. They don't like to be treated as ignoramuses, and yet if I assume the least scientific knowledge on their part they will not understand what I am saying.

Later on I went up to the place where the cattle died (you remember that Chamberlain brought me a plant supposed to have poisoned hem, some time ago?) to see what poisonous plants there might be. I found lots of larkspur growing there, but also some Umbelliferae which are more likely to be at fault. I looked out for the tracks of the three-legged bear but saw none. It begins to be quite a matter of doubt whether there *is* any bear about! Cress doesn't think there is. It is exceedingly likely that His Bearship has taken lodgings elsewhere. [Too many babies here!] So I'm afraid that Ward's bear hunt will not be a success.

Did I tell you that Frank Hamp is now in partnership with Beddoes?

The mail yesterday was (1.) Your letter, a delightfully long one. Am very glad you have gone (you will be there by now) to Swanage. I am sure you needed the change, and you will enjoy it. Someday we will go on a walking tour together for a holiday, say, a pilgrimage through Surrey and Hants to Swanage, putting up at the roadside inns. Don't you think it would be delightful?

It is nice of you to say you did not mean that I was unkind to you. I hope I am not, for if I am not kind to *you* I can never be kind atall. What you say about fiction is very interesting, because you are much more likely to be right than I in such a matter. I will think the whole matter over again.

You will hear that I did write to the Grannie after all, and now I am glad, for Mother writes, 'I can't tell you how pleased Grannie was with your little letter to her.' Yes, you were quite right to scold me, Yes, I hope Frederic will go to Swanage too for his holiday.

Nelly Allport is certainly a queer girl, but a very good one I think. Mrs. Cusack was talking last night of getting another 'help' out here, and I had just been reading your letter, so I suggested Nelly Allport! I don't suppose she would care to come, but she might like the change. She would make an excellent help, so excellent that I expect they need her at home. She would have to pay her own passage out, but once here Mrs. Cusack could probably find her wages. Anyhow, lots of other people would pay good wages. It's only a notion that struck me at the time, and Mrs. C. *may* go back to England, in which case she will need no help. You might mention it, perhaps, though, when next you see Nelly Allport.

By the way, what became of Douglas A. when he went back to Belgium? No, I don't remember Miss Stevenson, but what a girl! Yes, I remember Tucker. Poor Olive with her picture of you! Certainly, you *are* 'difficult'! We have discussed this over Louy's picture of you ages ago. Of course it is not extravagant of you to go to Swanage! What an idea! Alas, my spelling! I am a very illiterate person.

I am not so sure that men see mainly the *worst* side of women! It wants thinking over. Possibly it is so. But it is the men's fault if so, whereas women *cannot* always see the worst side of men.

I think your composite is *Leontodon autumnalis*, but cannot be sure without books. The leaves are very cut!

Other mail received: (2.) Letter from Mother. Poor Mother! She is having an awful time. A sale at Glen Druid seemed almost inevitable, and preparations were being made for moving Grannie to Bedford Park. But by great exertions on the part of Carlie and Uncle Douglas, it was put off. Grandpa is worse than ever and behaving as badly as it is possible to imagine. Mother has given Uncle Douglas Mrs. Cusack's address, that he may send consumptives out here to board.

(3.) A nice letter from Hy. Edwards, to say that his address for six or seven months will be Australia (at first, Theatre Royal, Melbourne) — he goes out professionally, being an actor. (4.) *Entom. Mags.* and reprints of last part of my variety paper (as usual I will of course send you one).

Aug. 22nd, 10:35 p.m. Here I am 23 years old! I don't seem to have celebrated the event in any notable way, for the day has been rather wasted, I am afraid. Ward turned up in the morning for his bear hunt. After breakfast I wrote up my notes for most of the evening. In the course of the morning Ward, Regy, and I went down to Brock's to see Wheatley (he is in the tent Mrs. Cox occupied), who is quite ill and unable to get about. He is supposed to have dysentery, but it is by no means certain. Tomorrow when I go to town I shall see what can be prescribed for him. My own notion is nourishing liquid food (e.g., milk) as often as possible, and not too much 'doctoring.' I had a great argument with Mrs. Cusack about this; she has great ideas of carbolic acid given internally, and she made him some beef tea of meat that had 'the bloom off', which I strongly condemned.

This afternoon Regy and I went out, partly to look at some fir trees that had been in dispute, and partly to discover and slay (if possible) the three-legged bear. We found our trees, but no sign whatever of the bear — no tracks, so it is almost certain it cannot have been round here very lately. We saw two grouse, and tracks of a deer. Lees is here tonight, and goes with Regy to Pueblo tomorrow; at least, they start tomorrow.

Aug. 23rd, 4:45 p.m. We were up early, and off by nine o'clock. Before starting I called on Wheatley, who is still ill, and promised to get him some medicine. I came to town with Regy, and when I arrived, having read my mail, went off to look for Dr. Patton, whom Wheatley wanted (he is a homeopath; I have no faith in him), but the doctor was away from town. Incidentally I called on Mrs. Freer, who is quite ill. Elsie informed me that she (Elsie) is now in decimal fractions. Then I went up to Silver Cliff and got some medicine from Dr. Ellis. This, on returning to Silver Cliff, I took to Mrs. Cox (who was lunching at the Humphrey's, having driven to town) that she might take it out to Wheatley.

At the Humphrey's I sat a little while taking notes from an interesting book on the North American Flora, by A. Wood. From it I gather that at one place in New York State there is a constant variety of the wild strawberry (*Fragaria vesca*) with white fruits. Humphrey paid me $1.00 for Bertha's attendance at the botany class.

Today's mail is: (1.) Your letter, a pleasant surprise. Thank you, love, for your good wishes and, although you do not say so, you *know* what will give me 'happiness in the future' and is giving me 'hope and courage in the present.' *Our Mutual Friend* and *Isleworth Magazine* are yet on the way.

I once traveled with a whole cargo (some thousand, perhaps) of those grey parrots with red tails. One could even sing 'Tommy Make Room for Your Uncle!' It was when I came back from Madeira. The parrots were from West Africa.

How I wish I were with you at Swanage! No, I have forgotten the Clifford Smiths, though I remember the name. Thank Kate Hemery for her kind remembrances. I have looked at the *Tussilago* fungi (I presume from Swanage) with the microscope and find they are a little too undeveloped for a high power. But the hand lens shows them well, and they are, no doubt: (1.) *Coleosporium tussilaginis,* and (2.) *Aecidium tussilaginis* (this has been said by some to be a variety of *Aecidium compositarum,* which we find here).

The other mail is (2, 3.) Two letters from Mother, one enclosing $5.00. (4.) Letter from Olive. (5, 6.) Letter and postcard from Carlie. Letter encloses $15.00 for a picture. I will do one, but expect to have to return most of the money. I shall estimate value by time. (7.) *Pall Mall Budget.* (8.) [inadvertently omitted words. Ed.] for C.B.A. Library, containing article by him on Steller's Sealion. (9.) 'Observations on the osteology of the orders Tubinares and Steganopodes' (Albatrosses etc.) by and from Shufeldt, for C.B.A. library.

It is possible that I cannot post another letter for over a week, as I may not be able to get away from looking after the Cox's, but I expect I can get Rev. Wright to come to town and post it.

1 p.m. The meeting of the Lit. and Sci. Society is over, but of this later. I must post this now. I am going to walk back to the Cusacks'

tonight. It is better than in the morning, being cool though late.

Most lovingly, your Theo.
Health. Excellent.

August 24th, 1889, 6:5 p.m.

Dear Annie,

Here I am, having walked up to the Cusacks' (it *was* hot) this morning. I was going yesterday evening, as I said in my last letter, but after I posted your letter I got so very sleepy that my resolution to walk out wavered, and finally I went to bed and to sleep and did not wake until six this morning.

The meeting last night went off all right. There was a better attendance than usual, Vetter read a paper on 'Placer Mining' and panned out some gold before the audience. I spoke about the mountain summits and their fauna and flora, reading from MS and partly speaking as I drew on the blackboard or exhibited butterflies. I went into the Glacial Period and the origin of the boreal fauna.

After the meeting the mail came in, bringing me a letter from Leslie, and (from Carlie) a photograph of Grannie. This morning I was a long time getting out here, as the sun was very hot and I felt a bit exhausted. On the way I found fungi on *Carex, Glycyrrhiza, Lupinus,* and *Euphorbia,* the first four new to me. I also got a pretty red beetle, *Chrysomela.*

Sunday, Aug. 25th, 8:5 p.m. Last night I walked up to Lees'. I did not start until after supper, so it was dark before I got there. In fact, it was nearly ten when I reached the cabin. Lees asked me to go up there, as he had been obliged to leave (to go to Pueblo) and there was a mountain rat in the cabin which *must* be killed; and the cattle might get into Smith's Park. The mountain rat is *Neotoma cinerea,* a large rat which I have written of before, very troublesome because it

452

steals all imaginable things (e.g., spoons, bottles, etc.) to put in its nest.

The Cox's rather wanted me here but Lees had been very anxious that I should go and look after the rat, so I went up. (Besides, he gave me a new pair of trousers for going! Fortunate, as my last pair was about worn out.) Well, I walked up to the mine and after some trouble finding a candle, searched for the rat. Under the floor I found its nest of leaves, etc., but no rat. Until eleven I was investigating, and setting a figure-of-four trap, and then I went to bed, but for another hour left the candle burning and had the gun by my side read to shoot, directly the rat might appear. However, no rat came, and though I have no doubt it was about, it did not enter the cabin while I was there. The cattle, too, were not in Smith's Park; I met them on the road, miles away. This morning, after breakfast, I felt quite out of sorts, no doubt the effect of the heat yesterday, so I did not leave Lees' place until about eleven.

The elder bushes are very pretty round there now (*Sambucus racemosa*). They have bright scarlet fruit, most of them, though there are varieties with the fruit dull crimson and others with pale yellowish fruit. These last are undescribed. On my way down from Lees' I caught several butterflies and found other things including a brown pseudoscorpion.

I had Mrs. Cusack's butterfly net, my own having mysteriously disappeared, much to my annoyance. Also, I collected many specimens of minerals which I shall take to Charlton to be identified. I met Beddoes, his boy (Edgeworth, 13) and Miss Bellaire riding up to the mine to fetch the teepee. The Ferrises are coming to *them* in a few days and some will sleep in the teepee.

When I got here in the afternoon early in the after noon I was quite 'done up' and feared I might be ill. But I lay down on my bed in the workshop, and Mrs. Cusack gave me some food, and I read some of Sutton's *Dermoids* and finally got up much better, and cut some wood. The girl (Bessie Taylor) is away, but Rev. Wright is going to town to fetch her again tomorrow, so I shall give him this to post, for although it is only a bit of a letter, I do not know whether I should be able to get one posted on Friday if I waited.

The other day I caught a *Hydroecia nictitans* var. *erythrostigma* in Regy's house. This is a common English moth, vide Newman.

Your own lover, Theo.

Aug. 26th, 8:25 p.m.

Dear Annie,

Last night, being Sunday, we had a little service but did not attempt any hymns. This morning the first event was a hawk. At about 6:30 a.m. I heard the chickens making a great noise and, looking out I saw them all seeking shelter in the stable while a hawk sat in a tree and pondered which it should take. So I hastily dressed and took a rifle (could not find a shotgun) and shot the bird dead. It was about the size of a peregrine. I do not know the species but have seen it before.

Rev. Wright went to town early this morning, so I hastily boiled the hawk and sent it off to Shufeldt in the flesh, for him to dissect and keep the bones. I reserved a wing and a leg for identification. I also gave Rev. Wright a letter to you, taking the opportunity of getting it posted now, as I might not have a chance later. Wright went in mainly to get that girl, Bessie Taylor, but he failed to find her (she had gone off somewhere) and returned without her. After he came back, I went up to Cress's to see if they would let Mrs. Cox have their eldest girl, but she could not come, so Mrs. Cox is girl-less.

One thing I did today was to look over the shells Douglas sent me, I found I could name about half of them at sight, but others must wait for comparison with descriptions when I go to town. Wright brought me some mail: *Our mutual Friend*, Vol. 1. Thank you. I will tell you what I think of it when I have read it. Letters from Morrison of Lexington, who says he is sending a lot more *Helix nemoralis* for me to look at. *Field and Farm* — they are sending me the paper now free of charge. The *Wet Mt. Tribune* of Saturday has a note, 'Prof. Cockerell, who has been rusticating in the mountains, has returned', though as a matter fact my 'return' was only for one night. Now some notes on *your* notes on the Academy. I see there is next to nothing to say, after all. We agree very well about them, and I daresay where we differ is mainly because I have not seen the real things.

Aug. 28th, 3:30 p.m. I have to go up to Lees' place again today, but it looks so stormy that I don't like to start. I don't want to get wet on the way up. This morning was mainly given to clearing up rubbish round Regy's house, to have it ready when they come. Otherwise I have not done much except identify one or two flowers and take descriptions of the colour varieties of Mrs. Cusack's fowls (12 varieties in all). I am going to pay more attention to variation in domestic animals in future. The last few days here have been so broken up with odd jobs that, although I have really had a good deal of spare time, I have never been able go properly set down to anything.

10:20 p.m. The storm cleared up, and at four I started for Lees', but when I got as far as the old Splann ranch I felt rather weak (not having quite got over the effects of the hot walk the other day) and concluded that I had better not attempt to walk to Lees' after all. (It was not so very neces-sary for me to go today, either.) So I came back up Willow Creek, through Brock's fields, finding a few flowers and insects on the way. In one place where Brock had once had a fire, a fine lot of *Epilobium angustifolium* had sprung up. The fondness for wood ashes shown by this plant is extraordinary. In a similar way I believe *Linaria minor* in England grows on cinders.

When about 1/4 mile from this place (the Cusacks') I put up eight or ten grouse. So when I got here I suggested to Wright to go after them with his shotgun, and he said he would. But he disappeared and was not to be found, so I took a rifle and went myself. I found the grouse again, but the best shot I could get was at one up in a fir tree, of which I could only see part of the body. When I fired, it flew away, a solitary feather fluttering to the ground. I must have barely hit it, perhaps not touched the flesh atall.

When I got back I found Rev. Wright had gone off after a hawk, which he shot — a fine specimen. But he came with me and we found the grouse still in the same place (nothing seems to scare them) and he had several shots and managed to bring one bird down.

After supper this evening I found Wright's hawk (it was outside under a tin) still alive. He had only half-killed it with his shot, so I put an end to the poor creature's misery with my knife. I had to make a small hole, and much blood came out, which I fear will not improve the specimen (Wright is going to have it stuffed), but I mopped most of the blood up with a sponge. One could not leave the hawk to die there all night. I might perhaps have killed it better by wringing its neck, but I feared that the skin would break.

Aug. 28th, 7;35 p.m. Lees' cabin. Am feeling very well today and have walked up to Lees' place. I must not stop to write now, as there is only a little bit of candle, about enough to cook supper by, and then I shall be left in utter darkness. Either Lees left no candles here (except this bit) or the rats have got away with them.

Aug. 29th, 8'15 p.m. At the Cusacks'. Well, I have come down from Lees' the second time and never seen the rat, though it certainly is or was about the place. When I started for Lees' yesterday it was stormy-looking, so I took a shawl or plaid to keep me dry. This was just as well, for it did rain before I got far. Near Oak Hollow I stopped to take notes on some cattle that were grazing there, and my appearance (kneeling with the shawl over my head) so amazed them that they all came round and stared, so that I got a very good view of them. When I went on they followed me (at a respectful distance) for quite a long way. I was afraid the cattle would be in Smith's Park, as I saw tracks leading that way, but they were not there.

T. D. A. C. and cattle

Arrived at the cabin, I easily found the key (Beddoes had it hidden under a rock by the chimney) and let myself in. There was very little candle, so I rather hastily cooked supper and, having made much search for the rat without success, went to bed. This morning I went down, getting here in time for lunch. I brought Lees' shotgun in case I should find the cattle in the Park. But I used it only to shoot a squirrel, and shoot *at* a small bird I wanted a skeleton of. The shot are too big and too few in Lees' cartridges for small birds, and they scatter too much for long distances. The squirrel I shot rather *too* much, somewhat spoiling the specimen. It seemed a pity to shoot the little animal, but I wanted to take a description, not being sure of the species, and Rev. Wright wanted the skin.

This afternoon we were in a great state of excitement because I saw through the telescope a waggon and a buckboard coming, and we made certain that it was the Urquharts coming from Pueblo. But when they had come part way across the prairie they actually turned back and disappeared. No doubt it was some other party that lost its way and turned back to go by a different road.

Brock comes tomorrow and I felt tempted to ask him to get my mail, as I want your letter (probably waiting for me) but I have concluded not to trust Brock with my mail, and I must go to town myself soon. Some attempts of Mrs. Cox to instill 'religion' into Isabel's brain have proved rather a failure, mainly provoking a host of questions. Today she wanted to know, 'Does God bite?'

Another 'sell' today. This afternoon, Mrs. Cox prospecting through the telescope, saw a waggon coming in the far distance, and these indeed seemed *surely* the Urquharts and company. So there was much hubbub, as yesterday only more, for we went to the extent of preparing food for them and

Aug. 31st, 10:5 p.m. The letter above was interrupted by the *arrival* of the multitude! Those we saw *were* the Urquharts, but they stopped off at Louis Howard's and hence disappeared mysteriously. Now I have to go to Beddoes', to Louis Howard's, and to town, so no time to tell you about anything. Everybody is greatly excited. Wedding to be tomorrow (Sunday).

5;30 p.m. In town. Here I am, in no end of hurry and bustle. Got your nice letter and have very much to say about all sorts of things, but cannot now. If nothing prevents I shall post a letter on Tuesday (today is Saturday).

Ever your lover, Theo.

Health. Feel exceedingly well and in good spirits.

Editors note: Unfortunately there is a gap in the correspondence, and the letter covering the marriage of Regy Cusack and Miss Urquhart was not found among the Cockerell letters. Considering the fact that the wedding must have been a major event, it is hardly likely that Cockerell wrote no letters to Anne describing this. (But see pp. 448-449)

There is another significant gap between the letters of Sept. 12-17, and October 28). Possibly these letters had been read and re-read and eventually were not returned to the main set.

Thursday, September 12th, 1889

My love,

Yesterday I went to town and took the opportunity of posting a letter to you. I took the horse, 'Joe', and the buckboard, and was not back here until after dark, as I had many errands. In West Cliff, after getting and reading the mail, I went to Charlton's to get some minerals named that I had found. He told me a good deal about them and named them as follows: Muscovite, Titanite, Quartz, Black Oxide of Manganese, Feldspar, Mica Schist, Hornblende, and Jasper. The manganese he thought might carry silver but if so I could get nothing of it as it was on Beddoes' land, and he would of course claim any ore found. I also looked up all those minerals in Dana's *Mineralogy*, which Charlton has.

After this, I did the shopping, and left and took washing for Mrs. Cox and Mrs. Regy, at Mrs. Cooley's (the washerwoman). Then, on the way home, I called at Louis Howard's to get 24 pounds of apples for Mrs. Cusack. I was very tired when I got home. I brought a letter and telegram from Cox, which were not satisfactory as he seems not to be coming here. Cox is a most abominable man.

I took the aneroid barometer belong to Rev. Wright with me to town and took a great many notes of altitudes of various places on the way

from it. This place (the Cusacks') appears to be about 8,192 feet above sea level. I had supposed it to be rather higher.

The mail I got was your letter, a letter from Mother ('Glen Druid' is sold), postcard from Shufeldt, a Chinese newspaper (!) from Carlie, *Naturalist* for September, and *Insect Life* for August. Today I have not done much, being tired and rather out of sorts. I was to have conducted Rev. Wright to the Lakes of the Clouds today, but have postponed it until tomorrow on this account. I have been greatly interested in reading in the weekly editions of the *Times* a full account of the strikes in London. I greatly sympathise with the men and wish I were there to help. (Now I must go to supper.)

7:35 p.m. Regy is a good deal better today and talks of going to town tomorrow. I am so glad the sea-bathing is doing you good. It is a thing I never took to, somehow, when I was at Margate. *Gentiana amarella* I used to have in my herbarium from Wetherby, Yorks. (F. A. Lees). In Colorado it is found in Custer Co., at Twin Lakes, and near Denver. The white *Erythraea centaurium* is interesting (it will be f. *albiflorum*, according to the way of naming these things: f. is 'form', that is, a grade less distinct than 'variety'). I fancy I have found it in Sussex, but I was quite a child and kept no notes, so I cannot be sure.

Sept. 13th, 8 p.m. Have been up to the Lakes of the Clouds, and come back, not too tired but with a headache.

Sept. 14th, 8:30 p.m. Am all right today though still a little tired. I will tell you about yesterday's excursions. Rev. Wright wanted to go and see the Lakes of the Clouds (at the head of Swift Creek, over 11,000 feet alt., as described in 1887), and I offered to take him there. Accordingly, we went yesterday, starting at about eight o'clock. He rode the Cusack horse, 'Joe', and I walked. We went through Cress's and up onto the hog-back beyond. Soon we got amongst the trees and had to make our way as best we could along cattle trails; the cattle always choose convenient paths. (I have just drawn a map of the route, but I think I shall have to finish the description tomorrow, as I have to wash my head and do not want to go to bed late).

Sept. 18th, 10:50 a.m. To continue: We went through a lot of quaking asp, up and down over a rough road until we got onto the hog-back north of Swift Creek, along which we traveled, looking for a trail that Regy said was there. Nothing, however, was visible, until at length, going a little down the hill to look for a path, we observed some branches which had long ago been cut with an axe — evidently an ancient trail. This we followed as best we could, for it was an exceedingly poor one, until finally we found ourselves at the bottom of the gulch at an old abandoned prospect hole! The trail, of course, went no further. To add to our misfortune, the grub bag had burst and all our bread was lost.

We had a very steep ascent to get back onto the top of the hog-back again, and Rev. Wright, having to walk (it was too steep to ride) got quite out of breath. But when we did get to the top, we found a good trail, the one Regy meant, and had no difficulty in following it until we got onto the main trail to the Lakes. (I have been interrupted any number of times writing this, and must now go and catch Ginger) . . . (letter continued at 2:20).

Close to where we joined the trail is the usual camping place of parties going to the lakes (where the road ends and the trail begins), and here we saw horses, buggies, a waggon, and some tents evidently belonging to quite a large party, and we noticed female footprints (easy to tell by the shape of the boots) going up the trail. Evidently they had gone up to the lakes on foot.

After a while we came to the heavy spruce timber which covers the steep ascent (perhaps

1,000 feet) below the lakes. Winding up through this is the very rocky trail until you come out just by the lower lake. The most interesting thing on the way was the extraordinary growth of 'old man's beard', which is a pale greenish lichen (*Usnea barbata*), growing on dead spruces and hanging from the branches. [These would be *Usnea lapponica* and *U. cavernosa*. Ed.] Some trees were almost covered with it.

Usnea *lichen*

When we got nearly to the lakes we came across the people whose camp was below. There were 18 of them, men, women, and boys. They came from Silver Cliff but I did not know any of them. Some time before we got to the lakes it clouded over and began to rain and hail. We took shelter under the trees and went on again when it abated. At the lakes it was blowing hard, and exceedingly cold. So we did not stay long at any spot. We had lunch at the lower lake. Some bread, etc., was kindly given us by the people we met, and we had plenty of mince of our own.

After lunch, Rev. Wright made a pencil sketch of the lake while I looked round for specimens, finding nothing very much, the only flower of note being *Swertia perennis*, a plant allied to the gentians. It was of course too late in the year for most of the flowers and insects.

Then we went up the trail to the other lake, or rather, the upper one, leaving the horse to feed. We were just going round to see the middle lake when a storm came down on us, rain and wind, bitterly cold, so we had to beat a hasty retreat and seek the shelter of the timber.

At the lower edge of the timber we met the greater part of the people we found at the lakes, huddled under the trees round a fire. They said they had seen a deer and a bear the day before, but we saw no game, and Rev. Wright did not once get a chance to use his gun.

Our journey down was uneventful, as Rev. Wright, being on horseback, had to go round by the road, while I made a short cut across Swift Creek when we reached the prairie. I was not very tired but, for some unknown reason, had a headache. Rev. Wright seemed pleased to have seen the lakes.

I found that Mrs. Cox and Mrs. Regy had been to town and brought me back a little mail: *Canadian Entomologist, Pall Mall Budget* (with interesting news of the strikes) and some papers about the Selbourne Society. Yesterday I was writing most of the time, letters and notes, but got less done that I had hoped. Today I have been doing all sorts of jobs. Just now Rev. Wright christened and baptised Mrs. Cox's baby. I had to take the place of one of the absent godfathers. Tomorrow I have to drive Rev. Wright down to Cotopaxi, so I must be getting things ready. 'Ginger' is the horse we are going to take. He was loose in the field, and I caught him, by a great piece of good luck, before lunch. He got into a corner and could not escape me.

9 p.m. We have just had service, today being Sunday.

Sept. 16th, 9:45 a.m. It is beautifully warm and fine today and the snow that fell on the top of the range a few days ago is nearly all melted. We are almost ready to go to Cotopaxi.

Our camp near Cotopaxi

Sept. 17th, 8:50 p.m. Have come back from Cotopaxi. Everything has gone right, and I have rather enjoyed the trip.

Sept. 18th, 11:15 a.m. Here has Regy gone to town and I never gave him this to post; I am so sorry. I fear it will be late. I was thinking I posted the last on Saturday. However, I will give it to Ward and he will see it off by the stage. Ward has just come up here. I will tell you about our journey to Cotopaxi. Rev. Wright, as you know, was going back to England and taking little Charlie Cox with him, to adopt him as his own son. One does not so much wonder at the parents parting with their son in this way, for he will be properly educated, etc. He was an outrageous boy with whom they could do nothing.

The West Cliff branch of the railroad Is washed out, and they talk of abandoning the line up Grape Creek altogether, and building a new one from Cotopaxi up the valley. However, the only way to get to the railroad is to go down on the coach to Cotopaxi or drive one's own rig. We chose the latter way, and I drove them down with 'Ginger' and the buckboard. Having packed up the luggage (three boxes, a bed, etc.) we got off about eleven. We stopped at the Moore's for butter, and then went on by way of the Beddoes' upper ranch, going quite slowly, as we had such a load.

It is about 20 miles to Cotopaxi and I think over 3,000 feet descent. Near Beddoes' we got on the main road, which goes down the valley to Salida, with a turning off to Cotopaxi at the bottom of a long hill. Then Dinsmore's, just on the

Custer-Fremont County line where was the landslide some months ago. One could see it very well. The ground was broken up, looking as if there had been an earthquake. There must have been two or three acres in the slide. Dinsmore's

is the last place of note before Hillside, which is a sort of half-way house where there is a store and postoffice, and the mail coach changes horses.

This place belongs to one Armstrong, but rather to my surprise we found Cox and Mrs. Cox (of the West Cliff Hotel) running the store and postoffice. We got some oats from Cox, and had our lunch (corned beef and bread) by the roadside. Opening the tin of corned beef I cut two of my fingers rather badly and have had them tied up ever since. (They will be all right in a day or two. Mrs. Cusack has given me fingers off an old glove for them.)

I think it was about three when we got off again and passed over less settled country, open and grassy, with piñons, junipers (the large kind that grows in gardens in England) and scrub oak. It was rather a hazy day and things had a soft look; the colours, light and dark greens, reds, browns, and blues, blended very beautifully. Rev. Wright was quite delighted with it all. Presently we passed down a hill which was tinged green with copper, and came to the turning to Cotopaxi and got into the cañon of Corral Creek, which flows into the Arkansas River four miles below at Cotopaxi. It was an exceedingly dusty and sandy road with a good deal of oak scrub by the wayside, in places covered by clematis (C. ligusticifolia) looking very like the English species and now in seed. Among the dead oak leaves I found little snails, Cochlicopa lubrica, etc.

We camped by the creek about half a mile from Cotopaxi. It was a suitable place, dry, with a little stream of clear water close by and with plenty of good wood. There were trees — cottonwoods (Populus angustifolia).

Having looked after the horse and made sort of a tent of a waggon-sheet for Rev. Wright and Charley to sleep under, I went down to Cotopaxi to look up the times of the trains, as it was about six and the office might close. I found Rev. Wright's train left at 11:30 a.m. (Next day of course). I also got the Report on the Zoölogy of the Wheeler Survey by express — a magnificent volume, now out of print, lent me by Nash. I had asked Nash to send it to Cotopaxi so that I could fetch it and save the coach charges.

On my way back to the camp I saw a large camping outfit with U.S.G.S. in coloured letters on the waggon cover. I had learned in Cotopaxi that this was the Geological Survey, so without ceremony I looked in and introduced myself as the secretary of the C.B.A. They received me with the greatest kindness and asked me to supper, but I had to go back, as Rev., Wright was expecting me. Johnson, the head man of the affair, seems to be one of the nicest men I ever met; of anyone else, he is most like Tutt.

After supper I went back to their camp for a moment to give them some notes, and found them just starting out for Wet Mountain Valley to survey Gibbs' Peak. What do you think that for energy! — riding about 20 miles at night and then surveying all next day. They wanted me to go with them but of course I could not. As a matter of fact they did do their surveying, as I met them coming back next day saying that they found it too misty for their work. This is not really a Geological Survey but is Topographical, its object being to make an inch-to-the-mile map of Colorado (like the English Government maps). There is altogether insufficient time allowed for the work, which Johnson bitterly complains of, as he will not be able to turn out a full and accurate map, and the errors will cause him to be blamed.

Next morning we got up at six, and after breakfast Rev. Wright made a sketch of the camp, while I looked for flowers and shells. Then we packed up, and I took Rev. Wright and Charlie to the station and said goodbye, starting off without waiting for their train. The journey back took the whole of that day. I lunched at Hillside, by the road. Mrs. Cox kindly brought me some tart baked apples, and I named some flowers for her. She makes up little books of pressed flowers and sells them.

At Dinsmore's I found some of the familiar *Plantago major*, the first I have seen in this country. It was about dusk when I reached the Cusacks'. Today I have been writing this since I finished the morning's chores. Miss Kitty Ferris is here, staying with Regy and Mrs. Regy for a week or so; she came from the Beddoes' the day before yesterday. Ward came here this morning, for the day. I will give him this to post.

> Most lovingly, Your Theo.
> Health. Very good.

Wednesday, Sept. 18th, 9:35 p.m.

Dear Annie,

At the Cusacks'. I am a little unhappy tonight, for two reasons. (1.) Regy has been to town, and the hoped-for letter from you has not come. (2.) Ward is staying here the night after all, so your letter will not be off by the morning coach tomorrow and will be a day late. I am very sorry, for it is really my fault, as I ought to have sent it by Regy this morning, although had I done so I could not have told you about the Cotopaxi journey. All this afternoon I have been writing up my Cotopaxi notes. I got some mail by Regy but won't write about it tonight, as everyone has gone to bed, and Ward is sleeping in the sitting-room here and wants the light put out.

Sept. 19th, 5:5 p.m. In town. Ward seemed uncertain when he could post this, so to make sure, I have walked to town to post it myself. I also hoped your letter would have come, but

alas! Nothing but a letter from *Field and Farm*. I send you the variety paper and also *Field and Farm* with letter from me on page 12. Also seeds of the white poppy [*Argemone*], gathered on the way to town. You will know it when it comes up, by the pale blue-green prickly leaves. There are enough to give a few away if you know anyone who wants them. You see this is the beginning of another letter, but I began it after I gave Ward the other, but I send this scrap and begin again. I enclose a slip of my field-record to show you how I take my notes on the road. The pencil mark across means I have entered it in my book.

Have seen no more of the Geological Survey people. Wish I could get on the Survey!

> Your own Theo.

Editor's Note: There is a large gap in the sequence of letters. The next letter we have is dated October 22nd, 1899.

Thursday, Oct. 22nd, 1889, 9:15 p.m.

Love,

I was very glad to get your nice letter this morning. Last night, I posted one to you, and at the same time a good deal of MSS to the *West American Scientist*, written that evening. I find I can sometimes work better at night than during the day, but I rarely sit up after 10:15. This morning, besides your letter, I got six reprints of the last part of my paper on Variation of Insects, and a *Pall Mall Budget*. The reprints except one, I sent away — one to you, and the rest to Edwards, Hamilton, Scudder, and Sutton.

After breakfast I read the *Pall Mall* for a while. It is an interesting number. Irving's play, 'The Dead Heart' at the Lyceum must be a wonderful thing, but for me *too* horrible. I should not like to see it. Would you? Perhaps the most interesting thing in this *Pall Mall* is an account of Sir W. MacGregor's explorations in New Guinea. Up on the mountains there, in quite unexplored country, he found a delightful temperate climate and a flora like that of the temperate regions. It sounds fascinating. Let's go and found a colony there! There are no natives, he says, above 4,000 feet.

Then there is an account of a model city, worked on more or less socialistic principles, in Mexico. But that may not be all it appears from the newspaper account. It seems that Rider Haggard 'cribbed' nearly the whole of the shipwreck account in *Mr. Meason's Will* from an old number of *Pall Mall*. I recollect the thing in *Pall Mall* myself, I think. It was in 1886. I will enclose the bit about it.

Having looked through the *Pall Mall* I wrote the addenda to Swanage list (from your letter) into my notebook and then proceeded to sort out my insects taken this year (they are in paper envelopes) according to their orders. Then I packed the Orthoptera (about 17 species off to L. Bruner) and wrote him a letter about them. Since then I have been working at the Hemiptera and Hymenoptera, and I got so interested that I did not get supper until it was quite late.

But I have not answered your letter. You are very courageous, going to bathe after it is too cold for everyone else. When I lived at Margate, I scarcely even bothered, I suppose on the principle that what was always at hand was never chosen. But I might wisely have done so. Your list of additional plants is most excellent. You must already know more about British botany than I ever did. Many of the plants would be new to me. It is really very nice of you to be working at the plants so well. I am so glad you take a pleasure in them.

I never could get along with Olive, mainly because she was so unappreciative of all such things, but then, if she had been like you, I should not have minded, though she did scoff at the plants. Yet she is one of the nicest of girls. It's queer. But for us two, though we love one another ever so much in our hearts, it is good for us to understand and like one another's headwork also. Is it not so? It always seemed so queer to me at Wimpole Street that, though the Uncle and Aunt were affectionate enough, she had no part whatever in his work, nor he in hers. The

greater part of the day they might have been any distance apart and it would not have made any difference. It seemed to me only a half-marriage.

'Mince' that we took up to the lakes is meat minced in a sausage machine. I thought the word was a common one. Possibly *Usnea barbata* may kill the limbs of spruces to some extent, but I will look the matter up. It was with the tin that I cut my fingers. They are now all right now. You see, the U.S.G.S. here at present is topographical. I might get on a real Geological Survey possibly, if there were one. It would be very nice work. Yes, Huxley is quite right about the importance of Physiology. The study of form without the study of functions is mostly wasted time. Only this, that one cannot study function without a knowledge of form. The true beauty of nature is less in appearance than in meaning.

No fungus on *Senecio vulgaris* was enclosed, but there was a lovely *Gentiana pneumonanthe* (apparently), though not quite like one I used to have, for which best thanks. By the way, you should gather what roses and Rubi you can and send them to Baker, who will tell you the species and varieties. The variation of these plants Is very interesting.

Oct. 23rd, 9:15 p.m. You see I was at Louis Howard's last night and so only wrote on a little scrap of paper, which I enclose. But really, everything about yesterday has still to be told.

Oct. 24th. As usual, the mail was the first thing I got: (1.) Letter from Douglas, who says he is going in seriously for conchology. It seems he is going (or has now gone) to near Winnipeg for the bank. Whether to stay or not he does not say. When he wrote he only had a telegram from the head office about it. (2.) Letter from Mother, from Boulogne. (3.) Two letters from Morrison of Virginia. (4.) Letter from Dr. Sterki (a shell man).

I was proceeding to reply to these when Regy appeared. He had kindly brought to town some things bought of Mrs. Cox (the Cox's went to Denver some time ago) and also the socks you sent me, kindly darned by Mrs. Cusack. Those socks, my dear, are the best I ever came across. They wore exceedingly well and I never once had sore feet when wearing them all over the mountains. Directly I took them off and put on another pair and walked to town, my feet got sore.

Regy was going up to Silver Cliff, and I went with him to ask whether there were any letters for me at the postoffice there. (There were not.) Three of my morning's letters had gone up to Silver Cliff and been sent down here after having been stamped, and I feared there might be some up there that they had not noticed as belonging to this town. After getting back from Silver Cliff I wrote some conchological postcards and letters.

About three p.m., getting tired of writing and wanting a walk (it was very fine) I walked out to Louis Howard's at Ula to do those accounts for him. On the way I got a few insects. When I got there, I found Mrs. Howard painting, while Louis had gone to town; I had missed him. Before very long he came back and after a while we got to the accounts, but were soon interrupted by supper.

Ward is still at the Howard's (Campion still being in England), and I was introduced to Louis' two pupils from Bedfordshire. The elder is a great fellow but not very old (perhaps 18 or 20), his name, I think, McDougall. The younger may be 17. He is smaller, lighter; his name is Pennycuick (a curious name), wherefore he is addressed as 'Penny.' They seem pretty ordinary, tolerably nice fellows, but I saw too little of them to really know much about them. The elder one has been in India.

9:30 p.m. Here I am at the Howard's. I write on this bit of paper because I thought I should be back in town tonight and didn't bring the letter. I came here to do Louis' accounts for him and am stopping for the night.

The accounts I had to write up for Louis were the whole *ranch* accounts from January.

Louis didn't know how to make up a proper balance sheet, and it was necessary to have the thing properly done because Lees, as I think I said, is going half-shares in the ranch with Louis and wants to know where the money goes and how much he has to pay. So I worked that evening at it (Louis looking on and helping) and, as it was getting late and there was no chance of finishing it there, I stopped the night at Louis' request, and this morning by about 9:30 had the whole thing settled up in good fashion so that the expenditures, etc., could be seen at a glance. Louis offered to pay me for the work but of course I would not take anything. So Mrs. Howard gave me two pots of their homemade jam, which is a great luxury to me.

Now we have come to today, the 25th. When I walked to town this morning I got mail as follows: (1.) Letter from Morrison of Virginia sending yet another box of *H. nemoralis* for me to examine. (2.) Picture from G. G. Cantwell. (3.) *Nautilus*. (4.) *Pall Mall Budget*. (5.) Photographs of [Henry] Irving and Ellen Terry, from Sherborn! These are excellent photos with advertisements on the back, published I suppose, as adv'ts. Anyway they are quite nice and I am glad to have them. (6.) Adv't. and sample pages of book: *Catalogue of British Fossil Vertebrata* by A. S. Woodward and Sherborn, to be published in December. This will apparently be a most excellent work.

Except reading the *Pall Mall* and *Nautilus*, I have been mostly writing the rest of the day. I named Morrison's vars. of *H. nemoralis* (nine were new) and sent them back to him. This evening I have written a long postcard to Sherborn. Among other things I have suggested to him to get published for me (if he thinks it will pay expenses) a check-list of the British Land and Freshwater Mollusca, up to date, with varieties. I have it all in manuscript and should like it published in same form as the London Catalogue of Plants. I told Sherborn he could have any profit there might be on it if he would take it up. What do you think of the idea? I think if 250 copies were sold at 6/. each, that would pay.

I enclose two cuttings in this letter. One is a poem out of *Pall Mall*, which I like; do not you? The other is Ashmead's description (the proof he sent of the *Vipis coloradensis*).

Saturday, Oct. 26th, 8:35 p.m. Have been a little out of sorts today. The mail this evening was (1.) Letter from R. D. Halsted about weeds. (2.) Letter from Binney, and also a box of slugs and (on loan) a pamphlet on Mollusca by Fischer, a French conchologist. The box of slugs included a lot of *Limax agrestis* and one *L. campestris*. The latter is an American slug I had not seen before. In the letter was a box with American examples of *Helix cantiana* and *H. hispida*. The *cantiana* was var. *minor*, and the *hispida* was *concinna*. All the morning I was writing notes from the Fischer pamphlet.

This afternoon I chiefly wrote to Binney, and went out in search of *Limax montanus* (I got only two) to send to one Gray in Massachusetts, who is drawing slugs for Binney. Binney wrote about the Mollusca common to Europe and America, 'The only thing I can say is, I hope you will elaborate the subject and publish an extensive treatise on it. As yet, no one has given it much attention. Indeed none of our authors have been in the position to do so.' What do you think? Shall I prepare an 'extensive treatise'? (And live on fried slugs meanwhile?) It would be a biggish work, but one worth the trouble.

That miserable Colorado Springs man has not yet written to say he got the seeds and enclose payment for them.

Sunday, Oct. 27th, 7:35 p.m. Quite seedy today and have done little. Got a *Field and Farm* by mail this morning. They have inserted a notice of the C.B.A. meeting I sent them and have also extracted from my letter an insect destroying corn (that is, maize). I have cut two bits out of the paper for you that are amusing — one about

a milk regulation in Denver and the other about Jay Gould.

Sam Lee, the Chinese washerman, tells me he is going to Pueblo this week.'No wash here, no money in country', he says, and he is not far wrong. As I told Doc Vetter when he was urging that one could live on so little out here, 'Yes, one can live on nothing, but one can't *get* the nothing to live on!'

Oct. 28th, 7:15 p.m. It is late, but I have not yet had supper. The fire is burning brightly and the potatoes are cooking. Outside it looks a little as if it would storm. I am all right again today, I feel glad to say.

Last night I wrote to Sutton and to Mother, and when I went round to the postoffice to post the letters at about 10:15 Lacy gave me my mail that had come that evening, though it was contrary to rules. The mail was: (1.) Letter from Riley.(2.) Bruner's report on insects in Nebraska for 1888 (he is the State Entomologist there). Riley's letter is a very nice one. The two letters I wrote to the Dept. of Agric. in the spring and which were supposed to be lost, have turned up! They arrived all right and were transferred to one of the assistants to help him in naming the specimens I enclosed, and after that forgotten. Riley quite seems to agree with me about the Ass'n. of Official Economic Entomologists. He says, 'Had I been home I should have fought the term 'official', and yet hope to get it voted down.' I had sent him some notes on insect pests in Colorado, and he says, 'I shall take great pleasure in publishing your brief report on Insect Pests in Colorado in *Insect Life*.'

This morning I wrote a longish letter to Riley and sent him some specimens. I also wrote to Ashmead and sent him specimens, the immediate object of my writing being the discovery of what seems to be a second species of *Vipis* among some things collected in Pueblo County and put aside. This afternoon I worked on Carlie's picture and finished it as far as I can. The foreground might be more elaborated, but away from the spot I am half afraid to go into details from memory. This evening I called on Charlton.

Have written some 'Bibliography' for *West American Scientist* and a further installment (Coleoptera) of the Wet Mountain Valley list. Now I must post this.

Ever lovingly, your Theo.
Health. Good.

Morning, Oct. 19th, 1889

Dear Annie,

Perhaps it is my fault. I have not seemed so loving as I should, but do believe that it is only the nature of the beast, and I do love you with all my heart, whatever that may be worth. Indeed, for being despondent and cold sometimes — I am that myself — for at times I love (or seem to love) nobody; but that is not really so, the love is hidden away out of sight. So forgive me and remember that I am yours forever.

And do not talk about anything preventing my coming back to you, else I shall turn up sooner than expected! But, about coming back, there is one thing I want to ask you. Don't be angry with me. I am sure you won't. And say no if you wish. I *might* (it is not very likely, but possible) have a good government scientific post offered me in the U. S. any day. Now if I came to England and fetched you, would you share such a post with me until we had enough money laid by to safely go back to England and look for something different, or start something on our own account? It is really a matter of £.s.d. It might be rash to throw away a good thing here when we know not what might be got in England.

I tell you about this because I might have to accept or refuse at once, and could not get enough into a cable to you to explain. If you

say no, I will not think of getting anything here. Anyway, I shall be in England next summer or earlier. I want to live in England as much as anybody could, but it is no use hiding the fact that good employment might be hard to get. I have written to Sutton and Carrington about it, asking them to keep an eye open for anything that offers. Perhaps I may put an adv't. in one of the magazines.

7:40 p.m. Well, dear, you will see from the above that I got your letter this morning. Now I will answer the other parts of it. It sounds very exciting getting down to that 'Dancing Lodge.' I was afraid you would fall as I read it, but you didn't! Very sorry about the pun! Won't do it again. Really, though, I don't make half the puns I think of. Alas, my 'biography' is not yet completed.

For all that we had early snow here, we have had sunshine since. Today I had to draw the curtain to keep the glare and heat of the sun off me as I wrote, and I daresay London is all in a fog. Your little old man preaching at Swanage makes me think of the late Archbishop of Canterbury. He preached once at Beckingham when I was at school there. The poor man did his best but could not raise his voice so that we at the other end of the church could hear him.

The other mail I got was (2.) Letter from Scudder, joining the C.B.A. He says he is now working on fossil insects, an interesting study. (3.) Letter from L. Bruner to say he got the Orthoptera I sent him. (4.) Letter from Binney enclosing a letter for me to send to the Secretary of the Smithsonian Institution asking them to send me Binney's work on shells which was published by the Smithsonian. I sent the letter off today, and I hope it will have the desired effect. It was kind of Binney to write the letter. (5.) Two postcards about beetles from Dr. John Hamilton. Two beetles I sent him are new species. (6.) Proc. Nat. Sci. Assn. of Staten Island for C.B.A. Library. I wrote to Scudder, a postcard to Nash, and a letter to Hamilton with a box of beetles to name.

A good part of this afternoon, though, I was writing letters for the Lit. and Sci. Society, as they 'instructed the secretary' at the last meeting to write to all those members who had not yet paid their subscriptions (about 75 per cent!). Before writing these letters I called on Miss Byington to get note of who had paid, and also to get money for secretary's expenses (postage and stationery) and my own fees for acting as janitor up to date. I cleaned out the treasury altogether!

Another thing I posted was Carlie's picture. I sent it inside a cardboard cylinder and put on a five-cent stamp, which I hope will take it there, for Mrs. Lacy was unable to discover what the postage on a picture was. We finally concluded it would fall under 'Commercial Papers.'

This evening I squandered five cents on a cabbage at Kettle & Walters'. A little green food is doubtless good at times. Did you ever eat tomato jam? It is the finest jam I know. Mrs. Howard gave me a pot of it. I didn't suppose I should like it, as I don't like raw tomatoes.

I shall post this this evening, although I did send a letter yesterday.

Your lover, Theo.

As I look back on my career, I seem to have been well treated on the whole, and it is not without a certain surprise that I find that I have not had to endure injurious or grinding poverty at any time, I have never been robust, but I have missed few days of work, and have never had a long, disabling illness. I have never been obliged to discontinue my researches, and while at the University of Colorado have found opportunity to open up new fields of work, such as fossil insects, fish scales, the genetics of sunflowers, and the anatomy of rodents. Paleobotany has also taken a good deal of my time. Perhaps it is legitimate to conclude that one needs enduring interests and a good deal of patience, not only with institutions and various people, but also with oneself. The people who achieve excellence or make substantial progress in science are those who keep at it, month after month, year after year, decade after

decade. They correct their own mistakes, which are likely to be numerous.

Recollections

Oct. 30th, 1889, 7:35 p.m.

Love,

It snoweth, just a little. The marvel is, it has not done so sooner, for it has been grey and snow-like all day. What do you think of a fellow with only about $5.00 in his pocket, going and squandering $1.25 on a MS book? That's what I did today, only it is really a very nice one with a stout cover, good ruled paper, and 356 pages. I want to put my notes in for my future book (!) on variation, so as to have everything orderly and ready for reference.

I did a small wash this morning (two towels, two handkerchiefs, and a necktie) before I bought the book, but since then I have done nothing (except cooking, etc.) but write up notes into it from Darwin's *Variations of Animals and Plants under Domestication*. I have fully written up my notes from the chapter on bud variation and graft hybrids. Some of these things are indeed marvelous! I have now all my correspondence written up to date, which is a blessing. Some notes I took during the summer in my pocket notebooks yet wait to be entered up.

There was not an atom of mail for me this morning. By the way, did those *Calochortus* bulbs I once sent ever come up? Are the cacti the only things from Colorado that ever came to anything?

Oct. 31st, 7:15 p.m. The moon looks like a grease spot — not altogether a bad thing, as it would be colder if the sky were clear. It had been snowing more or less all day, but the snow is now only a few inches deep. I suppose there would be a foot of it if none had melted. Louis Howard and one of the pupils came to town in the sleigh. As for your lover, he had just been at work on Darwin's book all the day (having only been to the postoffice, for water, and to cut wood.

It is almost hard work, condensing from Darwin. My plan is this: I make notes separately of anything special, and then again, reading each section (referring to a given subject) I make a summary and write the essence down in my MS book. Then I index up my notes. In this way I also remember most of what I read.

The only mail I got today was from Morrison of Virginia — a postcard about two varieties of *H. nemoralis* he had found. I wrote him today that, for a dollar, I would copy out for him all my manuscript on *H. nemoralis* with descriptions of all the varieties! I surmise it is worth a dollar, too. He could get the same from no published work.

Strange, how one makes one's money. Had this been a more civilised spot I might have earned some threepences this morning by sweeping away the snow, but the people here do that sort of thing for themselves! I shall have to get up a demonstration of the unemployed pretty soon, as I don't see my way to a lucrative job around here. All West Cliff being in the same box, I should think the demonstration ought to be a success. The trouble is, that when West Cliff starves, it has no rats or cab horses to fall back upon.

But, methinks I saw a *cat* in the back yard!

Friday, Nov. 1st, 7:5 p.m. Last night was the coldest one we had had. The water froze in my room, but tonight it is colder. And the meeting of the Lit. & Sci. Society comes off in about an hour. I must go round to the schoolhouse sooner, and light the fire.

There was some mail for me this morning: a *Punch* and two letters, (1.) from Mother — very sad. The dear Grannie seems near the end. 'She longs for it to be over', Mother says. Grandpa has not been nor written to her for a fortnight.

It seems that Uncle D. has sent an asthmatic man to Colorado and told him to find me and the Cusacks. I suppose he may turn up some day.

(2.) Letter from Ashmead. He takes my wrathful letter about the *Rhodites* very well, and says 'He who laughs last laughs best', and you have the laugh on me and I acknowledge the comment and make the 'amenda honorable'. I see I have been too hasty and trusted too much to my memory.' There are some more new species in the last letter; lots of Hymenoptera I sent him. He speaks very strongly of Carrington's proposed society for studying variation.

I asked him how he could get through so much work as he does, and he says 'It is only by burning the midnight oil that I am able to do so much work in entomology, and I am frequently completely played out before I retire. All last week I seldom retired before 2 o'clock in the morning. My wife tells me I shall kill myself, but next year I hope to go to Germany and France, and shall take a long rest and recuperate if I run down!' One would be inclined to agree with his wife! That sort of thing would kill *me* in six months, for the critical study of insects is very hard work. But Ashmead has a very strong constitution. Some men seem to need less sleep than others.

A good part of the day I was sorting out a lot of Hemiptera (and some few Hymenoptera) for Ashmead which I posted off to him together with a letter. He is arranging the Hemiptera at the U. S. National Museum just now. This evening I have been round to the schoolhouse to fill up the lamps with oil for the meeting; there was none in them. Filling lamps is not of *my* choice — Is it of yours? The moon looks in the window and remarks that I ought to be off to the meeting house, so I must close this for the present.

Nov. 2nd, 7:46 p.m. When I left off writing yesterday there was still something to say about yesterday, but I have almost forgotten what it was. Of course, there was the meeting of Lit. & Sci. Society in the evening afterwards. I went round to the schoolhouse at about 20 to eight and found that Sam Wright was already there and had lighted the fire (I had already set it, ready for lighting when I went round to fill the lamps). It is just a heating stove placed in the middle of the house. Sam Wright had mistaken the time, and that is why he was there so early.

It was bitterly cold, somewhere below zero, and as the people came in they clustered round the stove. Contrary to our expectations, quite a number came to the meeting, which was in a way a pity, as we had almost no entertainment to give them. The 'entertainment', in fact, consisted simply of two quartette songs, a recitation by Bertha Humphrey, and a guitar performance (which was encored) by a young man from Silver Cliff named Myles. But there was an election of officers, and so forth. The following were elected: President, Vetter; First Vice President, Sam Wright; Second Vice President, Samse; Secretary, Cockerell; Treasurer, Miss Lowther.

Then Vetter had to appoint committees, which he did as follows: For Science, Charlton, Rob. Stockton (the elder Stockton boy), and Cockerell. For Art and Literature, Mrs. Charlton, Miss Lowther, and Prof. Wright (the schoolmaster). For Entertainment, Mrs. Wright (wife of the 'professor'), Miss Etzel (daughter of the man who made that speech at the railway meeting), and Vetter. The meeting then adjourned feeling rather cold, the fire being scarcely sufficient to warm the big building. When I got back here I went into Vetter's room (he had a nice warm fire) and I sat talking with him there until an absurdly late hour — about eleven p.m.

This morning I found the ink all frozen solid, so it was certainly the coldest night we have had this autumn. All the mail I got was a postcard from Silver Cliff to say that one S. Bourne, who was supposed to belong to the Lit. & Sci. Society was away and therefore wished to resign. However, I was consoled by the hope of much mail tomorrow, for no mail came up on the coach last night, owing to some delay in the trains (I suppose on account of the snow).

All day I have been 'running round', partly on my own account and partly on that of the Lit. & Sci. Society. First I called on Mrs. Wright (wife of the prof.) to inform her that herself and the prof. were put on committees (they were not there last night). I was almost expecting they would refuse to serve, but not so, and I really believe they will work very well for us. I have never talked to Mrs. Wright before. I found her a very pleasant, sensible, and probably very nice woman. In appearance she is small and slight, with small features, rather good eyes, and a quantity of rather light hair.

Next I called on the Charltons. Poor Mrs. Charlton was suffering from a very bad headache. I told them about the meeting last night (they also were not there) and talked about the next (scientific) meeting a fortnight hence. We finally agreed to have a debate on 'The origin of the human race', of course involving Darwinism. Mrs. Charlton made me a present of some more cast-off (but excellent) things, viz., a pair of top boots which didn't fit Charlton, and a sort of hybrid between a shirt and a jersey.

Shortly after I left the Charltons I met Prof. Wright on the street and unfolded to him a little scheme I had hit upon while talking to Charlton. At the end of this month there will be appointments of schoolmasters, and my idea was this: To put in an application to the board of trustees (i.e., Stewart, Stockton, and another — I forget who) to teach science at all the schools round here, say once a week at each school. Prof. Wright said the idea was new to him, but it seemed to him a good thing and feasible, and he promised he would 'feel about' and see whether I should have any chance. I don't atall expect myself that the proposal will be accepted, but if it were I would be a good thing for me, as no doubt the job would last all the winter.

Then I went round to Mrs. Stockton's and talked a good while with her about the 'origin of man'. I took her my paper on varieties in the Torrey Club Bulletin to read, as we had discussed this matter at the C.B.A. meetings. By the way, Mrs. Prof. Wright says she will come to the

C.B.A. meetings. I also told her of my notion of teaching science at the schools,, but she seemed to think the 'board' was too primitive in its ideas to allow such a thing. As her husband is on the board I daresay she knows.

I broke the handle of my little axe today.

Sunday, Nov. 3rd, 1889, 6:35 p.m. A very horrid day. Snowing gently all the time (except short intervals) and an insidious little breeze taking the heat out of everything. I have had a fire going all day, but my feet got quite cold. Before the postoffice was open, I busied myself writing to Dr. Merriam of the Department of Agriculture and sending him the boiled corpse of a mouse Mrs. Charlton caught.

I didn't get much mail: A *Field and Farm*, and letters from Britton and Bethune, and a postcard from Hulst to say he received the moths I sent him. Bethune (editor of *Canadian Entomologist*) writes in reply to some remarks of mine about the Ass'n. of Official Economic Entomologists. His remarks are quite worth quoting, as illustrating the wiles of even 'scientific' gents to get hold of the dollars and cents. He says: 'I felt myself the same objections that you make to the constitution of the new society of Economic Entomologists, and brought them before the primary meeting at Toronto. I thought that I was myself excluded from membership. It was replied that the third clause was expressly framed to include me and others in a similar position, and that the main object in making it an 'official' organisation was to enable the members belonging to Experiment Stations to get *their expenses paid* when they attended the meetings! I do not know how they work it, but they evidently have some method of getting 'the needful' out of the station funds. This, of course, was information privately given. After receiving it I made no further objections.'

What do you think of that? I have no objection to their expenses being paid, but I do think this is an underhand way of going about it, and calculated to bring the whole lot of them into disrepute. I wrote a long letter to Bethune about this

and suggested that outsiders should become associate members, and then altogether raise their protest and resign in a body if necessary. How the 'official' chaps would squirm if the above extract from Bethune were published!

Lacy made me a present of the current number of the *Wet Mountain Tribune* today, to my vast astonishment. It contains the 'Republican Ticket' for the coming (next Thursday) county elections, and I suppose he thought I had a vote. Chetelat is going in for Sheriff (Democratic). He will be better than that man Evans who had to do with the shooting of Potter.

Nov. 4th, 8:25 p.m. As Lacy puts it in his paper, 'The beautiful, in luxuriant profusion, has pasted the earth', that is to say, it has snowed. I has been snowing more or less all day, though not so very cold. I have just been writing letters, making notes and so forth.

I got some mail this morning: (1.) Letter from Morrison of Virginia. (2) Circular from Dept. of Agriculture, announcing meeting of Ass'n. of Official Economic Entomologists at Washington on Nov. 12th, but as the moon is just as accessible to me as Washington, that doesn't help me much. (3.) Long letter from C. V. Riley, with names of insects I sent him. Some are new species.

'The 5th of November', 7:30 p.m. I hoped your letter would have turned up by this morning, but not so. I got only a letter from B. D. Halsted about weeds, and a postcard from Morrison of Virginia, with a box of slugs. These slugs are rather interesting, and were *Limax campestris, L. variegatus* var. *flavus, L. maximus* var. *vulgaris,* and *L. maximus* var. *collaris.* All English, you see, except the first. I wrote Morrison about these, and sent Halsted a rather long discourse on weeds. Are you interested in weeds?

Since than I have been continuing my work on Darwin. As it was cold, I improvised a table out of an old box, and sat near the stove. One thing I notice in Darwin is his courtesy. Whenever he quote's anyone's work, he always gives the name and place of publication unless it is to *adversely* criticise an opinion, when he merely says 'a well-known naturalist' and so on, to hurt nobody's feelings. One wishes all naturalists were as polite.

I came across a passage today which made me laugh very much, though I ought rather to have cried at such barbarity. 'When the Fijians are hard pressed by want, they kill their old women for food, rather than the dogs. For, as we were assured, 'Old women no use; dogs *catch others*.' Darwin continues 'The same *sound sense* would surely lead them to preserve their most useful dogs when still harder pressed by famine.' After all, though, the Fijians are not so far different from more civilised nations who starve their working-men but do not starve their valuable horses, and who turn men off their native land for the benefits of deer.

Frederic once asked for some cases of *Helicopsyche,* so I enclose for him a couple that were found by Douglas at Woodstock, Canada. And for you I enclose *Rhodites rosaefoliae* Ckll. — the gall — as you can see, only a swelling of the leaf, and *Pupa concinnula* Ckll. (MS). The gall is from West Cliff, and the shell from Lees'.

Vetter and Samse came in here and we were talking of things in general for a longish time. Since then I have been looking over 'Merely Friends' — how it does recall the old times! I love that story — it was so much to me when you might not write. I thought you wrote it partly for me. Was I right? I do so want to get your next letter.

> Lovingly, your Theo.
> Health. Very good.

How are you? I do hope the horrid November fogs won't hurt you.

Nov. 6th, 1889, 8:30 p.m.

Love,

Your letter came this morning. A nice long one, and with pictures. What a good effect you get from simple straight lines. In my drawing I think I have generally put too much crossing in. I must practice on this a little. I was quite taken aback when I read that Eva was nearly 17. I suppose I may not any longer regard her as a child. What has become of Kitty since I left England? What a sell! [A 'sell' is a planned deception, hoax, take-in. (Oxford English Dictionary). Ed.] Those Chudleighs never coming after all your preparations. Moral: Never prepare for guests.

Your account of the 'Gleaners' Union is at the same time amusing and depressing, for it *is* a sad thing that people can be such duffers. At the same time, they do very little harm and, strangely enough, in *other* departments of life are sometimes sensible and clever enough.

I remember old J. W. Hulke, one of the best surgeons and most renowned geologists in England, a man of great ability, used (and no doubt does still) to have sort of prayer meetings much like the one you describe, at his house, at which various doctors, professors, and medical students used to attend. I went to one myself once (being specially invited), and I think I must rather have scandalised them by my views after the meeting was over. Hulke, you know, is connected to the Middlesex Hospital.

Is the Bedford Park 'Gardening Society' doing anything about publishing a list of the fauna, as was proposed?

I rather like that bit from *The Return of the Native* about the undemonstrativeness of love. It is said that the French peasant, who loves his wife truly, only tells her so twice in his life — the first time — and when he or she is dying.

As for the 'well-proportioned mind', I say preserve us from such minds! It is the mind of a hog. I like a person with *opinions*, don't you?

Is Miss Shafer now in Detroit? Don't you flatter yourself; you will have a lot more time when the seas don't divide us! How do you know I shan't turn up and claim your company at a very inopportune moment? In fact, I will tell you beforehand that I *shall* do so! I shan't allow you an *atom* of time, except when I have to be about my business. (How you will shudder when you read this! Really, my dear, I'm very sorry, but you see I can't help it, *whatever*. But I 'deeply sympathise', as the walrus said to the oysters.)

Yes, no doubt you are right about Cox, and also Brock, It astonished me how well you 'size-up' these people. Of course, I only 'cut' Brock, and he could have nothing to say about it, though I daresay it riled him. I should be very sorry to come to blows with him. He could knock me into the middle of next week in no time.

I cannot think how I came to write 'Swansea' for 'Swanage', though no doubt some temporary mixture of ideas was the cause. I feel very much ashamed, because it is exactly that sort of thing I should have unmercifully abused anyone else for doing. In fact, inaccuracy is the one thing I am continually blaming people for.

The other mail I got was: (1.) Postcard from Ashmead with names of some Hymenoptera. (2.) *Pall Mall Budget*, (3.) Report of Dept. of Agriculture for 1888. (4.) A bulletin of the Entomological Dept., Dept. of Agriculture, on worms that infest the roots of plants in Florida.

(5.) Letter from Hutton of Colorado Springs. At last, he has been away on a fishing trip, and hence the delay. He is pleased with the seeds and encloses a cheque for $5.00 instead of the $3.20 I asked, which is rather liberal of him. He says the seeds are to be grown near Conway, in Wales. This money came in very usefully, and speedily vanished in payments as follows:

Rent for October	$2.50
Payment for MS book bought the other day	1.25
Money order to Pilsbry for Nautilus' to be sent to Douglas, and list of Land Shells for myself.	1.15
	$4.90

Balance in hand, ten cents!

It is one blessing, that however hard-up, I have never yet owed what I could not cover out of pocket, unless in the present case where I ought to return Carlie about $8.00 of the $15 he sent for the picture, and I have only $3.00 left, but *he* does not ask for any money to be returned, and I suppose I may pay it as convenient. It is merely a question of the proper price of the picture; he put it too high.

I wrote Hutton a letter and asked him to give me the address of his correspondent in Wales, that I might write him about the plants the seeds came from. He might make some interesting experiments if he would. I also wrote to Pilsbry and sent him the money as stated above, and also a paper on Binney's and Morrison's slugs for the *Nautilus*.

Regy and Mrs. Regy came to town and called on me today. They say they have 18 inches of snow up at their places. Mrs. Regy returned *Our Mutual Friend*, which I lent to her when I was too busy to read it, and she has kept it ever since. I began to read it today as soon as I got it, and like it very much. Have only got to Chapter V. I sent up word to Mrs. Cusack that I would go out and work for a day or so on her plants if she wished.

Of course there was much talk about the elections this morning. The Democrats seem to have carried the day. Chetelat is elected Sheriff by a large majority, of which I am glad. 'Art' Walters becomes School Superintendent in place of Prof. Wright. These elections are only local — county and town offices, and have nothing to do with Congress or the House of Representatives.

Nov. 7th, 6:5 p.m. I sat up reading *Our Mutual Friend* to about 11:20 last night, and consequently got up late this morning (not that that is any valid excuse for doing so.) The mail that came for me was (1.) *Pall Mall Budget.* (2.) *Lancet*, with Dutton's address at Middlesex Hospital in it, 'with every good wish, j.b.s.' (Whereby he infringes the postal regulations).

Sutton's address is quite interesting, being on 'Intellectual Blindness.' He points out how often seemingly good observers are erfectly blind to certain facts, or if they do see them, do not comprehend their meaning. There are cases of most obvious phenomena being wholly overlooked by naturalists for many generationss, and yet, when discovered, as plain as day to anyone. I am glad that Sutton should have thus insisted on this 'intellectual blindness', for in ghe history of the human race it is infinitely more important than mere physical blindness or loss of eyesight. Don't you think so yourself? In every subject I have studied, it has been amazing to me how obvious facts have been completely overlooked.

Professor Shaler, writing of his experiences as a student of Agassiz relates that he at first tried to follow the classification [of fishes] based on the structure of the scales. It was supposed that the fishes with cycloid (entire-margined) scales were a group quite apart form those with ctenoid (comb-like)scales. But Shaler found a flatfish with cycloid scales on one side, ctenoid on the other. He says: 'This not only shocked my sense of the value of classification in a way that permitted of no full recovery of my original respect for the process, but for a time shook my confidence in my master's knowledge.' Had he been a little keener-minded, he would have perceived that the flatfish was truly of the group with ctenoid scales, and that the cycloid scales of the underside were secondarily so, for adaptive reasons. There was thus no reason for his skeptical attitude, but Agassiz himself did not have the advantage of the evolutionary outlook which is so commonplace today.

Recollections

I was reading my papers down in the store below, and took up some American papers from the counter. In a *New York World* I find as monstrous a story of foolishness as ever I heard of. There is a German prince (name begins with H. — I forget just what it is) who formerly had money, but for years has gambled and carried on every find of blackguard-ism all over Europe. Now, being bankrupt, he paid his attention to a wealthy American girl in Paris, and she, wonderful to relate, accepted him. The father at first would not favour the marriage but, being strongly pressed by *his wife and daughter*, commenced to bargain with Prince H. The prince would not marry her unless the father paid all his debts and have him an enormous sum besides. So they fixed the thing up, and I believe the pair are married.

Now is it not marvelous that a girl should *sell herself* for a title, and that her own *mother* should most favour the arrangement! You may think, possibly the girl *loved* the man, but after reading the account of how they fixed the price and so forth, it is impossible to think that this was the case. Nor is the thing unique. It is only an exceptionally glaring case of what is being continually done.

Another prince or something, a Frenchman, broke off his engagement with an American girl the other day because she would only give him $10,000! One would think the Church, with its traditions of morality, might take up these things, but I suppose they are afraid to. There is a class of women at the other end of society that is always abused, but verily these 'highly respectable' ladies are worse. They seem to have lost all sense of the fitness of things whatever.

There is account in the *Pall Mall* (with portrait) of M. Bertrand, the old chap who used to teach me fencing. I cannot say I enjoyed his lessons, and I never finished the course.

After supper, 7:10 p.m. In the course of the morning I had an IDEA, which I speedily planned to put into execution. A vacant room up here, next to mine, seemed going to waste (being filled with dust and every kind of rubbish), and this suggested the notion: Why not take possession and start a PUBLIC LIBRARY and MUSEUM? No sooner said than done!

I conferred with Chetelat and Vetter, and got leave to use the room, and the desk and glass show-case that were therein, and to eject all garbage. The museum should be in the show-case, and the library on shelves to be put up. Books to be got by begging or stealing (as seemed most convenient) and to be loaned out at five cents a week or part of a week. Books to be taken on loan for library, and allowance made to lenders in consideration thereof. The whole, if you please, to be dubbed THE WEST CLIFF ACADEMY OF SCIENCE! Doesn't that sound enchanting?

Having the thing (in my mind's eye) in full working order, I went round to talk it over with the Charltons. They were less enthusiastic, doubting whether I could coerce the people here into improving their minds, but they were willing to take part in the undertaking. Mrs. C. says the Ladies' Literary Society is going to get me to write them a manuscript flora of Custer County, and pay me for the same. I offered to do it for nothing, but if they feel like paying me, I raise no objections. As I left, Mrs. Charlton gave me a bucket of genuine cow's milk, a great luxury. The Charltons now have a cow, who supplies a superfluity of milk

Coming back from the Charlton's, I worked like a nigger at cleaning out the Library-to-be, and after getting eyes, nose, and mouth full of dust, finally got it into fairly decent order — a blessing to humanity, even if there were to be no library. I find snow an excellent substitute for tea-leaves, not to make tea of, but to sprinkle it on the floor and gather up the dust. But it would hardly do on a carpet.

9:55. Have been on the grand tour. Great success everywhere! First to Mrs. Stockton, and extracted from her seven books. Then to the Humphreys, and got promise of volumes in-numerable. Next to Prof. Wright's, and there promise of more books. Finally to the Chetelats, and got seven books. All this takes a little time to relate, but it has taken all the evening to do. At each place I had to expound at length my project, and discourse on the immense benefit to the neighborhood, and so forth. But they all 'tumble to the racket' and will join in.

Nov. 8th, 10:20 p.m. Dyspepsia! No mail. Little work. Much consolation from *Our Mutual Friend*. That is today. No mail, because the train was, I presume, late to Cotopaxi. And no mail came on the coach. Dyspepsia, I know not why, but it has made me feel out of sorts all day. Little work — in fact nothing but putting up some shelves in the Library. (Got the lumber for them out of the back yard.) *Our Mutual Friend* all the rest of the time, so that I have finished volume I. I like the book exceedingly, but am a little oppressed by the number of shady characters. Eugene Wrayham is a miserable creature, and is practically identical with Langham in *Robert Elsmere*. I hope the girl Lizzie won't go and marry him, for I like Lizzie greatly. The Boffins are charming. I fear that in a generation or two such simplicity will be extinct. I guessed that the secretary would prove to be John Harmon.

Nov. 8th. Just off to the Cusacks'. Will post this in case I should not be in town at the proper time next week.

Ever yours lovingly, Theo.

Health. Still a little seedy. Shall be all right in a day or so.

Nov 9th, 1889, 9:30 p.m.

Love,

Here I am at the Cusacks'. I was quite seedy this morning but am now most excellently well. I got a great lot of mail this morning, of which later. Regy came to town with a load of wood and an invitation to me to go out to the ranch (to do the flowers), so here I am. But I will tell you all about it tomorrow.

Nov. 10th, 10 p.m. Have been at the flowers all day, and now too sleepy to write anything intelligible.

Nov. 11th, 8 p.m. A snowy day, but first of yesterday and the day before.

Nov. 9th. There was an astonishing lot of mail for me. (1.) Book on the *Land Snails of America* (illustrated) by Binney, sent me at his request by the Smithsonian Inst., which published it. This is an admirable work that I am exceedingly glad to get. It will greatly aid me in my conchological work. (2.) Letter from Binney, and some slugs which are unfortunately dead and decayed. (3.) Letter from Nash. (4.) Letter from Douglas, from Portage la Prairie, Manitoba. He says, 'I may stay here for years, and I may be moved tomorrow.' The bank has raised him $100, and he now gets $300 a year, not a very enormous sum for the responsible position he seems to occupy.

(4.) Very long letter from W. H. Edwards, about all sorts of questions relating to butterflies. Do you remember that caterpillar I sent him in the spring, that he wrote about so often? It is now going to have its portrait published. Edwards wants me to write to *Can. Ent.* controverting certain views of Scudder, but I don't feel inclined to do so. (5.) Some papers on fossil insects from Scudder for C.B.A. Library.

I went out to the Cusacks' with Regy, where I still am. I found them all (Mrs. Cusack, Regy and Mrs. Regy) living in Regy's house, and we have our meals there though I sleep in the old house, and Mrs. C. and I go over there in the daytime to work on the flowers.

Nov. 10th. Mrs. Cusack and I were busy over the flowers all day, and nothing special happened. It was windy and cold.

Nov. 11th (Friday). At the flowers again. Identified several I did not know before. It was snowing all the morning, but now it is clear, and consequently bitterly cold. Lees turned up in the course of the day. He has been down at Pueblo and Colorado Springs. He brought me a little mail — a box of slugs (all dead and decayed) from Binney, a *Field and Farm* and an interesting trade catalogue of fruit trees, etc.

Nov. 12th, 9:45 p.m. Regy has been to town and brought your letter, and one from Carlie with news of Grannie's death. I don't feel equal to writing now. How the wind blows! Shall go to bed.

Nov. 13th, 9 p.m. At the Howard's. Shall be in town tomorrow, and then some peace to write a proper letter. It is now snowing. This continual bad weather is extraordinary. I came here from the Cusacks' with Lees on the sleigh. I have not finished Mrs. Cusack's flowers but have promised to return and finish them as soon as I can. I meant to go on to town tonight, but Lees stopped here and this led to my doing so also. It is Mrs. Howard's birthday, and we were treated to plum-pudding at supper in celebration of that event.

Nov. 14th, 8 p.m. In town at last and able to write more fully. I came in with Lees and Pennycuick this morning (it was cold; thermometer at zero when I got up) in the sleigh. I got another great lot of mail, and having read it, I finally got settled down to work at noon and was busy until supper time writing. I have 17 letters to answer.

I sat in the library, as it was warmer than in my room. The Library today received several additional books, sent round by Mrs. Humphreys, some of them good ones, others indifferent. Now I must answer your letter.

I think I absolutely agree with you about the meals. Of course I was exaggerating when I spoke of a chunk of bread and a jack knife as the correct sort of a meal, but I do maintain that that is better than the oppressiveness of the Wimpole-ite meals. I think my own family conducts its meals on a fairly rational system at 5. Priory. What do you think? My own ideas on the subject would be to follow the wisdom of my father's in this matter, if in no other.

But to illustrate the distinction of which I was thinking: I should like a cup of tea much better if *you* would pour it out for me than if a servant appeared from nowhere and produced it on a tray. And in the unlikely event of our rolling in untold wealth, I shall still beg permission to cut you a slice of bread! And I think there is no harm in requesting your neighbor at table to pass the salt! You will laugh at these sage reflections, but then you have not dined at Wimpole Street. (By the way, lunch at Wimpole was moderately human, ditto breakfast. This because of the children; they were natural under all circumstances.)

No, when I thought of emigrating I had no idea what I should do. The wish seemed to be to get away and start fair at anything that turned up. I don't like leaving people and I hate to be alone, but in those times I was alone among so many people, and I always had a kind of fancy that I should form stronger attachments elsewhere. There was something fascinating in the thought of millions of people I had never met, and of the people there might be yet to meet. And the person I had most need to meet was all the time quite close, and I didn't know it! Now I have found *you* I no longer wish to search among the millions, but I commend the search to others. Did you never have that feeling of wonder as to who there might be among so many? About emigrating, again. You see, I was quite an expense to

the family and naturally wished to be earning an independent livelihood somehow.

I very much grudge the bit you cut out! I am glad to hear that about Lord Walsingham and his tenants; it shows him to be a reasonable man. I would *shake* that Miss Tuting. I am amazed to find that the Bedford Park-ites seem at times quite unable to behave in a gentlemanly manner. You remember how preposterous they were when Morris was there.

Payn is in England now, under a doctor who has special care of morphia cases (this *strictly* confidential). Mrs. Payn wrote Lees a letter about it which I read. Mrs. Payn was much distressed at Payn's appearance and health when he got back. He seems to be in a very bad way. I hear that shortly before Payn left for England, a man borrowed a team of horses from him (or hired them) and went away with them altogether.

About snails and insects, I think I only prefer the former because I know more about them. I am gradually working my way up in the entomology line.

Annie, why be troubled about the future? We will surmount the troubles when they come. You speak of trouble and worry for you; tell me, dear, just exactly what it is you dread. I believe people will be kind to both of us when it comes to the point. Can I do anything now to make things better? (Except what I *am* doing.) Perhaps I am a little selfish about it. It seems such a great joy to see you again that it occupies my thoughts. About a poor job. I might get something at Kew Garden *pro tem*. That would do, wouldn't it? Or if you are at Swanage, I would sell 'cockles and mussels alive-alive-o!' And you would be obliged to buy some even if you didn't want them!

I must say, I think Mr. Burt would as well confer an everlasting benefit (?) to Dorsetshire by instituting the said T.D.A. Cockerell as boss of Dorsetshire Museum! Pity he wouldn't see it in that light! Humphrey is getting up a whist club in town just now. Never heard of Frederic's K. before, that I can remember! No, none of the West Cliff galls are like yours. Yours was more in this wise, wasn't it? Yes, your creature would no doubt be *Aphrodite aculeata*. I used to find them at Margate. They are lovely things when alive.

No, love, you shall *not* copy out extracts for me! Do you supose I am such a helpless old creature that I shall let you tire yourself out at that sort of thing? I give you a kiss for offering to do so, and say no. It is very proper for everyone to make their own notes; they learn while doing it, and it is a test of their enthusiasm for it is apt to be dreary work. Am I not right?

I am grateful for loan of Louy's photo, but I *don't* like it. Actually, looking at it sideways as I took it out, I wondered who it might be. I hope it is not a good photo of her present appearance, for somehow it is not my notion of Louy a bit. Mrs. Cusack said that she looked thin, and I think so too. Comparing it with the Sutton photo (to be sure it is not my fancy) I am sure there is a difference. Now tell me, is this as you thought?

I have read very little Huxley. It is necessary that I *should* read some sooner or later. Likewise Herbert Spencer, whose works I have no natural fondness for. Possibly you prove too *much* about orthodox Christianity, but I think you are right except that I doubt the advantage. I think that prospectus of 'Gleaner's Union' is fairly reasonable, did I not think the union itself to be fundamentally unreasonable. It is a fair statement of a bad case.

I shall post this tonight (although I have any amount of other mail to tell you about) so that it may reach you about your birthday. *Many* happy returns, love, and much hope that the next birthday I may not have to *write* the greeting. I hope you will have a happy birthday, and a *happier* one (may I say?) Next year.

Ever your lover, Theo.
Health. Very good.

P.S. There is time just to enumerate the mail I got: November 12th. Letter from you. Letter from Carlie. Letter from Anderson (a botanist of Montana), Report of Botanist, Dept. of Agriculture, for 1888, *West American Scientist* (October).

Canadian Entomologist (November) has a note of mine in it on a moth called *Gnophasia*. *Young England* and *Little Folks*. Many thanks. I like your articles. I learned from the 'Art Industries' one. Wish you'd draw the pictures for your own articles though. Letter from Hamilton (with names of beetles I sent.

Nov. 14th. Letters from Denis Gale (about C.B.A.). Morrison of Virginia (sending $1.00 for MSS (to be written) about *Helix nemoralis*. By the way, Carlie says I am to make other sketches for the rest of his $15.00. Letter from Mortimer Woolf, the man Uncle Douglas sent out here. He writes from Denver; I think he will come here. Letter from Miss Eastwood (long letter, also shells and fungi). Letter from Ashmead. Letter from C. H. Merriam. Adv't. for *Memoirs of the Torrey Botanical Club*. West American Scientist (extra copies; I sent you one). *Orchard and Garden* (sample copy). *Bulletin 9*, Fort Collins Experiment Station (about soils).

It was a great event for me when on June 16, 1889, I met Miss Alice Eastwood, the first skilled botanist I had seen since I arrived in Colorado. She then lived in Denver, teaching in the High School. Last spring I lunched with her at the California Academy of Sciences, San Francisco, and today she is of course one of the leading botanists of America. When in 1889 we wandered in the meadows near West Cliff in search of plants, we could not know that we should be the last survivors of those then actively concerned with Colorado natural history.

Recollections

Nov. 15th, 1889

Love,

Must now go round to meeting of Lit. & Sci. Society. Have had a headache today and done nothing, which is very horrid, as I have so much to do. Am all right, I think, this evening, though.

Nov. 16th, 8:35 p.m. The meeting last night went off all right. We had more than enough to fill the programme, and there was a good attendance. Vetter gave an original paper of his own (the subject of the evening was 'The origin of Man'), taking the 'special creation' view, and extracts from Agassiz and Hugh Miller were read by Samse and Sam Wright, supporting the same view. Sam Wright also spoke on the subject. I gave the evolution theory, and afterwards replied *re* 'missing link' to Sam Wright. And finally Charlton discoursed at length on the Geological Record, with diagrams in illustration, contending for the evolution theory. I have no idea how much or how little people understood it all, but the subject is far too great to be explained, to those who were ignorant of it, in a single evening. It was nearly eleven when we adjourned. In future we will meet a half hour sooner, i.e., at 7:30.

Today I seem to have been busy all the time but have not done as much as I expected, apart from miscellaneous notes written up, and the common duties of cooking and cutting wood. I have written only two letters, namely to the man in Wales who is to grow the seeds I sent Hutton, and to Anderson of Montana. I got this morning a letter from Binney and the November *Torrey Bot. Club Bulletin*. Nobody has taken up the variety matter. I half expected this number would contain some article in opposition to mine. Considering how often I have written on controversial matters, my writings have hardly ever been criticised. I do not know why this should be.

Yesterday the mail was: (1.) Letter from B. D. Halsted, about weeds. (2.) Postcard from Packard, who is back in America. He wants larvae of *Gnophaela*. (3.) *Daily News* of Oct.31, with an amusing bit about Frederic in an account of the exhibition of South London Ent. Soc. (very prominently, on page three). You may not have seen this, so I quote:

'Amongst the shells must be prominently mentioned Mr. F. G. Fenn's British Land and Fresh Water specimens. Of the 130 species or thereabouts which we have,

he has found 110 and no doubt sighs for the balance, and as he is as earnest a naturalist as his father the novelist, the lost sheep will no doubt in due time be gathered into the fold, to fill in the few gaps staring upon the white cardboard.'

(4.) *Pall Mall Budget*. (5.) *Naturalist*. (6.) *Science Gossip*, in which a paper of mine on bees and flowers. Also more by Williams on variation. Having a headache, I read these papers, and this of Williams took me some time to master, not being very lucidly put, and now I find nothing very new or remarkable about it.

I was going to say a little more about the mail received earlier in the week. Miss Eastwood writes a lengthy epistle to say she is so occupied with school work that botany has at present to go to the wall. '150 boys and girls take my days and a good deal of my nights.' She was coming down here on her way from Durango, but could not do so on account of the washout on the line.

Ashmead quite astonished me by a paragraph in his letter about his English cousins. I recollect once seeing these said cousins at a demonstration in Hyde Park. I never thought much of either of them politically.

Overwhelmed by mail

Sunday, Nov. 17th, 7:40 p.m. Have done a little better today. In the morning I wrote to Douglas and Miss Eastwood, and wrote out a list of the shells of Manitoba, with notes, for

Douglas. This afternoon I made good progress with the MSS on *Helix nemoralis* for Morrison of Virginia. The mail I got when the postoffice opened at noon was *Field and Farm* and *Nautilus* (with five extra copies). The *Nautilus* has an article of mine on *H. nemoralis*, so I will send you a copy. Frederic will perhaps be astonished to find himself down as the author of one band-variety; probably he will have forgotten where he recorded it. It was in *Science Gossip* (Oct., 1883) in a list of Torcross shells.

I must be a very absent-minded person. I have a metal pen-holder which I commonly hold in my mouth in the intervals of writing (while I turn from the book I am writing from, and so forth), and yet I was almost totally unaware of this frequent habit of so holding the pen. A few days ago, a little sore place appeared on my lower lip, and I was totally at a loss to imagine what caused it, until the pen resting upon it began to hurt, and the cause flashed upon me all at once. Since then I have several times put the pen in my mouth, though I meant never to do it again! It is a small matter, but it illustrates the half-automatic way in which one does certain things.

Nov. 17th, 1:35 a.m. Good gracious! It is half past one. Here I have been sitting up reading *Our Mutual Friend*. I have not quite finished it but am too sleepy to continue. I am filled with amazement at the events in Vol. II. Hardly know what to think of it all.

Tuesday, Nov. 19th, 8 p.m. Yesterday, after lunch, I thought I would read just *one* chapter of *Our Mutual Friend*, and I continued reading 'just one chapter' until long past midnight. So this morning I felt a bit ashamed of myself, but then your letter came, with advice to read a novel or so, and immediately I felt exceedingly virtuous (having done right by accident, so to speak), and sat down and finished the book this morning. Certainly you are right in this matter. I already feel better since I read *Our Mutual Friend* — more human.

It is not desirable that one should become like Mr. Venus altogether, from too much attention to science. After all, I think we are both more interested in our own species than anything else. I feel sure you are; I hope I am. Looking the thing square in the face, I can not honestly believe that it is ever right to pursue abstract studies without thought of our fellow men. Can you? It is hard to say why it should be wrong, but there is something unnatural about it. Perhaps it is on the same sort of principle that it would be wrong to willingly isolate oneself physically and hold nothing in common with others, say, on a desert island. The matter wants thinking out. The proof would be this — that wherever men have practically isolated themselves in work or ideas from all others, they have finally come to harm, by madness or otherwise.

Here, you see, we touch on the 'monomaniac vs. pure specialist' question. Possibly the pure specialist is justified, but one fancies one would rather not be the fellow. Here the thought occurs, was not Christ a monomaniac or pure specialist in one sense? And if so, does it not justify all 'pure specialists' and such for ever and ever? Here we see, I believe, the real reason why people thought him divine. It seemed that a mere human being had gone mad or given up in his place. The *moral* strength seemed more than human, and hence seemed divine. And as divine it was yet too grandly alone; hence the trinity. You see I am writing this down as it occurs to me. I may think differently later on.

To come back to the scientific matter. The analogy between pure science and pure Christianity seems far-fetched. But not so much as it seems. Christ spends his early years considering moral and other questions. From long thought, at last he clearly sees his way, clearly sees what to him is certainly and everlastingly right. He preaches the truth — the gospel, and urges people, saying naturally, 'It is so. You cannot see it because you have not been through what I have been through, but believe me it is the TRUTH.' Which we now believe, that it is, but others just as earnest have been wrong.

477

Galileo, after much study in different matters, is likewise convinced of certain facts in science, and preaches accordingly. Now we know he was right, but people did not know it then, and they rightly argued that he might be wrong. So, in great things, so also perhaps in the smallest things of life.

I don't know anyone but yourself that I would write thus and make examples of the great for the guidance of the small — not because I lack the impudence to write anything I please but because I should certainly not be understood. Tell me what you think about it, and by then I may have more thought out on the subject, and clearer.

Some people would say, certain men are born heroes (as Carlyle calls them); most men are not. Leave the hero business to those who are qualified. It may be rightly so said, but I cannot persuade myself that the principle of the thing does not run through everything, and that the term 'hero' is not wrongly used in this connection. It is perhaps a question of the right of assertion. And before that, the right of independent knowledge, whereon to base an assertion. Society, at least, recognises nothing of the sort if put in practical form.

Jones thinks Smith (who is a millionaire) has no right to his money (and I agree with Jones). Jones proceeds to take the money away from him and immediately finds himself in gaol. Probably Herbert Spencer would say that was wrong — putting Jones in gaol, and here we have the great specialist sticking up for the right of assertion, but society does not see it in that light. The pilgrim wanders in search of heaven, or home, or whatever you please. Sometimes he keeps to the road and notes the footprints of others. Sometimes he takes short cuts across the country. Which is the better way?

The specialist invites us to take the short-cuts. He says, 'Believe what I have found out, and base your fresh conclusions on that.' So we never get to know the bit of road we missed; we trust him that the one we have cut across to is the same right road, and very likely he is right. But very likely, too, he is wrong. All the different theories of science and religion, are they not like false short-cuts to sell the innocent and ignorant? They cannot all be right. So our specialist had better have gone a little slower and taken us along with him, and we should then have the satisfaction of all being in the same box together, even if it was the wrong box!

Well, I will leave off now, for I know you must be asking me to, when you have read this far.

The commonplace events of yesterday were in this wise. In the morning I finished and sent off Morrison's MS about *Helix nemoralis*. Charlton came in and was talking for about an hour and a half. The afternoon, as you know, was given to the frivolous pursuit of novel-reading. Ditto the evening. Doc Vetter, in the course of the day, borrowed a book from my library — the first to go out. It was Thackeray's *Virginians*, (which I have not read). The sum total of mail was a letter from Ashmead, who says among other things:

'You were elected an associate member of the new Association of Economic Entomologists yesterday, and I had the pleasure of seconding the motion for your admittance.' So I suppose that was all right.

This morning, besides your nice letters, and Frederic's, I got a letter from Morrison of Virginia (who says he is sending more *H. nemoralis*), a letter from H. Wallis Kew, and letter from the Smithsonian Institution which, though late, is highly satisfactory:

Dear Sir:
    In reply to your letter of Sept. 30, in which you express your desire to receive for the Colorado Biological Association, copies of the Reports and Proceedings of the National Museum, I take pleasure in

informing you that the name of your association has been placed on our mailing list, and in future will receive copies of such papers as relate to the fauna and flora of Colorado.

Yours faithfully,
F. W. True, Acting Curator in Charge.

I will talk about your letter afterwards, only I must say that I am delighted with the change in Frederic's affairs and certain it will be good for him. And the teeth — well, up in the teeth as to say for certain, they are not human, certainly. I will try to find out more about them.

I was taking notes part of today from Scudder's paper on fossil insects. He gives a graphic description of the place (Florissant) where they are found. It is near Pikes Peak. It is strange and impressing to read all about it. In Eocene times, long before the advent of man, was a lake at Florissant, and on the borders of the lake were oaks, poplars, willows, walnuts, palms, elms, and flowers. In the lake were fishes. Birds flew about, and insects were in myriads. Everything indicated a warm and genial climate. Volcanic action was fierce in the neighbourhood. Insects would die, fishes and birds would die, leaves would fall into the soft mud at the sides of the lake, and volcanic ash would cover them up and preserve them for the long ages to come.

Now there is no longer any lake, but one can go there and take out insects, leaves, even sometimes birds and butterflies, all in the most beautiful state of preservation! Hundreds of species, perhaps, have been found. Is it not strange, to dig up so living a memory of the times before there was man atall? Charlton was talking about it yesterday and he is very anxious to go there. He seems to want me to go with him. It would be an interesting trip.

Now let us talk about *Our Mutual Friend*. I like the book exceedingly. There is something very charming about Dickens. Some things,

though, puzzle me. I can hardly comprehend the deception of Bella Wilfer by the Boffins and Harmon. It came out all right, but it seems a wild idea. Yet on second thoughts, I don't think it was likely to have come out other than right. More surprising, perhaps, is the way Bella takes the news that her husband is not Rikesmith. I expected her to be more astonished. There are some sad bits to the book, but I think the death of old Betty Higden is by far the saddest. I cried over that. Pa Wilfer is delightful, and so are the Boffins. The objectionable characters are also very true to life. About Eugene Wrayburn, I am still unconvinced that he is anything but a worthless fellow, and doubtful about his reform. I think he was more to blame than Headstone, for Wrayburn was clearly in possession of his wits, while Headstone was as clearly mad. I had nothing but pity for Headstone. Lizzie and Bella are both excellent. Now it's 10:20, and I'll go to bed. Goodnight, dear.

Wednesday, Nov. 20th, 8:30 p.m. The mail this morning was (1.) Letter from L. O. Howard. (2.) Letter from McDonald of U. S. Fish Commission, thanking me for some fish notes I sent. (3.) Letter from Woolf, who says he is going to Colorado Springs for a few weeks and will then come here. (4.) Letter from Morrison of Virginia, and box of *Helix nemoralis*. (5.) Journal of Mycology. I overhauled Morrison's *nemoralis* (some of them were interesting) and sent them back to him. I also wrote to Galloway and Ellis about fungi, a long shell letter to Binney and a letter to Woolf. I haven't answered your letter yet.

I will look out for Bishop of Peterborough on Socialism in *The Times*. But it may not be in the weekly station. I like what you say under Oct. 29, about the Grannie's death, and the lovely day. Thank you for the list of Swanage acquaintances. It gives me a much more complete notion of them. But I rather wonder that you seem to have come across nobody of very special interest. Yet it's not so strange, for in Margate, with all the time I lived there, I remember only one or two people above the general level.

I don't know whether I am proud or not. But as for accepting clothes from people, I think it is always right to take a kindly-meant gift kindly. Sometimes I have taken things I would willingly have refused because I feared a refusal would seem like pride or ill will. In this country we are all poor together, and small helps of any sort are acceptable. Don't you think that I am right? Some men, like Cox, instead of being honestly poor, *borrow* money and live in style on what they will never repay, which *looks* better to the public, perhaps, but *is* very much worse. Cox *might* have used his old clothes which he distributed to the public, but he was too 'high-toned' and hence either gave them away or left them at the Cusacks' to be 'attached' by anyone who needed them. His kindness to me was that he gave me 'first pick', so that I had the best of them.

Yes, the postoffice did look at the teeth to see whether they were dutiable! I am sorry Louy could not get down to Swanage. Respecting [my] paper in the *Torrey Bulletin*, I plead guilty to the clumsiness of the last sentence, and I like you to correct me. 'Behooves' astonished me as much as you. It is American for 'behoves', the word I wrote.

I think this is a most preposterous letter altogether. I shall post it tonight and try to start fair with something sensible tomorrow.

With much love, your Theo.
Health. Very good.

How are you? I will enclose a scrap for Frederic.

Nov. 21st, 1889, 8:30 p.m.

My love,

Last night a letter was posted to you. Today's work is not satisfactory, as I have been dyspeptic and hardly up to anything. There was no mail for me this morning.

After breakfast I made a little experiment in cooking which would have made you laugh. The Charlton's gave me some milk yesterday. Half of

it I took as bread and milk, but this morning the other half was sour. Now I remember Mrs. Cox used to make cakes out of sour milk, so I put some flour with mine to make a batter, and put it in the oven. Now it has turned out better than I expected, but I am in serious doubt as to what it is. It would be pretty good pudding, but very inferior cake or bread, being something of the consistency of a suet pudding without the suet. Query: Is it good to eat? It tastes pretty good. I think I shall cut it into slices and fry it.

During the day I wrote letters and sent some flowers off to Coulter to be named. Afterwards I took Carlyle's *Heroes*, *John Sterling*, and *Past and Present* round to Mrs. Charlton, as the next meeting of the Ladies' Society is to be devoted to Carlyle, and they wanted to make selections to read. Mrs. Charlton is getting the thing up. I had to cut most of *Past and Present* and *John Sterling*, not having read them myself, although I have had them so long. I think I shall read *John Sterling* soon. I read today Sterling's letter on *Sartor Resartus* (to Carlyle), and thought his remarks exceedingly to the point. I believe there is most virtue in plain English, and *Sartor Resartus* is anything but plain to me.

We are having warmer weather now, but still much snow remains on the ground. The wind blows tonight. I was looking at a magazine called *The Cosmopolitan* today. Some of the illustrations are remarkably well done. A group of people in an illustration of a story is extraordinarily natural. It is done by some photographic process. I fancy the original was a genuine photograph of a group.

If I have recently read too few story-books, I seem now in danger of reading too many. Today I have read a whole novel — *Looking Backward*, by Edward Bellamy, which came by post this morning from Mother. There was a good deal of mail for me this morning besides this book, viz., (1.) from Mother, writing from Margate. (2.) From Olive, who says, among other things, 'It will be lovely to see you again', which I take as an omen that the family have nothing against my return next summer. Nobody has raised any objection. It will be much nicer if I can return with the consent of all parties, don't you think so? (3.) Letter from Morrison of Virginia, with list of varieties of *H. nemoralis* he has taken this year, and the number of each. He has taken some 2,200 shells this year. (4.) Letter from H. F. Wickham of Iowa, who wants beetles, and says he is sending me a box of slugs by express. (5.) Postcard from Shufeldt.

No, I don't think I should agree with Mr. Burt! His speech would have been very offensive to me, had I been a quarryman. But then, if they put themselves in a position to be thus patronised, they cannot very well raise any objections when It comes to the point. I see my respected namesake had a hand in the pie.

I had the bliss to earn 35 cents and a little chunk of silver today. Cox of the Hotel (not now of the Hotel, but of Hillside) appeared about noon with seven books of pressed flowers done by his wife, and a request that I would write the names. My charge was ten cents a book (as arranged long ago), so 70 cents was due. He could make only 65 cents in change, and so Cox threw in the bit of silver to make up. I wrote the names in the books in the course of the afternoon. Two of the flowers, a gentian and a *Thelesperma*, were new to me, but I made them out all right from Coulter's *Manual*.

Looking Backward is a most interesting book. Have you read it? (If not, do!) It is long since I have laughed so heartily over anything as the account of the way music was supplied to every house. The essence of humour is said to be in contrast, not in absurdity, and here the rule applies. The whole book makes one laugh with pleasure. The story is, that one Julian West is mesmerised, and remains in a trance until the year 2,000, when he awakes ro find everything conducted on socialistic principles. The way in which the new society is explained to him is delightful, and really, when putting the book down, it gives one quite a shock to reflect that, after all, one is still in the 19th century, with all its barbarisms. Here are a few extracts:

'There is no such thing in civilised society as self-support. Every man, however solitary may seem his occupation, is a member of a vast industrial partnership as large as the nation, as large as humanity.'

'To talk of dignity attaching to labour of any sort under the [competitive] system then [i.e., now] prevailing was absurd. There is no way in which selling labour for the highest prices it will fetch is more dignified than selling goods for what can be got.'

'The cultured man in your [20th Century] age was like one up to the neck in a nauseous bog solacing himself with a smelling bottle.'

'We have no jails now [A. D. 2000]. All cases of atavism are treated in the hospitals.'

It was one of your [19th Century] fictions that the government and the banks authorised by it alone issued money, but everybody who gave a dollar's credit issued money to that extent.'

Saturday, Nov. 23rd, 7:55 p.m. A 'sluggy' day for me, which I have enjoyed. The *Entomologist* and *Ent. Mo. Mag.* represents the morning's mail, but by express there came the box of slugs from H. F. Wickham. These slugs are in alcohol, carefully packed in nice little bottles. They come from California, Washington Territory, Idaho, Vancouver Island, and Oregon, and represent at least five species. One tube contains the familiar *Limax agrestis*, new to the Pacific Coast. Practically the whole of today has been taken up in work on these slugs, although I first read the *Ent.* magazines and wrote Wickham a letter and sent him some beetles. The slugs will probably take at least two more days before I have done with them, but then I shall have material for a paper of western slugs that will throw fresh light on several points. Nearly all the specimens have to be dissected, and their jaws, etc., have to be examined under the microscope. One great fellow, blessed with the name of *Agriolimax californicus*, took me a long while to dissect today.

This afternoon I went round to Charlton's to get some caustic potash to dissolve out the lingual membranes of the slugs. At the same time I took *Looking Backward* to Mrs. Charlton to read. She had already heard of the book and was wishing to read it. I hear this book is creating quite a sensation in even the callous West.

I was sorry to read in the paper this morning that Prof. Cassidy of the Fort Collins Agricultural Station died the day before yesterday. It is the first member of C.B.A. we have lost by death.

Sunday, Nov. 24th, 9:10 p.m. Have been busy at the slugs all day except when I was writing a letter about them to Binney. Today's mail was *Field and Farm* and 'List of fungi collected in 1884 along the Northern Pacific Railroad' (from the author, A. B. Seymour). It has been cold and cloudy all day and is snowing a little this evening. Two of the slugs I have been examining seem to be new species, and so I am provisionally calling them *Prophysaon pacificum* and *Prophysaon humile*. The first is from Vancouver Island, the last from Idaho.

Nov. 25th, 7 p.m. Snow, snow, snow! At least six inches of it. Most of it fell last night, but it has been snowing a good deal of today. There was no mail for me this morning. I am now going round to call on the Charltons.

9:55 p.m. Today was given to writing letters (I have now got my correspondence well up to date again) and reading over the papers on melanism in *Entomologist* and the discussion on insects and flowers (Insect Selection) in *Science Gossip*. I had read these before but wanted to freshen my memory. I also read some of Darwin.

In the afternoon, Charlton came in to see the teeth of the slugs I received from Wickham. At the same time, I showed him some diatoms. Charlton declared that he was going to study entomology, and he is going to send for Packard's elementary book on the subject to commence

with. I hope, indeed, that he will take the matter up. We greatly need entomologists in this part of the world. This evening I went round and took Charlton a few insects I had sorted out for him. We also discussed the question of 'Women's Rights.' This is to be the subject for the next meeting of Lit. & Sci. Soc'y. At the Charlton's I saw a second notice of Prof. Cassidy's death, in the *Denver Republican*. It says that he originally came from Kew Gardens, which I did not know, though I knew he had been in England.

Nov. 26th, 7:55 p.m. It has been fine and warm today, I am glad to say. My mail this morning was a letter from Sterki about the shells of the genus *Pupa*. Before replying to him, I thought I might as well work up the *Pupae* I had on hand, which I did. With a glass I was able to make out the characteristics of the most minute species, but it took a lot of time.

In the afternoon I was looking over Heynemann's paper (in German) on slugs. Heynemann is that man who wrote me that long German letter at Bedford Park. Do you remember? I was much at a loss to decipher a certain rather important passage, so I took it round to Rosenstraugh, the butcher, who is a German, but he could not help me much, from the abundance of technical terms. I must work it out with the dictionary.

I also posted my formal application for the position of science teacher at the schools, as it is getting near the time for the examination and appointment of new teachers. I don't think it will come to anything, but there's no harm in trying.

This evening I have been taking notes on variation. I have found some facts which seem very strongly to confirm my theory of Seasonal Dimorphism. I hope there will be a letter from you tomorrow morning!

Nov.27th, 7:15 p.m. Your letter did come this morning, to my great satisfaction. The other mail was letters from Hulst, and Anderson (of

Montana), postcard from Carlie, and a sample copy of a rather trashy paper called *The Farmer's Voice*. Hulst gives the names of a lot of moths I sent him; two are new species. The first thing I did after reading the letters was to look over a *Popular Science Monthly* that was in the store below. The most interesting article was one by Grant Allen on the 'Woman Question' (copied, I think, from the *Fortnightly Reviews*). Much of what he says is doubtless true, though I do not altogether agree with him. The day has gone by rather unprofitably, taking notes, etc., and beginning an account of the insects of high altitudes for the *Canadian Entomologist*.

There is a *Chrysanthemum* plant in the post-office window here; it seems like an old friend. (This as you mention chrysanthemums in your letter.) Chrysanthemums don't seem to grow out of doors here, though I have seen them at Cañon City. I like that servant's letter; it sounds very genuine. I should like to know what has become of her and him since. The Etiquette book is ridiculous. I especially like 'Love. . . is a respectable feeling.' One wonders how anyone can have the face to publish such absurdities.

I was pleased to find that Louy came down after all. You must both have been glad of it. You say you feel rather disloyal to the family for telling me about the discord v. Louy, but I am glad you told me because I like to know how things are that concern you in any way. I will tell you lots of things at different times that I am supposed to keep quite secret, but I always feel justified in telling you all I know, and I believe nobody would expect me to keep secrets from you. If they wished me to do so, I should ask them not to bother me with secrets.

Certainly my coats are small because I have expanded! It is interesting about the Chinchens. Possibly they are a good deal happier than the people who scoff at them. I hope Carlie will never give me a book on architecture! If he does I shall present him with Coulter's *Manual of Rocky Mountain Botany* in revenge. Yes, dear, I hope we may several times visit the Natural History Museum together. I remember that time when we

met there very well. When I got home Carlie said he thought it a truly remarkable coincidence that we should happen to be there on the same day!

Thank Frederic for his scrap of letter. I see he is getting £100 a year — not a very mighty sum, but he thinks it will increase. Salaries are pitifully low. Carlie writes of Kelsall: 'Kelsall has been restored to the land of the living and spent yesterday evening with me. He wished to be remembered to you. He is on the point of going into the church, and looks much worried.' Kelsall is a nice fellow and I wish he had let the church alone, for I don't think he will be able to consciously swallow the dogmas, and the whole thing will bother him. As a lay-preacher on his own account he might do more good, I should think. I have heard nothing of Toynbee Hall for some time.

Yours lovingly, your Theo.
Health. Excellent.

Nov. 28th, 1889, 7:35 p.m.

Love,

I posted a letter to you last night. Today I have been writing my paper on the insects of high altitudes for the *Canadian Entomologist*. I got it finished before evening. This evening I have been reading some Darwin, so you can see the day has hardly been an exciting one. There was no mail for me this morning.

I see in the paper that there has been another land swindle on a very gigantic scale. A man at Chicago 'sold' land to settlers and speculators, and when he had made away with the money they discovered that the land was not his, and they had paid their money for nothing. It seems that a number of 'highly respectable' Chicago capitalists were aiders and abettors. It shows the rotten state of trade, anyway, that such a thing should be possible.

I wonder what has become of the Cusacks! I haven't seen any sign of them since I last came to town. And they cannot have been unknown to me, for I see their postoffice box is crammed full of letters. I was to go there again some time. I hope there is nothing wrong up there. I have not seen Lees either. I frequently notice Brock in town.

There was a man in the store below, yesterday, who amused me rather. It seems he quarreled with a man on a ranch near his, and when one day his neighbour came upon his ranch, he ordered him off in a rather threatening way. The result was that the neighbour brought an action against him, and yesterday they went before the judge who, after hearing their statements, settled the matter by binding them *both* over to *stay* on their own ranches, and if they wanted provisions in town, they must send in their wives or anyone else after them! It seems a queer way of settling the matter, but it should be effectual. However, the man who related the story said he was going away down south shortly, so the decision would not trouble him.

Tonight is the Lit. & Sci. Soc'y, and I must go round and start a fire in the school house, as last time the ladies complained of being cold. Mrs. Becker said she caught cold. I am not very sensitive to cold, so I daresay what would not be unpleasant for me would be very cold for them. The discussion is to be on 'Women's Rights' tonight. I have written a short essay on the subject.

9:55 p.m. We have had a rather amusing debate. I went round to the school house early and lit the fire so that the place was nice and warm for the meeting. I had to come back and fetch oil to fill the lamps after I had lit the fire, and when I had returned and the lamps were full, it was meeting-time. I ran round to the Stockton's to wash my hands (I had got them oily filling the lamps) and was surprised to find Freer there. I asked how he was getting on at Cañon City. He was not doing much, and had lately been to Chicago. He seemed to take a very despondent view of things and said he felt as if he could never put forth any fresh effort or embark on any undertaking. I Trust this feeling will wear off in a little while, for the children's sake. I had to leave abruptly and go off to my meeting, so I could not talk much with him.

We had a small meeting. Those present were Charlton, Mrs. C., Mrs. Becker, Miss Lowther, Mrs. Conway, Vetter, Sam Wright, Miss Etzel, and T.D.A.C. Sam Wright began with a speech in favour of women's suffrage. I followed with a rather lengthy discourse based on the enclosed sketch, which I partly read, and added much that was additional, in speaking, especially an account of differentiation. Charlton followed with some remarks, and Vetter read a paper. Then Wright replied, and finally I replied again to Wright. None of the women would speak, but after the meeting we gathered in a group and they talked with much vigour.

The rest of the day has not been very interesting. The morning mail was a letter from Douglas. Some papers on Minnesota shells from one Grant of that state, and the October *Ornithologist and Oölogist* (lent me by Nash, as it has a continuation of Morrison's list of Colorado birds in it). Then I took a lot of notes on Mollusca, and finally notes on Colorado birds from Nash's *O. & O.* so that I might return it. This took up most of the day, and nothing else to mention was done. I baked bread this afternoon and also called on Charlton to read to him my notes for tonight. I found the Charltons in the midst of a house cleaning. Mrs. Charlton kindly gave me some milk.

Nov. 30th, 8:35 p.m. The mail this morning was quite interesting, being as follows: (1.) Postcard from Carlie. (2.) *Pall Mall Budget.* (3.) Postcard from Horn, and Salticini paper. (4.) Postcard from Vilmorin-Andrieux & Co., and trade catalogues. To explain further. I had written to Vilmorin & Co. (the celebrated firm of seed-men in Paris) asking for a copy of their trade catalogues, and these they have kindly sent. They are very interesting to me and useful in my work on the variation of plants.

I had written to Dr. Horn (the coleopterist) asking the loan of his recently published monograph of the Salticini. Now he sends the paper (it is quite a book) and kindly says I may keep it, a gift which is very welcome to me. The Salticini, by the way, are those little beetles which hop, a notorious example of them being the turnip-flea which is so destructive in England. My *Longitarsus nitidellus*, described in first report of C.B.A. belongs to the same group and is duly entered and described in Horn's paper.

The *Pall Mall* is more interesting than usual, especially the interview with Owen (who talks good sense) and the account of Mrs. L. Sambourne. I am amazed to see that Sambourne's *Punch* pictures are done from photographs! I see, too, they are starting a daily 'Graphic.' I suppose Frederic will know all about that. I should think it might be a success.

Carlie's postcard is about the picture I did, which reached him safely. He remarks, 'I hope you will not look upon this picture painting as a little matter for odd hours and moments only, but will practice it consistently next spring, and here in England when you return. There are all kinds of technical tricks which water-colourists use, as sponging, stippling, etc. for getting softer tones and atmospheric effects, which you must learn, and if you care to persevere at it, I see no reason why you shouldn't compete with the best of them.'

By which I gather that he would have me turn artist in water-colours! It's a fascinating idea, for then *we* could work together. But, goodness gracious — the £.s.d.? I am afraid it would never, never pay. What do you think? And it would be ages before I learned enough to do any good at it. It wouldn't do atall!

I have just been reading and writing today, so there is nothing special to relate. The rest of the evening I shall take notes from Vilmorin.

Suday, Dec. 1st, 9:35 p.m. Have been busy taking notes on the varieties of cultivated plants, and learned much that was new to me. It is singular that horticulturists have raised a permanently yellow-leaved variety of poplar. The asps here go yellow in autumn, you know.

I went round to call on the Charltons this afternoon, but they were out. The snow is rapidly melting and it is very sloppy underfoot. By the way, my 'Early Rose' potato is described and figured in Vilmorin's catalogue, so it is evidently known in France. I got rather a lot of mail today: (1.) Letter from Binney. (2.) Letter from Morrison of Virginia. (3.) Letter from U. S. National Museum, with name of a fungus I sent them. (4.) Postcard from L. Bruner, with names of some Orthoptera. (5.) *Field and Farm.*

Dec. 2nd, 12:25. I am just off to the Cusacks for a few days, so will post this now. I got a letter from Pilsbry this morning, and drawings of some shells. No other mail.

Your lover, Theo.
Health. Very good.

Read before Literary and Sci. Society.

Human society consists or should consist of a number of individuals working for the greatest good of all. What is the greatest good? It is not essentially the greatest material wealth or even the greatest health or longevity — these are strictly means, not ends. The greatest good is the greatest happiness, which is the greatest harmony. Harmonious development is the object and end of mankind. What is the ideal position of members of such a society? Manifestly they should be all working for the mutual end in the manner most suited to their capabilities.

Now is it desirable that all should do the same kind of work? Obviously not, since capabilities are diverse, and development depends always on differentiation [explain differentiation]. Hence nature first, more lately aided by human effort, has set apart certain individuals for different works, and it is from the diversity of special capabilities, and the play given to such that modern civilisation has sprung, and in further and, we hope, better, developments in the same line lies our certainty of progress.

What are the divisions of labour thus fundamentally necessary to progress? They are endless, but in the beginning were few. The earliest differentiations were in parts of the same animal, but those hardly now concern us [argument of equal value of parts]. One of the earliest divisions of labour among individuals was effected by nature in the separation of the sexes. The principal duties [this long before man existed] were to procure food and nourish offspring. The male animal undertook the former, the female the latter. Is there any difference in the merits of the two functions? If so, the female is surely the higher.

This same differentiation holds good to the present day. It cannot be changed. Males cannot nourish offspring. Females cannot be the breadwinner without impairment to their duties as females. [cite Rickets, etc.] It is nonsense to suppose that it could be so. [Quote Grant Allen on number of births necessary, etc.] Differentiation, division of labour we insist on. Likewise we insist on equality of position, not similarity.

Many and increasingly more of the pleasures of this life are intellectual, scientific, artistic, etc., etc. Are these pleasures, the ability to cultivate which is the most precious fruit of labour, to be confined to one sex? Surely not. Is it evident that women are incapable of enjoying them? Not so! Therefore they should not be debarred from them. Judgment for the welfare of the community, lawgiving if you will, is this to be confined to one sex? Is one sex only concerned? Surely both are concerned equally, etc., etc.

Furthermore, many kinds of labour (especially that requiring deftness) are best done by females. Ought they to be allowed to do it? Yes, allowed, but hardly compelled. The care of children and the care of house (too much of it often) are amply fair exchange for a woman's right to life and livelihood in this world. But what of unmarried women? They indeed may not unprofitably turn to bread-winning for themselves, but this is only when and while unmarried. It is necessary that they should always have means of livelihood, and necessary that they should not be compelled to marry, for without such freedom half the marriages will be (as perhaps they are) unfortunate. But above all things they must be educated, refined, and cultivated, and to get this is worth any expense and trouble. Such education may be given them as will equally fit them on the other hand to work unmarried in those callings which are adapted for them: Literature, art, sewing, cooking, and a host of others.

Dec. 3rd, 1889, 8:55 p.m.

Love,

I had written a letter to Pilsbry and made drawings of some shells for him yesterday, when Regy and Mrs. R. came to town and invited me to go out with them to finish Mrs. Cusack's flowers. So I posted a letter to you, and went out with them. The only reason they had not sooner come to town was the bad weather and snow. I found Lees, Ward, and Pennicuick at the Cusacks' (living in the old house), working mainly at moving the house Frank built over to Regy's house (which they haven't yet done). You know (if I did not omit to describe it at the time) that Frank Cusack built a long time ago two additional rooms as a separate house by the old one. [People want to go to bed, so must leave off.]

Dec. 4th, 8:35 a.m. Well, as I was saying, those two rooms that Frank built used to be occupied by Mrs. Cusack until she moved into Regy's house. This latter being now the center of operations, it was deemed expedient to move the two rooms over here to form part of this (Regy's) house. Lees was to do the moving, but from various breakages of chains, ropes, etc., it has been delayed. Yesterday they got started again, but when the house had gone about its length, the basement of it broke, and today Lees is sending Ward after lumber to make it strong again. The way the house is moved is by getting two tree trunks under it, to act like the runners of a stage, and then with various arrangements of ropes, etc., the horses are able to pull it over the snow-covered ground. Pennnycuick has now returned to Louis' at Ula, but Lees and Ward propose to move the house over as soon as they can.

Dec. 5th, 10:15 p.m. Have been to town to-day, and coming back tired, have written nothing. I got your nice letter.

Dec, 6th, 9 p.m. This has been another day over the flowers, and tomorrow morning I go to town to stay. I have arranged the roses of the neighbourhood to my satisfaction, but find the geraniums still puzzling. The roses and geraniums are exceedingly variable.

Yesterday I rode to town on 'Ferris', being sent by Lees to post and get mail and groceries. I had to call at the Howard's on my way back, and had lunch there. I got mail for myself in town — your letter, letters from Mother and Coulter (with names of plants I sent him) and some slugs from Pilsbry. There was a *Queen* [that] Mother had sent to Mrs. Cusack, and when I got back tired I amused myself by reading it through and laughing at its absurdities for some time. The night before last I read some little stories by Bret Harte, and enjoyed them. I posted you two of the wedding photographs yesterday. They are presented to *you* by Mrs. Cusack.

Dec. 7th, 8:25 p.m. I am back in my room again. I came in with Regy today. The mail I got was (1.) Letter from one Evermann, wanting C.B.A. publications. (2.) Postcard from Hamilton. (3.) Plate of *Erebia episodea* (a butterfly) from W. H. Edwards. This is one of the beautiful plates from his book. (4.) *Pall mall Budget*. (5.) Diary for 1890, from Carlie. Unfortunately the cover had got broken in the post. This afternoon I examined the slugs I received from Pilsbry, and returned them to him with a report on them. They are all *Limax agrestis*, but of five varieties.

There are so many things to tell you about that I have got quite mixed up in my ideas of sequence, so I shall jot them down as I think of them:

(1.) COWS: The Cusacks have now got two cows and two calves, hence much milk, and Mrs. Regy makes beautiful butter.

(2.) CUSACKS: Regy and his wife seem to live very happily together so far; undoubtedly the marriage has improved Regy. Mrs. Cusack (the elder) is going to Santa Barbara to stay with the Charley Cusacks as soon as she can get away. There are rumours of Frank Cusack returning from Australia.

(3.) PHOTOGRAPHS: The photographs I sent are a present from Mrs. Cusack to you. The house in them is Regy's house, the one I lived in. I enclose an outline drawing to show you who the people are. I am afraid it does not flatter any of them. Mrs. Cox looks as if she were being tortured and little Charley ditto. I am sorry Mrs. Urquhart is so invisible, but from what there is of her you can see how she resembles her daughter. Mrs. Cusack was standing in the doorway and is invisible.

The wedding party. (left to right) Cardwell Lees, Mrs. Urquhart, Gertrude (Urquhart) Cusack, Isabel Cox, Reggie Cusack, Frank Hampe (best man), Mrs. Cusack

(4.) TEACHERSHIP: When I was in town on Thursday, Stockton came up to me and said the school trustees had considered my application for the post of Science Teacher, and were going to decide later on when they had consulted Prof. Wright. This looks rather hopeful; I had expected they would refuse point blank. Still, I do not really expect to get the post.

(5.) MAILS: The mails have been changed so that the coach now comes in at noon instead of at ten p.m. This will be much better for the postmistress and the stage driver, so I am quite in favour of the change, though we get our mails a few hours later in consequence.

(6.) WEATHER. We have been having most extraordinary and unheard-of weather the past week. It has been stormy, but although it is December, it has been very warm, not even freezing several nights, and of course the snow on the ground has been rapidly melting. Today it has been raining considerably. Everyone says they never heard of *rain* in December here before!

(7.) BROCK: Mrs. Turner departed, I believe, to Denver, some time ago. Last week, Brock and Wheatley likewise departed for Denver. Brock had a waggon and all his horses, etc., and Regy went with him as far as a place called Yorkville (about 20 miles along the road to Cañon City) to help drive the animals. Regy came back,

and Brock went on, and we supposed he was gone for good. But certain people here in West Cliff, storekeepers and others, had much money — they say $1,500 — owing to them from Brock, and they naturally objected to his going off with his property like that. The ranch of course was left behind, but as that was already mortgaged up to the fullest possible extent, that would not help them.

So the Sheriff departed after Brock and caught him up in Colorado Springs, and attached the property, which will be sold to pay the creditors. It is questionable whether Brock will have anything left atall, especially as they will of course charge to him all the expense of going after him, in addition to his debts.

Lees had received a cheque from Brock for $100 in payment of a debt (for money lent) of Turner's to be paid by Mrs. Turner, Mrs. Turner's money being all lodged in Brock's name in a bank at Denver. The creditors have sent word to the bank not to pay out Brock's money, and probably Lees will lose his $100, the cheque not being cashed as yet.

There is still another complication. Brock has mortgaged all his property to Mrs. Turner and says it is no longer his. Of course this is only a scheme to evade the creditors, and will not be allowed in a court of law, but I believe there is going to be a trial to settle the matter. So you see Brock is beginning to be handled roughly (and justly) at last.

I wonder what will become of Wheatley. He has hardly enough sense to earn a living. He talked of setting up a cigar shop when he got to Denver. (I found a photo of Wheatley lying about at the Cusacks', and as nobody wants it I enclose it that you may see what a duffer he looks).

COX: Here is another brilliant Englishman. He got some money from England and set up in Denver as a real estate agent, as you know. So far, the family has been living in a single room here, but I hear they are going into a house. (All this about Cox is between ourselves, as it was told me in *strict confidence*.)

Last week Cox suddenly appeared at the Cusacks' and had 'business' with Lees. Then he went back again to Denver. So much on the surface, but the facts are these. Cox tells a story that he drew $600 in gold from the bank one morning and went away with it in his pocket. Presently he looked, and found he had lost it; presumably it was stolen. As Lees remarks, 'It was so palpable a lie that I did not even question him about it.'

$600 in gold weighs about two pounds, I believe, and it is ridiculous that he could have lost it by accident, however careless he may have been. The presumption therefore is that he had to pay the money for some debt unknown to us, or he gambled it away, the former being the more likely supposition. However, having lost this money, he declared that he would be subject to proceedings at law for something or other if he could not raise more money at once. He would commit suicide if he could not raise the money, and so forth.

Further, he and Mrs. Cox had written to England to get money in legacies coming to them on the deaths of certain relatives. (This can be done in advance through the money-lenders) but the money would not come in time. Would Lees therefore back his note for $1,000? (Whereby Lees would be rendered liable for that sum if the note were not paid, with18 per cent interest, four months after the money was drawn on it.) Well, Lees did it, but with many doubts (and since, more) whether he was acting wisely and rightly. Cox promises that he shall not be made to suffer in any way, but what are his promises worth?

It is a miserable affair. But for Mrs. Cox and the children it would not matter particularly what became of Cox. I don't think he is essentially bad, but he is a hopeless fool and absolutely careless, and one can never expect any good of him. Lees has much more patience with him and generosity than I should ever have. Lees was almost going to Denver to see how things were tomorrow, but he has concluded to let the matter stand over for the present.

Could you not write a story and bring Cox in? Anonymously of course, to show how much misery may follow from sheer foolishness and carelessness and gambling. I think it would have a good effect. I do not remember seeing the thing worked out in fiction, common as it is in real life. Nobody knows all this about Cox here except Lees and myself, and of course it is not known in England.

Your letter: Mrs. Regy said she was sure I had received a letter from you, because I was in such good spirits when I came home (or rather, back to the Cusacks' on Thursday! I don't think

I shall answer it tonight after all, as I am sleepy and stupid. It is nearly 10 o'clock.

Sunday, Dec. 8th, 10:30 p.m. Now I will answer your letter, and then post this. I like what you say about head-work and marriage. I can very well understand that businessmen may not like to talk over their business to their wives, being themselves a little ashamed of their proceedings. But that is not of necessity. Men ought to do their work in such a way that they are ashamed of no detail of it. I am afraid, though, that some wives would not willingly forego extra profits for conscience sake. Do you think I am here unjust to the wives?

Supposing that women were forced to know and given control of the doings of all men, how far do you think they would act by principle, and how far by conscience? I believe they would be more honest than the men, but less honest than might be expected from their present standards of morality. Of course I know many excellent women who would flinch at nothing, but likewise many excellent men, and I do not think of these, because they are, I believe, in the minority.

However, all this doesn't immediately concern you and me, and we at least may share in one another's work and have no secrets. Happily, in scientific work there is not even any temporary advantage in 'shady' proceedings!

Perhaps you are right in saying that 'beauty' applies only to appearance. If so, I used the word wrongly. But then, 'beautiful' must not be applied to a poem or to music, as it commonly is. I don't wonder that the word 'type' puzzles you. It is very carelessly used and has given rise to much discussion. The 'type' of a species is generally the commonest or original form. Thus the 'type' of *Gallus ferrugineus* (= bankiva) is the wild Asiatic bird and not the domestic fowl. The 'type' of a genus is the first species referred to that genus. Author's 'types' are the specimens which he originally described from.

You are very nice about my letter you got on Nov. 15th. You say you don't doubt me. Well, I don't doubt *you*, even if you doubt yourself. So I always feel happy about you and hopeful for the future, I don't believe you half know what an excellent creature you are! You are so much more worthy of trust than I am, as anybody would admit. Very few men have the good fortune to be loved by and to love women like yourself, and I am glad accordingly. And dear Annie, you must not be hopeless about your health. You know how I wish for your sake that you were always quite strong and well, but if any illness can't be avoided, we must make the best of it, and to do so of *course* we must marry! How could it be 'for my sake' not to marry me under *any* circumstances? Should I not love you just the same? If so, you ought not to love *me*, for I shall never be a Hercules, to put it mildly! So promise me that you will never refuse to marry me because of your health, won't you?

As to the post in U. S., I don't think I am atall likely to be offered one, but I wait anxiously to hear what your mother will say. I shall 'take my chance' for nothing! But if it *should* come to the point, I could cable you and hear the result. I should not myself be altogether sorry to have to refuse an American post, as I should infinitely prefer living in England. But as I said, the £.s.d. is an item. Of course, it would not necessitate living out-of-the-world atall. The State University, for instance, is a center of much activity.

Louy evidently needs fresh air and exercise more than anything. I feel annoyed with Murray of the Museum for being cross about the fungi, but then these fellows will sometimes, and there is no accounting for it. In your list, should not '*prittacinus*' be '*psittacinus*', '*cericeus*' '*sericeus*', and '*Lepista*' '*Lepicta*'?

Ever your lover, Theo.
Health. Am very well.

Dec. 8th, 1889, 9:30 p.m.

Love,
I posted a letter to you about noon. Soon after, the mail came in and brought me letters from Binney, Nash, and J. B. Ellis, *Field and Farm*, and Parts 1 and 2 of *North American Fauna*, these last being papers on American Mammalia by C. H. Merriam, published by the Dept. of Agriculture. In them Dr. Merriam actually describes one new genus and 26 new species of American mammals! Binney's letter is about slugs. He thinks with me that two of the species I had from Wickham are new. Nearly all afternoon I have been working at the slugs and replying to Binney at length. Nash says he expects soon to have his paper on Colorado butterflies ready but does not know whether he can afford to have it printed just now.

Dec. 9th, 7:10 p.m. Quite a lot of mail, including your letter, came this morning, or rather, this noon — the mail, as I said in my last letter, not coming in until noon under the new arrangement. In the morning I was packing up slugs to Binney, fungi to Ellis, and writing to Nash. This afternoon I called on the Charlton's to fix a day for the next meeting of the C.B.A. Last Saturday was the proper day for it, but it was put off, and we have fixed on next Saturday instead.

Mrs. Charlton told me an amusing story. She was teaching at the Sunday School here, and having related all about Absalom, began to question the children. She asked a little girl (about five years old) named Morton 'what happened to Absalom after all his wickedness?' 'Guess they sued him', was the reply.

The day's mail, besides your letter, is: (1.) Letter from Mother. (2.) Letter from Dr. G. H. Horn. He says he is getting up a popular scientific paper, and asks me to contribute. (3.) Letter from Jenner Weir. (4.) Postcard from Elwes to ask what has become of me, that I have not written to him nor sent him any butterflies. (5.) Postcard from G. Roberts.

Jenner Weir begins his letter, 'I was at Tolhurst's yesterday and saw a cat belonging to your mother, now 15 years old and in good health!' The Tolhursts were our next door neighbors at Wayside, Beckenham. The Tolhurst boy used to go to school with Carlie.

To turn to another subject, Jenner Weir writes: 'I do not like this separation of Darwinites into two sections: One holds that acquired characters are *not* inherited (Weissmann, Meldola, and Poulton); others hold that they are. I am rather grieved to be in the latter category as a heretic, and find myself with St. George Mivart and others. I would rather hold with the former but *cannot* do so. It has been a dread with me that perhaps in my old age I should be unable to recognise a new truth. I have committed myself to that view in a letter to *Nature*. I trust I am not wrong, but am not easy in my mind, and find a coolness between myself and my old friends.'

There is something quite pathetic in all this, and you see how it touches on the 'intellectual blindness' question. I myself am strongly of Jenner Weir's view in this matter, however, and the opinion is backed by many eminent naturalists. Jenner Weir reminds me of Darwin in his modesty and fear of error. Would that all naturalists were like him.

Now your letter. I cannot help being pleased at the way your parents look at the American post question, although they think I should occupy the post some time first, and are averse to the idea of it on the whole. Indeed, were I in their position, I think I should be of their opinion, so I ought to be satisfied. I hope the difficulty will not occur, for an American post is no choice of mine. Altogether, I feel thankful to them and to you for being so reasonable about it. And not less thankful to you because I was already sure that for your part you would be kind. Except the West, I think England is more healthy than America.

Thank you for the Stevenson poems. I am not sure that I care very much for them. Possibly I have a latent prejudice against Stevenson though I am not conscious of it in this connec-tion. The ideas are rather pretty, some of them, and natural to a child. Reading them a second time, I like the poems better. What made you specially pick them out?

Your account of the domestic Ada tumbling out of bed and shaking the house made me laugh, though I suppose I should be sorry for her. I sleep long hours — about nine, being an exceptionally sleepy mortal. I don't know whether I could do on less, but any attempts that way have not succeeded. I get so sleepy at ten p.m. that if I remained up I should be unfit for work without an artificial stimulus or an interesting novel to read. I can read when I am too tired to write, and think when I am too tired to do either.

Yes, I will concoct some nonsense or other for the *Daily Graphic*. I thought of it directly I saw the announcement in *Pall Mall* but don't know whether they would approve of my work. Thank you for the address. The idea of the editor of *Saturday Journal* returning a story as not sensational enough! I rather agree with you about Ashmead and his health. When I spoke of *weeds*, I meant plants *as* weeds, and not from the botanical point of view.

I like your saying you wrote *Merely Friends* partly for me. Your remarks about my seeing you once a week in the presence of the family terrify me very much. No, I don't think you are so *meek* as I am, but then I am fearfully *obstinate*! Seriously, I fear I may not see so much of you as even you would permit, as I shall no doubt have to be quite busy getting work or doing it. What you say on 'intellectual blindness' is very true. Yes, I quite agree with you that men who marry for money are scoundrels, but somehow one less expects a woman to marry for a title.

The 'West Cliff Academy of Science' is latent at present. I *am* a little shocked at your liking Eugene Wrayburn! It makes me shudder to think of this.

Dec. 10th, 10:5 a.m. I shall post this today so that it will reach you about Christmas. And here's a Christmas greeting and wishes for much happiness in the new year for you and all at Syon Lodge. For *you only*, a kiss and my love. By way of a Christmas card, I enclose a reputed portrait of a lover of yours who will probably appear at the gate of Syon Lodge some time next June.

The artist wishes me to state that if it is not in all respects true to nature, it is entirely your lover's fault, as he could not be got to stand to have his portrait taken, and turned his face away from the artist all the time. Now that it is done, of course the gentleman protests that it is not atall like him, but that is the way with all portraits that are unflatteringly true to life.

With love, *your* Theo.

[There is a gap in the sequence of letters, from December 10th, to Feb. 4th. Ed.]

Feb. 4th, 1890

Love,

A letter to you went yesterday. Today I posted the photographs (returned). There is not much to be said about yesterday beyond what was in my last letter. In the afternoon, among other things, I packed up a lot of galls for the South London Ent. Society. In the evening I called at Charlton's, and later on wrote up a lot of notes.

Today is as warm as mid-summer. I sat writing this morning in my shirt sleeves with the window wide open. No letter yet from Fort Collins. The only mail today was from Merriam, and a postcard acknowledging subscription to *Canad. Entom.* I worked on shells this morning. I was out nearly all the afternoon, hunting shells in the Pleistocene deposit by Grape Creek. I found three species new to the deposit. Very curiously, the *Pupae* found there turn out to be *Pupa ovata*, a species common in some parts of the U. S., but not now known in Colorado. I took the shells up to Charlton's and sorted them. Regy was in town today. He brought me some brawn [possibly pickled boar's flesh. cf. O.E.D. Ed.], kindly sent for me by his wife.

9:45 p.m. It is a beautiful night, warm and moonlight. Partly for the walk, I went down to the Conways to talk to Sam Wright, Mrs. Conway and Miss Lowther about the Lit. & Sci. Society. If we cannot improve it somewhat I shall be inclined to give the society up. The *Play*, which had fallen into abeyance, was once more discussed, and we arranged to copy the parts out, since we could not get the extra copies of the paper.

I hear that Mrs. Cox has started for England! Hope she will get there safely!

Feb. 5th, 8:25 p.m. I have just been looking over *African Farm*. It affects me more than any book I know. This has been the finest day I ever remember. Clear and bright, with a warm sun, not too hot. After breakfast I went to Mrs.

Stockton's and told her she ought to go out, but she could not, but would come tomorrow. The I went over the road to Mrs. Humphrey's, and Mrs. H., being also busy today, would go out tomorrow if it were fine.

So we said we would get the hand-car (alias trolley)) and go down the railroad about four miles to a place called Dora, tomorrow morning. Anyone who would should come with us. Dora was once a postoffice; now there is nothing but a house or so there, and the postoffice is abolished. Then I went to the Charlton's, and they said they would come on the hand-car. They were just losing Minnie, the girl they had to work for them; she goes off to her father in Utah. Her uncle had come with a waggon to take her as far as Cañon City. Then I saw Mrs. Chetelat, and she also would come on the hand-car. We shall so have quite a little party. It will be a novelty and will do us good.

This much arranged, I started off on another matter. Mrs. Saxe, up toward Silver Cliff, was reputed to take *Harper's Bazaar*. Why not try to borrow from her the copy with our *Play* in it? It would save copying *one part*, at all events. So I went up there, and Mrs. Saxe at once found the desired copy and lent it to me. So I went to Dr. Ellis' but they had not got it. However, they told me there that Mrs. Johnson, wife of the superintendent of the Security Mine, had *Harper's Bazaar*. I went down there and was able to borrow a second copy. This was great good fortune. I left one copy in Chetelat's store to be sent out to Darling; the other copy I took myself down to Miss Byington. I found Miss B. quite ill with influenza. I gave her some advice as to treatment and suggested that it might do her some good to come with us on the hand-car, but she didn't feel strong enough for that.

But it was now one o'clock. When I got back I lay down for a while and lunched on biscuits, bring rather tired from my morning's gyrations. Presently Charlton paid me a call. The Ladies' Literary Society was meeting at his house, and the poor fellow had come away to escape them!

Afterwards I wrote, cut some wood, etc., until it was supper-time.

Feb. 6th, 6:35 p.m. The saying, 'Make hay while the sun shines' is perhaps of specially frequent application in Colorado. Yesterday it was beautifully fine, so that we arranged to go on the hand-car this morning. *This morning* there was 2 ½ inches of snow on the ground and our hand-car ride was impossible! All the day has been dull, with some hail in the afternoon, but it has not snowed any more, and such snow as fell last night is rapidly melting. I called on Mrs. Humphrey, Mrs. Stockton, and the Charltons, and we said we would go on the hand-car another day. I have examined the car, by the way, and see it will only hold six people. So I must be careful not to invite more than we can take.

This morning I also called at the Conway ranch and left *African Farm*, directing them to read Part II, Chapters 1, 11 (or the whole book if they wish). So that I was on my feet all the morning except intervals at the various houses I visited. At Mrs. Charlton's I was paid for the Custer County Flora list. I asked $1.00 for the work, but the Ladies' Society thought that was not enough and so voted me $2.50!

The mail was a letter and a box of shells from a man named Elliott. The shells are some he collected in Colorado. He wanted them named. Several of them are new for Colorado. I named them and posted them back to him this afternoon. Tonight I have to copy out Samse's part in the *Play*, as I promised to do so.

Feb. 7th, 7:15 p.m. Delightful letter from you today! Am just off to Lit. & Sci. Society.

Feb. 8th, 9:45 p.m. On Thursday night I copied out Samse's part in the play, and gave Samse the manuscript when he came to town today. Yesterday (Friday) I wrote 'Notes' in the morning; that is to say, I finished writing up my pencil notes of last summer in my record-books.

The mail came rather late, but there was your letter, and also letters from (1.) Mother, enclosing $5.00. Perhaps it is rather a pity she should send me money, though it is kind of her. When I don't earn anything it is proper for me to be poor; and just at present I am rich — for me! (2.) Letter from Miss E. L. Morton, an entomologist of New York State and corresponding member of C.B.A.

(3.) Letter from J. E. Robson of Hertlepool. I offered Robson my list of British Land and Freshwater Mollusca to publish as a supplement to *Young Naturalist*, the paper he edits. He writes to say he cannot tell until he sees the manuscript whether he can publish it, but if I send it he will return it safely if not used. No, 'sending the manuscript' involves copying it out from my books, and a lot of preparation and work, so I was half minded to leave the thing alone, but I shall publish the list somehow anyway, so I concluded to write it up and sent it off to Robson. So I worked at it all yesterday afternoon, and for an hour at night after returning from Lit. & Sci. Society, and again all today, and got it finished and posted to Robson by about 7 p.m. It was so big it cost me 15 cents postage. It is planned, as far as possible, after the model of the 'London Catalogue' of British plants.

Last night at the Lit. & Sci. Society we had a pretty full meeting. The subject was a discussion as to what constituted right and wrong. But nobody would discuss except Charlton and myself (I opened the debate), though Mrs. Becker did say a few words. Charlton and I had quite a little debate between us, and the company seemed satisfied to look on and listen, so it was not so bad as it might have been. Charlton had manuscripts prepared, but I had none. Mrs. Charlton took the chair. We arranged that in future the meetings should be on Saturdays so as not to conflict with the 'socials.'

Sunday, Feb. 9th, 10:10 p.m. I have taken a holiday altogether today, as is proper. It has been very fine, and after breakfast I went to hunt up the walking-club. But when I got to Mrs. Stockton's, she would not go out, and moreover she began talking about our 'right versus wrong' debate (of which she had an account though she was not there), and in a discussion on the *conscience* we used up most of the morning, or at least perhaps an hour and a half. Mrs. S. thinks 'conscience' teaches us only to do right in the abstract, and our intelligence and education decide each particular case. In this view I do not concur. I don't exactly see how right or wrong can exist in the abstract, without relation to some object or objects, or to some specified or imagined case. And I think the common term, 'conscience' includes two things, (1.) the inherited social instinct; (2.) The accumulated effect of environment during our lifetimes (e.g., religious training). Our conscience provides us with the axioms from which, in the ordinary way of reasoning, we deduce our code of everyday morality.

Afterwards I called on Mrs. Humphrey, but it was too late to go out for a walk. Then I went down to Charlton's. Charlton is thinking of publishing an article on the fossil wood at the Security (alias Geyser) Mine, and as this will be his maiden effort of the kind (except for the bare list of minerals he wrote for the C.B.A.) he had a great many questions to ask me about scientific writing, and the various points of etiquette to be observed therein.

Then I returned home and prepared a little meal of potatoes and bacon, and at about three I went round to the schoolhouse to give Miss Lowther her copy of *Harper's Bazaar* (with the Play), as I supposed she would be at Sunday School. I got these rather soon, and so went out on the prairie and looked for minerals.

While there, four girls (waiting like myself) joined me, and I walked with them and told them about the rocks, the galls on *Bigelovia*, and about a tiny grasshopper one of them caught. They seemed pleased and interested and, thinking it over afterwards, I fancied it might be possible to make naturalists out of some of these children. If they would study nature, how pleased I would be to help them! Somehow there is something refreshing about children that one misses so in many adults. They have not learned to be apathetic.

The saying, "study nature, not books" should not be interpreted to mean that books are to be ignored, but it is wise counsel for the beginning student who should learn to see things and to know their characters, instead of merely following what has been written. It may be actually detrimental to a young student to have his insects all named for him by experts. He is thereby excused from studying their characters, and unless he has a good deal of originality and initiative he may lose the chance of becoming competent. On the other hand, of course, if he lacks these qualities, he is likely to quit altogether when he runs into difficulties, and this may not always be a misfortune to science.

Recollections

At length Miss Lowther came and I gave her the paper and talked about the first rehearsal, which is to be on Saturday. After that I left, not staying to Sunday School. I read *Pall Mall Budget* for a while, but the afternoon was so lovely that I did not want to stay indoors. (I see in *Budget* that Lord Hartington has the honour to be ill in the house of a member of the C.B.A., Lord Walsingham! I suppose that explains why Lord W. has not written about some moths I sent him. Mother tells me (as a secret, so don't tell anyone) that Uncle Douglas went to attend Lord Hartington in his illness.

Well, I walked out to Louis Howard's, just for the walk and to pay a visit (I had not seen them for a long time). I found them at home, and stopped for supper and the evening, not getting back to West Cliff until about ten. Louis made a proposal to me that, if I should be here in March

and April, I should go and live up at Lees' cabin, for a consideration. The reason being that they are afraid that someone will 'jump' (that is, take possession of Smith's Park while Lees is away). When they get a crop in up there it will be all right, but in the early spring someone might appropriate the place if it was quite deserted. It would be rather more healthy for me than town life, so I said that if nothing prevented, I should be willing to do it on the following terms:

(1.) Payment of $8.50 per month (to cover my board). (2.) Buonaparte (the horse) to be there for my use (and food for him). (3.) I may come to town as often as I please, and stay three or four days if I wish. (4.) When I am in town, the horse is to be kept at Louis'.

Louis seemed to regard these terms as very reasonable (which in fact they are), and wrote off to Lees to get his consent to the arrangement. Of course I shall keep my room in town still, if I do go up to the cabin.

I meant to answer your letter tonight, but it is eleven o'clock, so I must put it off until tomorrow.

Feb. 10th, 8:55 p.m. I had meant to write a lot of letters today but so far they are unwritten. I took a few minerals to Charlton's after breakfast, and Mrs. C. asked me to draw some Valentines for the coming 'Valentine Social.' She gave me about 25 sheets of paper, and on each one I had to make some drawings suitable for various people. Most of them were comic, but I did a few flowers too. I only did four in colours. These took me all the morning and some of the afternoon. When I took them round to Mrs. Charlton she was quite pleased with them and thought they would do very well. Verses will have to be written under the drawings, but I leave that to the ladies.

Regy was in town about noon. My mail was only pens and paper (for the new drawings of shells) from Binney, and *Field & Farm*, containing a report of C.B.A. meeting.

Now I will answer your letter, and then post this. I wrote a letter to Frederic about his living in town, I am afraid he will think I do not take a sufficiently hopeful view of it all. Of course I say nothing about Fred and Kate Hemery to anyone.

As for Cox, I think he never was of much use in the world, but probably he has become worse as time has gone on. It is mainly the gambling mania that has ruined him.

Will you teach me to dance properly? Well, I will try to look respectable when I visit you, but you must be strict with me and tell me when I have a second-hand sort of appearance! You see, my dear, you have a natural faculty for looking nice, whereas your lover is by nature a sort of orang-utang and it is only under the influence of others that he can be got to look like a passable human being atall. However, from his memory of the past, he believes you will be able to control him in an effectual manner.

No, you are not a common type. Miss Harsch is not so *much* like you, after all, but there is more resemblance than I have noticed in anyone else since I came to America, by far. I shall try to find out what she is like, but with a knowledge of my own curiosity on the subject, I feel rather shy about trying to talk to her. Apparently she is not particularly admired in West Cliff, but with so good a face she must surely have something in her.

I believe Regy forwarded your letter to Mrs. Cusack; it got *here* all right, as I saw the envelope. No, I don't see why a woman shouldn't like to be admired; it seems right and proper that she *should*. So far as physical beauty goes, a beautiful woman is certainly the most beautiful thing in existence, and why otherwise than for the admiration of her fellows? I don't think beautiful faces and remarkable minds by any means always go together, but the beauty in itself is a good thing, just as the beauty of a flower is good.

Beauty, however, is not *lovable*, as I understand love. Men not rarely think they love when they only admire or covet, but if they would dissect their motives they would find there was no more *love* about the affair than there is when a man sees a picture at the Academy he likes, and desires to purchase it. Don't you agree with me? When a woman thinks of nothing else but her beauty, she is a fool. When a man sees nothing in woman except her beauty, he is also a fool. But since women *are* beautiful objects, let us enjoy a good thing in a rational way!

People, when they see your photograph, tell me (in various phrases) that I am fortunate to be engaged to so beautiful a woman, as if I had come to love you on account of your beauty! I know I am fortunate, but your looks have very little to do with that indeed — practically, have nothing to do with it. I might have admired you to any extent, but if you had been only beautiful, I should never have *loved* you. There is no one else like *you*, but as for simply beautiful women, there are plenty of them.

The girl you draw in your letter is like Ethel Allport.

I am glad to hear of your father's wrath about your not getting credit in *Ladies' Pictorial*. I heartily sympathise with him. I am sorry you had a headache. I wonder whether I could comfort you during an headache, or whether I should only worry you.

[It is beginning to snow.]

To tell the truth, I think the 'poor human nature' argument is a more foolish one than most that are advanced against Socialism! Some object that we appeal only to the baser motives, while others say just the reverse. It is very absurd. Why do people want gain? Simply to enable them to live in the first place, and to give them power in the second. What man would become a millionaire on the terms that he had to live with his millions on a desert island? Under Socialism necessities are provided for, and power and influence do not depend on money, hence the apparent inadequacy of reward does not exist. If you are puzzled about it, tell me and I will try to explain more fully and precisely.

By the way, the army illustrates the principle of honour and duty. Who will propose that Tommy Atkins is enrolled from the best part of the population? We know the reverse, yet he is always heroic when it comes to the point. This clearly is no matter of £.s.d.

Well, I will close now, though I have more in my head in a nebulous condition.

Ever lovingly, your own Theo.
Health. Excellent.

Tuesday, Feb. 11th, 1890, 3 p.m.

Love,

A letter was posted to you yesterday. Last evening and in the night it snowed and was very cold — the wind blowing at the same time. To-day it has been sunny but cold, and the snow lies in drifts which will not quickly melt.

I got up very late in the morning and have not done much today. For one thing, I wrote to Fort Collins to ask why they had written nothing more about my going there. Possibly a letter may have got lost in transit. This afternoon I called on Charlton, taking him some things to read.

The mail today was a paper on *Erebia epipsodea* (a butterfly) sent by W. H. Edwards, being really part of the book he is publishing on North American butterflies; and *Canadian Entomologist* for Feb. This last has a paper on insects of high altitudes and a note on *Erebia* by myself, of which they sent me plenty of extra copies. I posted one to you. I shall send them round to various people just to remind them I am still alive.

Talking of horrible plays (this is a horrible *pen!*), here is an extract from Mother's letter. She went to see *La Tosca* (Garrick Theatre) and says: 'It is horrid beyond description — agony piled up, and unrelieved until at least it is quite

a relief and comfort to see the heroine jump over a bridge into the Tiber, instead of killing herself in any more horrid and lingering way. A clown with a red-hot poker and a harlequinade would be an immense relief between the acts.'

Feb. 12th, 8:15 p.m. A sad thing happened today. There are some people (I forget their name) living in the house formerly occupied by the Gowdys. The husband has gone away and the wife and children are left very poor. One boy, aged 16, declared a few weeks ago he was too old to stay at home and be a burden to the family, and he would go away and get work. Fearing that they might try to prevent his going, he ran away without asking leave, and went off near Rosita and got employment among horses and cattle. On Sunday (I think it was) he returned to his home on foot, not to stay, he said, but only for fresh clothes. He seemed tired but ate a good supper, and immediately afterwards began to suffer in his left leg. Quickly he became seriously ill, with fever, etc., and the doctor was finally sent for. Dr. Ellis would not say what was the matter, but seemed to regard the case as hopeless.

I heard all the above today when I went round to the meeting of Ladies' Lit. & Sci. Society at Mrs. Humphrey's. Mrs. Stockton was at the house of the sick boy, helping. I went round and saw Mrs. Stockton about it, and from what she told me of the symptoms I had no doubt the boy had septicaemia (or perhaps anthrax), either disease being classable as 'blood-poisoning' and both equally hopeless. Then I saw the boy and felt his pulse, which was so weak I could hardly detect it. He breathed heavily and seemed to be dying.

I ran back to my room and read the subject up afresh, and became quite sure it was septicaemia or anthrax, as I had said. There was nothing to be done except what I had already told them to do — let in lots of fresh air. (The room was hot and stuffy.) I had hardly got back to the Humphrey's and was telling Mrs. Stockton and the others about it and what I thought they ought to do, when a man came from the place where the boy had been and told us he was dead.

Mrs. Stockton and Mrs. Humphrey went to comfort and help the family. I went for some carbolic acid and begged them to see that everything was disinfected, and to take every care that the infection was not carried to any other person. In their sorrow, those of the family would naturally forget the importance of taking care of such things. So I left them to do what they could.

The Ladies' Society held no meeting, after all, as for various reasons only Mrs. Humphrey, Mrs. Stockton, and Mrs. Charlton were present, and we were concerned for the dying boy.

The mail today was very nice — two letters from you, and the *Review of Reviews*, and also a very interesting letter from Ashmead (who fully endorses my theory about galls), a postcard from J. H. Durrant, and the *Young Naturalist* for January. Durrant is Entomological Assistant to Lord Walsingham, and writes to say that the names of the moths I sent Lord W. will soon be sent. I once met Durant at the British Museum; he was naming some beetles.

By the way, now I think of it, though it has nothing to do with the mail, Humphrey has got (contrary to expectations) the post of Surveyor General to the State of Colorado. It is a very good post and, although I don't imagine H. is the *best* man available, he is at least a man with some ability, and not a worthless man like McNeely, who got the cattle appointment a good while ago. All these things are settled on political grounds entirely, to the great harm of the public.

Now, your very nice letters. (No.1) So we *are* a little alike, it seems! This is strange. Perhaps it is some affinity. At all events, I am pleased to be thought like you, for whatever reason. A somewhat similar case was that of my mother and father. You know Mother's writing is so unlike most people's, yet it is very like my father's. She says she did not copy his writing, but it seems naturally so.

Yes, I did think the verses *very* pretty on the New Year card, but I liked them so, as they came from *you*. The elderly man you draw in your letter is a little like the Rev. Arthur Wright.

It seems as if Louy wants a little more freedom. My own instinct would be to let her do exactly as she likes. People *must* form their own lives; it cannot be done for them. If Louy does not soon find out what she will do, and set about it, she will in after years find herself severely handicapped in the struggle for success. I don't think people ought to *expect* any brilliant success until they are at least 40 or older, but I do think they ought to be knowing what they want to do as soon after 18 or 20 as possible, if not earlier. Don't you? Now, if Louy has certain ambitions, and these are stifled, and she forms no more, it is impossible to exaggerate the injury to her life as a whole. So I say, give her freedom at least.

You are different from Louy. I wish you had more freedom, very much indeed, but environment which may harm Louy has not harmed you. I could not wish you different from yourself. But you need a wider field. Someday, when we are together, we will see what our faculties are good for. To me now everything seems provisional and preparatory, compared with that time to come.

I am rather amused by Miss Rosie Pidger's secret. But I rather pity the Hibernian solicitor if she had no more idea whether she loves him than *that*. I judge, myself, that she *doesn't*. Very likely 'Aura' is short for 'Aurora.' I had not thought of that.

I have seen nothing of the Daltons for some time; I suppose Miss Dalton's paints have not yet come. I must go and look them up. Dalton, senior, seems to do all sorts of odd work. He goes about in rags, and looks a miserable object. But he is a big healthy man and seems a cheerful one.

About your ankle (I hope it is now well) and the doctors — I don't much believe in local doctors and prefer a London man who has his wits up to date. Am still more horrified at Fred's energy; he will surely break down. It is curious, your ghostly sensations. I have never experienced anything of the kind. But I am naturally nervous.

I am afraid, love, I made too much of my influenza. It is all over now and I am quite well. But your sympathy makes me feel happy.

(Letter No. 2.) With a primrose! What an idea! To write to me every day! But it is delightful to me! The mails, though, only come from England twice a week, I believe. I must write to you oftener. You *are* a dear creature.

Stead's new review is very interesting, and will I think be very useful, but I will write fully about it later.

No, it wasn't your fault about the *Entom. Mags.*, and I don't blame Fred, as he had 'other fish to fry' (as my father used to say). I wrote Carlie to send them in future.

Freer was in West Cliff today and showed me pictures of his girls. Elsie's was the best.

Feb. 13th, 4:30 p.m. Another letter today! You will spoil me! (But I like to be spoiled, all the same!) I have been indoors all day except when I cut some wood. I have a little attack of dyspepsia, which has been coming on for several days. (Otherwise, am excellently well.)

Today's mail was: (1.) Your letter. (2.) Letter from Mother. (3.) Notice from Tutt about his forthcoming Monograph of Varieties of British Noctuids. It will cost 10/. I must try to find money for it. (4.) *Science Gossip* (wonderfully early!). It contains Williams' reply to some criticisms of mine. (5.) *Daily Graphic* (from Mother). I have only just glanced at it but it looks interesting. I like its 'get-up' and the pictures are good. I am alarmed to read in Mother's letter that Douglas got frost-bitten up in Manitoba. I must write and ask him about it. I like what you say in your letter about 'our beliefs.' I quite agree with you. I would have come to your dance. *Wouldn't* I?

I read a good deal of Stead's *Review of Reviews* this morning. It has rather too much *Stead* about it, but I may fairly say it is the most interesting and useful magazine I ever saw. I believe Stead is a good fellow. At all events, he is a useful fellow and does good in the world. I shall certainly read *R. of R.* when I am in England. Conoul Johnson, pictured as a frontispiece, is very like Mr. Schopp, the man whose place I took at Klein's.

Stead's own effusion I have as yet only glanced at. Ditto Stanley. I read *Ellen Middleton* (but I object to hashed-up novels), and I think it must be a very powerful story, perhaps too powerful. At all events, I think I can understand Ellen's position. I very carefully read H. Spencer on page 57 and Huxley on page 35, and finally wrote a letter to Huxley, criticising his article. I think it would have been better to have published my criticism, but as if sent to 19th Century it would only be put in the waste paper basket, I concluded to write direct to Huxley. I wonder what he will say! I think Huxley errs in regarding the individual as the only practical unit. H. Spencer has it much more correctly (according to my view), and he has also given the subject more attention than Huxley.

Now, my own dear Annie, I will close, and post this.

Your Theo.

Feb. 14, 1890, 6:15 p.m.

My love,

It is Valentines Day, so I ought to write a letter to you.

Amo te:
Amas me?
Annie!

That is the best I can think of. I hope it is better Latin than poetry. Cannot write now, as I have to go and help about the 'social' this evening. Will probably write when I get home.

11:30 p.m. We have had an enjoyable evening, but how late it is! Must put off the account of it until tomorrow.

Feb. 15th, 7:15 p.m. It is the Lit. & Sci. Society tonight. Have filled and lit the lamps, and lit the fire in the schoolhouse and am back in my room for half an hour to wash my hands and get ready for the meeting.

Not much has happened today. Regy, Mrs. Regy, and Ward came to town. There was a big mail for me including some papers, of which I posted to you copies of *Nautilus, Entom. News,* and *Bull. Torr. Bot.Club* containing articles of mine. But there is lots to tell you about yesterday.

Feb. 13 (The day before yesterday) I posted a letter to you. The evening I spent at Charlton's. I took them Stead's *Review of Reviews* and the *Daily Graphic* to see. They were much pleased with Stead's paper, and I think they will take it in.

Feb. 14th. I read most of the morning, and later on worked at the list of North American Land Shells I am preparing. This list is to contain all the varieties, and be on the same plan as the list of British shells I wrote the other day. I sent the first part off to Binney for his opinion. The mail I got was *Pall Mall Budget* and *Naturalist.* (Now I really must be off to the meeting.)

(To continue where I left off, Feb. 14th). Just as I got my mail, I saw a procession coming down the road. It was the funeral of the poor boy that died. (Ashcroft was the name.) First came a light waggon with the coffin, then about half a dozen young men on foot, then about ten waggons, and at the end a few men on horseback.

In the evening we had the 'Valentine Social.' It was at the schoolhouse. I was asked to light the fire and lamps, which I did. At about six the people came — quite a number of them, most of the 'Aristocracy' of West Cliff. There was a 'post-office' set up, and everyone had to come and get their 'mail', which was of course a Valentine, for which they paid ten cents. In this way the King's Daughters Society collected $4.60, so I suppose there were 46 people present.

About half the Valentines were those I had drawn, the rest being partly drawn by Charlton and partly bought. The drawn ones, both Charlton's and mine, were a great success and caused much laughter. I got a Valentine from Charlton, representing me looking through a microscope, with insects crawling around.

Just as we were going, at the end of the social, Humphrey came round to a number of us and invited us over to his house. I was among those invited, and from ten to past eleven we talked and had music at Humphrey's. The music was very nice, and everyone was in a good temper. Harry Stockton played the violin, several people sang, and the sedate Mayor of West Cliff (Cassidy) astonished everyone by sitting down to the piano and playing some lively airs with great ability. Several songs were sung in chorus, as 'John Brown', 'Marching Through Georgia', etc.

Feb. 15th. This was yesterday. I finished reading Stead's *Review of Reviews.* Stead's appeal to all English-speaking folk is a little too much of a good thing. Stead is not a modest man! The account of Stanley is interesting, and I must allow, gives me a much *worse* opinion of Stanley than I had before. I think I should *not* like him.

The mail, as I said, was a big one, as follows: (1.) Letter from Binney. (2.) Letter from N. L. Britton. (3.) Letter from Dr. Cooper of California, with a very interesting box of living slugs. (4.) Letter from Dr. C. H. Merriam. (5.) Postcard acknowledging my subscriptions to *Ent. News.* (6.) A letter I wrote to John Fraser of West Cliff last October, returned through the dead letter office. This was a letter telling him his subscription to Lit. & Sci. Society was due, and it has been gone four months to Washington and now comes back to me! (7.) *Nautilus* for January, containing the first part of my list of Colorado Mollusca. (8.) *Bulletin of Torrey Bot. Club* with my notes on *Castilleja*.

The first article in this paper, as you will see (I sent you a copy) seems to be written by a husband and wife who went on a botanical tour (and enjoyed themselves). *We* must go on such a tour one of these days and see what we can find! (9.) *Entomological News*, Jan. and Feb. I sent you the Jan. number, as I have another copy, and it contains my paper on metallic colours. The February number contains (to my amusement) a letter I wrote to the Editor about the magazine. The Editor follows with some remarks in which he calls me 'one of the most active biologists interested in our science!' There are also reports on two meetings of the Colorado Biological Association.

In the afternoon I examined Cooper's slugs and wrote him a letter about them. In the evening we had a successful meeting of Lit. & Sci. Society, which is 'looking up' at last. Evidently it was a good move to make the meetings all public and to meet every week. We commenced with music by the Misses Etzel ('Adieu, Adieu, kind friend, Adieu', and a comic piece called 'The Grecian Bend') and others. Then we had a debate in which Art Walters and I had to affirm, and Charlton and Wright deny that 'Great Britain will adopt a republican form of government within the next 25 years.' We had a lively debate, and the three judges appointed gave two votes for the affirmative and one for the negative, so the former won the day. These votes were supposed to be given on the merits of the speeches, and not on the intrinsic merits of the question.

Feb. 17th, 10 a.m. Yesterday afternoon and evening I spent at the Charlton's. The wind blew very violently again yesterday.

I forgot to tell you that Martin accosted me the other day and asked me to go down to the cliff-dwellings in the southwestern part of Colorado with him this summer. Of course I could not go, but he was very urgent about it and said

that he would provide everything, and the trip should not cost me a nickel! It appears he has a commission from some firm to go and collect the ancient pottery, etc., that is to be found there. It would be interesting to go, and Martin's offer was a liberal one, but even if I were going to be in America all summer, I don't think I should care to go on such an arrangement. I would rather pay my way and be independent entirely, or else go and work all the time for wages. At the same time, in fairness to Martin, I should say I don't believe he would try to take advantage of the situation, under the terms he proposed.

7:45 p.m. I have been very busy over my list of Land Shells of North America today, and have finished the first rough copy. I have also written to Binney and to C. H. Merriam, sending the latter a mouse Charlton caught. The mail today was: *Field and Farm*, India ink, cardboard, and a letter from Binney, and (at last) a letter from Fort Collins, as follows:

'Dear Sir. Yours of Feb. 11th is at hand. In reply I will say that the finance committee of our Board at its last meeting did not consider the proposition which you made to us, for one or two important reasons, the chief of which was that we had a violent windstorm but a few days previous which had damaged our buildings to the extent of $1,200 or $1,500, and made them feel too poor to consider any outlay other than that of again putting our buildings in order for work. When they will be able to do anything of this kind I am unable to state. I will, however, bring the matter before them soon and let them formally decide the matter. The proposition which you make in reference to Entomological work I will consider, and especially with reference to the matter of bulletin of injurious insects of 1889.'

So I judge I shall not go to Fort Collins, as it will no doubt be too late to go by the time they can recover the loss to buildings and find the money for me. The bulletin referred to was a bulletin on insects I offered to write for them.

The India ink from Binney is a stick that will last for ages. It is the best quality and is covered with Japanese inscriptions and coloured figures of men and animals. I like the *smell* of India ink! Do you?

Charlton has written his first 'contribution to Science' (if we except his paper on fossils in Reports of the C.B.A.) — a paper on the charcoal of fossil wood I found up at the Security (Geyser) Mine. I read his MS yesterday. It is interesting but rather long. He will send it to a mining paper, and I hope they will publish it. (I have a notion they may *not*, though I don't tell Charlton so.)

Feb. 18th, 9 p.m. A cold, windy day. I wrote to Ingersoll and to Binney, and made India ink drawings of the living California slugs for Binney. The mail was letters from L. Bruner (with names of Orthoptera I sent him) and Binney (asking my opinion about a slug). This evening I have been to the Charlton's. I was there to tea — a real English tea such as I have not enjoyed for a long time.

I have a new idea respecting the Colorado Biological Association. People here come to our meetings but do not care to pay the dollar membership subscriptions. So I shall try to get them to form an affiliated society, The Custer County Biological Association, with each member subscribing only ten cents a year (for the use of that association), and having the privileges of coming to our regular C.B.A. meetings, using the C.B.A. Library, and having specimens named by the C.B.A. The 'affiliated' Society will thus consist virtually of associate members of the C.B.A. and will be an associated association! Its members will not vote in C.B.A. elections, nor will they receive the publications of the C.B.A. The subscriptions of the members of the Associated Society will be used for that society and will not go to the C.B.A. What do you think of the idea?

Feb. 19th, 5:10 p.m. Your letter has come today. It snowed a little last night, and today it has been cold. All this morning I worked on slugs and made very good progress. Soon I shall be able to prepare a good paper on American slugs. This afternoon I wrote to Binney and to Mother.

7:10 p.m. To answer your letter. I am so sorry you were worried about my influenza, because there was really nothing very wrong. I am all right now.

About offering my services cheaply, many people blame me for it, but I *think* I do rightly on the whole. I don't like to seem atall grasping, and I do not wish to get more than I deserve. It is rather a matter of principle than of policy. What do you think? And if it were a matter of policy, I think modesty in such things is good. At least I get this advantage, that everybody trusts me and treats me well.

No doubt I shall have to borrow money from home to get back to England again. In such a case I don't mind borrowing, and I don't think they will mind lending it to me.

Now I won't say anything about our health in the future! 'Sufficient unto the day is the evil thereof!' And don't let's imagine any future troubles. Your party must have been nice; it's too bad I couldn't come. There's a remarkable scarcity of Bedford Park-ites among the guests, is there not?

Well, I hope miss Rosie does like her Irishman, now she has got him! I am sorry to hear of Kitty's illness. Mr. Bale does seem to have been critical about your drawings — too critical.

Somehow it reminds me of a time when I made some menu cards and tried to sell them in all the shops that deal in such things, near Oxford Circus. The shop-men were polite but not encouraging, and I sold none. One shop in Regent Street would take *Christmas* cards if I brought them a few weeks before Christmas, but when Christmas came, for some reason or other I did no cards.

Yes, Olive's photo *does* look rather more independent. So Frederic has finally taken his room. Well, we shall see! I have great faith in him and expect him to distinguish himself in course of time. The Bullock's debating society sounds interesting. I like such things. We discussed exactly the same *novel* question here once, but it was one of the meetings I have missed. They told me there was a pretty good debate. Yes, that was a satisfactory letter from Griffith and Farran.

Feb. 20th, 5:45 p.m. It is snowing. Last night, and again this morning, I worked up my notes on the flora of high altitudes in Custer County, preparatory to writing a paper for the *Bull. Torr. Bot. Club* on the subject. The mail was very late today; it seems to come later every day. I hoped the *Entom. Mags.* would come, but I seem fated never to get them until I return to England. By the way, when I do return, how I shall enjoy a day at the library of the Zoological Society, looking at all the things published in the last three years!

The mail I did get is (1.) *Psyche* for Feb. (21.) 'A reply to Dr. C. V. Riley' by Dr. Geo. H. Horn. Horn's reply is a pamphlet, carrying on a dispute with Riley, because Riley failed to give Horn the 'credit' due to him in a paper he wrote. Riley is rather inclined to 'make hay with other people's grass', I am afraid. (3.) A letter and a box of beetles for names from H. G. Smith, Jr. of Denver. Smith's beetles took me most of this afternoon. I named seven and have packed the rest off to Horn to name. I have also sent some plants for names to Coulter.

Most lovingly, your Theo.
Health. Good.

Feb. 20th, 1890, 8:25 p.m.

Love,
A letter went to you this evening, and since then there is practically nothing to add.

I was rather amused today a the sudden appearance of Pennycuick up here, who said John

Burke had a steer that seemed to be dying, and wanted me to go and kill it and do the post mortem! J. Burke lives a mile and a half from here and, in any case I don't crave after post mortems of cattle. I'm not going to turn free 'vet' to this community, though I did once examine Cox's horses and Todd's cattle that died. So I sent out word to J. B., 'Certainly, but it would cost him five dollars.' Can imagine his disgust!

Feb. 21st. Perhaps I should call it 'Feb. 22nd, for it's about midnight! Have just returned from party at the Humphrey's.

Feb. 22nd, 6:45 p.m. Must eat supper and then be off to Lit. & Sci. Society. Have had lots of adventures since I began this letter. Must tell you about them tomorrow.

Sunday, Feb. 23rd, 6:30 p.m. Three days have passed, and I have hardly written to you atall! I must go back a little, to Feb. 21st.

Feb. 21st. All the morning I was running around, getting ready for the C.B.A. meeting, to be in the afternoon. I told Mrs. Prof. Wright to come, but she was ill, and didn't. I went down to the Conway ranch and told Mrs. Conway and Miss Lowther to come, and they did. I told Miss Byington to come, but she had hardly got over her attack of influenza, and didn't. I went down and told the Charltons, Mrs. Humphrey, and Mrs. Stockton to be there, and they were. So you see we had a pretty fair meeting. It was drizzling rain a good deal of the morning — queer weather for this place in February.

The C.B.A. meeting was at two p.m. at Mrs. Stockton's. We were 'meeting' all the afternoon, and then had more to do than time to do it in. We mounted a lot of flowers for the Ladies' Literary in the first place. The Charlton exhibited and spoke on the charcoal from the Geyser Mine, and other matters. I showed the living slugs from Cooper, the beetles from H. G. Smith, and a variety of other things, and sandwiched between was a great deal of talk. In fact we all enjoyed it, I think. At the end, I expounded my ideas of having an associate society (Custer Co. Biol. Assn.) to act with us, the members paying only ten cents per annum. And the idea was favourably received, so that the society organised on the spot, with the following members: Mrs. Humphrey, Mrs. Stockton, Mrs. Conway, Miss Lowther, and Mrs. Charlton. So much for the C.B.A. meeting.

In the course of that day I had been invited by Mrs. Humphrey to a party at her house that same evening, and rather rashly said I would go. Rashly, because I had no clean collar, and nothing but overalls to wear. I did not think of the gravity of the situation until Mrs. Charlton, hearing I was going, said I really *couldn't* go in overalls, for it was to be a real swell affair. I protested that if people *would* invite me out, they must stand the consequences, and after all, the overalls were *new*, and of a beautiful blue colour! But it 'wouldn't do', and so, after some discussion, the Charlton's asked me to have supper with them, and put on the best I could, and they would fix me up in the things I lacked, and we would all go to the Humphrey's together! It seemed quite absurd, but I consented.

So at supper time I donned black coat and waistcoat, and nice clean cuffs I found I had and, going down to the Charlton's, was provided with trousers, collar, tie, and white shirt, so that you might have taken me for the Prince of Wales. They were quite pleased with the transformation scene they had effected, and assured me that for once I looked quite nice!

When I got to the party (through rain and slush — it was a dreadful night) I found we needn't have been so particular after all. Even the great Falkenberg, who was there in all his glory, wore no collar, nor did some of the others. The world and his wife were there of course — I need not enumerate the guests. It was late when we came away.

By the way, I forgot to say that when I called at the Conway's, *African Farm* was returned to me and I was agreeably surprised to hear that both Mrs. Conway and Miss Lowther had read it and liked it very much. Miss L. had even copied a good many passages out of it. I have now lent them *Sesame and Lilies*, while *African Farm* has gone to the Charltons.

Feb. 22nd. Hearing that the Geyser (Security) Mine at Silver Cliff had struck new rock, I went up in the morning to see what it was. I found they were getting out the same kind of rock, but it was full of little bits of granite, mica, chlorite, etc. Very interesting from a geological point of view, though I fear their chances of finding mineral are very slight.

Being in Silver Cliff, I thought I might do a little for the Custer Co. Biol. Assn. (shall abbreviate this C.C.B.A. in future). I went into Ellis' drug store and asked for Dr. Bruce and Dr. Ellis to join this society. Bruce wouldn't, as he could not get away even in the evenings, but Ellis said he would. Neither of these men are of very much account, but we might as well have them.

Afterwards I called at the Daltons and got Miss D. to join. Her water-colours have not yet come, and she is busy over other matters, so the lessons are for a time postponed. I also called at the house of the Silver Cliff school-teacher, but he was out. Then I returned to West Cliff. At West Cliff I called on Prof. Wright and got him to join, and we also arranged that about the middle of the week I am to address the children on the subject in school. This will I hope do good and swell the list of C.C.B.A. I do want to get the thing going so that it won't collapse when I leave.

By this time I was a little tired, and I read part of the afternoon, besides writing reports of the C.B.A. meeting for *Field and Farm* and *Entom. News*. In the evening it was the meeting of the Lit. & Sci. Society. The people came quite late but we had a good meeting, and some came who have not been at our meetings before. First we had music, readings, and recitations. Music by Mrs. Lowe, Mrs. Conway, and Sam Wright. Readings by Mrs. Charlton, Bertha Humphrey and Rob. Stockton. Recitations by Miss Lowther and Mabel Conway.

Then followed the debate: 'Affirmed, that a spirit of discontent is more beneficial than a spirit of content.' I think, in most ways, it *is* taking discontent to mean dissatisfaction with present attainments, or rather, a negation of finality. However, I was appointed to speak on the negative side, and so did my best to pick holes in the speech of Sam Wright, who preceded me. The other speakers were: Pro, Charlton; Con: Ireland (a man I have not seen before, a brother, I think, to Miss Ireland; speaks very well). The judges gave two votes to the affirmative, and one to the negative.

That *play* still seems to remain in a state of abeyance. Samse has influenza or something, and doesn't know whether he will act. I don't think I will bother any more about it but leave it to the actors to arrange matters as best they can.

Feb. 22nd (today). Am a sort of invalid with sore throat and a cold. So have been in all day except that I went out to cut wood, rather to the disgust of Jim Aldrich who, passing by, asked if I didn't think I was breaking the Sabbath.

I have written some letters and read a little, and that's about all I have done today.

Yesterday's mail was a bulletin on cranberry-fungi, from Halsted, and a letter from Hulst with the names of some moths I sent him. On Friday my mail was a postcard from Elliott, a letter and a slug from Binney, and a letter and some fungi from Miss Eastwood,.

Miss Eastwood writes: You will be surprised at the news I have for you. I have given up my plans in the school for a time, and tomorrow I go to Florida with a dear friend who is very ill. I shall have my hands full with her and her eleven-months-old baby, but I guess I am equal to it.'

I am sorry she is going away just now, because she is needed to look after the C.B.A. when I leave.

The *Wet Mountain Tribune* has been a little more moderate of late, so I ventured to give Lacy reports of our C.B.A. and Lit. & Sci. Soc'y meetings. I will send you the paper to see what you think of it.

Feb. 24th, 10 p.m. The sore throat has gone, but the cold is worse, and I am dull and stupid in consequence. I have been at home all day, reading and writing. Ward appeared at noon. He told me he had the luck to shoot a deer last week. Charlton came in the afternoon and wanted to know why he saw nothing of me yesterday, and said he was afraid I was offended at something he said in debate on Saturday!

The mail today was a big and very interesting one. Letters from Mother, Carlie (very long, mostly about art), and Binney. Binney sends me some valuable notes for my List of American Land Shells, and also a box of rare shells for me to draw for him. I shall try to commence on them tomorrow. Then there are all the magazines, come at last, and exceedingly interesting. But alas! Here is a waste of some money, for Frederic sends *Entom.* and *Entom. Mo. Mag.* for Jan. and Dec., and Carlie sends them for December, so that of the December numbers I get two copies. The February numbers do not yet appear. I am not overjoyed to see that the *Entomologist* has changed hands. Carrington retires and South becomes Editor, with Leech as Proprietor. South is a better entomologist than Carrington, but as a man I like him less.

Then comes *Pall Mall Budget* and *Nature*, all the January numbers. Carlie is very nice about the papers and says, 'I am very pleased indeed to be asked to send anything and certainly shall not stop the *Pall Mall Budget. Journal of Conchology* and *Field and Farm* also came. I have read the *Ent. Mags.* and *J. of Conch.*, but the rest stand over. *Nature* will be the most interesting. These various papers contain a few notes of mine, as follows:

Thyatira batis var. *mexicana. Entom.*, Dec.

Colorado Entomology. *Entom.*, Jan.

Limax agrestis and *Cochlicopa lubrica* at St. Thomas, Canada. *J. of Conch.*

Is the Hawk a friend or foe? *Field and Farm* (An article in defence of hawks, in answer to one advocating their destruction.)

Feb. 25th, 6:10 p.m. Cold is better. It has been very windy today. I have been very busy but did not find time to commence the Binney drawings. Until two o'clock I was writing a paper, 'Critical notes on some land and fresh water shells' for *J. of Conchology*. Afterwards I dissected the slugs Cooper sent me, and when that was done, it was time to peel the potatoes for supper.

The mail today was a letter from L. N. Johnson (about plants) and a pamphlet on extinct mammals from Shufeldt (for C.B.A. Library). I think I will post this now, though it is not a week since the last.

> Your own loving Theo.
> Health. Good, except for cold.

Feb. 26th, 5:25 p.m.

Love,

You would have laughed if you could have been in the schoolhouse this afternoon, but you would have been interested too. As I said in my last letter (posted yesterday) I was to address the children in school this week. So I went round at about three this afternoon and found them all at lessons. Soon the *very* little ones were dismissed, and about 25 or 30 were left to me.

Prof. Wright got up and said I was going to make an announcement to them (about C.B.A.) And then said he had promised me I would first answer *any* questions they chose to put to me! You can suppose I was rather flabbergasted, as it was the first time I had heard of this, but I put a good face on it and announced my willingness to answer.

First, one of them enquired whether I could answer questions about the Bible! This I declined. Then a question came about the migratory birds, which I answered in some detail. Then — how do spiders breathe? How do spiders catch their prey? How does the water-spider make its nest? Are spiders insects? All of which I answered. How do you find the centre of oscillation? The Professor himself asked, but I did not feel able to explain this in a lucid manner at the moment. Then: What is the apex of a shell? How is it what we see a half-moon and a full sun at the same time? What is an eclipse of the sun? These I answered with diagrams on the blackboard. I think these were all the questions. I was very pleased with the intelligence of the children, and the quick way they understood my explanations.

After that, I told them about the C.B.A. and begged them to study natural history, and promised to help them as much as possible. They seemed interested, and I was very well satisfied with the result of my little endeavor. I also showed them a box of insects, and explained to them all about galls and gall-flies.

After I had done speaking, I waited and watched Prof. Wright conduct school. He does it very well and evidently has the confidence and esteem of the children. He was examining them on what they had learned. Some of the answers he got were very funny. In Physiology, one said 'digestion is taking food in the mouth.' Another thought it was taking it into the stomach. When he asked where the *brain* was, there came a chorus of answers. Some thought it was at the front of the head, some said at the back, some at the side! But many of the answers were very good indeed.

It has been *most* miserable weather today, cloudy, with a constant most *piercing* wind. I could not keep warm in my room this morning,

- so after writing a letter I went down to the Chetelat's store and sat there reading *Nature*, which I found *most* interesting. My mail was a letter from Douglas (who is not badly frostbitten) and a postcard and some shells from Binney. I have not yet begun Binney's drawings.

Feb. 27th, 6 p.m. Very nice mail today. Your letter, nice letters from Mother (sending $5.00) and Olive, postcards from Carlie and J. G., Cooper, a postcard from Romanes, and a delightful letter from [Alfred Russel] Wallace! I will copy out Wallace's and Romanes' epistles.

WALLACE

Theo. D. A. Cockerell, Esq.

Dear Sir:

I am very much obliged to you for your letter containing so many valuable commendations and suggestions on my *Darwinism*. They will be very useful to me in preparing another edition. Living in the country with but few books, I have often been unable to obtain the *latest* information, but for the purpose of the argument, the facts of a few years back are often as good as those of today, which in their turn will be modified a few years hence.

You refer to there being five species of *Aquilegia* in Colorado. But have they not each their stations, two seldom growing together? During a few weeks botanising in Colorado, I saw only two species, *coerulea* and *brevistyla* [*saximontana*. Ed.], each in their own area. Though the Andrenidae are not usually gayly coloured, yet they are not *inconspicuous*. The Chrysididae are I should think coloured so brilliantly partly perhaps to simulate stinging species and partly to prevent their being taken for fruits or seeds when rolled up. They are *very* hard, and like many hard beetles are coloured as a *warning of inedibility*.

In the Rocky Mountains I think there is a *real scarcity* of Monocotyledons, especially bulbous Liliaceae and Amaryllids and Orchises. This struck me as being the case. You appear to have so much knowledge of details in so many branches of natural history, and also to have thought so much on many of the more recondite problems, that I shall be much pleased to receive any further remarks or corrections on any other portions of my book.

I am devoted to gardening, and grow all the curious and interesting plants I can get. If you have any species of *Calochortus*, *Cypripedium*, or *Fritillaria* in your neighborhood, I should be glad of a few bulbs or tubers. They travel well packed tightly in moss, and come by sample post at a very low rate.

I have moved from Godalming to this place for a rather milder climate and more sheltered position.

Believe me, yours very truly
Alfred R. Wallace

ROMANES

18 Cornwall Terrace
Regents Park, London N.W.
Feb 10./90

Your suggestion about the galls appears to be an admirable one and well worth working out. Where are you going to publish it? If not in *Nature*, may I forward your communication to me to the Editor? If you do publish in *Nature* I wish you would point out that the last letter on the subject (*Nature*, Jan., 22nd,) shows that the writer does not understand the difficulty, while what he says about Natural Selection is merely a truism, viz., that the less fitted die.

10 p.m. I wrote to Romanes this afternoon, and have been writing to Wallace all evening. Don't you think that is a *very nice* letter from Wallace? I feel very much honoured by receiving such a letter from such a man. Wallace's handwriting is not so noteworthy as I should have expected. I enclose the envelope of his letter so that you may have a specimen of it.

Apparently I have converted Romanes to my gall-theory, which is very satisfactory.

Last night it snowed and was bitterly cold. Yesterday evening I spent at the Charlton's. I discussed Socialism with Charlton, but I don't like discussing with him, as I never can keep him to the point. This morning it was fine, and I was cold and wanted a walk to warm me up, so I went to the Conways, and afterward to Prof. Wright's, to fix a meeting of C.C.B.A. at the schoolhouse on Saturday next, at three. In this afternoon I also called at the Charlton's and at Mrs. Stockton's.

It is rather late, but I think I shall answer your letter. That debate on novel-reading sounds interesting; wish I had been there! Fancy Alice being thus addicted to bishops, etc.! What in the world will she think of *me* when I return? I shall be the incarnation of all abominableness in her eyes! (For I am not bishopy, you will allow!). As for the Bishop of Lincoln, without paying much attention to the case, it seemed to me a shame to prosecute an apparently good old man on such grounds. But possibly they know what they are about.

It will drive me out of my wits, that maid at 5 Priory being called *Annie*. How can I address anyone but you as Annie? Shall have to give the maid a new name when I return. It was clever of you to identify *Rissoa parva* — the Rissoas are not easy to name. Yes, we *will* go over these Swanage specimens together. I shall enjoy that.

That remark of the clergyman about practising for singing in the next world is, I think, the most absurd thing I ever heard, even in a pulpit! One wonders how a congregation can sit and listen to such nonsense, even in church, where they are expected to take what is given them without remark or protest.

Carlie tells me Frederic *won't* be paid for the magazines he has sent me. It is very kind of Fred, but he *ought* to be paid all the same. I must tackle him about it when I return. *Thank you* for our suggestions *re* face drawing — I think they will help me a lot. I had not a very lucid notion of the principles of the thing, though I knew about the three 'divisions.' Miss Marshall taught me that when I was a very little fellow. I must study this matter somewhat. I drew a little face on Olive's letter (i.e., a letter I wrote to her) and now she says 'They are so like the little faces Papa used to draw on bits of blotting-paper.' I suppose I inherit the drawing facility from my father a good deal — but he had a better notion of it than I.

It is eleven, and I expect I had best leave off, but there is more to answer tomorrow or another day.

Feb. 28th, 8:45 p.m. To continue answering your letter. Have I been in a downright rage lately? I have been rather angry at times, but it has soon evaporated. I am a much more dangerous person when I am *not* very angry. High altitudes favour heart disease, though they can hardly be said to originate it. No, there is no church here now. The clergyman went away and died, and the town won't support a new one. There is, however, a Roman Catholic priest.

Now for news. Last night and this morning I wrote to Wallace and posted a long letter to him at noon. This afternoon I have written a long letter to Binney and also done two drawings for him. Besides this, I have done some reading and have worked on some shells.

An interesting mail came today. There were three letters from Binney! Of the last slug drawings I sent him (from the living slugs) he says: 'Your drawings are perfect. It is too late to have them engraved with the main batch of drawings already sent to New York. We must, however, squeeze them in somehow. I must 'bang a sixpence' on a supplemental plate.'

Binney also sends three proof plates, but these are some done before my 'innings' and have none of my drawings on them. He also sends (on loan) a volume in parts, unbound, of Tryon's *Manual*, which has in it descriptions and figures of most of the known slugs. I must make copious extracts from it.

The other mail is: (1.) Reprints of some interesting papers by J. C. Cooper, on Western Mollusca. (2.) A reprinted paper on 'A tumour in the Freshwater Mussel' by J. W. Williams — 'with the author's compliments!' (3.) Postcard from H. G. Smith, Jr. (4.) Letter from E. T. Cresson, one of the staff of *Entomological News*. He says: 'Your contributions to the *News* are very interesting, and we hope you will often contribute to its pages. We want popular, newsy articles, such as those you give us, rather than dry scientific matter.'

March 1ˢᵗ, 7:10 p.m. Am just off to Lit. & Sci. Society.

March 2ⁿᵈ, 9:45 p.m. Much to tell about today and yesterday, but am tired and sleepy and shall go to bed now. Have been out with the Charltons most of the day.

March 3ʳᵈ, 8:30 p.m. Your letter came today, and I meant to post *this* today but could not find time to write it up to date. For there are three days to account for, as follows:

March 1ˢᵗ. A cold, unpleasant day. I wrote some letters, etc. In the afternoon at three there was to be a meeting of C.B.A. so I went round to the schoolhouse at the proper time and lit the fire and made everything ready. Then it turned

out that Prof. Wright had forgotten to announce the meeting at school, as he was to have done, so hardly any of the children knew of it! The Professor is quite unreliable, and I must not trust to him again.

I had my misgivings this time, but had a bad cold and was busy, so I did not go round and tell the children about it myself. So we didn't have much of a meeting. Nine of us were present, viz., Mrs. Stockton, Miss Byington, two others I don't know, and myself, to complete the number. We held a sort of little informal meeting and looked at some butterflies and shells I brought, and then dispersed.

In the evening we had the Lit. & Sci. Society meeting, which was a great success, I think about the best we have had. A large number of people came including several who had never been before. The first part of the meeting, as usual, was given to music, as follows:

An essay — Miss Ireland. (Not particularly good, but we are very glad to get someone to break the ice in this line.)

'Song of Welcome' — Mrs. Lowe, Miss Anna Etzel, Miss Maggie Etzel (quite a pretty girl, this)

Song — Mrs. Conway and Miss Lowther.

Violin and organ duette — Miss Maggie Etzel, organ, and Frank Paton, violin (very well done on the whole — was encored)

Recitation —Chas. Johnston (a comic piece, well done)

After this came the debate, 'Affirmed, that the natural tendency of the human family is upward, in a moral sense.' The speakers on the affirmative side were Price Walters and myself. On the negative, Sam Wright, Ireland, and Charlton. The judges appointed (Miss Ireland, Darling, and Deterding) decided for the negative by two votes to one. A show of hands seemed to go the same way, only people wouldn't hold up their hands properly.

We had a very good debate. You can imagine about what I said. Price Walters was vehement but rather illogical and damaging to his own side. I had to speak twice to make up for the deficiency of speakers on our side. The negative took the view that humanity was naturally bad, but Christianity, etc., etc., had interposed and saved it from going its natural way. Of course, in these debates, any very careful and close reasoning is avoided as more or less useless, and striking but often illogical statements are used. It ought not to be so, I suppose, but it seems unavoidable. I am afraid I am sometimes unintelligible to the multitude because I get talking as if I were seriously defending an argument in print or before a learned audience. There is one thing about these debates; they are splendid practice.

March 2nd, Sunday. A complete change in the weather. It was warm and fine and sunny. So much so that, abandoning all else, I persuaded the Charltons to come out for the day. We made the ascent of Round Mountain, a hill perhaps 1,000 feet high a short distance northeast of Silver Cliff. It is a bare, rocky hill, but with piñons (*Pinus edulis*) and cedars (*Juniperus virginiana*) on one side. Cacti grow numerously on it, and on the extreme summit is a mound of stones. The shape of the hill is just like that of a wash-basin turned upside down. Charlton and I walked while Mrs. Charlton came on after in the buggy, and brought also Mrs. Stockton with her.

At the foot of the hill the buggy was left, and we all made the ascent together. As we were going up, we took a rest, and I turned over a stone, when to my amazement I found a shell entirely new to me, called *Pupa arizonensis*. We at once searched for more and found plenty, some of them alive. This was most interesting, as it had been quite doubtful whether *P. arizonensis* was found in Colorado. Afterwards we found three other kinds of shells, one of which may be a new species. I had no idea we should find so much on such a dry hillside. From the top of the hill is a fine view of the country round, and I got a clearer idea of the geography of the neighbourhood

than I had before. It was getting late when we returned, and I went to supper and the evening at the Charlton's.

March 3rd, today. As fine as yesterday. I wrote letters all the morning. When the mail came in, I read in your letter that I was to go out this very day, so I walked down to the Conway's, reading my letters and papers all the way. As I went, Pennycuick caught me up — he had been to town. 'Penny' has left Louis Howard's and gone to live at the Cusack's! He told me how it had come about.

They were baling hay, and Louis for some reason got in a rage with Penny and abused him. Penny resented this and Louis, in his anger (not really meaning it in soberness) told him he didn't want him any longer. Now Louis is a good fellow enough, but I know how it is. He does get in a rage over merest trifles and seems to think he can abuse people just as he likes. He never treated me so, but I know how it is. Now, had I been in Penny's place, my own self-respect would have obliged me to do just as Penny did, so I don't blame him atall. Meanwhile, Louis, through his own fault, has lost his best 'pupil', which is a serious matter to him, as the pupils pay well for being 'taught.' At the Conway's, I planned an excursion to Round Mountain next Saturday, if it is fine, with the children and anyone who will come. We shall see how this turns out.

By the way, that wood Regy brought in didn't last nearly so long as I expected. I have been burning it all day, you see, this cold weather we have had, and it wasn't a very big load in the first place. So now the last sticks of it are cut up and I am going to have a new load tomorrow.

That is about all the news, but there is the mail to tell you about. Saturday: Letters from (1.) C. H. Merriam. (2.) J. H. Thomson, of Massachusetts, wants Idaho shells. As if I kept Idaho shells! (3.) Binney, and a box of interesting shells, to be drawn. (4.) Singley, of Texas, and a box of shells. Singley says the shells of his I returned never reached him, and he fears they were lost in the post. I am greatly distressed about this, as it was a very valuable lot of shells. (5.) Horn. This Horn vs. Riley business is getting serious. Horn writes:

'He [Riley] has been systematically building a reputation on the work of others. Notably his employees, but I do not intend he shall use my bricks. Mr. Riley made a deliberate attempt ro antedate me in print but failed by accident. That Riley is not the real author of either *Platyphyllus* paper is shown by comparing them. The first is good and is the work of Otto Lugger, who left him in May,1888, and who is a good coleopterist. The second is by Theo. Pergande who is no coleopterist and who is now there. Hence the outrageous blunders which Riley did not know enough to detect. All the Coleoptera (nominally) by Riley are named by Schwarz.'

I can't imagine that a man of Horn's standing would make such assertions without reason, and it looks pretty black for Riley. I have at times fancied Riley acted rather that way, before. However, I wrote Horn that it was his clear duty to leave off asserting or insinuating unless he meant to put the thing in black and white, with full proof. And writing to Riley, I said he (Riley) ought to take the thing seriously and prepare the best possible defence. It is a case rather like the *Times* vs. Parnell — but the 'Parnell' *may* not come out so well this time. At all events, I don't see how we can take any notice of or act on mere assumptions until they are proved.

Monday (today). The mail came in on Sunday, but being away on Round Mountain, I got it this morning. Then there was the usual day's mail. Including both lots, the mail is: (1.) Letter from you. (2.) Letter from Binney, and some slugs. (3.) Letter from Collinger of Leeds. He had found a new variety of *Limax flavus* and wants to call it var. *cockerelli*! (4.) Letter from Vasey. (5.) Letter from Horn, about a beetle. (6.) Letter from Galloway. (7.) Notice from Dr. P. Sclater of

Zoöl. Soc'y that the paper on galls I sent them has arrived. Sclater's writing is peculiar; I will send you a specimen. He is a well-known bird and mammal man. (8.) *Review of Reviews*. Thank you. Shall have more to say of this when I have read it. (9.) *Field and Farm*, containing report of the last C.B.A. meeting. (10.) Proc. Staten Is. Nat. Sci. for March. (13.) *Nature*, for Feb. 6 and 13. That for Feb. 13 has a note of mine on the gall-theory.

Now, lastly, I may answer your nice letter. I rather laughed at your description of Mrs. Farnell Watson. She sounds like a character in Dickens, doesn't she? You see *Ent. Mags.* turned up all right. But I still wait on Carlie for the February numbers, which I presume I shall not get until my reminder of them has had time to reach him. *Re* Walters being younger than his younger brother, I never thought of the pre-existence theory! I am so glad you agree about not rushing things. Oh, no, don't send me any ink and pens (but thank you all the same); Binney has sent me very nice ones.

What fearful names your Isleworth-ites do have, don't they? Ludlam, Odlum, Drabble, etc! Now do you think a person with a name like Odlum could be distinguished? Clive is a puzzle. I don't feel quite easy about him myself, but I don't see how you can help his going and doing as he pleases. Frederic will be all right wherever he goes, unless his health breaks down. Yes, people like that their own preference should meet the approval of others — certainly. (This *re* quotation from *Felix Holt*.)

I quite feel as you do about the strange mystery of fossils. There are such extraordinary possibilities. Yes, keep the Morris letter *yourself*, please. The enclosed Wallace and Sclater might be turned over to the General collection, but not being signatures I presume they are of no use. I just send them for you to see the writings. The Wallace letter we will keep for ourselves, as it is a bit of a treasure. If anyone wants (i.e., you or the family) the Romanes postcard I will send it on. Only I don't want such things to go out to unknown persons (i.e., in exchange). So much for autographs.

You say you dislike Americanisms so. They are not so bad, but I don't exactly like the Americans; as a nation I *dis*like them. Yet in this immediate vicinity I cannot say the *English* are a whit better than, if as good as, the Americans.

March 4th, 4 p.m. Went out this morning and found some slugs, which I dissected. Otherwise have been examining shells and writing letters. The mail was a letter, a postcard, and some slugs from Binney, and a postcard from Dr. Skinner, now Editor of *Entom. News*.

Regy came to town with a load of wood for me, for which I paid $3.00. It is a bigger load than the last. I enclose the Romanes postcard after all, for the autograph collection. I suppose Romanes is distinguished enough for this purpose.

Your loving lover, Theo.
Health. Am very well.

Tuesday, March 4th, 1890, 9:40 p.m.

Love,

A letter to you was posted today, and there is little fresh to be said. I did a drawing for Binney late this afternoon. While supper was cooking I read part of *Review of Reviews*. I think Stead is not strictly accurate in all his facts, but he writes well and interestingly.

March 3rd, 8:30 p.m. Last night I sat up till nearly twelve copying from Tryon. Today has been warm, but rather windy. In the morning I dissected some slugs, examined some shells, drew a slug for Binney, and wrote to Binney. This took till about one o'clock. Then the mail came in, and I got (1.) Letter and some slugs from Binney, (2.) Letter from Hulst. (3.) Some fungi, notes on a fungus I sent, and 'franks' from Galloway of the Department of Agriculture. The 'franks' enable me to send letters and parcels to the Department without paying postage. This afternoon I sorted out a lot of fungi and packed

them off to the Dept. of Agriculture. I am to be paid for them. I also wrote to Mother, and to J. B. Ellis, and sent him some fungi. Then came suppertime.

I met Darling this evening, and he told me that Sam Wright had had a bad accident. He got his news third-hand, so he did not know exactly how it was, but Sam Wright had been thrown off his horse and had fallen with his face against a fence, breaking his nose all up. Mrs. Conway tied it up (the nose) as best she could, and at once Sam rode off to Cañon City to be properly doctored. Now it is 30 miles to Cañon, and he will be five or six hours getting there, and suppose he should faint or fall off his horse on the way? It was right to go to Cañon, but he ought never to have gone alone. I feel quite anxious about him. Poor Sam! It is a great misfortune to have one's nose all broken up.

Hulst, in his letter, remarks on the Riley vs. Horn matter, as follows:

'I suppose I am prejudiced, but I have had many inside views of Prof. Riley's doings, and I have no respect for him. He has not, to my knowledge, a single friend among entomologists. Prof. Riley is a peculiar man, a remarkably fine politician and wire-puller with the ability, as he is situated, to choose the best assistants, who give him just as little as they can and retain their places. Pardon all this, but it is a thing which grinds us all. No one will have anything to do with Washington if he can avoid it. I am afraid the end of the Horn vs. Riley case is not ended. I think Dr. Horn will take off his gloves next time.'

What do you think of all this?

March 6th, 10 p.m. Last night I again sat up late, copying from Tryon. This morning I wrote an article: 'What are the uses of bright colours in Hymenoptera?' for *Entomological News*. It is in part a criticism of a passage in Wallace's *Darwin-*

ism. The only mail I got was an advertisement of some scientific books for sale.

This afternoon, not feeling quite up to the mark, I gave myself a half holiday and read *Review of Reviews*. Later on, as it was fine and warm, I walked up the street, still reading. I called on Prof. Wright to tell him about an excursion to Round Mountain I propose getting up on Saturday — but more of this later on.

This evening I called on Mrs. Stockton and lent her *Darwinism*, which she wanted to read. The February *Review of Reviews* I found interesting from cover to cover. Stead's remarks on the origin of the influenza I put down as 'bosh.' The 'sketch' of Parnell is interesting. Myers, on the dreams of dead men (!) is amazing enough and hardly plausible, but suggestive and not unintelligent. Dr. Charcot on Mesmerism is equally astonishing and more plausible. Huxley on 'Progress and Poverty' seems to me nonsense. Huxley is descending to the level of a common politician. I am greatly amused to see that Misart says Wallace's *Darwinism* contains nothing contrary to Catholic theology, and that it is 'one of the most anti-Darwinian publications which have appeared for a long time.' Misart is a queer fellow.

As for Mark Twain's new book, it may be all right, but from the extracts given I am disposed to agree with the 'Speaker's' criticism: 'He is not only dull when he is offensive, but perhaps even more dull when he is didactic.' But the three little pictures marked 'Brother to dirt like that' are considerably to the point.

March 7th, 9:35 p.m. Here is the account of today. Morning: Did four drawings for Binney. Afternoon: Read mail, wrote a little, etc. I called on the Charltons, and at half past three went round to the schoolhouse and announced to the assembled school that the C.B.A. would hold an excursion to Round Mountain tomorrow morning, starting at 9 a.m. from the schoolhouse. All invited to come. Round Mountain is the Prim-

rose Hill of this neighbourhood and, as I found it so interesting last Sunday, I concluded to get up this excursion there tomorrow if it were fine.

Frank Hunter showed me some fossil shells he said 'old Harsh' (or Harsch — am not sure how name is spelled) had found 'on the range.' Desirous of more information, I called on old Harsh himself, and found he had been down to Huerfano and found a lot of interesting fossils — ammonites, *Turritella*, oysters, etc., etc. It's queer to think that this country was once under sea; these are all marine shells. I told Harsh he should exhibit them at some C.B.A. meeting. On my way back, I looked in at the Charltons and told them about Harsh's find.

The mail today is (1.) Letter from Mother. (2.) Postcard from Carlie. (3.) Letter from Binney. (4.) Letter from Conradi. I think that he has written asking for a specimen of *Colias eriphyle*! I suppose I must send one and charge him 25 cents. (5.) Adv't. of books for sale by Harwood of Colchester. (6.) *Pall Mall Budget*. (7.) *Nature*. (8.) *Ent. Mo. Mag.* for February. (9.) *Entomologist* for January, which I already had — no February number!

Binney writes: 'I think it will be much best to incorporate all the figures in my 3rd Supplement. I shall then feel as if I can leave the subject [conchology], having done the best I can for it. I am rejoiced to leave the slugs in your hands. The fact is, I am not as young as I once was, and distrust my powers of observation and comparison.'

Of Cooper, who sent me the living slugs, Binney says: 'You will find Cooper a prompt and generous correspondent, and posted peculiarly in West Coast forms. I have known him well over these thirty-five years, and his father before him.'

Of Hemphill, who found most of the slugs I draw for Binney, he writes: 'The prince of conchologists and collectors is Hemphill, a bricklayer by trade, by nature a nobleman. He will send you any slugs you want.'

After Horn vs. Riley, and other like disputes, it is refreshing to find one good man speaking well of another.

Nature (Feb. 20th) contains a short note of mine on a greenish meteor I saw, and a very flattering letter by Romanes on my gall-theory. Romanes writes (p. 369):

'The interesting suggestion which has now been made on the subject by Mr. T.D.A. Cockerell induces me to withdraw the sentences that he quotes from my previous letters. Mr. Cockerell, however, has now furnished what seems to me an extremely plausible hypothesis. Mr. Cockerell informs me in a private communication that he has been verifying this hypothesis by observations in detail, but whether or not he will be able to establish it, I think at any rate he has done good service in thus suggesting another possibility.'

So I seem to have converted him! Am rather proud of the feat!

In *Ent. Mo. Mag.*, W. G. Blatch says he found 412 species of beetles on a single small mossy bank at Knowle, Warwickshire!

March 8th, 6:45 p.m. This morning was the excursion to Round Mountain. It turned out windy, and partly for this, and partly because many children were needed to work at home, the expedition nearly fell through. Harry Stockton went 'down town', supposing it too windy. Bertha Humphrey would come if Anna Gowdy would, but *Anna* wouldn't. The Etzel girl had to scrub their floors, and so forth. But three smallish boys — two sons of Rosenstraugh the butcher, and another whose name I forgot, wanted to go, so off we started, climbed the mountain, and got back by about 1:30. They were nice little boys and walked as well as could be desired.

In Silver Cliff I bought candles, and by their light we explored a tunnel (abandoned mine) in Round Mountain, but did not find it very interesting. The real find of the day was a profusion of lovely little *garnets* embedded in the rock at the very top of the mountain. There were plenty of them, looking every bit like rubies, but they are very small, hardly bigger than a pin's head and mostly smaller than that. It was an interesting find and of course pleased the boys greatly. It shows how things may stay undiscovered right under people's noses. Charlton tells me that old Harsh once found some up there, but of the many people who have been up the mountain, including our party last Sunday, hardly any discovered the garnets, and to the general public their occurrence there was quite unknown.

When I got back, there was the mail — a letter from Leslie. One part of his letter makes me rather anxious: 'What do you think of Mother's health and Bedford Park? Don't you notice a failing in the brightness of her letters of late? And I am sure she ought to move away from B. P. very quickly. I wrote to Carlie and he is of the same opinion. I also wrote to Douglas. He also noticed it.'

What do *you* think about it? Mother is *not* well, but whether this has anything to do with living at B. P., I don't know. I don't believe B. P. is worse than any other suburb, but perhaps she ought to move into the country altogether. Not being on the spot, I don't like to insist on anything, as she and Carlie ought to know what is best to be done. It might have been good for her to have been in Colorado three years, but she would so detest the lonesome life. [According to Wilfred Blunt, in *Cockerell*, p.116-118, Alice Cockerell had become bored with life. Having lost her husband and with the children grown, her family life was over. She died in July 1900, aged 55. Ed.]

10 p. m. To continue, after meeting of Lit. & Sci. Society. After my walk to Round Mountain I felt rather too tired for serious work, so I spent the first half of the afternoon at the Charlton's and the last half at home reading *Pall Mall Budget*. This evening, though it rained part of

the time, we had a good meeting. Here is the programme:

Mrs. Conway and Darling: Duette

Bertha Humphrey: Recitation

Darling: Reading

Mrs. Lowe: Recitation ('Mrs. Candle's curtain lecture')

Miss Ella Steel (organ) and Harry Stockton (violin)

Miss Lowther (reading ('Who stuffed that white owl')

Magic lantern show: It was Willie Falkenberg's lantern. Charlton managed it. and I did the explanatory lecturing. The pictures were German and not very interesting, but we managed to make the people laugh, which was the best we could expect.

Sunday, March 9th, 9:30 p.m. Have been quite dyspeptic today and rather melancholy in consequence.

Yesterday I was talking to Lacy about the *Tribune* and telling him I wished it could be changed altogether and made a better and more representative paper. He rather favoured the idea of a reformation in these matters, and I promised to get him up a sample in manuscript to show what I wanted. So this morning I prepared, on a largish sheet of paper, a page of a new newspaper, which I called *The Scarecrow*.

The headings of the articles were as follows: 'Parable.' 'Ten Cents for a Nickel.' 'The Latest.' ' Interviews with Local Celebrities: No. 1, Mr. Lacy of the *Tribune*.' 'Pilgrims on Round Mountain.' The thing was half a joke and may be described as serio-comic. I took it and showed it to the Charltons, who were amused by it, but didn't believe I could do any good at running, or helping to run, a paper here. But I *will* if I *can*, all the same. It would be good practice for me and (I hope) a benefit to the community. At noon I showed the production to Lacy, who thought all the articles were good and readable, and asked

me to talk the matter over with him tomorrow morning. So the matter rests. I will send you the MS if I don't get it printed, and of course you shall have a copy if I *do*.

This afternoon I called at Harsh's and made drawings of all his fossils. There were ten species of shells, a coral, and a fragment of a crinoid. Curiously, a piece of the rock he gave Mrs. Charlton contains two shells not represented in the larger collections he has kept.

Later on, I spent some time at the Charlton's. Then I came home and read the last *Pall Mall Budget* (a lot in it about Stanley), and while the potatoes were cooking for supper, I wrote a short article for *Nature* on 'The nesting habits of birds.'

I send you a few of the garnets I got on Round Mountain. Charlton found *topaz* also in the rock I brought down, but the topazes were too small to be of any use.

March 10th, 5:5 p.m. The first thing this morning I got the mail which came (but was not delivered) yesterday. There was a letter from Binney, and some shells and slugs to be drawn; a *Field and Farm*; *Insect Life*, a very interesting number; and a bundle of reprints of my article in the March *Canad. Entom.* One of these reprints I posted to you. Today's regular mail brought me a longish letter from Miss Eastwood in Florida (she is delighted with the semi-tropical climate and the sea), a postcard from L. Bruner, and a postcard from Binney Have just finished two drawings for Binney, but otherwise have not done much of a tangible character today. It has turned cold, with a sprinkle of snow.

Your loving Theo.

Health: Am a little out of sorts just now, but nothing really the matter.

P.S. No arrangement yet made with Lacy about the paper.

Tuesday, March 11th, 9:15 p.m.

Love,

My last letter was posted yesterday. Afterwards, I sat up late writing. In the night there was some snow, and today it has been cold. I am still a bit dyspeptic and have not done much except three drawings for Binney. I saw Lacy about the paper, and he talks of having a 'definite proposition' to make to me 'for our mutual benefit' in a day or so. He also said that no more abuse should appear in his paper, which is a radical reformation of which we may be thankful!

The mail was not very interesting: (1.) Letter from Binney, who also returned two of my shell drawings for alteration. I am afraid my shell drawings are not as good as they should be. I cannot manage them as well as the slugs. (2.) Postcard from Bethune of the *Canad. Entom.* to say some notes I sent him will appear in April number. (3.) Reprint of a paper on beetles, from Hamilton.

March 12, 9:10 p.m. I have done shockingly little today. Nearly all this afternoon I was at a meeting of the Ladies' Literary Society at Mrs. Stockton's, helping them with their flowers. We made good progress and rather enjoyed the afternoon. Those present were Mrs. Stockton, Mrs. Humphrey, Mrs. Charlton, Miss Byington, Mrs. Aldrich (who brought some nice flowers) and Miss Katie Aldrich.

I was greatly taken aback this afternoon by being invited to dine at 'Martha's' at one tomorrow, 'to turkey!' Martha, I should explain, is an elderly coloured damsel who goes round to various houses and works — a sort of charwoman, so to say. She is very pious and highly respected and respectable. Not a *genius*, but a good soul of simple ways. I have not rarely come across her at the Charlton's and elsewhere, and have chatted with her. Now it seems she got a turkey, and thinking it too bad to eat it all herself, concluded to give a dinner-party to three of her best friends! So she invited Mrs. Humphrey, Mrs. Charlton, and myself! I ought to think myself greatly hon-

oured and of course I shall go. But isn't it funny! This is a queer world. [This episode is continued below. Ed.]

There was a delightful letter from you today, and several other epistles, viz., (1.) Letter from Robson of the *Young Naturalist*, who will publish my List of British Mollusca, but not for some months, i.e., July to December, in parts. (2.) Letter from Horn, all about Riley, and enclosing another paper he has written criticising Riley! (3.) Letter from Binney. (4.) Postcard from Singley — the lost shells have not yet turned up. (5.) Letter from Tutt. Tutt is going to edit a new entomological paper and he wants me to write for it 'a series of short notes running to about one or one and a half pages of print so that I can print one a month.' I'll see what I can do for him.

I have already answered your letter in my thoughts (one of my imaginary conversations with you) but I won't write it down tonight, as I really must be doing a little work. The last few days have slipped through my fingers, leaving no result. I must bestir myself. It is hard to get much energy up all alone. Somehow I want someone to scold me!

March 13th, 9:55 p.m. Here are two items of news, before I forget them:

(1.) Sam Wright arrived in Cañon City all right, and the doctor says his accident will not disfigure him for life, as was feared.

(2.) Freer is going to get married to a school teacher in Cañon City! I was astonished to hear it. Perhaps it will be a good thing for the children. [The fate of Mrs. Freer may have been told in some of the missing letters. Ed.]

Last night I sat up until twelve writing an article for Tutt — a Bibliography of Middlesex Insects for 1887-1889, which he very likely won't publish. As a result, I got up late this morning and failed to do a good morning's work. I am very hoarse today. I wish this cold weather would finish. I want a little warmth to set me right.

I had a queer experience this afternoon at Martha's. At one I went there and found Mrs. Humphrey and Mrs. Stockton already there, and Mrs. Charlton presently arrived. After a while, we sat down to dinner — a huge turkey and various other things — most magnificent. To my blank amazement, Martha did not join in the meal herself, but when we were seated, handed round the things as a domestic servant in England would. However, I said nothing, and she seemed to prefer it that way — I was already resolved to take things as they came, the whole thing being so astonishing to me that I felt as if in a foreign country!

After dinner, we four sat round the stove and talked, and Martha joined us after having her own dinner in the kitchen and washing up the dishes. So we sat round talking all the afternoon and enjoyed ourselves pretty well. Martha said little, but looked on and listened. In these days, when everyone is elbowing everyone else to one side in the rush to the front, doesn't it seem strange to find a modest hostess who takes pleasure in providing the means of entertainment for four people, and retiring into the background herself? I am gasping at the thought of it yet. Martha is an interesting character. At her age she is *now* learning to read and write. She never learned while she was young, for she was a slave.

My mail today was a letter from Vasey, with the names of some plants I sent him, and a letter from Riley. Riley says, about the Riley vs. Horn matter:

'You are not the first who has expressed surprise at Dr. Horn's privately printed reply. I shall probably answer it in due time, though a number of my friends urge that it is beneath retort. But I agree with you. Dr. Horn's method of attack only shows how keenly he feels that he is in the wrong, and how small and narrow a specialist, however eminent, may become and is in danger of becoming.'

Now I will answer your letter. About Heatherly's, I don't really understand it properly, so as to know whether it would help you to go. But on the face of it I should say no. But you know best. I am sorry Olive could not paint you, but I don't wonder! You are not the sort of person to be painted. I could not even *describe* you — your individuality is too subtle to be rendered on paper or canvas. There is too much expression.

I am sorry about your Uncle Harry. When I saw the black-edged paper, I thought of the grandmother. I am glad if Fred will be near Emery Walker. Walker is a most excellent man, so genuinely and entirely true. No humbug about him. The end of your letter, about our meeting again, is very nice. Thank you, dear Annie. I think several times every day now of when we should meet. It is getting nearer every minute.

What will you think of *me*, I wonder? I am a fearful-looking specimen of humanity. In appearance, I have degraded, especially as most of my top teeth have come out. In knowledge, well, I seem to *know* less every day! When you present me to your friends and say, 'This is my lover' they will think, 'Well, if I couldn't get a better one than *that*, I'd have none at all!' So you see you will have every reason to be disappointed with *me* when I return. But as for *you*, I shall never be disappointed with *you*. Everyone allows you are a very superior person, and even if you weren't, I *love* you, which is a dispensation of nature or providence over which neither you nor I have any control. *Quod erat demonstrandum.* Had the matter been under my control, I should never have had the *impudence* to fall in love with you!

You enclose a newspaper cutting about gambling — advising the women to permit small gambling in their homes! I should advise them to do nothing of the kind. I would rather a man got drunk than gambled in my house. My experience in Colorado has led me to regard all cards much as a pious lady regards a whiskey bottle. I have a horror at the sight of a card. Does this seem queer to you?

March 14th, 7:50 p.m. I must be off to the 'social' at Mrs. Becker's, but just a line first. It has turned warm again, and already I feel the benefit of it. I dissected some interesting slugs today and made three drawings for Binney.

Three pieces of news are agitating the town today: (1.) A *new doctor* has arrived, named Williams. He will stay. (2.) We are shortly to have a parson (Presbyterian), so church will start up again. (3.) The Geyser Mine at Silver Cliff has 'shut down', as the company won't put up any more money looking for mineral that isn't there.

March 13th, 7:10 p.m. Lacy was very anxious I should write something for his paper today, but I had no time, so I gave him an article of mine in *A1* to reprint.

Sunday, March 16th, 1 p.m. Just off to Louis Howard's.

8:35 p.m. Have just walked from Howard's. It is a most lovely night, cloudless and starry, and the air is almost intoxicating. If you were here, I should ask you to take a walk with me and look at the stars. Would you come? When I return, perhaps, we will go for walks together in the evenings. Shall we be allowed to do so? But I must go back to Friday, to tell the news:

Friday, March 14th. Some of the news I already told you. The mail I got was quite interesting: (1.) Letter from Mother. (21.) Long and interesting letter from Tutt. (3.) Letter from Binney. (4. Letter from Singley. (5.) Letter from Wickham. (6.) Postcard from J. B. Ellis, with names of some fungi I sent. (7.) *Nature*, containing my article on Wallace's *Darwinism*, which takes a whole page, and also a criticism on my gall theory by one Wetterham, which I have since answered, and also in the 'Diary of Societies' an announcement of a paper on galls by me, to be read before the Zoological Society. (8.) *Pall Mall Budget*.

What do you think of this extract from Mother's letter? 'He (John Blow) came over to tell me that John Blow's engagement had been broken off, which I was wicked enough to be glad of, as were all the Blow family, John included. But as they are going in the same boat to the Cape and to the same spot when there, I don't think there is much chance of escape for John. He got engaged there about two years ago, when feeling dull. We shall see the sequel.' !!!! What lunatics some people are!

I told Tutt he could write me down as a subscriber to his new book on moths if he wished, but I didn't know when I could find money to pay him, so now he writes: 'I shall certainly put your name down. Bother the blessed money. Why isn't everyone supplied on Socialist lines with enough, without worrying, provided he is willing to do the best he can for the community? Do you know, if I wasn't a lepidopterist I believe I should become a Socialist lunatic!'

Talking of money, I now have but ten cents left, and owe for a few things. But I am not concerned, as sufficient money is owing me from Galloway, Binney, and the Lit. & Sci. Society.

In the evening (Friday) was the 'social' at Mrs. Becker's. It was pretty much as these things usually are, so there is not much to say about it. But we had rather a novelty in one way. Cards were provided for men and ladies, and we had to put one another down for *conversation* (as for a dance). Each conversation lasted five minutes, when a bell rang, and one had to pass on to the next. Here is a list of those I conversed with: Mrs. Lowe, Miss Bertha Humphrey, Miss Florence Aldrich, Miss Lowther, Miss Byington, Miss Kate Aldrich, Miss May Cassidy.

They were not very interesting to talk to, but we got sufficient amusement out of it. I interviewed them all on the subject of *ghosts* (having the Saturday night debate in view). Only one, Florence Aldrich, believed in ghosts, and she was able to defend her position in a much more sensible way than I should have expected.

Saturday, March 15th. In the morning there was supposed to have been an excursion like last Saturday's one to Round Mountain. It was beautifully fine but I hardly raised the thing abroad, so nobody came. The Charltons started off to the Huerfano and I went down and saw them off. They went with Harsh in his big waggon and will come out for a day or two and then return. They are having lovely weather and must be enjoying it.

Strictly, they are gone on 'business', Charlton having to work on a marble claim he has down there. He has to do so much work on it every year or the property would fall into other hands. I am afraid he rather looks for 'unearned increment' in the matter, hoping not to use the marble himself but to sell the claim to someone who needs it. In the meanwhile, they will examine the fossil beds down there and bring back lots of fossils, which will of course be very interesting.

The Charltons having started, it was so fine that I did not care to stay indoors, but took *Pall Mall Budget* and *Nature* and read them out of doors, sitting in the sun. The mail I got was: (1.) Letter from Binney. (2.) Note from S. Carson & Co. about *West American Scientist*. I am afraid it has practically suspended publication. (3.) Postcard from Thomson, a shell man. (4.) Postcard from Hemphill. (5.) Postcard from Dr. Cooper. (6.) *Weekly Globe Democrat*, a sample copy.

I wrote a little in the afternoon and spent some time preparing for the meeting of the Literary and Scientific Society. The meeting came off successfully in the evening. The music part of the programme was rather uninteresting, not worth enumerating. The debate was more amusing. It was: Affirmed, that 'the belief in ghosts is contrary to all reason.' Ireland and Sam Wright spoke for the affirmative, and Price Walters and myself for the negative (i.e., in favour of ghosts). Ireland made a very amusing speech, and Price Walters spoke well.

I don't know just how far *my* belief in ghosts may be said to go! But we are put on one or the other side of these debates in an entirely arbitrary manner by the committee, so I had to say all I could think of in favour of the ghostly ones. But my main point was the production of a *real* (?) ghost, visible to the whole company. I got the apparatus all ready in the afternoon, and by arrangement of glass, etc., reflected the face of Harry Stockton in a perfectly ghostly manner. Harry was hidden behind a blackboard so that the audience could not see him, (*vide* diagrams) and the ghost was what was known as 'Pepper's Ghost.' By an arrangement of cloths and a shawl the box was covered and the glass in it rendered invisible, so that with a proper arrangement of the lights a very ghostly effect was produced. I announced that I would show the audience the ghost of Rameses II, and having turned down the lights to let Harry get into position, turned up two lights on the stage, uncovered the box, and there was my ghost! Of course we did not take it seriously, and one or two even recognised Harry Stockton's face, but it was a good joke all the same. Later in the evening I explained the whole thing and the theory of it. The judges gave two votes to one for the affirmative, but a show of hands was overwhelmingly in favour of the ghosts.

The ghostly arrangement

The Geyser Mine did not 'shut down', after all, as I stated above. But I expect it will soon.

Sunday, March 16th, (today). Most of the morning I was preparing an article on galls for *Nature*, in answer to Wetterham's criticism. I also wrote to Horn, Vasey, and J. B. Ellis. This afternoon I had meant to stay at home and write letters, but it was so fine that I walked out to Louis Howard's, calling on my way at the Conway ranch. I had promised Louis some time and help him with his accounts again, and this seemed a suitable time. So I was there all the afternoon, and to supper. I settled up the accounts in proper fashion, and also named some flowers (or rather, drawings of flowers) for Mrs. Howard. When I came away, Louis and his wife, lured by the fine night, walked along the road with me for a bit. Louis is a queer sort of fellow, not a bad fellow atall but almost entirely through his own fault, falling out with nearly everyone. Now he tells me he had quarreled with Regy, and especially with Mrs. Regy!

Louis read me a long and very interesting letter from his brother, a doctor, who has just gone to Johannesburg in South Africa. You must have read of this place and its 'boom' in the papers. Now Howard's brother reports that the boom was a regular humbug and that the thousands who have flocked there are in most miserable condition, and the town is at the mercy of the worst kind of blackguards! It is just what one might expect, but from the description, Johannesburg does seem to be the 'hardest' town mortal man ever struck! It is awful!

Louis had a letter from Lees about my going up to the 'Micawber' [a mine. Ed.] to look after the place, as I wrote you about before. Lees said he would be glad of it if I could go. It would be an advantage to me from the dollars and cents point of view, and good for the fresh air, but there is so much that I *must* get done before I start for England, that as Louis did not seem very anxious about it, I decided to stay in town. I am very unwilling to give this thing up, but it seems a physical impossibility to carry on my other work in the limited time I have unless I remain in town.

March 17th, 6:30 p.m. I have only got some letters written today (four, and a postcard), as the morning was taken up by an entirely novel occupation for me. I was in the store below, and

someone had left the door open. I ran rather precipitately to shut it, and the Chetelat's dog, 'Carlo' got excited thereat and jumped upon me, causing me to lose my balance and fall into one of the great glass panes in the door! The Chetelat's were very kind about it and said they would pay for the glass if I would put it in. So I turned glazier, and cleaning out the old glass and putty, and putting the new one in, took me about all the morning.

Otherwise, nothing much has happened. Ward called on me about noon. Lacy's paper is out, and I send you a copy, containing a leading article, an account of the Round Mountain excursion, and a few odd notes copied out of my 'Scarecrow', with a few alterations in minor points by Lacy.

The mail today was (1.) *Field and Farm*. (2.) *Nautilus* of February with a paper of mine on slugs; I send you a copy. (3.) Letter from Galloway of the Dept. of Agriculture. They are going to send me $12.00 for the fungi I sent them, which is quite satisfactory. (4.) Letter and postcard from Binney, and also his photo. I sent him one of mine, a Stereoscopic Co. one, the only one I had, and he sends his in return. He has a nice face, not unlike General Gordon.

Lovingly, your own Theo

Health. very good, thanks to the grand weather.

March 25th, 1890, 6:35 p.m.

Love,

A letter went to you yesterday. Nothing particular happened after it was posted. In the evening I sat up copying from 'Tryon.' This morning, after having written two letters (one to Leslie) I walked down to the Conway ranch to get some money from Miss Lowther (Treasurer of Lit. & Sci. Soc.) which the Lit. & Sci. Soc. owed me for my services as janitor. $4.00 was my bill, but as there was only $2.00 in the treasury, I had to be content with that for the time being.

This money enabled me to pay a few little bills I had run up for groceries and stationery at Chetelat's ($1.25), Etzel's (60 cents), and Kettle & Walters (40 cents). I found Miss Lowther alone on the ranch, Mrs. Conway and Sam Wright having gone with Conway to Cañon City. I took her *A Dream of John Ball* to read. After I got back to town I called at the Charlton's, leaving a *Nature* for Charlton to read.

The mail came in due course. I got: (1.) Letter from Cresson about *Ent. Amer.* (2.) Two letters from Binney. (3.) Postcard from Horn. (4.) Postcard from Dr. Cooper. (5.) Advertisement of 'compressed cork.' (6.) Report on trip to Australia, by A. Koebele, published by Dept. of Agriculture.

Binney returned two drawings for slight corrections. Evidently he is not so pleased with the shell drawings as with those of the slugs, and that is not unreasonable, since I cannot do shells so well as slugs. In drawing shells I especially seem to feel the want of a properly *trained* hand, if you understand what I mean.

Koebele's Australian report is *exceedingly interesting*. There is a creature called *Icerya*, allied to the cochineal insect, which years ago was imported from Australia to California (of course by accident). It increased wonderfully and did enormous damage to the orange and other trees. Now Koebele was sent to Australia to find out what enemies (e.g., parasites, etc.) it had there, and to import those enemies to California. He found several, and among them a little ladybird (*Vedalia*), which he brought to California, and now it is decimating the *Icerya*, so that it is expected that in a few years California will be practically rid of that pest! Is not this wonderful?

March 26th, 8:20 p.m. Last night, after writing the above, I took some notes from Tryon and then did a little 'wash.' Today I am indifferently well, and it is *not* a nice day. Dry and windy, and the atmosphere full of smoke and dust, blown from some distant unknown spot. Except that I called on the Charltons, I have been writing all day, though this afternoon I did a little drawing, correcting some of the Binney drawings.

My mail today was: (1.) Postcard and some shells from Binney, (2.) Letter from one Truman in Dakota wanting insects. (3.) Letter from Singley. (4.) Letter from Packard, thanking me for a caterpillar I sent him. (5.) Letter from Pilsbry and also some MSS of his on shells for me to examine and comment upon, and a published paper of his on 'New and Little-known American Mollusks.'

Here are some rather amusing extracts from Pilsbry's letter:

'I have been afraid to tell you of a dire calamity that befell me some time ago, but I will now make a clean breast of it. I swallowed the specimen of *P. coloradensis* you sent me!! I was trying to get the dirt out of its aperture by washing it in my mouth — an old dodge — and it disappeared. I am perfectly aware that men have been shot for far less serious offenses out in that wild western country; but still I try to hope that you will fix the extreme penalty at sending me another of the shells.' [But I have only two left, so he *can't* have one. It is a new species and I can't risk losing the types.]

'I want to tell you that I appreciate the work you are doing on Western slugs. We need just such conscientious work!!'

March 27th, 10:35 p.m. Have been out on the hand-car again today, and this evening at the Charlton's. Am too tired to write sense or even nonsense now. Got your nice letter today.

March 28th, 9:35 p.m. First I must tell you about yesterday.

I had promised to take Martha, the Charltons, etc., out on the hand-car if it were fine. It turned out fine enough, though rather cold and windy, so after breakfast I went down to the 'round house' and got the car. I could not find the parties responsible for it, and so had to steal it, but nobody would be likely to object to that. Having got my car, I went to hunt up the people.

The Charltons would come, and also Martha. Mrs. Stockton was afraid of the wind. Mrs. Humphrey could not come because Bertha H. was not well and she couldn't leave her. Mrs. Chetelat could not leave the store. So we had a small party, viz., Charlton, Mrs. C., Martha, and myself. After a bit we started off, and went down to Dora. Half way there, Charlton declined to go on, saying there was too much work about pulling the car, but I protested vehemently, and he came. I was wroth at this backing out before we got there, because (1.) I had gone myself simply for the sake of the others. (2.) I detest giving up a thing like this when once undertaken.

So we got down there, and crossing Grape Creek on some convenient rocks in the stream, had lunch among the rocks (granite) and pine trees. Afterwards we wandered about, and I added a good deal to my list of Dora fauna and flora. We also found some *epidote*, a pretty green mineral. There is not much to say about the return journey. I had a rope and pulled, while Charlton pushed behind. The work was continuous but not hard. It was a great advantage to have a rope.

I got a very good mail on my return. After I read it I went down to the Charlton's, being invited there to supper, and I was there all evening, being too tired to do any work if I had been at home. It was a moonlight night, and at about nine we heard a waggon outside, and were astonished to find it was Sam Wright come with a load of hay (about 13 cwt.) for Charlton! There was nothing to be done but put it in the barn, which was not very easy in the night. However, Sam, Charlton, and I worked at it, and after a bit got it safely stored away. You will wonder that I

could pitch hay when I have just said I was too tired to work, but I can do manual work long after I am useless for brain-labour.

Today I have been writing letters and an article for *Nature* (which *may* be nonsense) on the 'Inheritance of Acquired Characters.' Today's mail was: (1.) *Review of Reviews* for March, thanks to you. (2.) *Journal of Mycology* for December.

I wrote today to Mother about money to get home with. I also wrote to Leslie for information about the Montreal route. I believe that way is as good as any, and it would allow me to see Leslie at Toronto on my way, a chance I may never get again.

Yesterday's mail was: (1.) Your letter. (2.) *Standard*. Thanks. Gladstone has got the better of Tyndall this time! Serves Tyndall right for interfering in politics. (3.) Letter from Jenner Weir. (4.) Letter from Leslie, enclosing a letter of Una's to Mother — most excellently written. Una is rapidly developing. (5.) Letter from W. J. Coulter of Texas, who says he is sending some slugs. The slugs have not yet come. (6.) Postcard from W. H. Edwards. (7.) *Pall Mall Budget*. (8.) *Nature*.

Jenner Weir is very complimentary about my Galls theory. This is what he says:

'My dear Cockerell:
    Your paper on galls which has appeared in the *Entomologist* has delighted me beyond all powers of expression. It is excellent, well argued, one of the best contributions to the Theory of Natural Selection that has been written since my revered friend Darwin's decease. It shows how easy it is for anyone to bring forward a carping objection to the great theory, and how there are disciples of the great 19th Century philosopher who can overcome such criticism. It was a difficult problem to solve, and you have solved it, in my opinion quite conclusively.'

I meant to answer your letter tonight but I don't think I will, as my brain is not very clear.

I have been reading a good deal of *Review of Reviews* and find it interesting as ever.

March 29th, 10:30 p.m. Now I will answer your letter. Yes, I hope you will take Frederic's bedroom. I have always said that yours was entirely too small.

We might seem to have a good deal of 'fun' here, but so far as I am concerned, only my mail really relieves the monotony. There are lots of nice people here, no doubt, but not one that I really care *much* about or can talk to with unalloyed pleasure.

I wonder why you thought your letter rec'd. Feb. 19th, did not please me! What a ridiculous idea! A nickel is five cents; it is a nickel coin rather bigger than a sixpence. I shall get out a C.B.A. report some time next month. You are a corresponding member (subscr., 25 cents). Members resident in Colorado pay a dollar.

I don't much expect the Cliff-ites will do much in the Natural History way after I am gone, but they may. There's no harm in trying to get them to.

About 'atavic' vs. 'atavistic', it sounds as if *atavic* would be right, but I have an idea that *atavistic* is the word to use. But we say Socialism, Socialistic, not Socialic!

I don't think Horn is really greedy of credit. For instance, I found a new beetle, but Horn is going to all the work on it, and yet by his special request *I* am to describe it (and incorporate Horn's work) as soon as its affinities are settled.

I have a lot to say about the *Review of Reviews*, but will postpone that, especially as I have not yet finished reading it.

Sunday, March 30th, 6:35 p.m. I must be off to look after the fire, etc., for the church. I have been out of sorts and lazy today, and done hardly anything.

March 31st, 5:30 p.m. Dear Me! There are three days gone and nothing written about them. Well, on Saturday nothing particular happened. I was not feeling quite up to the mark but had to spend a good deal of time over getting up and getting ready meetings of C.B.A. and Lit. & Sci. Society.

My mail was a long letter from Miss Eastwood, in which she says she will take the office of Secretary of C.B.A. if elected (I asked if I might nominate her). She says it is cold in Florida now, and very unpleasant as to weather.

I also got the April *Entom. News*, with a note of mine in it on *Erebia epipsoidea* (a butterfly) and a report of two C.B.A. meetings.

At four o'clock we had a C.B.A. meeting in the schoolhouse. Those present were Charlton and Mrs. C., Mrs. Stockton and Rob. Stockton, Mrs. Humphrey, and T.D.A.C. Charlton exhibited his Huerfano fossils and I brought a lot of miscellaneous objects, so we had quite enough to occupy the time.

In the evening we had the Lit. & Sci. Soc'y meeting, as usual. Here is the programme:

Music: Miss Lottie Byington

Reading: 'The Inventor's Wife' (a poor piece), Mrs. Charlton

Reading: Miss Jessie Lowther

Recitation: Chas. Johnson

Reading: Samse (too long a piece)

Organ and violin duette: Maggie Etzel and F. Paton (was encored, but violin string broke and couldn't play again)

The debate was: 'Affirmed, that Wet Mountain Valley is better without the Grape Creek Railroad branch.' Charlton, Sam Wright, and Ireland took the affirmative, and Beaumont (a ranchman) and I were appointed to speak on the negative. Price Walters was intending to speak, but through an unfortunate mistake the chairman (Sam Wright) did not call him. Ireland made a very clever and amusing speech. I spoke badly, or at least not well. The judges gave for the affirmative, and no doubt they were right, ruling according to the merits of the debate. The debate next week (or at the end of the present week) will be on 'Government Interference with Sunday Labour.'

So much for Saturday. Yesterday (Sunday) I was not atall up to the mark. I wrote a short paper on fungi for *Journal of Mycology* but otherwise did little but read. About noon I called on the Charltons and borrowed some geological pamphlets Charlton had. In the evening I had to light up, etc., etc., for the church. At the second bell, being a little late, I pulled the rope so vigorously that the bell turned right over, and it won't ring anymore until it is righted! I climbed up to the bell, but was unable to turn it back, so I left it. I believe those who understand it can get it back easily by moving the rope.

Church last night was a distinct improvement on the first. The sermon, if not very original, was almost entirely sensible, and a good deal needed. It was about being discouraged. One sentence deserves to be written in big letters: 'NO MAN OUGHT TO BE DISCOURAGED UNLESS HE HAS DYSPEPSIA!' He might have added, 'or La Grippe!'

Today (Monday) it has been snowing all day. I have only been out for water and wood. (I cut a lot of wood.) I have written Sunday letters and got a biggish mail, as follows: (1.) *Field and Farm*. (2.) *Psyche*, for March and April. (3.) Two old numbers of *Psyche* sent by Gillette, containing articles by him. (4.) Postcard from Gillette. This is an Iowa entomologist. I offered him some galls for 50 cents and he accepts the offer. (5.) Postcard from Skinner, now editor of *Ent. News*, apologising for misprints in my articles in that paper. (6.) Postcard from R.E.C. Stearns saying he will send me some slugs. (7.) Letter from Teator, a shell man. I sent him two shells inside a cork in an envelope, and on the way some postal official stole them. I am wroth. (8.) Letter from Nash. (9.) Letter from Galloway with notes on fungi. (10.) Letter from President of Colorado Agric. College, saying that committee will consider my offer to supply MSS for a bulletin on injurious insects. (11.) Letter from Conradi, the man who plagued me for butterflies. He sends $1.15, and I sent him in return six butterflies, such as he requires.

I meant to write a lot about *Review of Reviews*, but this must go now. But I will send another letter before the end of the week. Tomorrow is April 1st, — May — June!! It isn't such a very long while!

With a kiss, lovingly, your Theo.

Health. All right, but a bit dyspeptic.

April 5th, 1890, 6:30 p.m.

Love,

Summer is coming; the evenings are getting quite light. I now write by daylight. This morning I made extracts from a *Catalogue of North American Fishes*, to ascertain what variation there was among them, and afterwards I wrote to Scudder. Regy, Pennycuick and MacDougall were in town at noon. The only mail I got was a letter from Orcutt, who says, the *West American Scientist* is not dead after all, but will shortly reappear. In my last letter I said *Nature* was a fortnight late. I expected it today, but no English mail came. This afternoon I wrote letters. I must be off now to get things ready for Lit. & Sci. Society.

11 p.m. It is late, but before I go to bed I will relate the proceedings at the Lit. & Sci. Society. In the first place, we nominated officers for the next six months, as follows: Pres., Sam Wright. Vice Pres., Mrs. Becker and Mrs. Conway. Sec'y, T.D.A.C. (But I shall not be here six months!). Treas. Miss Lowther. The programme was:

Duette: Mrs. Conway and Miss Lowther

Reading: Miss Byington

Song: The Etzel girls

Reading: (On aluminism) Rob. Stockton (rather well read)

Organ and violin duette: Maggie Etzel and Harry Stockton (I never heard Harry play the violin so well)

Song: Darling (He sang well)

The debate was: 'Resolved, that Government should prohibit Sunday labour.' Affirmative: C. Ireland, Charlton, and S. Wright. Negative: Mackenzie (a little man from the Hardscrabble), Price Walters, T.D.A.C.

The judges decided by two to one for the affirmative, and a show of hands gave 20 for the affirmative against seven negative, but many did not vote. I was not much use to my side, as I gave just my opinion this time, reserving nothing. My opinion is that Government should leave every man free to work or not on Sunday, and should compel factories to shut down on Sunday where possible, so that freedom should not be tampered with. As most Sunday labour is really by compulsion, my view of the case was *practically* that government should prohibit Sunday labour, though *theoretically* otherwise.

Thus, had it been possible to move an amendment, I would have moved that 'Government should only prohibit compulsory Sunday labour', using the word *compulsion* in its widest sense. What is your idea on the subject?

Sunday, April 6th, 4:10 p.m. This morning, after breakfast, I went down to Charlton's to talk over various matters with C. We discussed the immortality of man (which is the subject for the next debate at the Lit. Society), the wages, etc., of coal miners, the habits of wasps, and other equally dissimilar matters. After a while, Mrs. Humphrey and Mrs. Stockton turned up. They had actually been enterprising enough to go out for a walk by the creek, and had found

some galls. They had called for me when passing through town, but if course I was not there.

Charlton told me about a patent he is just getting out, to cheapen a process for the concentration of ores. It is simple and ingenious, and the method works excellently. He hopes to make one or two thousand dollars over it. I hope he will succeed with it, as I think he deserves to. Don't tell anyone about this, as it was told to me in strict confidence, and I am the only one he has told. Of course, after the patent is fully secured, there will be no more secrecy. Charlton explained the thing fully to me, but I won't bother you with the details.

— p.m. (Watch stopped!) Have just come back from church. The sermon was well-delivered but (as I thought) highly illogical. Even Charlton, who is generally pretty orthodox, said he couldn't 'swallow it.' The sermon was on the resurrection, and the preacher tried to 'prove' from the Bible that we should arise in bodies like our present ones except that they would be immortal. Christ was supposed to have risen with such a body after his crucifixion. He gave us some science, part of which was inaccurate, and also quoted Ruskin about some mud from the road transforming into a sapphire, an opal, a diamond, and snow. Altogether the sermon was interesting, though apparently for the most part nonsense. It was very apropos to our next debate at the Lit. & Sci. Society.

My watch has suddenly declined to go! This will be a great inconvenience to me.

April 7th, evening. Regy, Mrs. Regy, and Pennycuick came to town this morning, and as they were going up to Silver Cliff, I drove up with them in order to get my watch put right by the old watch-mender who lives in that town. He examined it and said the only trouble was *dirt* (and with his magnifier I could see the dirt) and he would clean it for $2.00. So I gave it him to do, as although I can ill afford the money, I can less afford to be without the correct time. After all, it has gone well for about three years, so I ought not to complain.

Being in Silver Cliff, I took the opportunity of calling on Miss Dalton. She says she has been ill but wants to have lessons again in about a fortnight. After I returned to West Cliff I cut a lot of wood, and before I went, I had written up some notes on the Cephalopoda (cuttlefishes, etc.) and so the morning was gone.

The mail was not very interesting., viz., (1.) Letter from Leslie. He talks of going on a trip to England for about a *fortnight* and wants me to go with him! Wish I *could*, but must wait until June, and could not raise the money *now* anyhow. It seems a little soon for Leslie to be taking a home trip. Douglas would be the one who should go. (2.) Letter from H. G. Smith, Jr. of Denver, sending $5.00 of C.B.A. money to pay for printing membership list, etc. Smith volunteers to be secretary himself, but as Miss Eastwood is nominated, I suppose she will be elected. I certainly prefer Miss Eastwood myself, especially as I believe Smith is young and inexperienced. (3.) Postcard from W. H. Edwards. (4.) A box of Florida shells (*Donax*) from Miss Eastwood — pretty and variable. (5.) *Field and Farm* with report of the last C.B.A. meeting.

In the afternoon I called on Charlton and also wrote to Smith, and sent some fungi to Dept. of Agriculture. Charlton talks of removing to Denver in June. It appears that the painter, Landendorfer, who I mentioned in a former letter, is mainly a painter of carriages, fences, and so forth. How far an 'artist' is doubtful.

Late in evening. Have been at the Charlton's most of the evening. Went mainly to discuss Charlton's new patent and make some suggestions. It is blowing a hurricane. I think I forgot to tell you that I am now the regular janitor of the church, for which I get 25 cents a night.

April 8th, evening. This has been a very unsatisfactory day. I meant to do some drawings, but until late in the afternoon it has been blowing so violently that I had some difficulty in writing, from the shaking of the house, and drawing was impossible So I have been at home, reading and writing notes. The only mail was *Insect Life* for March. I have seen no English mail for some time. Very likely some was delayed on the *City of Paris,* which I hear came to grief.

The *Bothnia,* alas, seems late. A boy, a brother of Mrs. Regy, is coming out to the Cusack's on her, and they are concerned because they hear nothing of him or the vessel. Ward was in town today, hoping to get news. They have to meet this youth in Cañon City, so they expect a telegram from New York to say when he will be there.

April 9th, 8:55 p.m. It has been a nice fine day. In the morning I made a drawing of a shell for Binney, and afterwards went up to Silver Cliff and got my watch, which has been set right again by the old fellow.

Shortly after I returned, the mail came in. There was some English mail, but alas, no letter from you. The mail I got was: (1.) Letter from Mother. To my astonishment, they are moving from 5. Priory to Fairfax Road. I do not know why. Mother says, 'I am getting your room ready for you' — sounds like coming home, doesn't it? In a little while I shall be back, a sort of Rip van Winkle, and it will seem like a dream that I ever went away!

(2.) Letter from Romanes asking me to let him know of anything more I publish on galls, and sending me some circulars issued by him. (3.) Letter from W. G. Smith, of Loveland, Colorado, joining C.B.A. Glad to get a new Colorado member. (4.) *Ornithologist and Oölogist* for March, sent to me to look at by Nash, as it contains part of Morrison's list of Colorado birds.

Practically all this afternoon was taken up naming flowers at the meeting of the Ladies' Literary, which met at Mrs. Stockton's. We finished the mounting of all the flowers they have. The usual ones were present, and in addition two:

Mrs. McClellan and Mrs. (forget name), whom I had not before met.

In a *Popular Science Monthly* at Mrs. Humphrey's (where I went at first, supposing the meeting to be there) I saw a very well-seasoned article on the psychology of *prejudice*. The writer pointed out that what we actually *see* is small compared with what we infer. Hence, as different people *infer* differently, their prejudices affect their judgment perhaps more than the evidence of their senses.

This evening for supper I tried a novelty in the way of dried pears, which one boils. I don't think much of them. I find, from statistics given in a Fisheries Report, that though potatoes be cheaper per pound than flour, yet flour is really the cheapest food because the percentage of water is so much greater in potatoes. Hence in using so many potatoes as I do, I am really rather extravagant.

The C.B.A. membership list has been going into print today, and this evening I saw the proof. Tomorrow it will be printed. I have already addressed envelopes to all the members, ready to send out with the list.

April 10th, 7:20 p.m. I have been indoors all day. Not a scrap of mail for me. This morning I did a drawing for Binney. This afternoon I took notes from and read the volumes of the Fish Commission (in C.B.A. Library). At last the membership list of C.B.A. is out. I enclose your copy.

> Your own lover, Theo.
> Health. Excellent.

April 11th, 1890, 7:30 p.m.

Love,
Two glorious letters from you today! Am as happy as a lark. Must not write now, as I have to be off to 'social' at the Charlton's.

April 12th, 3:40 p.m. Now I can find some time to write to you. First the news.

Yesterday. I wrote and read in the morning and wrote several short articles to be printed in the *Tribune* and reprinted for the C.B.A. I wil not relate their contents, as you will receive the articles.

In the afternoon I went up to Silver Cliff and called on White, the parson. I went partly to ask him to go to the 'social' at the Charlton's (he didn't) but principally to see his library, said to consist of about 12,000 books. These books were brought in on waggons and were not yet arranged; in fact the whole parsonage was in a state of chaos. But the little man was very civil, and showed me what he had. Unfortunately they were nearly all theological works, with some historical; not one did I see of any special interest to me. I did not attempt to argue with him but let *him* talk. I gathered that he did not think much of the Darwinian theories. The scientific department of his library consisted of Gray's *Manual of Botany*. Wood's *Homes without Hands*, and one or two others. He said he was interested in mineralogy.

As I walked down the street on my way homeward, I heard my name called, and saw old Mrs. Dalton standing at her door. She called me in and talked to me for a while about her daughter's painting. They are very anxious to send the girl to England to study.

Returning to West Cliff, I went down to Charlton's, having promised to help them to remove furniture and make various preparations for the 'social.' Mrs. Becker was also down there helping. later I came home, had supper, wrote some letters, and at about eight went to the 'social.'

4:30 p.m. [Interruption to cut wood.] The 'social' was at first *fearfully* dull. All the men sat at one end of the room and talked nonsense, and all the women sat at the other end and talked nonsense. It was a degrading spectacle! A whole room full of people and not one able to make a sensible remark or give the conversation a sensible turn. I looked on gloomily and only answered when spoken to. A little girl named Gracie Morton was asked to 'recite', and when she gave 'Little Miss Muffet' and broke down half way through, she was clapped and told she had done splendidly. I think the poor child felt the mockery of it. Afterwards they got her to 'play', and breaking down on this also, she wept because they seemed to laugh at her.

However, the thing was given a better turn when charades were suggested. The company (which was small for a 'social') divided into two portions, and each set alternately gave a charade. Mrs. Charlton had charge of one lot, and I of the other. I had Charlton, Chetelat, etc., etc., in my lot. We acted several words, e.g., 'outlandish' — 'out' being a meeting, which I addressed, and Harry Stockton was uproarious, and we turned him 'out.' 'Land', a dispute over some land, and for 'dish' we all fed out of a dish. And so forth, the other words acted being incapacity, mutineer, champagne, etc. Altogether the charades were a decided success and put everyone in a good humour. Then the refreshments, which were rather elaborate, were handed round (I did most of the handing) and some time after eleven the 'social' broke up and we all went home.

This morning at eight I went round to the Charltons to help them get things in order again, wash the dishes, etc. Martha turned up there a little later. That took most of the morning. Since then I have been reading, and writing letters to Lees, Ashmead, Binney, and Sterki.

[Another interruption, to fill the lamps at the schoolhouse and peel potatoes for supper.] Yesterday your two very nice letters came at once, and I will now answer them. I am not atall sure I like Heatherley's. I am afraid it is all too much for you. Besides, don't you think it rather a mistake to work at drawing so long? It would kill *me*. Please don't work until you are 'played out', dear. It is much better to take things slowly and comfortably. I am naturally lazy, *very*, I know, but I think there is a certain advantage to it. I am rather amused at your account of the people at Heatherley's. I can very well imagine them.

I think Mrs. Nickels must be like Mrs. Aldrich of this place. What a name, too — it's as bad as Halfpenny!

I am so glad the girl at Bedford Park is named Martha, not Annie! I won't allow more than one Annie in my vocabulary.

I am glad you like Wallace's letter. It *was* an honour, certainly. Yes, let's call on Wallace if we get the chance, by all means. I think he would be kind to us. I pronounce Romanes 'Row-manes', but I don't know how it should be. Yes, I will remember Alice declaring me to be a positivist. I am glad she will think no worse of me. No, Sclater is not so very old, though he is elderly. Romanes simply signs his name at the end of his letters. I do not mind it so myself. I am pleased that you liked the garnets. I have the others in the rock, as found. [No time to write more now.]

11:20 p.m. The meeting is over and it is now very late, so I think I will postpone the account of it until tomorrow, No, I am not sleepy. I will write about it now, on second thought. Shortly before the meeting, the *Tribune* for the week was published, containing my articles which are to be reprinted. I did not see the proofs of them, as unfortunately I was away at he schoolhouse filling the lamps when the proof was brought over, but luckily there are not many mistakes.

The meeting was a very full one, the largest audience we have ever had. All the seats were filled, and the doorway was filled with men and boys standing. First we elected officers for the next six months, namely Pres. Sam Wright, Vice Pres., Mrs. Conway and Mrs. Becker, Sec'y and Treasurer re-elected. Sam Wright made a good little speech on the past, present, and future of the society on being elected president. The programme was a good one, viz.:

Music: Mrs. Conway (good)

Song: Miss Falkenberg, Miss Ella Etzel, Miss Maggie Etzel (good)

Reading: Chas. Johnson (not very good, but not bad)

Song: Darling (good)

Organ and violin: Maggie Etzel and Frank Paton (very good, was encored)

Reading: Price Walters (nothing notable)

Reading: Chas. Skevington (atrociously done; when he began I thought he must be drunk!)

Song: Miss Anna Etzel and Darling (good)

The affirmative of the debate was 'That science does not prove the immortality of man.' Several speakers were down, but only two spoke. I spoke first, then Charlton (both at some length) and then I replied. The judges were Prof. Wright (schoolmaster), Mrs. Becker, and one Ryan, unknown to me. They gave unanimously for me, but the Charltons were afterwards very wroth, declaring that the decision was outrageous and that Wright had influenced the others. Mrs. Becker allowed that Wright had influenced her. We had a show of hands, but hardly anyone voted. Sam Wright (in the chair) said the sides were about equal, but I *think* I had the advantage.

I spoke entirely from my convictions. I believe that we are immortal, but whether we will always be *man* I know not, and it is perhaps unlikely. Can you not imagine our growing, changing, and evolving, and yet being ourselves, just as we grow and change in this life? However, I don't see that science *proves* our immortality in any way. It leads us to suppose that soul force is not annihilated, but it says, and can say, nothing about its continued existence as a human unit.

Charlton, on the other hand, regarded it as self-evident that our souls are immortal units like atoms are supposed to be, and thought that I had no argument on my side atall. Here is of course a matter of opinion. I think I am right, and he thinks he is right. At the same time, I think I know little about it, and he knows less. The debate next time is on the Credit System. I ought to explain what you may not gather from the

above, that the Charltons' discontent was only expressed privately and after the meeting.

Sunday, April 13th, 6 p.m. Have a slight headache today. Have been a good part of the day at the Charltons' talking over various matters. Since I returned have been reading *Pall Mall Budget*, and have had supper. Before long I must go and see after the church.

But to continue answering your letters. I only wrote about the garnets in green ink because it happened to be on the pen. It was very nice of you to go and see Mother, and report so quickly. May I send you a kiss for it? I had never thought of her being troubled with the associations since the Grannie's death; no doubt that is the reason for moving, and now I think of it, quite a sufficient reason. I think — have no doubt, that socially Bedford Park suits her better than any place she has ever lived in.

I hope Fred's prophecy about me may come true, but I fear it is altogether unlikely. I may not have enough vital energy, say, to convince people that I have not been a fool to devote my energies to biology, in place of something 'more useful.' There are certainly wide possibilities. Whatever success I may have I shall attribute in some measure that I have studied science rather for its own sake than for gain.

I am afraid that in the original conception of the 'Scarecrow' I rather leveled *down* to the public, but nothing much came of it. I fear there is not the remotest prospect of finding any valuable gems here. I am amused at the account of the Haite's baby.

I have not told you about the other mail I got on Friday and Saturday. Friday's mail was: (1.) Letter from Collinge of Leeds, about shells. (2.) Letter from M. Goldstandt, reducing my rent from April 1 to $1.00 a month. I had written to ask for the reduction. $2.50 to $1.00 is rather a come-down, but I had been paying too much.

(3.) Postcard from Mrs. Oldroyd of Faversham, about shells. (4.) Letter from Gillette, who is pleased with the galls I sent him. (5.) Letter from Lees. He writes in pencil, having been in bed a month, recovering from operation. Mrs. Cox is safely in England, he says, and much better in health. (6.) *Pall Mall Budget* and *Nature*. These are well to date, but two intermediate numbers of each have never reached me. Ray Lankester is severe to Romanes in *Nature*. (7.) 'On new forms of *Vertigo*', a shell paper by Sterki.

On Saturday I got: (1.) Letter from Ashmead, who says he will have the list of Colorado Hymenoptera out before I leave. He says he will be in Washington in June, and wants me to go there on my way to England, but of course I can't. On the Horn vs. Riley matter he writes:

'Dr.Riley is entirely in the wrong in his controversy with Dr. Horn., and has treated him very shabbily, and I do not wonder that he is riled over it. I know all about it and never could have believed Riley capable of such a contemptible action, It shows a meanness and smallness of mind I never expected to see in a scientific man.'

So I am afraid we must give Riley up as a bad job. Ashmead knows all about it if anyone does.

(2.) Letter from Binney, who kindly makes me a present of the blocks of three engravings taken from my drawings. They were three drawings I made of things which he found he would not have to refer to in his work, so he had them engraved and sends me the engravings so that I can have pictures when I publish on them. I enclose the proofs of the three so that you will see what they are.

Have done nothing today, so am very tired and sleepy! Church is over; have just returned. There was a very good attendance, but the service and sermon were not remarkable. Darling and Mrs. Conway sang a hymn duette, a sort of thing I don't care for in church. The sermon was an ordinary orthodox one on the text, 'Watch.' Allowing some moral good from these services, there is so much in the whole thing I cannot agree with that I hardly think I am justified in attending and acting as janitor. What do you think?

April 14th, 4:15 p.m. Here is a pleasant surprise! Another letter from you so soon. I will answer it now, and post this. I no longer feel sorry for Miss de Gaja, since she has such atrocious ideas about love! I don't doubt I could find her a husband among the batchelors of Colorado, if she would think one worth emigrating for! Seriously, one wishes there *were* more wives for the Western batchelors; it would mend their manners and their morals. But it's a hard life for a woman, even when treated well.

As to Mrs. Brodie Clark and Mr. Scull, it *may* be all right, but I must confess that if *you* struck up such a very intimate relationship with some young man, I should be *fearfully* jealous. Would *you* wish me thus intimate with some woman? It seems to me that the 'purely intellectual' sort of friendship is rather an impossibility. Those who sympathise intellectually can have a purely intellectual *objection* to a person, perhaps, but that is different. I have met many people (e.g., several here in West Cliff) with whom I have been on excellent terms of friendship (using the word in its broadest sense), yet I have been every whit as far off from an 'intellectual' sympathy as any other. But we will talk this over the month after next.

I never saw a confirmation. I *quite* agree with you about people *learning* so much to be good that they never *are* good, or only in a negative sort of way. They should think more, as they repeat the confession, 'We have left *undone* those things we *ought* to have done.'

My health is really all right; the dyspepsia and such things being only temporary. As to my appearance, I must allow that you are right. However, except the missing teeth, I am 'all there', and presumably no *uglier* than formerly. My lower teeth are all right, but except two (or one and a half) incisors, all the upper teeth are gone. The trouble is the outcome of an accident when I was a little fellow at Beckenham. I fell against a bedpost and knocked my upper teeth all out of shape. I am very sorry, but I will have a false set put in after I get back. No, it does not particularly disturb my speech. I shall need a complete set of new teeth except the lower front teeth.

It *is* annoying about the disappearance of your picture.

My objection to Heatherley's was perhaps a sort of prejudice, but if you think it good, of course I have no objection. Partly, I had a sort of feeling that you should be left to paint according to your own ideas, and not perverted or 'bossed' by others.

I am glad to see the note from Carrington. Certainly I will take anything he has to offer, provided it is moral and honest.

The other mail today is: (1.) Letter from G. K. Gude, the Secretary of the Practical Naturalist's Society (I was once on the council of that institution), wanting shells. He offers to send me books of my own choosing in return, but I can't send him any. (2.) Letter from W. S. Teator, thanking me for a few shells I sent him. (3.) *Journal of Conchology* for Jan. and April. The January number has a short note on Colorado shells by myself. (4.) *Naturalist* for April. (5.) *Field and Farm*.

It is a dull day, threatening snow. I have not been out except for wood and water. In the morning I made a drawing for Binney. I see in *Journal of Conchology* that Binney has been elected an Honorary Member of the Conchological Society.

With much love, your own
Theo.
Health. Good.

April 15th, 1890, 6:40 p.m.

Love,
Have been hardly up to the mark today and have done little. It has been a dismal day, chilly, cloudy, and with some rain. It has snowed on the range.

There was a little mail for me, as follows: (1.) Letter from Leslie: 'I am off by 2:55 train to New York, and go intermediate passage on *Umbria*, so by the time this reaches you, you will probably have seen him in England. I wish I didn't have to wait until June! (2.) Letter from W. G. Smith of Loveland, Colo., enclosing a dollar subscription to C.B.A. (3.) Postcard from Dr, Cooper about slugs. (4.) Postcard from W. H. Edwards, asking whether I can get him certain caterpillars he wants. (5.) Letter from J. E. Bean, who lives up in Alberta, saying he will send me some shells.

I paid a month's rent today. In the morning I cut a lot of wood, before it rained, fortunately, so that I have it dry. This evening I called at the Charltons' to leave a *Pall Mall Budget* and *Naturalist* for them to read.

April 16th, 10:10 p.m. Last night it snowed heavily, and although today has been very warm, much snow remains unmelted on the ground, and it is very wet underfoot. This morning I partially cleaned out my room, using snow to take up the dust on the floor. Otherwise I have spent most of the day taking notes from the Bulletin of the U. S. Fish Commission.

This evening I got the reprints of my notes in the *Tribune*. the heading is wrong and the general 'get-up' is poor, but I trust they will be acceptable to members of the C.B.A, I send you one. What do you think of it? The mail today was: (1.) Letter from Nash. (2.) Letter from Binney. He says 'I am sorry you do not sail from New York, whence you could easily visit me. It would give Mrs. Binney and myself much pleasure.' Very likely I may sail from New York after all (supposing Leslie is not back in time for me to see him in Toronto), but really, I *cannot* stop anywhere unless from sheer necessity! (3.) Annual Report for 1889 of the Fort Collins Agric. College. (4.) *Canadian Entomologist* for April, with notes by me and reprints of same. I send you one.

April 17th, 6 p.m. Not a scrap of mail for me today. Have been busy all day but done little. This morning I spent a good deal of time getting the C.B.A. leaflets ready to mail, and afterwards wrote two letters, but was interrupted by Chetelat, who brought me several sheets full of figures which he asked me to add up. I assented, but after I got to work found I was quite out of practice in that line, and it took me a long time to finish the job. I don't know whether he proposes to pay me, but I believe it is connected with his work as County sheriff, for which *he* gets paid.

After the mail had come in I went down to Charlton's to discuss the Literary Society, etc. Soon after I got there they sat down to dinner (it was 2:30 p.m.!) But I did not partake. having already had my lunch of biscuits. Miss Anna Etzel was there, the eldest of the Etzel girls. After dinner she and I washed up the dishes. Soon after I got back to town I heard the fresh news that her father had died at Cañon City Everyone is sorry for the poor girls (three of them) for their loss. They are certainly the best girls in West Cliff, though I believe the father was not esteemed so highly.

This afternoon I have written some letters and also a little essay on Socialism for the *Tribune*. Lacy says he does not know whether he can reprint any more leaflets, as John Lacy (his son) who did the work, is going (or has gone) away today.

April 18th, 12 midnight. This morning, except that I cut some wood, I spent in making notes from the books of the Fisheries Commission. Later than usual the mail came, viz.: (1.) Letter from Mother, enclosing also $5.00. (2.) *Nautilus* for March, five copies, with my article

on the slug *Phenacarion*. I posted you a copy. (3.) *Pall Mall Budget*; as yet I have hardly looked at this. (4.) *Science Gossip*. This and *P.M.B.* were together; the wrapper (an ordinary postal wrapper) was hanging on by its eyebrows. It is quite too weak for such heavy papers. No doubt this accounts for the loss of the *Natures*. It is tiresome! (5.) *Entom.* and *Entom. Mo. Mag.* for April. The former has two notes of mine, on melanism and on moth-parasites. The latter contains my description of *Cecidomyia bigeloviae* n.sp. In both is an account of the exhibition of some of my galls at the South London Ent. Soc., but the names of several of the species are printed wrong.

In *Entomologist* are several references to my variation papers which appeared last year. F.H.P. Coste, especially, in taking up the subject of insect colours and the chemistry of them, differs from me in certain points. However, I think he is mistaken, and with Charlton's help I have found references to literature which I think will prove the soundness of my position. I have today written on the subject to the *Entomologist*. This evening I went down to Charlton's, mainly to talk over Coste's paper and insect chemistry.

April 19th, 6:55 p.m. After breakfast I went round to Charlton's to make some experiments on the effect of ammonia, etc., on the colours of butterflies, but was able to ascertain nothing new. Since then, I have been reading and writing at home. Charlton called on me this evening. The only mail I got was a short letter from Binney.

At 10:30 a.m. the funeral of the Etzel father (Gabriel Etzel) took place. He was the man I once told you about as speaking at the Railroad meeting over the Bank. The service (Roman Catholic) was held in Silver Cliff, and a very long procession of vehicles followed the coffin. The Etzels being Roman Catholics, are obliged especially to spend a good deal of money over the funeral and mourning, etc., which they can ill afford. It is wonderful how they live — the mother, an oldish brother (Tony Etzel) and the three girls, with no visible means of subsistence but a little shop where books, papers, fruit, cigars, and stationery are sold. They are Germans by origin and Roman Catholics by descent, but the eldest girl, Anna, wants to break loose from that faith, only they won't let her do so openly.

I have been very puzzled over an entomological point today. I had some whitish fluffy galls, unknown to science, from which the flies had never been bred. Not supposing the flies would emerge this month, I neglected to shut the galls up in a box. Then yesterday I noticed a lot of little flies, apparently gall-gnats, on the window and, looking at my galls, sure enough, there were the empty pupa shells on the surface of them, and the flies had escaped. So I kept one of the flies and today proceeded to write a description of it. But to my astonishment, when I came to look at it with a glass, it was not a gall-gnat (*Cecidomyia*) atall but something allied to *Phora*, a genus of flies that breeds in decaying food (e.g., cheese, vegetables, etc.)! Now you see, here is a puzzler. Where did the *Phora* come from, and where have the genuine gall-gnats gone to? I cannot find the true gall-gnats anywhere! I found one or two gall-gnats on the window, indeed, but they must belong to different galls, as they were too big to have come out of the pupa cases I found.

Sunday, April 20th, 4 p.m. There isn't much to tell about, except the Literary & Sci. Society last night. We had a good meeting. Here is the programme:

Reading: Miss Byington (not remarkable)

Recitation: Miss Doll Cassidy (ditto)

Quartette: Mrs. Conway, etc.

Recitation: Miss Bertha Humphrey (well done, but a poor piece)

Organ and violin duette: Mrs. Conway and Harry Stockton

Recitation: Mrs. (Prof.) Wright (very well given; a comic piece)

Song: Chetelat (Very good, comic, was encored, but he wouldn't sing again)

The debate was: 'Affirmed, that the credit system in business relations should be abolished.' Affirmative: Sam Wright and Charlton. Negative: Price Walters and Cockerell. It was a pretty good debate. I was really of course of the *affirmative* opinion, but being put on the other side I made fun of the question, this being the only way out of the difficulty. The judges gave for the affirmative.

At the suggestion of Price Walters, those present who were *not* members, subscribed to defray lighting expenses (oil) and $1.73 was raised. Mrs. Humphrey and Mrs. Conway were appointed as the next committee to arrange the programmes. At the next meeting, in place of a debate, we have decided on a novelty, which I suggested. Two sides were appointed, four on each side, to read selected bits of prose, and the others poetry, and the judges to decide on the relative merits of the two kinds of literature, according to the excellence of the pieces read. I am for prose, and I think I shall read the piece in *Sesame and Lilies* about novel-reading.

Today I went down to the Conway ranch to get *Sesame and Lilies* (which I had lent to them) and that led to my staying to lunch there, and part of the afternoon. We discussed the Lit. Society a good deal, as three of the principal members, Sam Wright, Mrs. Conway, and Miss Lowther, were there.

9:45 p.m. Have just returned from church. About an hour after I returned from the Conway ranch this afternoon, I took my oil-can and went round to fill the lamps in the church. But I found they were still at Sunday School, so I went on to Mrs. Stockton and talked there for a while with her and the Stockton boys. Rob. Stockton, by the way, is taking up chemistry quite seriously and

I believe he will make a success of it. He is one of those fellows who appear abnormally stupid, but every now and then make a remark showing that they have really more intelligence than the average. In some ways he reminds me a little of Frederic. Mrs. Stockton invited me to supper with them, so that I was there most of the latter part of the afternoon. And when, after that, I had called on Mrs. Humphrey (mainly to talk about Lit. & Sci. Society), it was church time.

We had a very small congregation in church, and the sermon was poor. It was an orthodox appeal, with little argument, to us to 'come unto Christ, who will no-wise cast us out.' To me, of course, it was almost meaningless, but the Charltons also did not like it. The trouble is that the parson has not *enthusiasm* in his work. He does his best as a sort of duty, but he himself seems to lack the faith he would instil into others.

April 21st, 7 p.m. The days are getting long. The sun still lights the top of the range. This morning it looked very stormy and actually snowed a little, but it has cleared up and is now fine. Ward came to town and called on me. Another call I had was a prospector named Jordan, a very intelligent and quite scientific man. He would be a great support to the various meetings we have, no doubt, were he not always away prospecting.

This morning I made a drawing for Binney, and cut some wood. This afternoon I have been reading and answering mail and examining slugs. The mail I got today was: (l.) *Field and Farm.* (2.) *Bulletin of Torrey Botanical Club.* (3.) A letter and some interesting slugs from Dr. Cooper of California. (4.) Letter from Binney with the proofs of my slug drawings. Some have turned out very well, but others are inferior. The 'half-tone' process is not well suited to the work, I think.

This is a miserably short and uninteresting letter. But it must go now.

> With much love, your own
> Theo.
> Health. Excellent.

April 29th, 1890, 10 p.m.

Love,
Yesterday a letter went to you. Today has not been eventful. In the morning I dissected some of Binney's slugs and made drawings of the anatomy, and wrote to Binney about it. That, and cutting wood took most of the morning. I read *Review of Reviews* and *Pall Mall Budget* moist of the afternoon, though I also called on the Charltons. I had supper early, and thus taking a long evening, commenced, and thought to finish, a paper on the Flora of High Altitudes for the *Torrey Bulletin.* However, it isn't done, and must be left to finish tomorrow. It proves longer than I expected. I have already written five pages of manuscript.

The only mail I got was a large package, which proved amazing enough. It is a big photograph of a group of seven young men (nice-looking fellows) in the uniform of what appears to be the Northwest Military Police, and *Douglas* in the midst of them, and one of them! Now what am I to understand by this? Has he enlisted, or is it merely some volunteer corps? There is no explanation, and I feel a bit uneasy about it. Possibly the N.W.T. Police work is as good as being a bank clerk, and I don't think I want Douglas to be a sort of soldier anyway. I anxiously await an explanation.

Regy and Pennycuick were in town today; also Louis and Mrs. Howard. Louis asked me to go and stay with his wife for three days while he and MacDougall are away on a projected trip to Cañon City. I told him I would do so.

April 30, 11 p.m. It is late. I have been at work all the evening taking notes on the fossil plants of Colorado, out of a book (by Lesquereux) that Charlton recently received, as I think I told you. I sat up late to finish it, and have done so and found it interesting. The willow leaves from the rocks near Rattlesnake Mountain seem likely a new species. In my notebook I have called it *Salix mons-crotalariae!* It took me all this morning and until mail time to finish my paper on the flora of high altitudes.

The mail I got was rather uninteresting. (1.) Letter from D. Gale, still wishing to back out of the presidency of C.B.A. and proposing *me* in his place, which is absurd, as I shall not be here. I wrote to Gale about it and sent Gale's letter to Nash, asking him what had best be done. (2.) Postcard about slugs from Dr. Cooper. (3.) *Ornithologist and Oölogist*, a sample copy. (4.) Harvard University Papers, i.e., a programme of lectures, account of degrees, scholarships, etc., etc., sent by some kind but unknown person who I suppose thinks I may go to Harvard to get *educated* a bit!

May 1st, 3 p.m. The first of May! And the next month is June! It is a very rainy day, but the rain has now ceased and I shall be able to go out to the Howards, as invited. Potatoes are cooking on the fire. I need a fire to keep warm, so may as well use it to cook something.

This morning I went round to Charlton's to return his book. I found he had been yesterday to Rattlesnake Mountain and had brought back many more of the fossil leaves. With this increased series, which I spent some time examining, I was able to make out that the leaves were not willows after all but belonged to *Planera longifolia* of Lesquereux, a plant with willow-like leaves allied to the elms. Most of the specimens represent a new variety, *integra*. These are of the same species and the same age as those of the insect-beds of Florissant, so perhaps some insects may turn up here.

I have been reading *Review of Reviews* and have got as far as the middle of the account of Bismarck. That workhouse-helping notion is not bad and will do good, but I should prefer to throw my energies into some enterprise for the *prevention* of the workhouse necessity, instead of trying to alleviate the symptoms which our competitive system has produced. It seems like elbowing one's neighbour into the ditch and then offering him one's handkerchief to wipe the dirt off his clothes.

My only mail was a query about snow-birds, sent on by *Field and Farm*, who want an answer to put in the paper. I have written a suitable reply.

May 2nd, 11 p.m. I walked out to Howard's yesterday towards evening. It was very damp underfoot and began to drizzle before I got there. I found things as usual, except that there was a novelty in the shape of a garden and a hotbed. We had supper, and afterwards spent the evening talking and looking over a pile of numbers of *The Graphic*. Louis asked me to stay the night, which I not unwillingly did on account of the weather, though it had cleared up by the time we went to bed.

This morning, after breakfast, Mrs. Howard took me over the garden and proudly showed and explained the sprouting peas, turnips, beets, onions, etc., etc. Then I went off with Louis and MacDougall in the waggon to where they had to plough (as it was on the way toward town). Some of the land on the ranch is so wet they cannot get on it to plough it.

Leaving them at their work, I walked on to town. On my way I called at the Conway ranch as I passed. On the table they had a little vase with five flowers of *Caltha leptosepala*, and they asked me to explain the botanical characters of the plant. Examining the plants for this purpose, I was surprised to find that the number of carpels in a flower varied from two to eight, and of the three flowers, only two had the same number of carpels. Quite a notable case of variability, this.

When I got to town I went to the Charltons'. I found Mrs. C. had a new idea, namely to have a garden by the creek. She was trying to dig up grass sod with a very blunt spade, and of course without much result. But going over the ground, we found a better place, and Charlton has undertaken to dig a little plot for her.

I got some rather interesting mail today. (1.) Two letters from Dr. J. Hamilton. The first letter was to tell me that a beetle I sent him, found in an ant's nest, was exceedingly rare; in fact, only one specimen was hitherto known, but that most unfortunately it had got crushed in the post so that it broke all up upon being touched. It is a great misfortune. The original specimen was from California. I wrote a note about it to *Ent. Mo. Mag.* this afternoon, headed 'An Entomological Tragedy.' Hamilton's second letter was about some other things I sent him. After he got composed after the beetle tragedy, he found there was more to write, but had already posted the first.

(2.) Letter from Gillette, asking when I described the new galls. I sent him the *Entom.* paper but told him to return it. (3.) *Pall Mall Budget.* (4.) *Nature*, containing my reply to Wetterham about the galls and also a report of an Entomological Society meeting where I see Billups exhibited some flies raised from the galls I sent to the South London Society,

This evening, feeling very restless, I went to the Charltons' and stopped all the evening talking.

May 3rd, 7:30 p.m. An uninteresting day. Have been rather dyspeptic and have been at home all day working on a paper, 'Contributions to the Nomenclature of the Pulmonata-Geophila [land shells] of America north of Mexico.' This will be quite an extensive paper and will probably take me nearly a week to prepare. Today's mail was simply a letter from Binney, a postcard from Scudder, and a leaflet of *Proc. Nat. Sci. Assn. of Staten I.*, for C.B.A. Library.

Sunday, May 4th, 5:30 p.m. Am down with 'mountain fever' (febricula).

May 5th, 7:10 p.m. Am considerably recovered but still in the 'knock me down with a feather' stage. Will proceed to recount events, and then post this. On Saturday we had a good meeting of the Literary Society. Here is the programme:

Music: Miss Falkenberg

Reading: Miss Mary Ormsby (a child)

Recitation: Miss Gracie Morton (a very small child)

Music: Fred Haskell (a young man of Silver Cliff) and May Cassidy). Miss Cassidy played the organ, and Mr. Haskell some sort of 'infernal machine', which I fancy is called a harmonica.

Reading: Miss Byington (well done)

Recitation: Miss Florence Aldrich (she didn't know it and had to be prompted)

Violin-organ duette: Frank Patton and Miss Falkenberg (was encored)

Recitation (Miss Lowther)

The debate was: Affirmed 'That the West will progress faster than the East in the next quarter of a century.' (West meaning west of the Mississippi.) Sam Wright and Beaumont took the affirmative, and I was left to defend the negative all alone. My opinions rather incline toward the negative on the whole, though I know little of the eastern states. The judges gave for the affirmative by two to one. Charlton, who was to have debated, did not attend the meeting, being unwell.

I also announced that I would give three botany lectures to complete the course broken off last summer, if eight or ten cared to attend. I owe them to those who attended before, but said I would let any others attend free. The first lecture is to be tomorrow at 2:30 p.m. (Hope I shall be well enough.) I don't know exactly who will come, but the Aldriches, Charltons, and the Conway people said they were going to. I shall not do much unless a fair number come. Florence Aldrich wants coaching in botany for an exam she is in for. I also described and drew on the blackboard those lost insects, *Rhizococcus* and *Hetaerius* (the Hamilton beetle) and requested the children to hunt for fresh specimens.

The debate next Saturday has it: Affirmed: 'That men are more polite than women!' The ladies ought to be got to speak on this, if on anything! I hear rumours that one or two will speak. I suppose it will be treated rather as a joke. I am on the affirmative.

Sunday. Yesterday morning I woke up very feverish, with a headache, etc. Once or twice I tried to get up but was almost too weak to stand. I had no food cooked, and could not cook any, and nobody came near my room. So I was in a rather sorry plight although I had nothing worse than the so-called 'mountain fever.' At 2 p.m. I began to think something must be done, and was feeling a little better, so I got up and went down with some eggs I had, meaning to ask Mrs. Chetelat to cook them for me. But the Chetelats were not at home , and so I contrived to walk down to the Charltons', and there was treated very kindly. Mrs. Charlton cooked my eggs and also made me some tea and toast.

After a while the parson turned up (being asked to dinner by the Charltons) and soon after that I left. Charlton promised to see to the lighting of the church, and I went to bed as soon as I got home. Mrs. Chetelat was denouncing the poor parson's last night sermon very vehemently this morning. I fear he is not atall popular with the people here on the whole, though I am not clear that he deserves to be.

Today I am a good deal better. Charlton called at about ten, bringing some tea and cakes. Soon after that I got up and, for the sake of warmth spent most of the day reading *Review of Reviews*, etc., by the stove in Chetelat's store.

While I was down there, Louis Howard called, as I found a paper on my table on which was written: 'I heard you were sick, so I came down to see what was up only to find you gone. E.L.B.H.'

There is a good deal of excitement here today, as they are electing the School Board.

Today's mail was: (1.) Postcard from Binney, and a rare slug, which unhappily had died and become decomposed on the way. (2.) Letter from Nash. (3.) Letter from J. H. Thomson, sending a *dollar* to repay me for examining his shells. (4.) Letter from Dr. White of Washington, in reply to some criticisms of mine to his papers on fossil shells. He admits my criticisms 'are not unreasonable.' (5.) *Field and Farm*.

In the next letter I shall have some remarks to make on the *Review of Reviews*. This is the last letter you can reply to to Colorado! Indeed, I may get away before the reply to this comes. The happy time is near now, love!

Your very own loving Theo.

Tuesday, May 6th, 1890, 9:25 p.m.

Love,

Am much better but still rather weak, of course. In the morning, having risen late, I read and wrote. Regy and Pennycuick came and called on me. At the usual time the mail came in and proved interesting, though unfortunately the mail from England did not appear. There were two items, viz.: (1.) A paper by Ashmead in pamphlet form, on new Ichneumonidae in the U. S. National Museum. In it are descriptions of four new species found here by me. (2.) A book of 454 pages from the Dept. of Agriculture, being the first part of a *Bibliography of Economic Entomology*. This book contains lists of the writings of Walsh (now dead) and Riley. Riley's effusions number 2,033! The book will be very useful, as even if Riley is entirely a black sheep, it is the more necessary to keep track of his doings.

At 2:30 I went round to the schoolhouse for the appointed botany lecture, but as I was not very fit for an elaborate dissertation, I was not sorry that only Charlton and the two Miss Aldriches turned up. I think the others supposed I should not be well enough to lecture anyway. However, I gave them some talk on the characteristics of the principal natural orders of plants, and the Aldrich girls, at all events, took notes and did their best to remember what was said. My remarks at the Literary the other night already seem to have effect, to my surprise.

I am getting rather in the way of expecting nothing in this town. A small girl came up to me at the postoffice and said she had been collecting bugs all morning and had found one of the lost varieties, but she had the bugs at home. I told her to bring them round to the schoolhouse at botany lecture time, but she never did. Then again, this afternoon that gorilla-like personage Mac Ormsby stopped me and from mentioning my remarks at the Literary, led on to such a lengthy account of his experience with scorpions that I had to rather break off the conversation to get away.

May 7th, 8:30 p.m. I will post this today just to let you know I have recovered. I am very well today indeed. It is fearfully windy, so that one can scarcely venture out of doors for the dust.

This morning I carefully examined, drew, and described some little Chalcididae bred from my *Cecidomyia alticola* galls. After that I continued work on my paper on the nomenclature of land shells, and so all the morning was used up. After breakfast, I forgot to say, I read from the *Bibliography of Econ. Ent.* for a while.

When I went to the postoffice at mail time, I was handed various things, including some English mail, but proceeded to look over what I had got in the office, when presently Mrs. Lacy called my name and handed me your little package with the letter enclosed. It had been overlooked. Now I will answer your letter before I proceed any further.

My thanks to Eva, but I fear I must decline the kitten! What could I do with it? About the scent of flowers in the evening, it *is* remarkable, and I don't know whether any rational explanation has been offered to account for it. One can well understand that its use may be to attract the moths. Shall we study the matter when I get back? Frederic's lodgings in London don't sound to me much more attractive than mine here, but I suppose they are. It used to seem to me that the only thing that made 'office' tolerable was the return each evening to home, not lodgings. But if Frederic likes it, it is all right.

Yes, I agree with you about Mrs. Cavid and marriage, But there is one trouble; what is to become of those who are not able to grasp the proper ideal of marriage. Should they not marry? What I meant by competition and so forth was that so many women marry just to get a living and a home, whereas if the condition of women were better, so that they were always able to get sufficient bread and butter by themselves, they would not be so careless about marrying.

Respecting my turning up at Syon Lodge in overalls, etc.! Of course not. I shall appear 'according to the latest fashions.' But there is a point I have been turning over in my mind long and carefully. I shall cross the sea in rough clothes (probably) and shall have to transform when I get to Bedford Park (unless I am delayed in Liverpool). Now I can't possibly wait to hunt the town for stylish clothes before I go to Syon Lodge, so I shall have to actually arrive in such plumes as I can borrow from Carlie at the moment. Will that do? They will certainly be of good quality and I presume they will fit. Only don't let out the secret!

Dear, I can very well understand your fears about your father and myself. I have my own anxieties upon the subject although I put a bold face on it. However, if we do quarrel or disagree it will not be my fault. I should think your father might be willing that we should 'agree to differ' and be silent on points like Socialism, or otherwise, discuss them in a rational and scientific spirit.

On the other hand, he is a gardener and takes an interest in nature and living things, so we should have something in common. He is of the old school of thought and probably never could accept more modern ideas. But there is much, even in that, that is excellent to those of the later times who think carefully. Of course, though, my views are my own and without adequate reasons I could not change them. Views will change as one ascertains new facts, but as a rule, opposing opinions do not affect anything in that direction.

Thanks for the vine beetle. It is one of the weevils (Curculionidae), but the species I do not know. Many species of this family are very injurious to fruit trees. There is a weevil called *Craponius inaequalis* injurious to grape vines in America.

The mail of today: (1.) Postcard from Ancey. He says he is sending a bundle of his manuscripts (in French) in Colorado shells, but it has not yet come. It will be useful to me in presenting my paper on nomenclature. (2.) Postcard from Elwes, at last acknowledging the butterflies. He says none I sent were new or rare, and says nothing about payment. I had been told that Elwes was a 'shabby fellow', and I begin to think so. (3.) 'Rural Notes', from the *Yorkshire Post*, from Geo. Roberts. (3.) List of rare, etc., books for sale by B. Quaritch of Picadilly. Why sent to *me*, I wonder. (5.) Scudder's paper on butterflies found fossil at Florissant — a large pamphlet with two plates. Very interesting. It is for the C.B.A.

Just a few remarks on the *Review of Reviews* before I post this. It is interesting, but there is little to remark on. I rather think I don't much like Bismarck after reading the account of him. I have a prejudice against him, I suppose, and certainly I don't like many of his ways and beliefs. But he is a great man, like Napoleon.

I should think Gladstone's remarks on the Bible would be worth reading, when he gets over the preface. Can quite believe Dr. Richardson's

statements about cycling. Dawkins is a villain to want to see a coal center in Kent. I certainly hope, myself, that it will never be. E. Simon's 'French City' (about the Chinaman) is not bad. Miss Brigham Young about polygamy is amazing enough! Don't like the looks of Zola, from portrait given. I never read any of his works. Mr. Geo. Chaney and his new religion (?) seem to me pure bosh. I don't like Spurgeon and don't care whether he was baptised or not.

Yes, I have little doubt Morell MacKenzie is quite right about the College of Surgeons. As he says, they certainly teach practically nothing, and sell the M.R.C.S. for pretty considerable fees to those who pass the exam. It is rather like one of the City companies. On the other hand, it is very useful as insisting on a certain standard of knowledge for those who are to practice in its name.

O. Schreiner's *Vision of Hell* must certainly be dismal. I don't want to read it either. I think she rather overdoes these things, thereby spoiling her point.

Tolstoi must be a queer sort of man, I began his story, as given by Stead, but have not yet finished it. I can't say I like it. I agree with Stead's remarks on Tolstoi in the preface.

I think the British delegates to the Berlin Conference, as reported in *Pall Mall*, did not behave in a very gentlemanly way. One of them, being interviewed, suggested that all the Emperor said to him was the result of 'coaching.' Surely rather a rude thing to say of one's host. However, the men they sent were no real representatives of labour.

I enclose *Phlox caespitosa*, which I gathered high up at timber line last year. You will see the flower is like the garden *Phlox* but the whole plant, how different! The effect of altitude.

Your loving Theo.

Thursday, May 15, 1890, 9:45 p.m.

Love,

This is the last day of my secretaryship of C.B.A. The polls close. Only ten have voted, and those nominated are all elected. Miss Eastwood is the new Secretary. May the Association have success in the next year!

Last night we had a 'prayer-meeting' at the church. Being janitor, of course I attended. These prayer-meetings are quite a feature in this country, but the thing was entirely new to me. I was interested and, I must admit, a little amused. The congregation consisted of Roberts (the Rosita stage-driver) and his wife, Williams (the new doctor) and his mother-in-law, May and Doll Cassidy, Mrs. Stockton, and myself — eight in all.

We began with hymns. The parson played the organ, and a desperate (and fairly successful) effort was made to sing. Then the parson prayed, and then read out of the Bible. After that, 'brother Williams' was requested to offer up a prayer, which he did. We were invited to get up and relate our thoughts, etc., but nobody had any ideas they wished to communicate.

Finally we went through the Sunday School lesson for next Sunday. It was the 'transfiguration' of Christ, where they go up on the mountain, and Moses and Elias appear, etc. This we discussed at length, Williams and his mother-in-law and Mrs. Roberts making many critical remarks, mostly to the point. Here the parson did well, being able to answer readily and generally satisfactorily, from his point of view.

The points that came up were such as these: How did the apostles *know* Moses and Elias when they saw them? Were Moses and Elias actually present, or only ghosts of them? What was the object of the 'transfiguration'? And so forth. I wisely refrained from commenting until at the end, when the parson began talking about our spiritual bodies hereafter. I felt moved to ask what *age* he supposed our spiritual bodies would appear. He thought, at the age we died. Would the babies thus appear babies for the rest of time?

I asked. He thought they would. Then would it not seem rather an advantage to die in the prime of life? (For he said he supposed we should retain our intelligent faculties much the same.) He allowed that it would.

I confessed that I could not see much reason in his ideas on the subject — it seemed to me unreasonable. So he asked, 'what did *I* think we should appear like in the hereafter?' I said I had no idea. 'Did I not believe the Bible?' Not entirely, certainly. 'What parts did I deem untrue?' I didn't know which were true and which not — wish I did. After that he said no more, but sat down and played the concluding hymn.

I suppose a prayer-meeting is hardly the place to make critical remarks on the veracity or otherwise of the Bible, and I therefore only answered what he asked when he got into such questions. Perhaps I should have said nothing in the first place, but his theory was so peculiar that I thought I might criticise it without offence.

When the people had gone away, the parson came up to me, and I had a long talk with him. He proved much more reasonable and sensible than I expected, and I was much more favourably impressed with him than heretofore. I shall talk again with him when I get an opportunity. I want to understand more fully his point of view, as I think it is typical of quite a class. And I think *he* has not yet comprehended my point of view, which in a way is perhaps as typical as his.

Almost all today I have been working in the nomenclature paper, and yet I wrote only seven pages. I called at the Charltons'. Mrs. C. is about well, and they talk of going down to Cañon City tomorrow.

The mail was: (1.) Letter from H. G. Smith, Jr., about the C.B.A. (2.) *Psyche* for May, containing a note of mine on the habits of a kind of wasp.

May 16th, 10:35 p.m. Am very tired tonight. Have been working all day on my nomenclature paper, except part of this afternoon. The mail today was: (1.) A nice letter from Carlie. (2.) Letter from Gillette, about galls. (3.) Letter from Collinge of Leeds. (4.) Letter and some slugs from Binney. (5.) Some interesting reprints of papers from Schwarz, an entomologist of Washington. Kind of him to send them, as I am not a correspondent of his.

At three I went round to the schoolhouse, as a sort of half-arrangement had been made for a botany lecture. We were going to have a C.B.A. meeting, and bring the lecture in as an item. Mrs. Charlton was supposed to announce the same at the King's Daughters meeting. However, the Charltons have gone off to Cañon City, and so the C.B.A. meeting fell through, and nobody turned up at the lecture today except Mrs. Humphrey, who didn't expect I was going to lecture. I was quite glad, as I didn't feel up to it.

Falkenberg gave me that 'note' for $88.55 today, so I sent it off to Lees, and it will be all right.

Am still worried by a cough. It is sort of a 'remainder' of the fever. Things like that always pull me down for a while.

May 17th, 7:50 p.m. Must be off to Lit. Soc. meeting.

11:50 p.m. We have had a good meeting of Lit. Soc., but won't write about it now, as it is late.

Sunday, May 18th, 7:40 p.m. Must be off to light up the church. Have lots to write. Will find time tomorrow.

May 19th, 8:55 p.m. I have finished my papers on the American shells, I am glad to say, for I was weary of them. The check-list I had prepared I sent to Binney today.

But to recount the events of these last three days:

Saturday. In the morning I found among some of my specimens a little shell of the genus *Pupa*, about so big — ( ), and examining it very carefully, found it was something new and very interesting. So I had to write a description of it, and finally I sent it off to Dr. Sterki, who knows more about these little shells than I do. All this took most of the morning, The rest of the day was nearly all taken up working on my paper on the nomenclature of shells, and I was able to send eight pages of the MS off to Binney in the evening.

The mail I got was a long and interesting letter from Dr. Hamilton (a beetle I sent him proves to be exceedingly rare), a postcard and a box of *Helix hortensis* from Massachusetts from Thomson of New Bedford, and *Naturalist* for May.

In the evening as usual we had the Literary Soc. meeting. The programme a good one) was:

Recitation: Mary Ormsby (a child)

Duette: Carmie Falkenberg and Ella Etzel (was encored)

Recitation: 'The Street Musician', Miss Byington (an ambitious piece, with two snatches of song in it, not badly done)

Recitation: Kate Aldrich (well done)

Reading: 'The Singer in Prison', Samse

Chorus song: Led by Mrs. Conway. (After the first verse, they *whistled*. The effect was very pretty indeed. It was a hunting song)

Debate: Affirmed, that 'Circumstances make the man.'

Affirmative: (1.) Beaumont (only he *spoke* more on the negative!) (2.) Cockerell (I didn't feel much like speaking but got along pretty well when I started.)

Negative: (1.) Sam Wright. (2.) Price Walters.

The judges gave for the affirmative by two votes to one. the house was full, as it always is now, many coming from Silver Cliff. I am sure our Literary Society is doing lots of good. It relieves the dull monotony of this place and gives people something to talk about. Furthermore, it develops those who have any abilities for singing, reciting, or whatnot.

Sunday. I Called on Mrs. Stockton, and afterwards on Mrs. Humphrey (and Miss Lowther, staying with her) to discuss who we should get for secretary of the Literary Society when I went. I myself was in favour of Miss Lowther, but she did not want to take the work, and they were all in favour of having Price Walters. So I suppose he will be elected, if he will serve. I should think he would do it very well; he has plenty of ability but is a little 'touchy.'

After this (it was in the morning) I filled the lamps at the schoolhouse and then returned to my room and worked on the shell paper until church-time. I got the nomenclature paper finished (36 pages of manuscript) and commenced on the check-list of American Land Shells, which I had to write in connection with the nomenclature paper.

There was but a small congregation at church, but the sermon, on prayer, was not bad from the preacher's point of view. Altogether, I was quite pleased with it.

Monday (today). Worked all this morning and most of the afternoon on the check-list, and finally got it done. I had supper and, weary in body and mind, took a short walk in the evening air, which made me feel better. Tomorrow I hope Regy will appear and take me out on the ranch for a few days.

Today's mail was: (1.) Letter from Binney. (2.) Letter and some slugs from W. I. Raymond of Oakland, California. (3.) Letter from Packard. (4.) *Bull. Torrey Bot. Club.* for May. (5.) *Insect Life* for April. It contains a short note of mine on some injurious beetles new to Colorado. (6.) *Field and Farm.*

Packard writes a kind letter, in which he says:

As I wrote you I sincerely hope you will return to Colorado. We can't afford to lose so good a naturalist! But if you will take a bit of advice from an older man, I would urge upon you, as you are young, to make a thorough study of Morphology, say, at Cambridge or Oxford, as it would afford the best foundation for future good work. 'Species work', unless as a basis for thorough phylogenetic work, is often a snare and a delusion. But if you could follow in the footsteps of Weismann and your countryman Poulton, whom I met last summer at Oxford, you would have an admirable start.

With best wishes, most cordially yours,

A. S. Packard

But of course I shall neither return to Colorado (I hope!) nor go to Oxford or Cambridge!

Tuesday, 2 p.m. Regy is here, and am going out to the ranch with him.

Your own lover, Theo.

Health. Pretty good but still some cough.

May 21st, 1890, 9:10 p.m.

Love,

Yesterday morning I had written a few letters and done various odd things when Regy turned up to take me out to the ranch to do Mrs. Cusack's flowers. I ha already purchased a book in which to write the required herbarium list. Mrs. Cusack, I hear, will not be back here until July, so I shall not see her until she goes to England.

Regy wanted to wait for the mail, so I had plenty of time to get ready to go. I took the minute-book of the Literary Society round to Mrs. Humphrey, in case I might not be in on Saturday. (Did I ever tell you I found *lots* of garnets in the stones the Humphrey's house is built of, right in the doorway? *They* had never noticed them.)

When the mail came in, all I got was a long letter from Morrison of Virginia — no English mail.

We drove out uneventfully to Will Kettle's ('The Hon. Wm. Kettle') where we stopped to pick up Mrs. Regy, who was giving music lessons to the Kettle girls. Mrs. Kettle (an excellent farmer's wife, formerly of Lincolnshire) was very hospitable and, learning that we had not had lunch (I had forgotten all about lunch) set a meal before us. We had to wait some time, as the music lessons were not finished.

Mrs. Kettle showed me her garden with great pride, and also introduced me to her daughters, with no less pride. Both garden and daughters are excellent. The daughters (called Seddy and Carrie) are big girls, perhaps 20 and 18. They are being very highly educated, at least as highly a the Kettles can contrive. They talk of moving to Denver for the benefit of their daughters. I fear they will not like it. They will become too 'superior' for the common folks and yet will remain too countrified for the 'high-toned' society in which they possibly hope to mix. You can understand how this may be. As a matter of fact they are doubtless more excellent in reality than said 'society' and, I should say, they had better leave it alone. Possibly, though, they have more sense in this matter than one gives them credit for.

The elder girl, Seddy, has been learning botany, and told me all about her studies with some enthusiasm. I pulled one or two flowers to pieces and explained the parts to her. Margery Beddoes, the little Beddoes girl, was at the Kettles with Mrs. Regy. She had come down with her, as she is staying at the Cusacks'. She is a nice child on the whole, and has talked a great deal to me since I got here.

I didn't attempt to do any work yesterday evening after getting up here. I found things a good deal improved — a new stable, a new chicken-house, and so forth. Evidently Regy is working well. He also has a new horse, several cows, a pig, etc., etc. Ward has departed to Campion, but Pennycuick is here, and also young Urquhart (Keith Urquhart, Mrs. Regy's brother). The latter is a nice boy, intelligent, good-mannered, and obliging. No doubt he will develop. Cress came in in the evening and stopped to talk with Regy and the rest.

This morning, Cress appeared in the middle of breakfast and imparted a secret to Regy, that he had been out at five this morning and killed a big buck. Cress is very successful in killing wild animals. He has killed several bears, and in the kitchen there hang the skins of two wildcats (lynx) shot by him. Regy got a telegram yesterday saying that Pellham, a new boarder-pupil, has got as far as New York. This is good for Regy, and meanwhile we are all very curious to see what the new man will be like. He is about 19 years old.

Before breakfast this morning I collected a few specimens. Everything is looking very green, and the butterflies and flowers are coming out. After breakfast until dusk this evening, and again a little after supper, I have been making a list of Mrs. Cusack's herbarium. I number every specimen and make a corresponding entry in the book. I made better progress than I expected, and hope to be done tomorrow so as to go to town on Friday. The book I have got for the list is too big really, but it was the only decent book I could get in town, so I suppose it will do. At all events, it is a nice book, well-bound.

Frank Cusack, Mrs. Regy tells me, expects to return here before very long. There is some talk of Frank and his mother living together in a separate house not yet built.

May 22nd, 10 p.m. Have finished the herbarium list, all except the index. Will not write now, as I am tired and rather out of sorts.

May 24th, 10 p.m. Am in town again. Got a very nice letter from you. Have *lots* to say, but am tired tonight and will wait until I can collect my wits tomorrow. Goodnight, and a kiss!

May 25th, Noon. Now why can't I get away this very minute? It's too bad. They are cutting rates, owing to railroad competition, and I hear one can go to New York for $5.00! The usual fare is about $50.00. I suppose by the time I get the money to go, the rates will have gone up again. Everyone is going east and the trains are said to be crammed, Mrs. Becker told me, about Cañon City. I could probably raise enough to get to New York now, but then I couldn't get across the sea.

4:30 p.m. Ever since noon, my mind has been in a state of chaotic ebullition, causing me to wander hither and thither like a lunatic, and it is only by an effort that I can so compose myself as to take a chair for the purpose of writing this letter. The more I thought about it, the more it seemed to me that I *must* take advantage of the cut rates and, raising money somehow or other, get away early next week.

First of all I thought of going off to Louis Howard's and getting him to lend me the cash, and collect the debt whenever my money arrived here. Then I thought I had better find out more about it, and I wandered around town seeking information. Mrs. Stockton, whom I called on, gave me good advice. It seems that one Vance and wife, formerly of West Cliff and now of Cañon City, are staying with Mrs. Charlton. Now Vance is employed by the railroad and would know all about it, and besides, he was going to Cañon City on Monday and could get me a ticket so that I should not be left by getting there too late to get a cheap rate. (Tickets are good for ten days, and rates may go up.) Obviously Vance was the very man. I rushed off to Charltons' but

found them all out, and so must wait. Meanwhile the mail coach came in with news that the rates had risen a little.

I got some mail: (1.) Postcard from Sterki. (2.) *Proc. Staten Is. Nat. Sci. Ass'n.* for C.B.A. Library. (3.) Letter from Ashmead, and three copies of the Bulletin on Colorado Hymenoptera (150 copies coming by express). Of course the Bulletin interests me greatly. I send you a copy. Ashmead is very complimentary in his preface, and I see he names the new *Dolichocephalus* after me, though I had asked him not to do so.

I don't know whether I can command my brain sufficiently to give a coherent account of the past few days, but will try.

On Thursday (at the Cusacks') nothing particular happened except that toward evening I was a good deal out of sorts and had to repose in an easy chair. I finished the Herbarium list by evening, except the Index. Friday I returned to town. Mrs. Regy urged me to stay on, and I felt much tempted to do so but thought I ought to get back, and besides, their new boarder, Pelham, was about to arrive, and I felt I should be rather in the way. Pelham was already in West Cliff when we got there. I didn't speak to him (being deep in my mail) and did not see enough of him to judge what he was like. He looks like an ordinary sort of man.

Later, I called at the Charltons' and found only Mrs. Charlton and Miss Anna Etzel there. Charlton had gone off to see his friends in Missouri, on account of the cheap rates. Mrs. Charlton had heard that one could go to New York for $27.00, but the rates have gone down a lot since then, according to Mrs. Becker and others.

Your letter was very nice! I will answer it. *Arum.* Yes, it is as often or oftener 'immaculatum' as *maculatum*, vide Bedford Park List. Of course I will help you with the things you can't name — that is, if I can! Yes, let's go to the Academy together. I remember once, when Sperling told me he went with May Morris. I wished *I* could go with *you!* Why didn't I talk at the Charltons' social? Well, I'm not sensible, and on such occasions I only gaze on in despair. However, I did conduct the charades to some extent. Yes, I know about *bachelors*, but I like to spell it with a 't' when they do batch, and without one when they don't. That's logic! Am glad you don't want me to be so intimate with some other young woman. I am very fond of young women, as a class, but don't want to be intimate with more than one! Really and seriously, I don't believe a man *can* love *two* women at once. That's why polygamy is so contrary to the true notion of matrimony.

Well, I will see how near to New York the Binney's are, but don't like stopping even for them. No, I don't think Frederic appears abnormally stupid, but he does hide his light under a bushel to some considerable extent. I remember we all wondered what he was really like when first we knew him. I know nothing of half-tone except that it is in some way produced by photography from drawings in a sort of sepia-tint. Bimetallism is always a puzzle to me. The fellows seem to want to have the coinage restricted to gold and silver (no coppers or notes). I don't believe it would really help us. There is more I might answer, were I in my right mind!

I got a great lot of mail, as follows: (1,2.) Two letters from Binney, with orders for some more drawings. I don't know whether I can do them. (3.) Letter and some reprints from W. H. Edwards. He writes favourably as to a new scheme of mine relative to generic nomenclature. The scheme is too long to explain now. I wrote an article on it and sent it to *Canadian Entomologist*. (4.) Postcard from Coste, that fellow who is writing in *Entom.* on the chemistry of insect colours. He has much bosh in the May *Entom.* (5.) A nice letter from Mrs. Cusack. She says, ' I hope you are well. I wish I were near to you to take a little care of you1' She says I can take her herbarium away and give it to the Kew Herbarium if I like. I think Kew would be very glad of them, but I want Mrs. Cusack to take them there herself and compare specimens with those at Kew. You and I shall help her!

(5.) Notice from C. Copineau, a French botanist, asking me to exchange plants. (6.) Reprint from Collinge, of a paper on snails. (7.) *Daily Graphic*. Many thanks. Have not yet found time to read it. (8.) *Entomologist* and *Ent. Mo. Mag.* for May. Both interesting. (9.) *Science Gossip* for May. Chiefly remarkable for being full of misprints. It contains a rather long paper by me on weeds, and three notes on Mollusca. (10.) *Nature* of March 13, 20, May 1, 8. The May 1 number has my letter on birds' nests. and in the May 8 number I have a letter on slugs eating thorns. (11.) *Pall Mall Budgets*. (12.) A box of all sorts of things (not yet examined) from W. P. Lowe. (13.) A lot of envelopes for packing insects, kindly sent me by Ward, who got them from a relative of his in the business.

I shall post this letter now. Will write again soon.

Your own loving Theo.

May 27th, 1890, 8:45 p.m.

Love,

I got a letter off to you by the outgoing coach this morning, as I thought you would like to know what I was doing about coming home. It has been a warm day, but with gusts of wind at intervals, throwing up blinding clouds of dust.

This morning I first examined some rather interesting specimens of various sorts sent by W. P. Lowe, and wrote Lowe about them. I also wrote to Dr. J. G. Cooper and Dr. C. H. Merriam. After that, I went out for an hour or so and hunted insects down by the creek. I was fairly successful. I didn't get any mail, but heard that some express had arrived for me at Silver Cliff by the mail coach that runs from Cañon City to that place.

I went up to Silver Cliff at once (got a ride up with a very companionable man whose name I knew not) and found it was the Hymenoptera bulletins from Ashmead — about 150 copies. I found Pennycuick and Pellham in Silver Cliff, so rode down in their waggon with them to West Cliff again. It took me nearly all the afternoon to get off the copies of the Bulletin. I sent away half of them, one to every C.B.A. member, and a few to libraries. I had to carry them over to the post-office in my butterfly-net, which they filled.

Later I went and filled the lamps in the schoolhouse, as they were almost empty.

May 28th, 10:5 p.m. This morning I went out again, but it was rather too windy for insects. However, I got a fair number by sweeping. To-day's mail was a pamphlet on fungi from Dept. of Agriculture, and two letters from Binney and a letter from Nash. Nash will be here next Tuesday, so I may see him before I go.

Binney writes a very nice letter, My nomenclature paper, which I sent him in MS, contains a good deal that is contrary to his views, and I therefore said he might edit it before publication if he would, and alter it conformably with his ideas — that he had done so, of course, being stated in a preface. To this he replies:

'I appreciate fully your kindness and delicacy in offering to submit it to my alterations so as to suit my views. This would make it *my* paper, not *yours*. No, my views have already been expressed in my books — founded, indeed, on very careful, laborious study, but liable to be mistaken. So, let my old fogy ideas stand, and do you forge ahead with *your* ideas, and let people follow which seems best. Of one thing you may be sure, I have no pride of opinion, and not the slightest personal feeling in the matter! I think only of elucidating the subject, and am sure you feel the same.'

As I wrote Binney, 'May I always have it in me to be equally liberal-minded!' Would that all men were like Binney! I wrote Binney a long letter this afternoon and did four drawings for him (the jaws and teeth of certain slugs).

This evening I went round to the school-house and opened for the prayer-meeting, but I got Harry Stockton to see after the closing, and he will look after all these meetings in future.

This evening I went round to the Stocktons and found they had returned from Cañon City. Charlton, as well as Mrs. Charlton, Tomkins the banker (his eyes are too close together for him to be a nice man) and a friend of his were there, so I didn't get much talk with the Charltons. However, the rate to New York is $27.00, and it seems probable that the $5.00 rate was mythical. I think I shall be away before the rates can go up, as I believe they have to give ten days notice before making a change. So everyone says here, and Nash writes from Pueblo that it is so. I wish my money would come quickly.

May 29th, 9:30 p.m. A pleasant, warm day. Went out collecting insects near the waterworks this morning, and also called in at Charltons'. Charlton showed me a splendid book by Cope on the fossil Vertebrata, which he had received through the influence of Congressman Townsend. He also showed me letters he had received from the Smithsonian Institution relative to the fossil shells from the Huerfano and the fossil leaves from Rattlesnake Mountain. They make the leaves to be a *Crataegus* (hawthorn, but I feel certain they are wrong.

This afternoon was all taken up by transferring the C.B.A. Library to Charlton's. I had to enter a lot of books in the Library catalogue, which I had not written up to date. I carried the library in a wheelbarrow; there were four (small) loads. Nash will take the library when he comes, to Pueblo, but I leave it at Charltons' for safety.

The mail was a letter from Douglas. He is evidently not a soldier or policeman, after all, but is in the bank at Brandon. He says he is expecting to be moved.

May 30th, 2:30 p.m. The money has come!

9:35 p.m. This morning I catalogued and took down to Charltons' a few remaining pamphlets of the C.B.A. Library. Charlton's *Mother* has arrived there! She is a little old lady who talks such very rustic (North Country) English that I can barely understand it. But she is a nice little old woman and I like her.

Leaving the Charltons, I walked along the creek and caught insects. On my way homeward I again called in at the Charltons' to explain an idea that had just occurred to me. It was to have collections of wild flowers exhibited at the Literary & Sci. meetings, and a prize given for them, just as used to be done at the Bedford Park Gardening Society. The Charltons thought well of the notion. What put it into my head was seeing many children gathering flowers in the meadows lately.

At the usual time, the mail came in — the *Review of Reviews* from you (many thanks. I will read it on the train). A letter from Miss Eastwood and a notice that there was a registered letter. Presently, having signed the book in due form, I got my registered epistle, and it proved to be from Carlie, and contained $150.00 in American paper money. Of course I was greatly elated and excited about it and am still hardly calm. Now I can go as soon as I will, and I certainly *will* quite soon.

Carlie wrote: 'I send you 150 dollars, about £31, for your journey. This must come off the sixth part of a thousand pounds which I owe you, and we will be quite business-like and you shall give me a stamped receipt on account. You will of course let us know what boat you propose to come by. Send me a telegram to 33 New Bridge Street when you arrive, and I will meet the train at Euston.'

I don't believe in his owing me any one-sixth of £1,000, but I sent a stamped receipt (he had enclosed a stamp for the purpose). I shall go by any boat I happen to catch. There will no doubt be one leaving any day. If I booked beforehand and missed my boat I should have to wait for the next on the same line. I will telegraph him from Liverpool, and of course also to you. I will also write you from Queenstown.

Miss Eastwood writes a rather effusive letter, as is her wont. She says she *may* come up here

and see me on her way to southwest Colorado. This will be tomorrow, as she was going down there at the end of the week. She says also:

'In case I do not again communicate with you before your departure, I wish you a most pleasant journey and great happiness and prosperity on the new journey which you begin at the end of this.'

Which is rather nice. She ends up:

'I have learned much from you, in some respects more than from anyone else. I do not hope to be able to return the obligation to you, but perhaps I can, to my fellow men.'

This I hardly comprehend. She says that if I go via Denver, her father and mother will be very pleased to have me stop over a bit at their house, though she will be away. However, even if I did go by Denver and could stop, I don't think I have the cheek to go and introduce myself as a guest to people I have barely heard of!

I went down to the Charltons, took them *Review of Reviews* to look at and told them I had my money. Mrs. Charlton asked me to go and take meals at their house after I have packed my things up. This is a kindness I will gladly accept. Returning to my room, I was busy all afternoon writing letters and packing off things that don't belong to me. I returned to Binney several shells which unfortunately I have not found time to draw.

I also ran round town a good deal, looking for a ranchman or anyone who might be driving down to Cañon City with an empty waggon. Could I find such, they could easily take me down, and it would be cheaper and in some ways better than the stage. Failing any such, I shall *probably* take the stage to Cotopaxi. Going into Chetelat's in the pursuit of these enquiries. I was presently face to face with a most magnificently-dressed company of ladies who turned out to be chiefly those Kettle girls, who look very different in town from on the ranch!

I also looked in today's papers, and find it therein stated that the present low rates will cease on June 10th. So I must get away next week anyhow. I should like to go on Monday and very likely will do so, but it seems rather too bad if I don't wait and see Nash, who comes up on Tuesday. At all events, don't *expect* me too soon after you get this, as delays are likely to occur. I will post another letter when I go, but I may arrive almost as soon as that.

This evening, after supper, I called at the Humphreys. I found Mrs. Humphrey and Mrs. Stockton there. I expounded my flower show (wild flowers) idea, but they were as enthusiastic about it as the Charltons. Humphrey himself is coming up from Denver tomorrow and he will know all about the rates.

Afterwards I called at Harsh's to see Lyman Harsh (who drives the stage) about his charges and the amount of luggage he could take. Lyman was not in though, and old Harsh commenced telling me all sorts of ridiculous stories about his and other people's experiences. Harsh senior said Lyman would take all the luggage he could lash on [Hence the American slang, 'latch onto'? Ed.], so I suppose he can tackle my little all. Now this shall be posted.

May 31st, 1890, about 8 p.m.

Love,

Have been packing all day, except that I went out for a short walk and caught some insects this morning, and spent some time reading the mail (some papers from the Smithsonian Institution, etc.) this afternoon. Now I must be off to my last 'Literary' meeting.

Sunday, June 1st, 9:55 p.m. Last night we had a poorish meeting of the Literary. It isn't worth while to give the programme. The debate was:

Affirmed, 'That women have more influence for good in the world than men.' I had to take the affirmative alone, while Price Walters and a young man from Dora named Lemmons took the negative. I was really too tired to talk, and I spoke poorly. The whole debate was an indifferent one. The judges of course gave for the affirmative. Will Thomson was elected secretary in my place. He is a young man who may or may not shine in this position; we have yet to see what he will be like. I expounded my idea about the flower show and it seemed generally approved.

I have been packing all day, except that I have been a little at the Charlton's where I had a meal this afternoon. I saw Bertha Humphrey, who has just come from Denver, and she says it is true about the rates staying down for ten days. I also saw Lyman Harsh, and he can take me and my boxes down on his coach to Cotopaxi. I have filled my tin box, but shall have to get a second box, as there is a considerable surplus.

I now think I may not go until Wednesday morning, for these reasons: (1.) I might get a letter from you on Tuesday if not on Monday. (2.) I might see Nash. (3.) I should be able then to go and see the Howards before leaving, as I had promised.

June 2nd, 10 p.m. I must be off to bed, as I have to be up early tomorrow. I start on Wednesday morning. I have nearly all the packing done. I went to lunch at Howard's at Ula today and had supper at the Charltons'. Humphrey has brought here an Englishman (of South Lincs.), Dr. Greswell, for a short visit (he goes tomorrow). Humphrey introduced me to him, and at the Dr.'s request, I talked long with him about the country, plants, etc., this evening. He thinks of starting a company for breeding horses here and says he would like me to come out later on for a while in his employ to help him on the scientific matters. I would gladly, if it were possible. I think I see a possibility for *us* to some day visit the scenes of my former wanderings without any loss of time or £.s.d. I should like to bring you on a visit to this country, some day! However, we will talk over this when we meet. He says that If I can't come, he wants (or probably will want) me to supply written information from England for which he will pay me.

I do hope a letter from you will come tomorrow.

June 3rd, 4:15 p.m. I am glad I waited. Your letter has come today. I had lunch today at Charltons', and shall have supper there. This evening I expect to see Nash. I have a lot to do, principally to call on various people and bid them good-bye.

Mother's postcard (received today) makes me rather anxious. It seems Leslie will probably have to come to Colorado. I must see about this on my return.

It is sad indeed about Mrs. Horsley's death. I am very sorry to hear of it. It will be a terrible thing for Horsley, more so I think than it is for most men.

I won't write more now, as I must not wait, but must post this. I am very well indeed.

Your very own loving Theo.

[New York City]
June 9th, 1890

Love,
I booked intermediate by the *Wisconsin*, Guion Line, this morning; it cost $30.00. I go on board at ten a.m. and we start at eleven. I have been busy again today and had a 'good time' in general. First I went to Columbia College and found Dr. Britton still away, but was directed up to the herbarium, where I was entertained very kindly by a young lady botanist, a Miss Thompson. Miss T. was amazed that I had been able to get up there, as it was a day when no strangers were allowed in the building. I suppose I must have put so bold a face on it that they thought

I had a natural right to the premises! However, while there, I was allowed to look at part of the herbarium and at various books, which were interesting. While there, one Hollick came in, a botanist I knew by name — a nice fellow. After that, I went on to the Museum of Natural History. There also I found it was not a public day, but I told the superintendent I was a distinguished naturalist or something to that effect, and was allowed to enter. A Prof. Sanderson Smith, a well-known conchologist, was very good to me and talked to me while I went over and made notes on a lot of shells. He accompanied me part of the way down, as he was going home and it was in his direction. After that I had supper and so forth, and here I am.

Your loving Theo.

S. S. *Wisconsin*
Tuesday, June 10th, 1890

Love,
Here I am, and we are off! It's past ten, and so I won't write now, but tomorrow.

Wednesday, June 11th. I posted a letter to you on Monday, It will go by a White Star boat, which leaves New York City only today, but which they say will reach Liverpool before this vessel.

We got off yesterday soon after eleven a.m. I was down at the docks a while earlier, and spent the time looking at the process of loading, and reading a pamphlet on seedless fruits Miss Thompson gave me at Columbia College. The Intermediate on this boat is good enough. I sleep in a cabin with seven more men, rather a tight fit. But we each have a good bunk and sufficient bedding provided.

One of the men, named Gray, has rather fraternised with me — an Englishman (aet. about 28) who has been in America about three years. Not a bad fellow and rather interesting but not very likeable., He quarreled with his father and came to America, where he has been journalist, book-agent and a thousand other things, mostly very successfully, and now he goes back in order to be reconciled with his father. He is one of the fellows who are excellent as far as they go, but lack depth of character and purpose in life. His greatest interest is fishing.

There are two Irishmen also in the cabin — *very* Irish. One amuses us by singing songs, comic and otherwise, late into the night. Last night we were treated to 'A Warrior Bold' and 'Michael Murphy.'

The food is excellent, but there are so many of us that they have to lay two tables for every meal — that is, the tables are occupied twice.

Nobody seems to have been sick yet, and we are having very calm weather, with the winds behind us. The petrels (*Procellaria pelagica*) follow us in great numbers. We sit up on the deck most of the time. I got drowsy this afternoon and slept, perhaps a couple of hours.

Yesterday evening a very charming little girl (age five?) from the saloon came and introduced herself to me and was very talkative. I carried her round the ship and explained the various things we saw.

We have a lunatic on board, and a dangerous one. This morning he came on deck and began asking all sorts of absurd questions (as they tell me; I did not see him) — and this afternoon, without any provocation, he stabbed a sailor in the back, wounding him dangerously. Of course, he (the lunatic) is now in irons and will be handed over to the authorities in Liverpool. There is also a prize-fighter of some note on board; I forget his name, On the whole, though, we have a fair lot of passengers. Some, however, are *deplorable* specimens of humanity. There are several who have gone to America for a little while, found they did not like it, and have concluded to return to England or Ireland. These seem to be all fools who are no use anywhere.

Thursday evening. Still fine weather, but colder. Life uneventful.

Friday evening. Rather affected by the sea, but not yet sick. Have been in my bunk nearly all day.

Saturday evening. Feeling miserable today. Saw an iceberg this morning.

Sunday evening. A wretched day. Rough sea.

Monday evening. Still rough and unpleasant. Rain nearly all day. Our cabin (eight men in it) is near the engine room, and very hot and stuffy. Port-holes cannot be opened because of the sea. I sit now in the second saloon where many passengers are assembled. The parties are playing 'Old Maid' and seem to be getting lots of fun out of it. We are now about 1,000 miles from Queenstown.

Tuesday evening. A rather better day. Uneventful. We expect to reach Queenstown the day after tomorrow, and Liverpool some time Friday night.

Wednesday evening. We had quite a concert here in the second cabin, last night after I had written the above. A man who is, I believe, a parson of some sort (looks like a Roman Catholic priest) got up and called for songs, and to my surprise quite a large number were induced to sing, though there was no musical accompaniment. The songs were not anything remarkable, but I was surprised at the ability shown by what I had regarded as an exceptionally idiotic lot of people. However, all joined in with such hearty good-will. Today it has been fine and the sea smooth. The day has passed without incident, except that a pale-faced little man attacked me just now and attempted to 'convert' me.

Thursday afternoon. We shall reach Queenstown some time in the night. I will post this to go in the Queenstown mail bag, and it will no doubt reach you before I do. We shall get to Liverpool some time tomorrow night, but probably cannot land and get off by train until morning. Then five hours or so of travel to London, and then via Bedford Park to Isleworth! My love!

I enclose the programme of a concert they had last night in the saloon. It was for the Aged Mariners, and programmes were sixpence. The Second cabin people didn't know about it, and it was almost by chance that I and some others went in. It's a pity so many missed it, as it was not all that bad. You will see by the programme how it was — and everyone did his or her part well.

The 'Double Bow Knots' by Gregory, D. D. was anecdotes about weddings; rather too facetious, I thought. 'Mr. J. Studley' was introduced by the chairman as one whose name was familiar to all Americans, but I couldn't find out what he was renowned for. Do *you* know?

'Mr. J. McAuliffe (Mr. 'McCauliflower' the Chairman called him) is the prize-fighter, a sort of Cashel Byron. He wouldn't sing — said he never sung in his life. He is a great big fellow, manners seem gentlemanly, and not a bad face. You see, while the fellow is dressed up neatly, and on good behavior, he may travel saloon, and is treated with respect by all the grandees — rather lionised in fact. But these same people will talk of him as a 'horrid man', 'brute', etc., etc., when they read in the papers of his next prize fight.! As a matter of fact, I daresay he *may* be a moderately good sort of fellow — at all events better than his patrons. He has a 'trainer' on board to look after him. Mrs. Madden, on the programme, is said trainer's wife.

Now, good-bye love, until we meet — *the day after tomorrow!* I will telegraph from Liverpool.

Your loving Theo.

3. Fairfax
Dec. 13th, Saturday, 10:15 a.m.

Dear love,
It is foggy again this morning — Oh, dear! It's dreadful — it looks as if the fog never *would* go! But there is a letter from you this morning, which is nice. To think, though, that you actually *came* to Bedford Park with that note! And I never saw you, alas! I suppose there was no help for it, but I do feel tantalised. If only I could have seen you out of the window it would have been something. ·

If this fog continues, and you happen to the Park again, don't you think I might call at the Hemery's — no, meet you at the station and go to the Hemery's with you, or something of that sort? It would be easy to arrange it by letter beforehand, and I suppose that little bit of even bad weather would do me as much good as harm. But this must be as *you* think right. I like *you* to judge for me, as I know you will do what is best.

I am *glad* your pictures are accepted. It is nice for you, the more so that C[live] and F[rederic] are proving so unsatisfactory in their ways. I mentioned something about the *Annals* paper on the British Museum slugs to Chambers. Give my love to Grandma.

That's all in answer to yours. I sent you a letter yesterday afternoon. Yesterday was a dull day for me, as nothing came from you. After your letter went, one or two things of small importance happened.

The *Journal of Conchology* turned up. It has in it the concluding part of an article of mine on shells. I wrote to the editor (Taylor) and sent him some notes for the next number. I also wrote to Wallace and sent him some notes on beetles.

This morning, besides your letter, I got: (1.) Letter from editor of *Field*, saying he would like notes on the food habits of birds. Now, if that perverse fellow Starting does not interfere, here is a chance to turn a penny. I had written to the editor about it. (2.) Letter from South, thanking me for the Middlesex list manuscripts I sent him.

I am going to write an article on the food habits of birds for the *Field* today and we shall see what comes of it.

I must get this posted this some time this morning so that you will get it tonight. I suppose I shall hear no more from you until Monday if the weather keeps bad?

Your own loving Theo.

P.S. Just got a long letter from Robson. He accepts my offer about the *B. Nat.* and says that if he gets 100 subscriptions in 1890 through my influence he will give me £10 as an honorarium, and a proportionate amount if they are fewer or more. This, he says, must be *strictly private*. So don't mention it to anyone. This makes it quite worth while, doesn't it? *Good* of him, I think.

3. Fairfax
Dec. 19th, 1890, 12:50

Love,

This is miserable. I ought to be at Syon Lodge by now, and *here* I am! Besides not being quite up to the mark today, I dare not venture out in all this wilderness of snow.

Your nice letter came last night after I had posted one to you. What a time you had going to the Dickinson's, etc.! I *ought* to have been there to stand the hansom-cab.

As to the J. W. Williams letter, I *like* you to say what you think , and am not at all vexed. Of course, there is something in what you say, only it would not be well for the world when people only stood up for the right when they were obliged to by force of circumstances! I am *sure* I can convince you I am quite right, when we argue it out. My only doubt is that I may have been too mild about it.

I rather agree with Père Jerome (wasn't he called?) in *Madame Delphine*, that we're all responsible for one another, and the one who stands by and consents is nearly as bad as the offender. I remember once at school, there was a fight between two boys, and the Rev. Phillips not only caned those who had fought (I am not sure he didn't let the boy off who got beaten) but also all those who looked on and made no protest. He was perfectly right. I fancy Payn was one of those who got caned for looking on. Read, also, Ruskin, on kindred matters in *Sesame and Lilies*, the Lilies part.

Yes, it is womanly to be timid and forgiving, but you know, your man must be willing to do battle in this world, if he is worth his salt. Never mind if he is too bold or if he gets knocked about — but be very jealous that he always is on the side of the right, against that which is wrong.

I trust you to do this always and you have not failed me. I don't think even you quite know what your influence has been in helping me. But I am only one rather insignificant person. If every woman would do her womanly duty in this manner, half the wickedness would be wiped out of the world.

But all this has been said before and better by Ruskin, who, if he has said many foolish things, has said enough wise ones to atone for them.

You will think this is quite like one of my sermons of long ago! Let's now be more commonplace —.

I have written to Lees this morning. I ought to have written before.

About the Heatons — at the present minute I can't say I feel like going, but perhaps it may prove feasible. We will talk it over.

The mail this morning was only a letter from J. C. Melville and a postcard from Geo. Roberts — neither interesting.

> With a kiss, your own loving
> Theo.

I think I must get out as far as the postoffice to post this. Of course I shall come tomorrow if the weather permits.

3. Fairfax
Feb. 24th, 5:20 p.m.

Dear love,

Two letters and a postcard, to console me for not seeing you. They are very nice. Thank you, dear. I ought now to be starting for Kew Bridge if it were not so foggy. What a *horrid* day you must have had of it in town! Did Louy go up? I *hope* so, so that you would not have to go home alone.

It was a good idea, sending a note by Miss Lance. I must thank her for bringing it when I see her. Yes, I will come tomorrow afternoon, weather permitting, thank you.

I am glad you were not disappointed about Maidstone. Let's watch for the announcement when it is decided, and see who is appointed. I suppose it will be mentioned in *Nature*.

Yes, the biliousness is gone and I am now well. How absurd of Fred! I suppose the fact is, he does not now give his mind to anything outside his work, so that it is hardly worth while to tell him about things.

Last night, after I posted my letter to you, I deciphered as much as I wanted to of Simroth's paper concerning an American slug. I found Simroth had mixed things up a good deal and given a wrong name to a slug, and so forth, so I wrote him a postcard to tell him so. I also sent (or rather wrote — I sent both cards this morning) a postcard to Pollonera, with a list of shells I had given Salvadori for him.

In the evening, notwithstanding the fog, several people came, viz., Mrs. Mathews, Mrs. Emerson (these two stopped until twelve!), Mr. Thompson, Miss Unwin, Mr. Osborne, Miss Way — I think that's all. I had to talk to Thompson a good deal; he has lived in India, and told me a lot about the animals of Sikkim, etc. Curiously, he met Elwes (the entomologist) when he was in India. The other man, Osborne, had been taught at the school of Rev. Bethune (editor of *Canadian Entomologist*) in Port Hope, Ontario. I didn't go to bed until the people went, after all, not liking to do so for fear of seeming rude. The evening was very dull and uninteresting to me.

This morning I got your letter, and two pages of the proofs of a book of Tutt's on moths, by the first post. Later there came a letter from C. H. Morris of Lewes, asking me to exchange and name varieties of *Helix nemoralis*. (I said I would name them, but not exchange.) Your postcard came by the three o'clock post, and the note at about five or a little before.

I have been at home writing all day. I wrote the following: (1.) Letter to Tutt, with criticisms of his proof, and other remarks. (2.) Postcard to C. H. Morris. (3.) Postcard to Robson, to ask why the *Brit. Nat.* proofs have not yet come. (4.) Letter to Jenner Weir, sending him three Colorado butterflies (some of those Sanson returned) and telling him that as it is so foggy this week I am not very likely to get to the South London Society on Thursday — this because he is vice-president and wanted me to apologise for him to the meeting because *he* would not be there. (5.) Letter to Butler of the British Museum, about some American moths he asked me about. (6.) Letter to Myles, enclosing the MS for the March Nature Notes, which I did finally get done this afternoon, exceedingly to my relief!

This doesn't seem, very much, but it has kept me busy all day.

I was reading an account of an Ibsen play in the *Pall Mall Budget Gazette* this evening which I think is quite disgusting. I am getting to detest the very name of Ibsen exceedingly.

Olive was up at Wimpole St. today painting Dorothy Rowell, and found the Uncle in court suit, knickerbockers and buckles, sword and all. She says he looked very well in them, but it sounds a queer combination. He was going to a reception at the Prince of Wales!

I do hope you are no worse for being out on such a horrid day, dear.

With my love, your own Theo.

P. S. If it is 'rather foggy' tomorrow, I think I will come over as early in the afternoon as I can, and not stop to tea.

3. Fairfax
Feb. 26th, 5:5 p.m.

Dear love!

Thank you for such a nice letter. I didn't think you were at all foolish last night, really, dear. You mustn't think so. I was so glad to be able to console you a little. When we are married, and you are so sorrowful, we will sit together and talk, and I will try my best to be nice to you until you are cheerful again — will you let me, dear?

I am sorry to hear that Mrs. Lance is so ill, poor thing! I took your note round but did not go in. The servant told me she was rather better. How unfortunate for Miss Lance, too!

About Maidstone! I would have said go in for it, if I had used my own judgment alone, but it seemed that in this case the father's opinion was sufficiently valuable to follow altogether, because (1) he has had so much experience of such things and (2) all of his private *wishes* and inclinations would be towards something English; so he would not advise Jamaica rashly [Evidently T.D.A.C. had already been recommended for the post by Wallace. Ed.] or without being strongly of the opinion that it was best. This is badly put, but you will see what I mean.

It was so foggy this morning that I gave up all idea of going to town, but now it has cleared up and is beautifully fine! It cleared up just in time for me to go up in the afternoon and see you at Waterloo, but I thought, even before your letter came, that very likely you would not go up as it was so bad in the morning, so I am merely going up to the South London meeting by a train about half past six. Yes, I will come tomorrow just after lunch.

Your letter came this afternoon, and just now, by the 5 p.m. post, I got a *Field and Farm*, but there were some letters last night and this morning also. Last night I got: (1.) A letter from Robson, with the *Brit. Nat.* proofs at last. I corrected them at once, and took them out to the post. (2.) letter from Jenner Weir. (3.) Letter from Butler, of the Museum. This morning there came: (1). Letter from a man named A. H. Shepherd, offering to send me records for my Middlesex List. (2.) Letter from C. H. Morris of Lewes, and a box of varieties of *Helix nemoralis*, three of which were new. I identified them for him and returned them, writing him a letter on the subject. (3.) Letter from Carrington, as follows:

35 Peak Hill Gardens, Sydenham, S. E.

23 Feb'y, 1891

My dear Mr. Cockerell:

I am back again in England. Shall I see you at the South London meeting tomorrow? If not, will you arrange an appointment for the coming week? I have brought back a goodly number of land shells and a very few slugs. The frost drove away many slugs, so that I could not find any for the month or six weeks leaving. I hope you are quite strong and well after the very trying winter weather. Please don't give this address to *any* person. It is only temporary anyhow, Don't answer this if you come to meeting. With kind regards,

Faithfully yours, John T. Carrington

So here he is back again! I wrote him a letter, with a bill of 15/. for the *Field* work, but shall give it to him tonight, as I can go to the meeting. It is well I can see him at the meeting, as it saves the bother of a special appointment. He's a queer chap, isn't he?

This afternoon I have been working at the Middlesex List, and by tomorrow noon I hope to have the part for April finished.

With a kiss, your loving Theo.

The following letter written by Annie's father to Cockerell [who was then living at Mesilla Park, New Mexico] a month before Annie's death. Ed.]

Syon Lodge, Isleworth
Aug. 8th, 1893

My dear Theo,

I most warmly congratulate you upon the successful way in which you have escaped from an unpleasant position [the Jamaica post. Ed.] and made a fresh start. Every success to you, and I sincerely hope that the high dry climate will prove all satisfactory as regards health.

I am a very poor correspondent for reasons that you well know, but though I do not write *in propria persona*, I do so regularly enough by deputy, and listen to the return letters with the keenest interest.

So the scale insects are your temporary object of research? I hope you destroyed all you could of the new kinds and that you will be careful not to send any more here. I have an abundance. That Cape Tortoise scale I'd guess has swarmed here this season and seems to make its home on the peach and nectarines and to migrate to the fig, while, when it moves to the vine, it develops to a far larger size. It has been most abundant during drought, every leaf being fouled up by the insect to a terrible degree.

'Professor' sounds well before the name, and a few capitals at the end: F.Z.S., F.L.S., and the like, balance it well. Go on and add to them. Darwin has gone; Wallace is getting passé, so there is plenty of room for a big man, and he can [illegible; prosper? Ed.] as well in the Rocky Mountains as in England. But while growing learned, don't neglect the dear little natural history specimen at home [Annie, of course. Ed.], and take all the care of her you can.

I have been reading Hudson's natural history books about Patagonia. Most interesting. So is Moxley's [or Morley? Ed.] *Notes of a Naturalist*. Of course, dealing with extra things during the *Challenger* Voyage. It is the best book I have read. You must buy and read it.

Annie will be grieved that I have just lost my best old friend, Louis Archer. He had been ailing for a long time. On Saturday he died, a true honest gentleman in every sense of the word.

My dear, could you both — or *can* both? Well, I suppose at present,

Yours, G. W. Fenn

Annie Sarah Fenn Cockerell, 3 Nov. 1857 - 14 Sept. 1893. Born Alford, Lincolnshire, England. From Records of Odd Fellows Cemetery, Las Cruces, New Mexico (compiled by Marcena Thompson)

WILMATTE P. COCKERELL
1869 – 1957
HUMANITARIAN
NATURALIST – TEACHER

Headstones in Columbia Cemetery, Boulder. The Cockerell's were interred in the burial plot of Professor John Gardiner (1863-1900) of the Biology Department at the University of Colorado with permission of Prof. Gardiner's daughter, Dorothy.

Index